THE MYTHOLOGY OF ALL RACES

—

Volume XIII
COMPLETE INDEX

VOLUME I. *Greek and Roman*
WILLIAM SHERWOOD FOX, Ph.D., University of Western Ontario.

VOLUME II. *Eddic*
CANON JOHN A. MACCULLOCH, D.D., Bridge of Allan, Scotland.

VOLUME III. *Celtic, Slavic*
CANON JOHN A. MACCULLOCH, D.D., Bridge of Allan, Scotland.
JAN MÁCHAL, Ph.D., Bohemian University.

VOLUME IV. *Finno-Ugric, Siberian*
UNO HOLMBERG, Ph.D., Turku University.

VOLUME V. *Semitic*
STEPHEN H. LANGDON, M.A., B.D., Ph.D., Oxford University.

VOLUME VI. *Indian, Iranian*
A. BERRIEDALE KEITH, D.C.L., Edinburgh University.
ALBERT J. CARNOY, Ph.D., University of Louvain.

VOLUME VII. *Armenian, African*
MARDIROS ANANIKIAN, B.D., Kennedy School of Missions.
ALICE WERNER, L.L.A. (St. Andrews), School of Oriental Studies.

VOLUME VIII. *Chinese, Japanese*
JOHN C. FERGUSON, Ph.D., Peking, China.
MASAHARU ANESAKI, Litt.D., University of Tokyo.

VOLUME IX. *Oceanic*
ROLAND BURRAGE DIXON, Ph.D., Harvard University.

VOLUME X. *North American*
HARTLEY BURR ALEXANDER, Ph.D., Scripps College.

VOLUME XI. *American (Latin)*
HARTLEY BURR ALEXANDER, Ph.D., Scripps College.

VOLUME XII. *Egypt, Far East*
W. MAX MÜLLER, Ph.D., University of Pennsylvania.
SIR (JAMES) GEORGE SCOTT, K.C.I.E., London.

VOLUME XIII. *Index*

THE MYTHOLOGY
OF ALL RACES

IN THIRTEEN VOLUMES

CANON JOHN ARNOTT MacCULLOCH, D.D., Editor

GEORGE FOOT MOORE, A.M., D.D., LL.D., Consulting Editor

COMPLETE INDEX

TO

VOLUMES I–XII

VOLUME XIII

ARCHAEOLOGICAL INSTITUTE OF AMERICA

MARSHALL JONES COMPANY · BOSTON

M DCCCC XXXII

PUBLISHER'S ACKNOWLEDGMENTS

THE publication of a scholarly work of the magnitude of *The Mythology of All Races* has not only involved arduous research and painstaking editing, but also the assistance of libraries and museums in supplying primitive material necessary for illustrations. The occurrence of the World War delayed the issuing of volumes, doubled their cost, temporarily limited their distribution, and placed a financial burden upon the publisher greater than he could carry. It seems fitting at the completion of an undertaking that has required eighteen years of persistent effort that recognition should be given those men and agencies who have made it possible. The publisher gratefully acknowledges his indebtedness to the following:

George Foot Moore, guide and counsellor.

Louis Herbert Gray, sole architect of the series and editor of volumes I, III, VI, IX, X, XI, and XII.

John Arnott MacCulloch, editor of volumes II, IV, V, VII, and VIII.

Each and every author.

George Lyman Kittredge, Andrew F. West, Dwight W. Morrow, A. Kingsley Porter, Ralph Adams Cram, Charles Cutler Torrey, David Moore Robinson, William Dana Orcutt, Alfred B. White, and Charles F. D. Belden, advisers and helpers.

The Peabody Museum, Harvard; The Smithsonian Institution, The Peabody Museum, Salem; The Museum of Fine Arts, Boston; The British Museum, The Boston Public Library, and Harvard University Library, for aid in illustrating.

Grace Webber Jones, whose financial aid in a crucial hour made it possible to continue publication.

Hugh Bancroft, Susan Minns, James C. T. Baldwin, Dartmouth College, and Amherst College, for financial assistance which insured the publication of seven volumes.

The Carnegie Corporation, for contributing a revolving publication fund which the Archaeological Institute of America has used to further this undertaking.

John D. Rockefeller, Jr., Edwin H. Hall, George D. Pratt, Otto H. Kahn, James R. Jewett, W. O. Wiley, H. W. Corbett, and Dan Everett Waid, for a combined loan; which, under the trusteeship of the Archaeological Institute of America and Rollin H. Tanner, Treasurer, has brought the work to completion.

The dream of the publisher was to produce an authoritative series of monographs covering the whole field of mythology, interestingly written, adequately and artistically illustrated, well printed and bound. The appeal was to be to the library, to the man of culture who selects only the best, and to the school boy and girl whose casual approach might be turned into a deeper interest in the classics, art, and the development of the human mind. To the extent that he has succeeded, credit is due to these men and institutions.

A. MARSHALL JONES

Boston, November 1, 1932

COMPLETE INDEX
TO VOLUMES I–XII

EXPLANATORY NOTE

SLIGHT inconsistencies occur at times, especially in the repeating of words in the entries for the Chinese section, but they are allowed to remain for added clearness. The alphabetical arrangement of Chinese words is that of the " Index to Chinese Terms " at the end of the Chinese-Japanese volume.

With so many authors using words with divergent meanings (e.g. " ancestor " as ancestor, " ancestor " as first man; " mediator " as intermediary; " messenger " as messenger, " messenger " as agent), and emphasizing different mythological motifs, it has not always been possible to group the items definitely under a single heading; but since all are noted, the information may readily be found.

Diverse systems of transcription have been used in the various volumes of the Series, but in the Index these have been made uniform.

In references under a common entry, the dashes indicate the repetition of the key word or words — one dash for one word, a double dash for two words, etc.

THE MYTHOLOGY

OF ALL RACES

INDEX

A

A-ab-ba (or ab), Sumerian word for salt sea, v. 288

Aarnion Haltia, flames seen over, iv. 173

Aaron, v. 356

Aasa, body of Queen, believed to be in tumulus at Oseberg, ii. pl. XVI, opp. p. 130

Ab, father, title of gods, v. 5, 7, 9

Aba, Great Spirit, x. 63

Abaia, magic eel, ix. 120

Abaangui and Zaguaguayu, hero-brothers, xi. 297

Abakan-Khan, rain-maker, iv. 448

Abartach, son of king of Land of Promise, iii. 173

Abasy, spirit long-ago deceased, iv. 479, 486

Abatwa, dwarfs, vii. 120, 262–263, 264, 399 [14]

Abbu probably Labbu, v. 287

Abdera, city of, founded by Herakles beside tomb of Abderos, i. 84

Abderos killed by man-eating horses of Diomedes, i. 84

Abdi-Ninurta, god-name survives in, v. 135

Abdihiba, king of Jerusalem, v. 45

Abel and Cain, v. 202

Abe-no, field of, viii. 385 [22]

Abhayākara, sage, said to have assumed form of a Garuḍa, vi. 210

Abiba'al, king of Gebal, v. 43

Abibalos, king of the Berutians, History of Phoenicia dedicated to, v. 43

Abikarib, personal name, v. 7

Abi-milki, fatherhood of god emphasized in name, v. 11

Abipone, xi. 317, 320, 321, 322

Abirá, creator god, xi. 197

Abode of dead, Finnish, iv. 78, 79

——Norrhem is Swedish, iv. 78

——gods in sky, vii. 123, 131, 132, 133

——Hel: see HEL, DEITY OF UNDERWORLD AND HER ABODE.

——Indra, vi. 131

Abodes of dead, i. 30, 37, 121, 137, 141–148, 194, 220, 229, 250, 305, 373 [60]

——ii. 42, 44, 45, 120, 122, 153, 156–157, 221, 303–323, 340

——iii. 10, 14, 15, 16, 17, 36, 38, 50, 85, 90, 93, 95, 102, 103, 105, 113, 114–123, 138, 173, 174, 183, 185, 194, 195, 197, 210, 212, 213, 273, 329, 334 [12]

——iv. 40, 72–82, 209; 307, 309, 402, 483–495

——vi. 15, 31, 34, 70, 86, 99–100, 101, 131, 145, 148, 149, 150, 152, 159–161, 194, 200–201, 211, 250; 315, 344–345

——vii. 31, 59, 60, 68–72, 96, 97, 98; 118, 129, 134, 138, 141, 159–161, 173–174, 176, 178, 179, 180, 184–185, 189, 195, 198, 199–212, pl. XIX, opp. p. 206, 344–347, 384 [50], 395 [58]

——viii. 29, 32, 46, 53, 114, 115, 128, 137, 146, 196; 223–224, 235, 237–240

——ix. 59, 70, 255

——x. 6, 7, 22, 41, 49–51, 104, 108, 117, 132, 198, 205, 249, 254, 263, 273 [8], 274 [10]–275

——xi. 27, 28, 39, 40, 49, 53, 80, 81, 83–84, 138–139, 141, 191, 192, 193, 198, 279, 335

——xii. 41, 49 (fig. 47), 173–183, 214, 366 [7], 417 [21]

Abodes of dwarfs, ii. 269, 270–271
—fairies, viii. 114–115
—giants, ii. 279
—gods, ii. 35, 175; v. 91, 94, 252
—separate, of individual gods, ii. 23, 329
Aboré, Warau hero, xi. 273
Aborigines and incoming Celts, tradition of war between, iii. 25
—analogy between austral and boreal, xi. 337, 343
—Indo-Chinese, xii. 256–257
Above, the, x. 185, 188, 287 31; xi. 51, 52, 53
Abraham, v. 153
—of Rostov, iii. 300
Abrokomu, v. 383 97
Absalon, Bishop, destroyed idol Rugievit, iii. 283
Absolute, the, vi. 101, 103, 105, 107–108, 109, 119, 179, 188, 193, 230, 231
Absolution, v. 148; xi. 78
Absolutism as represented by the Emperor, viii. 9
Abstinence, xi. 35–36
Abstract divinities among Greeks and Romans, i. 282–283; 299
Abstraction, viii. 147
"Abstraction," farce, viii. 360
Abšušu corresponds to Kilili, v. 33
Abtagigi, an evil spirit, title of Kilili, v. 33
Ābtīn (Thrita Āthwya) killed to feed serpents, vi. 322
Ab-ú (or Eš-ú) title of both Tammuz and Ninurta, v. 131
Abu, lord of vegetation, v. 201–202
Abu Nawâs, jester of Bagdad, popular on East Coast of Africa, vii. 121–122, 292, 293, 353, 357–358, 430 9
Abu-ṭâb, name emphasizing fatherhood of god, v. 7
Abū'l-Faḍl, vi. 248
Abum-ilum, name emphasizing fatherhood of god, v. 7
Abundance, gods of, xi. 34; xii. 66, 378 102
Abundia, Dame, may be Fulla, ii. 184
Abydos, connexion of Osiris-myth with, xii. 50–51
—head of Osiris worshipped at, xii. 395 81
—Ḥeqet worshipped at, xii. 50–52, 134
—home of Leandros, i. 202

Abydos, Khnûm and Ḥeqet as masters of the necropolis of, xii. 372 50
————transferred to, xii. 50, 51
—Osiris lord of, xii. 122
—perhaps seat of worship of Shentet, xii. 148, 408 95
—principal seat of cult of Osiris, xii. 98, 386 17
Abyrga, sea-monster, iv. 345
—snake, dwelling in "lake of milk," iv. 357
Abyss a form of Amen-Rê', xii. 221
—both Osirian and Satanic, xii. 105, 391 43
—chest containing dead Osiris or infant Horus floats in, xii. 116
—entrance and source of, localized at Abydos, xii. 50–51
—father of Khepri, xii. 69, 71
—four sons of Horus or Osiris come from, xii. 112
—Horus goes to, xii. 209
—interpreted as "the great god who became by himself," xii. 219
—lowest circle of water of, depicted as a god in circular form, xii. 96
—monsters and good gods dwell in, xii. 73
—Nekhbet stands at entrance to, xii. 46
—Nile and Ptaḥ (-Tatunen) equated with, xii. 47, 145
—(Nuu) identified with sun (Rê'), xii. 220, 221
—Osiris and his kingdom at night arise from, xii. 97
—Osiris identified with, xii. 95, 112
—outside ocean, ii. 324
—"Ox-Leg" celestial counterpart of dragon of, xii. 112
—pond at Abydos regarded as source of, xii. 98
—Rê' born in, xii. 74
—shades swimming in, xii. 180 (fig. 188)
—sun-god proceeds from, xii. 30
—trodden by cosmic deity, xii. 223
Abyssinia, v. 3
—a Semitic people in, vii. 115
Abyzu, demoness, v. 366
Acacitli, chieftain, xi. 117
Acala, a Dharmapāla, vi. 214
"Acallamh na Senórach," iii. 45, 116, 165, 168, 174, 180, 182, 209, 210

Acatl (reed), day-sign, xi. 100, 104
Acca Larentia, intrigue of Hercules with, i. 303
Accad, Accadian: see AKKAD, AK-KADIAN.
Accidental gods, iv. 107
Accomplishers, viii. 26
Achaios, son of Xouthos and Kreousa, i. 71
Achchel founded kingdom of Cheles, xi. 127
Achekanet-kanet, by turn genius of good and evil, xi. 334
Acheloös and a Muse, Sirens reputed children of, i. 262
—River appeared to men in animal shape, i. 256, 257
—river deity, in form of bull, Herakles wrestles with, i. 93
—Sirens born from drops of blood from horn of, i. 262
Acheri, ghosts of little girls, vi. 248
Acheron, death of some of Argonauts at mouth of river, i. 111
—Kerberos on guard at entrance to, i. 88
—river (of mourning) of Hades, i. 143
Achilles and Priam, i. pl. XXIX (1), opp. p. 116
——Thersites, i. pl. XXXII, opp. p. 128
—Aias still wrathful with, in Underworld, i. 142
—armour of, wrought by Hephaistos, i. 206
—ashes of, placed in golden jar by Thetis, i. 217
—besought Boreas and Zephyros to fan flames of Patroklos's pyre, i. 265
—death of, i. 130–131
—double of Poseidon, i. 212
—fights with Skamandros, i. 256
—Harpies mothers of swift steeds of, i. 266
—not admitted to Elysion, i. 147
—Polyxena, Priam's youngest daughter, sacrificed by Greeks at tomb of, i. 133
—receives Briseïs as prize at Troy, i. 126
—refuses overtures of Agamemnon, i. 128
—renounces wrath and re-enters battle in Trojan War, i. 129
—shade of, appears to Agamemnon, i. 134

Achilles, shade of, appears to Odysseus in Hades, i. 146
—slays Amazon Penthesilea, i. 130
——Hektor, i. 129–130
—son of Peleus and Thetis, i. 122
—spear of, wounds and heals Telephos, i. 125
—tired of ruling dead, Celtic parallel of, iii. 182
—wrath of, i. 126–130
Achitescatoueth, succession of two Seasons to each other's places called, x. 31
Achiyalatopa, knife-feathered monster, x. 187–188
Achtland, wife of Connla, iii. 150
Acolhua, founders of Tezcuco, xi. 109, 111
Acolnauacatl, god Mictlantecutli otherwise called, xi. 80
Acrobat following sacrificial animal, xii. 195 (fig. 207)
Acropolis besieged by Amazons to avenge capture of Antiope, i. 103
—salt spring and olive-tree produced by Poseidon and Athene on the, i. 172
—sisters of Pandrosos leap from cliffs of, i. 67
Acyuta, one class of divinities, vi. 227
Adab, seat of Mah cult, v. 111
Adad = Balmarcod, v. 383 108
—and Shala, Mîshāru associated with, v. 67
—as Shamash, v. 37
——Zeus, v. 37
—at Padda, v. 39
—Balshamîn is, v. 63
—bull of, v. 37
—conquers Zû, v. 40
—deity, v. 36, 37, 38, 39, 40, 41, 42, 43, 45, 46, 56, 59, 60, 64, 65, 86
—destruction of, prophesied, v. 141
—fled from Zû, v. 101
—god of Aleppo, v. 39
—god of divination in Babylonia and Assyria, v. 39, 63
—hymns, v. 40
—in Akkad, v. 41
—in flood story, v. 220
—lord of Lebanons, v. 39
—Marduk identified with, v. 155
—omen-god, v. 39, 381 58
—rain- and thunder-god, v. 39, 60, 271, 273

Adad-Ramman, Babylonian and Assyrian deity, v. 39
— -Rimmon, v. 39
—Semitic god of winds, rain, and lightning, v. 60, 61, 80, 101, 132, 172, 193, 252, 271, 274
— -Set-Sutek, thunder-god, v. 48
—(sky-god) in first heaven, v. 172
—son of Enlil, v. 61
—thunderbolt symbol of, v. 150
—Yāw identical with, v. 73, 77
Adadi-bi'di, Aramaic deity, v. 42
Adaheli, Sun, later God, xi. 262, 267
Adaher forms triangle with two dog-stars, vii. 65
Adam = Alulim = Aloros, Hebrew patriarch, v. 205
—and Adapa, myth of, v. 175–189
——Lilith, Elle-folk children of, ii. 224
—composition of body of, iv. 371–372
—creation of, from different materials, ii. 326–327
—in late Jewish mythology, v. 354
—legend of, not known to early Hebrew writers, v. 188, 205
—Lîlîth said to have been first wife of, v. 363
—story of fall of, v. 183–189
—supposed Sumerian temptation of, v. 179
—Yāw imposed penalty upon, v. 181, 183, 184, 185
Adam of Bremen and Helmold on idols in Radigast, iii. 286
——description of rites of Slavic tribe Lutici by, iii. 221
Adams, Mt., x. 134
Adapa and Adam, myth of, v. 175–189
—Atarhasis as a title used of, v. 270
—author of work on astronomy, v. 175
—brings mortality on man, v. 181
—myth, v. 94, 227
Ādarān, small shrine for fire, vi. 284
Adarmalk (Adrammelek), king of Gebal in Persian period, v. 71
Adbhut Nāth, aerolite worshipped as, vi. 233
Addumu, seal of, v. 48
Adekagagwaa, the Sun, x. 25
Adelgot, Archbishop of Magdeburg, iii. 289
Adiabene, Herakles (Vahagn?) adored in, vii. 365

Ādibuddha, conception of, vi. 202, 205, 213
Adils, king, attended Disablot at Upsala, ii. 244
Aditi (" Boundless "), vi. 18, 19, 26, 28, 29, 44, 54, 55, 62, 74, 75, 85, 92–93, 96, 106, 107, 121, 138, 149, 174
—with addition of sun, has eight children, vii. 381 [1] (ch. ii)
Āditya, vi. 75, 82, 86, 138, 182
Ādityas, iv. 403; vi. 18, 21, 23, 25, 28, 29, 54, 55, 56, 85, 86, 94, 99, 107, 120, 135, 137, 142–143, 149, 264
Admetos and Alkestis, i. 107
—Apollo slave of, i. 280
—flocks of, herded by Apollo, i. 180
—motif in Africa, vii. 356
—pique of Artemis at harvest-home sacrifices of Oineus and, i. 184
—took part in hunt of Kalydonian boar, i. 56
Adobe houses, xi. 211
Adon of Gebal, Canaanitish god, v. 13
Adōnāi, v. 43, 75, 76, 77
Adōnī, Eshmun called, v. 75, 76, 77
— -Eshmun Tammuz employed by Syriac writers for the Phoenician, v. 340
—(" my lord "), title of dying god, v. 75–76, 77, 339, 340
—of West Semitic mythology, Tammuz became the, v. 335
Adonis and Tammuz identified, v. 76, 335, 339
—Aphrodite in story of birth of, i. 198
—Attis parallel cult-figure to, i. 275
—birth of, from a myrtle-tree, vi. 295
—(called also Bêl), tomb of, at Aphaca, v. 322
—celebrations of death and resurrection of, adopted and identified with death and resurrection of Christ, vii. 41
—(Eshmun), statue of, v. 76
—gardens, Armenian parallel to, vii. 381 [9]
—hidden in chest by Aphrodite and entrusted to Persephone, i. 198
—killed by boar, v. 132, 339
——and from Adonis's blood grew red anemone, i. 198
—killing of, by boar perhaps borrowed from explanation of Sêth in animal form, xii. 399 [111]
—origin of Greek ceremony at the wailings of, v. 350

Adonis (Osiris), pillar of Osiris in temple of, v. 71
—Sandakos ancestor of, vii. 41
—Shwe Pyin Nāts suggest, xii. 353
—supposed Celtic parallels of, iii. 204
——Tammuz, similarity of myths of, to those of Osiris, xii. 120
—Zariadres said to be son of, vi. 340
Adonis of Gebal, v. 52, 344
——legend of death of Hypsistos based on cult of, v. 66
Adopted captives, replenishment of blood of stocks from, x. 102
Adopted maids and sons of Odin, ii. 248
—son had no claim on "gods" of adopting father, v. 35
Adoption, v. 64–65
Adraa, celebration of birth of Dusares at, v. 18–19
Adrammelek, god introduced into Samaria, received human sacrifice, v. 71–72
Adrasteia, epithet of Fate, i. 284
Adrastos and Amphiaraos, pact between, i. 52
——Eteokles, battle of, before Thebes, i. 52–53
—escaped from before Thebes on his divinely born horse, i. 53
—king of Argos, made Polyneikes and Tydeus his sons-in-law as fulfilment of prophecy, i. 51
—plans of, to restore Polyneikes to his rights, i. 51–53
Adultery, iv. 379; x. 160; xi. 230
—ordeal to determine, v. 161
Adunî, local title of Tammuz at Gebal, v. 340, 351
"Adventures of Nera," iii. 68
Adventures related by Thor and Odin, ii. 72
Aed, son of Dagda, slain by Conchean, iii. 72
——king of Connaught, King Mongan took shape of, iii. 59
Aed Abrat, iii. 86, 87–88
——daughters of, had healing song, iii. 86
—Ruad's champions took sureties of sea, etc., against him, iii. 132
Aedan and Fiachna join against Saxons, iii. 62
Aedh returned from síd of Bodb Dearg, iii. 90–91

Aëdon said to have been wife of Zethos, i. 44
—transformed into nightingale, i. 44, 70
Ægir, god of sea, ii. 6, 16, 86, 100, 101, 102, 105, 110, 142, 144, 154, 159, 160, 171–173, 178, 180, 190–191, 220, 280, 281
Aeife, woman of the Land of Promise, iii. 116
Aelia Capitolina = Jerusalem, v. 388 [223]
Aelian, late Greek writer, v. 227–228, 234
Aëllopous ("Storm-Foot"), one of the Harpies, i. 266
Aeneas [Aineias], son of Anchises and Venus [Aphrodite], i. 304–306
—Venus accorded homage as mother of, i. 294
"Aeneiad" of Vergil, i. 304–306
Aengaba of Norway, commander of Tuatha Dé Danann, iii. 25
Aeracura, goddess, iii. pl. xiv, opp. p. 120
Aerolites divine, vi. 233
Áes síde, inhabitants of hollow hills (síd), iii. 49, 50, 84
Aesclepius: see ASKLEPIOS.
Aëshma, vi. 261
Æsir, men of Asia, in Prologue to the "Edda," ii. 32
—(sing. Áss), gods, ii. 6, 19, 20, 21, 23, 25, 26, 27, 28, 33, 35, 46, 53, 54, 55, 61, 63, 81, 82, 99, 100, 101, 103, 108, 120, 121, 124, 129, 130, 139, 140, 141, 146, 150, 152, 159, 165, 172, 173, 174, 179, 181, 200, 219–220, 278, 326, 327, 337, 341
—Vanir associated in cult with, ii. 25–26, 27
Æsop's fables, viii. 217
Aestii, Baltic people may be, of Tacitus and Jordanes, iii. 317
—worshipped Mater deum, ii. 109
Æther, Aud perhaps is, ii. 201
Aëthlios, father of Endymion, i. 245
Aetna, Mt., placed upon Typhon, i. 9
Afanc, Welsh, akin to water-horses, iii. 129
Affinity, viii. 218
Afiti, wizards and hyenas, vii. 335
Afrāsiyāb (Phl. Frāsīyāv; Av. Frangrasyan), Turanian king, vi. 329, 332, 333, 334, 336, 337, 338, 339, 351

Africa, interior, possible connexion of Egyptian religion with, xii. 377 [86]
African race, both Bantu-speaking and Sudanic, have ideas, customs, and beliefs in common, vii. 109
Afterworld, i. 141–148
A-ga-de, Akkad of early inscriptions, v. 377 [1]
—empire founded by Sargon, v. 1, 88, 326
Agamemnon, i. pl. xxx, opp. p. 120, 135–136
—Achilles renounces anger against, i. 129
—aided by Poseidon against Trojans, i. 129
—drove Thyestes out of Mykenai, i. 120–121
—kills sacred hind of Artemis, i. 125, 184
—(Munon), ii. 32
—of Mykenai sets sail with Menelaos to recapture Helen, i. 125
—prompted by dream sent upon him by Zeus, musters army for assault on Troy, i. 127
—receives Chryseïs as prize, but later restores her to her father, i. 126, 127
—sceptre of, wrought by Hephaistos, i. 206
—sends embassy to Achilles confessing wrong, i. 128
—shade of, appears to Odysseus in Hades, i. 146
—stays at Troy to appease Athene, i. 134
—takes Briseïs from Achilles, i. 127
—wounded and forced to retreat to the ships, i. 129
Agasilikkû, weapon, v. 128
Agastya, legends of, vi. 134, 135, 144, 146, 153, 159, 190
Agathangelos on Armenian religion, vii. 26, 27–28, 34
Agathodaimon identified with Shay, xii. 52
Agave, daughter of Kadmos, wife of Echion, i. 45, 47
—tore Pentheus asunder, i. 270
Age, Ages:
Age, agricultural, viii. 25, 30, 33
—before the flood, v. 203
—cosmic, vi. 18, 193

Age, demons may be older in, than gods, v. 354
—myth of golden, ii. 113–114
—of animals, x. 105, 142, 159, 160–164, 216, 261
——Beginnings, x. 159
——dwarfs, ii. 271
——giants, x. 157
——gods, x. 159, 164–166
——kings of Heaven and Earth, Chinese, v. 205
——peace, ii. 282
——transformations, xi. 30
—old, and youth, v. 52
—paradisiac, vi. 269, 293, 294, 295, 304, 361 [19]
—patriarchal, x. 159
—permitted dragons, vii. 392 [21]
—shortening of, after Fall, iv. 385
—The, Aiōn personification of, v. 382 [78]
—warrior, xi. 240
Aged man, Shamash represented as, in art, v. 61
Ageing, freedom from, claimed by mystic, viii. 75
Ages, five, xi. 240
—of the gods, each marked by new ruler, xi. 227
——world, i. 17–18; vi. 103, 106, 107, 132, 148–149; xi. 133
Ageb, deity of Abyss, xii. 371 [44] and fig. 223
Agenor, great-grandson of Io, established himself in Phoinikia, i. 44
—sent his wife and sons in quest of Europe, i. 44
Agent: see MESSENGERS (vol. vii).
Aghora, epithet of Śiva, vi. 97
Aghorī, epithet of Śivā, vi. 184
Aghrēraṭ (Av. Aghraēratha; Pers. Ighrīrath), pious Turanian, vi. 329, 333
Agias of Troizen, author of "Returns," i. 133
Aglaia ("Splendour"), one of the Charites, i. 237
Aglauros, mother of Alkippe by Ares, i. 190
Agli-Bêl (-Bôl), moon-god of Palmyra, v. 56, 58, 61, 87
Agn, sick given ashes and water in, vii. 57
Agnar, son of Geirrod, ii. 9, 56, 61, 62, 175, 176, 228, 251, 260
Agnāyī, wife of Agni, vi. 53

Agne, Norwegian, hung from tree by Apollo, vii. 63, 365

Agni as goblin-slayer, vii. 45

—fire-god, vi. 15, 16, 17, 18, 19, 20, 24, 27, 28, 32, 33, 36, 38, 41, fig. 1, opp. p. 43, 43–45, 50, 52, 53, 54, 56, 57, 61, 62, 63, 64, 65, 66, 67, 69, 70, 77, 81, 82, 83, 87, 88, 91, 92, 94, 100, 114, 117, pl. x, opp. p. 118, 135–136, 140, 141, 145, 159, 182, 216; 264, 284, 285, 291, 313, 316, 342; vii. 44, 54, 363, 364

—identical with Apām Napāt, vii. 46

—myth, Norwegian form of, vii. 365–366

—resemblance of, to Vahagn, vii. 43, 44, 45, 46

—sea-born, associated with lightning, vii. 386 [11]

—slays Vṛtra, vii. 45

—Vedic myths of, confirmed by Vahagn-myth, vii. 46

Agnihotri Brāhmans preserve fire, vi. 233

Agnis stands for Hyagnis, vii. 364

Agohya ("not to be concealed"), name of Pūṣan, vi. 27, 58

Agra, the Dūnd visited, vi. 248

Ägräs, Agröi, deity of turnips or twin grains, iv. 244

Agraulos (Aglauros), daughter of Kekrops and Agraulos, i. 67

—wife of Ares, i. 69

—daughter of Aktaios, wife of Kekrops, i. 67

Agrestes feminae: see WILDIU WÎP, ETC.

Agreus, the Hunter, descendant of Samem-roumos, v. 54

Agricultural Age, Shên Nung typifies the, viii. 25, 30, 33

—festival, Armenian Navasard as, vii. 22

—labours, ghosts forced by ancient Armenians to take part in, vii. 75, 391 [6]

—ritual, survivals of, on St. John's Eve, iii. 47

Agriculture, x. 14, 55, 76, 183, 282 [24–283]; xi. 2, 17, 34, 212, 370 [23]

—Athene patroness of, i. 172

—dependent upon water which becomes object of sacrificial cult, iv. 194, 212

—gods of, iii. 21; viii. 62

—Heaven-god a god of, iv. 219

Agriculture introduced by Oannes, v. 103

——Pṛthu, vi. 166

—Osiris patron of, xii. 399 [111]

—porcupine originator of, iv. 421

—Tuatha Dé Danann had power over, iii. 40

—"wounding" of earth, iv. 459

—Zeus (of Attike) god of, i. 160, 163

Agriculturists, School of, viii. 8

Agros, Agrōtēs, or Agrouēros ("the Farmer"), deity, v. 54

Agrōtēs ("Hunter"), name applied to El of Gebal, v. 54

Aguŝaya, goddess sent to subdue Ŝaltu, v. 27

Aḫ, aḫu, brother, title of gods as brothers, v. 7–9, 11, 135

Aha, a Vasu, vi. 142

Ahalcana, one of lords of Underworld, xi. 173

Ahalpuh, one of lords of Underworld, xi. 173

Ahalyā, Indra seduced, vi. 133, 145

Aharaigichi (Queevèt), evil spirit, xi. 321

Ahat, Ahet, Ahit, names of cosmic cow, as nurse and protector of Sun-god, xii. 40

Ahatl, chieftain, xi. 117

Ahau-Chamahez, medicine-god, xi. 137

Āhavanīya fire, vi. 91

Ahhazu (the Seizer), devil, v. 362

Ahi and Indra, Ninurta and dragons parallel to, v. 130

—(Iranian Azhi), vi. 265, 271

—(serpent), form of demon Vṛtra, vi. 62

—snake, iv. 444

Ahi Budhnya ("Serpent of the Deep"), vi. 37, 89, 142

Aḥi, Egyptian deity: see EḤI.

Ahiqar, legend of, v. 64–65

Ahi-râm, mythological relation of god and man found in, v. 8

—of Gebal, tomb inscription of, v. 379 [29]

Ahi-ṣaduq, name describing a deity as "my brother," v. 7

Ahi-Yami, letter of, mentions Yāw, v. 44

Ahkin-Mai, chief priest of Mayapan, xi. 127

Ahkinshok, owner of days, guardian of bees, spirit of new fire, xi. 141

Ahkushtal, birth-deity, xi. 141
Aḥmad ibn Faḍlān describes funeral of
Russian chieftain, iii. 233–234
Ahmakiq locks up winds, xi. 141
Ahmucen-cab in cosmogonic fragment
of Book of Chilam Balam, xi. 153
Āhom (Assam), Shan province, xii. 275
Ahpuch, death-god, xi. pl. I, frontis-
piece, 138
Ahriman, iv. 317; vii. 86, 391 [13]
—twin brother of Ahura Mazda, vii. 23
—see ANGRA MAINYU, ETC.
Ahsonnutli: see ESTSANATLEHI.
Ahti, water-spirit, a mighty hero, iv.
207
Aḥu, Aḥuti, god, xii. 129, 405 [40]
Ahuitzotl brought Aztec power to its
zenith, xi. 44, 58, 111
Ahura, associated with Mithra in the
Avesta, vi. 56
Ahura Mazda (Ormazd), iv. 315, 317,
321, 379, 390; v. 130; vi. 24, 355 [5],
25, 28; 260, 261, 269, 270, 273–292,
293–303, 305, 306, 307–309, 311, 327–
328, 342, 346, pl. XXXIII, opp. p. 264,
pl. XXXIV, opp. p. 272; vii. 12, 96,
381 [1] (ch. ii)
——as creator, vii. 20
——as fertility-god, vii. 21
——relation of, to Armenian Aramazd,
vii. 20, 21
——son of Zrvan Akarana and twin
brother of Ahriman, vii. 23
Ah-uuc-chek-nale (" he who seven
times makes fruitful "), xi. 155
Äi (" old man "), Esthonian name for
Thunderer, iv. 228
Ai, plain of, iii. 37
Ai, poet, sent against sons of Carman,
iii. 35
Äiä-hoog (" thunder-shower "), Esthonian name for Thunderer, iv. 228
Aiakos, house of, i. 121–123
—judge in Underworld, i. 142, 143–144
—king of Aigina, i. 10
—of Aigina, origin of, i. 163
—son of Aigina by Zeus, i. 11, 157
Aïapakal, incantations in honour of, xi.
341
Aias and Hektor fight in single combat
till truce established for both armies,
i. 128
Aias, son of Oileus, cast up on coast of
Euboia, i. 135

Aias, son of Oileus, drags Kassandra
from altar of Athene, i. 133
——drowned by Poseidon for
boasting, i. 211
——inspired by Poseidon against
Trojans, i. 129
——ships of, struck by lightning by
Athene, i. 173
Aias (Ajax), son of Telemon, i. 121
——bears body of Achilles to the
Greek ships, i. 131
——death of, i. 146 (fig. 6)
——inspired by Poseidon against
Trojans, i. 129
——refused arms of Achilles, goes
mad and slays himself, i. 131–132
——shade of, appears to Odysseus
in Hades, i. 146
——still harbours wrath against
Achilles in Underworld, i. 142
Aid, divine, iii. 12, 13
Áide and her family drowned, iii. 133
" Aided Chlainne Lir," iii. 51, 210
" Aided Chlainne Tuirenn," version of
Lug's coming taken from, iii. 29, 40
Aïdes (" Hades "), born of Kronos and
Rhea, i. 6
Aidne made first camp-fire, iii. 136–137
Aidonœus, Hades, vii. 97
Aidos (" Modesty "), abstract divinity
of state of mind, i. 282
Aietes, city of, on bank of Phasis, i. 112
Aietes, demands of, on Argonauts as
price of Golden Fleece, i. 112
—king of Kolchis, i. 108
—restored to throne by Medeia, i. 115
—son of Perse and Helios, i. 242
Aife overcome by Cúchulainn, iii. 144,
145
Aigai, Poseidon's home in sea near, i. 210
Aigaion (hundred-handed Briareos),
Aegean personified by, i. 259
—Mt., reputed birthplace of Zeus, i. 155
——Zeus hidden in cave on, i. 7
Aigamuchab of the Nama Hottentots,
vii. 243
Aige transformed into fawn, iii. 60
Aigeus consults Delphic oracle regarding
offspring, i. 179
—death of, i. 102
—double of Poseidon, i. 212
—King, consults oracle, i. 97
—Medeia becomes wife of, in Athens,
i. 115

Aigeus, son of Pandion, i. 68, 69

Aigialeus, son of Inachos by an Okeanid, personification of southern shores of Gulf of Corinth, i. 28

Aigimios, king of Dorians, aided by Herakles against the Lapithai, i. 94

Aigina, creation of man from ants in island of, i. 10–11

—mother of Aiakos by Zeus, i. 11, 121

—wife of Zeus, i. 157

Aigisthos and Kassandra reign over Mykenai (or Argos), i. 134

—death of, i. pl. XXXIII, opp. p. 132

—foments trouble in kingdom of Agamemnon during his absence, i. 134

—killed by Orestes and Pylades, i. 135

—son of Thyestes, i. 120

Aigyptos and Danaos, families of, i. 30–32

—derivation of, i. 324 [8]

Aihyt-Aga, Ajy, creator gods, iv. 398

Äikene ("little old man"), Esthonian name for Thunderer, iv. 228

Aïkouch, name of cause of illness, visible as arrow or harpoon point, xi. 341

Ailill, iii. 56, 58, 68, 69, 78, 79, 80, 90, 124, 125, 130, 140, 146, 147, 150, 152, 154, 157

—the Fair, cow of, iii. 127

Aillén mac Midhna comes out of síd every year to burn Tara, iii. 72, 165

—of the Tuatha Dé Danann, loves Manannan's wife Uchtdelbh, iii. 89

Ailment, Darkness son of, iii. 35

Ailô, one of names of Lîlîth in Jewish mythology, v. 365

'Ain Shams ("the Sun's well"), xii. 31

Aina, spirit long-ago deceased, iv. 479

Aine, daughter of Cuailnge, iii. 168

—queen of fairies of South Munster, daughter of Eogabal, iii. 47, 73, 89

Aineias [Aeneas], son of Aphrodite [Venus], and Anchises, i. 118, 199

—cult-title of Aphrodite, i. 199

—saved by Aphrodite, i. 197

——from Achilles by Poseidon, i. 210

'Ainel, in Persian period kings of Gebal called, v. 67

Ainge, daughter of Dagda, iii. 136

Ainu parallel of primeval couple, viii. 378 [7]

Ainus, early inhabitants of Japan, viii. 209

Ainus subdued by Yamato and a miraculous sword, viii. 304

Aiolic stock, Poseidon ancestor of, i. 11

Aiolos, descendants of, i. 106

—master of the winds, Odysseus's sojourn at island of, i. 137

—myth of, derived from Sumerian conception of earth-god, v. 63

—son of Hellen, ruler of certain districts in Thessaly, i. 37

——Poseidon, i. 211

—steward of winds, i. 266

—"Wind man" identical with, iv. 233

Aiomun Kondi, the Dweller-on-High, xi. 273

Aiōn (personification of "The Age"), image of, v. 18, 382 [78]

Air, viii. 28–29; x. 98, 186, 206

—Amon misinterpreted as god of, xii. 130

—and fire, sacrifice thrown into, iv. 432

—and sky-gods, iv. 217–234; vi. 15–40

— -burial of lightning victims, iv. 445

— -form of Amen-Rê', xii. 221

— -god Podoga, iii. 355 [44]

— -hole, iv. 418

—man created partly from, iv. 371

—Mithra genius of, vii. 33

—protégés of Odin carried through, under his cloak, ii. 43

—Ptaḥ equated with, xii. 145

—spirits of, iii. 319

Airāvata, elephant-vehicle of Indra, vi. pl. IV, opp. p. 34, 131, 132

—part of Jain cosmography, vi. 221

Airem ("Ploughman"), cognomen of Eochaid, iii. 42, 81

Aireskouy Soutanditenr called on for aid in shipwreck, x. 16

Airi, bhūt, vi. 248

Airmed, sister of Miach, separated herbs which grew from her brother's grave, iii. 28

Airyana Vaējah, region in Iran, vi. 307, 333

Ais (cognate of Skt. asu and Teutonic as, aes), "breath," vii. 86

Aisa ("Fate"), i. 283

Aison, son of Kretheus and Tyro, i. 106

——deprived of throne of Iolkos by Pelias but regains it by craft, i. 108–109

Ai-Tojon, over-god, iv. 402

Aither ("heavenly light"), i. 5

Aithiopia, Menelaos touches at, i. 134

—ravaged by great monster, i. 34

—why people of, black, i. 244

Aithiopians dwell on eastern and western shores of Okeanos, i. 256

"Aithiopis," i. 130–131

Aithra and Atlas parents of Pleiades and Hyades, i. 248

—and Helen taken to Sparta, i. 105

—daughter of Pittheus and mother of Theseus by Aigeus, i. 97

—Helen left in charge of, i. 25

Aitnaios, child of Prometheus, i. 12

Aitolia and the mountains, adventures of Herakles in, i. 93

—Artemis survives as "Lady Kalo" in modern, i. 313

—founding of, i. 55–56

—legends of, interwoven with Argive myth, i. 28

Aitolians, Thestios king of, i. 24

Aitolos killed Apis the Argive and the Kouretes, i. 55

Aja Ekapād ("one-footed goat"), vi. 36–37, 89, 142

Ajas, tribal appellation, vi. 63

Ājīvika sect, vi. 223, 224, 358 [2]

Ajmer, king of, turned into a Rākṣasa, vi. 245

Ajy-Khotun (Birth-giving mistress), iv. 415

Ajysit, birth-deity, iv. 399, 415

Ajysyt-Ijäksit-Khotun (Birth-giving nourishing mother), iv. 415

Ajy-tangara, creator god, iv. 398

Aka Rawa, fire from, ix. 185

Aka Manah, demon, vi. 261, 276

Akambou, good spirit, xi. 38

Akarnania founded by sons of Alkmaion and Kalliroë, i. 55

Akastos accompanies Iason when he goes to recover the Golden Fleece, i. 109

—cleansed Peleus of his pollution at Iolkos, i. 121

—son of Pelias, i. 106

Akbar, Emperor, vi. 232

Ake, sea-deity, and Ookeu, conflict between, causes flood, ix. 39

Aker as double lion with two opposite heads, xii. 42 and fig. 36

——earth-god, xii. 42–43, 422 [13]

——gaoler of Sêth, xii. 390 [39], 401 [34]

Aker as lion accompanied by crocodile, xii. 90

—assimilated to Shu and Tefênet, disfigured representation of, xii. 43 (fig. 37)

—at later period as single lion and with two differentiated heads, xii. 368 [22], 369 (fig. 221)

—compared with Babylonian Nergal, xii. 368 [22]

—composite figure of, separated into two lions, xii. 43 and fig. 37

—confused with 'Apop (Satanic dragon), xii. 43

—depicted as black and representative of lower regions of earth, xii. 43

—deprives 'Apop of strength, xii. 127

—Nut, and Khepri, xii. 369 (fig. 221)

—Sun-god passes through body (earth) of, at night, xii. 43

—theologians sought to reconcile existence of Qêb and, xii. 43

Akh-en-aten ("splendour of the disk"), name adopted by Amen-ḥotep IV, xii. 225

Akhmîn, Kenemtef(i) localized at, or near, xii. 404 [38]

Akhtya, Yōishta preserved his town from devastations of, vi. 335

Akim Korsunyanin, idols destroyed by Archbishop, iii. 294

Akîtu festival, v. 156, 315, 411 [44]

—house of New Year's festival, v. 156, 157, 318, 320

Aki-yama no Shitabi-onoko, tale of, viii. 294–295

Akkad (modern ruins called ed-Deir), geographical term, v. 1–2, 55

Akkadian, meaning of, v. xvi

—names of kings of Kish, v. 1

—texts, philological reasons for arguments and translations based upon, v. xv–xvi

Akkadians adopted polytheistic Sumerian religion, v. 6

—shall profit from universal disorder, v. 145, 146

Akkruva, fish-god of the coasts, iv. 191

Akku found Sargon in basket on Euphrates, v. 157

Akkulu ("eater"), dog, vii. 395 [58]

Ako, chief, ix. 65

Akrisios, Danaë, and Perseus, i. 33–36

Akrisios, grandson of Lynkeus, exiled his brother Proitos, i. 32

Akrokorinthos, Asopos offered to provide spring on, i. 37

—citadel, awarded to Helios, i. 37

Akrūra sent to bring Kṛṣṇa to Kaṁsa, vi. 172

Aksak, name applied to certain people; also name of creator beetle, xi. 323

Akṣobhya, one of the five "Meditative" Buddhas, vi. 211

Aksum, Aksomites, v. 3, 11

Aktaion, Artemis punishes, i. 185

—changed into stag by Artemis, i. 46

—death of, i. pl. LIII, opp. p. 248, 252

—("gleaming one"), son of Aristaios and Autonoë, i. 46, 251, 252

Aktaios, Kekrops wedded daughter of, i. 67

Akte ("seaboard"), old name of Kekropia, i. 66

Aktiōphi, name for Hekate, v. 161

Al is Babylonian Alu, but Arm. and Pers. Al corresponds to Heb. Lîlîth and Gk. Lamia, vii. 88

—stone, vii. 369–370

Ala, bisexual demons, v. 357

"Âla isîru" ("the city they hated"), poem, v. 167

Alad = šêdu, v. 358, 360, 361

Alagabiæ of Romano-German inscriptions, Gefjun found in, ii. 182

Alagar = Alaparos = Seth, Sumerian antediluvian king, v. 205

Alaisiagae, altar dedicated to the two, ii. 98, pl. XII, opp. p. 98, 358 [7]

Alakā, lake of Kubera, vi. 158

Alalkomeneus believed to be first man by Boiotians near Lake Kopaïs, i. 10

—sprang from bosom of Gaia, i. 272

Alaparos = Alagar = Seth, Greek transcription of antediluvian king, v. 205

Alaung Sithu, monarch of Pagān, xii. 355

Alb (Alp) in sense of spirit, fairy, ghost, etc., ii. 219

Alba (Scotland), iii. 143, 149

Alba, stag carried off bride for hero, iv. 430

Alba Longa founded by Ascanius, i. 306–307

Albania, finger-cutters of, vii. 370–371

Albasta, evil forest-spirit, iv. 468

Alberich, king of dwarfs, ii. 266

Al-Bīrūnī concerning Navasard, vii. 21, 22, 23

Albin, Steppe master, iv. 468

Albūrz, mountain, vii. 98; see also HARA BEREZAITI.

Alchad, king of Land of Promise, iii. 173

Alchemy, viii. 13, 19, 75, 76, 94, 135, 144

Alcis, two brothers compared with Kastor and Pollux, ii. 17, 64

—worshipped in sacred grove, ii. 203

Alcor, star of Great Bear, iv. 426, 427–428

Aldafadir (Odin), ii. 61, 175

Aldebaran, as fixed star Nabû identified with, v. 160

—certain stars regarded as sandals and cloak of, vii. 229

Alder-bark juice used at bear hunt, iv. 87–99, 175

—man, iv. 175–176

Ale-bearer, Ygg's (Odin's), ii. 54

——brewer of all gods, Ægir called, ii. 173

—Goibniu's immortal (analogous to soma and wine of Dionysos), iii. 31, 51, 54, 120, 208

—of the Great Plain, iii. 81

—Valkyries serve, ii. 250

—vat of unfailing, iii. 87, 120

Alea, cult of Athene, i. 22

Alekto, one of the Erinyes, i. 277

Aleos, grandson of Arkas, founded city of Tegea and cult of Athene Alea, i. 22

Aleppo, god of, v. 39, 387 [184]

Alesia, according to Diodorus, a city founded by Hercules, iii. 13

Alexander Balas, v. 83

—the Great conquered Armenia, vii. 8

——Etana myth transferred to, after his death, v. 173–174

——head of, i. pl. IV (3), opp. p. 1

——in mediaeval Armenian tale, confined in bottle by dragons, vii. 80, 83

——myths of, i. 223

Alexandros ("Defender of Men"), later name of Paris, i. 118

Alf, dwarf, ii. 266

Álf-reka ("elf-driving"), ii. 227

Álfablót, religious or mythic aspect of older Alfar seen in, ii. 226, 227

Alfar: see ELVES (vol. ii).

Alfheim, Alfar dwell in, ii. 23, 108, 158, 221, 329

Alfhild, daughter of Siward, ii. 256

—performed the sacrifice at disablót at King Alf's, ii. 244

Alfrek (Alberich), dwarf, ii. 270

—king, ii. 121

Alfrodull, the Sun, will bear daughter before Wolf swallows her, ii. 346

Alhue, sprite who frightens men, xi. 328

Ali: see VALI, ETC.

Alien gods, x. 156; see also ANAYE, ETC.

Ālikhant, demon, vi. 98

Aliki: see KARIHI.

'Alilat, 'Alitta, Aphrodite's name, v. 15

Alittu, Babylonian title of mother-goddess, v. 15

Alkaios, son of Perseus, i. 76

Alkeides, original name of Herakles, i. 80

Alkestis and Admetos, i. 107

—daughter of Pelias, i. 106

—returns from Hades, i. 144

Alkha, monster who swallowed sun and moon, iv. 424, 425

Alkinoös, king of Phaiakians, i. 138

—Poseidon ancestor of, i. 211

Alkippe, daughter of Ares by Aglauros, i. 69, 190

Alkmaion, i. pl. XVII, opp. p. 54

—curse of, i. lii

—Erinyes' pursuit of, i. 277

—used Delphic oracle as sanction for murder of Eriphyle, i. 179

Alkmene, daughter of Elektryon, i. 76

—on vase paintings, i. 249

—primitively a war deity, i. 168

—wedded Rhadamanthys, i. 61

—wife of Zeus, i. 157

—with child by Zeus, i. 77–79

Alkuntam presides over creation of man, x. 253, 254

Alkyone and Anthedon parents of Glaukos, i. 261

—wife of Keÿx, changed into kingfisher after drowning, i. 15

Allah (al-ilah), supreme god of Muhammadanism, v. 5, 7

—created Jinns before men, v. 354

Allahābād, union of Ganges and Jumnā especially holy at, vi. 234

Allallu bird, v. 256

Allāt, Arabian, became goddess of fortune, v. 24, 384 [116]

Allāt as Venus, v. 24, 25

—equated with Athene, i. 169; v. 381 [63]

—four-sided stone worshipped as, v. 16

—goddess of lower world, v. 259

—identified with Korē and Tychē, v. 19, 20

—mother-goddess of South Arabic religion, v. 15, 16, 17

—of Petra becomes Fortuna or defender of her cities, v. 20

———on coins, v. 382 [85]

Allatu, Akkadian name of Ereshkigal, v. 161

Allegiance, drinking of water of, xii. 324

Allegorical method of interpreting myths, i. lviii

All Children's Hall, viii. 84

— -father, ii. 200

——hint of, vii. 133

— -God, Pan the, in certain philosophical circles, i. 267

—Medicine, vii. 260

—Saints and All Souls: see WANDERING NIGHT OF DEAD.

—Soul's Day, kutĭya food on, iii. 310

—Souls, feast of, v. 162, 335

Allia, battle of, iii. 12

Alloit and Lludd identical?, iii. 103

Almha (Hill of Allen), iii. 162, 164

Almond-tree and river Sangarios parents of Attis, i. 275

Aloros = Alulim = Adam, Greek transcription of Sumerian antediluvian king, v. 103, 205

Alp, in sense of nightmare; nightmare-spirit, ii. 219, 288

Alpan, Etruscan deity, survives as Alpena in modern Romagnola, i. 319

Alpena, survival of Etruscan Alpan in modern Romagnola, i. 319

Alphabets, x. 70; xi. 158–159; xii. 339

Alpheios River, i. 82

———Herakles sacrifices to, i. 92

—of Elis, tale of, i. 257

Als, demons at child-birth, vii. 88–89, pls. V, VI, opp. p. 88, 369–370, 394 [52]

Alsvid, horse of Sun, ii. 196

Alsvith, giant, ii. 277

Altai ("prince") Mountain, worship of, iv. 340

Altaic race, distribution, languages, religion, and culture of, iv. 299–305

Altair, star, ix. 142

Altar, Aulid, hind substituted for Iphigeneia on, i. 184
—bonfires on festivals kindled from candles on, vii. 58
—dedicated to Adōn Eshmun or Asklepios, v. 75
——Malak-Bêl and Sol sanctissimus, v. 58–59
—fire-, at Bagavan, vii. 56
—for human sacrifice found at Edfu, xii. 420 [22]
—in mystic rites at Eleusis, i. pl. L, opp. p. 230
——the open, first sacrifices on, viii. 30, 31
—of Earth at Temple of Heaven at Pekin, prayers by Chinese Emperor at, substitute for old Ploughing Festival, xii. 328
——Fairies, viii. 114
——Palmyra, eagle on, v. 119
—Palmyrene, v. 61, 62
—see also MER FESTIVALS; OFFERING-TABLE; SPINNING-WHEEL AND FLAX OFFERED, ETC.; TABLES IN LUD; TREES SMEARED WITH BLOOD TO SUPPORT SKY.
— -stones, ring attached to, ii. 156
—to Athene erected by Bellerophon, i. 40
——Mars Thingsus, ii. 98, pl. XII, opp. p. 98
—with crescent and disk, v. 3
Altars, iii. pl. IX, opp. p. 86, 158, pl. XX, opp. p. 158, pl. XXI, opp. p. 166, pl. XXV, opp. p. 204; vi. 108; viii. 33, 34–35, 37, 38, 43–44, 48, 66, 73; x. 85, 110, 124, 191, 197, 199, 200, pl. XXVII, opp. p. 200, 290 [35]; xi. pl. I, frontispiece, 23, 39, 47, pl. XXXIII, opp. p. 160
—fire came upon at noon, xi. 138
—of sun and moon, vii. 47
—prayer-, Canaanite shrines are probably movable, v. 32, 33
—seven, of Armenia, vii. 17, 18
—to Mercurio Channini and Regi in upper Ahr region, ii. 37
Alterations of beings from their first forms, xi. 30
Alternating gods, ii. 64, 158
Althaia causes death of Meleagros, i. 58
—daughter of Thestios, wife of Oineus, i. 56

Althaia delayed fulfilment of prophecy concerning Meleagros, i. 56
—hangs herself, i. 58
—sent curses on Meleagros for killing his uncle in war, i. 57
—wife of Dionysos, i. 219
Althaimenes, son of Katreus, declared by oracle destined to kill father, i. 63
Althjolf, dwarf, ii. 270
Alû Alû limnu, Ailô, demon, v. 362, 364, 365
Aluberi, god pre-eminent over all, xi. 259
Alulim = Aloros = Adam, Sumerian antediluvian king, v. 205
—ruler at Eridu, v. 166
Alvaldi, giant, ii. 279
Alvand, Mt., vi. 270
Alvasta, evil spirit, iv. 184
Alviss, dwarf, ii. 10, 74, 95–96, 265, 268, 269, 330
"Alvissmal," ii. 10, 20, 21, 25, 26, 95, 197, 200, 265, 329
Alvitr, Norn, ii. 254
Alv-myror, ant-spirit, iv. 185
Älvor, elves, ii. 225
Am, ghost of murdered man, xi. 328
'Am-'Ashtart, mother-goddess, v. 13
Amadhlozi (ancestral ghosts), central factor of Bantu religion, vii. 117, 181, 193, 272, 404 [5]
Amadubad, title of Mah, v. 110
Amæthon, son of Dôn, iii. 96, 97, 99–100
Ämägät, shaman-spirit, iv. 498
Amaiauva, cave in Hispaniola, xi. 28
Amairgen, singer of spells and giver of judgements, iii. 42, 43, 44, 111, 126
Amait worshipped in Memphis, xii. 157
Amaite aidgill ("Hags of Doom"), in battle of Mag-Tured, iii. 25
Amalivaca, supreme Being, xi. 259, 270–271
Amaltheia, goat which suckled Zeus, i. 155
Aman, El of Gebal on Egyptian monument as, 391 [322]
Amanki (Enki), water-god, Innini reporting to, v. 327, 328
Ama-no-Hashidate, god and goddess enshrined at: see BONTENKOKU, TALE OF.
Ama-no-kawa (Heaven's river), Herdsman and Weaver-Maid meet on two sides of, viii. 235–236

Ama-numun-zid, Sumerian name of Earth mother, v. 12

Amarga, divine calf, v. 96–97

Amarna Letters, v. 48

Amarok, giant wolf, x. 3

Amarudukku, v. 155

Ama-terasu, sun-goddess, viii. 224

Amatudda, title of Mah, v. 110

Ama-ušumgal-anna (" mother-great-serpent of Heaven "), title borne by Tammuz and his mother, v. 78, 349

Amanta, priest-king dynasty, xi. 216, 217

Amazimu, ogres, vii. 136, 334

Amazon, the, and Brazil, xi. 20, 254–315

Amazons, i. 85, 326 [5] (ch. v)

—Bellerophon sent out against the, i. 39

—daughters of Ares, i. 190

—discussions of identity and character of, i. 86, 326 [4] (ch. v)

—in battle, i. pl. xxiv, opp. p. 92

—of the New World, xi. 19–20, 32, 281–287, 349 [5], 373 [1]–374, 374 [4]

—queen of, Pleiades and Hyades children of, i. 248

—second expedition of Herakles against, i. 91

—Theseus's expedition against, i. 103

Amber, tears of Phaëthon's sisters turned into, i. 244

Ambikā, sister of Rudra, vi. 83, 150

Ambirīṣa, king whose sacrificial victim carried away by Indra, vi. 148

Ambrosia, vi. 47, 48, 50, 104, 106, 107, 139, 143, 151, 214; viii. 242

—Demeter anoints Demophon with, i. 228

—of gods, v. 180

Ambrosius Aurelianus connected with story of Merlin, iii. 200–201

Ambumabbakal, child of Muntalog, ix. 184

Amchimalghen, female powers of invisible world form class of beneficent nymphs called, xi. 330

Amēlōn = Enmeluanna = Enosh, Greek transcription of Sumerian antediluvian king, v. 205

Amempsinos = Ensibzianna = Jared, Greek transcription of antediluvian king, v. 205

Amenaber (" bringer of all [good] things "), epithet of Aramazd, vii. 21

Amenemapt, Egyptian temple builder, v. 46

Amen-em-ḥêt III received divine honours near his monument, xii. 171

Amen-ḥotep (Amenophis) of Egypt, Abdihiba of Jerusalem corresponds with, v. 45

—religious revolution of, xii. 224–231

—son of Ḥapu, author of a magical book, xii. 198, 421 [2]

——worshipped as famous scholar at memorial sanctuary at Dêr el-Medineh, xii. pl. iii, opp. p. 170, 171

Ame-no-minaka-nashi, deity, viii. 378 [2]

Amen-Rê' (as sun), union of, with Mut (as sky), xii. 34

—hymn to, xii. 236–238

—identified with many other deities, xii. 221

—imitation of Horus-Rê', xii. 215

—pantheistic tendencies attached to, xii. 220

—sometimes partially portrayed in pictures of nameless cosmic deity, xii. 223

Ameretāt, vi. 260, pl. xxxiv, opp. p. 272, 281

—survives in Armenian flower name, vii. 62

American Indian creation-myths, iv. 326–327

—negroes derive tales from the African, vii. 398 [3]

Amesha Spentas, iv. 403; vi. 25, 355 [8]; vi. 260, 261, 270, 276, 277, 342; vii. 20, 62, 381 [1] (ch. ii)

Ami(n)s, name of moon (or month), vii. 51

Amita, god, vi. 201

Amitābha, vi. 202, 208, 209, 211, 212, 213; viii. 194; xii. 261

Amitāyus (Amitābha), Dharmākara as, exists in Sukhāvatī heaven, vi. 200, 211

Amleth (Hamlet), ii. 83

'Amm, " ancestor," " uncle," title of gods, v. 5, 9, 379 [30]

—title of moon-god, v. 7

Amma bore Karl to Heimdall, ii. 153

Ammenōn = Enmengalanna = Kenan, Greek transcription of Sumerian antediluvian king, v. 103, 205

Ammiṣadugu, name describing a deity as " uncle," v. 7

Ammizaduga, king of Babylon, made statue of Shamash, v. 150

Ammon, Alexander the Great said to be son of, i. 223
—horn of, i. pl. IV (3), opp. p. 1
Ammonite (Śālagrām stone) said to be Viṣṇu's form as golden bee, vi. 240
Ammonites, v. 355
Amoghapāśa, Śaivite form of Dhyāni-bodhisattva of Gotama, vi. 212
Amoghasiddha, one of the five Meditative Buddhas, vi. 211
Amon, Amen-ḥotep IV suppresses worship of, xii. 224–225
—and Mîn, prehistoric identification of, xii. 21
——Triphis, spell of, against dog-bite, xii. 209
—as a ram, xii. 129, 164
—becomes chief deity in Libya, xii. 241
—blue, variant of Mîn, xii. 21, 129, 138, 406 59
—chief god of Thebes, i. 129–130
—daughters of kings dedicated to, xii. 192
—local god of Thebes, gains chief position in pantheon, xii. 19, 215
—lost his importance at Thebes, xii. 139
—Mut later wife of, xii. 140
—nomination of high-priest of, by aid of oracle, xii. 197
—official deity of Ethiopia, xii. 240
—or Ḥemen, readings instead of Men-ḥu(i) in old manuscripts, xii. 405 49
—registers royal name on Persea-tree, xii. 37 (fig. 24)
Amonet, Amon, Mut, Theban triad, xii. 362 6
—early consort of Amon, xii. 129, 130, 148
A-mong and Lan-yein, sister and brother ancestors of Karens, xii. 282–284
Amo-no-Waka-hiko ("Heavenly Youth"), viii. 235
Amon(u)-Amonet, division of deity into, xii. 365 20
Amor: see ANAR.
Amoru, witch put into, vii. 340–341
Amours of Odin, ii. 47–50, 64
Amoxoaque, wise men, xi. 112
Amphiaraos and Adrastos, pact between, to appeal mutual differences to wife of former, i. 52
—declared death of Lykourgos's son foretold failure of army, i. 52

Amphiaraos, departure of, i. pl. XVII, opp. p. 54
—("doubly holy"), a seer of Adrastos, predicts disaster to expedition into Thebes, i. 51
—enjoins his sons to kill their mother to avenge his certain death, i. 52
—escapes from before Thebes by being swallowed up in the earth, i. 53
Amphiktyon, autochthon, driven from throne of Attike by Erichthonios, i. 67
Amphiktyony, Demeter chief divinity of northern, i. 225
Amphilochos, i. 54, pl. XVII, opp. p. 54
Amphion and Zethos, i. 43–44
—son of Zeus, i. 157
—striving to subdue bull, i. pl. XV, opp. p. 42
Amphitrite and Theseus, i. pl. XXV, opp. p. 96
—aids Leto in giving birth to Apollo, i. 175
—threw magic herbs in bathing spring of Skylla, i. 263
—wife of Poseidon, i. 211, 214
Amphitryon invites Kephalos to Thebes to kill a she-fox by aid of his hound, but both animals turned to stone by Zeus, i. 73
—son of Alkaios, i. 76, 77
Amphoteros and Akarnan, sons of Alk-maion and Kalliroës, avenged father's death, i. 55
Amritsar, tanks at, vi. 236
Amṛta, draught of immortality, vi. 46
Aṁśa ("Apportioner"), vi. 28, 85, 86, 143
Amulet, bearded deity used as, xii. 22 (fig. 2)
—iron as, iv. 163
—made by Cao-bien destroyed at a clap of thunder, xii. 318
—solar eye as, xii. 91
—symbolizing Isis, possible meaning of, xii. 99 and fig. 91
Amulets, ii. 71, 79, 80, pl. XI, opp. p. 84, 110, 117; v. 366, 367, 369, 370, 371, 372, 417 54; viii. 105, 149; ix. pl. VI, opp. p. 36; xi. 32, 190, 261; xii. 61, 199, 205, 422 6
—Bês on, xii. 61
—dead must be equipped with, xii. 181

Amulets, protective, of Bês, on Phoenician ships, xii. 64

Amulius, king of Alba Longa, exposes Romulus and Remus, but is later slain by them, i. 307

Amuyao, mountain of flood tale, ix. 171, 180

Amyklai, body of Hyakinthos buried in temple of Apollo at, i. 24

—Herakles seeks purification at, i. 89

Amyklas, son of Sparta and Lakedaimon, i. 23

Amykos, king of the Bebrykians, challenges Argonauts to boxing contest, and is killed, i. 110–111

Amymone, connexion of, with myth of Danaïds cannot be original, i. 32

—gained knowledge of springs of Lerne through Poseidon, i. 30–31

—intrigue of Poseidon with, i. 211

Amythaon, child of Kretheus and Tyro, i. 106

An-Alai-Khotun, Earth mother, iv. 459

'An, 'Anen, manifestation of Horus fighting monster of northern sky, xii. 60–61

———stellarized as guardian of Great Bear, xii. 60

An-ch'i Shêng known as Pao P'o-tzŭ, viii. 115, 145, 146

An-Darkhan-Khotun, Earth mother, iv. 459

An Lu-shan established himself as Emperor Hsiung Wu, viii. 96

An Ti, Emperor, viii. 188

Anaghã, the " Furrow " Sītā replaced by, vi. 97

Anahit, Aramazd, and Mihr perhaps once triad in Armenia, vii. 33

———Vahagn form triad in Armenia, vii. 42

—Armenian worship of, vii. 17, 18, 24–29, pl. III, opp. p. 26, 63, 381 [1]

—Astłik confused with, vii. 39

—daughter of Aramazd, vii. 20

—identified with Artemis, Nane, Athene, Mihr, and Hephaistos, vii. 381 [2] (ch. iii)

———Sidonian Astarte, Syrian Kaukabhta, and Greek Aphrodite, vii. 27, 39

—Mihr brother of, vii. 33

—once termed wife of Aramazd, vii. 23

—rival of Astłik, vii. 38

Anahit, temple of, vii. 17

Anāhita, Aphrodite usual Greek translation of, vi. 340

—as war-goddess, vii. 28

—Auramazda, and Mithra form triad in ancient Persia, vii. 42

—genius of water, vi. 260

—nature and origin of, vii. 25

—wears crescent on head in Persianized Lydia, vii. 381 [2] (ch. ii)

Anahitian Akilisene, centre of cult of Anahit, vii. 26

Anahuac dominated in turn by Toltec, Chichimec, and Aztec, xi. 106

Anaideia (" Shamelessness "), abstract divinity of vice, i. 282

Anaitis, Artemis identified with, i. 183

Anala, a Vasu, vi. 142

Analogies, geographical and cultural, between Old and New Worlds, xi. 16–17

Anakhai, spirits who haunt their old homes, iv. 479

" Analects," Chinese book ascribed to Confucius, viii. 16

Anamaqkiu in deluge-myth, x. 43

Ānanda, disciple of the Buddha, vi. 192, 193

Ānanda, terracotta placques with serpents found at, xii. 271

Anaṅga (" bodiless "), god of love, vi. 116, 141

Ananke (" Necessity "), Moira as, i. 284

Anansesem, Ashanti name for a Spider story, vii. 426 [1]

Anansi, Twi name of Spider, vii. 426 [1]

Ananta, cosmic serpent, vi. pl. XI, opp. p. 120, pl. XX, opp. p. 164

Anāq, sons of, v. 358

Anāqim, v. 355, 358

Anar (Onar), Jörd daughter of, ii. 194, 200, 201

'Anat, xii. 156, 157 (fig. 165)

— -Bêthêl, deity of Hebrews, v. 44, 381 [58]

—(Ishtar, Astarte, Astarte-qadesh), war-goddess, v. 25, 26, 29, 30

— -Yāw, deity of Hebrews, v. 44, 381 [58]

Ānata, divinity, vi. 227

—(Hanata), name of Ishtar as war-goddess among Western Semites, v. 29

Anatu, epithet of Ishtar, vii. 25

Anatum title of Ašratu, Astart, v. 385 [141]

Anaur, snake, ix. 120

Anavatapta, serpent, vi. 216

Anawra-htā, king, conquers Tha-tun, xii. 285

——introduced Southern School of Buddhism into Burma, xii. 271

Anaye or Alien Gods, man-destroyers, x. 156, 163, 165, 268 [2], 281 [19]

Anbar, shorter form of Hambaruna, vii. 91

Ancestor, a god as, v. 7, 9, 10, 378 [21]

— -cult and nature worship, Shinto religion combination of, viii. 215

—death of Conaire result of injury to god Midir by his, iii. 74

—each clan sacrifices to first, who settled in Kilimanjaro country, vii. 183

——Inca clan had genius or tutelary for, xi. 245

— -god, viii. 251

— -gods, fowl of the ghosts emissary of, vii. 288

—human, turned into animal, vii. 272

—thought to dwell in a stone, ii. 312

—worship and spirits, iii. 233–239, 240; vii. 55, 56, 73; viii. 47, 50, 62; xi. 26, 223, 234; xii. 255, 260

——connected with lud-spirit, iv. 151

————Voršud, iv. 134

——importance of, in life of Finno-Ugrians, iv. 70–71, 113, 114

——less developed in Egypt than among some other peoples, xii. 172

——not basis of cult of dead, xii. 182

——Saturday candles and incense remnant of, vii. 95

——Seide-cult had origin in, iv. 104, 105

Ancestors, vi. 240, 241, 249; x. xxii, 10, 199

—as soul-animals, ii. 217

—deceased, remembered at feasts, iii. 313

—feasts for souls of, v. 334

—[first people], vii. 116, 128, 133, 150–151, 152, 155, 156, 222

—Fravashis originally manes of, vi. 261

—Kachin beliefs concerning, xii. 297

—of Maias (the Orang Utan), inferior creatures, ix. 175

——renovated world, ii. 168

—primal, survive their bodies as shadows or images, iv. 13

Ancestors, spirits of, in images, ix. pl. XIX, opp. p. 198, pl. XX, opp. p. 220

Ancestral aid invoked by means of medicine, viii. 154

—ghosts, vii. 179–194

—gods, council of: see RAIN-BRINGERS, RAIN-MAKERS.

—hero, tongue-joined masks may represent descent from, xi. 222

—shrines, xi. 224

—spirits, vii. 179–194

——masques during presence of, x. 310 [65]

——some of the White Women are, ii. 222

—Temple, spirits of, viii. 49–50

Ancestress, Aphrodite worshipped in Thebes as, i. 196–197

Ancestresses, totem-, vii. 417 [23]

Ancestry, direct divine, comparatively rare, ix. 167

Anchicocha, brother of Pariacaca built house on, xi. 230

Anchimalguen, Anchimallen, Wife-of-the-Sun, xi. 330

Anchises, grandson of Assarakos, i. 118

—lame doublet of Hephaistos, i. 207

—of Troy, Aphrodite's desire for, i. 197, 199

—shade of, seen by his son Aeneas, i. 305

—stricken dead by bolt of Zeus for telling of divine descent of Aineias, i. 199

Ancient-bodied One, x. 34

—of Heaven, good power, xi. 295

—the, Ptaḥ called, xii. 145

Ancients, intermediaries, tutelaries, or patrons of fraternities, x. 188

Andalma-Muus, water-giant, iv. 387

Andarta, bear-goddess, iii. 124

Andean North, civilizations of, xi. 187–209

—South, civilizations of, xi. 210–252

Andes, cultured peoples of the, xi. 187–189

Andhaka, an Asura, vi. 116, 165

Andhrimnir, cook in Valhalla, ii. 313

Ando-Peruvians, a group of South American peoples, xi. 254

Androgeos, son of Minos, i. 61, 62, 68–69, 102, 236

Androgynous, Ila becomes, vi. 147

—Śiva regarded as, vi. 179, 357 [6]

Andromache and Helenos, Aeneas comes to home of, in Epiros, i. 305
—Hektor's farewell to, i. pl. XXXI, opp. p. 124, 128
—taken by Neoptolemos as prize of war, i. 133
Andromeda and Perseus, i. pl. XIV (2), opp. p. 36
——Irish parallel to story of, iii. 144
—daughter of Kepheus, bound to rock to appease monster, but freed by Perseus, i. 34–35
Andurunna, title of Arallû, v. 147, 292, 400 160
Andvari, dwarf, ii. 139, 141, 151, 210, 240, 268
Anemone, red, grew from blood of slain Adonis, i. 198
'Anezti, ancient god, early identified with Osiris, xii. 130
—localized in eastern Delta, xii. 402 7
Aṅga and Sunīthā, tale of, vi. 165–166
Angakok, claims of Taliesin and Amairgen resemble those of Esquimo, iii. 111–112
—(shaman), x. 5, 6, 7
Angantyr and Norns, ii. 240
—daughter of, takes sword from barrow, ii. 308
Angel and St. Anne, iv. pl. XXVIII, opp. p. 228
—guarding Paradise, Heimdall compared to, ii. 156
—Nabû appears in writings as, v. 160
—of Death, old woman who led doomed wife to funeral pyre, iii. 234
—protecting, v. 108
—soul-taking, vii. 94
Angeλ Tun, Torch head of house of, vii. 393 34
Angelburga, Wieland marries, ii. 260
Angels, vii. 93; viii. 242
—child of; the child who brought rain called, vii. 241
—descend from Heaven to aid in childbirth, v. 98
—fallen, v. 373
—good and bad, belief in Fylgjukonur influenced by Christian conception of, ii. 237
————Iranian, iv. 395
—light elves possibly parallel to, ii. 221
—ordered to worship man, v. 354

Angels rebel, cast from Heaven fell into barrows, etc., ii. 286
——Danish legend connects elves with, ii. 224
—who married daughters of man, Azāzel transformed into one of, v. 357
—winged, v. 96
Anger, divine (of Thor), ii. 82, 85, 351 19
—of fire, iv. 235
Angerona, Italic goddess of winter solstice, i. 290
Angeyja, giantess, ii. 153
Aṅgiras, an ancient seer, vi. 64, 108, 144, 145
Aṅgirases, priestly family sprung directly from Agni, vi. 18, 21, 34, 64, 71, 82, 87, 99
Angles lived in Brittia, iii. 16
Anglesey, iii. 101, 191
Anglo-Norman, Arthur stories in, iii. 195–196
Angoi, deity that provided mankind with breath, ix. 176–177
—serpents, tigers, etc., grew from body of, ix. 176
Angra Mainyu (Ahriman), principle of evil, iv. 315; vi. 261, 265, 266, 270, 273–303, 312, 321, 328, 335, 343, 346
Angrboda, giantess, ii. 145, 150, 279
Anguta, creation of fishes from fingerbones of daughter of, xi. 30
—("man with something to cut"), father of Sedna, x. 6
Anhanga, devil, xi. 295, 301
An-ḥôret of This, Shu identified with, xii. 44
—see ONURIS, GOD LOCALIZED, ETC.
—Shu perhaps compared with, xii. 383 103
'An-Horus fighting the Ox-Leg, xii. 61 (fig. 62)
Anh-tong built temple to Trung sisters, xii. 314
Anhui, Province of, viii. 100
Ani, citations from "Maxims" of, xii. 178, 232, 233
Ani, sanctuary of Aramazd in, vii. 24
—site of mausoleums of Armenian kings, vii. 24, 95
Anikutani, massacre of, x. 70
Anila, a Vasu, vi. 135, 142
Anima of baby, mother returns to entice, xii. 297

Animal and plant names given to persons, tribes, and cities, v. 9-10, 11

—black, demon left statue of Svantovit in form of, iii. 281

— -beings earth's rulers in Age of Giants, x. 122

—burrows lead to abode of dead, vii. 173-174, 184, 185, 186, 195

—cake in shape of, iv. 248

—consecrated, instead of sacrificed, to Heaven-god, iv. 399, 432

—corn-spirit in form of, iv. 247

—creation of life from flesh of slain, x. 206

—cult, Egyptian, barbaric origin of, xii. 13

—cults, vi. 240-243

——varying fortunes of, xii. 167-168

—dialects, vii. 427 [11]

—disguise: see SHAPESHIFTING.

—Fire mother appears as, to warn against coming fire, iv. 236

—form and names of giants, ii. 279

——soul of sleeper may take on, iv. 473

—forms assumed by gods, iii. 56, 124

——demons take on, vi. 67

——in ornamentation and idols of, xi. 190-191

——of Jinns, v. 352

——Seides may appear in, iv. 106

—friends of Momotarō, viii. 313, 314

— -gods, x. 81, 188, 192; xi. 140

—holy, of many-coloured thighs, iv. 337

—kinds, Haida have double nomenclature for, x. 252

—life, religious conception of, v. 233

—lodges, x. 122-123

—magic stone in entrails of, iv. 458

—Mahr in form of, ii. 289

—mysteries taught to slain youth on restoration of life, x. 123

—names of persons, v. 9

——twelve divisions of time, iv. 436-438

— -powers, x. 122, 134, 141-145

—purification of, by water, at festival to nature-gods, iv. 270

—ritual eating of sacred, gives knowledge, iii. 166

—rivers of life pierce rocks resembling, iv. 359-360

—Sêth represented in form of, xii. 102-103, 389 [33]

Animal shapes, mistress of Fionn could assume, iii. 168

—signs, xi. 291

—sometimes inventor of fire, iv. 450

—soul of, may be saved by miraculous power of the scripture "Lotus," viii. 242

——sacrificial, enters into lud-spirit, iv. 150

——("shadow") may assume form of domestic, iii. 228

—souls, abode of, at primitive Chaos, x. 106

—stories, vii. 111, 120, 270-333; viii. 316-337; ix. 288-293, 297

—totem, death of, causes death of its clan, vii. 276-277, 278

——man may turn into his, vii. 279

—totems: see chap. Totemism and Animal Stories (vol. vii. 270-290)

—trait stories, x. 64-66, 67-68, 294 [41], 297 [46]

—type of shaman dress, iv. pl. LXII, opp. p. 518; see also COSTUMES, SHAMAN.

—used in connexion with ancestor worship, ix. pl. IX, opp. p. 68

—worship, iv. 83-99; xii. 85

Animals aid in finding Mabon's place of bondage, iii. 187

—and birds as emblems, v. 116-117

——human sacrifice to, x. 305

——men, worship of, xii. 159-172

—are born to transformed humans in animal state, iii. 96

—as messengers of witches, vii. 406 [7]

——owners of fire, ix. 281

——sacrifice: see SACRIFICIAL VICTIMS.

—Bechuana tribes named after certain, vii. 271, 416 [2]

—believed to be sent down by Heaven-god, iv. 219

—birds, and fish set free to obtain pardon for sins, xii. 298-299, 300

—black, sacrificed to Yabme-akka and dead in general, iv. 70, 75

—bones of, hung on trees at the half-way place, iv. 25

—bound alive to grave, iv. 483

—brought fire, ix. 48, 50, 114, 183

——from Annwfn, iii. 95, 98, 100, 120, 124

—buried alive at child-birth sacrifice, iv. 255

—can detect Jinns, v. 352

Animals, certain, origins of, i. 15–16
—change in, after flood, xi. 270
—created in cave on God's Hill, xi. 334
—dead return as, vii. 192, 193
—devoured Kachin plant of life, xii. 296–297
—diving, x. 36, 42–44, 60, 62, 99, 104, 105, 217, 218, 220, 293 [40], 299 [49], 300 [50]–301
—domestic, vi. 260; xi. 212–213
—encountered in quest of Coniraya, xi. 229–230
—female only, offered to Sun Virgin, iv. 224
—fish, or vegetables, tribal appellations from names of, vi. 63
—four, of Marduk, v. 300
——spiritual, viii. 98
—ghosts in shape of, steal grain from living at night, vii. 185
—gods appear as: see chaps. Forest-spirits and Water-spirits (vol. iv. 175–216)
——incarnate in, vi. 62–63
—grateful, tales of, ix. 216–218, 225–226
—guardian spirits in form of, ii. 233, 234, 236
—heart, liver, and blood of, sole food of Mukasa, vii. 130
—heroes may have been, vii. 215
—holy, iv. 139
—images of, as assistants to spirit images, iv. 141
——spirits of, iv. 114
—included in person-class, vii. 182, 404 [6]
—Indra likened to, vi. 41
—influencing human events, viii. 156–157
—initiating, x. 240–241
—in myth, viii. 103–104, 105
—loosening of, from cave, chest, or cosmic monster, x. 33, 62, 206, 294 [41]
—loved by Ishtar, v. 28
—magic, iii. 96
—male, except cock, not sacrificed to gods of birth, iv. 255
—may possess supernatural kindred, iii. 258
—monstrous or giant, and in art, ii. 216–218
—Mulungu driven from earth because of man's cruelty to, vii. 134
—mythical, and other beings, iii. 124–134

Animals, no distinction between clean and unclean in Kachin sacrifice, xii. 297
—of Nixen rendered prolific by ordinary animals, ii. 213
——Quarters, x. 203
—offerings to, vi. 96
—on amulets: see AMULETS (vol. v).
—peculiarities of, vii. 286
—regarded as vehicles of gods may be traced to totemism, vi. 241
—related to myths of thunderbird, iv. 439–441
—sacred and as sacrificial victims: see SACRED ANIMALS; SACRIFICIAL VICTIMS.
—sacrificed by Thai races, xii. 300
—sacrificial, buried alive, iv. 75, 76
—serve as steeds for the gods, vi. 62, 63
—serving as vehicles or embodiments of departed spirits, vii. 194
—seven, connected with Great Bear, iv. 339
—shaman- (saivo), iv. 285
—skeletons of, preserved intact may take on life again, iv. 99
—soul-, iv. 285, 286; see chap. Shamanism and Totemism (vol. iv. 496–523)
—souls may appear as, iv. 7
——of, come down from heaven, iv. 415
—spirits of dead visible to, iv. 24
—stories of chase of enchanted or monstrous, iii. 172
—three-horned, third horn denoting divinity, iii. 129
—transformation of, in early times, iv. 504, 506
—veneration of, xi. 289–290
—vengeance for wounding, xi. 192, 300
—which man eats in this world will devour him in the next, vi. 100
—winged, v. 358–360
—witches have power over, vii. 336
—within gourd dropped from sky by Hkun Hsang Löng, xii. 289
——síd, iii. 120
—wood-folk appear as, ii. 206
Animiṣa, demon, vi. 98
Animism, ii. 192, 207, 273–274; iii. 29; iv. 187; vii. 63; viii. 215, 217, 220, 316, 338; x. 17–18, 251, 268 [3]–269; xi. 296; xii. 15–16, 23; 255–256; see also ANIMAL STORIES.

Animism, basis of earliest stage of Egyptian religion, xii. 23
—Central African, Egyptian religion parallel with, xii. 10, 11–12
—in primitive Egypt, xii. 18
—original basis of Babylonian religion, xii. 362 [4]
—possible survivals of, in Pyramid Texts, xii. 204
—primitive, claim of scholars that all religions have sprung from, xii. 15
—progress of Greek mind from, to deism, i. 287
—survival of, into historic times, xii. 16, 214
Animistic beings or souls, Æsir originally, ii. 20
—foundation of Zemiism, xi. 24, 26
—mind, x. 225–226
—rune, iii. 44
—stage of Greek religion, i. xlviii
—view of nature, iii. 29, 34
Aniruddha ranks as Egoism to mystics, vi. 174
—Ūsā became enamoured of, vi. 174
Anishinabeg, human beings, x. 40
Anit, spouse of Mont(u), xii. 130, 139
—Tenenet identified with, xii. 130, 150
Añjanā, mother of Hanuman, vi. 128
Ankles, parents of Oidipous pierced his, and gave him to be exposed on Kitharion, i. 48
Anklets, brass, sent to A-mong by Lanyein, xii. 284
An-montu, modern Erment, xii. 139
An-mutef misreading of Kenemtef(i), xii. 404 [38]
Anna Perenna, Italic divinity of winter solstice, i. 290
" Annales Cambriae," iii. 184
—of Tacitus, ii. 12
" Annals," Cakchiquel, xi. 159
—of Tighernach, iii. 160
Annam, Indian Trickster Tales found in, ix. 242
—mouse-deer as trickster-hero in, ix. 203
Annamese of Chinese origin, xii. 287
Annancy (" Spider ") and Death, stories of, vii. 331–333, 426 [1]
Anne, daughter of Uther and Igerna, iii. 185

Annedotus, mythical monsters, legend of, v. 140
Annihilation, vi. 70
Annwfn, Brythonic Elysium, iii. 93, 95, 96, 103, 108, 111, 122, 192, 212
—equivalent to Hell, iii. 122, 192, 212
Anobret, son of Kronos, sacrificed, v. 342
Anoeth, Arthur imprisoned three nights in, iii. 189
Anointing of images by women, ii. 138
—with oil, v. 180, 181
Anos (Anu), v. 292
Anṛta (" disorder "), opponent of Ṛta, vi. 24
Anshar and Kishar, primeval couple, v. 92, 291, 296–297, 298, 302
Answerers, functions of, xii. 177
Answering by inanimate objects for persons, ix. 85, 224–227, 228, 229, 277
Antae, Procopius's and Helmold's accounts of, iii. 277
Antaeus (Antaios), worshipped in Antaiopolis, xii. 130, 240 (fig. 218)
Antaiopolis, Antaeus associated with Nephthys at, xii. 130
—battle between Horus and Sêth localized near, xii. 397 [101]
—Nephthys neighbour of Sêth at, xii. 392 [56]
Antaios, son of Poseidon, i. 211
——ruler of Libya, slain in wrestling with Herakles, i. 87
Antaka (" the Ender "), an abstract form of death-god Yama, vi. 99
Antardhāna, weapon of Kubera, vi. 158
Antares in Scorpio, god Nesu known by his star, v. 110
Anteia (or Stheneboia) wedded to Proitos, i. 32
Antelope and boar, tale of, ix. 199
—animal of Sêth regarded in rare instances as, xii. 389 [33]
—of the Apsû, v. 105, 106, 108
—(parallel of Brer Rabbit), vii. 121, 178, 282, 294
—Prajāpati pursued his daughter who took form of, vi. 76
—priests, x. 197, 198, 199
Anteros counterpart of Eros, i. 203
Anthedon, Glaukos of, i. 42, 261
Anthemoëssa, home of Sirens, i. 113, 262

Anthesteria, festival in honour of Dionysos, i. 221; v. 382 [79]
—Gaia associated with festival of, i. 273
—Zuñi parallel to Greek, x. 196
Ant-hill, offerings made to the forest-spirit at, iv. 185
Ant-hills, rainbow associated with, vii. 234, 235
Anthropological method of interpreting myths, i. lviii
Anthropomorphic figures of gods, iii. 34, 56, 58
—forms, gods conceived as, ii. 21; vi. 19, 21, 32, 61
—giants are, ii. 279
Anthropomorphism, ii. 192; vii. 144; viii. 58, 62–63, 73, 75, 82, 90; x. xv, xxi, 122, 141, 155, 189, 190–192, 216, 217, 226, 297 [47]; xi. 26, 298, 299
—of Azhi Dahāka, vi. 320
——myths, vi. 350
Anthropophagy, x. 246, 249, 281 [19]; xi. 303
'Anti identified with Osiris, xii. 130
Anti-Christ, v. 374
—except for his baptism Merlin would have been a sort of, iii. 201
Antigone, daughter of Oidipous and Iokaste, i. 49
—punishment of, for giving burial rites to her brother, i. 53
Antikleia mother of Periphetes by Hephaistos, i. 98
—Odysseus said to be son of, i. 123
—shade of, appears to her son Odysseus, i. 145
—violence of Sisyphos to, i. 37
Antikles, Greek leader in wooden horse of Troy, prevented by Odysseus from answering Helen's imitation of his wife's voice, i. 133
Antilles, the, xi. 15–40
Antioch, v. 19
Antiochia, Bishop of, vi. 175
Antiochus the Great, Artaxias, and Hannibal expelled Seleucids from Armenia, vii. 8
Antiope, an Amazon, won by Theseus, i. 103
—in Farnese Bull group, i. pl. xv, opp. p. 42
—mother of Amphion and Zethos, i. 43

Antiope said to have died at Theseus's side, i. 103, 104
—wife of Zeus, i. 157
Antipodes, suggestions of, x. 292 [39]
Antiquities, Land of, viii. 363
Antisuyu, eastern province of Inca empire, xi. 213
Antiu tribes, Mîn patron of, xii. 138
Ants, x. 63, 136–137, 159
—gnawed through bowstring of Vişnu, vi. 79–80, 89
—in Olofat tale, ix. 262
—knead clay and mend Tortoise's shell, vii. 426 [20]
—larvae of, Bushman rice, vii. 230, 231
—on island of Oinone turned into human beings, i. 121
—transformed into men in Aigina, i. 10–11
—world-building, xi. 259
Antu, v. 367
Antum, goddess, wife of Anu, v. 94
Antzevatz, Stone of Blacksmiths at, vii. 27
Anu (An) and Antu, sky-god and his wife, v. 66
——Enlil planned flood, v. 207, 218
——Anos in Greek, v. 292
——as god of water and bread of life, v. 94–98
——begets four winds, v. 294
——citizens of Erech compelled by Gilgamish to repair temple of, v. 267
——condemns man to mortality, v. 181
——created the Anunnaki, v. 190
——creator of heavens, v. 104
——crown of, veiled, v. 317
——cult of, described, v. 94–105
——descent of, v. 91–92, 291
——devils messengers of, v. 373
——Enlil, and Ea (Enki), Sumerian trinity, v. 89, 105, 106, 108, 172
———Ea, and Ninmah create the world, v. 314
———Enki, and Ninhursag created mankind, v. 206
——father of seven cruel gods, v. 138
———the gods, v. 94, 101
——festival of, v. 156
——first of gods of civilized man, v. 91, 92
——flees from Tiâmat, v. 297
——gardeners of, v. 385 [136]
——gate of, v. 178, 180

Anu (An) has title Gula (Aquarius), v. 86

——Heaven made for, v. 303

——heaven- (sky-) god of Sumerians, v. 28, 29, 78, 89, 109, 128, 144, 173, 176, 177, 181, 184, 191, 192, 256, 257, 291, 305, 308, 316, 330, 367, 369, 374

——heavenly bull sent by, to avenge goddess, vii. 69

——implored by Ishtar to create bull of Heaven to destroy Gilgamish, v. 267

——in Sumero-Babylonian mythology devils offspring of, v. 357

——Wagon Star, v. 94

——kept plant of birth in Heaven, v. 166

——monotheism of, v. 89, 93

——navel of sky as throne of, iv. 401

——receives sceptre from Nergal, v. 148

——sons of Enlil and, are dragons, v. 320–321

——symbol of, v. 105

——third Heaven of, v. 94–95, 173

——trees of, v. 97

——way of, in astronomy, v. 94, 96, 306

——weeps for man, v. 112–113

——with overflowing vase, v. 94, 95, 96, 395 21

Anu, Irish goddess, iii. 39, 40

Anuanaïtu and Maconaura, Carib story of, xi. 261–268, 286

Anubis and Ophoïs represented as Roman soldiers, xii. 240

—Anupet female form of, xii. 131

—as dog or jackal (identified with Ophoïs?), sole ruler of nether world, xii. 364 10

——embalmer, xii. 111 (fig. 112), 181, 393 62

——tiller of soil or neat-herd, xii. 399 111

—Bati received honour beside, at Saka, xii. 131, 393 60

—dog of, declines in importance, xii. 167

—guardians of captive 'Apop have heads of dogs or jackals like, xii. 105

—hearts of dead weighed by, xii. 111, 176

—in the Osirian cycle, xii. 93, 110–111, 114, 117

—judge of the dead, xii. 111, 366 3

Anubis leads dead to place of punishment, xii. 179–180

—Ophoïs confused with, xii. 144, 364 10

—Qebhet as daughter of, xii. 145

—Sop may be identified with, xii. 409 104

—symbol of, xii. 111 (fig. 113)

—takes care of infant Horus, xii. 117, 399 111

Anulap, Luk ordered Olofat killed by, ix. 260–261

Anumati, abstract goddess, vi. 54, 93

Anunnaki, gods of lower world, v. 94–95, 102, 112, 124–125, 136, 140, 147, 148, 167, 175, 190, 191, 200, 216, 220, 235, 297, 307, 312, 313, 320, 333, 334

Anupet, xii. 148

—female form of Anubis at Kynopolis, xii. 131

Anup(u)-Anupet, division of deity into, xii. 365 20

Anupu: see ANUBIS.

'Anuqet, xii. 20 (fig. 1)

—goddess associated with Khnûm(u), xii. 20 (fig. 1), 131

Anush in compound Armenian names connects anush with names of gods, e.g. Vartanush, etc., vii. 71, 390 18

—wife and mother of dragons, vii. 78

Anushat, Anmasht, transcriptions of Nin-ib give pronunciations, v. 132

Anuttaras, gods, vi. 227

Anvil, heart and liver of sacrifice beaten on, iv. 464

—thrown eastwards at evening, iii. 32

Anyiewo, snake, vii. 234

Aobh, wife of Ler, iii. 51

Aodh, Donn abducts a hundred maidens from síd of, iii. 172

—Morna's son, afterwards known as Goll, iii. 164

Aoife, wife of Ler, transformed her step-children into swans, iii. 51, 59, 72, 175

Aokeu and Ake, conflict between, causes flood, ix. 39

Ao-marama, daylight, ix. 6

Aonia, ancient name of Boiotia, i. 42

Aonians and Hyantes succeeded the Ektenes, i. 42

Ao-pouri ("world of darkness"), ix. 31

α-Orionis, vii. 229

Aos and Daauke, primeval couple, v. 293

—(Ea), v. 103, 292

Aoshnara, vi. 335, 350

Ao-tsê, occult sciences, viii. 133

Ao-tu-roa, long-standing light, ix. 6

Apām Napāt, vi. 36–37, 43, 89; pl. xxxii, opp. p. 260, 267, 340

——Indo-Iranian water-deity, vii. 63, 365

——suggests Vahagn, vii. 46

Apaosha, vi. 261, 267–271, 280, 350, 360 15; vii. 363

Aparājitas, class of Jain divinities, vi. 227

Āpas, a Vasu, vi. 142

Apasōn and Tauthe, primeval couple, v. 290

Apaukkyit Lôk causes death to enter the world, xii. 264–265

Ape, tarsier, in trickster tales, ix. 187, 191, 192–197, 199, 204–205

Apes as degenerate men, vii. 273

—Rāma allied with, under Sugrīva, vi. 128

—sacred, of India, vi. 236–237

—tailed, vi. 311

Apex, the great primordial principle, viii. 136

Aphaca, tomb of Ba'al at, v. 52

—traces of Marduk legend at, v. 322

Aphangak, ghosts of men, xi. 323

Aphareus, image of Hades on tomb of, i. 26

—son of Perieres and Gorgophone, i. 24

Alpheios, river of Elis, story of, i. 257

Amphiaraos and Ourania reputed parents of Linos, i. 253

Aphidnai in Attike, Helen carried off to, by Theseus, i. 25

Amphitrite and Poseidon parents of Triton, i. 259

Aphrodite, i. 196–203; pl. x (1), opp. p. 20

—and Adonis, Astarte and El in Semitic legend are, v. 67

——Hippolytos, i. 104

——Nike, Plutarch identifies Nephthys with, xii. 392 58

—apples of, i. 59

—Arabian, said by Herodotus to be called 'Alilat and 'Alitta, v. 15

—Ares in an intrigue with, i. 190

—Astλik identified with, vii. 39

Aphrodite awarded apple for beauty, i. 125

—caused by Eris to quarrel with Hera and Athene at marriage of Peleus and Thetis, i. 124

——madness in horses of Glaukos, i. 39

—daughter of Zeus, i. 157, 197

—Eros son of, i. 203

—goddess of love, born from the contact of the severed flesh of Ouranos with the sea, i. 6

—Greek identification of Astarte with, v. 15

—Hephaistos husband of, i. 205

—hid Adonis in chest in care of Persephone, v. 335

—identified with Astλik and Astarte, vii. 27

——Sidonian Astarte, Syrian Kaukabhta, and Armenian Anahit, vii. 27, 39

—induced by Hera and Athene to make Medeia fall in love with Iason, i. 112

—Ishtar is, v. 335

—Kybele parallel cult-figure to, i. 275

—mother, i. pl. 1, frontispiece

—name Mylitta used by Assyrians for, v. 13

—never identified with planet Venus, v. 15

—Parakyptousa, v. 32

—rescues Paris, i. 127–128

—seizes Eos and Kephalos to guard her temple by night, i. 244

—sent desire into wild animals, v. 412 11

—suggests that Paris build a ship, i. 125

—survivals of, in modern Greek folk-belief, i. 313–314

—transformed Melanion and Atalante into lions, i. 59

—Venus converted into double of, i. 294

—Vulgaris, figurines of, v. 34

—Zariadres said to be son of, vi. 340

Apia, i. 28–29

Apil-Adad, Aramaean deity, v. 383 108

— -Addu-ba'di, Aramaic deity, v. 42

— -ili-shu, fatherhood of god emphasized in name, v. 12

Apis, Argive killed by Aitolos, i. 55

—attempt to identify Sobk with Osiris in, xii. 409 100

Apis, Buchis, sacred bull of Mont(u), pictured much like, xii. 163
—bull, xii. 160, 161
——identification of Osiris with, xii. 98, 385 [4]
—of Memphis, cult of, xii. 160, 162–163
—son of Phoroneus, after whom the Peloponnesos was called Apia, i. 28–29
Apito, name of Earth mother, xi. 25
Aplu retains traces of Apollo and Artemis in modern Romagnola, i. 318
Apollo, i. pl. VIII (2), opp. p. 8, pl. XI, opp. p. 24, 175–182, 300–301; vi. 314; vii. 63
—and Herakles, i. pl. XXIII (3), opp. p. 88, 90
——separated by lightning of Zeus, i. 160
——Hermes, eternal friendship of, i. 193
——Marsyas, i. pl. IV (2), opp. p. l
——Psamanthe (or Kalliope) parents of Linos, i. 253
—advised Alkmaion to carry out his father's request that he kill his mother, i. 54
—Aristaios often confused with, i. 251
—arrows of, wrought by Hephaistos, i. 207
—Asklepios heir and successor of, in healing, i. 279
—associated with Muses at Delphoi, i. 239
—attempts to take Marpessa from Idas at Messene, i. 27
—Belvedere, i. pl. XLI, opp. p. 176
—birth of, i. 174–175
—brought to Rome as god of healing, i. 300–301
—Bull of Marathon sacrificed on altar of, i. 102
—carried off the nymph Kyrene, i. 251
—Chryses priest of, i. 126
—Delphian, given booty by victorious Argives, i. 54
—disputes right of Herakles to the Keryneian doe, i. 81
—father of Ion, i. 71
—forced by Zeus to serve Admetos as punishment for slaying Kyklopes, i. 107
—guides arrow of Paris which slays Achilles, i. 131

Apollo in Caesar's account of Gaulish gods, iii. 9
—Ion placed in temple of, at Delphoi, i. 71
—killed Koronis, i. 280
—sons of Niobe, i. 44
——the Kyklopes and had to make expiation by becoming slave of Admetos, i. 280
——Linos, i. 253
—Maponos equated with, iii. 188
—old Slavic texts seem to identify Chors with, iii. 299
—on Mt. Kynthos, i. 175
—oracle at shrine of, at Delos, i. 304
——of, foretold victory to Argives if they secured Alkmaion as leader, i. 54
—original of Aplu and perhaps of Boschet in modern Romagnola, i. 318
—Phol explained as, ii. 137
—(possibly Belenos), in Celtic myth, iii. 10, 106
—received instruction from Glaukos in prophecy, i. 261
—Reshep identified with, v. 45, 46, 48
—revives wounded Hektor, i. 129
—sacrifice to, before launching of Argo, i. 109
—sends plague on Troy, i. 85
—son of Zeus, i. 157, 174
—slays Tityos, i. 175, 176
—Theseus pays vows to, i. 102
—Tiur identified with, vii. 31
—tricks Artemis into killing Orion, i. 250
—unwittingly kills Hyakinthos, i. 23–24
—urges Trojans to greater resistance against Greek army because of insolence of mortals, i. 128
—vengeance of, against Greeks for seizure of Chryseïs, i. 127
—wooed Hestia in vain, i. 209
Apollodoros's account of Great Flood, i. 19
Apollōnia, Greek name of Ereş-Reshep, v. 45
Apollophanes knew Babylonian legend of plant of immortality, v. 228
Aponibolinayen and Ini-init (the sun), tale of, ix. 221–224
—Ligi, and tree of Matawitawen, tale of, ix. 232–235
'Apop, iii. 34

'Apop, Aker confused with, xii. 43
—as devourer of dead, xii. 179
—bound in lower world, xii. 104 (fig. 100)
—chained by children of Horus, i. 105
—confused with Sêth, xii. 72, 107, 108–109
—destruction of, xii. 127–128
—etymology of name, xii. 390 38
—god with ass's ears in fight against, xii. 108
—Ḥapet's serpent head possibly connected with, xii. 387 23
—hymn concerning overthrowing of, xii. 68–69
—Neḥa-ḥo(r) confused with, xii. 141, 406 65
—serpent of Abyss, in Osirian cycle, xii. 104, 118
—soul of, in Bekh, xii. 219–220
—war of, with sun-god, xii. 79, 209, 364 11
Apotheosis of king, hymn on, xii. 202–204
Apotropaic virtues, bodies and heads of warriors have, iii. 104
Apoyan Tachu (All-covering Father-sky), x. 207
Äppäräs, souls, especially of children, which remain in world as ghosts, iv. 82
Apparition, ghostly, viii. 239
—of disembowelled man prophesying, xi. 197
Apparitions appear at noon in hot countries, vii. 196
Appearance, original meaning of shadow-soul, iv. 12
Appearances, four heavenly, related to four elements, viii. 142; see also OMENS (viii. 135)
Apple, iii. 324, 326
—attribute of Aphrodite, i. 203
—Cúroi's soul in, and apple in a salmon which appeared every seven years in a well, iii. 151
—following track of, iii. 143
—(magic), given to Connla by goddess, iii. 84
—sent to Rerir, ii. 249
— -tree sacred to Apollo, i. 180
Apples, golden, Herakles in search of, i. 114
——offered to Gerd, ii. 111

Apples, Irish stories of magic, may have influenced Idunn myth, ii. 180
—Isle of, iii. 193, 194
—magic, grow in Green Isle, iii. 123
—of Aphrodite, i. 59
——Hesperides, i. 87, 88, 260; iii. 131
——immortality, ii. 22, pl. VI, opp. p. 32, 178, 179, 180; see also IDUNN, GODDESS, ETC.
Appolonios fled to Ashdod, v. 83
Apsarases, heavenly nymphs, vi. 18, 59, pl. V, opp. p. 60, 82, 94–95, 106, pl. X, opp. p. 118, 133, 143, 149, 159, 185, 233; 325
Apsû as rope, v. 309, 312
—astral identification for, v. 310
—dragon, Ea destroyed, v. 293, 295, 297, 333
—nether sea of fresh water, v. 91, 92, 102, 104, 105, 106, 139, 140, 289, 292, 293, 303, 309–310, 320
—of Ea, Marduk created in, v. 157
Apsyrtos, Argonauts' murder of, punished by delayed home-coming, i. 113, 158
Āptya, Trita son of, vi. 265
Aquarius Asiatic counterpart of Nile-god, xii. 396 93
—fish-man of Assyria identified with constellation, v. 86, 96, 282, 395 21
Aqueducts, Peruvian, xi. 212, 213
Aquila and Serpens, close connexion between, v. 170–171
—Ninurta as Zamama identified with constellation, v. 119
Aquileia, temple of Belenos at, iii. 10
Ara (Er), Armenak great-grandfather of, vii. 66
—myth, Arlez in, vii. 90
—the Beautiful, vii. 68–70
Ara Maxima, ancient altar of Hercules, near the Forum Boarium, i. 302
——ceremonies to Hercules at the, model for succeeding centuries, i. 303
Arab element in Indonesia, ix. 153
—influence on African mythology, vii. 121, 353, 357, 430 12
Arabia, Aigyptos king of, i. 30
—Felix (mod. Yemen), inscriptions from, v. 3
—myths concerning Bês in, xii. 62
—religion of, remained outside the culture and theology of Sumer and Akkad, v. xvii

Arabia, South, may have been the
"India" of Pantaenus, vi. 175
——original home of Semitic peoples,
v. 3
Arabian Nights, influence of, in Africa,
vii. 352-353
—plain, primeval twins settled on, vi.
298
Arabic sect (Ssabeans) worshipped
Tammuz, v. 336
Arabo-Muhammadan civilization en-
tered eastern Finno-Ugrian stocks
through Tatars, iv. xviii
Araçani (Murad Chay?), Nhangs in
the, vii. 90
Arachosia, land of, vi. 66
Aradā, the "Furrow" Sītā replaced by,
vi. 97
Aradda, god, v. 206
Aradgin = Ardates = Lamech, Sume-
rian antediluvian king, v. 205
Aradus, marine deity on coins of, v. 83,
86
Aragads (now Alagez), mountain abode
of Armenak, vii. 66
Arai ("Curses"), abstract divinity of
social institution, i. 282
Arakho: see ALKHA.
Aralezes, dog-spirits, of Semiramis, vii.
68
Arall Mountain possibly connected with
Aralez, vii. 395 [58]
Arallû, descent of Ishtar to, v. 326-335
—Enkidu's vision of, v. 260
—lower world, v. 99, 114, 136, 140, 147,
148, 161-162, 209, 400 [160]
—poem on condition of souls in, v. 263-
264
—possible explanation of Aralez, vii.
395 [58]
—sun shines on, vii. 50, 69
Aram, exploits of, may belong to Armenak, vii. 66, 67
—vanquishes Ba'al Shamîn, vii. 37
Aramati ("Devotion"), abstract goddess, vi. 54
Aramazd, Anahit, and Mihr perhaps
once triad in Armenia, vii. 33
——Vahagn form triad in Armenia,
vii. 42
—Anahit daughter of, vii. 26
—as creator and sustainer, vii. 28
—creator of heaven and earth, vii. 17,
20-24, 56, 93

Aramazd, deity, and temple of, vii. 17,
18
—issues divine decrees, vii. 30
—Mihr son of, vii. 33
—Nane daughter of, vii. 38
—Tiur scribe of, vii. 29, 31
Arame, Aram identified with, vii. 67
Āraṇa, vi. 227
"Āraṇyakas," treatises attached to the
"Brāhmaṇas," vi. 12
Araṇyānī, goddess of the jungle, vi. 60
Ararat, Mt., Ark rested on, v. 232
—see MASSIS, ETC.
Araru, demon, vi. 98
Arātis, personifications of illiberality,
vi. 67, 98
Araucanians, tribe of southern Andean
region, xi. 324-331
Aravan, possible connexion of, with
Atharvan, vii. 385 [8]
Aravius, Mt., combat of Arthur and
Ritho on, iii. 185
Arawn, king of Annwfn, iii. 95, 96, 100
————and Pwyll exchange forms and
kingdoms for a year, iii. 56, 93-94,
121-122
Araxes, sacred cities built around, vii.
59
Arazu, artisan-god, v. 104
Arbela, temple of Ishtar in, v. 108
Arbuda, serpent, vi. 67, 155
Arbudi, spirit, vi. 98
Arch, stone, Heaven as a, iv. 342
Archaic period, xi. 347 [1]
Archaistic tendencies in Egyptian re-
ligion, xii. 235-236
Archer, beaver once an, iv. 504
— -hero, iv. 428, 429, 441, 443
—Sêth an, xii. 103
—sun-god as, adapted to Greek my-
thology, xii. 239
Archery contest, Herakles wins Iole in,
i. 89
——to win wife, viii. 295, 308
Architecture, suggested influence of
Persia in Pāṭaliputra, vi. 153
Archives of divine decrees, temples of
Tiur and Nabû as, vii. 31, 384 [48]
Archon, symbolic marriage of wife of
King, to Dionysos, i. 221
Arctic Ocean, land of dead lies hidden
somewhere in, iv. 77, 78
Arcturus addressed in astral hymn to
Marduk, v. 317

Arcturus, when arrow of, shoots down North Star heavens will fall, iv. 221
Ard, land, field, vii. 14
Ardar, "righteous," in Armenian, vii. 21
Ardat Lillî, demoness, v. 362
Ardates = Aradgin = Lamech, Greek transcription of Sumerian antediluvian king, v. 205
Ardokhsho, vi. pl. xxxiv, opp. p. 272
Ardvī Sūra Anāhita, a spring, vi. 278–281, 299, 307, 311, 332, 337, 339, 365 4
——Lake, regarded by Iranians as goddess of birth, iv. 358, 414
Aré, a shadow, creates men from sand, xi. 200
Areca-palm, legend of, xii. 355–357
Areia, spring of, guarded by dragon, i. 45
Areion, divinely born horse of Adrastos, i. 53
—Poseidon father of, i. 213
Areitos (see also DANCES [vol. xi.]), xi. 26, 33–36, pl. IV, opp. p. 34, 76–77
Arejaṭaspa (Pers. Arjāsp), Vīshtāspa defeated, vi. 340, 341, 342
Arenavak, sister of Yima, made captive, vi. 311
Areop-Enap ("Ancient Spider"), ix. 249, 252
Areop-It-Eonin ("Young Spider"), born from boil on tortoise, ix. 255
Areopagos, Ares associated with, i. 190
—Kephalos adjudged guilty at, i. 73
—meaning of name, i. 70, 103, 326 4
—Orestes tried and acquitted on, i. 135
Ares, i. pl. VIII (2), opp. p. 8, 14 (fig. 2), 103, 189–190
—amour of Aphrodite with, i. 197; vii. 39
—Ba'alti loved, v. 340
—father of Alkippe, i. 69
—Greek counterpart of Mars, i. 293
—Greeks identified Onuris with, xii. 143
—Hebe prepares bath for, after battle, i. 241
—isle of, where sea-birds dropped shafts upon Argonauts, i. 111
—Kadmos bound in servitude to, i. 45
—Lafitau regards Areskoui as American reminiscence of, x. 283 25
—possible Armenian reminiscence of myth of relations of, with Aphrodite, vii. 39

Ares, Procopius speaks of, as a Scandinavian deity, i.e. Odin or Tyr, ii. 17, 98
—said to be true father of Meleagros, i. 56
—son of Zeus, i. 156, 166
—third day of Harranian week sacred to, v. 154
Areskoui, spirit, x. 20, 283 25
Aresthanas, goatherd who found Asklepios on Mt. Titthion, i. 280
Arete ("Excellence"), abstract divinity of virtue, i. 282
Arethousa, Alpheios in love with, i. 257
—Euboian, copy of personage in Cretan mythology, i. 42
—head of, i. pl. LXI (1), opp. p. 294
Arezō-shamana slain by Keresāspa, vi. 324, 326
Arezūra, demon, vi. 293
Argalan-Zon (prince of animals), iv. 362
Argante, queen in Avalon, iii. 194
Argavar, chief of chagons, vii. 78
Argeïphontes ("Argos-slayer"), i. 29
—Hermes, i. 193–194
Arges (thunderbolt), born of Ouranos and Gaia, i. 6
Argestes, a wind, born of Eos, i. 247
Argive dead secured by Theban army, i. 54
—myth, national origins of, i. 28
Argives punished by Apollo with plague for death of Linos or Psamathe, i. 253
—victorious over Thebans, i. 54
Argo (constellation), chest containing dead Osiris or infant Horus found in, xii. 116
——ferryman of Underworld can be found in, xii. 394 64
——Osiris connected with, xii. 57, 94
Argo (ship), Atalante said to have joined the heroes in the voyage of, i. 58–59
——Athene assisted in building the, and steered it past the Symplegades, i. 171, 172
——dedicated to Poseidon at Isthmus of Corinth, i. 114, 212
——Herakles sails on, in search of Golden Fleece, i. 91
——piece of talking oak of Zeus built into prow of the, i. 162
——prophesies course to Argonauts, i. 113

Argo (ship), voyage of the, i. 106-116
——Zetes and Kalaïs sailed on, i. 73
Argolis, a Pelasgic centre, " sacred marriage " of Zeus and Hera celebrated at, i. 165
—geographical situation of, i. 28
Argonauts, i. pl. xxvii, opp. p. 106
—and Boreas punish Phineus, i. 74
—interpretation of adventures of, i. 116
—intrigues of gods in favour of, i. 112
—voyage of, i. 113, 262
—Zeus retarded homecoming of, i. 158
Argos (district), cults of Hera and Dionysos in primitive, i. 32
——Danaos and his daughters fled to, i. 30
——Dionysos comes to, i. 216
——divided from rest of Peloponnesos and ruled by a Heraklid family, i. 95
——fifty sons and daughters of Aigyptos and Danaos married in, i. 31
——Inachos River worshipped in, i. 257
——Io divine patroness of, i. 29
——Kassandra and Agamemnon slain on return to, i. 134
——myths of, i. 28-36
——not Mykenai, made scene of the " Agamemnon " by Aischylos, i. 327 ¹⁴
——Polyneikes went to, upon exile, i. 51
——springs and streams of, dried up by Argos, i. 30
—old dog of Odysseus, recognizes him, i. 139
Argos Panoptes (" All-Seeing "), monster having body covered with eyes and guardian of Io, i. pl. xii, opp. p. 28, 29
——nameless Egyptian cosmic deity covered with eyes like, xii. 223
——possibly an earth-born monster controlled by Hermes and guarding Underworld, i. 194
——slain by Hermes at direction of Zeus, i. 29, 193-194
—son of Phrixos, commanded to build fifty-oared ship, i. 109
Ar źori corresponds to " Half Man," iv. 182
Archer-goddess, xii. 56, 374 ⁶⁷
Arhats, those who have attained final sanctification, vi. 191, 192, 210, 224, 225
Ari (manly, brave), Armenian reminscence of " Arya," vii. 21

Ari, priests, xii. 271-272
Ariadne and Theseus at Naxos, i. 101-102
—daughter of Minos, i. 61
—double of Aphrodite, i. 198
—falls in love with Theseus and helps him out of the Labyrinth, i. 101
—liberated by Dionysos from bondage in Underworld, i. 220
—said to have led Amazons against Athens, i. 104
—wife of Dionysos, turned into stone, i. 36
—yields to spell of Aphrodite, i. 199
Arianrhod, Math's " foot-holder," iii. 96, 97, 98-99, 100, 106
Aricia of Latium, cult of Diana at, i. 294
Aries, v. 304, 308, 309, 310
—possible connexion of Amon with, xii. 402 ⁴
—station of Shamash-Sun, v. 304
Ari-hems-nofer: see ERI-ḤEMS-NOFER.
Arihi, expedition of, to slay monsters, ix. 64-65
Arisbe, wife of Priam, i. 118
Ariṣṭa attacked Kṛṣṇa in the dance, vi. 172
Aristaios, i. 251-252
—epithet of Zeus, reason for, i. 252
—son of Apollo and Artemis (Kyrene), i. 184
Aristakes: see RISTAXEZ, ETC.
Ariṣṭanemi occurs in connexion with sun-horse, and is a precursor of Ariṣṭanemi as one of the Tīrthakaras of the Jains, vi. 96, 224
Aristias perhaps knew Babylonian legend of plant of immortality, v. 228
Arjuna, one of five Pāṇḍavas, vi. 111, 116-118, 124, 131, 138, 142, 143, 152, 155
Ark, v. 37, 38, 204, 208, 218, 219, 223, 231, 232, 275, 386 ¹⁷⁵
—believed still to be on high mountain, iv. 366
—of covenant of Yāw, v. 82
Arkadia, appellation of Artemis connected with root of name, i. 183
—importance of cult of Pan in, i. 267
—myths of, i. 20-23
—named after Arkas, i. 22
Arkadians believed Pelasgos to be first man, i. 10

Arkas (eponymous ancestor of Arkadians), teachings of, in beginnings of civilization, i. 16
—placed in heavens near his mother Kallisto, i. 251
—son of Kallisto and Zeus, i. 21–22
Arkona, centre of worship of Svantovit, iii. 279–281
Arktinos of Miletos, author of "Ilioupersis" and "Aithiopis," i. 130, 131
Arktophylax ("guardian of the bear"), i. 251
Arlez (Aralez, Jaralez), spirits who restored life of those slain, vii. 90, 395 58
Armais, father of Shara, vii. 67
Ārmaiti, goddess of earth, vi. 306
Armat, anc. Arm. for Mother-earth, now "root," vii. 14, 35
Armavir, Armenian respect for old Urartian capital, vii. 12
—temple of Anahit at, vii. 28
——Tiur at, vii. 29
Arm-bands, widower's, ix. 136, 142
Arm-bone of swine-herd, new arm for Nuada made from, iii. 28
Armenak, eponymous hero of Armenia, vii. 14
—son of Hayk, vii. 66, 67
Armenia, Ark stranded on mountain in, v. 204, 232
—Minor, vii. 8
—Mithraic mysteries not recorded in, vii. 34
—political background of, vii. 7–9
—St. George, legend of, famous in, v. 338
—Tīr migrates from Iran to, vii. 32
Armenius, father of Er, probably Armenak, vii. 66
Arming of sons of knights, xi. 250
Armorica, Arthur stories brought to, iii. 195–196
Armorican coins, iii. pl. II (6), opp. p. 8, pl. III (4), opp. p. 14
Armpit, a forest-spirit made powerless by touch on, iv. 183
—of mummy, magic formulae in books under, xii. 175
—Skrzatek may be hatched from egg of peculiar shape carried under, iii. 245
Arms, celestial, receiving sun-god, xii. 100 (fig. 94)
—Cúchulainn assumed, iii. 142–143

Arms (rays) of sun, ix. 276
—stretching from sky or ocean, or from west, to sun, xii. 99, 387 23
Armies, Heavens as god of, iv. 394
Armour made for Achilles in forge of Hephaistos and brought by Thetis, i. 129
Armti-kh, "cereal," may throw light on aramati and armaiti, vii. 14
Army, Hadding taught wedge formation of, ii. 56
—headless, of Sayyid Sālār, vi. 248
—invisible, Norther Ruler head of, iv. 156
—phantasmal, iii. 31, 100, 155
—priestess among ancient Cimbri accompanied, ii. pl. XXXII, opp. p. 246
Arnarksuagsak, Arnakuagsak, goddess, x. 273 7
Arohi-rohi ("Mirage"), ix. 312 50
Arranger of the Ancestral Temple, viii. 47
Arrhephoria (or Hersephoria), ritual of, i. 325 3
Arrival (a contingency), omens for, viii. 135
Arrow, constellation of three-pronged, vi. 76
— -chain, ix. 139, 294, 302, 327 19; x. 295 42
— -heads, axes, and celts believed to be thunderstones or lightning-bolts, x. 288 32
—in fire-ritual, ii. 201
—invisible, causes disease in cattle, ii. 302
—leads suitor to maid, ix. 75, 161
—sacrifice, xi. 79, 115, 182, 356 18
— -sacrifice Torem receives arrows shot into sky, iv. 404
Arrows associated with Nabû and Tīr, vii. 33
—dipped in bile, vii. 393 27
—of Apollo, origin of, i. 181
—Artemis, i. 183
—poisoned, i. 81, 82; vii. 151, 258, 263, 415 7
Arruns Veltymnius receives Etruscan law of limitation from Begoë, i. 289
Arṣā (Arṣu) at Palmyra used for Venus as Evening Star, v. 24, 35, 384 117
Arsacid Dynasty established in Armenia, vii. 9

Arsacids, Khosrau (Chosroës) honoured sanctuaries of his ancestors, the, vii. 17, 18

Arsan-Duolai, Ruler of dead, iv. 486

Arsinoë, daughter of Phegeus, married Alkmaion and received robe and necklace of Harmonia, i. 54

—reputed mother of Asklepios, i. 279

Är-soghotoch, ancestor of Yakuts, iv. 353, 354

Ar-sori ("half-human"), evil forest-spirit, iv. 468

Arsūf, Arabic name of Ereş-Reshep, v. 45

Art and myth, i. lvi–lvii, lxi–lxii

—animal forms in Norse, ii. 216

—Aztec religious, xi. 50

—Buddhist religious, vi. 198, 201, 204, 206, 211

—Chimu and Chincha, xi. 226

—combat of Marduk and dragons in, v. 280–281

—Egyptian, gods in sacred, xii. 212

——relations of, to Egyptian religion, xii. 12–13

Art, Greek, Amphitrite in, i. 214

——Aphrodite in, i. 202–203

——Apollo in, i. 182

——Ares in, i. 190

——Artemis in, i. 186

——Asklepios in, i. 281

——Athene in, i. 172

——Demeter in, i. 232–233

——Dionysos in, i. 223

——Eos in, i. 246

——Eosphoros in, i. 247

——Eros in, i. 204

——Glaukos in, i. 261

——Hades in, i. 234–235

——Hekate in, i. 188

——Hephaistos in, i. 208

——Hera in, i. 168

——Hermes in, i. 195

——Hestia in, i. 209

——Iris in, i. 241

——Kore in, i. 232–233

——Nereus in, i. 260

——Okeanos in, i. 255

——Pan in, i. 268

——Poseidon in, i. 213

——Rhya-Kybele in, i. 276

——Sirens in, i. 263

——Triton in, i. 259–260

——Zeus in, i. 163

Art, holy mountain in Indian, Chinese, Japanese, iv. 344

—Navaho, x. 154, 155

—Peruvian, of coast and highland at some time met, xi. 215, 216

—Pueblo, x. 183

—religious, x. xxi, xxiii, 86–87

——conservatism in Egyptian, xii. 212–213

—Siberian, iv. 520–523

—skaldic, ii. 160, 173

—sun in, v. 60

—Yunka, xi. 221–222

Art, son of Conn, High King, iii. 72, 162

Artaios, Celtic god equated with Mercury in Gaul, iii. 186

Artavasd, son of Artaxias, a changeling, vii. 78, 80, 83, 95, 98

Arţā Vīrāf, soul of, at Cinvat Bridge, vi. 344–345

——visions of, may have been influenced by other religions, vi. 346–347

Artaxata, capital of Artaxias, vii. 8

—temple of Anahit at, vii. 28, 29

Artaxerxes Mnemon, inscriptions of, vii. 33

Artaxias and Hannibal expelled Seleucids from Armenia, vii. 8

—poem of, on Navasard, vii. 22

—Sathenik Albanian wife of, vii. 78

—sends in illness to sanctuary of Anahit, vii. 28

—suicide of servants on grave of, vii. 95, 99

Artemis, i. 21, 182–186, pl. VIII (3), opp. p. 8, pl. XI, opp. p. 24, pl. XXX, opp. p. 120; vi. pl. XXXIV, opp. p. 272

—aids Leto in giving birth to Apollo, i. 175

—Anahit in later times identified with, vii. 26, 381 2 (ch. iii)

—angered at Admetos, i. 107

—and Hermes, Eros son of, i. 203

—appears as Artemisia in modern Romagnola, i. 319

—arrows of, wrought by Hephaistos, i. 207

—assumes moral qualities of Selene, i. 244

—attended by nymphs, i. 258

—birth of, i. 174–175

—daughter of Zeus, i. 157

Artemis deceived by trick of Apollo, kills Orion, i. 250
—Diana identified with, i. 294
—discovered bathing in spring Parthenios by Aktaion, i. 46
—disputes Herakles's rights to the Keryneian doe which is sacred to her, i. 81
—has given some traits to Aplu of modern Romagnola, i. 318
—Hekate identified with, v. 369
—identical with Kallisto, i. 21
—Iphigeneia priestess of, i. 135
—killed daughters of Niobe, i. 44
—kills Aktaion, i. pl. LIII, opp. p. 248, 252
——Kallisto (in bear form), i. 21
—(Minos in a divergent account) gives Prokris hunting-spear and dog, i. 72
—mother-goddess of Doura identified with, v. 20
—Nana of Elam, identified with, vii. 385 [5] (ch. iv)
—Nemesis first used as epithet of, i. 284
—Orion joined, in Crete, i. 251
—Pekhet identified with, xii. 144, 150
—represented by Diana in Roman mythology, i. 288
——in human form by Atalante, i. 59
—sacred image of, to be carried away from land of Tauroi by Orestes at direction of oracle, i. 135
—saves Iphigeneia and she becomes priestess of Artemis, i. 126
—sends storms on Greek hosts because Agamemnon had killed sacred hind, i. 125
—sent boar to destroy herds and men of Aitolia, i. 56
—statue of, brought from west and seized by Romans, vii. 29
—survivals of, in modern Greek folkbelief, i. 313
—temple of, at Sparta, Helen dancing in, i. 25
—thought to wander with demons at midday in Galatia, iii. 12
—Ubastet identified with, xii. 150
—Virgin Mary possibly associated with Ephesian, iv. 257
—worshipped by Hippolytos, i. 104
Artemisia a vampire in modern Romagnola, i. 319
Artemision, mountain, i. 81

Arthur disinterred Bran's head, iii. 105
—in Avalon possibly referred to by Demetrius, iii. 15
——Brythonic myth, iii. 64, 103, 108, 111, 120, 139
——Heroic Tales, iii. 184–205
Arthurian cycle purely Brythonic, iii. 93, 205
—romance valuable for source of myths, iii. 19
Arthur's hunt, iii. 125
Articles on which runes written, ii. 296–297
Artificers, divine, vi. 27
—giants in wide sense, ii. 282
Artinis, sun-god, vii. 11
Artio, bear-goddess, iii. 124, 186, pl. XXIII, opp. p. 186
Artisan gods, pantheon of, v. 291
Artisans, Athene patroness of, i. 171
Ar-tojon, Heaven-god, father of Lonely Man, iv. 354
Artor ("ploughman"), Artorius, possible source of name Arthur, iii. 186
Arts and crafts, Minerva teaches, iii. 9
—Athene patroness of, i. 170, 171
—graphic, origin of, viii. 35
—Lug possessed of many, iii. 29, 31
—of civilization, xi. 2, 17
—one hundred, vi. 226
Aruṇa, vi. 117, 139
Arunawati Ruang, fabled to have had silvan dragon for mother, xii. 277
Arundhatī, vi. 140, 144, 146
A-rungu, vii. 260
Arurmaghas (or Arunmukhas) slain by Indra, vi. 88
Aruru as creator, v. 112, 113, 114, 115, 236, 312
—goddess of child-birth, v. 91, 110
—sister or wife of Enlil, v. 14, 110, 111, 380 [50]
—Sumerian mother-goddess, v. 12, 13, 15, 182, 236, 314
Arusyak ("little bride"), modern Armenian name for planet Venus, vii. 17, 39
Arvak, horse of Sun, ii. 196
Arya, ari ("manly, brave") Armenian reminiscence of, vii. 21
Āryā, first of Jain female converts, vi. 221
Āryadeva elevated to rank of Bodhisattva, vi. 210

Aryaman, Armenak may be Vedic, vii. 14, 66
—("comrade"), vi. 27, 28, 54, 85, 86, 138, 143
Aryan influence on Indo-China, xii. 288
—migration, Indra patron of, vi. 35
Aryans, Indra chief aid of, against Dāsas, vi. 34
Aryenis, first queen of Astyages, vii. 390 [18]
Āśā, the "Furrow" Sītā replaced by, vi. 97
Asa-Thor, ii. 92
Asaheim, land of Æsir, ii. 33
Asakku, plague, title of Ninurta, v. 120, 398 [98]
—primeval dragon, v. 142, 264, 265, 283, 291, 295, 320, 321
—("the robber"), one of the devils, v. 364, 369, 372
Asan-Sagan-Tengeri, thunder-god, iv. 442
Asaṅga, vi. 202, 210, 216
Aśani, vi. 82
Asar, title of Marduk, v. 155
Asarhaddon, v. 108, 147, 187, 358
Asari may be Egyptian Osiris, v. 344
Asarludug, title of Marduk, v. 310
Asarri (Asaru), title of Marduk, v. 155, 344
Asbet ("Flaming One"), goddess perhaps in serpent-shape, xii. 131, 402 [12]
—Sebit possibly identical with, xii. 147
Ásbru, bridge of Æsir; rainbow, ii. 329
Ascalon, v. 83, 84
Ascanius, son of Aeneas and Lavinia, founded Alba Longa, i. 306–307
Ascension Eve associated with annual rendering of divine decrees, vii. 30
——cave of Zympzymps can be entered on, vii. 34
——Virgin reveals divine decrees on, vii. 30
Ascension into Heaven of Carib first man, xi. 39
—of Alexander the Great, v. 173–174
——dying gods to Heaven, v. 178
——-tide procession, expelling spirits at, ii. 231
Ascent from subterranean world, x. 62, 203, 205
——under to upper-world, xi. 200
—of woman of primitive period to the upper-world, x. 112–113

Ascent through world-storeys, x. 160–164, 175, 177, 209
—towards heaven, viii. 262
Ascents to, or descents from Heaven or sky, iv. 311, 442, 477; v. 95, 96, 97, 168, 172–174; vii. 81, 106, 124, 130, 131, 132, 135, 136, 137, 138, 139–140, 192, 195, 266, 268, 311, 321, 322, 400 [39]–401; viii. 262; ix. 58, 59, 60, 66, 67, 139, 209, 215–216, 221, 255, 293, 294, 295; x. 48–49, 63, 94, 96, 104, 112–115, 161, 203, 221, 234, 255, 257, 294 [42]–295, 300 [49]; xi. 96, 120, 132, 140, 153, 271; see also TREE, HEAVEN; items s.v. LADDER.
Ascetic Master, viii. 276
Ascetics, Asceticism, vi. 77–78, 105, 113, 116, 117, 118, 120, 121, 134, 146, 147, 153, 164, 166, 177, 190, 196, 223, 224, 226, 232; viii. 14, 20, 23, 28, 54, 108
Asdis, Dis appears in female names such as, ii. 244
Asgard, seat of gods, ii. 6, 16, 23, 27, 34, 35, 54, 66, 81, 88, 89, 90, 103, 122, 130, 140, 141, 172, 173, 175, 179, 266, 282, 314, 327, 329, 384 [21]
—(Troy of Prologue to "Edda"; also Byzantium), ii. 33, 35
Ash Iggdrasil: see YGGDRASIL, ETC.
—trees, men of bronze sprang from, i. 17
—women, Danish forest-elves, ii. 205
—worshippers applied to Armenians and Persians, vii. 54
Ash ("Lord of the Libyans"), god in human form, xii. 131, 410 [1]
Asha, Avestan, equivalent to Vedic Ṛta, vi. 23, 24, 355 [4]
—(of the Avesta), iv. 392, 393
—(or Arta), Amesha Spenta, vi. 260, 261, 266, pl. XXXIV, opp. p. 272
Ashārah, v. 78
Ashbury, Berkshire, Long Barrow at, ii. pl. I, frontispiece
Ashdar, mother-goddess and Semitic divine name, v. 2
—variant form of Astarte, v. 14
Ashdod (Azotus), seat of Dagan, v. 82, 83
Ashēra, wooden pillar, symbol of deity, v. 9
Asheroth, Sydyk and Misor represented by, vii. 40

Ashes, after cremation, placed in cairn, iii. 233, 234
—all mountains once reduced to, vi. 159
—black and white, rubbed on newly created male, ix. 273
—brought by bride to new home, iv. 452
—comet in shape of heap of, vi. 223
—eating of, brought about debasement of Hkun Hsang L'rong, xii. 290
—from bonfire to promote fertility of fields, vii. 58
—heaped in fire-enclosure, vii. 57
—identification by smearing, x. xxii
—Kāma burned to, vi. 116
—magic qualities of, vi. 234
—Nechtan turned into, iii. 116
—oak-fire, as medicine, vii. 57
—of dead cast into Ganges, vi. 234, 250
——creation from, xi. 90
——ghost contain vitality, ii. 309
——Quetzalcoatl, birds arose from, xi. 68
——sacred fire not thrown away, but added to water become healing, vii. 56, 57
——three hearts of son of Morrígan with serpents through them cast into streams killing all creatures, iii. 132
——Titans, man born from, v. 275
——purification in, iv. 180
—sacrificial, prayer for good luck to finder of, iv. 280
—save woman from monster, vii. 221
—sick given, in Agn, vii. 57
—smearing of, x. xxii
—sold as treasure, vii. 354
—sons of Sagara transformed into, by Kapila, vi. 115–116
—strewing of, or washing hands in, as protection against the dead, iv. 23, 24
—strewn before hut as trap, iv. 389
—transferred from old to new sacred grove, iv. 146, 236
—use of, in obtaining new Voršud, iv. 122–123
—when soul leaves no trace in, it realizes death, iv. 478
Ashi, vi. pl. xxxiv, opp. p. 272
Ashim-Bêthêl, father-mother deity, v. 22, 44
——worshipped by Jews of Elephantine, v. 381 [58]

Ashima, Syrian deity, identified with Shîmti, v. 22, 384 [111]
Ashimur, title of Sin, v. 152
Ashiwanni, rain priesthood, x. 191, 200
Ashiwi, ancestors of Zuñi, x. 199, 210
Ashnan, grain-goddess, v. 191, 193, 313
Ashō-zushta, bird, vi. 290–291
Ashtar feminized to Ashtart in West Semitic, v. 14
Ashtar-Kemosh a father-mother deity, v. 47
——Astarte worshipped in temple of Kemosh, v. 13
Ashtar: see also ASTARTE.
Ashtaroth: see ASTARTE.
'Ashtart: see also ASTARTE.
— -'Anat, Yāw associated with, v. 44
—Yāw, on coins, v. 44
Ashteroth Qarnaim, Rephâim smitten by Chedorlaomer at, v. 355
Ashtishat, temples of Astλik, Anahit, and Vahagn at, vii. 28, 29, 39, 42
Ashtoreth, Babylonian earth-goddess known in West as, v. 13
'Ashtoreth, Hebrew deformation of name 'Ashtart, Astarte, v. 14, 384 [110]
Ashur-Adad, type of Ashur who exercises functions of rain- and omen-god Adad, v. 381 [58]
Ashur (Marduk) and winged creatures, combat between, v. 279, 281
—Marduk replaced by, v. 293, 322
—(originally Ashir) borrowed character from Enlil and Marduk, v. 160
—pursuing the mušhuššû, v. 131
—reference to a son of, v. 323
—sun-god of Assyria, v. 70–71, 148
—symbol of, same as Enlil, v. 150
Ashur, city, v. 88, 289
Ashurbanipal, v. 154, 157, 204, 324
Ashurnazirpal, v. 150, 358
Asi ("the Sword"), creation of, vi. 109
Asia and Europe, separation of, due to a flood, i. 19
—Æsir connected with, ii. 32
—Eastern, similarity of myths and traditions in, xii. 258–259
—(epithet of earth-goddess) said to be wife of Prometheus, i. 11
—Minor, evidence of Indo-Iranians among Hittites of, vii. 379 [2]
—Orion in mythology of, xii. 57

Asia, possible influence of, on Egyptian religion, xii. 365 [19]
—relatively slight influence of Egyptian religion on, xii. 241
—symbolism of seven-rayed star possibly from, xii. 53
Asianic element in ancient Armenian religion, vii. 5
—myth of Marsyas connected with that of Osiris, xii. 393 [62]
Asiatic analogies to stellar manifestations of Isis as Queen of Heaven, xii. 101
—astral myth reflected in Egypt, xii. 84
—contacts with Egypt in myths of Osiris and of Tammuz-Adonis, xii. 120, 399 [111]
—doublets of Osiris and Isis, Melqart and Astarte of Byblos as, xii. 114
—influence, possible, on Osiris-myth, xii. 395 [76]
—motif of Queen of Heaven surrounded by flames in Osiris-myth, xii. 395 [84]
—motifs in Egyptian mythology, xii. 153–157, 239, 410 [1-3], 411 [4 6 9-11]
——————Egyptian tales, xii. 398 [106], 399 [111]
—myth of combat between god of Heaven and dragon of ocean penetrates Egypt, xii. 104, 106, 109
—myths of Queen of Heaven influence belief in death of Osiris, xii. 119
—signs of the Zodiac, xii. 57
—versions of finding infant floating in a chest, xii. 396 [93]
Asiatics, possible effect of, on development of Egyptian civilization, xii. 361 [3]
—Sêth as god of, xii. 390 [35]
Asiatizing theory not found in earlier strata of Egyptian theology, xii. 73
Asiknī, healing powers of Maruts brought from river, vi. 39
Asios, quotation from a fragment of, regarding Pelasgos, i. 20
'Asît treated as separate divinity, xii. 156, 157 (fig. 164)
Asita and Simeon tales may be parallels, vi. 206
Ask and Embla (ash and elm), mankind came from, ii. 327
—Hœnir associated with creation of, ii. 151, 204

Ask, Loki gives heat to, ii. 148
Askefruer (Ash-women), Danish forest-elves, ii. 205
Asklepios, i. pl. x (2), opp. p. 20, 279–281
—god of medicine, Eshmun of Sidon identified with, v. 74, 77
—healing shrine of, i. 301
—is Greek equivalent of Eshmun, v. 67
—see IMUTHES, GREEKS EXPLAINED, ETC.
—slain by Kyklopes, i. 107
Askles, King, healed by Asklepios, i. 281
Askr Yggdrasils ("ash of Yggdrasil" or of "Odin's steed"), ii. 43; see also YGGDRASIL, ETC.
Askul (corrupt survival of Esagila), feast of wailing in temple, v. 337, 339
Ásmodi, divine fury, ii. 82, 85
Asmund and Asvitus, ii. 309
—dream of, ii. 255
"Asmundar-saga," ii. 255
Asnavand, fire established on Mt., vi. 306, 337
Aso, Ethiopian queen, xii. 114
Asopos asks aid of Sisyphos in finding his daughter Aigina, i. 37
—river-god, reputed father of Antiope, i. 43
—River worshipped in Phlious and Sikyon, i. 257
Asp, fiery, xii. 25, 29
—on head of sun-god, Renenutet identified with, xii. 378 [98]
—see UBASTET, CAT-GODDESS, ETC.; URAEUS.
—solar, "Justice" as daughter of the Sun connected with, xii. 100
—Sun's eye as, xii. 88
—symbol of fire, xii. 26, 29
Aspect, twofold, of Grail, and Celtic parallels, iii. 203
Asperging a penitent, xi. pl. XXI, opp. p. 144
Ass aided by the Dead against dragon, xii. 107 (fig. 106)
—animal of Sêth compared to, xii. 389 [33]
—braying sign that it has seen a Jinn, v. 352
—Horus in form of, xii. 119 (fig. 121)
—Iblis enters Ark in guise of, iv. 363
—Midas given ears of, i. 220
—origin of slander that Jews (and later

Christians) worshipped an, xii.
390 35
— -Pairika, ass-bull, vii. 91, 92
—sun-god's name Eay, Ay, interpreted
as meaning, xii. 108
—three-legged, vi. 270–271, 288
'Assah of Gaza, Athene and Hera said
to be offshoots of, i. 169
Assam, Indonesian affiliations with, ix.
304
—Mahāyāna carried to Burma and
Siam from, xii. 260
Assarakos, son of Tros, i. 117–118
Assessors, forty-two, at judgement of
dead, correspond to nomes in Egypt,
xii. 176, 179, 416 8
Ašširgi, son of Mah, v. 114
Assiut (Lykopolis), xii. 144
Association of snakes and eels in deluge-
myths, ix. 120
Assōros and Kissarē, primeval couple,
v. 292
Assuan, cataracts of, mythological
source of Nile between, xii. 46
Assumption, blessing of grapes at, vii.
381 5 (ch. ii)
—feast of, united with Navasard, vii.
382 11
Assyrian mythology and religion, ori-
gin of, v. xvi–xvii
—New Year's festival replica of Baby-
lonian with Ashur for Marduk, v. 322
Assyro-Babylonian culture in early con-
tact with Indo-Iranian, vi. 263–264
'Astar, South Arabian god, v. 11
Astarte [Astarte is Canaanite equivalent
of Ishtar (q.v.)], Allāt the North
Semitic, v. 19
—and Adonis, Gebal centre of West
Semitic cult of, v. 8
——El are Aphrodite and Adonis in
Semitic legend, v. 67
—Artemis identified with, i. 183
—as mother-goddess on Egyptian bas-
relief, v. 30
—(Ba'alat or Beltis of Gebal), El married, v. 67
—Canaanite goddess at Salem, v. 46
—city-goddess of Byblos, Asiatic doublet of Isis, xii. 114
—designated by Kaukabhta, vii. 39
—functions of, i. 196
—Ilāt of North Arabians identified
with, v. 381 61

Astarte in Egyptian mythology, xii.
155–156, 411 9 10
—late association of Ptaḥ with, xii.
407 79, 411 9
—made Isis nurse to her child, v. 71
—not identified with planet Venus in
Canaanite religion, v. 15
—of Tyre principal deity of Carthage,
v. 53
—or Beltis of Gebal identified with
Tychē, v. 68
—possible Armenian reminiscence of
myth of relations of, with Ba'al, vii.
39
—represents in West Semitic the Sumero-Babylonian mother-goddess, v.
15
—Sidonian goddess, identified with
Syrian Kaukabhta, Greek Aphrodite,
and Armenian Anahit, vii. 27, 39
—statue of, v. 76
—temple of, v. 83
—war-goddess, v. 385 141; xii. 40
—West Semitic earth-goddess and sister
of all Canaanite deities, v. 8, 13–14,
252
— -Qedesh, Resheph associated with, xii.
155
— -Venus-Virgo as heroine in " Story of
the Haunted Prince," xii. 153
As-tar-tu: see Astarte.
Aṣṭāvakra and Bandin, competition of,
vi. 138
Aster, wine made from, viii. 130, 131
Asteria and Perses, Hekate daughter of,
in Hesiod, i. 187
——Zeus, Hekate daughter of, in Mousaios, i. 187
—changed into a quail, i. 15
Asterios, step-father of Minos, i. 61
—Zeus abandoned Europe to, i. 60
Āstīka intervened to save life of Takṣaka, vi. 155
Astλik (Astarte-Aphrodite), vii. 36, 38–
39
—devotion of Sathenik to, vii. 40
—identified with Aphrodite, vii. 27
—temple of, vii. 17, 24, 56, 60
—won by Vahagn, vii. 37, 38
Astō-Vīdhōtu, destroying being, vi. 294
Astraios and Eos, parents of the Winds,
i. 265
—(" Starry Heaven "), son of Krios
and Eurybia, i. 247

Astral bodies of witches hold orgies, vii. 337
—deities, three, in most primitive form of Semitic religion, v. 6, 11
—hymns and characters, v. 317
—myth, Asiatic, reflected in Egypt, xii. 84
——in Egyptian representation of Qedesh, xii. 411 [11]
—mythology fails to explain Gilgamish myth, v. 267–268
—myths of Epic of Creation known in Babylonian iconography before Neo-Babylonian period, v. 309
—names of deities, v. 91
Astrologer, Nektanebos became an, at court of Philip at Pella, i. 223
Astrological motif in creation- and death-myths of Pawnee, x. 108, 116–117
—oracles and horoscopes, xii. 200
Astrology, viii. 42–43, 135, 141, 142–144
—Babylonian, iv. 438
——mechanically copied in Egypt only in Graeco-Roman period, xii. 411 [4]
—Ninurta in, v. 135
—period of origin of, v. 160
Astronoë, Phoenician goddess, mother of the gods, v. 74
Astronomical and astrological systems of Greece borrowed from Babylonia, v. 304–305
—cycle, xii. 56
—interpretation of legend of Hayk, vii. 65
—myths, Polynesian, ix. 87–88
—origin of combat of eagle and serpent, v. 170
Astronomy, viii. 144
—in Mexican calendar, xi. 96–105, 358 [10]
—minor importance of, in Egyptian religion, xii. 54, 55
—poem of, contains astrology, v. 304
—sacred Egyptian, contrasted with Babylonian, xii. 56–57, 411 [4]
Astvat-ereta, one of three Saoshyants, vi. 343
Asu, breath, vi. 85
Asunīti ("Spirit Life"), abstract goddess, vi. 54
Asura, term given to Varuṇa, vi. 22, 24
Asuras, vi. 38, 65, 66, 67, 68, 74, 77, 78–79, 80, 82, 84, 88, 90, 97, 106, 107, 108, 116, 132, 146, 149, 150–153, 156, 168, 203, 244, 245
Aṣû-šu-namir, birth of, v. 332, 333
Aśvaghoṣa sometimes worshipped, vi. 238
Aśvaka country, cult of "Dionysos" in, vi. 110
Aśvapati of the Madras, vi. 160
Aśvattha (Ficus religiosa), tree dwelling-place, vi. 89, 239
Asvid made runes for giants, ii. 55
"Āśvina Śastra" sung to Aśvins, vi. 87
Aśvinī, a name of Sūryā, vi. 55
Aśvins (twin celestial "Horsemen"), iii. 325; iv. 433; vi. 21, 28, 30, 31–32, 49, 53, 55, 61, 62, 63, 64, 65, 68, 80, 86, 87, 93, 141, 142, 233; 295, 313
Asvitus and Asmund, tale of, ii. 309
Astwad, word for God, vii. 14, 380 [7]
Astyages, grandfather of Cyrus the Great, vii. 70, 390 [16] [17] [18]
Astyanax, Hektor's farewell to, i. 128
—son of Hektor, thrown from walls of Troy by Odysseus, i. 133
Asuras, furious spirits, iv. 355–356; viii. 282
Asynjur specific name for goddesses, ii. 21, 112, 144, 174, 178, 180, 183, 186, 194, 197
Atā assimilated to Ishtar, v. 38
Ataentsic, woman-being cast down from heaven, x. 35, 37, 39, 291 [37], 294 [42], 295 [43] [44]
Atahocan, Montagnais Great Spirit called, x. 20, 271 [6], 283 [25]
Atahualpa and Huascar, conflict of, xi. 214
Atalante, Artemis identified with, and impersonated by, i. 184, 185
—characteristics of, show her to be Artemis in human form, i. 59
—yields to spell of Aphrodite, i. 199
At'am, thunder-god, iv. 228
Ataman, head of Princes of death, iv. 491
At'amjonks, rainbow, iv. 228
Atanua ("Dawn"), ix. 11, 26, 37
Ātar battles with Azhi Dahāka, vii. 45
—genius of fire, vi. 260, pl. XXXII, opp. p. 260, 266–267, pl. XXXIV, opp. p. 272, 328, 344, 345
—dragon fighter, vii. 363
Atar-bi'di, Aramaic deity, v. 42
Atargatis, Artemis identified with, i. 183

Atargatis, 'Atar-'ate, 'Athtar-'ate, as earth-goddess of Syria, v. 37
——Greek transcription of, v. 36
—cult of, in Syria, v. 37
—god of Palmyra, v. 56
—mother-goddess, v. 36, 37
—(name corrupted to Derketo), Syrian goddess at Ascalon, tale of, v. 84
—on coin of Caracalla, v. 38
—Syrian god of the Hieropolitans, v. 37
—Tychē of Palmyra is, v. 20
—variant form of Astarte (Ishtar), v. 34
Atarhasis and Ea, poem of, v. 222, 270–276
'Ate ('Ata, 'Atta), Aramaic goddess, v. 36, 386 174
Ate banished by Zeus from Olympos, i. 78
Atea (Vatea, Wakea) a heaven-god, ix. 11, 14, 26, 37, 313 65
Aten (" Disk "), Amen-ḥotep IV's name for sun-god, xii. 225
Atfiyeh, local cult of Ḥesat on site of modern, xii. 134
Athamas and Ino, Hera sent madness upon, i. 46
——reared Dionysos, i. 46
—insanity of, i. 166
—killed his son Learchos through mad delusion, i. 46
—son of Aiolos, i. 107
Athapascan pantheon, x. 77–79
" Atharvaveda," vi. 11, 12
Atharvan, fire-priest, vi. 63–64, 71
—Vedic sage, vii. 44, 385 8
Athene, i. 14 (fig. 2), pl. VIII (3), opp. p. 8, pl. XIX, opp. p. 66, pl. XXI, opp. p. 76, pl. XXII, opp. p. 82, pl. XXIII (3), opp. p. 88, pl. XXV, opp. p. 96, pl. XXVII, opp. p. 106
—Aias, son of Oileus, drags Kassandra from altar of, i. 133
—Alea, cult of, i. 22
—altar to, erected by Bellerophon, i. 40
—Anahit identified with, vii. 381 2 (ch. iii)
—and Hera induce Aphrodite to make Medeia fall in love with Iason, i. 112
——Hermes led Perseus to the Graiai, i. 33
——Zeus overthrow giants, i. 9

Athene angered by sacrilege of Aias, delays homecoming of Greeks, i. 133
—caused by Eris to quarrel with Hera and Aphrodite at marriage of Peleus and Thetis, i. 124
—cursed with torture any one who picked up her discarded flute, i. 181
—daughter of Zeus, i. 157
—directs Odysseus to visit Eumaios in guise of beggar, i. 138
—faint survival of, in modern Greece, i. 314
—gives bridle to Bellerophon, i. 40
——Herakles cymbals for use against man-eating birds, i. 84
—guides Argonauts through Symplegades, i. 111
—helped Asklepios secure blood from Medousa, i. 280–281
—helps Argos to fashion the Argo, i. 109
——Odysseus gain arms of Achilles, i. 132
—in guise of Mentor, visits Odysseus's son Telemachos, i. 138
—instructs Epeios to make wooden horse of Troy, i. 132
—invention of flute by, i. 34, 171, 181
—made Kadmos king of Thebes, i. 45
—Minerva identified with, i. 299
—Nane identified with, vii. 38
—overthrows Ares, i. 189
—Parthenos, i. pl. IX, opp. p. 14
—provokes quarrel between sons of Atreus, i. 134
—receives Medousa's head from Perseus, i. 35
—reputed mother of Erichthonios, i. 67
—requests Zeus to allow Odysseus to return home, i. 138
—Seimia and Ishtar identified with, v. 22, 23, 56
—Soteira, 'Anat identical with, v. 30
—statue of, erected on sacred hill by her son Erichthonios, i. 67
—supersedes Poseidon as divinity of Athenians, i. 66–67
—war-goddess, v. 381 63
—watches Herakles slay Lernean hydra, i. pl. XXII, opp. p. 82
Athenians adopt Theseus as national hero, i. 96
—believed Kekrops to be first man, i. 10, 66

Athenians, Tuatha Dé Danann quickened dead, iii. 347 [61]

Athens aids children of Herakles against Eurystheus, i. 95

—and Thebes, war between, i. 70

—Athene patroness of, i. 173

—cult of Dionysos reaches, i. 216

—Gaia known as "Nourisher of Youths" at, i. 272

—Horai honoured at, i. 238

—Medeia in, i. 115

—Orestes pursued to, by Furies of Klytaimnestra, i. 135

—return of Theseus to, i. 105

—shrine of Asklepios at, i. 281

—Theseus in, i. 99–100

—view of creation prevailing in, in fifth and fourth centuries B.C., i. 4

—worship of Athene in, i. 169

Athi, Burmese for Brahmā, forfeits his head in bet, xii. 323

Athletics, Hermes patron of, i. 195

Athlone, tops of three mountains of, sheared by Cúchulainn, iii. 136

Āthravans, fire-priests of Iran, vi. 44–45, 64

Athribis, Ḥar-merti adored at, xii. 388 [28]

—or Xoïs, Ḥar-khent(i)-khet(?) worshipped at, xii. 388 [28]

'Athtar as Morning Star early replaced in Asia by Venus as "Queen of Heaven," xii. 54

—El occurs with, v. 66

—South Arabian god equivalent to Babylonian Astarte, v. 14, 36

————name of Venus, v. 2, 4

Āthwya, priest of Haoma sacrifice, vi. 282

—second man to prepare soma, vi. 36, 48

—(Skt. Āptya), Thraētaona son of, vi. 265

Ati-auru, woman made by Tii at, ix. 25

Atira (mother), earth, x. 91, 92, 108

Atithi, fire as the guest in human abodes, vi. 284

Atl ("water"), day-sign, xi. 104

Atla, giantess, ii. 153

"Atlakvitha," ii. 8, 43, 156, 256, 315

"Atlamal," ii. 8, 233, 299, 311

Atlantides (Hesperides), seven, children of Atlas and Hesperis, i. 248

Atlas and Pleione (or Aithra) parents of Pleiades and Hyades, i. 248

—brother of Prometheus, i. 12

—child of Ouranos and Gaia (Ge), v. 66, 67, 80

—connexion of, with the legend of the apples of the Hesperides, i. 88

—Hesperos said in myth to be brother or son of, i. 247

—myth of Chibchachum parallel to, xi. 203

—represents sea-billow rather than mountain, i. 259

Atlatonan, goddess-wife of victim of sacrifice to Tezcatlipoca, xi. 64

Atli (Attila; Etzel), ii. 189, 190, 209, 233, 278, 317

Atmosphere, vi. 15–16, 29, 32, 74, 91, 94, 96

—affected by death of great soul, iii. 14–15

—Indra god of, xii. 255

Atnatu, self-created deity of heavens, threw first creation down to earth, ix. 274

Atonatiuh, first age, terminated by flood, xi. 91, 94

Atonement, iv. 18; v. 342, 343

—between Æsir and Vanir, Hœnir becomes, ii. 26

—boar at Yule festival, ii. 109

—human sacrifice for, x. 305

—in Sun dance, x. 90

Atossa, wife of Darius, vi. 341

Atotarho, magician and war-chief, x. 52, pl. XI, opp. p. 52, 302 [55]

Atraioman, Kalinago reincarnated in the fish, xi. 39

Atramhasis, form of Atarhasis, v. 274

Atreus, failure of, to sacrifice to golden lamb of Artemis, i. 184

—Helios shrunk from murder of house of, i. 243

—kills Thyestes's children and serves their cooked flesh to their father, i. 120

—pact of, with his brother, i. 120

—promise of a sacrifice to Artemis, i. 120

—receives throne back from Thyestes, i. 120

—son of Pelops and Hippodameia, i. 120

Atri, Atris, seer and family, vi. 64–65, 99, 108, 136, 144
—penance of, brings about Viṣṇu's avatar Dattātreya, vi. 170
—replaces eye of sun after eclipse, vi. 67
—rescued from burning pit, vi. 31
Atropos cutting thread of life parallel to Bau severing cord of life, v. 398 101
—(singer of the future), one of the Moirai, i. 284
Atrushans, Persian fire-temples, vii. 56
Atse Hastin and Atse Estsan, first man and woman, x. 158, 160, 168
Atsuta, shrine of, contains sword of Dragon, viii. 304
Attabeira (Atabei) one of five names of mother of supreme Being, xi. 24, 25, 28
Attalos of Pergamon gave permission to bring stone embodying Magna Mater from Phrygia to Rome, i. 304
Atthis, daughter of Kranaos, i. 67
—reputed mother of Erichthonios, i. 67
Attike, festivals of Dionysos in, i. 221
—invaded by sons of Pandion, i. 68
—Kekrops changed name of, from Akte to Kekropia, i. 66
—myths of, i. 66–74
—name of, memorial to Atthis, i. 67
—ownership of, contested by Athene and Poseidon, i. 172
Attis, birth of, from an almond-tree, vi. 295
—parentage of, and parallel cult-figure to Adonis, i. 275
Attributes, shaman-, iv. 511
Atum, Amen-Rêʿ identified with, xii. 221
—Apis connected with, xii. 163
—as father of king, xii. 202
—associated with ancient deity Ruruti(?), xii. 370 31
—bitten by monster, xii. 381 58
—creates first beings from plants (and?) his eye, xii. 379 16
—earlier solarized god of Heliopolis, xii. 363 3, 364 13
—earliest solarization of a local god in Lower Egypt, xii. 364 13
—Ḥar-khent(i)-merti(?) identified with, xii. 388 28
—identified with Osiris, xii. 424 6
—name of sun towards evening, xii. 27–28 and fig. 11, 83, 165

Atum of Heliopolis, xii. 164, 165 (figs. 171, 172)
—old local deity at On, xii. 31
—parallel to, in American Indian, x. 89
—-Rêʿ and Osiris as double occurrence of sun, xii. 50
—registers king's name on celestial tree, xii. 53 (fig. 51)
—Rêʿ called, xii. 81, 237
—son of Ptaḥ-Nuu and Ptaḥ-Nekhbet, xii. 220
—Thout(i) gives order to, xii. 73
—tolerated in worship by Amen-ḥotep IV, xii. 226
Atum(a), female form of Edom, xii. 157
A-tu-ud, A-tu-tu(r), goddess, v. 414 32
Auaris, in eastern Delta, built by Hyksos kings, xii. 390 35
Aubin Tonalamatl, day-hour lords follow the, xi. 54
Auca Runa, Age of Warriors, xi. 240
Aud, air, weather, wind, vii. 14
—(Authr) perhaps is Æther, ii. 201
—burial-place of, ii. 310, 311
—son of Night, ii. 200
Audbjorga, witch, ii. 302
Audhubla (Audhumla), cow and Ymir, giant, produced at same time, vi. 294
—cow which nourished Ymir, ii. 276, 324
—mythic cow, gave origin out of ice-block to Buri, ii. 63
Auexotl, chief of tribe, xi. 117
Auge and Herakles, intrigue of, cause of plague, i. 22
——her son cast adrift on sea, i. 22
—("Sunlight"), daughter of Aleos, i. 22
—variation of tale of, i. 22
Augeias, king of Elis, stables of, cleaned by Herakles, i. 82
—retaliation of Herakles against, i. 91–92
Augsburg (Ciesburc), Ziu's town, ii. 98
Augurs, nine ancient, viii. 136
Augury, i. 16; iv. 12; xi. 115
Augustines in Truxillo in 1619, xi. 223
Augustus dedicated temple to Apollo on the Palatine, i. 301
Aulis, Achilles and Patroklos join Greek host at, i. 122
—Agamemnon kills sacred hind of Artemis at, i. 125

"Aunt's Wine," farce, viii. 361–362

Aura (Yin), a mother or female principle, viii. 56

Auramazda, Anāhita, and Mithra form triad in ancient Persia, vii. 42; see AHURA MAZDA.

Aurgelmir: see YMIR, GIANT.

Aurṇavābha, strides of Viṣṇu interpreted by, vi. 29

Aurnir, giant, ii. 283

Aurora and Eos, Uṣas one in origin with, vi. 32

—(Eos, "Dawn"), Roman, i. 245–246

Aurora Borealis, iii. 319; iv. 287; x. 35, 249

——beliefs on, iv. 79, 81–82, 287

——home of those who die violent death, iv. 488

——Sky said to give birth to son during phenomenon of, iv. 398

Aurvandill, stars made from toe of, ii. 328

—the Valiant, ii. 82, 83

Aurvangr, dwarfs proceed from Svarin's mound to, ii. 265

Aurvaṭ-aspa, epithet of Apām Napāt, vi. 340

—(Pers. Luhrāsp) succeeds Haosravah (Kai Khusrau), vi. 338, 340

Aus, tribe, worshippers of Manât, v. 21

Aūsīndōm, Mt., vi. 278

Ausonia, Argonauts to be purified at, i. 113

Australia as part of Oceania, ix. xii

—physical and ethnological characteristics of, ix. 267–269

—relationship of Melanesian mythology to, ix. 149

Australian mythology, summary of, ix. 301–303

Austre (East), dwarf, ii. 264

Austro-Asiatics, Mōn probably an independent branch of, xii. 268

Aut, Prince of the river, iv. 403

Authority, dragon symbol of Imperial, viii. 102

Autochthones, iii. 9

Autolykos, gifts of thievery and falsehood conferred by Hermes on, i. 192

—grandfather of Odysseus, i. 123

—steals cattle of Eurytos, i. 89

Autonoë, daughter of Kadmos, wife of Aristaios, i. 45, 46–47, 252

Autumn, genius of: see TATSUTA-HIME.

Autun, Diana regarded as midday demon in, iii. 12

Aut-(y?)êb, god of joy, xii. 67

Auuenau, ghoulish spirit, ix. pl. XXIII, opp. p. 284

Auxo ("Growth"), one of the Horai, i. 238

Avadānas, stories of causes of Buddha's attainment, viii. 217

Avagddu, ill-favoured son of Tegid the Bald, Gwion obtained inspiration intended for, iii. 109, 110, 166

Avallo (Avalloc), derivation of Avalon from, iii. 194, 195

Avalokiteśvara, Kuan-yin said to correspond to, xii. 262

—one of the Buddhas, vi. 201, pl. XXVII, opp. p. 202, 205, 208, 212, 213, 217

Avalon appears (in "Vita Merlini"), as "Isle of Apples", iii. 193

—Arthur mortally wounded and carried to, iii. 185

—bird-woman conveyed to, iii. 193

—departure of Arthur for, iii. 193, 194

—Elysium of Brythonic Celts, iii. 85, 122

—identified with Glastonbury, iii. 194–195

—sword of Arthur made in Isle of, iii. 185, 197

Avasarpiṇī, descending era, vi. 221, 225

Avatar play, xii. pl. XVIII, opp. p. 346

Avatars of Viṣṇu, vi. 121–122, 168–170, 241

Avenger, heaven-god as, iv. 395–396

—of the gods, Vidarr is, ii. 159

Aventine Hill, cult of Diana on, i. 294

Aventinus, child of Hercules, i. 303

Avernus, waters of Lake, retained in their basin by Hercules, i. 303

Avesta as source for knowledge of Iranian religion, vi. 259

—recited in language of birds, vi. 290

Avezuha sought to harm Virgin Mary, v. 363

Avīci, Hell, vi. 201

Avilix, god of Balam-Agab, xi. 166, 167

Awa, island, viii. 378 [13]

Awahokshu, dwelling-place of Tirawaatius, x. 276 [11]

Awam Samoyeds, one group of Samoyeds, iv. xvii

Awaré, pity, sympathy, viii. 296, 297

Awenhai, goddess Ataentsic, x. 295 [43]
Awig, ix. 224
Awitelin Tsita, Earth mother, x. 207
Awl, magic, ii. 267
Awonawilona, He-She, x. 187, 206, 207
Axayacatl, a predecessor of Montezuma, xi. 111
Axe, covenant of the, iii. 148, 149
—Double, Orion called, i. 249
—in dream, here employed for Enkidu, v. 242
—loan of, refused, unless secret name of animal known, vii. 321–322
—lord with the, iv. 442–443
—magic, used to cut boy in half to make two boys, x. 133
—of Tuirbe Trágmar beyond which he bade sea not to come, iii. 133
—on which heavens rested, xi. 86
—sacrificial, iv. 268, 273, 274
—see KEREMET, SPIRITS, SACRIFICE TO; METAL, ARTICLES OF, ETC.
—thunder-god's, vii. 237
—with trident-like handle, xi. 369 [16]
Axenthove, well at, ii. 163
Axolotl, Xolotl became an, xi. 83
Ay: see EAY, ETC.
Ayar Auca and Mama Huaco, pair who came through window Capac, xi. 248, 249, 250, 251
—Cachi and Mama Ipacura, pair who came through window Capac, xi. 249, 251
—Manco and Mama Ocllo, pair who came out of window Capac, xi. 244
—Uchu and Mama Raua, pair who came through window Capac, xi. 249, 250
Ayaviri refused to submit to Incas, xi. 244
Ayllu of Copara, Indians of the, still worship Choque Suso, xi. 231–232

Ayo, spirit helper of Aponibolinayen, ix. 234
Ayodhyā, capital of Daśaratha, vi. 127
Āyu, king of frogs, vi. 147
Azag-Bau, Semiramis legend has reminiscence of, vii. 367, 368
Azat (Yazata?), Mt. Ararat, vii. 62, 77, 389 [6]
Azâzel (Iblîs), leader of Jinns and primitive satyr of flocks, v. 352, 356, 357
Aždahak Byrasp, tale of, vii. 98
—of Media, vii. 70–71, 390 [16]
Azé and Nasé, story of, viii. 253, 380 [6] [7] (ch. ii)
Azelekel, Lake: see CHERLAK, STORY OF LAKE.
Azer-ava: see NISHKE-AVA ("GREAT BIRTH-GIVING MOTHER").
Azhi parallels serpent dragon Mušḫuššû, v. 130
—serpent, v. 357; vi. 279, 288, 295, 350
—Dahāka bound to rock parallel of bonds of Loki, ii. 147, 150
——(Dahhāk), demon, vi. 265–266, 267, 273, 305, 309, pl. XXXIX, opp. p. 310, 311–312, 315, 320–328, 331, 343, 350–351; vii. 45, 77, 79, 391 [13]
Azizā, hunter's god or forest-demon, vii. 242
Azizos ('Azizu), Morning Star, companion of sun, v. 35, 36
Azmaz, chief Iberian deity corresponding to Armenian Aramazd, vii. 382 [22]
Aztecs, xi. 42, 43, 44, 46, 47–123, 352 [2]
Aztlan, fabled first home of Aztecs, xi. 112, 116
Azuma dance, viii. 261
"Azure Dragon," Chinese, symbolizes Spring and wood, viii. 243

B

Ba'al (Akk. Bêl), became specific name for deity in Semitic, v. 65, 158
—Hamman, male deity of Carthage, v. 53
—identified with Sêth, xii. 155
—Lebanon, title of god of rain, thunder, and lightning, v. 39
— -malâk, v. 58

Ba'al Melqart, Minos explained as human representative of, i. 63
—of Gebal, El special name of, v. 67, 68
— -peor, Pripégala compared with Priapus and, iii. 289, 353 [25]
—possible Armenian reminiscence of myth of relations of, with Astarte, vii. 39

Ba'al (probably Adonis of Gebal), tomb of, v. 52
—pronunciation of, was Bôl, v. 58
Ba'al Shamîn, Balshamene, deity of Aramaeans and Phoenicians, v. 63, 64–65
——Greek translation of, on altar is Zeus megistos keraunios, v. 63
——Palmyrene inscription renders, by Helios, v. 64
——-rûm ("high lord of the heavens"), v. 390 265
——sun-god, vii. 17, 36, 37, 43, 67
Ba'alat, feminine counterpart of Ba'al, xii. 156
—of Gebal-Byblos identified with Hathôr, xii. 154
—or Beltis of Gebal, Astarte the, v. 67
Ba'albek, temple of sun at, v. 54
Ba'alt Zapuna, goddess, xii. 156
Ba'alti (title of Ishtar), Tamōzā loved, v. 339, 340
—translation of Belti "my lady," v. 340–341
Baba, Rê' gives light in island of, xii. 84
Babbar, Sumerian sun-god, v. 4, 60, 89, 148
Babel, tower of: see TOWER OF BABEL.
Babi (Babai, Bebi, Bibi[?]), god of Upper Egypt, xii. 131, 132, 403 18
—Bati confused with, xii. 132
Baboon as god of wisdom, xii. 33–34
—hearts of dead weighed by Thout(i) and his cynocephalous, xii. 176
—of Thout(i) as healer of sun-god's eye, xii. 90
——leads dead to place of punishment, xii. 180
——origin of, xii. 85
—one of four sons of Horus or Osiris has form of, xii. 112
—probably represented Thout(i), xii. 164
—sent on errands by wizards, vii. 336
—totem, vii. 272, 273, 275
Baboons, xii. 32 (figs. 12–14), 33 (fig. 17)
—are witches' familiars, vii. 429 18
—four, interchange with four sons of Osiris-Horus, xii. 417 20
——of Thout(i), xii. 365 27
—help guard captive 'Apop, xii. 105
—of sun dance and play before solar gods, xii. 377 86

Baboons salute and guide returning sun's eye, xii. 86
Babylon becomes first of cities, v. 307
—capital before Flood, v. 88, 150, 207
—constellation of, is Canal Star, v. 308
—influence of, on Marduk-Bêl, v. 155, 278
—Marduk city-god of, vii. 384 51
—prophecy of annihilation of, v. 141, 143, 144, 145
—seized from Marduk by Irra, v. 143
—Ssabean cult at, v. 336
Babylonia, Anāhita imported from, vii. 25
—astronomy of, contrasted with Egyptian, xii. 56–57
—destruction of, by Irra, v. 138, 141, 222
—influence of, on Northern and Western Semitic races, v. 7
—Nana goddess in, vii. 38
—original animistic basis of religion of, xii. 362 4
—triads in, vii. 11; xii. 362 5
Babylonian and Egyptian religions, relationship of, xii. 411 4
—art, lost stellar divinity has exact analogies in, xii. 64
—doctrines of communal responsibility and original sin, v. 223
—influence in South Arabia, v. 5
—Ishtar-myth parallel to explanation of Nile flood in summer, xii. 384 116
—light-god's spear influences sun-god's harpoon in Egyptian art, xii. 397 101
—mythology and religion, origin of, v. xvi–xvii
——basis of Harranian cult, v. 155
—origin of Nimrod, v. 55
—religion vs. Arabian, v. 15, 354
Babylonians, Egyptian religion less edifying than, and not to be compared with, religion of, xii. 245
Bacab, four, deities of the Quarters, xi. 137, 143, 144, 154
—second person of the trinity, xi. 143
Bacchanalia, Phrygian and Thracian, at winter solstice, vii. 13
Bacchantes, spirits of wild conceived as feminine, i. 269–270
Bacchus (Dionysos): see SATYRS ASSOCIATED, ETC.
—Min Kyawzwa has resemblance to Dionysos or, xii. 353

Bachelor married after his decease, iii. 234

Bach-ho (White Tiger), spirit of the West, xii. 307

— -ma Temple at Hanoi, connected with Trung sisters' shrine, xii. 316–318

Bachue, goddess of agriculture, xi. 204, 225

—(Turachogue), woman who emerged from Lake Iguaque, xi. 199

Back, ghosts who turn, vii. 180

—why new moon has bent, ix. 278

Backdoor, holy, iv. 84, 85, 87, 88, 94, 102, 113

Backwards, ferryman of lower world whose face is, xii. 58

—sacrifice, iv. 73, 152, 245

—spirit wanders, iv. 468

—walking, i. 192

Bad fetish caused death of hunter, vii. 344–345

Badabangisa and giant, tale of, ix. 236–237

Bādāmi, Jain sculptures at, vi. 226

Badb, Irish war-goddess, ii. 255, 342; iii. 24, 25, 39, 40, 70, 134, 155

Badba (Furies), in battle of Mag-Tured, iii. 25

Badda (Pāli bhadda, "good"), name of this world, xii. 291

Badger, uncanny power of, viii. 325, pl. xxxviii, opp. p. 326, 327, 329–330, 384 8

Badnjak, bŭdnik, Christmas log, ceremonies attending, iii. 308–310

Badon, Mt., battle at, iii. 184

Badtibira, city before Flood, v. 206, 207

Baduhenna, war-goddess, grove of, ii. 17, 203, 255

Bældæg (Balder), royal families of Bernicia and Wessex traced descent to, ii. 19

Ba'eru, Sobk's home, xii. 409 99

Baetyl (stone), of El at Jerusalem, v. 388 223

———Elagabal at Emesa, v. 54

———sacred, v. 9, 16, 24, 54

Bagajun River, reputed abode of cannibal witches, vii. 141, 203

Bagaron, town of gods, vii. 387 5

Bagavan, Navasard celebrated in, vii. 22

—Persianized fire-altar at, vii. 56, 61

—temple or altar of Aramazd at, vii. 24

Bagavan ("town of gods"), burial-place of priests, vii. 19, 61, 387 5

Bagayarij, chief temple of Mihr at, vii. 34

—town of gods, vii. 387 5

Bāgh Deo, tiger-god, vi. 242

Baghauts, ghosts of men slain by tigers, vi. 248

Bagin, altar; plural of, means temple, vii. 18

Bag-Mashtu (Bag-Mazda), Khaldi became identified with, vii. 12

Bagos Papaios, Phrygian sky-god, vii. 12

Ba'ḥ in Lower Egypt, Neḥem(t)-'auit and Thout(i) perhaps associated at, xii. 141

Bharata, Agni god of, vi. 44

Ba'ḥet, Abundance may be feminine as, xii. 378 102

Bāhīkas, Rudra called Bhava among, vi. 81

Bahrām fire, vi. 284

Bahrein (Dilmun), location of, v. 194

B(a)i, meaning of word, xii. 413 13

Baidrama, twined divinity, strength-giver, xi. 25

Baile's Wave, seaburst, iii. 89

Baine, síd, iii. 91

Baiti, trace of, as Osiris, xii. 403 18

Baitocaice, v. 35

Bai-Ylgön, heaven-god, iv. 341, 342, 349, 405, 406

Baiyuhibi caused his sons to rain for three days, ix. 179

Bajanai, Bai-Bajanai, forest-spirit, iv. 466

Bakchos, name Iakchos etymologically akin to, i. 220

Bake, ogress, and princess, tale of, ix. 227–229

Baked things, goddess of, xii. 66

Bakhalal, city, xi. 128

Bakht, "fortune," vii. 384 46

Bakhtagan, son of over-god, iv. 402

Baking (of bread) first taught by Arkas, i. 16

Bakororó, singing of, xi. 290–291

Baku, seven fire-springs of, vii. 56

Bâl (Bêl-Marduk), Jupiter, fifth day of Harranian calendar sacred to, v. 154

Bala, child of Parikṣit, vi. 147

Bala, Lake, iii. 109

Baladevas, class of Jain divine beings, vi. 225

Balagan Itshitä, Master of Yakut dwelling-place, iv. 466

Balāha, winged horse, vi. 202, 208, 209

Balam-Agab and Balam-Quitzé, two of four brothers created from maize, xi. 165, 166, 177

Balance of Osiris, xii. 100

Balarāma, avatar of Viṣṇu, vi. 169, 170, 171, 174, 225

—sacred being of Jains, vi. 225

Balavant, serpent, vi. 216

Balder (Beldeg, Bildr), god, ii. 9, 15, 17, 18, 19, 21, 22, 32, pl. VI, opp. p. 32, 33, 43, 45, 49, 62, 65, 66, 79, 103, 120, 127–138, 143, 146, 161, 164, 165, 166, 174–175, 243, 249, 265, 277, 278, 303, 304, 337–338, 345; iii. 55

—saga, solutions of, ii. 135–136, 137

—summer god, xii. 255

" Baldersbraa," an herb or plant, ii. 129, 138

Baldersbrönd, traces of spring opened by Balder found at, ii. 134

Baldershog in Norway, temple at, ii. 138

Balderslee, place connected with Balder, ii. 134

" Baldrs Draumar," ii. 7, 9, 43, 127, 128, 129, 133, 134, 164, 304, 311, 341

Balefires, Celtic, x. 196

Bali, Viṣṇu deprives, of sovereignty of the three worlds, vi. 122, 153

Balichù, devil, xi. 333

Balih, son of Etana, v. 167

Balioe, Dyak deity, ix. 176

Balios and Xanthos, immortal horses, i. 213

Balkash Sea, vi. 177

Balkh, city of Bactria, scene of Firdausī's epic shifts towards, vi. 340

Ball-carrier, an Indian Jack-the-giant-killer, x. 48

— -court at Chichen Itza, xi. 127

—game, x. 48, 137, 288 33

——symbolic of movements of stars and sun's course, xi. 68, 82; see also TLACHTLI, ETC.

—magic, x. 48

—man originally like, ix. 29

—soul conceived to be like a, viii. 237

—stone, Perkúnas's, iii. 319

Ballads, Irish and Scots Ossianic, iii. 212

Balls, featherdown, as cloud-symbols, xi. 60

—of fire, weapons shot, iii. 175

Balls, wooden, reference of Delphic oracle to, i. 328 4 (ch. iii)

Balmalagê, Phoenician god, v. 58

Balmarcod, god, temple of, v. 22, 383 106

Balmung, sword, ii. 268, 272

Balongahoya, one of Warrior Brothers, x. 205

Baloo, moon, and dogs, tale of, ix. 285

Balor, grandson of Nét, Fomorian war-god, iii. 25, 27, 32, 33, 46, 99, 172

Balsnes, place-name connected with Balder, ii. 134

Balthî (Bêlit), in Ssabean sect, v. 154

Baltic peoples and mythology, iii. 317–330

Baltîn, goddess who loved Tammuz, v. 341

Balungwana sometimes descend in thunder storm, vii. 127

Balustrade, dragon, xii. 272

Balyks, son of Nama, iv. 364

" Bamboo Books ": see " CHU SHU."

—brought to China by Huang Ti, viii. 21

— -hewer, tale of, viii. 262–263

—intermediary, xi. 298

—(or tree), mankind came from, ix. 168, 169; see also TREES, MANKIND CREATED FROM.

—slips in divination, vii. 138–139

—yarns tied to, offering to Weaver-maid, viii. 236

Bambyce said to have been founded by Sisythus, v. 36, 37, 38, 229

Bāṇa, Śiva intervenes and saves life of King, vi. 174–175

Banana-plant (bashō), in Japanese literature, viii. 300, 382 9, 385 4

— -tree, first, vii. 154

——Irimu took root as, vii. 256, 415 32

Banawasi, a clever trickster, vii. 122, 292, 353

Banba, queen, iii. 42, 43, 44

Band, great, of the holy house, v. 109

—leather, invisible, binding shaman and reindeer, iv. 506; see also COSTUMES, SHAMAN.

" Bandamanna-saga," ii. 286

Bandicoot, owner of fire, ix. 281

Bandin, son of Varuṇa, vi. 138

Banian-root grew on arrow-chain to sky, ix. 139

Banquets in honour of dead, iii. 233, 234, 235, 236
—to gods, xii. 195
Bantoid languages, vii. 110, 398 [4]
Bantu migration, intermarriage with Bushmen in earlier stages of, vii. 113
Banyā (Banjārā), tribe, vi. 242, 244
Baobab, sacred tree, vii. pl. ix, opp. p. 124
Baoisgne, clanna, iii. 160, 161
Baptism, xi. 74, 142
—at communal hearth, vii. 55
—in Fosite's spring, ii. 163
—Oceanic, ix. 52, 83
—of child with name of ancestor, iv. 15
——Finno-Ugric people, iv. xix-xx
——Merlin, iii. 201
——pagans, iii. 207, 208
——Vladimir in 988, destruction of Perun on, iii. 293-294
—renunciation of pagan gods at, ii. 18, 38, 68
—rituals of the house of, v. 106
Baptismal formula, setting free of unbaptized souls of children by the, iii. 253, 254
Baptized, tradition says Oisin, iii. 183
Bar-Adad, Barat-Adad, v. 384 [108]
—'Atā, Bath-'Atā, fatherhood of god emphasized in, v. 12
—Bahlul, Syriac lexicographer, on Tamōzā, v. 339
—Rakib, fatherhood of god emphasized in name, v. 12
—Rakkab, Aramaean king, v. 44
Baraguldu, Tagtug in, v. 198
Barasi-loeloe, creator-god, ix. 176
Barbatus, Hercules, on Rhenish inscriptions, ii. 69
Barber of gods, xii. 132
——Ninurta, v. 125, 398 [108]
Barbmo-akka, tutelary genius of migratory birds, iv. 176
Bard, messenger of Mongan to síd, iii. 119
Bardad, Adad of Padda had special name, v. 39
"Bardar-saga," ii. 20
Bardesanes, androgynous form of Śiva known to, vi. 357 [6]
Bardsey, Isle of, Treasures of Britain taken to, iii. 201
Barǝsman, possible origin of use of, vii. 386 [18]

Barǝsman, twigs held in hand of Iranian during the sacrifice, vi. 300
Barhis, sacrificial grass, vi. 61
Baris, mountain, vii. 389 [2] (ch. ix)
Bark, swine, fowl, and dogs grew from, ix. 176
Barley mother, name of Demeter explained as, i. 225
—see PEKKO (PELLON-), ETC.
Barrenness, milk of one-coloured cows to remove, iii. 26
Barri, secret wood, ii. 112
Barrow, Balder's, ii. 134
—Frey's, ii. 114
—Long, ii. pl. i, frontispiece
—Thorgrim's, ii. 119
— -wight, ii. 308, 309, 312
Barrows, ii. pl. xxxviii, opp. p. 306, pl. xxxix, opp. p. 310, 306-312, pl. xli, opp. p. 320
Barsai responsible for rain, vii. 411 [43]
Barsham, Aram conqueror of, vii. 67
Barshamina: see items s.v. BA'AL SHAMÎN.
Bartholomew: see PARTHOLAN.
Bashō, fairy of the banana-plant, viii. 343-345; see also BANANA-PLANT, ETC.
Basil, church of St., on old site of Perun's statue, iii. 294
Basil, holy, in myth, vi. 239
Basilinna, and Dionysos, cult of, v. 19
Basin rimmed with carbuncles in which fairy washed, iii. 120
Basket having property of magic carpet, vii. 358
—let down to earth by sky-cannibal to haul up human food, ix. 62
—of Gwyddneu, iii. 192
—Romulus and Remus set adrift by their father on the Tiber in a, i. 307
Basketry, x. 183, 214, 238
Baskets, bones of dead put in, xi. 27
Bašmu, viper (of Chaos), v. 127, 282
Bassak, conquered Chams centre around, xii. 287
Bast(et): see UBASTET.
—Ubastet not to be read, xii. 409 [109]
Bastvar avenged his father, vi. 340
Bāsuk Nāg, Vāsuki survives as, vi. 241
Basukund (anc. Kuṇḍagrāma), place of descent of Mahāvīra, vi. 222
Basutos, how witchcraft introduced among, vii. 338-340

Bat as soul in Votiak and Vogul belief, iv. 7–8, 11
—created of three races, vi. 291
—(fu), why symbol for happiness, viii. 104
Bat (god), double face of, xii. 368 16
——female deity of Diospolis Parva, xii. 40
——Naville identifies Bati with, xii. 403 17 18
——similarity of symbols for, with those of Ḥat-ḥôr, xii. 40–41, 368 16
Batara Guru (Skt. Bhaṭṭara Guru), highest deity in creation-myth, ix. 161–163, 173
Bath for purification, xi. 308
— -house man, Votiak god, iv. 162–163, 164–165, 167
— -houses occupied by water-spirits before Christmas, iv. 196
—of blood, iii. 150
——broth for Fraoch, iii. 130
—ritual, vi. 323; x. 58, 197
—sacrificial, vi. 85
—steam, giving Dziadys a, iii. 237
—sweat: see SWEAT-BATH.
—taken by sun at end of daily journey, vii. 50
Bathe, Soma directed to, vi. 137
Bathing, iv. 24, 48, 50, 62, 64–65, 129, 154, 265–266; vii. 202; see also PURIFICATION.
—as magical ablution, i. 185
—before festival, iii. 236
—ceremonial, i. pl. LXII, opp. p. 300
—facilities for Domovoy, iii. 241
—first man and woman destroyed in, xi. 85
—for purpose of fertility, i. 257
—forbidden in newly created lake, xi. 272
—in Ganges, vi. 234
——living waters of Tane, ix. 88
——sap of yucca for strength, xi. 25
—of Caer and Oengus, iii. 79
——Cormac, iii. 118
——new-born, xi. 73
—protection against water-spirits required while, iv. 206
—purificatory, vii. 60
—restores Half-Child, ix. 216
Bati, early god, worshipped later only in Saka, xii. 131–132, 393 60
—identified with Osiris, xii. 399 111

Baton, driver of Amphiaraos's chariot, i. pl. XVII, opp. p. 54
Bats, xi. 174, 177, 364 6
Battak, Sumatra, possible Indian influence among, ix. 243
Battle, Asuras are reborn personalities of those killed in, viii. 282
—future home of those killed in, iv. 80–82
— -gods (sig-tivar, val-tivar), ii. 21
—help of gods in, ii. 24
—hymning of first of all brave men on eve of, ii. 69
—of Ventry: see CATH FINNTRÁGA.
—precursors of, ii. 43, 250
— -slain shared by Odin and Freyja, ii. 120
—spells chanted before, iii. 30
—weaving fate of, ii. 254–255
Battles, Wood-maidens took part invisibly in, ii. 132
Bau (Gula), wife of Ninurta, in epic, v. 110, 115, 120–121
—severs cord of life parallel to Atropos who cuts threads of life, v. 398 101
—Sumerian earth-goddess, sister or daughter of Enlil, v. 14
—Sumero-Babylonian mother-goddess, v. 15, 22, 115
Bau-ama-mu, Sumerian name of Earth mother, v. 12
Baudihillie, one of the Alaisiagae, ii. 358 7
Baugi and Odin, tale of, ii. 53–54
Bawrī (Babylon), vi. 311
Baxbakualanuchsiwae, Cannibal-spirit, x. 248
Bay of Souls, at Raz, iii. 17
Bayazid (anc. Bagravand), old Armenian relief of altar found at, vii. 18, pl. II, opp. p. 18
Beach-Field-Master, viii. 248–249
Beacon lights kindled by Yu Wang, viii. 166–167
Beads as money, ix. 141
—at ends of rainbow, vii. 234
Bean, calendar and lucky, viii. 33, 35, 43
— -planting, x. 195
Beans, peas, etc.; see EGRES, CREATOR, ETC.
Bear, Bears:
Bear as component of names, viii. 210
—as Fylgja of Gunnar, ii. 234
——guardian, x. 5

Bear, Atalante nursed by, i. 56
—causes moon to wane by eating its disk, iv. 424
—chief of Underworld Manitos, x. 48, 302 [52]
—connected with north wind, x. 23
—constellation, vi. 102
— -Doe story, x. 233
— -feast, Lapp, iv. 3, 86–99
—frequently underground genius, x. 293 [40]
— -god, Nemcatacoa the, xi. 204
—Great: see URSA MAJOR.
—grizzly and Raven feed on eyes of Cannibal's victims, x. 246
—holiest of animals, secret names of, iv. 83, 85
—idol whose face resembled the snout of a, xi. 47
—Kallisto in form of, falls before bow of Artemis, i. 184
——turned into, by Hera, i. 16, 21
—Master, iv. 469
—of Heaven, iv. pl. XXVII, opp. p. 224
——guards place of sunrise, x. 254
—on Gaulish coins and statuettes, iii. pl. II (10), opp. p. 8, pl. XXIII, opp. p. 186
—or boar enemy of young nature-god in Phoenicia, xii. 397 [101]
—polar, worshipped by Lapps, iv. 94–95
— -race, legendary invaders, viii. 210
—remnants of totemism seen in ritual eating of Artemis under form of a, i. 183
— -skins used by Lapps and Northern Ostiaks for wrapping of dead, iv. 19
—slain Kallisto placed among constellations as, i. 21
—who carried off water, tale of, ix. 297–298
—Woman lives again in forms of several animals made from parts of her body as she is cut up, x. 164
— -worship of the Voguls, iv. pl. VI, opp. p. 84
Bears, ii. 234, 266, 293
—enemies recognized and persecuted by, after their death, iv. 85
—Leib-olmai protector of, iv. 175, pl. XXVII, opp. p. 224
Beard-Bragi, any long-bearded man called, from kennings for Bragi, ii. 160

Beard, false, Cúchulainn bidden to smear a, iii. 153, 158
—Guzu Tenno planted forests on Kii from hairs from his, viii. 228
—of Dillus Varvawc, leash made from, iii. 199
——Donar, ii. 69
——Odin, ii. 43, 161
——Thor, ii. 75, 80
——Thorkill, ii. 95
——Velos, plaiting of, at harvest time, iii. 300
——Ychdryt Varyvdraws, iii. 190
—perhaps symbol of descending rain, xi. 68
—refused by Arthur to giant, iii. 185
Bearer, Votiak god, iv. 172
Beas (Vipāś), river, vi. 48, 146
Beast marriage, ii. 258
Beasts and birds formed in opposition to other creatures, vi. 291–292
—bound, to be released before end of world, iv. 426
—called Mulungu's people, vii. 134
—held accountable for killing of men, v. 232–233
—language of, acquired by eating portion of animal, iii. 166
—world catastrophe by wild, v. 222
" Beating out " of homes on death, iv. 23
Beauty, Ḥat-ḥôr deity of, xii. 40
—idealized type of: see ONO-NO-KOMACHI.
— -spot of Diarmaid uí Duibhne, iii. 163
Bebhionn woman from Maiden's Land seeks protection of Fionn, iii. 117
Bébind, sister of Boann, iii. 130
Bebon, possible allusion to, in myth of why the moon rules night, xii. 383 [95]
Bebrykians, Argo reaches land of the, i. 110
Béchuille, witch, sent against sons of Carman, iii. 35, 39
Bécuma, goddess, iii. 72, 81, 202
Bé Find (White Women), goddesses survive as, iii. 133
Bed, Beds:
Bed, captives fitted to brigand's, i. 99
—symbol of Meskhenet, xii. 372 [52]
—the couple's, place where Dagda and Morrígan met, iii. 30

Beds of Diarmaid and Grainne, sepulchral monuments in Ireland known as, iii. 178–179

Bêd-El, Aramaic deity, v. 42

Bedd Gelert legend in India, vi. 242

Bede, altar dedicated to, ii. pl. XII, opp. p. 98

Bedr: see MEDR.

Bedwyr (Bedivere), personage in Arthurian cycle, iii. 188, 189, 191, 192, 198, 199, 200

Bee, vii. 275
—and Yogo, tale of, viii. 323
—as soul-animal, iv. 473
—golden, stone representing Viṣṇu's form as the, vi. 240
— -hives, prayer for luck for, iv. 188, 275
—prophetic powers of, ii. 253
— -spirit, iv. 169
—totem, vii. 275, 280
—Viṣṇu as, vi. 240
— -woman, tale of, ix. 218–220

Beech-tree, iii. 246

Beef-eating, impurity from, viii. 232–233

Beer: see MENQET, GODDESS.
—[used in nearly all FEASTS, FESTIVALS, etc., wh. see and also SACRIFICIAL VICTIMS, esp. vol. iv.] family-, ceremony of, performed every autumn, iv. 174

Beetle-creator, xi. 322, 323, 324
—primeval creature, vii. 144

Beetles, Ostiaks believe that dead dwindle to little, iv. 9, 73
—used as omens by Lan-yein, xii. 284

" Begets himself," meaning of, in relation to sun-god, xii. 38, 50, 220

Beggar body characteristic of Li T'iehkuai, viii. 120–121
—with magic bag, Pwyll appeared as, iii. 94

Beggars, Erinyes defenders of rights of, i. 277

Beginning, myths of the, i. 3–19; see also entries s.v. ORIGINS.

Begoë, Etruscan divinity, survives as Bergoia in modern Romagnola, i. 317
—nymph who revealed Etruscan sacred law of limitation to Arruns Veltymnius, i. 289

" Beguiling of Gylfi," ii. 5–6

Behbeit, modern name of Per-ḥebet, xii. 99

Beḥdet, goddess of Edfu, xii. 132

Beḥdeti identified with Horus, xii. 21

Being, definition of, x. 17

Beings, intervention of divine, at Zoroaster's birth, vi. 342
—screaming, who answered Cúchulainn's cry, iii. 134
—supernatural, viii. 108–132
—wild, iii. 266

Beisan (mod. Ta'annek), letter in cuneiform script found at, v. 44

Béist: see PÉIST, ETC.

Bekh: see BUCHIS, NAME OF, ETC.
—soul of 'Apop in, xii. 219–220

Bekhu, Sobk's home, xii. 409 [99]

Bekotshidi, deity, x. 157

Bêl and Beltis (Marduk and Zarpanit), prayers of priests to, v. 316, 317, 318–319
— -Dragon, v. 160–161, 286
—ascent of, from lower world, v. 324
—death and resurrection of, v. 322, 324–325
—designs of monsters of Chaos in temple of, v. 290
— -Dragon conflict known among Babylonians, v. 278
—Enlil never known as, by Babylonians, v. 102
—may have provided Greek Christian title Kyrios Christos, v. 341
— -Merodach, light of sun, xii. 254
—(Nimrod), Hayk led his people from tyranny of, vii. 64–65
—of Babylonian and Assyrian religion, Marduk is, v. 56–58, 156, 157
—poem to, recited by priest, v. 315
—see BA'AL, ETC.; MALAK-BÊL, ETC.
—tomb of, v. 323–325
—used for Marduk of Babylon, v. 65
— -Marduk, death and resurrection of, v. 322–325, 382 [77]
—festival of, v. 156
—Semitic god of heaven and light, xii. 104
—tomb of, at Babylon, v. 52
—šamê, v. 391 [310]

Belā, temple of, at Belaun, vi. 244

Bèlbôgh, divine name Phol connected with Slavic, ii. 137

Beldeg (Balder), son of Odin, ii. 32

Belemnite, small meteorite, iii. 319

Belemnites as fingers, iv. 198
—perhaps supposed to be testicles of Sêth, xii. 390 [87]

Belenus, Celtic god, having temple at Aquileia, iii. 10
—divine name Phol connected with Celtic, ii. 137
—perhaps identical with Beli or Belinus, iii. 93, 106, 135
Beli, Frey slays, ii. 110
—or Belinus, Belenus may correspond to, iii. 93, 101, 106
Belial chief enemy of God, v. 373
Bêlikbi, v. 187
Belili, title of Ishtar, v. 334
Bêlit-ilāni (Queen of the gods), Babylonian name of Aruru, v. 14, 17
Bêlit-ilî, mother-goddess, v. 41, 182
——Queen of gods, v. 109
Bêlit-ni (Our Lady), Zarbanit addressed as, v. 341
Bêlit-sêri, scribe of lower world, v. 259
Bella Marta, survival of Mater Matuta in modern Romagnola, i. 319
Bellerophon, Artemis slays daughter of, i. 183
—letter motif in Africa, vii. 356, 357
—receives bit and bridle to guide Pegasos, i. 172
—son of Glaukos and Eurymede, i. 39–40
Bellona, Bohemians worshipped deity similar to, iii. 301
—gloss of Wælcyrge, ii. 253
Bells, vii. 223, 426 20; viii. 36; 242, 315, 331
Belos, grandson of Epaphos, father of Danaos and Aigyptos, i. 30
Bêlos (Marduk) born, v. 293
Below, the, x. 185, 188, 287 31; xi. 51, 52, 53
Belt, magic, ii. 133
—metal wire, on drums, iv. 288
—ungirding of, ensures free passage in birth, death, etc., iv. 27, 253, 292; see also GIRDLE AT SACRIFICE; STRAW, BELT OF, ETC.
—wampum, x. pl. x, opp. p. 44
—with writing on dropped by swans, ii. 261
Beltane (May-day), iii. 26
Bêlti (my Lady), title of Ishtar, in address, v. 341
Beltiri, fermented liquor, xi. 264
Beltis, v. 316, 317, 318, 323, 324, 340
—Kilili is, v. 34

Beltis of Erech or Ishtar in Marduk legend, v. 323, 332
——Gebal, v. 68
Bêlun, field-spirit, iii. 269
Bêlup(?)ri, comrade of Nergal, v. 163
Ben (Befnet), a scorpion of Isis, xii. 210, 211
Ben Gulban, Diarmaid's combat with wild boar of, iii. 177
Benares, Dakṣa erected statue of liṅga at, vi. 179
—footsteps of Rāmānand revered at, vi. 240
—stratagem of king of, to end drought, viii. 276–277
Bendis, Artemis identified with, i. 183
—of Thrace, resemblance of Hekate to, i. 186
Benik, horse of Sun, vii. 51
Benin, vii. 165
Benkei, soldier monk, tale of, viii. 307, 310–312
Bennu ("plague"), v. 163
Benten (the Hindu Sarasvatī), tutelary deity of music and public speaking, viii. 268–271, 279–280, 331
Beorn, Land-vættir follow, ii. 230
"Beowulf," ii. 124, 209, 238, 255, 280, 282
Bêr, title of Adad, v. 387 187
Berār, totems in, vi. 240
Berde-Gabat, apparition of Maidere, iv. 385
Berejya, Camrōsh sent by the spirit, to save Iranians, vi. 289
Berezisavanh fire, vi. 285
Bergbui, mountain-giant, ii. 230, 276, 279
Bergelmir and his household saved from flood of blood, ii. 324
—son of Thrudgelmir, ii. 275, 276
Bergoia represents Etruscan Begoë in modern Romagnola, i. 317
Bernal Diaz del Castillo, narration of, xi. 46–49
Berne ("Bear-City"), traces of ancient Celtic bear cult in, iii. pl. xxiii, opp. p. 186
Bernicia, royal families of, traced descent to Bældæg (Balder), ii. 19
Berosus, v. 103, 106, 290
—source for Akkadian mythology, v. 203–204, 207, 307
Bêrouth, wife of Elioun, v. 66

Berries, certain, confer immortality, iii. 54-55
Bersa, Mair wife of, iii. 168
Berserker-rage, ii. 58
Berserkers, ii. 91, 136, 292
Bês and prototypes later symbolize most universal and primitive powers of nature, xii. 63, 64
—as guardian of young sun, xii. 64
——warrior, xii. 62, pl. II (2), opp. p. 116
—associated with Khepri-Sokari, xii. 377 90
—companion of Uêret-Êpet, xii. 62
—confused with Sêth, xii. 376 82
—corresponds to constellation Ophiuchos (Serpentarius) in stellar mythology, xii. 61
—description of, xii. 61, 62
—drinking, xii. 61, 62 (fig. 65)
—feather crown worn by, perhaps analogous to dress of red and brown African tribes on Red Sea, xii. 62
—female, xii. 63 and figs. 66, 67
—functions of, xii. 61-62
—in relation to destruction of serpents, xii. 63, 64
—influenced type of Silenos, xii. 63
— -like gods dance and play before solar gods, xii. 377 86
—localized at Bu-gem (or Bu-gemet) in Nubia, xii. 62
—nameless cosmic god partly in form of, xii. 222, 223
—not East African or Arabian deity, xii. 412 14
—old types of, xii. 61 (fig. 63)
—on amulets, xii. 61
——magic wands, xii. 63
—placed among stars at early period, xii. 61
—possibly a foreign god?, xii. 62
—protective functions of, xii. 62
—relatively late worship of, xii. 63
—serpent-strangling dwarf (or giant), description of, xii. 61
—Sopd(u) later pictured like a winged, xii. 149
—tail of (as stellar?), xii. 376 81
—with flowers, xii. 62 (fig. 64)
Bešomar, iii. 289
Bestla, Odin's mother, ii. 51, 63, 324
Bêt-Ninurta or Bêt-Anuššat, city name, v. 45, 133

Betel, ix. 207, 210, 212, 217, 221, 222, 223
— -vine, legend of, xii. 355-357
Betelgeux, star, hunter in first book of Gilgamish epic wrongly identified with, v. 267-268
Beth-'Anath, Beth-'Anôth, 'Anathôth, v. 30, 399 135
Beth-Lahama, v. 399 135
Beth-Ninurta, city, v. 133
Beth-Shan, temple of Astarte at, v. 30-32, 46
Bêthêl, shrine of El, v. 35
—sun-god, v. 44
Betting freedom away, x. 163
Betulos, child of Uranos and Gê, v. 66, 80
Beyggvir, Frey's servant, iv. 246
Beyla, wife of Bygvir, ii. 110, 144
Bhadrā stolen by Varuṇa while bathing, vi. 137
Bhadrakālī, form of Umā, vi. 179, 246
Bhaga, god, vi. 27, 28, 32, 53, 85, 86, 114, 138, 142, 143
Bhagīratha and Śiva, tale of, vi. 115-116
Bhairava, form of Śiva, god Bhairon being metamorphosed into, vi. 237
Bhairon (Bhaironnâth, Bhairoba [or Kāla Bhairava]), village deity, vi. 237, pl. XXXI, opp. p. 238
Bhaiṣajyaguru, a Buddha (master of healing), called, vi. 211
Bhangāsvana, androgynous nature of, vi. 147
Bhānu, daughter of Sūrya married to, vi. 138
Bharadvāja, sage, vi. 120, 144
Bharata, epic hero, vi. 97, 127, 128, 164
—part of Jain cosmography, vi. 221, 225
Bhāratī, sacrificial goddess, vi. 49
Bhārhut, sculptures at, vi. 198
Bhāruṇḍas, birds who carry away the dead, vi. 144
Bhaumeyikas (or Bhavanavāsins), class of Jain divinities, vi. 227
Bhava, Rudra called by Bāhīkas, vi. 81, 82
Bhavānī, wife of Śiva, Vajravarāhī as form of, vi. 219
Bhīma, epic hero, vi. 125, 155, 156, 237
Bhīmasen apparently a borrowing from Bhīma, vi. 237

Bhīṣma, sage and warrior of the Epic, vi. 142, 237

Bhogavatī, city of serpent king, vi. 154

Bhomkas can restrain tigers from appearing, vi. 242

Bhṛgu connected by some with Brig = Phrygians, vii. 385 8

——son of Brahmā and sage of the gods, vi. 118, 136, 145, 163

————Varuṇa, vi. 100

Bhṛgus, race of man and priestly family, vi. 63–64, 71, 87

Bhṛkuṭī, aspect of Tārā, vi. 217

Bhūḥ, Bhuvaḥ, Svar, earth, atmosphere, and sky, vi. 74

Bhujyu, son of Tugra, saved by Aśvins, vi. 31

Bhūkhī Mātā, personification of famine, vi. 238

Bhūmiya, shrine of earth-deity, vi. pl. xxx, opp. p. 234, 237

Bhūtas, class of Jain divinities, vi. 227

Bhūts, ghosts of dead, vi. 247, 248, 249

Bias wedded to one of the daughters of Proitos, i. 32

Bibbu (Mercury), offering to, in wailing of Gilgamish, v. 261

Bich-can, altar of, xii. 321

Bi'di employed with Aramaic deities, v. 42

Biflindi (Odin), ii. 58

Bifrost, rainbow-bridge, ii. 23, 153, 156, 278, 329, 339, 341, 343

Big-Fist the Siren, sons of, iii. 148

——-headed dwarfs, vii. 266

—Knife (Nitsikuts), one of old men of the Skidi, x. 305

Bihār, cult of "Dionysos" extended to, vi. 110

Bil follows moon in sky, ii. 16, 183–184

Bildr, a magician, ii. 136

Bile, Mile son of, iii. 10, 43, 46, 106

Bílé Paní (White Women), iii. 270–271

Bi'li-Rakkabi, name of sun-god found in proper name, v. 44

Billing, Odin and the daughter of, ii. 10, 48, 49

Bilskirnir, hall of Thor, ii. 77, 329

Bilu, ogre, xii. pl. VII (3), opp. p. 272

Bīnāk, healing fruit used by Ahura Mazda against Angra Mainyu, vi. 286

Binama, horn-bill, tale of, ix. 145–146

Binaye Ahani, limbless twins, x. 163

Bi-n-dêd(u): see RAM, SACRED, OF CITY OF MENDES, ETC.

Binding by Indra and Varuṇa, vi. 23

—or loosing fetters on prisoners of war, charm for, ii. 18

—with words, ii. 47

Bi-neb-dêd(u), sacred ram of Mendes, xii. 164

Biologist, modern evolutionary, supplies broad explanation of origin of myth, i. xliv

Bir-atar, fatherhood of god emphasized in name, v. 12

Bīr Badr, deity of boatmen, vi. 235

Birch-bark as old Lapp wrapping for dead, iv. 19

— -tree, iv. 231, 266, 267; 340, 349, 350, 364, 404, 450

Bird, air takes on form of, x. 206

—announces dawn, ix. 275

—as bait, ix. 44

——counsellor, ix. 73

——mark on sacrificial bread, iv. 267

——portent of death, iv. 10, 11

—Badb or Morrígan as black, iii. 70

—bamboos in which primeval pair were, pecked open by, ix. 169

—becomes second wife of chief, vii. 139

—black, changed into gem on altar, viii. 38

—blue, man-eating, x. 71

—brought seed of fire to trees, ix. 254

—came with message to man, vii. 169, 170

—(Che Mlanda), story, vii. 286

—child-soul comes in shape of, iv. 398

—combat, xi. 274

—convulsions called the, vii. 127

—divine form (for sun), vi. 19, 26

— -dress, iii. 79

—eclipse due to, xi. 319

—emitting sparks, Skrzatek as, iii. 245

—(erin-), mythical, "poisonous tooth" refers to, v. 129

—featherless sky-, birth of first man from, ix. 169

—fertilized tree which produced mankind, ix. 168

—fire of Heaven brought to earth by a, vi. 263, 264, 266

—flew from grave of Yamato, viii. 304

——to Isle of Women, ix. 140

— -footprints writing, viii. 31

Bird-form, deities of Eddas could assume, ii. 259, 261
—giant Thjazi as, ii. pl. VI, opp. p. 32
—given crest to show it was messenger, vii. 169
—half-, vii. 244
—hatched from sea-eagle's egg, ix. 141–142
— -headed god, primitive name of, xii. 21
—Imdugud or Zû the storm-bird, v. 117
—Imgig, always called a god, v. 117
—Karshiptar spread religion, vi. 290, 309
—kuala-spirit in form of, iv. 127
— -like deity from Etowah Mound, x. 71
— -made clothing of Shun, viii. 35
—magic, vi. 289–290, 331
— -man, v. 174
—metamorphosis of Yamato into, viii. 304–305
—Moshanyana after death became a, vii. 222
—of storm who stole tablets of fate, v. 40
——sun, eagle is, v. 119
—primeval deity in form of, ix. 250
—red, born from fire, viii. 43
——Chinese guardian of south symbolized as, viii. 243
—saivo-, iv. 285
—sent to boars, iii. 188, 189
— -serpent symbols in Maya art, xi. 134–135
— -spirit, x. 246
—supernatural, of god Ler killed by Caoilte, iii. 174
—swan often prophetic, ii. 262
— -symbolism: see SYMBOLISM (vol. x).
—tells girl Death's name, vii. 178
—that laid egg of world, ii. 363 [4]
——made milk, vii. 421 [20]
—three-headed, which wasted Erin, iii. 126
—transformed into man, came as lover of Mess Buachalla, iii. 75
— -type of shaman dress, iv. pl. LX, opp. p. 508, pl. LXI, opp. p. 512, 513, 515; see also COSTUMES, SHAMAN.
—who swallowed man, ix. 68
— -woman, x. 133; xi. 240
—woos Old Woman of the Sea, x. 5–6

Bird-zada, iv. 458
Birds, vi. 41, 62, 65, 87, 88, 144, 149, 242
—and animals as emblems, v. 115, 116–117
——sacrifice to, x. 305
——bull on monument, iii. 9
——Maui go to Hine-nui-te-po, ix. 52–53
—as avengers stories, vii. 210–212
——creators, ix. 174, 175
——forest-spirits, ix. 61
——intermediaries, x. xvii, 22, 92, 293 [40], 306 [60]
——messengers, ii. 65; vi. 290, 309, 312, 313; vii. 169, 170; 387 [1]; ix. 18, 19, 29, 139, 275; x. 21, 81
——nature daemons, await chance to descend into bodies of men, xi. 323
——portents, xi. 181
——servants of highest deity, ix. 160, 161, 163
——transmitters of revelation, vi. 291
—assigned proper time to sing, xi. 310
—at termination of St. Andrew's Cross, xi. 55, 56, 57
—became armed men after Conaire hunted them, iii. 75
—black, one of which turns into woman, iii. 193
—Caer and her maidens took form of, every second year, iii. 78
—caged, liberated, xii. 298, 300
—certain Finno-Ugric peoples believe dead appear as, iv. 9
—children born dumb receive speech from, xi. 95
—demons fly like, v. 330
—desecrate sacred head of Nikeu, ix. 90
—devouring, Dechtere and maidens returned as, iii. 82
—escaped rain of fire, xi. 94
—fire owned by, ix. 281, 282
—flock of, appeared in Ulster, iii. 86
—God and devil appear as, iv. 314, 317, 318, 322–323
—gods and goddesses in form of, iii. 56, 86, 121, 153, 158
—guidance of Segovesi by, iii. 13
—in beast-fables, vii. 284
——Celtic worship and divination, iii. 13
——deluge-myth, interpretations of, xii. 279, 280

Birds in sacrifice, purification, and on shrines, v. 32, 34
—joined two by two by silver chains, iii. 82
—kisses of Oengus transformed into, iii. 60
—lightning-, vii. 237
—little Tengu represented as, viii. 288, pl. xxix, opp. p. 288
—man-eating, x. 288 32; xi. 191, 192, 194
——killed by Herakles, i. 84
—migratory, Barbmo-akka tutelary genius of, iv. 176
—mythical, vi. 289–291
—nine sisters in form of, iii. 193
—nocturnal, live in Grotto of Caripe, xi. 279
—of Elysium were the " bird flock of Land of Promise," iii. 213
——iron, iv. 335, fig. 14; see also Cos-TUMES, SHAMAN.
——paradise, viii. 242
——Rhiannon, iii. 101, 104, 121
—(or duck's) way, stair, or road = Milky Way, iv. 434, 435
—origin of mankind from, ix. 108–109
—protecting young under wings as symbol of protective deity, v. 70
—quests in guise of, ix. 71–72, 85
—sacred, of Aphrodite: see HERO AND LEANDROS.
—Seides may appear as, or may originally have been, iv. 106
—sent from Ark, v. 221, 230, 232
—seven elders have form of, v. 140
—shaman, iv. 285; 500; see also Cos-TUMES, SHAMAN.
—slogan of, adapted by Spider, vii. 330
—Sosondowah in guise of, x. 26
—souls appear as, iii. 60
——continue life as, in world-tree, iv. 487, 494, 495
——of warriors metamorphosed into, xi. 61
—spirit-like, appeared under regency of Tan, viii. 43
—tabu to Conaire, iii. 75
—tell Maui secret of fire, ix. 49–50
—Tiri and Caru married, xi. 314–315
—to carry Light until all earth illuminated, xi. 199
—(turning into women) born of marriage of sun and moon, ix. 110–111

Birds, two, created sky and earth from egg-like objects, ix. 165
—two-headed lord of, iv. 511
—water-, iv. 196–197, 202
——rivers and sea prayed to for, iv. 214
—white, souls of living in form of, iii. 227, 229
—who eat human flesh, vii. 330
—Zeus reveals his will through flight of, i. 162
Birdu, i.e. Nergal as " cold," v. 49
Bīrs, heroes, village demons, vi. 244, 247
Birth, Births:
Birth and death not permitted to take place on Isle of the Temple, viii. 269
——ratio between, viii. 224, 233
—astral influences surrounding, viii. 143
— -bricks, two, symbol of Meskhenet, xii. 52, 372 52
— -charm for reindeer cows, moon plays part in, iv. 226
—connexion of Gandharas with, has disappeared, vi. 143
—control of Klotho over, i. 284
—cottages especially built for, viii. 266
—customs, ii. 195–196; iii. 83; iv. 416; viii. 149
— -deity, Heqet is later consort of Khnûm, transformed into, xii. 52
transformed into, xii. 52
—deity of, iv. 357, 358, 397, 398, 399, 413, 414, 415, 416, 459–460
—from various causes, i. 6, pl. XLIV, opp. p. 194, 262; iii. 57, 207; vi. 166; vii. 156, 157, 222; viii. 27; ix. 107, 112–113, 157, 234, 251, 255, 272, 338 44; xii. 115
—gods who are decreers of, iv. 394, 413
—Heqet protector of, xii. 50–52, 134
—legends, viii. 217, 223
—magical plant of, v. 94, 95, 166, 171
—marvellous, of Marduk, v. 157
—Meskhenet goddess of, xii. 52, 137
—mortals give, to embryo only, iv. 415
—mother, iv. 413–416
—myths of Heimdall's, ii. 153, 154, 155
—navel symbol of, xi. 27
—of child, original shape (woman dragon) taken at, viii. 266
——children from Loki in woman-form, ii. 143, 145
——Helen, various versions of, i. 24–25
——wind, in Finnish poem, iv. 457

Birth pangs begin with entrance of shadow-soul into child in womb, iv. 473
—plant of, v. 166–174; vi. 283
———see further PLANT OF BIRTH.
——rate, connexion of Demeter with, i. 227
—reeds stuck in thatch of house on new, vii. 146
——star, iii. 273
—star descends in human form at a, x. 96
——stories, Jātakas are, viii. 217
—supernatural, caused by rays of sun, xi. 201
——temples, xii. 171
—Thracians mourned at, but joyful at death, vii. 397 [4]
—Zodiac, signs of, for, vii. 52–53
Births, miraculous, iii. 80, 81, 83, 140; v. 27, 158, 167; vii. 156, 157, 213, 214, 222, 223, 224; viii. 6, 27, 29, 35, 37, 38, 41, 111, 154
—royal, four gods with crocodiles' heads (probably sons of Horus or Osiris) assist at, xii. 394 [67]
Birthday celebrations, viii. 81, 82, 128
Birthdays of gods on epagomenal days, xii. 394 [70]
Bisexual demons, v. 357
Bishamon-ten (Vaiśravaṇa), guardian of north, viii. 243, 279
Bishop of Greenland, x. 2
Bison, black, national emblem of the Rhetarii, iii. 286
Bit and bridle first contrived by Athene, i. 172
Bit, Bita, Serpent of Underworld, confused with Sêth-'Apop, xii. 403 [18]
Bit-gimil-Dagan, v. 79
" Biterolf," ii. 170
Biton, story of death of, i. 167
Bitsitsi, jester to Sun Father, x. 200
Biwa, Lake, viii. 254–255, 270–271, 340
Biwa (Skt. vinā), a kind of banjo, viii. 269
Bjarka songs, ii. 314
Bjarki, bear the Fylgja of, ii. 234
Bjarmar apparently old Norse name for Russian Karelians, iv. xv
Bjerg-trolds or -folk, ii. 224
Bjorn changed into bear, ii. 293
bKra-shis-lhun-po (Ṭa-shi-lhun-po), monastery at, vi. 209
Black Arcan, Cumhal's murderer, iii. 168

Black art [magic], viii. 155–156; xii. 109; 207, 348, 349
—as sacred colour in connexion with Osiris, xii. 94, 97
—Book of Caermarthen, iii. 191, 199
—cannibals, ix. 67
—cat foretells weather, viii. 327
—Dragon, a dog, viii. 107
—Prince: see KARA-KHAN, ETC.
—race subjected to Aryans by Indra, vi. 34–35
—regarded as the same colour as blue, xii. 367 [10], 386 [14]
—River of Tuonela, dead must cross, iv. 74, 78
—sacrificial animal, iv. 70, 75, 148, 151, 153, 160, 161, 165, 202, 210, 211, 212, 215, 235, 239, 243; see also SACRIFICIAL VICTIMS.
—son of Carman, tale of, iii. 35–36
—stone, object of Dusares's worship, v. 16
—Tengeri (gods), iv. 411
—Water, Fraoch warned not to swim, iii. 67
—why most sacred animals in Egypt are, xii. 413 [11]
Blackbird born of flesh of Pünegusse, iv. 386–387
Blacksmith, Ruler (nature-god), believed to dwell in tools of, iv. 464, 465
—thunder made by, vii. 238
Blacksmiths, vii. 27, 28, 85, 99; 115, 345, 399 [10]
—Boshintoi deity of, iv. 337, 464
—stars of Great Bear skulls of seven, iv. 426–427
—supposed to turn into hyenas, vii. 345
Blaenn, dwarf-race from bones of, ii. 264
Blai, mother of Oisin, iii. 168, 180
Bláthnat, wife of Cúroi, iii. 148, 151, 152, 155, 156
Bledhericus: see BLIHIS, ETC.
Bledlochtana (monsters), in battle of Mag-Tured, iii. 25
Bleeding of stones, x. 283 [27]
Blemmyians cling to Egyptian religion long after spread of Christianity, xii. 244
Blenyiba, fetish of Cavalla, vii. 178
Blessing of gods and not-gods, pronouncing of, iii. 71

Blessing of Noah, v. 232
Blest, Islands of the, i. 147–148
Blight, conception of Fomorians as powers of, iii. 33
Blihis (Bleheris, Bledhericus, Breri?), source of Grail story, iii. 196, 198
Blind guardian in Underworld, ix. 75
—men who met with an Elephant, tale of, viii. 355–356
—ogress, stealing of food from, ix. 45, 46, 59, 65
Blindness as punishment of swearing falsely by Ptaḥ, xii. 234
—cured through dream, vii. 349
—sent by devil on slothful followers, vii. 371
Blizzard caused if Seide not honoured, iv. 103
Blodeuwedd, bride for Lleu, made out of flowers, iii. 97, 100, 152
Blodughofi, horse of Frey, ii. 109
Blood, xi. 47, 48, 51, 55, pl. IX, opp. p. 70, 79, 80, 88, 90, 94, 122, 142, 144, 148, 153
—abhorrent to dragon folk, viii. 272
—and earth combined in rites, ii. 196
——honey blended to form mead, ii. 53
——lungs of ox, eating of, made ancestors of Nama red, vii. 150–151
——wounds of Bêl, v. 323
—as fertilizer, iv. 239; xi. 79
—bath of, to wash away shame, iii. 150
—bowl of, of Bhairon, vi. pl. XXXI, opp. p. 238
—bowlful of earth became, and blood became the Rabbit, x. 40
— -brotherhood, ii. 140, 142, 145, 160, 196
—bull's, in oath, i. 190
—circulation of, basis of Cheremiss belief that the soul or life wanders through the body, iv. 4
— -clot, origin of man and deities from, ix. 30, 109, 110, 121, 251
—coloured clay red for creation, ix. 24
— -covenant, saliva-rite analogous to, ii. 53
—created from water, iv. 371
—Cúchulainn drank Emer's, iii. 144
—directed on post in slaughtering sacrifice, iv. 339
—dragon's, vii. 76, 82
—dreams of, ii. 250, 254, 255

Blood-Drinker, monster judge of dead, xii. 176
— -drinking god, iv. 173
—drinking of, iv. 5; vi. 157; vii. 242, 252; viii. 156
— -dripping garments of those killed without sickness, iv. 81
—drops of, in Grail romances, iii. 202–203
—dwarf race from Brimir's, ii. 264, 265, 278
—eyebrows of dead painted with, iv. 18
—feuds, vi. 242; x. 4
—flood of, ii. 324
—from corpse of Osiris, Isis gathering, xii. 114 (fig. 118)
——Medousa used by Asklepios both in killing and restoring life, i. 280–281
——Osiris, Isis conceives Horus from, xii. 115, 397 97
——serpent (tree-trunk), ix. 181
——wind, magic spear-head could draw, iii. 199
—Heaven-reaching thornbush from, x. 104
—hook baited with, ix. 43
—in creation, x. 56, 219, 229, 263
——divination, ii. 171
—Mora sucks, iii. 228
—oak's, iii. 322
—of bear contains magic, and is smeared about, iv. 90
——bullock to redden hill at álfablót and disablót, ii. 226, 244
——cock as purification, iii. 242
——criminals used as charms, viii. 156
——eagle sprinkled on people, ii. 233
——elephant for Baboon, vii. 423 29
——fawn for purification, x. 21
——gods, creation from, v. 275, 276, 307, 313
——Gorgon gives rise to poisonous serpents in Libya, i. 34
——Indech's heart given to men of knowledge, iii. 30
——Kvasir collected in kettle Odrörir and vats Son and Bodn, ii. 53, 54
——river Vaitaraṇī, vi. 235
——sacrifice flows into hollow on hearth which is then smeared with clay, iii. 238
——sacrifices on trees in tabued grove, iii. 11

Blood of sacrificial victim, smearing of, viii. 135
——serpent and tapir to knead maize at creation, xi. 179
——sorceress Gorddu obtained by Arthur, iii. 188
——swine sacrificial blood, ii. 155
——three kings, Fionn released with, iii. 170
——Tiamat and Labbu, v. 303
——Ymir drowns frost-giants, ii. 276, 324
—offered to ghosts in Hades, i. 145
— -offerings, vi. 89, 96
——Asgard place of, ii. 33
——demanded by lud-spirit, iv. 148
——Odin erected temple with, ii. 29, 30
—promise must be sealed in, iii. 246
—rain used for, in creation-myth, ix. 174
—rains before war, ii. 250
— -Red River, the Lohū, vi. 245
— -revenge, ii. 164–165
— -sacrifice in autumn to earth-spirit, iv. 460
—sacrifices becoming obsolete, iv. 131, 139, 142
——offered to world-pillar, iv. 333–334, 338, 339
—sacrificial, disposal of, iv. 130, 148, 154, 160, 163, 215, 232
——smearing of, on various objects, iv. 38, 67, 107, 108, 110, 114, 139, 142, 188, 222, 223, 224, 231, 233, 250
—singing of, before battle, ii. 250
—Sirens born of drops of, from horn of Acheloös, i. 262
—six streams of, from which all evil spirits came, ix. 160
—smearing of, iv. 90, 188; 464, 467; see also BLOOD, SACRIFICIAL, SMEARING OF, ETC.; viii. 135
—sprinkled from trough in dream, ii. 250
—sprinkling Heaven and air with, by Managarm, ii. 200
——of, on drawings, creates mankind, ix. 107
———restores to life, ix. 279
—stones sprang from, x. 296 45
—streams of, conjured against Firbolgs, iii. 24
—tabu, xii. 362 3
—used to colour runes, ii. 50, 295

Blood, uses of, in mer festival, iv. 271, 273, 277
Bloodless sacrifices, iv. 139, 142
Bloodletting, vi. 185
Bloodshed, expiation for, xi. 138
—necessary to memorial feasts, iv. 44
Bloom Lady: see LADY-WHO-MAKES-THE-TREES-BLOOM.
Blotgud Svia ("sacrificial god of Sweden"), ii. 29, 114
Blow from Govannon caused death of Dylan, iii. 99
— -gun, xi. 177
—received on magic mound, iii. 94
Blows given Guinevere, iii. 192
——Medraut, iii. 193
—one would kill; two resuscitate, iii. 93
Blue, Amon as man has skin of, xii. 129
—(and Eternal) Tengri, denote two different stages of development, iv. 391–392
—Huitzilopochtli born with limbs painted, xi. 60
—mantle of forest-spirits, iv. 190
—men exist in Sweden, ii. 276
——see KUMUSH, BLUE MAN; MAN, BLUE (SKY-GOD), ETC.
—not to be worn near holy place, iv. 102
—regarded as the same colour as black, xii. 367 10, 386 14
—Rutu sometimes appeared as man dressed in, iv. 76
—shield, xi. 60
Bö = shaman, iv. 496
Boahje-naste, north nail or star, iv. 221
Boann, goddess, iii. 50, 52, 67, 73, 78, 121, 130
Boar, Adonis killed by, i. 198
—and antelope, tale of, ix. 199
—animal of Sêth possibly likened to, xii. 124, 389 33
—annual wounding by, legend of, v. 132, 133
—atonement, at Yule festival, ii. 109
—avatar of Viṣṇu, vi. 30, 121, 168
—black, earth raised on back of, vi. 75, 121–122, pl. XII, opp. p. 122
—Erymanthian, conquered by Herakles, i. 82, 83 (fig. 3A)
—Freyja rides on, ii. 22, 120, 125
—hunt for Kalydonian, cause of war between Kalydonians and people of Pleuron, i. 56–57

Boar incarnation, older attribution of, to Brahmā or Prajāpati, vi. 170
—killing of Adonis by, perhaps borrowed from explanation of Sêth in animal form, xii. 399 111
—Kirghis descended from, iv. 502, 503
—length of life of, same as that of Diarmaid, iii. 67, 177
—of Gulban, iii. 177
——Mac Dáthó, tale of, iii. 124, 145, 157
—or bear enemy of young nature-god in Phoenicia, xii. 397 101
—Prajāpati took form of, vi. 75, 79, 96
—Rākṣasa in form of, vi. 118
—Rudra the, vi. 82
—Tuan Mac Cairill as, iii. 207
—Vṛtra as, vi. 30
—white, as sacrifice, viii. 233
—with three valuable possessions, knight as, iii. 125, 187, 188, 189
Board, sacrifice: see SACRIFICE-BOARD.
Boars, ii. 10, pl. VI, opp. p. 32, 109; iii. pl. III, opp. p. 8, 65, 108, 125, 172, 184, 187–188, pl. XXIV, opp. p. 188, 199
—Maruts as four-tusked, vi. 39
Boat, animals and men saved in, at deluge, x. 63
—burial in, among Ugrians and Karelian Finns, iv. 32–33
—dead taken over river of Tuonela in, iv. 75
—drawn by swan, ii. 262–263
—dream of blood-stained women in, portent of war, ii. 250
—Earth-supporter rests on copper box conceived as, x. 250
—floating, meaning of name of princess, viii. 302
—for descent to Underworld, iv. 292
—god of the, v. 152
— -gods and boats, iv. pl. XLI, opp. p. 308
—golden, of Sun's daughter, iii. 328
—in which souls ferried to spirit-land, ix. pl. XVIII, opp. p. 182
—made of fingernails in which Evil One carries off dead, iv. 75
—miraculous, viii. 364
—of Eternities, throne of Osiris in, xii. 72
——Frey: see SKIDBLADNIR, ETC.
——Khin-ort's son, iv. 78

Boat of Prince of Sickness, iv. 78
——Yü borne by dragons, viii. 38
—rowed by shaman in Heaven, iv. 307
—see FUNERAL, DESCRIPTION OF, ETC.
—trough shaped like, used at Lapp Christmas festival, iv. 67
—witch-, xi. 328
Boatman across waters of death, v. 148
—of Utnapishtim: see URSANAPI, ETC.
Boats, ii. pl. XXVII, opp. p. 204, 275, 276, 281; iii. 25, 72, 84, 87, 89, 96, 116, 117, 133, 151, 192, 194; xi. 207
—found in graveyards in Russian Karelia, iv. 33
—in village of dead, iv. 485
—living and mouth-prowed, x. 274 9
—of dead, iii. 16, 17
——fir dedicated to Christmas Master, iv. 67
—offered to wind-god, iv. 233
—phantom women's, x. 7
Bocánachs and Banánachs, iii. 134
Bochica, god, xi. 202, 203, 204, 240, 293, 370 23
Bodaw Payā, King, presented golden heads to shrine of Mahāgiri Nāts, xii. 344, 345
Bodb, king of síd of Munster, iii. 32, 57, 58, 72, 78, 79, 91
—Dearg, war-god and commander of Tuatha Dé Danann, iii. 25, 33, 40, 51, 54, 55, 60, 90, 168, 174
Bodh Gayā, Māra assailed the Buddha at, vi. 226
——sculptures at, vi. 198
Bodhidharma, Indian patriarch, viii. 188
Bodhisattva Avalokiteśvara, after death King Sroṅ-btsan-sgam-po took up abode in statue of, vi. 208
—" Buddha To Be," vi. 194, 197, 202, 205, 208, 209
—female, vi. 202
—Hkun Hsang L'röng a, xii. 290
—one destined to become a Buddha, xii. 261, 262
Bodhisattvas, viii. 194–196
Bodhmhall, sister of Muirne, iii. 165
Bodies, Body:
Bodies cut in pieces form animal creation, ix. 177
—of first beings undeveloped, ix. 159, 164, 166

Bodies, transformation and retransformation of, x. 30
Body, double or astral, viii. 120
—killing " life " of, ix. 237
—material, of Li T'ieh-kuai left with his disciple, viii. 120
—of Cian buried seven times before earth ceased to reject it, iii. 40
——food-goddess, play on words of products coming from, viii. 232, 379 16
——ghost undecayed while it haunted, ii. 309
——owner, fire obtained from, ix. 47, 49, 115, 283
—parts of, in Indian worship, x. xx–xxi
—silhouette of the, symbol of the shadow [soul], xii. 174
—soul with material, iv. 478
—White-, Blue-, Yellow-, and Black-, gods of fourth world-storey, x. 160, 162
Bodily conditions, abstract divinities of, i. 282
Bodn, blood of Kvasir collected in vat, ii. 53, 54
Bodvar, Egil's son, ii. 191
Boghaz Kyoi, discoveries at, vi. 5, 263
Bogies, ix. 142; x. 145–149, 291 37
—gods, and ghosts, xi. 295–300, 327–328
Bogomil sect, legends of, iv. 316–317, 321, 326
Bogotá, Zipa of, xi. 196
Bogs, creation of, iv. 315, 318
Bogŭ (Old Church Slavic " god "), Bagha corresponds to, vi. 28
Bohinavlle (nail of the north), iv. 221
Bohutis, boii, bovites, both doctors and priests, xi. 38, 351 10
Boil, child born from, vii. 222
Boils, Adapa covered with, v. 177
Boiocalus, king of the Ansivari, invoked sun and stars, ii. 197
Boiotia, cult centre of Poseidon, i. 210
—Dionysos comes to, i. 216
—Kephisos River worshipped in, i. 257
—legends of, interwoven with Argive myth, i. 28
—oldest Hellenic conception of Artemis found in, i. 183
—origin of name of, i. 42–43
—Orion in legends of, i. 250
—Pelasgic centre, " sacred marriage " of Zeus and Hera celebrated at, i. 165

Boiotian Mountain of the Muses, i. 40
Boiotians near Lake Kopaïs believed Alalkomeneus to be first man, i. 10
Boiotos, son of Poseidon, eponymous hero of Boiotia, i. 42, 211
——possible meaning of name of, i. 330 3 (ch. viii)
Bojabi-tree, vii. 317–319, 425 19 20
Bokenyane, abnormal birth of, vii. 222
Bokh: see BUCHIS, NAME OF, ETC.
Bokholdoi, spirit long-ago deceased, iv. 479
Bolgars, Volga, chief focus of Turco-Tatar civilization in Eastern Europe, iv. xviii
Bolnay-tree in Philippine tale, ix. 232–235
Bolon-ti-ku (nine gods), xi. 154
Bolon-tsac-cab (nine orders of world), xi. 154
Bolon-Zacab, idol at entrance to chief's house, xi. 144, 145
Bolster of down, person dying on, must reckon, in afterworld, number of feathers contained therein, iv. 21; see also HAIR MATS, ETC.
Bolthorn, giant, ii. 51, 63, 170
Bolverk (Odin), ii. 49, 53–54
" Bonaouaci," vii. 357–358
Bon-dancing, songs of, viii. 369, 373–374
Bonds fastened on enemy prisoners, ii. 252
—magic, iii. 170
—of Loki have Iranian parallel, ii. 147
Bone and flesh created out of earth, iv. 371
—-breaker, monster judge of dead, xii. 176
—-construction, soul of man intimately connected with, iv. 480
—marked with runes, Ollerus (Ull) travelled overseas on, ii. 157
Bones, ghosts so called because they have no, vii. 180
—Giaiael's, change into fishes, xi. 29
—new flesh grows on sacrificial victim's, iv. 3
—of beasts and fish, preservation and disposal of, iv. 25, 98–99, 109–110, 130, 150, 200
——deer and fish reborn, x. 292 40–293
——forefathers, various peoples created from broken, xi. 83, 90

Bones of sacrifice placed in god-chest at memorial feast, iv. 38, 120
——sacrificial victim not broken according to Finnish Lapps, iv. 7, 92
——Tammuz ground in mill, v. 336, 337
—throwing of, by diviner, vii. 190
Bonfires, ii. 124, 202; iv. 237; 451; vii. 57-58, 60; viii. 226; x. 194; xi. 146
Bongabong, creator-god, ix. 179
Boniface on Christian priests who sacrificed to Jupiter, ii. 68
Bonnes dames, goddesses survive as, iii. 133
Bontenkoku, tale of, viii. 356-359
Bonto and Onto, divine couple, iv. 157-158
Book-goddess, Sekha(u)it is the, xii. 200
" Book of Burial Customs," viii. 140
——Changes: see " I King."
——Chilam Balam," cosmogonic fragment from, xi. 128, 129, 153, 360 2
——Dead," xii. 72-73, 175, 178, 179, 199
——Fate, sky as, iv. 393
——Fermoy," iii. 50, 51
——Gates," xii. 26
——Good and Bad Days," xi. 100; see also Tonalamatl, etc.
——Invasions," iii. 36, 38, 42
——Lecan," iii. 154
——Leinster " and " Book of the Dun Cow," sources for study of Irish mythology, iii. 19
——Odes," viii. 62
——Rites ": see " Li Ki."
——Taliesin," iii. 109
—(or Table) of Life, iv. 408, 410
Books, Classical, burned by Shih Huang, viii. 134
—of Adam and Eve, v. 354
——deerskin parchment, xi. 190
—similar to " Book of the Dead," xii. 415 7
Boor's form, Cúroi in, iii. 149
Boot, ancestors of white men put in sole of, x. 10
—shaman, iv. 513, 517; see also Costumes, Shaman.
Boötes, constellation, addressed in hymn to Marduk, v. 317
——guardian of malevolent Ox-Leg, xii. 60
—(" Ox-Driver "), i. 251, 331 9 (ch. xi)

Bootoolgah, crane, tale of, ix. 284
Bope, spirit, xi. 296, 297
Bor, sons of, iv. 372
Boreas and Argonauts punish Phineus, i. 73
——Oreithyia, i. pl. lvi, opp. p. 266
—north wind, carries off Oreithyia, i. 73
——son of Astraios and Eos, i. 247, 265
Borg in Iceland, ii. pl. ii, opp. p. 4
Borghese Ares (of the Louvre), i. 190
Borgrund, runic inscription on church at, ii. 241
Borneo, mouse-deer as trickster-hero in, ix. 203
—southern, Indian influence in, ix. 242
Borr, son of Buri, ii. 24, 63, 324
Borre, tumuli at, ii. pl. xvi, opp. p. 130
Borrowed saucepan, joke about, vii. 354-355
Borrowing of myths, x. xxi-xxii
Borsippa (Barsippa), cult of Nabû at, v. 20, 158, 318
—Nabû city-god of, vii. 384 51
—Nabû's temple in, archive of divine decrees, vii. 384 48
Börtö, household image, said to be forefather of the Khangin clan, iv. 501
Boschet, companion of Téramó in modern Romagnola, i. 318
Boshintoi (deity of blacksmiths), nine sons of, taught preparation of iron, iv. 337, 464
Bothvild, daughter of Nithud, ii. pl. xxxiv, opp. p. 266, pl. xxxv, opp. p. 272
Botuto, sacred trumpet, xi. 275
Boulders, erratic, frequently associated with Gargantua, iii. 135
Boundaries, bhūts at, vi. 249
Boundary man, iv. 173
—stone of Melishipak, v. 106
—stones, i. 316-317; v. 182
Bouphonia, ritual of the, i. 160
Bous (Vali), son of Odin and Rinda, ii. 48, 135, 164
Bousiris, son of Poseidon, i. 87, 211
Boutes, son of Pandion, i. 67-68
Bow and arrow, v. 126
——arms of Tiermes, iv. 230-231

Bow and arrow in porridge, or in placenta basket (if a boy), for new-born child, iv. 254, 261
——offered to Leib-olmai, iv. 175, 178
——one of three precious things of Susa-no-wo, viii. 229
——see APOLLO, BIRTH OF.
——used on images by Lapps to injure enemies, iv. 13
—(and net) of Enlil (Marduk), three names of, v. 308
—given by Apollo to Herakles, i. 80, 126
——god, Ull is, ii. 156
—old woman; see JUKSAKKA, ETC.
—Priesthood, x. 189, 191
—see RAINBOW, SIGN OF, ETC.
—star, v. 135, 233, 308, 317
Bowels, binding Loki with son's, ii. 144, 146
Bowl, charm on Jewish, Lîlîth legend of, v. 363–364
—emblem of Demeter, i. 233
—for ritual use, ii. pl. XXXI, opp. p. 238, pl. XXXII, op. p. 246
Bowls, x. 40, 61, 106, 208, 209, 249, 310 66; see also KETTLES, TWO, ETC.
—earth likened to two, vi. 16; x. 106
—serpents on, v. 179
Box, Pandora's, i. 15
Boxes, calf-skin, iv. 42
Boy buried alive, tale of, vii. 280–281
—corps of Conchobar, Cúchulainn joined, iii. 141, 153
—magic ceremony at birth of, iv. 416
—Mirage-, White-Corn, Rock-Crystal, Pollen-, x. 158
Boyan, minstrel, called grandson of Veles, iii. 300
Boyar mistress, iv. 212
"Boyish Deeds of Fionn": see "MAC-GNÍMARTHA FINN."
Boyne, battle at the, iii. 44, 49
Bracan, warrior of Tuatha Dé Danann, iii. 164
Bracelet of Miming, ii. 132
Bracelets, finding of jade, viii. 171
Braciaca, goddess of cuirm or braccat, iii. 120
Braga-lund (Bragi's Wood), ii. 162
"Bragaraedur," ii. 6, 15, 52, 161, 173
Brager-full ("cup of the foremost"), ii. 162
Bragi Boddason, god Bragi may have been poet, ii. 161

Bragi, Odin's son, husband of Idunn, ii. 6, 15, 65, 140, 142, 143, 160–162, 173, 178, 220, 240, 250, 286, 315
"Bragi's Shield-lay," poem, ii. 88
Bragr-man, one who excels in skaldic art, ii. 160
Brahm, malignant ghost of a Brāhman, vi. 243
Brahmā, vi. 51, 52, 78, pl. VI, opp. p. 78, 94, 100, 104, 107, 108, pl. IX, opp. p. 108, 109, 116, 117, pl. X, opp. p. 118, 120, pl. XI, opp. p. 120, 121, 127, 134, 136, 143, 145, 147, 148, 152, 153, 158, 163, 165, 170, 174, 179, 180, 182, 192, 193, 199, 203, 208, 212, 213, 215, 216, 232, 235–236, 239; viii. 356; xii. 323, 327
Brahmadatta, one of the Cakravartins, vi. 225
Brahmaloka, vi. 227
Brahman Svayambhū ("Self-Existent prayer"), Prajāpati becomes the, vi. 77–78
"Brāhmaṇas," explanatory prose texts of the Vedas, vi. 11, 12, 13
—mythology of, vi. 73–102, 190
Brahmaṇaspati, epithet of Bṛhaspati, vi. 45, 50
Brāhmanism accepts worship of Mother-earth, vi. 230
—Buddhism in the beginning a reformed, xii. 259–260
Brāhmans, vi. 40, 107, 108, 127, 133, 136, 146, 147, 155, 190, 229
Brahmarṣis, Brāhman seers, vi. 145
Brain-sucking, iv. 67; x. 246, 253
Bralgah, native companion to emu, ix. 275
Brams, two, tale of, ix. 296–297
Bran, head of, ii. 46; iii. 109, 203
—hound of Fionn, iii. 126, 169, 172
—son of Febal, iii. 64, 114–116, 178, 197
——Llyr, iii. 56, 100, 101, 104–106, 112, 191, 203
Branch, musical, given Bran, iii. 114–115
—taken by Fraoch from rowan-tree but guardian of it attacked him, iii. 130
—with nine apples of gold, iii. 117, 118, 119
Branches, joining of ten cyclical, with Eight Diagrams, viii. 144
Branchidai, offshoot of Apollo's shrine at Delphoi, i. 178

Brand, horse of, ii. 118, 216
Brandenburg, Slavs of, worshipped Triglav, iii. 285
Brandy, Sarakka's, iv. 253
Branginoco: see HANTHAWADI SINBYU-YIN.
Branwen (or Bronwen, Brangwaine), daughter of Llyr, iii. 100, 101, 102, 104, 106
Brasilio-Guaranian, a group of South American peoples, xi. 254
Brass, body of Gaya Maretan became molten, vi. 293
Brāṭrō-rēsh, Zoroaster slain by, vi. 342
Brats, wild, changelings, iii. 264
Bravalla battle, ii. 256
Brazen serpent raised by Moses, parallel to, xi. 202
Braziers, iii. 31, 40
Brazil and the Amazon, xi. 254–317
Brea built first house and cauldron, iii. 137
Bread and water of life eternal, v. 94, 95, 97, 178, 180, 181, 184
——put on head of dead cacique, xi. 27
—Arkas taught Arkadians how to make, i. 16
—barley, strewn on graves, iv. 3
—from earth-goddess festival retained all year, xi. 34
—of death, v. 180
— -Para, iv. 172
—sacrificial, iv. 131, 136, 148, 154, 179, 184, 196, 197, 267–279
—see KEKRI-FEAST OF FINNS, ETC.; LOAVES, LARGE AND SMALL, ETC.
—use of, in obtaining new Voršud, iv. 122, 123
Breads in magic ceremony to waken Gilgamish, v. 224–225
Breast aflame, name of a strong passion, viii. 262, 380 [3] (ch. iii)
— -cloth of shaman, iv. pl. LIX, opp. p. 504; see also COSTUMES, SHAMAN.
— -plate given by Hephaistos to Herakles, i. 80
—see MILK-BREASTED GODDESS.
Breasts, iii. 142, 144; 264, 265; iv. 414, 467, 468; vii. 396 [63]; ix. 131; x. 8, 10, 114, 242; xii. 142, 177
—growths on gingko-tree said to resemble woman's, viii. 342
—milk of, refused by Goll, iii. 179

Breasts mutilated by Amazons, xi. 282–283
—of ogress, ix. 131
——children sucked by Vetter, ii. 225
Breath (Ais), vii. 86
— -clouds of gods, x. 206
—connexion of, with four winds, xii. 65
—Control, The Classic of, viii. 56
—desecration of deity by exhalation of, iii. 281
—Finno-Ugric belief that it is another soul, iv. 7
—human, desecrates fire, vii. 54
—life-, viii. 140
—magic, iii. 59
—master of, x. 59
—of horse of Iddawc, iii. 190
——life, x. 22, 59, 92, 210
——first child of Earth and Sky, x. 35
——to new-born child carried by Quetzalcoatl, xi. 89
——maidens warmed magic cauldron, iii. 95, 193
——man is life, ix. 107, 170, 172–173, 174, 273
——monster, destruction of animals, trees, etc., by, x. 139
——red birds withered everything, iii. 126
——serpent caused skin irritation, vii. 148
—plumes, x. 190; see also FEATHER SYMBOLISM.
— -spirit, xi. 342
— -tabu, where found, iii. 11
Breathing, control of, viii. 56-57, 147
" Breath's departure " synonym for death, iv. 7
Bregia, Conaire went in tabued direction around, iii. 76
—three herdsmen of, iii. 148
Bregon, descendant of Scythian noble, iii. 43
Breidablik, abode of Balder at, ii. 33, 127, 129, 329
Breidafjord, guardians of, ii. 229
Breit-hut (Broad Hat), name of leader of Host, ii. 42
Breith seems to be connected with Me-rui, xii. 406 [55]
Brennus, Bran euhemerized into a British king who was confused with, iii. 105–106

Brer Fox, Brer Wolf, Brer B'ar, vii. 285, 292, 307

Brer Rabbit, vii. 292, 307; see also AN-TELOPE, PARALLEL, ETC.; HARE (vol. vii).

——Great Hare reappears as, in negro lore, x. 121, 297 [47]

——stories appear as Cherokee saga cycle, x. 67

—Terrapin, tortoise becomes, vii. 284; see also TORTOISE, TORTOISE STORIES.

Breri, iii. 196

Bres, one of Three Finns of Emuin, iii. 90, 156

—son of Elatha and his sister Eri, warrior of Tuatha Dé Danann, iii. 24, 25–28, 29, 32, 33, 34, 39

Břetislav II of Bohemia, sacred groves destroyed in reign of, iii. 305, 306

Bṛhaddivā, goddess, vi. 53

Bṛhadratha, two wives of, each bore half a child, vi. 156

Bṛhaspati (Lord of Devotion), vi. 16, 21, 45, 57, 88, 92, 100, 122, 132, 133, 145, 168

Bri loved by Liath, iii. 91

Bri Léith, hosts from síd of, came to Conaire, iii. 75

——síd of Midir, iii. 80

Brian, god of Danu, iii. 39, 40

Briareos awards Akrokorinthos, the citadel at Corinth, to Helios, i. 36–37

——Isthmus of Corinth to Poseidon, i. 36–37, 212

—born of Ouranos and Gaia, i. 6

—guards Kronos who is imprisoned on island, iii. 15

—personifies Aegean Sea, i. 259

Brick, earth and water united as a, vi. 76

—represents divinity of Mami and is symbol of clay of creation, v. 274, 276

Bricriu, hero, iii. 83, 140, 145–146, 199

" Bricriu's Feast," iii. 145–146, 149, 151

Bridal fee, ii. 89

—veil of Freyja put on Thor, ii. 88–89

Bride, Brides:

Bride drives away dragon, vii. 393 [24]–394

—from the South, tale of, x. 31

— -price, iii. 130

—spirit, x. 119–120, 276 [12]

—tale of chief's son and, vii. 139

Brides blessed with Thor's hammer, ii. 79

—of berserkers in Hlesey slain, ii. 91

Brides, perpetual, name of nymphs, vii. 84–85, 393 [32]

—sacrifices of, to water, iv. 213–214

—who died after betrothal, fairies souls of, iii. 256

Bridegroom, earth, iv. 240, 243

—of Earth mother in Finnish poems, iv. 462

——see EARTH STOLEN, ETC.

Bridge, ii. 278, 320, 321, 329; x. 6, 35, 48, 134, 138, 236, 254; see also SOULS, BALANCE OF.

—Cinvat, vi. 344, 346

——dog at, vi. 69

——known as hair-, vii. 100

—Floating, of Heaven, viii. 223

—from Heaven to earth, ii. 156

——mountain to mountain built by gods and demons, viii. 276

—Great Oak as, for those killed without sickness, iv. 82

—made by magpies over Milky Way for Weaving Damsel and Shepherd Boy, viii. 132

—magic, iii. 59

—of deceased, iv. 54, 74, 82

——Gojō, viii. 310

——leaps, hag guarded, iii. 144

——Nemda god, iv. 155

——ox as, vi. 289, 298, 303

—punishment-, iv. 494

—rainbow-: see BIFROST, ETC.; ÁSBRU, ETC.

—sky-, x. 277 [13], 294 [42]

—souls of dead must cross a, xii. 265, 429 [7]

—sword a, iii. 197

—to island of Scátlach, iii. 143

—under-water, iii. 197

—Yatsu-hashi, viii. 349

Bridle given to Bellerophon by Athene, i. 40

—silver, iv. 266, 268, 271

Brig, daughter of Dagda, iii. 32

Brig: see PHRYGIANS EQUATED, ETC.

Brigands, the, viii. 168, 169

Brigantes, Brythonic tribe, iii. 157

Bright Star, commander of the elements, x. 111–112, 116

Brigit (Brigindo, Brigantia), goddess of poetry and culture; goddess to whose ritual St. Brigit succeeded, iii. 11, 13, 39, 112, 137

Brigit, St.: see ST. BRIGIT.
Brimir, hall, ii. 318
—sword, ii. 169, 278
Brimir's blood, dwarf race from, ii. 264, 265, 278
Briseïs given as prize to, and taken from, Achilles, i. 126, 127
Brisinga-men, the necklace of Freyja, ii. 88, 120, 121, 123, 124, 140, 142, 149, 155, 180, 267
Brisings, necklace of the: see BRISINGA-MEN, ETC.
Britain, three blessed or white ladies of, iii. 98
Britannia confused by Procopius with area between Brittany and mouths of Scheldt and Rhine, iii. 16
British ancestry for Cúchulainn, iii. 157
—Celts (Brythons), myths of, iii. 92–113
——the sources for the mythology of, iii. 19
Britomartis, Artemis identified with, i. 183
Britons, iii. 16, 23, 194
Brittany, Arthur in, iii. 187
—Egyptian cults spread as far as, xii. 242
Brittia (Britain), Procopius's account of, iii. 15–16
Brocade-Weaving-Lady: see TATSUTA-HIME, ETC.
Brokk, dwarf, ii. 266–267
Brontes, a Kyklops, father of Athene by Metis, i. 170
—(Thunder-roar), born of Ouranos and Gaia, i. 6
Bronze Age, Scandinavian, ii. pl. xx, opp. p. 160
—creation of men of, i. 17
—Race of, i. 114, 326 4 (ch. vii)
—vessels for religious worship, viii. 7, 47, 48
——melted by Shih Huang to make statues, viii. 134
Brooch, Nordendorf, name of Donar on, ii. 70
Brook, worship of, iv. 212–214
Broom, fiery, Škrat comes in form of, iii. 246
Brosinga mene: see BRISINGA-MEN, ETC.
Brothel, kin of Siward put in, ii. 115
Brother, god described as, v. 12

Brother-gods called Alcis, ii. 64; see also ALTERNATING GODS.
—in personal names; as creator; in relationship of god and man, v. 7, 8, 9, 10, 12, 379 22 26, 380 50
—of Cross, xii. 302
——First Man drowned and resuscitated by sweat-bath, x. 106
—tales, ix. 41–42, 107–108, 122–129, 296–297
—title of gods as brothers, v. 7–9, 11
—Underworld-, of sky deity, ix. 163
—Yāw appears as Tammuz or, v. 135
" Brothers," gods as, v. 14, 15
—(pair), demiurgic, x. 106, 107, 295 44; see FLINT; SAPLING; HERO BROTHERS; HERO - TRANSFORMER - TRICKSTER; TWINS.
—separation of, in different worlds, x. 137
—seven, tales of, iv. 427–428
—Story of the Two, xii. 153, 398 106
—Warrior, x. 205
—who divided their crops on threshing floor, Milky Way formed by, vii. 386 14
—younger, x. 169
Broths, nine, in creation, xi. 165
Brown Bull, iii. 58, 127
Brown or red animals or reptiles symbolize Sêth, xii. 196
Brownies (Toumte), ii. 204, 225, 226, 231
Brug Maic Ind Óc, síd took name of, iii. 50
—na Boinne, iii. pl. i, frontispiece, 41, 50, pl. vi. opp. p. 50, 66, 67, 79, 177
" Bruighean Caorthuinn," Irish tale, iii. 170
Brun, Odin disguised as, ii. 56, 57
Brunnakr's brook, Idunn dwelt at, ii. 178
" Brut," Grail first appears in Wace's, iii. 186
Brynhild, daughter of Budli, ii. 251
—(Sigrdrifa), ii. 56, 112, 168, 195, 229, 239–240, 251, 252, 254, 260, 279, 297, 305
Bryniar (dead) invites Thorstan to his barrow, ii. 308
Brythons: see BRITISH CELTS, ETC.
bSam-ldin, priestess of monastery at, vi. 218

bSam-yas, oldest Tibetan monastery of, vi. 209

Bu, star-group known as the Dolphin, ix. 142

Buan, Samera's daughter, iii. 147

Bubastos, sacrifice before sacred pillars of, xii. 190 (fig. 196)

—Ubastet cat-goddess of, xii. 150

Bubble or bladder, creation of earth from, iv. 313, 316

Bubembe Island, temple to Mukasa on, vii. 129, 130

Buchis bull, identification of Osiris with, only late, xii. 385 [4]

—name of Mon$t$(u)'s sacred bull, xii. 139, 163

Buck, universal god designated as, xii. 413 [14]

Buckeye Bush, parent of flame, x. 223, 224

Bucranium used for religious decoration, xii. 367 [11]

Buču, spirit-bird, iv. 509

Buddha Amita, Buddha of Infinite Light and Life, viii. 242

—Gotama, vi. 168, 169, 187–219, 220; viii. 216, 217, 219, 332; xii. 259, 260–261

——equated with Burkhan, iv. 315, 330, 401

——finger-bone of, viii. 200–201

——image of, reflected in a crystal, viii. 272

——miracle in connexion with, at Plowing Festival, xii. 328

——predecessors of, worshipped Rukmiṇī, vi. 126

——received title " The Golden Immortal of Great Knowledge," viii. 194

——sacred images of, xii. 327

——visits and converts Tha-tun, xii. 285

Buddhaḍākinī, female divinity, vi. 218

Buddhaghoṣa, commentator, vi. 203

Buddhakṣetra, Buddha realm, viii. 240, 379 [24]

Buddhism, iv. 315, 318, 321, 327; viii. 13, 14–16, 19, 20, 24, 104, 188–198, 200–201; 237, 238, 240–243, 264, 266, 267, 273, 278, 279, 287, 296, 297, 298, 301, 316, 335, 336, 339, 345, 346, 350–351

—adapted itself to Chinese opinions, viii. 193–197

Buddhism and Jainism, similarity of, vi. 13, 220

—enters Indo-China through Burma and Mèkhong Valley, xii. 288

—in Indo-China, xii. 259–260

—only faint traces of, in India itself, vi. 13

—Southern School of, introduced into Burma, xii. 271

Buddhist fairies: see TENNIN, HEAVENLY MAIDENS, ETC.; RYŪJIN, HEAVENLY MAIDENS, ETC.

—influence on Indonesian Trickster Tales, ix. 242

——Japanese mythology, viii. 214, 216–219, 221

—monk, badger in disguise of, viii. pl. XXXVIII, opp. p. 326

—mythology and religion in India and Tibet, vi. 187–219

—text in China translated in A.D. 781, vi. 176

Buddhistic practices absorbed into Taoist ceremonials, viii. 135

Buddhists, Dragon King tutelary deity of, viii. 268, 273

—polemics against, vi. 163, 164

—some Wa are, xii. 296

Bude took form of bird, iii. 56

Budi slain by Sigi, ii. 358 [21]

Budli, Brynhild daughter of, ii. 251

Buds, first pairs of beings from, ix. 166–167

Budu, temple of python-god at, vii. 271

Buffalo and ape, tale of, ix. 191, 196, 198

——newly married wife, tale of, vii. 278

—clay figure of, carried before temple at Thangh-long, xii. 319

—golden, xii. 321

—see DURGĀ (frontispiece, vol. vi).

—totem, vii. 278

Buffaloes, vi. 29–30, 33; x. 109, 115, 116, 118, 119, 122, 123, 124, 127, 128

Buffoon at funeral, xii. 182 (fig. 191)

Buga, heaven-god, iv. 371, 399

Bu-gaku, dance, viii. pl. XL, opp. p. 336

Bugan and Wigan, brother and sister, survived flood, ix. 170–171, pl. XVII, opp. p. 170, 180, 183

Bu-gem(et), Bês localized at, xii. 62
—birthplace of sun and Osiris, xii. 376 [84]
—sun's eye discovered in, xii. 86
Bugimamusi, place where heaven touches earth, vii. 130
Buhuitihu a name for priest or medicine-man, xi. 25
Buichet in charge of children turned into swine, iii. 127
Builders, mythical, of city walls, originally storm-daemons, i. 267
Building, ceremony for laying foundation of, v. 147
—kuala, removed and rebuilt, iv. 125
Buildings, customs connected with erection of, and removal to, new, iii. 243–244
—Indian and Burmese influence in architecture of ancient, xii. 327
—souls of, iv. 169
Builth, Caball left print of paw on stone near, iii. 184
Buj, river, sacrifice to, iv. pl. xxi, opp. p. 200
Bujuruktši, Tatar term for heaven-god, iv. 394
Bukha-Nojon (Bull Lord), iv. 502–503, 506
Bulagat, son of a bull and maiden, iv. 503
Bull, vi. 16, 19, 21, 26, 33, 37, 43, 47, 62, 111, 242
—Acheloös in form of, i. 93
—ancestor of Mongols, iv. 502, 503
—and Gilgamish, v. 28, 29, 98, 238, 385 [139]
— -calf, young man impersonates, at Votiak spring festival, iv. 242
—celestial, Sêth identified with, xii. 390 [36]
—(constellation of Taurus) associated with seven Hat-hôr cows, xii. 40
—Cretan, and Herakles, i. pl. xxiii (2), opp. p. 88
——mastered by Herakles and slain by Theseus, i. 84
—difficult rapids called, iv. 471
—Dirke bound to, i. pl. xv, opp. p. 42, 43
—double, and bull-god, xii. 22 (fig. 2), 34, 169, 368 [16]
——connected with constellations, xii. 366 [6]

Bull-feast, divination for new king at, iii. 75
—four-horned, for cardinal points, xii. 367 [10]
—grey, breath of, gives birth to wind, iv. 457–458
—head of, and two birds on altar, iii. 157–158; see also TARVOS TRIGARANOS.
——as religious symbol, xii. 367 [11]
—heavenly wild, xii. 367 [10]
—horns characteristic of Sumerian, Babylonian, and Assyrian deities, v. 46, 47, 48
—human-headed, v. 238
—in Cretan myth and ritual, i. 325 [1]
——myth, vi. 264, pl. xxxiii, opp. p. 264, 269, 273, 286
—made to eat silk containing mysterious sayings, viii. 75
—of Cúalnge, iii. 58, 69, 70, 134, 152, 158; see also TÁIN BÓ CÚALNGE.
——Heaven, v. 28, 238, 239, 256–257, 319, 385 [139] [140]
———Ishtar implores Anu to create, to destroy Gilgamish, v. 267
———his mother, meaning of, in relation to sun-god, xii. 38
————Rê' as, xii. 82, 383 [87]
———Marathon, i. 69, 102
———Poseidon, i. 65
—on monument, iii. 9
—or cow, celestial, most sacred animals sought in, xii. 413 [11]
———ox, primeval, vii. 93
—Osiris as, xii. 94, 385 [4], 399 [111]
—Poseidon in form of, when he begat Boiotos, i. 330 [3] (ch. viii)
—ravaging Arkadia, killed by Argos, i. 29
—represents Adad in Semitic symbolism, v. 47
—rock shaped like mouth of, from which flows river, iv. 360
—sacred animal of Mîn and Mont(u), xii. 139
—sea-born, ravaged lands about Marathon, i. 62
—šêdu as, v. 361
—see MYTHS OF MINOS.
—symbol of thunder-god and rain-god, v. 60
—title belonging to Dionysos, vii. 15

Bull, water-spirit can show himself in form of, iv. 199
—world-supporting, iv. 311–312
Bulls and S-Symbols, iii. pl. XIX, opp. p. 152
—black, iv. 210; xii. 160, 367 [10]
—carvings of, from Burghhead, iii. pl. XIX, opp. p. 152
—Iason's brazen-footed, made by Hephaistos, i. 207
—mythic, reincarnations of divinities, iii. 124, 127, 152
—on Gaulish coins and monuments, iii. pl. II (4, 5, 9), opp. p. 8; pl. III (5), opp. p. 14; pl. IX (B), opp. p. 86; pl. XX (B), opp. p. 158; pl. XXI, opp. p. 166
—sacred to Anahit, vii. 383 [39]
—winged, v. 358–359
—with brazen feet and flaming breath, Iason ploughs field with, i. 112
Bulrushes, Moses in, v. 158–159
Bumba [also verb bumba, "make," in sense of shaping], a high god, vii. 125, 131–132, 144, 145, 155, 399 [7]
"Bûndahishn" on stars, iv. 344
Bundle of Years, Aztec, xi. 146, 148
Bundles, ceremonial and sacred, x. 109, 111, 269 [4]; xi. 90–91, 167
Bunene, Sumerian god, v. 44
Buninka, the devil, iv. 329
Bunjel sliced earth into creeks and valleys, iii. 136
Bunyip, mythical man-eating animal, ix. 280
—water monster of Australian blacks, vii. 396 [62]
Bur-Sin, v. 327
——as Tammuz, v. 345, 346
——of Ur, shrine of, v. 170
Burbot drowned human beings, iv. 504
Burghhead, carvings of bulls from, iii. pl. XIX, opp. p. 152
Buri, father of Borr, ii. 24, 63, 324
Burial, iv. 480–481, 498, 501, 508; vi. 243, 246; vii. 95; see also entries s.v. FUNERAL.
— -ale, ii. 191
—alive, ii. 309; iii. 130, 233; vii. 280–281; viii. 155; xi. 192
—boat, iv. 32–33
—custom associated with Milky Way, xi. 323

Burial customs, vii. 170, 403 [27]; xii. 182, 418 [23]
——among all Finno-Ugric peoples possess general affinities, iv. 17
——(book of), viii. 140
——costly, extended from kings to common people, xii. 178
——in time of Kuo P'o, viii. 141
——flood and drought may be caused by improper, xii. 298
——in funeral chamber in ship enclosed in tumulus, ii. pl. XVI, opp. p. 130
——last rites of, v. 162
——laying-out oldest method of, as traced by philologists, iv. 34
——methods of, iv. 31–32
——mock, to entice soul back to its home burial-place, iv. 73–74
——of animals upright, iv. 93
——Balder, ii. 135
——bones of bear, iv. 92–93
————animals so that Earth may produce corn and grass, iv. 239, 250–251
————sacrifice to the dead, iv. 38, 136
——dead children, x. 281 [18]
——flesh and bones of sacrifice under floor, iv. 160, 163
——Ludek, iii. 248
——memorial dolls, iv. 42
——totems with Incas, xi. 245
— -place for chiefs and their families, fire temple as, x. 57
——priests: see BAGAVAN ("TOWN OF GODS"), ETC.
— -places, sacred groves are ancient, vii. 190
—preparation for, xi. 80–81
——rites among pagan Slavs, iii. 233
——of Pite Lapps, iv. 3
————Slavic people, water in, vii. 75–76
—scaffold, x. 34
—see, further, items s.v. COFFIN.
—shroud of daughter of Kumush, x. 229–230
—souls denied Christian, iii. 231
—white cloth used in, ix. 237
Burials, orientation to the rising sun indicated to some degree in, x. 287 [31]
Burkhan equated with Buddha, iv. 315, 330, 401

Burkhan, Siberian term for God, iv.
318, 324, 329, 361–362, 375, 379,
420
Burkhans, road of, later Mongol name
for Milky Way, iv. 435
—seven, Mongols called Great Bear the,
iv. 427
Burkhatu-Khan, mountain, iv. 453
Burma, Buddhism enters Indo-China
by way of, xii. 288
—Indonesian affiliations with, ix. 304
—southern, held by Talaings for thousand years, xii. 253
Burmese hostile attitude to neighbours,
xii. 339
—uncertain origin of race and religion
of, xii. 249
Burner Period, xi. 146
Burning ground, ghosts of, vi. 248
—of corpses, iv. 4, 34
——dead, rite of, vi. 70
——ghost, ii. 309
——Gollveig, ii. 27
——Heidrik, ii. 63
——images, iv. 42, 149–150
——man, vii. 222
——sacrifice to Cattleyard man, iv. 162
—with Roses, festival, vii. 59–61
Burnt offerings, v. 221
——for heaven-god, iv. 220–221
——see, further, s. v. OFFERINGS; SAC-
RIFICE, HUMAN; SACRIFICIAL VICTIMS.
—sacrifice, viii. 43
——and utensils, iv. 278–279
——offered by Hermes, i. 192, 193
—sacrifices not offered by Lapps to
their idols, except to sun, iv. 238
Burto, dog of Dogedoi, iv. 433
Būrzhīn Mitrō fire, vi. 306
Buschfrauen, ii. 205, 206
Buschgrossmütter, ii. 206
Bush-demon, Dodo, vii. 325–326
— -fire, why hawk hovers over, vii. 177
—Heaven-reaching, x. 104
— -jumpers, vii. 243
— -rope, vii. 315
— -soul, vii. 279
Bushman rice (ants' larvae), vii. 230,
231
Bushmen aborigines, vii. 109, 112, 113,
115, 120, 264
—treatment of South African, by colon-
ists, vii. 113
Būshyāsta, demon of sloth, vi. 261, 294

Busiris, cult of Osiris spreads over all
Egypt from, xii. 98
—Dêdet worshipped at, xii. 132
—(Home of Osiris), Greek name of
Dêd(u), xii. 92
—Mendes ram embodies soul of Osiris
of, xii. 164
—perhaps centre of cult of Tait as goddess of weaving, xii. 150
—pillar-god of, fused with Mendes-
" spirit," xii. 413 12
Busk, ceremony at maturing of maize,
x. 57–59, 292 39
Bussurman-Mozhga, village home of
Mardan, iv. 151–152
Bustards and emu, tale of, ix. 288–
289
Buth, spring at, vii. 56
Buto and Nekhbet, Merets representatives of two divine kingdoms of, xii.
136–137
—birth and education of Horus localized at or near, xii. 116
—earliest capital of Lower Egypt, xii.
132
—(Egyptian Uazit, Uzoit) serpent-
shaped goddess of Pe(r)-uzoit, xii.
132
—Nekhbet counterpart of, xii. 132, 142
—Nesret identified with, xii. 143
—(Pe-Dep) had " souls " instead of
" gods," xii. 361 2 (ch. i)
—soul (god) of, xii. 32
—two serpents of, belong to Mîn-
Amon, xii. 236
Butter-cat, iv. 172
—offering of, iv. 167
—smeared on doors for return of sun in
spring, iv. 224
—smearing of, as fertility rite, iv. 416
Butterflies come at playing of flute, x.
200
—dance of, viii. 335–336, pl. XL, opp.
p. 336
Butterfly, vii. 418 41
—ghost rises from parted waters as, x.
263
—grey, soul as, iv. 8–9, 13, 240, 241
—insignia, earth-goddesses share, with
fire-gods, xi. 74
—Kawelu becomes a, ix. 76
—Mr., and his flowers, tale of, viii. 345–
346
—Rigi in creation-myth a, ix. 250

Butterfly, soul may leave body as, iii. 229; iv. 473
—of corn assumes shape of, iv. 13
—spirit of, appears in spring night, viii. 213
—tales of, viii. 335–337
—three sons born from three eggs laid by, ix. 328 [25]
Byak-ko, Japanese name for one of Chinese world-guardians, viii. 379 [28]
Byamee, creator-deity, wives of, swallowed by monster, ix. 296
Byat Ta and Byat Twe became skilled in black art, xii. 348
Byblos, body of Osiris received by Melqart and Astarte at, xii. 114
—(Gebal), v. 66

Byblos, mistress of, identified with Ḥathôr, xii. 154
—Osiris-Horus worshipped under name of Tammuz-Adonis at, xii. 241, 395 [84]
—Osiris-myth associated with, xii. 120, 399 [110]
—pillar worshipped at, apparently Egyptian symbol of Dêd, xii. 399 [111]
Byggvir and Beyla, servants of Frey, ii. 110, 144
Byleipt, Loki brother of, ii. 139, 340
Byrgir, well from which came children of Vidfinn, ii. 184
Bytes, Manetho refers to Bati as mythical king, xii. 132
Byzantium (here Asgard), gods dwelt first in, ii. 35, 175

C

Caball (or Cavall), dog of Arthur, iii. 184, 188, 192, 199
Cabiri: see KABIRS.
Cabrakan overcome by hero-brothers, xi. 168, 169–170, 177
Cacao-tree, xi. 193
Cacce-olmai (Cacce-jielle or -jienne), (Water man), iv. 192, 193
Cachimana, Good Spirit of the Orinoco, xi. 259
Cacibagiagua, cave in Hispaniola, xi. 28
Cacus, legends of, vi. 263
—shepherd who stole cattle of Geryoneus from Hercules, i. 303
Cadmus: see KADMOS.
Caduceus, attribute of Hermes, i. 191
Caēcasta, Lake, vi. 337
Caer, maiden of Oengus's dream, iii. 78–82
Caer Ludd, London, iii. 107
—Oeth, Arthur imprisoned three nights in, iii. 189
—Sidi, a part of Annwfn, iii. 95, 96, 111, 122, 192, 339 [4]
Caesar on Gaulish gods, iii. 9
Caesarean operation, xi. 29, 303, 312
Cagn, divine or quasi-divine being, vii. 134–135, 288–290, 418 [47]
Caibell and Etar, tale of, iii. 38
Cain and Abel in Hebrew tradition, v. 202
——Maui and Maru perhaps parallel of, ix. 315 [8]

Cain and Abel story, Surinam parallel of, xi. 274–275
Cairbre, high king of Ireland, iii. 162, 179
—Niaper slain at Ros na Rígh, iii. 155
Cairn, ashes after cremation placed in, or scattered over, iii. 233, 234
—made of heads and arms of slain, iii. 149
—of layer of gold and silver (sacrificial money), raised over Hölgi, ii. 187
Cairns, as distinct from barrows, piled over criminals, ii. 311
Caitraratha, grove of Kubera, vi. 158
Cakchiquel and Quiché, tribes, xi. 156–159
—Annals of the, xi. 177–183, 364 [7]
Cake at festival of Svantovit, iii. 282
—cut into four parts at festival for Stopan, iii. 238
—in shape of animal, preserved in granary until sowing time, iv. 248
—stone thrown to Näkk for protection called a, iv. 203
Cakes baked in shape of boar survival of sacrifice, ii. 109
Cakix, deity of Zotzil, xi. 181
Cakradharman, chief of Vidyādharas, vi. 144
Cakravartin, the "universal monarch," vi. 195–196, 225
Calabash, bones put in, xi. 29
—magic, swallows creation, vii. 223

Calabash, night-, to prolong darkness,
vii. 341
— -tree, xi. 193, 261
Caladbolg, sword of Cúchulainn, iii.
136, 197
Calah, Nimurta principal deity of, v. 55
Calatin, children of, help cause death
of Cúchulainn, iii. 155
Calchaqui, civilization of, xi. 220
—Diaguité, potsherds found in region
of, xi. 235
Calculations, good luck, for marriage,
viii. 143
Caledonius (Merlin the Wild), iii. 201
Calendar, v. 152–153, 154, 400 [164]; vi.
58; viii. 21, 348; x. 30–31, 89, pl. xx,
opp. p. 128, 192–196, 292 [39], 310 [65];
see also YEAR-COUNTS; xi. 52–57, 58,
61, 74, 92, 96–105, 106, 107, 146–152,
158, 184, 329, 358 [9], 363 [22]; xii. 57
Calf owed to Thor, ii. 77; calves
watched over by Orion, xii. 399 [111]
Caliban, xi. 332
Caliburnus, sword of Arthur, iii. 185,
197
Calli ("House"), day-sign, xi. 100
Calligraphy, origin of, viii. 35
Calling or touching clothes of one
"away" would prevent return, vii.
187
Calneh: see KULLABA, ETC.
Calumet ceremony, x. xvi, 20–22, 83,
141, 271 [6], 286 [30], 287 [31]
—on raft personified as "Flatpipe"
representing the palladium, x. 308 [63]
Camahueto may cause wrecks, xi. 328
Camalotz, bird, xi. 164
Camaxtli similar to Huitzilopochtli, xi.
59, 92
Camazotz, House of, a place of ordeal,
xi. 174, 177
Cambodia, Aryan infusion in Indo-
China from, xii. 288
—Indian Trickster Tales found in, ix.
242
—mouse-deer as trickster-hero in, ix.
203
Camel and riders in sky cause of rain,
iv. 444
Camenae, Roman muses, i. 295
Camese, Ianus associated with, i. 297
Cam-hke River, in Province of Son-tay,
columns erected by Ma-vien near, xii.
314

Camlan, battle at, iii. 184, 189, 190–
191, 192
Camoodi, Mt. Roraima guarded by an
enormous, xi. 277
Camp, form of, x. 80
Campāpurī, Vāsupūjya obtained release
at, vi. 222
Camrōsh, bird, vi. 289
Cam-thin, a monk, offered prayers for
rain at temple of Trung sisters, xii.
314
Camudi, constellation, xi. 278
Camulodunum (? Colchester), name of
god Camulos found in, iii. 164
Camulos (warrior-god), Cumhal iden-
tified with, iii. 164
Cana submitted to Incas, xi. 244
Canaan, customs and language of,
spread throughout the Nile-land in
New Empire, xii. 154–155
Canal of flames: see ISLAND OF FLAMES.
Canal star, v. 308, 309, 316
Cancer station of Marduk-Jupiter, v.
304
Caṇḍakauśika, Indian sage, vi. 156
Cāṇḍāla, Viśvāmitra debates with, vi.
146
Cāṇḍālikā, a form of Śiva's wife, vi.
205
Candir, shaper of land and father of
men, xi. 297
Candle, Candles:
Candle lighted and, after prayer, extinguished, at feast for dead, iii. 236,
238
—see, further, items s. v. WAX TAPERS.
Candles, ii. 213, 214, 215, 241–242; vii.
56, 58, 59, 94–95, 388 [10]
—for lud-worship made in sacred grove,
iv. 150
—held at night by fairylike genii of
fate, iii. 250
—on rim of Tōnni vakk, iv. 137
Candlemas, bonfires and New Fires on,
vii. 57, 388 [11]
Candlestick at foot of sacrifice tree, iv.
266, 267, 269, 274, 279
Candra, Candramas, the moon, vi. 82,
91, 117, 136
Candrabhāgā (modern Chenab), vi.
183
Cane with white feathers, a symbol of
breath of life, x. 59
Canens, son of Ianus and Venilia, i. 297

Canicubá, evil spirit, xi. 197
Canis Major, v. 135, 233, 317
——(name of bow of Marduk), bow of hunter Orion, v. 308
Cannibal Babe, x. 10, 146, 281 [19]
—concealing victim from, x. 132, 138
—demons, vi. 244
—feast, vii. 337, 340–341
—heads, x. 290 [37]–291
— -myths, iv. 494–495
—Society, x. 246, 286 [29]
— -spirits, iv. 484
—tutelary of secret society, x. 246–249, 254
—Woman, x. 243–244
Cannibals, cannibalism, i. 119; ii. 211; iv. 386–389, 423; vi. 112, 156, 157; vii. 136, 141, 156, 177–178, 203, 219, 242, 243, 249, 252, 254, 259, 260, 337, 399 [11], 414 [24 25], 414 [29]; viii. 155; ix. 57–58, 59, 60, 61, 62, 63, 65, 67, 69, 74, 79, 84–86, 123, 130–138, 148, 178, 227–232, 271, 298–300; x. xx, 10, 29, 176, 246–249, 281 [19]; xi. 17, 19, 36, 37, 72, 76, 197–198, 242, 300–304, 348 [2], 349 [5]; xii. 202, 213; see also items s. v. OGRES.
—water-, x. 68, 274 [9]
Canoe paddle as sacred emblem of Mukasa, vii. 129
Canoes, ix. 55, 61, 62–63, 68, 124–125, 257
Canola connected with discovery of harp, iii. 137
Canopic vases, viscera of dead placed in, xii. 112
Canopus (star), Osiris connected with, xii. 57, 94
——perhaps identified with ferryman of Underworld, xii. 58
——regarded as Horus, xii. 116
——Shou Hsing, God of Longevity, takes his name from, viii. 81
Canton, people of, still called "Men of T'ang," viii. 5–6
Cantul-ti-ku (four gods), xi. 154
Canul, Mexican mercenaries settled at, xi. 127
Canum-Lum, successor of Votan, xi. 133
Canute, laws of, ii. 198, 201
Canzienal, omen under Muluc, xi. 145
Cao-bien, celestial white horse appears to, xii. 317

Cao-bien, General, King, and protector-spirit of Annam, worshipped at Bach-ma Temple, xii. 316
—guardian-protector of Thanh-long, xii. 318–319
—portent appeared to, xii. 317–318
Caoilte, Irish hero, iii. 32, 45, 55, 89, 126, 129, 169, 174, 180, 182, 209–210, 212
Caoilte mac Ronan, Fionn's nephew, famed for fleetness, iii. 162, 163
Cap of darkness belongs to Hades, i. 34
——rushes (resembling crown of Upper Egypt) characteristic head-dress of most Asiatic gods, xii. 155, 400 [111], 411 [6]
Capac, a window through which came four Ayars with their wives, xi. 248
Cape Province, some Bushmen in, vii. 113
Capital of Silence, viii. 22
Cappadocia, Tīr migrates from Iran to, vii. 32
Capricorn, v. 95, 106, 108, 283, 395 [21]
—station of Nergal-Mars, v. 304
Captive, offer of reward for tying withe around foot of, iii. 68
—women, Caribs ate children of, xi. 349 [5]
Captives adopted, x. 102
—sacrificed and bodies eaten, xi. 76
——that blood might fertilize earth, xi. 79
—taken in war, sacrifice of, x. 285 [29]
Captivity, souls in, iv. 477
Capture, marriage by, viii. 229
Car, Eos rides in, i. 246
—Eosphoros rides in, i. 247
—see items s.v. CHARIOT; WAGGONS OF GODS.
—Selene rides across heavens in, i. 245
Cara, Caraques, city of, xi. 206–207
Caracalla, coin of, with moon-god, v. 154
Caracaracol (Mangy), son of Itiba Tahuvava, cause of flood, xi. 29
Caracarols (Haitian), shell people who caused flood, xi. 272
Caradawc (historic Caractacus), son of Bran, iii. 106, 191
Cāraṇas, minstrels or troubadours, vi. 143
Carapucu, meaning of, xi. 239
Caravaya, cross erected in mountains of, xi. 239

Cardinal points, ii. 264–265; iv. 308, 344, 347–348, 359–360, 371, 445, 457, 486; vi. 16, 134, 196, 203, 215; 276, pl. xxxv, opp. p. 284; viii. 46, 50, 64, 142; 242–243; x. 19, 22, 23, 37, 40, 41, 48, 58, 60, 63, 81, 97, 98, 99, 100, 101, 108–109, 135, 159, 160, 161, 162, 167, 168, 179, 185, 203, 275 [11], 287 [31], 308 [63]; xi. 52, 55, 122, 126, 139, 141; xii. 37, 39, 46, 112, 363 [4], 367 [10]

Carib, *caniba,* is the source of cannibal, xi. 17, 37, 348 [2]

—description and customs of, xi. 36–38

Caricatures of themselves, fighting demons by, v. 255

Caripe, beliefs connected with Grotto of, xi. 279

Carman and her sons, tale of, iii. 35–36

Carmenta, functions of, survive in modern Romagnola, i. 319

Carmentis (or Carmenta), Roman muse, i. 295

Carna (Cardea, Cardo), goddess of hinges, passion of Ianus for, i. 297

*Carnoglovy, "black-headed," Leger regards Tiernoglav as error for, iii. 353 [27]

Carnutes, coin of the, iii. pl. II (11), opp. p. 8, pl. III (5), opp. p. 14

Carpenter-god, v. 263

Carrhae, city, v. 19, 154

Carrying off of people in dreams, vii. 184

Carthage, Aeneas at, i. 305

—Ṣêd-Melqart at, v. 53

Caru, brother of Tiri, xi. 314–315

Carvings, x. 238, 245, 264

Cascade, name of, not to be spoken, xi. 267–268

Case, sacrifice: see SACRIFICE CASE.

Cashel, dynastic family reigning at, iii. 45

Casket, Anglo-Saxon, ii. pl. xxxiv, opp. p. 266, pl. xxxv, opp. p. 272

—magic, of Urashima, viii. 264–265

—miraculous, viii. 320

Cassava (manioc), song of, xi. 291, 292, 293

Cassiopeia, constellation, associated with "Dôn's Court," iii. 100

Cassivellaunus, Caswallawn confused with, iii. 106

"Castaway," name of Ch'i, viii. 41

Castes, institution of, vi. 103, 105, 108, 216; 317–318

Casting lots, v. 356

—of skin brings life, ix. 182

Castle of Cúroi guarded by spells, iii. 148–149

Castor: see KASTOR.

Castration: see EMASCULATION.

Caswallawn, son of Beli, iii. 101, 106

Cat, Cats:

Cat, iv. 362; vi. 242

—and deer, tale of, ix. 202

—animal form of Ubastet, xii. 29

—"Bearer" resembles a, iv. 172

—butter-, iv. 172

—dancing, vii. 276–277

—demon, iii. 191

—fire, iv. 236

—-god cuts a serpent into fragments at foot of celestial tree, xii. 106–107

—-goddess, Ubastet a, xii. 150

—"golden flower," viii. 327, 328

—haltia appears as, iv. 169, 170

—Ketuiti has head of, xii. 417 [21]

—knife-bearing, xii. 107

—-like god, xii. 106 (fig. 105)

—of Utgard-Loki the Midgard-serpent, ii. 92–93

—Paluc, Arthur clove the, iii. 191

—(totem) taken by Titishana, tale of, vii. 276–278

—uncanny power of, viii. 325, 327, 328–329

—who gave birth to girl child, tale of, ix. 238–239

Cats draw waggon of Freyja, ii. 22, 120

—sacred, not divine, xii. 169

—three, Druidic creatures, iii. 147

Cataclysm, Celts' fear of a, iii. 12

Cataclysms, x. 221–225, 228, 294 [41]; xi. 91, 94, pl. XIII, opp. p. 94, 230, 240, 268–275, 311–315, 342; see also SUNS, EARLY WORLD EPOCHS; WORLD, DESTRUCTION OF.

Cataleptics believed to return from spirit-world, vii. 184

Cataract, First, place where sun's eye was lost, xii. 90

—region, Khnûm(u) deity of, xii. 135

Caterpillars, sacrifice to departed without kin on appearance of, iv. 9

Cath Finntrága ("Battle of Ventry"), iii. 175

—Godeu, mythic battle of, iii. 96

Cathbad, Druid, iii. 140, 142
—sang of births of Christ and Conchobar, iii. 208
Cathedral of City of Mexico, xi. 59
Cattle and rainbow, vii. 236
—brought to earth by Uldda, iv. 178
——gods' land by heroes, iii. 127, 128
—coming of, myth, vii. 373-374
—driven through fire at time of cattle-plague, ii. 202
— -fructifier, sacrifice to, iv. 259
—herding of Death's, vii. 174-175
—hind quarters of, taken in some nomes, xii. 362 ³
—horned, Karneian Apollo as god of, i. 180
— -luck, iv. 275
—of Apollo stolen by the infant Hermes, i. 192, 193
——Oilill, iii. 73
——síd of Cruachan, iii. 69
——Sun, i. 113
——Water-maid, grey and blue, iv. 202
—owned by Maahiset may be captured by throwing steel upon them, iv. 205
— -plague, ii. 202
— -Raid of Cúalnge: see "TÁIN BÓ CÚALNGE."
——Fráich: see "TÁIN BÓ FRÁICH."
——Regamon: see "TÁIN BÓ REGAMNA."
—recovered from dún, iii. 130-131
—red, owned by Geryoneus, i. 86, 303
—ritual passing of, through fires at Beltane possibly connected with the passing through fire of kine of Munster, iii. 26
—sacred, of the Sun, slain by Odysseus's men, i. 137
—spell cast by Lug on, iii. 28, 29
— -Spoil of Cúalnge: see "TÁIN BÓ CÚALNGE."
—stolen by Charybdis from Herakles, i. 264
—stories of how they came to earth, vii. 149-150
—troll-ridden, ii. 302
—Tuatha Dé Danann had power over, iii. 40
Cattleyard man, Votiak god, iv. 161, 166
Cau, title, later adopted as family name, xii. 355
Cauac years, xi. 145

Cauca valley, inhabitants of, xi. 196-197
Caucasus, Io wanders through, i. 29
—Prometheus imprisoned in, i. 13
Caul, a meaning of, ii. 235
—Cian born with, iii. 132
Cauldron and cows taken from dún, iii. 132, 151
— -bearer, Salic Law of Franks condemns calling any one, ii. 301
—boiling, containing seals, x. 6
—Dagda's, iii. 120, 192, 204
—first, iii. 137
— -holder, iv. 266
—of Diwrnach, iii. 192
——giant pair out of lake restored life to dead although they remained dumb, iii. 100-101, 105, 112
——inspiration and science to boil one year, iii. 109, 111, 112
——knowledge of Cerridwen, iii. 112
——Ogyrven, iii. 112
Cauldrons, divine, iii. 203
—Ketuiti god of, xii. 417 ²¹
—magic, iii. 95, 100, 101, 111, pl. XIV, opp. p. 120, 192, 193, 203
Causation, bond of moral, viii. 218
—law of, viii. 221-222
Causes, nine and thirteen, xi. 354 ⁷-355
Causeway to be built, iii. 81
Caut and Cautopat, vi. pl. XXXVI, opp. p. 288
Cavall, Arthur's horse, iii. 192
Cavalla, fetish of, vii. 178
Cave, Artavazd confined in, vii. 98, 99
—disobedient spirit confined in, viii. 276
—dragons confined in, cause drought, viii. 276-277
—dwellings, vii. 258, 259
—heavenly, viii. 226-227, pl. VIII, opp. p. 226
—Loki bound to stones in, ii. 146
—Mher confined in, vii. 34, 370
—of winds, myth of, v. 99
—Oisin entered, and lived there three hundred years, iii. 181
—painted, in which earth-goddess worshipped, xi. 270
—paintings, vii. 418 ⁴⁰
—under waterfall, giant slain in, ii. 280
—Wayland Smith's, ii. pl. I, frontispiece

Cavern which swallowed the Flood, v. 37, 38

Caves, iii. 60, 126, 147
—believed entrances to Underworld, i. 143
—burial, watched over by priests and vestals, xi. 217, 218
—first people came out of, vii. 147, 184; xi. 28, 29, 30
—lead to spirit-world, vii. 184, 195
—Seven, at Tulan-Zuiva, xi. 166
——whence Aztecs came, identified with Seven Cities of Cibola, xi. 20

Cavillaca (a virgin) pregnant from eating fruit containing seed of Coniraya, xi. 228–229

Caybatz and Caynoh, sons of Gagavitz, xi. 182

Cayman, people of both sexes born from, xi. 262, 267

Cazziva, tale of, xi. 35

Cecisemi, priests, xi. 351

Cedar forest guarded by Humbaba, v. 247, 248, 252, 253, 255
—god in, xii. 80, 382 [72]
—Mountain of Syrian coast, " Story of the Two Brothers " laid on, xii. 153

Cedars, forest of, vii. 69

Ceiba growing through holes in heavens, path of souls, xi. 140

Ceiuci, tale of, xi. 303–304

Celebes, ape or tortoise as trickster-hero in, ix. 203, 204
—Indian influence in parts of, ix. 242

" Celebration of Birthday of Hsi Wang Wu, etc.," viii. 128–130

Celenderis founded by Sandakos, vii. 41

Celestial affairs, Jupiter sways, iii. 9
—beings, viii. 256–280
—deities, xi. 38, 138, 245
—divinities, Shu and Tefênet as, xii. 70
—four sons of Horus or Osiris interpreted as, xii. 112
—goddess, Neith as, xii. 142 (fig. 144)
—King of the Ox's Head (god Guzu Tenno), identified with Indra, viii. 228
—maiden, sun, moon, and stars originated from, ix. 177
—nature, feather patterns of dress of deities as indication of, xii. 212
—origin of Yamato people, viii. 211, 212

Celestial Teacher, Chang called himself, viii. 14
——mystical characters of, as charms, viii. 153–154

Celt, prehistoric, iii. 319

Celtchar, daughter of Calatin, took form of daughter of, and bade Cúchulainn fight, iii. 155

Celtic influence on Eddic poems, ii. 8

Celtica, giant daughter of king of, and Hercules, northern Gauls descended from, iii. 13

Cemeteries, Mātṛs inhabit, vi. 156
—village, and special, Finno-Ugric, iv. 35, 36

Cemetery, half-way place between house and, where belongings of dead are left, iv. 25

Cemis (Zemis), wooden images, xi. 22–26, 350 [9]

Cenn Crúaich (" Head of the Mound "), image of, at Mag Slecht, iii. 45
——sacrifice to, iii. 46–47

Cenomani, coin of the, iii. pl. II (3), opp. p. 8

Centaur (Nessos) killed by Herakles because of attack on Deianeira, i. 93
—see JUSHKAPARIK.
—water-spirit (Iceland and Sweden) may be a sort of, ii. 210

Centaurs and Lapiths, i. pl. XXVI, opp. p. 100
—fight with Herakles, i. 82
—Greek, name " Gandharvas " identified with, vi. 59
—Herakles purified of blood of, i. 88
—(Kentauroi), i. 270–271
—perhaps survive in modern Greek Kallikantzaroi, i. 315
—Thessalian, attack the Lapith women, i. 105, 270
—two, slain by Atalante, i. 57

Centipede, killing of, by Tōda, viii. 314
—Sop's name written with sign of, xii. 409 [104]

Central America, mythology of, xi. 156–186
—Park, Peking, viii. 64
—Polynesia as a myth-centre, ix. 93–94

Centre of the House, xi. 176
—worship of, viii. 64

Centzonuitznaua (" the Four Hundred Southerners "), xi. 60, 77

Cerberus: see KERBEROS.

Cerds (braziers), iii. 31

Cereals, omens from, planted at Plough-ing Festival, xii. 331–332

Ceremonial cleanliness, xii. 193, 419 [17]

—precinct or plaza, xi. pl. XXIII, opp. p. 160

Ceremonies, Master of Religious, viii. 46

—observance of family and tribal, viii. 7, 8

Ceres, Cerus, old Italic gods, i. 291–292

—in Roman mythology, represents Demeter in Greek, i. 288

—Marzyana identified with, iii. 355 [44]

Cerna, Conaire's pursuit of beasts of, a broken tabu, iii. 76

Černobog, god of evil, iii. 288, pl. XXXIV (3), opp. p. 288

Cernunnos, Celtic, ii. pl. XXXI, opp. p. 238, pl. XXXII, opp. p. 246

—Dispater perhaps Roman name for, iii. 9

—horned deity, iii. pl. XVI, opp. p. 128, 129, 158, pl. XXV, opp. p. 204

—triple-headed god [squatting god] may be another form of, iii. pl. VII, opp. p. 56, pl. VIII, opp. p. 72, 104–105

Cerridwen, Brythonic goddess, iii. 57, 109, 110, 111, 112

Cessair, Noah's granddaughter, fable of coming of, to Ireland, iii. 23, 206

Cet, son of Scáthach, iii. 144, 145, 157

Ceterni, wife of Naymlap, xi. 208

Céthlionn, wife of Balor, iii. 29

Cetus, v. 308

Ceylon, Buddhists in, vi. 187

—Hīnayāna carried to Burma and Siam from, xii. 260

Cezalcouati, a prince who became the god, xi. 126

Cha (La), harvest sacrifice, viii. 61

Chaabou (Ka'bu), identified with Korē, v. 16, 18, 382 [68]

Chac Xib Chac, ruler of Chichen Itza, xi. 128

Chacanputun occupied by the Itza, xi. 128

Chacnouiton (Chacnabiton), Xiu so-journ at, xi. 128

Chaco, mythology of, xi. 322–323

—physical and ethnological conditions of, xi. 316–318

Chacs, gods of abundance, xi. 137, 138, 140

Chac-u-Uayeyab, idol, xi. 145

Chad, Lake, vii. 145

Chaddanta, phrase denoting one who has the six organs of sense under control, vi. 358 [6]

Chagan-Shukuty, assistant to creator, iv. 319–320, 329, 377

Chains, iii. 10, 11, 78, 79, 82

—in Swan-maiden myths, ii. 261, 263

—on drums, iv. 288

—Ugarthilocus bound with, ii. 95

Chair fastened to pygmies, vii. 260

—moving, given to Thor, ii. 84

—of Taliesin, iii. 104, 111

—song of, that was defended from Cer-ridwen's cauldron, iii. 112

—with invisible snares, i. 206

Chakekenapok, Fire-stone man, x. pl. IX, opp. p. 38, 41, 44, 298 [47]

Chalchiuhtlicue, goddess of water, xi. 54, 56, 71–73, 92, 93

Chalcuitl, stone from heaven, destroyed pyramid, xi. 96

Chaldean method of reckoning time, iv. 438

Chalice and paten, pagan image of viper made into, ii. 216

Chalkidike, perhaps home of giant-chil-dren of Ouranos and Gaia, i. 9

Chalkis native habitat of Proteus, i. 332 [4] (ch. xii)

Chalybes (nation of iron-workers), Argonauts sail to, i. 111

Cham, Indian Trickster Tales found among, ix. 242

Chameleons, vii. 106, 121, 129, 134, 160–166, 168, 171, 172, 280, 284

Chamiabak, one of lords of Underworld, xi. 173

Chamiaholom, one of lords of Under-world, xi. 173

Champa Sak, Lao Shan name of area once occupied by Chams, xii. 287

Champion's light projected from fore-head of Cúchulainn, iii. 11

—portion at feasts, iii. 146, 147

Champions of the Red Branch, iii. 139–140

Chams conquered by Annamese and Shans, xii. 287–288

—mouse-deer as trickster-hero among, ix. 203

Chams of Cambodia, myths of, have influenced those of Siamese, xii. 268
Chan huo, viii. 143, 144
—Kuo ("Warring States"), origin of astrology should be placed during time of the, viii. 143
—Serpent, Votan of house of, xi. 132
—yao kuai, viii. 123
Ch'an Tzŭ-fang, name of Prince of Furnace in human form, viii. 75–76
Chancay, seat of Chincha Confederacy, xi. 220
Chance, Tychē divinity of, i. 283–284
Chandraprabha River, cataract of the, vi. 235
Chang, jade tablet, viii. 46
Chang and Li, tale of, viii. 150–151
—Chio, viii. 174
—Chiu-ling, littérateur, viii. 68
—Êr-ch'i, viii. 70
—Fei, viii. 174, 176, 177
—Hsien (Chang Yüan-hsiao), viii. 82–84
—Hua, viii. 70
—Kuo(-lao), one of Eight Immortals, viii. 124–125
—Liang, hero, viii. 92–93, 94
—Shan-Chün, viii. 106–107
—Shuo, littérateur, viii. 68
—Tao-ling, ascetic, viii. 13–14, 16, 19, 20, 21, 22, 24, 55, 94, 103, 134, 145, 153, 154
—Ya-tzŭ, viii. 112
—Yüan hsiao, viii. 83
Ch'ang-an, arms discovered in temple at, viii. 189, 190
Ch'ang Ch'un, viii. 23
—Kiang River, viii. 191
—(Wên Wang), son of Chi Li, viii. 41, 42
Changelings, ii. 212, 272; iii. 262, 264, 265, 266; iv. 11; vii. 74, 78, 80, 391 [12], 395 [52]
Channels disappearing underground behind entrance to Underworld, i. 143
Channini, altar to, ii. 37
Chants of ceremonials learned only by sons of chiefs, xi. 35, 351 [10]
Chanum and Woi-shun, parents of all things, xii. 263, 264
Chao Chung, magistrate of Pao Ch'ing, in tale of Li Chi, viii. 184–187
—Kung-ming, origin of god of riches traced back to, viii. 79, 80
—Mêng-fu, statesman, viii. 23, 24

Chao Yün, General of Liu Pei, viii, 175, 179
Ch'ao-chou (Canton Province), Han Yü Prefect of, viii. 201
—(Kuantung Province), Han Hsiang banished to, viii. 127
—serpent destroyed in, viii. 203
Ch'ao Yang Mên, viii. 23, 71, 135
Chaos, i. 5, 203; ii. 321; vi. 264; viii. 57; 222; ix. 5, 8, 9, 10, 12, 15, 26, 166–167, 169; x. 45, 61, 106
—dragons of, v. 86, 102, 108, 117–118, 127, 130, 233, 277, 282, 288, 325
—watery, male and female principles of, v. 289, 290
Chapels, memorial, foundations for maintenance of, xii. 183
—of dead, purpose of, xii. 172
Char, Armenian ruler of power of evil, vii. 86
Character of owner, animal Fylgja had corresponding aspect to, ii. 234
—tests in tales, vii. 204–205
Characters, eight, examination of, to determine astral influence at birth, viii. 143
——marriages arranged by comparison of, viii. 149
—seventy-six, on scroll, viii. 129
Charchasham used by Nhangs, vii. 90
Chariot, Car, vi. 19, 27, 30, 33, 37, 38, 39, 41, 45, 55, 57, 58, 61, 108, 120, 138, 140, 144, 158
—and horses seen by Greeks in sun, i. 243
—given by Poseidon to Pelops, i. 119, 213
—invented by Erechtheus, i. 68
—of Babylonian Ishtar, v. 27, 385 [131]
——sun made from sparks from Muspell, ii. 343
——sun-god, temple drawn by oxen refers to, v. 54
— -race, suitors challenged to, i. 119
—sun-symbol of Tyre in, v. 54
—symbol, v. 388 [223]
—Triton drives, over sea, i. 260
—Ursa Major known to Homer as the, i. 251
— -wheels, thunder-clap rumbling noise of, ii. 78
—wind-driven, of sun and moon, v. 55
—with winged dragon, Marduk driving, v. 118

Charioteer of sun-god, Rakīb El is, v. 44

Chariots, iii. 70, 71, 74, 90, 115
—in tombs of kings at Kish and Ur, v. 346, 414 [29]
—see also WAGGONS OF GODS.

Charissa (Charonissa), wife of Charos in modern Greek folk-belief, i. 314

Charites (Graces), i. 236–237
——affinity of Aphrodite with, i. 198, 329 [2] (ch. vi)
——three, i. pl. XLIII, opp. p. 188

Charlemagne desired to know what Frisian law was, ii. 163

Charles's Wain: see URSA MAJOR.

Charm, hemp, viii. 380 [7] (ch. ii)
—see MERSEBURG CHARM.

Charms, i. 31; ii. 17–18, 24, 38, 45, 46, 70, 124, 137, 165, 195, 201, 252, 253, 260, 283, 298, 300, 301, 351 [6]; iii. 149, 168; 262; iv. 226; v. 74, 302, 353, 363, 415 [7]; vi. 96, 203; vii. 60; 178, 237, 267, pl. XXXVI, opp. p. 340; viii. 149–150, 153, 156, 157, 158, 159; 226, pl. VIII, opp. p. 226, 251, 380 [7] (ch. ii); ix. 48, 59, 61, 63, 64, 67, 84, 85, 213, 249, 336 [10]; x. 100, 104, 269 [4], 293 [40], 302 [55], 308 [62]; xii. 83, 299, 300, 335, 348

Charon, ferryman to Underworld, i. 142, pl. XXXV, opp. p. 142
—survivals of, in modern Greek folk-belief, i. 314

Charos (Charondas), represents Charon in modern Greek folk-belief, i. 314

Charpan buried with young virgin, iv. 29

Charrhae, coins of, v. 154

Charthoλ, Hambaru defined as, vii. 91

Charybdis and Skylla, i. 113, 263–264
—daughter of Gaia and Poseidon, i. 264
—Odysseus driven to, by Notos and Euros, i. 265–266

Chase, Celtic divinities of the, iii. 21

Chastity, Indian women make vow of, xi. 282
—of Artemis, i. 185

Chautury (from chartularium, charter, record), festival for dead, iii. 235–236

Chavin de Huantar, monolith at, xi. 215, pl. XXXI, opp. p. 218, 226, 235

Chay Abah, obsidian stone, xi. 179

Chayanpur, Harṣu Pānre local god of, vi. 243

Chazrag, tribe, worshippers of Manât, v. 21

Chê ch'i shan, viii. 89

Chedorlaomer, v. 355

Cheiron accidentally wounded by Herakles and dies, i. 82
—Aktaion's picture before cave of centaur, pacified his hounds, i. 47
—and the Muses instruct Aristaios, i. 252
—eternal immunity of, from death conferred on Prometheus, i. 88, 158
—Iason educated by, i. 108
—noble attributes of, i. 270
—Peleus places Achilles in care of, i. 122
——saved from death by, i. 121, 122
—son of Philyra by Kronos, i. 11
—trained Aktaion to be a huntsman, i. 46
——Asklepios in the hunt and healing, i. 280

Chekechani, Morning Star, vii. 228

Cheleule, lesser devils, xi. 332

Chelone changed by Hermes into tortoise-shell and then lyre, i. 195

Chembe: see BUMBA.

Chemin, sky-god, xi. 38

Chemmis, Babi associated with, xii. 403 [15]
—Horus born in island of, xii. 116
—Pans and Satyrs of, xii. 114
—shrew-mouse dedicated to Horus of, xii. 165
—site of cult of Mîn(u), xii. 137–138

Chên, viii. 113, 134
—Jên (" Perfect Ones "), viii. 108, 113
—Kuang-jui, tale of, viii. 190–193
—Tsung, Emperor, viii. 70, 71, 112, 154
——ceded territory to Kitan Tatars, viii. 58
—Wu reincarnation of Yüan Shih, viii. 111

Ch'ên, capital city of Fu Hsi, viii. 30

Ch'êng Chi, divination before birth of, viii. 138
—Ch'ing, guardian of portal, viii. 78
—Huang, god of city, viii. 67–70
—T'ang, Emperor, viii. 9, 38, 48
—Ts'ui, eunuch, viii. 202
— -tu, capital of Liu Pei, viii. 176
—Wang, successor of Wu Wang, viii. 43, 66

Cheops and Thôth in inscriptions, v. 378 [14]
Cherchez la femme, i. 15
Cheremiss, a people akin to the Finns, iv. xvi, xix
Cherlak, story of Lake, iv. 210–211
Cherruve, man-headed serpents, xi. 327
Cherry: see LADY YAYE-ZAKURA, ETC.
Cherry-blossoms, fairy of, viii. 257; see also FLOWERS, PLANTS, TREES, TALES OF.
Cherub, v. 108
Cherubim guard tree of life, v. 186
Chess, vii. 356
—game between Arthur and Owein, iii. 190
——Eochaid and Midir, iii. 81
— -men of Bécuma and Art stolen, iii. 72
Chest, Adonis hidden in, by Aphrodite, i. 198
—Auge and her son set adrift on sea in, i. 22
—cave, or cosmic monster, animals released from, x. 294 [41]
—containing infant Erichthonios, Pandrosos entrusted with, i. 67
—Danaë and her son Perseus set adrift on Aegean by Akrisios in, i. 33
—eternal life kept in, x. 262
—god-, iv. 38, 120
—god in floating, richly developed in Asia, xii. 399 [111]
—infant Horus placed in floating, xii. 116
—Loki shut up in, ii. 83
—money, prayers for, iv. 275
—mystic, iv. 441
——represented in marble relief of Elusinian rites, i. pl. L, opp. p. 230
—Osiris floats in, as a child or as dead, xii. 94, 385 [6]
—sun-god represented in, xii. 71, 105
—sun or daylight imprisoned in, x. 256
—Ukko's, iv. 228–229
—young Horus sits in, xii. 396 [93]
Chestnut of Kurita, viii. 339
— -tree, mythical, viii. 339–340
"Chevalier de la Charette," French poem of Arthurian cycle, iii. 195, 197
Chi Li, Ch'ang son of, viii. 41
Ch'i, aura, viii. 56
—("Castaway"), Minister of Agriculture to Yao, viii. 41
—palace at, viii. 39
—state of, viii. 9, 11, 32

Ch'i Hou, set of bronze vessels, viii. 48
— -lin, unicorn, viii. 98
—Po, viii. 14, 29
Chia ("moon"), wife of Bochica, xi. 202
—Chang and Yüeh Hsiang, tale of, viii. 172–173
—chia, viii. 138
—Ching, Emperor, viii. 73
—Hsien pavilion, home of Chang Hsien, viii. 83–84
—I, viii. 138
—Yü Hsien, viii. 175
Chiang Ko, person who left example of filial piety, viii. 163
—Shan, name of Purple Mountain changed to, viii. 65
—shih, rigid corpse, which may come to life and waylay people, viii. 150
—Shih, viii. 165
—T'ai Kung Tsai Tz'ŭ put over doors, etc., to frighten evil spirits, viii. 153
—Tzŭ-wên, tale of, viii. 65
—Tzŭ-ya destroys Chao Kung-ming by magic, viii. 79–80, 153
—Yüan, father of Hou-chi, viii. 6
Chiao sacrifice to Heaven and earth, viii. 61
Chibcha, myths of, xi. 197, 198–204
Chibchachum, tutelary of natives of Bogotá, xi. 203, 204
Chibiabos, Algonquian prototype of Huron Iouskeha, x. 39, 47, 297 [47]–298
Chibirias, virgin mother of (Yucatec) second person of trinity, xi. 143
Chichen Itza, capital of the Itza, xi. 126, 128, 129, 136
Chichimec tribe, xi. 108–109, 111
Chicken bones as omens, xii. 335
—drenched (or bird), Škrata conceived as, iii. 245
—live, cast on coffin to prevent dead taking poultry-luck, iv. 18
Chicomecoatl (seven snakes), female counterpart of Cinteotl, xi. 75
Chicomoxtoc (seven caves), xi. 89, 112
Chiconamictlan, ninth hell, xi. 81
Chiconauapan, nine-fold stream of Underworld, xi. 81
Chicuna, lord of all things, xi. 193
Chicunauhmictlan, ninth pit, xi. 53
Chie (Huytaca, Xubchasgagua), woman who taught doctrines opposed to Chiminizagagua, xi. 202, 203

Chief, Bushongo Paramount, vii. 132
—of Heaven, x. 35
—Wealthy, x. 256
Chiefs, female, vii. 198
—Gothic word ansis used in titles of dead ancestral, ii. 20
Chieh Kuei to be superseded by T'ang, viii. 38
Ch'ien, viii. 136, 141
—bamboo slips, viii. 138
—Lung, Emperor, viii. 17, 88, 95
—shih, viii. 139
Chieng Mai, remains of Wa forts still found at, xii. 295
Chih, viii. 168
—Nü (" The Weaving Damsel "), viii. 97, 132, 162
Ch'ih Pi (modern Chia Yü Hsien), battle at, viii. 175
—Sung Tzŭ, arbiter of rain, viii. 94
—Yu, country ravished by, viii. 28
Chihli, Province of, viii. 39, 96
Chikamasi, sea-spirit (also North Wind) of Congo Bavili, vii. 411 46
Chikubu-shima, shrine at, viii. 270
Child, acceptance of newly born, by father, ii. 80
—born from boil on shin-bone, vii. 222
——to woman abandoned in tree or pit, ix. 233, 338 43
—dug up from base of two roots (mandrake superstition), x. 232
—duties of fate-deities at birth of, x. 253
—fish by day human at night, xi. 286
—in boar form, iii. 125
—legend of Weeping, x. 146
—must take over spirit of a Bodhisattva on its death, vi. 209
—new-born, laid on earth for strength, ii. 195–196
——shaped by Khnûm, xii. 51
—of sky-maiden and mortal cut in two and animals, birds, etc., made from, ix. 177
——Sun, title of Goranchacha who, born as an emerald, later became human, xi. 201
——Wasserkopf left in place of a stolen child, ii. 212
——Waters mentioned in magic Mandaean inscriptions as Nbat, vi. 360 14

Child of woman who died in child-birth lives in grave and is nourished by mother's body, x. 260
—receives shadow-soul from outside at birth, iv. 472
—soul of dead relative may enter new-born, x. 10
—spirit of ancestor comes into unborn, through name chosen, iv. 15
—to carry on line begged of ghosts, vii. 195–196
—water-spirit may appear as, iv. 197–198, 201
—without father, blood of, used in Foundation Sacrifice, iii. 200
Childbed, Näck desires women in, ii. 211
—Navi trouble women in, iii. 254
Child-birth, angels descend from Heaven to aid in, v. 98
—birth-runes aid, ii. 240
—branch of laurus nobilis supposed to aid in, v. 97
—connexion of Hekate and Artemis with, i. 185, 187
—demons [Als] at, vii. 88–89
—earth-goddess is goddess of, v. 91
—Êpet helpful at, xii. 60, 62
—fruit of Mimameid good in, ii. 331
—images of deity of, iv. 260–261
—incantations for, v. 96–97, 366
—Ixchel invoked at, xi. 143
—magic ritual for delivery of woman in, v. 274, 276
—Mar goddess of, v. 110
—Norn groats first food eaten after, ii. 245
—of Nintur, v. 196–197
—prohibitions issued by medicine-man before, vii. 280
—see also GODS OF BIRTH; LÎLÎTH IN JUDAISM AND CHRISTIANITY.
—separate abode for those dying in, x. 7, 198, 274 10
—sky-goddess guardian spirit of, iv. 220
—three Destinies at, iii. 251
—ungirding of belt at, iv. 27
—use of obsidian knives in, ix. 78–79
—Vätter ask help of women in, ii. 231–232
—woman condemned to pains of, v. 185
——cut open at, xi. 29
—Zeus as god of, i. 163
Child-souls, limbo of, xi. 83

Child-stealers, Lîlîth and Gallû as, v. 363, 365
Children, abandonment of, xi. 31–32
—as gifts of Demeter, i. 227
—begetting of, by Sun-goddess and Storm-god, viii. 226
—custom to destroy male, xi. 285
—devouring of, through love for them, vi. 297
—Egyptians desired, to provide sacrifices for souls of parents, xii. 178
—especially tormented by Mora, iii. 228
—exchange of, to learn language of different tribes, x. 102
—exposure of: see EXPOSURE OF CHILDREN.
—first, of primeval pair devoured by them, vi. 297
—Hera protectress of, i. 167
—immersed in fairy wells, vii. 393 ³²
—killed by mothers remain as ghosts in living world, iv. 82
—may be consecrated to some god, iv. 142
—of captive women eaten, xi. 349 ⁵
——human wife eaten by Nix, ii. 211
——Ler: see "AIDED CHLAINNE LIR."
——Sun, xi. 242–248
——Tuirenn: see "AIDED CHLAINNE TUIRENN."
—only, said to be reincarnated, x. 146
—Pleiades lost, x. 96
—prayers for, iv. 260; v. 64, 171
—sacrifice of, x. 72, 286 ²⁹
——at the feast of the Tlaloque, xi. 72
——to Seides, iv. 111
——under new watermill, iv. 174
—slaughter of all male, vi. 171
—souls of certain, personified as Navky, iii. 253–254
——dead, viii. 239–240
—spirits of, wander for year after death, iv. 479
—stealing of unborn, vii. 89, 394 ⁴⁹
—still-born, amulets for protection against spirits of, ix. pl. VI, opp. p. 38
—strange fish said to be water-spirits', iv. 192
—substitution of dwarf for human, ii. 272
—superstitions about moon's effect on, vii. 48
—two, born from swelling on knee of old man, vii. 156

Chilenga (Leza) is institutor of custom, vii. 126
Chiliāwāla, ghosts of, vi. 248
Chilwa Plain, vii. 144
Chimaira, a storm-divinity, i. 40
—Bellerophon commissioned to kill the, i. 39
Chimaireus, child of Prometheus, i. 12
Chimalmat, wife of Vukub-Cakix, xi. 169
Chimalmatl (Chimalma), second wife of Ixtacmixcoatl, xi. 112
Chimera, Egyptian, xii. 169 (fig. 178)
Chimeras and spirits, vii. 91–92
Chiminigagua, supreme god, xi. 199, 202
Chiminizagagua, messenger of Chiminigagua, xi. 202
Chimpanzee, Azizā an intensified, vii. 242
Chimu, xi. 220
—and Chincha pantheons, xi. 223–224
"Chin-chin Ko-bakama," tale of, viii. 355
Chin-chow, in Shansi Province, viii. 124
Chin dynasty, viii. 97, 112, 118, 188
—-hua, prefecture of, viii. 101
—Ku Ch'i Kuan, viii. 169
—Shan monastery, Chên's son rescued by Abbot of, viii. 192
—T'ung, statue of, viii. 71
—wên, "modern text" of sayings of Confucius, viii. 11
Ch'in Ch'iung, early guardian of the portal, viii. 78
—Dynasty, events in, viii. 10, 44, 61, 70, 81, 92, 93, 114, 115, 133, 145, 194
—Kuei murdered Yo Fei, viii. 97
—Prince of, viii. 78
—T'ien Chien, inspector of astrology, viii. 143–144
—Tsung, viii. 95
China, Buddhism carried to Annam from, xii. 260
—Central, Karens probably came from, xii. 269
—date of historical period of, viii. 7
—southern, prototypes of Malay perhaps to be sought among wilder tribes of, ix. 244
Chincha Camac, creator and guardian of all Chincha, xi. 224
—Confederacy, xi. 220
—myths of the, xi. 227–232

Chinchasuyu, province, xi. 213
Chinese counterpart of Buddhist guardians, viii. 243
—expand towards Indo-China, ix. 244
—influence on Japanese myth, viii. 256-257
—origin of Annamese, xii. 287
—terms, index of, viii. 403-416
—type in Japan, viii. 210
—world-guardians, viii. 243
Ching, viii. 18
—ch'êng chih chih, viii. 113
—Chow, in modern Hupeh Province, viii. 95
—K'ê, early guardian of the portal, viii. 78
—Shan (Prospect Hill), viii. 182
— -tê, father of Yü Huang, viii. 59
—Ti, Emperor, viii. 11
—Yang, host of Sun, viii. 106
Ching-tu, the Pure Land, the Western Paradise, xii. 261
Ch'ing Ch'êng Mountain, viii. 83
—ching, control of emotions, viii. 147
—Peak, viii. 126
Chinun-way-shun (Wakyet-wa), deity worshipped in Kachin festival, xii. 338
Chione, intrigue of Poseidon with, i. 211
—(" Snow-White "), daughter of Boreas and Oreithyia, i. 73
Chios and Lesbos, Phaon ferryman between, i. 200
—Orion married daughter of King Oinopion of, i. 250-251
Chipiapoos, presider over country of the souls, x. 41, 298 47
Chipiripa, rain-god, xi. 191
Chipoka sent locusts to Mlanje, vii. 182
Chips, Loki's, ii. 149
—sacrificial, ii. 52
Chiruwi, half-men, vii. 244, 245, 258
Chi-sach, execution of, by To-dinh cause of uprising of the Tongkingese, xii. 313
Chitagah, xi. 182
Chitowe (pl. Itowe), the " little people," vii. 261
Chitowi (of Yao): see CHIRUWI, ETC.
Chiu-hua, sacred hill, viii. 72, 193
—I, abode of fairies, viii. 114
—Kung (" Nine Palaces "), abode of fairies, viii. 114
—T'ang Shih, viii. 143

Chiu Ti, first epoch, viii. 25
Ch'iu, viii. 168
—Chên-jên, Yo Wang pupil of, viii. 106
—Ch'u-chi (Ch'iu Ch'ang Ch'un), noted recluse, viii. 23, 190
Chiung Chow, deity resides at, viii. 84
Chiuta of Nyasaland, vii. 116, 126
Chivim, Votan took his origin from, xi. 132
Chloris (" Verdant Herbage "), Zephyros husband of, i. 266
Choice of husband, methods of, ii. 103, 104
Cholera, god of, viii. 66
Cholula, pyramid to Quetzalcoatl at, xi. 71, 96, 108
Chonchoñ, vampire, xi. 329
Choosers of the slain (Valkyries, wh. see), ii. 45, 248, 250, 254
Choque Suso, tale of love of Pariacaca for, xi. 231-232
Chors, Slavic deity, iii. 293, 295, 297
Chosroës, sacrifices of, vii. 17, 18
Chot, temple, xi. 208
Chotā Nāgpur, cobra seal of, vi. 240
Choughs of Valkyries, ravens, ii. 255
Ch'o Wo, T'ai Yüan lived on mountain of, viii. 111
Chou Hsin, cruelty of, brought about downfall of Shang Dynasty, viii. 39-40, 43, 66, 111, 137
——may be smitten, characters meaning, on fish, viii. 43
— -i, a system of divination, viii. 137
—Yü, statesman of K'ung Ming, viii. 178
Chow, Duke of Chow Kung, viii. 40, 41, 44, 61
—Dynasty, events in, viii. 6, 7, 9, 11, 27, 40, 42, 51, 61, 63, 66, 67, 79, 122, 135, 194
— -Kung, son of Wên Wang, viii. 44
—Li, viii. 44, 45, 46, 47, 73, 135, 136
—Principality of, viii. 40
Chozyain, Russian " Master of the House," iii. 246
Christ, Balder identified with, ii. 137
—called Shahapet of graveyards, vii. 75
—death and resurrection of, identified with those of Adonis, vii. 41
—Nativity of, Conchobar born at hour of, in Cúchulainn saga, iii. 208
—tale of Thor challenging, ii. 76-77

Christening feasts, sacrifices left for spirits of destiny at, iii. 251

Christian associations rob Navasard of many original traits, vii. 382 [11]

—faith, after disenchantment children of Ler died in, iii. 60

—ideas of successive Heavens, Eddic parallel to, ii. 221

—influence on Eddic ideas, ii. 317–320, 326, 327, 342, 343–344

——seen in Balder myth, ii. 137

—mystery in Grail romances, iii. 202–205

—symbols for four Evangelists and Archangels, guardians correspond loosely to, viii. 379 [28]

—Syrians visit Chinese court in 639 A.D., vi. 176

—times, cult of Sin (of Harran) persisted up to, v. 154

Christianity, vi. 347

—abolished sacred groves, wells, etc., ii. 203, 208, 214–215

—and paganism, iii. 206–213

—brought to the Cymry, iii. 106

—expels spirits, ii. 231

—Finno-Ugric contacts with, iv. xix–xx

—in Andean North, xi. 202

——Armenia, vii. 9

——India, vi. 175, 176, 177–178

——Scandinavia, ii. 8

—influence of, on Indian mythology, vi. 176, 206–207

————Maya pantheon, xi. 140, 142, 143

————mythology in Wales and Ireland, iii. 17–18

————Tammuz-Ishtar cult on, v. 413 [16]

—introduction of, into Africa, vii. 351, 352

—Isiac religion formidable competitor of rising, xii. 242

—South Arabian people converted to, v. 3

—supersession of Egyptian religion by, xii. 244

—vs. worship of Thor, ii. 76–77

Christians, persecution of, v. 338

Christmas, corn-deity brought into house at, iv. 247

—Eve, foretelling future on, iii. 283

——revels of water-elves, ii. 211

—festivals among Swedish Lapps, iv. 67–68

Christmas, lords of, iv. pl. xxviii, opp. p. 228

— -master, iv. 67

—moon, iv. 226

—mothers, iv. 66

—night, shamans on, iv. 66

——stones raised on pillars on, ii. 287

—old man (Jul-gubbe), iv. 248

—people, iv. 67, 68

—pig, or bull, iv. 248

—Russians believe that water-spirits wander on land at, iv. 470

—spirits walk at, iv. 66–67

Christmastide, names for, iii. 307, 308

" Chronicle " of Nakuk Pech, xi. 360 [2]

" Chronology of the Han Dynasty," viii. 25

Chronos (" Time "), abstract divinity of time, i. 282

Chrysanthemums, Kiku-jidō genius of, viii. 275

Chrysaor, father of Geryoneus, i. 86

—sprang from severed neck of Medousa, i. 34

Chryseïs given as prize to Agamemnon, i. 126, 127

Chryses, priest of Apollo, i. 126

Chrysōr, inventor of hook, bait, etc., v. 54

Chrysothemis, i. pl. xxxiii, opp. p. 132

Chthonic deity, Zeus as, i. 163

—nature of Asklepios, i. 279

—powers, monstrous beings have affinities with, vii. 74

Chthonios, Zeus, i. 163

Chu, viii. 105

— -dieu (Red Sparrow), Spirit of the South, xii. 307

—Hsi, commentator and scholar of Sung Dynasty, viii. 49, 56, 77, 118, 144

—Jung (" furnace, hearth "), god of Fourth Month, viii. 32, 76, 77

— -ko Liang (K'ung Ming), viii. 175, 176, 177–178, 179

— -kong-thuc, Governor of Ky-chao, statue to, in Dong-do, xii. 320

—Show-ch'ang, one of persons leaving example of filial piety, viii. 164

—Shu, viii. 33, 35, 37, 44, 116

" Chū-u " existence, tale of, viii. 239

Ch'u, nine heroes of State of, viii. 85, 86, 88

—Ch'ieh, viii. 169

INDEX

Ch'u-ch'iu, master of divinations, viii. 138
—Fu, birthplace of Confucius and capital of Shên Nung, viii. 30
—Yüan, author of poem " Falling into Trouble," viii. 85–86, 91
Chua-hai-ba, two sisters deified and commemorated in temple at, xii. 312–314
Chuan Hsü, Emperor, viii. 62, 76
Ch'uan Hou, goddess of streams, viii. 72–73
Chuang-Chu, Japanese hero of " Wanderings," viii. 362–363
—Tzŭ, philosopher, viii. 14, 19, 22, 54, 90, 113, 133, 134, 168, 169
Chuchaviva, rainbow, honoured as deity, xi. 203, 204
Chukem, god of boundaries and foot-races, xi. 204
Chulavete, Morning Star, x. 176
Ch'un Ch'iu, viii. 8, 11, 138, 199
—Hua, Emperor, viii. 100
Chung K'uei, tale of, viii. 152–153
—Li arranged marriage for Yüeh Hsiang, viii. 173
— -li Ch'üan, one of the Eight Immortals, viii. 121–123, 128
— -liu [air-shaft], household god came to be called, viii. 74, 80
—Shan, Purple Mountain, viii. 65
—T'iao Mountain, viii. 124
—Wu (" Imperial Father "), posthumous title of Kuo Tzŭ-i, viii. 96
—Yu (Tzŭ-lu), viii. 162
Ch'ung Chêng T'an, viii. 181
—Hsü Chên King, viii. 134
—Hui, Duke of, Kuan Yü ennobled as, viii. 95
Church, Haltia of, iv. 171
—Indian [East], vi. 175
—Nestorian, fate of, vi. 176
—rites, Armenian, vii. 381 5 (ch. ii)
—see COMMUNAL HEARTH, ETC.
Churel, ghost, vi. 248–249
Churning, method of Wakonyingo, vii. 269
—string, Vāsuki served as, at churning of ocean, vi. 155
Chūtiā Nāgpur, mythical genealogy of Raja of, xii. 270–271
Chuvalete, Morning Star, xi. 120–121
Chuvashes, descendants of Turks who settled on the Volga, iv. xviii

Chwimbian, the Viviane of romance, iii. 201
Ciabhan, Clidna eloped with, iii. 116
Cian born with caul, iii. 132
—changed into pig at stroke of Druidic wand, iii. 40
—married Ethne whose son was Lug, iii. 25, 28
Cibas, shells, xi. 32
Cibola, Seven Cities of, x. 187, 310 67–311; xi. 4, 20
Cicada, Eos changed Tithonos in his old age into a, i. 246
Ciesburc (Augsburg), ii. 98
Cilicia, Sandakos goes to, vii. 41
Cimbri used shields as primitive toboggan, ii. 157, pl. XXXII, opp. p. 246
Cinders and metals, man created from, xi. 85
Cinteotl, maize-god, xi. 54, 56, 75, 77
Cinvat Bridge, vi. 344, 346
—dog at, vi. 69
—known to Armenians as hair-bridge, vii. 100
Cipactli, sea-monster from which earth was shaped, xi. 92, 101–102, 103
Cipactonal, first woman, xi. 92, 102, 112, 120, 184
Çipattoval and Tamagostad equivalent to Oxomoco and Cipactonal, xi. 120, 184
Circle, quartered, in Siouan stock, x. 98
—tribal, of the Omaha, x. 97–98
—with cross, symbolizes Plains Indians' conception of physical world, x. 97
—women form a, as they pray in earth-goddess festival, xi. 34
Circles, conjoined, on Gaulish coins, iii. pl. II (2), opp. p. 8
—fairy, ii. 225
—dryad, nymph, iii. 255, 259, 262
—magic, x. 290 36; xi. 277
—of Visions, Sun, Father Heaven, x. 275 11
Circular form, ocean-god depicted in, xii. 49, 96
Circumcision, xii. 186
Citadel for the gods, tale of building a, ii. 89–90
Cit-Bolon-Tum, medicine-god, xi. 137
Cities, five, founded by Enlil(?), v. 206
—sacred, vii. 59; xii. 189
Citlalachtli, " the Star Ball-Ground," xi. 98

Citlallatonac and Citlalicue, " Lord and Lady of the Starry Zones," xi. 88, 89, 95, 98

Citlalxonecuilli identified with Southern Cross, xi. 98–99

Citli (Hare) shot Sun with arrow, xi. 90

Citragupta, Dharma's spy, vi. 180

City-goddess, Tyche is the, v. 20

City gods, viii. 67–68; xii. 17, 18, 19

—moat, Ch'eng Huang and Shui Jung both have the meaning of, viii. 69

—prison in lower world, v. 323

Ciuacoatl ("Snake Woman"), earth-goddess, xi. 75

Ciuateteo (Ciuapipiltin), ghostly women who struck children with epilepsy, xi. 77–78, 82

Cium, successor of Naymlap, xi. 208

Civilization, beginnings of, i. 16

—decline of, in southern centres, xi. 361 [8]

—established by Osiris, xii. 113–114

—of China, viii. 7–8, 27

—origin of, v. 190–193, 194, 237

—value of mythology for knowledge of history of, i. ix–x

Civilizations of Middle and South America show parallels, xi. 44

Clams, ix. 69, 271, 276, 278

Clan, deity as father of a, v. 378 [19]

— -groves, ghosts live in, vii. 188, 189, 190

—on death one goes to one's own, in Underworld, vii. 180

—Seide protector of, iv. 104

—totem-myths, reminiscence of, in Conaire tale, iii. 75

Clans, x. 241–245

—conflict of two, descended from sun-goddess and storm-god, viii. 230

—division into, viii. 245–246

—six, in Yakut realm of dead, iv. 485

Classes of deities, formation of, x. 241

—To-Kabinana divided mankind into two, ix. 108

Classical references to Celtic gods, iii. 9

—world, influence of Egyptian religion on, xii. 242–243

——success of Osirian circle in religion of, xii. 120–121

—writers give no clear idea of vanished Egyptian religion, xii. 244–245

Claw (iron nail) of Ngojama, vii. 242

Clay, Allah created men from, v. 354

—believed to be used in fashioning man and beast, i. 13–14; xi. 200, 322

—creation from, v. 12, 104, 112, 113, 274, 275, 276, 403 [4]; ix. 24, 27, 106, 172, 174, 175, 273

—giant of, with mare's heart, ii. 81–82

—nebulous spots of Milky Way the track of spirits whose feet are smeared with, xi. 278

—Pandora created from, i. 14–15

—red ferruginous, vi. 245

—seals of, protected sacred rooms in temples at night, xii. 193

—white man created from clean white, with Indian and negro following as it became dirtier, xi. 271

Cleanliness essential for hunting and fishing, as well as worship in lud, iv. 82–84, 145, 148

—necessary to the sky, iv. 400

Cleansing measures after removal of corpse, iv. 23, 24

Cléars, bunches of straw tied on poles and lit, iii. 47

Cleon, v. 75

Cliach, harper, sought hand of Bodb's daughter, iii. 79, 91

Clidna the Shapely, tale of, parallel to Tuag story, iii. 89, 116

Clidna's Wave, iii. 89, 116

Cliff dwellings, x. 182, 184

Climatic conditions, myths concerning, viii. 254

Cloak, magic, of Odin, ii. 41, 42, 43

—of invisibility, Siegfried acquires, ii. 268

Clontarf, battle of, ii. 254

Closed Man, chief, x. 111

Cloth, Cloths:

Cloth, iii. 237, 242

—Master and Mistress of fire covered with red, iv. 455

—(perineal band), xii. 296

— -sacrifice Tōrem, iv. 404

—tearing of, denotes wish for only partial severance of living and dead, iv. 30

—white, in burial, ix. 237

——placed over animal's back at sacrifice if victim not white, iv. 220

Cloths on sacrifice post, iv. 339

—sacrificed as clothing for Fire-girl, iv. 235

Cloths, various uses of, iv. 29, 43, 68, 122, 131, 148, 267, 276, 278; see, further, items s.v. LINEN.
—which have absorbed personality from contact, vii. 337
Clothed and bearded stranger stories, xi. 36, 67, 241, 370 [23]
Clothes and shoes provided for dead, ii. 305; iv. 486
—may not be taken to abode of dead, x. 148
—of deceased, disposal of, after final memorial feast, iv. 56–57
——visible representation of himself, iv. 43
——one "away," calling or touching, would prevent return, vii. 187
—sacrifice, iv. 193
—soiled, of deceased brought out at memorial feasts, iv. 43, 56
—white linen, worn by enquirer in geomancy, viii. 140
—winged, aid in transformation to a god of thunder, iv. 441–442
Clothing hung on sacred tree to cure disease, vii. 62
—of living, dweller in Underworld may cause illness by obtaining, iv. 5
——Sky, ix. 36–37
—the dead, iv. 18–19, 29
Clothru, mother of Lugaid Red-Stripes, iii. 90, 156
Cloud-gallants, viii. 296, 299
— -gatherer, Zeus as, i. 159
— -god, viii. 88
—mother, iv. 234
—Parjana personifies the, vi. 37
— -snake, vi. 155
—song, viii. 36–37
— -symbols, featherdown balls as, xi. 60
Clouds, vi. 15, 62, 129, 137; 263, 264, 265, 267, 269, 291, 301, 303, 317, 320, 323, 350; viii. 102–103; ix. 58, 179; x. xvii, 92, 98, 109–112, 156, 190, 194, 206, 225, 233, 243, 255, 261, 309 [65]; xi. 68
—feather-dress of Freyja may be, ii. 126
—made of Ymir's brain, ii. 325, 326
—of five colours surrounded Yüan Shih at birth, viii. 111
——sent forth by ground, xii. 318
—rain-bearing, Pegasos may have originally stood for, i. 41
—ship of Frey may typify, ii. 109

Clouds soiled by people rose higher for cleanliness, iv. 400
—thought of Adam made from, ii. 326
Clowns, "Mudheads," x. 195
Club cut by Herakles in Nemea, i. 80, 81
—magic, ix. 45, 46
—of Herakles, ii. 69
——Periphetes captured by Theseus, i, 98
—Searbhan killed by his own, iii. 55, 152
—track of Dagda's, iii. 30
Cmok, snake, iii. 247
Cnoc Aine (Knockainy), dwelling of Aine, fairy-queen, iii. 47
—Miodhchaoin, hill on which shouting was prohibited, iii. 40
Cnucha, Cumhal fell at, iii. 161
Coagulation, cosmogonic, viii. 223
Coal, burning, x. 41
—Hill, viii. 182
—live, purged from sin, v. 98
—story of fallen oak explained as origin of, viii. 339
Coatepec, "Serpent Mountain," xi. 60
Coatl ("Snake"), day-sign, xi. 104
Coatlicamac (the South), in ancient painting of Aztec migration, xi. 115
Coatlicue, Aztec goddess, xi. pl. v, opp. p. 46, 58, 60, 74, 116, 118, 354 [5]
Coatrischie, tempest-raiser, xi. 25
Coba, trapper to Erem, iii. 137
Cobweb personified, vii. 322
Cock, Cocks:
Cock, ii. 276, 303, 307, 313, 331; vii. 302–304
—and hen, black, sacrifice to evil spirits, vii. 82, 393 [26]
—crowing sign that it has seen a Jinn, v. 352
— -fighting, xii. 354, 355
— -fire, iv. 236
—follows course of sun, xi. 122
—golden, of dawn, iii. 329
—guards against evil influences, viii. 104
—magic, xii. 309
—see HKUN LAI AND HKUN LU, ETC.
—white, as sacrifice, viii. 233
Cocks ("long singing birds of the Eternal Land"), iii. 226, pl. VIII, opp. p. 226
Cock's foot, Orion called, i. 249
Cockroach totem, vii. 279
Cocomes, family of, ruled Mayapan, xi. 126–127

Coco-nut hung in porch of Burmese houses in honour of Mahāgiri Nāt, xii. 344–345
Coco-nuts, ix. 55–56, 71, 72, 75, 76, 106, 107, 108, 126, 127, 131–132, 137, 211
Codal, foster-father of Ériu, iii. 136
Codex Borbonicus, xi. 54
—Borgia, xi. 56
—Boturini, xi. 114, 359 [16]
—Dresdensis, xi. 151, 360 [2]
—Ferjérváry-Mayer, xi. 55–56, pl. VI, opp. p. 56
—Peresianus, xi. 360 [2]
—Regius, ms. of Poetic " Edda," ii. 7
—Tro-Cortensianus, xi. 360 [2]
—Vaticanus B, xi. 56
Codical deities, xi. 139
Codran worshipped ancestor-stone, ii. 312
Coffin and grave, preparation of, iv. 21–22, 29
—glass, with corpse in oil found at Babylon, v. 323
—of late origin, iv. 31
—shavings of, may not be burned, lest corpse be blistered, iv. 25
—spinning about of, to deceive corpse, iv. 23
Coffins, hollowed tree-trunks as, iv. 34
—of dead in Underworld villages their houses, iv. 73
——stone, holy men buried in Ganges in, vi. 243
—see BOATS, BURIAL IN, ETC.; PUNTS, BURIAL IN, ETC.; SLEIGHS USED, ETC.
—windows in, iv. 29, 31, 32
Cogioba, an offering of tobacco, xi. 25, 26
Cohabitation, symbolic, to fertilize a field, i. 226, 331 [2] (ch. x)
Cohabiting of demons and human beings, v. 357
Coin, naked hand defiles, iv. 276
—of Gaza with 'Ashtart-Yāw or Yāw, v. 43, 44
——Trajan Decius with baetyl or stone pillar of Dusares, v. 16
Coins, androgynous form of Śiva on so-called Scythian, vi. 179
—Astarte's chariot on, v. 385 [131]
—buttons, or stones used to cover eyes of dead among Cheremiss and Ostiaks, iv. 21, 22
—cast into water in which corpse washed, iv. 21

Coins, Gaulish, iii, pl. II, opp. p. 8, pl. III, opp. p. 14
—gold, put into rations of Cridenbél, iii. 27
—head of Ogmios on Gaulish, iii. 11
—Iranian deities on, vi. pl. XXXII, opp. p. 260, pl. XXXIV, opp. p. 272
—myths depicted on, iii. 13
—of Charrhae bear symbols of Sin, v. 154
——Nabataean cities with Dusares, v. 17
——South Arabian people, symbolism on, v. 3, 4
——Tyre with head of Greek Herakles, v. 52, 53
—Rhodian Helios on, i. 243
—sacrificial, ii. 187; iv. 132–133, 140, 147, 193, 266, 276, 279
—silver, decorate watermill-goddess, iv. 167
——Water-master, iv. 199
—to buy place beyond the tomb buried with dead, iii. 230
—with Tychē, v. 19
" Cóir Anmann," iii. 85
Coirpre, Doel's brother, iii. 150
Cold, x. 78
—and frost, Stribog probably god of, iii. 301
Colhuatzincatl (the Winged), deity, xi. 77
Coll, guardian of demon cat, iii. 191
Collars: see STONES, ANTILLEAN, ETC.
Collasuyu, province, xi. 213
" Colloquy with the Ancients ": see " ACALLAMH NA SENÓRACH."
Colocolo, invisible bird or animal whose saliva is poison, xi. 328
Colonies, Apollo divine founder of, i. 180
Colotlixayac (" Scorpion-face "), star, xi. 98
Colour, changes of, connect chameleon with moon, vii. 166
—idea of cardinal points, iv. 347, 348
—in creation-myths, iv. 323, 324, 371
—of first peoples determined by parts of ox eaten, vii. 150–151
——sacrifices and pieces of silk correspond with colours of jade tablets used in sacrificial rites, viii. 46
— -symbolism, x. 92, 93, 96, 158, 166–167, 186, 206, 286 [31]–287, 290 [35]; xi. 52

Colouring of runes, ii. 50, 295
Colours assigned to Jain saints, vi. 221
—how birds obtained their various, vii. 287
—representing planets on seven stages of Ezida, v. 159–160
—the art of the mixing of, x. 173
Colours sacred or significant follow:
Black, i. 32, 62, 101, 102, 145, 223
—ii. 41, 79, 211, 221, 224, 235, 236, 304
—iii. 27, 28, 63, 67, 168, 191, 193; 238, 246, 254, 260, 263, 265, 268, 271, 281, 285, 286, 288
—iv. 38, 70, 74, 75, 78, 148, 151, 153, 160, 161, 165, 177, 193, 195, 202, 210, 211, 212, 215, 232, 235, 239, 243, 253, 257; 318, 323, 324, 325, 348, 359, 371, 406, 411, 440, 446, 449, 455, 460, 467, 469, 486, 487, 488, 489, 494, 501
—v. 16, 159, 160
—vi. 21, 39, 41, 68, 75, 82, 89, 97, 111, 114, 126, 139, 237; 302, 315
—vii. 82, 393 [26]; 144, 150, 208, 226, 239, 248, 339, 411 [43]
—viii. 35, 38, 46, 107, 113, 140, 155; 279, 327, 379 [17], 381 [15]
—ix. 67, 273
—x. 61, 63, 72, 111, 115, 127, 138, 158, 162, 165, 166, 186, 206, 225, pls. III, VI
—xi. 33, 62, 92, 122, 138, 139, 145, 170, 173
—xii. 43, 94, 97, 138, 139, 195, 363 [5], 367 [10], 386 [14]; 277, 279, 300, 306, 406 [59], 413 [11]
Blue, i. 223
—ii. 223, 276
—iv. 10, 76, 102, 190, 202, 247, 257; 346, 347, 348, 353, 360, 391, 392, 459, 467, 479
—v. 159
—vi. 45, 81, 109, 111, 132, 138, 154, 205
—vii. 50, 392 [19]; 411 [43]
—viii. 106; 282, 288, 345
—ix. 226
—x. 36, 63, 71, 72, 80, 92, 96, 128, 157, 158, 160, 162, 165, 166, 186, 201, 206, 252
—xi. 33, 47, 56, 60, 72, 122, 184, 199, 201, 208, 300

Blue, xii. 25, 39, 50, 129, 189, 367 [10], 386 [14]; 277, 307, 321
Blue-black, iv. 365
—xii. 39, 129
Blue-green, viii. 65
—x. 206
Blue-grey, iv. 425, 503
Brown, iii. 26, 58, 127; 323
—iv. 202, 215; 371, 405, 459, 460, 464, 467
—vi. 38, 46, 69
—vii. 339
—viii. 327
—xi. 334
—xii. 62, 196
Brown-red, v. 159
Copper, iv. 226; 501(?)
Crimson, iii. 130 (crimson-brown, 128)
Dun, i. 52
Gold, v. 159
Golden, i. 77, 81, 87, 108, 114, 120, 144, 146
—iii. 258, 262; 323, 326, 328, 329
—iv. 337, 341, 342, 343, 346, 347, 351, 353, 356, 360, 373, 378, 379, 415
—vi. 22, 30, 45, 158; 313
—viii. 274
—xii. 318, 321, 330, 344, 345
Green, ii. 210, 223
—iii. 63, 64, 67, 86, 130, 138, 143; 254, 261, 262, 270; 323, pl. XXXVII
—iv. 156, 197–201; 348
—vi. 217
—viii. 34, 35, 37, 38, 43, 46; 336, 345
—x. 35
—xi. 56, 67, 76, 90, 96, 145, 161, 173, 180, 208, 209, 284
—xii. 38, 39, 142, 189, 367 [12], 386 [14]; 284, 306, 352
Grey, ii. 43, 211, 223, 224
—iii. 128, 129; 326
—iv. 8, 9, 171, 202, 203, 231, 233, 240; 356, 357, 460, 466, 508
—viii. 282
Pink, viii. 282, 336, 346
Purple, i. 23, 69
—iii. 32, 37, 86, 87
—iv. 396
—vii. 70
—viii. 294, 345, 346, 356, 357
Red, i. 62, 86, 198
—ii. 75, 80, 190, 224, 278, 286, 303, 329

Red, iii. 65, 70, 76, 90, 139, 200; 240, 247, 263; 309, 322, 323
—iv. 156, 235, 238, 257; 323, 324, 325, 346, 347, 348, 350, 360, 370, 371, 373, 375, 429, 441, 453, 455, 458, 465
—v. 147, 316
—vi. 24, 30, 140, 154, 159, 160 (reddish-yellow, 132)
—vii. 150, 208, 226, 231, 235, 237, 238, 239, 325, 411 [43]
—viii. 34, 35, 37, 38, 42, 44, 46, 111, 167; 274, 287, 288, 327, 335
—ix. 24, 27, 36, 106, 114, 226, 275
—x. 48, 60, 63, 71, 72, 73, 93, 111, 128, 138, 147, 159, 186, 206, 219, 221, 225, 249, 287 [31], pls. III, IV, VI
—xi. 33, 55, 56, 62, 81, 116, 122, 139, 170, 173, 174, 181, 182, 199, 200, 230, 272, 277, 313
—xii. 30, 55, 62, 142, 195, 196; 277, 294, 300, 307, 315, 321, 330, 345, 351–352, 354
Scarlet, viii. 270, 309
Silver, iii. 323, 328, 329
—iv. 347, 351, 353, 360, 501(?)
—v. 159
—x. 206
Vermilion, xii. 306
White, i. 62, 73, 102, 143, 147, 247
—ii. 41, 58, 100, 118, 129, 137, 138, 152, 153, 190, 211, 235, 236, 245
—iii. 57, 70, 193; 227, 242, 250, 251, 253, 254, 258, 260, 262, 264, 267, 268; 280
—iv. 155, 156, 198, 202, 204, 209, 220, 221, 223, 224, 228, 232, 233, 240–241, 242, 243, 244, 253, 255, 257, 258, 267, 272, 276, pl. XXIII; 318, 323, 337, 340, 341, 346, 348, 349, 350, 351, 353, 358, 359, 360, 365, 371, 394, 397, 398, 399, 403, 404, 405, 413, 415, 422, 425, 429, 449, 453, 454, 460, 494, 503 (milk-white, 449)
—v. 319 (white-gold, 159)
—vi. 24, 81, 85, 111, 131, 139, 154, 169, 215, 217, 228; 265, 268, 270, 272, 281, 291, 293, 296, pl. XL
—vii. 18; 133, 144, 189, 191, 208, 231, 238, 287, 349
—viii. 35, 37, 38, 43, 46, 65, 106, 112; 233, 275, 280, 304, 305, 317, 327, 346
—ix. 119, 168, 216, 218, 220, 226, 228, 237, 238, 260, 273
—x. xx, 21, 39, 40, 41, 52, 59, 63, 71,

72, 107, 111, 127, 156, 157, 158, 162, 166, 186, 199, 204, 206, 225, 284 [27], 287 [31]
—xi. 32, 68, 98, 116, 122, 154, 165, 170, 173, 261, 277, 313, 323, 340
—xii. 131, 142, 144, 195; 277, 279, 300, 307, 317, 321, 329, 342, 345, 347, 351, pl. XII (A)
Yellow, iii. 64, 65
—iv. 201, 241; 346, 348, 351, 353, 516 (yellowish-white, 446)
—vi. 41, 45, 46, 69, 85, 120, 138; 271, 281, 324
—viii. 27, 35, 37, 38, 46, 76
—x. 48, 63, 94, 111, 127, 152, 156, 158, 160, 162, 165, 166, 186, 200, 201, 206, 209, pls. VI, XXII
—xi. 55, 56, 76, 113, 116, 144, 165, 170, 200, 230
—xii. 142, 407 [74]; 315
Colts disappear on May Eve, iii. 95
Columbus, first encounters of, with natives, xi. 18–21, 348 [4]–349
Columcille's cowl, Mongan went to Heaven with his head under, iii. 211
Column primitive symbol of Hekate-Artemis and Hermes, i. pl. XLIII, opp. p. 188, 195
Columns, old Irish belief that earth rests on, iii. 12–13
Coma Bereneces, v. 317
Comb between ears of Twrch Trwyth, iii. 187, 188, 189
Combabus and Huwawa, no mythological nor philological connexion between, v. 253
—myth of, v. 75
Combat between Enkidu and Gilgamish, v. 243–244
—by incantation, v. 293
Combats, gladiatorial, xi. 59
—of Cúchulainn, iii. 153, 155, 156
—ritual, between summer and winter, iii. 108–109
—transformation, ii. 155
Comet, horn-shaped, appearing at battle of Salamis may be identical with that at death of Mahāvīra, vi. 223
Comets as portents, xi. 98
—foretold evil, vii. 48
Commoner, king becomes, v. 318–319
Communal hearth may become substitute for church in marriage or baptism, vii. 55, 56

Communal heredities and legends, viii. 244

Communities, Phoroneus first taught life in, i. 16

Comox myth, x. 284 [27]

Compass, beetles set free to each point of, xii. 284

—bowing to points of, to reconcile angry Domovoy, iii. 242

—colours of four points of, iv. 346, 347, 348, 360, 371

—of the dead, point of, points downwards, iv. 486

—points of, doubled in tale of octagonal earth, iv. 308, 371

————represented by animals, iv. 360

—used in selection of burial sites, viii. 141, 142

Composite character of Polynesian myths, ix. 4

Compromise characterized Japanese philosophy of life, viii. 231

Conaire Mór, doom of, iii. 74–77, 82

Conaire's Druid Tulchainde helped by Morrígan, iii. 67

Conall Cernach (epithet means victorious), iii. 125, 131, 134, 140, 143, 145, 146, 147, 148, 149, 152, 156, 157, 158

Conan, Celtic hero, iii. 169, 170, 173, 199

—Loki parallel to, ii. 149

—Maol, Fionn put fine on, iii. 163

—tried to ride mythic horse, iii. 128

Conapa (Coniraya; Tonapa), Peruvian equivalent of Quetzalcoatl and Bochica, xi. 241

Conaran, chief of Tuatha Dé Danann, iii. 170

Conception: see BIRTHS, MIRACULOUS.

Concert of gods, viii. 270

Conch shell blown to drive away ghost, ix. 118

Conchean slew Aed, iii. 72

Conchenn, Cliach loved, iii. 91

Conchobar caused Macha to run against his chariot, iii. 74

—king of Ulster, iii. 82, 83, 84, 88, 90, 124, 136, 139, 140, 141, 143, 144, 146, 147, 148, 152, 153, 155, 157, 188, 196, 198, 208

—River, iii. 140

Concordia ("Harmony"), abstract divinity, i. 299

Concubines, xi. 19, 31, 349 [5]

—of dead, "dolls" buried provide, xii. 416 [14]

Condor in carving of ancient gods, xi. 234

——coto, mountain birthplace of Pariacaca, xi. 230

Confederacy of Araucanians, xi. 324–325

Confession, xi. 78–79

—Negative, read by dead in judgement hall, xii. 176, 184, 185, 187

Conflagration, cosmic or eschatological, possible allusion to, xii. 209, 424 [43]

—final, ii. 202

Confucius, Confucianism, viii. 8, 9, 10, 13, 16, 19, 20, 24, 33, 44, 70, 98, 133, 161, 162, 168, 189, 199, 219, 220, 256

Coniapuyara, Amazons, xi. 285

Coniraya, idol, xi. 226, 228–229, 241

Conjugal fidelity, pine-trees connected with, viii. 254

Conjuror, O'Donnell's Kern a, iii. 60

Conjurors, xi. 25

Conlaoch slays own son, iii. 145

—son of Aife and Cúchulainn, iii. 144, 169

Conn bound by spells, iii. 72

—high king, iii. 87, 127, 161, 162, 164, 165, 175

Connaught, province of, accepted after battle by Firbolgs, iii. 25

—síd of, iii. 57, 58, 78

—tale of son of king of, iii. 37

Connla had head in west, feet in east, iii. 150

—son of Conn, and goddess from "Land of the Living," story of, iii. 50, 84–85, 116, 197

Connla's Well in Land under Waves, iii. 120

Conopa, household gods, xi. 223

Conqueror, Selqet as the, xii. 411 (fig. 229)

Conquerors, Maidu mythic pair, x. 232

Conquest of Mexico, xi. 45–49, 354 [4]

——the Síd, iii. 50

Conquistadores, xi. 44–49

Consecration of images, ix. pl. XIX, opp. p. 198

——shaman, iv. 512

——wine with different symbols, ii. 77, 79

Conservatism, viii. 8, 9, 10, 11, 19, 20, 21, 52
—Egyptian religious, impressed Classical world, xii. 242–243
—in Egyptian religion and religious art, xii. 212–213
Constantine, Arthur resigned crown to, iii. 185
Constellation, knife-bearing cat may once have been explained as a, xii. 107
Constellations, vi. 70; 276; vii. 94; viii. 73; 235; x. xxii, 8, 96, 206, 278 14; xii. 112, 366 6
—monsters of Chaos identified with, v. 108
—watchmen of Heaven are figures of monsters and animals in, v. 303, 306
Consus, purely Italic god, i. 292
" Conte del Graal," French poem of Arthurian cycle, iii. 195
Contests, athletic, held by Danaos, i. 31
—between living and dead, iv. 4
—different sorts of, x. 228
—Huathiacuri challenged to series of, xi. 231
—pole-climbing, xii. 138
Continents, four, iv. 344, 347
Contingencies, eight, viii. 135–136
Continuity, serial and collateral, viii. 218
" Contortion " of Cúchulainn, iii. 141, 153–154, 198
Contracts, Mithra god of, vii. 33
—violation of, v. 108
Contradictory teachings in Egyptian religious texts, xii. 213–214
Convector (" Garnerer "), Roman divinity, i. 300
Conway, noise of water pouring into, traditionally groans of Dylan, iii. 99
Con-y chant sung to Nguyen-hu'u-do, xii. 321
Cook Group, cosmogonic ideas of, ix. 13–14
—Islands, Indonesian myth-elements in, ix. 97
——Melanesian myth-elements in, ix. 95, 96
——relation of myths of, to those of Hawaii, New Zealand, and Society Group, ix. 93, 94
Cooking, ix. 185, 281
— -hearth tabu to Cúchulainn, iii. 156

Coosaw, Cussitaw dwelt at, x. 71
Copper, v. 147
—associated with sun, x. 254–255
—banknote, x. 239
—box (boat), Earth-supporter rests on, x. 250
—rings of, in moon-worship, iv. 225, 226
—sacred to Semitic Queen of Heaven, xii. 367 12
Copts of Egypt, vii. 115
Coqui-Xèe (Coqui-Cilla), creator god, xi. 87
Còr, Welsh (" dwarf "), Coranians connected with, iii. 108
Cora, Mexican tribe, x. 176
Coral thresholds of palace of Annunaki, v. 333
Coranians, plague of, iii. 107–108
Cord, Cords:
Cord, severing of, means to determine fate, v. 398 101
—with magic knots, xii. 199, 421 6
Cords, earth suspended by seven, ix. 163
—reckoning by, xi. 217
Cordelia, Llyr (in Welsh tradition), father of, iii. 102, 103, 108
Corfu (Kerkyra), perhaps home of giant-children of Ouranos and Gaia, i. 9
Corinth, Aphrodite still associated with modern, i. 314
—cult centre of Poseidon, i. 210
—divine patrons of, i. 36–37
—(Ephyra) said to have been founded by Sisyphos, i. 37
—festivals of Dionysos in, i. 221
—fountains of Peirene and Glauke at, i. 258
—Glaukos king of, i. 38
—Gulf of, Aigialeus personification of southern shores of, i. 28
—Iason and Medeia in, i. 115
—Isthmus of, place of dedication of the Argos to Poseidon, i. 212
——Poseidon patron of, i. 37, 212
—legends of, interwoven with Argive myth, i. 28
—Medeia at, i. pl. xxviii, opp. p. 110
—myths of, i. 36–41
—Oidipous reared in court of, i. 48
—Poseidon chief deity of, i. 212

Corinth, Sinis highwayman and murderer at, i. 98

Cormac, Celtic adventurer, ii. 94

—high king, iii. 162

—mac Art, tale of, iii. 117–119, 121, 152, 175

—ordered infant daughter slain, iii. 74

Corn and flax, straw figure erected on Shrove Tuesday to gain good growth of, iv. 248

——game, coming of, to earth, x. 62

—Daughter, x. 91–93

— -deity, last sheaf cut regarded as, and seed obtained therefrom, iv. 247–248

—Demeter divinity of, i. 226

—depends on gods or on sacrifice, mythic belief that, iii. 36, 46–47

—destruction of, as punishment, iii. 71, 72

—Father, x. 188

—Girl, x. 162

— -goddess, x. 198

— -luck, horns believed to carry, iv. 247

—Maidens, x. 199–201, 210

—Mother, iv. 241; x. xvii, 81, 92, 107–108, 188; xi. 121–122

—Mountain, x. 193

— -seeds, Freyja's tears may be, ii. 126

—soul of, assumes shape of butterfly, iv. 13

— -spirit, x. 27, 289 [35]–290

—supreme symbol in Eleusinian Mysteries, x. 92

—Virgin, iv. 247

—Wolf, iv. 247

Cornfield, how soul of, is sought, iv. 240–241

—protected by tutelary spirit, and customs concerning, iv. 246

Cornucopia emblem of Hades, i. 235

Cornwall, iii. 190

Corona Borealis, v. 317

——Arianrhod connected with, iii. 100

——(Aurora Borealis), x. xxii, 96

Coronado went to Seven Cities of Cibola, x. 187, 310 [67]–311

Corpre, poet, chants first satire [on Bres] in Ireland, iii. 27, 137

Corpse, Corpses:

Corpse-boat (made of fingernails), iv. 75

—carrying of, as punishment, iii. 72

Corpse, cleansing after removal of, iv. 23, 24

—coins cast into washing water of, iv. 21

—deduction of length of life from threads laid on, iv. 28

—divided in pieces, xii. 181

—good wishes to, iv. 29, 30, 53

— -hungry giantess, ii. 281

—leading astray of, iv. 22

—of vampire does not decay, iii. 232

—ordinary occupations may not be followed during presence of, iv. 22, 61

—rigid, leaves coffin moonlight nights, viii. 150

—sewed in skin in prehistoric period, xii. 418 [23], 420 [23]

— -ship, ii. 200

— -spirit, x. 156

— -strand, ii. 318

—tables, benches, etc., thrown on sides at removal of, iv. 23

—(who caused epidemic in life), bones of, burned after years, iv. 4

Corpses, animated, ii. 309

—believed to injure living at night, iv. 4

—contests between living and, iv. 4

—earlier dead relatives come to remove, iv. 23

—Nasu makes, impure, vi. 261

—of dangerous people, disposal of, iv. 4

—pinned to ground by stake, iv. 4

—restored to life to become familiars, vii. 338

—significance of covering bodies of, iv. 21

" Corpus Poeticum Boreale," ii. 11

" Corrector ": see PENITENTIAL OF " CORRECTOR."

Cortez, third expedition to Yucatan under, xi. 45, 119

Corvus, constellation, v. 305

Cosmas, chronicler, iii. 301

—on religion of Czechs, iii. 222, 240

—states that Christians were in India in A.D. 525–530, vi. 175

Cosmetic usage and implements, xii. 420 [18]

Cosmetics, Bês with, xii. 61

Cosmic and cosmogonic myths, xii. 68–91

—chamber, flocks and grain thrived only in, v. 192

Cosmic conflagration, possible allusion to, xii. 209, 424 [43]
—cycles, Hindu, v. 205
—deity, Osiris rather early became, xii. 93
—dramas, xi. 105
—forces, personification and divinization of, xii. 23
—functions often attributed to nome-god, xii. 18
—god, nameless, xii. 221–224
—gods especially likely to be divided into male divinities and female consorts, xii. 365 [20]
——misinterpreted as, xii. 15
—ideas of the Osirian circle, xii. 167
—myth, fragments of a Mocobi, xi. 319
—number, seventy a, xii. 413 [7]
—phenomena, Tilo associated with, vii. 127
—powers, general absence of worship of, xii. 24
—rôle, local gods have little mythology until given, xii. 20
——of certain deities, xii. 167
—space, arbiter of, viii. 51
—tendency to make gods, xii. 214, 215
—tree, xii. 35, 36
Cosmogony, i. 3–4, 11, 289; ii. 9, 10, 181, 182, 202, 324–347; iii. 12; vii. 93; viii. 52–60; 221–237; ix. 4–38, 50, 51, 148, 155, 240, 248, 263, 302; x. 8–10, 34–42, 60–64, 98, 99, 102–112, 113, 124, 138, 177–179, 202–211, 216, 217–229, 259–262, 278 [15]–279, 307 [62], 311 [70]–312; xi. 28–32, 85–91, 152–155, 159–167, 178–179, 185, 193, 194, 199–200, 239–240, 262, 269, 271, 308–309, 311, 313, 323–324, 330, 342, 376 [27], 377 [9]; see, further, items s.v. ORIGINS, MYTHS OF.
Cosmological conception of world, Babylonian, v. 216, 217
—theories, viii. 52–60
Cosmology, vii. 93–94; x. xxiii–xxiv, 21–23, 185–187, 249–254, 275 [11]–276, 293 [40], 294 [42]
Cosmos, self-evolving, ix. 5
Costume, fish, of priests, at rituals, v. 84–85
—interchange of, x. 309 [64]; xi. 282
—match in splendour of, xi. 231
—of Nāga, xii. 277
——Siamese Shans, xii. 296

Costume, priestly, xii. 193 and fig. 202
Costumes, shaman, iv. 512–519, 522
Cottages specially built for birth of children, viii. 266
Cotton, bands of, as charms, xii. 299, 300, 335
—image of plaited, xi. 23, 27
— -wood log, first people emerged from, x. 105
Cotzbalam, bird, xi. 164
Council of Vanir and Æsir, ii. 27
Counsel, Artemis as goddess of, i. 329 [6]
Counting, vigesimal system of, xi. 97
Countries, Horus the Uniter of Both: see ḤAR-SAM-TAUI, ETC.
Country-side, Pan divinity of, i. 267
Couples, primeval: see PRIMEVAL PAIRS.
Courage among North American Indians, x. 15
—Vahagn god of, vii. 43
Courland, iii. 317
Courser, heavenly, given by Yama, vi. 69
Couvade, xi. 37–38
Covenant of the axe, iii. 148, 149
——Unity: see "TS'AN T'UNG CH'I."
Covenants, iii. 72
Cow, Cows:
Cow, archer hero born of, iv. 429
—body of, covered with lines representing water, xii. 39
—born from head of food-goddess, viii. 232
—celestial, Meḥt-uêret a name of, xii. 136
——Osiris as neat-herd originally associated with, xii. 399 [111]
——sun-god between horns of, xii. 38 (fig. 27)
——sun-god on back of, xii. 50, 78
——sun's relation to, xii. 38, 39
—cosmic, xii. 40
— -footed Men, iv. 181, 182
—head of, as religious symbol, xii. 367 [11]
——indication of female divinities, xii. 38
—heavenly, xii. 78 (fig. 77)
—(heifer), Kadmos bidden to follow, and to build city where she should first rest, i. 44–45
—Isis assumes form of, xii. 116
——bears horns of, on her human head, xii. 99
— -maid, Loki as, ii. 143, 145, 146, 149

Cow, Neith often appears as, xii. 142
—Nekhbet called " great, wild," xii.
407 71
—or bull, celestial, most sacred animals
sought in, xii. 413 11
——ox given to clergyman at a death,
survival of funeral sacrifice, iv. 46–47
—priestess painting eyes of sacred, xii.
420 18
—primeval, vi. 48, 52
—reclining in ship, Sothis-Sirius pictured as, xii. 54 (fig. 53), 56
—sacrificed by Kadmos to Athene, i.
45
— -shape of sky, xii. 37–40, 56
—Shenṭet appears in form of, xii. 148
—sky compared to, xii. 37, 39
— -stall, Kṛṣṇa born in, vi. 178
Cowherd, Kṛṣṇa as, vi. 357 5
Cowherd's foster-child: see MESS BUA-
CHALLA.
Cowherds of Britain, Gwydion one of
three, iii. 98
Cows, ii. 63, 102, 216, 276, 309, 324;
iii. 26, 58, 63, 69, 70, 71, 72, 98, 118,
120, 127, 128, 132, 151, 192, 208;
iv. 205, 259; vi. 15, 16, 22, 28, 29, 33,
34, 35, 37, 47, 54, 55, 57, 61, 62, 63,
64, 65, 66, 67, 86, 90, 93, 96, 98, 129,
134, 142, 145–146, 147–148, 235, 242;
263, 264, 265, 288, 315, 335; vii. 148,
152, 154, 199, 236, 324–326, 337, 373–
374; xii. 40, 57, 368 14
Co-walker (double of fairy), seen by
people with second-sight, resembles
the Vardögr, ii. 237
Cowards condemned in future world to
be slaves, xi. 39
Cowrie-shell became first woman, ix.
110
Coxcox, Mexican Noah, xi. 95
Coyolxauhqui (" She whose Face is
Painted with Bells "), moon-goddess,
xi. 60, pl. VII, opp. p. 60
Coyote, x. xvi, 121–122, 136, 139, 140–
145, 159, 160, 161, 162, 163–164, 175,
176, 178, 179, 180, 181, 217, 218, 227,
230–231, 234, 298 47 48, 308 63; xi.
119
—and crow, xi. 178
—Xolotl may only be a special form of,
xi. 83
Coyote's son, myth of, x. 136, 234
Cozaana, creator god, xi. 87

Cozumel, xi. 136
Crab aids hydra against Herakles, i. 81
—and monkey, tale of, viii. 330–331
—in creation of earth, iv. 325
—Ko Pala returned to Kēngtüng reincarnated as a, xii. 279
—which entered Hill, xii. 279
—world-bull stands on, iv. 312
Crabs, ix. 138, 159, 182, 206
—why bloodless animals, xii. 291
Crack in grave for soul to move
through, iv. 30
——sky, iv. 336
Cradles, deities with seven, iv. 460
Craftiness, Sisyphos interpreted as personification of, i. 38
Craftsmen, divine, iii. 32–33
Crane, Aoife in shape of, iii. 59
— -bag of Manannan, iii. 175
—born from rock washed by waves, ix.
157
—crowned, vii. 418 35
—(hsien ho) symbol for longevity, viii.
104, pls. XLIII–XLIV, opp. p. 348
—married to benefactor, viii. 323–324
—meaning of tortoise-crane emblem,
xii. 307–308
—or ibis, Nephthys once represented
with head of, xii. 392 57
—Urashima metamorphosed into a, viii.
265
Cranes, Megaros rescued from flood by
following cry of flock of, i. 19
—three, on monument, meaning of?, iii.
9, pl. XX (B), opp. p. 158
Crann buidhe, magic spear, iii. 65
Creation, vii. 116–117, 134, 145, 146,
147, 149–150, 152, 156, 184, 372–373,
375, 400 24, 402 22; xi. 152–155, 268–
275; see, further, items s.v. ORIGINS
and COSMOLOGY.
—Armenian Navasard as commemo-
rating, vii. 21
—Babylonian epic of, and similar Semitic myths, v. 277–325
—Egyptian theories of, xii. 48
—epic of, v. 91–92, 102, 118, 127, 156,
157, 160, 278, 279
—Greek myths of, basic principles of,
i. 9–10
—gross interpretation of spontaneous,
xii. 372 48
—in Etruscan cosmogony, i. 289
——Genesis, v. 303–304

Creation in Genesis admittedly of Babylonian origin, v. 73
— -legends, detailed, lacking in Micronesia, ix. 263
— -myth from the Sumerian, v. 313–314
— -myths, iv. 312–332, 345, 371–385; v. 104, 112, 190–192; vi. 74, 75, 76, 108–109; 275–304; vii. 143–159; viii. 220–243; xii. 282–284, 285–286, 288–289, 379 16
—of Adam and Eve, v. 183–184
——Heaven and earth out of body of Tiâmat, v. 286, 303–304
——man, i. 10–12, 18
——men and women from stones on Mt. Parnassos, after the Flood, i. 19
——world, i. 4–5
————and men, xii. 68–73
————by sun-god, xii. 30
————Kachin traditions of, xii. 263
—often attributed to nome-god, xii. 18
—old Heliopolitan doctrine of, xii. 50
—speculations of priests on, xii. 372 48
— -struggle, reminiscence of Babylonian doctrine of, xii. 106
— -tale, Asiatic, faint traces of, found in Egypt, xii. 104
—theory of, viii. 56–57
Creative agents, hare, coyote, and raven as, x. 217, 259–262, 293 40, 308 63
—force, hammer (of god) symbol of, iii. pl. XIII, opp. p. 116
—type of origin-myths, ix. 18–27, 105–108, 111–112, 157–158, 159–163, 165, 172–177, 248–250, 251–252, 253, 270, 273–274
Creator being, Australian, ix. 286
—god, Cagn as, vii. 134–135, 288–290
——Katonda as, vii. 129
——Lubumba as, vii. 126, 399 7
——Tonacatecutli as, xi. 75
—gods, Khnûm and Ḥeqet transformed from cataract-deities into, xii. 51
——Yakut, iv. 398–399
—Great, viii. 110–111
—high god not always the, vii. 125
— -myths, viii. 210
—Odin a, ii. 61
— -of-All-Things, the Mixtec, xi. 87
—(Pacific Coast, West), x. 217–221
—Rêʻ as, xii. 238
—Zeus as, i. 328 9
Creators, Ahura Mazda and Aramazd as, vii. 20

Creators, gods and goddesses as, v. 7, 9, 11
Creed, Incas apostles of new, xi. 242–248
Creek, migration legend of, x. 70–73
Creidne, divine brazier, iii. 361 90
—god of smith-work, iii. 28, 31, 40
Creidylad (Cordelia), myth of, iii. 108, 188, 191
Creirwy, daughter of Tegid the Bald, iii. 109
Cremation, ii. 15, 27, 34, 63, 114, 130, 135, 309, pl. XVI, opp. p. 130; iii. 233, 234, 248; iv. 4, 34–35, 42, 130, 481; v. 338; vi. 69–70, 150, 246; vii. 95; viii. 120, 121; x. 179, 181, 214, 280 18; xi. 27; xii. 415 4
—self-, in order to become deified, vii. 390 14
Creosote bush, x. 177
Crescent of sky, fish may typify, xi. 234, 235
—symbol, iii. pl. XVII, opp. p. 134
—worn by Anahit west of Armenia, vii. 29
Crest given bird to show it was a messenger, vii. 169
Crests, x. 238, 239, 241–243, 244, pl. XXXII, opp. p. 256
Crete, according to one account, wife of Minos, i. 61
—Aeneas at, i. 304
—bull of Minos taken from, to Mykenai by Herakles, i. 84
—connexion of Rhea-cult with, i. 274
—cult centre of Aphrodite, i. 196
—Dionysos comes to, i. 216
—herds of Helios located in, i. 242
—legends of, interwoven with Argive myth, i. 28
—Menelaos touches at, i. 134
—Minos claimed crown of, on death of Asterios, i. 61
——explained as pre-Hellenic god of, i. 63
—myths of, i. 60–65
—name of Zeus still survives in, i. 312
—oldest cults and myths of Boiotia and Euboia can be traced back to, i. 42
—reputed birthplace of Zeus, i. 7, 155
—sistrum used in religious ceremonies in, xii. 241

Crete, supposed connexion of Perseus legend with, i. 36
—Talos not allowed by Argonauts to land at, i. 114
—Theseus in, i. 100
—Zeus carried Europe away to, i. 44
——wedded Europe on, i. 60
Crichie Stone, iii. pl. xvii, opp. p. 134
Cridenbél, lampooner, iii. 27, 35
Criminals, cairns piled over, ii. 311
Crimthann Nia Náir, tale of, iii. 90
" Cristne-saga," ii. 312
" Critical Catalogue," viii. 17
Cróchan and Etain carried off by Midir, iii. 80
Crocodile accompanies Aker in form of a lion, xii. 90
—became Typhonic animal of Sêth, xii. 390 35
—birth on a certain day condemns to death by, xii. 200
—carried on back of Êpet, xii. 59
—character in beast-fables, vii. 284
—evil spirit Maga represented as, xii. 111
—" fish " from which earth made, xi. 57, pl. ix, opp. p. 70, 102
—form may be taken by spirits, xii. 175
—four male gods (probably sons of Horus and Osiris) with heads of, assist at royal births, xii. 394 67
—Ḥar-khent(i)-khet(?) once represented with head of, xii. 388 28
—" Horus in Three Hundred " sometimes depicted as composed of, and other animals, xii. 388 28
—idol half man half, xi. 48
—in form of 'Apop-Sêth fights against Horus, xii. 107
——trickster tales, ix. 190, 197–198
—lover, water monster as, xi. 286
—Nhang and Hambaru mean, vii. 89, 91
—primeval animal, vii. 144
—see Horus kills Sêth, etc.; Sobk (crocodile-god).
—Sêth later often appears as, xii. 398 102
—tame, of Sobk-Suchos at Arsinoë, xii. 166
—totem, vii. 272
Crocodiles, address to, viii. 201, 202–203
—Neith giving breast to, xii. 142
—souls of Sobks, xii. 219
Cronia, festival of, v. 18

Cronnchu, Sainred came to house of, iii. 73–74
Cronus: see Kronos.
Crops and weather influenced by zodiacal signs, vii. 53
Cross, x. 57, 97, 115, 177, 203, 307 61, 310 66
—an object of veneration on island of Cozumel, xi. 45, 142
—and Heaven, association of Bacabs with, xi. 143
—as a charm, viii. 159
——world-tree, ii. 335, 336
—at Carabuco, xi. 239
—carved on memorial-tree, iv. 25–26
— -forms, explanations of, xi. 55–57
—Hakon signed cup with a, but was accused of making hammer-sign of Thor, ii. 77
—lowered into water to induce water-spirits to return to their homes, iv. 470
—made in Jerusalem carried on Arthur's shoulder, iii. 184
—Maltese, of Babylonian origin, v. 150
—of archangel Michael, vii. 391 4
—on boats and trees in Christmas festival, iv. 67
——reindeer's forehead at bear hunt, iv. 88
— -pieces on world-pillar, iv. 335, 339
— -roads and forests, Diana (in Autun) haunted, iii. 12
——bhūts at, vi. 249
——games at, iii. 234
——Hekate as goddess of, i. 187, 188
——images of Hermes at, i. 194
——of souls, guardian of, viii. pl. xii, opp. p. 240
——offerings at, ii. 213, 214
———to Itowe at, vii. 261
—sculptured, containing Loki and Sigyn, ii. pl. xviii, opp. p. 146
—sign of, Kikimoras tangle and tear the tow of women who do not make, iii. 228
———made in liquor on forehead, by Norwegian Lapps before Lord's Supper, iv. 38
———over cup at autumnal festival, iii. 282
—sun represented as, v. 61, 377 9
—tablet of the foliated, and of the sun, xi. pl. xx, opp. p. 136, 144

Cross, veiling of, survival of veiling of shrine, v. 160
—within circle symbolizes physical world, x. 97
Crosses, xi. 66–67, 70, pl. IX, opp. p. 70, 201
—at Bewcastle, Ruthwell, and Dearham, ii. pl. XLII, opp. p. 324, pl. XLIII, opp. p. 326, 332, pl. XLIV, opp. p. 332, pl. XLV, opp. p. 336
——entrances of pueblos, spirits at, xi. 141
—mark graves of those who die of snake-bite, xi. 198, 202
—sewn with metal wire on cloth for bear hunters, iv. 93
—skulls on, xii. 297
—used against Wild Huntsman, ii. 207
—wayside, vampires on, iii. 232
Crossing-place, river's, on road to village of dead, iv. 484–485
Crown, conical and gazelle head characterize Reshef, v. 46, 47, 48
—feather, xii. 62, 131
—Ishtar with mural, v. 23
—mural, v. 19, 20, 23, 68
—name of Babi written with white, xii. 131, 403 18
—of cord, v. 386 161
—(of Lower Egypt), Amonet wears, xii. 130
——the sun, xii. 29
—royal, filled with maize, xi. 75
—taken from síd of Cruachan, iii. 68
Crowns, Ḥepḥep wears, xii. 64
—worn by gods and goddesses, xii. 131, 132, 142, 144, 146, 150, 155, 156
Crows, iii. 190; iv. 364–365; ix. 292
Cruachan, cave and síd of, iii. 60, 68, 71, 147, 152
—hunting of magic swine from cave of, iii. 125
—Medb sent bull to, iii. 154
Crucible, sacrifice to, viii. 146
Crucifixion and resurrection of Bacab, xi. 143
—Conchobar died just after the, iii. 209
—Odin's hanging on the tree may be reflexion from Christian belief on the, ii. 52
—our Lord's, earthquake at time of, iii. 157
Cruelty, viii. 155–156

Cruind River in Ulster, swineherd became worm in, iii. 58
Cruithne, wife of Fionn, iii. 168
Crusades, Esthonians returned to old beliefs during, iv. 34
Cryptomeria-tree and fox, tale of, viii. 326–327
—in folk-lore, viii. 288, 341–342
Crystal-gazing, x. 262, 284 27; xi. 180, 245, 247
Crystal in head of serpent, x. 68, 300 50
—vision of sun in, xi. 244–245
Crystals, magic, viii. 271–273
—symbolic and magic properties of, x. 284 27
Cuailnge, smith to Tuatha Dé Danann, iii. 168
Cuare, son of Scáthach, iii. 144
Cúchulainn and Conall Cernach may be Castor and Pollux, iii. 158
——his circle (heroic myths), iii. 139–159
—cycle relatively unaffected by alien elements, iii. 18
—Ulster hero, iii. 11, 36, 55, 56, 64–65, 67, 69, 70, 74, 82–84, 86–88, 90, 98, 120, 128, 131–132, 134, 136, 142, 165, 169, 185, 191, 192, 196, 197, 198, 208–209, 212
Cuchumaquiq, one of lords of Underworld, xi. 173
Cuckoo of wood placed on graves, iv. 35
—sacred to Hera, i. 166, 168
Cuculcan, Prince, who was regarded as a god, xi. 126
Cuernavaca, city, xi. 108
Cuero, monster, sort of octopus, xi. 328
Cuextecatlichocayan (East), in myth of world-quarters, xi. 115
Cuirass brought by dragon-horse, viii. 34–35
Cúldub stole food of the Féinn, iii. 167
Culenn Wide-Maw, "phantoms" revenge their sister, iii. 170
Culhuacan ("crooked hill"), dwelling-place of Aztec ancestors, xi. 116–117
Culprit, Haltia as a, iv. 11
Cult and ethics, xii. 184–197
——festivals, iii. 305–314
—astral, served by women only, v. 25
—bear, iii. pl. XXIII, opp. p. 186
— -centres of Poseidon, i. 210
—earth, survival of, ii. 195

Cult (hero-), of Mordvins, iv. 157–158
—kuala, iv. 114–134, 144, 149, 165, 174
—lud-, iv. 143–151
—moon, v. 6, 378 14; xi. 224
—mystery, iii. 204–205
—nature: see TANTRIC RITES.
—objects used in lamenting of Gilgamish, v. 261
—of Adad, v. xvii
——Adonis, i. 275; v. 8, 9, 66, 76, 133, 135
——Æsir, ii. 25–26, 27
——Agni, vi. 65
——Anahit, vii. 26, 29
——ancestral or tutelary deities, viii. 246
——animals, ii. 216, 218; vi. 240–243; xii. 13, 159–160, 167–168
——Anu, v. 94
——Aphrodite, i. 196, 199, 275; v. 32–33
——Apis of Memphis, xii. 160, 162–163
——Artemis, i. 182, 183, 184
——Astarte, v. 8
——Astλik, vii. 38, 39
——Atargatis, v. 37
——Athene Alea, i. 22
——Balder, traces of, ii. 138
——Dagon, v. 82
——dead, i. 31, 324 9 (ch. ii); iv. 3, 4, 186–187, 198, 199; xii. 254–255
———at barrows, ii. 309–310, 311
——Demeter, development of, i. 231
——Diana, i. 294
——Dionysos, i. 32, 216, 217, 330 8; v. 19; vi. 110
———and Basilinna, v. 19
——divinized men, xii. 415 32
——drowned, i. 48
——dying god, v. 75–77, 133, 336, 346
——Ea, v. 103, 107
——earth, iv. 198
——earth-goddess, Sumerian, v. 90–91
——El, v. 135
——Enki: see ERIDU, SEAT OF ENKI CULT.
——Enlil and Ninlil of Nippur, v. 109
——Eshmun, v. 75
——fire: see items s.v. FIRE-CULT.
——Fortuna, i. 295
——Fosite (Forseti) passed from Frisians to Norsemen, ii. 163
——Frey, ii. 114–115, 118–119; iv. 243, 246, 249–250, 251
——Germanic deities, ii. 203

Cult of Hades, i. 234
——Ḥeqet, xii. 134
——Hera, i. 32
——" Herakles " (Kṛṣṇa), vi. 110
——Ḥesat, xii. 134
——holy men after death, vi. 243, 244
——Horus, xii. 101–102, 387 27, 388 28
——household snake, iii. pl. xxxvii, opp. p. 304
——Innini and Dumuzi, v. 113
——Irmin, ii. 336
——Ishtar, v. 8; vii. 38
———and Tammuz, v. 19, 113
——Isis, xii. 244
——Kṛṣṇa, vi. 171
——life, iii. 204, 205
——Mah, v. 111
——Malik, v. 50, 51
——Manât, v. 21
——Melqart, v. 51
——Mihr, vii. 34
——Mîn(u), xii. 138
——moon, v. 87, 153
——mountains, ii. 202
——Muses, i. 239
——Nabû, v. 158, 318
——Nebo at Borsippa, v. 20
——Nergal, v. 47, 49–50
——Nerthus, ii. 28; see also NERTHUS, TACITUS, ETC.
——Nikilim, v. 132
——Ninurta, v. 45, 132, 135, 136, 137
——Norns suggested, ii. 242, 244
——Odin, ii. 64
——Osiris, xii. 98, 386 17
———and Isis, v. 19
——Pan, i. 267
——peyote (plant), x. 177
——Poseidon, i. 210, 213
——procreation, iv. 259–260
——Ptaḥ, xii. 145
——Quarters, x. 111–112, 275 11, 311 67; xi. 51
——" Queen of Heaven," v. 25
——Reshep, v. 44–45
——Rhea, i. 274
——Serapis, xii. 239
——sister-goddesses, ii. 186–189
——Śiva, vi. 119
——Soma, vi. 65
——souls of deceased kings, xii. 189
——spirits dwelling in stones, ii. 203
——spiritual powers, vii. 179
——sun, vi. 183; see also SUN DEITIES.

Cult of sun and moon in Scandinavia, ii. 197, 198
——Tait, xii. 150
——Tammuz, v. xvii, 77, 131, 132, 336–337, 340, 351
——Tammuz-Ishtar, v. 351
——T'ang dynasty, viii. 69
——Thor, ii. 68
——Ull and Frey contained ritual marriage, ii. 158
————widespread, ii. 157
——Veralden-olmai (Norse Frey), iv. 250–251
——virgin earth-goddess, v. 108, 110
——Vulcan, ii. 201–202
——water, ii. 208; iv. 194, 212
——water-god of Eridu, v. 176
——weapons, iii. pl. ii (6), opp. p. 8, 33–34
——whole species of animals, xii. 169
——Wodan, spread of, ii. 29, 38, 59
——worship of dying god, v. 17
——Zamama, v. 117
——Zeus, i. 20, 159, 160
—phallus, iv. 398; vi. 63, 119; xii. 138
—solar, xii. 364 13
——in Peru, xi. 242–248
—Spartan, i. 26
—Ssabean, v. 336
— -symbols of Navaho arranged according to colour-symbolism, x. 158
— -titles of Aphrodite, i. 199, 202
—Vanir associated with Æsir in, ii. 25–26, 27
—vegetation, xi. 25
—Voršud, iv. 134
—war, ii. 28–29, 64, 106; see also WAR BETWEEN ÆSIR AND VANIR.
—water, iv. 194, 210, 211–215
Cults and myths, oldest, of Boiotia and Euboia can be traced back to Crete, i. 42
—animal, vi. 240–243; xii. 13, 167–168
—Aramaean, v. xvii
—Canaanite, v. xvii
—communal, viii. 244–255
—in Crete, i. 42
—Moabite, v. xvii
—Nabataean, v. xvii, 16
—of Frey and Njord associated, ii. 106–107
——Sin and Ningal, v. 153, 154
——Zeus on mountain peaks, i. 159
—Phoenician, v. xvii

Cults, sacrificial, iv. 407
—spread of Egyptian, to Italy, xii. 242
—Sumero-Babylonian, v. xvi–xvii
Cultural relationships of the Americas, xi. 343
—traits, grouping by, in South America, xi. 254–256
Culture areas of Mexico and Central America, xi. 41–43, 352 1
— -hero, applied to Trickster-Transformer, x. 311 69
——tales: see HERO-BROTHERS.
— -heroes, vii. 219, 220; xi. 361 9–362
—Peruvian, background of, xi. 367 6
—renaissance of, in Peru, xi. 219
Cumae, Apollo brought to Rome by way of, i. 300
—home of Sibyl, and place where Aeneas makes descent into Hades, i. 305
—slaughter of giants at, by Hercules, i. 303
Cumhal, chief, father of Fionn, iii. 160–161, 162, 163, 164, 165, 167, 168, 175, 176
Cumuri sent to sleep by Indra, vi. 68
Cuneiform script, v. xvi; see, further, Cuneiform Tablets, etc., v. 438
Cunnie Rabbit, antelope called, by English-speaking negroes, vii. 282–283, 284, 294
Cuntisuyu, province, xi. 213
Cup, Cups:
Cup drunk by heir after death of a king, ii. 162
—glass, of Hymir, ii. 87
—glowing, of ruler of China, while in captivity, iv. 396
—god with a, iii. pl. xiv, opp. p. 120
—golden, of Helios, given Herakles, i. 86
—in Grail romances, iii. 202, 203, 205
—magic, which Pryderi touched, iii. 102
—never-failing, x. 133, 307 62
—of Tvaṣṭr, vi. 57, 58
——victory captured from the Féinn, iii. 171
—or shell, Odin's pledged eye as, ii. 167
—presented to worshipper, v. 188
— -sacrifice Tōrem, iv. 404
—which would break when a lie was told, iii. 118–119
Cups consecrated at banquets, ii. 77
—given to three heroes, iii. 147–148
—golden, ii. 50

Cups, golden, may represent useful things brought from island of gods, iii. 15

—of gold to prolong life, viii. 146

——skulls of seven blacksmiths (seven stars of Great Bear), iv. 426–427

Cupid (Cupido), Roman counterpart of Eros, i. 294; vi. 141

Curcog, Manannan's daughter, iii. 207, 208

Curicaveri similar to Huitzilopochtli, xi. 60

Curiosity, iv. 360–361; vii. 163, 170, 174, 209; viii. 223, 227, 266; ix. 209; x. 49, 50; xi. 308

" Curious Tales of the Present and Past," viii. 169

Curlew, red legs of, ix. 291–292

Cúroi mac Daire, iii. 140, 146, 148, 151, 155, 156, 157, 188

Curses, i. lii, lvi, 48, 50, 51, 53, 57, 106, 120, 181, 189, 233, 234, 331 ⁵ (ch. x) ; ii. 111, 112, 206, 230, 268, 277, 285, 298, 299; iii. 74, 79, 149, 152; 254, 256; iv. 364–365, 376, 378, 444; v. 29, 33, 72, 82, 107, 122, 129, 142, 143, 161, 168, 185–186, 200, 252, 256, 258, 293, 295, 297, 302, 330, 333, 354, 372; vi. 134, 137, 139, 142, 143, 145, 146, 147, 150, 168; vii. 168, 175, 190; viii. 295, 382 ³; ix. 88; xii. 125, 205

Cursing-bell and cursing-pot used by childless man to drive out ghosts, vii. 187, 188

Cursing (one's self) spells, ii. 299

Curupira (Korupira) Devil, xi. 295, 300

Cushi-ant, Emisiwaddo identified with, xi. 259

Cushion, use of, in memorial feasts, iv. 49–54, 55

Cuso, Thora daughter of, ii. 187

Cussitaw (Creek) came forth from Earth in far West, x. 71

Customs, ancient sacrificial, traces of, among Finno-Ugric peoples inhabiting Russia, iv. xix, xx

Customs and beliefs of ancient heathen Finno-Ugrian people, previous studies of, iv. xx–xxv

—burial: see items s.v. BURIAL CUSTOMS.

Cutha (Arallû), v. 331

Cutting of air to rout Devs and Als, vii. 87, 89

——bodies (of survivors) and hair at time of death, vii. 95

—one's self in time averts capture by ghost, vii. 186

—way out of animals, vii. 221, 224

Cuzco, capital of Peru, xi. 213, 215, 216, 217, 219, 238, 247, 249, 250–251

—sun ritual reminiscent of, x. 89

Cyavana, demon, vi. 31, 87, 98, 141–142

Cycle, viii. 29

—Osirian, xii. 92–121

Cycles, Maya, xi. 146–152

" Cycles " of Battiste Good, x. 128

Cyclic Epics, i. 326 ² (ch. viii)

Cyclical period, viii. 21

Cyclone, v. 118

Cyclops (Kyklopes), vii. 369

—Aeneas at land of the, i. 305

—see also Kyklopes.

—Telchins sometimes confused with, vii. 85

Cymbals, brazen, given by Athene to Herakles for use against man-eating birds, i. 84

Cymry (Welsh), Christianity brought to the, iii. 106

Cyprus, cult centre of Aphrodite, i. 196

——of Reshep at, v. 45

—Menelaos touches at, i. 134

—named from Paphos, i. 200

Cyrus conquered Armenia, vii. 8

—the Great, vii. 70

Cyuuari, Suabian descendants of Semnones, ii. 98

Czar, silvan, iii. 261

—Sun = Dažbog, iii. 297

Czech: see RZIP, ETC.

Czechs, " Chronicle " of Cosmas, source for religion of, iii. 222

D

Daaukĕ, Damkina as, v. 293

Dabage, tortoise, tale of Spider born from boil on, ix. 255

Dabaiba, name of river and divinity, xi. 191

Dabeciba (Dabaiba), mother of Creator, xi. 197

Dabhīti, man favoured by Indra, vi. 68

Dabir (" writer "), epithet of Tīr, vii. 32, 384 ⁵⁶

" Da Derga's Hostel," tale of, iii. 74–77

Dadhīca, seer, Tvaṣṭṛ made thunderbolt from bones of, vi. 132

Dadhikrā (Dadhikrāvan), winged horse, vi. 61

Dadhyañc, horse's head given to, vi. 31, 64

Dâdyâne (Diocletian), v. 338–339

Daemon, generative, of flocks and herds, Pan at first a, i. 268

Daemons, xi. 295, 327
—as guardians, x. 145
—Chaco class of nature-, xi. 322–323
—harpy-like, xi. 238
—of death, winged, Sirens are, i. 262
—(or familiars) of shamans, x. 79

Daenn, dwarf, carved runes for Alfar, ii. 220, 265

Daēva contrasted with Vedic deva, vi. 84

Daēvas and drujas, myth of, v. 415 [15]
—(demons), vi. 261, 300, 302, 303, 305, 309, 333, 335, 342

Dag sacrificed to Odin, ii. 56

Dagan-takala, king of southern Palestine, v. 83

Dagda of Tuatha Dé Danann, iii. 24, 25, 27, 28, 30–31, 32, 34, 39, 40, 41, 46, 50, 51, 52, 53, 66, 72, 78, 112, 121, 136, 174, 204

Dagolayan and Kanag, fight of, ix. 234

Dagon, child of Uranos and Gê, v. 66
—Dagan, Dagun, West Semitic god, deity representing deification of corn and agriculture, v. 78–87, 141, 143
—Saul's head placed in temple of, v. 385 [146]
— -Ashur, v. 381 [58]

Daguna, Arad-, v. 393 [383]

Dahae perhaps equated with Dāsas, vi. 66

Ḍaḥḥāk: see AZHI DAHĀKA.

Dahlmann on Mahāyāna system, vi. 205

Daida-Delkhe-Edzhin, spirit of earth, iv. 460

Daidalos, i. 64–65
—aids Ariadne in her love for Theseus, i. 101
—connexion of, with Pasiphaë myth, i. 61
—erects statue of Herakles at Olympia, i. 91

Daikoku (Great Black Deity), viii. 279

Daimyō and badger, tale of, viii. 330

Dainà, etymology of, iii. 357 [6]

Dainn made runes for the Alfar, ii. 55
—name shared by dwarfs and elves, ii. 266

Dainslef, Hogni's sword, ii. 267

Daire, son of Fionn, swallowed by dragon, iii. 131

Dāitya, mythical land and river, vi. 307, 340

Daityas, vi. 108, 111, 118, 122, 151, 152, 180, 244

Ḍāka, male deity, vi. 218

Ḍākinīs, female deities, wives of Ḍāka, vi. 205, 208, 215, 217–219

Dakṣa, creator god, vi. 18, 28, 54, 74, 75, 86, 114, 149, 178–179
—Prajāpati, gods, and Asuras sprung from daughters of, vi. 106, 134, 136, 139, 151
—Satī daughter of, vi. 184

Dakṣiṇāgni fire, vi. 91

Daktyloi and Korybantes, ritual of, i. 275–276
—Lares Roman counterparts of, i. 299

Dala, child of Parikṣit, vi. 147

Dalai Lama resides in Potala, xii. 262

Dalbhyeśvara replaces Indra as rain-god in Benares, vi. 233

Dam, Urartian, in Van, ascribed to Semiramis, vii. 368

Damascius, Greek philosopher, v. 290, 291, 292, 293
—head of Neo-Platonic school at Athens, v. 102

Damascus, v. 16, 19

Damastes, brigand who fitted captives to his bed, i. 99

Damāvand, Mt., vi. 271, 320, 323, 327, 343; vii. 98
—rock, ii. 147

Damayantī able to recognize deities, vi. 149

Dam-can rDo-rje-legs, local Tibetan divinity, vi. 216

Dames blanches, goddesses survive as, iii. 133

Damgalnunna, epithet of Enki's wife, v. 107, 196

Damkina, wife of Ea, v. 157, 194, 293

Daṁśa, Asura, vi. 154

" Damsel, The Weaving," viii. 97, 132, 162

Damu, title of Tammuz, deity of Gebal, v. 133, 345, 347, 348, 349

Da-mu-ya ("my god Damu"), title of
Tammuz, v. 340, 343
Dán, meaning of, iii. 39
Danaë, Akrisios, and Perseus, i. 33–36
—mother of Perseus by Zeus, i. 11
—wife of Zeus, i. 157
Danaïds, connexion of myth of, with
Amymone and springs of Lerne cannot be original, i. 32
—myth of the, i. 30–32
—task of, to carry water in a basket-
sieve, xi. 269
Danann, commander of Tuatha Dé
Danann, iii. 25
Danaos and Aigyptos, families of, i.
30–32
—crime of daughters of, i. 167
Dānavas, demons, vi. 98, 108, 116, 118,
122, 151, 152, 244
Dance, xii. 325, 326, 336, 342, 345, 347,
348, 351, 354
—as magic device, i. lii
—connected with totemism, vii. 271,
416 2
—death, x. 133; xi. 308; xii. 265
—ghost, x. 149–153
— -house of the gods, x. 147, 188, 191,
210, 275 10
———spirits, x. 50
—in lion's skin as magic, xi. 231
—medicine, x. 269 4
—of butterflies, viii. 335–336, pl. XL,
opp. p. 336
———heavenly peacock, viii. 357
———Satyrs, i. 14 (fig. 2)
———shaman, iv. 294
———Śiva, vi. 180
———Spider transfers sores of man to
himself, vii. 330–331
———Yaos, vii. pl. xxv, opp. p. 250
—shade of deceased invited to, iv. 52
—sparrow-, viii. 320
—Spartan military, Kastor and Polydeukes invented, i. 26
—to greet new moon, vii. pl. xxxiii,
opp. p. 314
—when eleventh variation of Strömkarl's lay played by mortal, every
person and thing must, ii. 211
Dancers at funeral, xii. 182 (fig. 191),
265
—spirit, x. 119
—wedding-, at feast to Utumö, iv. 69
Dances, viii. 226–227, pl. VIII, opp. p.

226, 258, 261, 274, 298, 300, 356, 369;
xi. 21, 26, pl. IV, opp. p. 34, 64, 83,
145, 199, 200, 222, 231, 290–295; see
also AREITOS.
—ceremonial, x. pl. I, frontispiece, xvi-
xvii, 58–59, 169, 194, 197–201, 216,
292 39
—Rāsa or Hallīśa, vi. 172
—sacred, ix. 107
——dwarfs in, xii. 377 86
Dancing, ii. 104, 225; iii. 308, 311, 313,
327; vi. 143, 172, 212
—and singing of sheep, vii. 248
—animals, viii. 314
—at bear feast games, iv. 96
—before newly created images, ix. 106,
273
—Bês, patron of, xii. 61
—by Nāt-kadaw, xii. 345–346
——Nāt-thein, xii. 342, 351, 354
—cat, vii. 276–277
—death by, iii. 262; iv. 181, 183, 189;
468
—fairy, iii. 256–260, 262
—of ghosts, vii. 188
——water-nymphs, iii. 255
——-place of Elle-folk bad grazing for
cattle, ii. 225
Daṇḍaka forest, vi. 128
Dandur, shay and "Osiris, much praised
in the Underworld," worshipped at,
xii. 171–172
Danes, Skjoldings (or kings) of, ii.
32
Dañh-bi, python-god, vii. 272
Daniel, vision of, v. 156
Dānos, demon, vi. 244
Dante, like Arṭā Vīrāf, visits other
world, vi. 344
Danu (Danand; Brythonic equivalent,
Dôn), goddess, iii. 39, 40, 97, 106
Dānu, parent of Vṛtra, vi. 67
Dao-ly, sons of Cau took service with,
xii. 355
Daozos = god-Dumuzi = Mahalalel,
Greek transcription of antediluvian
king, v. 205
Daphne changed into the laurel, i. 16
Daphni, Aphrodite still associated with
modern, i. 313–314
Darabzu, conception of form of Enki as
monster, v. 105
d'Arbois on saga of Cúchulainn, iii.
157–159

Dardania, country settled and named by Dardanos, i. 117
Dardanos (son of Zeus), i. 117–119, 157
Darius conquered Armenia, vii. 8
Dark Warrior (Chinese), a tortoise, symbol of Yin, viii. 243
Darkness, ii. 201; vi. 263–274, 317; viii. 137; xi. 51
—caused by the fall in paradise, iv. 419
—Chên Wu ruler of abode of, viii. 111
—controlled by Fei Ch'ang-fang, viii. 132
—deification of, xii. 48
—distinguishing feature of house of Lie, vii. 397 [7]
—Extinction son of, iii. 35–36
—fire potent against powers of, vii. 55
—first man created to fight against, vi. 295
—killed by Varuṇa, vi. 137
—magically prolonged, vii. 341
—world of, ix. 31–32, 33
Dart, fairies', vii. 393 [30]
Dāsa denotes slave, vi. 66, 67
—destroyed by Indra, vi. 68
Daśagvas, seers, vi. 65
Dasahra festival, worship of plough at the, vi. 239
Daśaratha, king of Kosala, performed horse sacrifice, vi. 127, 128
Dāsas (Dasyus), human enemies who rank as demons, vi. 34, 66, 154
Dāshtāyani, sons of, slain by Keresāspa, vi. 324
Dasra (Wonder-workers), vi. 30, 141
Datanus, Samogitian god, Dažbog to be compared with, iii. 354 [14]
Date of Egyptian religious texts, xii. 213
——Flood, v. 205
——founding of Kish, v. 203
——historical period of China, viii. 7
Date-palm, iv. 357; v. 98, 179, 187; viii. 105
Dates, ceremonial, x. 193, 194, 276 [13]–277; xi. 53, 55
Dating systems, xi. 129–131
Datta, Viṣṇu partly incorporated in, vi. 170
Dattātreya authority on Yoga or an incarnation of Viṣṇu, vi. 168, 170, 244
Daugawa, " Great Water " identified with, iii. 328, 329, 330
Daughter of the Sun, planet Venus as, xii. 365 [19]

Daughter of the Sun, Tefênet as, xii. 45
—Sun bears a, ii. 199
Daughters of the sun-god, xii. 29, 30
Daurrud, vision of, ii. 254
David and giants, v. 355
—(Scriptural) and Nezahualcoyotl, parallels in lives of, xi. 109–110
Davis, John, discoverer of Davis Strait, x. 2
Dawn, vi. 18, 20, 21, 26, 28, 30, 34, 60, 62, 76
—announced by bird and fowls, ix. 114, 117, 275
—called grief of Alfar, ii. 222
—captured Sosondowah the hunter, x. 26
—(Eos), i. 245–246
—mother of sun, vii. 49
——people, x. 48
—Qat taught to make, ix. 113–114
—(Te Ata), ix. 7
—water-elves fear, ii. 211
Dawn's Heart (Jupiter), tale of, vii. 229–231
Day, vi. 31, 69, 85, 86
——counts, xi. 148
—Delling father of, ii. 200, 201
—name of fifth, of week attests widespread Thor cult, ii. 68
—(of danger; evil day), v. 153
——Judgement, ii. 343
——week, fourth, named for Odin, ii. 37
——Frigg occurs in sixth, ii. 176, 177
——third, names of Tyr deduced from, ii. 97, 98
—origin of, ix. 276
—Osiris master of the sixth, xii. 123
—River, temple to Trung sisters on banks of, xii. 314, 315
——signs, xi. 55, 99, 100, 101, 102, 103, 104, 146–148
Daybreak, places vanishing at, found in Fionn and Grail romances, iii. 119–120
Daylight and dawn drive away ghosts, ix. 327 [24]
—fatal to underground beings, ii. 96
—perpetual, ix. 113
Days, lucky and unlucky, viii. 34, 101, 143; xii. 197, 200, 422 [7]; 337
—names of Maya, xi. 147
—of week, Anglo-Saxon names of, evidence of gods, ii. 19

Days of week, German names of, show where gods found, ii. 18
——year defined by stellar signs, v. 306
Dažbog, " the Giving God," son of Svarog, iii. 277, 297, 299
Dazimā, goddess, v. 201–202
Dea Hludana, inscriptions to, ii. 194
—Quartana and Dea Tertiana, fever-goddesses, i. 296
—Tacita and Mercury, parents of Lares, i. 299
Dead, abodes of: see ABODES OF DEAD.
—after living in Underworld, may die second time, iv. 72
—Agni eater of the, in one aspect, vi. 44
—aid sun in journey through nether world, xii. 27
—aiding ass against dragon, xii. 107 (fig. 106)
—Alfar connected with, ii. 226
—alive in their barrows or mounds, ii. 306–307
—amusement of, iv. 61
—and Night, Nephthys as queen of, xii. 110
—annual rite in commemoration of, x. 215
—Anubis and Thout(i) judges of Egyptian, xii. 366 [3]
——general god of, xii. 111
——predecessor of Osiris as god of the, xii. 399 [111]
—appear as birds, iv. 9
——beautiful by night, skeletons by day, x. 230, 276 [12]
—Armenian Navasard as commemoration of, vii. 22
—aroused for special purposes, ii. 9, 11, 45, 49, 124, 299, 300
—as herdsmen, iv. 39, 286; vii. 174–175
—Asklepios raised people from the, i. 280
—at celestial tree and at tree and spring of life, xii. 35 (fig. 21), 36 (fig. 23), 39 and fig. 28
—attain to different worlds according to what caused death, iv. 80–81
—banquets in honour of, iii. 233, 234, 235, 236
—become members of crew of sun-god, xii. 415 [2]
—belief in an orifice by which they descend into earth and arise for re-birth, x. 289 [34]

Dead, black animals sacrificed to, iv. 75
—boats of, iii. 16, 17
—bodies thrown to dogs, iv. 481
—body desecrates fire, vii. 54
—bones of, powerful fetishes, xi. 27
—breaking-up of objects for, iv. 14, 20, 40, 53
—brought to life: see items s.v. LIFE, RESTORATION OF.
—buried in standing position because soul still alive, xi. 278
——to be born again, x. 289 [34]
——towards east, vii. 47
—" burning," " cry," or " dance " of, an annual rite, x. 215
——of, ii. 34; iv. 4, 34; vi. 69–70, 243; x. 179; see also items s.v. BURIAL; CREMATION.
—candle at feast for, iii. 236, 238
—care for the, xii. 172
—carried off by birds, vi. 144
——in boat made of fingernails, i. 75
—carry off domestic animals with them, iv. 365
—certain, go to Tlalocan, xi. 81
—chieftains, faces of, blackened, x. 189
—children born of, x. 120, 146, 147, 262, 276 [12]
—classification of abodes of, ii. 306
—clothes of, calling or touching, would prevent return of, vii. 187
——taken away by Yamī, vi. 215
—clothing and outfitting of the, iv. 19–20, 72
—coins, buttons, etc., to cover eyes of, iv. 21, 22
——food, and drink buried with, iii. 230
—come to earth to tell what killed them, vii. 176
—connexion of bones of, with abundance of food and minerals, x. 256
—cotton masks over faces of, x. 189, 190
—covering of mirror in presence of, iv. 22
—cult of, i. 31, 324 [9] (ch. ii); ii. 309–310, 311; iv. 3, 4, 186–187, 199; xii. 254–255
—descent to Underworld of, ix. 72
—Dharma takes place of Yama as judge of, vi. 180
—disasters sent by, to remind living of neglect of, vii. 182
—disposal of: see DEAD, BURNING OF.

Dead dragged down in sea to house of Sedna by Anguta, x. 6
—early, meet newly deceased and join in funeral feast, iv. 44, 45–46
—entrance to realm of, ii. pl. v, opp. p. 22
—epithets of Odin show connexion with, ii. 44–45, 217
—equipment buried with, aids journey to Hel, ii. 305
—Eumenides the avenging spirits of, i. 50
—eyebrows of, painted in blood from slain hen, iv. 18
—feasts and festivals for the, ii. 310, 311; iii. 235, 236, 352 7; iv. 37–59, 60–71, 237; v. 122, 398 105; ix. 118
—ferrymen of, iv. 75; xii. 58 (fig. 59), 176
—first cup and food for, at feasts, iv. 45
—food of, xii. 177, 178
——set aside for, at Christmas meal, iii. 308
—forgiveness implored of, iv. 17, 58
—forgotten, reveal themselves, ii. 307
—forms of, x. 276 12
—future of, vi. 160–161
—Fylgjukona passes from, to a kinsman, ii. 235
—Gandharvas connected with souls of, vi. 59
—gave revelations to Volva, ii. 299
—general nature of worship of, xii. 172
—gifts to, iii. 233, 234, 235
—Gilgamish visits land of, v. 263–265
—goats of Thor made to live again, ii. 79
—god of, xi. 54
—gods as leaders of the, ii. 39–40
——land wrongly regarded as realm of, iii. 338 10
——of earth, demons, and, vi. 41–72
—Grand Lama, spirit of, descends on another, vi. 216
—grave as house of, vii. 189
—graves of, iv. 31–32
—great city of, v. 235
—greeted by Bragi, ii. 161
—guardians of, x. 236
—Ḥat-ḥôr divinity of, xii. 42
—have knowledge of earthly life, viii. 47
——no navels, xi. 27

Dead, headless goddess as personification of regions of, xii. 99, 100
—hearts of, weighed by Thout(i) and his baboon, xii. 176
—Hel denotes general Underworld of, ii. 303
—Hel-ride performed to gain tidings of, ii. 305
—Hindu idea of, vi. 249–250
—how custom of offerings to, arose, vii. 185–186
—husband, marriage of widow to obtain son for, vi. 150
—images buried with, provide servants, concubines, etc., xii. 177, 416 14
—in their barrows, ii. 306–312
——Underworld become younger and dwindle until they are born again into the family, i. 73
—inquiries of, ii. 311; iv. 28, 79
—Inue of their graves, x. 5
—invitation to, to return for feasts, iv. 47, 48, 49, 54, 56, 63, 68
—invite living to barrows, ii. 308
—islands of the, in Celtic belief, iii. 16, 17
—jade used in burial of, viii. 47
—Jaik-Khan (Flood prince) ruler of, iv. 365
—judges of: see items s.v. JUDGE.
—killing of objects deposited with, xii. 418 23
—kindly (class of the fathers), vi. 15, 57, 67, 159–161
—Klickitat buried the, on islands, x. 146
—land of, believed to lie hidden in Northern Arctic Ocean, or under earth, iv. 77
—Land-vættir may have included spirits of, ii. 228
—led to place of punishment by baboon, xii. 180
—life of, in the hereafter, xii. 176–177
——parallels that of living, iv. 61, 72
—lighted to other world by sacred fire, x. 47
—live together in villages, iv. 73
—living man resembling, chosen to represent him at memorial feast, iv. 43, 52, 53, 55
—maidens, Gefjun mistress of, ii. 180
—male or female, invocations against, xii. 415 6

Dead, man created from bones of, x. 236, 312 [70]

——heart of, inserted in image, which then talked and walked, ii. 188

——sacrifices to, iv. 25, 38–39; see also SACRIFICING TO DECEASED, ETC.

—Maruts may be souls of, vi. 102

—may assume solar, lunar, or stellar character with Osiris, xii. 178

——become assimilated to Masters, iv. 465–466

——rejoin living, ii. 307

—men ride to their barrow, ii. 342

—might come from Underworld to Heaven, iv. 75

—moon abode of souls of, iii. 273

—Moqwaio given charge of, x. 43

—mother, breasts of, nourish her offspring, x. 114

—Mothers may be angry spirits of the, vi. 238

—mourned at Sun-dance festival, x. 90

—Mulungu sometimes used for spirits of the, vii. 116

—music dedicated to spiritual welfare of, viii. 356

—must cross " black river " of Tuonela, iv. 74, 78

——water, iv. 33, 78

——seek aid of cow over Vaitaraṇī River, vi. 235

——travel 86,000 yojanas, vi. 159

—need care of relatives until shaman takes their shadow to otherworld, iv. 39

—" Negative Confession " read by, in judgement hall, xii. 176, 184, 185, 187

—Nergal is judge of souls of, v. 49, 50, 147

—no change in position of, in the " Purāṇas," vi. 185–186

—November month of, iv. 64

—objects intended for, broken, for admission to invisible world, iv. 14, 20, 53

—Odin learned scornful language from, ii. 46

——perhaps god of, ii. 40–41, 42, 44, 45, 65

—offerings to, vii. 95–96, 98

——made towards north, iv. 77

—Osiris as divinity of the, xii. 93, 94–95, 96–97, 100, 111

——judge of the, xii. 118, 120

Dead passed to another world and were not reborn on earth, iii. 14

—pastimes of, xii. 177

—perhaps legend of, partaking of water and plant of life in Arallû, v. 333

—person as local deity, viii. 64, 65, 66, 67

—pillars of Hel-gate made of bones of, ii. pl. XIII, opp. p. 106

—place by door residence of, at memorial feast, iv. 46

—poem recited as incantation to recall souls of, to the parentalia, v. 334

—portion of the, setting sun as, vii. 98

—prayers to, x. 310 [65]

—preparation of, for burial, xi. 27

—presents sent with, to relatives, iv. 20

—promises to, iv. 69–70

—property of, iv. 20

——the Devil, iv. 316

—protection demanded from, iv. 38, 44, 51, 52, 53, 62

—provided with water-jars, v. 111

—provisions for, for use in otherworld, iv. 19–20, 72

—Ptaḥ opens mouths of the, xii. 407 [77]

—quest for, x. 50, 118–119, 147, 236, 264, 276 [12]

—raising of, i. 280; xi. 134

—realm of the: see ABODES OF DEAD.

—reaping " upside down " for, iv. 73

—receive eternal life from Ḥat-ḥôr, xii. 39

—received by Nut, xii. 41 (fig. 31)

—red kangaroo skin presented to sun in land of, ix. 275

—relative, pregnant woman is given charm of hair to induce rebirth of, x. 100, 302 [55]

—restoration of, from spirit world at entreaty of living, vii. 184

—restored to life by magic cauldron, iii. 100, 101, 203; see, further, items s.v. LIFE, RESTORATION OF.

—resurrection of, symbolizes personification of plant life in Osiris, xii. 66

—return as animals, vii. 192, 193, 344

——of, x. 50, 137, 302 [53]

—returned to earth to eat living, xi. 340

—returning to old homes, red dragonfly associated with, viii. 335

—rider of the, ii. 257

—rising of, at end of world, iv. 370

Dead, rites in honour of the, x. xvii
—Roman Junones originally souls of, iii. 249
—roof-boards raised by Russian Karelians to allow for passing of, iv. 17
—rowed by sun-god, xii. 26 (fig. 7)
—ruled by Odin in hills, ii. 202
—Ruler of kingdom of, remembered at funeral feasts, iv. 45, 49, 77
—Russian Lapps have same idea of their Seides as of their, iv. 106
—sacrifice offered to those, whose names are given to children, iv. 15
—sacrifice trees of, must be dark, iv. 152, 158, 220
—Sea of, iii. 17
—see, further, items under ABODES OF DEAD; BURIAL; CLOTHES; CLOTH; CORPSE; CREMATION; G R A V E S ; TROUGH.
—seeing of, with special preparations, iv. 61
—serpent-keeper of resting-place of, vii. 75
—serving of the, iv. 22
—shoes provided for, ii. 305; iv. 486
—signs in house for, ix. 141
—sleigh to convey, to memorial feast, iv. 56
—smoke-outlets opened for passing of the, iv. 17
—Sokar(i) became god of, xii. 149
—solar myths of, vi. 312, 314, 315, 350
—soul of, believed to stay under table forty days, iv. 48
——dwells forty days on earth, iii. 230
——supposed to enter memorial doll, iv. 41
—souls of, iii. 319
——as snakes, ii. 217
——borne on wind, ii. 193
——fairies are, iii. 256–257
——fed from celestial tree, xii. 39
——have motion like living, iv. 9
——held captive in Hell by Nergal, v. 72
——see, further, items s.v. SOUL.
——wandering, v. 361
—spirits of, dwelt in trees, ii. 204, 207
——Ostiaks sacrificed to, for luck in fishing, iv. 193
——resemblance of kuala cult to worship of the, iv. 115

Dead, spirits of, supposed to wander in wind, ii. 40, 41, 42
———watch over morality of the people, iv. 220
—stars associated with the, x. 96
—stoop for, at forty-day feast, iv. 51–52
—Sumerian mythology attributes origin of demons to wandering souls of, v. 354–355
—Sun as woman nightly visits land of, ix. 275
——sails through regions of the, xii. 27
——shines on world of, vii. 50
—swing of the, iv. 30
—table of, iv. 54
—tabus connected with, x. 215
—threat to call, from Hell to consume living, v. 28, 330
—three regions of the, vii. 137, 180–181; see also GHOSTS, THREE ORDERS OF, ETC.
—Tiur guides souls of, to nether world, vii. 31
—to return no more, x. 144, 147
—tortured by Rutu or Rota, iv. 75–76
—trees connected with souls of the, vi. 239
—unmarried, i. 324 9 (ch. ii); iv. 19, 29
—viscera of, placed in Canopic vases, xii. 112
—visited by wives, ii. 307
—wailing for: see items s.v. WAILING.
—waked by Odin, ii. 47
—walking, xi. 197
—wandering-nights of, iv. 61–62, 63–64, 66
—warriors resuscitated each night, ii. 316
—washing of, iv. 18, 21, 25, 73
—watched by an idol, x. 57
—weapons placed beside the, xii. 174
—wedding of, or horse-wedding, memorial feast, iv. 57–58
—weeping-songs to, iv. 27, 30, 56, 68, 74
—who died in strange places, tables set up in memory of, iv. 25
——go in the wind, Maruts souls of, vi. 39
—witches feed on bodies of those recently, vii. 335
—witness birth of sun, xii. 35 (fig. 21)
—woman, figure of, appears from a flower, viii. 301
—Woman's Land, iii. 138

Dead, work of, described by his impersonator, iv. 55
——performed with pious intention, affects the, viii. 386 ³
——worship of, ii. 310; iii. 233–239; vi. 249
——wrappings for, of reindeer skins, iv. 19
——Yima's legend combines first man and the, vi. 316–317
——Zuñis water the earth, x. 189–190
Deaf One, Celestial, viii. 113
" Dean of Lismore's Book," iii. 131
Death, iv. 472–482
——abandonment of habitation after a, x. 154
——Absolute may be identified with Time and, vi. 107
——an eight-headed monster, vii. 177
——and birth not permitted to take place on Isle of the Temple, viii. 269
————ratio between, viii. 233
——burial, Finno-Ugric, iv. 17–36
——ghost-world, x. 233–236
——life, viii. 221–224
——tree of, iv. 383
——old age, Connla invited to escape, iii. 234
——Angel of, iii. 234
——Annancy marries his daughter to, and sends her as servant to Death's house, vii. 331–333
——appearance of House-man (god) sign of, iv. 159
————umkovu in kraal means, vii. 338
——articles used for protection against, iv. 23
——as cannibal, vii. 178
——decision of Norns, ii. 239
——associated with owl, god of war, and a divinity of frost and sin, xi. 139
——beating out of homes on, iv. 23
——because of broken tabu, vii. 189, 190
——beetle flying to graveyard as omen of, iv. 9
——bird as portent of, iv. 10, 11
——body ordered to return to respective sources at, iv. 372
——bound about neck of Sisyphos by Zeus, i. 37
——bread and water of, v. 180
——breath's departure synonym for, iv. 7
— -bringing powers, xi. 38

Death brought into world by eating of gourd, xii. 289–290
——by sacrifice, Tlahuicol offered citizenship in place of, xi. 59
——ticklings, wrestling, or dancing, iv. 181, 183, 189
——came to man because of touch of devil, iv. 376
——caused by ancestors among Kachins, xii. 297
————death of animal totem, vii. 276–279
————eating rice in which is found finger-print of departed relative, xii. 297
——comes to master of house when snake guardian dies, iii. 246
——connexion of dog with, vi. 242
——conquered by Herakles on behalf of Alkestis, i. 107
——considered beginning of life, xi. 112–113
——control of Atropos over, i. 284
——creation of, vi. 76
— -dance, xi. 308; xii. 265
——denoted by falling star, iv. 395
——disposal of articles infected with, iv. 25
——doctrine of life after, xii. 172–183
——does not sever bond between soul and corpse, iv. 7
——door or window left open for ingress and egress of soul while corpse remains in house, iii. 229
——driving out of, iii. 312; iv. 23
——extraction of soul, vii. 94
——folk-myth of introduction of, xii. 264–265
——foretelling of, by dead, ii. 311–312
——from childbirth, ix. 78–79
——the Kenaima, xi. 260–261
——future lot dependent on nature of, ii. 317–318
——gives both good and evil fortune, vii. 175
——goddess " West " personifies, xii. 99
——Greek view of, i. 141–143
——Hel appears before, ii. 304
——Hubur river of, v. 235
——in battle, souls who met, x. 249; see also VIOLENCE, SEPARATE ABODE, ETC.
————certain cases remediable, vii. 171
————forest: see chap. Forest-spirits (vol. iv. 175–190)
————home necessitates new fire, vii. 95

Death, Ishtar a goddess of, vii. 38
—kāla originally, viii. 381 [15]
— -keen, first, in Ireland, iii. 32, 137
—marking place of, iv. 23
—Marta an omen of, iv. 205
—met with in strange locality great calamity, iv. 25, 73–74
—mystery of, x. 115–120, 121, 276 [12], 302 [53]
—not annihilation in Piman ideas, x. 176
—of all parts of witch must be absolute because any surviving part may kill, vii. 334
——great soul causes atmospheric change and pestilences, iii. 14–15
——Heavenly Youth, reference to star in, viii. 235
——man followed that of his Fylgja, ii. 234–235
——master and mistress of house, two house snakes reveal themselves at, then die, ii. 217
——one man for another, viii. 312
——Seide if it became annoying, iv. 107
——shaman follows that of his spirit-animal, iv. 507–508
——temporary incarnation of the Bodhisattva, vi. 209
—omens of, x. 5
—only want of Land of Immortality, viii. 363
—origin of, vii. 106, 125, 154, 160–178, 332–333; ix. 54, 106, 117–119, 122, 170, 182, 252–253, 285; x. xviii–xix, xxiii, 9, 10–12, 50, 115–120, 121, 161, 180, 205, 218, 220, 233–235, 260, 262–263, 279 [16]–280; see also IMMORTALITY FOR MAN.
—outwitting of, by Spider, vii. 332
—overcome by Hero Brothers, xi. 159
—path of Yama, vi. 69
—personifications of, under different names, vii. 117
—powers of, xi. 79–84
—predestined by deities of winter solstice, x. 253
—presaged by appearance of daemon, xi. 323
—Prince of, iv. 367
—purification after, iv. 365
—rainbow portent of, xi. 203
—region of, termed " daughter of the great god," xii. 386 [22]

Death, repeated escapes from; see chap. Heroes (vol. vii. 64–71).
—repetition of name of god, or use of sacred water and plants efficacious at, vi. 250
— -river, iv. 74, 78
—Sea, iv. 486
—second in Underworld, for wicked dead, xii. 179
—shackled by Sisyphos, i. 37–38
—shooting star sign of, vii. 94
—signs of Zodiac caused, vii. 52
—song and dance, x. 133
—songs, iv. 79–82
—soul remains about house some time after, iii. 230; iv. 48, 49, 53; 478
—souls after, abide near human beings, viii. 237
—Spider brought, into world, vii. 329
— -stone of Nasu-no, viii. 325
—sudden, caused by Artemis, i. 183
—Sunīthā daughter of, vi. 165
—Tena-ranide is, x. 78–79
—those dying violent, haunt upper earth, vii. 179
—to see mysterious fire sign of, x. 47
—warning of, viii. 158
—warrior-aristocracy at, went to Odin, and folk to Thor, ii. 72
—warrior's, xi. 59, 60, 61
—waters of, v. 214, 215, 218
—worship of, believed by some scholars basis of all religions, xii. 254–255
—" Writer " confused with angel of, vii. 384 [50]
—Yucatec have excessive fear of, xi. 138
Death's body, half of (also a boy's), in state of decay (typifying life and death), vii. 175, 281, 404 [34]
—Head god of Underworld, xi. pl. v, opp. p. 46, 57
— -heads in tree, xi. 171
De-Babou and De-Ai, primeval pair, ix. 254
" De Gabail int sída," iii. 50
Debility, Ulstermen's: see ILLNESS, PERIODIC, ETC.
Decanal stars, xii. 57, 112, 378 [94]
Decans, stellar, v. 306
Decapitated mummies point to human sacrifice, xi. 222
Decapitation, x. 104, 290 [37]–291, 302 [55]
December 25th festival, v. 16, 18

Dechtire or Dechtere, Conchobar's sister, iii. 140, 141, 155, 198
——love of Lug for, iii. 82–84, 117
Decreeing, punishing activity of Heaven related to its, iv. 395
Decrees, collection of, made by Burchard of Worms, ii. 69
—divine, issued by Aramazd, vii. 30, 384 [48] [51]
Decrepitude, Gaokerena-tree produced to avert, vi. 281
Děd, dědek, děduška, ancestor raised to rank of family genius, iii. 240, 244
Dedication of animals to gods, iv. 399, 432
—practice of, viii. 386 [3]
Dêd(u), Osiris originally local god of, xii. 92, 222, 385 [3]
—ram (or goat?) of Mendes as "soul" of, xii. 385 [4]
—symbol of, apparently pillar worshipped at Byblos, xii. 399 [111]
Dêdet, goddess at Busiris and Mendes, xii. 132
Dedun (Dedunti) worshipped at Semneh in Nubia, xii. 157, 411 [12]
—mentioned among Egyptian gods, xii. 412 [13]
Dĕduška Domovoy (Grandfather House-lord), description of, iii. 240–242
—Vodyanoy, water-spirit, iii. 270
Deep, Horus and Osiris born from, xii. 389 [29]
—western, nightly resting-place of sun, xii. 96
Deer-horn, flute invented by Athene out of, i. 181
Deer, horned, sacrifice-Tōrem, iv. 404
—king of the, xi. 167
—Learchos changed into, i. 46
—(lu), why symbol for promotion, viii. 104
—mortals transformed into, iii. 129
—mouse, and cat, tale of, ix. 202
—Prajāpati in form of, vi. 76
—relation of, to gods and generation, xi. 74, 75, 86
—sacred, viii. 269
—side took form of, iii. 38, 56, 129
—substituted as sacrifice for Iphigeneia, i. 126
— -tail, fire-god and singing shaman, xi. 121

Deer, woman transformed into, eats people and is in turn eaten, xi. 231
— -zada, iv. 458
Deewa Deenes, Lettish name for October, iii. 352 [7]
Defilement of man by devil, iv. 374–377
Degenerations of a god, xi. 297
Degradation, conception of, xi. 302
Deianeira, attempted outrage by centaur Nessos on, i. 270
—Herakles suitor for hand of, i. 93
—uses love philtre on garment of Herakles with disastrous effect, i. 94, 95
—wife of Pelasgos, i. 20
Deïdameia, wife of Peirithoös, i. 104–105
Deification, i. 295; v. 78
—of departed not to be overestimated in importance, xii. 183
——heavens, iv. 391
——humans into gods, vii. 117, 119
——lake, iv. 413–414
——peyote into god, x. 177
—process of, xii. 17
—self-cremation in order to attain to, vii. 390 [14]
Deifications, viii. 62, 64, 82, 95, 107, 111, 112
—of weapons as gods, v. 128, 146
Deimne, Fionn at first called, iii. 165
Deimos ("Panic"), steed of Ares, i. 189–190
Deinolochus knew Babylonian legend of plant of immortality, v. 228
Deïphobos, brother of Paris, i. 119
—Helen's husband, slain by Menelaos, i. 133
—removes pollution from Herakles, i. 89
Deir el-Baḥri, birth-temple at, xii. 414 [29]
Deism, Greek mind emerged from animism to, i. 287
Deities, ancestral and tutelary, viii. 246
—animal beings rarely to be regarded as, x. 293 [40]
——Egyptian, of barbaric origin, xii. 13
—animistic, viii. 215
—Asiatic, popular in black magic, xii. 207
—borrowed from Asia by sorcerers, xii. 157, 207–209
—chief, of Armenians, vii. 17–19
—combination of male and female, v. 22, 44, 50, 53, 381 [58]

Deities, constellations, fixed stars, and planets identified with, v. 91
—creation of, xi. 335
—descendants of first people became, ix. 159
—explanations of origins of Scandinavian, ii. 31
—good and bad, ix. 118
—Iranian, vii. 20–35
——on Indo-Scythian coins, vi. pl. XXXII, opp. p. 260, pl. XXXIV, opp. p. 272
—local, iii. 8, 9; viii. 63, 64, 65, 66, 67
——assimilation of, into Buddhism, vi. 209, 216, 219
—mixed representations of, xii. 160, 161, 412 [4]
—more than 5,000 Sumerian, v. 88
—of Elbe Slavs, iii. 277–289
——flowers, dancing, games, and feasting, xi. 77
——Good Fortune, viii. 279–280
——pagan Russians, iii. 293–301
—Pan-Teutonic, ii. 19
—primitive, xii. 255–256
——develop into tutelary spirits, fetishes, and gods, xii. 15
—Semitic, v. 2–87
—seven, may have been genii of the seven planets, vii. 17
—special names to diverse functions of, v. 91
—temporary eclipse of, iii. 28
—three classes of, vi. 15
—Urartian, secondary and local, vii. 11
—whose deaths recorded appear again in Christian times, iii. 55
Deity, a, not necessarily a creature existing from birth or all time, vi. 190
—actual making of man by, ix. 167
—as father of clan, v. 10, 378 [19], 379 [21]
—astral, Semitic tribes appear to have started with single tribal, v. 11
—bearded, xii. 22 (fig. 2)
—clan, viii. 215
—eponymous, of elements of language, poetry, and letters, Ogyrven perhaps, iii. 12
—father-mother, v. 22
—fire as, iv. 452
——female, vii. 55
——given to first man by, ix. 184
—male, half serpent half human, v. 90

Deity, male, sky-, associated with sun; female with earth, ix. 166
—of medicine, viii. 230
——Tzŭ-t'ung, viii. 112
——Underworld, sex of, ix. 48
——original Khaldian pantheon had no female, vii. 11
——without arms or legs created birds, ix. 165
—primitive Semitic tribes believed in descent from patron, v. 7
—serpent symbol of, xii. 301
—supreme, nome-god treated as, xii. 18
—with mask and bolts, xi. pl. XXXI, opp. p. 218, 235
Dekanawida, x. 52, pl. XI, opp. p. 52
Delbaeth, Danu daughter of, iii. 39
Delbchaem, iii. 72
Delling (Day-spring), father of Day, ii. 200, 201
—magic song before, ii. 265
Delos, i. 250
—Aeneas at, i. 304
—Apollo and Artemis born on, i. 174–175
Delphian Apollo: see APOLLO.
Delphinios ("Dolphin-like"), title under which Apollo was to be worshipped, i. 178
Delphoi, Apollo in, i. 177
—Galatian Celts vanquished at, because of breach of tabu, iii. 12
—god of, necklace and robe of Harmonia deposited with, i. 55
—Helen consults oracle at, concerning marriage, i. 25
—Herakles goes to, seeking cure for disease, i. 89
——sacks shrine at, i. 89–90
—Hestia dwells in Apollo's sacred house in, i. 209
—influence of oracle of, on development of legend of Herakles, i. 76
—Ion placed in temple of Apollo at, i. 71
—Kadmos enquired of oracle at, concerning Europe, i. 44–45
—Muses attached to Apollo at, i. 239
—Neoptolemos killed at, i. 135
—oracle of, warns Oidipous against entering his own country, i. 49
—pre-Apolline shrine of Gaia at, i. 273
—prophecy regarding Herakles, from shrine of Apollo at, i. 80

Delphoi, sacred tripod at, desecrated by Herakles, i. 90

Delta, Ash perhaps worshipped in western part of, xii. 131

—eastern, Sêth old local god in, xii. 390 [35]

—Neith worshipped in the, xii. 142

—Sekhmet adored at, xii. 146

—Sêth worshipped in, xii. 389 [32]

—worship of Osiris and Isis long local in, xii. 120

Deluge: see FLOOD.

Delusion, art of, ii. 35, 280; see also GLAMOUR.

—cosmic principle, vi. 184

—to Milesians, magic army a, iii. 44

Dementia, ii. 211

Demeter and Demophon, analogue of, in Osiris myth, xii. 115, 395 [84]

——Iasion, union of, magic device to bring fertility to soil, i. lii

——Persephone, Iroquois story of Onatah parallel of, x. 27

—connexion of, with fertility, i. 198

—daughter of Rhea and Kronos, i. 225, 274

—earth-goddess of Eleusis, Dionysos affiliated with, i. 219

—Gaia as, i. 273

—Italic Ceres double of Greek, i. 288, 291

—partakes of flesh of Pelops, i. 119

—sickle of, wrought by Hephaistos, i. 207

—survivals of, in modern Greek folk-belief, i. 313

—the Black of Arkadia reverse of Demeter the Beautiful, vii. 97

—use of phallic emblem in rites of, ix. 330 [7]

—wife of Zeus, i. 156

Demetrius's Eve, autumnal dziady on, iii. 235, 237

Demi-gods, vii. 118–119

Demiurge, vii. 213, 322

Demon, Demons:

Demon, Bush: see DODO, ETC.

—cursed for crying at window of a harlot, v. 33

— -guarded sanctuary on Mt. Roraima, xi. 277

—Humbaba in later mythology a, v. 253

—in idol of Perun exorcised, iii. 294

Demon, Katsumbakazi the Giryama, vii. 243–244, 258

—Loki a fire-, ii. 148

—midday, iii. 12

——Mahr in form of, ii. 289

—Morvran seemed a, iii. 189

—Namzimu a, vii. 409 [36]

—of air, Bodb changed Aoife into a, iii. 51

——darkness and sun-god, conflict between, v. 118

—will not enter house on which his name is written, v. 366

—worship, iii. 278; xi. 182

Demons, vi. 33, 34, 36, 44, 66–72, 77, 97–98, 104, 120, 132, 150–151, 180, 244, 245; vii. 48, 73; viii. 90–91, 105; 242, 243; xi. 48, 49; see also chap. Spirits and Monsters (vol. vii. 72–92).

—and gods, wars of, vi. 263–274

—ogres, tales of, vii. 242–257

—as shades of wicked from Hell, v. 162

—Christians think of old gods as, iii. 208

—corpse-devouring, ii. 281

—dead escaping from Arallû become, v. 330

—devils, good and evil spirits, v. 352–374

—dispersed by St. Patrick, iii. 210

—divinities regarded by Christians as, ii. 18, 41, 68

—figures covered with pitch in forest clearings as protection against, vii. 421 [20]; see also TAR-BABY.

—gods of earth, and dead, vi. 41–72

——regarded as, on Hallowe'en, iii. 68

—haunting-, vii. 119, 241, 242

—images brought to exorcise, xii. 199

—indwelling, of images, iii. 45

—magic ritual for protection against, v. 182

—marriage custom probably indicates exorcising of, iii. 322

—masks of Humbaba as protection against, v. 255

—nightmare, ii. 256

—of air, iii. 134

——the Dark, xi. 82

—prevented by Oscar's flail and sand from tormenting Féinn, iii. 183

—pursued Thorkill, ii. 95

—sent into dead Athenians, iii. 347 [61]

—seven, v. 287, 361, 364, 371, 372, 373

Demons, seven, death of Tammuz attributed to, v. 337
—tailed, vii. 242–243
—Tuatha Dé Danann regarded by some as, iii. 38–39
—twelve, v. 362, 364
—vampires, and other ghostly beings, viii. 281–292
Demoniac being of waters, Ran is, ii. 191
—guise, those hostile to gods of growth and light depicted in, iii. 34
—one story of Tuatha Dé Danann regards them as almost, iii. 170
Demonology, v. xviii; vi. 184–185
—Arabian and Persian, v. 357
—Christian, Jewish, and Mohammedan, v. 353–354
Demonstrations of sky (comets, meteors, etc.), iv. 396
Demophon, magic rites to cause immortality of, practised by Demeter, i. 228
—son of Theseus, marries Phyllis and is later killed, i. 136
Demos (" the People "), abstract divinity of social institution, i. 283
Denderah, Ḥar-sam-taui perhaps mentioned especially at, xii. 388 28
—loss of name of deity once worshipped at, xii. 362 8
—prominent goddess associated with lesser male divinity as her son at, xii. 20
—Ṭentet at, xii. 165
—Unut worshipped at, xii. 151
" Denial " (in law-suits, etc.), Syn is, ii. 186
Denmark, paganism in, ii. 16
—strife for, ii. 133, 135
" Deor's Lament " refers to Volund story, ii. pl. 1, frontispiece
Dep (Depet), the One of, xii. 403 19
Dêr el-Medineh, memorial sanctuary of Amen-ḥotep at, xii. 171
Derbrenn's swine fashioned by magic, iii. 127
Derketo (Atargatis), v. 36, 84
Descent, divine, Classical evidence for Celtic belief in, iii. 14
—fate of man depended on his, iii. 249
—how counted, x. 184, 238, 240
—stories of, from fictitious personages, iii. 10
Descents, vi. 170

Desecration of fire, vii. 54
Desert, Osiris lord of the, xii. 399 110
Deserts dwelling-places of evil spirits, iv. 479
—ghosts haunt, vi. 249
Desire, first seed of the mind, vi. 17
Desmond, Lord, captured and married Aine, iii. 47
Destinies, three, iii. 251
Destruction of effigies in creation by evil spirit, ix. 172
Detsyovi, friend of Spider, vii. 327–329
Deukalion and Pyrrha alone survived from Iron Age and became parents of our race, i. 18
——flood of, i. 18–19
—child of Prometheus, i. 12
—flood of, in reign of Kranaos, i. 18, 67
—myth of ark of, v. 37, 38
—son of Minos, i. 63
—teachings of, in beginnings of civilization, i. 16
Deusoniensis, Hercules, ii. 69
Deus Requalivahanus, Vidarr the, ii. 160
Deva, viii. 281
Devadatta, conch of Indra, vi. 132
Devak, or guardian deity, in Bombay held to be ancestor, vi. 240
Devakī, mother of Kṛṣṇa, vi. 171, 224
Devānandā and Triśalā, foetuses in wombs of, interchanged, vi. 222–223
Devarddhigaṇa, vi. 220
Devarṣis, divine seers, vi. 145
Devas, vi. 108, 244
—tivar (gods) related to Sanskrit, ii. 21
Devaśarman, vi. 133
Devasena, vi. 140
Devatās (Jap. Tennyo, Tennin), viii. 266, 267
Devayāna (Way of the Gods), vi. 71
Developmental type of creation-myths, ix. 7–8, 10–11, 15–18
Devī, female counterpart of Śiva, vi. 116, 215, 219, 230, 233, 236, 238, 239, 241, 246, 247
—Mātā, disease-goddess, vi. 246
Devil, x. 176, 285 28
—as spoiler of people, iv. 374–379
—Azāzel later became a, v. 356
—child sent to, for washing of rice-stick, vii. 141
—(Curupira, Taguain, Pigtangua, Machchera, Anhanga), xi. 295

Devil ("debble"), Zimwi becomes, in West Africa, vii. 251
—errand to, vii. 203
—evil by will, not by nature, vii. 82, 393 25
—(Iblisi) imprisons girls in tree, vii. 414 24
—in creation-tales, v. 319
—king of the south sea escaped by means of miraculous rice, viii. 358, 359
—mediaeval, distorted form of Utgard-Loki with traits of, ii. 94, 150
—of mediaeval lore, Coyote resembles, x. 142
—(or Satan), in fish, vii. 244
—priests of Cuna communed with, xi. 191
—suitor, vii. 346
—took over features of old evil deities under influence of Christianity, iii. 288
—tree becomes a, xi. 26
—whose body breaks into stony fragments, x. 68
—wife of, and disease-devil, iv. pl. XXVIII, opp. p. 228
—worship and witchcraft, finger-cutters sect has affinities with, vii. 370–371
Devils, belief that gods were really, ii. 30
—demons, and good and evil spirits, v. 352–374
—expelled by Marduk, v. 106
—Isle of, Momotarō visits, viii. 313
—Magic Eggs, tale of, vii. 204–205
—Masai, vii. 243
—of Sumero-Babylonian mythology sons of heaven-god, v. 358
—possessed of, v. 84, 85
—with tails of snakes, xi. 47
Devorgilla and her handmaid appear as birds, iii. 56, 144
Devs, vii. 80, 83, 86–88, 90, 91, 394 45 52
Dew, ii. 133, 200; viii. 130; ix. 33, 34
—as spittle of stars, xi. 278
—Eagle, x. 24, 288 32
—Isis called, by magician of Roman period, xii. 95
—Tefênet not to be compared to, xii. 45
—Zeus sender of, i. 160
Dhana, a Rudra, vi. 142
Dhanapati, vi. 97

Dhanuṣākṣa reduced all mountains to ashes, vi. 159
Dhanvantari, avatar of Viṣṇu, vi. 168
—physician, vi. 106, 151
Dhara, a Vasu, vi. 142
Dharaṇendra, snake born as, vi. 226
Dhāraṇī, spell containing name of Uṣṇīṣavijayā, vi. 217
Dharma, vi. 112, 124, 141, 142, 149–150, 152, 159, 168, 180, 186, 189
Dharmadhātuvāgīśvara, vi. 213
Dharmākara, a monk who determined to become a Buddha, vi. 200
Dharmakīrti, vi. 210
Dharmapāla of gNas-c'un, diviner, incarnation of god Pe-har, vi. 209–210
Dharmapālas, Hindu or local Tibetan gods brought into the Buddhist system, vi. 213–214, 215, 217
Dharṇā (starvation) performed by Harṣu Pānre, vi. 243
Dhartī Māī ("Mother who Supports"), vi. 234
Dhātakīkhaṇḍa, part of Jain cosmography, vi. 221
Dhātṛ, v. 50, 85, 93, 97, 138, 143
Dhenuka, Kṛṣṇa destroys, vi. 172
Dhiṣaṇā, goddess, vi. 53
Dhouti, earlier name of Thout(i), xii. 33
Dhṛtarāṣṭra, vi. 125, 150, 155, 215, 246; viii. 242–243
Dhruva, a Vasu, vi. 142, 165
Dhūmaprabhā, vi. 228
Dhūmrākṣa, leader of Daityas, vi. 180
Dhuni sent to sleep by Indra, vi. 68
Dhyānibodhisattvas, vi. 211, 212, 216
Dhyānibuddhas, vi. 210, 211, 213
Di Penates, i. 298
Dia ("Divine Earth"), mother of Peirithoös by Zeus, i. 11
—wife of Zeus, i. 157
Diagrams, eight and sixty-four, viii. 8, 16, 22, 29–30, 44, 67, 101, 136, 137–138, 141, 142, 144–145
Dialects, special, for each animal among Bushmen, vii. 427 11
—variety of Chin, accounted for, xii. 266–267
Diamichius, Chrysōr deified as, v. 54
Diana, i. 294
—associated with witchcraft in modern Romagnola, i. 319
—Dzewana identified with, iii. 355 44

Diana in Roman mythology, represents Artemis in Greek, i. 288
—of the Crossways, Hekate known as, i. 187
—perhaps originally a greenwood goddess, i. 332 ⁴ (ch. xiv)
—regarded as midday demon in Autun, iii. 12
Diancecht, commander of Tuatha Dé Danann; divinity of leech-craft, iii. 25, 28, 32, 40
Diar (or Drotnar), temple-priests, ii. 26, 33
Diarbekir, sick given ashes and water at, vii. 57
Diarmaid aided by Oengus, iii. 174–175
—and Fionn leap into magic well, iii. 173
——Grainne, iii. 121
——pursuit of, iii. 175–179, 185
—ascended cliff by magic staves, iii. 173
—had weapons of Manannan, iii. 65–67
—head of, demanded by Fionn, iii. 55
—hunted Wild Boar of Gulban, iii. 125
—magic spear of, killed monstrous worm, iii. 132
—nurtured and taught by Manannan, iii. 103
—obtained magic ring, iii. 172
—slew giant guarding quicken-tree, iii. 131, 170
—uí Duibhne possessed " beauty spot," iii. 162–163
Dibobe, Duala word for Sun and Spider, vii. 284
Didactic tales, viii. 317, 354–359
Didi (half man half monkey), wild man of woods, xi. 276, 277
Didko or Domovyk, family genius of Little Russians, iii. 244
Dido, queen of Carthage, loves Aeneas, i. 305
Diermes, iv. pl. xxviii, opp. p. 228
Dies, Day parallels, ii. 201
—Jovis, names [of Thursday] equivalents of Roman, ii. 68
Diespiter, Diovis, Dius: see IUPPITER.
Differentiation, local, of deities, xii. 21
Digambara, oldest Jain sect, vi. pl. xxviii, opp. p. 220
Digger Indians, x. 131
Digging stick, x. 94–95, 114–115
Digichibi, xi. 297

Digini, half wizard half sprite, x. 156–157
Dikaiosyne (" Righteousness "), abstract divinity of virtue, i. 282
Dike (" Law "), one of the Horai, i. 237
—(" Precedent "), abstract divinity of social institution, i. 283
Di-kh (gods), Armenian word, vii. 13, 14, 380 ⁶
Dikte, cult of Zeus on, i. 159
—Mt., reputed birthplace of Zeus, i. 155
Diktynna, Artemis identified with, i. 183, 184
Diktys made king of Seriphos, i. 35
—releases Danaë and Perseus from chest at Seriphos, i. 33
Dil, daughter of Lugmannair, iii. 67
Diligina, palace of Anunnaki, v. 333
Dillus Varvawc, leash made from beard of, iii. 199
Dilmun (location of Paradise), v. 158, 184, 193–194, 195, 196, 208, 224
Dilwāra temple, vi. pl. xxix, opp. p. 226
Dim-me, v. 416
Dinas Emreis in Snowden, dragons placed in cistvaen at, iii. 130
—Emrys, obtained as citadel by Merlin, iii. 200
Dinay, tale of, ix. 221
" Dindšenchas," iii. 81, 93, 116, 121, 125, 132, 135, 151, 175
Dinewan, emu, ix. 275, 288–289
Dingir, digir, word for " god," v. 93
Diniktu, Nikilim worshipped at, v. 132
Dinsdag, ii. 98
Dio of Dionysos explained as " god," vii. 380 ⁶
Diocletian persecuted Christians, v. 338–339
Diodorus on origin of northern Gauls, iii. 13
Diokles, a minister of rites of Demeter, i. 230
Diomedes, i. pl. xxx, opp. p. 120
—and Glaukos exchange armour, i. 128, 158
——Odysseus, i. 123–124
—Ares wounded by, i. 189
—armour of, wrought by Hephaistos, i. 206

Diomedes brings Philoktetes from Lemnos to Troy, i. 132
—seeks to aid dying Penthesilea, i. 131 (fig. 5)
—son of Ares and king of Bistonians, i. 84, 190
—wanderings of, after return to Argos, i. 136
—wounded and forced to retreat to ships, i. 129
——by Pandaros, but wounds Aphrodite and Ares, i. 128
—wounds Aphrodite, i. 197
Dione, earth-goddess, wife of Zeus at Dodona, i. pl. IV (5), opp. p. l, 156, 165, 197
—El married, v. 67
—Hebe early supposed to be equivalent of, i. 241
Dionysos, iii. 55; xii. 353
—afflicted by Hera with frenzy for discovering vine, i. 47, 222
—Alexander the Great said to have been descendant of, i. 223
—and Liber, i. 292
——a Maïnad, i. pl. III, opp. p. xlvi
—Aramazd identified with, vii. 21, 22
—Artemis associated with, i. 184
—attendants of infant, identified with Hyades, i. 248
—birth of, from thigh of Zeus, i. pl. XLIV, opp. p. 194
—changed into kid by Zeus and taken to Mt. Nysa, i. 46
—character and functions of, transferred to St. Dionysos in modern Greek folk-belief, i. 313
—confused with Spantaramet, vii. 35
—connexion of Maïnads and Bacchantes with rites of, i. 270
——with fertility, i. 198
—cult of, in primitive Argos, i. 32
—Dušurā (Gk. Dousares) identified with, v. 16, 17, 18
—emblems of, i. pl. VI, opp. p. lx
—given battle by Argives and Perseus, i. 35–36
—Hermes and the infant, i. pl. XLIV, opp. p. 194
—identified with Indian gods, vi. 109–110, 119
——Soma, vii. 380 [11]
—in connexion with lightning, vii. 15

Dionysos, infant, nursed by nymphs, i. 258
—influence of, over women, i. 47
—mythically foisted on Zeus as son, i. 165
—Ninkasi corresponds to, v. 202
—' Orotalt Arabic name of, v. 382 [79]
—Osiris as Egyptian, xii. 377 [86], 385 [8]
—probably represented by Faflon in modern Romagnola, i. 318
—reared by Ino and Athamas, i. 46
—represented on marble relief of Eleusinian rites, i. pl. L, opp. p. 230
—rescued women of Tanagra from Triton, i. 260
—returned to Thebes while Pentheus was king, i. 47
—rites instituted by Argives in honour of, i. 36
——of, celebrated on Kithairon, i. 47
—said to have carried Ariadne to Lemnos and married her, i. 101
—St., assumes character and functions of god Dionysos in modern Greek folk-belief, i. 313
—Satyrs and Silenoi in circle of, i. 268
—son of Zeus, i. 157
—spell cast over, by Hera, i. 166
—Thraco-Phrygian, called Sabazios, vii. 13, 364
—votaries of, driven into sea by Lykourgos, i. 190
—weds daughter of Kybele and Sangarios, i. 275
—Yāw had been identified with, v. 43
Dioskouroi, i. pl. XXVII, opp. p. 106; iii. 325
—and Helen, i. 246–247
—(Dioscuri), gods most worshipped by Celts in west of Gaul, iii. 158
—Harpies mothers of steeds of, i. 266
—Idas and Lynkeus Messenian doubles of, i. 27
—in essence Aśvins one with the, vi. 31
—Kastor and Polydeukes known as, i. 26
—sons of Zeus, i. 157
Diospolis Parva, goddess (Bat?) of, xii. 40 (fig. 30)
Dīpaṁkara, one of the Buddhas, vi. 194, 199, 211
Dipsas, tale of the snake, v. 227–228
Directors of the House, six rain priests as, x. 191
Dirge-mothers, vii. 95

Dirges, peculiar, chanted at spring dziadys, iii. 237

Diridotis (Teredon), "given to Mercury," city built by Nebuchadnezzar, vii. 32

Dirke bound to the bull, i. pl. xv, opp. p. 42, 43

—wife of Lykos, i. 43

Dirt, goddess of, xi. 54

Dis in proper names, ii. 244

—Pater, attempts to equate Bile with, iii. 46, 106

——Gauls declare themselves descended from, iii. 9

——great Celtic god of Underworld, iii. pl. xiv, opp. p. 120

——(Orcus), i. 303

——with hammer, iii. pl. xiii, opp. p. 116

—the southern, Sigrun called, ii. 251, 255

Disablót, sacrifice to Disir, ii. 226, 244

Disarsalr (hall of Disir), ii. 244

Disathing, court, ii. 244

Discontent, age of, and satire, viii. 362–365

Discord, goddess of, v. 27

Disease, v. 182, 247, 363, 364, 365, 372

—cause and cure of, viii. 29, 31, 105, 121, 147

—clothes hung on sacred tree to cure, vii. 62

—cow's flesh cure for, iii. 63

—cure of, viii. 229

— -demons, vi. 112, 185, 232, 238, 239, 243, 244–247

——Als formerly, vii. 88

—fire used in cure of, ii. 202

—inflicted for nonworship by Varuṇa and Mitra, vi. 23, 25

—magic twigs cause and cure, ii. 206

—rainbow as, vii. 235, 236

—regarded as divine punishment in case of Herakles, i. 89

—skin, caused by fire, iv. 453

Diseases, xi. 76, 230

—Apollo repels, iii. 9

—as weapons, vi. 83

—caused by moon, vii. 48

—cured by wood-fire or friction-fire, iv. 451

—demoniac, must flee before fire, vii. 55

—images of points of compass to prevent, iv. 360

Diseases, internal, caused by defilement of devil, iv. 374–377, 383

—released from Pandora's jar, i. 15

—under control of Artemis as goddess-physician, i. 184–185

—wife of Manitou cause of all, x. 285 28

—Yama accompanied by, vi. 160

Disembodiment, x. 8

Disguise, vii. 297, 420 19

—assumed by gods, iii. 56

Dish placed for deceased at funeral place, iv. 45, 47

Dishes, ceremonial, xi. pl. xxviii, opp. p. 200

Disir, class of female supernatural beings, ii. 18, 188, 189, 226, 236, 240, 244, 248, 252, 255

Dísirs, spirits of deceased mothers who have become dispensers of fate, iii. 249

Disk, divine, x. 89

—of earth, iv. 308, 310, 319, 330, 341, 343, 344, 349, 358, 487

——heaven, iv. 351, 405, 410–411

——moon, x. 162

——bear eats, iv. 424

——sun, i. 332 9 (ch. xii); v. 47, 69, 377 9; x. 162, 166

—on head of sun-god, Tefênet as, xii. 45

—rayed, on head of Viracocha, xi. pl. xxxvi, opp. p. 236

——solar, iii. 327

——worn by goddesses, xii. 136, 146

—winged, Beḥdeti identified with Horus, xii. 21

——Horus battles in form of, xii. 117

——of Edfu, xii. 363 1

Disks, double, iii. pl. x, opp. p. 94; pl. xvii, opp. p. 134

Disorder: see Anṛta, etc.

Dispersion of mankind, ix. 274

Distingen, fair, ii. 244

"Distortion" of Cúchulainn, iii. 141, 153–154, 198

District serpents, vii. 76

Diti, artificial counterpart of Aditi, vi. 55, 106, 151

Dius Fidius, witness of fidelity to oaths, Iuppiter as, i. 290

Diva-ta Žena (Wild Woman), iii. 265

Diver, Apollo in form of, i. 180

Divination, i. 16, 244; ii. 34, 171, 295, 299; iii. 13, 75, 81; 277, 279, 280, 281, 282, 285; iv.: see entries s.v.

OMENS (vol. iv); v. 39, 63, 92, 140,
150, 152, 203; vi. 209; vii. 12, 31,
48, 58, 59, 62, 99; 288, 366–367; viii.
7, 8, 17, 44, 48, 100, 135–147; 230,
233; x. xxi, 161, 280 [16], 293 [40]; xi. 55,
74, 92, 100, 102, 147, 180, 217, 312,
350 [9]
Divine beings, ancient Slavs often derived their origin from, iii. 297
—efficacy, things of, viii. 226
—help in Irish myths, iii. 13
—land, iii. 37–38, 114–123
—life, bread and water elements of, v.
178
—nature of kings, v. 41, 42, 327
—or semi-divine offspring are result of
incestuous union, ix. 170
—order, evil spirits belonged to, v. 373
—powers, contest of, with hostile po-
tencies of blight; origin of tale of
plagues probably in, iii. 107
— -producing-goddess, viii. 229
—spouse, xi. 40
Diviners, vii. 187–188, 190, 196, 272
Divining-twigs used to discover more
drink for banquet, ii. 86
Divinities, Celtic, apt to be local, iii.
93
—female (or demons), worship of, vi.
184–185
—ordinary Jain, names of classes of, vi.
227
—regarded as demons by Christians, ii.
18, 41, 68
—semi-, may be reborn as bulls, iii. 152
Divinity, Demeter Hellenic, i. 225
—Marduk given double, v. 294
—of articles, vi. 61
—or first Principle existed unconsciously
amongst Indians, x. 16–17, 283 [25]
—size an indication of, in Celtic myth,
iii. 30, 56, 58, 104, 127, 150, 163
Divja Žena (Wild Woman), iii. 265
Divji Mož (Wild Man), iii. 265
Divodāsa, Agni god of, vi. 44
Divous (Wild Brats), iii. 264
Divoženky, Džiwje Žony, etc. (Wild
Women), iii. 263–266
Diwrnach the Irishman, cauldron of, iii.
192
Djadeks, guardian genii of family in
Silesia, iii. 244, pl. XXVIII, opp. p. 244
Djanbasien, Tammuz said to be a, v.
339

Djati-plant, ix. 191, 195
Djirdjîs, Arabic name of George of
Lydda, v. 338
Djiwao (João), adventures of, vii. 358
Długosz on old Polish religion, iii. 222,
301
Dobrizhoffer, Jesuit missionary, quota-
tions from, xi. 320, 321–322
Dobrynya, uncle of Vladimir, set up
idol of Perun at Novgorod, iii. 293
Docetism, vi. 199
Doctors, professional, make the inkata,
vii. 110
Doctrine of Five Pecks of Rice, viii.
14
—School of, viii. 8, 10, 13
Dodo, Bush-demon, vii. 325–326, 334,
427 [13 14 16]
Dodona, Dione, not Hera, regarded as
wife of Zeus at, i. 165
—oracle of Zeus at, i. 23
—talking oak of Zeus at, i. 109
—Zeus coupled with Gaia at, i. 272
Doe, Keryneian, captured by Herakles,
i. 81
——sacred to Artemis, i. 184
—Telephos said to have been suckled
by, i. 22
Doel, sons of, iii. 149–150
Dog, Dogs:
Dog and hermit, tale of, xi. 274
——kangaroo, tale of, ix. 146–147
——mouse-deer, tale of, ix. 191
——Mukosala, tale of, vii. 252–256
——spear given to Prokris by Artemis,
i. 184
—appearance of Pörthozjin as, iv. 159
—as guardian, x. 6
——of creation, iv. 373–378, 379, 381,
382
—(as Nzasi) disappears in explosion
(of thunder), vii. 238
—associated with Gula as protector of
homes, v. 182, 183
—at Cinvat Bridge, vi. 69
—(Black Dragon), viii. 107
—Culann's, iii. 142
— -days, vi. 267, 270
—death comes through, vii. 162, 168,
169
—deceit of, caused death, iv. 481
— -eater who reveres Śiva ranks above
a Brāhman who does not, vi. 180
— -eating spirit, x. 246

Dog, Europe's brazen, made by Hephaistos, i. 207
—girl who bore children to the, x. xxii, 10, 103
—given birth to by tree, forefather of Mongols, iv. 502
—gnaws heart of shaman, iv. 507
—-god Makedon companion of Osiris according to Greeks, xii. 393 61
—hair-covering of, iv. 373–378
—haltia appears as, iv. 169, 170
—-headed battle-trumpets, xi. 276.
—heavenly, devours sun, viii. 84, 103
—kept from time of conception and sacrificed at time of confinement, iv. 255, 257
—kindles fire, x. 231
—of Anubis declines in importance, xii. 167
——Mac Dáthó, iii. 125, 145
——Odysseus recognized him, i. 139
——Tuila causes earthquakes, iv. 312
—or black jackal, Anubis originally, xii. 110
—sacrificed at grave enters into eternal house of the dead, xi. 81
—spell for bite of, xii. 209
—-spirits, vii. 395 58
—symbol of goddess of healing, v. 182
—transformed into human being to till soil, xi. 274
—votive offering at Spring Feast at Kēngtūng, xii. 333
—which ate silk-worm, tale of, viii. 322
—Xolotl presides over ball-game, xi. 82
——sent to Underworld for bones of the forefathers, xi. 83
Dogs, ii. 111; iii. 142, 156, 184, 199, 208; v. 367, 368, 369; vi. 58, 62, 69, 146, 149, 237, 242, 248; 292, 297; vii. 106, 200, 212, 220, 418 35; ix. 55, 70, 86–87, 114, 156–157, 172–173, 183, 216, 285; see also items s.v. HOUNDS.
—Arlez derived from, vii. 90, 395 58
—at funeral-meals, omens from behaviour of, iv. 45
—belief that daemons of heat and drought ran about like ravening, i. 252
—cause eclipse of moon, xi. 319
—fish transformed into, xi. 95
—four, of Marduk, vii. 395 58
—gnaw fetters of Artavazd, vii. 99

Dogs, gold and silver, of Alkinoös, made by Hephaistos, i. 207
—Indo-Chinese races claim to be sprung from, xii. 293
—men born, iv. 504
—tear Linos to pieces, i. 253
Dogai (female bogey and group of stars), ix. 142
Dogedoi, horse-herd, groom of Solbon, iv. 432, 433
Doh, Great Shaman, iv. 323, 522
Dokekaoros, iv. 438
Dökkalfar (dark elves), ii. 221, 266
Doliones, people on island of Kyzikos, i. 110
Doll, Dolls:
Doll, iii. 311–312
—of wood represents family god, iv. 137, 138
Dolls, iv. 141
—buried with dead provide concubines, xii. 416 14
—memorial, of deceased, iv. 41–42, 43
—Samoyed gods, iv. 113
—straw, iv. 248
Dolmen, ii. pl. 1, frontispiece
Dolorous Stroke in Grail cycle, iii. 203
Dolphin, Apollo takes form of, i. 178, 180
—attribute of Eros, i. 204
—bears Theseus to Poseidon and Amphitrite, i. 101
—emblem of Triton, i. 260
—star-group, ix. 142
—symbol of Poseidon, i. 7 (fig. 1)
Dolphins, captain and crew of Dionysos's ship changed into, i. 219
Dolya, name of personification of fate bestowed at birth, iii. 251–252
Dom occasionally devours sun and moon, vi. 233
Dominae, ii. 206
Domnal the Warlike in Alba, Cúchulainn sent to find, iii. 143
Domovníček, house snake, iii. 246
Domovoy, Russian god, iv. 164, 168
Dôn (Brythonic equivalent of Goidelic Danu), iii. 96, 97, 100, 106
—Court of, stars associated with, iii. 100
Doṇa questions Buddha, vi. 191
Donalitius, Christian, Lithuanian poet, iii. 319

Donar, axe from which well sprang suggests, ii. 163
— -Thor (Loud-sounder; Thunderer), thunder-god, ii. 18, 24, 68, 69, 70
Dong-co Mountain, spirits of, aid Ministers of State in debate, xii. 319
Do-nguyen-khoi, Governor of Kinhchu, statue to, near Han-thuy River, xii. 320
Donn, one of the síde, iii. 172, 174
—Tetscorach, steeds of, iii. 76
Donnotaurus equivalent of Donn Tarb found in Gaul, iii. 158
Doom of the gods, ii. 46, 50, 74, 81, 99, 100, 110, 127, 128, 137, 146, 147, 148, 150, 153, 155, 158, 159, 168, 169, 200, 276, 278, 279, 313, 320, 331, 336–347
——world, Njord given as pledge until, ii. 23, 25
Dooms given by Thor at ash, ii. 23
Doomsmen, twelve, ii. 33
Doon Buidhe, minstrel goddess of síd of, iii. 121
Door as person, address to, v. 252
—Delling's, ii. 201
—Elysium lost through opening, iii. 105
—of Heaven, iv. 336
—opened to invite soul to feast, iv. 47
—place by, is residence of dead who arrive at memorial feast, iv. 46
—woman, Uksakka, receives new born baby, iv. 254, 256
Doors, concealed, ii. 269
—leading to sacrificial places are divine, vi. 61
—opened by Esthonians to allow for passing of dead, iv. 17
—seven, open at shots at bottom of pool, vii. 188
Doorways, white thorn to banish evil from, i. 297
Doppel-gänger, shadow-souls transformed into, iv. 10, 14
Dorians beseiged by the Lapithai, i. 94
—Herakles the hero of, i. 76
Doris and Nereus, Amphitrite daughter of, i. 214
—wife of Nereus, i. 260
Dornolla, Cúchulainn refused love of, iii. 143, 153
Dorobo, "helot" tribe among the Masai, vii. 148–151
Dörr-Käring (Door old woman), iv. 256

Double-headed god, Ḥar-akhti as, xii. 388 [28]
Double names of gods, v. 381 [58]
—or astral, body, viii. 120
—soul, viii. 237, 238
Doubles, ii. 233, 237; x. 78–79
—of kings, xii. 170
Doura, mother-goddess of, v. 20
Dove, attribute of Aphrodite, i. 203
—in Flood stories, v. 38, 221, 230
—returns to Ark with birch twig, iv. 364
—sacred bird of Ishtar, Semiramis disappears in form of, vii. 367, 368
—symbol of Astarte, v. 30–31
Doves above battlefield good omen, viii. 305
—and turtle doves only birds admitted in Hebrew sacrifices and purifications, v. 31–32
—early Greeks saw swarm of wood-, in the Pleiades, i. 249
—figures of, on shrines, v. 30, 34, 37
—flying, form part of Vartavar celebrations, vii. 60, 71
Downward, point of compass of dead points, iv. 486
Dpir (Dipsar), name Tīr doubtfully derived from, vii. 384 [56]
Drag-gshhed, group of dreadful gods, vi. 214
Dragon, ass aided by the Dead against the, xii. 107 (fig. 106)
—balustrades, xii. 272
—beliefs of Macedonia, vii. 392 [24]–393
—Blue, spirit of the east was Thanglong the, xii. 307
—bound and given to god of Underworld, v. 321
—Chimaira compounded of lion, goat, and, i. 39
—Chinese, Kinkō Sennin riding on, viii. pl. XXI, opp. p. 276
—condemned dead before the, xii. 179 and fig. 187
—Festival, viii. 86
—fire-, viii. 123
— -fly, red, associated with dead returning to old homes, viii. 335
—golden, and spirit appear in portent to Cao-bien, xii. 318
—guards apples of Hesperides, i. 87, 88
— -horse, viii. 8, 34–35, 101
—human sacrifice to, viii. 249

Dragon in art, ii. 216
——Karen myth of fall of man, xii. 269, 270
——myth, vi. 263, 264, 265, 266, 328, 330, 340, pl. XLIII, opp. p. 340
—issue of Ares, guards spring of Areia, i. 45
—issued from earth at harp music, iii. 91
—King, viii. 250, 264, 268, 272, 273, 314, 315
——in body of fish, viii. 191, 193
—lady and Tōda, viii. 314
—legend, vii. 70–71
—lion type of, v. 278
—Lonely Man fights with, iv. 354
— -made clothing of Shun, viii. 35
—magic rod becomes a, viii. 132
——sword of Le-loi changes into, xii. 303
—meteorological and eschatological, fused, vii. 81, 392 23
—myths, xii. 272–278, 302–303, 310, 311, 318, 327
—of abyss, 'Apop as, xii. 104
——Quirigua, xi. pl. I, frontispiece, pl. XXIV, opp. p. 168
—once inhabited lake at Pokhar, vi. 235
—origin of, xii. 302
—Palace, viii. 264, 269, 272
—plain snake becomes the ornate, xii. 301
— -slaying associated with fire, vii. 45
——of, x. 44–45
—spirits, viii. 266
—spiritual animal, viii. 98, 101–103
—Temple at Thanh-long, xii. 318–319
—Theban, son of Ares, i. 190
—trace of the flying, above water, viii. 253
— -worship existed in India and beyond, xii. 270–273
Dragons, iii. 67, 107; 325; iv. 425; v. 91, 101, 102, 118, 127, 361; vi. 33, 37, 88; 320–323, 324; viii. 25, 37, 38, 43–44, 141
—conquered by Vahagn, vii. 43, 46
—eleven, became gods of lower world, v. 302
——identified with constellations, v. 316
—endeavour to swallow sun and moon, vii. 48
—fight of, iii. 200

Dragons infesting lochs and as guardians of trees, iii. 129–130, 131
—male, little mentioned, xii. 278
—of Chaos, v. 86, 117–118, 130, 134, 233, 395 21
—water-, disturbing of, the cause of drought, viii. 155
—winged, draw Triptolemos in car given him by Demeter, i. 230
——Medeia flees to Athens in chariot drawn by, i. 115
Dragon's teeth sown broadcast, men germinated from, i. 10, 112
Drakht (Pers. dirakht), vii. 100
Drama enacted in Nāt worship, xii. 342, 345
—lyric, constructed around dance of Bashō, viii. 343–345
Dramas, viii. 297, 298
—folk-, ii. 9
Draughts, dead sometimes play, xii. 177
—peasant lost son to giant in game of, ii. 151
Draugr, same as Ravgga, iv. 192
Draupnir: see RING OF ODIN.
Dravidian tribes worship Earth, vi. 234
Dravidians, influence of, possibly seen in idea of female Bodhisattva, xii. 261–262
—possibly carried some traditions to Indo-China, xii. 257
Drawings sprinkled with blood, mankind from, ix. 107
Dṛdhasyu drank up ocean and burnt Asuras, vi. 146
Dream adventures, viii. 363–365
—blindness cured through, vii. 349
—death predicted in a, vi. 321, 322
—of A-mong anent the wish-drum, xii. 283
——Oengus, iii. 78
——Rhonabwy, iii. 190
— -oracles, classification of, as necromantic, i. 194
— -Vision-Man, viii. 363–365
— -voyages, iv. 495
—warning conveyed to Aeneas in, i. 304
— -women, ii. 236, 237, 250
Dreams, i. 113–114, 127; ii. 234, 235, 250, 251, 254, 255, 311–312; iv. 472–482; v. 95, 209, 222, 241, 242, 250, 251, 252, 257, 259, 262, 267; vi. 226; vii. 184, 349; viii. 28, 35, 37, 42, 58, 59–60, 70, 128, 154–155, 169, 173; 321,

323, 326, 337; x. 18, 24, 81, 85, 87, 135, 137, 229–230, 231, 291 37, 309 64; xi. 307–308, 341; xii. 283

Dreams as omens, ii. 234–235, 250, 251, 255

—oracles, xii. 197

—bad, sent by Mora, iii. 228

—Balder's: see " BALDRS DRAUMAR "; BALDER; VOLVA.

—Cheremiss, of a city, indicate that his soul has visited it, iv. 6

—consultation of sibyl to explain Balder's, ii. 9, 43, 127

—creation of, i. 6

—Devs assumed forms of wild beasts in, vii. 87

—divination by, after eating flesh of sacrificial bull, iii. 75

—ghosts appear in, vii. 181

—guardian spirit appears in, iv. 10

—Gudrun's, ii. 240

—Hermes as god of, i. 194

—high gods communicate their will to earth in, vii. 125, 132

—indicate position of lud, iv. 145

—kudo-, Vodyž appears to family in, iv. 135

—lud-spirit appears in human form in, iv. 151

—Nabû god of, vii. 32

—Odin believed to appear before battle in, ii. 34, 40

—spirits may carry off one in, vii. 183

—temptation of men in, by Drujes, vii. 87

—Thor threatens a Christian in, ii. 77

—Tiur's temple famed for interpretation of, vii. 31

Dreamers, a sect, x. 149

Drem, supernatural keenness of sight of, iii. 189–190

Dress, dwarfs divided into white, brown, and black according to their, ii. 266

Dresses, ten, of daughter of Kumush, x. 229–230

Drink, dwarf's: see MEAD.

—given to wife of hero of flood to obtain secret of ship, iv. 363

—magic, viii. 306

——composed of earth, sea, and swine's blood, ii. 155

—memorial, iv. 26, 37–38, 39, 44, 45, 46, 47, 49, 50, 51, 54

Drink-names, vii. 428 26

—of gods, divine smiths associated with, iii. 31

——spirits honours Seides at holy places, iv. 103

— -offering to Cloud mother, iv. 234

— -offerings, ii. 63

—poured into grave for corpse, iv. 46

— -sacrifice at mer festival, iv. 278

—shaman-, iv. 283

—Tenemet patroness of intoxicating, xii. 66

Drinker, Kei a great, iii. 199

Drinking bout, challenge to a, xi. 231

—horn emblem of Triton, i. 260

——for restoring youth, iii. 169

—mead (magic drink) containing scrapings of runes, ii. 297

—of liquid in which written charm has been washed off, xii. 83, 119

— -vessel of the gods, vi. 57

Drinks, strong, preparation of, iv. 366

Droṇa, teacher of Pāṇḍavas, vi. 124, 244

Droṇāsa, vi. 98

Dropsy, vi. 25

Drotnar, ii. 26, 33

Drought, v. 271, 273; vi. 332, 333, 334; viii. 70, 155; 276–277; xi. 74, 191; xii. 298

—caused by land Zduhaczs, iii. 227

—ceremonies to avert, x. 106

—incantations at grave of rain-maker in times of, vii. 238

—may be caused by improper burial, xii. 298

Drowned property of water-spirits, ii. 212

—Ran goddess of, ii. 190, 191

—water-spirits originate in the, iv. 198, 207, 208–209, 216; 466, 469, 470

Drowning a blessed death, xii. 415 4

—as punishment, xii. 180, 415 4, 417 19

—by water-spirit, ii. 211

—death by, iii. 253, 255, 259, 260

—ghost captures men by, vii. 186

—in well produces loch, iii. 136

—of children by trickery, tales of, vii. 139, 196, 204

—tradition of, of Apis, xii. 412 6

Dṛṣadvatī, river, vi. 49

Drugs, Medeia's, i. 41

Druhs, hostile spirits, vi. 67

Druid, Fer Fídail a divine, iii. 89

Druids, iii. 14, 20, 29, 30, 32, 36, 40, 42, 43, 52, 54, 60, 65, 67, 72, 79, 81, 84, 88, 140, 147, 157, 164, 167, 168, 175
—religion of, assimilated to that of Rome, iii. 8
—sacred verse of, iii. 8, 9
Druj, vi. 261, 296, 343
Drum, calling of animals by signal-, vii. 322
—divine, vi. 97
—friction, vii. pl. xxxiii, opp. p. 314
—Hare makes chief's skull into, vii. 297
—of temple of Cao-bien at Thanh-long beaten to extinguish flames, xii. 319
—royal, vii. 191
—sacred, x. 270 4
—said to be stretched with serpent skins, xi. 48
—shaman, in moon, iv. 424
—singing girl in, vii. 250
—used to drive evil spirits from sick person, xi. 333
—wish, xii. 282, 283
Drums, ix. 71, 106, 141, 181, 224, 225
—magic, iv. 86, 92, 175, 224, pl. xxvii, opp. p. 224, pl. xxviii, opp. p. 228, 230, 231, 232, 233, 250, 252, 256, 286–295; xii. 282–283, 284, 319
—shaman, iv. 335 (fig. 14), 424, pl. xlviii, opp. p. 432, pl. xlix, opp. p. 444, pl. l, opp. p. 452, pl. li, opp. p. 458, pl. lii, opp. p. 462, 477, pl. lix, opp. p. 504, 510, 512, 519, 520 (fig. 26), pl. lxiii, opp. p. 522, 523
—shaman's bowl- and sieve-, iv. pl. xxxvii, opp. p. 284, 286, 287–288
—signal-, vii. 322
—spirit-, vii. 189
Drunkard Boy, viii. pl. xxxiv, opp. p. 306, 306–307, 313
Drunkenness, vi. 185; xii. 185, 200, 419 6
—cured by Earth, ii. 195
—of Buu tribe, vii. 349–351
—permitted to Persian King at Mithrakana festival, vii. 34
Družes (Av. Drujes), lewd female spirits, vii. 87
Dryads, iii. 262–263
—and Hamadryads, i. 270
—tree-spirits, i. 258
Drych, a swift runner, iii. 199
Dryope and Hermes, parents of Pan, i. 267

Dryopians, Herakles wars against, because of their inhospitality, i. 94
Dsovean (sea-born), storm-god, vii. 46
Dsovinar (sea-born), storm-goddess, vii. 46
Dsung, temple to Kaches at, vii. 84
Du aided in catching boar, iii. 108
Dua-'Anu, identified with Morning Star and connected with four sons of Horus, xii. 376 80
Dualism, ii. 337; v. 130, 291, 373, 374; vi. 261, 262, 327, 349; vii. 86; ix. 122, 126, 148, 172, 302; x. 98, 176, 285 28, 295 44; xi. 62, 159, 193, 194, 202, 259–260, 295, 333
—apparent, reflected in life of beings who represent nature powers, iii. 34
—cycle of antithesis did not develop into, viii. 225, 231
—in creation-myths, iv. 313–323, 326, 329
—old nature-, mythical story of Bres's sovereignty may parallel, iii. 28
—school of, viii. 8
Dualistic conceptions, ii. 89, 154
Dualities, vi. 56
Duality in creation-myths, ix. 7
Dua-mut-f, one of the four sons of Horus or Osiris, xii. 112
Duat ("Rising Abode of the Stars"), Underworld, varying localization of, xii. 386 16
— -star as parent of Orion, xii. 373 61
Dua(u), perhaps adored at Herakleopolis, xii. 132, 403 21
Dua[-uêr] confused with Morning Star and Orion-Horus, xii. 132–133, 404 22
Dub, wife of Enna, chanted spells over sea, iii. 132–133
Dubbisag, oldest title of Nabû, v. 158
Dubh Lacha, daughter of Fiachna the Black, iii. 63, 64
Dubhros, quicken-tree of, iii. 66, 131
Dubhthach, skin-changers, ii. 293
Dubo, snake, ix. 120
Dubsainglend, mythic horse, iii. 128
Duck, mandarin, tale of, viii. 320–322
Ducks' wings hide Corn Maidens, x. 200
Dudugera became the sun, ix. 113
Duel, i. 53
Duels, x. 11, 231, 282 21
Duezenna, v. 195
Dug-from-the-ground, x. 232
Dughdhōva, vi. 342

Duḥsaha, son of a Brāhman mother and Śūdra father, vi. 180–181
Duḥśalā, Christian parallels in bringing to life son of, vi. 178
Duiker totem, vii. 280
Dukug ("holy chamber"), v. 155, 191, 192
Dumb speak by aid of magic ring, ii. 308
Dumbness inflicted for wounding animals, xi. 192
Dumuzi and Innini, cult of, v. 112
— = Daozos = Mahalalel, Sumerian antediluvian king, v. 205
Dumu-zi occurs in personal name Ur-dumu-zi, v. 346
—(Tammûzî), v. 339, 341, 344
Dumuzida, v. 342
Dumûzu-Dûzu, Babylonian form of Tammuz-Adonis, xii. 120
Dūnd, headless ghost, vi. 248
Dunga, patron of singers, v. 105
Dungi as Tammuz, v. 345
—of Ur, v. 2
Dunlaing's shirt, iii. 69
Dunlang O'Hartigan, tale of, iii. 123
Dúns, iii. 130, 131, 132
Duodna ("the dead one"; "death"; "life beyond"), iv. 74
Durgā, vi. frontispiece, 83, 118, 184, 246, 247
Durin, creation of dwarf, ii. 264
Durvāsas, form of Śiva, vi. 170, 183
Duryodhana, vi. 125, 130
Dusādh tribe, vi. 233
Dushmata, duzhūkhta, duzhvarshta, vi. 285
Dusii, demons who lusted after women, iii. 14
Dust, vi. 37, 39
—Leza as cloud of, vii. 133
—of earth, uses of, vi. 234
Dušurā (Gk. Dousares), male deity of Nabataeans, v. 16, 17, 18
Duty, vi. 105
Dvalin, Sun deceives, ii. 197
—dwarf, ii. 265
—made runes for dwarfs, ii. 55, 220
Dvāpara Age, vi. 105
Dvārakā, vi. 125, 127, 173, 174, 183, 225
Dvärg, dwarf, akin to trolls, ii. 287
Dvergar, ii. 223
Dvergemål-kletten ("Dwarf-speech summit"), ii. 269

Dvina, iii. 317, 329
Dvita ("second"), brother of Trita Āptya, vi. 36, 176
Dwarf, Bês as, xii. 61
—deity, xii. 22 (fig. 2)
—divinities usually feminine, xii. 377 [86]
—fairy-folk, iii. 108
—gods, Plutarch confuses Harpokrates with, xii. 117
—incarnation of Viṣṇu, vi. 29, 79, 80, 168, 169
—nameless cosmic god under form of, xii. 222
—people, x. 28
—roasted heart of dragon for, iii. 166
—types, combination of two — Bês and Khepri-Sokari, xii. 377 [90]
—water-spirit as, iv. 204
Dwarfie stone, ii. 270
Dwarfs, ii. 9, 10, 35, 46, 53, 55, 66, 78, 95–96, 99, 108, 109, 123, 141, 149, 170, 197, 205, 207, 210, 219, 220, 221, 224, 239, 264–274, 325, 327, 337; vii. 120, 136, 141–142, 145, 243, 258–269, 399 [14], 416 [19]; viii. 229–230, 286; x. 68; xi. 32, 71, 72, 82, 153
—and dwarf-shaped gods of earliest period, xii. 63, 377 [88]
—as goldsmiths, xii. 377 [86]
—in sacred dances, xii. 377 [86]
—Loch of, iii. 116
—mythic hermaphrodite, appear as denizens of moon, x. 257, 309 [64]
—myths concerning, xii. 63, 377 [86]
—perhaps identified with Satyrs, xii. 377 [86]
—sea-dwelling, iii. 134
—worship of family genii associated with myths about, iii. 247–248
Dwelling-places of dwarfs, ii. 265
Dwellings for Votiak and other gods, iv. 114–115, 140, 141
—kinds of, x. 76, 80, 97
—magic, iii. 83
—of spirits preserved in India, vi. 249
Dyadya ("Uncle"), iv. 181
Dyaus, ii. 97; xii. 340
—fire son of, vi. 284
—god of sky, vi. 16, 21, 26, 53, 62, 75–76, 86, 134, 142
—Pitar, war-god, vii. 13
—-Tiwaz, vii. 14
Dyāvāpṛthivī, gods of sky and earth, vi. 16, 21, 86

Dyfed, Manawyddan given land (which became enchanted) in, iii. 101, 102

Dying goddess, v. 113

——myth of, xii. 100–101, 396 98

—gods, i. 218; v. 17, 28, 75–76, 113, 114, 131, 179, 180, 188, 322, 325, 326, 335, 340, 343–344, 345, 346, 351; xii. 99, 101, 119, 120, 410 2, 413 12; see also TAMMUZ AS DYING GOD; LIL.

—" to reach the mountain " expression for, v. 161

Dylan, son of the wave, ii. 191

—twin son of Arianrhod, iii. 96, 97, 99

Dymas(?), Hekabe daughter of, i. 118

Dzajaga, Dzajagatši, iv. 392, 393, 394

Dzajan, iv. 394

Dzewana identified with Diana, iii. 355 44

Dzhe Manito, x. 40

Dziady, festival to Svantovit shows resemblance to Russian autumnal, iii. 282

Dziadys, deceased ancestors whose memory honoured four times annually; also festivals of same name, iii. 235–237, 305

Dzimwe, butt and victim of Hare, vii. 249

Dziwozony, Polish term for superhuman females, iii. 264

Dzoavits, stone giants, x. 134

Džokh in sense of Hades from Persian Duzakh, Hell, vii. 97

Dzol-Dzajagatši, guardian spirit, iv. 395

Dzydzilelya identified with Venus, iii. 355 44

E

Ea and Atarhasis, poem of, v. 270–276

—as antelope of the sea, v. 105

——creator of man, v. 175, 307, 396 46

——Lahmu of the sea, description of, v. 103

—charged gods to slay a god in order to obtain flesh and blood for creation, v. 112

—friend of men, v. 141, 270

—gave Namtaru comrades to go with him to Ereshkigal, v. 163

—god of purification, v. 106, 107, 167, 172, 176, 184, 218, 221, 222, 223, 257, 265, 271, 272, 274, 292, 293, 297, 303, 332, 333, 370

——Tigris and Euphrates, of rivers and fountains, v. 105, 106

—in Adapa legend, v. 175 ff.

—laments over world catastrophe, v. 141

—Marduk created in Apsû of, v. 157

——identified with, v. 155

—patron deity of 'Anat, v. 26, 27, 102, 395 21

—see ENKI, WATER-DEITY.

—Sumerian hymn on temple and cult of, v. 107

——patron of arts and philosophy, v. 103, 104

—Tammuz and Innini (Ishtar) son and daughter of, v. 344

—Way of, in astronomy, v. 94, 306

Eä, invisible nature-god, iv. 464

Eabani, vii. 69

Eachtach made war on Fionn, iii. 178

Eagle and owl, tale of, viii. 334–335

——serpent, alliance and strife between, v. 168–173

—as dragon in battle with Ninurta, v. 131

—ascends (an augury) to sun with serpent in its talons, xi. 115

—associated with rising sun, v. 119

—bird of sun, clearly distinct from Zû, v. 119

——Zeus, i. 162

—crested, primeval bird, vii. 144

—dew-, related to thunderbird idea, x. 24, 288 32

—emblem of Hades, i. 235

— -dragon (Imgig) associated with constellation Pegasus, v. 119

—form, ghostly women in, xi. 77–78

—Ganymedes borne aloft by, i. 118, 240

— -headed lion may be Zû, v. 281, 283

—images of, on fire-temple, x. 57

—in West Semitic, v. 398 94

—lion-headed, emblem of all types of war-god, v. 116–117

—Lleu as, iii. 56, 97

—of " Edda," iv. 357

——Hako ceremony, x. xx

——Mountain Chant, x. 174

Eagle on pillar called twin gods of battle, v. 115
——roof of temple of Yāw, v. 117
—primarily the sun, xi. 74
—rescued man and woman from flood, ix. 180
—stands for Ninurta as Sol invictus, v. 119
—symbol of sun-god, v. 35, 60, 61, 62, 115
—(*yin*), why symbol for answer to prayer, viii. 104
Eagles, ii. 179, 193, 216, 233, 332; iv. 360, 500, 501, 504, 505, 508; vi. 47, 48, 61, 62, 65, 91, 94; 264, 283, 289, 291, 336; x. 122, 179, 204, 229, 252
Eaḥes ("patron of the South"), xii. 152
Eanna, Anu's temple, examined by Gilgamish, v. 235–236
—("house of heaven"), Anu worshipped in, v. 94, 143
—King, iii. 172
Eaochaid ua Flainn, iii. 38
Ea-pe (Jehovah?), creed of supreme deity (of Red Karens), xii. 270
Earendel, constellation, ii. 83
Ear-rings, vi. 145, 154, 174; xi. 245
Ears, piercing of, x. 90; xi. 250
—ringing of, as portent, iv. 12
Earth, iv. 459–462; vi. 15–16, 17, 18, 21, 29, 31, 34, 37, 49, 74, 77, 79, 80, 86, 91, 94, 96, pl. XII, opp. p. 122, 140, 197, 216; viii. 27, 29, 32, 46, 50, 51, 53, 137, 141–142; x. xvi, xvii, 22, 27, 35, 39, 42, 43, 44, 62–63, 98, 179, 186, 187
—a form of Amen-Rê', xii. 221
—and Heaven, ceremony of union of, x. 92–93
——first separation of, gives rise to Osiris, xii. 30
——made by Rê', xii. 82
——separation of, xii. 78
——Peneios, parents of Daphne, i. 180
——Zeus capture Persephone, i. 227
—[as animal?] walking [creation-myth], x. 222–223
—as gaping jaws, xi. 54
—body of Aker, xii. 43
——born, Choctaw and Creek regard themselves as, x. 63
—cavernous, Lord of Death, xi. 79

Earth contains replicas of what is in Heaven, v. 308, 310, 411 [33]
—creation of, vi. 280–281; x. 9, 34–42, 60–64, 278 [15]–279; see also COSMOGONY.
——deity, Ethiopic, is sun-goddess of South Arabia, v. 380 [39]
—depths of, represented by Khnûm on back of lion, xii. 369 [22]
—Devil lives in, iv. 481
—Doctor, x. 176, 178
—dragon bound beneath, xii. 104
——dwellers, ii. 308
—Elysium created by glamour on surface of, iii. 122
——lost through contact with, iii. 105
—Eyatahentsik goddess of, x. 295 [43]
—female, birth-deity, iv. 397
—fifth element, rules Middle Kingdom, viii. 379 [27]
—first sacrificial victim to Sun, xi. 74
—foundation of, vii. 93
—founded by Horus, xii. 209
——fructifier, sacrifice to, iv. 259
——giants: see GIANTS (vol. xi).
——gnomes, vii. 259
——god, Dagda in one place a, iii. 40
——Enlil identified with Babbar-Shamash, v. 380 [39]
——Osiris not treated as, xii. 95
——Sokar(i) became, xii. 149
——Sumerian Enlil, v. 14
——goddess, Aphrodite the mother, as, i. pl. I, frontispiece
——as female principle of Anu, special titles of, v. 91
——Astarte as, v. 15, 91, 108
——Ciuacoatl as, xi. 75
——epithets of, i. 12
——idea of, dim among Armenians, vii. 21
——of Syria, Atargatis as, v. 37
——Pandora as form of, i. 12, 324 [8]
——Semele (Pers. Zamin) a Phrygian, vii. 12
——Sumerian Aruru (Gula, Bau, Ninhursag, Nintud, Bêlit-ilāni), v. 14
——Teutonic, vii. 14
——West Semitic 'Ashtart (Ashtar), v. 14
——goddesses, ii. 194; vi. 128, 237, 238; xi. 26, 33, pl. IV, opp. p. 34, 57, pl. IX, opp. p. 70, 122
—gods of, vi. 41–72, 236

Earth, gods of birth live in, under Lapp tents, iv. 252, 254
——demons and dead, vi. 41–72
—increased, vi. 306–307
—inhabited by Jinns before creation of Adam, v. 355
—Lapp sacrifice to, iv. 251
—life beyond is under the, iv. 72
— -lodge, xi. 74
——dwellings, x. 76
—made of Ymir's body, ii. 325, 326
—(Mama Pacha), xi. 224, 246
—man created from, i. 11; ix. 24, 25, 27, 74, 172, 173, 174, 175; see various items s.v. CLAY.
——partly from, iv. 371
—marriage of Heaven and, vii. 124
—may be reckoned as thirteenth heaven, xi. 53
—men's beliefs on form of, x. 135
—mother, earth took shape and was personified as, ix. 5, 9, 16, 30, 32, 33, 34, 35, 38, 166
——goddess, primitive pictograph of, v. 90
——only sacrificed to up to winter, iv. 219
—mothers, iii. 8, 39, 98; iv. 239, 240, 243; v. 12, 131; vii. 124, 125; xi. 24, 25, 74, 79
—mountain, iv. 340–348
——of Ekur, v. 100
—new, at end of old, iv. 370
—opens and swallows people, vii. 200, 406 8
—origin of, iv. 313–332
— -people, x. 97
—Power = Tunkan, x. 98
— -priest determines who shall begin sowing, xii. 338
—Python dragon-offspring of, i. 177
—refounded after destruction, ix. 161, 163
—rejects Cian's body seven times, iii. 40
—reputed mother of Erichthonios, i. 67
—rite of going under the, ii. 196
—sacrifices to Four Quarters of, viii. 61
—see JORD.
—sent dream-oracles to visitors at shrine of Apollo, i. 178
—shapes of, iv. 308, 310
—Sirens created from drop of blood from broken horn of Acheloös that fell upon, i. 262

Earth sliced into creeks and valleys, iii. 136
— -soul, iv. 13, 14
—soul dwells on, for forty days, iii. 230
—Spenta Ārmaiti presides over, vi. 260
— -spiders, viii. 211
— -spirit, blood sacrifice in Autumn to, iv. 460
—stolen with wedding-like ceremonies, iv. 240
—stretching of, x. 168, 218–219
—superstitions about, ii. 195–196
—supported by Poseidon, i. 211
— -supporter, x. 250
—survivals of spirits and guardians of, iii. 133
—taken for granted, vii. 143
——to new home or on journey, iv. 124
—throne of Osiris later sought in depths of, xii. 97
— -Titaness, Chalcuitl the jealous, xi. 96
—Toad, xi. 75
—Vahagn son of, vii. 44
—Vasus doomed to be born on, vi. 142
— -watching Man, iv. 403
—what exists on, pre-existed in Heaven, v. 192
—withdrawal of sun-god from, xii. 76–79, 84
— -worship in Armenia, vii. 35
—worship offered to spirits of, viii. 61
——of Mother, vi. 230, 234
Earthquake caused by dragon of Abyss raging against his fetters, xii. 104
—ended Age of Giants, xi. 91, 94
—Poseidon causes, i. 211, 212–213
—was caused by our Lord's crucifixion, Druid told Conchobar that the, iii. 157
Earthquakes, ii. 92, 145, 147, 150, 363 38; vii. 93; 118, 130; ix. 163; x. 232, 250
—restlessness of Chibchachum causes, xi. 203
—Supporter of earth causer of, iv. 310, 311, 312
Earths, three, prayer that enemy may lie below, vi. 71
Earu, Osiris supervises dead working in fields of, xii. 97
East, Blue Dragon spirit of, xii. 307
—ceremonial lodge door faces, x. 88, 97

East, doors of house of the world are the portals of the, vi. 17
—facing, in praying to gods, iv. 111, 262
— -gate entrance to spirit-world, vii. 184
—god of sun rising in, viii. 90
—guardian of, viii. 242
—head of sacrificial victim towards, iv. 221
—homage to, viii. 46, 50
—in colours of the compass, iv. 346, 347, 348, 360
—man created partly from iron brought from the, iv. 371, 447
—orientation towards, vi. 47
—Prime Man of the, v. 275
—representative of dead man placed on grave with back to the, iv. 55
—represented by Blue Dragon, iv. 360
—sacrifices towards, iv. 399
—Spring came from, viii. 234, 235
—"the before," x. 287 31
—to west, at end of world a river of fire (igniting the earth) will flow from, iv. 370
—Yima appears in the, vi. 315
Easter celebrations, vii. 381 5 (ch. ii)
—kuala sacrifice at, iv. 129–130, 132
—termed "festival of Zatik," vii. 40
—Tuesday, spring dziadys on, iii. 236–237
— -week memorial feasts, iv. 61, 63
Eastern Emperor, viii. 88
—Han Dynasty, viii. 65
—Sea, Island Mountains supposed to be in, viii. 115, 117
—Tengeri, iv. 411, 412
Eastertide, iii. 307
Eastward branches of tree for nourishment, iv. 381, 383
Eastwards, anvil cast, iii. 32
—Earth moves, viii. 29
Eataentsic, Eyatahentsik, x. 295 43
Eater of cattle: see RYANG'OMBE, etc.
Eating flesh of son by father, i. 70
—land bare, iii. 193
—mystic claimed freedom from necessity of, viii. 75
—of elephant from the inside, vii. 199, 313
Eay, Ay, name of sun-god, interpreted as meaning "ass," xii. 108, 109

Ebarra, statue of Shamash in temple, v. 150–151
Ebb-tides, cause of, ii. 93, 94
Eb'ebta, Ebta, Ebi(?)u, monkey-shaped genius, xii. 403 18
Eber, Milesian hero, iii. 42, 44
Ebisu, deity of good fortune, viii. 279
Ecatonatiuh, sun of destruction by winds, xi. 94
Ecclesiastical decrees, ii. 198
Echedoros, river, i. 87
Echemos kills Hyllos in duel, i. 95
Echidna and Typhon, parents of the Chimaira, i. 39
—said to have been trapped by Argos Panoptes, i. 29
"Echinus," legend of a fossil, iii. 14
Echion, father of Pentheus, i. 47
Echo, ix. 312 50, 313 63
—heard at cliff, iii. 133
—literally "speech of dwarfs," ii. 269
— -spear, iv. 421
—when "Boundary man" shouts there is no, iv. 173
—work of Lĕšiy, iii. 262
"Echtra Nerai," iii. 68
Echuac, Maya Holy Ghost, xi. 143
Echumech, iii. 30
Eçka, x. 19
Eclectic School, viii. 8
Eclecticism, age of, viii. 279
Eclipse, Yugo-Slav tradition of, iii. 229
—thorn-tree rising from body of the dragon of the, xi. 56, 62
Eclipses, ii. 198, 200, 338; iii. 325; iv. 223–224; 424, 425; v. 106; vi. 65, 67, 99, 137, 139, 151, 192, 232, 233, 234; vii. 48; 220; viii. 84; x. 25, 150, 277 13, 255, 257; xi. 82, 94, 135, 277–278, 319
—moon regulates, xii. 33
—myth of pig in sun's eye probably referred originally to, xii. 125
Ecstacy, x. 249, 254
—hikuli plant induces, xi. 123
—of votaries of Dionysos, i. 221–222
Edaein, woman of the Land of Promise, iii. 116
Edda had son by Heimdall, ii. 153
"Edda" of Snorri, iv. 372, 423
"Eddas," ii. 3–8, 12, 16, 25, 26, 31, 39, 45, 58, 63, 64, 68, 74, 77, 81, 91, 98, 101, 103, 115, 123, 124, 127, 150, 157, 164, 165, 171, 181, 198, 219, 220, 221,

223, 233, 239, 251, 254, 259, 270, 275, 280, 285, 286, 292, 296, 311, 312, 317, 336, 343, 344

Eddic poems, dates, origin, and forms of, ii. 8–9

Edessa, v. 35–36

Edfu, altar for human sacrifice found at, xii. 420 22

—birth-temple at, xii. 414 29

—cult of Horus at, xii. 101, 388 28

—Horus battles in form of winged disk of, xii. 117, 363 1

—Men'et at, xii. 101, 136

Edji, first woman, iv. 381

Edom, Canaanitish god, xii. 157

—desolation of, v. 363

Edomite divine name, v. 58

Edzhi, invisible nature-god, iv. 464

Eel (serpent), Morrígan vanquished as an, iii. 158

Eels, ix. 55, 56, 120

Ef, Euf, special name of ram-headed form of sun, xii. 364 15

Effigies and Masks, x. 309 65–310

—death and torture by, common throughout world, xii. 205

—of straw used for magic destruction of Chao Kung-ming, viii. 79–80

—probably represented Hrungnir, ii. 96

Egalmah, temple of Ninsun, v. 249

Egeria, affiliation of Diana with, i. 294

—connexion of, with child-birth, i. 294, 295

Egerton Manuscript, iii. 79, 80, 81, 82

Egg, vi. 74, 75, 138

—all birds sprung from, ix. 25

—birth of Nāga child, Tüng Hkam, from, xii. 273

—carried beneath armpit, Šetek (Škrat, etc.) may be bred from, iii. 244, 245, 246

—cosmic, ix. 20, 22, 242

——bird laid, ii. 363 4

—dragon's or serpent's, vii. 76–77, 391 8

—Egyptian sun-god born from, vii. 385 9

—emu's, sun created from, ix. 274

—external soul of fairy or dragon sometimes hidden in, vii. 391 8

—Hsêng Nya hatched from, xii. 276

—laid in teak forest by Nāga princess with whom Mang Kyaw Sa had an amour, hatched by tiger, xii. 292

—lightning-bird's, vii. 237

Egg, sea spume in shape of, from which boy born, ix. 157

—symbolism of, xii. 71

Eggs containing human beings hatched by serpent, ix. 109, 121

——lifeless beings later vivified, 170

—Devil's magic, vii. 204–205

—five, on Mt. Condor-coto, birthplace of Pariacaca, xi. 230

—Indo-Chinese races claim to be sprung from, xii. 293

—Kadrū's serpent sons hatched from, vi. 139

—laid by Nāga, children hatched from, xii. 285

—mankind originated from, ix. 169

—of the hyena, vii. 408 9

—offerings in form of yolks of, xi. 145

—put on mountain, x. 162

—rolling of, at spring dziadys, iii. 237

—solar and lunar, turned by Ptaḥ on potter's wheel, xii. 145

—sowing of, iv. 241–242

—sun and moon as, xii. 208, 423 34

—three hens', produced three maidens, ix. 160

Eggther, warder of giants, ii. 276

Egil, ii. 86, 191, 259, 267, pl. xxxv, opp. p. 272, 286

—Skallagrimsson, poet, ii. pl. ii, opp. p. 4, 230

"Egils-saga," ii. 121, 122, 191, 240, 292

Egime, sister of Lil, v. 114

Egoism, vi. 174, 179

Egres, creator of vegetables, flax, and hemp, iv. 244

Egypt, account of Israelite captivity in, not influenced by Gilgamish epic, v. 267

—as two countries, xii. 39 (fig. 29), 370 33

—early boundaries of, xii. 158

—influence of, on Semitic religion, i. 6

—Io wanders to, i. 29

—Lower, Buto earliest capital of, xii. 132

—Menelaos sacrifices to gods of the Nile when storms detain him in, i. 134

—sun's eye brought back from Nubia to, xii. 86

—Syria apparently borrowed killing of Adonis by boar from, xii. 399 111

Egypt, Upper, worship of Osiris and Isis scarcely recognized officially in, before Second Dynasty, xii. 120

Egyptian religion, development and propagation of, xii. 212–245

——peculiar value of, xii. 22, 245

——possible Asiatic influence of, xii. 365 [19]

Egyptians associated sun with celestial tree, vii. 49

Ehcatonatiuh, sun of Air, xi. 91

Ehet (Ehat) as primeval cow-form of sky, xii. 371 [46]

——" development of the members of Khepri," xii. 71

——names of cosmic cow, as nurse and protector of sun-god, xii. 40

Ehi (Ahi) associated with Hat-hôr of Denderah, xii. 133

Ehulhul, temple of Sin at Harran, v. 153–154

Eidothea forced Proteus to reveal to Menelaos state of affairs at Sparta, i. 261

Eight-banners (god Hachiman), viii. 252

—diagrams: see DIAGRAMS, EIGHT AND SIXTY-FOUR.

—divine treasures, Grace-maiden born from, viii. 294

—Gentlemen, viii. 118, 119

—Immortals, viii. 118, 119–130

—living creatures from which all others grew, vii. 144

—Spirits, viii. 68, 69

Eighty-owls, viii. 211

Eikthyrnir, ii. pl. VI, opp. p. 32

Eildon Hills, iii. 195

Eileithyia, goddess of child-birth, i. 78

—helps Leto in child-birth, i. 175

—likeness of Roman Mater Matuta to, i. 290

—-Lucina, Nekhbet identified with, xii. 143

Eileithyiai, the, Hera's daughters, control birth of Herakles and Eurystheus, i. 164, 166

Eileithyiaspolis, human victims burned at, xii. 196

—(modern el-Kâb), Nekhbet goddess at, xii. 142

E-imhursag, state tower of Ekur, v. 99

Einar, shepherd, ii. 118, 234

Einarr slays Halfdan, ii. 240

Eing Saung Nãt, household spirit, xii. 344

Einhere, Thor called, ii. 315

Einherjar, warriors in Valhalla, ii. pl. VI, opp. p. 32, 57, 313, 314, 315, 321, 341

Eir, goddess, ii. 15, 186

Eirik, king, ii. 57, 77, 107, 230, 251, 280, 310, 315, 322

" Eiriksmal," ii. 57, 161, 251, 315, 342

" Eiriks-saga," ii. 75

Eistla, giantess, ii. 153

Eithinoha, " Our Mother " = Earth, x. 27

Ek Ahau (Black Captain), xi. 138

Ekajatā, vi. 217

Ekalgina, palace of Anunnaki, v. 333

Ekar in Twi, head-pad, vii. 111

Eirene (" Peace "), abstract divinity of social institution, i. 283

——one of the Horai, i. 237–238

Eka-śrnga, Skt. for Ikkaku Sennin, viii. 381 [11]

Ekata (" One "), went to Śvetadvīpa, vi. 176

Ekchuah, god of travellers, xi. 137, 139

Ekerit, an ancestor, iv. 503

Ekhutet, ancient goddess, xii. 133

Ekisiga (House of sacrifices), temple of Tirga, v. 80

Ektenes, entire people of the, perished by plague, i. 42

—Oxygos king of, i. 42

Ek-u-Mayeyab, idol, xi. 145

Ekur, demons ascended from house of, v. 365

—house of Enlil, v. 265

—world named, v. 99, 100

El and Jacob, wrestling of, v. 244–245

—creates heaven and earth, v. 303

— -ba'al, name of ancient king, v. 67

—Elôah, myths of war-god of Sumer and Babylonia attached by Hebrews to, v. 133, 134

—Elōhim, deities Ilâh and Yâw correspond to, v. 5, 11, 43, 245

—Ilâh (Bab. Anu, Gk. Zeus), sky-god, Semitic religion had as first deity, v. 93

—(Ilos) depicted as cruel tyrant of Gebal, v. 66, 67

—of West Semitic races, Babylonian influence on, v. 71

—special name of Ba'al of Gebal, v. 67

El specific name for Shamash (sun-god), v. 65–66
—statue of, v. 76
—sun-god of Phoenicians, v. 342, 351
—West Semitic deity, v. 14, 35, 37, 39, 41, 42, 43, 44, 45, 46, 54, 66, 67, 68, 69, 70, 71, 72, 73, 80, 389 242
El Caleuche, witch-boat, xi. 328
—Chaco and the Pampeans, xi. 319–324
—Destolanado, Meulen appears as, in modern folk-lore, xi. 327
—Dorado, xi. 194–198, 199
—El, daemon, xi. 333
—Gran Dios, home of, xi. 140
—Kāb modern name of Hierakonpolis, xii. 101
— -lal, creator-hero, xi. 335–336
— -malak, Aramaic transcription of Il-ma-la-[ku], v. 58
Ela, ancestors of Karens came from, xii. 282
Elagabal, sacred baetyl of, stands on chariot, v. 54, 55
Elam, temple of Ishtar in, vii. 38
Elamite goddess Nahunta, vii. 25
Elamites capture statue of Ishtar, vii. 38
Eland made by Mantis, killed and restored to life, vii. 289
Elāpattra, serpent, vi. 216
Elatha, Fomorian king, Bres son of, iii. 24, 25, 26, 27
Elattipuu, tree to which first-fruits were offered, iv. 26
Elbe, elber, friendly spirits, ii. 219, 222
—Slavs, religion of, contains the best evidences of Slavonic religions, iii. 221, 222
Elbisch, mental unsoundness caused by ghostly beings, ii. 219
Elbjungfer, ii. 213
Elbow stones, xi. 23, 350 9
Elcmar, foster-father of Oengus, iii. 51, 52, 53, 79, 207
Elder Brother, x. 176, 178, 179
— -mother, asking permission of, to cut tree, ii. 207
Elders (of animal-kind), x. xvii, 31–32, 39, 62, 69, 81, 99, 156, 254, 292 40–293
—of the kinds, x. 30–33, 35, 39, 62, 104, 298 48; xi. 192, 289
——Underworld, iv. 74

Eldhrimnir, cauldron, ii. 313
Eldir, "Fire-man" servant of Ægir, ii. 142, 172, 220, 280
Elegy, origin and meaning of, vii. 385 4 (ch. v)
Elektra, daughter of Agamemnon, takes Orestes to Strophios, i. 135
—one of Pleiades, iv. 428
Elektryon, son of Perseus, i. 76
Elements, five, viii. 29, 55, 135, 142; 243
—gods of four, attempted representation of, as rams, xii. 65–66
—masculine and feminine, xi. 122
Eleos ("Pity"), abstract divinity of state of mind, i. 282
Elephant, iv. 360; vi. pl. iv, opp. p. 34, 194, 195, 242; vii. 121, 148–149, 151, 284
—and Blind Men, tale of, viii. 355–356
—in trickster tales, ix. 188, 189
—see LAO, SIAMESE SHANS, ETC.
—swallows mother and child, vii. 198–199
—symbol, iii. pl. xvii, opp. p. 134
—totem, vii. 272, 274, 279, 345
—White, pagoda in Laihka, xii. pl. xii (A), opp. p. 316
Elephantine, deeper sources of Nile at, four in number, xii. 46, 370 35
—god had two wives at, xii. 20
—Khnûm(u) god of, xii. 50, 135
—triad of, xii. 20 (fig. 1)
Eleusinia, the, i. pl. L, opp. p. 230, 231, 232
Eleusinian Mysteries, analogies to, in Hako ceremonial, x. 92–93
Eleusis, Demeter earth-goddess of, i. 219
—Erechtheus conducted Athenians against people of, i. 68
—in Attike, Demeter at, i. 228
—Kerkyon killed by Theseus at, i. 99
—mystic rites at, i. pl. L, opp. p. 230
—St. Demetra now replaces Demeter at, i. 313
Eleutherai, cultic practice at, in connexion with introduction of Dionysos into Attike, i. 217, 221
Elf-beam or -ray, ii. 197, 222
— -driving (álf-reka), form of defilement known as, ii. 227
Elfin host, Nera merely in presence of, iii. 68–69

Elfin traits, ii. 133, 148–149, 150, 170, 207, 223, 254, 286
Elfins, water-, ii. 209, 223
Elicius, name of Iuppiter as rain-god, i. 290
Elidurus taken to visit dwarf fairy-folk, iii. 108
Elijah and Lîlîth, v. 363
Elilli, wife of Ndabu, vii. 340
'Elioun (Hypsistos), god, v. 66
Elis, Augeias king of, i. 82
—cult of Hades and temple of, at, i. 234
—invaded and captured by Herakles, i. 91–92
—Odysseus inspects his herds at, i. 140
Eλishe, on Sassanian Mihr, vii. 381 [1] (ch. ii)
—voice of dragon, vii. 79
Elivagar (icy stream), Thor waded over, ii. 82
—(stormy waves), ii. 275, 276, 324
—where Hymir dwelt, ii. 86
Elixir of Æsir, apples of immortality are, ii. 178
——life: see LIFE, ELIXIR OF, ETC.
Elk commanded the winds, x. 99
Ellasar, a centre of sun-worship, v. 150, 153
—capital before Flood, v. 207
Elle-folk, Elver-folk, origin of, ii. 224, 231, 286
Elli (Old Age), Thor tried to throw, ii. 93, 94
Elm and ash = Ask and Embla, ii. 327
Elms, mistress of fire descended from, iv. 453
—planted at tomb of Andromache's father, i. 258
Elōeim (elōhim), " gods," v. 66, 70, 72, 73–74
Elōhim for monotheistic deity in second Hebrew account of Flood, v. 231, 232
—in creation of Genesis, v. 303–304
—sons of, demons, v. 358, 373
Eloquence, Hercules native god of, iii. 10
—Tiur patron of, vii. 31
Elpaʻal, in Persian period kings of Gebal called, v. 67
Elpenor, shade of, appears to Odysseus, i. 145
Elphin rescued Taliesin, iii. 57, 110
" Elucidation," iii. 196

Elullo, Okuni chief, vii. 340–341
Elurā, Jain sculptures at, vi. 226
Elves (Alfar), ii. 20, 23, 25, 35, 42, 46, 55, 108, 141, 143, 183, 197, 204, 205, 209, 219–227, 239, 266
—(siabhra) transformed Aige into fawn, iii. 60
Elyōn applied to Yāw, v. 66, 70
Elysian Fields, Kadmos and Harmonia sent to dwell in, by Zeus, i. 47
—Island, iii. 72
Elysium, i. 147–148
—a sort of Japanese, viii. 269
—Aeneas visits, i. 305
—Brythonic, iii. 14, 15, 17, 36, pl. v, opp. p. 40, 50, 90, 93, 95, 102, 103, 105, 113, 114, 117, 121, 122, 138, 173, 174, 185, 194, 195, 197, 210, 212, 213, 334 [12]
—Irish, influences Eddic beliefs, ii. 321, 322–323
—of Brythonic Celts, Avalon is, iii. 85, 122
—parallel between early Greek and Celtic, iii. 123
—water-world, iii. 194
Emah, temple to Mah, v. 110
Emain Macha, Conchobar's palace, iii. 71, 140, 141, 143, 147, 149, 150, 153, 155, 157, 209
Emakong brings fire, birds, crickets, etc., from underwater city, ix. 117
Emanation of gods from primeval couple, v. 291
Emasculation, i. 6, 197; v. 74, 75, 76, 293
—cause of death of Shwe Pyin, xii. 351
—self-, of Osiris (or Rê'), xii. 398 [106]
Emathion, child of Eos and Tithonos, i. 246
Embalmer: see ANUBIS AS EMBALMER.
Embalming of Mimir's head, ii. 46
Embalmment, xii. 173, 175
—four sons of Horus or Osiris as guardians of, xii. 111–112
—in Pyramid Period, xii. 172
—necessary to secure bliss for dead, xii. 181
Embers, carrying of, outside village fence said to protect from fever and sickness, xii. 337
Embla (elm), Hœnir associated with creation of, ii. 151, 204
—Loki gives heat to, ii. 148

Emblem, Mexican, xi. 115
Emblems-totem painted in cave of chiefs, vii. 418 [40]
Embryo, in Indian belief, father became an, and was reincarnated in his first-born son, iii. 83
Embryos, interchange of, vi. 222, 223–224, 228
Emen and Emenet ("the Hidden") sometimes replace third pair of ogdoad, xii. 371 [46]
Emer, wife of Cúchulainn, iii. 87, 88, 143, 144, 146, 149
Emerald born of virgin becomes living creature, xi. 201
—veneration of great, xi. 207–208, 209
Emergence, story of the, x. 63, 175, 210; see also ASCENT THROUGH WORLD-STOREYS; LOG, HOLLOW; REED, HOLLOW; SIPAPU; MIDDLE PLACE; NAVEL, EARTH'S.
Emeslam, v. 141, 146
Emesti, one of the four sons of Horus or Osiris, xii. 112
Emigrants, Artemis protectress of, i. 186
Emigration tale, ix. 86–87
Emim, legendary race of giants, v. 355, 358
Emisiwaddo, wife of Kururumany, xi. 259
Emi-uet ("the One [in the city of (?)] Uet"), term applied to symbol of Anubis, xii. 393 [62]
Em-Ku ("Descent of God"), baptismal festival, xi. 142
Emma (Skt. Yama-rājā), king-judge in hells, viii. 238, pl. xiv, opp. p. 240
Emotions, control of, viii. 147
Emperors, mythical Three, viii. 7, 25–32
Empire, discussion of use of term, xi. 352 [2]
Empousa, monster, i. 278
—vampire, v. 365
Empty Days unlucky, xi. 99
Emu and bustards, tale of, ix. 288–289
Emu, origin of priestesses of Ḥat-ḥôr at, xii. 76
Emuin, Three Finns of, iii. 90
Enarsphoros, son of Hippokoön, Kastor and Polydeukes fought against, at Sparta, i. 26
Enbarr, Lug rode Manannan's steed, iii. 29, 128

Enchanted castle and serpent, vii. 358
—cup in Fionn tales, iii. 203
—fleet, iii. 97
—sleep of Arthur and his knights, iii. 195
Enchantment, fairy, ii. 204
—of Dyfed, iii. 102
——Loch Guirr and tale of tree of, iii. 138
——trees, stones, etc., to become combatants in battle, iii. 31, 100, 155
Enchantments, Féinn overcome by, iii. 172
—Pryderi defeated and slain by Gwydion's, iii. 96
End of world, Meher will come from cave of Zympzymps at, vii. 34
Endashurimma, watchman of Ereshkigal, v. 164
"Ender," gods fear the, vi. 77, 99
Endukugga, watchman of Ereshkigal, v. 164
Endushuba, watchman of Ereshkigal, v. 164
Endymion, i. pl. XIV (1), opp. p. 36
—grandson of Aiolos, led Aiolians from Thessaly to Elis, i. 55
—story of Selene's love for, i. 245
—wedded a nymph, Iphianassa, i. 55
Eneene seeks wife in Underworld, ix. 74
Enemies recognized and persecuted by bears after their death, iv. 85
—totems influenced to attack clan-, vii. 278, 279
Enemy, charm for keeping back, ii. 18
Engur, title of Ea, v. 105
Enik, horse of Sun, vii. 51
Enim, xi. 194
Eninnû (falcon of hostile land), temple of Ningirsu at Lagash, v. 122, 126, 398 [104]
Enit (Anit), xii. 130
—wife of Mont(u), xii. 139
Enkar, temple, v. 126
Enkata (Inkata), in Uganda, meaning of, vii. 110–111
Enkelados, Athene in conflict with, i. 172
—giant born of blood of Ouranos, i. pl. VIII (3), opp. p. 8, 9
Enki and Damkina, poem on, almost parallel to Adam and Garden of Eden, v. 194–195
—curse in name of, v. 82

Enki-Ea, water-god, v. 190, 344
—fashioned man, v. 104
—Innini (Ishtar) and Tammuz daughter and son of, v. 329
—(later Ea), water-deity, v. 84, 88, 89, 92, 102–103, 109, 151, 152, 155, 175, 193, 196–197, 198, 199, 206, 275, 291, 310, 327–328, 329, 357
—titles of, as patron of arts, v. 105
Enkidu (a hostile offspring), also Enkimdu, Enkita, v. 236–266, 268, 407 [23]
—and Gilgamish slew celestial bull, v. 29
—created by Aruru, v. 115
—death of, v. 209, 212, 257, 258, 260
—in epic of Gilgamish, v. 209, 210, 211, 212, 234, 242, 246–255, 256, 257, 258, 259, 263, 264, 265
En-lil and Zû, contest between, vi. 264
—advocacy of, of Irra's plan to destroy Babylon, v. 141
—and Marduk, Ashur borrowed character from, v. 160–161
—as Aeolus, v. 63
——earth-god prophesied destruction of man, v. 270, 271, 272, 274, 365
——god of storms, rain, and agriculture, and as creator, v. 99, 100–101, 102, 193, 200, 201, 206, 221, 222, 223, 257, 265, 287, 288, 303, 307, 357, 367
—author of world catastrophes, v. 141–142
—Dagan identified with, v. 82
—decrees that Humbaba should keep safely cedar forest, v. 247
—devils messengers of, v. 365
—identified with Shamash, v. 63
—lord of both upper and Underworld, v. 63, 99, 400 [144]
—man created to serve, v. 314
—Marduk identified with, v. 155
—Ninamaškug shepherd and psalmist of, v. 356
—of Nippur not meant by Bêl, v. 65
——Susa, Elamitic god Humba described as, v. 255
—omitted in cosmological list, v. 292
—pantheon, Sin belongs to, v. 152
—receives sceptre from Nergal, v. 148
—Shamash sometimes called son of, v. 150
—Shulpae =, v. 114
—stands on winged lion, v. 396 [42]
—Sumerian earth-god, v. 12, 14, 55, 61, 79, 80, 89, 92, 99, 107, 109, 172, 292, 317, 380 [39] [50]
En-lil, survival of, in west, only in account of Babylonian theogony, v. 102
—symbol of, v. 105
—tablets of fate stolen from temple of, v. 40–41
—translates Ziûsudra to a paradise, v. 208, 224
—Way of, in astronomy, v. 94, 306
—with Anu in Arallû, v. 259
Enlilbanda, title of Ea, v. 107
Enlilbani of Isin, magic ritual of expiation copied during reign of, v. 204
Enmeluanna = Amêlôn = Enosh, Sumerian antediluvian king, v. 205
Enmenduranna = Euedorachos = Enoch, Sumerian antediluvian king, v. 203, 205
Enmengalanna = Ammenôn = Kenan, Sumerian antediluvian king, v. 205
Enmesharra, god of lower world; title of Nergal, v. 82, 147, 296, 342
Enmity and punishment, divine, iii. 68–77
—fights of two heroes at, iii. 59
Ennammasht (Enmasht), Nimurta's title may be, v. 132
Ennead, development of, xii. 20, 216
—Heliopolitan, xii. 26
Ennius, i. 304
E-no-shima, shrine of, viii. 271
En-no-Ozuna (Gyōja, "the Ascetic Master"), viii. 276
Ennugi, god, v. 218
En-nugigi, watchman of Ereshkigal, v. 164
Ennunsilimma, god in service of Anu, v. 385 [136]
Enoch = Enmenduranna = Euedorachos, Hebrew patriarch, v. 205
—descendant of Cain, v. 95, 160, 202, 205
Enosh = Enmeluanna = Amêlôn, Hebrew patriarch, v. 205
Enshagme, lord of Dilmun, v. 202
Ensibzianna = Amempsinos = Jared, Sumerian antediluvian king, v. 205
Entrails in omen literature, v. 254–255
Enyeus, king of Skyros, son of Ares, i. 190
Enyo pronounced in oath of the "Seven Generals," i. 190
En-zu: see Zu-EN.
Enzulla, watchman of Ereshkigal, v. 164

Eochaid, iii. 25, 36, 56, 73, 74, 81, 208
—Airem, Etain married by, iii. 80
—Bres, " the beautiful," miserliness of, iii. 26
—Ollathair, a name of Dagda, iii. 40
Eocho Glas arrived to fight Coirpre, iii. 150
—Rond, Cúchulainn cursed by, iii. 149, 150
Eogabal, father of Aine, iii. 47, 73, 89
Eogan, Fand dwells in bower of, iii. 335 [32]
—heard music from yew-tree, iii. 73
—the Stream, iii. 36
Eol, supernatural foe of Labraid, iii. 36
Eolus, son of King of Greece, iii. 116
Eopuco scourged and crowned with thorns the Mayan Christ, xi. 143
Eormanric, ii. 124
Eos, abstract divinity of time, i. 282
—and Astraios parents of the Winds, i. 265
——Aurora, Uṣas one in origin with, vi. 32
——Kephalos, i. pl. xx, opp. p. 72
————parents of Phaëthon, i. 244
—carries Orion away to her dwelling, i. 250
—(" Dawn "), i. 245–246
——enamoured of Kephalos, i. 71–72
—mother of Memnon, i. 130
Eosphoros and Phosphoros, two names for Morning Star, i. 247
Eoten, water-giants, ii. 280
Epagomenal day, Osiris and Isis born on first, xii. 113
—days, sun yields to moon, xii. 373 [57]
Epaphos (" Touch "), son of Io by Zeus, taken by Hera and hidden, i. 29–30
Epeios endowed with skill by Athene, i. 170
—makes wooden horse of Troy, i. 132
Êpet appears at birth and death of sun each day, xii. 60
—as divine nurse, xii. 376 [79]
—assists Horus-Orion fight Ox-Leg, xii. 110 (fig. 110)
—helpful at child-birth, xii. 60
—hippopotamus-deity, lives in water, but does not represent it, xii. 15, 412 [2]
—(later " she who bears the sun "), identified with Nut and bears head of Ḥat-ḥôr-Isis, xii. 60

Êpet, mistress of talismans, xii. 60
—month Epiphi sacred to, xii. 60
—names of, xii. 60, 376 [79]
—originally local divinity but later identified with constellation Boötes, xii. 60
—representation of, xii. 59–60 and figs. 60, 61, 376 [79]
— -Tuêris sometimes identified with Meskhenet, xii. 372 [52]
—Urt-ḥekau epithet of, xii. 151
Ephesos [Ephesus], v. 19
—Artemis of, i. 183
Ephialtes and Otos bound Ares in vase, i. 189, 329 [1] (ch. iv)
—giant born of blood of Ouranos, i. pl. viii (2), opp. p. 8, 9, 250
—nightmare demon, ii. 288
—punishment of, in Hades, i. 144
Ephka, genius of the holy fountain of Palmyra, v. 20
Ephods, v. 35
Ephyra, cave believed to lead to Underworld, i. 143
— = Corinth, i. 37
Epics, Cyclic, i. 326 [2] (ch. viii)
Epidauros in Lakonia and also in Argos, shrines of Asklepios at, i. 281, 301
—mythical relationship of Apollo and Asklepios at cult-shrine at, i. 279
—Periphetes slain by Theseus at, i. 98
Epidemics, offerings to Rutu during, iv. 76
Epigonoi consult Delphic oracle, i. 179
—(" Later Born "), sons of seven generals who had fought against Thebes, i. 54
Epikaste = Iokaste, i. 48, 49, 50
Epilepsy, xi. 77
—caused by moon, vii. 48
—charm against, ii. 70
Epimetheus (" Afterthinker "), brother of Prometheus, i. 12
—Pandora brought to, by Hermes, i. 15
—warned to accept nothing from the gods, i. 15
Epione, wife or daughter of Asklepios, i. 281
Epios, Asklepios first known as, according to Epidaurians, i. 281
Epiphanius, v. 16
Epiphany is called " the following of the water-spirit," iv. 196

Epiphany, water-spirits dwell among humans at, iv. 198

Epiros, belief in Moirai in modern, i. 315

—(Epirus), Aeneas at coast of, i. 305

Epochs, ten, in Chinese chronology, viii. 25–27

Epona, horse-goddess, iii. 9, 124, pl. xv, opp. p. 124, 129

Epopeus, Antiope wedded to, in Sikyon, i. 43

Epunamun, Evil, war-god, xi. 327

Equality, School of, viii. 8

Equinox, Apollo appeared in sky near vernal, iii. 10

Equinoxes, v. 306, 308, 315

—symbolized by twin obelisques, xii. 31

Er, vii. 66, 68, 69, 100, 390 15

Erato (" Loveliness "), one of the Lyric Muses, i. 240

—wife of Arkas, i. 22

Erazamuyn, temple of Tiur at, and meaning of name, vii. 29, 383 43

Erc, son of Cairbre, iii. 155

Erce, part of spoken spell, ii. 195

Ercol, iii. 147

Erebos, abode of, in Underworld, i. 278

—(" Lower Darkness "), i. 5

—Nor parallels, ii. 201

" Erec," French poem of Arthurian cycle, iii. 195

Erech, Astλik goddess in, vii. 38

—(Badanki), city of Anu and Ishtar, v. 143, 144, 240, 242, 243, 312, 351

—citizens of, compelled by Gilgamish to build their city walls, v. 267

—cult of Anu at, v. 94

—in Tammuz myth, v. 326

—may be connected with exploits of Gilgamish, v. 55, 227

—return of Gilgamish and Enkidu to, v. 256

—wall of, built by Gilgamish, v. 235

Erechtheus, daughters of, i. 71–73

—Harpies mothers of steeds of, i. 266

—son of Pandion, i. 67–68

Erem, son of Mile, iii. 137

Ereṣ-Reshep, name of section of Sidon, v. 45

Ereshkigal (Akk. Allatu), goddess of Underworld, v. 99, 109, 110, 161, 162, 163, 164, 259, 262, 328, 330, 331, 332, 333, 334, 335, 357

—Babylonian goddess popular in black magic, xii. 207

Erez (Eriza), Anahit worshipped at, vii. 17, 28, 29

—sacred prostitution in honour of Anahit at, vii. 26

Erginos battles against, and is killed by, Herakles, i. 79

" Êrh-shih-ssŭ Hsiao," viii. 161

Eri, vii. 70

—of the Tuatha Dé Danann through succession of female line, iii. 25

Eri-ḥems-nofer, local deity of island near Philae and manifestation of Shu, xii. 86, 133

Eric, a fine, iii. 81

Eric the Red discovered Greenland, x. 1

Erica-tree grew and enveloped coffin of Osiris, v. 71

Erichthonios, birth of, i. pl. xix, opp. p. 66

—finds doublet in Erechtheus, i. 68

—mares of, Boreas in form of horse begat foals by, i. 265

—Poseidon later identified with, i. 66

—son of Athene, fertility-rites in connexion with birth of, i. 172

——Dardanos, succeeds father on throne of Dardania, i. 117

——Hephaistos, i. 67, 208

Eridanos [Eridanus], Apollonius on Celtic myth of waters of, iii. 10

—constellation, v. 317

—Eridu identified with, v. 310

—given place among constellations, i. 244

—Phaëthon fell from chariot into river, i. 244

—river, i. 87

Eridu, v. 175, 176, 194, 312, 327

—in astronomy, v. 310

—magic tree in, v. 152

—Marduk of, v. 155

—School, v. 103, 104, 175

—seat of Enki cult, v. 102, 103, 107, 112, 140, 152, 206, 207, 310

——first king, v. 166

Erigena, Duns Scotus, iii. 43

Erigone, daughter of Ikarios, hanged herself at father's grave, i. 217

Erimanutuk, god, v. 128

Erin-bird called poisonous tooth, v. 129

Erin, Bran not to visit, iii. 115

—Fand made tryst with Cúchulainn in, iii. 88

Erin, nobles of, satirized by transformed birds, iii. 60
—Oisin's visit to, iii. 181
—sometimes hazels of wisdom thought to grow at heads of rivers of, iii. 121
—wasted by birds, iii. 126
Erinyes ("Furies"), born from the blood of Ouranos, i. 6
—Hades father of, i. 233
—lesser divinities of Underworld, i. 276–277
—of Klytaimnestra pursue Orestes, i. 135
—punish violations of marriage vow, i. 167
—Sirens akin to, i. 262
—translation of Wælcyrge, ii. 253.
Erinys, or Fury, drove Alkmaion mad, i. 54
—of Tilphossa, similarity of story of Saranyū to, vi. 53
Eriphyle beguiled by necklace of Harmonia to decide in favour of Adrastos's expedition, i. 52
—bribed with Harmonia's robe, i. 54
—holding fatal necklace, i. pl. XVII, opp. p. 54
—to decide mutual differences between Adrastos and Amphiaraos, i. 52
—slain by her son Alkmaion, i. 54, 179
Eris causes strife at wedding of Peleus and Thetis, i. 124
—("Strife"), steed of Ares, i. 189
Ériu (still surviving as Erin), queen, iii. 42, 43, 44, 136
Erkhe-Mergen, iv. 420
Erkin, Heaven, vii. 14
Erkir, earth, vii. 14
—(Perkunas), Armenian earth-goddess, vii. 35
Erlen-Khan ("Prince of Death"), iv. 477
Erlik, first man, iv. 316, 370, 373–374, 378, 387, 411–412
Erlik-Khan, on black throne, with court of evil spirits, iv. 487
Erment, modern Hermonthis, xii. 139
Eros, abstract divinity of state of mind, i. 282
—Aphrodite still known as mother of, in modern Zakynthos, i. 314
—child of Hephaistos and Aphrodite, i. 197
—Cupido (Cupid) Roman counterpart of, i. 294

Eros ("Love"), i. pl. iii, opp. p. xlvi, 5, pl. x (1), opp. p. 20, pl. XLV, opp. p. 200, 203–204
Erotes, i. pl. XIX, opp. p. 66
Erotic elements in customs of St. John's Day, iii. 313
Erp slain by Hamther, ii. 240
Eruption (disease) caused by Vetehinen, iv. 207
Erwand, King, confined in rivers and mist by dragons, vii. 80, 83, 84
Erymanthos, Artemis hunted over, i. 183
—boar of, conquered by Herakles, i. 82, 83
—Centaurs especially associated with range of, i. 271
Erysichthon, son of Kekrops and Agraulos, i. 67
Erytheia, island, whereon lived Geryoneus's red cattle, i. 86
Eryx, king of Sicily, wrestles with Herakles for possession of hill, and is killed, i. 86
Erzya, a dialect of the Mordvins, iv. xvi
Es, Heaven-god, iv. 399, 401, 481
Ésa (sing. ós), supernatural beings hostile to men, ii. 20
Esagila, Askul corrupt survival of, v. 337, 339
—temple of Marduk, v. 112, 139, 142, 143, 157, 307–308, 309, 312, 316, 320, 321, 322, 337
Esau, Ousōos is probably, v. 389 [252]
Esbus, v. 19
Eschatological reference in Irish mythology, iii. 34
Eschatology, vii. 96–100
—association of Mihr with, vii. 34
—Iranian, vi. 344–347
—no evidence of Egyptian speculations on, xii. 398 [104]
Esden, later name for baboon-form of Thout(i), xii. 366 [3]
Esdes, xii. 133, 366 [3]
—(Esden?), god mentioned with Thout(i), xii. 366 [3]
Esege-Burkhan, creator, iv. 375
— -Malan-Tengeri, god of Heaven, iv. 442, 477
Êset, Egyptian form of name of Isis, xii. 98, 386 [20]
Esgeir Oervel, Ireland, iii. 190
Esharra, earth, made for En-lil, v. 303

Eshmun, altar to, v. 75
—as god of generative heat, v. 74, 76
— -'Ashtart, name of deity at Carthage, v. 13, 44, 381 [58]
—Canaanitish god, v. 13
—(Esmounos, " healer of sick "), one of eight Kabirs, v. 74-75
—(" healer "), v. 77, 78
—in Phoenician pantheon, vii. 41, 381 [1] (ch. ii)
—of Sidon identified with Asklepios, v. 67, 74
—Paeōn name for, v. 74, 392 [353]
—Sydyk father of, vii. 41
—West Semitic deity, v. 14
—with serpents on coins, v. 77
Eshmun'azar of Sidon, inscription of, v. 72
Eshumera, temple of Ninurta in Nippur, v. 120, 398 [100]
Esikilla (" holy house "), v. 109
Eskimos, x. 2-12
Esneh, Khnûm deity of, xii. 135
—Menhu(i) confused with Menehtet at, xii. 136
—Nebt-uu worshipped at, xii. 140
Esoterism largely absent from Celtic mythology, iii. 20, 21
Esplumeor, Merlin disappears in an, iii. 201
Ess, daughter of Eochaid, iii. 74, 82
——Etain, iii. 81
Essence of the Great Centre, viii. 55
Essex, Seaxneat son of Bældæg (Balder) in, ii. 19
Esta, survival of Vesta in modern Romagnola, i. 319
Estas, trickster, x. 122
Esthonians akin to Finns in linguistic and geographical aspects, iv. xv, xvii, xix
—orthodox, certain saints replacing ancient gods among, iv. xix
—return of, to old beliefs, during Crusades, iv. 34
Estsanatlehi (" Woman Who Changes " [back into youth]), x. 157, 164, 166, 167, 169, 273 [7], 296 [46]
Eš-ú (or Ab-ú), title of Tammuz and Ninurta, v. 131
Esus, Cúchulainn identified with, iii. pl. XVIII, opp. p. 140, 157, pl. XX, opp. p. 158

Esus cutting down a tree, to what myths related?, iii. 9, pl. XX (A), opp. p. 158, pl. XXI, opp. p. 166
Etain, Irish goddess, iii. 40, 52, 56, 59, 69, 74, 79-80, 82, 193
Etair, Etain fell into golden cup of wife of, iii. 80
Etalak and Latarak stood at gate of sunrise, v. 134
Etan, Cúchulainn gave ring to, iii. 150
Etana and eagle, myth of, v. 129
—in Arallû, v. 259
—king of Kish, v. 166
— -myth, vi. 283, 347
—sought plant of birth, v. 94, 166-174
Etar and Caibell, tale of, iii. 38
—king of cavalcade from síd, iii. 74
Etaśa, celestial steed, vi. 34, 61
Eteokles and Adrastos, battle of, before Thebes, i. 52-53
——Polyneikes kill each other in duel, i. 53
——plan of, to reign singly in alternate years unsuccessful, i. 51
—son of Oidipous and Iokaste, i. 49
Eternal fires recall sacred fire of St. Brigit at Kildare, iii. 11
—life beyond Western Sea for four inmates of Ark, v. 204
——lost through jealousy, v. 175
— -Ruling-Lord grew out of Chaos, viii. 222
Eternity, Neheh deity of, xii. 378 [102]
Eterscel, King, iii. 74-75
Ethal of síd Uaman, iii. 78
Ethelbert, St., church of, on site of temple of Triglav, iii. 285
Ether, Shu and Tefênet gods of, xii. 44
Ethical aspects of Zeus, i. 160
Ethics, viii. 16, 17, 19, 20; xii. 184-197
—and myths, i. liii-lvi
—Confucian, viii. 220
Ethiopia as region or type of lower world, xii. 395 [76]
—influence of Egyptian religion on, xii. 240
Ethne, daughter of Balor and mother of Lug, iii. 25, 29, 86, 90, 207, 208
Ethnography, American, xi. 2, 347 [2]
—of Mexico and Central America, xi. 41-42, 352 [1]
—South American, xi. 254, 371 [2]
Etimmu, ghost, v. 162, 362
—limnu, v. 364

Etna, Arthur in, iii. 195
Etnar, ii. 285
Etowah Mound, birdlike deity from, x. 71
Etruscan mythology, i. 289
Etruscans, survivals of divinities and myths of, in Romagnola, i. 316, 317, 318, 319
Etuda, mother of Tammuz, v. 347
E-u, first woman in Karen myth, xii. 269
Eua, first land, ix. 19
Euboia, a Pelasgic centre, " sacred marriage " of Zeus and Hera celebrated at, i. 165
—adventures of Herakles in, i. 89
—Aias, son of Oileus, cast up on coast of, i. 135
—legends of, interwoven with Argive myth, i. 28
Euechoros (Ga-ur), v. 203
Euedorachos = Enmenduranna = Enoch, Greek transcription of Sumerian antediluvian king, v. 203, 205
Euhemerism in Eddic mythology, ii. 6, 12, 16, 23, 25, 26, 27, 28, 31–36, 58, 106, 114, 120, 135, 181, 205, 223, 281, 310, 329
—influence of, on Celtic mythology, iii. 18, 19, 24, 31, 35, 38, 39, 46, 49, 92, 94, 106
Euhemeristic method of interpreting myths, i. lviii
Eumaios, Odysseus visits, in guise of beggar, i. 138
Eumenides, i. 277
—Oidipous a suppliant at shrine of, i. 50
Eumolpos, a minister of rites of Demeter, i. 230
—legendary founder of Elusinian priesthood, of Thracian origin, i. 219
—possible origin of, i. 74
—purifies Herakles of Centaurs' blood, i. 88
—slain by Erechtheus, i. 68
—(" Sweet Singer "), son of Poseidon and Chione, i. 73, 88
Eunomia, ancient abstract deity, i. 282
—(" Order "), one of the Horai, i. 237
Eun[u?], Un[u?], early forms of On, xii. 31
Eunuchs, v. 147, 332, 333; vi. 143; viii. 174, 202
Euphrates, v. 157, 312, 313, 314, 316, 317, 318

Euphrates, Ea god of, v. 105
—horses sacrificed to, and sources worshipped, vii. 59
—Nhangs in the, vii. 90
—Tammuz cast upon, and sunk in sign of failing summer stream, v. 348
Euphrosyne, abstract divinity of state of mind, i. 282
—(" Good Cheer "), one of the Charites, i. 237
Eurmeiminanki, stage tower of Ezida, v. 159
Euro carried fire in its body, ix. 282
Europe and Asia, separation of, due to a flood, i. 19
——Peru, likeness of development of civilization in, at same period, xi. 219–220
—influence of Egyptian religion on, xii. 241
Europe appears in Boiotia as Io, i. 42
—daughter of Agenor, carried away by Zeus to Crete, i. 44
——(or of Phoinix), i. 60–61
—[Europa] and the bull, i. pl. xviii, opp. p. 60
—Idama form of, i. 42
—Kadmos consults Delphic oracle for help in finding, i. 179
—Minos explained as sun-god in conjunction with moon-goddess, i. 63
—search for, i. 44
—wife of Zeus, i. 157
Euros (south-east wind), son of Astraios and Eos, i. 265–266
Eurotas River worshipped in Sparta, i. 257
—son of Myles, i. 23
Euryale and Poseidon, reputed parents of Orion, i. 250
Eurydike and Orpheus theme, x. 50, 118–119, 236, 264, 302 [53]
—hangs herself on learning of death of Haimon and Antigone, i. 53
—soul of, passes into Hades, i. 146, 147
Eurykleia, nurse of Odysseus, recognizes him, i. 139
Eurymede (or Eurynome), wife of Glaukos, i. 39
Eurymedon, king of giants, born of blood of Ouranos, i. 9
Eurynome and Thetis, Hephaistos takes refuge with, i. 206
—daughter of Okeanos, i. 236

Eurynome ("Wide Rule"), wife of Zeus, i. 156

Euryphaëssa and Hyperion, parents of Helios, i. 242

Eurypylos, Herakles engages in battle with, at Kos, i. 91

Eurystheus, birth of, i. 78, 164
—flight of, i. 83 (fig. 3B)
—slain by Hyllos, i. 95
—son of Sthenelos, i. 76, 80, 81, 82, 84, 85, 87, 88, 89

Eurytion guards cattle of Geryoneus, i. 86

Eurytos, Herakles punishes faithlessness of, i. 94
—lord of Oichalia, i. 89
—refuses money from sale of Herakles, i. 90

Eusebius, v. 341

Euterpe ("Delight"), one of the Lyric Muses, i. 240

Euxine, Io crosses, i. 29

Evadne burned herself on husband's funeral pyre, i. 54

Evaki claps lid on pot in which sun is, xi. 306

Evander becomes an ally of Aeneas, i. 306
—dedicated Ara Maxima to Hercules who married his daughter, i. 303

Eve (Hawwā), v. 402 [16]

Evening and Morning Stars sometimes called Moon's wife, vii. 228
— -glory, story of, viii. 301, 385 [7]
—Star, Ishtar goddess of, vii. 38

Evenos River, Centaur Nessos ferryman at, i. 93
—uncle of Leda, father of Marpessa, i. pl. xi, opp. p. 24, 27

Evil, vi. 261, 262
—Aramazd less marked antagonist of, than Ahura Mazda, vii. 21
—aspect of dwarfs, ii. 268-269
—being destroyed creation, ix. 172-173
——Forest-master, iv. 467
—comes from Maruts, vi. 39
—creation of, vi. 74
—day, rules for, v. 153
—devils, incantations against, v. 106, 366-369
— -doers, place of, vi. 70-71
—eclipses and comets signs of, vii. 48
—enters life of men, i. 14
—existence of third place for, vi. 101

Evil eye, Balor possessed the, iii. 32
—is blue, vii. 392 [19]
—of woman cast on Conaire, iii. 76
—god of (contrasted with good), Černobog as, iii. 288
—influences, cock guards against, viii. 104
—magic, Freyja said to have introduced, to Æsir, ii. 120
—Power must be placated, xi. 260, 295
—Powers, head- and shoulder-souls wander about as, xi. 39
—son of Carman, tale of, iii. 35-36
—spirit, dragon in sense of, vii. 77, 391 [9]
—spirits, viii. 78; 211, 226, 349
——fire drives away, vii. 54-55
——seize souls, iv. 474
—star, vii. 48
—warding off of, viii. 105

Evils, how they befall mankind, xi. 261-268
—origins of, from Pandora's jar, i. 15

Evnissyen, half-brother of Bran, iii. 100, 101

Evolutionary type of creation-myths, ix. 5-18, 21, 23, 30, 166-167

Excalibur, sword, iii. 194, 197

Excavations near Santa Elena, xi. 206
—of Bingham, xi. 218

Exchange of possessions between sun-goddess and storm-god, viii. 226

Exchanges, series of, carried out by Hlakanyana, vii. 219-220

Excitation, drums as means of, iv. 291, 293, 295

Excrement, man made from, ix. 274, 293

Exemplars, four, viii. 136, 137

Exile as punishment for murder, i. 93
—of the Sons of Doel the Forgotten, iii. 149

Existence, finite, produced by great self-existent, viii. 56

Exogamy, sacred prostitution explained as modification of, vii. 382 [26]

Exorcism, iii. 294, 322; v. 161; vi. 241, 243, 247; xii. 199

Expiation, x. 282 [21]
—dish containing emblems of, xi. 56
—doves in ritual of, v. 34
—rituals, v. 88, 204, 235, 354, 356, 361

Exposure of children, i. 43, 48, 56, 118, 253, 280, 307; ii. 196, 263; v. 157, 234, 349; vii. 89; viii. 41; ix. 42, 208, 315 [6]

Exposure of dead, vii. 170, 403 [27]

"Expulsion and Return" formula, iii. 168, 202

Extinction, tale of three sons of, iii. 35–36

Eyafjord, temple of Frey at, ii. 117, 119

Eyatahentsik goddess of night, x. 295 [43]

Eye disease punishment for neglecting rites to idols, xi. 145

—evil, vii. 80, 392 [19]; xii. 205

— -illusions, ii. 93

—of Atumu, first beings created from plants and, iii. 379 [16]

——dead child kept in water till whole body (restoration to life) grows, vii. 289–290

——God's son torn out by squirrel, iv. 440

——Horus injured or put out by Sêth, xii. 117

——Ingcel, iii. 76

——Khepri, xii. 69, 70, 379 [14] [17]

——Odin pledged for drink from well, ii. 50, 167, 168

——Ogmios, ray from, suggests parallel to Cúchulainn, iii. 11

——Rê' aids him in destruction of mankind, xii. 74

——sun-god, myth of lost, xii. 85–91, 214

——sun in religious poetry, xii. 30

———Tefênet as, xii. 45

—pig in sun's, xii. 124–125

—Pölöznitza's, a blue flower of cornfields, iv. 247

—ruler of dead has only one, iv. 479–480

—Sekhmet as a solar, xii. 146–147

—solar, in watery depth, xii. 89 (figs. 80, 81)

—soul is fled when no reflexion is seen in pupil of, xi. 26

—stones, v. 334

—sun as an, xii. 25

—third stride of Viṣṇu described as an, vi. 29

—Thout(i) heals sun's, xii. 33

Eyebrows, bushy black, meeting above nose indicate a Mora, iii. 228

—of dead painted in blood from slain hen by Cheremiss, iv. 18

——Qat blackened, ix. 113

Eyebrows of Ymir, circle surrounding Midgard created from, iv. 372

Eyelash, certain plant called Balder's, ii. 129

Eyelids of Balor, iii. 32–33, 187

——Ispaddaden, iii. 187

—tree made to grow by lifting of, x. 136

Eyes, creation from, iv. 372

—disease of, tales of, v. 363

—given to restore sight, ix. 318 [5]

—gorgoneus, ii. 253

—Horus with, or before, Two, xii. 388 [28]

—in feet of Aigamuchab, vii. 243

—itching of, as portent, iv. 12

—nameless cosmic deity, like Argos, covered with, xii. 223

—of Adam made of the sun, iv. 371

——all except two who approached secret well burst, iii. 121

——Cannibal's victims, Bear and Raven feed on, x. 246

——celestial god, xii. 29, 30

——Heaven, sun and moon as, x. 257; xii. 38

——Indra, vi. pl. IV, opp. p. 34

——soul of shamans, Heaven picture seen by, iv. 403–404

——spider put out, vii. 132

——sun-god, men proceed from, xii. 30, 50

——sun, myth of two, xii. 87–88

—Oidipous put out his own, i. 50

—sun and moon as, ix. 37, 314 [98]

—two, as guardians of righteousness, xii. 418 [3]

Eyjafjord, ii. 75, 230

Eyjolf lamed by fall caused by Fylgjur of enemy's kinsfolk, ii. 234

Eylimi, king, ii. 251

"Eyrbyggja-saga," ii. 169, 191, 293, 300, 307

Eyrgjafa, giantess, ii. 153

Eywind settled Flatey-dale, ii. 203

Ezekiel, dirge of, on Tyre, v. 188

—says Tammuz wailings known in temple at Jerusalem, v. 336

—vision of, v. 160

Ezen-Ninazu ("Festival of Ninazu"), month name, v. 162

Ezida, temple of Nabû, v. 158, 159

—wailing in temple of, v. 342

F

Fa (Wu Wang), son of Ch'ang, viii. 41
Fa Hien, vi. 201
Fa Hsien, viii. 188
Fabulous beings, xii. 169
——Bushmen considered in light of purely, vii. 120
Face-painting, x. 80, 86, 252; xi. 115
——preceded tatuing, ix. 73
Faces, shapes of, correspond to shapes of four continents, iv. 347
Fachtna Fathach, king of Ulster, Nessa's lover, iii. 140
Facing the Sun, region of Himukai, viii. 211
Faebor beg-beoil cuimdiuir folt scenbgairit sceo uath, gibberish name of sorceress, iii. 70
Faflon probably represents Dionysos in modern Romagnola, i. 318–319
Fafnir, dragon, ii. 216, 267
——Sigurd obtained wisdom through tasting roasted heart of, iii. 166
"Fafnismal," ii. 220, 239, 244, 343
Fa-get, Nekhbet worshipped at, xii. 407 [71]
Faggot and Meleagros, tale of, i. 56
Faggots, bundle of, attached to dead, vi. 70
Fainting fit caused by sun, iv. 222
——soul leaves body in, and returns with consciousness, iii. 227
Fair roof and wheel, ii. 221
——Weather, conquest of Tlaik by sons of, x. 243
——Yellow son of, iii. 148
Fairs, Vu-murt may seek company of humans at, iv. 195
Fairies, ii. 204, 223, 226; iii. 256–260; vi. 228; vii. 80, 83, 391 [7], 393 [32]; viii. 103, 114–115; 256–280, 335, 342–348, 385 [7]; see also IMMORTALS (vol. viii).
——dart of, in Scottish folklore, vii. 393 [30]
——food and milk left out for, survival of sacrifice for corn and milk, iii. 47
——Insects as, viii. 335
——mischievous, Welsh Coranians still known as, iii. 108
——of the Toothpicks, tale of, viii. 355
——see PUKWUDJIES.
——serpent-, vii. 73

Fairies who befriend mortals when human aid fails, iii. 65
Fairy as wild boar, iii. 126
——Bloom Lady conceived as, viii. 234
——boy transformed into, at concert of gods, viii. 270
——fell in love with Lanval, iii. 85
— -folk(síde), iii. 38, 47, 49–53, 121
——god-father, Hippopotamus as, vii. 285–286
——music induces sleep, iii. 165
——of the Floating Veil (Rafu-sen), viii. 275, 348–349
——Palace of the Quicken-Trees, iii. 170
——race, Christianized tribes regarded old gods as a, iii. 45
— -rings, iii. 255, 259
——stories of New Empire employed Asiatic motifs, xii. 153, 398 [106]
— -tales of animals, viii. 104
——sources of, viii. 256–257
— -week, iii. 253
Faith, new, Oisin's paganism prevailed over, iii. 182–183
——souls in Jainism develop into, vi. 228
Faizābād, vi. 248
Fal, Stone of, iii. 41, 204
Falcon of Horus, xii. 101
— -men, legendary invaders, viii. 210
——or hawk, hieroglyph of, as class-sign for all male divinities, xii. 102
——Sopd(u) shown as, xii. 149
Falcon's plumage, ii. 22
Falerii, Minerva originally a goddess of the, i. 299
Falga, Isle of (Isle of Man) as Land of Promise, iii. 67, 151
Falias, Stone of Fal brought from, iii. 41
Fall of man, i. 18; v. 181, 184–187
——Karen myth of, xii. 269–270
——myth of eye of sun-god possibly connected with, xii. 383 [106]
——of Babylonian origin, v. 73
Fallen Sennins, viii. 276–277
"Falling into Trouble," poem, viii. 85–91
Falsehood, vi. 23, 24; viii. 263
Familiar spirit, help of, iii. 126
Familiars, animal, of witches, vii. 336, 338, 339

Familiars, corpses restored to life to become, vii. 338
—of shamans a class of personal spirits,
x. 79
Family and village name same among
Votiaks, iv. 116–117
— -beer, ceremony of, iv. 174
—god known in primitive Egypt, xii. 18
—Seide protector of, iv. 104, 106–107
Famine, v. 29; x. 200
—man destroyed by, v. 271, 272, 273
—Sun of, xi. 94
Famines, cannibalism at times of, viii.
155
Fan Ch'êng-ta, viii. 76
Fan, Tengu, viii. 287, 309
Fand, Cúchulainn's journey to, iii. 145
—daughter of Flidais, iii. 32
—goddess, iii. 36, 55, 56, 86–88, 145,
155, 194, 335 32
Fang sacrifices, viii. 61
Fang-chang, viii. 115
Fang-ming, emblematic cube, viii. 47
Fang shih, viii. 54, 194
Fangge, life of, bound up with tree, ii.
207
Fanggen, wood-elf, ii. 205, 206
Fanio successor of Faunus in modern
Romagnola, i. 317
Fantasy, imported, xi. 4–5
Fara: see SHURUPPAK, ETC.
Faraguvaol (zemi), tree-trunk with
power of wandering, xi. 25
Farbauti ("storm"), giant, father of
Loki; also peasant, ii. 139, 140, 148
Farīdūn: see THRAĒTAONA.
Farma-tyr, Odin as god of cargoes, ii.
42
Farm-yard, soul of, iv. 14
Farnese Bull, i. pl. xv, opp. p. 42
Faroe Island's ballad of Ouvin, Honir,
and Lokkji, ii. 151
Fast, xi. 245, 356 15
"Fastenings and bands" or "fetters,"
gods described as hopt ok bond mean-
ing, ii. 21
Fasting, iii. 88; vi. 196, 197; viii. 33, 94,
147
—after creation, ix. 182
—against, obtaining entrance to fortress
of warrior by, iii. 207
—and vigil, x. xvi, 58, 85, 86, 215, 241,
282 21
—at grave of Fergus mac Róich, iii. 211

Fasting during couvade, xi. 37
Fata morgana, iii. 268
Fatalism, x. 83
Fatalists, old Armenians, vii. 94
Fate, Fates:
Fate, arbiter of, viii. 51
—Book of, or Table, iv. 366, 408, 409,
410, 415
—deity of, iv. 357, 358, 392, 394–395
—Destinies decide, iii. 251
—different, for different deaths, xi. 28
—(Dzajaga) of heavens, iv. 392–393,
394, 395, 396
—each mortal has arbiter of, in Heaven,
iv. 395
— , Fates, ii. 47, 64, 73–74, 154, 174, 180,
238–247, 254, 255, 259, 278, 327, 331,
337; see also NORNS.
—foretold, iv. 419, 432
—genii of, iii. 249–252
—god of, iv. 358
—goddess of, iv. 260
———Ḥat-ḥôr in leopard-skin garment
assimilated to, xii. 368 13
—goddesses of, v. 19, 20, 21, 22, 23, 24,
383 97, 384 123, 398 101
—Heimdall's, ii. 154
—hymns to planet of, v. 25
—inevitable operation of, iii. 74
—Ishtar as goddess of, v. 21, 398 101
—Marduk possessed power to decree, v.
300
—Meskhenet goddess of, xii. 52, 137
—(Moira), Fates (Moirai), i. 5, 283–284
—names of, have Babylonian origin, v.
23
—of Adapa, v. 181
———child written down by Kaltes
mother, iv. 260
———dead, Mars called star of judgement
of, v. 147
———to be cast on Ishtar, v. 334
———Gilgamish, v. 243
———man, "net and trap" may refer
to, v. 263
———plants, v. 199
———Tagtug, v. 201
—or Providence connected with sky, iv.
392–393
—Pleiades constellation of, xii. 40, 376 78
—see also items s.v. MOIRA.
—Sekha(u)it as, xii. 52, 53
—Selqet analogous to goddess of, xii.
147

Fate, severing of cord of life by goddess of, v. 20, 398 [101]

—(Shay, the male principle), counterpart of birth-goddess, xii. 52

— -spirits, iii. 250

—tablets of, v. 40, 101–102, 130–131, 158, 160, 296, 297; vi. 264

—the goddess, v. 22

—tree of, xii. 36, 53

— -tree, Yggdrasil the, ii. 331

—Zeus as, i. 162–163

—Zeus's will is, i. 153

Fates, x. 117, 143–145, 249, 252–253, 254; xi. 51, 53, 97

—Ea creator of, v. 107

—for year determined in Marduk's temple, v. 157, 307, 320, 337

—foretold by lines on heated tortoise shell, viii. 100

—grant boon to Admetos at Apollo's request, i. 107

—of gods written for each year, v. 102, 307

——stones decreed by Ninurta, v. 122–124, 129

—seven, v. 22, 138

——identical with seven Ḥat-ḥôrs, xii. 40

——originally Pleiades, xii. 40, 376 [78]

—three, in Aischylos, limit dominion of Zeus, i. 162

Father, divine, Parjanya the, vi. 37

— -god, viii. 225

——Aramazd as, vii. 20, 381 [2] (ch. iii)

——birth of sun-goddess from left eye of, viii. 224

—Heaven, circle of, x. 80, 271 [6], 275 [11]

—human, not given to hero, vii. 223

—of Fathers, setting sun as, vi. 317

——Heaven, the sky-god, iv. 220

——home, sacrifice to, iv. 173, 174

——magic, Odin as, ii. 45

—Sun, x. 87–90

Fatherhood of god to man, v. 5, 7, 9, 10, 11, 12

Fathers, vi. 15, 21, 57, 67, 70, 71, 82, 91, 92, 101, 157, 159, 248

—serpent, of remarkable men, vii. 79, 80

—Yama ruler of, vi. 312

Fathir, Rig's host, ii. 153

Fat-Neck refused to fulfil his part of covenant, iii. 149

Fa-tsang, name of Amitābha when he became an ascetic, xii. 261

Fauna, Hercules said to be husband of, i. 303

—wife or sister of Faunus, i. 293

Fauns, Schrat akin to, ii. 205, 206

Faunus, i. 293, 306

—represented by Fanio in modern Romagnola, i. 317

Faustulus, a shepherd, found and brought up Romulus and Remus, i. 307

Faustus of Byzantium on survivals of cult of Anahit, vii. 26–27

Fawn, blood of, for purification, x. 21

—connected with south wind, x. 23

— -skin, emblem of Dionysos, i. 222

Fawns associated with fire, x. 233

—conveyed to heaven by stone, x. 233

Faxabrand, ii. 118

Fayûm, Neith worshipped in, xii. 142

—Pharoahs of Twelfth Dynasty built their residence in the, xii. 408 [99]

—Sobk ruled over country of the, xii. 148

Fear of Celts (based on myth) of a future cataclysm, iii. 12

——Heaven unnecessary, when it does not direct fate, iv. 397

Feast, beer, iv. 96

—before and at time of sowing, xii. 337

——flood, ix. 180, 181

——bull-, iii. 75

——cow's milk, iv. 259

—farewell, on anniversary of death, iv. 56

——to deceased at the end of forty days, iv. 49–53, 237

—Fifth Moon, viii. 86

—fifty years' common, iv. 68

—for dead, iii. 236, 238

——souls of dead, v. 122, 162

—funeral, ix. 118

—gods found food and drink for, v. 299

—harvest, viii. 225

—in honour of unknown dead who have no relatives, iv. 68–69

—Kekri-, iv. 64–66, 248

—memorial, iv. 68, 70

—New Year's, x. 57–59

—of Assumption, vii. 382 [11]

——Bricriu, iii. 134, 145–146

——dead, Lithuanian autumnal, iii. 352 [7]

Feast of full moon of Babylonian calendar, v. 152
——Man-flaying, xi. 76
——mourning for Ba'alti, v. 339–340
——Pekko, iv. 244–245, 246
——Pergrubrius, iii. 356 [14]
——St. Iliya's Day, iii. 295
——St. John the Baptist, iii. 313
——Tapana, xi. 266
——Transfiguration, vii. 22
——Winding Stream, viii. 352
—planting-, ix. 212–213
—prepared by Luk, ix. 260
—to Utumö, iv. 69
Feasting on sacrifice to Jupiter by Christian priests, ii. 68
Feasts at Whitsuntide, iii. 306, 311–312
—bears and bear, iv. 83–98
—dates of, xii. 90–91, 113, 195
—funeral, ii. 311; iv. 39–40, 44–59
—in honour of dead, ii. 310, 311
—memorial, and kuala ceremonies similar, iv. 134
——general, iv. 60–71
——special, iv. 37–59
——to dead who cause illness, iv. 58, 133
—of first-fruits, vii. pl. xxiii, opp. p. 238
——long-deceased and newly deceased celebrated together, iv. 44
—sacrificial, ii. 162, 226; iv. 263–264
—see also items s.v. Festivals.
—taper, iv. 60
—to Jengk-tongk, iv. 193
Feather-bearing deities present at judgement of Osiris, xii. 101
—crowns, xii. 62, 131
— -dress of Freyja or Frigg, ii. 22, 83, 88, 120, 121, 126, 140, 141, 149, 174, 179
——Swan-maidens, ii. 258, 259, 260, 261
——see Swan-maiden parallels in Oceanic mythology.
—jackal (?) with a, xii. 393 (fig. 226)
—Khenset wears, xii. 135
—magic, cured Rustam, vi. 290
—Ma'et wears, xii. 100, 135
—of magic bird used in conjuring, vi. 289–290, 331
—patterns of dress of deities, xii. 212
—rope, x. 220
— -snake, green, xi. 57

Feather supposed to symbolize conquest of Sêth by Horus, xii. 362 [8]
—symbolism, x. 109, 190, 232, 306 [60]
—Woman, x. 95, 96
Feathers, viii. 229, 287; xi. 59, 60, 67, 68, 313, 336
—Amon wears, xii. 129
—'Anezti wears, xii. 130
—Antaeus wears, xii. 130
—exchanged between fowl and parrot, vii. 286
—flint, x. 291 [38]
—gods with two, at Judgement, xii. 101
—head, turn into bird, vii. 210
—Horus with two, xii. 388 [28]
—house built of, xi. 264–265
——haunted by, x. 262, 306 [60]
—in open lotus flower emblem of Nefertêm, xii. 140, 141
—iron, iv. 495, 519
—life preserving, x. 164
—magic, vi. 290, 331; x. 133
—Mîn wears, xii. 138, 219
—Mont̬(u) wears, xii. 139
—Nefer-têm wears, xii. 140
—ostrich, xii. 47, 99, 100, 386 [22]
—pall of, to cover corpse, xi. 265
—replace brains in restoration to life of Ready-to-Give, x. 306 [60]
—robe of, property of all celestial maidens, viii. 260
—Shu with four, xii. 144, 369 (fig. 222)
—Sopd(u) wears, xii. 149
—tale of Robe of, viii. 257–260
—Tatunen wears, xii. 150
—Tekhi wears, xii. 150
—two, symbol of Amon, xii. 129
—white, symbol of breath of life, x. 59, 92
Febris, i. 296
February and January, Finnish tale concerning, iv. 226
—fire-festivals in, vii. 33–34
—moon, iv. 226
—thirteenth, festival on, vii. 58, 75
Fecundity, Anāhita goddess of, vii. 25, 28
Fedelm the prophetess, iii. 152, 153
Feeding of fire at mealtime, iv. 452, 454, 455
—soul, iv. 478
" Feelers " symbol of Meskhenet, xii. 372 [52]
Fées, ii. 204, 206, 207, 222, 242, 245

Fées of mediaeval French, side resemble, iii. 49, 133
—prophesied at Arthur's birth, iii. 187
Feet, choosing husband by seeing, ii. 103, 104
—loss of, in Mexican pantheon, xi. 61
—rapid, of servants of Guinevere, iii. 190
—skin sometimes removed from mummy's, xii. 418 22
—turned backwards, iv. 183; xi. 300, 327
——churel may be recognized by, vi. 248
Fe-fo-fum episode of English folklore occurs in American Indian, x. 281 19
Fei Ch'ang-fang, viii. 131–132
Fei, Lady, viii. 82
Féinn, iii. 32, 56, 66, 125, 126, 128, 160–183, 209–210, 212
—and Tuatha Dé Danann, match of, iii. 54
—Diarmaid's form given to each of nine, iii. 176
—possessed some of weapons of Manannan, iii. 65
Female, Absolute conceived as, in the " Tantras," vi. 231–232
—consort and male divinity, tendency to divide deities into, xii. 365 20
—deity, Sun as, v. 4
—demons, v. 357
—divinities of Egypt, xii. 155
—element plays part in Tibetan mythology, vi. 202, 217–219
—form, daemons in, xi. 141
—line, succession through, iii. 25
— -male (mother-father) deity, v. 44, 50, 381 58
—personifications, xii. 46, 67, 378 102
——of the sun, xii. 29–30
— -Who-Invites, viii. 222–224
Femen, síd of, iii. 91
Fên-chow, viii. 124
— -yang, viii. 96
—Yen Chien Wên Chi, viii. 14
Fence about Iud, iv. 143–144
Fêng, capital city of Wên Wang, viii. 41–42
—Hsiang, finger-bone of Buddha in temple at, viii. 200
— -huang, phoenix, viii. 21, 98
—I, god of waters, viii. 90
—Po (Fêng Shih), wind-god, viii. 73

Fêng Shan ceremony, viii. 199
—Shên Yen I, viii. 66, 80, 112
—Shih, viii. 73
—Shui, popular name of geomancy, viii. 140, 141
—Su Chi, viii. 131
—T'ung, viii. 78, 105
— -yang, appearance of phoenix at grave of father of Hung Wu at, viii. 100
——Kuo Tzŭ-i ennobled as Prince of, viii. 96, 179
Fenja, giantess, ii. 114, 282–283
Fenris-wolf, ii. pl. v, opp. p. 22, 99, 100, pl. xiii, opp. p. 106, 143, 144, 145, 159, pl. xxi, opp. p. 168, 174, 199, 216, 279, 280, 313, 314, 328, 339, 340, 341, 342, 346; vi. 302; x. 121
Fensalir, dwelling of Frigg, ii. 129, 174, 175, 183
Fer Fídail, Manannan's slaying of, iii. 72
——son of Eogabal, iii. 89
Fercertne, prophecy of, ii. 342
Ferchess, Eogabal slain by, iii. 73
Ferdia, opponent of Cúchulainn, iii. 65, 134, 140, 153, 154
Ferdiad, iii. 144
Feretrius, Fulgur (" Lightning "), Fulmen (" Thunderbolt "), epithets of Iuppiter, i. 290
Fergna, king of síd of Nento-fo-hiuscne, iii. 58
Fergne, leech, iii. 78
Fergunna, mountain of oaks, ii. 194
Fergus mac Róich, hero of the Cúchulainn cycle, iii. 128, 134, 136, 140, 141, 144, 152, 210
—True-lips, iii. 163
Feridun (Hruden, Thraētaona) bound Aždahak, vii. 98
Feronia, functions of, in modern Romagnola, i. 319
Ferry of souls of dead to " Brittia," iii. 16
—to realm of Osiris, situation of, xii. 176
Ferryman, Kipanawazi (kind of hare) ferries souls over a river, vii. 419 4
—of dead, xii. 58 (fig. 59), 176, 187
——Odin once acted as, ii. 45, 72–73
——Underworld, xii. 394 64
—Pāurva is, vi. 365 4
—Phaon the, between Chios and Lesbos, i. 200

Fertility, ii. 102–103, 104, 109, 115, 116,
122, 123, 125, 126, 158, 181–182, 195,
198; xi. 24, 34, 79, 286, 288, 292, 350 [9]
—cauldron symbol of, iii. 112
—chief function of Rivers, i. 256–257
—connexion of Demeter with, i. 198,
226–227, 331 [2] [3] (ch. x)
——Dionysos with, i. 198
——Hephaistos with, i. 208
——Hermes with, i. 195
——Hyades with, i. 249
——Poseidon with, i. 213
——Satyrs and Silenoi with, i. 268
——Thesmophoria with, i. 331 [3]
(ch. x)
—deities, vii. 48, 379 [1] (ch. i)
—Dionysos as god of, in Phrygia, i. 216
—fires to prevent disease and to secure,
vii. 388 [11]
—fish and tortoise symbols of, xi. 286
—formulae for restoring fields to, ii.
195
—Frey god of, ii. 114–115, 126, 158, 218
—functions of some divinities as controllers of, iii. 47
— -god, Aramazd as, vii. 21, 28
——Dagda probably, iii. 40
——Hermes as, i. 195
— -goddess, Aphrodite as, i. 198, 329 [3]
(ch. vi)
— -goddesses apt to possess a double
character, iii. 98
— -gods, v. 179
—magic, vi. 231
—of land, preservation of, by rituals,
iii. 204
——souls interested in, vii. 22
——lands connected with lives of rulers,
v. 326, 327
——nature, Dionysos represented, vii.
12–13
—Priapus god of, iii. 353 [25]
—rite, bathing as a, i. 257
——butter used in, iv. 416
—rites, i. 172; vii. 13, 75, 379 [4]
——human heart in, x. 203
——trees, branches, and twigs in, ii. 204
—sacrifice of virgin to Morning Star
for, x. 76, 94, 286 [29], 306 [58]; xi. 79
—Śiva as god of, vi. 119
—suggestion of Fomorians being pre-
Celtic gods of, iii. 33
—symbols of, x. 188, 290 [35], 293 [40],
300 [50]

Fertility, thunder storm regarded as
beneficent aspect of, ii. 75
—was Branwen a goddess of?, iii. 104
—Zeus god of, i. 160
Fertilization, magic, of grain, by sacrifice
of a virgin, x. 76, 94, 286 [29]; xi. 225;
see also MORNING STAR, SACRIFICE TO.
Ferzol, sculpture of sun-god at, v. 36
Festa calendarum, iii. 307
Festival after couvade, xi. 38
—Akitu, v. 156, 315, 411 [44]
—and feast to Anahit, vii. 28–29
—April, on banks of Havola, iii. 306
—Armenian New Year's, vii. 21–23
—autumn, iii. 282
—baptismal, xi. 142
—boy's doll, viii. 349–350
—Bulgarian, in honour of deceased an-
cestors, iii. 237
—Busk, x. 58
—Carib, xi. 38
—Celtic (Lugnasad), iii. 99, 138
—Chautury, iii. 235–236
—Dasahra, vi. 239
—dragon, viii. 86
—for Gerovit, iii. 306, 356 [14]
——increasing (sheep), iv. 259–260
——Magna Mater, i. 304
——Stopan, iii. 238
—Genesia, i. 273
—harvest, iii. 235–236, 237
—Hyakinthia, i. 24
—(January), Lenaia, i. 221
—July ("marriage of virgins"), at
Kēngtūng, xii. 334–335
—Knot of the Years, xi. 101
—Kupalo, iii. 313–314
—Lapp Christmas, iv. 67
—Lugnasad, iii. 99, 138
—medicine, xi. 137
—mer, iv. 265
—Mithrakana, vii. 34
—New Year's, for Bacabs, xi. 144
—Nga-hlut Pwé, xii. 298
—nine years', songs at, ii. 115
—of Anu, v. 156
——Cronia, v. 18
——Kikēllia, v. 18
——mourning death of vegetation, i.
244
——Nanâ-Ishtar, v. 156
——Ninazu, v. 162
——Pamelia, xii. 396 [93]
——Roses: see VARTAVAR, ETC.

Festival of Svantovit in Arkona, iii. 305, pl. XXXII, opp. p. 280, 281–282
——Ta-ūz, v. 336
——Thesmophoria, i. 331 [8] (ch. x)
——Varuṇa, vi. 85
——weeping women, v. 336
——Yule, evil powers ascendant in, ii. 96, 109, 191, 233
——Zatik (Jewish Passover), vii. 40
—on Peritios, v. 52
—Panathenaïc, i. 68
—Pax, xi. 138
—ploughing, viii. 63–64; xii. 328–332
—potlatch, x. 239
—Rek Na, xii. 329–330
—Saturnalia, i. 292
—spring, connexion of Wa with, xii. 281
——of Marduk, v. 18, 156
——to follow the ice a, iv. 214–215
—star, viii. 235–237, pl. x, opp. p. 236
—summer, iii. 306
—sun-dance, x. 89
—swing, i. 217; xii. 277, 324–326
—Tana-bata, viii. 235, 369, 372–373
—Thagyan, xii. 323
—throwing water at Persian New Year's, vii. 60
—to earth-goddess, xi. 33–34
—Vartavar: see VARTAVAR, ETC.
—water, vii. 60–61; xii. 298–300, 324, 333
—Yurupari, xi. 293–294
Festivals, ii. 38, 102, 103, 115, 121, 158, 191, 195, 198, 202; iii. 36, 99, 145–146, 147, 157, 238; 306, 311, 313, 356 [14]; vii. 13, 28–29, 33–34, 57–58, 59–61, 75, 96, 388 [10], 397 [4]; viii. 235–237, 286, 301, 305, 338, 348, pls. XLI–XLIV, opp. p. 348, 353; x. XX, 57–59, 89–90, 92–93, 97, 123, 170, 184, 191, 193, 194, 195, 197, 215, 239, 246, 272 [6], 292 [39], 300 [50], 307 [61]; xi. 33–34, pl. IV, opp. p. 34, 38, 52, 72, 75, 76, 78, 99, 101, 134, 135, 137, 138, 142, 144, 145, 182, 223, 266, 293–294, 307, 322, 323, 355 [15]–356; xii. 189, 194–195, 323, 419 [13]; see also DANCES, CEREMONIAL.
—Akitu or Zagmuk, v. 315, 411 [44]; see also ZAGMUK, ETC. (vols. v, vii).
—and cult, iii. 305–314
——feasts, xii. 272, 277, 281, 298–300,
pl. x, opp. p. 302, 310, pl. XI, opp. p. 310, 319, 322–326, 328–357
Festivals and plants, New Year's days', viii. 348
—autumn, xii. 336
—celebrating Virgin conception, v. 18
—fire-, vii. 33–34, 57–58
—first toast drunk at, ii. 60
—for dead, iii. 235; see also DEAD, FEASTS, ETC.
——Rusalky and Vily, iii. 257
—gods instituted, iii. 138
—harvest, Lityerses connected with, i. 253–254
—Indo-Chinese, xii. 323–338
—May Day, iii. 108–109
—mer-, iv. 262, 263, 265, 267, 269, 272
—New Year's, iv. 227, 248; v. 52, 148, 153, 156, 160, 307, 309, 315–325, 337; vii. 21–23, 60; xi. 144; xii. 76; 298–300, 324, 341, 381 [43]; see also FESTIVALS AND FEASTS.
—of Dionysos, i. 217, 221–222
——Indo-Chinese, xii. 323–338
——Kikēllia and Cronia, v. 18
——resurrection of Melqart and Marduk, v. 52
—on which women anointed images, ii. 138
—seed, iv. 241–242
—sixth and fifteenth days of each month as, xii. 384 [115]
—spring, iv. 242; 402; v. 18; xii. 323, 332, 333, 335
—summer, xii. 334
—water, iv. 242; vii. 60; xii. 272, 298
"Féth Fiada" ("Deer's Cry"), Manannan's spell, iii. 55, 65, 208
Fetish-construction, West African, making of wooden zemis analogous to, xi. 25
Fetishes, vi. 211, 239, 240; vii. 178, 279, 344–345, 407 [7], 421 [20]; x. 189, 191, 216, 270 [4], 284 [27], 290 [35]; xi. 23, 26, 27, 179, 224, 275; xii. 15; 340
Fetishism, vi. 61
—of Central Africa, Pietschmann regarded beginnings of Egyptian religion as parallel with, xii. 10, 11–12
Fetishistic form, "medicine" in some, x. 269 [4], 270
Fetters, unloosening of, ii. 252, 253, 298
Feuds among gods, vi. 19–20
Fever from meeting invisible elves, ii. 225

Fever demon, vi. 157
Feyness, ii. 45
Ffergll (Vergil), books of, iii. 109
Fiacha, Ulster hero, iii. 143, 152
Fiachna and Loegaire, tale of, iii. 37–38
—Dub (" the Black "), wife of, bore a daughter Dubh Lacha, iii. 63
—Manannan appeared as, to Fiachna's wife, iii. 56, 63
—tales of, iii. 62–64
—worm spoke to, iii. 58
Fiadr-hamr: see FEATHER-DRESS.
Fianna, troops, iii. 160, 161, 162
Fidga, Plain of, iii. 87
Field-god, songs of, viii. 370–372
— -goddess, xii. 66, 67 (fig. 74)
— -gods, Cheremiss sacrifice to, iv. pl. XXX, opp. p. 242
—Lord of the, vi. 60
—mother, iv. 239, 240, 243
—of Sacrifices (sky), xii. 36, 416 12
— -rites as associated with Demeter, i. 226, 227
Fields, divine, xii. 176
—formulae for restoring fertility to, ii. 195
—genii of, vii. 73–74
—Holy Water sprinkled on, to expel spirits, ii. 231
—of the Blessed, magic plant from, iii. 131
—tutelary spirits ascribed to, xii. 15–16
Fifteenth and sixth day of each month " fill the sacred eye " of sun, xii. 90–91, 238
Fifth Moon Feast, viii. 86
Fifty years' common feast, iv. 68
Fight between two groups of dead, ii. 308
—of Thor and Hrungnir, ii. 81–82
—till doom for Creidylad, iii. 108
Fighting of dead warriors, ii. 316
— -shaman animals, iv. 503, 507
—the waves with weapons at high tide, Muireartach story may be romantic treatment of, iii. 171
Fights with barrow-wight, ii. 308, 309
Figol the Druid, iii. 30
Figure-head on ship, law against approaching land with, ii. 229
File, man of letters, iii. 92
Fillet of Amon, xii. 129
—transferred from goat's to man's head, v. 356

Filth inside man, iv. 374–377
Fimafeng slain by Loki, ii. 142, 172
Fimbul-tyr, rune, ii. 345
— -winter, ii. 168
Fimmilene, ii. pl. XII, opp. p. 98
Fin mac Cumhal, name of Fionn, iii. 167
Findabair, daughter of Ailill, iii. 130–131, 147, 154
Findbennach (" White-Horn "), Medb's cow bore, iii. 58, 69, 152, 154
Findchoém, mother of Conall Cernach, iii. 150, 158
Findgoll and Lug advise Nechtan to singe kine to trick Bres, iii. 26
Findias, Nuada's sword came from, iii. 41
Finding lost things by means of magic mirror, iv. 419
Fines, iii. 55, 81, 165, 173, 176
Finger, biting of, v. 333
— -cutters, Albanian, vii. 370–371
— -marks, three, made on beasts at memorial feasts to get protection from dead, iv. 38; see also BREAD, SACRIFICIAL.
— -nail boat, iv. 75
— -nails, parings of, desecrate fire, vii. 54
——of deceased gathered by slain hen in afterworld, iv. 18
—people came from hole in, vii. 236
Fingers and toes, fire concealed in, ix. 47, 49, 316 33
—of Vu-murt stones resembling thunder-bolts, iv. 195
Finnabair and Riangabair, castle of, iii. 149–150
—corresponds to Welsh Gwenhwyfar (Guinevere), iii. 193
Finnéces, salmon of knowledge caught by, iii. 166, 167, 168
Finno-Ugrians, contacts of, with Turco-Tatars, iv. xviii
Finns, Baltic, iv. xv, xvi, xviii–xix
——Teutonic influence upon, iv. xviii–xix
—certain saints have replaced ancient gods among, iv. xix
Finntain, all Cessair's company perished except, iii. 206
Finuweigh, creator-god, ix. 175
Fionn, iii. 15, 33, 38, 56, 64, 66, 67, 74, 116, 117, 125, 126, 128, 131, 139, 160–183, 185, 195, 198, 205, 210, 212

Fionn and giant daughter of king of Maidens' Land, story of, iii. 13
—cycle relatively unaffected by alien elements, iii. 18
—demanded head of Diarmaid or berries of immortality as fine, iii. 55
—King Mongan regarded as rebirth of, iii. 62, 112
Fionnghula, iii. 60
Fir, branches of, represent Votiak family god, iv. 129
—sacrifice animal must be killed on twigs of, iv. 161
—striking with, at cemetery gates, iv. 24
— -tree, iv. 152, 158, 179, 220; 339, 349
——offerings to forest-spirits under, iv. 179–180
——symbolizes ritual of annual death and rebirth of god of wild vegetation, i. 275
Fir Dea ("Men of the God") suggested earlier name of Tuatha Dé Danann, iii. 39
— -Donnann, Nemedian survivors who returned to Ireland, iii. 23, 161
—síde, iii. 49
Firbolgs, ii. 30
—Nemedian survivors who returned to Ireland, iii. 23, 24, 35, 137, 161
Fire, iv. 449–456; vi. 233; vii. 44, 59, 60, 61; x. 58, 88, 98, 100, 110, 140, 179, 186, 221, 223, 230–233, 256, 299 [49]
—about barrows, ii. 308
——place of confinement of Brynhild, ii. 251
—Agni god of, vii. 43, 44
—Āhavanīya, vi. 91
— -altar and -temple, vi. pl. xxxiv, opp. p. 272
—among Ostiaks, may not be allowed to go out on death, iv. 23
—an eye of Śiva, vi. 110–111
—and air, sacrifice thrown into, for Solbon, iv. 432
——heat sources of life and its destruction, ii. 339–341
——water are children of octopus, ix. 17
—anger of, causes skin disease, iv. 235
—art of making, xi. 93
—as cause and cure of disease, ii. 202; iv. 451, 453; vii. 55

Fire as divine weapon of first man, vi. 295
——gift of the sea, x. 256
——means of transmission of offerings, iv. 142, 154
——such, not Armenian main deity, vii. 56
—Asha spirit of, vi. 260
—associated with sun, vii. 44, 49
—at end of world foretold, iv. 367–368
——spring festivals, iv. 402
——time of creation of man ordered to return to its source on death, iv. 372
—Atharvan associated with production of, vi. 64
—birds incarnation of, vi. 291
—birth of gods of, fatal to Izanami, viii. 223
—blood and portion of flesh of offering thrown into, iv. 148, 154
—bound in bowels of red salmon, iv. 238
—Branwen's child thrown into, iii. 101
—breath tabu in connexion with, iii. 11
— -bringer of Moody, quotation from, i. 255
—brought from Heaven by Spider, vii. 321
——old to new home, iv. 236
——village to light sacrificial fire, iv. 154, 267
—built within sea-monster, ix. 69
—burst from girl's body in Maruwa tale, vii. 208
—came upon altars at noon, xi. 138
—captive in the stone Gak Chog, xi. 180
—cattle driven through, in time of cattle-plague, ii. 202
—caused by red stone from mystic chest, iv. 441
—claimed by Argives to have been discovered by Phoroneus, i. 16
—coming of, to earth, vi. 47, 104
—Conaire broke tabus to avoid, iii. 76
—cosmic, Agni represents, and is fire in man, vi. 135, 136
—could not destroy great shaman, iv. 283
— -cult, ii. 201–202; vi. 44, 64, 233–234
——of Finno-Ugric peoples, Iranian influence on, iv. 237
—Demeter bathes Demophon in, i. 228
— -demon, Loki a, ii. 148

Fire derived from the ocean or from ghosts, x. 301 [51]
—destroyed giants for sin of sodomy, xi. 205–206
—divine, as souls of men, i. 14
— -dragon, x. 35, 294 [42]
——who presents magic sword, viii. 123
—dragon-slaying associated with, vii. 45
—dragons cast into, v. 315, 316, 320
— -drill, ii. 148
——kinds of wood to be used for, vi. 239
——parent of flame, x. 223, 224
—(ēsh), v. 74
—established on Mt. Asnavand, vi. 306, 337
—feeding of, at mealtime, iv. 452, 454, 455
— -festivals, vii. 33–34
—Fire-gods, iv. 235–238
———in mer sacrifice, iv. 271–281
—(Fire-Lapp), shaman may fly in form of, iv. 286–287
—first gift of Tohil, xi. 166
—flood, and transformation, xi. 311–315
—food and drink sacrificed in, iv. 130, 139; see also BLOOD, SACRIFICIAL, ETC.
—Gārhapatya, vi. 91
— -giants, ii. 279–280, 344
—gift of, to Chipiapoos, x. 41
—giving no heat, ii. 179
— -god, Marduk described as a, v. 157
——Seven gods (addressed as one), identified with, v. 147
—god of, viii. 76–77; xi. 54, 74
———devours army of Sahadeva, vi. 136
— -gods, v. 100
—gold as Ægir's, ii. 172
—Greeks believed all natural, originally divine, i. 14
—Head passed through wall of, x. 104
—hearth of universe, created, xi. 92
—hearth-, one of the lesser powers, x. 81
—heavenly, brought down by Spider and others, vii. 135
—Hephaistos held to be god of, i. 205, 206, 207, 208
—house of, vii. 56
—importance of, in family life, iii. 298
—impure, vii. 54
—in barrows, ii. 308
———primordial ocean, iv. 328, 329, 330

Fire in tent at shaman ceremonies, iv. 510
—Inue at times appear in form of, x. 5
—invented by infant Hermes, i. 192
———Laki Oi, ix. 184
—Irish story of first camp-, iii. 136–137
—Jinns created from, v. 352, 354
—jumping over, iii. 314; iv. 24, 63, 83, 237; see also FIRE, LEAPING, ETC.
—Keresāspa's sin against, vi. 327, 328
—knowledge of, vii. 134, 137, 142, 155
—lake of, xii. 179 (fig. 186)
—leaping or casting things across, vii. 58, 60
—Loki subterranean, ii. 145
—luminous, on graves, vii. 336
—magic shower of, iii. 32
—making of, xii. 200
—man created partly from, iv. 371
——half of, iv. 447
—Manabush the, x. 40
—men punished for accepting, i. 14
—Mihr god of, vii. 33, 34
—mother, medium of keremet sacrifice, iv. 154
— -myths, Kuhn's comments on, vii. 387 [1]
——Norwegian tale of Agne and King Dag an echo of, vii. 365
—myths of, vi. 263, 264, 265, 266, 267, 283, 284–286, 299, 301, 303, 306; vii. 44–45, 46
—name of Loki connected with, ii. 147–148, 149
—necklace of Freyja connected with, ii. 124
—new, vii. 388 [11]; x. 58, 59, 301 [51]
——at death in home, vii. 95
——kindling of, xi. 101, 115, 118, 141
—obtained from owner's body, ix. 47, 49, 115, 283
—Odin tortured by, ii. 9, 62, 156, 175
—Odin's, sword is, ii. 59
—of bracken, Bres caused kine of Munster to pass through, iii. 26
——moon and sun, vii. 51, 52
——sacrifice lit at dawn, Uṣas associated with Agni as, vi. 32
——Surt will destroy world, ii. 159, 168, 279–280, 339, 341, 343, 346
—one of the elements, viii. 29, 142
—or bright light marks presence of beautiful woman, ix. 222, 337 [26]
——light at child-birth, vii. 394 [50]

Fire, origin of, iii. 136–137; ix. 112, 114–117, 182–185, 254–256, 278, 281–285, 286
——in Finnish poem, iv. 343, 445, 450
——mankind from, ix. 252
—passing through, v. 52
——of Sītā, vi. 128
— -people, x. 7, 28, 274 [9]
—perpetual, in temple of Sul, iii. 11
——maintained at sacred oak, iii. pl. XXXVII, opp. p. 304
——of oak, before statue of Perun, iii. 354
—placed in waters by Varuṇa, vi. 22
—porcupine inventor of, iv. 421
— -powers, x. 99
—priests walk through, at offering, vi. 232–233
— -producers, viii. 26
—Prometheus god of, i. 324 [7]
—pursuit by, ix. 293
—quenched by magic song, ii. 46, 47
— -quest of Maui, ix. 43, 47–51
—rain of, xi. 72, 94
——conjured against Firbolgs, iii. 24, 30
—red bird born from, viii. 43
— -rite, two snakes cut to pieces in felling of tree for, vi. 226
— -ritual in land claims, ii. 201
—Rudra the, in its dread form, vi. 83
—sacred, vii. 15, 54–58, 387 [1 2]; x. 47, 56–57, 194
——in the sacrificial ritual, vi. 76
——of Nīla, tended by his daughter, vi. 136
——St. Brigit at Kildare, iii. 11
— -sacrifice by primeval pair, vi. 297
—sacrificial, ii. 83; iv. 131, 132, 237, 280
——entering the, xi. 88–89, 90
——in India, vi. 284
——must be lighted even if only bread sacrificed, iv. 131
— -serpent (meteor), living, as well as dead, souls may fly about as, iv. 10
—shaman-bird becomes flame of, iv. 495
—shows establishment of Aryan civilization, vi. 92
—singing, on King of Mountains, x. 63
—signs of, iv. 170
—sister and Spring brother, vii. 56, 57, 58

Fire snake, xi. pl. VII, opp. p. 60, pl. xiv, opp. p. 100
——as source of, ix. 116, 121
—snapped up by bush-fowl, therefore his red wattle, xi. 270
— -soul, iv. 13, 14, 236
—Spider mistakes sun for, vii. 325
—spirit of forest, xi. 182
— -spirits destroying earth's verdure conquered by dew, x. 24
—spirits which do not burn in, viii. 28
— -stick (or twig) stuck in ground as walking-stick for dead, iv. 56
— -sticks, vi. 41, 233
— -stone man, x. 41, 44
—sun created from, iv. 421
—(sun), daily lighting of, for world, ix. 275
—supernatural, vi. 337, 338
—surrounding the ambrosia extinguished by Garuḍa, vi. 139
—Svarožič god of, iii. 298
— -temple, x. [a temple of fire, 46] 56–57
— -temples, vi. 284, pl. XXXV, opp. p. 284
—terrestrial, Hephaistos principally concerned with, i. 207
—theft of, x. xvii, xxiii, 46–47, 56, 61, 104, 134, 140, 162–163, 223, 224, 230, 231, 256, 257, 293 [40], 301 [51]; xi. 95, 313
——by Prometheus from Zeus, i. 13
—thrown after followers of hearse, iv. 23
—to consume body of Kāśyapa when hill miraculously opens, vi. 212
——guide souls of dead, x. 43
—Underworld people of Polynesia unacquainted with use of, vii. 137
—undying, on altars of solar god, xi. 247
—used in creation of Adam, iv. 371
—uraeus asp symbol of, xii. 26, 29
—Vahagn a god of, vii. 34, 37, 44, 46
—(Vulcan), worshipped by Germans, ii. 197
—water, and salt as elements in old Germanic cosmogonic myth, ii. 326
—will consume hall of Ægir, ii. 144
—wine poured into, at festival, iii. 238
—within ghost's gate, vii. 184
— -world, ii. 279
—worship of, iii. 273

Fire-worship, possible origin of use of barəsman in, vii. 386 [13]
— -worshippers, vi. 260, 284–285
Fireplace, abode of gods under, or on hearth of, iv. 159, 164, 236
—bestowed on woman, x. 110
—first ray of sun over, x. 88
—stone over, entrance to lower world, x. 137
Firesteel used against fish-god, iv. 191–192
Fires as symbol of life of Gisli, ii. 236
—at Beltane, iii. 26
—built by birds destroyed giants, x. 134
—enumeration of, vi. 285, 306
—Kekri-, iv. 66
—made by wandering spirits may be stolen and thief then becomes rich, iv. 479
—of straw, coffin carried between two, to cemetery, iv. 24
—three, vi. 91; 306
—to prevent disease and to secure fertility, vii. 388 [11]
First-born, Erinyes defenders of rights of, i. 277
——sacrificed in fire, v. 52
— -fruits, x. 20, 22, 58
——feasts of, vii. pl. xxiii, opp. p. 238
——must be garnered and offered to Nāts before reaping begins, xii. 338
——of harvest dedicated to Demeter, i. 226–227
——offering of, to tree, iv. 26, 174
——sacrifices of, i. 56
—man, iv. 351–352, 355–356, 358, 359, 366; x. 160, 162
—people, x. 217, 223, 225–230
——degeneration of, xii. 265
——emergence of, xi. 30, 31
Fish, v. 83, 84, 85; viii. 38, 43, 73; xi. 29, 234, 235, 288–289, 290
—Andvari took form of, ii. 141, 210
—blind, as soul, iv. 508
—(Brahmā or Viṣṇu) saves Manu from the deluge, vi. 75, 99, 124, 147
—devil in, vii. 244
—earth-supporting, iv. 310–311, 328
—eating of, prohibited, xii. 169
—flying, men shot by sea-spirit with, ix. 135
— -god, Dagon described as, v. 83, 84
——Seide stone sometimes, iv. 191
—guardian spirit in form of, iv. 15

Fish-hawk and pheasant, tale of, ix. 290
— -hook, lost, viii. 265–266
——by Parpara, tale of, ix. 156, 328 [6]
—in cannibal tale, ix. 133–134
—incarnation, older attribution of, to Brahmā or Prajāpati, vi. 170
—Loki as, ii. 144, 146, pl. vi, opp. p. 32
— -man, v. 83–86, 103, 106, 282, 283, 395 [21]
—miraculous, bearing texts of Koran on its sides, vii. 348
— -net invented by Loki, ii. 146
—ocean adored in form of a, xi. 223
—of Maui, ix. 43
—(or spirit possessing such), devouring mankind, vii. 244
—parent of all other fish, vii. 144
—people transformed into, xi. 93, 94
— -ram, v. 105, 106, 108, 395 [21]
—reports of monstrous, inhabiting depths of Great Lakes, vii. 151
—rescued from falling floods by Buddhists, xii. 298, 300
—returned to water by Chên contained the Dragon King, viii. 191
— -robe, v. 84, 367
—sacrifice for foals, iv. 162
——of, to Seides, iv. 111, 191
—saivo-, used in journeying to Underworld, iv. 285–286
— -scale house, viii. 90
—seven elders have form of, v. 140
—Skylla changed into, i. 69
—son of Kṛṣṇa swallowed by a great, vi. 173
— -stick, magic, ix. 221
—strange, said to be children of water-spirit, iv. 192
—swallowing man, legends of, x. 44–45, 51, 79, 274 [9]
—(the sun), ii. 313
— -trap, Chameleon finds man and woman in, vii. 134
—water-spirits may appear as, iv. 195, 198, 199, 202, 205, 216
—why considered unclean, xii. 395 [80]
—woman's leg pregnant by a, ix. 112–113
—worshipped, vi. 242–243
Fisherman, Glaukos (sea-god) a, i. 261
Fishermen swore in name of Zaden, vii. 40
Fisher-woman and lost crystal, viii. 272–273

Fishes, creation of, from finger-bones of daughter of Anguta, xi. 30
—god of, viii. 90
—(mazomba), vii. 140
—of underground rivers, iv. 487
Fishing, luck in, iv. 339
—regarded as holy and has vocabulary of its own, iv. 83–84
—rules for, iv. 84
—sacrifice to wind-god while, iv. 233
—up of land, ix. 20, 43–44, 105
"Fitness of Names," iii. 85
Five Brigands, viii. 168, 169
—Nations, x. 14, 282 23
—sacred mountains, viii. 70, 71, 193
—Tact dance ascribed to fairies of the cherry-blossoms, viii. 261
Fjalar, another name of Skyrmir, ii. 93
—cock, wakens giants at Doom of gods, ii. 276
—dwarf, made poetic mead, ii. 53, 265, 269
Fjallar, epithet of Suttung, ii. 49
Fjolnir (Odin), ii. 47, 121
Fjolsvid, giant, ii. 124
"Fjolsvinnsmal," ii. 7, 11
Fjorgyn, Thor's mother, Frigg daughter of, ii. 174, 194
Fjorgynn, Frigg's husband, ii. 194
—Scandinavian thunder-god, iv. 228
Fjörgynn, Teutonic goddess of earth, vii. 14
Flag in temple of Svantovit, iii. 279
—of Huyen-vu represents seven stars of the north, xii. 307
Flags, three, of grave of Lugaid called Murder, Disgrace, and Treachery, iii. 156
Flagstaffs, xii. 188
Flail and sand spread on earth by Oscar to keep demons from tormenting Féinn, iii. 183, 212
Flame, blue, soul may manifest itself as, iv. 10
Flame-flash and Flame-fade, tale of, viii. 265–266
—Forest mother sometimes takes form of, iv. 184
—phosphorescent, ghost with, viii. pl. XI, opp. p. 240
—spirit-bird shot and falling to ground became a, iv. 495
—tongue of, Lope de Aguirre haunts savannahs in form of, xi. 279

Flames, flickering, protection about Gerd's abode, ii. 111, 112
—horse of Frey can go through, ii. 109
—Isis and other deities surrounded by, xii. 395 84
—seen over Aarnion Haltia on Midsummer Eve, iv. 173
Flaming Island: see ISLAND OF FLAMES.
Flat, earth, ix. 178–179
Flatey-dale, ii. 203
Flax mother, iv. 246
—Shrove Tuesday offering for good crop of, iv. 248
Flaying alive, vii. 63, 370
—of captive, xi. 76, pl. X, opp. p. 76
"Fled Bricrend," iii. 134, 145–146
Flesh, Agni as eater of raw, distinguished from the Agni who carries oblations, vi. 70
—and bone created out of earth, iv. 371
—Brāhmans made to eat human, vi. 146
— -eating class who came from gourd, xii. 292
—human, madness of Glaukos's horses said to be caused by eating of, i. 39
—Lapp belief that new, grows on bones of sacrificial victims, iv. 3
—of Ningyo, women eating of, gain perpetual youth and beauty, viii. 273
—raw, devoured by Maïnads, i. 270, pl. LVII, opp. p. 272
— -sticks (also meat-), iv. 273, 274, 276, 281
Flidais and her cow, iii. 127–128
—mother of Fand, iii. 32
Flies, Fly:
Flies, vii. 325
—evil spirits rioted like, viii. 211
Fly in temple of Śiva, Pulaha was, vi. 180
—why it rubs its hands together, x. 180
Flight, magic, ix. 235; x. 308 62; xi. 304
—of witches and sorcerers, ii. 48, 300–301
—on earthen jars, vii. 84, 393 31
—swift, depends on falcon's plumage or feather-dress, ii. 22
Flint, vii. 54, 55
— -making, x. 44
—(Tawiscara, "Warty"), x. 36–37, 40, 44, 68, 231, 291 37 38, 295 44, 296 45
—theft of, x. 223
Flintstone and steel, iv. 450, 453

Floci, Viking, set out to seek Snowland, ii. 216

Flocks, Veles (and St. Blasius) guardians of, iii. 300

Flogging, x. 282 [21]

—ceremonial, x. 194

Flood, iv. 197; 322–323, 361–370, 420; v. 36–38, 112; vi. 75, 99, 104, 124, 147; vii. 124; viii. 32, 33, 37; x. xxiv, 9, 42–44, 63, 104, 105, 108, 125, 136, 160, 161–162, 164, 177, 178, 180, 203, 204, 205, 210, 221, 224, 250, 261, 274 [9], 299 [49]–300, 300 [50]; xi. 29, 30, 38, 85, 87, 91, 93, 94, 95, 96, 119, 153, 154, 164, 191, 197, 203, 230, 239, 269–270, 271, 311–315, 330, 342, 357 [7], 358 [8]; see also FLOOD-LEGENDS; FLOOD-MYTHS.

—ages before, v. 166, 167

—Babylonian high gods cowered in terror before the, iii. 28

—dead may cause a, xii. 298

— -episode, birth from incestuous union follows the, in Philippine area, ix. 170, 171–172, 178

—Great, xii. 39, 390 [36]

——caused by Rêʻ, xii. 82, 383 [87]

——Zeus punishes world with, i. 158

— -legend, Iranian equivalent of, vi. 307–309

— -legends, v. 203–233, 237, 262, 270, 274, 275

——considerably developed in Indonesian mythology, ix. 240

——found all over Indo-China, xii. 267–268

—magic, from Balder's barrow, ii. 134

—Marduk, or Irra, or Enlil, sent, v. 139, 140

—may be caused by improper burial, xii. 298

— -myths, i. 18–19; ix. 17, 38–40, 58, 111, 119–121, 170–171, 178–183, 256–257, 279–280; xii. 278–282, 286; see also FLOOD-LEGENDS.

—of Babylonian origin, v. 73

——blood, ii. 276, 324

——Deukalion, i. 67, 244

——Zeus, i. 158

—Poseidon covered plain of Attike with, i. 67

—possible allusion to, xii. 73, 75, 76

—primeval, sacred lake as remnant of, xii. 31

Flood prince, iv. 365, 402

—Samothracian, i. 19

—strata at Kish, v. 203

—tale of coming of Noah's granddaughter to Ireland before the, iii. 206

— -tales may be influenced by Christianity, ix. 40, 119

Floods believed to be caused by demons who are elaborately propitiated, vi. 235

Floor, friendly (Vingolf), ii. 45

—living beings rooted to the, x. 243, 245

—sacrifice killed and buried in home of god under the, iv. 160, 161

—stone should not be cast across a, as it stirs stone in Thor's head, ii. 82

Flora, i. 294

—functions of, partly absorbed by Floria in modern Romagnola, i. 319

Floral Calendar, viii. 338, 348–353

Floria in modern Romagnola a contamination of Flora and Pomona, i. 319

Flower, attribute of Aphrodite, i. 203

—enchanted, dragon-killers born from, vii. 45, 385 [9]

—form may be taken by spirits, xii. 175

— -god as maize-god, xi. 54

— -gods, xi. 77

— -maidens, viii. 296

—special, sacred to Osiris, xii. 385 [8]

Flowers, Bês with, xii. 61, 62 (fig. 64)

—comparison between Buddha and the, vi. 191

—may be infested by bhūts, vi. 249

—plants, trees, tales of, viii. 338–353

—rain of, on warriors, vi. 144

Flute calls dwarfs, ii. 272

— -dance, x. 194–195, 199

—invented by Athene, i. 34, 171, 181

—music of, dedicated to the dead, viii. 356

—of reed, attribute of Pan, i. 269

Flutes, vii. 62, 364; viii. 36; 359; x. 95, 231; xi. 64, 294

—spirit-, vii. 189

"Flying, go thither," command to Ayar Auca, xi. 251

—gods, iv. 172–173

—of people before creation of sun and moon, iv. 419

— -palace, ix. 208

Flyting, abusive dialogue between gods, ii. 10, 81, 143, 249

Foal (also as offering) ridden by magician to find site for new lud, iv. 145

—demanded as offering, iv. 156, 157

Foals, birth of two, iii. 83

Foam from mouth of boar resembled waterfall, iii. 125

—Woman, x. 242, 273 [7]

Foaming Water and Sun parents of Divine Ones (Twins), x. 199

Fog, ix. 179

—in creation, x. 229, 233

Fölgie like Fylgja, ii. 237

Folk-belief, Russian, penetrated Finno-Ugrians along with Russian colonization, iv. xviii

— -customs descended from rituals of vanished paganism, iii. 8

— -lore, Chinese, viii. 148–160

——of civilization corresponds with savage ideas out of which it has grown, xii. 357

——people, land, and climate in relation to, viii. 220, 245, 246

— -songs, iii. 318, 319, 320, 321, 324, 325–326, 327–328

——folk-lore in, viii. 369–374

— -tale, story of Perseus in its bearing on primitive, i. 325 [12] (ch. ii)

— -tales, diffusion of five groups of, vii. 357–359

Folkvaldi-god (Frey), ii. 119

Folkvang, dwelling of Freyja, ii. 120, 314

Folkvitr (Battle-wight), ii. 248

Follower (Fylgja), ii. 233

Followers of gods, xii. 179, 417 [17]

——Rata multiplied, ix. 61

Following woman (Fylgjukona), ii. 235

Fomorians, ii. 30

—descendants of Ham, iii. 23, 24, 25, 30, 33, 34, 35, 144

Fongasigde, xi. 208

Fons (Fontus), son of Ianus and Iuturna, i. 295, 297

Food, cooking, in sun's rays, ix. 46, 316 [30]

—disappearance of year's, iii. 107

—Dish, x. 5–6, 273 [7], 289 [34]

—divine, makes one unfit for earth, iii. 90

Food, eating easily perishable, brings mortality to man, ix. 182

—festival, must not be reserved, iv. 53

—for chief's son bewitched, vii. 340

——mortals, debate of Wolf and his brother on, x. 143–144

— -genius, viii. 232

— -giver of the sea, xi. 223

—gods jealous of man's sharing their, iii. 131

—inexhaustible vessel of, ix. 127, 209, 325 [23]

—magic, from the Grail, iii. 203

——in Isle of Joy, iii. 115

——rejuvenation may be influenced by, ii. 180

——replenishment of, iii. 84, 118, 119, 120

——unsalted pork, new milk, mead, iii. 81

—makers and dance masks, xi. 287–295

—Melanesian tale of stealing of, presents parallels with Indonesian tales, ix. 134–136

—Menḥu(i) special giver of, xii. 136

—miraculous, ix. 218–220, 221–224, 237–238

—of Balder contained magic strength, ii. 133, 134, 135, 243

——dead, xii. 177, 178

——fathers and gods, vi. 71

——gods, iii. 126

——Underworld tabu to mortals, ix. 77

—offered to tree by harvesters, xii. 16

—offerings to dead, xii. 175

—raiment, etc., in hereafter furnished to dead in proportion to that presented at funeral, iv. 483

—restrictions on clean and unclean, xii. 185–186

—rubbed into mouth of image, iv. 178

—sacrificed and buried together with image at memorial feasts, iv. 39

—sacrificial, xii. 195, 196

——on anniversary of death, iv. 25

— -stage, ix. 80, 134

—stealing of, from blind person, ix. 45, 46, 59

—various kinds of, used at funeral feasts, iv. 39–40, 44–59

Fool-Coyote, a star, x. 116

Foolish tales, vi. 145

Foot-holders of Math, iii. 96

—in back of neck, vii. 252

Foot of Balder's colt charmed by goddess, ii. 18

Footmarks in funeral ashes indicate whether next death animal or human, iv. 28

—of funeral procession swept away, iv. 23, 24

Footprints of first creations, vii. 147

Footsnare, iv. 268, 271

Footsteps of Viṣṇu and Rāmānand revered, vi. 240

Force, meaning of term, xii. 220

Forehead, divine decrees written on, vii. 30

Foreign god, worship of, viii. 82, 84

—influence on Egyptian religion, xii. 239–240

——Japanese mythology, viii. 212, 213, 214–220

—lands, Ḥat-ḥôr rules over, xii. 367 [12]

Foreknowledge, ii. 25, 47, 60, 209

Forest at Breag to be cut down, iii. 81

—common representative of all trees, iv. 189

—demons, ix. 188

—fire spirit of the, xi. 182

— -game-sharing man, sky-god, iv. 403, 404

— -god, sacrifice to, iv. 99

—guarded by one-eyed black giant, iii. 191

—magic creation of a, iii. 136

—man, iv. 232

—region and tribes, x. 13–52

—soul, iv. 14

— -spirit, protector of cattle, same height as grass, iv. 243

— -spirit-berry forbidden to man, iv. 384

— -spirits, iv. 178–190, 232

——elfin beings earlier, ii. 204, 205

——sometimes in guise of birds, ix. 61

Forests in charge of genius ("shadow"), iii. 228

—planted from hairs of Guzu Tenno, viii. 228

—storm-god transformed into genius of, viii. 228

—tropical, of the Orinoco and Guiana, and of the Amazon and Brazil, xi. 253–315

—Underworld, iv. 484, 485

Forgall, Emer daughter of, iii. 143

Forge, ii. pl. 1, frontispiece

Forge of Hephaistos, i. 129

Forgiveness implored of dead, iv. 17, 58

Forgotten deities, revival of, xii. 207

Formalism in Egypt after 1000 B.C., xii. 235

Formula, magic, said over images to create life, ix. 173

Formulae, language of magic, xii. 206–207

Fornjöt (old giant), ii. 171, 281

Forseti (Fosite), god; son of Balder, ii. 15, 19, 162–164, 197, 209

Forts, Dagda required to build, iii. 27, 28

Fortuna, i. 283, 295

—coins with figure of, v. 19, 20

—prototype of goddess of fate, v. 22

—Roman deity, influences development of Greek goddess Tychē, i. 283

Fortune, deities of good, viii. 279–280

—good and evil, given by Death, vii. 175

—precedes and announces the coming of the man, iv. 11–12

—wheel of, turned by Meher, vii. 34

Fortunes, divination for, viii. 140–141

Forty days' time on earth for soul of dead, iii. 230; iv. 48, 49, 53

Forum Boarium, i. 302

—Ianus and Vesta connected with, i. 297, 298

Fossegrim: see GRIM, WATER-SPIRIT.

Fothad Airglech, death of, iii. 180

Fotla, queen, iii. 42, 43, 44

Foundation boxes, clay figurines in, v. 176–177

—sacrifice, iii. 200; xii. 196

Foundling, taunts on being, ix. 68

Fount (Well of Connla) overwhelms seeker of wisdom, iii. 121

Fountain, Arethousa changed into a, i. 257

—of Youth, i. 261; ii. 205; viii. 351, 352; x. 234–235; xi. 4, 20, 349 [6]; see also REJUVENATION.

—with five streams seen by Cormac, iii. 121

Fountains, holy, v. 20

—sacred, ii. 208; viii. 247, 251, 252, 267

Four Beautiful Objects of Emperor Ch'ien Lung, viii. 88

—celestial number, xii. 39, 52, 65, 368 [12]

Four corners of earth, blessing of, vii. 381 [5] (ch. ii)
—guardians: see FOUR LOKAPĀLAS.
— -headed god of Underworld, xii. 394 [67]
— -watchmen, viii. 104
—Heavenly Kings, viii. 14, 110
—Horuses or "sons of Horus," xii. 387 [27]
—Hundred Southerners, xi. 169, 176
—Lokapālas, viii. 14, 110
—Meskhenets of Osiris apparently symbolize four sources of Nile, xii. 95
—(or five) sons of Horus or Osiris, xii. 104, 105, 110–113, 111 (fig. 114), 112 (fig. 115), 375 [77 80], 387 [27], 391 [42], 394 [67], 424 [39]
Fourfold serpent of the Abyss, xii. 105 (fig. 101)
Fourteen as mystic number, xii. 395 [78]
—(six, sixty-four) pieces, solar eye of Osiris torn into, xii. 90
—souls (manifestations) of the sun-god, xii. 384 [115]
Fowl of the Ghosts emissary of ancestor-gods, vii. 288
Fowls and birds brought to announce dawn, ix. 114, 117, 275
Fox, viii. 37, 156–157
— -day, vii. 53
— -god, xi. 204
—in story of horse sacrificed at funeral, iv. 488–489
—nine-tailed, xii. 309
—ravages Thebes and is changed into stone, i. 73
—star, v. 310
—uncanny powers of, viii. 324–327, 329–330
Frācīh, vi. 335
Franang's waterfall, Loki as salmon hid in, ii. 144, 146
Fraoch, Irish hero, iii. 67, 127, 130–131, 144, 154
Frashaoshtra, father-in-law of Zoroaster, vi. 341
Fraternities, x. 184–185, 188, 191–192, 196–197, 245, 249
Frau Holle, African variants of Grimm's, vii. 118, 138, 141, 196, 202–203, 204, 265
Fravāk and Fravākaīn, twin children of primeval twins, vi. 298, 299

Fravarti, month of, consecrated to ancestral souls, vii. 22
Fravashi, double; external soul or self, vii. 94
Fravashis, vi. 261, pl. XXXIV, opp. p. 272, 286, 300, 327, 342
—have some affinity to conception of Dhyānibuddhas, vi. 211, 358 [8]
Frea Ingwina, king of East Danes, ii. 113
Free will in cuneiform literature, v. 314
Freki (the Glutton), wolf of Odin, ii. 65
Frenzy, Dionysos afflicted by Hera with, i. 47, 219, 222
—Gerd's, ii. 298
—giant's, ii. 66, 90, 182, 277–278, 292
—Mongan's, iii. 119
—potion given Fionn causes, iii. 168
—Rinda's, ii. 45–46, 48
Frey, cult of, iv. 243, 246, 249–250, 251
—god, ii. 7, 10, 15, 16, 17, 20, 22, 24, 25, 26, 28, 29, 30, pl. VI, opp. p. 32, 33, 34, 35, 60, 66, 71, 72, 100, 102, 103, 108–119, 126, 143, 144, 158, 162, 165, 166, 188, 266, 278, 329, 341, 343
Freydis, ii. 244
Freyfaxi, horse of Hrafnkell, ii. 118, 216
Freyja, goddess, ii. 7, 10, 15, 17, 20, 22, 25, 27, 28, 56, 79, 81, 88, 89, 90, 91, 102, 110, 120–126, 140, 143, 153, 155, 176, 180, 182, 186, 194, 220, 229, 244, 249, 250, 265, 270, 278, 314, 337
Freyjuhar, fern, ii. 177
Friagabi, ii. 358 [7]
Fricco: see FREY.
Friction Drum, sacred, vii. pl. XXXIII, opp. p. 314
Fridleif, king of Denmark, ii. 242, 244, 261
"Fridthjofs-saga," ii. 138, 191
Friendship, creation of, i. 6
—Kastor and Polydeukes guardians of divine, i. 26
Frigg (Frea, Freya, Fri, Frîa, Frigida, Frija), goddess, wife of Odin, ii. 15, 16, 18, 19, 22, 32, 38, 50, 60, 61, 62, 63, 65, 83, 121, 122, 124, 126, 129, 130, 143, 174–177, 180, 183, 184, 185, 229, 249, 340
Friggjargras, orchis, from which love-philtres made is called, ii. 177
Frijszhög, hill, ii. 158
Frisians, ii. 17; iii. 16
Friuch, herd of god Bodb, iii. 57

Fro, king of Sweden, ii. 115
Frobag, fröbak, or farnbag (Pers.) fire, vi. 306; vii. 56
Fröblot (sacrifice to Frey), ii. 113
Frodi, myth of, ii. 114, 282–283, 378 49
Frog, vii. 284, 418 34
—advises Ülgen to allow his creation to live, iv. 377
—earth-supporting, iv. 311, 319–320, 327
—form of evil spirit, in Shan belief, which swallows moon in eclipse, xii. 333
—Ḥeqet has head of, xii. 50
—no positive knowledge of cult of Ḥeqet as incarnate in, xii. 167
—Nuu has head of, xii. 47
—used in rain-making, xii. 430 26
—who drank all the water, tale of, ix. 279
— -woman, xi. 273
Frogs, abandoned children turned into, xi. 32
—born from burnt bones of man-eating giant, iv. 388
—compared to priests and are connected with rain, vi. 62, 63, 89
—conjured against Firbolgs, iii. 24
—Parikṣit orders massacre of, vi. 147
—Yatawm and Yatai as, xii. 293
Frost feared by Northern people, ii. 96
— -giants, ii. 49, 96, 111, 147, 167–168, 266, 275, 276, 278, 279, 324, 340
—man and woman, iv. 233–234
——of the Autumn Mountain, viii. 294
—song of origin of, iv. 207
Fruit, eating of forbidden, vii. 316–319, 424 16, 425 20
—forbidden, ii. 322; iv. 381–382, 383, 384, 419
—god of, xi. 48
—of tora'a-tree, man originated from, ix. 169
—thrown at primeval man transforms him into woman, ix. 107
Fruitfulness, ring symbol of, ii. 66
Fruits of tree, man made from, ix. 176
Fryanas, vi. 335
Fu, viii. 104
Fu ch'i, control of breath, viii. 147
Fu Hsi evolved the Eight Diagrams, viii. 8, 137
——mythical Emperor, viii. 25, 26, 27, 29–30, 55, 136

Fu-pao, magical pregnancy of, viii. 27
Fu Shan, viii. 30
Fu-shou-lu, spirits of longevity, happiness, and prosperity, viii. 82
Fu-ti, viii. 115
Fu Yü Tai, P'an Ku's spirit went to, viii. 111
Fuamnach transformed Etain into an insect preliminary to rebirth, iii. 59
—wife of Midir, iii. 79, 80
Fubito, chief of Fujiwara family, viii. 272–273
"Fudo-ki," viii. 245
Fuegians, xi. 338–344
Fuego de Aguirre, phosphorescence of swamp, believed to be tortured soul, xi. 195–196
Fuel lost in sea by Ogma because of hunger, iii. 26, 27
Fufluns, Fuflunu, Etruscan deity, survives as Faflon in modern Romagnola, i. 318
Fuji, Mt., viii. 233–234, 258, 262, 263, 383 12
Fujiwara-no-Fusazaki, a minister of state, story of mother of, viii. 271, 381 9
Fukien, viii. 5
Fukuji, Mt., viii. 251
Fukuro, owl, tale of, viii. 334–335
Fuku-roku-ju, genius of fortune, etc.; also incarnation of southern pole stars, viii. 280
Fulla, goddess, ii. 15, 18, 61, 130, 174, 184–185
Fünen, ii. 143
Funeral, iii. 312, 314
—ceremonies, tree played part in, vii. 401 6
—customs because of fear of witches, vii. 336
—description of Russian chieftain's, iii. 233–235
—feasts, ii. 311
—games, i. 35, 39, 57, 69
—meals, vii. 95
—phantom, vii. 342–343
—processions, superstitions on, iv. 24, 30–31
—pyre of Burmese monk, xii. 326, pl. XIII, opp. p. 326
—rites, vii. 95–96, 397 4; xi. 23, 27
——denied to foes of Thebes by Kreon, i. 53

Funeral rites performed, in fifth month of pregnancy, for father, iii. 83
—sacrifices, xii. 196–197, 420 [22]
—services, Babylonian, v. 262
—urns, xi. 286–287
Funerary pictures, Nut in, xii. 41
Fur, giant's, made of beards of kings, iii. 185
Furies, Fury:
Furies in battle of Mag-Tured, iii. 25
—of Hades, viii. 224
——Klytaimnestra, i. 135
Fury, divine, ii. 82, 85
— -giants, viii. 211
—of Adad, v. 40–41
Furious Host (Storm personified), names of leader of, ii. 40–44, 56, 255
—Spirit, viii. 287
Furnace, tsao means both hearth and, viii. 76

Furo-No-Yashiro, Shinto shrine, viii. pl. xv, opp. p. 246
Furrows, iron cleansed at ends of, iii. 99
Futsu-nushi, General of sun-goddess, viii. 230
Future, Domovoy able to foretell, iii. 242
—foretelling the, by water divinities, i. 258
—foretold, xii. 40, 53
—knowledge of, iii. 144
—life is eternal, xi. 139
Fylgja, kind of guardian spirit in animal form, ii. 217, 228, 230, 233–237, 286
—(Scandinavian " guide "), corresponds to Finnish Saattaja, iv. 12
Fylgjukona (Following woman), ii. 235, 372 [10]

G

Gabhra, battle of, iii. 161, 179, 181, 182
Gabiæ of Romano-German inscriptions, Gefjun found in, ii. 182
Gad, deity of fate, v. 21, 23, 383 [95]
Gad-fly sent by Hera to madden the cattle of Geryoneus, i. 86
——————pursue Io, i. 29
Gaga, messenger of Anshar, v. 298, 299
Gagavitz, xi. 178, 179, 180, 181, 182
Gagnrath (Odin), ii. 62
Gā-gorib, enemy of mankind, vii. 214
Gagua (light-giver), Spaniards called, xi. 202
Gahonga, stone throwers, x. 28, 283 [27]–284
Gaí bolga, spear, iii. 145, 150, 200, 212
—dearg, magic spear, iii. 65, 177
Gaia: see GE.
Gaible, son of Nuada, iii. 136
Gail (Wolf), underground river, vii. 370
Gaion, i. pl. VIII (3), opp. p. 8
Gajomartan: see GAYA MARETAN, ETC.
Gak Chog, fire captive in form of the stone, xi. 180
Gaki, hungry ghosts, viii. 282, 287
Galahad, iii. 198, 202
Galai-Khan, ruler of fire, iv. 456
Galarr, dwarf, ii. 53, 265, 268–269
Galateia and Pygmalion, legend of, i. 200

Galateia, double of Aphrodite, i. 198
Galatia, Artemis thought to wander with demons at midday in, iii. 12
Gali-Edzin, Master of fire, iv. 456
Galibi, legend of origin of Carib from among the, xi. 39
Galikalangye, miraculous birth and tale of, vii. 223, 224
—mother of, promises him to demon, vii. 214
Galindae, a division of the Baltic peoples, iii. 317
Galióin, Nemedian survivors who returned to Ireland, iii. 23
—suggestion that Fionn was hero of the subject race, iii. 161
Gall, Herakles dipped his arrows in hydra-, i. 81
—of bear sucked in hardens one's nature, iv. 91
Gallows called Odin's steed, ii. 43, 334, 336
—of Odin, Yggdrasil possibly, ii. 52
Gallû, demon, v. 337, 359–360, 362, 363, 364, 415 [20]; see also GELLÔ.
Galōn (Garuḍa), Khrut name for the, xii. 323
—heraldic bird of Burmese, corresponds to Indian Garuḍa, xii. pl. VII (2), opp. p. 272

Galta-Ulan-Tengeri, god of fire, heat, and drought, iv. 449

‡Gama ‡Goub, evil spirit almost identical with ||Gaunab, vii. 159

Gama Sennin (" Toad-master "), viii. 276

Gamal, men's house, ix. 133

Gambara, mother of Lombard leaders, ii. 38

Gambler sent back into world to rule Mexicans, x. 163

Gamblers, 179, 204, 303 56

Gambula, v. 187

Game and Corn, entrance of, into world, x. 62, 289 35, 294 41

Games, iii. 307, 308, 312; ix. 42, 76, 77
—bear-feast, iv. 96
—first Olympian, celebrated by Herakles, i. 92
—funeral, at Pelias, i. 39, 57, 69
——Perseus contestant in, i. 35
—in honour of Dusares, v. 16, 18
—Isthmian, in honour of Poseidon founded by Theseus, i. 103
——said to have been established in honour of Melikertes, i. 37, 46
—Nemean, instituted in honour of infant son of Lykourgos, i. 52
—Pythian, instituted by Apollo, i. 177
—(scenae), performed with pagan rites at crossroads, iii. 234

Ganadhara, Jain leader of disciples, vi. 221

Ganapati, vi. 358 7

Ganas vi. 204, 217

Ganaskidi, or Humpbacks, harvest-deities, x. 156

Gandak River, sacred stone in, vi. 240

Gandalf, dwarf, ii. 266

Gandarewa, dragon-like monster, vi. 58, 59
—(Gandharva), vi. 273, 279, 324, 325, 328, 350

Gandayah, one of three tribes of Jogaoh, x. 28

Gandhamādana Mountain, vi. 158

Gāndhārī, vi. 217
—mother of the Kauravas, vi. 125, 145
—smallpox-goddess, vi. 246

Gandharvas, vi. 18, 58–59, 90, 94, 95, 97, 108, pl. x, opp. p. 118, 143, 149, 157, 158, 159, 185, 191, 203, 215, 227

Gāṇḍīva, bow, vi. 138

Gaṇeśa, vi. 141, 181–182, pl. xx, opp. p. 182, 237–238, 242
—sacred images of, xii. 327

Ganges, heavenly birth of, vi. 48
—Mother (Gaṅgā Māī), most holy river, vi. 234, 235
—Nāgas dwell on northern banks of, vi. 154, 155
—one of the Buddhas born on mystic island in the, vi. 194
—received in Śiva's hair, vi. 115
—Śiva connected with, vi. 115
—valley, " Herakles " worshipped in, vi. 110
—Vasus children of, vi. 142

Gang-i-Dizhhūkht, Ḍahhāk's capital, vi. 365 4

Gangler (Odin), ii. 42

Gangleri, ii. 6, pl. III, opp. p. 12, 199

Gangr, giant, ii. 279

Gangways (of the sky), two and four, xii. 363 4

Ganiš (Gidne), forest-maiden, iv. 177

Gansām Deo metamorphosed into Ghana-śyāma, vi. 238

Ganÿklos, Veles corresponds to Lithuanian, iii. pl. xxxv, opp. p. 300

Ganymedes and the eagle, i. pl. LII, opp. p. 242
—horses given by Zeus to Laomedon for theft of, i. 86
—son of Tros, i. 117–118, 240

Ganzir, name of Ereshkigal; also of Arallû, v. 161

Ga-oh, wind giant, x. 23, 26

Gaokerena-tree, vi. 265, 281, 286, 288, 289

Gaping Jaws of Earth, xi. 54, 80

Garawada, tale of, ix. 136–138

Garden of Eden, v. 184–185, 186, 188, 189, 314
——Yāw, v. 402 21

Gardener in Dilmun, v. 198

Gardeners of Anu, v. 385 136

Gardens of Adonis, v. 350
——Egyptian parallels to, xii. 399 111

Gargantua, natural features associated with, iii. 135

Gārhapatya fire, vi. 91

Garland as symbol of divine birth given to Theseus by Amphitrite, i. 101
—poisoned, sent to Glauke by Medeia, i. 115

Garm, dog of Hel, ii. 100, 303, 304, 339, 341
—Icelandic dog, x. 121
Garman, son of Glas, iii. 136
—took Bodb's daughter Mesca, iii. 91
Garment, indestructible, promised by devil to man, iv. 374
—(of Bêl), ceremony with a, v. 324
—swan-, iv. 501
Garments, Arkas taught Arkadians how to weave, i. 16
—exchange of, between sexes, vi. 185; x. 309 64
—magic, conferring invisibility, viii. pl. XXXVI, opp. p. 314
—mourners', v. 332
—Pelasgos first to contrive fashioning of, i. 16
—rending of, v. 261
—theft of: see SWAN-MAIDENS.
Garmna, iii. 147
Garôṭmān, paradise, vi. 328, 345
Garse-tree, vii. 401 6
Garshāsp: see KERESĀSPA.
Garsīvaz: see KERESAVADAH.
Gartuk, mopoke, and two Brams, tale of, ix. 296–297
Garuḍa dwells in tree, ii. 334
—(Galōn), xii. 323
—(Garide), iv. 345, 357
—(robber of Soma), iv. 356, 357, 413, 447
—Tengus resemble Hindu, viii. 288
Garuḍas, vi. pl. x, opp. p. 118, 120, 139, 140, pl. XVI, opp. p. 140, 149, 183, 203, 210, 214, 216; ix. 224, 242, 319 7, 337 30
Garutmant ("winged"), sun called, vi. 140, 291
Garz (Korenice), iii. 283
Gashansubur, messenger of Innini, v. 327, 328
Gatamdug, goddess, v. 404 15
Gate gives entrance to Pohjola, iv. 79
Gates, charms against pestilence put on, viii. 251
—leading to spirit-world, vii. 184, 195
—to Underworld, iv. 75; v. 329, 330, 331, 334
Gateway leading to Wakonyingo country, vii. 268
—monolithic, xi. pl. XXXI, opp. p. 218, 233–234, pl. XXXV, opp. p. 234

Gaul, saga of Cúchulainn perhaps known in, iii. 157–158
Gaulish coins, iii. pl. II, opp. p. 8, pl. III, opp. p. 14
Gauls, account of origin of Northern, by Diodorus, iii. 13
||Gaunab, Hottentot evil spirit, vii. 157, 158, 214, 215, 344
Gaunu-Tsachau, child of Mantis, vii. 289
Ga-ur (Gk. Euechoros), founded first dynasty at Kish, v. 203
Gaurī, another name for Umā, vi. 118, 138, 183
Gaut, Gautatyr, Odin called, ii. 59
Gautama, adventure of, with Arundhatī, vi. 144
—cursed Indra, vi. 134
—rejuvenates Utaṅka, vi. 145
Gautland or Götland, Odin perhaps first worshipped in, ii. 59
"Gautreks-saga," ii. 52
Gavida, uncle of Lug, iii. 99
Gawain, Arthur's nephew, iii. 188, 196, 197, 198, 202, 203
Gayā, vi. 211
—footsteps of Viṣṇu revered at, vi. 240
Gaya Maretan (Gayōmart), first man, iv. 358; vi. 293, 298, 299, 313, 316
—Sukumāla, vi. 224
Gayāl, sonless ghost, vi. 247
Gāyatrī, bird and metres, vi. 91, 140, 233
Gaza, v. 82
—Yāw of, v. 43
Gazelle, Brer Rabbit may be the, vii. 282
—head of, symbol of Reshef, v. 46, 48
—Mārīca killed in form of, vi. 156
—Resheph's head-dress ornamented with, xii. 155
—tabus connected with, xii. 362 3
Gazelles, Antaeus as hunter of, xii. 130, 240 (fig. 218)
Ge (Gaia), i. 5, pl. VIII (1), opp. p. 8, 20, pl. XIX, opp. p. 66, 272–273
—and Ouranos, Eros son of, i. 203
——founders of "first royal house of gods," i. 5
——parents of Hyperion and Euryphaëssa, i. 242
——Okeanos according to Hesiod, i. 256
——Rhea daughter of, i. 274

Ge and Pontos parents of Nereus, i. 260
——Poseidon parents of Charybdis, i. 264
—Demeter form of, i. 225
—earth-goddess, v. 66
—Greek identification of 'Ashtart with, v. 15
—mother and wife of Ouranos, i. 5, 272
—Persephone offshoot of, i. 230
—said to be mother of Prometheus by Iapetos, i. 12
—see BACHUE, ETC.
—Tellus Mater stood for, in myth, i. 292
Gê Hinnom, Canaanitish centre of worship of Malik, v. 50
Geasa: see TABUS (vol. iii).
Gebal, coffin of Osiris drifted to, v. 71
—cult of Ninurta at, v. 135
——Tammuz at, v. xvii, 351
—founded by Ilos, v. 66–67
—Ninurta and swine at, v. 132
—sacred city, v. 351
—Tammuz at, v. 340
—temple of Ninurta at, v. 132
—West Semitic cult of Adonis and Astarte (Tammuz and Ishtar) at, v. 8
—Yāw worshipped as early as 1000 B.C. at, v. 44
Gefjun, goddess, ii. 15, 23, 60, 143, 180–182, 278
Gefn (Freyja), ii. 125, 181
Gehenna, how myth of, arose, v. 50
Geide the Loud-voiced, iii. 137
Gëinos, inventor of brick making, v. 54
Geirhild, wife of Alfrek, ii. 121
Geirrid summoned to the Moot as a Dark-rider, ii. 300
Geirrod, king, ii. 9, 61, 62, 81, 83, 84–85, 95, 139, 141, 175, 176, 184, 321, 322, 323
Geirronul (Spear-bearer), Valkyrie, ii. 249
Geirstadar-álf, sacrifice to, ii. 226
Geirvimul, river in Hel, ii. 383 83
Geirvor, singing skull found on a scree called, ii. 169
Geismar, sacred oak at, ii. 68
Geite, second sight of, ii. 234
Gelanor, king of Argos, yielded crown to Danaos, i. 30
Gelder, king of Saxony, ii. 132, 135

Gellô (Gelou, Gilou, Gelu), v. 363, 365, 366, 369, 416 34; see also GALLÛ.
Gem, Gems:
Gem containing inscription fished up by Lü Shang, viii. 42
—of sky, Sūrya as, vi. 26
Gems, magic properties of, xii. 421 6
——shower of purple, iii. 32
—nine, vi. 104, 107, 120, 151
—thrown into water, viii. 38, 43
Gem-bu, Japanese name for one of Chinese world-guardians, viii. 379 28
Gem-Pei, Minamoto and Taira clans collectively called, viii. 307
Gemini, xi. 98
—Gilgamish wrongly identified with, v. 268
Gendenwitha the star-maiden which is the Morning Star, x. 26
Gender of sun, moon, and stars, iii. 320
Genealogical lists of Anglo-Saxon royal families trace back to Woden, ii. 19
—type of myths of origin, ix. 5–18, 21–22, 30, 166–167
Genealogy of Chichimec, xi. pl. XVI, opp. p. 112
——giants, ii. 281
" General of the Five Ways," viii. 169
Generation, cult of Frey connected with, ii. 115
—(life and death), spontaneous, viii. 221–224
—male and female powers of, xi. 53
—serpents associated with, xi. 74
—turtle symbol of, xi. 288
Generations, Wachaga do not sacrifice to ghosts of more than three, vii. 183
Generative powers, serpent symbolic of, v. 90
Genesia, Gaia associated with the festival, i. 273
Genesis, Biblical, Pawnee myth suggests, x. 112
—Navaho, x. 159–166
—Pueblo, x. 185
Genghis Khan, first Yüan emperor, viii. 23, 190
——Yoshitsune said to have become, viii. 383
Genii, vii. 62, 73, 74–76
—ancestral spirits, may appear as serpents, vii. 73

Genii, belief in, iii. 227–232, 243, 244–245, 247–252, 254
—eight, viii. pl. 1, frontispiece
—female, of trees and fountains, viii. 267
—fighting with nets or snares, xii. 109 (fig. 109)
—four, at birth of Osiris, parallel four harvest-goddesses, xii. 378 98
—Fravashis are, in Zoroastrian creed, vi. 261
—of earth, air, water, xi. 234
——plants and trees, viii. 340–342
——Quarters, four old men represent the, xi. 137, 143
——rivers, v. 19, 20
——world beyond, viii. 238, 239–240, 242–243, pls. XII, XIII, XIV, opp. p. 240
—(" souls ") assemble on mountain-tops and battle for their countrymen, iii. 227
—worship of, iii. 277, 305–306
Genitals of mummy cut off and wrapped with it, xii. 418 22
Geniti Glinni (" spirits of the Glens "), iii. 134, 147
Genius and Lares, i. pl. LX, opp. p. 290
—bear as underground, x. 293 40
—family, iii. 240
—Iuno, i. 291
Genji, Prince, stories of, viii. 297, 300–301
" Genji Monogatari," romance, viii. 297, 298, 301
Gentlemen of the Wood, viii. 114
Geoffrey of Monmouth euhemerizes Celtic myths, iii. 93
——reports Arthurian legend as known in South Wales, iii. 184, 185–186
Geomancy, viii. 135, 140, 141
Geometric qualities and construction of images, viii. 50–51
Georgia, region named for St. George, v. 338
Geraistios, Athenians sacrifice four maidens on tomb of, i. 69
Geras (" Old Age "), abstract divinity of time, i. 282
Gerasa, coins bearing figure of Fortuna at, v. 19
Gerd, giantess, ii. 10, 16, 66, 110, 111, 112, 114, 144, 220, 278, 279, 298

Geri (" the Ravener "), wolf of Odin, ii. 65
" Germania " of Tacitus, ii. 12
Germanic tribes, few references to gods of pagan, ii. 17–18
Germany in Lettish folk-songs, iii. 328, 359 56
Germinating powers, viii. 222
Germs, three, of Zoroaster left in world, vi. 342–343
Gerovit, festival for, iii. 306, 356 14
—(Herovit), Pomeranians worshipped, iii. 283
Gerraei, land of, v. 4
Gersimi, daughter of Freyja, ii. 120
Geruthus: see GEIRROD, KING.
Geryoneus, cattle of, stolen from Hercules by Cacus, i. 303
—killed by Herakles, i. 86
—legends of, vi. 263
—son of Chrysaor and Kalliroë, i. 86
—three-bodied, i. 34
Geshtinanna, goddess, v. 349
" Gesta Danorum," ii. 12, 34
Gestation, 260 days approximate period of, xi. 102
Gestumblindi, Odin as, ii. 62, 190, 201
Gēush Urvan (" soul of the ox "), vi. 286, 288, 328, 362 26
Gewar, king of Norway, ii. 131, 132
Ghanaśyāma, Gansām Deo metamorphosed into, vi. 238
Gharma, sacrificial kettle, vi. 80
Ghat, burning, Śiva at the, vi. 113
Ghaṭotkaca, vi. 156
Ghora Āṅgirasa was teacher of Kṛṣṇa son of Devakī, vi. 126
Ghoṣā befriended by Aśvins, vi. 31
Ghost baby, vii. 189, 190, pl. XVII, opp. p. 190
—Bushman idea of a, vii. pl. XXX, opp. p. 290
—comes to drink Yule-ale, ii. 191
—derivation of, in Semitic, v. 355
—gallû is a, v. 359
—hand of, disease laid to, v. 364
—of Chên became general in bodyguard of Dragon King, viii. 191
——Etana invoked, v. 173
—(or Satan), in fish, vii. 244
——sword taken from, ii. 136
— -world and death, x. 233–236
— -worshippers, heathen Armenians, vii. 94

Ghostly beings, vampires, and demons, viii. 281–292

Ghosts, ii. 308, 309, 315; vi. 203, 228, 243, 245, 246, 247–250; vii. 117, 118, 125, 128, 141, 180, 181, 183, 185, 186, 187, 188, 189, 190, 193, 196–197, 198, 242, 244, 288, 399 [11]; viii. 150, 151, 152, 154, 184; 224, 238, 239, pl. xi, opp. p. 240, 282, 287, 299, 301; ix. pl. xiii, opp. p. 116, 118, 142–144, 148, 226, 327 [24]; x. 117–120, 133, 145–153, 162, 230, 246, 262, 263, 264, 275 [10], 276 [12], 281 [20]; xi. 328; xii. 293; see also SHADE; SHADES; SHADOW; SHADOWS; SPIRITS, ANCESTRAL.

—ancestral, ii. 204, 208
—clothed like birds and fly, v. 329
—Eskimo, are men in front, skeletons behind, x. 8, 146
—fire derived from, x. 301 [51]
—gods, bogies, xi. 295–300, 323, 342
—Haltias appear as, iv. 11
—harvest withheld by, vii. 198
—in living world, children killed by mothers remain as, iv. 82
——shape of hills, v. 361
—interest of, in human welfare, vii. 73–74
—Kukuwazuka the fowl of the, vii. 288
—man fearing extinction of his line applies to, vii. 195–196
—of family, prayers to, for protection against tormenting demons, v. 162
——Hades, viii. 224
——strong men, xi. 279
—prayers against, v. 235
—present race sprang from bones of, x. 230
—property burned to supply, x. 215
—receive fire, x. 256
—scalped men become, x. 117–118, 275 [10], 276 [12]
—shield-maids and their, ii. 256
—three orders of; three orders of beings correspond to, vii. 136
—(urvakan), vii. 94

Ghoul, Arabian, v. 352, 353
Ghoulish spirit, ix. pl. xxiii, opp. p. 284
Ghṛtācī, an Apsaras, vi. 143
Giadruvava, companion of Guagugiana, xi. 30–32
Giaia and Giaiael in origin of sea-myth, xi. 29
Giant, Bês as, xii. 61

Giant, Great Hare as a, x. 49
— -killer (Thor), ii. 75, 81
—power, Utgard-Loki abstraction of, ii. 94
—race preceded gods, ii. 324
Giantesses as consorts of gods reckoned with deities, ii. 16, 106, 186
—Heimdall son of nine, ii. 153, 154
Giants, ii. 9, 10, 16, 23, pl. vi, opp. p. 32, 34, 46, 48, 49, 53, 55, 62, 63, 73, 78, 81–82, 83, 85–87, 88–90, 91, 92, 100, 101, 104, 110, 111, 114, 123, 124, 130, 131, 139, 151, 170, 171, 173, 175, 181, 182, 193, 199, 230, 241, 265, 266, 275–284, 324, 326, 351 [19], 384 [21]; iii. 55, 70, 131, 146, 148, 167, 169, 172, 173, 175, 176, 181, 185, 191, 200; vii. 86, 87; viii. 285–286; ix. 60, 61, 62, 63, 188, 189, 236–237; xi. 91, 92, 93, 94, 159, 168, 182, 204–209, 240, 331–332
—and gods, i. pl. viii (1), opp. p. 8
——Zeus conquer Titans and drive them into depths of earth, i. 8
—armed, born from blood of Ouranos, i. 6
—Aśvins as succouring, vi. 31
—born by blood of Ouranos perhaps forefathers of human race, i. 9
——of Gaia and Ouranos, i. 272
—challenge Zeus, i. 9
—Dance erected as memorial, iii. 201
—freed by Zeus, i. 8
—in Hebrew mythology may be wandering souls of dead, v. 355
—Land of, viii. 363
—offspring of angels, v. 357
—overthrown by Zeus and Athene, i. 9
—primitive race of, x. 108, 163, 228
—stone, x. 29, pl. ix, opp. p. 38, 132, 133, 134, 268 [2], 291 [38]–292, 297 [46]
—struggle of, replica of battle of Titans, i. 9
—volcanoes piled upon, i. 9
Gibbôrim, ancient Hebrew heroes, v. 358
Gibil, fire-god, and god of lustration, v. 100, 102–103, 296, 317
Gid-kuźo (Cattle man), iv. 161–162
Gifts, Arthur distributed, iii. 191
—at creation to Indian and white man, x. 70
—of Odin, ii. 56
—sacrificial, left at memorial tree, iv. 25–26

Gifts to dead, iii. 233, 234, 235

Gigim, gidim, ghosts, Semitic giants and demons correspond to Sumerian, v. 355, 364

Gihon, river, v. 315

Gīlān, vi. 363 22

Gilded Man, legend of, xi. 194, 196

Gilgamish, iii. 131
—an historical character, v. 234
—became Underworld deity, v. 235
—created by Aruru, v. 114–115, 236
—epic, v. 209–218, 224, 225, 226, 227, 234–269, 274, 330; vii. 69, 390 14
——Ishtar heroine of, vii. 38
—exposed, v. 234
—fills his jar from overflowing vase, v. 95, 96, 98
—legend of, and bull, v. 28, 29, 98, 238, 385 139
—Nimrod the Babylonian, v. 55
—prayer to, v. 162
—scanty fragments of original Sumerian Epic of, v. 234–235, 406 2
—with Tammuz, v. 235, 407 5

Gilla Caemhain, traces of annalistic scheme in chronological poem of, iii. 160
—Dacker and his Horse, tale of, iii. 173
—Decair brought horse to Fionn, iii. 128, 173

Gilling drowned by dwarfs, ii. 53

Gilvæthwy, iii. 96, 97

Gimil-ili-shu, v. 346
— -Sin as Tammuz, v. 345
——promulgated a date by completion of ship of antelope of Apsû, v. 106

Gimle, hall in Heaven, ii. 221, 318, 346, 347

Gina, tale of, ix. 277–278
—teiga is Haida designation for animals as such, x. 252

Ginabai, daughter of Bake, ix. 228–229

Ginn-regen, high, or holy gods, ii. 20–21

Ginnunga-gap, ii. 275, 324

Giocauvaghama, prophecy from, xi. 36

Giovava, grotto from which sun and moon emerged, xi. 28–29

Gir, Gira (" fire "; also god), Girra (fire-god) early title of Nergal, v. 49, 93, 136, 137, 259

Girdle at sacrifice, iv. 266, 271, 272, 273–274, 276, 280, pl. XXXVIII, opp. p. 288
—Parsi, vi. 184
—sacred, vi. pl. III, opp. p. 26

Girdle: see BELT, UNGIRDING OF, ETC.

Girdles, ii. 22, 77, 80, 84, 133, 272

" Girl and the Cannibals," Zulu tale, vii. 136
—Ground-Heat, Yellow-Corn, etc., x. 158
—in moon, with yoke and buckets, iv. 423
—sun, moon, and stars made from body of, ix. 314 103
—who Ate Pork, vii. 424 10
——married a star: see POÏA, ETC.
——Plaited Devil's Beard, vii. 251

Girnār, Neminātha became a Kevalin and attained final bliss at, vi. 221, 222

Girtablili (Sagittarius), scorpion-man, dragon of Tiâmat, v. 282

Gir-unu-gal, title of Lugalmeslam, v. 135, 136

Gishgimmash, Hittite pronunciation of Gilgamish, v. 253

Gishzida and Tammuz disappeared, v. 178, 180

Gisla, dream-women appear to, ii. 236

" Gisla-saga," ii. 119, 236, 302

" Gītagovinda " of Jayadeva, vi. 185

Gitche (Kitshi) Manito, x. 19, 40, 82, 284 28–285

Gīv, son of Gūdarz, companion of Haosravah, vi. 339

Gjallar-horn, ii. 50, 152–153, 154, 168, 340

Gjalp, daughter of Geirrod, caused Vimur to rise, ii. 84

Gjoll River and Gjoll-bridge, ii. 130, 304–305, 321

Gjolp, giantess, ii. 153

Gladiatorial sacrifices, xi. 59, 76, 356 18

Gladsheim (" world of joy "), ii. 45, 313, 327, 329

Glam haunts farm, ii. 308–309

Glamour, ii. 6, 22, 29, 93, 94, 132, 149, 254, 280; iii. 87, 122, 172

Glas, father of Garman, iii. 136

Glasir, tree in Valhalla, ii. 333

Glasisvellir, Gudmund dwells in, ii. 322

Glass house, Merlin went to sea in a, iii. 201
—stones on altar fused into, ii. 121

Glastonbury, identification of, with Avalon, iii. 194–195

Glauke, fountain of, at Corinth, i. 258
—Medeia dismisses her children with fatal gifts for, i. pl. XXVIII, opp. p. 110

Glauke, poisoned robe and garland sent by Medeia to, i. 115
—quenched flame caused by Medeia's drugs in spring, i. 41
—wife of Iason, in succession to Medeia, i. 115
Glaukos and Diomedes exchange golden and bronze armour, i. 128, 158
—of Anthedon duplicates son of Minos, i. 42
——Potniai, son of Sisyphos or of Poseidon, i. 38–39, 211
—said to have died in collision of chariots at Olympia, i. 39
—sea-god, i. 261
—son of Minos, i. 61, 62–63
———raised from dead by Asklepios, i. 280
———returns from Hades, i. 144
Glaumvor, ii. 311
Gleipnir, fetter made of non-existent things, ii. 99
Glen of the Deaf, Cúchulainn concealed in, iii. 155
Glen, Sol married, ii. 183
Glitnir (sky), hall of Forseti, ii. 162, 197
Globes, dying fire in temple of Sul turns into stony, iii. 11
Glooscap: see MANIBOZHO.
Glory (Av. Khvarenanh; Old Pers. farnah), vi. pl. XXXII, opp. p. 260, 271, 285, 289, 300, 304, 305, 309, 311, 314, 322, 324, 327, 332–333, 336, 337, 341, 342, 343
Gloucester, nine witches of, iii. 191
Glove of Skrymir, ii. 92, 144
—wolf-skin, causes transformation, ii. 293
Gloves of Thor, ii. 22, 77, 78–79, 80, 84
Glum, ii. 117, 119, 235
Gluttony, ii. 88, 89, 92
—poetry of Northwest tribes pervaded by spirit in, x. 248
Gna, goddess, ii. 15, 174, 185
Gnæfa, ii. 185
gNas-c'un, vi. 209, 216
Gnat which rises with sun, iii. 190
" Gnawer," auger, ii. 54
Gnipahellir, cliff cave in Hel, ii. 304
Gnomes, ii. 223

Gnosticism, Babylonian influence on, v. 156
—Harranian elements in, v. 154
—myth and ritual of Bêl-Marduk known to, v. 323
Gnostics, iv. 321, 322
—Patagonian principles in common with, xi. 333
Goat, vi. 27, 36, 56, 58, 62, 70, 91
—Chimaira compounded of lion, dragon, and, i. 39
— -fish, v. 105, 106
—is a good šêdu, v. 359
—Khurmusta's daughter in form of, iv. 503
—of Odin, ii. pl. VI, opp. p. 32, 125
—part of materia medica of Artemis, i. 185
—primeval animal, vii. 144
—six-headed wild, legend of, v. 129
— -skin, babies carried in, vii. 190
— -star (Lyra), v. 317
—upon whom sin poured out is sacred to Ninamaškug, v. 356
—with seven horns, iv. 492
Goatskin attribute of Pan, i. 269
Goats of Thor, ii. 22, 71, 77–78, 79, 87, 92, 93, 94, 100
—satyrs as, v. 355, 356
Goat's stomach, contents of, favourite medicine, vii. 231
Gobharaṇa, Buddhist priest, viii. 188
Gobi, Desert of, hints of, in Karen myths, xii. 269
Goblet-bearers, iv. 277–278
—golden, Helios believed to be conveyed in, i. 243
——sun embarks in, vii. 49
—Ukko's, iv. 228–229
Goblin captors of Tawhaki's mother killed, ix. 58–59
— -slayers, Agni and Indra as, vii. 45
Goblins, ii. 205
—three, of Sescind Uairbeoil, iii. 148
God, Gods:
God as modern equivalent for ancient Zeus in Greece, i. 312
—becomes incarnate in his votaries, vii. 13
—chief, divided their various spheres among divinities, iii. 50
—cult of a local, on hill within which his abode was, iii. 122
—desertion of, ii. 312

God-Father, iv. pl. xxviii, opp. p. 228

—four-faced, x. 177

—frost-, iv. 233

—general use of word, iv. 391

—goddess, low conception of, in Pyramid Age and later, xii. 16

—Greek, when conceived not reality but symbol, i. xlviii

—Heaven as synonym for, viii. 51; see also Heaven, " The Supreme Ruler."

—heaven-: see Heaven-god.

— -house, spirits of drowned escorted to, by priest, iv. 209

—(Iruwa) seen by woman as large body white one side red other, vii. 238

—Kalunga one of the names for, vii. 117

— -kings, v. 326

—male, of Thracians gradually usurped certain functions of the Asianic goddess, vii. 12

— -man, semi-divine nature of mankind, v. 276

— -Mash, name of Ninurta, v. 116

—meaning of, v. 65, 93

—name for, borrowed by Mordvins from Indo-European source, iv. xix

—Norse use of tyr in general sense of, ii. 97

—of death and resurrection of religions that preceded Christianity was Dumu-zi, " the faithful son," v. 346

——hot springs, Suku-na-biko sometimes called, viii. 230

——plenty, horned deity with bag of grain, iii. 9

——the Sun, existence of, in pagan Russia, iii. 273

——waters, Varuṇa as, vi. 137

—one, among Elbe Slavs, iii. 277

—or king, Lykaon may represent old Pelasgic, i. 21

—owns [forbidden] fruit tree, vii. 316

—sons, horses, steeds, daughter of, iii. 320, 322, 324, 326, 328–329, 330, 359 52 56, 360 62

——of, iv. 402–412

—supreme, xii. 256

——and eternal, xi. 24

—(Taaroa) assumes substance of man, ix. 27

—three-headed, iii. pl. vii, opp. p. 56

—throne of, in seventh Heaven, v. 95

God who had child by mortal reborn while still existing himself, iii. 83

—wind-, iv. 232, 233

—with ass's ears, xii. 108 (fig. 107), 109 (fig. 108)

——overflowing waters, v. 95

——rayed head and wands or bolts in hands in monolithic gateway, xi. 234, pl. xxxv, opp. p. 234

—Zeus as supreme, i. 157

Gods A, B, C, D [p. 134], E, F, G, H, I, K, L, M, N, O, P, xi. 139–140

—abandoned?, how were the old, iii. 45

—above, belief in pre-existing world of, ix. 19

—abstract, i. 299

—Agni benefactor to, vi. 44

—alternating twin-, ii. 64, 106, 158

—and Asuras, enmity between, vi. 150–151

——sprung from one father, vi. 106

——demons, wars of, vi. 263–274

——giants, i. pl. viii (1), opp. p. 8

—(and goddesses), dying: see Dying gods.

——katcinas, x. 187–192

——men formed by Khnûm(u) and Ḥeqet, xii. 50

——mortals, signs distinguishing, vi. 149

—animals associated with, ii. 218

—arise by emanation from primeval pair, v. 291

—as patrons of upper and underworlds and as rulers and tutelaries, xi. 54

——supposed mortals, deified and worshipped after death, ii. 310

—assembly of, at Kitsuki, viii. 250

—beliefs of Egyptians of historical period concerning, xii. 15

—birth of, vi. 17–18

—Celtic, iii. 7, 8, 9, 54–61

—citadel of, built by giant, ii. 278

—connected with nature, xii. 33–67

—cosmic, not conceived as human beings, viii. 50–51

——emphasized by earliest Egyptian theology, xii. 46

—could transform each other and mortals, iii. 59, 60

—council of, ii. 264; x. 191

—cutting down trees, iii. 157, 158, pl. xx, opp. p. 158

Gods, deification of aspects and ac-
tivities of, v. 128
—deifications of humans into, vii. 117,
119
—departmental and momentary, i. 300
—descriptions of, ii. 21
—developed from buds on *top* of tree,
ix. 176
—development of, from spirits, xii.
16–17
——in Greek religion, i. xlviii
—direct descent of man from, ix. 26,
27, 167, 169
—disappearance of, into the air, vii.
132, 133
—dragons [hostile to man and fer-
tility] conquered by, iii. 130
—earthly, surrendered to heavenly gods,
viii. 211
—Egyptian, prehistoric, xii. 22 (fig. 2)
—embodiment of, in human form common to Tibet, vi. 208
—family, iv. 113–138
—Féinn possessed magic articles once
belonging to, iii. 175
—fertility-, sun-, thunder-, and wind-,
iv. 250 (fig. 9), 280
—foreign, xii. 153–158, 410 [1]
—further principal, xii. 129–152
—Gaulish, iii. 8, 9
—general survey of the, ii. 15–24
—ghosts, and bogies, xi. 295–300
——of chiefs or famous medicine-men
may become, vii. 183
—giant wishes to gain the power of the,
ii. 89
—given to clans, xi. 166, 181
—good, dwell in Abyss, xii. 73
—great, xi. 57–73
——of the Epic, vi. 103–130
————Plains, x. 80–81
—greater, i. 151–235; ii. 37–100
——personalized parts of nature eventu-
ally became the, iii. 133
—Greek, influence of community on
development of, i. xlix
——intimate relations of, to life-interests
of men, i. xlix
——rise of, from one stage to another,
i. xlviii–xlix
—having abode in sky, vii. 123, 131, 132,
133
—helping mortals, iii. 62–67
—heroic, v. 147

Gods, household, iii. 228, 240–248; iv.
136–137; v. 34–35; viii. 74–84; xi. 223
—hymn by, to Marduk, v. 308
—identification of, with other gods,
vi. 170
—in men's power, iii. 73
—incarnate in animals, vi. 63
—irreverent stories of, iii. 30
—jealousy of, against man, v. 167
—(Jumala, Jumo), sky, iv. 217
—Kronos assumed kingship over, i. 6
—land of, bestowing of knowledge,
plenty, etc., property of a, iii. 112;
see also LAND, GODS', ETC.
——never associated with dead, but
living invited there, iii. 114
——pigs associated with, iii. 127
—lesser, i. 236–284
—local, xii. 15–22
—Loki brings trouble upon, ii. 139, 140,
146, 148
—loves of the, iii. 78–91
—many tutelary spirits never developed
into, xii. 16
—minor, of the Epic, vi. 131–159
—momentary and departmental, i. 300
—mythic powers of, iii. 54–61
—native Italic, i. 289–300
—nature: of fire, Underworld, disease,
i. 296
——human life, earth, agriculture,
herding, i. 291–295
————sky, atmosphere, time, i. 289–290
————water, i. 295–296
——sacrifice to, indicated in Seide
sacrifice, iv. 111
—Navaho, x. 154–159
—of birth, iv. 252–261; see also JUMON-
AVA, ETC.
——conqueror and conquered tend to
coalesce, iii. 35
——earth and vegetation, iv. 239–251
——elements, x. 97–101
——foreign origin in Italic mythology,
i. 300–304
——human society, i. 297–299
——mountains, x. 132–135
——order, v. 291, 296
——Quarters, xi. 57
——war, v. 130; x. 191, 200
—offerings to, vi. 19–20
—old, associated with mounds, iii. 49
——of the land worshipped by Yaos
along with own ancestors, vii. 117

Gods, process of creating, for one's own uses, iv. 172
—product of, or emanation from, universe, ix. 16
—rank and functions of, ii. 23
—ransom, ii. 141
—reckoning of, and prayers to groups of, vi. 19
—regarded as brothers and sisters of men, v. 7, 8, 9
—Roman, equation of Celtic gods with, iii. 8, 9
—Romano-British, iii. 8
—sacrifices to nature, among Volga Finns, iv. 262–281
—servitude of beings who are, parallels to, iii. 28
—Sompio Lake Lapps worshipped first sighted objects on leaving tent in morning as, iv. 107
—special, represented each hour, xii. 66
—stations of, v. 304
—story of advance of, at Doom, ii. 340–341
—strife of the, iii. 23–41
—subjected to mortals, iii. 82
—Sumerian kings not infrequently assumed title of, v. 158
—things shared in common by the, vi. 148–149
—travelled through air or appeared over men's heads, iii. 56
—two heavenly, as creators, viii. 210
—various, xi. 50–51
—worship of the, iii. 305–306
—Yucatec, xi. 136–142
Goddess, Ashtar-Kemosh a father-mother, v. 47
—from Land of Living appears to Connla, iii. 84
—mother in Sumerian, v. 17
—of baked things, xii. 66
—sun as, ii. 196
Goddesses associated with gods, viii. 66, 67, 68
—Asynjur (sing. Asynja), specific name for, ii. 21
—eager for love of man, iii. 85–86
—in North American mythology, x. 5, 6, 273 7
—keys in form of, found in a temple, vii. 395 58
—lesser, ii. 178–189
—of the Ṛgveda, vi. 52–56, 92–93

Goddesses, virgin Earth mothers, v. 12
—worshipped by Elbe Slavs, iii. 289
Godeu, battle of, iii. 100
Godheim, Odin goes to, ii. 34
Godmund, ii. 292
Go(d)vetter, a good spirit, iv. 177
Goewin, Math's foot-holder, iii. 96
Goga, fire from body of, ix. 115
Gohone, winter, x. 26
Goibniu, Irish celestial smith, iii. 31, 32, 40, 51, 54, 97, 99, 361 90
Goidels: see IRISH CELTS.
Gojō, bridge of, over river Kamo, viii. 310
Gokarṇa, cult of " Dionysos " prevalent round, vi. 110
Gokuraku, Buddhist paradise, viii. 241
—Jōdo (Skt. Sukhāvatī), one of three chief paradises, viii. 241, 242
Gold, vi. 32, 145, 149; viii. 75, 146, 155; xi. 20–21, 44, 45
—a curse, ii. 141
—as solar, xii. 30, 140
—associated with Anahit, vii. 26, 29
——Ascension Eve, vii. 30
—citadel made of, vi. 116, 152
—Colombian, work of, xi. 196, pl. xxvii, opp. p. 196
—creation of men of, i. 17
—first smelting of, iii. 137
—found by watching flight of butterfly (as soul), iv. 8–9
—Gjoll-bridge thatched with, ii. 130
—Gollveig thought to embody power of, and its refining by fire, ii. 27, 28
—ground from mill, ii. 114, 283
—hair of, ii. 141
—in place of fire, gave light in Ægir's hall, ii. 172, 314
——possession when drowning good, ii. 191
——religious symbolism, xii. 30
—Īṣatprāgbhāra consists of pure, vi. 228
—Midas receives from Dionysos power to transmute objects into, i. 220
—pounded, resource against poison, ii. 378 49
—Rê"s members of, xii. 74
—same number of mouthfuls of, method of dividing inheritance, ii. 279
— -smiths, myth that dwarfs best, xii. 377 86
—(sunlight), theft of, x. 48
—tears of, ii. 27, 125, 126

Gold was Gaya Maretan's seed, vi. 294
—-workers, Xipe Totec patron of, xi. 76
—Zeus approaches Danaë in form of shower of, i. 11
Golden Age, vii. 103
——descriptions of, influence early Christian delineations of Heaven, i. 18
——of gods, ii. 241, 327, 378 49
——Saturnus ruler of the, i. 292
—cities, search for, xi. 194–196
—Fleece, i. 108, 109, 112
——Herakles sails on Argo in search of, i. 91
——ram of the, offspring of Poseidon, i. 211
—flower cat, viii. 327, 328
—Germ, vi. 50
—Hordes of Tatars, viii. 66
—Immortal of Great Knowledge, Buddha's title, viii. 194
—Lad, statue of, viii. 71
—table service which gave immortality to those eating therefrom, viii. 75
—the, as epithet of Kaltes mother, iv. 260–261
Goldun, Valkyrie, ii. 250
Goll, head of Féinn, iii. 161, 163, 164, 165, 168, 170–171, 173, 179
—nephew of Fiachna, iii. 37, 117
—Valkyrie, ii. 249
Gollinkambi, cock, ii. 313
Gollrond, witch, ii. 229
Gollveig ("Gold-might") is burned and comes alive again, ii. 27, 28
Goloka, a world given to Nandinī, vi. 134
Goλthn, persistence of paganism in, vii. 43, 385 6 (ch. v)
Gomatī, Nāgas dwell on shores of the, vi. 154
Gōmēz, bull's urine, vi. 302
Gondatti, iv. 403
Goṇḍs propitiate souls for one year, vi. 249
Gondul, Valkyrie, ii. 250
Good, vi. 261
—and Evil, contest of, iv. 370, 373
——god of, iii. 288
—as well as evil, said by late poets to have been contained in Pandora's jar, i. 15
—People, vii. 258

Good Spirit the creator in Guiana, xi. 256–257
—spirits recognized by Caribs, xi. 38
—thought, word, and deed, vi. 345
Goomblegubbons, bustards, ix. 288–289
Goonur, kangaroo-rat, tale of, ix. 284
Goose as sacrifice, iv. 160, 163
—association of, with Qêb, xii. 42
—early sacred animal of Amon, xii. 129
—Pairekse travels in form of, iv. 409
Gōpatshah, bull-man, vi. 333
Gopīs, Kṛṣṇa dances with, vi. 172, 177, 185
Gorakhpur, sacred fire at, vi. 234
Goranchacha, child born of virgin, xi. 201
Gorddu, sorceress, iii. 188
Gordias, in myth husband of Kybele, i. 275
Goreu, cousin of Arthur, iii. 189
Gorget, x. pl. iii, opp. p. 8.
Gorgo, type of, influenced by Bês, xii. 63
Gorgon, Athene invented flute on witnessing death of, i. 34
—head of, used to turn monster to stone, i. 35
—Perseus's quest for head of, i. 33–34
" Gorgoneion " of Athene, i. pl. viii (3), opp. p. 8
Gorgons, Athene imitated lamentations of the, on flute, i. 171
—represented a phase of the sea, i. 259
—three, after flight of Perseus with Medousa's head, i. pl. ii (2), opp. p. xlii
Gorgophone, daughter of Perseus, queen of Perieres, i. 24, 35
Gorias, Lug's spear brought from, iii. 41
Gorilla, vii. 418 35
Gorlois, Duke of Cornwall, iii. 184
Gorm, ii. 84–85, 94, 95, 321
Gortyna, mythical relationship of Apollo and Asklepios at cult-shrine at, i. 279
Gosāla, vi. 223
Goset dance (Five Tact Dance), ascribed to fairies of cherry blossoms, viii. 261
Goshy-e, giant, xi. 336
Gospels, Christian, said to be influenced by Buddhism, vi. 206
Gotama Rāhūgaṇa, vi. 92
—Śākyamuni: see BUDDHA.

Goþ (neuter), gods, with epithets "holy," "blessed," ii. 20

Gourd, viii. 121, 132; 319, 382 [10], 385 [7]
—in Wa creation-myths, xii. 288–289
—Wa race sprang from seeds of a, xii. 281

Gourds grew on place where Zimwi died, vii. 251
—splitting of, by successful suitor of Nang Pyek-kha Yek-khi, xii. 290–292

Gourgourgahgah, bird who laughs to announce dawn, ix. 275

Govannon, Brythonic equivalent of Goidelic Goibniu, iii. 97, 99

Govardhana, Kṛṣṇa upraises Mt., vi. 172, 236

Government, "Chow Li" treats of, viii. 45
—of Pacific North-west, x. 238–239

Grace-maiden, tale of, viii. 294–295

Graces at creation of Pandora, i. 15
—Hephaistos said to be married to one of the, i. 205
—see CHARITES.

Graeco-Roman accounts of Egyptian religion, xii. 92
——exaggeration of value of Egyptian mythology, xii. 7–8
——influence on Egyptian religion, xii. 239–240
——types of divinities, adaptations to, in late Egyptian religious art, xii. 212

Grahas, or "Seizers," vi. 157

Graiai, ancient daughters of Phorkys and Keto, i. 33–34
—the, represented a phase of the sea, i. 259

Grail romances, iii. 120, 186, 196, 198, 202–205

Grain-god: see NEPRI, ETC.
— -goddess created, v. 191, 193
——in Sumerian creation poem, v. 313, 314
——on primitive seals, v. 90
—Hou-chi and Yin Hung patrons of, viii. 66, 67
—images of Osiris in sprouting, symbolize resurrection, xii. 399 [111]
—sacrifice, iv. 405
——to, viii. 61
—staple, Triptolemos first taught cultivation of, i. 16
—under protection of Demeter, i. 226

Grainne and Diarmaid, pursuit of, iii. 65–66, 175–179, 185
—as deer, tale of, iii. 168

Graiveyakas, vi. 227

Gram, Sigurd's sword, ii. 267

Grammarian in myth, Linos a, i. 253

Grand Buddha = Tran-vu Pagoda, xii. 306–310

Grandfather Above, xi. 134

Grandmother, magic, x. 289 [34]

Grapes, blessing of, at Assumption of the Virgin, vii. 381 [5] (ch. ii.)

Grapevine extended from world above to underground village, x. 105

Grasper of Locks, Underworld being, xii. 202

Grass-folk and tree-folk, battle of, viii. 347–348

Grass, as hair, of Earth mother, x. 91
—man made from, ix. 176
—mother, iv. 249
—Mower, magic sword, viii. 304
—rings, importance of topmost of, supporting thatch, vii. 110–111
—sacred, Vena slain with the, vi. 166
—sacrifice for, iv. 242
—sacrificial, vi. 61
—twines around feet of belated travellers, vii. 338

Grasshopper form may be taken by spirits, xii. 175
—Girl, x. 162
—people, x. 160

Grasshoppers called "mother dead," x. 63

Gratitude, virtue of, viii. 317, 318–324, 354

Grave, iv. pl. xxviii, opp. p. 228
—Armenian and Avestan words for, vii. 96
—as house of dead, vii. 189
— -hills, ancestral, ii. 311
— -house of dead, iv. 31–32, 42
— -houses in Russian Karelia, iv. pl. i, frontispiece
—man (Merlin) who speaks from, iii. 201
— -mound at Indeóin na nDése, iii. 32
—of unmarried, water-jar placed on, i. 324 [9] (ch. ii)
——Urashima, viii. 265, 381 [5] (ch. iii)
—participants of memorial feast go to, to invite deceased, iv. 48, 49–50
— -plate, ii. pl. xxii, opp. p. 176

Grave-stone, Swedish, ii. pl. viii, opp. p. 60
—water pouring out at digging of, forms loch, iii. 136
Graves, cairns found in South Africa called Haitsi-aibeb's, vii. 216, 217
—ceremonies at, iii. 234
—cuckoos of wood placed on, iv. 35
—lucky or unlucky sites of, viii. 140–141
—of Armenian kings violated, vii. 95, 396 ³–397
——Gwythur, March, and Arthur, iii. 192
——Lapps and Northern Ostiaks, iv. pl. iii, opp. p. 36
——those who died of snake-bite marked by crosses, xi. 198, 202
—opened at cannibal feast, vii. 337
—ringed about to prevent dead from trampling down fields, iv. 35
—swept with birch sprigs called " giving Dziadys steam bath," iii. 237
—themselves become luminous, vii. 336
—three, of Yamato, viii. 305
——Unai and her lovers, viii. 295, 296
Gravestones, vii. 75, 95–96
Graveyard, ruler of, remembered at funeral feasts, iv. 45, 62, 73
—serpent-ghost genius of the, vii. 74, 75
Gravitation, dead in Celtic belief not subject to laws of, iii. 56
Greasing of hoes in flesh of human victim to acquire good crops, x. 306
Great Bear: see Ursa Major.
—Destroyer, x. 38
—Dipper, in United States, seven principal stars of Ursa Major, wh. see.
—Divide, x. 129–132
—Fear, giant, iii. 148
—God, the, xi. 54
——who became by himself, commentary of " Book of the Dead " on meaning of, xii. 219
—Hare, x. 39, 40, 43, 44, 46, 48, 49–50, 67, 121, 143, 296 ⁴⁵, 297 ⁴⁷–298, 298 ⁴⁸; see also Coyote; Manibozho.
—Heads, x. 29, pl. viii, opp. p. 30, 56, 104, 290 ³⁷–291
— -Land-Master: see Oh-kuni-nushi, successor, etc.

Great Learning, viii. 161
—Medicine, creator, x. 124, 284 ²⁸, 308 ⁶³
—Mother, Artemis of Ephesos a hybrid form of, i. 183
——influenced Classical mind more deeply than Isiac mysteries, xii. 121
—Mountain, x. 194
—Plain (gods' land), iii. 80
—Plains, x. 74–128
—Sea Serpent = dragon of Chaos, v. 118
—Serpent married a human, xi. 309–310
—Shining Heaven, sky-being, x. 257
—Spirit, x. xxvii, 5, 19–21, 22, 63, 82, 90, 105–106, 141, 271 ⁶–272, 308 ⁶³
——list of indigenous appellations of the, xi. 258
—Star, Venus, xi. 54, 57–58
—Tortoise of Zulus, vii. 320
—Turtle of Quirigua, xi. pl. i, frontispiece
—Uncle, Votiak spirit, iv. 179
—Vehicle: see Mahāyāna.
—Wain, xi. 319; see also Ursa Major.
Greater Dionysia, March festival in honour of Dionysos, i. 221
Greatest Mountain, ancestress of the Eagle clan, x. 242
Grebes and Locust, magic contest of, x. 161
Greece, approach of cult of Dionysos to, i. 216
—influence of Egyptian religion on, xii. 241, 242
——religion of, on Italic religion, i. 288–289
—Modern, survivals of Ancient Greek divinities and myths in, i. 311–315
—southern, Ishtar's cult in, vii. 38
Greek and Celtic myth of Apollo mingled, iii. 10
—astronomical systems borrowed from Babylonia, v. 304–305
—doctrines, echo of, found in Hawaii, ix. 5
—gods exercised relatively little influence on Egyptian pantheon, xii. 158
—influence on Armenia, vii. 16
—religion, nature of the, i. xlviii–xlix
Greeks, Egyptian religion less edifying than, and not to be compared with, religion of, xii. 245
Green, colour, in Egyptian mythology, xii. 367 ¹²

Green Feather Snake, xi. pl. vii, opp. p. 60, 67
—Isle, now above, now below waters, iii. 123
—ocean, the great, xii. 46, 400 [10]
—Osiris sometimes represented as, xii. 386 [14]
Greenland colonized by Icelanders, x. 1–2
Gregorian calendar, Floral Calendar adjusted to meet changes in, viii. 348
Gregory Magistros quotes fragment of poem of Artaxias, vii. 22
—the Illuminator substitutes festival of St. John Baptist for Navasard, vii. 382 [11]
——wages campaign against paganism in Armenia, vii. 24, 28, 34
Greip, giantess, ii. 84, 153
Greit, Little Dog of, iii. 199
—one of three notable prisoners of Britain, iii. 103
Grendel, x. 44
—female monster, ii. 209, 280
Grettir, ii. 230, 280, 285, 286, 308, 309
" Grettis-saga," ii. 280, 285, 286, 308
Grey of Macha, horse out of Grey Lake, iii. 128, 147, 156
Gṛhapati, Agni bears title of, vi. 44
—domestic fire, vi. 284
Grianan (bower) of Etain, iii. 79, 80
Grid, mother of Vidarr, ii. 48, 84, 158, 174, 278
Grief, three drops of, became lochs, iii. 135
Griffin, xii. 169
—became Typhonic animal of Sêth, xii. 390 [35]
Grijalva, Juan de, commanded second expedition to Yucatan, xi. 45
Grim, son of Stein, dedicated to Thor as Thorgrim, ii. 76, 119
—water-spirit, ii. 210, 211
Grimhild, ii. 155
Grimnir, Odin as, ii. 9, 61
" Grimnismal," ii. 6, 9, 15, 16, 23, 45, 61, 65, 77, 104, 127, 152, 156, 157, 158, 175, 176, 184, 199, 217, 220, 248, 313, 319, 321, 325, 326, 330, 331, 332, 333, 339, 341, 343
Grims River, ii. 229
Gringalet, steed of Gawain, iii. 197
Grjotunagard, Thor and Hrungnir fight at, ii. 81

Groa called from grave, ii. 124
—sang spells and recited charms, ii. 82, 165, 243
Groats, Norn, ii. 245
Grodno, iii. 317
Gromovnik, St. Iliya as, the dispenser of good harvests, iii. 296
Gronw Pebyr, lover of Blodeuwedd, iii. 97
" Grotta-song " (" Grottasongr "), ii. 7, 282, 283
Grotti, mill, ii. 283
Grotto, painted, of Sun and Moon, xi. 34
Grottoes as dwelling-place of dead, iv. 486; xi. 279
" Grougaldr," ii. 7, 10–11
Ground cut from under Muireartach, iii. 171
—first men came out of, ix. 169
—lying on, to avert evil from bhūts, vi. 247
Grove-folk, ii. 225
—tabued, near Marseilles, iii. 11–12
Groves and trees, sacred, ii. 203–208
—people have access to ghosts dwelling in sacred, vii. 196–197
—sacred, iii. 305–306
——and sacrificial, iv. 143–158, pl. xvii, opp. p. 146, 184, 189, 262–281
——connected with tailed Heaven-dwellers, vii. 191
Grunau, Simon, historian of 16th cent., iii. pl. xxxvii, opp. p. 304
Grus (Adad), v. 317
Guabancex, goddess of wind and water, xi. 25
Guabonito taught use of amulets, etc., xi. 32, 261
Guacarapita, one of five names of mother of supreme Being, xi. 24
" Guacharos, to join the," equivalent to being gathered to one's fathers in the tomb, xi. 279
Guagugiana (Vagoniona), parallel of HERO-TRANSFORMER-TRICKSTER (wh. see), xi. 30–32, 261, 285
Gualicho, evil spirit, xi. 333, 335
Guamaonocon and Iocauna, two names for one supreme Being, xi. 24
Guami, ruler, xi. 24
Guañape, decapitated mummies found on island of, xi. 222
Guanhumara, form of name Guinevere in Geoffrey of Monmouth, iii. 185

Guarantee of sun, moon, etc., of Bres, against fighting points to animistic view of nature, iii. 29

Guardian deities, vi. 210–211, 213, 215, 237, 240

—deity of Eneene, ix. 75

—domestic snake as, vi. 241

—female, watches souls in ovens of Hell, xii. 180 (fig. 189)

—goddess against poison, Sigyn may have been, ii. 150

——of children, vi. 246

—gods of Balder's barrow, ii. 134

—of Heavens, Thunderer as, x. 24

——image-house of Siryans, iv. 149

——kuala, iv. 117, 118, 121

——lud, iv. 145, 148, 150, 151

——Moonlight Night, viii. 224

——sacred groves (burial places) has charge of sacrifices, vii. 190, 191

—péists, iii. 131

—sea-dwelling, of yellow shells of the West, xi. 32

—spirit, Nāga as, xii. 280, 281

——of name of ancestor descends to child, iv. 15

——understood by Siryan ört, iv. 10

—spirits, ii. 20, 204, 255, 346, 347; iv. 394–395; ix. pl. XII, opp. p. 104; x. 11

——Saivo spirits originally, iv. 105

Guardians, v. 20

—bear, serpent, lightning, x. 5, 164

—Chinese counterpart of Buddhist, viii. 243

—daemons as, x. 145

—Fravashis as, vi. 261, pl. XXXIV, opp. p. 272, 286, 300, 327

—(of animal-kind), x. xvii, 292 40

—of dead, x. 236

——fire, x. 230–233

——king's crown in well, iii. 68

——men, x. 5, 145, 270 4

——portals, viii. 77–78, 103

——Sun, x. 255

——waters, dragons as embodiment of, iii. 130

——world, viii. 242–247, 279, 379 28, 383 5

—see also VÆTTIR; FYLGJA; NORNS (vol. ii).

Guatauva, messenger of goddess of wind and water, xi. 25

Guatavita, famous shrine, xi. 196

Guatemotzin, xi. 45

Guayarakunny, lord of the dead, xi. 335

Gucumatz, xi. 134, 161–163, 182

Gudanna, celestial bull, v. 28, 98, 256, 319

Gūdarz, vi. 339

Gudatrigakwitl (" Old-Man-Above "), x. 221, 229

Gudea, birth of, v. 404 15

—expelled the ú-dug-ga, v. 364

—inscriptions of, v. 170

—of Lagash, Sumerian priest-king, v. 68, 126

Gudenesberg, ii. 44

Gudmund killed by Illugi, ii. 252, 321, 322

—ox as Fylgja of, ii. 234

Gudrun, ii. 44, 155, 240, 241; iii. 104

Gueggiahora, supreme Being, xi. 297

Gufittar, underground dwarfish creature who brings cattle to earth, iv. 177

Gūga, snake-god, vi. 241

Guhyakas, vi. 141, 157, 158, 204

Guiana and the Orinoco, xi. 253–280

—leg-bands worn by Carib of, xi. 37

Guianos, yellowish shells, xi. 32

Guide (rare), the Saattaja is, iv. 11, 12

Guilds, actors' and musicians', Dionysos patron of, i. 221

Guillotine and its inventor, story of, resembles that of first trap in Ireland, iii. 137

Guimazoa, one of five names of mother of supreme Being, xi. 24

Guinea-fowl associated with cult of Artemis, i. 184

——sisters of Meleagros changed into, i. 16

Guinevere (Guanhumara; Gwenhwyfar), iii. 185, 188, 190, 192–193, 197, 199

Guineveres, a triad speaks of three, all wives of Arthur, with different fathers, iii. 193

Gujarāt, " Mothers " in, vi. 238

Gula (Aquarius), v. 86, 395 22

—(Bau), wife of Ninurta, in epic, v. 120–121

—Damu appears for, v. 133

—Earth mother, v. 13, 115

—name of earth-goddess as patroness of medicine, v. 91, 110, 182, 183

—Sumerian earth-goddess, sister of En-lil, v. 14

—Sumero-Babylonian mother-goddess, v. 15

Gulf Region, x. 53–73
Gull, Apollo in form of, i. 180
—forms the sky, ix. 249
Gullfaxi (" Golden-mane "), horse of Hrungnir, ii. 66
Gullinbursti, boar of Frey, ii. pl. VI, opp. p. 32, 109
Gullintani (Heimdall), ii. 153
Gulliver, Japanese, by Bakin, viii. 381
—motif, viii. 363–364
Gulltop, horse of Heimdall, ii. 153
Gullveig, slaying of, by the gods, ii. 337
Gulu, "Heaven," vii. 117, 129, 152, 172
Gulumpambe, name of chameleon in Nyasaland, vii. 160, 161
Gum of wattle-tree, origin of man from, ix. 272
Gumba, cannibal dwarf race followed by the, vii. 259
Guṇakeśī, daughter of Mātali, vi. 132
Gund stones, ii. 203
Gundlaug ridden, ii. 300
Gungnir, spear of Odin, ii. 43, 66, 266
Guṅgū, goddess, vi. 53
Gunn and Gondul sing of blood before battle, ii. 250
Gunnar Helming and image of Frey, tale of, ii. 115–116
Gunnar's barrow open, ii. 308, 311
Gunnhild, queen, ii. 230
Gunnlod, giantess, ii. 10, 48, 49, 53, 54, 174, 279
Gunnodoyah, once mortal, now a lesser Thunderer, x. 24
Gunthram and snake as soul-animal, tale of, ii. 217
Gunwald the Thul or "Reciter," ii. pl. XXXI, opp. p. 238
Gurguntius, son of Belinus, Gargantua may have been, iii. 135
Gurikhoisib, First Ancestor, vii. 158
Gūshasp fire, vi. 306
Gushtāsp kills dragon, vi. pl. XLIII, opp. p. 340, 341
Gusts-of-wind, x. 35, 36
Guth, Valkyrie, ii. 248
"Guthrunarkvitha," ii. 155, 195
Gūzhak and Haoshyangha, Iranians descendants of, vi. 298
Guzu Tenno, another name of storm-god, viii. 228
Gwadyn Odyeith, sparks from foot of, iii. 190

Gwadyn Ossol, highest mountains became a plain under feet of, iii. 190
Gwalchmei (GAWAIN, wh. see), iii. 188, 191
Gwales, Bran's head-bearers remained at, iii. 101
Gwanazi, chief of Maputa, vii. 358
Gwawl, iii. 94, 95, 102
Gwchyvar, iii. 191
Gwddawc, Kei died at hands of, iii. 199
Gweir imprisoned in Caer Sidi, iii. 96
—one of three notable prisoners of Britain, iii. 103, 188, 192, 339 [4]
Gwenhwyfach, sister (in "Kulhwch") of Guinevere, iii. 192
Gwenhwyfar, Welsh form of name Guinevere, iii. 185, 188, 190, 193
Gwenn Pendragon, Arthur three nights in prison near, iii. 189
Gwevyl, strange lips of, iii. 190
Gwiawm, marvellous powers of, iii. 190
Gwion Bach obtained inspiration intended for Avagddu, iii. 57, 110, 166
—parallel to Tuan MacCairill, iii. 207
—reborn as Taliesin, iii. 112
Gwoden [Godan] (Odin) called Mercury by Romans, ii. 37
Gwrhyr Gwalstawt sent to boars in form of bird, iii. 188, 189
Gwri Golden-Hair, son of Rhiannon and Pwyll, became Pryderi and succeeded Pwyll, iii. 94–95
Gwrnach Gawr, killed by Kei, iii. 198–199
Gwyddneu, basket of, iii. 192
Gwydion, iii. 96–97, 98, 100, 155
Gwydion's Castle name for Milky Way, iii. 100
Gwydno's weir, wealth found at, on May-day, iii. 110
Gwyn, magician and warrior, iii. 108, 122, 191, 194, 212
Gwynedd governed by magic, iii. 98
Gwythur, Creidylad affianced to, iii. 108
—grave of, iii. 192
Gyes born of Ouranos and Gaia, i. 6
"Gylfaginning," ii. 5–6
Gylfi, king of Sweden, ii. 6, 24, 29, 32, 33, 181, 314
Gymir (Ægir), Gerd daughter of, ii. 110, 111, 171, 276–277
Gyōja (the Ascetic Master), viii. 276
Gyrd, dream woman, ii. 250

H

Ḥa(?), xii. 133, 405 [40]
Ha-ak, cannibal monster, x. 179
Haamu, "shadow-soul," iv. 12
Habiru and their god Ilāni, v. 72–73, 392 [351]
—introduced cults of Sin and Ningal at Harran, v. 153
Habonde, Dame, may be Fulla, ii. 184
Ḥabnutu, vessel, v. 333
Habur (Eridu), city of water-god Enki-Ea, v. 207, 344
—River, v. 287, 288
Hacavitz, god of Mahucutah, xi. 166, 167
Hachiman ("Eight Banners"), viii. 252, 383 [3], 387 [4]
Hackelberg, leader of Furious Host often bears some form of the name, ii. 42
Hadad, male deity, v. 39, 42
Hadba'd, Aramaic deity, v. 42
Hadding ("slayer of a benignant god"), ii. 56, 102–103, 105, 113, 278, 306, 311, 320
Hades, iii. 105; vii. 50, 69, 96–98; viii. 223–224, 238; xi. 80
—Aeneas descends into, i. 305
—Aiakos accorded high place after death in kingdom of, i. 121
—all dead must go to same, xii. 417 [21]
—(Babylonian Arallû), vii. 50, 69
—dead remembered during first period in, iv. 40
—Dionysos as releaser from, i. 220
—Harrowing of, iii. 209
—Hermes conductor of souls to, i. 194
—inside of elephant's stomach the Zulu, vii. 198
—Jaik-Khan escort for souls bound to, iv. 402
—Odysseus's descent into, i. 137
—or Arallû possible explanation of Aralez, vii. 395 [58]
——Hell, Annwfn later equated with, iii. 122
—place, not person, in modern Greek folk-belief, i. 314
—punishment of Danaïds in, i. 30
—punishments of, i. 144
—seven gates must be passed to enter, v. 328–329, 330, 331
—shade of Orion in, i. 250

Hades, storeys in, iv. 309
—visits of living to, i. 144
Hades binds Theseus and Peirithoös to Seat of Lethe, i. 105
—born of Rhea and Kronos, i. 274
—cap of, rendered Perseus invisible, i. 34
—carried Persephone off in his golden chariot, i. 227–228
—condemns Sisyphos to roll a stone uphill, i. 38
—fighting on side of Pylians wounded by Herakles, i. 92
—image of, on tomb of Aphareus, i. 26
—kine of, i. 88
—king of Underworld, i. 142
—meaning of Persephone's espousal to, i. 231
—Peirithoös and Theseus go to home of, to capture Persephone, i. 105
—releases Persephone from Underworld, i. 229
—see PLOUTON.
—sometimes called Zeus, i. 152
—Zeus consigned Sisyphos to, i. 37
Hadramut, inscriptions from, v. 3
—map of, v. 377 [8]
Hadrian constructed temple of Venus and Rome, i. 294
Hadui episode, x. 37, 285 [28]
Hadyayōsh, ox, vi. 289
Hafgygr ("sea-giantess"), ii. 209
Hafra drottin (Thor, "lord of goats"), ii. 78
Hafsman, water-spirit, ii. 210
Hagen seized garments of merewîf, ii. 212
Hagene compelled water-women to prophesy, ii. 261
Hag-ridden men, ii. 289, 290, 300, 302
Hags of Doom in battle of Mag-Tured, iii. 25
—supernatural, iii. 169, 170, 171
Hāhāhūhū, vi. 97
Hai-chow, viii. 190
Hai-uri (Bush-jumpers), vii. 243
"Hai Yü Ch'ung K'ao," viii. 127
Hail, prayer against, iv. 245, 246
—soul of Tanshikai came as, iv. 398
Haimon, death of, before cavern in which Antigone sealed, i. 53

Hair, ii. 38, 80, 95, 141, 191, 266; v. 256, 261; viii. 228, 229; x. 29, 49, 85, 91, 100, 215, 302 55
—attaches giant to a rock, x. 163
— -bridge, vii. 100
—burnt in fire desecrates it, vii. 54
—catching in tree saved woman from flood, ix. 257
—colours of: i. (golden) 77; (purple) 69; iv. (black) 193, 195; (green) 197, 201; (white) 198; (yellow) 201
— -covered man, iv. 374–376, 380, 383–384
—cutting as sign of mourning, vii. 95
—deceased by river side combing her, x. 162
—from mother-deer's lick, on forehead of Oisin, iii. 168
—Ganges received in Śiva's, vi. 115
—how Fionn's, turned grey, iii. 168–169
—ladder of, sorcerers climbed to tie moon and sun, vii. 367
— -mats, persons dying on, must reckon number of hairs in afterworld, iv. 21
—of bear, biting of, as one swears oath, iv. 85
——Xochiquetzal, woman formed from, xi. 92, 93
—primitive pair meet through finding of, ix. 169
—removing all, from body, xi. 302
—soul in, iv. 5
—straight and curly on first two males, ix. 273
—strength of fairy in her, iii. 258
—surrendered as token of devotion of life to a deity, i. 97
—tearing of, expression of sorrow for dead, iv. 27
—Thanatos clips lock of, from head of dying to hasten last breath, i. 278
—unbound, ensures free passage of dead, iv. 27
Hairs, golden, promised to dog, iv. 373, 374, 375
Haiti (Hispaniola), myths of, xi. 28–32
Haitsi-aibeb of the Hottentots, vii. 119, 158, 159, 214, 215, 216
Hakalanileo, husband of Hina, ix. 89
Hakama, viii. 355
Ḥa-ka-Ptaḥ, sacred name of Memphis, i. 324 8
Hakemann, water-spirit, ii. 210

Hakkas, a raiding sept who turned the Tashōns out of their capital, xii. 267
Hako ceremony, x. xx, 92–93, 97, 170, 272 6, 292 39; see also FEATHER-SYMBOLISM.
Hakon, Earl, ii. 65
—king, ii. 77, 104, 161, 187–188, 250–251, 315, 342
" Hakonarmal," ii. 161, 250, 315, 342
" Hakonar-saga," ii. 113
Halāhala, form of Dhyānibodhisattva of Gotama, vi. 212
Hālāhala, poison which burned all creation, vi. 106
Haldja, Ruler, household god, iv. 169–170
Half-child, tale of, ix. 215–216
— -man (Pales-murt), iv. 181, 182
— -men, vii. 138, 244, 245, 249, 251, 252, 413 13 18 19
— -sun created, xi. 92
— -trolls, ii. 286
Halfdan slain by Einarr, ii. 240, 280
" Hálfs-saga," ii. 121
Halfway between Heaven and earth, wicked spirits stop, iv. 479
Halieus, the Fisherman, descendant of Samem-roumos, v. 54
Halirrhothios, son of Poseidon, attacks Alkippe and is killed by Ares, i. 69
Hall and kinsmen, Fylgjur of, ii. 236, 237
—Odin's, Gollveig burned in, ii. 27
—of slain (Valhalla), ii. 45
——the Thirty-third Heaven, viii. 196
Halla, sorcerer's stool, xi. 264
Hallāt (Allāt), mother-goddess of South Arabic religion, v. 15
Hallfred, skald, ii. 194, 235
Hallinskidi (Heimdall), ii. 153
Hallīśa dances, vi. 172
Hallmund, a Land-vættir, ii. 230
Hallowe'en, Cúchulainn active from, until Spring, iii. 141
—gods regarded as demons on, iii. 68, 69
—(Samhain), four Fomorians expelled on, iii. 33
Halmahera, ape or tortoise as trickster-hero in, ix. 203, 204
—Indian influence in, ix. 242
Halman perhaps Aleppo, v. 387 184
Halogaland, ii. 106, 186, 187
Haltia, tutelary genius of man which may precede him, iv. 11, 169–171, 173

Hâlu, uncle, ancestor, v. 10
Halwanli and his brothers (Cain and Abel story), xi. 274–275
Halziqu, leather water-jar, v. 332, 333
Ham, Fomorians descendants of, iii. 23
Hama, necklace carried off by, ii. 124
Hamadryads and Dryads, i. 270
—tree-spirits, i. 258
Hāmāravān, vi. 336
Hamatsa songs, x. 248–249
Hambarus, chimeras, vii. 91
Hamingjur, weapon-bearing guardian spirits, ii. 255
Hamīstakān, resting-place for those whose sins and good works counterbalance, vi. 344–345
Hamitic, moon-myth characteristically, vii. 168
—speech, vii. 108, 109
Hamlet (Amleth), ii. 83
Hamlet, god of, known in primitive Egypt, xii. 18
Hammer, god with a, iii. 8, 9, pl. ix (b), opp. p. 86, pl. xiii, opp. p. 116, pl. xiv, opp. p. 120, pl. xxvi, opp. p. 208
—iron, reason for veneration of, by a Lithuanian people, iii. 318
—may denote creative power, iii. 8
—Ngawn-wa Magam shaped earth with, xii. 263–264
—of Donar, ii. 69
——Thor, ii. 10, 22, 60, 69, 71, 74, 77, 78, 79, 80, 84, pl. xi, opp. p. 84, 87, 88, 89, 92, 130, 142, pl. xxxi, opp. p. 238, 266, 346, 384 [21]
—shaman, iv. 288, 289
—weapon of, and offering to, thunder-gods, iv. 230, 231
Hammurabi and sun-god, v. 149, 150
—calls himself " establisher of holy repasts for Ninazu," v. 163
—conquered Mari by might of god Dagan, v. 80
—hymn on 'Anat by, v. 26, 27
—is Amraphêl, king of Kingin, in opinion of Langdon, v. 384 [128]
Hamr (sing. Hamingja), skin, covering, ii. 233, 235
Hamramr, wolf-form, ii. 293
Haṁsikā, vi. 134
Hamther slays Erp, ii. 240
" Hamthesmal," ii. 222
Hana, Dagan appears in, v. 80

Hanaçiruka of Mata, vii. 389 [10]
Han Ch'i, statesman, viii. 106
Han Chung-li, viii. 122
Han Dynasty, viii. 10, 19, 20, 25, 32, 44, 55, 62, 70–71, 73, 75, 76, 81, 93, 94, 117, 122, 134, 144, 174, 176
Han Fei Tzŭ, viii. 19
Han History, viii. 140
Han Hsiang, one of the Eight Immortals, viii. 126–127
" Han Li Chih," viii. 25
Han Yü, scholar, viii. 126, 200, 201, 202, 203
Hand, fire obtained from, iii. 137
—left, used in washing or sacrificing to dead, iv. 18, 67, 73
—loss of, ii. 99, 100
—of glory caused invisibility and sleep, iii. 107
——silver made for Nuada, but a spell restored the flesh hand, iii. 28
—open, symbol of, xii. 422 [6]
— -writing, dexterity in, viii. 387 [8]
Hands, black, iv. 502
—in creation, x. 221, 228
—of Bêl, priest prepares to take, to lead him to the Akîtu, v. 318
" Hanes Taliesin," iii. 109, 111
Hangchow, viii. 66, 95, 97
Hanged go to Paradise, xi. 139
—men talk, ii. 46, 47
—Odin god of the, ii. 43
Hanhau, lord of Mitnal, xi. 139
Hankow, viii. 5
Hannibal and Artaxias expelled Seleucids from Armenia, vii. 8
—expelled from Italy by Magna Mater, i. 303, 304
Hannouch, wild beings, xi. 340
Hannouchmachaaïnan stolen by the Hannouch, xi. 340
Hanoi, Le-loi crowned king in, xii. 303
—Mountain of Jade and Pagoda of Tran-vu in, xii. 304–307
Hanpa, Pazuzu son of, v. 371, 372
Hanthawadi Sinbyuyin (Branginoco) ordered sacrifices to Mahāgiri Nāts stopped, xii. 345
Ha-nui-o-rangi, child of Rangi by his first wife, ix. 8
Hanumān, monkey-god, vi. 128, pl. xv, opp. p. 128, 129, 236
" Hao Ang Hsien Hua," viii. 70
Hao T'ien Yü Huang Shang Ti, viii. 59

Haoma, iv. 447; vi. 28, 59; 265, 280, 281–283, 291, 295, 325, 338, 342, 350 —as tree of life, iv. 356

— -plant, Zarathushtra's soul comes to earth in stalk of, vii. 45

—(a god), vi. 269, 270, 282, 333, 337, 338, 341, 342

Haoshyangha (Phl. Hōshang) and Gūzhak, Iranians descendants of, vi. 298, 299–300, 302

Haosravah (Phl. Kai Khusrau), vi. 333, 336, 337, 338, 339, 340, 350

Ḥapet (Embracer), arms which hold the sun, xii. 387 [23]

Ḥaʻpi, Apis compared secondarily with, xii. 163, 412 [6]

—fertility-god, xii. 46

—(the Nile), nearest representative of element of water, description of, xii. 45–46, 370 [32]

Hapikern, Nohochakyum will wear serpent, at end of world, xi. 141–142

Hapi-ñuños, harpy-like daemons, xi. 238

Happiness (fu), why symbolized by bat, viii. 104

—Ḥetpet deity of, xii. 67

—spirit of, viii. 82

" Happy Land " (Fu-ti), viii. 115

Haptōk Rīng (Ursa Major), vi. 276

Har ("high"; Odin), one of lords of Asgard, ii. 6, pl. III, opp. p. 12, 24, 199, 243

Ḥar-akhti and Horus retained in worship by Amen-ḥotep IV, xii. 226

—"Horus of the Horizon," xii. 27, 55, 388 [28]

—hymn of penitence to, xii. 235

—Iu-s-ʻa-s wife of, xii. 134

Ḥar-em-akhet: see HARMACHIS.

Ḥar-ḥekenu, Rēʻ called, xii. 81, 388 [28]

Ḥar-khent(i)-khet(?), local form of Horus worshipped at Athribis or Xoïs, xii. 388 [28]

Ḥar-khent(i)-merti(?) (" Horus before the Two Eyes ") honoured at Panopolis, xii. 388 [28]

Ḥar-merti (" Horus with Two Eyes "), local form of Horus at Athribis, xii. 388 [28]

Ḥar-pe-khrad (" Horus the Child ") later most popular form of young Horus, xii. 117; see HARPOKRATES.

Ḥar-sam-taui (" Horus the Uniter of

Both Countries "), local form of Horus especially at Denderah(?), xii. 388 [28]

Ḥar-shaf, Amen-Rēʻ identified with, xii. 221

Ḥar-shuti (" Horus with Two Feathers "), local form of Horus, xii. 388 [28]

Ḥar-si-êset (" Horus, son of Isis ") later form of Horus, xii. 117

Ḥar-teḥen (" Bright Horus "), local form of Horus, xii. 388 [28]

Ḥar-uêr (" Great Horus "), later form of young Horus, xii. 117, 397 [96]

Hara, appellative of Rudra or Śiva, vi. 84, 112

—Śiva invoked as, in words āhara and prahara, vi. 180

Hara Berezaiti, vi. 278, 280, 282, 299, 302, 330, 331, 334, 335, 350

——sacred mountain, vii. 389 [2] (ch. ix)

——world-mountain of the Iranians, iv. 344, 356, 358, 414

Harahey, x. 311 [67]

Harahvaiti: see SARASVATĪ.

Harald Gormsson and Rolf, quarrel of, ii. 76

——horse and chariot of, burned on his pyre, ii. 305

——king of Denmark, ii. 118, 229

——learns wedge-formation of army, ii. 56–57

——offers Odin souls of slain, ii. 57–58

—Hardradi, ii. 250

—seeks to open Balder's barrow, ii. 134

Harbard, ii. 10, 93, 285, 311

—Odin as, ii. 10, 43, 45, 72–73, 351 [4]

" Harbardsljod," ii. 10, 45, 46, 48, 55, 56, 60, 72, 81, 83, 91, 93, 179, 182, 311, 314

Harbour-mark, Hrimgerd turned into stone and mocked as, ii. 277

" Hardar-saga," ii. 252

Hardaul Lāla, cholera-god, vi. 246–247

Hardgrep, giantess, ii. 278, 311

Hare, vii. 121, 162, 166, 167, 168, 213, 215, 219, 220, 226, 227, 282–284, 285, 286, 291, 292, 293–304, 309, 316, 353, 355, 419 [4], 420 [19 20 21 22], 422 [23 24 25 26], 423 [29 33], 424 [14], 425 [20]

—and tortoise, tale of, ix. 192

— -City (Hermopolis), xii. 151

—corn-spirit as a, iv. 247

—escaped from cut gourd, xii. 291

—in moon, iv. 424; vi. 137, 232

Hare-lip, xi. 224
—White, of Inaba, tale of, viii. 317–318
Hari, name of Viṣṇu, vi. 121, 165
Hariasa, war-goddess, ii. 255
Harihara, name of Viṣṇu and Śiva in one person, vi. 121
Harimella, war-goddess, ii. 255
Hariṇaigamaiṣin, vi. 228
Hariṇegamesi, vi. 224, 228
Harivaṁśa family, two Tīrthakaras belonged to the, vi. 221
Harke (Herke), Frau, erce connected with, ii. 195
Harlech, Bran at, iii. 100, 101, 105
Harlot and Enkidu, v. 239–240, 241, 242, 243, 246, 256–257, 258, 259
Harlots, v. 32, 33, 256–257, 258, 334
Harma (" Chariot "), city of, founded on site of Amphiaros's disappearance into the earth, i. 53
Harma, father of Aram, vii. 67
Harmachis (Ḥar-em-akhet), local form of Horus at Great Sphinx, xii. 388 28
Harmonia and Kadmos sent to dwell in the Elysian Fields by Zeus, i. 47, 158
———withdrew to land of the Illyrians, i. 47
—daughter of Ares and Aphrodite, given in marriage to Kadmos, i. 45, 190, 197–198
—double of Aphrodite, i. 198
—necklace and robe of, given to Eriphyle as bribe, i. 52, 54
———wedding-robe of, symbol of kingship in Thebes, i. 51
Harold the Fair-haired, ii. 8
Harp, Dagda's, iii. 34
—High Man with a, viii. 275
—invention of, iii. 137
—magic, one of three precious things of Susa-no-wo, viii. 229
—of Teirtu in Welsh tale, iii. 34
—played in honour of Star Lovers, viii. pl. x, opp. p. 236
—strains, three magic, iii. 29
Harper Cliach kept from Caer by magic, iii. 79
—of yew-tree made contention between Eogan and Lugaid, iii. 73
Harpies, Aeneas at the island of the, i. 305
—of the Strophades, parallel to, xi. 191–192, 238

Harpies (Snatchers), i. 266
—steal food of Phineus but later made to cease by Argonauts, i. 111
—Zetes and Kalaïs killed in pursuit of, i. 73
Harpokrates, classical misinterpretation of picture of, xii. 243
—Ḥat-meḥit termed mother of, xii. 133
—parallel to, in American Indian, x. 87–88
—see ḤAR-PE-KHRAD.
Harpoon, x. pl. iii, opp. p. 8
— -bearers in battle against 'Apop, xii. 109
—hieroglyphic symbol of Mîn(u) looks like, xii. 137
—of Horus, xii. 391 47, 397 101
Harran (Carrhae), centre of moon worship, v. 19, 153–154
Harranian Tammuz cult, v. 336–337, 338, 339
Harranians, adherents of cult of Sin at Harran known as Ssabeans or, v. 154–155
Harṣu Pānre, local god of Chayanpur, vi. 243
Hart of Odin, ii. pl. vi, opp. p. 32
Hartebeest, story of, vii. 289
Haru-yama no Kasumi-onoko (" Mist Man of the Spring Mountain "), tale of, viii. 294–295
Harun-al-Rashid, vii. 353–354
Harvest, Erinyes sometimes entreated for good, i. 276
— -feast, viii. 225
—festival, iii. 235–236, 237
—festivals, Lityerses connected with, i. 253–254
— -god (Mi-toshi-no-kami), story of, viii. 232–233
— -goddesses, four, parallel four genii at birth of Osiris, xii. 378 98
—Meḥt-uêret brought into connexion with, xii. 39–40
—Mîn god of, xii. 139, 406 61
—of the dead, iv. 55, 58
—Pharaoh's dream of seven cows to indicate nature of coming, xii. 368 14
— -serpent, xii. 66, 378 98
—withheld by ghosts, vii. 198
—Zeus god of, i. 160
Harvests, patron of good, viii. 67
Haryakṣa, vi. 98

Haselwurm, snake found under hazels of knowledge, iii. 166

Hastsheyalti, talking god, god of dawn, x. 156, 163, 164, 166, 170; xi. 370 23

Hastsshehogan, house-god and god of evening, x. 156, 163

Hastvads, vii. 380 7

Hat, iv. 47, 96, 109, 148, 171, 190
—flood-bringing, x. 261
—of Odin, ii. 41, 42, 43
—use of, in sacred dances, ix. 107

Ha-thanh, birthplace of Nguyen-hu'u-do, xii. 321

Ḥat-ḥôr, xii. 29, 30, 366 5
—among flowers and plants, xii. 38
—and Rê', attempt to connect myth of lost eye of sun-god with battle of, against rebellious men, xii. 86
—apparently goddess of Ḥôt, xii. 392 56
—Beḥdet resembles, xii. 132
—bestows eternal life upon dead, xii. 39
—connected with sun by epithet " golden," xii. 30
—description of, in cow-form, xii. 38
—divinity of the West and of the dead, xii. 42
—double emblems of, borne by Ehet, xii. 71
—early assimilated other goddesses, xii. 40
——identified with cow-shaped goddess, xii. 37
—entering western mountain and green thicket, xii. 38 (fig. 26)
—eye of Rê' in form of, xii. 74
—feeds dead from celestial tree, xii. 39, 136
—foreign countries thought to be under protection of, xii. 410 1
—four sons of Horus or Osiris become an interpretation of blue-black tresses of, xii. 394 67
——tresses of, marking cardinal points, xii. 39, 366 7
—functions of, xii. 40, 42, 45
—goddess of third, sixth, seventh, tenth, and twenty-second nomes, xii. 19
—Horus male counterpart of, xii. 39
—identified with many local goddesses, xii. 41
——Sothis-Sirius, xii. 56
—in cow-form, assumed functions of Asiatic Queen of Heaven, xii. 40

Ḥat-ḥôr in leopard-skin garment assimilated to goddess of fate, xii. 368 13
—Isis identified with, xii. 99
—Justice associated with, xii. 386 22
—long existence of human and bovine personifications of, xii. 38
—Matit and Ma(t)-si-s compared with, xii. 135
—meaning of, xii. 367 11
—Men'et compared with, as wife of Horus, xii. 101, 136
—Nebet local form of, xii. 140
—Nebt-ḥotep and Nebt-uu forms of, xii. 140
—Neḥem(t)-'auit identified with, at early date, xii. 141
—NN., female dead addressed as, xii. 178
—of Byblos, xii. 154 (fig. 157)
——Denderah, Eḥi associated with, xii. 37, 133
—patroness of malachite mines and of Malachite City, xii. 367 12
——women and deity of love, beauty, joy, music, ornaments, xii. 40
—represents sun as principal eye of heaven, xii. 38
—Saṭet compared with, xii. 146
—seven cows with bull, identified with Pleiades, xii. 40, 57
—similarity of Bat's (?) symbols with, xii. 40–41, 368 16
—sitting amid green rays identical with celestial tree, xii. 39
—Sobk associated with, at Ombos, xii. 148
—sometimes mistress of war, xii. 40
—sun's eye as, xii. 86
—symbol of, xii. 37 and fig. 25, 38
—Tefênet identified with, xii. 87
—tresses of, attributed to Horus as celestial god, xii. 39
—wife of Horus, xii. 40, 102
——Mont(u), xii. 139
—worshipped in Emu, 381 41
— -Isis, Êpet bears head of, xii. 60

Hathor [Ḥat-ḥôr], v. 69
—in inscriptions, v. 378 14

Ḥat-ḥôrs, " the seven," foretell future, xii. 40

Ḥat-meḥit, goddess of nome of Mendes, xii. 133

Hati, giant, ii. 209, 278
—wolf, ii. 199, 201, 279

Hātim Tāī, Nhang appears as sea-monster in tale of, vii. 89

Hattatal (enumeration of metres), ii. 7

Hatuey, cacique, story of, xi. 20, 350 [7]

Haumea, female deity, ix. 62

Haumia-tikitiki, god of uncultivated food, ix. 32

"Haunted Prince, Story of," Asiatic motifs in, xii. 153, 398 [106]

Haunting by certain souls, iv. 479

Haupu, high cliff, ix. 89, 90

Haurochiri, myths of the, xi. 226

Haurut, name of flower, vii. 62

Haurvatāt, vi. 260, pl. xxxiv, opp. p. 272; vii. 62

Hauskuld, dream of, ii. 234

"Haustlong," ii. 78, 178

"Havamal," ii. 9, 20, 43, 46, 49, 50, 54, 55, 195, 201, 202, 220, 243, 252, 296, 297, 298, 300, 328, 329

"Havardar-saga," ii. 65

Havfolk, water-spirit, ii. 210

Havgan, rival of Arawn, iii. 93

Havola (Havel), April festival on banks of, iii. 306

Hawaii, Indonesian myth-incidents in, ix. 96, 97

—Melanesian myth-incidents in, ix. 95, 96, 97

—relation of myths of, to those of New Zealand and Cook and Society Groups, ix. 93, 94

—resemblances of early doctrines of, to those of Greece and India, ix. 5

—shows close myth-relationship to Micronesia, but little with Melanesia, ix. 98

Hawaiki, image of Woman made at, ix. 25

Hawk, xii. 32

—City: see HIERAKONPOLIS.

—divergence of some local forms of Horus from shape of, xii. 388 [28]

—east wind as, xii. 65

—eye of, symbolizes lost eye of sun-god, xii. 89

— -god, earliest identification with sun, xii. 24

——Sokari a, xii. 98

—Horus a solarized deity with head of, xii. 101

—one of four sons of Horus or Osiris has form of, xii. 112

Hawk or falcon, hieroglyph of, as class-sign for all male divinities, xii. 102

— -plumage of Frigg, Loki flies in, ii. 83; see also FEATHER-DRESS OF FREYJA OR FRIGG.

—sanctity of, xii. 362 [3]

—sea-, malignant winds thought to reside in, i. 265

—solar, Amon as, xii. 402 [4]

—soul of boy escapes in form of, vii. 177

—sun as egg of, xii. 208, 423 [34]

Hawks of Horus at Edfu, xii. 167

—three, from Buto (Pe-Dep), xii. 365 [26]

Hawthorn in moon, iv. 423–424

Haxige, x. 298 [47]

Hay, Hayastan, vii. 65

Haya-to, legendary invaders, viii. 210

Hayagrīva, god with horse's head, vi. 214

Hayk, hero; giant, vii. 64–66, 389 [4] [6]

—Orion and Sirius may be involved in myths concerning, vii. 49

Haykanush, vii. 390 [18]

Hayowentha, x. 52

Haze, primeval, viii. 223

Hazel-pole with horse's head, ii. 230

— -tree, head of Balor split, iii. 33

Hazels of wisdom grew above Connla's Well, iii. 121, 166

He, He of Seven Syllables, gods, vi. 205

—of the Sun, xi. 163

Head-band, Amon Master of the, xii. 129

—Bran's, iii. 105

—bringing in of boar's, ii. 109

—buried, of Bran protected land from invasion, iii. 101, 104, 203

—called Heimdall's fate, ii. 154

—decapitated, followed sons, x. 104

— -dress, x. 123–124, 140, 303 [55]

——Nāga, worn at Swing Festival at Bangkok, xii. 277

——of shaman, reindeer or stag type, iv. 513

——removed as greeting to lud-spirit, iv. 148

— -hunters, Wa, xii. 293, 294

— -hunting, ix. 234–235

——coco-nut reminiscence of, xii. 345

——expedition of egg, snake, etc., ix. 202–203

—of Balor, tree split by, iii. 33

Head of Brahmā, *rôle* of, in Burmese
Spring Festival, xii. 323
——Connaughtman under knee of Conall while he slept, iii. 145
——Drunken Boy after death tried to
attack Raikō, viii. 307
——Gorgon Medousa, i. 33–34, 35, 36
——Komdei-Mirgan, quest for, iv. 489–
494
——Mim consulted, ii. 340
——Mimir, ii. 46, 66, 168, 169, 240
——Osiris worshipped, xii. 395 81
——Ruad's child hurled after him, iii.
133
— -pad, vii. 111
—passed through wall of fire, x. 104
—rings, vii. 420 19
—sea flowed from Pele's, ix. 39
—singing, iii. 105
— -soul, heart-soul, xi. 39
—soul of shamans in, iv. 498–499
—tabu, xii. 362 3
— -taking, xi. 303, pl. XLII, opp. p. 304
—wager of Loki's, ii. 267
Headless goddess as personification of
regions of dead, xii. 99, 100
——explained as Isis, xii. 118
Heads, ix. 56, 70, 81
—as seats of life, burning of, xii. 180
—buried in spring of Lerne, i. 31
—cannibal, also great, x. 290 37–291
—Celtic myths and customs about, ii. 46
—divine, iii. 104–105
—gaping, ii. 229, 230, pl. XXX, opp. p.
230
—in Yunka art, xi. 222
—many, of giants, ii. 173, 277
—Odin and giant wager their, ii. 62
—of father and uncle of hero-brothers
become sun and moon, xi. 176
——victims placed in caves, xi. 39
—on fork of tree set in ford, iii. 153
—travelling, xi. 329
—unharmed by flame, xii. 343
—washing of, in new river, iv. 210
Healer, deified, Trita Āptya held to be
a, vi. 36
—Zeus as, i. 162–163
Healing, i. 279, 280, 300–301; ii. 18,
44, 57, 202, 205, 206, 208, 226, 231,
313, pl. XLI, opp. p. 320; iii. 70, 71,
153, 155; vi. 286, 323, 361 26; x. 5,
173, 184, 284 27; xi. 25
—Anahit as goddess of, vii. 28

Healing, Apollo and Artemis as gods
of, i. 177, 179, 182
—Asklepios's function of, i. 279, 280,
281
—emerald as god of, xi. 207–208
—founder of art of, viii. 14
—from sacred springs, vii. 59
—god of, viii. 66
—hill of, ii. 186
—incantation for, v. 182
—magic pig's skin, iii. 40
——tree of, v. 152
—miraculous, of axe-cuts on chestnut-
tree, viii. 340
—of Fraoch, iii. 131
—powers, vi. 38, 39
——of rivers, i. 257
—remedy of Rudra, vi. 38
—song, iii. 86
—virtue of ashes and water among Armenians, Belgians, and Letts, vii. 57,
388 9
—*vs.* magic, xii. 199
—wells, iii. 24, 32, 65
—Wodan as god of, ii. 39
Heaps of Gold, vii. 353
Hearing, incantation against, iii. 84
—of Klust, iii. 190
—Sozem (Sodem, Sotem) god of, xii. 67
Hearn, Lafcadio, viii. 248, 249
Heart, Hearts:
Heart as seat of life, symbolism of, x.
195, 203, 285 29, 302 55
—created from iron, iv. 371
—eating of, to obtain courage of slain
man, x. 285 29
—green gem to serve as a, xi. 90
—giant with mare's, ii. 81–82
—human, in fertility rites, x. 203
—of a primeval being, tree with buds
sprang from, ix. 166, 169, 176, 177
——Danish crusader eaten by Sakkala
peasants, iv. 5
——dead father eaten causes madness,
iii. 108
——earth, xi. 162, 166
——Liu Hung burned, viii. 193
——sacrifice buried with bones at memorial feast, iv. 38
——the sky, xi. 161, 162, 166
——woman eaten by Loki, ii. 145
—parti-coloured, of the Red Man, x.
72–73
—presented as sacrifice to sun, xi. 65

Heart Revelation, Classic of, viii. 57
—theft of, from burning corpse, x. 180
Hearts burned as incense, xi. 48
—of animals and reptiles offered for rain, xi. 137
——bread-dough, offerings of, xi. 144
——captives eaten for various reasons, iv. 5
—three, of son of Morrígan, with shapes of serpents through them, iii. 132
Hearth, bhūts on the, vi. 249
—fire of, vi. 284
—god of, viii. 74, 76
—Hestia the, i. 208–209
—of the universe world's centre, xi. 53; see also items s.v. MIDDLE PLACE.
—sanctuary of home, iv. 452
—Tsao means both furnace and, viii. 76, 77
— -worship associated with ancestor spirits, vii. 55, 387 [4]
Hearths have fire maidens, iv. 236
Heat, vi. 17, 26; x. 78, 167–168
Heater, the, a torture, viii. 39
Heathen, dwarfs called, ii. 271
Heaven, ii. 42, 120, 153, 156–157, 221, 318, 340; vi. 15, 31, 34, 70, 86, 99–100, 101, 131, 145, 148, 149, 150, 152, 160, 194, 200–201, 211, 250; viii. 29, 32, 46, 53, 128, 137; see also UPPER-WORLD.
—and earth, ceremony of union of, x. 92–93
——divine pair, worshipped on wooded mountain, ii. 194
——made by Rê‘, xii. 82
——originally one, or earth let down from, iv. 330–331
——separation of, xii. 78
——(first), of, gives rise to Osiris, xii. 30
——two lines separating, iv. pl. xxvii, opp. p. 224
—high gods, vii. 123–142
—Apollo driven from, iii. 10
—as a stone arch, iv. 342
—ascent to: see items s.v. ASCENTS TO OR DESCENTS, ETC.
—attempt to fly to, vi. 336, pl. xLII, opp. p. 336, 347
—Babylonian picture of, iv. 309
—bull of, v. 238, 239, 256–257, 330
—conception of, vi. 344, 345

Heaven, Conchobar said to have been first pagan who went to, iii. 209
—daughter of, Spider marries, vii. 427 [13]
—deities of birth also deities of, iv. 258, 265–266
—description of, in early writings, xii. 417 [21]
— -dwellers, tales of, vii. 138
——tailed, vii. 192, 238, 241
——unacquainted with use of fire though in Polynesia this is told of people of Underworld, vii. 137
——Wakonyingo resemble, vii. 269
—early Christian delineations of, influenced by descriptions of Golden Age, i. 18
—eastern and western gates of, xii. 24 (fig. 3), 28 (fig. 11)
—entrance to, by gate in east, vii. 184
— -father, vii. 124
——sky personified into, ix. 5, 9, 16, 166
—fire of, vi. 263
—first people and animals from, vii. 149–150
—forefathers of Buriats came from, iv. 503
—funeral of Waka-hiko took place in, viii. 235
— -god, iv. 219–223; 390–401; vii. 14
——Heimdall a poetic form of old, ii. 152
——" Writer man " may be of late origin and sprung from, iv. 408–409
— -goddess, Freyja as, ii. 124
—(Gulu), Walumbe son of, vii. 117, 129
— -Illuminating Deity, viii. 224
—Isis represents, xii. 99
—land of, ancient Babylonian belief that Zodiac is, iv. 347
—life in, resembles that of earth, iv. 487–488
—meaning of, iv. 391
— -mountain, iv. 344–345, 401
—of Contentment, viii. 241
—personified as female, xii. 37
— -propper, ix. 35
— -quarters, xi. 54, 56
—Queen of, vii. 235
—Rockies regarded as pillars of, x. 132
—ruled by sun-goddess, viii. 225
—shadows [souls] may ascend to, during sleep, iv. 6

Heaven, special orders from, viii. 35
—storeys in, iv. 307
—sun and moon symbolize eyes of, xii. 38
——sometimes regarded as life of, x. 277 [13]
—symbolized by arms stretched from sky or ocean, xii. 99
—tendency to remove local spirits and fetishes from earth to, xii. 214
—the supreme Ruler, viii. 49–51, 52, 63, 66, 89
—third, vi. 315
—thirty-third, viii. 196
— -throne from which Odin and Frey overlook worlds, ii. 22
—translation to, of family of Hsü Hsün, viii. 114
—trees and plants from, transferred to earth, ix. 248
—trees: see TREE, HEAVEN.
—Tuatha Dé Danann banished from, on account of their knowledge, iii. 38
—upheld by dwarfs at cardinal points, ii. 264–265
—Vahagn son of, vii. 44
—vault of, iii. 324
—wife of god of, bore son whose body became the earth, iv. 330
—Yamato race descended from, viii. 212
Heavenly bodies, viii. 51
——figures representing, xi. pl. XII, opp. p. 88
—caves, wells, rivers, etc.; see CAVE, HEAVENLY.
—Consort, T'ien Hou canonized as, viii. 72
—Father, Biblical epithet, x. 272 [6]
—tree of Buddhism, viii. 339
—Youth, Amo-no-Waka-hiko is the, viii. 235
Heavens a solid cube hanging on nothing, vii. 93
—and paradises, difference between, viii. 282
—band of, v. 109
—deification of, iv. 391
—falling of, xi. 93
—made from half of Tiâmat's body, v. 303
—numbers of, xi. 53
—origin of: see items s.v. ORIGINS, MYTHS OF.

Heavens, raising of, x. 179; see also SKY, RAISING OF.
—received power of creation, ix. 12
—series of, v. 94, 95; ix. 59, 70, 255
—seven, above earth, xi. 140–141
—superimposed, xii. 49 (fig. 47), 366 [7]
—supported on four corners by four daughters of Sarvakāmadughā, vi. 134
—supporters of, xi. pl. IX, opp. p. 70
—thunder guardian of the, x. 24
—two (opposed skies of upper and lower worlds), xii. 41, 367 [7]
—Young Spider visits all series of, ix. 255
—Zeus as god of, i. 159
Heaven's river, Ama-no-kawa is, viii. 235–236
Hebe, abstract divinity of time, i. 282
—daughter of Hera and Zeus, i. 166
—Herakles weds, in Heaven, i. 95
—(" Youth "), i. 240–241
Ḥebet, uncertain if Sop worshipped in, xii. 409 [104]
Hebrew belief, Babylonian influence on, v. 156
—religion stands apart from Semitic, v. xviii
—tradition uninfluenced by Gilgamish epic, v. 266–267
Hebrews, Habiru probably identical with, v. 72–73, 74
Hedin, ii. 286
—King, ii. 123, 162
Ḥeḥ, air-god, xii. 89
—and Ḥeḥet (Ḥeḥut), lift sun (Khepri) over eastern horizon, xii. 48, 49 (fig. 45)
—blended with Shu, xii. 44, 65 (fig. 71), 369 [26]
—created to support Nut, xii. 77
—Shu soul of, xii. 219
Heid, magic-wielder, ii. 27, 117
Heiddraupnir's head, runes from fluid from, ii. 168
Heidrik, king, ii. 62, 109, 190
Heidrun, goat of Valhalla, ii. 313–314
Heifer, black-maned, of Dagda, by its lowing brought cattle demanded by Fomorians, iii. 28
—Ilos guided by, to found Ilion, i. 118
—sacred to Anahit, vii. 29
—Spartoi grew from teeth (scattered broadcast) of, i. 45

Heifer, white, Io changed into, by Zeus, i. 29
Heifer's Glen, Brown Bull of Cúalnge flees to, iii. 153
Height, increasing or diminishing of, iv. 467
" Heike Monogatari," Kiyomori hero of epic, viii. 270
" Heimdalar-galdr," ii. 153, 154
Heimdall (Vindler), god, ii. 10, 15, 21, 25, 33, 65, 88, 111, 123, 142, 144, 147, 152–156, 160, 278, 329, 340, 341, 385 [63]
" Heimskringla," ii. 5, 33, 106, 140, 181, 229, 244, 281, 290
Heir occupied high-seat first at funeral feast, ii. 311
Heith, child of Hrimnir, ii. 278
Heithdraupnir, thought-runes arranged from draught from head of, ii. 46
Heithiurun, British idol, suggests Taran, iii. 93
Hei-tiki, amulet, ix. pl. VI, opp. p. 38
Ḥeka, god of magic, in myth of sun-god's withdrawal from earth, xii. 79
—in solar ship, xii. 96
—may accompany sun-god in his ship, xii. 67, 378 [101]
—reason for yellow skin of, xii. 407 [74]
—Shu early identified with, xii. 27 (fig. 10), 44 and fig. 39, 133
Hekabe, dream of, and its interpretation, i. 118
—taken by Odysseus as prize of war, i. 133
—wife of Priam, i. 118
Hekataion, an Attic, i. pl. XLIII, opp. p. 188
Hekate, i. 186–188
—and Sun saw capture of Persephone, i. 228, 243
—assumes moral qualities of Selene, i. 244
—connexion of Artemis with, i. 185
—curse in name of, v. 161
—description of, v. 164–165
—identified with Selene, Artemis, and Persephone, v. 369
—Medeia priestess of, i. 112
—probably represented on marble relief of Eleusinian rites, i. pl. L, opp. p. 230
Heke-heke-i-papa, third wife of Rangi, ix. 9
Ḥeken, hawk-god, xii. 133
Ḥeknet, goddess, xii. 133
Hektor, i. pl. XXIX (1), opp. p. 116

Hektor and Aias fight in single combat until truce established for both armies, i. 128
—farewell of, to wife and child, i. 128
—healed by Apollo, i. 177
—kills Protesilaos, i. 126
—proposes that Paris and Menelaos fight a duel with Helen as prize, i. 127
—slain by Achilles, i. 129–130
—slays Patroklos, i. 129
—son of Hekabe and Priam, i. 118
—taking leave of Andromache, i. pl. XXXI, opp. p. 124
—wounded by Greeks but revived by Apollo, i. 129
Hel, deity of Underworld and her abode, ii. pl. II, opp. p. 4, 16, 17, 43, 65, 66, 111, 127, 129, 130, 135, 145, 147, 184, 265, 276, 278, 303–306, 315, 317, 318, 340, 341, 343, 386 [64]
Hel-gate, ii. pl. XIII, opp. p. 106
—road to, ii. 304; iii. 340; iv. 78
Helblindi, brother of Loki, ii. 139
Hêlêl, Jupiter, v. 144, 145
Helen, i. pl. XXXI, opp. p. 124; iii. 325
—Achilles (after restoration to life) dwells with, in White Isle, i. 131
—admitted to Elysion, i. 147
—and Dioskouroi, i. 246–247
——Menelaos, i. 133–134
——Paris, i. pl. X (1), opp. p. 20
—birth and beauty of, i. 124
—consents to Paris carrying her to Troy, i. 125
—daughter of Tyndareos, i. 24–27
——Zeus by Nike, i. 284
—imitates voices of wives of Greek leaders in wooden horse of Troy, i. 132–133
—inspired by Aphrodite to go with Paris, i. 197
—kidnapped, i. 25, 105
—released by brothers, i. 105
—tomb of, i. 134
—wife of Menelaos, i. 121
Helena, niece of Duke Hoel, iii. 185
Helenos and Andromache, Aeneas comes to home of, in Epirus, i. 305
—prophetic son of Priam, captured by Odysseus and forced to tell outcome of Trojan war, i. 132
Helga-fell (" Holy fell "), sacred hill, ii. 227, 307, 310, pl. XL, opp. p. 316, 317

"Helgakvitha Hjorvardssonar," ii. 11, 24, 162, 189, 190, 228, 256, 300

"Helgakvitha Hundingsbana," ii. 11, 183, 190, 249

Helgi (Helgo, Hölgi), king of Halogaland, ii. 132, 186, 187, 188, 189

—hero of Helgi poetic cycle, ii. 11, 56, 162, 190, 209, 228, 233, 235, 240, 251, 260, 279, 307, 342

—Hundingsbana, ii. 55, 240, 307

—the Thin sought help of Thor, ii. 75

—Thoreson met Ingibjord, ii. 322

Helgoland, Fosite said to be worshipped on sacred island of, ii. 19, 162

Helgrindr, Tuonen-portii (Underworld's gate), corresponds to, iv. 75

Helike, tidal wave which submerged, demonstration of Poseidon's power, i. 330 [2] (ch. viii)

Helikon, Linos buried on Mt., i. 253

—Mt., in Boiotia, southern centre of cult of Muses, i. 239

—Pegasos returned once to earth and created spring of Hippoukrene on, i. 40

Heliopolis as place where sun's eye was lost, xii. 384 [114]

—centre of solar cult, xii. 364 [13]

—ennead of, xii. 26, 50, 215–216

—Ḥar-akhti lord of, xii. 235, 388 [28]

—local god of, xii. 27, 363 [3], 364 [13]

—parallels to sacred tree of, xii. 31

—localization of Khepri at, scarcely original, xii. 363 [3]

—Menehtet worshipped at or near, xii. 136

—Nefer-têm associated with, xii. 140

—On of the Egyptians, xii. 31

—phoenix came to temple at, xii. 166

—seat of worship of Shentet, xii. 148 [8]

—Sekha(u)it sometimes localized at Persea of, xii. 53

—Ser localized at, xii. 147

—sun's eye reconciled to father at, xii. 86

—worship of Osiris at, xii. 98, 400 [3]

Heliopolitan as epithet of Osiris, xii. 400 [3], 425 [23]

—doctrine, double occurrence of sun in, xii. 50

Helios, i. pl. XXVIII, opp. p. 110, pl. LI, opp. p. 236

Helios and Kurios ouranou identified, v. 64

—Perse, Aietes son of, i. 242

—Apollo as, i. 181

—association of, with Eos, i. 246

—cup of, wrought by Hephaistos, i. 207

—father of Lampetië, i. 281

—Phaëthon, i. 244

—frequently translated by Dažbog in early Russian texts, iii. 297

—gives Herakles golden cup, i. 86

—grandfather of Medeia, gives her a chariot drawn by winged dragons, i. 115

—Palmyrene inscription renders Ba'al Shamîn by, v. 64

—Phaëthon recognized as person of, i. 243–244

—(Sun), rival of Poseidon for lordship of Corinth, i. 36–37

—son of Hyperion and Euryphaëssa, i. 241–243

—with chariot, v. 54

—witnesses seizure of Persephone, i. 228, 243

Helkappe, ii. 269

Hell, Hells:

Hell, ii. 42, 305; iii. 209, 212; v. 49, 50, 72, 162, 330, 367; vi. 71, pl. VIII, opp. p. 100, 101, 106, 145, 150, 154, 160, 186, 201, 212, 214–215, 250; viii. 238

—called Mitnal, xi. 138

—Cave of Cruachan regarded as Ireland's gate of, iii. 126

—conception of, vi. 344, 345

—dead in, xii. 180 and figs. 188, 189, 417 [21]

—descent into, x. 108

—Diaz's description of idol-house as, xi. 49

—fire, v. 156

—and tar-kettle of, iv. pl. XXVIII, opp. p. 228

—Hel may have borrowed traits from Christian, ii. 304

—in some ballads Féinn shown to be in, iii. 183

—supreme Ruler of, viii. 196

Hells, doctrine of, in Purāṇas, vi. 186

—Jain, names of, vi. 228

—nine, xi. 53

Hellas, native abode of the Muses, i. 238–239

Helle, daughter of Athamas, i. 107–108

Hellebore in materia medica of Artemis,
i. 185

Hellen (son of Deukalion and Pyrrha),
name of, perpetuated in Hellenic race,
i. 37

—son of Zeus, i. 11, 157

Hellenizing, possible, in Armenian mythology, vii. 381 [2] (ch. iii)

Hellespont (Helle's Sea), i. 108

Helluland, x. 1

Helmet in grave at Vendel, Sweden, believed to represent Odin, ii. 58

Helmets, boar-shaped, as protectives, ii.
110

—snakes on, added to strength, ii. 216,
217

Helmold on Černobog, etc., iii. 288, 289

——religion of Elbe Slavs, iii. 222, 240

Helmund, identification of Sarasvatī
uncertain, but connected with Harahvaiti and, vi. 49

Helper, Zeus as, i. 162–163

Helpers, x. 5, 7

Helveg, road to Hel, ii. 304

Helyas, Knight of the Swan, ii. 263

Hema, son of Whaitari, ix. 58, 59, 63,
64, 66, 67

Hemādpant, Rākṣasa, minister of Mahādeva, vi. 245

Ḥemen, hawk-god of Upper Egypt, xii.
133

—or Amon, readings instead of
Menḫu(i) in old manuscripts, xii.
405 [49]

Hemera, abstract divinity of time, i. 5,
282

—child of Eos and Tithonos, i. 246

Ḥem(?)-ḥor, lion-headed god, xii. 133

Hemispheres, sky believed to contain,
iv. 309

Hemp as charm, viii. 380 [7] (ch. ii)

Ḥemset ("sitting, resting force"),
once recorded as consort of Ni(u),
xii. 371 [46]

Hen, Cerridwen as a, swallowed Gwion
as grain, later giving birth to him,
iii. 57, 110

—throat of, cut, when death occurs,
iv. 17–18

Ḥenmemtiu, a class of mankind, xii.
379 [18]

Henotheism, vi. 355 [2] (ch. i) ; viii. 63

—approximation to, xii. 18

Hephaistos, i. pl. xix, opp. p. 66

Hephaistos, amulet figures of Bês at
prow of Phoenician ships are called
representations of, xii. 64

—Anahit identified with, vii. 381 [2] (ch.
iii)

—and Prometheus, curiously allied in
relations to human culture, i. 12

—Aphrodite wife of, i. 197

—armour of Achilles wrought in forge
of, i. 129

—Athene associated with, i. 171

—attacks Skamandros, i. 256

—Baltic celestial smith compared to,
iii. 330

—created Pandora from image of clay,
i. 14–15

—depicts Pleiades on shield of Achilles,
i. 248

—father of Erichthonios, i. 67

——Periphetes by Antikleia, i. 98

—fires of, quell waters of Skamandros, i.
129

—Goibniu equivalent of, iii. 31

—husband of Ba'alti, v. 339, 340

—makes armour of Memnon, i. 130

—Mihr identified with, vii. 33

—parallel with Weyland the Smith, ii.
271

—Ptaḥ compared by Greeks to, xii.
145

—robe and necklace wrought by, i. 45

—son of Zeus, i. 157, 166

—Svarog often identified with, iii. 277,
298

—Volcanus wore mask of, i. 296

Ḥepḥep, god in human form, wearing
crowns, xii. 64

Ḥepi, Apis sometimes confused with,
xii. 412 [5]

—one of the four sons of Horus or Osiris, xii. 112

Ḥeqes, stellar character of, xii. 64, 377 [92]

Ḥeqet and Khnûm(u) transferred to
Abydos, xii. 50, 51

——transformed from cataract-gods
to creators, xii. 51

—as a birth-genius of Osiris, xii. 385 [12]

——master of necropolis of Abydos, xii.
372 [50]

—frog-headed and frog-shaped goddess
and wife of Khnûm(u), xii. 50, 133,
404 [33]

—gives children life, xii. 51 (fig. 51)

—lake of, xii. 364 [11]

INDEX

189

Ḥeget later consort of Khnûm(u) transformed into birth-deity, xii. 52
—no positive knowledge of cult of, as
incarnate in frog, xii. 167
—one of the two first gods who formed
men and gods, xii. 50
—sometimes parallel to Meskhenet, xii.
52
Hera, i. pl. vii, opp. p. lxii, pl. viii (2),
opp. p. 8, 14 (fig. 2), 83 (fig. 3B),
85, 163–168
—and Athene induce Aphrodite to
make Medeia fall in love with Iason,
i. 112
——Herakles reconciled in Heaven, i.
95
—appears to Semele in guise of her
nurse and prompts request to Zeus,
i. 45–46
—as goddess of wedlock, Hypermnestra
probably a priestess of, i. 30
——protector of wedlock, vii. 27
—awarded divine supremacy of Argos
by Inachos, i. 30
—born of Kronos and Rhea, i. 5, 6,
274
—cattle of Geryoneus sacrificed to, i.
87
—caused by Eris to quarrel with Athene
and Aphrodite at marriage of Peleus
and Thetis, i. 124
—cult of, in primitive Argos, i. 32
—curses Pelias in his youth, i. 106
—dedication of temple to, v. 22
—equated with Atargatis, v. 37
—hastens birth of Eurystheus and delays
that of Herakles, i. 78
—in form of Melampous, i. 35
—inflicts frenzy on Dionysos for discovering vine, i. 47, 219, 222
—Io priestess of temple of, i. 29
——probably identical with, i. 30
——surrendered to, i. 29
—Milky Way formed when breasts of,
were snatched from infant Herakles,
iv. 414
—origin and name of, i. 163–164
—represented by Iuno in Roman mythology, i. 288, 299
—rouses wind against those who incur
her anger, i. 153, 328 ⁴ (ch. i)
—sacrifice to, by Argonauts, i. 110
—said to be offshoot of ʿAṣṣah of Gaza,
i. 169

Hera sends gadfly to pursue Io from
land to land, i. 29
——madness on Herakles, i. 80
—sent plague of madness on Ino and
Athamas, i. 46
——the Sphinx to destroy citizens of
Thebes, i. 49
—stood for government of household,
i. 209
—suspended from Heaven by Zeus, i. 91
—turns Kallisto into a bear, i. 16, 21
—wedded to Zeus, i. 5, 7–8
—wife and sister of Zeus, i. 156, 157
Heraion, temple of Hera near Argos,
source of earliest form of Io-myth, i.
30
Herakleia, cave believed to lead to Underworld at, i. 143
Herakleopolis, association of Ḥat-ḥôr-
Sekhmet with, xii. 75
—Dua(u) perhaps adored at, xii. 132,
403 ²¹
—Ḥer-shef worshipped at, xii. 135
—Khnûm(u) deity of, xii. 135
—Magna, Nekhbet worshipped at, xii.
407 ⁷¹
Herakles, i. 75–95, pl. xxvii, opp. p.
106; iii. 131; iv. 414
—Alexander the Great said to be reincarnation of, i. 223
—and Apollo separated by lightning of
Zeus, i. 160
——Auge, intrigue of, cause of plague,
i. 22
——boar, i. 83 (fig. 3A)
——hydra, i. pl. xxii, opp. p. 82
——lion of Nemea, i. pl. xxi, opp. p.
76
—arrows of, dipped in bile, vii. 393 ²⁷
—as original husband of Hera, i. 165
—birth of, retarded by Hera, i. 164
—bow of, i. 126, 132
—breaks shackles of Prometheus, i. 13
—challenged to wrestling match by
Polygonos and Telegonos, i. 261
—Charybdis stole cattle from, i. 264
—conquers Death on behalf of Alkestis,
i. 107
—consults Delphic oracle regarding a
cure for disease, i. 179
—dedicates lock of his hair to Apollo,
i. 180
—development of, as mythological
character, i. 326 ¹ (ch. v)

Herakles, Dua(u) perhaps identified
with, xii. 132
—forced Nereus to point out way to
Apples of Hesperides, i. 260
—founded feast of mourning for his
daughter Ba'alti, v. 339–340
—given Horn of Plenty by Acheloös, i.
257
—granted invisibility by Zeus, i. 158
—identified with Indian gods, vi. 109–
110, 126
—insanity of, i. 166
—in search of Golden Apples, i. 114
—Khôns(u) identified with, xii. 34
—killed Linos, i. 253, pl. LIV, opp. p.
254
—left on coast of Mysia by crew of
Argo, i. 110
—legends of, vi. 263
—restored Tyndareos to his kingdom, i.
24
—see also HERCULES.
—sends men of the Argo on their way
from Lemnos, i. 110
—sets Theseus free from Seat of Lethe,
i. 105
—slays Autochthons attacking Argonauts at Kyzikos, i. 110
——Laomedon, i. 91, 118
——Lityerses and throws his body into
Maeander River, i. 253
——Nereus and his children at Pylos,
i. 106
—son of Zeus, i. 157
—strangles serpents, vii. 45
—taught music by Linos, i. 253
—took sea-born bull to Argolis from
whence it escaped and ravaged lands
about Marathon, i. 62
—Vahagn and Verethraghna identified
with, vii. 43, 363, 365
—visits Hades, i. 145
Herald of gods, Hermes as, i. 191
Heraldry, viii. 353
Heralds protected by Hermes (as herald of the gods), i. 194
Herb, cleansing, xi. 31
—fish eat of certain, and regain life, i.
261
—magic, madness of Glaukos's horses
said to be caused by, i. 39
— -symbolism, xi. 52
—white, ii. 129
Herbs grew from grave of Miach, iii. 28

Herbs, knowledge of, given, x. 63
—magic, in spring changed Skylla into
monster, i. 263
—medicinal, iii. 24, 32, 65, 110
——in China, viii. 105
Hercules, i. 302–303; ii. 17, 37, 69, 70
—and daughter of king of Celtica progenitors of northern Gauls, iii. 13
——Sanda identical, vii. 379 [1] (ch. i)
—as god of eloquence, Gaulish explanation of, iii. 10
—Ba'al-Hamman identified with, v. 53
—founding of city Alesia by, native
myth given by Diodorus in terms of
Greek mythology, iii. 13
—Germanic, placated with animal victims, ii. 69
—Indian parallel to, x. 232
—Keresāspa and Rustam parallel, vi.
324, 329
—Melek of Tyre identified with, v. 52
—Melqart the Tyrian, v. 52, 53
—of the Armenians, Verethraghna be-
came the, vi. 271
—Ogmios possesses attributes of, iii. 10
—sacred grove of, near the Weser, ii.
203
—see also HERAKLES.
Herding song, vii. 268
Herds, Apollo protector of, i. 180
Herdsman, constellation, viii. 235, 236
Herdsmen, dead are, for Death, vii. 175
—returned dead as, iv. 39, 286
—three, of Bregia, iii. 148
Here, the, x. 287 [31]
Ḥerem-Bethel worshipped by Jews of
Elephantine, v. 381 [58]
Herfadir (Odin), ii. 58
Herfjotur, Valkyrie, ii. 249, 252, 253,
256
Herjan's Disir, ii. 248, 255
Hermanubis ("Hermes-Anubis"), the
Greek term for Anubis, xii. 393 [61]
Hermaphrodites, vii. 367; x. 160, 257,
308 [64]–309
Hermes, i. 14 (fig. 2), pl. XXII, opp. p.
82, pl. XXIII (1), (2), (3), opp. p. 88,
191–195, pl. XLIV, opp. p. 194; 301;
xi. 204
Hermes and Artemis, Eros son of, i. 203
——Athene led Perseus to the Graiai, i.
33
——Dryope, parents of Pan, i. 267
—brought Pandora to Epimetheus, i. 15

Hermes, child of Hephaistos and Aphrodite, i. 197
—credited with invention of flute, i. 181
—developed on pattern of Nabû, vii. 31
—Dionysos distinguished from, in art, i. 222
—entrusts infant Dionysos to nymphs of Mt. Nysa, i. 217–218
—gave Aristaios to care of Gaia, i. 252
—Greeks compared Anubis with, xii. 393 61
—Mercurius identified with, i. 301
—mustered immigrants for Underworld, i. 142
—of Kyllene, temple of, erected by Lakaon, i. 20
—Perseus supposed to have been identified with, at Thronion in Lokria, i. 36
—replaced by Archangel Michael in modern Greek folk-belief, i. 312
—sells Herakles to Omphale, i. 90
—sent with message by Zeus to Underworld to release Persephone, i. 228–229
—slew Argos, earning for himself title of Argeïphontes (" Argos-slayer "), i. 29
—son of Zeus, i. 157
—takes unborn child of Kallistos to his mother Maia, i. 21
—Tiur identified with, vii. 31
—Trismegistos, Tīr possible component of name, vii. 384 56
—watches Herakles slay Lernean hydra, i. pl. XXII, opp. p. 82
Hermione, cave at, believed to lead to Underworld, i. 143
Hermione, wife of Orestes, seized by Neoptolemos, i. 135
Herminones, son of Mannus progenitor of, ii. 328
Hermod (son of Odin), subordinate god, servant of higher gods, ii. 16, pl. vi, opp. p. 32, 65, 129–130, 131, 161, 304, 315
Her-monthis, Buchis, bull of Mont̬(u) worshipped at, xii. 139, 163
—Sobk worshipped at, xii. 148
—Tenenet adored at, xii. 150
Hermopolis, Neḥem(t)-'auit associated with Thout(i) at, xii. 141
—Unut worshipped at, xii. 151

Hermund, ii. 286
Hermunduri, ii. 357 2
Hernandez de Cordova discovered Yucatan, xi. 44–45
Hero and Leandros, i. 201–202
Hero, Heroes, Heroic:
Hero, Aren, iv. 156–157
—Artaxias became legendary, vii. 8–9
— -brothers, the, ix. 41–42, 105, 107–108, 122–129; x. 39, 104, 133, 164, 231, 277 13, 295 44, 298 48; xi. 159, 164, 165, 166, 168–177, 297, 312–313, 330
— -cult of the Mordvins, iv. 157–158
—culture-, x. 52, 113, 121, 311 69
— -deliverer rescues mankind from the stomach of monster, vii. 119, 399 12
—demiurge, serpent an antagonist of, x. 300 50
— -transformer-trickster, x. 136, 258, 298 48–299
—Trita as beneficent, vi. 265
Heroes, iv. 42, 70, 139–158 [used in different senses in different volumes of this series]; vii. 64–71; 118–119, 213–224
—and kings, Odin patron of, ii. 56
—birth of, from god and human mother in Irish myth, iii. 13
—created to aid dwarfs, ii. 265
—Gilgamish had charge, in month of Ab, of souls of, v. 235
—Gods seek help of, iii. 36–37
—great national, viii. 85–97
—inspired by birds to build towns, iii. 13
—or divinities converted to Christianity, iii. 207–208
—primeval, vi. 292
—race of, placed on earth by Zeus, i. 17
—sleeping in hills, iii. 202
—survive their bodies as " shadows " or images, iv. 13
Heroic myths, iii. 139–205
—stories, viii. 303–315
Herodotus confuses Osiris with Mykerinos, builder of the Pyramids, xii. 398 106
Heron, ii. 49
—and ape, tale of, ix. 192–193
——snake, fight of, ix. 68
—lightning-bird identified as, vii. 237
—primeval bird, vii. 144
—Utet̬ possibly had form of, xii. 151

Heron's Feather, tale of, vii. 210–212
Herovit (Gerovit), iii. 283
Herse, i. pl. LVI, opp. p. 266
—(" Dew," or " Offspring "), daughter of Kekrops and Agraulos, i. 67
—union of Hermes with, in Attic legend, i. 329 [5] (ch. v)
—wife of Hermes, i. 70
Hersephoria, ritual of, i. 325 [3]
Ḥer-shef worshipped at Herakleopolis, xii. 134
Hertyr (Odin), ii. 58
Ḥer-uret, Ḥeqet worshipped at, xii. 133
" Hervarar-saga," ii. 109, 201, 244, 308
Hervey Group, cosmogonic ideas of, ix. 13–14
Hervor takes sword from barrow, ii. 308
—the All-wise, ii. 259, 260
Heryan (Odin), ii. 58
Ḥesat, cow-goddess, xii. 134
He-She, Zuñi bisexed Creator, x. 187, 206, 309 [64]
He-Who-Holds-the-Earth, Chief, x. 34–35
Hesi-Nekht Astarte, v. fig. 14, opp. p. 32
Hesiod, four ages set forth in, vi. 103
Hesiodic story of creation, i. 5
Hesione, daughter of Laomedon, offered as sacrifice, but saved by Herakles, i. 85–86
—given to Telamon as prize of war, i. 91
—said to be wife of Prometheus, i. 12
—wife of Telamon, i. 121
Hesperia (Italy), Aeneas bidden to establish his colony in, i. 304, 305
Hesperides children of Atlas and Hesperis, i. 248
—gardens of, i. 5
—Golden Apples of, taken by Herakles, i. 87, 88
—Herakles in search of Golden Apples of, i. 114
—myth of Garden of, influenced Idunn myth, ii. 180
Hesperis, wife of Atlas and mother of the Hesperides, i. 248
Hesperos (Latin Vesper), i. 247–248
—and Phosphoros, v. 36
——identification of, xi. 97
Hessians at Geismar revere sacred oak, ii. 68

Hestia, i. 208–209; vii. 55
—'Anuqet compared by Greeks with, xii. 131
—born of Rhea and Kronos, i. 274
—fire adored in Greece as, vi. 284
Hestiaia founded by defeated Thebans, i. 54
Hetaera, Semiramis a, vii. 367
Hethin, brother of Helgi, ii. 233, 235
Ḥetmet, Egyptian goddess, xii. 134
Ḥetpet, god of happiness, xii. 67
Hetu (Hetet), name of baboons associated with sun, xii. 365 [27]
Hevajra, a Yi-dam, vi. 215
Heveidd Hên, father of Rhiannon, iii. 94
Hi, river, viii. 249
Hian, tale of, ix. 156
Hi-asa, blood of, origin of a primeval pair, ix. 109
Hiawatha, x. 51–52, pl. XI, opp. p. 52, 302 [54 55]
Hidaka-gawa, tale of, viii. 331, 384 [12]
Hides of Buriat offerings, iv. pl. XLVII, opp. p. 410
—used in shamanizing, iv. pl. LVII, opp. p. 488, 512
Hiḍimba, a Rākṣasa, attacked the Pāṇḍavas, vi. 156
Hiding of boy by means of transformation, ii. 151
— -places of Arthur and Fionn, traditions of, iii. 180
Hiei, Benkei belonged at monastery of, viii. 310
Hierakonpolis (City of Hawks), cult of Horus at, xii. 101–102, 387 [27]
—(Nekhen) had " souls " instead of " gods," xii. 32, 361 [2] (ch. i)
Hierodules in worship of Anahit, vii. 26
Hieroglyphic writings, xi. 43, 352 [3]–354
Hieroglyphs of Dedun and Selqet, xii. 158 (fig. 166), 411 [12 13]
—plant, xii. 370 [33]
Hieropolis, old names of, v. 36, 387 [176]
High God idea, vii. 115–116, 117, 123–142, 157, 232
—gods, iii. 28, 98
—priest could force king to abdicate, v. 319
— -producing-god and Divine-producing-goddess, primeval couple, viii. 222, 231, 378 [3]
Highroad, Hermes as god of, i. 194

Highwaymen destroyed by Keresāspa, vi. 326

Hiho, forest of, viii. 258

Hiiden väki = Huldre-folk, iv. 77, 178

Hiisi, evil spirit, iv. 158, 189

Hiko-Hohodemi, tale of, viii. 265–266

Hiku and Kawelu, tale of, ix. 75–76

Hikuli [four-faced god], peyote deified as, x. 177

—[plant], adoration of, xi. 123

Hilaeira, daughter of Leukippos, i. 24

Hild ("Warrior"), Valkyrie, ii. 249

Hilde, king, ii. 123

Hildisvini ("battle swine"), boar of Frey, and Freyja's lover Ottarr in that form, ii. 109, 120

—boar made for Freyja, ii. 265

Hili, Zulu water-sprite, vii. 244

Hilib synonym of Ganzir, v. 161

Hill-Damara came out of a rock, vii. 147

—dying into the, ii. 310, 315

— -giants, ii. 153, 202, 278, 279

—of Allen (Almha), iii. 162

——Ares, i. 70

——the Axe, iii. 133

———Two Wheels, iii. 89

—totem, vii. 270, 271

Hillock near Pagān raised from river-bed by a Nāga, xii. 271

Hills, ii. 202–203, 227

—armed men came out of, ii. 316

—four sacred, of Buddhism, viii. 71–72

—hollow, known as síd, iii. 49

—many, associated with Gargantua, iii. 135

—(mountains), dwelling-place of wind, Host, and dead, ii. 44

—origin of, iii. 136

—regarded as petrified giants, ii. 279

—split by stones from a sling, xi. 249

Himālayas, Kaimūr and Vindhya ranges fabled to be offshoots of the, vi. 236

Himavant as father of Gaurī, vi. 182–183

—Mt., Brahmā sacrificed on, vi. 108

Himawunta (Himālayas), Hkun Hsang L'röng journeys through, xii. 290

Himeros ("Longing"), abstract divinity of state of mind, i. 282

—River of Sicily, healing powers of, i. 257

Himinbjorg, abode of Heimdall at, ii. 33, 152, 153

Himinbjorg, heaven-mountain, ii. 336; iv. 343

Himinbrjot, Hymir's largest ox, head of, used for bait, ii. 85

Himmel, vii. 14

Himukai, mounds at, viii. 211

Himyaritic, Akkadian language allied to, v. 2, 4

Hina and Kapipikauila, tale of, ix. 89–91

—daughter-wife of Taaroa, ix. 26–27

Hina-ua, mankind derived from, ix. 26

Hina-uri, Maui's sister, ix. 70

Hīnayāna has displaced Mahāyāna in Burma and Siam, xii. 260

—"Little Vehicle," vi. 189, 202, 203–204, 205, 206, 207

Hind, sacred, of Artemis killed by Agamemnon, i. 125

Hindu cosmogonic ideas, New Zealand parallels, ii. 20–21, 22

—mythology and religion, vi. 13

Hinduism, Buddhism of Tibet penetrated with, vi. 207

—mythology of modern, vi. 230–250

Hine and Tinirau, tale of, ix. 82–84

Hine-ahu-one ("earth-formed maid"), ix. 25

Hine-i-tau-ira became Hine-nui-te-po, ix. 74, 165

Hine-maki-moe (Daughter of Troubled Sleep), ix. 7

Hine-nui-te-po, guardian and goddess of Underworld; goddess of night, ix. 27, 52, 74, 77, 182

Hine-tu-a-maunga, wife of Tane, ix. 24

Hinges, goddess of, i. 297

Hino, the Thunderer, x. 24, 26

Hip-bone, ruler of spirits changed into, iv. 480

Hippios ("Equestrian"), Poseidon's title at Corinth, i. 213

Hippocamp, fabulous, included in materia medica of Artemis, i. 185

Hippodameia, Pelops suitor for, i. 119

—yields to spell of Aphrodite, i. 199

Hippolyte, queen of Amazons, whose girdle Herakles was directed to, and did, obtain, i. 85

Hippolytos and Aphrodite, i. 104

—Artemis patronizes, i. 185

—bull maddening horses of, offspring of Poseidon, i. 211

—destroyed by Poseidon, i. 104

Hyppolytos raised from dead by Asklepios, i. 280
—sent to death for spurning love of
Aphrodite, i. 199
—son of Theseus and Ariadne, i. 104
Hippopotami, Horus and Sêth change
themselves into, xii. 117, 126
Hippopotamus, vii. 284
—Armenian translators of Bible use
Nhangs in sense of, vii. 89
—as god-father, vii. 285–286
—became Typhonic animal of Sêth, xii.
390 [35]
—Êpet as, xii. 59, 412 [2]
—" Horus in Three Hundred " sometimes depicted as composed of, and
other animals, xii. 388 [28]
—in form of 'Apop-Sêth fights against
Horus, xii. 107
—tabus connected with, xii. 362 [3]
—totem, vii. 276
Hippoukrene (" Horse's Fount "), cre-
ated by Pegasos, i. 40, 213
Hir Atrym and Hir Erwn, Medraut re-
sembled, iii. 193
Hira hurricane, story of, viii. 254–255
Hiraṇyagarbha, creator-god, vi. 50–51,
74, 93
Hiraṇyakaśipu, vi. 122, 123, 146, 154,
164–165
Hiraṇyapura, vi. 151, 152
Hiraṇyatīrtha, Soma directed to bathe
at, vi. 137
Hirata, viii. 381 [1]
Hi-son, Mt., Trung-trac carried to
heaven from, xii. 314
Hischen, mother of the virgin Chibirias,
xi. 143
" Historia Danica," ii. 12
" Historical Record " of Ssŭ-ma Ch'ien,
viii. 145, 199
—Records of Shantung, account of
" Jade Lady " in, viii. 71
History, legendary Mexican, influenced
by cosmogonic and calendric cycles,
xi. 105–111
—mythic, x. 69–73
—Nennius's, on Arthur, iii. 184
—reconstruction of Yucatec, xi. 129
Hitachi, viii. 251, 253
Hitāspa, vi. 324, 326
Ḥitpu, sacrificial kid, v. 153, 400 [164]
Hittavainen, game-spirit, iv. 185
Hittites, Indo-Iranians among, vii. 379 [2]

Hittites, original models of Amazons
may have been, i. 86
Hiwanama, tale of, xi. 274–275
Hjadnings' strife, ii. 316, 342
Hjallti Skeggjason outlawed by Thing,
ii. 122
Hjalmgunnar slain in battle, ii. 251
Hjalmmeyjar (" helmet-maids "), ii.
248
Hjalmvitr (" helmet-wight "), ii. 248
Hjalprek, king, ii. 267
Hjalti, sons of, thought by Icelanders
to be Æsir, ii. 21
Hjorvard, Helgi's father, ii. 189
Hjuki, child of Vidfinn, ii. 184
Hka-chè, race of northern Lao country,
xii. 296
Hkas (meaning " slaves "), name ap-
plied by Shans to all savage tribes,
xii. 278
Hkè (Chinamen), six clans of, xii. 292
Hkmēr (Khmēr), language perhaps
originally spoken throughout Farther
India, xii. 253
Hkrip Hkrawp, male spirit representing
earth, xii. 263
Hkun Ai married a Nāga princess, xii.
272–273
—Hsak hatched from the egg of Nāga
princess but later called Hsö Hkan
Hpa, xii. 292
—Hsang Lōng, creator spirit, xii. 289
——L'röng, debasement and pilgrim-
ages of, xii. 290
—Lai and Hkun Lu (sons of Tüng
Hkam), first Shan kings, and variant
beliefs, xii. 274–275
—Lu founded kingdom at Möng
Kawng, xii. 275
—Sakya (Indra) invoked by Hkun
Hsang L'röng, xii. 290
Hladgud the Swan-white, ii. 259, 260
Hlakanyana, trickster and transformer,
vii. 213, 219–220, 222, 224, 283, 292,
295, 316, 353, 358, 425 [16]
Hlebard gave Odin magic wand, ii. 46
Hleidra, Gefjun's dwelling-place, ii. 181
Hler (Ægir), ii. 173
——sea, in genealogy of giants, ii. 281
Hlesey, island, dwelling of Hler, ii. 91,
173
Hlethjolf, dwarf, ii. 270
Hlidskjalf, seat of Odin, ii. 38, 60, 61,
110, 119, 146, 174, 175, 329

Hlin, goddess, ii. 15, 174, 176, 185
Hlodver, king, ii. 259
Hlodyn, Jörd called, ii. 194
Hlok ("Shrieker"), Valkyrie, ii. 249, 252
Hlolo, a rabbit, foil to Hare, vii. 293, 419 [8]
Hlorrithi (Thor), ii. 75
Hludana (Jörd), ii. 194
Hnikar (Odin), ii. 44, 58, 240
Hnitbjorg, Suttung hid mead in rock, ii. 53
Hnit-ma-dawgyi Nāt, xii. pl. 1, frontispiece
Hnit-ma Taunggyi-shin, xii. 342
Hnoss, goddess, ii. 15, 120
Ho, island and river, viii. 33–34, 37, 43
—chêng, officer of fire, viii. 77
—Hsien-ku, woman, one of Eight Immortals, viii. 128
— -ling, Stork Peak, viii. 123
—po, viii. 77
—Po, god of Yellow River, viii. 90
—Shên, god of fire, viii. 76–77
—Ti, Emperor, viii. 134
—T'u, viii. 34
—t'u, origin of, viii. 35
Ho-no-susari, tale of, viii. 265–266
Hoakils, spirit, xi. 341
Hoan-kiem-ho (the Lake of the Great Sword), ii. 302, 303–309
Hobby-horses, shaman with, iv. pl. LVII, opp. p. 488, 521
Hobgoblin: see Skřítek, etc.
Hobgoblins, dwarf races of America, Scotland, and Deccan believed to have become, xii. 255
Hobnil, omen of Kan year, xi. 144
Hobowakan, calumet, x. 21
Hockey, x. 232; see also Lacrosse.
Hod (Hotherus), god, ii. 15, 17, 21, 65, 127, 128, 129, 131, 132, 133, 134, 135, 164, 165–166, 187, 243, 254, 345
Hodbrodd, king of Sweden, ii. 131
Hoddmimir, Mimir called, ii. 168
Hoddrofnir, thought-runes from horn of, ii. 46, 168
Hoe-handles, talking, vii. 205
Hoeing Star, vii. 410 [15]
Hoel, Duke, iii. 185
Hœnir (Honir), god, ii. 15, 24, 26, 49, 61, 139, 141, 151–152, 160, 178, 179, 327, 345, 363 [4]

Hoes, sacrificed to "World's man," iv. 251
—wooden, exchanged for iron, vii. 220
Hofvarpnir, horse of Gna, ii. 185
Hog and woman came from tree, ix. 168
Hogeatz vank', convent, vii. 27
Hög-folk, ii. 225
Hogni, Dag avenged, ii. 56, 240
—king, ii. 251, 308
"Hokke-kyō," viii. 336, 344
Hokomata, x. 179, 180
Holda or Hulda, tale of, vii. 202–203
Hole, first people came from a, vii. 147
—(opening) in earth, vii. 175
—under waterfall, ghosts ascend through, to seize sheep, etc., vii. 186
Holes in earth lead to spirit-world, vii. 184, 195
——sky, iv. 336
—on gravestones for food offerings, vii. 96
—stars as, iv. 336, 417–418, 487
Hölgi: see Helgi, hero, etc.
Holkan-Okot, Dance of the Warriors, xi. 138
Holly sticks, yarn on, for magic binding of Fionn, iii. 170
Hollyhock, Lady, viii. 300
Hoλm ("wind"), vii. 14
Holocaustic offerings, xii. 195, 196
Holy animal, bear a, iv. 85
—(cosmic) chamber, v. 191
—figure 613 in Lîlîth myth, v. 364
—Gebal, title of sacred city of West Semitic religion, v. 351
—location of Seides considered, iv. 101, 104
—men, vi. 243, 244
—places, animals caught near the, iv. 85, 143
——Lapp, superstitions about behaviour near, iv. 102–103, 104
—the, highest grade of supernatural beings, viii. 108, 109
—water, ii. 231, 309, 312; iii. 209, 212; v. 176, 318; xii. 193
—Water connects three parts (sky, earth, Hades) of world, iv. 307–308
Holzfrauen, forest-elves, ii. 205, 206
Holzmuoja, forest-elf, ii. 205
Holzrûna, forest-elf, ii. 205
Holzweibel, forest-elf, ii. 206
Home left open after death by Russian Lapps, iv. 23

Home, new fire carried to, iv. 451
—of the Moon, x. 257
— -visitors (Kodukäiat), dead who return, iv. 37
Homeric poems, "blameless Ethio-
pians" mentioned in, xii. 428 [86]
"Homilia de Sacrilegiis," ii. 68
Homonoia ("Unanimity"), abstract
divinity of social institution, i. 283
Homs (Emesa), the temple to κυρια
Σημεα at, v. 22, 54
Hon, Brāhman priests of Bangkok,
prognostications of, xii. 323
Honan, viii. 80
Honduras, xi. 183–186
Hone of Odin, ii. 53
Honey, vi. 29, 30
—and blood blended to form mead, ii.
53
—drink, iv. 266, 267, 269
— -guide, vii. 245, 418 [35]
—miraculous properties of jar of, be-
longing to Kubera, vi. 158
—sprinkling with drink of, during
prayer for rain, iv. 188
—tabu in one nome, xii. 362 [3]
Honotato kako, x. 305
Hood, magic, made in Land of Promise,
iii. 175
Hood, Mt., x. 134
Hook, Hakemann seized children with
a, ii. 210
—magic, ix. 43, 44, 65
Hooks, baiting of, with various things,
ix. 43, 44, 315 [13]
—Samoa drawn from under sea with,
ix. 40
Hoop, marvellous, x. 125, 165
Hoopoe, Tereus changed into, i. 16, 70
Hop-field master, iv. 246
Hope alone remained in Pandora's jar,
i. 15
Hopt ok bond ("fastenings and bands,"
or "fetters"), gods described as, ii.
21
Hor (Odin), ii. 49
Hora-galles (Thor-man), thunder-god,
iv. pl. xxvii, opp. p. 224, 230, 231
Horai ("Hours"), i. 237–238
—("Seasons," "Hours"), affinity of
Aphrodite with, i. 197
—the, i. pl. li, opp. p. 236
Horeb, Mt., may have been ancient cen-
tre of moon worship, v. 6

Horiuzi, old manuscripts in Japanese
monastery at, vi. 217
Horizon, vii. 131
—Horus of the (Ḥar-akhti), xii. 27, 55,
388 [28]
Horizons, Horus of the Two, xii. 388
(fig. 225)
Horn-bill, tale of, ix. 145
— -blowing to banish evil spirits, xi. 276
— -covered man spoiled so that only
finger- and toe-nails remain, iv.
376
—end of, in sea, so that Thor could not
empty it, ii. 93
—(Freyja), ii. 125
—Gjallar-, ii. 50, 152–153, 154, 168
—if Fionn drank from, death would
follow, iii. 179
—in hand of statue for annual offering
of mead, iii. 279
—of Acheloös, drops of blood from, i.
262
——restored by Herakles in return
for Deianeira, i. 93
——Ammon, i. pl. iv (3), opp. p. l
——Plenty given to Herakles, i. 93, 94
——presented to Herakles by Acheloös, i. 257
——stag, horn implement, x. 44
—sign of fertility, x. 199
—used as synonym of might, especially
divine power, iii. 129
——on Midsummer Day, ii. pl. xx,
opp. p. 160
— -yard at sacrifice to Seides, iv. 109
Horned gods, ii. pl. xxxi, opp. p. 238,
pl. xxxii, opp. p. 246; iii. 8, 9, pl.
viii, opp. p. 72, pl. xii, opp. p. 112,
pl. xvi, opp. p. 124, 129, 158, pl. xxv,
opp. p. 204
Horns, blowing of, iv. 246–247
—breaking of last of world-bull's, indicates end of world, iv. 312
—golden, containing representations of
mythic deities, ii. pl. iv, opp. p. 16, pl.
v, opp. p. 22, pl. vi, opp. p. 32, pl.
xiii, opp. p. 106
—Ḥat-ḥôr's, symbolize limits of sun's
course, xii. 38
—indicate connexion of Sekha(u)it
with subterranean sky, xii. 53
—indication of female divinities, xii. 37
—interlaced sign of Odin, ii. pl. xxxi,
opp. p. 238

Horns, magic, buried in hut to prevent escape, vii. 246, 248
—may suggest divine strength or early beast-god, iii. 8, pl. VIII, opp, p. 72, 129
—musical instruments, vii. 295
—of Sekha(u)it mistaken by Plutarch for lunar crescent, xii. 373 57
——wise hare, vii. 294
—spirit-, vii. 189
—three, of divine animals, cranes may be rebus for, iii. 157
Horoscopes, xi. 102; xii. 200
Horse and horsemanship under patronage of Poseidon, i. 211
—Angra Mainyu ridden as a, vi. 302, 303
—as component of names, viii. 210
—black, offered in praying for cessation of rain, viii. 379 17
—Boreas in form of, begat twelve foals, i. 265
—born from head of food-goddess, viii. 232
—buried or burned with dead to ride over Hel-way, ii. 305
—celestial white, appeared to Cao-bien, xii. 317
—divine, Pegasos a, i. 40
—dragon-, marks on back of, viii. 8
—drawing hearse, omen of further death if it raise left foot first, iv. 28
—eaten by Abatwa, vii. 262–263
—enchanted, vii. 347, 358, 431 19a
—first, produced by Poseidon, i. 213
—foretold in Iason's dream, guides Argonauts to Tritonian Lake, i. 114
— -god, Poseidon as, i. 213
——Usching, iii. 329–330
—grey, of giantesses, term for wolf, ii. 286
—head of, doctrine of Madhu told by a, vi. 122, 124
———given to Dadhyañc, vi. 64
———on hazel-pole called insulting-post, ii. 230
—in worship of Triglav, iii. 285
—iron, xii. 314
—lake formed from well produced from micturation of, drowned Eochaid, iii. 73
—miraculous, viii. 358
—miraculously cured, vi. 341

Horse of Gwyn, iii. 108
——Iddawc, iii. 190
—on Gaulish coins and monuments, iii. 13, pl. II (1–3), opp. p. 8, pl. III (2, 4), opp. p. 14, pl. XV, opp. p. 124
—which none could be killed, iii. 29, 128
—one-legged, with chariot-pole through its body, iii. 70
— -post ruler = world-pillar, iv. 337
—provided for journey to afterworld, iv. 486
— -racing, iii. 73–74
—rejected suitors took oath over severed pieces of, to defend Helen, i. 25
—sacrifice of, in ritual of Poseidon, i. 213
— -sacrifice to keremet-spirit, iv. 156–157, pl. XIX, opp. p. 156
—Votiak, iv. 410
—sacrificed at funeral demanded back, iv. 488–489
—sacrificial, iv. pl. XXVII, opp. p. 224
—sun-, vi. 96
— -Targeldeš, iv. 185
—Tishtrya enters contest as, vi. 268–269
— -water, viii. 104
— -wedding, iv. 57–58
—white, altar of, xii. 321
——as sacrifice, viii. 233, 379 17
——consecrated to Svantovit, iii. 280
—winged, a form of Zû, v. 283
——battle of, with Ninurta, v. 131
——Pegasos the, i. 34
—wooden, of Troy, i. 132–133
Horseman, Kastor type of expert, i. 26
Horsemen: see Aśvins.
Horses, ii. 18, 22, 43, pl. VIII, opp. p. 60, 82, 90, 109, 111, 131, 134, 137, 138, 153, 157, 185, 196, 197, 200, 251; iv. 360, 431, 432–433; vi. 56, 61, 62, 63, 106, 115, 125, 127, 128, 132, 133, 147
—associated with Mithra-Meher, vii. 34
—Astarte mistress of, xii. 155, 156 (fig. 160)
—at Jerusalem, v. 388 223
—Ercol's, Loegaire's, and Cúchulainn's, iii. 147
—first trained by Athene, i. 171–172
—given by Zeus to Laomedon for theft of Ganymedes, i. 86

Horses, Glaukos famous for swiftness of his, i. 38–39
—gravestones in shape of, vii. 95–96
—introduction of, and horse-stealing, x. 76–77, 205
—Lykourgos drawn asunder by, on Mt. Pangaion, i. 218
—man-eating, of Diomedes, i. 84–85
—mythic, iii. 128, 129
—of Achilles deprived of speech by Erinyes, i. 277
——Glaukos, cause of madness of, i. 37–38
——Manannan personifications of waves or locks of his wife, ii. 191
——the sun, v. 36, 54, 61; see also HORSE, SUN-.
————four, vii. 50–51
—patrons of, iv. 244
—ridden by night by Cattleyard ruler, iv. 166–167
—sacred, kept in Frey's temple, ii. 118
—sacrificed at breaking up of ice, iv. 214
——to sun (or Mithra) by Armenians, vii. 15, 47
—shaman's, iv. 521–522
—stars as drove of, iv. 337
—swift, of Oinomaos, i. 119
—tethered to heaven-post, iv. 337, 340, 349
—tutelary genii of, iv. 402
—war-, of King Setho, v. 30
—warnings not to dismount from, iii. 90, 128, 181
Horvendillus, father of Amleth (Hamlet), ii. 83
Horus, xii. 24, 26, 27, 29–30, 34, 54, 55, 69, 209
—and Har-akhti retained in worship by Amen-hotep IV, xii. 226
——Isis, statues of, interpreted as representing Child and Madonna, xii. 244
——Khnûm draw net to capture dragon, xii. 391 [52]
——Sêth, conflict between, merged with myth of Rê' and serpent, xii. 107
——Isis in combat of, xii. 126–127
——Sonet-nofret, Neb-taui son of, xii. 140
——Sothis-Sirius, association of, unexplained, xii. 56
——Thout(i) come from Ptah, xii. 220

Horus, Antaeus compared with, xii. 130
—as god of ocean, xii. 373 [60]
——male counterpart of Hat-hôr, xii. 39
—begotten by Qêb and Nut, xii. 69
—binds a great serpent, xii. 391 [43]
—blended with Shu, xii. 44
—(celestial), house of, xii. 367 [11]
—children of, bind 'Apop, xii. 104–105
—connected with Morning Star, xii. 94
—conquest of Sêth by, supposed to be symbolized by feather, xii. 362 [8]
—cosmic explanation of, xii. 215
—earthly reigns of, listed by Turin Historical Papyrus, xii. 399 [108]
—Ehi represented like, xii. 133
—eye of, xii. 384 [109]
—fetters 'Apop, xii. 127
—fighting monster of northern sky, xii. 61
—followers of, xii. 179
—four (or five) sons of, xii. 104, 105, 110–113, 111 (fig. 114), 112 (fig. 115), 375 [77 80], 387 [27], 391 [42], 394 [67]
—god of light, regarded as ruler of place of torture, xii. 417 [21]
—harpoon of, xii. 397 (fig. 227)
—Hat-mehit wife of, xii. 133
—(Hor, Horu) in the Osirian cycle, xii. 101–102, 115–118, 124–125, 126–127
—husband of Hat-hôr, male ruler of sky, xii. 40
—identified with Behdeti, xii. 21
——Mîn, xii. 219
——Orion, xii. 57, 58
—in the Underworld and Khnûm hold infernal monster down, xii. 391 [51]
——Three Hundred produced by late speculation, xii. 388 [28]
—infant, nursed by Nephthys, xii. 110, 117
—instructs Sêth in fighting with spear, xii. 103 (fig. 99)
—Kenemtef(i) sometimes identified with, xii. 134
—Khasti identified with, xii. 134
—kills Sêth in form of ass and as crocodile, xii. 119 (figs. 121, 122)
—later rôle of, in Osiris-myth, xii. 363 [1]
—legend of, as parallel to deluge-myth, xii. 76
—local forms of, xii. 388 [28]
—lord of the four greens, xii. 400 [10]

Horus, Men'et compared with Ḥat-ḥôr as wife of, xii. 101, 136

—Merui called " son of," xii. 137

—Nefer-têm identified with, xii. 141

—Nephthys sister of, xii. 394 71

—nursed by Isis in the marshes, xii. 116 (fig. 119)

—of Chemmis, shrew-mouse dedicated to, xii. 165

——Edfu, Beḥdet consort of, xii. 132

——symbol of, xii. 101 (fig. 96)

——Mesen(?), lion-headed local form of Horus, xii. 388 28

——Ombos, Sonet-nofret wife of, xii. 140, 149

——Praises, xii. 81, 388 28

——Shesmet, Shesemtet seems to have been companion of, xii. 375 76

——the Horizon, xii. 27, 55, 388 28

——star-abode (abode of dead, Underworld), xii. 373 60

——Two Eyes, xii. 28, 29

——Horizons, xii. 388 (fig. 225)

—on his green, xii. 125, 400 10, 401 (fig. 228)

—one of smiths of, xii. 101 (fig. 97)

—Onuris regarded as same as, xii. 143

—parallel to, in American Indian, x. 87–88, 89

—partially portrayed in pictures of nameless cosmic deity, xii. 223

—patron of the races of man, xii. 426 38

—pig abomination to, xii. 124

—rides in sledge-bark, xii. 409 102

—Selqet sometimes termed wife of, xii. 147

—Sêth originally adversary (and brother) of, xii. 103, 390 34, 394 71

——perhaps confused with, xii. 391 47

—Shu assumes form of, xii. 86

—Sokar(i) at first regarded as manifestation of, xii. 149, 409 102

—son and doublet of Osiris, xii. 113, 394 71

—Sopd(u) compared with, xii. 149

—Sothis mother of, xii. 398 105

—spear or harpoon of, xii. 109

—temporarily half blinded by pig entering his eye, xii. 124–125

—to be heir of Osiris, xii. 72

—tresses of Ḥat-ḥôr attributed to, xii. 39

—violates his mother Isis, xii. 125, 398 104

Horus-Orion fights the Ox-Leg, xii. 110 (fig. 110)

——Osiris, sons of, near Orion, xii. 112 (fig. 116)

——Rê' as renascent Osiris, xii. 54

Hoshangābād, vi. 242, 246

Hosi ("chief; lord"), Tilo sometimes called, vii. 127

Hospitality, story of, viii. 250–251, 252

—to deceased, iv. 47–49

Hospitallers, Oengus and Midir appeared as, iii. 56

Hospodář, house-snake, iii. 246

Hospodáříček, Bohemian " Master of the House," whose symbol is snake, iii. 246

Host, iv. 123, 131

—see Furious Host, etc.

—Wodan's, ii. 41

Hostages, iii. 36, 174

—given by Æsir and Vanir, ii. 26, 27, 101, 143, 152

Hostius, vii. 380 7

Ḥôt, capital of seventh nome of Upper Egypt, Ḥat-ḥôr apparently goddess of, xii. 392 56

Hotei, deity of good fortune, viii. 280

Hotherus: see Hod.

Hotots, spirits who lure people to death by drowning, vii. 396 63

Hótt (Odin), ii. 121

Hottentot god, Mantis called the, vii. 288

Hottentots, discussion of supreme Being of, vii. 157–159

Hotu-papa, fourth wife of Rangi, ix. 9

Hoturu, winds, x. 91

Hou-chi, legendary founder of Chow Dynasty, patron of grain, viii. 6, 66

——t'u (Hou-t'u nai-nai), myth of, viii. 62, 67

——Shên, Ko Lung deified as national god of soil, viii. 62

Houmai-tawaiti, tale of dog of, ix. 86–87

Houmea, tale of, ix. 84–86

Hound, venomous, turned against sheep, iii. 63

—Underworld's, iv. 75, 76

Hounds of Aktaion, stricken with madness by Artemis, killed master, i. 46–47

——Fionn, nephews of his own, iii. 126, 169, 172

Hounds of Norns, wolves as, ii. 241
——Odin, ii. 41, 65
Hour, an, xii. 66 (fig. 72)
Hourglass, iv. 344
Hours at creation of Pandora, i. 15
—care for Aristaios, i. 252
—each of twenty-four represented by special gods, xii. 66
—gods of, xi. 53
—of day, four sons of Horus or Osiris patrons of first four, xii. 113
House, bhūts on roof of, vi. 249
— -building contest in which animals aided, xi. 231
—built of feathers demanded by Anuanaïtu's father, xi. 264–265
—fire carried to new, vii. 55
—first, in Ireland, iii. 137
—haunted, tale of, viii. 151–152
—man, god of the dwelling, iv. 159–161, 165
—of Birth, xi. 114
——Dark Cliffs, x. 166
——Descent, xi. 114
——God, xi. 132
——Myths, x. 253, 254
——sacrifices (to dead), a temple to Dagan, v. 80
——Serpent, xi. 107
——Seven Caves, xi. 112, 113
——Sun, journey of song-seeker to, xi. 90–91
——Thirteen Serpents, xi. 132
——world, vi. 17
—offerings to all previous tenants of, viii. 81
— -riders, ii. 46, 300, 301
— -serpent, vii. 76, 391 16
— -spirits, ii. 208, 224, 226; vii. 91
—to be built in air, vii. 354
—where names of Lîlîth written unapproached by her, v. 363
Housecleaning, ceremonial, vii. 56
Household genii: see chap. The World of Spirits and Monsters (vol. vii. 72–92)
—gods: see GODS, HOUSEHOLD.
—spirits, iv. 499–500
Houses, communal, x. 214
—conceived as animate forerunner of household spirits, iv. 168
—excavated, people still live in, viii. 80
—for cemis, xi. 22, 26

Houses, Hopi speak of solstitial points as, x. 194
—in charge of genius ("shadow"), iii. 228
——Tuonela, iv. 74
—mysterious, iii. 119, 169–170
—of Gloom, Lances, Cold, Tigers, Fire, Bats, etc., xi. 171, 174
—partitions in, to guard sacrifice shelf, iv. 135
—tutelary spirits ascribed to, xii. 15–16
Housesteads on Hadrian's Wall, old altars found at, ii. 98
"How the Ill-treated Maiden became Rich," vii. 141, 205
"How Wives Restored Husbands to Life," vii. 359
"Howard the Halt, Story of," ii. 292
Howler, the, Rudra, vi. 38
Hoy in Orkney, ii. 316
Hoza, invisible nature-god, iv. 464
Hozanek, omen of Cauac years, xi. 145
Hpai, ten clans of, xii. 292
Hpaung-daw-u, guardian of the lake, xii. pl. xx, opp. p. 352
—image carried around Lake Yawnghwe on raft, xii. pl. x, opp. p. 302
Hpi Hpai = ogres, xii. 294
——and Hpi Lu, kings at Nawng Kōng, xii. 292
Hpilu Yek-kha, thirteen clans of, xii. 292
Hræsvelg ("Corpse-eater"), giant in eagle form, ii. 193, 276, 279, 340
Hrafna-god (raven-god), Odin as, ii. 65
Hrafnkell, half-share of horse of, dedicated to Frey, ii. 118
Hranush, vii. 390 18
Hrapp, ii. 188
Hraudung, king, ii. 176
Hreidmar, ii. 49, 141
Hrimfaxi, horse which brings night, ii. 200
Hrimgerd, daughter of Hati, ii. 190, 209, 228, 269, 277, 278, 279, 281
Hrimgrimnir, giant, ii. 111, 278–279
Hrimnir, frost-giant, ii. 111, 278
Hrimthursar, frost-giants, ii. 279
Hringhorni, funeral ship of Balder, ii. 130
Hrist ("Shaker"), Valkyrie, ii. 248
Hrod, slayer of, ii. 91
Hrodvitnir (Fenris-wolf), ii. 199

Hrolf Kraki, bear fought by side of, ii. 234
——(Mysing), sea-king, ii. 283
" Hrolfs-saga kraka," ii. 293
Hromund and Helgi, fight of, ii. 260
—possesses Mistelteinn, ii. 136
" Hromundar-saga Greipssonar," ii. 136
Hropt (Odin) arranged thought-runes, ii. 46, 128, 168
Hroptatyr (Odin), ii. 46, 201
Hross, daughter of Freyja, ii. 120
— -thjof, child of Hrimnir, ii. 278
Hrosshars-grani (" Horse-hair-beard "), Starkad called, ii. 73
Hrotic, Armenian name of month Fravarti, vii. 22
Hruden (Thraetaona, Farīdūn) bound Aždahak, vii. 98
Hrungnir (" Blusterer "), giant, ii. 21–22, 65, 66, 74, 81, 82, 83, 96, 122, 123, 182, 279, 283
Hrym, giant, ii. 147, 278, 340, 384 [21]
Hsen-wi, chronicle of, gives chronicle of ancestry of first kings of Möng Mao country, xii. 272
Hsēng Nya hatched from egg and became Udibwa, xii. 276
Hsi-an, viii. 40
—Hai (" Western Sea "), viii. 70
— -hua, abode of female fairies, viii. 114
— -ling Shih, viii. 28
—Pien Mên, viii. 23, 135
—Po, Wên Wang chief of, viii. 41
—Wang Mu, fairy queen, viii. 104, 114, 116, 117, 118, 128, 129
— -yü, viii. 120
—Yu Chi, viii. 190
Hsia, viii. 35
—Dynasty, events in, viii. 9, 27, 37, 49, 66, 76, 137
— -p'i (modern Hsü Chow), viii. 94–95
Hsiang, half-brother of Emperor Shun, viii. 161
—Ch'êng, viii. 14
—Chi, military leader, viii. 92
—Chün, hero, god of waterways of Hsiang (modern Hunan), viii. 86, 88, 90
—Fu-jên, two daughters of Yao, viii. 86, 88, 90, 161
—mien, viii. 139
—Shan, island, viii. 89
—Yang, viii. 95

Hsiao, Duke of Chow Dynasty, viii. 122
—Hsüeh, viii. 118
—Kan, viii. 163
—King, viii. 100
Hsieh t'ien hu kuo chung i ta ti, viii. 95
Hsien, Hsien Jên, viii. 108
—(" Immortals "), viii. 114
—Ching, viii. 114
—ho, viii. 104
—introduced into Japanese, viii. 266
—Shan, viii. 114
—T'an (Altar of the Fairies), viii. 114
—Tsung, Emperor, viii. 200
— -yüan given name of Yellow Emperor, viii. 27
Hsin-ch'ou day, viii. 34
—Yin King, viii. 57
Hsing, viii. 74
—ch'i, control of the breath, viii. 147
—Shên, viii. 82
Hsiu-chi, mother of Yü, viii. 37
Hsiung Wu, An Lu-shan established himself as, viii. 96
Hsö Hkan Hpa, hatched from egg of Nāga princess, founded Wing Mai, xii. 292
Hsü Chow (ancient Hsia-p'i), viii. 94–95
—Hsün (Hsü Chên-jên), one of the " Perfect Ones," viii. 113–114
—Shên, viii. 140
—Shih, viii. 115
—Wu, tale of, viii. 169–171
—Yen and Hsü P'u, brothers of Hsü Wu, viii. 169–171
—Yu, viii. 167–168
Hsüan Chiao, Taoism referred to as, on tablet, viii. 23
—Ti, Emperor, viii. 75–76, 105
—T'ien Shang Ti, viii. 111
—Tsung, seventh Emperor of T'ang Dynasty, viii. 18, 96, 112, 134
—Wang, viii. 167
— -yang, viii. 113
—Yüan Huang Ti (Emperor of Mysterious Origin), viii. 22
Hsüeh Shan, Snowy Mountain, viii. 23
Hsün Tzŭ, viii. 139
Hsuriya (Skt. Sūrya), prince, fell in love with serpent princess Thusandi, xii. 276
H'Uraru, the earth, x. 91, 92

Ḥu associated with birth of sun-god, xii. 71
—connected with Nile-god, xii. 66
—(" Feeling, Wisdom," frequently confused with Ḥu, " Abundance ") one of sense-gods, xii. 66
—god in form of man or sphinx, xii. 66–67, 96, 134
——of abundance, xii. 66
—in solar ship, xii. 96
Hu, viii. 46
—Ching-tê, early guardian of the portal, viii. 78
—(house), viii. 74, 80
—jade tablet, viii. 46
— -k'ou, P'êng Yü-lin protector of, viii. 66
—Kung, magician, viii. 131–132
—li, viii. 103
—sisters, tale of, viii. 156–158
—(tiger), viii. 103
—Yin destroys serpent with mysterious powers, viii. 203
—Ying-lin, critic, viii. 128
Hu, dog, sky-region, ix. 178–179
Hu, Gadarn, oxen of, iii. 129
Hua T'o, viii. 107
Huacas applied to anything wonderful, xi. 224, 227, 246
Huai-nan Tzŭ, viii. 19, 54–55
—Wang song, viii. 115–116
Huaillepeñ (Guallipén), causes birth of deformed children, xi. 328
Huallallo Caruincho, idol, xi. 227, 228
Huaman Poma, xi. 370 23
Huan, Duke, viii. 138
Hüan Tsang on cult of sun in India, vi. 183
Huanacauri (Guanacaure), Ayar Cachi, altars to, xi. 249–250
Huang, jade tablet, viii. 46
—Chin, viii. 174
— -chow, viii. 154
—Hsiang, viii. 164–165
—Lao, viii. 144
—Li, viii. 143
—Ti (Yellow Emperor), first of Five Sovereigns, viii. 7, 17, 21, 25, 26, 27, 28, 32, 33, 41, 75, 82, 94, 98, 99, 100, 133, 135, 144
——Ping King Su Wên, viii. 28
—T'ien (Imperial Heaven), viii. 49
——Shang Ti (Supreme Ruler of Imperial Heaven), viii. 49

Huang T'ing-chien, viii. 165–166
—Yao, viii. 34
Huari Runa, xi. 240
Huarochico, arming of sons of knights of, xi. 250
Huas or ᶜUas, explained as Hayk, vii. 389 4
Huascar and Atahualpa, conflict of, xi. 214
—replaced symbol of creator by image of sun, xi. 246–247
Huasi-camayoc, household gods, xi. 223
Huastec, sacrifice of, xi. 79
Huathiacuri cured brother of Pariacaca of disease, xi. 230–231
Huayna Capac gave Inca empire greatest extent, xi. 44, 110
——Quito subdued by, xi. 207
Hubeane, vii. 119, 213, 214, 217, 219, 223, 224, 353, 355
Hubur, designer of all things, v. 295
—legendary river, v. 261
—river of death, Gilgamish crossed, v. 235
Huecuvu (Guecubu), daemons able to assume human form, xi. 327
Hūgar, Mt., vi. 278
Hugi, ii. 81, 93
Huginn (Thought), raven of Odin, ii. 65
Hui Tsung, Emperor, viii. 59, 95, 135, 194
Huichaana, creator god, xi. 87
Huichilobos, god of war, description of, xi. 47, 354 5
Huitranalhue, friend of strangers and protector of herds, xi. 329
Huitzilopochtli, Aztec war-god, xi. pl. v, opp. p. 46, 47, 57, 58–61, pl. vii, opp. p. 60, 65, 66, 74, 87, 92, 114, 116–118
Hukairya, a summit of Mt. Albūrz, vi. 280
Huldra, mountain fairy, possesses tail or is hollow behind, ii. 223
Huldre-folk, ii. 223–224, 231; iv. 77, 178
Huldreslaat, music, ii. 223
Hūm, a god, vi. 205
—Haoma has become the hermit, vi. 338
Human aid required by dwarfs, ii. 271–272
—being, Hare once a, vii. 168, 291
——porcupine a, iv. 450

Human beings, anthropomorphic forest-
spirits originally, iv. 186
——kuala-spirits appear as, iv. 127
——metamorphosis of, into animals and
trees, i. 15
——within gourd dropped from sky by
Hkun Hsang Lōng, xii. 289
—character of pair surviving flood emphasized, ix. 172
—flesh fed to serpents, vi. 320
—form, figures (of earth) of, ii. 264
——fire-spirit may take on, iv. 236
——ghosts may live their life in, vii.
189-190
——Seide may appear in, iv. 105
—Leopards, society for protection
against witches, vii. 342
—origin of Tammuz almost entirely
suppressed, v. 347
—race descended from Spider, vii. 322, 323
—Sacred Pack, x. 305-306
—sacrifice: see SACRIFICE, HUMAN.
—shape, Devil in, in creation-myth, iv.
317, 318, 326
——ghosts in, vii. 73-74, 75
——Master of fire may take on, iv.
455
—snakes, vii. 192, 193, 194
—Thunderer originally, iv. 442
—Valkyries, ii. 251, 252
Humans and birds (or animals) hatched
from same setting of eggs, ix. 109
Humayaka, demon-worshipper, vi. 340
Humba (variant of Hubaba), Elamitic
god, described as the Enlil of Susa, v.
255
Humbaba, conflict of Gilgamish with,
v. 28
—(Huwawa), monster, attack on, v.
246-255, 257, 260, 268
—monster of Lebanons, v. 211, 212
—wrongly identified with star Procyon,
v. 268
Humming-bird dies with dry and revives with wet season, xi. 56
Humorous and irreverent tales of gods,
ii. 48; iii. 30
Humour and satire, tales of, viii. 360-365
Humpbacks sacrificed, xi. 82
Ḥumuṣiru (Akk. pig), title for Ninurta,
v. 132
Hun Camé and Vukub Camé send challenge to upperworld for ball game, xi.
170, 173, 174-177

Hun Ytzamna son of Hunab-Ku, xi. 134
Hunab-Ku, a supreme god, xi. 134
Hunac Ceel, xi. 128
Hunahpu and Xbalanqué, hero-brothers,
xi. 164, 168, 169, 172, 174, 177
Hunan, viii. 88, 89
Hunbatz, one of hero-brothers, xi. 172,
177
Hunchouen, one of hero-brothers, xi.
172
Hung-chow (modern Nanch'ang), viii.
113
—Lieh Chuan, viii. 54
— -têh, viii. 166
—Vuong instituted worship of Lien,
Tan, and Lang, xii. 357
—Wu, Emperor, viii. 68, 99, 117
Hungarians, or Magyars, a Finno-Ugric
people, iv. xvii
Hunger used to threaten the gods, xii.
200
Hunhun-Ahpu, one of hero-brothers, xi.
170, 173
Hunter and monkeys, tale of the, viii.
355
—bear a, iv. 504
—gods and goddess of, x. 669
—sun-god as, v. 55-56, 60
Hunting Age, Fu Hsi typifies the, viii.
25, 33
— -cry, iii. 178
—dragons and Kaches went, vii. 80,
393 30
— -god, Ull is, ii. 156
—in preparation for Busk festival, x.
58
—regarded as holy and has special vocabulary, iv. 83-84
—rules for, iv. 84
—Vahagn patron of, vii. 365
—white cloth at birch-tree sacrificed
for luck in, iv. 233
Huntress, Artemis a, i. 186
—Diana a, i. 183
Huong-vien, inhabitants of, dedicated
to service of Temple of Trung sisters,
xii. 316
Hupeh, old State of Ch'u the modern,
viii. 86, 95
Hur, word for fire, vii. 55
Hurakan, Mayan storm-god, xi. 38, 161,
162, 163, 177
Hurbak (Arm.), fire, vii. 56
Hurling match, iii. 24, 167

Ḫurra-stone with head of panther, weapon, v. 126

Hurricane, vii. 133; xi. 38

Ḫursag, dwelling-place of winds, v. 99

—used for place of judgement, v. 161

Hursagkalamma, temple of Mah, v. 111

Huruing Wuhti of the East and West, visited by sun, x. 204

Husbandry, Father of, viii. 62

"Husdrapa," ii. 88, 109, 128, 131, 155

Hushbishag, wife of Namtar, who keeps tablets of Arallû, v. 161

Hûshêṭar, vi. 343

— -mãh, vi. 343

Hut of straw as shrine of small village deity, xii. 17

—wedding, iv. 123

Hutaosa, same name as Darius's wife Atossa, vi. 341, 342

Huts, Galla, vii. pl. IX, opp. p. 124

—Pelasgos first to contrive fashioning of, i. 16

Hutu and Pare, tale of, ix. 76–78

Hu'u-vong, section of Hanoi, xii. 304

Huyen-thien temple at Hanoi, xii. 308–309, 320

— -vu, statue in Pagoda of Tran-vu represents, xii. 306–310

—temple of, xii. 308

—worship of, xii. 307–310

Huytaca transformed into owl, xi. 202

Hvanîrâthra (earth), central Karshvar, v. 217

Hvergelmir, serpents dwell in, ii. 217, 318

Hvōgvas, family of the, vi. 341, 342

Hvōvī, wife of Zoroaster, vi. 341

Hwyvar, Welsh word cognate with Irish siabur, siabhra, iii. 193

Hyacinth flower grew from blood of Hyakinthos, i. 23–24

Hyades, vii. 229

—and Pleiades, i. 248–249, 250

—nymphs of Nysa transformed into, i. 46

—rain-god associated with, viii. 73

Hyagnis, name of a Phrygian satyr, vii. 15, 62, 364, 379 [6]–380

Hyakinthia, Lakonian festival, i. 24

Hyakinthos resembles Dionysos in alternately dying and coming to life, i. 218

—son of Amyklas, i. 23–24

Hyantes and Aonians succeeded the Ektenes, i. 42

Hyas, death of, i. 248

—identical with Hayk, vii. 379 [6]–380

—Phrygian sky-god, vii. 66

Hybris (" Offensive Presumption "), abstract divinity of vice, i. 282

—sin of, xi. 168

Hydra and Herakles, i. 81, pl. XXII, opp. p. 82

—as serpent in " Story of the Haunted Prince," xii. 153

—Ereshkigal identified with, v. 164

—Lernean, slain by Herakles, i. 81, pl. XXII, opp. p. 82

—Mušḫuššû identified with, v. 277, 278, 282, 286, 288, 409 [2]

—Ningishzida identified with, v. 164, 178, 284, 286

—Virgo, and Orion associated in Asiatic astral myth, xii. 84

Hyena totem, vii. 275–276

Hyenas, vii. 171, 223–224, 226, 230, 284, 336, 337, 344, 345, 346, 347, 404 [31], 406 [7], 408 [9], 428 [11]

Hygieia, abstract divinity of state of body, i. 282

—(" Health "), daughter of Asklepios, i. 281

—Salus recognized as same as, i. 301

Hyksos kings gave special honour to Sêth, xii. 390 [35]

Hylas captured by water-nymphs, i. 110

Hyldehög, hill, ii. 158

Hyllos dies in duel with Echemos, i. 95

—slays Eurystheus, i. 95

—son of Herakles and Deianeira, king of Dorians, i. 95

Hylozoism, viii. 220

Hymir, giant, ii. 10, pl. X, opp. p. 76, 85, 86, 87, 100, 172; see also MID-GARD-SERPENT.

—sea, ii. 281

" Hymiskvitha," ii. 10, 20, 85, 86, 89, 93, 100, 171

Hymn on apotheosis of king, xii. 202–204

—to Amen-Rê', xii. 236–238

——Hermes, summary of, i. 192–193

——nameless cosmic god, xii. 222

——the sun by Amen-ḥotep IV, xii. 227–231

Hymns, x. 110–112, 151–153

Hyndla, giantess; seeress, ii. 10, 125, 279

"Hyndluljod," ii. 7, 10, 15, 39, 56, 91, 110, 121, 124, 128, 131, 145, 152, 153, 155, 164, 182, 195, 205, 280, 338, 346

Hyperbios, giant born of blood of Ouranos, i. 9

Hyperboreans (a Celtic people), circular temple to Apollo in island of the, iii. 10

Hyperion and Euryphaëssa, parents of Helios, i. 242

—born of Ouranos and Gaia, i. 6

—Eos daughter of, i. 246

Hypermnestra, origin of, i. 167

—wife of Lynkeus and priestess of Hera, i. 31

Hypnos, abode of, in Underworld, i. 278

Hypnos, abstract divinity of state of body, i. 282

—("Sleep"), creation of, i. 6, pl. LVIII, opp. p. 278

Hypnotic power of wizards and witches, vii. 335, 336, 337

Hypnotism in magic, xii. 206

Hypsipyle, nurse of infant son of King Lykourgos, i. 52

—ruler of race of women on Lemnos, i. 109

Hypsistos ('Elioun) slain by beasts and deified, v. 66

Hypsomata, v. 304

Hypsouranios, inventor of huts, v. 51, 389 252

Hyrokkin, giantess, ii. 128, 130, 277, 280, 361 10

Hythin, ii. 261

I

"I King," viii. 8, 14, 16, 44, 45, 136, 142, 144

I-Qong, Night, ix. 113

I Yin, viii. 9

Iahes (Eahes), probably worshipped near southern frontier, xii. 152

Iakchos, a form of Dionysos, i. 220

—represented in marble relief of Eleusinian rites, i. pl. L, opp. p. 230

Iamet (Eamet), goddess who nurses young divinities, xii. 152

Ianiculum, Mt., Ianus said to have dwelt on, i. 297

Iano, survival of Ianus in modern Romagnola, i. 317

Ianus Bifrons, i. pl. LXI (2), opp. p. 294, 295, 297–298

—survives as Iano in modern Romagnola, i. 317

Iapetos, born of Ouranos and Gaia, i. 6

—the Titan, father of Prometheus by Gaia (or of Themis), i. 12

Iarnvith ("Iron-wood"), old forest, ii. 199, 280

Iarnvithjur ("Iron-wood women"), ii. 199, 205, 280

Iasion killed by Zeus because of amour with Demeter, i. 226

—struck dead by thunderbolt, i. 117

Iason and Medeia in Corinth, i. 115

——wedded, i. 113

Iason, commander of Argo, i. 109, 111

—dedicates the Argo to Poseidon at Isthmus of Corinth, i. 212

—dream of, i. 113–114

—exposed Atalante in forest, i. 56

—Medeia falls in love with, i. 112

—Pelias plots against, i. 114

—said to have restrained Atalante from going on the voyage of the Argo, i. 59

—took part in hunt of Kalydonian boar, i. 56

Iasos and Klymene said to have been parents of Atalante, i. 56

Iath n'Anann, Ireland called, iii. 39

Iberia, Vahagn worshipped and sacrificed to in, vii. 365

Iberian deity Azmaz, vii. 382 22

——Zaden, vii. 40

Ibhell, hag transformed into shape of, iii. 59

Ibibio (Calabar), head-pad in magical ceremonies of the, vii. 111

Ibik-Ishtar, v. 404 16

Ibis-god, xii. 33 and fig. 15

Ibis, moon as egg of, xii. 208, 423 34

—of Thout(i), xii. 33–34

——origin of, xii. 84–85

—or crane, Nephthys once represented with head of, xii. 392 57

Ibi-Sin as Tammuz, v. 345

Iblîs (Azâzel), v. 352, 354, 355

Iblîs enters ark in guise of ass, iv. 363
Iblisi imprisons girls in tree, vii. 414 24
Ibnisharri, seal of, v. 98
Iboroquiamio, the Devil, xi. 257
Ibrāhīm ibn Vāsīfshāh on religion of southern and eastern Slavs, iii. 222
Ibycus knew Babylonian legend of plant of immortality, v. 228
Ice, x. 41, 43, 138, 139, 178, 292 38, 296 45
—ceremony at breaking-up of, iv. 470
— -covered sea regarded as spongy mixture of earth, water, air, iii. 17
—Jengk-tongk sacrificed to on the, iv. 193
—Man, x. 68
—origin of, ix. 34
—to follow the, a spring festival, iv. 214–215
—venom congealed into, ii. 275
Iceblock, mythic cow gave origin to Buri out of an, ii. 63
Iceland, ancient paganism of, ii. 16
—colonization of, ii. 8
—cult of Frey in, ii. 119
—settlers in, dedicated their land to Thor, ii. 75–76
Icelanders colonized Greenland, x. 1
Ichaumra (Ighamba), xi. 297
Icheiri, a kind of Lares and Penates, xi. 39–40
Ichiki-shima-hime, Benten the ancient Japanese, viii. 270
Ichneumon advises and assists Mantis, vii. 289
—Ḥar-khent(i)-merti(?) depicted as, xii. 388 28
—"Horus in Three Hundred" sometimes depicted as composed of, and other animals, xii. 388 28
—once embodied soul of Atum, xii. 165
Ichō, gingko-tree, tale of genius of the, viii. 342
Içona, first person of the trinity, xi. 143
Ida, cult of Zeus on, i. 159
—Mt., Cretans went to, every ninth year, i. 64
——reputed birthplace of Zeus, i. 155
Iḍā (Iḷā), sacrificial goddess, vi. 49, 53, 92, 96, 99, 143, 147
Idaia of Troy, loved by Phineus, i. 73
Idama ("Healer of the People"), a form of Europe, i. 42

Idas and Lynkeus as Messenian doubles of the Dioskouroi, i. 27
——story of encounter of Kastor and Polydeukes with, i. 26–27
—son of Aphareus, i. 24, pl. XI, opp. p. 24, 26, 27–28
—took part in hunt of Kalydonian boar, i. 56
Iddahedu, ship of Nabû, v. 318
Iddawc, horse of, iii. 190
Ideal, the ultimate, viii. 218
"Ideas" of things, x. 30
Idem-kuguza and -kuva, Threshing-barn man and woman, iv. 167
Identification motif, ii. 103, 104
—of secret lover by smearing of ashes or paint, x. xxii
Identifications of most non-cosmic deities with sun, xii. 28
Ideogram becomes dragon, viii. 253
Ideograms, name Yamato written in Chinese, viii. 377 3
Ideographs, viii. 7, 38, 44, 100, 138, 139, 140
Idhlozi, ancestral spirit, vii. 116, 272, 404 5
Idi, giant, ii. 279, 283
Idin-Dagon, v. 327, 346
— -Ishtar, v. 346
Idiptu (whirlwind), v. 163
Idisi, charm concerning group of beings called, ii. 18, 24, 198, 244
—correspond to Disir, ii. 252, 253, 256
Idisiaviso, perhaps place called after Idisi, ii. 253
Idleness, ritual, ii. 68
Idmibi, xi. 297
Idol, anointment of, with one's own blood, xi. 144
—car, vi. pl. II, opp. p. 22
—golden, of sun in temple Askul, v. 339
—head of Bishop of Mecklenburg offered to, iii. 287
— -house for drowned, and sacrifices therein, iv. 208–209
—oaken, at Korenice, iii. 283
—of green stone called Llampallec, xi. 208
—tree becomes an, xi. 26
—which gave oracles, xi. 224
——watches the dead, x. 57
—whose face resembles face of a bear, xi. 47
Idolatry, iii. 234–235

Idolatry of Elbe Slavs, iii. 222, 277, 278
—see ZEMIISM.
Idols, and their emblems, in sacred oak, iii. pl. XXXVII, opp. p. 304
—at Kiev, iii. 293, 297, 299, 301
—care of, xii. 194
—Chibcha offerings to, xi. 198
—description of jewelled, xi. 47–48, 49
—devil- and cat-, xi. 197
—fabrication of new, xi. 137, 144
—household, xi. 136, 206
—(huacas) supposed to have walked in the form of man, xi. 227
—in animal form, xi. 191
—of rare occurrence in forest regions of tropical America, xi. 275
——vanquished peoples imprisoned so that they may not assist former owners, xi. 50
—on islands of Zapatero and Pensacola, xi. 184
—presiding over elements, war, and sowings, xi. 193, 287
—sending of, to cure disease, xii. 199, 421 5
—three-headed, xi. 198
—two lesser, of earth-goddess, xi. 34, pl. IV, opp. p. 34
Idomeneus, son of Deukalion, i. 63
Idunn, goddess, guards apples of immortality, ii. 15, 22, pl. VI, opp. p. 32, 139, 140, 141, 142, 143, 151, 160, 161, 178–180, 278
Idurmer, Semitic deity, v. 80
Iella, one of five names of mother of supreme Being, xi. 24
Iermaoguacar, name of Earth mother, xi. 25
Ifing River separates giants and gods, ii. 276
Igay, leading god of Theban nome, xii. 152
Igerna, wife of Gorlois, iii. 184, 185, 201
Iggdrasil tree of " Edda," iv. 357; see also YGGDRASIL, ETC.
Igigi, gods of upper world, v. 94, 95, 140, 167, 192, 299, 311, 313
Igihegal, god, v. 152
Igi-sig-sig, god in service of Anu, v. 385
Igisub, title of Tammuz, v. 345
Igor and his people take oath before Perun, iii. 293

Iguaque, lake, xi. 199
Ihoiho, god, ix. 20
Ihuaivilu, seven-headed fire-monster, xi. 327
Ijä-kyl, shaman animal, iv. 507, 510, 519
Ikarian Sea, i. 65
Ikarios, Dionysos presented vine to, i. 216–217
——sends epidemic upon people of, as penalty, i. 217
—killed by shepherds to whom he had presented wine, i. 216–217
—of Lakedaimon, Penelope daughter of, i. 123
—son of Perieres and Gorgophone, i. 24
Ikaros and Daidalos, thrown into prison by Minos, escape by means of wings, i. 65
—Herakles finds and buries body of, i. 91
—survival of, in folk-tale from Zakynthos, i. 312
Ikat, x. 2
Ikh = soul, xii. 174, 415 3
Ikhnaton, uncertain pronunciation of name Akh-en-aten, xii. 426 31
Ikkaku Sennin (" One-horned "), viii. 276
Ikom, how witchcraft became known to, vii. 340
Ikšuda (" Snatcher "), vii. 395 58
Ikšumatī, Nāgas dwell in river, vi. 154
Ikṣvāku family, most of Tīrthakaras belonged to the, vi. 221
Iku, Canal Star, said to be star of Babylon, v. 308
Ila (Iḍā), androgynous nature of, vi. 147
Ilabrat (Ili-abrat) messenger of Anu, v. 176, 177
Ilâh (Il), one of names of moon-god, v. 5, 7, 93
Ilamatecutli, mother of the gods, xi. 54, 75
Ilancue, wife of Iztacmixcoatl, xi. 112
Ilāni Habiri (" the Habiru gods "), v. 72–73, 392 349
Ilāt (al-Ilāt, Allat), North Arabian sun-goddess, identified with Athena the war-goddess, v. 381 63
—mother-goddess of North Arabic religion, v. 15, 381 61

Ilāt of South Arabia is the sun-goddess, v. 15, 381 [61] [63]

Ilavilā, mother of Kubera, vi. 157

Ildathach drowned by Clidna's wave, iii. 116

Ilem, Item, sky-god, iv. 217

Ilgi, Lithuanian name for autumnal feast of the dead, iii. 352 [7]

" Iliad," i. 126–130

Ilībiśa may be aboriginal name of foe of Aryans, vi. 68

Ilimu a beast in form of man, vii. 252

Ilion, city founded by Ilos, i. 118

—Odysseus leaves, i. 136

—Poseidon's attitude in war at, i. 210

—Zeus caused strife at, to decrease race of men, i. 124

Ilios (Gk. Helios), first day of Harranian week sacred to, v. 154

" Ilioupersis " recounts overthrow of Troy, i. 131

Ilisos River, i. 73

Illa Tici Uiracocha, meaning of, xi. 236, 241

Illad, god, or Ildu, son of Etana, v. 167

Illan, husband of Tuirrean, iii. 169

Illinos (Enlil), v. 292

Illness as punishment for ill-treating the Voršud, iv. 126

—brought by ghosts to obtain offerings, vii. 180

—caused by getting in way of " invisible army," iv. 156

———sight of Katsumbakazi and Sikulokobuzuka, vii. 243–244, 246

———spirit of the lud, iv. 143, 147

———" whole of life " not being eaten by witches, but if whole eaten death ensues, vii. 338

—dead may cause, iv. 291–292

—household gods removed to neighbour's house because of, iv. 136–137

—Lapp belief on, iv. 5, 76, 292

—lurking spirits believed cause of, xii. 415 [6]

—medicine-bag exposed in, x. 85

—memorial feasts to dead who cause, iv. 58, 133

—of women on nearing Seide, iv. 103

———Rê', xii. 76–77

—periodic, of men of Ulster, iii. 64, 74, 141, 152, 154, 155

—result of ill-treating Tõnni case, iv. 138

Illness, sacrifice at the " uttermost kuala " in case of severe, iv. 128

Illugi, ii. 252

Illuminated, first beings, iv. 385

Illusion and tricks of Odin and Gylfi, ii. 29

—magic, iii. 155

Illusions, eye-, ii. 93

—magical, xi. 113, 115

" Illustrated Guidebook to Famous Places ": see MEISHO-ZUYE.

Illyrikon, Io wanders through, i. 29

Il-ma-la-(ku), personal name in Assyrian contract (Aramaic transcription: El-malak), v. 58

Ilmarinen, Baltic celestial smith compared to, iii. 330

—sky-god, iv. 217, 232, 238

Ilmaris, iv. pl. XXVIII, opp. p. 228, 232

Ilmasamba, Esthonian term for pillar of the sky, iv. 222

Ilmuqah, name of moon-god, v. 5, 7, 66, 378 [13]

Ilos (El), v. 80

—(Kronos), child of Ouranos and Gê, v. 66, 67

—son of Tros, i. 117–118

Iltepu (" satisfier "), dog, vii. 395 [58]

Ilu, el, elōah, elāh, ilāh, all words for god, v. 65

Ilu-Salmān, El called, v. 45

Ilumarru, Adad called, v. 39, 42, 45

Ilumer, iturmer, idurmer connected with, v. 80

Iluwir, Adad called, at Hamath, v. 39, 387 [187]

Ilvala seeks to destroy Agastya, vi. 146

Image, birchwood, of Veralden-olmai, iv. 250–251

—food rubbed into mouth of, iv. 178

—golden, of Shamash, v. 150–151

——house of Siryans, iv. 149

—memorial, old Turkish, iv. pl. XLIII, opp. p. 352, pl. XLIV, opp. p. 372

—miraculously found by Sāmba, vi. 183

—of fire-god, iv. 455

———Frey enchanted so that he spoke out of it, ii. 115

———god made of grain eaten as sacramental rite, xi. 60–61

———gold called sēmēios (a symbol), v. 37, 386 [175]

———loom of shaman, iv. 498

Image of Melqart (Tyrian Hercules), burning of, v. 52
——Porenutius, iii. 283
——Porevit, iii. 283
——Rugievit (Rinvit), iii. 283
——Svantovit, description of, iii. 279
——Thor made of stumps of birch, iv. 231
——thunder, iv. 439
——thunderbird, iv. 227
——wood-spirit at Vasyugan, iv. 178
—old Turkish, iv. pl. XL, opp. p. 302
—placed on chest containing bones of sacrifice at memorial feast, iv. 38
—(" shadow ") made of sun and moon smeared with blood and worshipped by Yuraks, iv. 223
—soul originally meant both shadow and, iv. 12, 13, 476, 477
—wax, of Pekko, god of barley, iv. 245
—with heart of dead man in it made, by magic, to talk and walk, ii. 188
Images, ii. 24, 35, 70, 71, 76, 83, 106, 110, pl. XIV, opp. p. 114, 115, 116, 117–118, 138, 175, pl. XXII, opp. p. 176, 187, 216, 327–328, 333; v. 18, 108, 367; vi. 61; vii. 16, 47; viii. 50, 75, 80; 274, 276, 288; x. 57, 189, 191, 244, pls. XXVIII, XXIX, opp. p. 216; 269 [4], 309 [65], 312 [70]; xi. 22–28, 136, 350 [9]
—animal-, of time, iv. 436–438
—at Mag Slecht, iii. 45
—brought to exorcise demons, xii. 199
—buried with dead for servants, concubines, etc., xii. 177, 416 [14]
——food at memorial feasts, iv. 39
—carved on trees, iv. pl. XIX, opp. p. 156, 178
—destruction of, by St. Stephen, iv. 149–150
—fouled by devil, iv. 374
—iron, of children of Boshintoi, iv. 464
—kinds of, at shaman ceremonies, iv. 508–512, 519, 522
—lud-spirits materialized as, iv. 149
—made and burned in ritual of New Year's festival, v. 316
—of animal gods, iii. 124
——dead, iv. 478
——deceased in form of memorial dolls, iv. 41, 42, 43
——deity of child-birth, iv. 260–261
——divine heads, iii. 104, 105

Images of family spirits, inheritance of, iv. 124
——fish gods, iv. 191–192
——gods in Ehulhul, v. 154
——Lakṣmī, xii. 327
——Masters, iv. 465, 467
——points of compass to prevent disease, iv. 360
——python made of straw, vii. 271
——Seven gods to protect man's house against demons in ritual, v. 147
———wise ones, v. 84–86
——shamans, iv. pl. LVI, opp. p. 482, 499
———kept in calf-skin box, iv. 42
——Silesian Djadeks and Šetek, iii. 244, 245, pls. XXVIII and XXIX, opp. p. 244
——various materials, man created from, ix. 18, 24, 25, 27, 30, 74, 106, 107, 110, 157, 158–159, 160, 167, 168, 172, 173, 174, 175, 176
——water-spirit, iv. 469
——world-pillar, iv. 333–334
—Ostiak Samoyed, description of, iv. 140
—put into crevices, iv. 192
—sacred, found in ancient cities and pagodas, xii. 299, pl. X, opp. p. 302, 306–310, 327
—see DEITIES OF PAGAN RUSSIA; plates in vol. ix; SPIRITS AT FIXED HOLY PLACES, ETC.
—shamans must conjure spirit into, iv. 114
—stone, of Lapps, iv. 100–112
—subconscious, vii. 238
—use of, to injure people, iv. 12–13
—Votiak and Siryan, iv. 120
—formerly in sacred groves, iv. 146
—wood, of Lapps, iv. 113–114
Imana, supreme Being, ancestor of race, and chief of ancestral spirits, vii. 129
Imastun, cognate of Avesta mazdao, vii. 21
Imbulu, large lizard, vii. 201
Imbunche, babies stolen by witches changed into, xi. 328
Imd, giantess, ii. 153
Imdugud, bird, late name of Zû, v. 117
Imgig identified with Pegasos, v. 119
— = Zû, v. 117
I-m-ḥotep, xii. pl. III, opp. p. 170
—later son of Ptaḥ, xii. 171, 407 [79]
—patron of all scholars, xii. 171

Imhullu wind, v. 302
Imhursag ("wind of Underworld mountain"), title of Enlil, v. 99
Imi, Adad identified with, v. 39
Imikovu, vii. 429 [18]
Immer (Adad), v. 60
—son of Enlil, v. 61
Immersion of children in fairy wells, vii. 393 [32]
Immigration, Polynesians blend of several waves of, ix. 3
Immigrations into Japan, viii. 210
Immorality in Tantric rites, vi. 184–185
Immortal, flesh of resuscitated swine of Manannan makes gods, ii. 94
—ghosts not, vii. 180, 181
—gods not absolutely, ii. 22
—life, bread and water of, v. 94, 95, 178, 184
Immortality, vi. 18, 23, 27, 76–77, 139; 281, 283, 284; viii. 20, 28, 31, 54, 75, 94, 105, 106, 115, 145, 146; 219
—belief in, vii. 96, 100
—Celtic belief in, iii. 14, 181, 206, 208
—certain berries confer, iii. 54–55
—conferred by ale of Goibniu and rowan berries, iii. 54, 55
——on Dionysos, i. 218
——Ganymedes, i. 240
——Herakles in Heaven, i. 95
—defeated, i. 228
—food of, v. 179, 180, 184
—for man, ix. 51–54, 174, 182, 252, 253, 332 [146]
—gift of, in package to be kept unopened, x. 49
—Gilgamish seeks, v. 216, 218, 224
—Gorm troubled about, ii. 94
—Idunn goddess of, ii. 178
—in Elysian wonder-lands, ii. 322
—Land of, viii. 363
—loss of, xii. 115, 396 [85]
—Menelaos and Helen attain, i. 134
—Moon sends Hare to man with message of, vii. 227
—obtained by fairy through marriage with mortal, vii. 393 [32]
—of tree, ix. 253
—pills of, viii. 145
—plant of, v. 228; viii. 115
Immortals, iii. 14, 31, 85, 111, 189; viii. 114, 118–132, 145, 156, 157, 196–197; 274–280
Imos, Votan descended from, xi. 132

Impaling, ii. 309, 382 [31]
"Imperial Calendar," lucky, unlucky, and uncertain days published in, viii. 143
—Father, title conferred on Kuo Tzŭ-i, viii. 96
—princes, story of short life of, viii. 233
—rule, reappearance of light said by Shintoists to celebrate triumph of, viii. 227
Implements, giants apparently personifications of stone, x. 291 [38]
—worship of, by users, vi. 239–240
Imprecations uttered at sacrifices to Herakles, i. 88
Impregnation of bisexual demon by man, v. 357
——Nintur by Enki, poem on, v. 196–197
Imprisonment in tree, vii. 414 [24]
—magical, i. 189, 329 [1] (ch. iv)
Improvements introduced by Hare and Hlakanyana, vii. 219–220
Imps, were-beasts, cannibals, xi. 300–304
Impure fire, vii. 54
Impurities of fields caused by beef-eating, viii. 232
Imuthes, Greeks explained, as Egyptian Asklepios, xii. 171
Ina and the eel Tuna, ix. 55–56
—(Hina) and Nanga, tale of, ix. 71, 72
Inaba, White Hare of, tale of, viii. 317–318
Inachos awarded divine supremacy of Argos to Hera, i. 30
—principal river and river-god of the Argolid, i. 28, 257
Inada-princess to be sacrificed to dragon, but married storm-god, viii. 249, 250
Inang-i-Bake, tale of, ix. 227–229
Inanimate objects become persons or act as such, ix. 141–142; see also ANSWERING BY INANIMATE, ETC.
Inapertwa, rudimentary human beings, ix. 272–273
Inca, Incas:
Inca conquests, xi. 244
—dynasty, xi. 216–218
—rule, the Fifth Age, xi. 240
Incas, xi. 43, 44
—apostles of a new creed, xi. 242–248
—empire of the, xi. 210–220

Incas, legends of, xi. 248–252
Incantations, ii. 295, 308; iii. 35, 84; v.
96–97, 106, 107, 112, 116, 152, 175,
182, 194, 227, 293, 302, 317, 318, 324,
333, 334, 366, 369, 370, 371, 416 [36] [37];
vi. 226; vii. 32; 136, 202, 238, 239;
viii. 79, 156; ix. 8, 59; xii. 199, 201
—myths used as: see MYTHS USED AS
INCANTATIONS.
Incarnate in bull, buck, or man, deity
at Bacchanalia held to be, vii. 13
Incarnation, vi. 209–210, 213, 218, 226
—divine, Pharaohs claimed, xii. 170
—[East Indian] doctrine of, not necessarily borrowed from Christianity,
vi. 176
—of celestial beings, xii. 160, 161, 164,
166, 167, 414 [29]
——deities, vi. 171
—quasi-parallel to, xi. 201
—Spider Woman mythic, of Earth, x.
289 [34]
Incarnations, birds as, vi. 291
—twenty-eight, of Śiva, vi. 178
Incense, v. 25, 67, 221, 231, 249, 310,
318, 334; vii. 56, 59, 94–95; viii. 80;
xi. 47, 48, 137, 144, 145, 146; xii. 194
—sun described as fragrant flame of,
xii. 28
—symbolic patterns originally used in a
game of discriminating the several
varieties of, viii. 382 [7] (ch. v)
Incest, i. 6, 16, 50, 119, 164, 198; ii. 26–
27, 29, 102, 108, 110, 143; iii. 25, 74,
75, 82, 84, 90, 98, 156, 201; vi. 24,
68, 75–76; ix. 26, 70, 74, 109, 158,
164, 165, 170, 171, 172, 180; x. 210;
xi. 192, 275
Incestuous relations of Sun and Moon,
x. xxii, 8, 277 [13], 280 [17]
—unions, vi. 310–311
Incubation (sleep-cure) a rite of healing, i. 281
Incubi, souls return in form of, xi.
26–27
Incubo, nightmare-demon, sent by
Faunus, i. 293
Incubus (Celtic dusius), iii. 14, 200
—(demon lover) at first nightmare, ii.
288
Indech, Fomorian king, iii. 27, 30, 31,
33
Indech's daughter and Dagda, amour
of, iii. 31

Indeóin na nDése, anvil cast showers
of water, fire, and gems toward grave-
mound at, iii. 32
Indi, or Inti, name of sun-god, xi. 249
India, close relations of mythology of,
to Jainism, vi. 220, 229
—Dionysos reaches, i. 219
—Indo-Chinese mythology almost entirely borrowed from, xii. 249
—North, sun worship in, vi. 232
—Tibet borrowed chief and minor
deities from, vi. 216
Indian doctrines, echo of, found in
Hawaii, ix. 5, 22
—element in Indonesia, ix. 153, 203–
204, 209–210, 218, 242–243, 306,
328 [20]
—influence on African mythology, vii.
121, 353
——Japanese myth, viii. 214, 216,
219, 256–257
—" Middle Country," vi. 66
—religion influenced by outside forces?,
vi. 175
——question of relation of, to Iran, vi. 84
Indians, Egyptian religion less edifying
than, and not to be compared with,
religion of, xii. 245
—fears of, of natural objects, xi. 276–
277
—so called by Columbus, x. 13
" Indiculus Superstitionum," ii. 68, 198,
202, 214
Indigenes, xi. 240
Individual, rites for the, xi. 35
Individualized, only recent ghosts, vii.
118
Indo-China common refuge for fugitive
tribes from India and China, xii. 258
—general character of mythology of,
xii. 249
—Indonesian affiliations with, ix. 304
—peoples and religions of, xii. 253–262
—probably populated originally by
dark-skinned race, xii. 286
Indo-Chinese transcription and pronunciation, xii. 251
Indo-Europeans, early contact of Finno-
Ugric peoples with, iv. xix
Indo-Iranian culture in early contact
with Assyro-Babylonian, vi. 263–264
—mythology, Lettish parallel to, iii.
329, 360 [88]
—origin of Vahagn-myth, vii. 46

Indo-Iranians, vii. 12, 379 [2]
Indonesia, area and ethnic composition of, ix. xi, 153
—Indian influence on, ix. 153, 203–204, 209–210, 242–243, 306
—Polynesians migrated from, ix. 3, 153
—relationship of Melanesian mythology to, ix. 149, 150
——Micronesian mythology to, ix. 263
Indonesian element in Polynesian myths, ix. 96–97, 98, 153
—mythology, affiliations of, ix. 304
——summary of, ix. 240–244
Indo-Scythian coins, Tīr's name found on, vii. 32
Indra, ii. 54; vi. 264–265, 271, 291, 351; vii. 44, 393 [24]
—as goblin-slayer, vii. 45
—Asuras warred against, iv. 356
—corresponds to Indo-Chinese Sek-ya (Sanskrit Śakra), xii. 285
—god of atmosphere, xii. 255
——storm, vi. 15, 16, 17, 18, 19, 20, 22, 25, 26, 27, 28, 29, 30, 32–34, pl. IV, opp. p. 34, 35–36, 37, 39, 41–43, 45, 46, 47, 49, 50, 52, 53, 55, 56, 57, 59, 60, 61, 62, 64, 65, 66, 67, 68, 77, 79, 80, 85, 87, 88, 89, 93, 94, 100, 107, 111, 115, 117, 118, pl. X, opp. p. 118, 120, 122, 129, 131, 132, 133, 134, 135, 139, 140, 142, 143, 145, 148, 150, 152, 153, 159, 166, 168, 172, 174, 180, 181, 182, 184, 190, 203, 204, 213, 214, 216, 222, 228, 233, 236
—Japanese storm-god as Guzu Tenno identified with, viii. 228
—(lightning), Agni (fire), and Sūrya (sun) form triad in India, vii. 43
—likeness of Perkúnas to, iii. 322
—(Phra In), xii. 323, 324, 326
—(Sek-ya), of Indian Olympos, Brahmā loses head to, xii. 323
—slaying Ahi parallel with Ninurta slaying dragons, v. 130
—slays Vṛtra, vii. 45
—thunder-god, iv. 444, 447
—Verethraghna reminds one of, vii. 363, 364
Indrabhūti, vi. 208
Indrajit assisted Rāvaṇa in battle, vi. 156
Indrāṇī, Dsovinar perhaps reminiscence of, vii. 46

Indrāṇī wife of Indra, vi. 33, 39, 53, 134
Indu, name for Soma, vi. 136
Indus River, vi. 48, 49
——Sāmbha crossed, vi. 183
Ine-shki-ava, heavenly deity, iv. 258
Infant may make its own Haltia within three days, iv. 11
Infants, bodies of, believed to be created by Madderakka and Sarakka, iv. 252, 253
Infernum stands for hellia, ii. 306
Infinity, Chinese dragon symbol of, viii. pl. xxi, opp. p. 276
Influences, xi. 97
Ing, tribal ancestor of Ingwines, ii. 113
Ingcel, with three-pupiled single eye, invaded Ireland, iii. 76
Ingibjorg, Helgi Thoreson met, ii. 322
Ingimund, Volva's prophecy to, ii. 117–118, 119
Ingnersuit, Fire-people, x. 7
Ingolf, Thorgrim grandson of, ii. 76
Ingrians of Ingermanland included among Karelian stocks, iv. xv
Ingun, ii. 112, 126
Ingunar-Frey, ii. 126
Ingvaeones, son of Mannus progenitor of, ii. 328
—tribes of Schleswig-Holstein, ii. 28, 112, 113
Ingvi-Frey or Ingunar-Frey, Frey sometimes called, ii. 112
Ingw, tribal ancestor of Ingvaeones, ii. 112
Ingwines, East Danes, ii. 113
Inhabitants, first, of Boiotia, i. 42–43
Inheritance, iv. 452–453
—calling of shaman goes on through, iv. 498, 506, 519
—of earthly possessions in the hereafter, iv. 483
——Seides by children, iv. 104
—through eldest son, iv. 117
—totem may be transmitted by, x. 241
Ini-init (sun) and Aponibolinayen, tale of, ix. 221–224
Initiation, x. 100, 194, 197, 215–216, 241, 242, 243, 244, 246, 247, 282 [21]; xi. 250, 251
—ceremony, vii. pl. xxxii, opp. p. 306
—" medicine " revealed in religious, x. 85
Inkata (Enkata), Zulu word, meaning of, vii. 110–111

Ink-slab, representation and description of, on arch on " Mountain of Jade," xii. 304–305

Inkstand characterizes office of goddess Sekha(u)it, xii. 53

Inktonmi, trickster-hero, x. 105, 122

Inmar, god of Heaven, sky-god, iv. 217, 219, 220, 242, 258; 420

Innana, title of moon-god, v. 152

Innini, descent of, to Arallû, v. 326–335

—garments of, v. 327, 331, 334

—is planet Venus at sunrise, v. 328

—Lamashtu is, v. 369

—meditation of, v. 350

—Morning Star, v. 60, 94

—see IRNINA.

—Sumerian equivalent of Ishtar, v. 14, 326–329, 333

——mother-goddess, v. 5, 91, 92, 108, 109, 206

—weeps for Tammuz, v. 347

Innini-Ishtar, Earth-mother goddess, v. 12

— -Ninsianna-Ishtar both planet Venus and mother-goddess, v. 15

Ino and Athamas, Hera sent madness upon, i. 46

——reared Dionysos, i. 46

—infant Dionysos delivered to, i. 248

—insanity of, i. 166

—(Leukothea), daughter of Kadmos, i. 45, 46, 261–262

—wife of Athamas, plots to destroy his children by an earlier marriage, i. 107–108

Inoaeman, mother of Olofat, ix. 259

Inquiries of dead, iv. 28, 79

——Seides, iv. 100

Insanity, vii. 74, 84, 87; see various items s.v. MADNESS.

—caused by painted heart, x. 262

—Hera's power to cause, i. 166

Insatiable, in flood-tale, ix. 256–257

Inscription, Greek, on South Arabian coin, v. 3, 4

—of Shamshi-Rammon of Assyria, vii. 389 10

—tomb-, of Ahi-râm of Gebal, v. 379 29

—Yorkshire, " to god who invented roads and paths," iii. 9

Inscriptions, viii. 7, 23–24, 32, 48

—as source for knowledge of Celtic religion, iii. 7, 8

—at Warka, Koweit, and Ur, v. 379 10

Inscriptions, cuneiform, vii. 7

—from altars, ii. 12, 17

——Arabia Felix and Hadramut mention sun, Venus, and moon, v. 3

——Magharah, v. 378 14

—of Achaemenian kings, vi. 259

—on Tuxtla Statuette and Leiden Plate, xi. 130

—Phoenician, v. xix

—runic, ii. 70

—South Arabian, v. 4

—Urartian, vii. 389 4

—Vannic, vii. 70

Insect as Moon's messenger, vii. 167

—Etain changed into, iii. 79

Insects born from body of slain giants, iv. 386, 387, 388

—souls find concealment in guise of, iv. 9

—tales of, viii. 335–337

Inspector of Astrology appointed under T'ang Dynasty, viii. 143

Inspiration of Taliesin, and goddesses of, iii. 109, 112

——wisdom by drinking from well or eating salmon in it, iii. 120

———eating snake, iii. 166

Institutions established by Tan, viii. 43

" Instruction of Youth," viii. 118

Insula Pomorum (" Isle of Apples "), Avalon appears as, iii. 193, 194

Insulting-poles, ii. 298

Interchange of dress: see COSTUME, INTERCHANGE OF.

Intercourse, iv. 58, 166, 177, 185

Intermarriage, vi. 144, 240

—in " pair " period, vi. 144, 225, 226

Intermediaries, x. xvii, xx, 22, 42, 87, 92, 188, 192, 272 6, 277 13, 293 40, 306 60; xi. 24, 40, 298; see also BIRDS AS INTERMEDIARIES.

Intermediary between Arthur and Mordred at Camlan, Iddawc an, iii. 190–191

—fire as, vi. 284

——or fire-god as, iv. 142, 154, 237, 273

—see also MEDIATOR.

—Spider as, vii. 135, 321

Interment of dead in crouching position in prehistoric period, xii. 420 23

Interpretation of myths, xi. 6–10

Interpreters or " Watchmen of Heaven," iv. 404, 407–408

Inti, falcon, tutelary of Manco Capac, xi. 245
Intoxication, iv. 488; viii. 129-130; xi. 77, 115, 146, 190, 275, 322
—of Ulstermen: see " MESCA ULAD."
Intulwa (intulo) considered unlucky, vii. 164
Inue, x. 5, 6, 8, 10, 18, 268 ³
Invasions, Irish, chronology of, iii. 42, 46
Invention, Huang Ti typifies Age of, viii. 33
Inver Umaill, salmon of, iii. 127
Invisible but stationary elves, sickness caused by touching, ii. 225
—walls around fairy circles, iii. 51
Invisibility, xi. 328, 329
—a divine power, iii. 55-56, 61, 64, 65, 66, 80, 84, 88, 106, 107
—charm of, laid aside by Ethne, iii. 208
—garments and staff of, ii. 268, 269, 301
——of, viii. pl. xxxvi, opp. p. 314
—granted Herakles by Zeus, i. 158
—jewel of, iii. 129
—mantle of, x. 133
—of Arthur and his men, iii. 189
——Daityas and Dānavas must be met with invisible weapons, vi. 152
——Perseus, i. 34
——witches, vii. 336
—secured by unguents, iii. 263
—(to attack enemies) of man who changes into his totem animal, vii. 279
Invisibly unladen, boats of dead, iii. 16
Invitation by dead to living to visit barrow, ii. 308
—to deceased to return for feasts, iv. 47, 48, 49, 54, 56, 63, 68
Invocations of deities, xii. 207
Invoking powers of nature to do harm, iii. 132
Invulnerable coat, ii. 133
Invulnerability, gift of, granted to Rāvaṇa, vi. 127
Io, i. pl. xii, opp. p. 28
—changed into heifer by Zeus, i. 158
—child of Prometheus, i. 12
—crown restored to line of, by Gelanor through Danaos, i. 30
—daughter of Inachos (or of Peiren), priestess of temple of Hera and divine patroness of Argos, i. 29

Io, Europe appears as, i. 42
—Hermes forbidden to release, i. 193
—insanity of, i. 166
—primeval god, ix. 11
—wife of Zeus, i. 157
Iobates commissioned Bellerophon to kill the Chimaira, i. 39
—King, gives his daughter Anteia in marriage to Proitos, i. 32
Iocauna and Guamaonocon, two names for one supreme Being, xi. 24
—" yucca " appears in form, xi. 34
Iodama, wife of Zeus, i. 157
Iohdi, spirit, iii. 319, 323
Iokaste (Epikaste), daughter of Menoikeus, wife of Laios, and later of her son Oidipous, i. 48, 49-50
—hanged herself through remorse at having married her son, i. 50
Iökul, icicle, ii. 281
Iolaos aids Herakles to kill Lernean hydra, i. 81, pl. xxii, opp. p. 82
—Herakles turns his wife over to, i. 89
Iole taken captive by Herakles, i. 94
—wife of Hyllos, i. 95
—won by Herakles in archery contest, i. 89
Iolkos, city founded by Kretheus, i. 106, 107
—Peleus cleansed of pollution by Akastos at, i. 121
—Poseidon chief deity of, i. 212
—return of Iason to, i. 108
Iolokiamo (" Lord of Darkness "), evil spirit of the Orinoco, xi. 259
Ion according to some accounts founder of Ionian stock, i. 71
—son of Apollo and Kreousa, i. 71, 180
Ioskeha, demiurge, vii. 322
Iouskeha, x. 32-33, 38, 39
Iowahine, female of primeval pair, ix. 24
Iphianassa, wife of Endymion, mother of Aitolos, i. 55
Iphigeneia, Agamemnon slain by Klytaimnestra in ostensible punishment for sacrifice of, i. pl. xxx, opp. p. 120, 125-126, 134
—becomes priestess of Artemis among the Tauroi, i. 126
—hind placed by Artemis on Aulid altar in lieu of, i. 184, 186
—in Tauris, i. 326 ⁵ (ch. viii), 327 ¹⁵
—priestess of Artemis at Tauroi rescued by Orestes, i. 135

Iphikles, children of, killed by Herakles, i. 80
—son of Amphitryon and Alkmene, i. 79
Iphitos gave Odysseus bow, i. 123
—son of Eurytos, killed by Herakles in fit of madness, i. 89
Iqi-Balam, one of four brothers created from maize, xi. 165, 166, 177
Irā, an Apsaras, vi. 143
Ira, Irra myth, v. 139–140, 141, 142–146, 222, 322
Irad, descendant of Cain, v. 202
Īraj, son of Farīdūn, vi. 323, 324, 329
Iran, question of relation of Indian religion to, vi. 84
—Tīr migrates from, to Armenia, Cappadocia, and Scythia, vii. 32
Iranian deities in Armenia, vii. 20–35
—element in ancient Armenian religion, viii. 5
—influence in fire-worship, iv. 456
——on Armenians, vii. 15
———development of Amitābha in Tibet, vi. 211
—myth of conflict of light and darkness, v. 130
—religion, vi. 259
Ireland, annalistic accounts of people who went to, iii. 23
—called Iath n'Anann, iii. 39
—Morrígan proclaimed victory to royal heights of [reminiscence of animistic view of nature], iii. 34
—to be afflicted by dragon at end of world, iii. 91
Iri, creator bird, ix. 174
Irimu, vii. 249, 250, 252–256, 346, 413 23
Iris, i. 14 (fig. 2)
—and Zephyros, Eros son of, i. 203
—personification of rainbow, i. 241
—saves Harpies, i. 111
—sent by Zeus to plead with Demeter for people of Eleusis, i. 228
Irish Celts (Goidels), iii. 92, 205
—mythology, sources for, iii. 19
Irkalla, goddess of lower world, v. 259
Irlek-Khan, daughter of Ruler of dead, iv. 489, 494
Īrmān (Airyaman), medical art ascribed to, vi. 318
Irmin, Armenak may be Teutonic, vii. 14, 66
—cult of a god, ii. 336

Irminsul, sanctuary, image, pillar, ii. 335–336
Irnina (Innini), v. 366, 368, 369
—cedar mountain abode of goddess, v. 252
Iron, vii. 55, 387 2; vii. 220, 242; viii. 30
—and stone father and mother of fire, iv. 450
—art of smelting of, vii. 259, 261
—as amulet, iv. 163, 166
—bar, white-hot, thrown at Thor, ii. 84
—bird = thunderbird, iv. 439
—birds of, iv. 335 (fig. 14)
—birth-deities in songs on origin of, iv. 257
—boat, ii. 202
—bonds of Loki changed to, ii. 146
—castle of the sky, vi. 283
—citadel made of, vi. 116, 152
—club, Searbhan killed by his, iii. 55, 152
— -coolness, ii. 196
—creation of men of, i. 18
—explanation of, xii. 35
—feathers, iv. 495
—gloves: see Gloves of Thor.
—house, descendants of people from cauldron imprisoned in white-hot, iii. 101
—images, iv. 464
—kettle on back of Srvara, vi. 325
—later regarded as sacred metal of Sêth, xii. 390 35
—leg, ii. 100
——given to Viśpalā, vi. 31
—made into tools by primeval pair, vi. 297
—man created partly from, iv. 371, 447
—mountain, sacrifice on the, vi. 299, 300–301
—must be cleaned at end of furrow, iii. 99
—nail containing flint in head of images of Thor, ii. 83
—palisades of dún, iii. 132
—pillar, ii. 84
——tree, man, post, mountain, iv. 333, 334, 337, 338, 340, 346, 349, 358, 425
———with cross-beams supported world, ix. 163
—provision-bag bound with, ii. 93
—rod, iv. 328
—shoe, Vidarr possessor of, ii. 159
—statue substituted for Bhīma, vi. 125

Iron totem, vii. 271
—used to obtain cattle from gods, iv. 177
—vase, haoma kept in, vi. 282
—vessel of, iv. 362
——tribute collected in, iii. 27
—" Water master's daughter " and cattle may be captured by use of, iv. 200, 205
—weapons at child-birth to fight off Als, vii. 89
— -wood women: see IARNVITHJUR, ETC.
— -workers in Abyssinia a race apart, vii. 345
Iroquoian stock, x. 13–14, 15
Irpa, local goddess, ii. 15, 186–189
Irrigation, x. 183; xi. 211, 231
—only son of water-deity became god of, v. 344, 348
I-ruwa, sun, vii. 116, 171, 232, 233, 238
Is (Vogul, " soul "), applied to shadows of trees, etc., iv. 12
Īšāna, vi. 81, 82, 112, 227
Isänen (" little father "), Finnish name for Thunderer, iv. 228
Īṣatprāgbhāra, home of finally perfected souls, vi. 227–228
Ise, songs of speeding and return of pilgrims to, viii. 369
—supposed to be made up of chestnuts, viii. 339
Iseion, Greek name of Per-ḥebet, xii. 99
Iseru, antelope, vii. 321
Isfandyār, vi. 342
Ishar title of Adad and Nergal, v. 41, 132
— -badan, apparently Ishar of Padan, v. 41–42
— -padda (-padan), name of Nergal, v. 41–42, 387 [197]
Išhara, goddess, v. 244
Ishbi-Girra, as Tammuz, v. 346
Ishkur, Mir, Mur (Adad, Ramman), control of winds given to, v. 99
—son of Enlil, v. 61
Ishme-Dagan, v. 327, 346
Ishri-el occurs on seal of Gilgamish and Enkidu, v. 244
Ishtar aided by angels in child-birth, v. 98 [Ishtar is Babylonian equivalent of Astarte (q. v.)]
—Anāhita identified with, vi. 280; vii. 25
—and Asari, v. 344
——Marduk, myth of, v. 131, 324

Ishtar and Tammuz, v. 336–351
—Anu bestows divine powers upon, v. 177
—as earth-goddess, v. 8
——female principle of Anu in highest heaven, v. 173
——goddess of fate has titles Minû-anni (or Minû-ullu) and Shimti, v. 21, 384 [123]
———water, vegetation, love, and maternity, vii. 382 [23]
——Lamashtu, v. 368
——protector of wedlock, vii. 27
——war-goddess, v. 23, 25, 26, 27, 381 [63]; vii. 28
—(Astλik) festival, the flying dove of Vartavar celebration may have reference to, vii. 60
—Babylonian, identical with Canaanitish Ashtoreth, goddess of fate, v. 21
—came into Urartu as Sharis, vii. 11, 379[1], 383 [31]
—curse in name of, v. 82
—daughter of Moon, v. 329
—descent of, to house of Ereshkigal, v. 164, 326 ff.
—desired shepherd for men, v. 167
—equated with Allāt, v. 17, 19, 24–25
—explanation of Nile flood in summer parallel to Babylonian myth of, xii. 384 [116]
—Gilgamish, and Enkidu on cylinder, v. 245
—goddess of discord and faithless, v. 28, 256
—god-kings husbands of, v. 326
—hypsoma of, is Pisces, v. 304
—implores Anu to create bull of Heaven to destroy Gilgamish, v. 267
—in Gilgamish epic, vii. 69
—(Innini), descent of, to Arallû, v. 326–335
—is Sumerian goddess of planet Venus, v. 29, 172
—known as twin sister of Shamash, v. 36, 151
—love of, for Gilgamish, v. 256 ff.
—loved Sargon, v. 157
—maid of Sin, as cow, v. 97, 395 [25]
—name of virgin mother-goddess, v. 368
—nude, v. 34
—of Assur called Shulmanîtu, v. 45
——Nineveh sent to Egypt, v. 34
—Parakyptousa, v. 32

Ishtar patroness of priestesses and harlots, v. 25, 384 [123]
—sacred prostitution in honour of, vii.
382 [26]
—see SIDURI (WEST SEMITIC NAME OF,
ETC.).
—Semiramis has characteristics of, vii.
367, 368
—Siduri West Semitic name of, v. 211
—Siouan parallel to descent to hell of,
x. 108
—" sister " in personal names may
refer to, v. 7
——of Ereshkigal, v. 330
—sixty maladies inflicted on, v. 332
—star symbol of, v. 150
—tends heavenly " sheep," iv. 433
—to be washed with " water of life,"
v. 334
—Urartian, vii. 71 (fig. 3)
—Uttukku as title given to, v. 190
—variant form of Astarte, v. 14
—weeps for destruction of men, v.
220
—with mural crown, v. 23
—yearly sends Tammuz to his doom,
v. 28
—Zaden perhaps northern representative of, vii. 40
Ishtar-Venus, Pisces station of, v. 304
Ishullanu the gardener, Ishtar's love for,
v. 256
—turned into hog by Ishtar, v. 28,
385 [136]
Ishum, messenger of Irra, revealed
poem to scribe, v. 137-139, 141, 142,
144, 145, 146, 148
Išḫura, v. 155
Isiac mysteries less influential in Classical religion than Great Mother or
Mithra, xii. 121
—religion a formidable competitor of
rising Christianity, xii. 242
—societies in Classical world, xii. 243
Isikqukqumadevu, Izimu akin to, vii.
249
Isilo used of leopard instead of word;
also title of Zulu kings, vii. 406 [7]
Isimu, messenger of Enki, v. 197, 199
Isin, hymn on dead kings of, v. 326-
327
—kings of, become dying gods, v. 345
Isiququmadevu, vii. 320
Isir, god, v. 347, 348, 349

Isirana, title of Tammuz (Isir-ana), v.
345
Isis, xii. 98 (figs. 90, 91), 117 (fig. 120)
—and Horus, statues of, interpreted as
representing Madonna and Child, xii.
244
——Nephthys accompany sun as
scarab, xii. 96
———dirge of, xii. 122-124
———explained as the feathers on head
of Mîn, xii. 219
———tears of, cause inundation of
Nile, xii. 95
——Osiris, Min son of, xii. 139
——scorpion, legend of, xii. 210-211
—as a birth-genius of Osiris, xii. 385 [12]
——Lady of Gebal, v. 391 [322]
——mother of Osiris, xii. 408 [82]
——sky, identified with Sekha(u)it,
xii. 53
—begotten by Qêb and Nut, xii. 69
—brings Nile back from Nubia, xii. 90
—called " dew " by magician of Roman
period, xii. 95
—celestial goddess, xii. 29, 37, 45
—colourless as compared with her
original, the Asiatic goddess of love,
xii. 120
—cult of, long survived at Philae, xii.
244
—frequently identified with Ḥat-ḥôr
and solarized, xii. 41
—gathering blood from corpse of Osiris,
xii. 114 (fig. 118)
—Ḥat-meḥit assimilated to, xii. 133
—hunts body of Osiris, v. 71
—identified with Sothis-Sirius, xii. 55
(fig. 54), 56
—in the Osirian cycle, xii. 98-101,
113-119, 122-123, 125-127
—member of ennead of Heliopolis, xii.
216
—Menkhet identified with, xii. 136
—Meskhenet sometimes identified with,
xii. 137
—mistress of sorcery among female
divinities, xii. 80-83, 200, 201
—Nephthys as rival of, xii. 395 [76]
——associated with, xii. 110
—nursing Horus in the marshes, xii. 116
(fig. 119)
——protected by sting of Selqet, xii. 147
—question whether name Osiris is really
connected with, xii. 384 [2]

Isis, Rê'-Ḥor identified with, xii. 221
—retained little more than name and
forms of worship in Classical world,
xii. 243
—retention of Egyptian type of, in
Classical world, xii. 243
—Saṭet compared with, xii. 146
—Sekha(i)t-ḥor often identified with,
xii. 146
—Sêth persecutor of, xii. 103
—Shenṭet variant of, xii. 148, 408 ⁹⁵
—sister and wife of Osiris, xii. 122, 123
—Smentet parallel to, xii. 148
—sun-god, and serpent, myth of, xii.
79–84
—tears of, xii. 90, 125
—Tenenet identified with, xii. 150
—Ûrt-ḥekau compared with, xii. 151
——epithet of, xii. 151
—worshipped by division of Suebi, ii. 17
— -Ḥat-ḥôr, xii. 99 (fig. 92)
——Êpet bears head of, xii. 60
— -Tait, xii. 149
Iškur, title of Adad, v. 39–40, 61, 99,
193
Islam, Bolgars embraced, in 922, iv.
xviii
Islamic writers, legend of St. George
famous among, v. 338
Island, creation of, iv. 323
—Elysium, iii. 122
— -Maker, Dīpaṁkara signifies, vi. 194
—Mountains, viii. 115
—of Dreams, i. 278
——Flames, xii. 27, 72, 180, 202, 364 ¹¹,
395 ⁸⁴, 417 ²¹, 426 ³⁰
——Scáthach, iii. 143
Islanders (Antillean), xi. 15–18
Islands, dead buried on, x. 146
—gods dwelt on, iii. 49
—Oceania composed entirely of, ix. xii
—of the Blest, i. 147–148
————Achilles after death said to
consort with Medeia in, i. 131
————Menelaos and Helen given immortality in, i. 134
—rest on pillars in romantic Irish voy-
ages, iii. 13
—round Britain named after gods and
heroes, iii. 14, 15
—sacred, visited by Demetrius, iii.
14–15
—twelve, surrounding centre of world,
iv. 347

Isle, Isles:
Isle of Apples, iii. 193
——Joy, iii. 115
——Man, iii. 67, 103, 117
——the Temple, viii. 269–270
——Women, iii. 117; ix. 66, 140–141
Isles of gods, dead, etc., xi. 18
——the Blest, Three, viii. 115, 146
" Islendinga-bók," ii. 113
" Islendinga Sögur," ii. 60
Ismaros sacked by Odysseus, i. 136
—son of Eumolpos, i. 74
Ismene, daughter of Oidipous and
Iokaste, i. 49
—joined Oidipous and Antigone in exile,
i. 50
Israël, explanation of name, v. 244, 245
Israel, lost tribe of, Jesuits conceived
Indians to be, x. 17
Issun-bōshi (One-inch Dwarf), viii. 286
Istaevones, son of Mannus progenitor
of, ii. 328
Iṣṭāpūrta, sacrifice and baksheesh, vi.
356 ¹⁷
Isthmian games, horses frightened at,
said to be haunted by Glaukos, i. 39
Isthmians, linguistic and cultural affini-
ties of, xi. 189–194
Isthmus of Corinth awarded to Posei-
don, i. 37
————Melikertes body washed ashore
at, i. 46
—(Panama), xi. 15, 16
Istwo of Teutonic mythology, vii. 14,
380 ⁷
Īśvara, vi. 112, 142
Italy, mythology of ancient, i. 289–307
—spread of Egyptian cults to, xii.
242
Ith came to Ireland, iii. 43
Ithake, Naiads inhabited, i. 258
—Telemachos born to Odysseus and
Penelope at, i. 123
Ithavoll, ii. 159, 327
Ithoba'al and Tyre, dirge on destruc-
tion of, v. 188
Ithome (nymph and mountain), the
baby Zeus placed in care of, i. 155
Itiba Tahuvava, xi. 29
Itje, iv. 386
Itóki (Mother Scorpion), Ituána iden-
tical with, xi. 185
Itongo-snake, vii. 194
Itowe (sing. Chitowe), vii. 261, 269

Itse, Finnish "self" (soul), applied to shadows of trees, etc., iv. 12

Itshi, invisible nature-god, iv. 464

Itsuku-shima (Miya-jima), shrine of, viii. 269–270

Ituána: see ITÓKI, ETC.

Itylos, son of Zethos and Aëdon, i. 44, 70

Itys, flesh of, given by his mother to his father at a banquet, i. 70

Itzam-kab-ain (female whale with alligator feet), xi. 155

Itzamna, god of rain, xi. 134, 137, 138

Itzcueye, form of earth-goddess, xi. 184

Itzeecayan ("Place of Cool Winds"), xi. 77

Itzpapalotl, earth-goddess, xi. 75

Itztli, stone-knife god, xi. 54, 56, 63

Iuchar and Iucharba, gods of Danu, iii. 39, 40

Iuchna Curly-Locks, iii. 89

Iuchra transformed Aoife into a crane, iii. 59

Iulus, son of Aeneas, i. 304

Iuno (Juno), i. 156, pl. LVIII, opp. p. 278, 291

—by a storm drove Aeneas to Carthage, i. 305

—causes war between Turnus and Latinus, i. 306

—Hercules said to be husband of, i. 303

—in Roman mythology, represents Hera in Greek, i. 288

Iuppiter (Jupiter), vi. 21

—in Roman mythology represents Zeus in Greek, i. 288, 289

—Indiges, title given Aeneas after his death by his subjects, i. 306

—(Iovis, Diovis, Dius, Diespiter), sky-god, i. 289–290, 296

—Liber epithet of, i. 292

—unknown by name in modern Romagnola, i. 316

—urges Aeneas to complete his journey to Italy, i. 305

Iu-s-'a-s, goddess of Heliopolis, xii. 134, 404 [37]

Iuturna, Castor and Pollux water horses at fountain of, i. 302

—wife of Ianus, i. 295, 297

Ivaldi, dwarfs called sons of, ii. 221

Ivithjar, wood-giantesses, ii. 205, 280

Ivory shoulder of Pelops, i. 119

Ivy ascribed to Osiris, xii. 385 [8]

—attachment of poet for poetess embodied in, viii. 347

—emblem of Dionysos, i. 222, pl. XLIX, opp. p. 224

—revenges itself on chestnut-tree, viii. 340

—shade of, protected infant Dionysos, and is used at shrine of his mother Semele, i. 217

Iwa-naga-hime, "Lady-of-Rock-Perpetuity," viii. 233

Iwa-shimizu, shrine at, viii. 252

Iwaya (pseud. "Uncle Sazanami"), viii. 377 [6]

Ix years, xi. 145

Ixchel, goddess of fecundity, xi. 143

Ixcuiname ("the Four-faced"), Earth mother, xi. 79

Iximche, Cakchiquel capital, xi. 179, 183

Ixion on the wheel, i. pl. XXXVI, opp. p. 146

—punishment of, in Hades, i. 142, 144, 145, 147

—shade of, appears to Odysseus in Hades, i. 146, 327 [6]

Ixtab, goddess of the hanged, xi. 139

Ixtlilton ("Little Black-face"), xi. 77

Izamal (Itzamna, Itzmatul), tomb-temple of Zamna at, xi. 133

Izanagi and Izanami, primeval couple, viii. 222–224

—pursuit of, in Hades, viii. 223–224

Izidwedwe, cloths which have absorbed personality from contact, vii. 337

Izimu (IRIMU, wh. see), vii. 120, 249

—(Lelimo), usually cannibal or ogre, vii. 414 [25]

Izrah-Dagan, v. 79

Iztacmixcoatl (White Cloud Serpent), xi. 112

Izumo, Oh-kuni-nushi became ruler of, viii. 318

—oldest of local legends concerned with topographical feature of, viii. 247–251

—Ryū-tō heralds approach of dragons bringing offerings to deities at shrine of, viii. 271

—storm-god descended in region of, viii. 228–229, 230, 248

Izushio-tome ("Grace Maiden"), tale of, viii. 294

J

Jaafar, vii. 353, 354

Jabal, patron of tents and flocks, v. 105, 202

Jabbok, stream, v. 244

Jabme-akka (Yabme-akka), iv. 75, 79

Jáburu, evil divinity, who ate seeds of life, xi. 193, 194

Jack and Jill may be linked with Bil and Hjuki, ii. 184

Jack-and-the-Beanstalk, ii. 335; iii. 325, 359 [56]; vii. 131; x. 48–49, 113, 136, 138, 294 [42]

Jackal, vii. 121, 215, 231, 283, 293, 302, 304–308, 309, 336, 420 [19], 423 [32]; xii. 32

—black, or dog, Anubis originally, xii. 110

—Esdes has head of, xii. 366 [3]

— -gods, rope about necks of, refers to towing of solar ship, xii. 364 [10]

—Khent(i)-amentiu perhaps originally a, xii. 21

—Lake, pond at Abydos regarded as, xii. 98

—of the South, Ophoïs in older form is the, xii. 144

—one of four sons of Horus or Osiris has form of, xii. 112

—totem, vii. 279

—(?) with a feather, xii. 393 (fig. 226)

Jackals associated with sun and Underworld, xii. 364 [10]

—at "lake of life," xii. 364 [10]

—three, from Nekhen (Hierakonpolis), xii. 365 [26]

Jack-o'-lanterns, souls appear as, to lead people astray, iii. 231

Jacob and Rachel, tale of, v. 34–35

—wrestling with El, v. 244–245

Jadatshy, rain-makers, iv. 447

Jade Emperor, viii. 58

—Field of, viii. 171

—green, used to cure epilepsy and colic, xi. 284

—Lady, statue of, viii. 71

—Mountain of, xii. 304, 305

—symbolic objects of, viii. 46–47, 50, 116

—tablet, mother of Confucius vomited up, viii. 98

Jafnhar, one of lords of Asgard, ii. 6, pl. III, opp. p. 12, 24

Jagatī metre, vi. 91

Jaguar, xi. 62, 69, 79–80, 93, 177, 264, 266, 268

—brothers, xi. 314

— -snake, the deer-goddess, xi. 86

—sun, xi. 94

Jahi, female demon, vi. 276–277, 293

Jahnu, vi. 116

Jahveh, position of Shang Ti similar to that of, viii. 49; see also Yāw.

Jaik, son of over-god, iv. 402

— -Khan (Flood Prince), iv. 365

Jain and Kṛṣṇa mythologies closely connected, vi. 225

Jainism, vi. 13, 14

Jains, Ariṣṭanemi one of the Tīrthakaras of the, vi. 96

—mythology of, vi. 220–229

—polemics against, vi. 163, 164

Jaiwas, Kachin priests, xii. 263

Jajutši (" Orderer "), guardian spirit, iv. 366, 394, 395, 406, 413

Jalandharāyaṇa family, vi. 222

Jalang's heath, ii. 114

Jalāṣa (rain?), special healing remedy of Rudra, vi. 38

Jama, in Maco, means supreme Deity, sun, and moon, xi. 278

Jamadagni, adventure of, with Arundhatī, vi. 144

—Kaśyapa, and the gods, triple life of, vi. 81

—son of, struck off his mother's head, vi. 169

Jāmāspa husband of Zoroaster's daughter Pourucista, vi. 341

Jambha, vi. 154

Jambi, a high god, vii. 125, 131

Jambudvīpa, continent on which we live in Jain belief, vi. 220–221

—" the world," vi. 192

Jambūnadasaras, lake of Kubera, vi. 158

Jamshīd: see Yima.

Jan Menecius describes idolatry of ancient Prussians, Lithuanians, and Russians, iii. 234–235

Janaka, king of Videha, vi. 127, 138

Janamejaya, snakes sacrificed by, in revenge for his father's death, vi. 154–155

Jáṅgulī, vi. 205

January and February, Finnish tale concerning, iv. 226

Janus figure of deity El of Gebal, v. 68, 69

——headed, Marduk is, v. 294

—nature of Nergal, v. 49, 136

Japan, ape or tortoise as trickster-hero in, ix. 204, 205

—Indian Trickster Tales found in, ix. 242

——Warrior-Hero conferred on Yamato, viii. 304

Jar, bottomless, in Hades, Danaïds condemned to fill, with water drawn in leaky vessels, i. 30

—children of Byat Ta launched in, xii. 349

—earthen, flying on, vii. 84, 393 [31]

—golden, given by Dionysos to Thetis, i. 217

—Pandora's, origin of evils from, i. 15

—storage, of Eurystheus, i. 82 (fig. 3B), 83

—water, placed on grave of unmarried, i. 324 [9] (ch. ii)

Jär-Sub, earth-deity, iv. 462

Jarā, a female Rākṣasa, vi. 156

—(" Old Age "), death of Kṛṣṇa from arrow of, vi. 125, 225

Jarākumāra, vi. 225

Jaralez, spirits to restore life, vii. 90, 395 [58]

Jarāsandha, one of the anti-Vāsudevas, vi. 225

—seeks to avenge death of Kamsa, vi. 173

Jared = Ensibzianna = Amempsinos, Hebrew patriarch, v. 205

Jarilo, iii. 313–314

Jarl, son of Heimdall, first of jarls, ii. 10, 153, 155

Jarnsaxa, giantess, mother of Magni, ii. 74, 82, 153, 278

Järv-elaj (" Sea-dweller "), iv. 207

Jashar may be title of Adad and Nergal, v. 41, 387 [197]

Jashigan, son of over-god, iv. 402

Jātaka literature, vi. 207

—story at Zanzibar, vii. 121

Jātakas, birth-stories, viii. 217

—influence Indonesian trickster tales, ix. 242

Jātavedas, Agni is, vi. 44, 136

Java, Indian influence in, ix. 242, 306

—mouse-deer as the trickster-hero in, ix. 203

Javelin wrought during Mass to kill Lleu, iii. 97

Javerzaharses (nymphs), vii. 84–85

Jaw-bones, magic fish-hooks made from, ix. 43, 45

Jaya, snake, vi. 155

Jayantas, vi. 227

Jayantī, Śukra lived with, vi. 168

Jealousy, divine, at man's obtaining knowledge, iii. 28

—of gods, v. 167, 175, 180, 183, 184, 185, 200, 223

Jehovah, v. 43

—see JEWS, GOD OF THE; YAHWEH; YĀW.

Jemdat Nasr, v. 1, 89

Jemmy Button, superstitions of, xi. 338–339

Jen, the Christian God, iv. 217

Jên Fang, viii. 58

—Tsung, viii. 127, 139

Jenghiz Khan, iv. 390, 392, 396, 398

Jengk-tongk (" water-spirit "), sacrificial feasts to, iv. 193

Jeroboam divinely appointed king, v. 42

Jerusalem, ii. 32

—(Aelia Capitolina), v. 45, 388 [223]

Jesus Christ, Book of Generation of, v. 347

——New Testament account of, not influenced by Gilgamish epic, v. 266

Jewel, a chosen, condition of Cúchulainn, iii. 151

——crystal which makes ebb and flow of tide, viii. 271, 305

—one of three insignia of ruling family, viii. 226, 228

——symbolism, xi. 52

Jewelled idols, xi. 47–48

Jewellery, vii. 300

Jewels of Mah, v. 221

——the Quarters, x. 158

Jewish Exile, v. 134

Jews, Chinese, Karen myths suggest acquaintance with, xii. 269

—God of the, xii. 207, 209, 423 [32]

Jězě, Jězěnky, etc., silvan spirits, iii. 265–266

Jezreel equivalent in meaning to Izrah-Dagan, v. 79

Jhajhār Singh, vi. 246

Jikoku-ten (Dhṛtarāṣṭra), guardian of east, viii. 242–243
Jimmu Tenno, legendary founder of Imperial dynasty, viii. 211
Jina, vi. 226, 229
Jingō, Empress, subjugated Korea, viii. 305
Jini, vii. 250
Jinn, Milhoi originated with, vii. 412 4
Jinns, vi. 208
—(abstract noun meaning "the hidden"), v. 352
Jinroku and the fox, tale of, viii. 325–326
Jizō, protector of children, quotation from hymn dedicated to, viii. 239–240, pl. xiii, opp. p. 240, 379 23
Jñātṛs, clan of, vi. 223
Jocakuvague, appellation of Sky-father, xi. 24
—"yucca" appears in form, xi. 34
Jōdo, Buddhist paradise, viii. 241
Joe Kull, spirit living in a river, iv. 208
Jogaoh, Dwarf People, x. 28
Joha, anecdotes of, vii. 355
Joḥḥa (Hâjj Joḥḥa), vii. 430 9
Johilā River, vi. 234
John, Bishop of Mecklenburg, head of, offered to idol in 1066, iii. 287
—little, breaks solar jug, iii. 329
—the Baptist, St., festival of Kupalo coincides with that of, iii. 313–314
Jokes, profane, practised at grave by masked men, iii. 234
Jolasveinar, Icelandic spirits who moved about at Christmas, iv. 68
Jomsvikings, naval battle with the, ii. 187
"Jomsvikings-saga," ii. 187
Jonathan, v. 83
Jörd ("Earth"), co-wife with Frigg to Odin, ii. 16, 174, 194–196, 200
——Thor said to be Odin's son by, ii. 65, 74, 75
—erd ("earth") seems to survive in ard "land," "field," vii. 14
—lifranda Manna (Land of living Men), visits to, ii. 320, 322
—parallel of Terra, ii. 201
Jordan, life-renewing (Fountain of Youth), xi. 20
Jordegumma ("Old woman of the earth"), midwife but, earlier, deity of child-birth, iv. 257

Jöruplain, ii. 265
Joseph motif, vi. 336
Josephus calls Pharaoh's daughter Thermuthis, xii. 397 94
Jötunheim, giants dwell in, ii. 23, 65, 66, 78, 81, 82, 88, 89, 92, 106, 110, 111, 123, 130, 140, 145, 179, 181, 241, 276, 281, 322
Jötuns, ii. 83, 104, 180, 281; iii. 34
Journeys, spirit, iv. 509–512, 519, 523
Jove's bolt, xi. 235
Joy at death, mourning at birth, Thracian, vii. 397 4
—Aut-[y?]êb deity of, xii. 67
—Ḥat-ḥôr deity of, xii. 40
Jrag, candle, vii. 55
Ju [Ru] Chia (School of Letters), viii. 8, 24
Jubal, patron of music, v. 105, 202
Judaeo-Christian beliefs, traces of, in Karen myth, xii. 269–270
Judaism, vi. 347
Judge, Judges, Judgements:
Judge of dead, vi. 69, 100, 160, 180; xii. 97, 118, 120, 176, 366 3
——Dharma takes place of Yama as, vi. 180
——Egyptian, Anubis, xii. 366 3
——Osiris as, xii. 97, 176
——Thout(i) is, xii. 366 3
—trickster as, ix. 197–199
Judges examined souls at various posts, viii. 238
—forty-two, in afterworld, xii. 176, 179
—in Hades, i. 143–144
Judgement (and judges) of souls of dead, v. 49, 50, 80, 135, 147, 148
—concerning champion's portion, iii. 146–149
—day, iv. 221
—deity of, Sebg(u)-Mercury as, xii. 373 63
—first, given in Ireland, iii. 44
—gods with two feathers present at, xii. 101
—hall, xii. 176, 179 (cuts)
—of dead, xii. 118
——on bridge, iv. 74
——Nascakiyetl, x. 275 10
—place of, v. 161
—tablets found at Susa prove Babylonians believed in, v. 148
Judgements, Heaven neutral in its, iv. 396

Judy, female evil spirits, iii. 260

Jug, solar, iii. 328, 329

Jui (tablet), Yellow Emperor awarded the, viii. 27

Juju man: see WITCH-DOCTORS.

Juksakka, deity of birth, iv. pl. xxvii, opp. p. 224, 252–257

Jul-gubbe (" Christmas old man "), iv. 248

Julian family, Venus divine ancestress of, i. 294

Julius Caesar constructed temple of Venus Genetrix, i. 294

Jumala (Jumo), sky-god, iv. 217

Jumnā a sacred river, vi. 234

—Kṛṣṇa kills Kāliya in the, vi. 172

Jumo, great, sacrifices at tree of, iv. 265–280

—sacrifice to messenger of, iv. 272–273

Jumon-ava, deity of child-birth and Heaven, iv. 258, 265–266

Jungle Gate in Rek Na Festival, xii. 329–330

Juniper: see MATERIA MEDICA.

Juno (Iuno), identified with Sima (Sîmî), fate-goddess, v. 22

—temple of, erected over cavern at flood, v. 37

Junones, Roman (protectors of women), originally souls of dead, iii. 249

Junuvī (or Janamī) Mātā, birth-goddess, vi. 238

Jupiter, viii. 228, 229; xi. 278; see also IUPPITER.

—Balmarcod identified with, v. 383 [106]

—Bohemians worshipped deities similar to, iii. 301

—Christian priests sacrificed to, ii. 68

—(Diespiter), *Tiwaz equivalent of, ii. 97

—Donar regarded as Teutonic, ii. 68, 69

—fifth day of Harranian week sacred to, v. 154

—Hêlêl is, v. 144

Jupiter in Caesar's account of Gaulish gods, iii. 9

——Plutarch's account of a Celtic island, iii. 15

—Mercury (Wodan) mentioned with, in eighth century, ii. 37–38

—on tablet, v. 286

—paralleled by Tangaloa, ix. 29

—Thagya Min may be paired off with, xii. 340

—undoubtedly Thor, ii. 68, 69, 70, 74

—planet, Aramazd probably lord of, vii. 17

——beneficent, vii. 52

——Bṛhaspati regent of planet, vi. 92

——" Horus the Opener of Secrets " equals, xii. 388 [28]

——Marduk as, v. 110, 317

——Osiris identified with, xii. 94

——readings of names of, xii. 54–55

——representative of wood, viii. 142

——represented by brown-red in Ezida, v. 159

——see POÏA, ETC.

——Sydyk deity of, vii. 41

Ju-rōjin (" Aged Man of Longevity "), viii. 280

Jurt-ava and -azerava (Dwelling-place mother and mistress), iv. 168

Jushkaparik (Vushkaparik), chimera, vii. 91–92

Jus primae noctis possessed by Conchobar, iii. 140, 144

Justice, v. 193

—Balance of, xii. 179 (fig. 186)

—double, xii. 100 (fig. 95), 101, 387 [23]

—Ma'et female personification of, xii. 67

—pedestal which was hieroglyph of, xii. 145, 407 [76]

—Sydycos title of sun-god as, v. 74

Justinian suppresses old Egyptian religion, xii. 244

Jutland, Odin came to, ii. 32

Jyotiṣkas, vi. 227

Jyotsnākālī, wife of Puṣkara, vi. 137

K

Ka = soul, xii. 174, 415 [3]

—of a king, xii. 170, 171

Ka (" Who "), vi. 74

Käbä, god of fate, iv. 393, 409

Kabeiroi, Kubera may be Indian coun-

terpart of Greek, vi. pl. xix, opp. p. 158

Kabigat, son of Wigan, tale of, ix. 178–179, 183

Kabirs, Esmounos one of eight, v. 74–75

Kabirs, seven, with Eshmun as eighth, vii. 381 [1] (ch. ii)
—Sydyk father of, v. 74; vii. 41
Kablunait, white men, legends of, x. 2
Kabti-ilāni-Marduk, poem revealed to the scribe, v. 137–138
Kābul, vi. 328, 331
Kab-ul ("the Potent Hand"), shrine, xi. 134
Kaca, vi. 153
Kaches claimed and held captive those coming from their stock, vii. 80, 83–84
Kachi-kachi Yami, tale of, viii. 384 [8]
"Kachirambe," Nyanja tale, vii. 224, 402 [31]
Kachpikh, wild beings, xi. 340
Kadalayapan, spring at, ix. 233, 235
Kadmos, i. 44–45
—and Harmonia sent to dwell in the Elysian Fields by Zeus, i. 47, 158
——withdrew to land of the Illyrians, i. 47
—connexion of, with Boiotian myth, i. 43
—consults Delphic oracle for aid in finding Europe, i. 179
—daughters of, i. 45–48
—grandson of Hayk, vii. 65
—Ino daughter of, i. 261
—Linos first to use alphabet brought from Phoinikia by, i. 253
—not admitted to Elysion, i. 147
—value of story of, i. 47–48
Kadrū, vi. 139, 155
Kadulubare, house of King's first wife, ceremonies at building of, vii. III
Kae scalded to death, ix. 84
Kaggen: see CAGN, ETC.
Kaguya-hime ("Lady of Brilliancy"), viii. 262, 360
Kahegal, god, v. 152
Kahil, title of moon-god, v. 5
Kahinalii, Sea of, ix. 39
Kahit ("Wind"), x. 223–225
Kai Khusrau: see HAOSRAVAH.
K'ai Yüan, Emperor, viii. 125
Kaiānians, vi. 334
K'ai-fêng, Sungs fled from, viii. 95
Kaikasī, vi. 157
Kaikeyī, vi. 127
Kaïkos, river of Mysia, healing powers of, i. 257

Kaikoutji, father of Anuanaïtu, xi. 264, 265
Kaikuzi sent to earth to take back Death to Gulu, vii. 172–173
Kailāsa, vi. 131, 158
Kaimūr range fabled to be offshoot of Himālaya, vi. 236
Kaira-Khan, iv. 401
—spirit of one of upper storeys of Heaven, iv. 406, 448
Kairos ("Opportunity"), abstract divinity of time, i. 282
Kaiṭabha, demon, vi. pl. xx, opp. p. 164
—stole Vedas from Brahmā, vi. 122–124
Kai-tangata ("Man-Eater"), ix. 57
Kāla, god, vi. 93, 118
—originally meant "death," but kala is "black," viii. 381 [15]
——Śiva, vi. pl. VII, opp. p. 82, 112, 118
Kalabsheh, Merui worshipped at, xii. 137, 406 [55]
Kalaïs and Zetes free Phineus from depredations of Harpies, i. III
—son of Boreas and Oreithyia, i. 73
Kālakā, vi. 152–153
Kālakañjas, vi. 152
Kālanemi, vi. 154
Kālapṛṣṭha, snake, vi. 155
Kalauitan, mountain of flood tale, ix. 171, 180, 183
Kālayavana advances against Mathurā, vi. 173
Kalchas, i. pl. xxx, opp. p. 120
—consults oracle on behalf of Agamemnon, i. 125
—gives seizure of Chryseïs as reason for plague which came upon Greek army, i. 127
—prophesies about Achilles, i. 122
Kaldyni-mumas, goddess, iv. 258
"Kalevala," iii. 135
—Aino episode in, iv. pl. xx, opp. p. 192, 210
Kālī, vi. 118, 184, 246, 247
Kali Age, vi. 105, 235
Kālidāsa, divinity of, vi. 244
Kalikalanje, vii. 409 [36]
Kalinago, ancestor of Carib, xi. 39
Kaliṅga, cult of "Dionysos" extended to, vi. 110
Kāliya, serpent, slain by Kṛṣṇa, vi. 172
Kali-yuga, one of four Indian ages of world, v. 205
Kalki, avatar of Viṣṇu, vi. 168, 169

Kalliana (probably Kalyāṇ), Christian bishop appointed from Persia in, vi. 175

Kallidike, Odysseus weds, i. 140

Kallikantzaroi, type of monsters in modern Greek folk-belief, i. 314–315

Kalliope and Apollo parents of Linos, i. 253

—("Sweet-Voiced"), one of the Epic Muses, i. 240

Kalliroë, daughter of Acheloös, married Alkmaion, and later demanded robe and necklace of Harmonia, i. 55

—mother of Geryoneus, i. 86

Kallisto and Zeus, parents of Pan, i. 267

—Artemis identified with, i. 21, 184

—changed into a bear, i. 16

—daughter of Lykaon, i. 21

—may not bathe in Okeanos, i. 21

—placed in heavens near her son Arkas, i. 251

Kalmāṣapāda eats sons of Vasiṣṭha, vi. 146

Kalmuk world-picture, iv. 347 (fig. 15)

Kalo, Lady, Artemis survives as, in modern Aitolia, i. 313

Kalpas, gods born in and above the, vi. 227

Kältas (Kaltes) mother, birth- and fate-deity, iv. 260

Kalunga (or Kalunga-ngombe), Death personified as, vii. 117, 175–177

Kalydon, great hunt at, i. 56

—Oineus ruled over, i. 56

—son of Aitolos, i. 56

Kalypso and Odysseus, episode of Gilgamish and Siduri wrongly supposed to be connected with, v. 266

—Hermes carries command of Zeus to, i. 191

—Odysseus cast on island of goddess, but later released by order of Zeus, i. 137, 138

Kam = shaman, iv. 496

Kāma, vi. 93–94, 116, pl. x, opp. p. 118, 141, 183, 197

Kāmadeva, vi. 218

Kamak, bird, vi. 326

Kamalākṣa, an Asura, vi. 116, 154

Kamaluluwalu, hero half stone and half flesh, ix. 89

Kamass Samoyeds, iv. xviii

Kamaṭha and Marubhūti, brothers, born enemies in eight incarnations, vi. 226

Kame and Keri, twins and heroes, xi. 312–313

Kami, deity or spirit in Japanese animism, viii. 215

Kamikos, Daidalos flew to, i. 65

Kami-nashi-zuki [tenth month], "month without gods"; Kami-ari-zuki, called in Izumo "month with gods," viii. 250

Kami-shimo, garment, viii. 355

Kampaneus, wife of, threw herself on his funeral pyre, i. 54

—Zeus sends thunderbolt on, for temerity in scaling wall, i. 53, 158

Kāmpti, battle of, vi. 234

Kaṁsa and Kṛṣṇa deadly foes in 150 B.C., vi. 177

———protagonists in a ritual contest, vi. 126

—plots death of Kṛṣṇa, vi. 172–173

—warned that death awaited him, vi. 171

"Kamucu" ("We behold"), a song, xi. 167

Kan Pas (god prince), iv. 158

Kan years, xi. 144

K'an yü, classical name of geomancy, viii. 140

Kanag, son of Aponibolinayen, ix. 234

Kanagawa, grave mound of Urashima at, viii. 381 [5] (ch. iii)

Kanaima, xi. 276

Kanakamuni, Mānuṣibuddha of present period, vi. 211

Kanakuk, prophet, x. 149

Kanal-Acantun, idol, xi. 144

Kanaloa: see TANGAROA.

Kanati, x. 69

Kandarpa, name of Kāma, vi. 141

Kande, lizard, vii. 165

Kandralekel Lake, iv. 210–211

Kane, god, ix. 24

K'ang Hsi, viii. 153–154

Kangaroo and dog, tale of, ix. 146–147

———wombat, tale of, ix. 289–290

—skin, red, presented to sun in land of dead, ix. 275

Kangha, Mt., vi. 339

K'ang-hsi, Emperor of China, restoration of worship of Cao-bien under, xii. 317

Kaniki, waist-cloth [of Katsumbakazi], obtaining piece of, brings riches, vii. 244

Kankhal, vi. 245
Kan-lu, heavenly dew, viii. 130
Kansa, religious feeling of, x. 17
Kan-su, Province of, viii. 29
Kantharos (kind of drinking vessel), emblem of Dionysos, i. 222
Kantjil = mouse-deer, ix. 186
Kan-u-Uayeyab, fabrication of statue of, xi. 144
Kaṇva, blind seer, vi. 65
Kan-xib-yúi to order world after flood, xi. 154
Kanyakubja (modern Kanauj), vi. 145
Kanyanga and Mkunare, tale of, vii. 266–268
Kanym, son of over-god; wife of Ülgen, iv. 402, 405
Kao Hsin, emperor, viii. 40–41
Kao Huang, viii. 128
Kao Tsung, Emperor, viii. 76, 124, 134
Kao, Yüeh Hsiang married to son of, viii. 173
Kaodanan, ix. 224
Kaoko veld, actual tree which produced human race in, vii. 146
Kaoru, son of Genji, story of, viii. 301–302
Kapālin, a Rudra, vi. 142
Kapaneus raised from dead by Asklepios, i. 280
Kapapitoe, parakeet and maiden, ix. 207, 211–213
Kapila, avatar of Viṣṇu, vi. 168
—sage, vi. 115
Kapipikauila, tale of, ix. 89–91
Kapirimtiya, hole from which first people came, at, vii. 147, 184
Kapūṭ (or Pēhīn), wolf killed by Keresāspa, vi. 327
Kar-fish, vi. 272, 281, 288
Kar-Ninurta ("Wall of Ninurta"), city, v. 128
Kara, Sigrun reborn as the Valkyrie, ii. 251, 260
Kara, son of over-god, iv. 402
— -Khan, son of creator, iv. 405, 406
Karakarook, sister of Pallyang, ix. 282
Karamnāśā river of ill omen, vi. 235
Karaty-Khan kills demon from whom insects are born, iv. 388
Kardas-śarko, god living beneath stone, iv. 168

Karelians, one of Finnish linguistic groups, iv. xv, xix
—Russian, certain saints replacing ancient gods among, iv. xix
Karens migrated peaceably into Indo-China, xii. 268–269
Karevel, Torem-, iv. 404–405
Kari, wind, ii. 281
Karia, i. 245
Karihi (Aliki), son of Hema, ix. 58, 59, 66
Karkoṭaka, king of Nāgas, vi. 155, 241
Karl, peasant, birth of first, ii. 10, 153
Karma, viii. 218, 238, 296, 384 [15]
Karmaḍākinī, vi. 218
Karṇa, brother of Yudhiṣṭhira, vi. 138, 155
Karneian Apollo, i. 180
Karonis bore son to Apollo, iii. 10
Karpo ("Fruitfulness"), child of Zephyros and Chloris, i. 266
—one of the Horai, i. 238
Karr, fire in barrow of, ii. 308
Karshiptar, bird, vi. 290, 309
Karshit, son of over-god, iv. 402
Karshvars (Keshvars), six Persian regions of earth, v. 217; vi. 280.
Karsikko, a piece of white paper used on funeral day containing name and dates of birth and death, iv. 43
—memorial tree or thicket, iv. 25–26, pl. II, opp. p. 26, 35
Kart, priests, iv. 264–265, 268–281
Kartavirya succeeded Jamadagni, vi. 169
Kārttikeya, possibly Indian prototype of lCam-srin, vi. 214
Karubu, protecting spirit, v. 108
Kasai country, Bumba god in, vii. 125
Kashtiliash, king of Babylon, v. 400 [155]
Kaśmīr, cult of "Dionysos" in, vi. 110
—home of magic arts, vi. 208
Kassandra and Aigisthos reign over Mykenai (or Argos), i. 134
—dragged by Aias, son of Oileus, from altar of Athene, i. 133
—endowed by Apollo with power to foresee future, i. 179
—killed on return to Mykenai, i. 134
—sister of Paris, i. 119
Kassiepeia, Queen, boast of, i. 34
Kassus, Indo-Iranians among, vii. 379 [2]
Kastor, i. pl. IV (1), opp. p. l
—and Pollux, i. 301–302

Kastor and Pollux, Alcis compared with, ii. 17
——likeness of Indian belief to fable of, x. 31
——stars, Gilgamish wrongly identified with, v. 268
——worshipped by Celts, iii. 158
——Polydeukes at home, i. pl. XLIX, opp. p. 224
——invented Spartan dance, i. 26
——took part in hunt of Kalydonian boar, i. 56
—son of Tyndareos, i. 24–27
—Temple of, erected at fountain of Iuturna, i. 302
Kāsu (Hāmūn Swamp), Lake, germs of Zoroaster in, vi. 342
Kasuga, shrine of, monk has vision at, viii. 273
Kaśyapa, adventure of, with Arundhatī, vi. 144
—all creatures descendants of, vi. 75, 122, 139
—came to heal Parikṣit of snake-bite, vi. 155
—lies at hill Kukkuṭapada, vi. 211–212
—Mārīca, father of gods and Asuras, vi. 106
—Prajāpati, vi. 107, 151
—received the earth, vi. 169
—triple life of, vi. 81
Kāśyapa family, vi. 223
Kaśyapas, numbers of Buddhas called, vi. 200, 211, 212
Katcinas and gods, x. 187–192, 195
—masques during season of presence of, x. 310 65
Kathatakanave, first man, x. 180
Kātilu ("slayer"), v. 417 41
Katō-Saemon, tale of, viii. 331, 384 13
Katonda, the creator, vii. 129
Katreus, son of Minos, i. 61, 63
Katsumbakazi, Giryama demon, vii. 243–244, 258
Katsura, kind of laurel, viii. 232, 339, 378 15
Katuns, periods of 7,200 days, xi. 129
Kaua, hero, ix. 90
Kaukabhta, Astλik translation of, and designation of Ishtar, vii. 39
—Syrian (Chaldaean, Mesopotamian) goddess, identified with Sidonian Astarte, Greek Aphrodite, and Armenian Anahit, vii. 27, 39

Kaun'ápa, rock with sign of umbilical cord, xi. 185
Kauravas, vi. 125, 246
Kausalyā, vi. 127
Kaustubha gem, vi. 107, 151
Kava-Jumo, iv. 393
— -plant, ix. 64
Kavi Kavāta (Pers. Kai Qubād), vi. 334, 350
—Usan (Pers. Kai Kāūs), vi. 334–335, 336, 350
Kavis, vi. 84
Kāvya Uśanas, Indra aided by, vi. 65, 84
——seer, vi. 335
Kāvyas, vi. 101
Kāwaj, modern Indian deity of boatmen, vi. 235
Kawelu and Hiku, tale of, ix. 75
Kayak-men, x. 7
Kayan, Borneo, possible Indian influence among, ix. 243
Kāyotsarga posture, Tīrthakaras obtain release in, vi. 222, 226
Kayurankuba, god of storms, vii. 237, 410 35–411
Kchemnito ("goodness itself"), x. 285 28
Kebriones, chariot driver of Hektor, i. pl. XXXI, opp. p. 124
Kè-buoi (Village du Papier), temple to a fisherman at, xii. 312
Keening, first, heard in Ireland, iii. 32, 137
Kei, iii. 188, 189, 191, 198, 199
Kekeko, bird in wonder-tree tale, ix. 237–238
Kekri-feast of Finns corresponds to All Saints' Day, and is celebrated in two ways, iv. 64–66, 248
Kekritär, masked people at Kekri-feast, iv. 65
Kekropia, i. 66
Kekrops, i. 66–67
—believed to be first man by Athenians, i. 10
—daughters of, i. 69–70
—son of Erechtheus, i. 68, 71
—sprang from bosom of Gaia, i. 272
Kek(u) (or Kekui) and Keket (or Kekut) ("Darkness"), two members of primeval ogdoad, xii. 48
Kelaino, said to be wife of Prometheus, i. 12

Keleos, a minister of rites of Demeter, i. 230
—built temple to Demeter at Eleusis, i. 228
—daughters of, place their brother Demophon in care of Demeter, i. 228
—son of Keleos, taught agriculture by Demeter, i. 230
Kelliwic, Cornwall, iii. 190, 192
Kelok, giant, x. 228, 232
Kemosh, West Semitic deity, v. 11, 13, 14, 47, 444
Kenaima, a member of a class of death-bringing powers, xi. 38
—avengers of murder and death bringers, xi. 258, 260, 262, 266
Kenan = Enmengalanna = Ammenōn, Hebrew patriarch, v. 205
Kenemtef(i), one of four sons of Horus, xii. 134, 404 38
Kenemt(i), Kenemtef(i) perhaps identical with, xii. 134, 404 39-405
—vanished divinity who fills first three decanal stations, xii. 134
Keneu chief representative of thunderbird, x. 25
Kengida, messenger of Enlil, v. 100
Kēngtūng, deluge-myth concerning, xii. 278–280
—founded by Mang Rai, xii. 281
—July ("marriage of virgins") festival at, xii. 334–335
—spring feast at, originally had human sacrifice, xii. 332–334
Kenharingan, creator god, ix. 182
Kennings, ii. 6–7, 58, 83, 95, 99, 131, 147, 157, 160, 166, 171, 184, 185, 186, 194, 196, 249, 255, 326, 334
Kentauroi (Centaurs), i. 270–271
"Kentils-saga," ii. 301
Keos, Aristaios ends plague on, i. 252
Kephallenia, island from which Kephalos committed suicide, i. 73
Kephalos and Eos, i. pl. xx, opp. p. 72
——parents of Phaëthon, i. 244
—banished from Attike, i. 73
—husband of Prokris, i. 71–73
—penchant of Eos for, i. 246
—slays his wife by accident, i. 72, 73
—son of Hermes and Herse, i. 70
Kepheus endeavours to appease monster sent to ravage Aithiopia, i. 34–35
Kephisos River worshipped in Boiotia, i. 257

Keraunō ("thunderbolt"), v. 56
Kerberos, i. pl. iv (1), opp. p. l, 86, 88
—dog of Hades, brother of Orthos, i. 86
—guard at main entrance to Underworld, i. 142–143, 327 4
—return of, from Hades, i. 145
—survival of, in modern Macedonia, i. 314
—taken from and returned to Hades by Herakles, i. 88, 89
Kerchief, iv. 31, 47
—of Frigg, ii. 130
Keremet, Devil, iv. 317
—sanctuaries of Cheremiss, iv. 152–156, 262
—spirits, sacrifice to, iv. 153–156
Keres, i. 278
—Sirens akin to, i. 262
Keresāspa, vi. 273, 311, 322, 324, 325–328, 329, 343, 350
—dragon fighter, vii. 363
—overcomes Gandarewa, vi. 59
—unwittingly kindled fire on sea-monster, vii. 57
Keresavadah (Pers. Garsīvaz), vi. 336, 338, 350
Keri and Kame, labours of, xi. 313
Kerkopes, Herakles captures two, near Ephesos, i. 90
Kerkyon of Arkadia killed by Theseus in wrestling bout, i. 99
Kerkyra (Corfu), perhaps home of giant-children of Ouranos and Gaia, i. 9
Kernitou, Breton tradition that church at, stands on four columns in congealed sea which will liquefy, iii. 13
Kernuz, menhir of, iii. pl. xviii, opp. p. 140
Kernyu (Cornwall), boar fled to, iii. 188
Kerry, two hills in, called "paps of Anu," iii. 39
Kervadel, standing-stone at, iii. 159
Keryneian doe captured by Herakles, i. 81
Keryx, son of Hermes and Pandrosos, i. 70
Keśava, vi. 106
Kesh, seat of Mah cult, v. 111, 140
Keśin, vi. 152
—destroyed by Kṛṣṇa, vi. 172
Keśinī, vi. 115
Ketil, ii. 301

Keto represented a phase of the sea, i. 259

Ketsi Niouask, x. 285 [28]

Kettle covers roof-opening of Heaven, ii. 156–157

—Odrörir, ii. 53

—of Hymir, ii. 10, 86, 87, 100, 172

Kettledrum, ceremony of, v. 153, 400 [164]

Kettles over consecrated fire in temples, ii. 201

—two, tribal fetish; may also be " bowls of earth and sky," x. 106

Kettu (" Righteousness "), a son of Shamash, vii. 40

Ketu, vi. 232, 233

Ketuiti, god of cauldrons, master of Hell, xii. 417 [21]

—Rê'-Ḥor identified with, xii. 221

Kevalin, one possessed of highest knowledge, vi. 221

Keyri old man (Keyri ukko), iv. 248

Keys, golden, found in temple of Khaldis in Mutzatzir, vii. 395 [58]

—of Hades, i. 144

Keÿx, of Trachis, Herakles takes up abode with, i. 93

—son of Hesperos, changed into kingfisher after drowning, i. 15

Kezer-Tshingis-Kaira-Khan, flood hero, iv. 366

Khadiravanatārā, vi. 217

Khaldi, supreme Being of Urartians, and possibly a moon-god, vii. 11, 12, 67, 395 [58]

Khan-Budal-Tengeri, iv. 446

— -Iti, youngest son of, iv. 403

Khangai-Khan, mountain, iv. 453

Khara assisted Rāvaṇa in battle, vi. 156

Khar-'aḥaut, combat of Horus and Sêth localized at, xii. 126

Khargi, shaman-spirit, iv. 497

Khas (" slaves "), ethnological composition of, xii. 287

Khasti worshipped at Sheta, xii. 134

Khatuli-Shedeti, xii. 165 (fig. 174)

Khaturi, Semitic name of Shed after 2000 B.C., xii. 165

Khava, demon, vi. 291

Khây-taou, local (Egyptian) name of dying god of Gebal, v. 76

Khenset, wife of Sopd(u), xii. 135, 149

Khent(i)-amentiu, variant of Ophoïs, xii. 21, 98, 362 [7]

Khepri, Amen-Rê' identified with, xii. 221

—and Rê' identified with Osiris, xii. 96

—Ehet as " development of members of," xii. 71

—explained by later theologians as weaker sun, xii. 25, 28

—forming and creating work of, xii. 68–69

—identified with Nuu, xii. 63–64

——Rê', xii. 237

—infant sun-god, 'Apop wraps himself around, xii. 105

—in human form, xii. 24, 25 (figs. 4, 5)

—(Kheprer), etymology of, xii. 363 [2]

—(?), lake of, xii. 364 [11]

—morning name of Rê', xii. 83

—not originally localized at Heliopolis, xii. 363 [3]

—Nut, and Aker, xii. 369 (fig. 221)

—representations of, xii. 43 (fig. 36), 369 (fig. 221)

—(" Scarab-Like "), xii. 25

— -Sokari associated with Bês, xii. 377 [90]

—(sun) in lower world, xii. 43 (fig. 36)

—with sun in double appearance, xii. 25 (fig. 6)

Khiḍr, vi. 235, 359 [3]

Khikuptakh, form in Tell-el-Armana letters of Egyptian Ḥa-ka-Ptaḥ (" temple of the ka of Ptaḥ "), sacred name of Egyptian city of Memphis, i. 324 [8]

Khin-ort's son, boat of, iv. 78

Khmun(u), " City of Eight," in Middle Egypt, believed scene or beginning of creation, xii. 48

—eight ancestors of sun-god connected with, xii. 48

— -Hermopolis, Ṭhout(i) local divinity of, xii. 33

Khnāthaiti conquered Keresāspa, vi. 327

Khnemtet, nursing-goddess; later of bread and cakes, xii. 135

Khnûm(u), xii. 20 (fig. 1)

—and Ḥeqet transferred to Abydos, xii. 50, 51

——transformed from cataract-gods to creators, xii. 51

——Horus draw net to capture dragon, xii. 391 [52]

Khnûm(u) and Horus in the Underworld hold infernal monster down, xii. 391 [51]
——Shu, Ḥeḥ identified with, xii. 381 [49]
—'Anuqet associated with, xii. 131
—as creator of human race, xii. 379 [18]
——master of necropolis of Abydos, xii. 372 [50]
——source-god treated as localized variant of Nuu, xii. 50
—fanciful Egyptian etymology of name of, xii. 51
—forms children, xii. 51 (fig. 49)
—four sons of Horus or Osiris associated with, xii. 112
—god of first and eleventh nomes, xii. 19
—guardian of waters coming from the Underworld, xii. 28
—Ḥeqet associated with, xii. 134
—lost eye of sun-god disappears in watery realm of, xii. 89, 90, 384 [112]
—on back of lion represents depths of earth, xii. 369 [22]
—one of the two first gods who formed men and gods, xii. 50
—possible allusion to, in 'Apop-myth, xii. 104
—possibly represented in association with Nuu (Nûn?), xii. 47 (fig. 43), 371 [44]
—ram-headed god, xii. 135, 405 [43]
—Satet associated with, xii. 146
—soul of Shu, xii. 219
Khoja Nasreddin, Turkish jester, vii. 353
Kholumodumo, Izimu akin to, vii. 249
Kholumolumo swallowed all people of world, vii. 220
Khon, bird, iv. 508
Khonds (of India), Morning Star sacrifice of Skidi Pawnee akin to similar rite of, x. 76
Khongjais (or Kukis), Chin tribesmen of Maṇipūr, xii. 267
Khôns(u), xii. 22 (fig. 2), 34 and fig. 18
—Amon associated with, xii. 129
—as moon-god, xii. 34 and fig. 18, 44
——son of Sobk and Ḥat-ḥôr, xii. 366 [5]
—equated with Tḥout(i), xii. 34, 366 [4]
—ibis-head for, rare, xii. 34
—identified with Herakles, xii. 34
—lunarized god, Shu identified with, xii. 44
—meaning of name of, xii. 34

Khôns(u),Neb-taui depicted like, xii. 140
—Nefer-ḥotep local form of, xii. 140
—possibly alluded to in hymn on apotheosis of king, xii. 422 [18]
—replaced by Amonet in Theban triad, xii. 362 [6]
—(" Roamer," " Wanderer "), xii. 34
—unexplained symbol for, xii. 34
Khorton, forefather of Khangin clan, iv. 500
Khosadam, cannibalistic demon woman, creator of mosquitoes, iv. 386
—female ruler of dead, tried to swallow soul of Doh, iv. 522
Khosrau (Chosroës) and the reorganizing of Armenian pantheon, vii. 17
Khoto, eagle, iv. 508
Khrut (Skt. Garuḍa), name for the Galōn, xii. 323
Khshathra Vairya, vi. 260, pl. xxxiv, opp. p. 272
Khshathrō-Suka, pass of, vi. 339
Khubilgan, animal- or bird-protector of shamans, iv. 499, 506, 508, 512
Khudjana, son of Ribimbi, vii. 128
Khulater, ruler of dead, iv. 77
Khumbaba, vii. 69
Khun-Khorel bird, iv. 500
Khuran-Nojon, rain-god, iv. 448
Khurbystan: see AHURA MAZDA.
Khuri Edzhin, master of musical instrument, iv. 465
Khurmusta's daughter in form of goat, iv. 503
Khvanīras, vi. 298, 303
Khvārizm, vi. 306
Khwai-hemm, monster, father of Porcupine, vii. 289
Kiaklo visited Pautiwa, x. 210
Kianda, spirit who rules over water, etc., vii. 177
Kiang Chow, viii. 190, 191, 192
Kiangsi Province, viii. 95, 113
Kiang-su Province, viii. 93
Kiara, supreme God, addressed as " Father," vii. 133
" Kibaraka," vii. 257
—magic horse, vii. 358, 431 [19a]
Kibi, culture-hero, dogs of, vii. 220
Kibo, mountain, tale of poor man's son and, vii. 266–268
Kichalundu and the heaven tree, vii. 137
Kicva, Pryderi's wife, iii. 101, 102
Kid, Dionysos changed into, i. 46

Kidnapping, ix. 141
Kidneys of bear eaten to awaken love, iv. 91
——Indech, valour from, iii. 30
Kiehtan, a great spirit, x. 20, 271 [6]
Kiev, idols at, iii. 293, 297, 299, 301
Kii, Susa-no-wo said to have planted forests of, viii. 228
Kii (= Tii = Tiki), ix. 26
Kikēllia, festival of, v. 18
Kikimora, Slavic nocturnal demon, steals unborn children, vii. 394 [49]
Kikimoras play rôle of household gods, iii. 228
Kiku-jidō, genius of chrysanthemum, viii. 275
Kildare, sacred fire of St. Brigit at, iii. 11
Kildisin, birth-deity, mother or wife of Inmar, iv. 242, 258, 260, 399
Kildis-Vordis, Heaven-god, iv. 399
Kiliboban, a first woman, ix. 168
Kilili, Ishtar the harlot known in Babylonia and Assyria as, v. 33–34
Kililu, kulilu, some kind of bird, v. 34, 386 [161]
Kilimanjaro, vii. 136, 141, 183, 184, 266
Kilix settled in Kilikia, i. 44
Kill-crop required milk, vii. 391 [16]
Killing an object to release its soul, iv. 14, 20, 40, 53
——ceremonial, x. 247
——of objects deposited with the dead, xii. 418 [23]
Kilyikhama, class of nature daemons, xi. 322–323
Kimanawezi, vii. 321
Kimīdins, goblins, vi. 67
Kimmeria (Crimea), Io wanders through, i. 29
Kimmerians dwell on northern shore of Okeanos, i. 256
Kimpuruṣas, vi. 157, 227
Kiṁvadanta, vi. 98
Kinder-brunnen, iv. 214
Kindred, supernatural, iii. 258
Kinds, x. 30–33
Kine of King of Leinster, Dubh Lacha exchanged for, iii. 64
——offered to a black hag for her cow, iii. 63
——seven fat and seven lean, of Pharaoh's dream not influenced by Gilgamish epic, v. 267

Kine, story of Bres and the, iii. 26
Kine-kine-boro, ogre, ix. 230–231
Kineun, chief of Thunderers, x. 48
King, Kings:
King, birth of, protected by gods, xii. 170 (fig. 179)
——books of sorcery do no harm when used by, xii. 205
——Conaire divinely assisted to become, iii. 75
——Egyptian, primitive reminiscences in costumes of, xii. 361 [4]
——hymn on apotheosis of, xii. 202–204
——in myth represents delivering son of a god, v. 158
——of all habitations, myth, v. 137
——Babylon at New Year's ritual, v. 318–319
——or god, Lykaon may represent old Pelasgic, i. 21
——Pelasgos first Arkadian, i. 20
——prayer at crowning and death of, xi. 63–64
——Rêʿ-Horus as protector, type, ancestor, and soul of, xii. 215
——sacred, a marine deity, xi. 209
——soul of, lives by cannibalism, xii. 202, 213
——takes place of Marduk in combats with winged monsters, v. 281
——Tammuz slain by a, v. 336, 337
——who Opens the Heavens, sky-deity, ix. 26
Kings (as redeemers), marvellous birth of Marduk made precedent for births of, v. 157
——Aśvins sometimes regarded as two, vi. 31
——authority of, descended from Anu, v. 94
——chosen by oracles in Ethiopia, xii. 240
——deification and worship of, v. 326–327, 341
——descended from warrior-nobles, ii. 10
——divine appointment of, v. 41, 42, 327
——lists of pre-Inca, xi. 214
——of cities, in West Semitic religion, killed to satisfy powers of Hades, as sacrifice and atonement, v. 341–342, 343, 345
——dwarfs, ii. 271
——seven, Cúchulainn went against, iii. 150

Kings subject to ordinary rules of virtue and piety, xii. 180, 213, 235
—ten, before flood, v. 166, 205
—traditions of, vi. 320–343
—worship of, xii. 170–171, 414 27
Kingaludda, messenger of Enlil, v. 100
Kingdom for heavenly paradise, vii. 100
Kingfisher, spirit of midwinter calm dwelt in, i. 265
Kingfishers, Keÿx and Alkyone changed into, i. 15
Kingship, connexion of Wa with, in Kēngtüng, xii. 281
—hereditary and divine rights of kings, v. 166, 167, 206
Kingu, bearded beast with legs and body of lion may be, v. 283
—given Tablets of Fate by Tiâmat, v. 102
—Marduk burned, v. 156
—(Qingu, Kingugu), monster, v. 295, 296, 297, 302, 303, 307
—was cast into fire, tradition that, v. 315, 320
Kinich-Ahau, deity presiding at chief's house, xi. 145
—Kakmo, the Fiery Visaged Sun, xi. 138
Kinkō Sennin ("High Man with an Harp"), viii. 275, pl. XXI, opp. p. 276
Kinnaras, vi. 143, 149, 158, 203, 227
Kinship between Armenians and Thracians, vii. 12, 364, 379 1
—possible suggestion of change of, from male to female, vii. 278
Kintarō, son of Mountain-woman, viii. pl. XXXII, opp. p. 288, 290–292
Kintu, vii. 119, 129, 152–154, 155, 172–173, 402 22
Kiousa (Oki), an idol which watches the dead, x. 57
Kipanawazi ferries souls over river, vii. 419 4
Kirämät (? holy), iv. 151
Kirasa, magic life-restoring staff, vii. 171
Kirāta (mountaineer), Śiva assumes form of, vi. 118
Kirke, daughter of Helios and Perse, i. 242
—described Sirens to Odysseus, i. 262–263
—fountain of, at Thebes, i. 258
—sorceress-goddess, daughter of Helios, changes Odysseus's men into swine, i. 137

Kirke to purify Argonauts at Ausonia, i. 113
Kisagan-Tengri, god of war, iv. 406
Kisangada, vii. 186
Kisani, inhabitants of fourth world, x. 160
Kish, v. 89, 111, 117, 136, 166, 326, 331
—Azag-Bau founded dynasty of, vii. 367
—Bau wife of Zamama at, v. 14
—excavations at, v. 1
—flood stratum at, v. 203
—founding of first dynasty at, v. 203
——kingdom of, v. 168
—seals of Marduk at, v. 280
—with Gilgamish and Enkidu found at, v. 237, 238
Kishar and Anshar, primeval couple, v. 92, 291
—watchman of Ereshkigal, v. 164
Kisig-Ninazu ("Feast of parentalia of Ninazu"), month name, v. 162
Kisin, the evil one, xi. 141
Kiškānû, tree and plant of healing, v. 152, 226
Kiskil lilla and kiskil-uddakarra, devils, v. 362
Kislev, a month, v. 160
Kiss changed into bird, iii. 60
—of Angra Mainyu, serpents grew from, vi. 312, 320
—throwing of, to statue of deity, v. 378 17
Kissarē and Assōros, primeval couple, v. 292
Kisseus(?), Hekabe daughter of, i. 118
Kissing of Seide, iv. 111
Kite, vii. 144, 145; viii. 131
—miraculous, viii. 364
Kites, wine associated with flying of, viii. 130, 131
Kithairon, cult of Zeus on, i. 159
Kitimil and Magigi in flood-myth, ix. 256–257
Kitsawitsak, animal-lodge, x. 123
Kitshi Manitou: see GITCHE MANITO.
Kitsuki, great shrine of, viii. 229, 248, 249–250
Kittu, attendant of Shamash, v. 67, 151
Kitunusi, vii. 243, 244, 258
Kituta spirit, Ngunza turned into a, vii. 177

Kiu-kiang (old Tê-hua), viii. 123
Kiva, x. 184
Kiyamat-tora = Prince of Death, and his assistant Kiyamat-saus, iv. 75
Kiyomizu Kwannon, temple, viii. 286, 310
Kiyomori, hero of an epic, viii. 270
Kiyyūn, false vocalization for Kaywān, v. 134, 135
" Kjalnesinga-saga," ii. 76
Klashun (Tashōns), xii. 266
Klehanoai, moon-carrier, x. 157
Kleio ("Praise"), one of the Epic Muses, i. 240
Kleisobora, probably Greek name for city of Kṛṣṇa on Jumnā, vi. 110
Kleobis, story of death of, i. 167–168
Kleoboia (or Philonis) united in marriage with Eosphoros, i. 247
Kleopatra, daughter of Boreas and Oreithyia, i. 74
—wife of Meleagros, i. 57, 58
Klepsydra ("Stolen Water"), spring in which Zeus was washed, i. 155
Klickitat, chief, x. 134
Klotho ("singer of the present"), one of the Moirai, i. 284
Klust, marvellous keenness of hearing possessed by, iii. 190
Klymene and Iasos said to have been parents of Atalante, i. 56
—mother of Phaëthon by Helios, i. 244
Klytaimestra, i. pl. xxxiii, opp. p. 132
—daughter of Tyndareos, i. 24
—killed by Orestes and Pylades, i. 135
—lives in adultery with Aigisthos during absence of her husband, i. 134
—murder of, causes Orestes to appeal to Helios as witness, i. 243
—wife of Agamemnon, i. 121
Klytia, wife of Helios, i. 242
Klytios killed by Hekate, i. 187
K'mukamtch, "Old Man," x. 220
Knee, birth from, i. 156, 157
—Wounded, supreme Being of Hottentots, vii. 157, 158, 214
Knife, Knives:
Knife-bearers: see OSIRIS, REALM OF.
——spirits mentioned in hymn on apotheosis of king, xii. 175, 203
—(or crescent-) -shaped symbol may be symbol of moon cult, xi. 224
—thrown into whirlwind (as soul), iv. 9–10

Knife thrust into wall, promise to Keremet spirit accompanied by, iv. 153
Knives, flint, x. 291 [38]
—obsidian, used in child-birth, ix. 78
Knight in boar form, iii. 125, 187
Knights of the Swan, ii. 262, 263
Knossos founded by Minos, i. 64
—labyrinth of, i. 62, 65
Knot of the Year's festival, xi. 101
Knots, magic, xii. 199, 421 [6]
" Knowledge " as a function of " three gods of dán " may be personified as Danu, iii. 39
—Gwion becomes master of, by tasting from cauldron of inspiration and science, iii. 110
—hazels of, iii. 166
—men of, iii. 30
—Odin seeks, ii. 49, 50
—often associated with springs and streams, iii. 169, 208–209, 210, 211
—ritual eating of sacred animal gives, iii. 166
—some kinds of, tabu, iii. 120
—souls in Jainism develop into, vi. 228
—thumb and salmon of, iii. 120, 121, 162, 166, 167, 168
—Tuatha Dé Danann banished from Heaven on account of their, iii. 38
Ko Hung, viii. 144, 145, 147
—Lung deified as national god of soil, viii. 62
—Pala, Hka neatherd who became Chief of Kēngtūng, xii. 278–279
Kobine and Nareau created Heaven and earth, ix. 248
Kōbō Daishi by miraculous power set free a fountain, viii. 251, 252–253
Kobold: see BROWNIES.
Kobolds, vi. 228
Kobu-tori, viii. 283–284
Koḍāla, family of, vi. 222
Kodojezä, Esthonian god, iv. 173
Kodukäiat, dead who return, iv. 37
Kogniuntara, Jupiter's wife, vii. 229–231
Koios and Phoibe, parents of Leto, i. 174
Kokalos, king of Kamikos, i. 65
Kokamomako and Sunrise, tale of, ix. 225–227
Koki ("Praying Mantis"), wife of Spider, vii. 323
Kokko, entire group of anthropic gods worshipped by the Zuñi, x. 191–192

Koko, owner of [forbidden] fruit-tree, vii. 316, 425 [20]

Kokytos, river (of lamentation) of Hades, i. 143

Kola Lapmark, Seide at, iv. 102

Koleda, iii. 307–310

Kolga, daughter of Ægir, ii. 190

Kolonos, in Attike, Oïdipous and Antigone went to, i. 50

Koloowisi, Zuñi plumed serpent, x. 188

Kols, Muṇḍāri, totems of, vi. 242–243

Kombu and yorokobu, play of words connecting, viii. pl. xxxix, opp. p. 332

Komdei-Mirgan sent to hunt Irlek-Khan, iv. 489

Komokoa, protector of seals, x. 244

Kōmoku-ten (Virūpākṣa), guardian of west, viii. 243

Köndös, reclaimer of land and tilled fields, iv. 244

Konkel and Pediu, hero-brothers, xi. 330

Ko-no-hana-sakuya-hime ("Bloom Lady"), viii. 233, 234, 257

Koori, spirit-bird, iv. 509–510

Kopaïs, Lake, special home of Triton, i. 259

Koppa Tengu, viii. 288

Koptos, site of cult of Mîn(u), xii. 138

Koran, v. 354

Korē and Chaabou identical, v. 382 [68]

—("Daughter"), Persephone known in cult as, i. 230, pl. L, opp. p. 230

—festival before image of, v. 18

—Greek Underworld goddess, v. 18

—Libera equated with, i. 292

Korea, viii. 248

—Susa-no-wo regarded as pioneer in colonization of, viii. 228

Koreans, affinity of, with Japanese, viii. 209, 377 [1]

Korenice (modern Garz), oaken idol Rugievit at, iii. 283

Kore-te-whiwhia in genealogy, ix. 6

Korinthos, Sisyphos said to be royal successor of, i. 37

Korka-kuźo and -murt, House-ruler and -man, iv. 159, 163–164

Korka-śuan, hut wedding, iv. 123, 161

"Kormaks-saga," ii. 45, 226

Körmös, lifelong evil spirit, iv. 395

Korobo-na and -náko, two sisters, xi. 272

Koronis ("Sea-gull"), reputed mother of Asklepios, i. 279, 280

Kororo-ma, -mana, -matu, -matítu, four brothers, xi. 272

Korybantes and Daktyloi attend Kybele, i. 275

——ritual of, i. 275–276

—born as a tree, vi. 295

—Lares Roman counterparts of, i. 299

Kos, Herakles engages in battle with Eurypylos at, i. 91

—shrine of Asklepios at, i. 281

Kosala, vi. 127

Kosamba forest, Kṛṣṇa wounded in the, vi. 225

Košla-Kuguza and -kuva, Old Man and Woman of Forest, iv. 184

Kostbera interpreted eagle as hamr of Atli, ii. 233

Kostroma, funereal elements in burial of, iii. 314

Kotan-Shōrai, viii. 250

Kothluwalawa, dance-house of gods, x. 191, 210

Kotikili, x. 188, 191, 275 [10]

Koto, musical instrument, viii. 261

K'o-tou wên, "tadpole" characters, viii. 11

Kotowake, Lake, viii. 332

Kött, giant, ii. 279

Kottos, born of Ouranos and Gaia, i. 6

Kou(k), Esthonian term for thunder, cognate with Lithuanian kaukas (ghost) and kauk-spennis (thunderbolt), iv. 228

Kouretes, dance of, magic device for averting evil spirits, i. lii

—defeated by Meleagros, i. 57–58

—killed by Aitolos, i. 55–56

—Lares Roman counterpart of, i. 299

—origin of Cretan priesthood of, i. 274

—placed Zeus in care of Neda and Ithome, i. 155

—the, and Zeus, i. pl. xxxviii, opp. p. 158

Kovno, iii. 317

Koweit, South Arabian inscriptions found at, v. 4

Kowwituma and Watsusi, twins of Sun and Foam, x. 209

Koźla-ia, a forest-spirit, iv. 182, 183

Kōzuke, viii. 252

Kraal (of moon), vii. 136, 401 [44]

Krak, word for fire, vii. 55

Krakucchanda, forerunner of Gotama, vi. 211

Krakucchanda, Mānuṣibuddha of present period, vi. 211

Kranaos, autochthon, native chief of Attike, i. 67

—driven from throne of Attike by Amphiktyon, i. 67

—of Athens, i. 18

Kraoko Hreidarr asked Thor for site on which to land in Iceland, ii. 75

Krasnoludi, Polish household genii, iii. 248

Krataiïs ("Mighty") and Phorkys, parents of Skylla, i. 263

Kratt = Money-Para, iv. 173

Kratti, god caring for property, iv. 173

Kratu, vi. 108, 144

Krauñca, Skanda split the rock, vi. 141, 159

Kreon assumed powers of king (of Thebes) on death of Eteokles, i. 53

—brother of Iokaste, succeeded Laion as king of Thebes, i. 49

—father of Glauke, i. pl. xxviii, opp. p. 110

—regent for Polyneikes and Eteokles, i. 51

—sealed Antigone alive in cave, i. 53

Kreousa consults Delphic oracle at Delphoi, i. 179

—daughter of Erechtheus, i. 68, 71

Kretheus, Tyro wedded to, i. 106

Kriemhild, iii. 104

Krios, born of Ouranos and Gaia, i. 6

Krisa, port of Delphoi, Apollo reveals himself to Cretan sailors at, i. 178

K'ri-sroñ-lde-btsan invited to contend with demons who hindered Buddhism in Tibet, vi. 209

Kriwe, head priest at Romowe, iii. pl. xxxvii, opp. p. 304

Krodhavaśa Rākṣasas, lake of Kubera guarded by, vi. 158

Krommyon, i. 98

Kronos, iii. 15, 35, 53; vi. pl. xxxiii, opp. p. 264

—and Poseidon, Olympias, mother of Alexander the Great, traces descent to, i. 223

——Rhea, Demeter daughter of, i. 225

——Hera daughter of, i. 164

——Hestia daughter of, i. 208

——Poseidon son of, i. 210, 211

—born of Okeanos and Tethys, i. 5

——Ouranos and Gaia, i. 6

Kronos devours his children, xii. 423 [24]

—equated with Rê', xii. 364 [14]

—father of Cheiron by Philyra, i. 11

——Eros, i. 203

——Zeus, i. 155

—human sacrifice to Melqart as, v. 52

—identification of Saturnus with, i. 292

—identified with El, v. 80, 342, 389 [242]

—(Ilos), child of Uranos and Gê, v. 66

—meaning of stone given by Rhea to, i. 274

—mutilated his father Ouranos, i. 6

—(Ninurta), v. 154

—parallels in Celtic myth to, iii. 202

—régime of, i. 6–8

—Rhea gives stone to, to swallow instead of infant Zeus, i. 155, 159

—sacrificed son when danger beset his land, v. 342

—scythe of, vii. 85

—warned Xisuthros of Flood, v. 204

—weds his sister Rhea, i. 6

Kṛśānu shot at eagle bearing soma, vi. 47, 94

Kṛṣṇa, vi. 121, 124–127, pl. xiv, opp. p. 126, 130, 145, 169, 170, 171–175, 177, 178, 183, 185, 188–189, 191, 224, 225, 231, 236, 237, 238, 239

Krsnik (Kresnik, Karsnik), good genius who combats the Vukodlak, iii. 229

Kṛṣṭa, pronunciation of Kṛṣṇa in parts of India, vi. 178

Kṛta Age, vi. 103, 105, 106, 137

Kṛttikās, wives of Seven Seers become stars in the constellation, vi. 140

Krŭvnik (Bulgarian), vampire, iii. 232

Kṣātrāṇa, vi. 97

Kṣatriya, term, given to Varuṇa, vi. 22

Kṣatriyas, vi. 40, 169

Kṣetrasya Pati, vi. 96

Ku game, vii. 230

—god, ix. 24

—poison, viii. 156

—Shên ("spirits of the valley"), viii. 53

—wên, viii. 11

Kua yao, three hundred and eighty-four diagrams, viii. 138

Kuai, introducer of mask dances, xi. 294

Kuala cult, iv. 114–134, 144, 149, 165, 174

—feast, presents at, iv. 123, 132

Kualas, great, had guardians for treasure therein, iv. 132

Kuan, viii. 83
— -de, supreme architect of universe, pagoda founded in honour of, xii. 305
—hsiang, viii. 142
—Hsiang T'ai, the Observatory in Peking, viii. 144
—I-wu, Chief Minister of Ch'i, viii. 9
— -t'an, drought in, viii. 70
—Ti (Kuan Yü), national god of war, viii. 196
—Wu, Emperor, viii. 76
—Yin, Buddhist deity, goddess of mercy, viii. 82, 84, 113, 194–196
——female Bodhisattva, xii. 261–262
—Yü, god of war, viii. 94, 95, 97, 174, 176, 177, 196
Kuang Ch'êng-tzŭ, recluse, viii. 22
—Wu terms of peace, viii. 92, 93
Kuangsi Province, viii. 139
Kuangtung, viii. 5
Kuanip, mythic hero, xi. 342
Kuara, xi. 312
Kubaiko, sister of Komdei-Mirgan, iv. 489
Kubera, vi. 97, 112, 116, 157–158, pl. xix, opp. p. 158, 159, 180, 204, 214, 215, 229, 356 [4]
Kubjā, healing of, vi. 173, 178
Kuda, tortoise, vii. 317
Kudai Bai-Ülgön, iv. 405
— -Bakshy, tutelary genius of blacksmiths, iv. 464
—Jajutshi, iv. 406
—seven gods, iv. 343, 373–374, 402, 408, 490
Kud-ava and -azerava, House mother and mistress, iv. 168
Kudo-spirit (Kudo-Vodyž), iv. 135–138, 168
—totem, vii. 271
Kudos, great and little, iv. 135, 174
Kuei, jade tablet, viii. 46
—sacrifice against evil influences, viii. 61
—Shê painting of tortoise and snake, viii. 100
—tortoise, viii. 98
— -fu, viii. 100
— -ts'ang, collection system, viii. 137
K'uei niu, viii. 111
Kugsugga, mighty priest of gods, v. 104
Kugu shotshen-ava (" Great birthgiving mother "), iv. 258

Kuguldei-Matyr, hero who became star, iv. 429
Kuhaka, snake, vi. 165
Ku-hkan, city built by Sithu and Kyawzwa, xii. 353–354
Kuhū, goddess, vi. 93
Kui the Blind, ogress, ix. 65, 66, 88
Kuila-moku, patron deity of medicine, ix. pl. i, frontispiece
Kukkuṭapada, hill where Kāśyapa lies, vi. 211–212
Kukulcan, hero-deity, xi. 125, 131, 134–136, 137, 139, 140
Kukumatz, x. 179
Kukuwazuka, fowl of the ghosts, vii. 288
Kul, evil water-spirit, iv. 194, 198–199
Küläjumal, village-god, iv. 174
Kulakaras, first lawgivers, vi. 225–226
Kulhweh and Olwen, iii. 99, 125, 187, 189, 190, 191, 192, 197, 198, 202
—hero of the Arthurian cycle, iii. 99, 100, 108, 187, 188, 198
Kulili, one of dragons of Chaos, v. 86
Kulilu (" the Fish-man "), dragon, constellation Aquarius, v. 282
Kulimina, Arawak creator of women, xi. 259
Kuling, viii. 123
Kulitara, parent of Śambara, vi. 68
Kul jungk, fish-spirit, iv. 194
Kull (or Koll), water-spirit, original meaning was " spirit of dead," iv. 208
Kulla of Babylon, v. 104, 390 [267]
Kullaba may be connected with exploits of Gilgamish, v. 55, 140, 342
Kul-oter, devil, iv. 376
Kultur-mythus, viii. 227
Kumāra, born of Prajāpati and Uṣas, vi. 82
Kumāras, ten subdivisions of, vi. 227
Kumaso, legendary invaders, viii. 210
Kumbhakarṇa, vi. 129, 157
Kumbhāṇḍas, a species of goblin, vi. 203, 215
Kumbhin, vi. 98
Kumé-dera, Buddhist temple, viii. 277
Kumé-no-Sennin, ascetic, viii. 277
Kumush, blue man, x. 229, 236, 277 [13]
Kund Aramazd, vii. 24, 382 [21]
Kuṇḍagrāma (Basukund), place of descent of Mahāvīra, vi. 222

Kundrav (Skt. Gandharva; Avesta Gandarewa), mythical creature, vi. 322
Kunene River, vii. 146
K'un, viii. 136
K'un-lun Mountains, viii. 99, 116
Kung-ch'ang, Fu Hsi born near, viii. 29
—Kung rebelled against Nü Kua, viii. 31
—Lao, one of the "Three Venerable Ones," viii. 109
—Liu, grandson of C'hi, viii. 41
— -sun, family name of Yellow Emperor, viii. 27
——Chao, viii. 179
——Shu, viii. 139
—Wang, viii. 10–11
K'ung An-kuo, viii. 10
—Ch'iu, viii. 168
—Ming, viii. 177, 178, 179
—Shên ("Spirit of Vacuity"), viii. 56–57
— -t'ung Mountain, viii. 22
Kuni-toko-tachi, viii. 378 [2]
Kuntī, wife of Sūrya, and mother of Pāṇḍavas, vi. 138, 149, 155
Kunugi, kind of oak, viii. 339
Kuo, Duke of, viii. 166
—Ai of T'ang Dynasty, viii. 179–180
—Chü, viii. 163–164
—Chü-yeh, viii. 161
—Kung, viii. 140
—P'o, viii. 140, 141
—Shang, patriot who died for country, viii. 91
—Shou-ching, viii. 142
—Tzŭ-i, general, viii. 96, 179, 180
Kuova-manno, February moon, iv. 226
Kupalo, iii. 313–314
Kura, tale of, ix. 74–75
— -waka, image of man made at, ix. 25
Kurama Mountain, monastery on, viii. 309
Kurdalägon, Ossete divine smith, iii. 361 [90]
Kurds, origin of, vi. 320
Kurgal ("great mountain"), title of Enlil, v. 213
Kuribu, v. 396 [57]
—Karubu, Karibu, mythical being of Ea, image of, v. 108
Kurios ouranou identified with Helios, v. 64
Kurita, chestnut of, viii. 339
Kūrkura, vi. 98
Kurm, vii. 19

Kūrma, avatar of Viṣṇu, vi. 104
Kurozaemon, crow, viii. 334
Kurrashurur, god, v. 128
Kurukṣetra, home of Nāgas, vi. 154
Kurukullā, vi. 218
Kururumany, Arawak creator of men, xi. 259, 272
Kurus, overthrow of, vi. 125
Kurusakahiby, xi. 308–309
Kuśa and Lava, children of Sītā, vi. 128
Kusa-nagi ("grass mower"), miraculous sword, viii. 304
Kusarikku ("fish-ram"), conception of form of Enki as, v. 105, 106
Kusariqqu ("the Fish-man"), dragon, constellation Capricorn, v. 283
Kûsh, v. 55
Kushkan, son of over-god, iv. 402
Kuśīlava, wandering minstrels, vi. 128
Küsle, stringed instrument, to the accompaniment of which priests pray, iv. pl. xxxv, opp. p. 274
Küs-oto, sacrifice-grove, iv. 262
Kusu-no-ki, camphor-tree, tale of, viii. 347–348
Kut, soul, happiness, health, etc., iv. 463, 472
Kutar, king of Phoenicians, v. 340
Kutīya, etc., names for Christmas Eve, iii. 307
—food on Christmas Eve, iii. 307–308, 310
Kutku, god of Heaven, iv. 330
Kutsa, seer, vi. 65, 67
Kutywa, death of Shwe Pyin Nāts at, xii. 351
Kuvan Pas, iv. 158
Kuzimu, Underworld, vii. 118, 181, 195
Kuzu-no-ha, fox who married warrior, viii. 333
Kvasir, man created from saliva and possessed of great wisdom, ii. 26, 53, 146
—slain by dwarfs, ii. 265
Kveldrida ("night-rider"), ii. 300
Kveldulf accused Norns of taking Thorolf, ii. 240
—("Evening Wolf"), Ulf called, ii. 292–293
Kwammang'a in rainbow, vii. 289, 290
Kwang-loi-vu'o'ng, title given to Caobien by King Thaitōn, xii. 318–319
Kwang-vu, Emperor, had To-dinh imprisoned, xii. 313

Kwannon, goddess of mercy, prayed to, viii. 310, 358
Kwei Chi, viii. 183–187
Kweku Anansi, son of Spider, vii. 323
Kyanyittha, King of Pagăn, xii. 344
Kyatpyin (centre of ruby mines district of Burma), shattering of Thusandi's third egg at, is the origin of rubies and precious stones, xii. 277
Kyawzwa dies and becomes a Năt, xii. 354
Kyazimba, tale of, vii. 233
Kybäi-Khotun, mother of "Lonely Man," iv. 354, 358
Kybele, earth-goddess, vii. 12
Kydonia, city of Crete, i. 64
Kyklopes and Typhon, i. 267
—forge trident of Poseidon, i. 211
—Hephaistos and Athene instructors of, in their trade, i. 207
—killed by Apollo, i. 280
—Odysseus at country of, i. 136
—one-eyed, incarnation of disk of sun, i. 332 9 (ch. xii)
—("powers of the air"), born of Ouranos and Gaia, i. 6, 272
—see also CYCLOPS.
—slain by Apollo in revenge for Asklepios, i. 107
—smiths of Zeus, i. 159–160
Kyknos and Herakles separated by thunderbolt of Zeus, i. 87
——Tennes, story of, parallel to that of Bellerophon and Stheneboia, i. 325 15
—son of Ares, i. 190

Kyknos, son of Ares, waylays Delphian pilgrims, but slain by Herakles, i. 94
Kyllene in Arkadia, birthplace of Hermes, i. 192
—sea-nymph, i. 20
—temple of Hermes of, erected by Lykaon, i. 20
Kyn-fylgja, family guardian-spirit, ii. 235, 236
Kynon, iii. 191
Kynopolis, Anupet female form of Anubis at, xii. 131
Kynthos, Apollo on, Mt., i. 175
Kynyr Keinvarvawc, Kei passed as offspring of, iii. 198
Kyöde jielle, Russian Lapland god, iv. 159
Kyögen, farces, viii. 360
"Kypria," epic, i. 124–126, 326 2 (ch. viii)
Kyrene, Artemis identified with, i. 184
—conveyed to Africa in chariot drawn by swans, i. 180
—nymph, borne in golden car from Mt. Pelion by Apollo, i. 251
—worship of Athene in, i. 169
Kyrgys-Khan, protective spirit, iv. 405
Kyrios Christos, v. 341
Kysagan-Tengere, spirit of ninth heaven, iv. 406
Kythera, cult centre of Aphrodite, i. 196
—Odysseus sails past, i. 136
Kyūshū, island, viii. 211, 254
Kyzikos, Argo arrives at, i. 110

L

La Bella Marta, i. 319
—fille du roi, vii. 358
—Mort, Dodo called by French, vii. 427 13
—Plata, shrine at, xi. 207
—Route du Ciel, tale, vii. 136, 138, 140
La (Cha) harvest sacrifice, viii. 61
—chia, system of alchemy, viii. 144–145
Labaṣu, devil, v. 362, 364
Labat, Père, xi. 279
Labbu, Labu, dragon, v. 286–288, 303
Labdakos, sorrows of the house of, i. 48–51

Labours: see TASKS.
Labraid, a god, iii. 36, 86–88
—Lamfhada, iii. 175
Labyrinth in Cretan ritual, i. 61–62, 325 1
—of Knossos, i. 62, 65
Laceration of skin at festival after couvade, xi. 38
Lachē and Lachos (Lahmu and Lahamu), v. 291
Lachesis ("singer of the past"), one of the Moirai, i. 284
Lachrymatories, iii. 248
Lacrosse, x. 136–137, 232

Ladder assists dead to ascend to Heaven, xii. 175
—of Heaven, xii. 366 7
—to Heaven, x. 221, 234, 255, 257, 300 49
Ladders, Heaven-reaching, vii. 136, 266, 268; see also ASCENTS TO, OR DESCENTS, ETC.
Ladies in Romantic stories having names of flowers, seasons, etc., viii. 297, 300, 301, 302, 382 6 (ch. v)
Ladle, handle of, turns with sun, iv. 350
Ladon, river, i. 81
Ladru's Wave, iii. 89
Lady Abundance-Jewel, tale of, viii. 266
—of Brilliancy, tale of, viii. 262, 360
——Mt. Sano, genius of spring, viii. 349
——Rock-perpetuity, viii. 232
——T'ai Shan, viii. 70
——the Beasts, origin and statue of, i. pl. XLII, opp. p. 182, 184
——Fountain, Welsh tale, iii. 191
——Lake (Nimue), in Arthurian tradition, Morrígan resembles, iii. 67
——-Who-Makes-the-Trees-Bloom, viii. 213, pl. IX, opp. p. 232, 233, 234, 257
——-Weaves-the-Brocade, viii. 213, 234, 379 17
—Yaye-zakura, tale of, viii. 347–348
Læ, giant, Hler may be, ii. 173
Laeg, visitor to Elysium, iii. 128
Lærad, tree, ii. 204, 330, 333, 335
Laërtes, Odysseus said to be son of, i. 37, 123
Lævateinn, sword, ii. 136, 149
Lagash, Bau wife of Ningirsu at, v. 14
—image of six-headed ram in the portico of " gate of battle " at, v. 129
—Ninurta called Ningirsu at, v. 116, 117, 126
Laguna de Términos, xi. 131
Lahama-abzu, god, v. 152
Lahamu, v. 92
—dragon of Tiâmat, v. 282, 291
Lahar, goddess of sheep, v. 191, 193
—mother-goddess, v. 313
Lahmu and Lahamu created, v. 92
——first pair of gods of order, v. 291, 293, 298, 299
—god, v. 154
—image of, v. 108

Lahmu of the Sea, Ea as, v. 103
Lahu, spirit of Kēngtūng, votive offering to, xii. 333
Laikha, elephant-supported pagoda at, xii. pl. XII (A), opp. p. 316
La'i-la'i begotten of Po, ix. 26
Lailaps, dog given to Prokris by Artemis (or Minos), i. 72
Laimos (" Pestilence "), abstract divinity of state of body, i. 282
Laios carried off Chrysippos, son of Pelops, and was cursed, i. 48
—curse of, i. lii
—killed by his son Oidipous, i. 49
—son of Labdakos, banished by Amphion, but later returned, i. 48
—wedded to Iokaste, i. 48
" Lais " of Marie de France, parallel of Connla myth in, iii. 85, 195
Laistrygonians, Odysseus at land of, i. 137
Laitian, ix. 261
Lajnan (" cliff " or " rock "), female worm in creation-myth, ix. 250
Lake, Lakes:
Lake, belief that man issued from, xi. 200
—cauldron obtained from two mystery people of the, iii. 100
—deified as great mother, iv. 413–414
—found where shell of crab from the gourd fell, xii. 291
—goddess washed in secret, ii. 103
—guardian of the, xii. pl. X, opp. p. 302, 303, 305
—healing, horse went into, iii. 128
—holy, by which Seides stood, iv. 101
—made by gods, bathing in, caused grey hair, iii. 169
—new Haltia brought to, iv. 216
—of fire, xii. 180
——flames: see ISLAND OF FLAMES.
——Gems, viii. 117
——life, jackals at, xii. 364 10
——Purification of Millions, name of ocean as holding the lost eye of the sun-god, xii. 89
——-spirits, xi. 184
—survivals of spirits and goddesses of, iii. 133
—whirling, x. 173
Lakes, creation of, iv. 319, 331
—four, as sources of Nile and birthplace of sun, xii. 364 11

Lakes give entrance to spirit-world, vii. 186, 196
—in charge of genius ("shadow"), iii. 228
—personified, vii. 188
—sacred, vi. 235–236; xii. 31, 194
—spoke in time of wars, vii. 188
—subterranean, guarded by water-gods, xii. 89
—synonymous with fields in celestial sense, xii. 416 12
Lakedaimon divided from rest of Peloponnesos and ruled by a Heraklid family, i. 95
—son of Taÿgete by Zeus, i. 11
—Sparta bride of, i. 23
—son of Zeus, i. 157
Laki Oi, fire invented by, ix. 184
Lakonia and Messene, myths of, i. 23–28
Lakṣmaṇa, vi. 127, 128, 225
Lakṣmī, vi. pl. x, opp. p. 118, pl. xi, opp. p. 120, 124, pl. xiii, opp. p. 124, 151, 158, pl. xxi, opp. p. 170
—sacred images of, xii. 327
Lalakoñti, x. 199
Lama, Grand, vi. 216
Lamaitic creation-myth, iv. 328
Lamas, Dalai and Ṭashi, reputed to be incarnations of Bodhisattvas, vi. 209, 210, 213, 218
Lamassu of mercy, v. 358, 365
Lamaštu, demoness, v. 112, 175, 358, 362, 363, 364, 366–371, 416 34
Lamb, golden, Atreus failed to sacrifice, i. 184
——found by Atreus among his flock, i. 120, 326 1 (ch. viii)
Lambs, gravestones in shape of, vii. 95–96
Lambton Worm required milk, vii. 391 16
Lamech = Aradgin = Ardates, Hebrew patriarch, v. 205
— = Lumha, v. 105
—(probably Lumha, title of Enki), descendant of Cain, v. 202
Lameness, cause of, iii. 255
Lament, singing of, iii. 67
"Lamentation of Ch'ung Chêng," viii. 181
—see items s.v. WAILING.
Lamga, lord of the net, v. 349
Lamia, i. 278
—corresponds to Arm. Al, vii. 88

Lamia (Lam-me-a), v. 365, 366, 369, 371
Lamma, lamassu, winged female animals, v. 358, 360
Lammae (Labaṣu), v. 364, 416 34
Lamme: see LAMAŠTU.
Lampetië, daughter of Helios and Neaira, i. 242
—wife of Asklepios, i. 281
Lamps in Śiva's temple, vi. 181
——temple worship, xii. 193
Lamu, vii. 165
Lamyang, language of, xii. 267
Lan Pass, viii. 126
Lan Ts'ai-ho, one of the Eight Immortals, viii. 123, 129
Lance, magic, iii. 199–200, 202, 203, 204
Lancelot, iii. 197, 198
Land, divine, iii. 37–38, 114–123, 182
—enlarged by theft of land, viii. 248–249
—fishing up of, ix. 20, 43
— -gods, iv. 173
—gods', or Elysium, to which living were invited by Immortals, iii. 14, 36, 37, 54, 55, 69, 80–81, 90, 111, 114, 173
—of blessed, v. 223
——Eternity, viii. 230, 378 13
——the Living, iii. 84, 85, 181
——perpetual green of Sea King, viii. 213
——Promise, iii. 29, 63, 64, 65, 67, 89, 116, 118, 121, 128, 151, 173, 175, 177, 210, 213
——Purity, Jōdo is the, viii. 241
—(of Purity, etc., etc.), visited by Wa-Sō, viii. 363–365
——Women, iii. 72, 84–86, 87, 89, 115, 116, 117, 194
——Youth, iii. 180, 181
—under Waves, iii. 120, 173
—use of fire-ritual in claim to, ii. 201
— -vættir, guardian land-spirit, ii. 228, 321
— -water spirit, iv. 462
Landing-stick (wood), Êpet termed the great, 376 79
"Landnáma-bók," ii. 44, 76, 202, 203, 210, 216
Lang, dead body of, changed into betel-tree, xii. 356
—son of Cau, xii. 355
—twins, "Perfect Ones," viii. 113

Lang Ya, viii. 139
Langbard (Odin), ii. 161
Lang-son Hills, battle at, xii. 313
Language, vii. 109, 112, 114, 115, 126–127, 145
—Akkadian, v. 2
—animal, knowledge of, iii. 166
—Armenian, vii. 13–14, 379 [1] (introd.), 380 [9]
—Celtic and aboriginal, iii. 7
—dual, for men and women, xi. 17, 20, 282, 349 [5]
—each created pair had different, x. 219
— -map, Struck's, vii. 114
—no foreign, may be spoken in keremet, iv. 152, 157
—of Chimu, xi. 224
——Lapps and their underground spirits believed to be same, iv. 71
——Lesser Antilles, xi. 17, 20, 349 [5]
—scornful, Odin learned from the dead, ii. 46
—secret, to mislead Master of a place, iv. 471
—sign-, developed on Plains, x. 102
—snake eaten to acquire knowledge of beast-, iii. 166
—tabu, ii. 95, 357 [80]
—Toltec, xi. 107, 108
—Wa, evolution of, xii. 294
Languages, Chin legends of beginning of, xii. 266, 267
—Indo-Chinese, xii. 253–254
Laṅkā = Ceylon, vi. 128, 157, 158, 236
Lāntaka, vi. 227
Lanterns of the dragons, viii. 271
Lanval, knight, fairy fell in love with, parallel of Connla tale, iii. 85
Lan-yein and A-mong, brother and sister ancestors of Karens, xii. 282–284
Lao country, invaders from Turkistan founded brief dynasty in, xii. 287
—Lai-tzŭ, viii. 164
—Ngu tricks first two Shan kings and becomes Governor of Mithilā, xii. 275
—origin of, xii. 277
—Siamese Shans, and Hka-chè, tradition of brotherhood of, xii. 296
— -Tai carry Mahāyāna to Burma and Siam, xii. 260
—Tan, viii. 113

Lao Tzŭ philosophic founder of Taoism, viii. 8, 9, 10, 13, 14, 16–24, 52, 53, 54, 56, 59–60, 94, 103, 105, 106, 110, 112, 119–120, 129, 134, 144, 189
Laodameia, grief of, on death of Protesilaos, i. 126
Laokoon detects ruse of wooden horse of Troy, but, with his sons, is crushed to death by two serpents from the sea, i. 132
Laomedon, king of Troy, i. 85
—slain by Herakles, i. 91, 118
—son of Ilos, i. 118
Laos, prototypes of Malay perhaps to be sought among wilder tribes of, ix. 244
Lapis lazuli, celestial origin of, xii. 367 [12]
——Rê"s hair of, xii. 74
Lapithai besiege Dorians, i. 94
Lapiths and Centaurs, i. pl. xxvi, opp. p. 100
—outrage of Centaurs on women of the, i. 105, 270
Lappers of " Ara " or " brave men " or ever-lappers, vii. 90
Lapps, vii. 114
—belong anthropologically to different race than Finns, iv. xvi, xvii
—Finnish loan-words among the, iv. xvi
—language of, held to be Finno-Ugric, iv. xvi
—religious beliefs and usages of, largely of Teutonic influence, iv. xviii–xix
Lara and Mercury, parents of Lares, i. 299
Larak, city of Pabilhursag, v. 206, 207
Larches, iv. 490
Lares, i. 298–299
—and Genius, i. pl. lx, opp. p. 290
——Penates, xi. 39–40, 224
—represented by Lassi in modern Romagnola, i. 317
Laronda, barrack-spirit, represents Larunda in modern Romagnola, i. 317
Larunda represented by Laronda in modern Romagnola, i. 317
Larvae, men came out of ground as, ix. 169
Lasciviousness, serpent symbol of, viii. 332
Lash, Apollo presents Hermes with, to control cattle, i. 193

Lassi modern representatives of Lares in Romagnola, i. 317

Last Judgement, v. 147, 148

—word, one having, prevails, ix. 118

Lat, occurrence of Ba'al Shamîn with goddess, v. 64

Latarak and Etalak stood at gate of sunrise, v. 134

Látawci, souls of unbaptised children become, after seven years, iii. 254

Latin America, use of term, xi. 1–2

Latinus, child of Hercules, i. 303

—son of Faunus, grandson of Saturn, i. 306

Latium, Aeneas arrives at, i. 306

—Ianus arrives at, i. 297

Latmos, Mt., in Karia, i. 245

Latoere, creator-god, ix. 176

Laufey (or Nal), giantess, mother of Loki; also a peasant, ii. 139, 140, 148

Laughing Buddha, viii. 194

—folk of Isle of Joy, iii. 115

Laughter, ix. 274, 275, 279, 281, 283, 284, 293

—of Skadi, ii. 103, 141

— -strain, magic, played on harp by Lug, iii. 29

—tempting wayfarers on way to moon to, x. 8

Laurel, Daphne changed into, i. 16

—dark spots on moon, viii. 339

— -tree guards sanctuary in rites at Eleusis, i. pl. L, opp. p. 230

——sacred to Apollo, i. 180–181, 182

— -wood, Hermes invented fire by rubbing pieces of, i. 192

Laurus nobilis (êru), branch of, supposed to aid in child-birth, v. 97

Lava, vi. 128

Lavinia according to prophecy to marry Aeneas, i. 306

Lavinium, city founded in Latium by Aeneas, i. 306

Law, vi. 12, 109

—code of, received by Minos from Zeus, i. 64

— -court of Osiris, assessors in, xii. 141

— -givers, vi. 225–226

—international, Hermes important in early stages of, i. 194

—of Babylon revealed to Hammurabi by Shamash, v. 150

——limitation, Etruscan, revealed to Arruns Veltymnius by Begoë, i. 289

Law, tale of Charlemagne's demand to be told of Frisian, ii. 163–164

Laws given for earth-people, x. 258

—of Arallû defied by Gilgamish, v. 264

——Canute, ii. 198, 201, 293

—School of, viii. 8

Lawson, J. C., criticism of " Modern Greek Folklore and Ancient Greek Religion " of, i. 311

Laxha, deity, x. 252

Laying of ghosts, ii. 308, 309

—on of hands, by Odin, before war, ii. 58

lCam-sriṅ, war-god, vi. 214

" Leabhar Gabála," iii. 36, 38, 42

—na hUidre, iii. 79, 80, 81, 82, 164, 165

Lead in ritual of destruction of Namuci, vi. 97

Leaflet Tengu, viii. 288; see also TENGU, ETC.

League, x. 52

—triple, xi. 128

Leander (Leandros) and Hero, i. 201–202

Leannan sighe, fairies who befriend mortals when human powers fail, iii. 65

Leap, Glaukos's, i. 261

Lear, iii. 106

Learchos, son of Athamas, killed by father through mad delusion, i. 46

Leash which alone could hold Little Dog of Greit, iii. 199

Leaves, rustling, in divination, vii. 12

—talking, of tree of life, iv. 351

—withered, Sumerians recognized dead body of Tammuz in, v. 349, 350

Lebadeia in Boiotia, Trophonios (Hades) dispensed oracles in his cave at, i. 234

Lebanons, v. 39, 145, 400 [154]

—cedar mountain probably the, v. 252, 255

Leda at home, i. pl. XLIX, opp. p. 224

—daughter of Thestios, wife of Tyndareos, i. 24

—wife of Zeus, i. 157

Ledimo cannibal, vii. 414 [24]

" Le Gambadeur de la Plaine," translation of " Matlangua wa libala," tale of, vii. 278

Le-Loi, founder of later Le Dynasty, becomes king by gaining magic sword, xii. 302–303

Leechcraft, ii. 280
—Diancecht divinity of, iii. 28
Leeches consulted by gods, iii. 30
Leg-bands of Carib women, xi. 37
—birth from woman's, ix. 113
Legal Code of Manchu Dynasty, viii. 156
—problem stories, vii. 359
Legends and myths, xii. 263–322
—Celtic, must contain remnants of aboriginal mythology, iii. 7
—growth of, viii. 245–255
—Hebrew national, v. 74
—local, viii. 244–255
—of Minamoto and Taira clans, historical background of, viii. 307–308
——Old World gain footing in New, xi. 20
——Tammuz and St. George compared, v. 338
—similarity of universal, xii. 357
Lei deified as protector of wayfarers, viii. 82
—Chên K'on, viii. 155
—Yu-chung, Wên Ch'ang appeared to General, viii. 112
Leib-olmai, Alder-man, iv. 175–176, pl. XXVII, opp. p. 224
Leiden Plate, xi. 130
Leif the Lucky discovered and named Vinland, x. 1
Leikn, Thor broke leg of, ii. 91
Leil, Esthonian coul, iv. 7
Leinster, recovery of wife of King Mongan from King of, iii. 59, 64
Leira, Ull and Frey worshipped on two hills near, ii. 158
Leire (Hleidra), ii. 181
Lekek, Hungarian soul, iv. 7
Leland, C. G., criticism of "Etrusco-Roman Remains" of, i. 316
Lelegia, country named for Lelex, i. 23
Lelex, first man and first king of Lakonia, i. 23
Lelimo (Izimu), vii. 120
Lemnos chief volcanic centre of Hephaistos, i. 207
—men on Argo beguiled to linger at, i. 109–110
—sight of Orion restored on, i. 251
Lén Linfiaclach, cerd of god Bodb, Creidne may be compared with, iii. 31–32
Lena, grandson of MacDáthó, iii. 125

Lenaia (feast of wild women), January festival in honour of Dionysos, i. 221
Length of periods of time, v. 166
Lengthening of bodies by spirits: see TREES, SPIRITS APPEAR AS TALL AS.
Lenni-Lennapi, x. 21
Lent, abjuration of Devil in, vii. 381 [5] (ch. ii)
—water-spirit as musician may be approached on eve before, iv. 206
Leo (Ugallu, dragon), is, v. 282, 286
Leochares, sculpture of, representing Ganymedes and the eagle, i. pl. LII, opp. p. 242
Leontocephalous goddess, Menehtet a, xii. 136
Leopard, vii. 144, 200, 201, 252–256, 284, 336, 337, 346, 406 [7], 428 [11]
—totem, vii. 272, 275
Leopard's skin priestly costume of Sekha(u)it, xii. 53, 193
Leprosy, vi. 183
—Meleagros may have been demon of, i. 182
—Min Shwe Thè afflicted with a kind of, xii. 276
—sent by devil on slothful followers, vii. 371
Ler, children of, changed into swans, iii. 51, 59, 104
—Irish sea-god, iii. 40, 51, 73, 99, 102, 121, 174
Lerne, connexion of springs of, with myth of Danaïds cannot be original, i. 31, 32
—springs of, revealed by Poseidon to Amymone, i. 213
"Les Trois Vaisseaux," vii. 358
Lesbos and Chios, Phaon ferryman between, i. 200
Lesches of Lesbos author of "Little Iliad," i. 131
Lěšiy, Lěsovik, silvan spirit in animal or human form, iii. 261–266; iv. 177
Lesní Ženka may formerly have corresponded to Meschamaat, iii. pl. XXX, opp. p. 260
Lesser gods in Eddic mythology, ii. 151–166
Lethe, river (of forgetfulness) of Hades, i. 143
—Seat of, Theseus and Peirithoös bound to, by Hades, i. 105

Lethet Oidni, síd of, iii. 119
Leto and Artemis associated at childbirth, i. 185
———set Orion among the stars, i. 250
—daughter of Koios and Phoibe, i. 174–175
—mother of Apollo and Artemis, i. 174
—Niobe offended, i. 44
—parallelism in birth of Buddha to myth of, vi. 194
—wife of Zeus, i. 156
Letter of Uso-dori, interpretation of, viii. 334–335
Letters, School of, viii. 8, 9
Lettic god, vi. 31
Letto-Slavic character of Armenian language, vii. 380 9
Letts and Lithuanians akin to Slavs, iii. 317
—associated sun with celestial tree, vii. 49
Lettuce, Hebe child of Hera and a leaf of, i. 241
Lè-twin Mingala, Ploughing Festival at Mandalay, xii. 328
Leuke, Elysion identified with island of, i. 147
Leukippos, father of Koronis, i. 279
—son of Perieres and Gorgophone, i. 24
Leukothea, double of Aphrodite, i. 198
—(Ino), i. 261–262
———"White Sea-Spirit," marine goddess, i. 46
—likeness of Roman Mater Matuta to, i. 290
Leukothoë, wife of Helios, i. 242
Levarcham, prophetess, iii. 142, 153
Level Earth, xi. 176
Leviathan, v. 134
Leza, vii. 116, 126, 132, 133, 162, 179, 239, 316, 426 20
Lha-sa, vi. 208
Li, viii. 14, 49
—district, viii. 131
—Chi, viii. 183–187
—Chih-ch'ang, viii. 190
—Erh, viii. 18
—Hsü-chung, astrologer, viii. 143
—Hun, ceremonialist, viii. 91
—Hung-chang ordered to make sacrifice to tortoise, viii. 100
—Ki, viii. 61, 68, 69, 76, 98, 109, 135, 140
—Ku killed, viii. 193

Li Kung-lin, artist, painter of "Nine Songs," viii. 88
—Sao, viii. 85–91
—Shao-chün, viii. 75, 145, 146
—Shê, place where worship paid to god of soil, viii. 62
—Shih-min, viii. 14
—Ssŭ, viii. 10
—su, viii. 143
—T'ieh-kuai, one of Eight Immortals, viii. 119–122, 124
—Tzŭ-ch'êng captured Peking, viii. 181–182
—Ying, viii. 174
Liang Dynasty, viii. 188
—i, Apex evolved the two principles, viii. 136
"Liao Chai Chih I," viii. 156
Liath loved Bri, iii. 91
—Luchra, protector of Fionn in childhood, iii. 165
Liban, Irish goddess, iii. 36, 56, 73, 86, 90, 194, 208
Libations, ii. 117; v. 248, 249
—withheld from dead by Merope, i. 38
Liber first arose as epithet of Iuppiter, i. 292
—has disappeared from folk-belief of modern Romagnola, i. 318
"Liber Hymnorum," hymn and gloss of, on saints, iii. 13
Libera equated with Korē, i. 292
Liberalism, viii. 8, 9, 10, 11, 19, 194
Libombo forest, Chief of, vii. 191, 192
Libra, xi. 98
—Hayk older name for zodiacal sign, vii. 65
—station of Ninurta-Mars and house of Saturn, v. 305, 410 31
Librarian of the gods, Sekha(u)it as, xii. 52
Lîbu ("ague"), v. 163
Libya, Amon becomes chief deity in, xii. 241
—Apollo and Kyrene wedded at, i. 251
—Argo driven by gale to, i. 113
—became a desert, i. 244
—Danaos sovereign of, i. 30
—Menelaos touches at, i. 134
Libyan, Neith of Saïs and Ash not truly, xii. 410 1
Libyans, Ḥat-ḥôr goddess of, xii. 410 1
—Neith patroness of all, xii. 142
Libye, intrigue of Poseidon with, i. 211

Lice on infant's head "its soul," vii. 417 [22]

Lichen, forest-spirit has coat of, iv. 184

Licho, evil Dolya, iii. 252

Licking wounds to heal them, vii. 90, 395 [58]

Licko, Polyphemos appears in Russian folk-lore as, vii. 369

Lie, house of, darkness distinguishing feature of, vii. 397 [7]

Lieh, mountain birthplace of Shên Nung, viii. 30

Lieh Hou, Empress, viii. 76

—Hsien Chuan, viii. 94, 106

—Tzŭ, viii. 19, 28, 54, 117, 133

—Tzu, a classic, viii. 133, 134

Liekkiö, spirit, iv. 82

Lien, daughter of Dao-ly, wife of Tan, xii. 356

—transformed into betel vine, xii. 356

—hua, viii. 105

— -shan, the "connexion system," viii. 137

Lif and Lifthrasir, human pair, ii. 168, 338, 341, 346

Life after death, xii. 173–183

——bedrock fact of Bantu and Negro religion, vii. 179

—and death, viii. 221–224; x. 6, 10–12

——tree of, iv. 383

—aster-scented wine and kite-flying associated with lengthening of, viii. 131

—beyond, iv. 72–82

—breath, viii. 140

—ceremony of birth of, x. 92

—continuity of, viii. 217–218

—control of Lachesis over, i. 284

—cord of, v. 398 [101]

—created from the eye of the sun, xii. 30

— -cult, triple mysteries of a, iii. 204, 205

—deity of, iii. 355 [44]

—elixir of, viii. 103, 144, 145, 202

——(white) of, iv. 415

—eternal bestowed on dead by Ḥat-ḥôr, xii. 39

——bread and water of, v. 94, 95, 97, 178, 181, 184

——Gilgamish seeks, v. 214

——Osiris as lord of, xii. 93, 97

—fire emblem of, x. 46–47

—fountain of, often identified with source of Nile, xii. 177

Life, future, vi. 344–347; vii. 69, 390 [14]

—given by devil to God-created man, iv. 377

—heat of, Esmoun (Eshmun) so called because of, v. 74

—Heaven as giver of, iv. 397

—in sky parallels life on earth, iv. 400

—Indian tree of, iv. 356, 357, 359

—lake of, xii. 364 [10]

—length of child's, determined by distance between knot and staff on birth thread, iv. 260

—of dead, manner of, iv. 483

——King Mu, viii. 116, 117

—plant of, v. 97, 98–99, 188, 210, 234, 328, 333; vii. 69, 390 [14]; xii. 97 (fig. 89), 112, 296, 297

—pool of, vi. 87

—powers of, xi. 74–79

—prolongation of, viii. 29, 146–147

—red colour of, x. 93

—restoration of, i. 62–63, 119, 281; iii. 93, 347 [61]; vi. 178; vii. 68, 69, 90, 390 [14], 395 [58]; 158–159, 163, 167, 169, 170, 171, 210, 216, 217, 289–290, 337, 338, 339, 358, 407 [22]; viii. 121, 124, 145, 191, 193; ix. 49, 63, 70, 76, 78, 82, 279; x. 106, 123, 229, 243, 306 [60]; xi. 227

——by Asklepios, i. 280

——bathing in "living waters of Tane," ix. 88

——ghosts after death by slaying, x. 246

——Kaca and Uśanas, vi. 153

——magic cauldron, iii. 100, 101, 104, 105, 112, 203

——medicines, i. 281; vii. 163

——runes, ii. 297–298

——see also DEAD, RAISING OF; RE-VIVIFICATION.

——swine of Manannan to, ii. 51, 94

——Thor's goats to, ii. 92, 94

——to Osiris, xii. 397 [67]

——Poshaiyanne by Eagle, x. 204, 311 [69]

—serpent and sons of Horus guarding, xii. 112 (fig. 115)

— -span, vi. 20, 23

— -spirits of heart, head, etc., received by child through its mother's food in womb, iv. 472

Life, superstition that wood carvings of supernatural beings manifest, x. 244–245
—symbol of, xii. 32 (fig. 14)
—symbolized by water and vegetation, vii. 382 [23]
— -time writing man one name of Heaven-god, iv. 409
— -token, ix. 133, 234–235, 339 [46]
——cup of Hymir reminiscent of, ii. 87
——in Meleagros-legend, i. 56, 58
— -tokens, and tales in which they occur, ii. 241, 242
—tree of: see items s.v. TREE OF LIFE.
—(Tšon), Cheremiss, iv. 4
—water and plant of, Osiris guards and is often identified with, xii. 97
——of, iv. 354, 357, 358, 359, 424, 494; v. 178, 180, 184, 188, 328, 334; ix. 174, 252–253; x. 22; xii. 46
—Živa goddess of, iii. pl. XXXIV, opp. p. 288
Lifting power, rainbow as, iv. 444
Light, vi. 33, 34, 55, 137, 138; 263–274, 288, 295; viii. 37, 111, 137; ix. 6, 34, 162, 275; x. 9, 22, 35, 39, 45, 104, 116, 166–167, 206, 230–233, 256, 260, 294 [42], 296 [45]; xi. 51, 86, 89, 161, 199
—and darkness, combat between, basis of myth of Ninurta and Zû, v. 282, 286
——contests of, v. 130, 302, 304
——day-light, Shamash god of, v. 150, 151–152
——Life, Buddha of Infinite, viii. 241
—Apollo as god of, i. 177
—Babylonian god of, carries short spear with three points at each end, xii. 397 [101]
—birth of god of, viii. 226
—created, iv. 419, 420
—crystal symbolizes, x. 284 [27]
—descending ray of, as fructifying agent in birth, iv. 398
—from gold, ii. 172, 314
——mane of boar of Frey, ii. 109
——rotted trees only in Underworld grottoes, iv. 487
——swords in Valhalla, ii. 314
—given to world, vii. 144
—Heimdall may be god of, ii. 154
—History of the Great, viii. 54
—Inue at times appear in form of, x. 5, 8

Light, Mithra genius of, vii. 33
—or fire at child-birth, vii. 394 [50]
—phenomenon, iv. 336
—phoenix symbol of, xii. 413 [17]–414
—shines from Balder, ii. 129
—Sisyphos interpreted as god of, i. 38
—soul associated with, vii. 94
—source of, disappeared, viii. 226–227
—springs of, healing springs, vii. 59
Lighthouse destroyed by storm, tale of, viii. 255
Lighting world from glowing matter, ii. 196
Lightning, ii. 79, 80, 81, 148; iii. 319, 322; iv. 227, 228, 238; vi. 15, 36, 37, 38, 43, 44, 47, 62, 64, 132, 135, 234; 264, 283, 285, 291, 361 [30]; vii. 50, 387 [1], 392 [21], 392 [24]–393; 119, 126, 140, 237, 238, 239, 411 [43]; ix. 59, 250, 255; x. pl. XVI, opp. p. 84, 109–112, 116, 138, 162, 165, 188, 231, 281 [19], 288 [32], 294 [42], 300 [50]; xi. 68, 121, 161, 246, 295
—Agni associated with, vii. 46, 386 [11]
—and thunderbolt, Pegasos bearer of, i. 34
— -bird, vii. 237
—caused by thunderbird, iv. 439, 440
—Christian Armenian successor of Aramazd hurls, vii. 381 [6]
—creator of, iii. 277
— -doctors, vii. pl. XXII, opp. p. 230
—form of fire, vii. 44
— -god had place in Thracian religion, vii. 15
—god of, v. 39
——Vahagn-Hyagnis originally a, vii. 34, 44, 46, 365
—Indra god of, vii. 43, 44
— -makers, x. 191
—raising of house struck by, iv. 445–446
—" Sharpshooter god " an ancient god (?) of, iv. 406
—spear of Horus, xii. 104
—strikes places where evil or filth hidden, iv. 400
—striking of, creates a sacred person and place, iv. 445
—thunderbolts talismans against, iv. 443
— -worship, Slavic, vii. 15
—Zeus god of, i. 159

Lightning (a beast like black leopard), primeval animal, vii. 144

Lights (Aurora Borealis), fight of, iv. 287

—confining and liberating of heavenly, iv. 421

—mysterious, seen at sea, viii. 271

—of Heaven made of sparks from Muspell, ii. 343

—over marshlands, viii. 384 16

—to lead one astray, iv. 468

Ligi and Aponibolinayen, tale of, ix. 232–235

Ligiršagkušašša, title of Marduk, v. 310

Lignum vitae trees upholding the earth, Chibchachum made to take place of, xi. 203

Ligoapup sister of Olofat, ix. 251, 258

Ligobund, female deity, commanded trees, etc., to grow on earth, ix. 248, 250

Lihlanga, reed; nhlanga, reed bed, vii. 146

Lihyanians, Ilāt probably sun-goddess among, v. 15, 379 26

Likeness, appearing in another's, iii. 56, 63, 80, 82, 184, 201; vi. 67

—between Fionn and Arthur, iii. 185

Likymnios, natural son of Elektryon, i. 76

Lil and Nintur, myth of, v. 131

—god, v. 113, 114, 131

Lil, Ostiak soul, iv. 7

Lili, Vogul soul, iv. 7

Lîlîth, Armenian and Persian Al corresponds somewhat to, vii. 88

—as child destroyer, v. 363

—demoness, v. 353, 361, 362

—Elle-folk children of, ii. 224

—in Judaism and Christianity, v. 363

Lilîtu (Ardat Lillî), demoness of the wind, v. 362, 365

Lilla, fool, v. 234

Lillu, son of Mah, v. 114

Lilû, Lillû, Babylonian demon, v. 361–362, 364, 414 32, 416 25

——man, v. 112, 275, 396 66

Lily, viii. 385 7

Lima, xi. 224–225

Limbo of infants, xi. 83, 94

Lime, Udibwa's face smeared with, xii. 350

Limestone in betel-vine legend, xii. 355–357

Limos ("Famine"), abstract divinity of state of body, i. 282

Lin Yüan, viii. 72

Linden-tree, Philyra changed into, i. 16

Lindgadan, story of, iii. 133

Linen bound on head of sacrificial victim, iv. 255, 256

——goddess (Menkhet), xii. 136

—hung on trees at Whitsuntide sacrifice to water-nymphs (Rusalky), iii. 254

—white, placed in passage as invitation to Domovoy to join family meals, iii. 242

—woven by water-nymphs causes weakness and lameness if walked on by man, iii. 255

"Ling Ch'ien Shu," viii. 138

—Pao popular name of Tao Chün, viii. 109

—Ti, viii. 174

Linga worship, vi. 119, 178–179; see also items s.v. PHALLIC; PHALLICISM.

Linguistic divisions of Mexico and Central America, xi. 43, 352 1

—stocks along Pacific coast, x. 212–213

——of Honduras and Nicaragua, xi. 183

———North America, x. 75

———North-west coast, x. 237–238

———Pueblo tribes, x. 183

———South America, xi. 256, 371 3

Linh-lanh (Pagode Balny), Temple of, believed to stand on head of dragon, xii. 310

——Temple, spirits of, aid Ministers of State in debate, xii. 319

Linos, i. 252–253

—teacher on zither of Herakles, by whom he is killed, i. 79

Lion, iv. 360

—as symbol of 'Ate, v. 36

———sun, v. 60

—attended Kybele, i. 275

—Chimaira compounded of dragon, goat, and, i. 39

—double, Aker as, xii. 42, 43, 169; single, xii. 90, 368 22, 369 (fig. 221)

—Ḥar-ḥekenu often has body of, xii. 388 28

—hawk-headed, xii. 24, 29

—"Horus in Three Hundred" sometimes depicted as composed of, and other animals, xii. 388 28

Lion, " Horus of Mesen(?) " has head of, xii. 388 [28]
—kept at Leontopolis for god Shu, xii. 164
—Khnûm on back of, xii. 369 [22]
—killed by Herakles on slopes of Kithairon, i. 79
—Labbu used for, v. 287
—man-eating, x. 72
—Nefer-têm in form of, xii. 141
—Nergal as single, xii. 368 [22]
—of Nemea, i. 80, pl. xxi, opp. p. 76
———skin of, as protective cloak, i. 81
—old mediaeval story of the, vi. 212
—one of the Merets had head of a, xii. 137
—or leopard with serpent's neck, xii. 64, 65, 169
—probably Ugallu, v. 278, 283
—(shih), why symbol for teacher, viii. 104
—south wind has head or body of, xii. 65 and fig. 71
—winged, v. 279, 280, 396 [42]
Lioness, animal form of Tefênet and Sekhmet, xii. 29
—Men'et a, xii. 101
—sun's eye in form of, xii. 86
Lions, vii. 215, 216, 230, 236, 284, 292, 319-320, 323, 337, 344, 425 [20]
—(Aker) as " the morning " and " yesterday " in commentaries, xii. 43
———carry two mountains between which sun rises, xii. 43
———confused with Shu and Tefênet, xii. 43
———represented seated in bushes (the horizon) or as sustaining sky, xii. 43 and fig. 37
—as traditional guardians of temple, xii. 414 [21]
—depicted with Artemis in art, i. 186
—Enkidu in conflict with, v. 237-238
—Melanion and Atalante changed into, i. 59
—Shu and Tefênet represented as, xii. 43, 87 (fig. 78)
Lipit-Ishtar, v. 327, 346
Lips of Gwevyl, iii. 190
Liquor, xi. 77, 113
—ocean derived from amniotic, ix. 37
—poured on ground at health drinking in honour of spirits, iv. 39

Liquor, pouring of, for heroes, ii. 122
Lirufu: see LUFU.
Lise, sister of Kapapitoe, ix. 210-213
Lisi dialectic for Nesu, god, v. 110
Lisp, Spider speaks with, vii. 324
Litai (" Prayers "), abstract divinities of social institution, i. 282
Litanies, v. 88
Litaolane, tale of, vii. 220-222
Literature based on mythology in Ireland and Wales, iii. 7
—compilation of, viii. 245
—of Mexico, xi. 352 [3]-354
Lithuanian loan-words found among the Mordvins, iv. xvi, xix
Lithuanians, Baltic Finns in close contact with, iv. xix
Litr, dwarf whom Thor kicked into Balder's funeral pyre, ii. 130, 265
Little Bear, iv. 425-426
———God C perhaps identified with, xi. 139
—Dog of Greit, iii. 199
—Fawn: see OISIN, ETC.
—Iliad narrates siege of Troy, i. 131
—People (Bushmen or Pygmy): see DWARFS (vol. vii).
—people, souls in Heaven resemble, iv. 488
—Star, son of the Moon, x. 114
—Vehicle: see HĪNAYĀNA.
Liturgical formula into which names of five kings of Ur are cast, v. 345
Liturgies, v. 88
Liturgy, Ethiopic, possible survival of Egyptian sacred number forty-two in, xii. 416 [8]
Lityerses (" Prayer for Dew "), i. 253-254
Liu, viii. 113
—An: see HUAI-NAN TZŬ.
—Chih, viii. 168
—Hsia-hui, viii. 168
—Hsiang, viii. 55
—Hsiao-hsiang adopts Kwei Chi, viii. 183, 184
—Hung impersonated Chên, viii. 191, 192, 193
—Pang, military leader, viii. 92-93
—Pei, viii. 94, 95, 174, 175, 176, 177
—pu, viii. 45
—Shu, viii. 58
—Ssŭ Ch'in, viii. 183
—Sung Dynasty, viii. 188

Liu Tsung ("Six Honoured Ones"), viii. 51

Liuflingar, elves called, ii. 223

Liver of elephant eaten by those it had swallowed, vii. 199, 313

——Liu Hung burned, viii. 193

——mothers, food of Als, vii. 88, 369

——ox, eating of, makes ancestors of Hereros black, vii. 150

—tabu in some nomes, xii. 362 ³

Livers of captives eaten for various reasons, iv. 5

Living, ghosts influenced by, vii. 183

Livonians akin to Finns in linguistic and geographical aspects, iv. xv

Lizard and Kapapitoe, tale of, ix. 210

—as messenger, vii. 163

—created to injure the Gaokerena tree, vi. 281, 288

—poses as chief's daughter, vii. 201

Lizards, vii. 106, 160, 163, 164–165, 171

Ljod, " wish-maid " of Odin, ii. 249

Ljösalfar (" light elves "), ii. 221

Llacheu, son of Arthur, iii. 191, 199

Llama, speaking, saved one man from flood, xi. 230

Llapchilulli, xi. 208

Llautu, fringe, symbol of sun's rays, xi. 245

Llech Echymeint, Arthur imprisoned three nights under, iii. 189

Lleu, slaying of Cúroi compared with that of, iii. 152

—took form of eagle, iii. 56, 97

—Llaw Gyffes, twin son of Arianrhod, iii. 96–97, 98, 99

Llevelys, son of Beli, iii. 106

Lloque Yupanqui, third Inca, xi. 244

" Lludd and Llevelys," story of, iii. 107

—as King, rebuilt London (Caer Ludd), iii. 107

—buried serpent and its live opponent after stupification with mead, iii. 130

—father of Cordelia, iii. 103

—Llaw Ereint (" Silver-Hand "), Llyr sometimes confused with, iii. 102–103

—son of Beli, iii. 106

—suggested change from Nudd (for earlier Nodens Lāmargentios), iii. 103

Llwyd, bishop who raised enchantment on Dyfed, iii. 102

Llychlyn, a mysterious country in the lochs or sea, iii. 171

Llyr, family of, iii. 100

—in Welsh literature and Romances, iii. 191

—Half-Speech equivalent of Ler, iii. 102

—Lledyeith, one of the three notable prisoners of Britain, iii. 189

—Marini, Welsh sea-god, iii. 102, 106

—(Shakespeare's Lear), father of Cordelia, iii. 102, 103

" Llyvyr Taliesin," iii. 339 ⁴

Lo River, viii. 33, 35, 38, 43, 100

— -fou, viii. 145

— -han, viii. 196

—hu, viii. 101

—Kuan-chung, viii. 174

— -p'an, compass, viii. 141–142

—shu, origin of, viii. 35

— -yang, viii. 27, 188

Loa, creator being, ix. 248–249

Loaves left for forest-elves, ii. 206, 207

—see BREAD, SACRIFICIAL.

Local cults, preservation of, xii. 217–218

—deities mostly explained ultimately as manifestations of sun, xii. 28

—forms of Horus, xii. 388 ²⁸

—goddesses, frequently identified with Ḥat-ḥôr and solarized, xii. 41

—gods, xii. 15–22, 98

——nearer to man than cosmic gods, xii. 23

Localized, non-cosmic primitive gods develop little mythology, xii. 384 ¹

Loch Bél Draccan (" Lake of Dragon's Mouths "), Caer as bird at, iii. 78

—Gile, tears made, iii. 135

—Guirr, Aine still seen in, iii. 47

——tree in, iii. 138

—Léin, Lén Linfiaclach lived in, iii. 32

—Medb's warrior, iii. 153

—of the Birds, iii. 37

—Riach, white sheep cast into, become crimson, iii. 38

Lochlann, King of, iii. 63, 170, 171

—may have been supernatural region with superhuman people, iii. 171

Lochs and seas, secret of passing under, iii. 134

—origin of, iii. 135–136

Locomotion, seven forms of Platonic, xi. 52

Locust, magic contest of, with Grebes, x. 161
Locusts, vii. 182
—sent to rice-fields by harvest-god, viii. 233
Lodan, son of King of India, iii. 116
Lodbrok, Bragi's song of, ii. 250
Lodderaiddaras, bird's stair = Milky Way, iv. 434
Loddfafnir owes magic knowledge to Odin, ii. 46, 243, 296
Loddiš-edne, bird-mother, iv. 177
Lodens Lāmargentios, suggested change of Nodens Lāmargentios to, iii. 103
Lodge, ceremonial, at Sun-dance festival, x. 89
Lodges, animal, x. 122
—form of, x. 80
—in festivals, x. 57–58, 170
Lodur (Loki), ii. 24, 147, 151, 327
Loeg, Cúchulainn's charioteer, iii. 64, 86–88, 146, 147, 149, 150, 209
Loegaire the Triumphant, son of King of Connaught, iii. 37, 49, 69, 70, 90, 134, 140, 143, 145, 146, 147, 148, 149, 209
Löfjerskor, elves, ii. 226
Lofn, goddess, ii. 15, 174, 185
Lofoden islands, Ran came to fires on, ii. 191
Löfviska, ii. 205
Log, hollow, x. 105, 173, 180, 198; xi. 95
—place occupied by Seeland became water called, ii. 181
—whirling, x. 173
Logi ("Fire"), ii. 92, 93, 94, 147, 280, 281
Logos, creative Word, v. 105
Logres destroyed by Dolorous Stroke, iii. 203
Lohū, "Blood-Red River," vi. 245
Loi Hsao Möng apparently Wa equivalent of Mt. Meru, xii. 290
—Lông Tawng Peng, Min Shwe Thè becomes chief of, xii. 276
—Pu Kao ("Hill which the Crab Entered"), death of Ko Pala in crab incarnation at, xii. 279
Lokapālas, four, in Taoism, viii. 14
—four, vi. 159, 215, 216
"Lokasenna," ii. 10, 15, 49, 56, 60, 73, 75, 90, 91, 93, 101, 105, 124, 128, 139, 140, 141, 142, 145, 146, 153, 161, 171, 172, 174, 178, 220, 336

Lokeśvararāja, one of the Buddhas, vi. 200
Loki (Lopt), god, son of giants, ii. 10, 15, 17, 22, 24, pl. vi, opp. p. 32, 43, 45, 49, 56, 61, 63, 64, 73, 74, 79, 83–84, 87, 88, 89, 90, 91, 92, 93, 94, 95, 100, 101, 102, 103, 105, 110, 112, 121, 123, 124, 127, 128, 129, 131, 134, 139–150, 153, 155, 159, 160, 161, 165, 172, 174, 175, 178, 179, 180, 182, 220, 221, 229, 265, 266–267, 268, 278, 338, 339, 340, 341, 343, 351 [4], 386 [64]
Lokkji, Faroe Island's ballad of, ii. 151
Lokria, Perseus supposed to have been identified with Hermes at Thronion in, i. 36
Lol, Siryan soul, iv. 7
Lombards (Longbeards), legend of, ii. 38
—Wodan and Frija known to the, ii. 18
Lón láith ("champion's light"?), light projecting from Cúchulainn's forehead, iii. 11
Löndaung, village where Shwe Pyin brothers were taken but could not be killed, xii. 350
London, Bran's head buried at, iii. 101
Lonely Man, iv. 353, 354
Long Count, specimen on lintel at Chichen Itza, xi. 129
— -legged-fellow, viii. 211
— -lived personages, iii. 206–207
—wood, name of bow of Marduk, v. 308
Long-do, guardian spirit of Thanh-long, appeared to Cao-bien, xii. 318
—Pagoda to the dragon-spirit erected by Cao-bien, xii. 318
—village; temple of Cao-bien formerly in, xii. 317, 318
"Longes mac nDuil Dermait," iii. 149
"Longes mac nUsnig," iii. 65
Longevity, viii. 104, 105, 265, 278, 280, pl. xxxix, opp. p. 332, pl. xliii–xliv, opp. p. 348, 352
—deities of, viii. 279–280
—god of, viii. 81, 82, 97; see also LIFE, PROLONGATION OF.
—(tho), sign of, carved on altar, xii. 311
—tortoise and crane emblems of, viii. 100, 104

Longevity, trees as symbols of, viii. 104, 105
—wine and kites associated with, viii. 131
Lono, god, ix. 24
Loochoo Islands, Tametomo called first king of, viii. 309
Loom, wandering soul of shaman, iv. 498, 506
Loon Woman, sorcery practised by, x. 228–229
Loosening chains or fetters, ii. 252
Loowit, witch, guardian of bridge, x. 134
Lopamudrā, Agastya created, vi. 146
Lope de Aguirre, soul of, haunts savannahs in form of tongue of flame, xi. 279
Lopmus, Old Man of village, iv. 403
Lord-in-Centre-of-Heaven, viii. 378 2
Lord of Arallû, Nergal and Tammuz have title, v. 351
——the Heavens, v. 63–64, 390 280
——Lebanon, v. 39
——sun, xii. 264, 265
Lords of Day capture those of Night, xi. 153–155
——and Night, xi. 53–54, 55, 56, 100
——Death, hero-brothers triumph over, xi. 170
Lord's Prayer, Indian, x. 153
—Supper, wetting of fingers in liquor before, iv. 38
" Lordship has fallen " refers to death of Tammuz, v. 326
Lorica of Manannan preserved wearer from wounds, iii. 29
Loscuinn, iii. 30
Losy, giant snake of ocean, iv. 345
Lot, v. 153
—wife of, iv. 363
Lothar, one of Three Finns of Emuin, iii. 90, 156
Lothen, giant, ii. 279
Lo-tlhaka, a reed, vii. 402 9
Lots cast for possession of Helen in marriage, i. 25
Lotus, vi. 109, pl. XI, opp. p. 120, 133, 145, 146, 191, 192, 208, 212; viii. 385 7
—blue, birth of sun from, xii. 39
——symbolizes ocean, and sun-god grows in, xii. 50 and fig. 48
— -eaters, Odysseus at land of, i. 136
—Egyptian sun-god associated with, vii. 385 9

Lotus flower, emblem of Nefer-têm, xii. 140
—flowers, viii. 240, 242
—of Truth, Śākyamuni preached the, viii. 241, 242, 297, 332, 336, 344, 385 11
—Serpent ancestor of Raja of Chūtiā Nāgpur; married to Pārvatī, xii. 270–271
—stalk carried by Egyptian goddesses, xii. 13
—symbolic of offspring, viii. 105
— -throne, three Tīrthakaras obtain release on, vi. 222
Louquo, first man, xi. 38–39
Louse answers in place of Ginabai, ix. 229
Loutrophoros, water jar, placed on grave of unmarried, i. 324 9
Love, Aphrodite divinity of, i. 197, 198
—charms and philtres, xii. 205, 423 25
—god of, vi. 174
— -goddess, Asiatic, original of Isis, xii. 120
—Ḥat-ḥôr deity of, xii. 40
—in romantic stories, viii. 293–302
—Ishtar a goddess of, vii. 38, 382 23
—kidneys of bear eaten awaken, iv. 91
—of gods, ii. 22–23
— -philtre given by Nessos to Deianeira, i. 93, 94
— -philtres, ii. 177
—Xochiquetzal goddess of, xi. 77
Lovers, monsters as, xi. 286
—star, viii. 235–237, pl. x, opp. p. 236
—transformed into twin pine-trees, viii. 253–254
Loves of Ishtar, v. 256
Low, Odin made temple at the, ii. 33
Lowalangi, creator god, ix. 176
Lower Egypt, Merḥi worshipped in, xii. 137
Lozva-water, Holy Prince of the, iv. 403
Lu, viii. 104
—ancient Principality of, viii. 11, 29, 70, 168
—ho, system of alchemy, viii. 144–145
—Hsü, viii. 163
—Hsün, viii. 178
—Shêng, viii. 115
—Shih, viii. 142
Lü ceremony, viii. 61
—Mountain, viii. 123
—Shang (Tai Wang Kung), viii. 42

Lü Ts'ai, astrologer, viii. 143
—Tsu, viii. 123
—Tung-pin (also known as Lü Yen, Lü Tsu), one of Eight Immortals, viii. 123, 126, 128
Luagni, clanna, iii. 161, 164
Luang Prabang, festival of the New Year at, xii. 298–300
——limit of Aryan infiltration of Indo-China, xii. 288
Lübeck, iii. 305
Lubumba, the creator, Leza as, vii. 126, 399 7
Luchorpáin, sea-dwarfs, iii. 134
Luchta, carpenter, iii. 32, 33
Luchtine, smith, iii. 31
Lucifer, Devil, ii. 148
—Latin name of planet Venus, i. 247
Luck, iv. 18, 29, 275, 276
—connexion of Hermes with, i. 195
—deities of, viii. 279–280
—demand that corpse leave, with survivors, iv. 29
—earth- or field- may be stolen, iv. 240
——protector (Voršud) lives near sacrifice shelf, iv. 119, 121–122; see also VORŠUD, LUCK-PROTECTOR.
Lud-cult, iv. 143–151
Ludgate Hill, Lludd buried at, iii. 107
Ludki (Lútki), dwarf genii, description and language of, iii. 247–248
Ludzen, Usching worshipped in vicinity of, iii. 330
Luete-muor, sacrifice-tree, iv. 110
Lufu (Lirufu), Death, vii. 174–175, 404 34
Lug, Irish god, iii. 25, 26, 28–29, 30, 31, 32, 33, 34, 40, 41, 55, 56, 65, 82–84, 97, 99, 117, 122, 127, 138, 140, 153, 158, 159, 178, 188, 203
Lugaid, Cúroi's son, called Mac na Tri Con ("Son of the Three Dogs"), iii. 149, 155, 156
—Devorgilla given as wife to, iii. 144
—slaying of, caused battle of Mag Mucrime, iii. 73
—Red-Stripes, son of all Three Finns of Emuin, iii. 90, 156
Lugal (Marduk), v. 274
Lugalbanda (Ninurta) conquered Zû, v. 281, 396 41
——deified ancient king of Erech, god who recovered Tablets of Fate, v. 40, 102, 235, 241, 248

Lugalbanda (Ninurta) given bull's horn, v. 257
Lugaldimmerankia, title of Marduk, v. 311
Lugaldukug, Marduk called, v. 312, 342
Lugalgirra and Meslamtaea, names of Nergal as twin gods, v. 69
—i.e. Nergal as pest-god, v. 49
Lugalkurdub, minor deity in court of Ningirsu, v. 126
Lugalmeslam (king of Underworld), Nergal as, v. 93, 135, 136
Lugh Laebach, wizard sent against sons of Carman, iii. 35
Lugmannair, father of Dil, iii. 67
Lugnasad, Celtic festival (Aug. 1), iii. 99, 138
Lugus, equivalent of Lug in Gaul, iii. 158
Luhräsp: see AURVAṬ-ASPA.
Luhthurar ("fire-bringer"), ii. 147
Lujara Marete, dwarfs, vii. 416 19
Luk, creator of earth, ix. 250–251, 253, 259–262
Lukelang, highest deity, ix. 248, 258
Lul, Votiak soul, iv. 7
Luleå, Seide stones at, iv. 100
Lullaby song, viii. 372
Lulubu, Ishtar on monument of a king of, v. 187
Lumawig in fire tale, ix. 183
Lumbinī grove, Buddha born in the, vi. 194
Lumha, patron of singers, v. 105
Lumimu-ut, female deity born of sweat of rock, ix. 157–158, 165
Luminous beings, people living before the fall, iv. 419
Lun Yü, viii. 16
——Hsün Tz'ŭ, ("Analects"), viii. 10
Lunar myths dubious in Oceania and Polynesia, ix. xiv, 99
Lunarization of divinities rare, xii. 215
Lund-folk, ii. 225
Lundjungfrur ("grove-damsels"), ii. 226
Lung, dragon, viii. 98
—fei, viii. 103
—Lao, one of the "Three Venerable Ones," viii. 109
Lung-fish clan, vii. 130, 155
Lungs of sacrifice buried with bones at memorial feast, iv. 38
——woman taken by evil spirit, iv. 468
Luonnotar, deity of birth, iv. 257

Luot-hozjik, reindeer-goddess, iv. 176

Lupercalia, Zuñi parallel to Roman, x. 196

Lupercus, Faunus in aspect of, i. 293

Lupus (constellation) is dragon Uridimmû, v. 282

Lusin, name of moon, vii. 51

Lustration for building of temple, Marduk's creation of world as introduction to ritual of, v. 312

Lutici, description of rites of Slavic tribe of, iii. 221

Lu'u-huyen, sons of Cau took service with, xii. 355

Luxor, birth-temple at, xii. 414 [29]

Ly, Hill of the Standard of the, xii. 311

Lyada identified with Mars, iii. 301, 355 [44]

Lycanthropy, ii. 291, 294

Lydda (Ludd), St. George born at, v. 337

Lydia, adventures of Herakles in, i. 90

—Anāhita has crescent on head in Persianized, vii. 381 [2] (ch. ii)

—Herakles crushes enemies of, during slavery, i. 91

Lyfjaberg ("hill of healing"), ii. 186

Lykaion, Arkadian mountain, birthplace of Pan, i. 267

—Mt., reputed birthplace of Zeus, i. 155

Lykaios, Mt., worship of Zeus established on, i. 20, 159

Lykaon changed into prowling wolf, i. 16, 158

—son of Pelasgos and Meliboia, i. 20–21

Lyke-wake dirge, ii. 305

Lykeion in Athens founded by Lykos, i. 69

Lykia, throne of, won by Sarpedon, i. 61

Lykomedes, Achilles sent dressed as girl to court of, i. 122

Lykopolis (Assiut), Ophoïs wolf-god of, xii. 144

Lykos ("Light"), brother of Nykteus, directed to punish Antiope, i. 43

Lykos killed by Amphion and Zethos, i. 43–44

—king of Mysia, territory of, increased by Herakles, i. 85

—River connected with cult of Anahit, vii. 29

—son of Pandion, i. 68, 69

Lykosoura, founded and built by Lakaon, i. 20–21

Lykourgos drawn asunder by horses on Mt. Pangaion, i. 218

—Homer's account of attack of, on Dionysos, i. 215–216

—pursues attendants of infant Dionysos, i. 248

—smitten with madness by Dionysos, kills his own son, i. 218

—son of Ares, i. 190

——killed by serpent, i. 52

Lyktos, Mt., reputed birthplace of Zeus, i. 155

Lynkeus and Idas as Messenian doubles of the Dioskouroi, i. 27

——story of encounter of Kastor and Polydeukes with, i. 26–27

—avenged murders of his brothers, i. 31

—son of Aphareus, i. 24, 26–27

—succeeds Danaos as king, i. 32

—took part in hunt of Kalydonian boar, i. 56

Lynkia, in Asia Minor, Proitos received in, i. 32

Lynx, vii. 229, 231

—Messou and the, x. 39

—sun's eye in form of, xii. 86

Lyra (Goat-star), v. 317

Lyre, alternate stories of invention of, i. 192, 193, 195

—Apollo and the, i. 181

—attribute of Eros, i. 204

—Hermes credited with invention of, i. 181, 192, 193

—miraculous power of, charmed stones in walls of Thebes into place, i. 44, 47

Ly-thanh-tong, builder of temple of Huyen-vu, xii. 308

M

Ma, Anāhita identified with, vii. 25
—earth-goddess, vii. 12
—Magur, Magula-anna, title of Sin, v. 152
—sacred prostitution in honour of, vii. 382 26
Ma Bo Mè, wife of Kyawzwa, xii. 354
Ma Tuan-lin, viii. 200
Maa(?) ("Sight"), sense-god, xii. 67
Maahiset, small anthropomorphic beings living under earth, iv. 185, 205
Maailmanpatsas, Finnish term for "pillar of the world," iv. 222
Maasampa, Finnish term for "pillar of the world," iv. 222
Maasewe and Uyuuyewe, twin warriors, x. 204
Mabinog, aspirant to position of qualified bard, iii. 92
"Mabinogion," value of, for mythology of British Celts, iii. 19, 92, 93, 95, 96, 100, 106, 122
Mabon in Welsh literature and Romances, iii. 191
—one of three notable prisoners of Britain, iii. 103, 199
—son of Modron, iii. 187, 189
—Welsh equivalent of Maponos on British and Gaulish inscriptions, iii. 93, 188, 189
Mabouya, priesthood, xi. 351 10
Maboya (or Mapoia), tutelary of snakes and sender of hurricane, xi. 38
Maboyas may be insular equivalent for Kenaima, xi. 38
Mac an Daimh, birth of, iii. 63
—Cecht slew son of Morrígan, iii. 132
——("Son of the Plough"), king of the Tuatha Dé Danann, iii. 42, 76–77
—Cuill ("Son of the Hazel"), king of the Tuatha Dé Danann, iii. 42
—Dáthó, king of Leinster, tale of, iii. 124–125
—Dáthó's Boar: see "Scél Mucci Maic Dáthó."
—Gréine ("Son of the Sun"), king of the Tuatha Dé Danann, iii. 42
—Lugach of the Terrible Hand, iii. 163
—na Tri Con ("Son of the Three Dogs"), epithet of Lugaid, son of Cúroi, iii. 156

Macabi, decapitated mummies found on island of, xi. 222
Macaw, xi. 138
—(Cakix), deity of Zotzil, xi. 181
Mace, viii. 37
"Macgnímartha Finn," iii. 161, 164, 168
Macha slain, iii. 32
—("sun of women-folk"), daughter of Midir, iii. 73–74
—war-goddess, iii. 24, 25, 39, 40
Machaon heals Philoktetes, i. 132
—hero-physician, son of Asklepios, i. 281
Machchera, devil, xi. 295
Machira, souls go to a lake called, xi. 279
Machu Picchu, ruins at, xi. pl. xxx, opp. p. 212, 218, pl. xxxviii, opp. p. 248
Maconaholo, xi. 274
Maconaura and Anuanaïtu, Carib story of, xi. 261–268, 286
—tale of, incidents resembling the, xi. 273–274
Macrocosmus, Microcosmus, iv. 371, 372, 373
Macuilxochitl ("the Five Flowers"), deity of music and dancing, xi. 57, pl. ix, opp. p. 70, 77
Mada, vi. 154
Madagascar, mythical island Menuthias identified with, xii. 397 94
Madali Wi-hsa-kyung Nāt invoked by Hkun Hsang L'röng, xii. 290
Madana, one of the names of Kāma, vi. 141
Madari-Burkhan, creator, iv. 375
Madderakka, deity of birth, iv. pl. xxvii, opp. p. 224, 252–257
Madderatshe, male counterpart of Madderakka, iv. 252
Mādhavi, divinity, vi. 128
Madhu defeated by Viṣṇu, vi. 153, pl. xx, opp. p. 164
—("mead"), doctrine of, vi. 122
Madness, vi. 95, 98
—caused by eating heart of dead father, iii. 108
—Dionysos smites Lykourgos with, i. 218

Madness divinely sent on Alkmaion, i. 54
—from a god sent on Celts after battle of Delphoi, iii. 12
—guests at wedding of Attis stricken with, i. 275
—of cattle of Geryoneus, i. 86
——daughters of Minyas and of Dionysos, i. 215, 219, 222
————Proitos, i. 32, 215, 222
——Dionysos, Hera causes, i. 219
——Herakles, i. 80, 89
——horses of Glaukos, i. 38–39
——Io, i. 166
—sent by divinities on daughters of Proitos, i. 32; on hounds of Aktaion, i. 46; on Ino and Athamas, i. 46; on steeds of Glaukos, i. 38–39
Madonna and Child, statues of Isis and Horus interpreted as representing, xii. 244
Mādrī, vi. 142
Madurā (Paṇḍumahurā), vi. 225
Maeander River, Lityerses slain by Herakles and thrown into, i. 253
" Maelduin, Voyage of," iii. 85, 116
Maelstrom, iv. 78–79
Ma'et, earthly reign of, listed by Turin Historical Papyrus, xii. 399 [108]
—goddess of justice, xii. 67, 100, 135, 386 [22]
—Isis identified with, xii. 118, 119
—Nephthys identified with, xii. 110
Mafdet sometimes described as fighting on behalf of the sun, xii. 106
—warlike goddess, symbol of, xii. 135 (fig. 131)
Mafuike, owner and guardian of fire, ix. 47, 48
Mag mBreg, ox brought to, iii. 67
—Mell, fort of, iii. 37–38
——(" Pleasant Plain "), iii. 84, 85, 86
—Mesca, plain where Mesca was buried, iii. 91
—Mór (" Great Plain "), gods' land, iii. 80–81
—Mucrime, battle of, iii. 73
— -Rein in Connaught, Tuatha Dé Danann established themselves at, iii. 24
—Slecht, chief image bowed to St. Patrick at, iii. 45
— -Tured, two battles of, iii. 24–25, 32–34, 107, 137, 164, 188

Maga, evil spirit, xii. 111
Magadha, vi. 173
Māgadha (" Minstrel "), brought forth at birth sacrifice of Pṛthu, vi. 166
Magan probably identical with land of Gerraei, v. 4
Magas, vi. 183–184
—Magians, vi. pl. III, opp. p. 26
Maga-tsumi, wicked spirits, viii. 381 [1]
Mageba, Senzangakona escapes from spirits of house, vii. 135
Magharah, moon-god on inscriptions at, v. 378 [14]
Maghavan, epithet of Indra, vi. 35
—one of the Cakravartins, vi. 225
Magi, vii. 9, 52
Magic, ii. 6, 26, 27, 31, 33–34, 35, 39, 42, 45, 46, 47, 50, 55, 56, 58, 79, 96, 108, 110, 112, 120, 133, 143, 155, 168, 173, 188, 195, 197, 206, 230, 243, 246, 251, 252, 254, 265, 266, 267, 271, 295–302, 313, 321, 322
—iii. 14, 23–24, 28, 29, 30, 31, 32, 33, 35, 40, 41, 42, 43, 44, 46, 51, 56, 59, 64, 65, 73, 76, 79, 80, 81, 82, 83, 84, 87, 89, 90, 91, 94, 96, 97, 98, 101–102, 103, 118, 119, 122, 123, 125, 127, 141, 151, 155, 160, 161, 170, 173, 188, 201, 229
—v. 33, 106, 107, 114, 182, 224, 235, 272, 274, 276, 300, 318, 333, 353, 354, 356, 365, 366, 367
—vi. 44, 95, 96, 98, 107, 152, 166, 204, 205, 208, 209, 214, 226, 231, 233, 234, 365 [4]
—vii. 60, 74, 99, 366–367; 136, 178, 200, 246, 253, 264, 268, 278, 313, 329, 341, 350–351, 358, 414 [25], 417 [15], 421 [20 22]
—viii. 229, 274
—ix. 64, 70, 85, 173, 209, 223, 235, 259–260
—x. 4, 5, 18, 29, 48, 52, 59, 61, 66, 76, 92, 94, 100, 104, 116, 117, 126, 132, 133, 136, 157, 161, 163, 164, 168–169, 173, 177, 189, 192, 198, 203, 205, 215, 216, 231, 243, 252, 256, 261, 262, 269 [4], 282 [21], 283 [27], 286 [29], 289 [34], 295 [42 44], 302 [55], 307 [62]–308
—xi. 25, 65, 66, 76, 82, 86, 113, 171–172, 174, 181, 208, 209, 231, 249, 260, 261, 276, 277, 290, 291, 300, 308, 313, 350 [9], 351 [10]
—xii. 61, 63, 90–91, 125–126, 198–211,

239; 282, 283, 284, 290–291, 302, 303, 309, 348, 349, 350
Magic aids to dead, xii. 176
—animals, x. 136, 141–145, 252, 293 [40], 297 [47], 300 [50]
—arts, secrets of, written, v. 140
—Babi belongs to realm of, xii. 403
—Babylonian, mechanically copied in Egypt only in Graeco-Roman period, xii. 411 [4]
—beings, men slain in battle become, x. 117
—bird, Vāreghna a, vi. 289–290
—birth ceremony, iv. 416
—black, viii. 155, 156; xii. 109, 205, 207; 348, 349
—books, xii. 205
—ceremonies connected with cult of procreation, iv. 259–260
—claimed to be forerunner of all religions and mythologies of civilized races, v. 354
—custom of renewing a dry well with water from a full one, iv. 215
—drums: see DRUMS, MAGIC.
—early Hellenes addicted to, i. lii
—feathers, vi. 290, 331
—flight, xi. 304
——tale of, ix. 235–237
—formulae and pictures placed with mummies, xii. 175
—Ḥeka deity of, xii. 44, 67
—herb, i. 39
—Hermes as god of, i. 194
—homoeopathic, Artemis's methods of treatment suggest, i. 185
—in child-birth, iv. 252–253
——metals, i. 207
——solar ship, xii. 27 (fig. 10)
—knots, Neith tied, xii. 142
—magical development, viii. 13, 14, 16, 17, 19, 20, 21, 79–80, 106, 107, 123, 124, 126, 131–132, 178–179, 194
—many local gods survive only in, xii. 17
—method to obtain Zada-weather, iv. 458
—mirrors, iv. 419
—objects, ii. 46, 60, 62, 79, 108, 109, 111, 114, 132, 133, 134, 136, 170, 260, 266, 267, 268, 272, 301, 308; iii. 14, 24, 28, 29, 31, 32, 33, 40, 41, 65, 66, 76, 90, 94, 95, 96, 100–101, 109, 111, 112, 114, 117, 118–119, 123, 131, 132, 136,

145, 152, 165, 172, 173, 175, 177, 198, 199–200, 203; v. 94, 95; vii. 136, 171, 189, 204–205, 223, 246, 248, 327, 328, 347, 358, 414 [25]; ix. 43, 44, 45, 46, 61, 64, 75, 90, 91, 163, 208, 221
Magic of god more potent than that of goddess, ii. 18
—ogdoad important in, xii. 371 [45]
—powers given by vulture to girl, iv. 505
——in metals, i. 207
——inherent in gods, ii. 22
—prayers, iv. 211–212, 232, 244
—protective purposes, rings of brass and alder bark and copper used for, iv. 89–99, 226
——Wakonyingo taught, vii. 142, 268
—Qêb master of, xii. 368 [20]
—rain ceremonies, iv. 229
—religious foundations of, xii. 207–208
—rites in "raising" of house struck by lightning, iv. 445–446
——of Demeter to attain immortality, i. 228
—runes and songs, ii. 265
—Selqet connected with, xii. 147
—songs, iv. 77, 78, 79, 81, 110, 230, 234, 238, 243, 257, 290, 292, 294
—sword, xii. 303
—symbols, ii. pl. XLVI, opp. p. 338
—sympathetic, xii. 325
——water-pouring to ensure rain, vii. 22
—to still thunderstorm, iv. 227
—tree of healing, v. 152
—used in planting corn, iv. 241–242
—wands, xii. 366 [6]
—wind-, iv. 233
—words to overcome crab, iv. 325
Magical ceremonies in presence of moon to avert evil from children, vii. 48
—rod, viii. 132
Magician aid required to locate soul and to find new lud and appoint guardian, iv. 6, 145
—Gyōja condemned as, viii. 276
—Merlin may be old god degraded to mere, iii. 202
—Odin's coming as a, ii. 175
Magicians, v. 318, 330, 367; xi. 65, 116, 172, 175
—Bildr and Voli, ii. 136
Magico-medical skill, beliefs on, iii. 28

Magico-miraculous powers flourish in myth, not ritual, iii. 204

Magigi and Kitimil in flood-myth, ix. 256-257

Magna Mater, i. pl. LXII, opp. p. 300, 303-304

——Anāhita identified with, vii. 25

Magni, son of Thor, by giantess Jarnsaxa, ii. 21, 69, 74, 80, 82, 346

Magnus Nicholasson, ii. 80

Magoenggoelota stole parakeet's feather dress, ix. 206-207

Magoma, Chief, vii. 248

Magombe, kingdom of dead, vii. 174

Magonga, Nambi and Kintu came to earth at, vii. 154

Magpies make bridge over Milky Way, viii. 132

Magurmuntaë, ship of Ninurta, v. 120

Magusanus, Hercules, ii. 69

Magyars, or Hungarians, a Finno-Ugric people, iv. xvii

—subjected to Turco-Tatar, Slavic, and Teutonic influences, iv. xix

Mah, earth mother goddess, v. 109-III, 182, 220, 221

"Mahā Gītā Medanī," discussion of Nāts in, xii. 340, 341, 345, 353, 354, 357

"Mahābhārata," great epic of India, vi. 12

—influence of, on Java, ix. 242

Mahādeva, vi. 81, 82, 83, 112, 114, 168, 236, 245

—Bhūmiśvara, vi. 237

Mahāgiri (Magari, Magayē) Nāt, xii. 340, 342, pl. XVII, opp. p. 344

Mahājāṅgulītārā, vi. 217

Mahājaya, snake, vi. 155

Mahākāla, Daikoku, "the Great Black Deity," was a modification of, viii. 279

—Gaya Sukumāla performs meditation in graveyard of, vi. 224-225

—Rudra appears beside, vi. 216

—white, one of the two forms of Śiva enumerated among the dreadful deities, vi. 215

Mahākālī, vi. 118, 246

Mahākrodharāja, name of Acala, vi. 214

Mahalalel = god-Dumuzi = Daozos, Hebrew patriarch, v. 205

Mahāmayūrī, vi. 217

Mahāpuruṣa, "Great Male," vi. 195, 196, 198

Mahārāṇī Vindhyeśvarī, goddess of the Vindhya worshipped under name of, vi. 236

Mahāsiddhas, vi. 210

Mahātamaḥprabhā, vi. 228

Mahāvīra descended in lion-form, and took form of embryo in womb of Devānandā, vi. 221, 222, 223, 224

—"pot of great strength," vi. 80

Mahāyāna displaced by Hīnayāna in Burma and Siam, xii. 260

—"Great Vehicle," vi. 13, 199, 200, 201, 202, 204, 205, 206, 207, 210

—School, viii. 216

——Śaivite pantheon introduced into Buddhism of the, vi. 216

Mahdeo and the jackal, vii. 307

Mahendra, vi. 131, 169, 227

Mahendrāṇī, wife of Indra, vi. 134

Maheśvara, vi. 112

Mahiṣa defeated by Skanda, vi. 153

—mountain weapon of, vi. 152

—seeks to grasp chariot of Viṣṇu, vi. 140

—slain by Durgā, vi. pl. 1, frontispiece, 118

Mahodaya, vi. 148

Mahoragas, vi. 108, 203, 227

Ma-hora-nui-a-rangi, one of primeval pair, ix. 7

Ma-hora-nui-a-tea, spreading light, ix. 6

Ma-ḥos (Mi-ḥos), xii. 137

Mahr, nightmare-spirit, ii. 205, 208, 288-289

Mahrkūsha (Malqôs) will destroy mankind by snow and frost, vi. 309, 315

Mahucutah, one of four brothers created from maize, xi. 165, 166, 177

Maia, Hermes son of, i. 191

—rears Arkas on Mt. Kyllene, i. 21

—wife of Zeus, i. 156

Maid of lilla, v. 362

Maidenhood, fountain of, at Eleusis, i. 228

Maidens, all who die, attend on Gefjun, ii. 180

—celestial, viii. 257-260, 261, 262, 263, 269

—female forms, vi. 205

—golden, made by Hephaistos, i. 207

Maidens' Land, giant daughter of king of, and Fionn, story of, iii. 13

Maiden's Land in the west, iii. 117

Maidere, the eighth man, iv. 377, 379, 385

Maidhyōi-māongha, disciple of Zoroaster, vi. 342

Ma'in, map of, v. 377 [8]

Maïnad, Dionysos and a, i. pl. III, opp. p. xlvi

Maïnads, i. pl. XVI, opp. p. 48, 269–270, pl. LVII, opp. p. 272

—and Silenoi, i. pl. VI, opp. p. lx

—Artemis associated with, i. 184

—associated with Dionysos, i. 35, 36

—Korybantes classed as male, i. 275

Maināka retained its wings, vi. 159

Mair, wife of Bersa, sent love charms to Fionn, iii. 168

Maisahána and Ituána, Great Father and Mother, xi. 185

Maithoachiana, race of cannibal dwarfs, vii. 259, 260

Maitreya, viii. 194

—future Buddha, vi. 211

—(Jap. Miroku), viii. 241

—legend of, with Iranian affinities, vi. 211–212

—(Metteya), only Bodhisattva recognized by the Buddha of the Hīnayāna canon, vi. 202, 212

Maize, x. 14, 35, 37, 57–59, 62, 92, 108, 127, 156, 158, 160, 166, 173, 188, 199–201, 209, 283 [24], 289 [35]; xi. 34, 83, 92, 93, 95, 144, 145, 164–165, 166, 177, 178, 180, 212, 225, 230, 231, 278, 350 [9]; see also CORN.

— -eating class who came from gourd, xii. 292

— -gods, xi. 54, 75, 139, 180, 224

Majaje, rain-maker, vii. pl. XXIII, opp. p. 238

Majesty Enveloped, sacred bundle, xi. 167

Majoi Shingra Pum, mountain home of Ngawn-wa Magam, xii. 264

Maka, tale of, vii. 176–177

Makame, mysterious being, vii. 411 [46]

Makaravaktrā, a Ḍākinī, vi. 215

Makedon, dog-god companion of Osiris according to Greeks, xii. 393 [61]

Makha, demon, vi. 63, 98

—headless sacrifice, vi. 80

Maknongan, old man in Bugan-Wigan tale, ix. 171

Makonaima, creator god and hero of a cosmogony, xi. 258–259, 269, 271

Maksameri (Lebermeer), gathering-place for sorcerers and witches, iv. 78

Maku, damp, moisture, ix. 6, 7

Malabar coast, Christians on, in A.D. 525–530, vi. 175

Malachite associated with divinities, xii. 367 [12]

Maladies, sixty, inflicted on Ishtar, v. 332

Malâk, messenger-god, v. 58, 390 [291]

— -Bêl, Adad, Ramman, Ilumer often confused with, v. 63

——depicted on altar, v. 61

——("messenger of Bêl"), identified with Zeus, v. 58, 60, 390 [279]

——of Palmyra, sun-god of Aramaeans, v. 37, 39

——Yaribôlos another name for sun-god, v. 56

— -Bôl identified with Mercury, v. 58

Malar, Lake (Log), in Sweden, ii. 181

Malaria, i. 296

Malay element in Indonesia, ix. 153, 205, 240–241, 243–244, 263, 306

——Micronesian mythology, ix. 247

—Peninsula, mouse-deer as trickster-hero in, ix. 203

——Negritos in, ix. 154

Malays invade Indo-China by Mèkhong valley, xii. 287

Malaysian type in Japan, viii. 210

Malcandros (Malcander), title of El, god of Underworld, v. 71

Male divinity and female consort, tendency to divide deities into, xii. 365 [20]

— -female (father-mother) deity, v. 44, 50, 381 [58]

— -Who-Invites, viii. 222–224

Malea, Cape, Odysseus shapes course for, i. 136

Males, in most versions of "Transformation Combat" opponents are, iii. 57

Malice and goodness in Melanesian myths contrasted, ix. 258–262

Malietoa, genealogy of, ix. 17

Malik, Makil the god of Beth-Shan may be, v. 50

—(Moloch), god of plague, fiery heat, and Inferno, v. 361

——sun-god of Babylonia, Syria, and Canaan, v. 51, 52, 134

—Nergal defined as god, v. 50, 58

Malimluca, vi. 98

Malivaran-fish, tale of, ix. 123

Malkaddir, v. 72

Malkîzedek, king and priest of god El, v. 45

Malkōsh: see MAHRKŪSHA.

Malleos joviales, Thor's hammers, used in ancient faith, ii. 80

Mallet, miraculous, viii. 279, 286, pl. xxxvi, opp. p. 314, 381 [5] (ch. iv)

Malliator, Hercules, ii. 69

Maltai, reliefs of, v. 396 [42]

Maltese cross, v. 150

Mām, me, vi. 357 [1]

Mama Cocha (" Mother Sea "), xi. 223

—Huaco, wife of Ayar Auca, xi. 248–249

—Ipacura, wife of Ayar Cachi, xi. 249

—Mami, title of Mah, v. 110

—Ocllo, wife of Ayar Manco, xi. 248

—Oella and Manco Capac, primeval pair, vii. 151–152

—Pacha (Earth), xi. 224

—Raua, wife of Ayar Uchu, xi. 249

Māmā Devī, mother of gods, vi. 238

Mamalhuaztli (" the Fire-Sticks "), xi. 98

Mambrui, women of, heard spirits of old Sheikhs chanting, vii. 348

Mami, goddess, v. 12

—recreated man after destruction, v. 112, 113, 273–274, 275, 276

—wife of Irra, v. 138

Mamit (" the curse "), v. 372

Mammit, maker of fate, v. 216

Mamona, one of five names of mother of supreme Being, xi. 24

Man, Men:

Man and shepherd alternate in liturgical formula, v. 345–346

—animal (were-) turns into, to get wife, vii. 346–347

—antiquity of, in South America, xi. 253–254, 371 [1]

—as a woman bearing children, ii. 143

—blue (sky-god), twelve red men dance about, a solar rite, xi. 199, 200

—coming of, myth, vii. 372–373, 375

—created by sun, xii. 30

——from clay and blood of a god, v. 112, 275, 307, 313

—creation and fall of, i. 10–12, 18

——of, iv. 371–380

—destruction of, v. 112

Man-eater, wife of Saudāsa had become, vi. 145

—fall of, iv. 381–385

—first, iv. 351, 371–380

——develops into the Devil, iv. 316

—Great or Old, name of keremet-spirit, iv. 154–156

— -headed bulls, vi. 333–334, 367 [41]

——serpent on vases, xi. 226

—in moon, iv. 423

—is meaning of Ainu, viii. 209

— -lion avatar of Viṣṇu, vi. 122, 123, 168

—necessary to happiness of gods, v. 112, 192, 314

—Ngojama has shape of, vii. 242

—of Cold, of Heat, of Wind, x. 78

——the mountain roams in air and lives immortal life, viii. 219, 274–280

———world, iv. pl. xxvii, opp. p. 224

—one of four sons of Horus or Osiris has form of, xii. 112

—plan to decide which of three creators shall be life-giver and guardian to, iv. 375

—primeval, and primeval ox invoked together, vi. 294

—primitive, thoughts of, about world, i. xliv–xlv

—reduction of size of, after Fall, iv. 385

—said to be made of different materials, ii. 326–327

— -serpent, Kekrops as, i. 66–67

—tale of Euro, who rose out of ground as a child-, ix. 271

—Tammuz may have been, v. 341

—torn to pieces by Lion joined together to become Spider, vii. 323

—turning inside out of, iv. 374

— -Who-Never-Dies, x. 106

——rose into sky, moon regarded as, ix. 276

Men and animals, worship of, xii. 159–172

——gods formed by Khnûm(u) and Ḥeqet, xii. 50

——world, creation of, xii. 68–73

—Aphrodite among, i. 199–202

—assume ways of women, xi. 282

—belief that gods were deified, ii. 31, 33, 34, 35–36

—created for benefit of gods, v. 192

—creation of, vi. 18

Men derived from rocks and trees belief of hill and forest stocks, i. 11

—description, food, language, and classes of sixty races who came from gourd, xii. 292

—festival-, iv. pl. xxvii, opp. p. 224

—four old, annually chosen to help priests at festivals, xi. 137

—from the sea, xi. 204–209

—gods as helpers of, ii. 75

—holy, cult of, after death, vi. 243, 244

—hymn on creation of, xii. 68–69

—Kachin story of how mortality came to, xii. 296–297

—mortal, lured by underwater people, x. 29

—noble or princely, sometimes regarded as gods, ii. 21

—of captive tribe killed, xi. 20, 349 [5]

——gold, silver, iron, and bronze, creation of, i. 17, 18

——knowledge summoned before battle, iii. 30

——T'ang, viii. 5

——the Mountains, viii. 266–267

——síd had love affairs with goddesses, iii. 91

—originally died and rose monthly like moon, ix. 253

—rudimentary, completed by gods, ix. 272–273

—size of, determined by size of bones from which they were created, xi. 90

—some snakes may become, vii. 193–194

—sun, moon, and stars were once, vii. 225, 227

—swallowed by worm, iii. 132

—wild, bind sheaves in return for food, iii. 264–265

—worship of, xii. 170

Man I, barbarians, viii. 176

—Maw (Bhamo), first egg of Thusandi found at, xii. 276

— -Pai, vii. 92

—Sè on banks of Lake Nawng Put, xii. 272, 273

Managarm (" Moon-hound "), sprinkles Heaven and air with blood, ii. 200

Manala, Finnish name for " world beyond," iv. 74

Manalaiset (" deceased "), cows of the, iv. 205

Manalan-rakki, Underworld's hound, iv. 75

Manannan, Irish sea-god, ii. 94, 191; iii. 29, 33, 36, 40, 51, 52, 54, 55, 59, 60–61, 62, 63, 64, 65, 66, 72, 80, 86, 88–89, 99, 102, 103, 115, 116, 118, 121, 122, 125, 128, 135, 136, 172, 175, 180, 185, 204, 207, 208, 210, 211, 335 [32]

Mänäriks, heaven of, iv. 498–499

Mānasa, Lake, Gandharvas live near, vi. 143

Mānasarovara, lake formed from mind of Brahmā, vi. 235–236

Manât worshipped throughout South Arabia, v. 21

Manawātu (plu. of form Manât), Nabataean goddess of fate, v. 20–21, 382 [91]

Manawyddan, husband of Rhiannon, iii. 95, 188

—son of Llyr, name derived from Manaw, the Isle of Man, iii. 100, 101, 102, 103, 106, 191

Manchu Dynasty, viii. 68, 95, 102, 118

Manco Capac and Mama Oella, primeval pair, vii. 151–152

——founder of Incas, xi. 218, 244, 245, 246, 248, 249, 251

Mandaean sect believe fire played part in creation, iv. 329–330

Mandākinī, river of Kubera, vi. 158

Mandara, Mt., vi. 104, 106, 155

Mandāravā, incarnation of a Ḍākinī, accompanies Padmasambhava, vi. 209

Māṇḍavya cursed Dharma to be born of Śūdra woman, vi. 150

—impaling of, vi. 177

—sage, goes to question Dharma, vi. 159

Māndhātṛ, avatar of Viṣṇu, vi. 168

—birth of, vi. 166

—trident of Śiva slays King, vi. 111

Mandishire creator of earth, iv. 327, 387

—Bodhisattva, in care of ropes attached to earth-supporting fish, iv. 311

Mandrake superstition, x. 232

Mandulis, xii. 135

Mane of Skinfaxi burns brightly, ii. 200

Mane steers course of moon, ii. 183

Maneros, prince, origin of Plutarch's story of, xii. 396 [85]

Manes of dead, sacrifice of war captives partly a propitiation of, x. 285 [29]–286

Manes of Mahāgiri Nāts, xii. 344, 347

Mang Kyaw Sa, son of Mang Lön, xii. 292

—Lai, Lön, and Lu, three sons of Hkun Hsang L'röng, xii. 292

—Rai founder of Chieng Rai and Chieng Hsen and State of Kēngtūng, xii. 281

Mangaia, sons of Rongo ancestors of people of, ix. 26

—tale of flood from, ix. 39

"Mangwe, Mangwe, our king," salute to sun, vii. 133

Mangy cause of flood, xi. 29

Mani, iv. 315

— -Khan, iv. 466

Mani and manioc plant, xi. 292, 315

— -oka, manioc root, xi. 292

Mania ("Madness"), abstract divinity of state of body, i. 282

Maniai, i. 277

Maṇibhadra, king of Krodhavaśa Rākṣasas, vi. 158

Manibozho (Glooscap, Manabush, Messou, Michabo, Nanaboojoo), the GREAT HARE, wh. see, x. 23, 32, 40, 41, 42, 45, 46, 48, 49, 51–52, 121, 297 [47]

Manichaeans, Patagonian principles in common with, xi. 333

Manichaeism, iv. 390

Manikins, destruction of, xi. 162–163, 168

—souls regarded as, x. 146, 281 [20]

Maṇikopa, precious stone sent by parrot messengers by Hsuriya to Thusandi, xii. 276

Maṇipūr, Chin tribesmen migrated into, xii. 267

Manito, a dog may have been Cúchulainn's, iii. 142

—see GITCHE MANITO.

Manitos, x. 17–19, 28, 41, 45, 48, 82, 269 [3], 284 [28]–285, 302 [52]

Mañjughoṣa, form of Mañjuśrī, vi. 213

Mañjuśrī, viii. 196

—Bodhisattva, vi. 202, 212–213, 215, 216, 218

—Mandishire equals the Buddhist Bodhisattva, iv. 327, 328, 372

Mankind, classification of, xii. 379 [18]

—myth of destruction of, xii. 73–76

—origin of: see ORIGINS, MYTHS OF.

Mankind rescued from stomach of monster who had swallowed it, vii. 119

—Sumerian Enlil father of, v. 14

Manmatha, name of Kāma, vi. 141

Manna, an Eastern dependency of Urartu, vii. 12

Manna-hugir alternative name of Fylgja, ii. 234

Manna, origin of, v. 97

Mannheim, ii. 106

Mannus, member of triad, ii. 24

Manoa, xi. 194

Mansions in the sky, v. 310

Mantineia, Arkas buried near, i. 22

Mantis, Cagn originally the, vii. 135, 227, 287–290, pl. xxx, opp. p. 290, 418 [40] [41] [46]

Mantle, donning of, confers invisibility, iii. 55, 65, 66, 106

—magic, of Oengus, iii. 177

—of invisibility of Arthur, iii. 190

——Loegaire, taken from síd of Cruachan, iii. 69

—shaking of, parted Cúchulainn and Fand, iii. 88

— -wearer, ii. 42

Mantus, Etruscan god of the Underworld, i. 289

Manu, first man, vi. 294

—Minos said to be of same primitive origin as, i. 63

—son of Vivasvant, vi. 18, 28, 53–54, 57, 65, 75, 99, 109, 124, 143, 147, 166

Manuai creates wife from wooden image, ix. 106

Manuscript, Armenian gospel, page from, vii. pl. i, frontispiece, pl. iv, opp. p. 72

Manuscripts, ritual, xi. 112

Mānūsh, Mt., vi. 329

Manushchithra (Minūcihr), successor of Farīdūn, vi. 323–324, 329, 348

Mānuṣibuddhas, five, vi. 211

Manyu, origin of Rudra from, vi. 82

—("Wrath"), abstract god, vi. 52

Manzai dancers, viii. pl. xli, opp. p. 348

Manzan Görmö, Heaven-goddess, iv. 414, 434

Mao (Pleiades), viii. 34

Maobogan, ix. 234

Maorocon (Maorocoti), appellation of Sky-father, xi. 24

Map of Yucatan, xi. pl. xix, opp. p. 130

Map of world, Babylonian, v. 216, 217; see also s.v. Map, vol. v, p. 446.
—Tlotzin, xi. pl. XVI, opp. p. 112, 359 ¹⁶
" Maple Itinerary," story of, viii. 289–290
— -log as bridge, x. 35
— -trees, viii. 213
Maponos on British and Gaulish inscriptions identical with Welsh Mabon, equated with Apollo, iii. 93, 188, 189
Mar Ebedishu bound Lîlîth, v. 363
Māra, Buddha's contest with, vi. 192, 193, 196–197, 209, 226
— -Namuci, demon, vi. 204
Mara, oppressive nightmare spirit, ii. 290, 306
Māradhvājas, numbers of Buddhas called, vi. 199
Marajo, mounds on island of, xi. 286–287, pl. XL, opp. p. 286
Maras, a window through which came the Maras tribe, xi. 248
Marat-Adad, Aramaean deity, v. 383 ¹⁰⁸–384
Marathon, bull of, i. 69
——and Theseus, i. 102
——offspring of Poseidon, i. 211
—Pan at battle of, drove Persians into mad rout, i. 267
—spirit of Theseus aids Athenians at battle of, i. 105
—Theseus slays Cretan bull at, i. 84
Marawa, Spider, created mankind, ix. 106, 124–125
Marbendill, water-spirit, ii. 210
Mar-bi'di, Aramaic deity, v. 42
March Malaen, plague of Coranians called that of, iii. 107–108
—(Mark, King of Cornwall), son of Meirchion, iii. 191
Marcos of Niza, x. 310 ⁶⁷
Mardan, hero-founder of the Votiaks, sacrifice to, iv. 151–152
Mardoll (Freyja), ii. 125, 126
Marduk and Irra, v. 139–140, 141, 142–145
——Ishtar, myth of, v. 131
——the ostrich, v. 283, 352
——Tiâmat, battle between, vi. 264
——winged creatures, combat between, v. 279–280, 281, 282, 283, 286
—as creator, v. 101
——Jupiter, Shulpae in reality name of, v. 110

Marduk, avenger, v. 297–298, 299, 300, 302
—Babylonian, iii. 34, 50
——priesthood placed rôles of all principal gods on, v. 325
—" band " employed of, v. 109
—(Bêlos) born, v. 293
—bore Tablets of Fate on his breast, v. 102
—champion of gods of order, v. 296
—chapel of, in New Year's festival, v. 318
—city-god of Babylon, exalted into rôles of Ninurta and Enlil, v. 292
—created stations of gods, v. 304
—creates the earth, v. 112, 303
—death and resurrection of, v. 337
—destruction of, prophesied, v. 141, 142
—Epic of Creation glorified, v. 277–325
—fifty sacred titles of, v. 289, 310–312
—first-born son of Ea, v. 344
—four dogs of, vii. 395 ⁵⁸
——wings of, v. 409 ³
—gains ascendancy over Nabû, vii. 384 ⁵¹
—in Akkadian, the " faithful son," v. 342
——Babylonian religion, v. 155–157, 158, 159, 160
—incantation of, against Lamaštu, v. 370
—infancy of, v. 320, 324
—Janus-headed, v. 294
— -Jupiter, Cancer station of, v. 286, 304
—Nabû messenger of sun-god, v. 58
—obtains power of divinity and kingship, v. 300
—of Eridu originally an agricultural and vegetation deity, v. 155–156
—(or Bêlu), god of Babylon, v. 56, 95
—originally same as Tammuz of Eridu, v. 344
—regarded as conqueror of dragons of darkness, v. 286
—replaces Enki-Ea in creation-myth, v. 112
—said to recall dead to life, vii. 395 ⁵⁸
—sent to expel devils by magic, v. 106, 370
—sometimes sun-god; also associated with Taurus, vii. 225
—spring festivities at Babylon for, v. 18, 156

Marduk subdued female dragon of Chaos, v. 118, 131
—symbol of, v. 109, 155
—throne of, with spade, v. 127
—tomb of, v. 52
—two-headed, on seal, v. 68, 69
Mardukzakirshum, king of Babylonia, v. 300
Mareba, spirit, xi. 296
Marena, funereal elements in destruction of, iii. 313
Marérewána, Arawak Noachian hero, xi. 273
Margidda, constellation, v. 109
Margygr (" Sea-giantess "), ii. 209
Marī Bhavānī, cholera-goddess, vi. 246–247
Mari, Dagon appears first in kingdom of, v. 78, 80
Mārica aided Rāvaṇa in plot to steal Sītā, vi. 156
Marīcī, an aspect of the Tārā, vi. 217
—one of the Prajāpatis, vi. 108, 109, 142, 144
Ma-riko-riko, a first woman, ix. 312 50
Marimatle, cave from which first people came, also entrance to spirit-world, vii. 184
Marine beings, viii. 268–274
—myths, x. 274 9
Marital relations of Devs and humans, vii. 87, 393 37
Mark set upon those abhorring wickedness, v. 160
Marka, demon, vi. 84, 98, 168
Markasu (" band of the universe "), v. 109, 309
Markland, x. 1
Marks, birth-, on Buddha, vi. 191, 195, 196
—family, son inherits, iv. 117
—made by supernatural beings on skin of humans, iv. 10, 15
—ownership, iv. 504
Marmin, man's body, vii. 94
Marmosets, female, surround Morning Star, xii. 365 27
Marne, name of, equals Gaulish Matrona, iii. 189
Marocael (Machchael) transformed into a stone, xi. 28
Marpessa, daughter of Evenos, i. pl. XI, opp. p. 24, 27–28
Marras, iv. 205

Marriage, viii. 30, 31, 149; x. 49, 98, 146, 178, 276 12, 280 17; xi. 37
—after separation (incest motif), ix. 158, 164
—Anāhita concerned with, vii. 25
—and love of animals, viii. pl. XXXIX, opp. p. 332, 333–335
—at communal hearth, vii. 55
—between celestial being and a mortal, viii. 257–263, 266, 277, 357
——human maidens and river-gods, i. 257
——maiden of deep sea and a mortal, viii. 257, 332–333
— -bond, Var has to do with the, ii. 186
—classes, two, in New Britain, ix. 108
—connexion of Demeter with institution of, i. 227
—customs, iii. 321–322; vii. 55
—explanation of mixed, between Brāhman and warrior caste, vi. 146
—good luck calculations for, viii. 143
—Hera patroness of, i. pl. VII, opp. p. lxi
—impediments to, iv. 116
—inter-, of twins, vi. 144, 225
—Lapps came into possession of tutelary spirits by, iv. 76
—Lofn gives permission for, ii. 185
—lots cast for possession of Helen in, i. 25
—miraculous, between Brahmā's daughter and Bontenkoku, viii. 357
—of animals and human beings, viii. 333
——Baboon and woman, tale of, vii. 273–274, 416 9
——brother and sister to keep dynasty pure, iii. 25
——fairies and mortals, vii. 393 82
——girl, sacrifice on, iv. 133
——gods and giants, ii. 278
——Heaven and Earth, vii. 124
——human hero and sky-girl, x. 290 36
——Iuno and Hercules, i. 302 (fig. 11)
——men and female water-spirits, ii. 211, 212
——mortal and ghost, x. 146
——Nambi and Kintu, vii. 154
——North and South, x. 138
——Sea-maidens to mortals, viii. 263–264
——Śiva and Pārvatī, vi. pl. X, opp. p. 118
——Sky-maiden and mortal, ix. 177

Marriage of Sun and Moon produced stones and birds, ix. 110, 177
——Vily and young men, iii. 258
——Zeus and Hera, i. 164–165
—on second, woman must propitiate spirit of first husband, vi. 247
—portion of the dead unmarried girls, iv. 19
—primeval, viii. 223, 229
—prohibited degrees of, vi. 240
—restrictions on, xii. 186
—rites, naked foot incident connected with, ii. 103, 104
—ritual, found in cult of Ull and Frey, ii. 158
—sacred, of a god of fertility, ii. pl. xiv, opp. p. 114, 116
—Svarog founder of legal, iii. 298
—to creator, ix. 24, 25
—tree-, vi. 238, 239
—tree played part in, vii. 401 6
—with fairy princesses, battle for, iii. 38
Marriages, deities of Japan assemble at Shrine of Kitsuki to arrange, viii. 249–250
—next-of-kin, vi. 345
—of Zeus, i. 156, 157, 328 7
Marru, Marri, Adad called, v. 39
—spade, symbol of Marduk, v. 156
Marrying again for purpose of securing a son for a dead husband, vi. 150.
Mars addressed as fire-god Gibil, v. 317
—and Rea Silvia parents of Romulus and Remus, ii. 307
—British Nodons possibly equated with, iii. 103
—Camulos equated with, iii. 164
—had high place in certain tribes, ii. 97, 98
—image of Odin resembled, ii. 40, 58
—in Caesar's account of Gaulish gods, iii. 9
—(Marspiter, Maspiter, Mavors), i. 293
—mentioned with Mercury, ii. 39
—perhaps survives in modern Maso of Romagnola, i. 317
—received animal and human sacrifice, ii. 69, 98
—representative of fire, viii. 142
—sings song predicting downfall of kingdom, viii. 167

Mars Thingsus, altar to, ii. 98, pl. xii, opp. p. 98
Mars, planet, vii. 52, 65
—of Nergal, called "star of judgement of fate of dead," v. 136, 147
—readings of name of, xii. 55
—"Red Horus" equals, xii. 388 28
Marseilles, tabued grove near, described by Lucan, iii. 11–12
Marshes of Arkadian Stymphalos cleared of man-eating birds by Herakles, i. 84
Marsi, temple of Tamfana among the, ii. 17
Marsyas, vii. 364
—and Apollo, i. pl. iv (2), opp. p. l
—Asianic myth of, connected with that of Osiris, xii. 393 62
—contest of Apollo with, i. 181
— -Masses, Phrygian god, vii. 62–63, 380 6
Marta as omen of death, iv. 205
Mārtāṇḍa, the setting sun, vi. 28, 141
Marten as sacrifice, iv. 404
—Glooscap and the, x. 39
Martwiec (Polish), vampire, iii. 232
Mārtyava, vi. 97
Martyrological writing, dragon worship in, vii. 82
Mārtyuṁjaya, vi. 97
Maru, brother of Maui, ix. 42
Marubhūti and Kamaṭha, brothers, born enemies in eight incarnations, vi. 226
Marudvṛdhā, river on earth, vi. 39
Marut, name of Vāyu, vi. 135
Māruta, father of Hanumān, vi. 128
Maruts, storm-deities, vi. 17, 20, 21, 29, 33, 34, 36, 37, 38, 39, 40, 45, 47, 52, 56, 63, 88, 89, 94, 142
Maruwa, tale of, vii. 196, 206–208
Marvellous Valley, horse of, iii. 128
Marvo Sea, Zambu-tree rises out of, iv. 359
Mary (planet Venus ?), waggon of, iii. 323, 329
—Virgin, substituted for Perkune Tete, iii. 357 11
Marzyana, Ceres identified with, iii. 301, 355 44
Masai, story of cattle given to the, vii. 150
Masān, ghosts who haunt the burning grounds, vi. 248
Masaya, volcano, xi. 184

Masculine personifications, xii. 66–67, 378 [102]

Mash, god, Ninurta, v. 116

Mashambwa, tale of, vii. 245–246

Mashenomak, monster who devoured fishermen, x. 45

Mâshu Mountains, v. 209, 210, 262

Mašḫuldubbû, goat, Sumerian origin of, v. 356

Māshya and Māshyōī, first human pair, vi. 294, 295, 296, 316, 350

Masked men in drama of bear feast games, iv. 96, pl. vii, opp. p. 96

Masking at Kekri-feast and at Christmas, iv. 65, 66

Masks, iv. 512; ix. pl. xii, opp. p. 104, pl. xiii, opp. p. 116, pl. xiv, opp. p. 124, pl. xv, opp. p. 138, pl. xvi, opp. p. 158; x. pl. i, frontispiece, xxi, pl. iv, opp. p. 14, pl. vii, opp. p. 26, 171, pl. xxv, opp. p. 188, 190, 216, 244, pl. xxxi, opp. p. 246, 250, 251, 269 [4], 309 [65]–310; xi. pl. i, frontispiece, 23, pl. ii, opp. p. 24, 47, 67, 68, 71, pl. x, opp. p. 76, 199, pl. xxxi, opp. p. 218, 221, 222, pl. xxxii, opp. p. 222, pl. xxxiv, opp. p. 230, 235, 287–295

—cotton, over faces of dead, x. 189, 190

—of Humbaba, v. 254–255

—used at initiations, vii. pl. xxiv, opp. p. 244

Maso, protector of crops in modern Romagnola, perhaps survival of Mars, i. 317

Masques, x. 154, 155, 159, 171, 187, 194, 310 [65]

Mass, javelin wrought during, iii. 97

Massis (Ararat) sacred mountain, vii. 62, 70, 71, 77, 78, 79, 80, 83, 98, 99, 380 [6], 389 [2] (ch. ix)

Mast of ship made from tree through which sick child passed, ii. 204

Master Carpenter, x. 254

—of forest and spirit of "holy places," connexion between, iv. 178

——image of, iv. pl. xix, opp. p. 156, 177, 178

——Life (Gitche Manito), x. 19, 22

——the Head-band, Amon called, xii. 129

——water, iv. 193

Masters, anthropomorphism and dwelling-places of, iv. 465–466

Masters of Nature, iv. 463–471

——Recipes, meditation practised by the, viii. 194

Mas'ûdî on cremation and worship of dead, iii. 234

——religion of eastern and southern Slavs, iii. 222

Matabele of Basuto, vii. 246–249

Mātali, charioteer of Indra, vi. 132

Matanga, Buddhist priest, viii. 188

Mātaṅgī, Mātaṅgīs, vi. 204, 205

—Śakti, Śītalā one form of, vi. 246

Mataora and the Turehu, tale of, ix. 72–73

Mātariśvan, vi. 19, 28, 36, 43, 63, 89

Matawitawen, bolnay-tree of, ix. 232–235

Matchimanitou, medicine spirit, x. 285 [28]

Mate (" Death "), ix. 118–119

Matenino, women of island of, xi. 19, 31, 32, 285–286

Mater deum, Aestii worshipped the, and wore boar as emblem, ii. 109

—Matuta, Italic goddess of dawn and of birth, connected with Greek Leukothea and Eileithyia, i. 290

——survives as La Bella Marta in modern Romagnola, i. 319

Materia medica of Artemis, i. 185

Maternal principle in earth, Rhea early Cretan conception of, i. 274

Maternity-goddess, Ishtar as, vii. 382 [23]

Matet, goddess connected with tree or shrub, xii. 135

Matet, scorpion of Isis, xii. 210, 211

Math, son of Mathonwy, iii. 96–97, 99

Math Hên (" the Ancient "), Welsh high god, iii. 98

Mathgen, wizard, iii. 30

Matholwych, king of Ireland, suitor for Branwen, iii. 100, 101, 104

Mathurā (modern Muttra), land of Kṛṣṇa cult, vi. 171, 172, 178

—seat of cult of " Herakles " (Kṛṣṇa), vi. 110

Mating, desire for, dead in man and beast, v. 332, 412 [11]

Matit, goddess under form of lioness, xii. 135

" Matlangua wa libala," tale of, vii. 278

Matrae, Celtic, ii. 242, 245

Matres (Mothers), Celtic earth mothers or fertility goddesses, iii. 8, 98

—prophesied at Arthur's birth, iii. 187

Matrilinear descent, x. 184, 238, 240
Matronae, goddesses akin to the Matres, iii. 189
Mātṛs, or "Mothers," vi. 156-157, 185, 205, 238; see also items s.v. MOTHERS.
Mats of Dread and Sacred Holding, ix. 37
Matshehawaituk, x. 285 [28]
Matsi Niouask, x. 285 [28]
Ma(t)-si-s, worshipped in Upper Egypt, xii. 135
Matsu-mushi, pine insect, viii. 335, 385 [22]
Matsura, tale of standing rock of, viii. 234
Matsya, "fish" avatar of Viṣṇu, vi. 167
Matsyas, tribal appellation, vi. 63
Matter, origin of, viii. 128
Matthias in time of Herod, v. 117
Matuku, cannibal giant, ix. 60, 61
Matura, goddess of ripening of grain, i. 300
Matu'u-ta'u-ta'uo, bird who swallowed man, ix. 68
Matyavela, x. 181
Maui, demigod, ix. 20, 36, 41-56, 116, 128, 182, 184, 186, 256
Maung-la, A-mong settled in, and from her are descended White Karens, xii. 283-284
Maung Tin Daw, father of Queen of Tagaung, xii. 347
Maurut, name of flowers, vii. 62
Mauṣil (Mossul), v. 338
Ma-vien, general under Emperor Kwang-vu, in attack on Tongking, xii. 313
—or Phuc-ba, substituted for Cao-bien in worship at Bach-ma Temple, xii. 316, 317
Mavky, iii. 253
Mawa, children of God, came to earth in time of famine, vii. 329, 331
Mawanda, Kintu revealed himself to King, vii. 155
Maweza, owner of [forbidden] fruit tree, vii. 316, 426 [20]
Maya, art, culture, myth, ritual, calendar, etc., of the, xi. 124-131
—cycles, xi. 146-152
—nations, xi. 43, 44
Maya the architect appears as an Asura, vi. 152, 153

Māyā, Asura connected with word, vi. 84
—Buddha entered womb of, as six-tusked elephant, vi. 194
—occult power, vi. 22, 107, 151, 184
—often accepted as village deity, vi. 238
Māyādevī reared Pradyumna, vi. 173-174
Mayapan, xi. 126-127, 128-129
May-day (Beltane), fires at, iii. 26
—folk-survivals seen in Isle of Man festivals on, iii. 108-109
—wealth found at Gwydno's weir on, iii. 110
May-eve, dragon's shriek on, made land desolate until burial, iii. 130
—foals disappear on, iii. 95
—shriek on, caused by foreign dragon attacking dragon of the land, iii. 107
Mayo, battle of Mag-Tured in, iii. 24
Mayta Capac renewed gold plate, xi. 246
Māzainyan demons, vi. 300
Mazdaism, iv. 390; vi. 261, 342, 349
Mazimwi, vii. 427 [13]
Mbama, python, tale of, vii. 317
Mbamba, supreme God, addressed as Father, vii. 133
Mbanga-njo, tiger-cat, vii. 321
Mbasi of the Wankonde, vii. 159
Mbega, founder of Wakilindi house of chiefs, vii. 220
Mbiracucha, xi. 297
Mbirikimo, member of rumoured race of pygmies, vii. 260
Mbodze, incantations at grave of, for rain, vii. 239
Mbu, sea called, vii. 411 [46]
Mchemnito, "wickedness personified," x. 285 [28]
Mdskhit, Iberian capital, statue of Azmaz at, vii. 382 [22]
Mê, Nabû translation of old Sumerian title, v. 158
Mead, ii. 6, 10, 22, 48, 49, 51, 52, 53, 54, 220, 265, 269, 277, 297, 304, 313
—of Tvaṣṭṛ, vi. 31
Meadow mother and man, iv. 239, 242-243
Meander, perhaps symbol of earth, xi. 234, 368 [15]
Measles, process of curing, xi. 334
Meat, vi. 134

Meat, fat, iv. 476
—rule against eating, v. 153
—Yima gave, to men, vi. 310
Meath, plains of, to be cleared, iii. 81
Meath's three bare ones [mountains], iii. 136
Mecca, Black Stone of, x. 288 32
Medaba, copper coins at, v. 19
Medals, xii. 327
Medb, Queen, iii. 58, 64, 65, 69, 78, 90, 124, 125, 127, 130, 131, 134, 140, 141, 147, 150, 152, 153, 154, 155, 156, 157
Medeia, Achilles said to consort with, after death, i. 131
—and Iason exiled from Iolkos, i. 115
———in Corinth, i. 115
———wedded, i. 113
—at Corinth, i. pl. xxviii, opp. p. 110
—banished from Athens for plotting against life of Theseus, i. 115
—becomes wife of Aigeus in Athens, i. 115
—daughter of Aietes, falls in love with Iason, i. 112, 242
—drugs of, i. 41
—escapes to Athens in chariot drawn by winged dragons, i. 115
—gives Iason drug which makes him immune from fire and iron, i. 112
—healed Atalante of battle wound, i. 59
—in myth, a priestess of Hekate, i. 187
—kills brother to check father's pursuit of her on the Argo, i. 112–113
———her children after they deliver poisoned robe to Glauke, i. 115
—plots of, to destroy Pelias, i. 114–115
—puts Talos under spell and causes his death, i. 114
—restoration of, demanded of Argonauts by Kolchians, i. 113
—returns to native land in disguise, expels Perses and restores Aietes to throne, i. 115
—sends poisoned robe and garland to Glauke, i. 115
—Sisyphos said to have been royal successor of, i. 37
—wife of Aigeus, plots against Aigeus at Athens, i. 100
—yields to spell of Aphrodite, i. 199
Medes, vii. 12

Medes honour everything sacred to Persians, vii. 17
Medhāvin, life of, to last as long as mountains endured, vi. 159
Media named after Medos, son of Medeia, i. 115
Mediator, fire as the, iv. 455, 456
—Nanaboojoo, x. 41
Mediators, iv. 503
Medical art, vi. 317, 318
—material in papyri, xii. 206
Medicinal herbs, v. 74
———shown victor over Chiruwi, vii. 245
Medicine, vii. 231, 245, 246, 260, 315, 336, 340; x. xvii, 18, 41, 85–87, 189, 191, 269 4, 270 5, 284 27, 291 37, 309 65; xi. 260, 287
—Babylonians regarded Enmenduranna as founder of, v. 204
——bag, x. 85, 269 4
——bonnet, x. 95
—brewing of, at end of Busk festival, x. 58
—dance, x. 269 4
—Diancecht god of, iii. 40
—festival, xi. 137
—Gula patroness of, v. 91, 110
—Kuila-moku patron deity of, ix. pl. 1, frontispiece
—lodge, x. 269 4, 307 61
——man, x. 221, 270 5; 350 9 10–351
———attitude of savage, iii. 32, 43
——men, Celtic deities have powers possessed by, iii. 54
———representations of, with reptile tongue attached to their own, iii. 166
—Mexican Earth mothers goddesses of, xi. 74
——mystery, story of, xi. 261
—oak-fire ashes as, vii. 57
—obtained in vision, x. 145
—one of primeval twins becomes, x. 115
——powers, x. 293 40, 295 44, 300 50
—secret of, obtained by Sapling from Hadui, x. 37
——shirt, x. pl. xxiv, opp. p. 178
—Society, x. 40, 216
——spirit, x. 306 59
—Suku-na-biko familiar with, viii. 229, 230
—symbol of superhuman power, x. 85
Medicines, viii. 28–29, 31, 105, 106, 107, 154, 156

Medicines burnt on Fuji origin of smoke, viii. 263
—ensure that persons shall change into certain animals on death, vii. 344
—gave Uther Pendragon form of Gorlois, iii. 184
—inkata impregnated with powerful, vii. 110
—to restore life, vii. 163
Medicus, ii. 69
Meditation, practice of, viii. 194
Medos conquered barbarians and named their country Media, i. 115
—son of Aigeus and Medeia, i. 115
Medousa beheaded, i. pl. ii (2), opp. p. xlii, 34, 35, 36
—blood from, used by Asklepios both in killing and restoring life, i. 281
—Pegasos leaps forth from severed neck of, i. 34
Medr (Behr), earth-god of South Arabia, v. 11
Medraut: see MORDRED.
Medyr, marvellous swiftness of, iii. 190
Me'enzet, day ship of sun-god, xii. 27
Mefkat ("Malachite City"), Ḥat-hôr patroness of, xii. 367 [12]
Megaira, one of the Erinyes, i. 277
Megalithic Age in Peru, xi. 215, 216, 218, 219, 220, 233, 252
Megara annexed by Theseus, i. 103
—daughter of Kreon, wife of Herakles, i. 80
—Gulf of, i. 46
—highwayman Skiron killed by Theseus near, i. 99
—Pandion takes refuge in, i. 68
—taken by Minos, i. 69
Megaris, legends of, interwoven with Argive myth, i. 28
Megaros rescued from flood by following cry of cranes, i. 19
Megasthenes, dance of Śiva recorded as early as, vi. 180
—on Indian religion, vi. 109–110
Mega(y), xii. 111
Mehekan, fire-festival in month of, vii. 58
—month dedicated to Mihr, vii. 33
Meḥen, mythological serpent, xii. 135
—solar serpent, Meneḥtet confused with, xii. 136
Meher legendary hero of Tarauntis, vii. 34

Meḥet, lioness worshipped at This, xii. 136
Meḥ(e)t-uêreʾ connected with harvest by parallel of inundation, xii. 39–40
—"Great Flood," xii. 39, 136, 390 [36]
—mistress of sky and both countries (i.e. Egypt), xii. 39 (fig. 29)
—sun called child of, xii. 39
Mehi (Meḥui?), perhaps identified with Ṭhout(i), xii. 136
Meḥit different from Meḥet, xii. 405 [47]
Mehiyyā-El, descendant of Cain, v. 202
Mehrem, South Arabian god, v. 11
Mehryan apparently derived from name Mihr, vii. 34
Meḥti, perhaps component of appellation of King Menenrêʿ, xii. 411 [12]
Meḥyan, word for temple, vii. 18
Meido, viii. 239–240
Meili, brother of Thor, ii. 74
Meilichios, Zeus, i. 163
Meïr, Ukhukh worshipped near modern, xii. 152
Meirchion, father of March, iii. 191
Mei-shan, viii. 83
"Meisho-Zuye," viii. 245
Mekel (Reshef), god of Bêth-Shan, v. 46, 48, 49
Mèkhong, valley of, route of Mongolian and Malay invaders of Indo-China, and of Buddhism, xii. 286–287, 288
Melampodes ("Black Feet"), named Aigyptos after himself, i. 30
Melampos, serpents on shoulders of Aždahak, told of, vii. 99
Melampous becomes founder of family of seers, i. 32
—cured daughters of Proitos of madness, i. 32
—Hera in form of, i. 35
Melanesia, ape or tortoise as trickster-hero in, ix. 204
—composition and mythology of, ix. xi, 103–150
—Polynesian migration through, ix. 3, 98, 243, 305
—relationship of Australian mythology and ethnology to, ix. 286, 302, 303
———Indonesian mythology to, ix. 243, 304
———Micronesian mythology to, ix. 263
Melanesian element in Polynesian myths, ix. 94–96, 98, 153, 305–306

Melanesian mythology, summary of, ix. 148–150

Melanesians, ethnic origin of, ix. 305

Melanion changed into a lion, i. 59

—won the race and Atalante as his wife, through aid of apples of Aphrodite, i. 59

Melanippos, son of Theseus, whose descendants worshipped asparagus plant, i. 98

Meléagant (Melwas), Guinevere abducted by, iii. 197, 199

Meleagar and the three Parcae, Nornagest tale may be influenced by that of, ii. 242

Meleagros and Atalante, i. 56–59

—cursed for killing his uncle in war, i. 57

—("Hunter of Members"), cult-title of Artemis, i. 182

—sisters of, changed into guinea-fowl, i. 15–16

Melek of Tyre identified with Herakles, v. 52

Meliboia, sea-nymph, i. 20

Melikertes, Isthmian games instituted in honour of, i. 46

—legend of, grew up about cult of drowned, i. 48

—Melqart passed into Greek mythology as, v. 51, 52

—nephew of Sisyphos, i. 37

—(originally called Palaimon), likened to Roman Portunas, i. 290

Melk, Milk, West Semitic for maliku, cstr. malik, Heb. melek, title of sungods, v. 50–51, 71

— -'Ashtart, name of deity at Hammon, v. 13, 53

— -Astarte, father-mother deity, v. 44, 50

Melon in Lao creation-myths, xii. 285–286

Melos, nymphs of, born from blood of Ouranos, i. 258

Melpomene ("Song"), one of the Dramatic Muses, i. 240

Melqart, city-god of Byblos, Asiatic doublet of Osiris, xii. 114

—Malik has name of, in Tyre, v. 50, 52

—tomb of, at Tyre, v. 322

—West Semitic deity, v. 11, 13, 14, 46, 51, 52, 53, 54, 55

—with chariot and four horses, v. 54

Melqart-Hypsouranios corresponds to El of Gebal, v. 67

— -Reṣef, god, v. 46

Melu, creator god, ix. 175

Meluhha of Sumerian geography, v. 4

Melusine, serpent-wife of Count Raymond of Poitiers, vii. 73

Melwas: see MELÉAGANT.

Mem Loimis, x. 223–225

"Members" denote various manifestations of same divine force, xii. 379 [14]

Memnon aids Trojans, slain by Achilles, and made immortal by Zeus, i. 130

—arms of, wrought by Hephaistos, i. 207

—child of Eos and Tithonos, i. 246

—tomb of, called memorial of, v. 322

Memorial feasts and kuala ceremonies similar, iv. 134

——reasons for preparing, iv. 58

—temples, xii. 171

—trees, iv. 25, pl. II, opp. p. 26, 35

Memory-beer, ii. 125

Memphis, Apis of, xii. 162–163

—chief temple of Astarte at, xii. 155, 411 [9]

—ennead at, xii. 216

—Ḥa-ka-Ptaḥ sacred name of city of, i. 324 [8]

—head of Osiris worshipped at, xii. 395 [81]

—Kenemtef(i) appears in, xii. 404 [38]

—Menkhet worshipped at, xii. 136

—Nefer-ḥo(r) special form of Ptaḥ at, xii. 140

—Osiris identified with Sokar(i), local god of Necropolis of, xii. 98

—Ptaḥ (Sokar[i]) god of, xii. 63, 144

—Sekhmet adored at, xii. 146

—sun ritual reminiscent of, x. 89

Mên, viii. 74

Mên Shên, guardians of the portals, viii. 77–78

Menai Strait, iii. 191

Menakā, an Apsaras, vi. 95, 143, 146

Mènam, valley of, as connected with migrations in Indo-China, xii. 286, 287

Mencius, viii. 133

Menders of Men, vii. 141, 414 [24]

Mendes, Dêdet worshipped at, xii. 132

—Ḥat-meḥit associated with Osiris ram of, xii. 133

——goddess of nome of, xii. 133

Mendes, ram of, xii. 66, 164
——(or goat[?]) of, called "soul of Dêd(u)," xii. 385 [4]
—soul of Osiris, xii. 219
— -"spirit" fused with pillar-god of Busiris, xii. 413 [12]
Menehtet (Menhet, Menhit), leonto-cephalous goddess, xii. 136
Menelaos abuses corpse of Paris, i. 132
—admitted to Elysion, i. 147–148
—and Helen, i. 133–134
——Telemachos visits court of, in Sparta, i. 138
——Paris fight duel for Helen, i. 127
—entreats aid of Odysseus against Troy, i. 123–124
—leaves Troy, i. 134
—of Argos, Helen becomes, by lot, wife of, i. 25–26
—Proteus reveals state of affairs at Sparta to, i. 261
—sets out to bring Helen back to Sparta, i. 125
—slays Deïphobos, Helen's husband, and takes her to his ships, i. 133
—son of Atreus, drove Thyestes out of Mykenai, i. 121
—wounded by Pandaros, i. 128
Menenrê', reading of appellation of King, xii. 411 [12]
Menes, King, ivory tablet of, xii. 26
Men'et, lioness, as nurse of Horus, xii. 101, 136
Mêng Ch'ang, viii. 82
—K'ang, viii. 51, 140
—River, viii. 29, 43
—Tsung, viii. 165
Mengk, evil spirit, iv. 179
Menglod, ii. 11, 112, 124, 186, 265
Menhet, Unut worshipped at, xii. 151
Menhir of Kernuz, iii. pl. xviii, opp. p. 140
Menhu(i) (Menhiu), god in human form, xii. 136, 405 [49]
Menî, goddess of fate, v. 21, 22; see also Meni, vol. v, p. 446
Menik, horse of Sun, vii. 51
Menja, giantess, ii. 114, 282–283
Menkhet, identified with Isis, xii. 136
—("Kind One") as name of Neph-thys, xii. 393 [59]
Menoikeus sacrificed himself to Ares to save Thebes, i. 52

Menoites, herdsman of Hades's kine, overpowered by Herakles, i. 88
Menqet, goddess producing vegetation, xii. 136
Menstruation, iv. 400, 504; x. 216
—protection of Sarakka sought in, iv. 253
Mentality, Chinese, viii. 45
Mentor, Athene in guise of, visits Telemachos, i. 138
Menuthias, mythical island in south, home of divine nurse of Horus, xii. 397 [94]
Menw took bird-shape, iii. 189
Mèpu, White Karens, creation-myths of, xii. 282–284
Mer festivals, iv. 262, 263, 265
Mer, Mermer, Adad identified with, v. 39, 42
Meragbuto, brother of Tagaro, ix. 126–128
"Merchant of Venice," vii. 353
Mercurio Regi and Channini, altars to, ii. 37
Mercurius, i. 301
—cultor, Artaios equivalent to, iii. 186
—represented by Téramó in modern Romagnola, i. 318
Mercury and child equated with Lug and his son, iii. pl. xviii, opp. p. 140
—Artaios equated with, iii. 186
—as messenger of Iuppiter bids Aeneas complete his journey to Italy, i. 305
—chiefly worshipped by Gauls, iii. 9
—father of Lares by Lara or Dea Tacita, i. 299
—(god Bibbu), v. 261
—identified with Thout(i) (?), xii. 55, 366 [2]
—interpretatio Romana of Wodan as, not clear, ii. 39–40
—Lugus may be Gaulish god equated by Caesar with, iii. 158–159
—(Nabûg, Nebo), fourth day of Har-ranian week sacred to, v. 154
—Odin identified with, ii. 37, 42, 55, 69
—received human sacrifice from Rhine-land tribes, ii. 37
—'Utârid identified with, vii. 384 [53]
—Wotan identified with, vii. 384 [50]
—(planet) dedicated to Sêth, xii. 55, 373 [63]
——identified with Sebg(u), xii. 55

Mercury (planet) malicious, vii. 52
——Nabû identified with, iv. 410; v. 58, 160, 317, 401 [177]; vii. 32
——representative of water, viii. 142
——represented by dark blue in Ezida, v. 159
——Tîr genius presiding over, vii. 32, 384 [54]
——Tiur corresponded to, vii. 17
Mercy, goddess of, viii. 82, 84, 113, 194
Mere-ema (" Sea mother "), iv. 211
Mereneiu, female human-like water-spirit, iv. 201
Meret in double form; water-goddess, xii. 136–137 (fig. 132)
—possibly a birth-genius of Osiris, xii. 385 [12]
Merfolk tales, x. 66
Mergen-khara, first shaman, iv. 477
— -Tengere, iv. 406
Merhi, bull-shaped or -headed divinity, xii. 137
Meriraukka, fish-god and spirit of drowned, iv. 191, 192
" Merlin," iii. 191
Merlin, iii. 52, 56, 130, 201
—in Arthurian legend, iii. 184, 200, 201, 202
Mermaid, Nāga princess as a, xii. 272
—Ran like to, ii. 191
Mermaid-like creature, Fisher-woman is a, viii. 273
Mermaids, iv. 197, 199–200, 201
—beings like, existed in early Irish belief, iii. 133
—caught by sticking needle into one's clothes, vii. 394 [37]
—otters transformed into, xi. 276
Mermen, ii. 210; x. 6, 274 [9]
Mer-mut-f disfigured form of Kenemtef(i), xii. 404 [38]
Mero, xi. 303, 312
Merodachbaladan, monument of, v. 309, 409 [2]
Meroë and Napata, Amon becomes official god of, xii. 240
Merope, wife of Sisyphos, withheld libations from dead, forcing Hades to release her husband, i. 38
Mêrrê, Me'arrêh, title of Eshmun, v. 75
Merseburg charm, ii. 17–18, 38, 46, 137, 184, 198, 243, 252
Merti (= Muit, Muut), name of Meret in dual number, xii. 136, 405 [51]

Mert-seger, goddess in human or serpent form, xii. 137
Meru, dwelling-place of Asura giants, iv. 356
—Mt., vi. 108, 149, 152, 176, 203, 215
——Loi Hsao Möng is Wa equivalent of, xii. 290
——Myimmo Taung Burmese name for, xii. 259
Merui (Murui), god in human (or originally, lion) form, xii. 137, 406 [55]
Merwîp, female water-beings, ii. 210, 212
Mer-woman, ii. 42
Mes, god, v. 138
— -tree, Mesu-tree, v. 140
Mesca taken by Garman, iii. 91
—Ulad, iii. 50, 101
Meschamaat, Lettish forest-goddess, iii. pl. xxx, opp. p. 260
Mesekhti, Egyptian name of Ursa Major, xii. 59
Mesen(?), lion-headed Horus of, xii. 388 [28]
Mesgegra, sling-ball made of brain of, iii. 157
Mesha', Kemosh mentioned on stele of, v. 47
Meshekenabek, the Great Serpent, x. 301 [50]
Meskhenet as a birth-genius of Osiris, xii. 385 [12]
——birth-goddess sometimes identified with Êpet-Tuêris, xii. 372 [52]
—explanation of name of, xii. 52, 372 [50]
—goddess of fate and birth, xii. 52 and fig. 50, 137
—symbols of, xii. 52, 372 [52]
—watches beginning of second life in realm of Osiris, xii. 378 [98]
Meskhenets, four, of Osiris, xii. 95, 385 [12]
——sun and Osiris, symbolism of, xii. 52
Meslam, mythical chamber in Underworld, v. 135
Meslamtae, god of Assyrians, v. 49
Meslamtaea and Lugalgirra, names of Nergal as twin gods, v. 69
Mesniu, mesentiu, smiths, xii. 101
Mesopotamia, vii. 379 [2]
—earliest inhabitants of, v. xvi, 1–2
—South Arabian inscriptions found in, v. 4

Mess Buachalla, child of incest, iii. 74, 75, 82

Messages, divine, brought by animals, viii. 35, 37, 38, 42, 43

—from ghosts to humans, vii. 185, 187

—to living from dead, x. 148, 149

Messene and Lakonia, myths of, i. 23–28

—divided from rest of Peloponnesos and ruled by a Heraklid family, i. 95

—Idas and Lynkeus doubles of the Dioskouroi at, i. 27

Messenger, bird as, vii. 169; viii. 321; x. 21, 81; xi. 89–90; see also BIRDS AS MESSENGERS.

—crest given bird to show he was a, vii. 169

—first ray of sun as, x. 88, 89

—fowl of the ghosts as, vii. 288

—hare as, vii. 168

—Morning Star as, x. 116–117

—of goddess of wind and water, xi. 25

——gods, v. 332

———Hermes is, i. 191

———Nabû as, vii. 384 [51]

———Juno, sacrifice to, iv. 272–273

———Light, culture-hero, xi. 202–203

———Night, shooting star as, x. 167

—snake as, to Powers Below, x. 197

—who brings offerings of man to the gods, vi. 284, 291

Messengers, devils as, v. 365, 373

—[mostly in sense of " agent "], vii. 163, 165, 166, 167, 168, 169, 170, 172, 321, 403 [25]

—of gods, v. 176–177

——seventh heaven, iv. 405

——witches, animals as, vii. 336

——Yama, the god of death, crow and pigeon are, vi. 62

—ravens as, ii. 65

—sent to ask name of forbidden fruit tree, vii. 316–319, 425 [20]

—Tlotli, Xolotl, and Tamats as, xi. 89–90, 122

Messenia, Polykaon ruler of, i. 23

Messina, Straits of, Skylla and Charybdis localized at, i. 264

Messor (" harvester "), i. 300

Messou: see MANIBOZHO.

Mestet, a scorpion of Isis, xii. 210, 211

Mestor, son of Perseus, i. 76

Mest-(yo?)tef, a scorpion of Isis, xii. 210, 211

Metal, articles of, used as protection against dead, iv. 21–22, 23, 66, 89–99, 122; see also MAGIC, PROTECTIVE PURPOSES, ETC.

—earth considered a, by Burmese, xii. 291

—may not be used in eating bear-meat, iv. 91

—molten, as purification, vi. 262

—objects representing sun and moon on shaman's dress, iv. 419, 437, 514; see also COSTUMES, SHAMAN.

—one of the elements, viii. 29, 142

—(sky), solar ship sailing over, xii. 35

—used as protection against water-spirits, iv. 206, 207

— -workers, iv. 490

— -working, vii. 259

——invented by Athene, i. 171

Metals and cinders, man created from, xi. 85

—four ages of, according to Ovid, i. 18

—Hephaistos early identified with magic powers residing in, i. 207

—in Möng Wa, xii. 291

—Khshathra Vairya patron of, vi. 260

—Numa introduced use of, vi. 299

—plentiful in Shang Dynasty, viii. 38

—transmutation of, viii. 54

Metamorphosis, x. 296 [46]–297

—in Shinto animism, viii. 221–222, 316

—spectres of shamans, liable to, iv. 11

Metaneira, mother of Demophon, rescues him from magic rites of Demeter, i. 228

Metempsychosis, vi. 71–72, 100; vii. 272; xi. 301

Meteor, fire-serpent as, iv. 10

—Gandarewa as a, vi. 325

—gods flying like a, iv. 172–173

—omen of death, x. 96

Meteorites, xii. 34

Meteorology, viii. 144

Meteors as portents, xi. 98

—flight of (when sky-cover opened), iv. 336

Methora, probably Greek name for Mathurā, vi. 110

Methusaleh = Ubardudu = Opartes, Hebrew patriarch, v. 205

Methūshā-El, descendant of Cain, v. 202

Methusuphis, Manetho's reading of appellation of King Menenrê', xii. 411 [12]

Metion, sons of, take throne of Attike from Pandion, i. 68

Metis, abstract divinity of spiritual faculty, i. 282

—(Constructive Thought), wife of Zeus, i. 156

—mother of Athene, swallowed by Zeus, i. 170

Metod, measure or fate, ii. 238

Metres, vi. 91, 92

—enumeration of, ii. 7

Metroön, shrine to Rhea containing state archives, i. 273

Mets-haldijas (Forest ruler), iv. 185

Metsänhaltia (Forest ruler), iv. 184, 185

Metsänneitsyt (Forest virgin), iv. 185, 189

Metshin, iv. 430–431

Metsmees (Forest man), iv. 232

Metta, "friendship" of the Buddha for all beings, vi. 198

Metternich Stele, xii. 207 (fig. 212), 208

Metteya, one of the Buddhas, vi. 198, 202, 206

Meulen, spirit of whirlwind, xi. 327

Mexican and Andean aboriginal civilizations, resemblances between, x. 1

—myths, rituals, etc., North American parallels to, xi. 120

Mexicatl ("mescal hare"), xi. 114

Mexico, xi. 41–123

Mexolotl, Xolotl became a, xi. 83

Mezentius, king of Etruria, slain by Aeneas, i. 306

Mfiti must not be answered at night, vii. 429 [18]

Mher, legend of hero, vii. 370

Miach, son of Diancecht, caused hand of Nuada to become whole by magic, iii. 28

Miao Ku Shê, viii. 168

Michael and Satan, strife of, parallels that of Loki and Heimdall, ii. 156

—archangel, v. 338, 354, 363, 366

——replaces Hermes in modern Greek folk-belief, i. 312–313

Micronesia, area of, ix. xi–xii

—ethnic composition of, ix. 247

—relationship of Indonesian mythology to, ix. 243, 247, 304

——Melanesian mythology to, ix. 149, 150, 247, 305

Micronesian element in Polynesian myths, ix. 98

—mythology, summary of, ix. 263

Mictecaciuatl, goddess, xi. 80

Mictlan, xi. 61, 184

Mictlanciuatl consort of skeleton god of death, xi. 53, 92

Mictlantecutli, god of the dead, and lord of the midnight hour, xi. 53, 54, 55, 56, 57, 80, pl. XI, opp. p. 80, 83, 90, 92

Midac, son of King of Lochlann, iii. 170

Midas given ears of an ass, i. 220

—Kybele and Gordias parents of, i. 275

—Lityerses son of, i. 253

—receives power from Dionysos of turning whatever he touched into gold, i. 220

Midday demons, iii. 12

—spirit, iii. 266

Middle America, xi. 41

—earth, human dwellers on, vii. 137

—Kingdom, Kachin vault of heaven, xii. 263

—Lands where Reeds Grow Luxuriantly, Japanese archipelago, viii. 210–211

—Path, viii. 385 [5]

—Place, xi. 53, 55, 57, pl. IX, opp. p. 70, 115, 140

—— = Earth, iv. 309

——navel of earth, x. 178, 185, 186, 187, 191, 193, 203, 204, 220, 287 [31]

Mideia founded by Perseus, i. 35

Midewiwin, sacred Medicine Society, x. 40, 302 [52]

Midgard, circle surrounding, iv. 372

—made of Ymir's eyebrows, ii. 325, 326

— -serpent, ii. 10, pl. X, opp. p. 76, 81, 85, 86, 87–88, 93, 94, 145, 193, 216, 279, 313, 328–329, 340, 341, 345; iv. 345

—Thor as defender of, ii. 81, 85, 96

Midir, god of Tuatha Dé Danann, iii. 25, 33, 40, 41, 50, 52, 55, 56, 73, 74, 75, 76, 79, 80, 81, 82, 91, 121, 151, 174

Midsummer Day celebrations, ii. 158, pl. XX, opp. p. 160, 202

—Eve, flames seen on, iv. 173

—Night, strength of "Wild Women" most apparent on, iii. 264

——sun's position on, ii. 197

——water-spirit as musician may be approached on, iv. 206

Midsummer water festival in Europe and Armenia, vii. 60–61
Midwife, iv. 257
—Scandinavian terms for, mean Earth mother, ii. 196
Midwives, dwarfs seek aid of human, ii. 272
—human, required for human wives of water-elves, ii. 211–212
Miehts-hozjin (Master of forest), iv. 177
Mientuš, Mintyš, genius of reindeer, iv. 176
Mier-iema (" Sea mother "), iv. 211
Might, Ṛbhus grandchildren of, vi. 57
Migir-Dagan, king of Mari, v. 78
Migrating, taking down of temples before, ii. 76
Migration and culture of native races, xi. 16–18, 348 [2]
—legends, x. 62–63, 70–73, 124–128, 210
— -myth, Mosquito, xi. 185
— -myths, Aztec, xi. 111–118, 359 [13]
——see " POPUL VUH."
—waves of, viii. 211
Migrations in Oceania, ix. xiii, 9–10, 21, 22, 304–306
—of Maya, xi. 128–131
—Polynesian, ix. 98, 150, 153, 205, 243
Miho, fairy dance on beach of, viii. 261
Mi-hos, lion-god, xii. 137 (fig. 133)
—Nefer-têm identified with, xii. 141
Mihr, vii. 33–35; see also MITHRA; MITRA.
—Anahit identified with, vii. 381 [2] (ch. iii)
——sister of, vii. 26
—deity, and temple of, vi. 17, 58, 381 [1] (ch. ii)
——son of Aramazd, vii. 20
—sun-god, vii. 43
—Vahagn probably rival of, vii. 43
Mi-ib of Anu, v. 126
Mikal, Makkal, Mukal, v. 50
—of Beisan, stele of, v. fig. 25, opp. p. 44
Mile, son of Bile, iii. 10, 43, 46, 65, 137
Mi-lê-fo, viii. 194
Milesians, Tuatha Dé Danann and the, iii. 24, 42–48, 49
Miletos founded city in Asia Minor bearing his name, i. 60
—legends of, interwoven with Argive myth, i. 28

Miletos, sons of Zeus and Europe quarrelled over, i. 60
Milfoil plant used in divination, viii. 135
Milhoi, Lamu name for Ngoloko, vii. 412 [4]
Mili'ar, tale of mortality of, ix. 253
Militia, Féinn regarded as hireling, iii. 160, 162
Milk, iv. 256, 257; vii. 74, 79, 391 [16]
— -breasted goddess, iv. 354, 355, 359
—caused to flow downstream, iii. 151
—churning of ocean of, vi. 104, 106, 111, 132, 139, 151
—depends on gods, or on sacrifice, mythic belief that, iii. 26, 46–47
—destruction of, as punishment, iii. 71, 72
—first-, iv. 446–447
—Lake mother, iv. 413–416
——of, iv. 352, 353, 357, 395, 413–414
—of all brown, hairless cows claimed by Bres, iii. 26
— -offering to cobras, xii. 301
— -Para, iv. 172
—poured ceaselessly from vessel to vessel, iv. 490, 492
—sacrificed to thunder in spring, and to earth, iv. 445, 446, 460
—saved gingko-tree in Tōkyō, viii. 342
—skin of, offered to fire, ii. 149
—sweet, of Mary, supposed to cure all disease, iv. 257
— -vessel, symbol of mysterious god, xii. 371 [44]
Milking of moon, vii. 48
Milkmaid: see COW-MAID, LOKI AS.
Milky Way, iv. 336, 414, 434–436; v. 178, 317; vii. 37, 49, 386 [14] (ch. vi.); 231–232; viii. 132; 378 [8]; x. 50, 95, 96, 117, 200, 274 [10], 294 [42]; xi. 76, 98, 278, 307, 323, 336, 356 [24]
——as trunk of celestial tree, x. 294 [42]
——cannibal pole sometimes the, x. 249
——Mother Scorpion receives souls at end of, xi. 185
——regarded by Arctic tribes as tree-trunk, iv. 82
——termed " Gwydion's Castle," iii. 100
Mill, first in Ireland, iii. 137
—magic, giantesses ground army from, ii. 114
— -spirit, iv. 167, 168
— -stone of Frodi, ii. 283, 284

Millenniums, three, the period between Angra Mainyu's invasion and Zarathushtra's reform, vi. 305

Miller (?) apparently the name of a goddess, xii. 75, 380 38

Millet given by Hou-chi, viii. 6
—grew on forehead of food-goddess, viii. 232
—stalk, climbing of, viii. 229

Millions of Millions, sun-bark called, placed in charge of Shu, xii. 77–78
—[of years], Rê' receives place in ship called, xii. 83

Millipede, vii. 286

Millstone grinding by itself, vii. 327, 328

Milómaki, singer who was burned and from whose ashes grew the paxiuba palm, xi. 294

Miluchradh, daughter of Cuailnge, iii. 168–169

Mimameid ("tree of Mimir"), world-tree, ii. 168, 331, 346

Mime the Old, master-smith, ii. 170

Mimes, ii. 115

Mimesā, Mimir's name found in, ii. 169, 170

Mimetic magic, ii. 96

Miming, satyr, ii. 132, 170

Mimir, dwarf, ii. 267
—(Mim, Mimi), water-spirit, ii. 26, 49, 50, 52, 66, 78, 167–170, 240, 340, 341, 346, 385 63
—Saga may be female counterpart of, ii. 183

Mimir's head embalmed and charmed by Odin so that it might impart wisdom, ii. 46, 50

Mimling, Mimir's name found in, ii. 169

Mimon, i. pl. VIII (2), opp. p. 8

Mîn, v. 30; xii. 160
—Amen-Rê' identified with, xii. 221
—and Amon, prehistoric differentiation of, xii. 21
—described in hymn to Amen-Rê', xii. 236
—earliest statues of Amon like those of, xii. 129
—god worshipped at many places in Upper Egypt, xii. 137–139
—interpretation of feathers on head of, xii. 219
—mother of, Usret once known as, xii. 151

Mîn of Koptos not a Troglodyte god, xii. 410 1
—represents Tammuz-Adonis, xii. 156
—sacred bull of, xii. 163
—Sanctuary of, xii. 138

Min, Duke of, viii. 138
—Kyawzwa, son of king of Pagān, resemblance of, to Bacchus or Dionysos, xii. 353
——variant version about, xii. 354
—Rama (afterwards king of Pagān), child hatched from second egg of Thusandi, xii. 277
—Shwe Thè, ancestor of all the chiefs of the Palaungs, xii. 276
——Yo, emperor of China who took title Udibwa, xii. 276
—Sun, viii. 162

Minaean, Akkadian language allied to, v. 2

Minaeans sons of Wadd (moon-god), v. 7

Minamoto clan, Hachiman patron deity of, viii. 305, 306, 307, 312, 353, 383 37

Mind, abstract divinities of states of, i. 282
—and throat, same word to designate, x. 262
—(Manas), vi. 173, 179

Mineral "men" and "women," x. 188

Minerals arose from Gaya Maretan's members, vi. 294

Minerva, i. 299
—equated with British goddess Sul, iii. 11
——Celtic goddess (Brigit, Brigindo, Brigantia), iii. 11
—in Caesar's account of Gaulish gods, iii. 9

Ming (a name), viii. 18
—Dynasty, events in, viii. 62, 66, 67, 70, 72, 81, 95, 96, 113, 143
—Huang, Emperor, viii. 125, 134
—Ti, Emperor, viii. 134, 169, 188

Mink (son of the Sun), story of, x. 255, 256

Minoa founded on site of burial-place of Minos, i. 65

Minos (Artemis in a divergent account) gave spear and dog to Prokris, i. 72
—bewitched with drug by Pasiphaë, i. 72

Minos, character, achievements, and date of, i. 63–64
—device of, to trace Daidalos, i. 65
—Glaukos of Anthedon duplicates son of, i. 42
—grief-stricken while sacrificing to Charites on Paros, i. 236
—interpretations of, i. 63–64
—judge in Hades, i. 143–144
—killed by daughters of Kokalas, i. 65
—remained in Crete and drew up code of laws, i. 61, 64
—shade of, appears to Odysseus in Hades, i. 146
—son of Zeus, i. 157
———and Europe, i. 60
—tests parentage of Theseus, i. 101
—tribute of Attic youths to, i. 100
—Triton directs Argonauts to Sea of, i. 114
—war with, i. 68–69
Minotaur and Theseus, i. 102 (fig. 4)
—birth and death of, i. 61–62
—seven youths and maidens annually sacrificed to, i. 69
—Theseus offers himself as victim to the, but killed him, i. 100–101
Minû-anni or Minû-ullu, titles of Ishtar as goddess of fate, v. 21
Minyas and Proitos, madness of daughters of, due to ecstasy of Dionysiac ritual, i. 32, 215, 222
Miodhchaoin, iii. 40
Mi-oya-no-kami, ancestor-god, viii. 251
Miqtu ("prostration by heat"), v. 163
Mirabilia on Twrch Trwyth appended to Nennius's "History," iii. 125, 184
Miracle-plays, xii. 194–195
Miracles, viii. 106, 123; 219
—concerning the Buddha, vi. 194, 196, 199, 212
—healing, iii. 60
—Ikkaku Sennin performed, viii. 276
—performed by Christian saints at pagan wells, ii. 208
———Tonapa, xi. 239
—power to do, sign of divinity, v. 300
—tombs of saints deemed to work, vi. 244
Miraculous articles, viii. 123, 132, 229, 262, 264–265, 271–273, 279, 286, 304, 306, pl. XXXVI, opp. p. 314, 315, 319, 320, 329, 358, 364, 381 [5] (ch. iv); see also MAGIC OBJECTS.

Miraculous births: see BIRTHS, MIRACU-LOUS.
—growth, vii. 221
—origin of mankind, ix. 167, 168, 169, 170
—powers of medicine-bag, x. 85
Mirage created by Pan, i. 268
— -horse, iv. 421
Miroku (Maitreya), viii. 241
Mirror, covering of, in presence of dead, iv. 22
—magic, vii. 358; viii. 262, 325, 329
———of shamans, iv. 419, 436–437
—one of three insignia of ruling family and sympathetic magic to welcome the sun, viii. pl. VIII, opp. p. 226, 228
—reflecting, xi. 61, 62, 70
Mirrors, Cheremiss, superstitions about, iv. 12–13
—two metal = sun and moon, iv. 419
Mirsi, title of Tammuz, v. 191, 403 [5]
Mirsu, god of irrigation, v. 191
Miru, lord of dead, ix. 76
Mirzāpur District, Karamnāśā River traverses, vi. 235
Mîśâru, attendant of Shamash, v. 67, 151
Miscanthus grass grew from grave of Yorikaze, viii. 347
Miscegenation, x. 55–56, 280 [17]
Miserliness of Bres, iii. 26
Misfortune, personification of, iii. 252
Misharu, judge of souls in Underworld, v. 80
—("Rectitude"), a son of Shamash, vii. 40
Misikinebik, monster, x. 45
Mis-khum, a Vogul spirit, iv. 179
Misōr in genealogy of gods of Tyre, v. 67
—(Misharu), culture-hero, vii. 40–41
Miśrakeśī, an Apsaras, vi. 143
Mission, ancestral spirits do not live in sky but go on some, vii. 195
Mist, Astλik wraps herself in morning, vii. 39
—Erwand confined in, vii. 80, 83
—magic, divinities hid in, iii. 37, 56, 177
———surrounds Cormac, iii. 118
———wall-less tower hidden by, iii. 201
— -man of the Spring Mountain, viii. 294–295
—("Mist"), Valkyrie, ii. 249
—Notos spreads, i. 265
—origin of, ix. 34

Mist, Trojans enveloped in, by Hera, i. 164, 166

Mistelteinn, sword, ii. 136

Mistletoe kills Balder, ii. 129, 134, 136

Mistress of Both Countries, Amonet also called Nebt-taui, xii. 130

——Life and Death, Sedna as, x. 6

Mistresses, fairy and divine, are the wooers, iii. 181–182

—of Fionn, iii. 168

Mists, magic: see GLAMOUR.

Mitanni inscription, gods listed on the, vi. 25, 30, 32

Mithilā (northern Bihār, India), Lao Ngu governor of, xii. 275

Mithra, vi. 260–261, pl. XXXII, opp. p. 260, pl. XXXIII, opp. p. 264, 273, 287, 289, pl. XLIV, opp. p. 342, 346; see also MIHR; MITRA.

—(Armenian), a fire-god, vii. 58

—Armenians perhaps sacrificed to, vii. 15

—Auramazda, and Anāhita form triad in ancient Persia, vii. 42

—fails to find secure position in Armenia, vii. 42

—influenced Classical mind more deeply than "Isiac mysteries," xii. 121

—Persian, undoubted solar nature of, vi. 24, 27, 56

Mithraic mysteries not recorded in Armenia, vii. 34

Mithrakana festival, vii. 34

Mitnal, a hell, xi. 138–139

Mi-toshi-no-kami, god of harvest, viii. 232–233

Mit-othin may have been Loki, ii. 140

—story, ii. 61, 63–64, 175, 176

Mitra, vi. 18, 20, 22–23, 24, 25, 26, 27, 28, 29, 43, 53, 54, 56, 85, 137, 143, 183, 355 [5]; see also MIHR; MITHRA.

Mitsima, x. 11

Mitsotsozini taught Vere to make fire, vii. 155–156

Mittanis, Indo-Iranians among, vii. 379 [2]

Mitthu Bhūkhiya, saint consulted before a crime, vi. 244

Miwa, sanctuary of, dedicated to Great-Land-Master, viii. 341–342

Mixcoatl of the Zenith, Milky Way was white hair of, xi. 98

—similar to Huitzilopochtli, xi. 60, 87

Mimixcoua, xi. 144

Miya-jima (Itsuku-shima), shrine of, viii. 269–270

Miyako, viii. 307, 308, 309, 310, 312

—Issun-bōshi in, viii. 286

—tale of pine-tree which stretches branches towards, viii. 254

Mjöllnir, hammer of Thor, made by dwarf Sindri, ii. 78, 83, 88, 346; see also HAMMER OF THOR.

Mjotudr-inn, or Mit-othin, connected with fate, ii. 64

Mjotvid, tree thought to be Yggdrasil, ii. 167

Mkunare and Kanyanga, tale of, vii. 266–268

Mkupa-tree, vii. 401 [6]

Mlanje, vii. 182

Mlecchas (Barbarians) produced by Nandinī, vi. 145

Mná síde (women of the síd), iii. 49

Mnemosyne, ancient abstract deity of spiritual faculty, i. 282

—("Memory"), i. 6

——mother, by Zeus, of the Muses, i. 156, 238

Mnevis bull, identification of Osiris with, only late, xii. 385 [4]

—sacred animal of Heliopolis, xii. 163

Moab, only deity of, v. 46–47

Mobed, a class of priest, vi. 285

Moccasins, red-hot, x. 231, 232

Moccus, swine-god, iii. 124

Mochica language of Chimu, xi. 224

Módgud guarded Gjoll-bridge, ii. 130, 304–305

Modi, son of Thor, ii. 74, 80, 346

Modron, father of Mabon, iii. 187

Mod's hounds pursued boar, iii. 125

Mœrthöll (form of Mardoll) wept tears of gold, ii. 126

Mogan-Khan, iv. 396

Mogōk Hills, Thusandi lived in spirit lake in, xii. 276

Mogthrasir's dwelling-place, maidens descend over, ii. 346, 347

Mohilev, autumnal dziady in government of, iii. 282

Moi clan tradition of first man, vii. 156

Moira, Moirai (Fates), i. 283–284; iv. 392, 393; v. 22, 383 [99]; vi. 24

Moirai bridesmaids to Hera, i. 5

—influence Eddic concept of Norns, ii. 243

Moirai prophesied Meleagros's death, i. 56
—survive in modern Greek folk-belief, i. 315
—three, daughters of Zeus and Themis, i. 284
Moisture, Zeus Ikmaios divinity of, i. 252
Mökkurkálfi, clay giant, ii. 82, 96
Moksha, a dialect of the Mordvins, iv. xvi
Molama clan, tale of ancestors (as heaven-dwellers) of, vii. 138
Molokai, island of, ix. 89
Molossians, country of, captured by Neoptolemos, i. 135
Molourian rocks, Ino with Melikertes in her arms, leapt from, into Gulf of Megara, i. 46
Moluccas, mouse-deer as trickster-hero in, ix. 203
Mombo-wa-Ndlopfu, snake Master of forest, vii. 192, 194
Momemphis, sacred cow of, xii. 163
Momiji-gari (Maple Itinerary), viii. 289–290
Momotarō (Peachling Boy), story of, viii. 313–314
Mon (Anglesey), iii. 191
Mōn, language of Talaings, perhaps originally spoken throughout Farther India, xii. 253
—myths of, have influenced those of Siamese, xii. 268
— -Hkmēr, affiliation of non-Negrito Indonesians with, ix. 155
——incest theme of Indonesia compared with occurrence among, ix. 165
—relation of, to Indonesian mythology, ix. 241, 244
Monastery, White Horse, viii. 188
Mondamin, myth of, x. 27–28, 283 24, 289 35
Money, x. 228, 239
—bags of, in Swing Festival, xii. 325
—chest, prayers for, iv. 275
— -Para, iv. 172–173
—sacrifice, iv. 147, 193
—sacrificial, ii. 187
—see also items s.v. COINS.
Möng Hsang, dwelling-place of the creator spirit, xii. 289
——sky-abode of Hkun Hsang L'röng, xii. 290

Möng Kawng (Mogaung in Upper Burma), Hkun Lu established kingdom at, xii. 275
—Mai, city built by Hkun Hsang L'röng, xii. 291
—Mang-lün Sampula, capital of Hkun Hsang L'röng, xii. 292
—Mao, home of Pappawadi and Tüng Hkam, xii. 274
—Wa, country of the Wa, xii. 291
Mongan, Fionn reborn as, iii. 112, 180
—King, iii. 59, 62–64, 175, 180, 185, 210–211
—tale of, iii. 119
Mongolian invasion of Indo-China along Mèkhong, xii. 287
Monimos, Evening Star, companion of Sun, v. 35
Monkey and crab, tale of, viii. 330–331
—as solar archer, xii. 428 85
—Indra's, vi. 62
—nameless cosmic god in form of, xii. 222
—put to fetch water in sieve, xi. 269
—red, viii. 154
Monkeys, xi. 91, 93, 164, 172
—and hunter, tale of, viii. 355
—didis may be personifications of, xi. 277
—inferior creation ancestors of, ix. 175
—sacred, xii. 365 27
Monks, Buddhistic, formula for protection of, vi. 203
—cutting of hair of, vii. 95
—origin of Christian community of, said to be in Buddhism, vi. 207
—visions of, viii. 273
Monotheism, iv. 390; vi. 19; viii. 49; 221; xi. 241
—in Sumerian and Semitic religions, v. xviii, 89, 91, 93
—late and rare in Egyptian religion, xii. 8–9, 10, 361 1
Monotheistic deities, Enlil and Marduk are, v. 155
—in spirit and teaching, Hebrew tale of Flood is, v. 231, 232
Mons angel, example of how myths grow, vii. 348
Monsoon, Hanumān may be connected with, vi. 129, 236
—mating of male with female deity at time of, ix. 166

Monster, armless and legless, grew from mating of sword-handle and spindle, ix. 159, 176, 177
—judge of dead, xii. 176
—of pool, how European tries to kill, vii. 188
—sea, carrying tablet on back, viii. 30
—water, ix. 280
Monsters, x. 10, pl. VIII, opp. p. 30, 44–45, 79, 99, 104, 106, 115, 132–133, 139, 156, 159, 163, 165, 179, 187–188, 205, 206, 244, 251, 261, 268 ², 274 ⁹, 301 ⁵⁰
—animal-headed, ii. pl. v, opp. p. 22, pl. XXIX, opp. p. 218
—chained, free at end of world, ii. 339–340, 341
—constitute oldest generation of divine beings, xii. 73
—(dragons, serpents, etc.) and spirits, world of, vii. 72–92
—in art, xi. 221–222, 368 ⁸
——battle of Mag-Tured, iii. 25
—of Chaos, v. 86, 102, 108, 290
—see vol. vii. 242–257
Montezuma, Aztec empire under, fell to Cortez, xi. 44, 45–49, 111–112, 116–118
—Xocoyotzin emperor of Mexico in 1502, xi. 118–120
Month, days of, not personified but placed under protection of gods, xii. 66
—eighth, and first day of every month, consecrated to sun, vii. 47
——dedicated to Renenutet, xii. 66
—first Egyptian, under protection of Thout(i), xii. 66
—god of fourth, viii. 76
— -signs, xi. 148
—(tenth), with and without gods, viii. 250
—twenty-fourth day, consecrated to moon, vii. 47
Months of Zuñi year, names of, x. 192
—twelve, of year, Gilgamish epic not based on, v. 268
——spokes of wheel equal the, vi. 24
Mont(u), Amen-Rê' identified with, xii. 221
—Anit spouse of, xii. 130
—black bull (Buchis) of, xii. 163
—deity of Hermonthis, xii. 139
—oldest type of, xii. 140 (fig. 139)

Monuments, inscriptions and symbols on, iii. 7, 8, 9
—numeral and dating systems on, xi. 129–131
Moods, nine, iv. 378
Moon, ii. 89, 90, 124, 183–184, 196–201, 279, 385 ⁵⁹
—iii. 319, 320, 321, 324, 325, 326, 328, 359 ³⁸ ⁴⁶, 360 ⁶² ⁷⁵ ⁸⁰
—iv. 417, 419–425
—vi. 22, 25, 31, 36, 47, 50, 55, 58, 59, 67, 69, 91, 93, 101, 110, 136, 137, 149, 151, 192, 232, 233, 234, 239; 276, 278, 287, 293, 316, 317, 348
—vii. 11, 17, 47–53; 119, 144, 166, 167, 168, 169, 170, 220, 225, 226, 227, 228, 232, 289, 290, 291, 321
—viii. 29, 42, 51, 103, 137, 142, 143
—ix. 37, 54, 79, 88, 110, 111–112, 159, 177, 239, 250, 253–254, 273, 276–278, 286, 314 ⁹⁸ ¹⁰³, 342 ²⁶
—x. xxii, 8, 25, 36, 37, 81, 108, 113–114, 176, 187, 205, 231, 254–258, 273 ⁸, 276 ⁶³–278, 291 ³⁷, 300 ⁵⁰, 309 ⁶⁴ ⁶⁵
—xi. 28, 51, 57, 58, 60, 61, 69, 82, pl. XII, opp. p. 88, 89, 93, 97, 121, 139, 167, 176, 193, 197, 198, 199, 200, 202, 207, 223, 224, 234, 235, 240, 241, 246, 277, 278, 304–311, 313, 319, 330, 342
—address to, v. 317
—and katsura-tree, connexion between, viii. 232, 378 ¹⁵
——sun called "eyes of Horus," xii. 102
——children of Ormazd, vii. 33
——placed in different storeys of sky, iv. 309, 405
—Artemis equated with, i. 186
—as eye of Heaven, xii. 38
——father of heavenly god, xii. 366 ¹
——ibis-egg, xii. 208, 423 ³⁴
——second eye of heavenly god, xii. 33
—astral deity of primitive Semitic religion, v. 6, 11
—Bil one of two beings who follow, ii. 16, 184
—born of Nut and Qêb, xii. 42
—bringing down of, vii. 366–367
— -carrier, x. 157, 162
—child of Amen-Rê' and Mut, xii. 34
—Chins built tower to capture the, xii. 266
—confusion of earth-goddess with, in nearer East, vii. 12

Moon cult, v. 6, 378 [14]
—darkness of, caused by seven devils, v. 287
—day of full, v. 152
—diseases caused by, vii. 48
— -disk created, x. 162
—Egyptian, usually masculine in theology, xii. 372 [57]–373
—giving of, after Fall, iv. 385
— -god, Allah and El supposed by some to be ancient, v. 5
——birth of, from right eye of Father-God, viii. 224
——[Khôns(u)], xii. 34 and fig. 18
——some say Yāw a, v. 43
——story of, viii. 232
——[Thout(i)], xii. 33 (fig. 17)
——wandering, iv. 223
— -goddess, xi. pl. vii, opp. p. 60
——Hekate as, in fifth century b.c., i. 187
— -gods, v. 3, 5, 56, 57, 87, 92, 106, 154, 201
——Sydyk and Misōr as, vii. 40
—grows every month by swallowing stars, xii. 423 [24]
—horns of, and man in the, iv. 223–224
—how night came to be ruled by, xii. 84–85
—identified with Soma, vi. 47–48, 90, 136
—importance of, among Semites of South Arabia, v. 87
—in eclipse swallowed by frog according to Shans, xii. 333
——period of darkness belonged to realm of Nergal, v. 136
—Io identified with, i. 30
—katsura dark spots on the, viii. 339
—King, viii. 263
—lover of Endymion, i. pl. xiv (1), opp. p. 36
—Mane steers course of, ii. 183
—may have been adjudged to Anahit or Nane, vii. 17
—men become wolves at changing of, ii. 293
—Mîn identified with, xii. 139
—mother, x. 206
—never rival of sun in Egypt, xii. 33
—old man and mother, iv. 222, 223
—Osiris connected with, xii. 94, 123
—palace, viii. 258

Moon regulator of time for primitive man, xii. 33
—represented by silver in Ezida, v. 159
—scanty attention paid to, xii. 24
—semi-mythical description of, vii. 52
—state-minister of first two Shan kings descended from, xii. 275
—sun parallel with, xii. 28
—tale of Mrile's search for, vii. 136–137
—tradition of wolf swallowing, iii. 229
—weaker reappearance of sun at night, xii. 33
— -worship, iii. 273; iv. 225–227, pl. xxviii, opp. p. 228; v. 152–153
——Hebrew Sabbath and Babylonian Šapattu originated in, v. 153
Moose connected with east wind, x. 23
Moosweibel, forest-elf, ii. 205, 206
Moot, Geirrid summoned to the, ii. 300
Moqwaio, the Wolf, x. 43
Mora, living being whose soul leaves body at night, thus allowing other souls to enter in, iii. 228
Moral basis largely lacking for Egyptian divinities, xii. 204
—causation, viii. 217
—demands of gods, necessity of obedience to, xii. 233
—tales with a, viii. 161–173
Morality, judgement of Greek myths on, i. lv–lvi
Moralltach, sword of Manannan or of Oengus, iii. 66
Morals, code of, among Egyptians, xii. 184–185, 418 [5], 419 [6]
Moras, or Kikimoras, play rôle of household gods, iii. 228
Morc (probably March) taxed Nemedians, iii. 108
Mordo-Khan, rain-maker, iv. 448
Mordred, nephew and enemy of Arthur, iii. 184, 185, 190, 191, 192, 193, 197, 198
Mordu, iii. 110
Mordvins, a Finno-Ugric people, iv. xvi, xix
—description of hero-cult of, iv. 157–158
—influenced by some Indo-European people who gave them their name for " God," iv. xix
Morgen, chief of nine sisters, rules Isle of Apples, iii. 193, 194

Morimarusam (= Mortuum Mare), sea which the dead crossed, or possibly calm sea, or ice-covered sea, iii. 17

Moriori records of myths, ix. 9–10

Morna, clan-chief, iii. 164

—clanna, iii. 160, 161, 163, 168

Morning Star, vii. 228; xi. pl. xii, opp. p. 88, 97, 102, 120, 166–167, 193, 234, 241, 360 23

——Angel (Myojo-tenshi), viii. 289

——Dua[-uêr] confused with, xii. 132, 404 22

——herald of the sun, x. 81, 88, 90, 93–96, 110, 116–117, 176, 278 14

——Quetzalcoatl associated with, xi. 68

——sacrifice to, x. 76, pl. xiv, opp. p. 76, 88, 90, 94, 176, 286 29, 305–306; xi. 79

—theft of, x. 230

Morrígan, war-goddess, iii. 24, 25, 30, 33, 39, 56, 60, 67, 69, 70, 132, 136, 153, 154, 156, 158, 174

Mortality, v. 113

—lot of man, v. 186

—of man theme of Gilgamish legend, v. 234

—see IMMORTALITY FOR MAN.

Mortals abducted daughters of gods, iii. 91

—gods appeared as particular, iii. 56

—helping, iii. 62–67

—tire of divine land, iii. 182

—transformed by gods, iii. 60

Mortars and pestle, vii. 124, 130

Morvran, son of Tegid the Bald, iii. 109, 188, 189

Moschi, god of, vii. 66

Moses, birth of, v. 157–158

—called Osarsyph by Manetho, xii. 149, 409 104

—of Khoren on Armenian religion, vii. 22, 24, 26, 29, 42–43, 47

Moshanyana (Litaolane), tale of, vii. 220–222

Mosquitoes, iv. 386–389; x. 253–254, 291 37

Moss-wives, ii. 42, 206, 207, 208

Mossynoikoi (people of topsy-turvy morals), Argonauts sail to, i. 111

Most, temple of Thor at, ii. 76

Mother-earth, ii. 102, 126, 195; iii. 329; x. xvi, xvii, 22, 81, 90, 91–93, 207, 285 28, 289 34

Mother-earth, Demeter wrongly explained as, i. 225

— -goddess, vii. 5, 11

——argument that human kings married with, v. 380 48

——astral connexion of Sumerian and Semitic, v. 29

——death of, beginning of antitheses between life and death, etc., viii. 222–224

——son, and husband died yearly and descended to Underworld, v. 113

——Sumerian, became many distinct goddesses, v. 108

——three types of, v. 109

— -goddesses, v. 13, 14, 15, 17, 19, 20, 21, 30, 36, 41, 44, 56, 75, 108, 151, 167, 182, 188, 196, 200, 236, 275, 313, 368

—great, iv. 413–416

——Rhea-Kybele is the, i. 273–276

—large river called, iv. 210, 211–212

—miraculous aid of own, against stepmother, ix. 89

—of Als, vii. 88, 394 47

——Earth invoked, ii. 195

——God, as creatress, iv. 324

——gods, xi. 54

——Allāt as, v. 16, 17

——wrongly applied to Anahit, vii. 382 15

——heaven, sky-goddess, later merged into Virgin Mary, iv. 220

—— -pearl, powder of, viii. 128

——sun and fire, vii. 49, 50, 54

—Scorpion, xi. 185

—serpent-, of Scythian race, vii. 73

Motherhood of goddess (Earth), basis of school of theology, v. 12

——Semitic deities, v. 12

Mothers (apparently the diseases of children), vi. 359 4

—as dispensers of fate, iii. 249

—see MĀTṚS (vol. vi).

—seven, who represent and control diseases similar to smallpox, vi. 246

—spirits of deceased, become dispensers of fate, iii. 249

Mothir bore Jarl to Heimdall, ii. 153

Motifs, Asiatic, xii. 153, 154, 398 106, 410 3

Mot'ša-oza, bath-house god, iv. 167

Motsognir, creation of dwarf, ii. 264

Mound, magic, Pwyll sat on a, iii. 94

—sleeping on, to gain inspiration, ii. 311

Mound to heaven, men tried to build, x. 63
Mounds of elves, ii. 224, 225, 226
——Himukai being excavated, viii. 211
—regarded as retreats of Tuatha Dé Danann or places of sepulture, iii. 49, 51
—seen on red pillars on St. John's Eve, ii. 286
Mountain and desert, x. 129–181
" Mountain and Sea Classic," viii. 17
——valley, how created, x. 62
—as land of dead, v. 168, 401 ³
—Chant, x. 173–174
—cosmic, in Old Testament, iv. 343
—demon of, viii. 90–91
—diamond, of paradise, iv. 384
—earth conceived of as a, x. 43, 44
— -giant, sea is a, ii. 171
— -giants, ii. 276
—golden, iv. 378, 379
—iron, iv. 340
—Maid, tale of, viii. 220
— -man (Hsien), viii. 114
—man of, ii. 44
— -names, ii. 44
—of sunrise, 'Apop rises behind, to attack solar bark, xii. 106
——eastern, sun's eye discovered in, xii. 86
——the west, xii. 28
—Pijaos ancestors come from, xi. 200
—quietness required when passing high, to prevent storm, iv. 457
—smoking, x. 63, 64
— -spirits protectors of living, iv. 76–77
—splitting of, x. 243
—the holy, location of Seides, iv. 101, 103, 104
—upshooting, x. 294 ⁴²
—Ukko's, iv. 229
— -woman: see YAMA-UBA.
—world-, iv. 341–348
Mountains abodes of dwarfs, ii. 269
——giants, ii. 276
—and valleys, origin of, ix. 159, 165, 179, 180
—as supports of sky, xii. 35
—become plains under feet of Gwadyn Ossol, iii. 190
—clefts in, place of sacrifice to thunder-gods, iv. 231–232
—conquest of, by animal-powers, x. 134

Mountains, cosmic, in relation to the sun, xii. 38
——sun rises between, xii. 43
—creation of, iv. 314, 318, 319, 321, 325, 332, 420
—five sacred, viii. 70, 71, 193
—gods dwell on, ii. 23
—held in veneration, x. 132
—holy, customs of dead dwelling in, iv. 76–77; see also UNDERGROUND INHABITANTS OF HOLY MOUNTAINS.
—home of wind, iv. 457
—in charge of genius (" shadow "), iii. 228
——Eddic mythology, ii. 202–203
—of the Immortals, viii. 114
—raised by Rê', xii. 82
—require offerings, x. 135
—sacred, vii. 62–63, 77; see also MASSIS.
—saivo-animals live in holy, iv. 285
—seven sacred, earth from, x. 161, 162
—Śiva dwells in, vi. 81
—snow-covered at cardinal points, x. 160
—Soma's abode in, vi. 47
—some Nāga tribes live in, viii. 268
—strife of, ix. 181–182
—with wings in Vedic legend, vi. 159
—worship of, iii. 273; vi. 236
Mourning chants, iii. 32
—customs as ordeals, x. 282 ²¹
—feast of, for Ba'alti, v. 340
—signs of, ix. 136
—ungirding belt sign of, iv. 27
Mouse as soul in Siryan tradition, iv. 7
— -deer in trickster tales, ix. 187–195, 203–204
—Devil changes into, in Ark, iv. 362, 363
—frees sun, x. 49
—Insatiable a, ix. 256–257
—wedding of, viii. 333–334
—why cat at enmity with, ix. 202
Mouseia established in Greek states, i. 239
Mouth at back of head, vii. 346, 413 ²³
Mouths, many, of witches, vii. 334
Mower, Lityerses as a, i. 253–254
Mōymis, intelligible world, begotten by Tauthe and Apasōn, v. 290
Možga pijos (" možga sons "), iv. 118
Mpambe, local name for " God " in a part of Nyasaland, vii. 126, 161

Mpembe, white stranger appears to, vii. 349–351, 429 [2]–430

Mpobe the hunter followed animal into burrow and reached Country of Dead, vii. 173–174, 177, 184

Mṛda, appellative of Rudra or Śiva, vi. 85

Mṛga, constellation, vi. 76

Mṛgavyādha, constellation, vi. 76

—one of the Rudras, vi. 142

Mrile of the Wachaga, vii. 119, 136

Mṛtyu ("Death"), vi. 99, 161, 196–197

——an abstract form of Death-god Yama, vi. 99

Mrule, tale of, vii. 138

Msalulu, lizard, vii. 160

Mtanga shapes the earth, vii. 143

Mu Kung ("Gentlemen of the Wood"), viii. 114

——Tung Wang Kung known as, viii. 116, 117

— -ling, viii. 65

—T'ien Tzŭ Chuan, viii. 116

—Tsung poisoned, viii. 202

—Wang, viii. 105, 116

Mu'allittu, origin of Babylonian earth-goddess Mylitta, v. 13

Muang T'eng (Dien Bien-phu), melon of the Lao beginnings grew at, xii. 286

Mucca Mhanannain ("pigs of Manannan"), gods' food, iii. 119, 120

Muc-thai-uy, shrine of, in Kè-buoi, xii. 312

Mucukunda destroys Kālayavana, vi. 173

Mudheads, clowns, x. 195

Mudor wedding, iv. 123, 124, 125, 128, 145

Mugasha (Mukasa), lake-spirit, vii. 410 [35]

Mugna, oak of, iii. 138

Muhafa palms, vii. 450, 451

Muhammad admitted power of demons, v. 353–354

Muhammadan element in Indonesian tales, ix. 153, 243, 306

Muhammadans of Gorakhpur, sacred fire of, vi. 234

Muic-Inis ("Pig Island"), iii. 43, 125

Muireartach, one-eyed hag, may be embodiment of tempestuous waters, iii. 171

Muirne, daughter of Tadg, sought in marriage by Cumhal, iii. 164, 165

Muit-Nekhbet possibly a birth-genius of Osiris, xii. 385 [12]

Mūjavant, mountain abode of Soma, vi. 47, 81

Mukasa, a god of Uganda, vii. 129–130, 131

Mukosala and dog, tale of, vii. 252–256

Mükš-ört, bee-soul, iv. 169

Mukunga Mbura, rainbow, vii. 236, 237

Mukuru, Father, vii. 147

Mula Dyadi, highest deity, in creation-myth, ix. 160–161, 328 [25]

Mulberry-tree, dog who ate silk-worm buried under, viii. 322

——why berries of, turned from white to red, i. 201

Mullo, mule-god, iii. 124

Muluc years, xi. 145

Mu-lu-lil, title of dying god, v. 113

Mulungu, vii. 116, 118, 125–126, 127, 133–134, 139, 140, 143, 150, 155, 181, 287

—anena ("Mulungu [thunder] is speaking"), vii. 126

Mumba'an dried up earth after flood, ix. 179

Mumbonang, father of Muntalog, ix. 183–184

Mumbonelekwapi, dwarfs, vii. 261

Mumboniag, mother of Muntalog, ix. 183

Mummies, Chincha peoples brought, to festivals, xi. 223

—decapitated, xi. 222

—of ichneumons found in Delta, xii. 165

Mummification = purification, xii. 174

Mumming, iii. 307, 308

Mummu bound by Ea, v. 293, 294

—creative word personified, v. 104, 290

—Ea and Marduk are the, v. 104, 396 [48]

—messenger of Apsû, v. 292

—Nabû as, v. 158

—name of Ea's symbol, v. 396 [52]

—of Ea, v. 104, 396 [48] [49] [52]

Mu-monto, journey of, to realm of dead, iv. 488–489

Mumuhango, wife of Tane, ix. 24

Muṇḍā languages spoken across Continental India today, xii. 253

Muṇḍās possibly carried some traditions to Indo-China, xii. 257

Mundilfari, father of Sol (sun) and Bil (moon), ii. 183, 196

Muninn (Memory), raven of Odin, ii. 65

Munisuvrata, twentieth Tīrthakara, vi. 221

Munon (Agamemnon), ii. 32

Munster, kine of, caused to pass through fire by Bres, iii. 26

—síd of, iii. 57, 78

Muntalog, Kabigat's father, ix. 183–184

Munt'śo-murt and -kuźo, bath-house gods, iv. 163

Muong Nan, pagoda at, xii. pl. XII (A), opp. p. 316

Mur, son of Enlil, v. 61

Mural decoration, xi. xx, pl. XVII, opp. p. 118

Murder, avengers of, xi. 258, 260

—made known, and avenged by, birds, stories of, vii. 210–212

—of man by beast, v. 232–233

Murderers, souls of, iii. 231

Murgi or Iohdi (spirits of air and souls of dead), iii. 319

Murias, Dagda's cauldron came from, iii. 41

Murough dives down and reaches land of King Under-Waves, iii. 113

Murtaznu, Murta'imu, names of "the Thunderer," v. 39

Muscle in leg of hare not eaten, vii. 291

Muses, i. 238–240

—and Dionysos, relation between, dates back to Thracian period, i. 220

—Benten added to company of, viii. 269

—Boiotian mountain of the, i. 40

—chorus of, led by Apollo, i. 181

—Pegasos associated with, i. 40

—Sekha(u)it identified with one of the, xii. 372 [57]

—three, from cauldron of Ogyrven, iii. 112

Mush, serpent-god, v. 90

Musheg Mamigonian, tale of murder of, vii. 90

Mushirtu (harlot), v. 33

Mushrooms, origin of sun and moon from, ix. 111–112

Mušḫuššû, serpent-dragon, v. 127, 130, 131, 158, 277, 278, 282, 283, 284, 285, 286, 288, 289, 293, 300, 301, 305, 316

Music, ii. 210–211, 223, 224, 225; iii. 247–248, 255; iv. 52, 54, 58, 69, 122, 123, 131, 151, 206; 461; vi. 68

—Apollo god of, i. 181

—Bês patron of, xii. 61

—bewitching, played by Manannan, iii. 60

—celestial, viii. 267

—Cheremiss priest prays to accompaniment of, iv. pl. XXXV, opp. p. 276

—dedicated to spiritual welfare of dead, viii. 356

—established by Tan, viii. 43

—goddess of, viii. 268–269, 270

—Ḥat-ḥôr deity of, xii. 40

—in Mag Mór, iii. 80

—Linos teacher of, i. 253

—magic, from yew-tree, iii. 73

—of birds, iii. 121

——Hotherus, ii. 133

Musical instrument broken, iv. 329

——Master of, iv. 465

—instruments, iii. 33–34, 284

—Kaches, vii. 84

—rites, xi. 90–91

Musician, water-spirit as, iv. 206

Musicians and bards, Bran may have been divinity of, iii. 105

—heavenly, the Gandharvas as, vi. 143

—insect, viii. 351

—two Merets described as, xii. 137

Musisi causes earthquakes, vii. 130

Muskhogean stock, x. 53

"Musō-Byōye," viii. 363–365

Muspell, sons of, will break rainbow bridge, ii. 329, 343–344

Muspell's sons, Frey must await, ii. 144

Muspellheim, ii. 275, 279, 324, 325, 339, 344

—conception, fire in the, ii. 202

Mussel-shell, Aphrodite's birth from, i. 196

——attribute of Eros, i. 204

——in which "Ancient Spider" crawled, ix. 249–250

Mustamho, x. 180

Mut, Amon, Amonet, Theban triad, xii. 362 [6]

——associated with, xii. 129

—Amonet confused with, xii. 402 [6]

—appropriated sanctuary of Ubastet at Thebes, xii. 150

—frequently identified with Ḥat-ḥôr and solarized, xii. 41

Mut-Khôns(u), Amen-Rê' perhaps identified with, xii. 221

—later wife of Amon, xii. 129–130, 140 (fig. 140)

—name of, obliterated from all old monuments by Amen-ḥotep IV, xii. 225

—(sky), union of, with Amen-Rê' (sun), xii. 34

Mutabriqu (lightning-maker), v. 163

Mute, earthly, viii. 113

Mutenia River, Seide near, iv. 103

Mutilated person not permitted to reign, iii. 25, 28

Mutilation of Boann by secret well, iii. 121

——living bodies for use in witchcraft, viii. 156

——their bodies practised by Korybantes, i. 275–276

'Mutla, Hottentot for Hare, vii. 293

Mutuhei, one of primeval pair, ix. 11

Mutzatzir, temple of Khaldis at, vii. 395 [58]

Mu(u)t (Muit) (" Watery One," " Water Flood "), original nature of, xii. 46, 49

Mwana Mbeu's tale, vii. 355–357

Mwavi ordeal, vii. 429 [18]

Mwawa of the Wakuluwe, vii. 159

Mwenembago (Lord of Forest), ghost who haunted wild places, vii. 242

Myaungtu-ywa, city built by Sithu and Kyawzwa, xii. 354

Myimmo Taung, Burmese name of Indian Mt. Meru, xii. 259

Mykenai founded by Perseus, i. 35

—golden lamb regarded by Atreus as emblem of kingship at, i. 120

—grove of, Io tethered to tree in, i. 29

—Kassandra and Agamemnon slain on return to, i. 134

—reign of Elektryon in, i. 76

Mykerinos, builder of Pyramids, confused with Osiris by Herodotus, xii. 398 [106]

Myles, son of Lelex, succeeded his father as king of Lakonia, i. 23

Mylitta, Babylonian earth-goddess, v. 13

Myojo-tenshi (" Morning-star Angel "), viii. 289

Myrddin: see MERLIN.

Myrkrida (" Dark-rider "), ii. 300

Myrkwood, ii. 144, 259, 260, 343

Myrmidons (ant-men), play on Greek word for ant, i. 121

Myrrha (Smyrna), tale of, i. 198

Myrrh-tree, birth of Adonis from, i. 198

——Smyrna changed into, i. 16, 198

Myrtilos, Oinomaos's charioteer, bribed by Pelops, i. 119

Mysia, Argo arrives at, i. 110

—Auge and her son cast upon shores of, i. 22

Mysing (Hrolf Kraki), sea-king, ii. 283

Mysteries, Egyptian theological speculations not, xii. 218

—Mithraic, not recorded in Armenia, vii. 34

—of Eleusis, i. pl. L, opp. p. 230, 231–232

—Samothracian, Argonauts initiated into, i. 110

Mysterious gods, Nuu (Nûn ?) father of, xii. 47

—Tally, viii. 17

Mystery-cult, iii. 204–205

—of the Lord, Hebrew legend of Lîlîth in, v. 363

—plays, Babylonian festival including, v. 315, 411 [44]

—translation of Manito, x. 18, 20, 284 [28]

Mystic meaning of each act of New Year's festival, v. 320

Mysticism, viii. 219, 274

—scarcely present in Egyptian mythology, xii. 8

Myth and art, i. lvi–lvii, lxi–lxii

——ethics, i. liii–lvi

—myth material, x. xvii–xxiv

—criticism of, viii. 199–203

—definition of, i. xliii

—evolution of, towards historical legend, vi. 348

—explanatory, viii. 233

—form of, i. xli–xlii

—Greek, unique character of, i. xlix–l

— -incidents, distribution and resemblances of, ix. xiv

—kinds of, i. l–li

—lack of abstractions in, i. xlv

— -making, recent products of, vii. 121

—methods of interpreting, i. lvii–lix

—origin of, i. xliii–xlvi

—relation of, to fact, i. xliii

Myth, religious appeal of, i. xlvii
—sanction and persistence of, i. xlvi–xlviii
—subject-matter of, i. xlii–xliii
—time of, i. xlii
—what is, i. xli–xliii
Mythic Dance Drama People, x. 187
Mythical plants and food, v. 166
Mythological family relation of god and man, v. 7–9, 10, 11, 12, 378 21
—scenes from a procession, xii. 194 (fig. 206)
Mythologies, individual, within tribes, clans, and societies, x. xv
Mythology, v. xvi–xvii, xviii
—Apache, x. 175–179
—attitude of mind to be maintained in study of, i. xi–xii
—Celtic, difficulties of, and methods of discussing, iii. 19–21
—concepts of Asiatic, passed into religion of Egypt, xii. 153
—Egyptian, excessive value attached to, xii. 7–8
——fragmentary and conflicting character of, xii. 3, 7–8
——general characteristics of, xii. 7–13
—general world-wide resemblances, xii. 253
—Iranian and Vedic, vi. 349–351
—paucity of, in the case of most gods, xii. 20
—people, land, and climate of Japan in relation to, viii. 209–220
—perhaps once a common, iii. 93
—Piman, x. 175
—plate [description of], key to Peruvian, xi. 246
—reasons for ascendancy of Babylonian, in Old Testament, v. 74
—scantily developed from primitive localized, non-cosmic gods, xii. 384 1
—Sumerian, contained basis of Babylonian idea of origin of universe from water, v. 288
—Yuman, x. 179–181
Mythopoeia among mediaeval and later Welsh Druidists, iii. 19, 20
Mythopoeic faculty still exists in Africa, vii. 120
Myths, ii. 12–13
—African, recent and imported, vii. 348–359

Myths and legends, Indo-Chinese, xii. 263–322
—Attic, growth of, i. 66
—author's (W. F. Fox) object and method of presentation of, i. lix–lx
—belief that most, have arisen from misunderstandings of rituals, i. xlv
—Buddhist, viii. 188–198
—concerning house of Labdakos, interpretations of, i. 55
—corrupting and disintegrating of, iii. 17–18
—cosmic and cosmogonic, xii. 68–91
—Greek and Roman, interchangeability of, i. 288–289
——kinds of, i. l–li
——possibility of employing, for variety of purposes, i. l
—House of, x. 253, 254
—in state of flux, ix. xv, 9
—interchange of, x. 103, 113
—mythology, xi. 5–10
—of: Boiotia and Euboia, i. 42–55; Aitolia, 55–59; Crete and Attike, 60–74
——Continental Celts not written but taught in verse by Druids, iii. 8
——early days of Rome, i. 304–307
——Fuegians meagre, xi. 342
——Minos and his sons, i. 61–65
——the beginning, i. 3–19
———northern mainland of Greece, i. 42–59
———Peloponnesos, i. 20–41; Arkadia, 20–23; Lakonia and Messene, 23–28; Argos, 28–36; Corinth, 36–41
—Pawnee, divided into four classes, x. 121
—purely Hebrew and purely Babylonian, v. 74
—reflex of life of a people, i. lii
—ritual, x. 169–175
—sources for Greek and Roman, i. lx–lxii
—Taïno, xi. 28–32
—traceable to time of Yellow Emperor, viii. 133
—two strata exist in, iii. 18–19
—used as incantations, xii. 79–83, 125–126, 127–128
—useful in determination of dates, i. lii
—what we may learn from, i. li–liii
Mzimu, place in which offerings made to spirits, vii. 181

N

Na Reau and Kobine created heaven and earth, ix. 248
——commanded his creation not to increase, ix. 254
—Rena (Rigi) came out of a rock, ix. 251
Nabataean kingdom, Babylonian influence in, v. 15
Nabataeans ancient Arabian people mentioned in Genesis and Deutero-Isaiah, v. 381 64
—North Arabic race, v. 16
—sun-worshippers, v. 381 67
Nabbe, dwarf, ii. 265
Nābhānediṣṭha asks boon of Aṅgirases, vi. 82–83
Nābhi, last of the lawgivers, vi. 226
Nabû, vii. 70
—carried Tablets of Fate, v. 102
—messenger of Bêl, v. 58, 316
— -Mercury, Virgo station of, v. 305
—(" prophet," " herald "), god of writing, v. 158, 159, 160, 161, 285, 318, 323, 324
—resemblance of Tiur to, vii. 31–33
—scribe of gods, iv. 410
—temple of, in Borsippa archive of divine decrees, vii. 384 48
—Yanbûshâd corruption of some name beginning with, v. 339
Nabuapaliddin recovered image of Shamash, v. 150
Nabuaplauṣur made clay box for statue of Shamash, v. 150–151
Nabûg (Nebo), v. 154
Nabunidus, king of Babylonia, v. 5, 154
Nachan (" House of Snakes "), older name of Palenque, xi. 131
Näck desires women in childbed, ii. 211
Nacon, war-chief, xi. 138
Nadir, mask of warrior of the, x. pl. 1, frontispiece, 185
Nadiyā, vi. 238
Nadzikambe (Gulumpambe) chameleon, vii. 160–161
Naevius, i. 304
Nāga people still in India, vi. 155
Nāgā, tribe, head-hunters, xii. 266
Nāga, Nāgas:
Nāga found by sons of Wōng Ti-fang in lake near Sawm Hsak Hill, xii. 280

Nāga Min, serpent-king, xii. pl. VII (1), opp. p. 272
Nāgas, viii. 266, 268, 269; see also RYŪJIN.
—not prominent in deluge-myths, xii. 278
—(serpents), vi. 96, 108, 132, 138, 154, 155, 203, 214, 216, 235, 241
—usually feminine in Burmese myth, xii. 271
—worship of, vi. 154–155, 203; xii. 271
Nagaitcho, x. 222–223, 229
Nāgaloka, snake-world, vi. 154
Nāgārjuna elevated to rank of Bodhi-sattva, vi. 210
Nagasaki, viii. 363
Naggadah or Naqqadah, modern name of Ombos, xii. 102
Naglfar, ship made from dead mens' nails, ii. 159, 200, 340, 343, 386 64
Naglfari, first man, ii. 200
Nahanarvali, brother-gods worshipped in grove of the, ii. 64
Nāhar Khān revered, vi. 243
Naharina, Haunted Prince wanders to, xii. 153
Nahid, Persian name for planet Venus, vii. 25
Nahuatlans, xi. 132
Nahunta, Elamite goddess, Anāhita identified with, vii. 25
Nahurak, Pawnee animal-powers, x. 122
Nahuṣa, vi. 133, 134, 144, 145, 146, 154, 190
Naiads, spirits of springs, i. 257
Nail as support of sky, iv. 221, 222
—copper, hammered in spear, gun, or drum, commemorates bear killed, iv. 94
— -cutting, formula at, vi. 290–291
—driven in at place of death, iv. 23
——memorial tree prevents dead passing beyond it, iv. 26
——into place of death prevents sickness, iv. 23
—in head of images of Thor, ii. 83
— -matter as first covering for man, iv. 376, 381, 384
—(or ray) from eye of Ogmios on Gaulish coins, iii. 11

Nails driven for deceased to hang clothes, iv. 68
—found on site of grounding of Ark, iv. 366
—Norns supposed to put marks on infants', ii. 245
—ship made of dead men's: see NAGL-FAR, ETC.
—soul in, iv. 5
Naimiṣa forest, Nāgas dwell in, vi. 154
Nainī Tāl, lake sacred to Devī, vi. 236
Nairyōsangha, divine messenger, vi. 285, 336, 342
Náisi, iii. 144
—helped by Manannan, iii. 65
Nāk dancers, xii. 325, 326
Näk, water-spirit, ii. 210, 211
Naka-samuta, another name of Nasé, viii. 380 6 7 (ch. ii)
Nakedness, iii. 75
—and silence required in Underworld, v. 264
Nakht ("giant," "strong man"), xii. 57
Nakiskat, animal-lodge, x. 122–123
Näkk (Nakineitsi, Näkineiu, Näkki), spirit inhabiting all deeper waters, iv. 200–208
Nakṣatras, lunar mansions, vi. 136, 233
Nakula regarded as rebirth of an Aśvin, vi. 142
Nal (Needle): see LAUFEY, ETC.
Nala, vi. 149
Nalakūvara, Jain deity, vi. 229
Nalinī, lake of Kubera, vi. 158
Nam Hka, river, xii. 293
—Hkön, human sacrifice at stream of, xii. 333
—Kiu (Irrawaddy) crossed by Hkun Hsang L'röng, xii. 290
—Kōng (Salween) crossed by Hkun Hsang L'röng, xii. 290
—Tao, hill where Yatawm and Yatai lived as frogs, xii. 293
Nama, builder of ark, iv. 364–365
Nambi and sons of Heaven, vii. 152–154, 155, 172
Nambubi, mother of Mukasa, vii. 130
Name, Death demands girl's telling his, vii. 178
—divine, no fear regarding utterance of, xii. 362 8
—fruit may be eaten only by those knowing its, vii. 316, 317, 425 19

Name given at puberty, iii. 142
—importance of knowledge of correct, xii. 82, 83
—many deities differ only in, xii. 217
—not to be spoken, xi. 267–268
—obtained in vision, x. 145
—of deceased made into visible object, iv. 25, 43
——king registered on celestial tree, xii. 53 (fig. 51)
——Loki, derivation of, ii. 147–148
——Odin given to children, ii. 34
——one must not answer to, vii. 338
——royal, registered on Persea-tree, xii. 37 (fig. 24)
—secret, of animal must be known to obtain loan of axe, vii. 321
Nameless, gods may be (as in Yorkshire inscription), iii. 9
Names, xi. 22, 24, 76
—additional, for deities as they were given special functions, v. 91
—ama-, v. 380 51
—ancient Canaanite city-, contain title of 'Anat, v. 29–30
—and souls, x. 10, 146, 264, 281 20–282
—avoidance of real, ii. 95
—Ba'al as component of proper, in Gebal, v. 67
—" brother," " sister," and " uncle " in personal, v. 7, 8, 378 21, 379 26
—change of, from clan to spirit, x. 246
—concealment of divine, iii. 70
—containing Dagan, v. 79, 83
—different, for souls in living and dead bodies, xi. 27
—discovered, foes not vanquished until, iii. 100
—emphasize fatherhood of god, v. 7, 11–12
—family, among Votiaks, iv. 116–117
——derived from animal kingdom, iv. 504
——system of giving, in Burma, xii. pl. XI, opp. p. 310
—for magic, ii. 299
——sea-monsters and water-spirits, ii. 210, 212
—given descriptive of patches of hair left after scalping, x. 118
——to night, new moon, etc., ii. 197
—Hebrew, composed with ab, ben, bath, v. 380 48
—in Japan, viii. 210

Names, Lîlîth and Abyzu forced to tell all their, v. 363, 364, 366
—Malik survives in proper, v. 51
—Melqart in proper, v. 53
—of dwarfs in Teutonic countries, ii. 270
——Eight Diagrams in divination, viii. 136
——first creatures obtained by bird-like being, ix. 252
——giants, ii. 275
——Indra, vi. 131
——Lamaštu, v. 367
——nightmare, ii. 288
——Šiva, vi. 111–112
—personal, meaning "son of" some animal, iii. 124
—place-, associated with Balder, ii. 134
——plant-, and star-, formed from Odin not found in Upper Germany, ii. 37
——Sîmî survives in Syrian, v. 22
—planetary, of Harranian week, v. 154–155
—power of knowledge of, in magic, xii. 201
—proper, cosmic nature of, xi. 177
——reveal idea of a god as ancestor, v. 7
—secret, of bear, iv. 83, 85
—Semitic, in period of Ur and Isin, v. 393 379
—some gods have no real, xii. 20–21
—symbolic, of priestly offices, xii. 192
—theophorous, in Armenia, vii. 32, 34
—Yāw and Yāh in proper, v. 42
Namesake, feats of King Mongan originally those of divine, iii. 59, 62
Namesakes in underwater city, ix. 117
Namī Sāpya helped Indra in vanquishing Namuci, vi. 68
Naming men from animals, trees, etc., Semitic custom of, v. 9–10, 11
—of a child, iv. 14–16
——all concepts by Adapa and of animals and birds by Adam, v. 175
—(of Fionn), incident of, iii. 167
Namru, Asarludug called the god, v. 311
Namtar ("Fate"), chief of seven devils, v. 161, 162, 163, 164, 332
—messenger of Ereshkigal, v. 333, 334
Namtaru, son of Enlil and Ereshkigal, v. 264, 265, 357, 364, 372
Namtilaku ("Life"), Asarludug called, v. 311

Namuci, demon famous in later literature, vi. 68, 97, 134, 153, 197
Namzimu, demon, vii. 409 36
"Nan Hua Shêng King," viii. 134
Nana of Elam identified with Artemis, vii. 385 5 (ch. iv)
—rival of Astλik, vii. 38
Nanā as star of venery, v. 317
— -Ishtar, festival of, v. 156
—mother-goddess of Doura bears Babylonian name, v. 20, 368
—sister of Tammuz also wife of Nebɔ, v. 382 90
Nanaboojoo: see MANIBOZHO.
Nanabozhu, iv. 326
Nanauatzin, xi. 88–89
Nanch'ang (ancient Hung-Chow), viii. 113
Nan-chao, Shan kingdom, xii. 268
— -chi lao-jên, viii. 82
Nancy, West Indian corruption of Tŵi Anansi ("spider"), vii. 426 1
Nanda Bhairon, village deity, vi. 237
—Christian parallels in story of, vi. 178
—Devī, mountain peak, identified with Pārvatī, vi. 236
—herdsman, saved Kṛṣṇa, vi. 118, 171
—serpent, vi. 216
Nandana, forest of Kubera, vi. 158
Nandin, guard of Šiva's palace, vi. 181
Nandinī, wish-cow of Indra, vi. 134, 145–146
Nandivardhana gave permission to Mahāvīra to become an ascetic, vi. 223
Nane, vii. 38
—Anahit identified with, vii. 381 2 (ch. iii)
——sister of, vii. 26
—daughter of Aramazd, vii. 20
—deity and temple of, vi. 17, 381 1
—Mihr brother of, vii. 33
Nane Chaha ("high hill") from which Choctaws believe they came, x. 63
Nang Pyek-kha Yek-khi, child (with ears and legs of tiger) of Ya-hsang Ka-hsi, xii. 289–290
Nanga and Ina, tale of, ix. 71
Nankilstlas, raven, x. 260, 261
Nanking, viii. 65
Nanna, goddess; wife of Balder, ii. 15, 17, 129, 130, 132, 133, 184
—title of moon-god, v. 92, 93, 152
Nannar for Nanna, v. 152, 195
—god of Ur, v. 100, 343

Nansō-bō, tale of, viii. 332–333, 384 [14]
Nāonghaithya, demon, vi. 30; vii. 364
Naotara (Pers. Naudhar), vi. 333, 334
Naotara's sons, epic of, vi. 339
Napata and Meroë, Amon becomes official god of, xii. 240
Nappigi, v. 36, 37
Naqqadah or Naggadah, modern name of Ombos, xii. 102
Nár, one of Three Finns of Emuin, iii. 56, 90, 156
Nara, vi. 151, 168; viii. 234
Nārada, vi. 132, 137, 145, 160, 168, 171
—Muni, divinity of, vi. 244
Naraka, apparently a personified hell, vi. 154
—infernal regions, viii. 282
—of Prāgjyotiṣa, Kṛṣṇa destroyed, vi. 174
Nāraka Loka, vi. 100
Narâm-Sin conqueror of Phoenician coast, v. 78, 79
Naras classed with Gandharvas, vi. 143
Narāśaṁsa, epithet of Agni, vi. 44, 45, 92
—Indian counterpart of Nairyōsangha, vi. 285
—sacrificial fire in India, vi. 284
Narasiṁha ascribed to Viṣṇu, vi. 81
Nārāyaṇa, Ājīvika sect brought into connexion with worship of, vi. 224
—becomes definitely identified with the Buddha, vi. 204
—development of, in " Brāhmaṇas " and Epic, vi. 80–81
—mystic name of Viṣṇu, vi. 121, 124, 151, 168, 196
Narcissus used as snare by Zeus and Earth to entrap Persephone, i. 227–228
Narcotics to induce visions, xi. 26
Nareua set fire to trees from whose ashes and sparks came mankind, ix. 252
Narfi, father of Night, ii. 200
—(Nari), son of Loki, ii. 139, 144, 145, 146
Naridimmeranki, title of Marduk, v. 311
Narihira, Ono-no-Komachi appeared to the poet, viii. 299
Narīmān, vi. 329
Narmadā River, vi. 234, 235
Narran Lake, origin of, ix. 296

Nâru, river of death (also " a singer "), v. 261
Naručnici, genii of fate, iii. 250
Narudu, sister of Seven gods, v. 147
Nāsatya, vii. 364
—listed on Mitanni inscription, vi. 30
—old name of Aśvins, vi. 141
Nasca, vases of, repeat motifs on monolith of Chavin de Huantar, xi. 215, 219, 220, 221, 222, 230, 235
Nascakiyetl, raven, x. 260, 275 [10]
Nasé and Azé, story of, viii. 253, 380 [6] (ch. ii)
Nashāk and Sīyākmak, primeval twins, vi. 298
Nasilele, wife of Nyambe, vii. 162
Nasr-ed-din, Hubeane recalls, vii. 213
Nastrand (" corpse-strand "), ii. 318
Nasu, vi. 261
— -no, death-stone of, viii. 325
Nata and Nena saved from flood, xi. 95
Nāteśa, form of Dhyānibodhisattva of Gotama, vi. 212
Natigai, earth-god, iv. 460
National element in ancient Armenian religion, viii. 5
Nativity, Christ's, iii. 208, 213
Nāt-kadaw, spirit wives, dance and sing the Nāt-than, xii. 345, 354
Nāt-than, spirit melodies recited by mediums, xii. 341, 342, 345–346
Nāt-thein, spirit mediums, xii. 341, 342, 347
Nāts, the Thirty-Seven, of Burma, xii. 271, 339–357
Natural forces personified, xii. 255
—method of interpreting myths, i. lvii
—phenomena, episodes of Thor myths may represent, ii. 93–94
—myth of Idunn and Thjazi explained as, ii. 179–180
Nature, ii. 192–215; viii. 54–55, 56, 58
—and human nature, xi. 275–280
—cult: see TANTRIC RITES, ETC.
—dualism, mythical story of Bres's sovereignty may parallel old, iii. 28
—forces of, apparently unworshipped in primitive Egypt, xii. 18
— -god, bear or boar enemy of young, in Phoenicia, xii. 397 [101]
— -goddess, Ishtar a, vii. 38
—gods conceived of as forces of, viii. 50
—connected with, xii. 33–67

Nature, influence of, on Japanese folk-lore, viii. 213–216, 219
—itself rarely personified, vii. 81
—masters of, iv. 463–471
— -myth, Buddha's conflict with Māra may be a, vi. 197
——Loki as cow-maid a, ii. 145
— -myths, vii. 220, 225–241, 269; viii. 227
—Osiris as god of changing, xii. 93, 96
—parts of, regarded mythologically, iii. 132
— -powers, iii. 34; vii. 119, 179; x. 155
——brothers represent upper and under-world, x. 295
——lodge of, x. 123
——worship of, on the Orinoco, xi. 257
——worshipped by Incas, xi. 246
—Ptaḥ god of all, xii. 145
— -soul, Pamaš-oza apparently a, iv. 215, 216
— -souls, iv. 14
— -spirits, vii. 116, 117, 179
—spirits of, viii. 61–73
— -worship, viii. 51; xi. 26
——almost all names of deities in Sumerian express, v. 89
——and myths, vii. 18, 47–63
Naubandhana, Mt., vi. 124, 147
Nauplios, Auge given to, to be killed, i. 22
Naurūz, feast of, vi. 315; see also NAVASARD.
Nausikaa, princess of Phaiakians, finds Odysseus on shores of Scheria, i. 138
Navagrahas, minor sky-gods, vi. 233
Navagvas, race of man, vi. 71
—seers, vi. 65
Navahos, gods, genesis, myths, etc., x. 154–175, 202–203, 283 24
Navasard, Armenian New Year's festival, vii. 21–23, 60, 61
Navel, dead have no, xi. 27
—of earth, iv. 349; xi. 55, 115, 213; see MIDDLE PLACE (vol. x).
——sky and of earth-bearing turtle, iv. 343, 401
Navels of images, breath blown into, ix. 273
Navi, invisible genii, in bird-shape, iii. 254
Navigation, x. 213–214
—Apollo divine guardian of, i. 179
—protectress of, Isis as, xii. 387 26

Navky, souls of unbaptised children or those born of mothers who meet violent death are personified as, iii. 253–254
Navskiy velikden (naviy den), vernal funeral rites, iii. 237
Nawng Awng Pu and Nawng Hkeo, two cities built by Hkun Hsang L'röng, xii. 292
—Hkeo, lake formed from falling of the crab shell; sacred mere of the Wa, home of Yatawm and Yatai in the tadpole state, xii. 291, 293–294
—Kong, Hpi Hpai and Hpi Lu kings at, xii. 292
—Put, lake, xii. 272, 273
—Taripu, source of the Nam Kōng (Salween), xii. 292
—Tung, lake in Kēngtūng, xii. 334
Nawrahtā Minzaw, Byat Ta takes service under King, xii. 348
——king of Pagān, who demanded tooth of Buddha Gotama, xii. 349–350
Naxos, Amphitrite first seen by Poseidon in, i. 214
—island of, Theseus and Ariadne at, i. 101
—modern Greek folk-tale of St. Dionysos in, i. 313
Nayanezgani, male deity, x. 157, 164
Naymlap, tale of coming of, to Lambeyeque, xi. 208, 209, 215
Nazi, divinity, v. 201
Nbat (" child of waters "), vi. 360 14; see also APĀM NAPĀT.
Ndabu consults witch-doctor to obtain child, vii. 340
Ndengei, great serpent, ix. 109
Ndonga country, vii. 146
Ndyambi Karunga distinct from ancestral ghosts, vii. 125
Neaira, wife of Helios, i. 242
Ñeambiú, vegetation-spirit, xi. 375 11
Nebājōth, Hebrew, Nabataeans are, v. 381 64
Nebel, darkness, ii. 268
Nebelkappe, dwarf's hat or cloak of invisibility, ii. 269
Neb-er-Zer (" lord of everything ") as title of Osiris, xii. 96
Nebet, local form of Ḥat-ḥôr, xii. 140
Nebo (Nabû), Antares assoc' ted with, v. 110
—" band " employed of, v. 109

Nebo in Greek magical texts, v. 161
—Nanā connected with cult of, v. 20, 382 90
Neboutosoulēth, deity, v. 161
Neb-taui, local god of Ombos, xii. 140
Nebt-hôt (" Mistress of the Temple "): see NEPHTHYS.
— -hotep, later explained as form of Hat-hôr, xii. 140
— -meret as a birth-genius of Osiris, xii. 385 12
— -taui (" Mistress of Both Countries "), variant name of Amonet, xii. 130
— -uu, form of Hat-hôr, worshipped at Esneh, xii. 140
Nebuchadnezzar devoted to Nabû, vii. 32
Nechtan, Boann wife of, iii. 52
—in Isle of Joy, iii. 115
—king of Munster, singes kine to trick Bres, iii. 26
—secret well stood in green of síd of, iii. 121
Necklace of Ashurnazirpal, five emblems on, v. 150
——Freyja: see BRISINGA-MEN, ETC.
——Gefjun, ii. 180
——Harmonia given to Arsinoë, i. 54
——hearts, x. 229
Necromancy, Hekate in, i. 187, 329 7
—Hermes in, i. 194
Nectanebo, Egyptian monarch, scholar, and magician, xii. 236
Neda (nymph and river), the baby Zeus placed in care of, i. 155
Nedolya, evil Dolya, iii. 252
Nedu, watchman of Ereshkigal, v. 162, 164
Needfire in rites, ii. 202
Needle, mermaids caught by, vii. 394 37
— -throwing, iii. 147
Nefer-ho(r), special form of Ptah at Memphis, xii. 140
— -hotep, local form of Theban Khôns(u); also a deity in Upper Egypt, xii. 140
— -khepru-rê' (" best of the forms of the sun "), a name of Amen-hotep IV, xii. 170, 231
— -nefru-aten, a name of the queen of Amen-hotep IV, xii. 231
— -têm adored at Memphis, xii. 140, 141 (fig. 142)

Nefer-têm and Sokhmet, son and wife of Ptah, xii. 145
——Mi-hos identified with, xii. 137
Nefert-iti, a name of the queen of Amen-hotep IV, xii. 231
Negative Confessions: see CONFESSION, NEGATIVE, READ, ETC.
Negrito element in Indonesia, ix. 153, 154, 205
—mythology in Oceania unknown, ix. 104, 304
Negritos in Melanesia, ix. 103
Negro sources for animal stories, x. 64
Negúruvila (Guirivilo), cat-like monster, xi. 328
Neha-ho(r), a serpent, confused with Sêth-'Apop, xii. 141, 392 54
Neheb-kau, evil spirit in form of serpent, xii. 141
——four sons of Horus or Osiris guard souls against subterranean serpent, xii. 394 67
—— (" overthrower of souls "), xii. 391 43, 416 9
——Selqet associated with, xii. 147
Neheh, god of eternity, xii. 378 102
Nehem(t)-'auit, goddess associated with Thout(i) at Hermopolis, xii. 141
Nehes, abstract deity, companion of sun-god, xii. 67, 141
—(" Wakefulness ") may accompany sun-god in his ship, xii. 67
Nehushtan, serpent, worship of, v. 78
Neith, xii. 148, 409 100
—ancient goddess of Saïs, xii. 136, 141–142, 393 58
—as a birth-genius of Osiris, xii. 385 12
——wife of Sêth, xii. 392 58
——Menehtet identified with, xii. 136
—of Saïs not Libyan, xii. 410 1
—Urt-hekau epithet of, xii. 151
Nejameṣa (Nejameya), vi. 358 4
Nekedzaltara, servants of death-bringer, x. 79
Nekhbet and Buto, Merets representatives of two divine kingdoms of, xii. 137
—connected with prehistoric capital of Upper Egypt, xii. 46
—no positive knowledge of cult of, as incarnate in vulture, xii. 167
—Sekha(u)it perhaps localized at, xii. 53
—stands at entrance to Abyss, xii. 46

Nekhbet, vulture-goddess, of earliest capital of Upper Egypt, xii. 142
——symbolizes Upper Egypt, xii. 132
—water-goddess, joined to Nile, xii. 46
—wife of Nile, xii. 45 (fig. 41)
Nekhen, Egyptian name for Hierakonpolis, xii. 365 26
—why called "white city," xii. 142
Nekke (Nik, Näcken), evil water-spirit, iv. 192
Nektanebos became astrologer at Pella, i. 223
Neman, Némain, war-goddess, iii. 40, 134
Nemanus (Gk.): see NEḤEM(T)-ʿAUIT.
Nemcatacoa, bear-god, xi. 204
Nemda, dwelling-place of keremet-spirit, iv. 155
Nemea, Adrastos's army halted at, and became cause of death of King Lykourgos's son, i. 52
Nemean games instituted in honour of infant son of Lykourgos, i. 52
Nemed, eponymous hero of Nemedians, iii. 207
Nemedians of stock of Noah, iii. 23, 207
Nemesis, an early greenwood goddess, i. 284, 332 4 (ch. xiv)
—creation of, i. 6
—said to be mother of Helen, i. 24, 284
Nemglan, king of birds, and father of Conaire, iii. 75
Nemi, a Tīrthakara, vi. 222
Neminātha, twenty-second Tīrthakara, vi. 221, 222, 224
Nemnach, first mill in Ireland at, iii. 137
Nemontemi, "Empty Days" of Aztec year, xi. 99, 100
Nempterequeteva (Nemquetheba), culture-hero worshipped as the god Bochica, xi. 202
Nenígo, xi. 297
Nennius, iii. 93
Nennius's "History," iii. 125
Nento-fo-hiuscne, síd of, iii. 58
Neoptolemos conquers country of Molossians, i. 135
—killed by Orestes, i. 135
—(or Pyrrhos), son of Achilles, brought from Skyros and confines Trojans to their city, i. 132
—slays Priam, i. 133
—takes Andromache as prize of war, i. 133

Nep, Nanna daughter of, ii. 129
Nepāl, vi. 213, 237, 242
Nepelle, tale of wives of, and Wyungare, ix. 293
Nephele saves Phrixos and Helle from Ino, i. 108
Nephîlim, giants, v. 358
Nephthys and Isis accompany sun as scarab, xii. 96
——dirge of, xii. 122–124
——explained as the feathers on head of Mîn, xii. 219
——identified with "double Justice," xii. 101
——tears of, cause inundation of Nile, xii. 95
—Antaeus associated with, at Antaiopolis, xii. 130
—as a birth-genius of Osiris, xii. 385 12
——mother of Osiris, xii. 408 82
——rival of Isis, xii. 395 76
——sky, identified with Sekha(u)it, xii. 53, 110
—begotten by Qêb and Nut, xii. 69
—confused with Isis, xii. 117
—frequently identified with Ḥat-ḥôr and solarized, xii. 41, 392 56
—helps to protect and nurse Isis and infant Horus, xii. 116
—in the Osirian cycle, xii. 110, 123
—member of ennead of Heliopolis, xii. 216
—Menkhet sometimes identified with, xii. 136, 393 59
—Rê'-Ḥor identified with, xii. 221
—sister of Horus, xii. 394 71
——Osiris, xii. 123
—takes care of infant Horus, xii. 117
—Urt-ḥekau epithet of, xii. 151
Nepri connected with Nile-god, xii. 66
—(fem. Nepret), grain-god, xii. 66 and fig. 73
—sometimes identified with Renenutet, xii. 66
Neptunalia, i. 295
—in mare, ii. 214
Neptune, equation of British Nodons with, iii. 103
—protects Trojans in voyage to Italy, i. 305
Neptunus, i. 295
Nera, adventures of, iii. 68–69
Nereïds guide Argonauts home to Hellas, i. 113

Nereïds, nymphs of inner sea, i. 258, 260
—survivals of, in modern Greek folk-
belief, i. 314
Nereus and Doris, Amphitrite daughter
of, i. 214
——Herakles, i. pl. xxiii (1), opp. p. 88
—(Neleus), Ancient of the Sea, i. 87,
260
——Herakles seeks purification from,
i. 89
——son of Poseidon and Tyro, i. 106,
211
—received instruction in prophecy from
Glaukos, i. 261
—tells Herakles where apples of Hesperides to be found, i. 87
Nergal (Babylonian), god of lower
world, may parallel Aker, xii. 368 22
—connected with Shamash, v. 351
—god of land of dead and judge of
souls, v. 49, 50, 147, 148, 342, 361
—husband of Ereshkigal, v. 163, 164
—image of, v. 147
—Ishar appears as title of Adad and,
v. 41, 132
—Marduk identified with, v. 155
— -Malik, sun-god of Tyre, v. 53
— -Mars, Capricorn station of, v. 304
—(Mars), counterpart(?) of Kisagan-
Tengri, iv. 406
—originally same as Ninurta, v. 400 152
—Sharrapu identified with, v. 49
—sun-god, v. 47, 49–50, 58, 61, 68, 69,
71, 93, 99, 115, 116, 135, 136, 137,
144, 146, 148, 265, 321
Neri's kinswoman a Norn, ii. 240
Nerrivik, x. 5–6
Nerthus, Gefjun may be form of, ii. 182
—island sacred grove of, ii. 203
—likeness of Frey procession to that of,
ii. 116
— -Njord, fertility-deities, ii. 104, 126
—sex of, ii. 103
—Tacitus mentions goddess, and her
cult, ii. 17, 24, 28, 102–103, 113, 194
Nervii, coin of, iii. pl. ii (1), opp. p. 8
Nesaru, x. 108
Nesi-Amsu, creation-hymn from Papy-
rus of, xii. 68–69
Nesjar, smith of, ii. 43
Neške-pas and Neškeper-ava, beegarden
mother and beehive-god, iv. 169
Nesreča, evil Sreča, iii. 252
Nesret, identified with Buto, xii. 143

Nessa, mother of Conchobar, iii. 140
Nessos, Centaur, and Deianeira, i. 93,
270
Nest-Builders, viii. 26
Nestor, " Chronicle " of, on Russian religion, iii. 222
—in Pylos, Telemachos went to, i. 138
—son of Nereus, spared by Herakles, i.
92
Nestorian, Indian Church, vi. 175, 176
—pillar at Si-ngan-fu, Karen myths
suggest acquaintance with, xii. 269
Nestorianism, iv. 390
—possible contact of Karens with, xii.
270
Nesu, as son of Mah, v. 114
—Ninsikilla wife of her son, v. 110, 113
" Net and trap," poetical description of
fate of man, v. 263, 265
—baboons of Thout(i) catch souls of
dead in, xii. 180
—genii fighting with snares or, xii.
109 (fig. 109)
—in battle against dragon or enemies
of sun-god, xii. 109, 397 101
—prepared to catch " red (fire) salmon," iv. 238
—Sêth caught in, xii. 118
—to catch seafarers, ii. 190
——enmesh Tiâmat, v. 300, 302
Nét, Fomorian war-god, iii. 27
Neti, god, v. 328
Neva and Navena, good and evil spirits,
xi. 298–299
New-comer may be excluded by deceased unless anniversary feast celebrated, iv. 57
—Fire, iv. 236–237
——ceremony, x. 194
—Guinea, character of mythology of,
ix. 149
—World, discovery of, x. 1
—Yam ceremony, vii. pl. xxiii, opp. p.
238
—Year, conclave of gods at beginning
of, v. 102
——Indian, x. 27
——sacrifice for favour in the, ii. 109
——Year's consecration of idols, xi. 137
——Day, 'Apop thrown into ocean on,
xii. 106
——songs, viii. 369
——domestic rites, viii. 74, 77, 79, 105,
106

New Year's Eve and Twelfth Night, water-spirits rise on to the land between, iv. 469
——names for, iii. 307
——Festivals: see FESTIVALS, NEW YEAR'S.
—Zealand believed to be land fished up by Maui, ix. 43
——Indonesian myth-elements in, ix. 96, 97
——Melanesian myth-elements in, ix. 95, 96, 97
——relation of myths of, to those of Hawaii and Cook and Society Groups, ix. 93, 94
——shows little relationship with Melanesia, ix. 98
Newton Stone, iii. pl. x, opp. p. 94
Nezahualcoyotl, King, elegy of, xi. 109–111, 359 ¹²
Nezahualpilli, last of great Tezcucan kings, xi. 109, 119
NE-zil-la, goddess, v. 317
Nga Tin Daw, father of Tin Dè, xii. 343
— -hlut Pwé festival of the Burmese, xii. 298
Ngai, vii. 116, 149, 150
Ng'ai, personification of rain, vii. 411 ⁴³
Nga-i-tahu of South Island, creation-myth of, ix. 6
Nganaoa concealed in gourd in sea, ix. 68–69
Ngaore, wife of Tane, ix. 24
Ngawn-wa Magam shaped earth with a hammer, xii. 263–264
Ngilin to give fire to the Ifugaos, ix. 184
Ngoc-ho, altar of, xii. 321
— -so'n ("Mountain of Jade"), small island on northern side of Lake Hoan-kiem-ho, xii. 304
Ngojama (ape?) of the Pokomo, vii. 242–243, 412 ⁴
Ngoloko (serpent?) of the Pokomo, vii. 412 ⁴
Ngulwe (local equivalent of Mulungu) caused child to come from woman's knee, vii. 157
Ngúnemapun, xi. 329
Ngunza Kilundu kia Ngunza, tale of, vii. 176–177
Nguyen-hu'u-do, viceroy of Tongking, shrine to, xii. 319–321

Nguyen-quan ("Greatest of Spirits"), epithet of Huyen-thien and Tran-vu, xii. 309
Nhangs, monster spirits, vii. 89–90
Nhlanga, Thonga for reed-bed, vii. 146
Ni (ocean), xi. 223
Niamh, daughter of Celtchar, iii. 155, 181
Niang Niang, goddess of T'ai-Shan, viii. 154
Niao chi-wên, bird footprints writing, viii. 31
Nibelung, dwarf king, ii. 272
"Nibelungenlied," ii. 261, 272
Nibelungs, ii. 212
—children of Nebel (darkness), ii. 268
Nicahtagah, god of Iqi-Balam, xi. 166
Nicander records variant version of Babylonian legend of plant of immortality, v. 228–229
Nicaragua, xi. 183–186
Niceras, sea monsters and water-spirits, ii. 210
Nicomedia in Bithynia, St. George martyred at, v. 338
Nicotine poisoning of Chameleon, vii. 161, 164
Nidaba, grain-goddess, v. 78, 193, 194, 271
—patroness of letters, v. 158
Nidafell, hall of gold in, possessed by dwarf race, ii. 265, 318
Nidānas, viii. 217
Nidhogg, serpent at root of Yggdrasil, ii. pl. VI, opp. p. 32, 217, 319, 346; iv. 357
Nidud, king, ii. 267
Niflhel or Niflheim (Underworld), ii. 9, 43, 145, 303, 304, 318, 324
Niggard, name Paṇis denotes, vi. 66
Night, vi. 25, 26, 31, 32, 69, 85, 86
—and dead, Nephthys as queen of, xii. 110
— -calabash, vii. 341
—Chant, x. 170–173
—concept that originally there was no, ix. 113–114, 117
—Eros hatched from egg of, i. 203
—Eyatahentsik goddess of, x. 295 ⁴³
—how moon became ruler of, xii. 84–85
—Isis symbolizes sky of, xii. 99
—Jörd daughter of, ii. 194
—Nor father of, ii. 200, 201
—origin of, ix. 276

Night, personification of primeval, x. 260; xi. 306
—release of, xi. 310
— -riders (witches), ii. 48, 300–301
—serpent sometimes husband of, x. 300 [50]
—shooting star messenger of, x. 167
—symbolized by black stones, x. 284 [27]
—(Te Po), ix. 6, 7
—Thick, x. 35
Nightingale, xi. 31
—heavenly, gives music for dance of peacock, viii. 357
—Japanese, has different associations than the western, viii. 385 [11]
—Philomele changed into, i. 16
—Prokne changed into, i. 70
Nightmare demons, ii. 256, 288; viii. 156
—(Incubo) sent by Faunus, i. 293
—phantoms, vii. 242
—spirit, ii. 205, 208, 288–290
Nightmares, v. 371
—spirits as, iv. 160, 164, 166
Nights, calculations for memorial feasts made according to, by Volga Finns, iv. 44, 49
—not days, counted, ii. 201
—of license, Teutonic twelve, vi. 58
Nihançan, trickster, x. 122
Nik (neyet), " obscene (?) serpent," designation of Sêth, xii. 109, 392 [53]
Nike and Aphrodite, Plutarch identifies Nephthys with, xii. 392 [58]
—(" Victory "), abstract divinity of war, i. 283, plate LIX, opp. p. 284
Nikeu surnamed the Rogue, ix. 90–91
Nikolai the miracle-worker, iv. 404
Nikumbha, vi. 153
Nīla, vi. 136
Nīlagrīva, vi. 81
Nīlakaṇṭha, name of Śiva, vi. 111, 212
Nile, xii. 25, 27, 45 (fig. 41)
—a form of Amen-Rê', xii. 221
—Apis compared secondarily with the, xii. 163, 412 [6]
—'Apop placed near source of, xii. 391 [43]
—as manifestation of Osiris-Horus and lost eye of sun, xii. 90
—birth of Osiris as, xii. 143
—counterpart of Ocean, chest containing dead Osiris or infant Horus floats in, xii. 116

Nile flood in summer parallel to Babylonian Ishtar-myth, xii. 384 [116]
—of, caused by Rê', xii. 83
—fountain of life often identified with source of, xii. 177
—four sons of Horus or Osiris interpreted as, xii. 112
—sources of, as part of, or as hostile to, Osiris, xii. 105
—symbolic interpretations of, xii. 52
— -god, Aquarius Asiatic counterpart of, xii. 396 [93]
—Nekhbet as wife of, xii. 46, 143
—Nepri, Ḥu, and Zefa connected with, xii. 66
—has four sources, xii. 95, 105
—hieroglyphs of, xii. 46, 370 [33]
—his wife Nekhbet, and the ocean, xii. 45 (fig. 41)
—Horus born in four lakes or sources of, xii. 400 [10]
—in Amen-ḥotep IV's hymn to the sun, xii. 229
—largely identified with Nuu (Nûn?), xii. 47
—Menelaos sacrifices to gods of, i. 134
—mythological explanations of origin and rise of, xii. 46, 94–95, 116, 125
—source of, on frontier of Egypt, xii. 46
—origin of all waters sought in mythological source of, xii. 50
—Osiris identical with, xii. 46, 105, 124, 394 [67], 395 [81]
—Ptaḥ equated with, xii. 145
—religious benefits of pilgrimage to, in Classical world, xii. 243
—rise of, connected with Osiris, xii. 95, 396 [93]
—rising of, caused by tears of Isis, xii. 90, 95, 125
—reminds faithful of Osiris, xii. 94, 395 [75]
—see also ḤA'PI (THE NILE), ETC.
—source of, xii. 47, 106, 417 [20]
—two water-goddesses joined to, xii. 46
Niles, four, xii. 370 [35]
—Merets compared to the two, xii. 46, 136, 137
Niltshi, wind, x. 158, 160, 164
Niman, x. 195
Nimbārak sect worships sun in a nīm-tree, vi. 232

Nimgirgirri, Nimgigri, Nigir, Adad identified with, v. 39
Nimrod, vii. 64
—(Nimurta probably origin of name), founder of cities, v. 55
Nimue, the Lady of the Lake, iii. 194
Nimurta dialectic Sumerian form for Ninurta, v. 55
Nīn Ella as prototype of Anāhita, vi. 280
— -Shushinak, god of Elam, identified with Ninurta, v. 117
Ninacolla, xi. 208
Ninagentue, xi. 208
Ninamaškug, Azāzel corresponds to, v. 356
Ninanasīanna, Ninsīanna, Ninsinna, names of earth-goddess as the planet Venus, v. 91
Ninanna, Nininni, Innini, earth-goddess as female principle of An, v. 91, 92, 108–109
Ninazu (Ereshkigal), mother-goddess in Arallû, v. 264
—husband of Ereshkigal, and lord of Arallû, v. 162–163, 202, 285, 349
Ninbubu, patron of sailors, v. 105
Nindubarra, patron of ship-menders, v. 105
Nindulla, lord of Magan, v. 201, 202
Nine Palaces, viii. 115
—Songs, part of poem, viii. 86, 88
—Sovereigns, viii. 25
—Tripods, emblem of Imperial authority, viii. 8, 100
Ninefold (and twelvefold) conception of universe, xi. 52, 53
Ninepins, gnomes playing at, x. 288 33
NIN(e)tud, mother-goddess, both mother and sister of Tammuz, v. 414 32
Nineveh, v. 55, 88
Ning Sang, xii. 263
Ningal, Babylonian deity of Underworld, xii. 157
——goddess popular in black magic, xii. 207
—moon-goddess, v. 150, 153, 154
Ningirda, queen of Arallû, v. 285
Ningirsu and Ninsubur, earlier titles of Ninurta, v. 93, 126
—god of irrigation, v. 147
—(lord of floods), v. 99, 116
—name of Ninurta at Lagash, v. 116

Ningirsu, son of Enlil, Bau wife of, at Lagash, v. 14, 99
Ningishzida and Gilgamish mentioned in omens, v. 235
——Umunmuzida identical, v. 345
—among gods of agriculture, v. 104
—as dying god, v. 188, 284
——title of Tammuz, v. 349
—guards gate of Anu, v. 177, 180
—identified with Hydra, v. 178, 284
—name of god as principle of arboreal life, v. 77, 78
—throne-bearer of wide nether world, son of Ereshkigal, v. 162, 164
—tree-god, v. 90, 94
Ningyo, the Fisher-woman, viii. 273
Ninhursag, goddess of child-birth, v. 91
—hymn of Lil and, v. 397 70
—Sumerian earth-goddess, sister of Enlil, v. 12, 14, 110, 112, 113, 114, 196, 200, 201, 275
—temple of, at Kish, v. 203
Nini-anteh and cat seen in full moon, ix. 239
Nin-ib, Aramaic transcriptions of, give pronunciation Anushat, etc., v. 132
Ninigi, grandson of sun-goddess, viii. 230, 231, 233
Ninigikug (Ea), a creator, v. 104, 218
Ninine cast down oak of Mugna, iii. 138
Ninkarnunna, god, barber of Ninurta, v. 125, 398 108
Ninkarraka, demoness and goddess of healing, v. 368
—goddess of child-birth, v. 91
—(Gula), divine physician, v. 182
—invoked against slanderers, v. 182–183
Ninkasi (corresponds to Dionysos), wine-goddess, v. 102, 201–202
Ni(n)kilim (Lord of Swine), title of Ninurta, v. 132, 133
Ninlil, Aruru as wife of Enlil at Nippur, v. 14
—Earth mother goddess, v. 12
—identified with Mah, v. 109, 111
—(Ninurta) mother of Marduk, v. 320, 367
—Ursa Major identified with, v. 317
Ninmah, v. 110, 314, 317
—mother-goddess, v. 30, 182, 317
Ninmar-ama-dīm, Sumerian name for Earth mother, v. 12
Ninmea or Nunusešmea (queen who allots the fates), v. 110

Ninsar among gods of agriculture, v. 104

Ninsīanna (Ninansīanna), title of earth-goddess as Venus, v. 91; see also s.v. Ninsīanna, vol. v, p. 448

Ninsikilla, daughter of Enki, v. 110, 195, 396 [58], 403 [10]

Ninsinna, v. 91

Ninsubur and Tammuz identified with Orion, v. 178

—as dying god, v. 188, 342

—is deity to whom titles of Papsukkal and Iliabrat really belong, v. 177

—to obtain report on Şaltu Ishtar sent her messenger, v. 26

Ninsun, mother of Gilgamish, v. 115, 241, 242, 246, 249, 265, 397 [73]

Ninsu-utud, divinity, v. 201–202

Ninth century, first mention of Arthur in, iii. 184

Nintil, divinity, v. 202

Nintud, Ishtar represented as Babylonian, v. 34

—Ninhursag, Ninkarraka, Aruru, names of earth-goddess as goddess of childbirth, v. 91

—Sumerian earth-goddess, sister of Enlil, v. 12, 14, 91

—title of Mah, v. 110

Nintur and Lil, myth of, v. 131

—hymn of Ašširgi, v. 397 [70]

—in Flood tale, v. 206

—(Ninkur), mother-goddess, poem on, v. 196–197, 198, 200

—Ninmea (or Nunusešmea), Ninsikilla, names of Mah, v. 110, 113

Ninudzalli, title of wife of Nintud, v. 115

Ninurta, address of, to stones, v. 121–124

—aids Anu in sending Flood, v. 218, 220, 221

—Bêl-Marduk represents the older, v. 156

—god of spring sun, v. 93, 116

——termed Şa-i-id nakirim ("hunter of the foe"), v. 53, 55, 61, 390 [274]

——war and Sol invictus, v. 99, 115, 119, 126, 131–132, 136, 281

——who opened gate of sunrise, v. 134–135

—identified with Saturn (not with Mars), v. 134

Ninurta in astrology, v. 135

——epics and hymns, v. 119–126

—Malik is Babylonian, v. 58

—Marduk identified with, v. 155

— -Mars, Libra station of, v. 305

—Nergal counterpart of, v. 135

—original hero of combat with dragons, v. 297

—originally also Tammuz, son of Earth mother, v. 131

—(originally Ninurash), as creator, v. 101

—regent of month Tammuz, v. 131

—slaying of six-headed goat by, v. 129

—slew dragon of Chaos, v. 102, 117–118, 131

—son of Enlil, v. 61, 115

——regarded as a dying god, v. 344

—Sumerian war-god, v. 45, 116

—sun-god, v. 55–56

—war-god, sun-god, Saturn, and brother of Astarte or Ashtoreth, v. 135, 146, 286, 287, 288, 289, 292, 296, 316, 320, 321

—weapons of, v. 115, 127–128

— -Zamama, symbol of, v. 136

Ninus, King, and Semiramis, vii. 367

—king of Assyria, vii. 68

Niobe and Leto, i. 175

—Artemis slays daughters of, i. 183

—boast of, i. 44

—children of, slain by Artemis and Apollo, i. 175

—daughter of Phoroneus, i. 29

—(earth-goddess?), mother of Pelasgos, i. 20

—turned into stone, i. 44, 175

—wife of Amphion, daughter of Tantalos, i. 44

Niou, story of, viii. 302

Nipinoukhe, x. 31, 283 [26]

Nippur, v. 12, 124, 125, 140, 312, 326

—assault of stones upon, v. 120

—Ninlil wife of Enlil at, v. 14

Niraya, vi. 154

Nirmocana, vi. 151

Nirrti, a Rudra, vi. 142

—("Decease"), an abstract form of Death-god Yama, vi. 54, 97, 99, 149

Nirukta of Yāska, oldest extant Vedic commentary, vi. 15

Nirvāṇa, vi. 191, 193, 196, 199, 200, 204; viii. 194

Niṣādas born from thigh of corpse of Vena, vi. 166

Niṣadha district, Nāgas dwell in, vi. 154

—Mt., Gandharvas live on, vi. 143

Nisan, month, v. 160

Niṣir, Mt., on which Ark rested, v. 221

Niske-ava (" Great birth-giving mother "), iv. 258–259

Nisonin, Buddhist monastery, viii. 347

Nisos of Megara changed into sea-eagle, i. 16

—son of Pandion, i. 68, 69

—survival of, in folk-tale from Zakynthos, i. 312

Nisse, elves, ii. 224, 225, 231

Nissyen, half-brother of Bran, iii. 100

Niṣṭigrī, mother of Indra, vi. 33

N[i]t, Nrt: see NEITH.

Nithud, king, ii. 11

Niti, game, ix. 42, 76

Ni(u) and Nit (" Sultry Air "), two members of primeval ogdoad, xii. 48

Niu Lang (" Shepherd Boy "), viii. 132

Nivātakavacas, vi. 152

Nivika, sons of, slain by Keresāspa, vi. 324

Nixen, water-elves, ii. 210, 211, 212, 213

Nixie, water-spirit, ii. 210, 211

Nixies lured men into the abyss, vii. 395 [54]

Njal and goat, ii. 234

" Njals-saga," ii. 76, 188, 234, 237, 254, 308

Njord, god, ii. 7, 15, 16, 20, 25, 26, 28, 29, 30, 33, 34, 71, 100–107, 108, 126, 143, 162, 278, 341

Nkanyan, brother of Elullo, vii. 341

Nkondi, Tar-Baby may be fetish, vii. 421 [20]

Nō dramas, viii. 257, 258, 261, 298, 300, 335, 381 [9] (ch. iii)

" No " sacrifice against evil influence, viii. 61

Noah, iv. 363

—Jamshīd confused with, vi. 319

— = Ziûsudra = Xisuthros (Sisythes), Hebrew patriarch, v. 205, 209, 223, 229, 230, 231, 232, 233; see also s.v. Noah, vol. v, p. 449

Noah's lineage, three groups of, arrived in Ireland, iii. 23

Noatun, dwelling-place of Njord, ii. 33, 101, 104, 105, 106

Nobadians cling to Egyptian religion long after spread of Christianity, xii. 244

Nodens Lāmargentios (" Nudd Silver-Hand "), suggested as changed to Lodens (Lludd) Lāmargentios, iii. 103

Nodons, British god, iii. 93, 103

Nodutus, god of nodation of grain, i. 300

Nofret, headless goddess of regions of the dead, xii. 100

Noh Ek, Venus, xi. 138

Nohochakyum, the Great Father, xi. 135, 141

Noidde, shaman, iv. 282–295

Noises, omens from, iv. 470

Noj, builder of ark, iv. 362

Nokomis, the Earth, x. 27, 39, 40, 46

Nome, capital of each, seat of special great divinity or group of gods, xii. 17

—every, contains holy tree, xii. 37

— -god, Sêth worshipped as, xii. 389 [32]

— -gods, xii. 17–18

—local tabus in, xii. 362 [3]

Nomos (" Law "), abstract divinity of social institution, i. 283

Nona (Rona), name of Haumea after restoration to life, ix. 63

Non-cosmic, localized primitive gods develop little mythology, xii. 384 [1]

Nonnos localizes Flood in Thessaly, i. 19

Nonoualcat, combat with people of, xi. 181

Noogumee, x. 45

Nor father of Night, ii. 200

—parallels Erebos, ii. 201

Nordre (North), dwarf, ii. 264–265

Normandy, Bedwyr Duke of, iii. 199

Nornagest, tale of, ii. 241–242, 246

" Nornagests-thattr," ii. 62, 241

Nornaspor, Norn-marks, ii. 245

Norns, ii. 18, 24, 74, 220, 236, 238–247, 254, 255, 262, 265, 331, 337; iv. 257; 357

Norrhem, Swedish home of dead, iv. 78

Norse influence on Celtic Elysium where gods are at war, iii. 123

Norseman and Skraeling, x. 1–3

Norsemen, invasion of Ireland by, iii. 171

North and its Wheel, xi. 98

—Arsan-Duolai, ruler of dead, lives in, iv. 486

—called " that below," iv. 308

North dwelling-place of powers of evil, vi. 297
—end of world home of " Cannibal," x. 249
—gateway erected to the, to mislead corpse, iv. 24
—guardian of, viii. 243
—homage to, viii. 46, 50
—" left," x. 287
—Mandaeans prayed towards, iv. 343
—mythical conceptions of, in Thor-Skrymir story, ii. 93
—nine women in black from, ii. 236
—Pole, god of the, viii. 111
—prayers read with face to, iv. 150, 151
—priests face, during prayer, v. 316
—region of Rudra, vi. 82
—represented by black turtle, iv. 360
—see COMPASS, COLOURS OF, ETC.
—Underworld lies towards, and offerings made towards, iv. 77
— -west Sea, viii. 130
—Wind (Chikamasi), indwelling sea-spirit, vii. 411 46
—world-mountain in, iv. 342, 343
North Star a hole in the sky, x. 95–96
——(as pillar or post), iv. 333, 339, 342, 343, 401, 487
——God C identified with, xi. 139
——("nail of sky"), round which heavens seem to revolve, iv. 221, 222
——to preside at end of all things, x. 116–117
Northern Ch'i Dynasty, viii. 67
—Crown, x. 96
—Lights: see AURORA BOREALIS.
—Ruler, Nemda Old Man, head of invisible army, iv. 156
Norway, cult of Frey in, ii. 118–119
—Odin came to, ii. 33
—paganism in, ii. 16
Nose, how it got its shape, ix. 175
—itching of, as portent, iv. 12
Noses on sacrifice bread, iv. 154
Nosjthej, xi. 335, 336
Nostalgia, earth as protection against, iv. 124
Nostoi ("Returns"), i. 133–136
Not-world, iii. 122
Notos, South Wind, son of Astraios and Eos, i. 247, 265
Notre Dame, Paris, Smertullos portrayed on altar found in, iii. pl. v, opp. p. 40

Noun, in most typical Bantu languages name for ghost not personal, vii. 118
Nouns of human speech originated in Adapa, v. 175
"Nourisher of Youths," Gaia known as, at Athens, i. 272
—see PŪṢAN.
November Eve: see HALLOWE'EN.
Novgorod, Finnish Karelians migrated to, iv. xv
—idol of Perun at, iii. 293, 294
Nowutset, parent of non-Indian men, conjured from magic parcel, x. 203
Nox parallels Night, ii. 201
Npat, Mt. (seat of Apām Napāt), 26th day of each Armenian month dedicated to, vii. 63
Nphan Wa, Kachin all-supreme Being, xii. 263
Ntehe, ghost mothers carry babies head downward in the, vii. 190
Ntotwatsana, tale of, vii. 246–249
Nü-chên Tatars, viii. 97, 181
Nü Kua, sister[?] of Fu Hsi, viii. 31–32
—Ying, daughter of Yao, viii. 88–89
Nuada Argentlám ("Silver-Hand"), king of Tuatha Dé Danann, iii. 25, 28, 30, 32, 41, 103, 136, 204
—Druid, father of Tadg, iii. 164, 175
—hand of, replaced by one of silver, ii. 100
Nubia, cosmic meaning of, forgotten, xii. 91
—cult of divinized men apparently especially flourishing in, xii. 415 32
—cults in, xii. 171, 415 32
—Ḥat-ḥôr in, xii. 410 1
—influence of Egyptian religion on, xii. 240
—Isis flees to, xii. 125
—Merui worshipped at Kalabsheh in, xii. 137, 406 55
—myths concerning Bês in, xii. 62
—sun's eye retires from Egypt to, xii. 86, 88
Nubian gods, Egyptians of earliest times worshipped, xii. 157
Nubians, Justinian propagates Christianity among, xii. 244
Nudd in Welsh literature and the Romances, iii. 191
—suggested change of name of, to Lludd, iii. 103

Nudimmud ("creator of form of man"), Anu begat, v. 92, 104, 107, 291, 292, 344, 396 [45]

Nudity rites, vii. 13

Nukara (or Nugara), the Babylonian Ningal, xii. 157

Nukuchyumchakob, lord of rain, xi. 140, 141

Nules-murt, a forest-spirit, iv. 179

Nuliajoq, x. 273 [7]

Num, sky- and heaven-god, iv. 218, 221

Numa, Roman parallel to the organizer of Iranian nation, vi. 299

Number, cosmic, seventy-two as, xii. 395 [75]

—in American Indian mythology, x. 311 [68]

——Mayan calendar, xi. 146–152, 153, 155; Mexican calendar, 97–105; Yucatan calendar, 128

—mystic, fourteen as, xii. 395 [78]

—of gods, ii. 15–16

Numbers, days: third, seventh, ninth, sixteenth, thirty-sixth, fortieth, iv. 41, 43, 44, 47, 54, 295; weeks: sixth, ninth, 48, 56, 68

—heaping up of, iv. 385, 419; vi. 199–200, 221, 227; 275, 276, 277, 281, 293, 299, 304, 305, 306, 309, 327, 346; xi. 93; xii. 280, 318, 342

—influence of, xi. 52–53, 354 [7]–355

——sacred, sacrificial cults influenced by old, iv. 407

—sacred or significant follow:

one, iii. 251; 283; iv. 38, 39, 68, 70, 179, 182, 206; 310, 311, 357, 430, 464; vi. 57, 138, 140; 270, 294, 315

two, i. 25, 26, 27, 43, 247, 301–302; iii. 13, 26, 36, 78, 117, 120, 238, 247; 280; iv. 34, 38; 310, 355, 356, 381, 383, 388, 422, 429, 434, 449, 457; vi. 16, pl. III, 43, 57, 69; 270; ix. 109, 156, 160, 170, 273; x. 58, 311 [68]; xi. 175; xii. 38, 43, 46, 52, 129, 136, 149, 150, 174, 363 [4], 372 [52], 418 [3]; 276, 285, 289, 290, 291, 296, 352; xii. 46, 47; see also TWINS.

three, i. 22, 33–34, 39, 86, 88, 95, 104, 188, 314; ii. 24, 27, 54, 81, 82, 83, 88, 92, 93, 111, 146, 207, 216, 228, 235, 241, 242, 243, 244, 245, 249, 261, 262, 266, 268, 294, 333, 335; see also TRIADS; iii. 27, 29, 31, 32, 33, 34, 39, 40, 55, 58, 65, 79, 82, 85, 87, 88, 89,

97, 120, 125, 126, 133, 135, 136, 147, 148, 149, 151, 154, pl. xx, 169, 172, 175, 187, 189, 203, 227, 233, 235, 238, 245, 251; 280, 284, 285, 309, 322, 323, 324, 365 [26]; iv. 20, 23, 24, 25, 30, 31, 38, 39–40, 42, 44, 46, 47, 50, 51, 57, 69, 70, 77, 80, 87, 94, 95, 126, 129, 130, 169, 179, 180, 181, 206, 213, 242, 253, 256, 257, 259, 263, 267, 268, 272, 274, 278; 307, 309, 310, 311, 318, 338, 341, 344, 345, 351, 353, 354, 355, 357, 358, 365, 379, 395, 402, 413, 416, 420, 429, 433, 441, 444, 445, 447, 448, 449, 465, 472, 475, 478, 482, 501, 507, 509, 516; v. 40, 94; vi. 15, 19, 22, 30, 33, 36, 38, 41 (fig. 1), 43, 45, 50, 55, 57, 61, 71, 79, 80, 88, 91, 93, 98, 110, 111, 116, 122, 154, 180, 212, 220, 226; 268, 270, 278, 284, 285, 297, 303, 306, 309, 311, 315, 328, 345, 346, 360 [10], 365 [4]; vii. 55; 132, 204, 209, 224, 229, 282, 304, 341; ix. 24, 43, 106, 156, 160, 163, 166, 167, 250, 261, 273; x. 35, 56, 95, 148, 177, 311 [68]; xi. 39, 47, 94, 137, 234, 251, 309; xii. 365 [26]; 273, 274, 284, 289, 318, 331, 345, 347, 352

four, ii. 133, 146, 181, 332; iii. 13, 32, 60, 63, 74, 81, 153, 235, 237, 238, 251; 279, 283, 284; iv. 23, 27, 34, 42; 308, 310, 344, 347, 353, 359, 360, 379, 381, 383, 388, 420, 435, 441, 444, 445; v. 54, 61, 191, 388 [223]; vi. 16, 19, 39, 52, 57, 58, 69, 77, 98, 103, 107, 110, 118, 120, 131, 134, 159, 193, 205, 215; 266, 336; vii. 51, 392 [21]; 232, 256, 306, 383 [5]; viii. 4, 135; ix. 213, 256; x. xxii, 7, 19, 23, 37, 50, 58, 59, 100, 116, 118, 128, 137, 165, 168, 173, 177, 185, 207, 250, 253, 254, 257, 263, 275 [11]–276, 308 [63], 311 [68]; xi. 29, 48, 52, 53, 55, 56, 61, 64, 71, 81, 88, 90, 91, 94, 106, 134, 144, 155, 164, 165, 166, 170, 174, 232, 239, 355 [7]; xii. 35, 39, 44, 46, 48, 52, 65, 66, 135, 143, 147, 180, 195, 199, 363 [4], 364 [11], 367 [10], 368 [12], 369, 370 [35], 378 [98], 417 [20]; 282, 286, 342, 349

five, iii. 25, 37, 74, 121, 130, 237, 251; 283, 323, 325; iv. 23, 27, 42, 70, 180, 263, 272, 274, 275; 309, 310, 381, 383, 394, 407, 516; vi. 16, 57, 98, 159, 169, 205, 216; 282, 285, 295; vii. 256, 273; viii. 135; ix. 14, 207; x. 250,

275 [11], 311 [68]; xi. pl. VI, 52, 53, 55, 64, 114, 136, 175, 227, 228, 230, 232; xii. 318, 352

six, i. 98; ii. 99; iii. 230; iv. 275; 307, 309, 310, 338, 427, 428, 431, 432, 435, 485; v. 219; vi. 17, 36, 137, 140, 194, 205, 215; 270, 280, 284, 298; ix. 8, 14, 106, 156, 167; x. 72, 190, 209, 286 [31], 311 [68]; xi. 38, 52, 53, 93; xii. 206

seven, i. 56, 242; ii. 79, 236, 242, 259, 260, 261, 262, 263, 294, 316, 335; iii. 11, 30, 31, 36, 38, 40, 79, 118, 119, 121, 125, 128, 132, 138, 143, 150, 192, 235, 251, 253, 254, 268; 283; 322; iv. 47, 70, 180, 260, 272, 275; 309, 322, 328, 338, 340, 341, 343, 346, 349, 351, 353, 359, 364, 367, 374, 378, 379, 382, 400, 401, 402, 404, 405, 406, 407, 408, 415, 425, 426–428, 432, 481, 486, 487, 492, 508; v. 18, 28, 29, 38, 84, 94, 112, 116, 126, 138, 146, 159, 161, 164, 167, 176, 217, 219, 224, 274, 364, 366, 367, 372, 373; vi. 25, 28, fig. 1, 45, 48, 49, 56, 65, 79, 105, 111, 115, 134, 138, 154, 168, 172, 186, 192, 194, 196, 205, 236; 269, 280, 282, 297, 298, 311, 326; vii. 17, 56; 188, 273, 356, 358; ix. 19, 106, 160, 162, 163, 170, 173, 178, 206, 207, 211, 212, 214, 215, 220, 226, 230, 231, 236, 237, 253, 257; x. 19, 50, 56, 60, 61, 72, 161, 162, 209, 287 [31], 311 [68]; xi. 52, 53, 93, 140, 155, 181; xii. 28, 40, 53, 57, 206, 364 [16], 368 [14], 376 [78]; 278, 279, 284, 289, 291, 298, 323, 324, 342

eight, ii. 43, pl. VIII, 66, 86, 88, 89, 143, 145, 146; iii. 283; iv. 275; 351, 364, 371, 378, 443, 445, 485, 491; v. 350; vi. 28, 56, 85, 120, 142, 205, 226; 340; vii. 144, 176, 177; 228, 303, 325, 347, 356; viii. 116; ix. 15–16, 34, 75, 162; x. 58, 89, 173, 203; xi. 64, 68, 81, 90, 234; xii. 48, 49, 167, 372 [56]

nine, i. 57, 64, 238, 240; ii. 27, 43, 66, 81, 91, 104, 130, 153, 154, 155, 158, 190, 228, 235, 236, 249, 251, 283, 294, 304, 318, 329–330, 331, 335, 341; iii. 34, 44, 52, 57, 82, 95, 116, 168, 169, 176, 188, 191, 193, 201, 235, 244, 251; 285, 321, 322, 325, 358 [26]; iv. 70, 206, 245, 267, 270, 272, 274; 309, 310, 337, 340, 351, 353, 354, 378,

381, 382, 400, 406, 407, 442, 448, 458, 464, 485, 487, 490, 491, 508, 509; v. 126, 219, 235; vi. 65; 225; 270, 298; viii. 35, 114, 117, 136; ix. 171, 182, 237; x. 170, 203, 311 [68]; xi. 52, 53, 56, 69, 73, 81, 165, 354 [7]; xii. 26, 264, 292, 294, 309, 324

ten, ii. 56, pl. XXVI, 199; iii. 116, 233; iv. 385; vi. 43, 61, 65, 110, 122, 154, 168, 181, 220, 221; 268, 270, 281, 296, 298; vii. 254; ix. 35, 107; xi. 251; xii. 294

eleven, ii. 73, 128, 211, 308; vi. 19, 142, 212; ix. 109, 220

twelve, i. 80, 110, 139; ii. 32, 33, 34, 73, 254, 327; iii. 96, 267; 282, 319; iv. 273; 329, 347, 436–438; vi. 24, 57, 85, 107, 225, 287; 348; vii. 392 [21]; x. 58, 167, 169; xii. 57, 199, 421 [4]; 284, 289

thirteen, ii. 242, 327; iii. 15, 128; v. 366, 370; vi. 138; xi. 52, 53, 92, 155, 179, 354 [7]

fourteen, v. 163; vi. 294, 325; xi. 179; xii. 28, 364 [16]

fifteen, iii. 235; vi. 269, 293, 294, 295, 303, 361 [19]

sixteen, iii. 125; iv. 356, 406; vi. 284

seventeen, iii. 85; iv. 405, 406

nineteen, iii. 11

twenty, iii. 235; vi. 33, 180; xi. 52, 64

twenty-one, vi. 56, 169

twenty-three, vi. 278

twenty-four, vi. 220, 225; vii. 238; x. 160

twenty-five, vi. 205; xi. 53–54

twenty-seven, iii. 115; vi. 136

twenty-eight, vi. 178

thirty, iv. 353, 435, 453; vi. 32, 33; 293, 296, 298, 302, 339, 348

thirty-two, vi. 195, 199

thirty-three, iv. 355, 356, 410; vi. 19, 63, 193; 280; viii. 196

thirty-six, iv. 412

thirty-seven, xii. 292, 339–357

thrice seven, vi. 39; thrice sixty, vi. 39

forty, iii. 230, 235; iv. 27, 40, 47, 48; 353, 365, 453, 490; v. 366; vi. 294, 309; xi. 37

forty-two, xii. 176, 179

forty-three, iv. 411

forty-four, iv. 411, 412

forty-eight, xi. 234

forty-nine, vi. 209

fifty, i. 21, 30–32, 118, 132, 242; iii. 27,
  82, 87, 125; iv. 27, 40, 68; 353; vi.
  297, 346
fifty-two, vii. 382 ⁷; xi. 92, 93, 95
fifty-four, iv. 382 ⁷, 411
fifty-five, iv. 411; vi. 286
sixty, iii. 82, 87, 125, 129; xii. 292
sixty-four, vi. 226
seventy, ix. 313 ⁷⁹
seventy-two, iv. 412; vi. 225, 226
eighty, iv. 364; vi. 195
ninety, vi. 29
ninety-nine, iv. 411; vi. 37, 68
one hundred, ii. 316; iv. 473; vi. 29, 32,
  33, 75, 114, 122, 131, 226; 297, 299, 312
one hundred and one, iii. 126; vi. 31
one hundred and eleven, iii. 271
one hundred and fifty, iii. 79
one hundred and eighty, vi. 56
one-third, v. 364
two-thirds, v. 213, 364
three hundred, iii. 59; 280
three hundred and twelve, xi. 93
three hundred and sixty-four, xi. 93
three hundred and sixty-five, xii. 35,
  38, 56
five hundred and forty, ii. 77
six hundred, xi. 92
six hundred and thirteen, v. 364
six hundred and seventy-six, xi. 92
seven hundred and twenty, vi. 220
nine hundred, ii. 86, 100; iii. 51
one thousand, vi. 22, 32, 33, 37, 41, 46,
  82, 86, 112, 131, 134, 168, 299, 305,
  346
eleven hundred, vi. 33
eleven hundred and eight, vi. 112
sixteen hundred, xi. 89
ten thousand, vi. 132, 134
eleven thousand, vi. 142, 144
sixteen thousand, one hundred, vi. 174
fifty thousand, vi. 68
one hundred thousand, vi. 68
six hundred thousand, vi. 137
Numen, life-potency, regarded in Roman religion as a living will, i. 287
Numitor, king of Alba Longa, i. 307
Numi-Tōrem, iv. 330, 404, 435
——Num-Tūrem, sky-gods, iv. 218, 219
—— -paireks, iv. 394
Nunamnir, v. 136
Nunda, eater of people, vii. 358
Nung Chih-kao, viii. 139
Nungungulu, vii. 127

Nunnehi, helpful spirit warriors, x. 68
Nuns serve in temple of Huyen-thien,
  xii. 309, 315
Nunu, weapon, v. 128
Nunurra, title of Ea, v. 106
Nunusešmea, v. 110
Nunyenunc, bird who carries off men,
  x. 139
Nur-Dagan crossed sea of death, v. 218
Nurra, patron of potters, v. 105
Nurse, divine, xii. 116, 376 ⁷⁹, 397 ⁹⁴
—Men'et the lion-headed, xii. 101, 136
—(of sun-god) at creation of world,
  xii. 40
—(Tethys), i. 5
Nursing mothers, gingko-tree has espe-
  cial care over, viii. 342
Nuru, Incantation of house of, v. 106
Nusku, fire-god, v. 107, 124, 125
—god of new moon, v. 154
Nut, Aker, and Khepri, xii. 369 (fig.
  221)
—and Qêb begotten of Shu and Tefênet,
  and parents of Osiris, Horus, Sêth,
  Isis, and Nephthys, xii. 69
————Heaven and Earth, created by
  Sun, xii. 50
————Osiris child of, xii. 113
—as a birth-genius of Osiris, xii. 385 ¹²
————primeval sky, xii. 49
————watery Chaos, xii. 49
—called into consultation by Rê', xii.
  74
—celestial counterpart of the abyss Nuu
  (or Nûn?), xii. 41, 372 ⁵⁵
—children of, as name of celestial beings, xii. 72, 380 ²⁴
————Egyptian beliefs concerning, xii.
  41, 42, 55
—(Egyptian), Connla's position resembles that of, iii. 150
—explained as sky of Underworld, xii.
  41
—gives birth to sun every morning, xii.
  41, 42 and figs. 33, 34, 35, 49
—heavenly flood, represented in picture
  by ornamented box, xii. 71
—hieroglyphic sign of, xii. 372 ⁵⁵
—identified with Êpet, xii. 60
————Isis, xii. 99
—member of ennead of Heliopolis, xii.
  216
—mother of all life, xii. 41
————stars, xii. 42

Nut, not clearly distinguished from sky in day-time, xii. 42, 45
—of ogdoad, relation of, to celestial Nut, xii. 49
—opens way to divinities, xii. 384 [116]
—personification of nocturnal sky, xii. 41
—pronunciation of, xii. 368 [17]
—Rêʿ places himself on back of, xii. 77
—receives sun at night, xii. 96
—receiving the dead, xii. 41 (fig. 31)
—representation of, xii. 41
—Sêth son of, xii. 103, 390 [34]
—(sky) upheld by Shu, xii. 43 (fig. 38)
—united with stellar tree of heaven, xii. 42
—wife of the earth-god, xii. 41, 42 and figs. 33, 34, 35
—with sun in scarab-form bends over Aker, xii. 368 [22]–369 and fig. 221
——symbols of sky in day-time, xii. 41 (fig. 32)
Nut, Idunn transformed into a, ii. 141, 179
Nuter Dua ("the Rising God"), the Morning Star, xii. 54
Nuts, nine, with love charms, iii. 168
—part of food of gods, bright folk, and fairy-folk of Erin, iii. 121
Nuu (Abyss) identified with Rêʿ (sun), xii. 220
—aided by Selqet and three other goddesses in protecting or representing the four subterranean sources, xii. 147
—and Nut (abysmal forces), two members of primeval ogdoad, xii. 48
——as parents of sun-god, xii. 49
—bidden to guard against reptiles, xii. 78–79
—comes to Ombos to avenge his father Rêʿ again, xii. 86
—cosmogonic idea of, xii. 47
—counsels Rêʿ, xii. 74, 77
—fertility-god, xii. 370 [41]
—god of Abyss, had no temples in New Empire, xii. 23
—identified with Khepri, xii. 63–64
——Ptaḥ-Sokari, as primeval god, xii. 63–64
——Ptaḥ-Tatunen, xii. 47
——Rêʿ-Hor, xii. 221
— -Khnûm, Ptaḥ perhaps confused with, xii. 407 [77]

Nuu, Khnûm treated as localized variant of, xii. 50
—lifts solar ship from depths in the morning, xii. 95
—(Nûn?), ocean identified with, xii. 47, 48
—pronunciation of, xii. 368 [17], 370 [38]
— -Ptaḥ identical with Bês and Sokari, xii. 223
—Rêʿ soul of, xii. 219
—representation of, xii. 47–48
—sends his springs to "the two mysterious ones," xii. 47–48 and fig. 43, 371 [44]
—soul of, identified with sun-god, xii. 372 [48]
—Tatunen identified with, xii. 47, 145, 150
—with head of ox, xii. 47 (fig. 42)
Nuvarahu, Turehu woman, ix. 72–73
Nvard, wife of Ara, vii. 68
Nwachisiana, honorary title of Hare, vii. 293
Nwali, vii. 128
Nyali, vii. 128
Nyamatsanes, tale of the, vii. 257
Nyambe, vii. 131, 132, 133, 162
Nyanku[o]pong of Gold Coast tribes, vii. 116, 123, 124, 399 [6]
Nyasa, Lake, vii. 133, 147
Nychar Mades (Nychar the Median), vii. 67
—perhaps Nakru, vii. 389 [10]
Nyja identified with Pluto, iii. 355 [44]
Nykr as horse drowns riders, ii. 211
Nykteus, death of, i. 43
—(Night), reputed father of Antiope, i. 43
Nyktimos of Arkadia, flood of Deukalion and Pyrrha in reign of, i. 18–19
—son of Lykaon, saved by Zeus at instigation of Ge, and succeeds his father, i. 20–21
—succeeded as king of Arkadia by Arkas, i. 22
Nymph, heavenly, vi. 18
—water-, vi. 18
Nymphs, ii. 133, 135, 242; vii. 84–85
—classed as Dryads and Hamadryads, i. 270
—Melian, born from the blood of Ouranos, i. 6
—of fountains as ministrants of Dionysos, i. 220

Nymphs of Mt. Nysa rewarded with place among constellations for care of Dionysos, i. 46, 217–218
—wood-, iii. 262–263
—worship of, iii. 277
Nynnyaw and Peibaw transformed into oxen for their sins, iii. 71
—son of Beli, iii. 106
Nyrckes (Nyyrikki), game-spirit, iv. 185
Nysa, Mt., possible connexion of, with name of Dionysos, i. 217

Nyx, abode of twins of, in Underworld, i. 278
—abstract divinity of time, i. 282
—Moirai sometimes daughters of, i. 332 ³ (ch. xiv)
—(Night), i. 4–5
Nzambi, a high god, vii. 116, 125, 131
—Mpungu, man translated to Heaven saw, vii. 238–239
— -si, Earth mother, vii. 125
Nzasi (Thunder) and his dogs, vii. 238

O

O, Prince of, viii. 66
Oak, ii. 68, 260, 333, 335; v. 35; vi. 90; x. 294 ⁴²
—and water in rites of sacred fire, vii. 15
—asked for rain, iv. 188
—blood of, iii. 322
—dedicated to Donar at Geismar, ii. 203
— -fire ashes for healing of sick, vii. 57
—great, iv. 82
—Kunugi a kind of, viii. 339
—of Mugna, iii. 138
—sacred, iii. pl. xxxvii, opp. p. 304, 305–306, 354 ¹⁰
——to god of Heaven and storm, vii. 57, 62
—sanctity of, iii. 358 ²⁴
— -sapling ring placed on pillar-stone, iii. 152
—talking, of Zeus, i. 109, 162
—tree of thunder-god, iv. 230
— -trees borne by giant, iii. 148
Oaks, dragons entwined round, iii. 11, 131
Oakum and straw, Kekri-fires made of, iv. 66
Oannes emerged from sea to reveal to men science and letters, v. 86, 103, 105, 106, 290, 395 ²¹
Oases, Osiris dwells in, xii. 399 ¹¹⁰
Oath by sun, iv. 422
—Leto's, by the Styx, i. 174
—Peach-orchard, viii. 174, 176
Oaths, i. 25, 125, 190, 290, 303; ii. 58, 71, 90, 106, 109, 117, 129, 134, 135, 156, 162, 164, 180, 186, 337, 338; iii. 293, 295, 300; v. 168, 333; vi. 128; vii. 40, 47, 54, 393 ³²; x. 141

Oaths, Ganges water for use in, vi. 234
—Helios invoked in, i. 243, 273
—invoked in name of Hades, i. 233
—of the Seven Generals of the Argive host, i. 190
—Ptaḥ sometimes god who watches over, xii. 407 ⁷⁶
—public, Gaia was invoked at, i. 273
—sworn in name of bear, iv. 85
—taken before sun, iv. 223
—Zeus invoked in, i. 273
Oats, Virankannos tender of, iv. 244
Ob, god of upper field of the, and of the Little Ob, iv. 403
—River, entrance at mouth of, into Underworld, iv. 77, 78
Obagat desired immortality for mankind, ix. 252
Obe, fabulous animal, carries girl to witches, vii. 339–340
Obedience, rulers must give, to spirits of ancestors, viii. 50
Obelisk, xii. 188, 189, 419 ¹¹
— -like structures erected by kings of Fifth Dynasty to Rê', xii. 31
—of the Pen, xii. 304, 305
Obelisques before Egyptian temples symbolize limits of sun's course, xii. 30–31, 38
—in Heaven, two, misinterpreted as two sceptres, xii. 365 ²²
—Osiris stands between two, symbolizing time, xii. 93 (fig. 84)
—two each in earth and Heaven, xii. 31
—worshipped as sign of sun's presence, xii. 31
Obi rites, vii. 335
Obiń-murt, iv. 163

Objects, ceremonial and votive, xi. 236, pl. XXXVI, opp. p. 236; see also SACRED OBJECTS (vol. xi).
—divine, vi. 97
—inanimate, replying in place of fugitive, ix. 85, 277, 322 [91]; see also ANSWERING BY INANIMATE, ETC.
Oblations, vi. 70
—made during first period after death are intended to create a body for deceased, vi. 250
Oblivion, draught of, iii. 88
—many local gods sink into, xii. 17
Obol of the dead, i. 142, 143, 327 [3]
Oboroten (Russian), vampire, iii. 232
Observatory in Peking, viii. 144
Obsidian Stone, xi. 178, 179, 180, 181
Obsolescence of old divine names, xii. 21, 362 [8]
Obyda, evil forest-spirit, iv. 468
Occult power, vi. 22
Occultism, viii. 44, 54, 57, 113, 133–147
—not explanation of Grail story, iii. 205
—practised by witches, vii. 336
Occupations, three, vi. 226
Ocean, vi. 30, 146
—adored in form of fish, xi. 223
—ancestor of Tane, ix. 25
—and sky, little distinction between, xii. 113
—apparently indicated in picture containing Ehet, xii. 380 [21]
—as enemy of the sun, xii. 237, 428 [77]
—both Osirian and Typhonic, xii. 95, 106, 108
—chest containing dead Osiris or infant Horus floats in, xii. 116
—churning of the, vi. 104, 106, 111, 124, 132, 139, 151, 155, pl. XXI, opp. p. 170, 214
—cosmic, idea of world-supporting being connected with, iv. 312, 366
—daily descent of sun's eye to and return from, xii. 89
—dragon bound in, xii. 104
—fire as gift of, x. 256
—" Great Green," xii. 46, 400 [10]
—heavenly, iv. 418
—Horus connected with, xii. 389 [29]
—identified with Nuu (Nûn?), xii. 47, 48
—in human circular form, xii. 49 (fig. 46), 96

Ocean, Midgard-serpent personification of, ii. 193
—Morning Star as god of the, xii. 373 [60]
—Mu(u)t wife of, xii. 46
—origin of, sought in mythological source of Nile, xii. 50
—Osiris born from, xii. 113
——identified with, xii. 95, 105
—primordial, iv. 313, 316, 317, 322, 323, 328, 331, 345, 361, 419, 420
—represents 'Apop in captivity, xii. 106
——smith, iii. 171, 175
—subterranean, sun and the, vii. 50
—sun-god grows in, and is symbolized by blue lotus, xii. 50
—Underworld, v. 226
Oceania, use of term; natural features; environment; ethnology, and myths gathered from all parts of, ii. ix, xi–xv
Oceanic mythology, summary of, ix. 304–307
Oçelopan, xi. 117
Ocelotonatiuh, epoch of giants and solar eclipse, xi. 94
Ochall Oichni, king of síd of Connaught, iii. 57–58
Ochocalo, xi. 208
Ocna, renovation of the temple in honour of gods of the fields, xi. 138
Ocpatli, the peyote, xi. 77
October, iii. 352 [7]
Octopus, ix. 15, 17, 37, 69
Od, Freyja's husband, ii. 120, 125–126
Odainsakr (" Acre of Not-dead "), visits to, ii. 320, 322
Odakōn, Dagōn connected with, v. 86
Odatis, daughter of King Omartes, vi. 341
Oddi, " Edda " said to be derived from, ii. 4
Oddibjorg, prophesying woman, ii. 246–247
Oddrun, ii. 251
" Oddrunargratr," ii. 121, 184, 228
Odendonnia (Sapling), x. 296 [45]
Odensberg, ii. 44
Odin (Odhin, Voden, Wodan, Woden, Vodan, Gwoden, Godan), ii. 5, 6, 9, 10, pl. III, opp. p. 12, 15, 16, 17, 18, 19, 20, 21, 22, 23, 24, 26, 27, 28, 29, 32, pl. VI, opp. p. 32, 33–34, 35, 37–67, 70, 71, 72, 73, 74, 77, 81, 90, 91, 98, 99, 101, 106, 112, 115, 120, 121, 122, 123, 126, 127, 129, 130, 133, 134, 137, 139,

140, 141, 142, 143, 145, 147, 151, 155, 156, 157, 158, 159, 160, 161, 162, 164, 165, 166, 167, 168, 169, 170, 174, 175, 176, 178, 181, 183, 184, 185, 193, 201, 202, 217, 220, 236, 240, 243, 248, 249, 250, 251, 256, 265, 266, 269, 278, 296, 297, 299, 300, 303, 305, 311, 313, 314, 315, 316, 324, 326, 327, 337, 340, 341, 342, 346, 351 4; iii. 35; iv. 479; vi. 37, 48, 288, 291, 302

Odin's island, Odin journeys to, ii. 33

O'Donnell's Kern, tale of, iii. 60–61

Odrörir, blood of Kvasir collected in kettle, ii. 53, 54

—magic mead of poesy, ii. 22, 48, 52, 53, 54

Odrus changed into pool of water, iii. 60, 136

Ods-mær (Freyja), ii. 120

Oduyen (modern Son-tay), capital of Trung-trac at, xii. 313

Odysseus, i. pl. xxx, opp. p. 120, 136–140

—aided when wrecked by Leukothea, i. 262

—and Cyclops, Irish parallel to, iii. 167

——Diomedes, i. 123–124

——shades confused by Claudian with Gaulish myth of the dead, iii. 16

——Sirens, i. pl. lv, opp. p. 260

—by trickery, takes Iphigeneia from her mother for sacrifice on altar, i. 126

—centre of themes of "Little Iliad" and "Ilioupersis," i. 131

—departure of, from Thrinakia hindered by Notos and Euros, i. 265–266

—descent of, to Hades, i. 145–146

—gains arms of Achilles by Athene's help, i. 131–132

—harassed by Poseidon for killing Polyphemos, i. 211

—like Arţā Vīrāf, visits other world, vi. 344

—reason of Athene's affinity for, i. 170

—ruse of, when he was deputed to bring Achilles to Troy, i. 122

—said to be son of Sisyphos, i. 37

—seeks to aid dying Penthesilea, i. 131 (fig. 5)

—slaying suitors, i. pl. xxxiv, opp. p. 138

—steals palladion from Troy, i. 132

—takes Hekabe as prize of war, i. 133

Odysseus throws Astyanax, son of Hektor, from walls of Troy, i. 133

—wounded and forced to retreat to ships, i. 129

"Odyssey, the," i. 136–139

—no trace of Gilgamish epic in, v. 266

Oedipus: see Oidipous.

Oengus Mac ind Óc, son of Dagda and Boann, iii. pl. i, frontispiece, 27, 28, 33, 40, 41, 50, 51–52, 53, 55, 56, 66, 67, 73, 78–82, 89, 120, 121, 126, 127, 174, 175, 176, 177, 178, 179, 202, 207, 208

—son of Aed Abrat, iii. 86

Œttar-fylgja, family guardian spirit, ii. 235

Offering-board, iv. 224, 230 (fig. 8), 231

— -girdle, iv. 271; see also Girdle at Sacrifice.

— -table, iv. 144

Offerings, blood-, at Asgard, ii. 33

—food, to fées and the like, ii. 244–246

—for sick in round holes in rocks, ii. 225

—from living to keep ghosts alive, vii. 180, 181, 189

—of foreigners required for Svantovit, iii. 280

——fruits, etc., at cross-roads to save crops from Itowe, vii. 261

——porridge at sacrifice-tree, iv. 267

—paid to memorials erected to satīs, vi. 244

—required according to one's ability, viii. 62, 63

—sacrificial, xi. 26, 34; see also items s.v. Sacrifice.

—see items s.v. Burnt, etc.

—to dead, iv. 77; vii. 95–96, 98; see also chap. Death and Burial (vol. iv, 17–36)

——deities, vi. 19, 97, 156

——household gods: see chap. Household spirits (vol. iv, 159–174)

——Pool accepted and human victim returned dead, vii. 188

——Seides, iv. 102, 112

——spirits at shrines poured into a pot sunk in the ground, vii. pl. xvi, opp. p. 182

——Thor, ii. 75

—withheld caused ghosts to withhold harvest, vii. 197–198

Offspring, viii. 82, 83, 105

—plants as symbols of, viii. 105

Offspring, prayers for, ii. 174, 249
Ofnir, serpent, ii. 217
O-fo, viii. 194
Ofoti, troll-king, attends troll-thing, ii. 301
Ofurunye, vii. 186
Og, king of Bashan, tale of, v. 355
Ogdoad, association of sun with, xii. 49
—cosmic deity wears shoes of, xii. 223
—doctrine of, xii. 50
—members of, xii. 48, 371 45 46
—primeval, two members of, xii. 48 (fig. 44)
Ogma, commander of Tuatha Dé Danann, iii. 24, 26, 27, 33, 34, 39, 40, 98, 111
—Ogmios, Bragi parallels, ii. 161
—whose name is akin to that of Ogmios, a divine warrior and a god of poetry and speech, iii. 10–11
Ogmios, Gaulish god, iii. 10, 98
—parallel (?) of, found in "Táin Bó Cúalnge," iii. 11
Ogre chief's daughter summoned by Brahmā's daughter, viii. 357
Ogres, vii. 204, 237, 242–257, 335, 346, 399 11, 427 13; viii. 306; see also items s.v. MONSTERS.
—Yatawm and Yatai as, have children only after eating human flesh, xii. 293, 294
Ogvald sacrificed to cow, ii. 216
Ogygos, autochthonous king of Ektenes, i. 42
Ogyrven from whose cauldron came three muses, iii. 112
—meanings of word, iii. 112
Ohdowas, underground people, x. 28
Oh-kuni-nushi, successor of Susa-no-wo, viii. 229, 230, 232–233, 237, 279, 317, 318, 341, 381 1
Oh-maga-tsumi, Great Evil-doer, viii. 381 1
Oh-yama-tsumi, mountain-god, viii. 233
Oichalia, Euboian city, i. 89
—sacked by Herakles, i. 94
Oidipous, i. 48–51
—Iranian parallel to solution of riddles by, vi. 335
—sons of, and the seven against Thebes, i. 51–54
Oil, anointing with rancid, to smell like corpse, ix. 76
—causes flood to abate, ix. 257

Oil, coffin of glass with corpse laid in, v. 323
— -seller, Lü Tung-pin as, viii. 123
Oilill (Bare Ear), punishment of, iii. 73
Oineus and Thestios supreme in Aitolia's councils, i. 56
—of Kalydon, duplicate of Dionysos, i. 219
——father of Deianeira, i. 93
—overlooked Artemis while offering sacrifices of first-fruits, i. 56
—pique of Artemis at harvest-home sacrifice of, i. 184
—ruled over Kalydon and married Althaia, i. 56
—summoned spearmen of the Greeks to kill the boar sent by Artemis against Aitolia, i. 56–57
Oinomaos challenges suitors for daughter to chariot-race, i. 119
—death of, i. 120
—king of Pisa, i. 119
Oinone, ex-wife of Paris, refuses to aid him when dying, i. 132
—island of, hiding-place of Aigina, i. 37
—prophetess, weds Paris, i. 119
Oinopion blinded Orion, i. 250–251
Oisin, son of Fionn by Saar (transformed into a fawn), iii. 91, 112, 124, 132, 162, 168, 169, 170, 172, 176, 178, 179, 180, 181, 182, 194, 209
Oita, Mt., funeral pyre of Herakles upon, i. 94
Öjä, invisible nature-god, iv. 464
Ojun = shaman, iv. 496
Oka, tale of, xi. 312
Okamsweli, vii. 164
Okeanos, Amphitrite daughter of, i. 214
—and Okeanids, i. 255–256, 258, 260
——Tethys purge Glaukos of imperfections before admitting him as sea-god, i. 261
——Rhea daughter of, i. 274
——Thetis, Philip of Macedon traces descent to, i. 223
—as creative source in Homer, i. 153
—nymphs offspring of, i. 258
—(" Ocean "), i. 5
—river, i. 86
—rivers usually regarded as sons of, i. 256
Oki, island of, viii. 317
—(Kiousa), idol which watches the dead, x. 57

Oki, Oke, Okeus, indwelling power of things, x. 18, 283 26

Okolnir, volcano in frost regions, ii. 278, 318

Okonorote, descent of, from sky-world, xi. 271

Öku-Thor (Wagon-Thor), ii. 78

Okypete (swift-flying), one of the Harpies, i. 266

Ol possessed marvellous power of tracking swine, iii. 190

Olaf Gudrudsson known as Geirstadar-álf, ii. 226

—son of Fridleif, ii. 242

—Tryggvason, king, ii. 42, 66, 241, 286, 322

" Olafs-saga Tryggvasonar," ii. 115

Old age came to Oisin through touching ground, iii. 181

——creation of, i. 6

——Elli is, ii. 93, 94

—Eagle, captor of Cheyenne woman, x. 305

—Hags of the Swamps, spirits, lure people to death by drowning, vii. 396 63

—Man, x. 115, 136, 142, 299 48, 308 63

——Acorn, x. 224

——and His Knee, myth of, vii. 156

——of the Sea, x. 251, 254

——Woman Below who jars world, xi. 203

——Night cares for Little Star, x. 114

——of the Sea, x. 5–6

——spirit of volcano Masaya, xi. 184–185

—— -Underneath, x. 250

—— -Who-Never-Dies, the Earth, x. 106, 115

Olelbis myth, x. 220, 223, 225, 228, 234–235, 272 6, 292 39, 294 42

Olelpanti, x. 220, 224, 234

Olin (motion), day-sign, xi. 104

Olive branch, symbol of Athene, i. pl. XXII, opp. p. 82

—created by Athene, i. 172

— -tree planted on the Acropolis by Athene, i. 67

Olkhon Island, iv. 500

Ollerus story, ii. 61, 64

—(Ull), god, ii. 15, 17, 64

Olofat, son of Luke-lang, tales of, ix. 254, 258–262

Olrun, daughter of Kjar, ii. 259

Olumbe (Orumbe), Death, vii. 173

Olver occupied haunted land, ii. 229

" Olwen and Lunet," iii. 199

—Kulhwch bade to seek as wife, iii. 187, 198

Olympia, Daidalos erects statue of Herakles at, i. 91

—Glaukos said to have died at, i. 39

—hippodrome at, i. 26

Olympian games, i. 92

Olympians, Aphrodite one of, i. 197

Olympias receives reading of her future from Nektanebos, i. 223

Olympos, i. pl. IV (2), opp. p. l

—cult of Zeus on, i. 159

—Dioskouroi dwell alternately in Underworld and on, i. 27

—Ganymedes cup-bearer to king of gods on, i. 118

—Mt., centre of gods of the circle of Zeus, i. 8

—nymphs appear on, i. 258

—queen of, patroness of wedlock, i. pl. VII, opp. p. lxii

—return of Hephaistos to, i. pl. XLVI, opp. p. 206

—universe supposed to be ruled from, i. 236

Omacatl (Two Reed), xi. 62

Omagua, xi. 194

Omaha, x. 19, 283 24

Omartes, King, vi. 341

Ombos, Neb-taui local deity of, xii. 140

—Sêth comes from " golden city " of, xii. 365 21

——divinity of, xii. 102, 107, 389 30, 392 56

—Sobk worshipped in early period at, xii. 148

—temple of, refuge of Rê', xii. 86

—worship of Khôns(u) at, xii. 366 5

Omeciuatl (Twofold Lady), female power of generation, xi. 53, 69, 88

Omega symbol, v. 109

O-mei, sacred hill, viii. 72, 79, 194

Omen-god, Adad is, v. 39, 381 58

—literature, v. 254–255

—Marta an, of death, iv. 205

— -tablets, vii. 367

Omens, i. 153, 154; ii. 42, 115, 117, 169, 212, 233, 234, pl. XXXII, opp. p. 246, 250, 255, 304; iii. 228, 236, 242, 271, 280, 285, 313–314; iv. 8, 9, 10, 11, 12, 17–18, 28, 45, 65, 66, 89, 90, 157, 163, 170, 180, 183, 191, 192, 195, 198, 199,

202, 205, 236, 241, 247, 253, 256, 264, 268, 269–271, 275, 289–290, 291, 293, 294; 395, 422, 432, 434, 446, 470, 500; v. 78, 152, 235, 254, 342, 384 [123]; vi. 226, 233, 235; vii. 48, 53, 89, 94; 164, 291, 338; viii. 27, 37, 42, 43, 44, 48, 98, 99, 100, 103, 135, 136, 169; 237, 305, 373; x. 2, 5, 32, 47, 90, 96, 116, 161, 162, 190; xi. 26, 74, 96, 98, 101, 118–119, 144, 145, 181, 203, 249, 323, 330, 341, 359 [18]; xii. 279, 284, 317–318, 323–324, 326, 328, 331–332, 335, 337, 345

Ometecutli (Twofold Lord), male power of generation, xi. 53, 69, 88

Ometochtli (Two Rabbit), xi. 77

Omeyocan (Place of the Twofold), xi. 53

Ómi (Odin), ii. 42

Ominameshi ("woman flower"), viii. 346–347, 385 [7] [8]

O-mi-t'o-fo, celestial Buddha, viii. 194

Omito-fu, Chinese name of Amitābha, xii. 261

Omi-tsu-nu (Beach-field-master), viii. 248–249

Omorōka (Omorka), ruler of primeval monsters, v. 290

Omowuhs, group of gods, x. 190

Omphale, Hermes sells Herakles to, i. 90, 161

Omumborombonga, sacred tree from which Herero people sprang, vii. 146, 147

On ("City of the Sun"), (Gk. Heliopolis), principal seat of solar mythology, xii. 31

— -Heliopolis, earliest centre of Egyptian religion, xii. 153

Ona, xi. 332

Onapu-oksa, sacrifice-tree coins, iv. 279

Onatah (corn-spirit) = Earth's daughter, story of, x. 27

Ondoutaete, x. 16

Öndurdis (Skadi), ii. 244

One-horned, Ikkaku Sennin is, viii. 276

— -legged beings: see HALF-MEN.

—on the Willows (?), an Underworld-being, xii. 203

—Road; oneness of life, viii. 296, 297

— -sided beings, vii. 204

— -Who-Stands-Perpetually-over-the-World, viii. 378 [2]

Oneness of existence, viii. 217, 218

Oni, devils, viii. 282–286, 287, 288

Onni (fortune) remains with man until death, iv. 11

Ono ("Sound"), ix. 11

Onokoro, primeval islet, viii. 223

Onomancy, viii. 139

Ono-no-Komachi, story of, viii. 298–299

— -Yorikaze, tale of, viii. 346–347

Onophris, xii. 97

Onto and Bonto, iv. 157–158

Onuris, god localized in This, Sebennytos, etc., xii. 143

Onyankopong, variant spelling of Nyankupon, vii. 123, 124, 399 [6]

Opartes = Ubardudu = Methusaleh, Greek transcription of Sumerian antediluvian king, v. 205

Open Sesame incidents, ix. 48, 63

Opening from sky-world, ix. 156

—to Underworld, ix. 48, 119

Opet, goddess of a quarter of eastern Thebes, xii. 144

Ophion and Eurynome supposed to have ruled universe from Olympos, i. 236

Ophiuchos, Bês corresponds to, in stellar mythology, xii. 61

Ophoïs and Anubis represented as Roman soldiers, xii. 240

—Anubis possibly identified with, xii. 364 [10]

—follower of, xii. 417 [17]

—(Up-uaut), xii. 21, 98

—wolf of, declines in importance, xii. 167

Opia, xi. 31

Opigielguoviran (zemi), dog-like being, xi. 25

Opium, v. 187

Opposition between gods of light and war, ii. 29

"Opr," song, poem, "Edda" said to be derived from, ii. 4–5

Ops, companion of Consus in cult, i. 292

—wife of Saturnus, i. 292

Opulence, Land of, viii. 363

Oracle of Spider, other animals consulted, vii. 321–322

—probable survival of, vii. 146

Oracles, i. 23, 25, 34, 35, 44, 45, 49, 50, 54, 61, 63, 68, 69, 71, 76, 80, 89, 90, 95, 97, 105, 108, 119, 120, 125, 135, 177, 178, 179, 181, 194, 218, 223–224, 234, 237, 273, 303, 304, 328 [4] (ch. iii);

ii. 9, 43, 58, 127, 208, 242, 333; vi. 210, 216; viii. 305, 326, 332; xi. 22–23, 180, 181, 184, 220, 224, 225, 351 [10]; xii. 162, 195, 197, 200, 206, 240

Oracles, Nabû god of, vii. 32

—Sibylline, books of, brought to Rome, i. 300, 301

—use of, in Ethiopia until Persian period, xii. 240

Oral traditions, compilation of, viii. 244–245

Orang Utan, ix. 175

Oratory, Hermes god of, i. 194

Orboda, giantess, mother of Gerd, ii. 110

Orchards as purified spot where sacrifices made, iv. 173

Orchestra of deities and fairies at Chikubu-shima in Spring, viii. 270

Orco, survival of Orcus in modern Romagnola, i. 319

Orcus (Dis Pater), i. 303

—Hell, ii. 305

—survives as Orco in modern Romagnola, i. 319

Ord, fight between two groups of dead at barrow of, ii. 308

Ordañh-do, snake clan, vii. 272

Ordeal, v. 161

—house of, v. 80, 393 [384]

—mwavi, vii. 429 [18]

Ordeals, vi. 262; x. 11, 35, 119, 132, 147, 164–165, 198, 231–232, 282 [21]; xi. 61, 170, 171, 174, 177; see also TASKS.

—of St. George, v. 338

Order, gods of, descended through a series of divine pairs, v. 291, 296

—Holy, vi. 23–24, 29, 32, 45

Orderer: see JAJUTSHI.

Oreads, mountain-spirits, i. 258

Orehu, evil spirit and water-sprites, xi. 261, 262

Oreithyia and Boreas, i. pl. LVI, opp. p. 266

—daughter of Erechtheus, i. 68, 73

—mother of Kleopatra, i. 74

Orejones (Big Ears), xi. 250

Orenda, indwelling power of things, x. 18, 38, 269 [3]

Orendil, Aurvandill the Valiant, is the hero, ii. 328

Orestes and Pylades kill Klytaimestra and Aigisthos, i. 135

—appealed to Helios as witness after murder of Klytaimestra, i. 243

Orestes, Erinyes' pursuit of, i. 277

—kills Aigisthos, i. pl. XXXIII, opp. p. 132

—Neoptolemos, i. 135

—pursued by mother's avenging Furies, i. 135

—son of Agamemnon, i. 135

Organs, viii. 36

Orgiastic worship of Anahit, vii. 27

Orient, possible influence of, on Cretan mythology, i. 42

Oriental vegetation-rites, ship in, possibly influenced Dionysos-myth, i. 330 [5] (ch. ix)

Origen, iii. 211

Origin of elves and fairies, ii. 226

—giants, theories of, ii. 281

Original land in Lumimu-ut tale, ix. 158

—sin, v. 183, 223, 231

—The Great, viii. 111

Origins, ii. 176–177; vii. 143–159; x. 63–66, 206, 294 [41]

—myths of, iii. 135–138; vii. 143–159; ix. 4–38, 105–119, 155–185, 248–256, 270–274

—of certain animals and trees, i. 15–16

—Inca race, xi. 242–244, 248

—tales of, viii. 221–243, 245

Orinoco, the, and Guiana, xi. 253–280

Orion, Artemis hunting partner of, i. 184

—as female, xii. 374 [70]

—hero in "Story of the Haunted Prince," xii. 153

—Asiatic types of, xii. 374 [70]

—companion of Sothis, xii. 58

——-Sirius when in human form, xii. 56

—compared with Morning Star, xii. 54

—constellation and mythical personage, i. 249–251

—double, xii. 58 (fig. 58)

—nature of, perhaps alluded to in two male heads of planet Venus, xii. 373 [60]

—early picture of, xii. 57 (fig. 57)

—father of the gods, xii. 374 [70]

—grants position to divinized king, xii. 203

——-Horus, Dua[-uêr] confused with, xii. 132–133

—Horus regarded as, xii. 102

—identified with Horus and son of Osiris, xii. 57

Orion identified with Osiris at early period, xii. 374 [70]
—in Asia, called " Hero," " Giant," xii. 57
—Osiris equated with, xii. 94, 385 [5]
—*penchant* of Eos for, i. 246
—perhaps identified with ferryman of Underworld, xii. 58
—representations of, xii. 57–58, 374 [70]
—shade of, appears to Odysseus in Hades, i. 146
—slain by Artemis, i. 183
—sons of Horus-Osiris near, xii. 112 (fig. 116)
—Sothis sister of, xii. 398 [104]
—still hunts in Underworld, i. 142
—watches over calves as parallel to Tammuz, xii. 399 [111]
Orion (constellation), ii. 177; iv. 426, 429–430; v. 308; vii. 49; 228, 229; x. 8–9, 104
—and Puppis, v. 135
—as ruler of sky, xii. 54
—Belt of, xi. 278
—born of duat-star, xii. 373 [61]
—constellation Earendel thought to be, ii. 83
—Hayk Armenian name for constellation, vii. 65
—Horus and Osiris confused as both represented in, xii. 389 [29]
—Hydra, and Virgo associated in Asiatic astral myth, xii. 84
—Osiris seen in, xii. 124
—Tammuz and Ninsubur identified with, v. 178
Orion's Belt, vii. 229
Orions, two, as celestial twins, xii. 58, 375 [72]
———year-myth, xii. 58
———correspond to Osiris-Sêth myth, xii. 58
Orisnici, genii of fate, iii. 250
Orissa, ill-omened river in, vi. 235
—small Buddhist colony surviving in, xii. 260
Orkhon stone inscriptions, iv. 394, 459, 460
Ormazd: see AHURA MAZDA (vol. iv).
Ormizd variant form of name of Aramazd, vii. 23
Ormzdakan, god: see ARAMAZD.
Ornamentation, symbolic, xi. 190
Ornaments, Ḥat-ḥôr deity of, xii. 40

Ornytos replaces Teuthis in some versions of legend of plague at Teuthis, i. 22
Orolek, iv. 273, 274, 279
Orontes River, youth symbol of, v. 19
'Orotalt, Arabic name of Dionysos, v. 382 [79]; see also s.v. 'Orotalt, vol. v, p. 449
Orphans, viii. 313; x. 8, 63, 72, 127, 282 [22], 286 [29]
Orpheus and Eurydike theme, x. 50, 118–119, 236, 264, 302 [53]
—author of philosophical books, i. 253
—descent of, to Hades, i. 145
—Izanagi parallel to, viii. 223
—parallels in Oceanic myths, ix. 72–78
—reason for association of Muses with, i. 238–239
—song of, drowns voices of Sirens, i. 113
—violates condition under which he might have rescued Eurydike from Hades, i. 146–147
Orpheus's singing head, iii. 105
Orphic philosophy, Zeus in, i. 328 [9]
—poems, value attributed to, in Athens, i. 4
—story of the creation, i. 4–5
Ört, after death, soul is blended with, iv. 10
—Cheremiss " shadow," iv. 6
—fire of, iv. 10
—reveals itself in the form of the deceased for forty days, iv. 10
—see also URT.
—soul, iv. 10, 168, 169, 188, 208, 215, 236, 240
Orthos, two-headed dog, brother of Kerberos, i. 86, 89
Ortiki, goose-spirit, iv. 409
Ortygia, Arethousa changed into fountain at, i. 257
—(Delos), Orion killed at, i. 250
" Orvar-Odds-saga," ii. 299
O'Ryū, spirit of willow-tree married warrior, viii. 333
Osarsyph, name given to Moses by Manetho, xii. 149, 409 [104]
Oscar, grandson of Fionn, iii. 125, 162, 173, 174, 177, 178, 179, 182, 183, 212
Oshadagea, Dew Eagle, x. 24
Osirian cycle, xii. 92–121
———deities of, in Classical world, xii. 242, 243

Osirian myth, connexion of lost eye of
sun-god with, xii. 90–91
—triad, Sêth becomes enemy of, xii.
103
Osiris, iii. 55; xii. 28, 36, 160, 164,
413 ¹²
—after death the Pharaoh held to be
manifestation of, xii. 171
—and Atum-Rê' as double occurrence
of sun, xii. 50
——Isis, Mîn son of, xii. 139
——myth of, may be borrowing from
Asari and Ishtar, v. 344
—'Anti identified with, xii. 130
—Apis compared with (?), xii. 163,
412 ⁶
—as black god, xii. 92 (fig. 82)
——god of the dead, Anubis predecessor
of, xii. 399 ¹¹¹
——judge on his stairs, xii. 97 (fig. 88)
——new sun, xii. 50
—Asiatic character of, xii. 399 ¹¹¹
—association of Anubis with, xii. 111
—attempts to identify Sobk with, xii.
148, 409 ¹⁰⁰
—Atum is identified with, xii. 424 ⁶
—Babi mentioned as "the first-born
son" of, xii. 131
—(Bacchus) met by Satyrs with music in Ethiopia, xii. 377 ⁸⁶
—Bati regarded as celestial and solar
divinity synonymous with, xii. 132
—before the West witnesses binding of
'Apop-serpents, xii. 104–105
—begotten by Qêb and Nut, xii. 69
—birth of, as Nile, xii. 143
—birthplace of, at Bu-gemet, xii. 376 ⁸⁴
—Buchis, bull of Mont(u), called "living soul" of, xii. 163
—burial-place of, localized at Abydos,
xii. 50–51
—confused by Herodotus with Mykerinos, builder of the Pyramids, xii.
398 ¹⁰⁶
——connected astronomically with Argo
or Canopus, xii. 57
——with a great serpent, xii. 391 ⁴³
—connexion between Asari and, suggested, v. 344
——of, with Dionysos-cult, i. 330 ⁸
—court of, in which dead are judged,
xii. 176, 179 (fig. 186)
—dead or unborn form of Horus, xii.
57

Osiris, dead, protected by sting of Selqet,
xii. 147
——wanders over mountain to seat of,
xii. 176 (fig. 185)
—earthly reign of, xii. 119–120, 399 ¹⁰⁸
—exact pronunciation and source of
name of, uncertain, xii. 384 ²
—exalted above all gods, xii. 72
—explained as yesterday, xii. 219
—father of Orion, xii. 57
—ferryman of Underworld may be explained as, xii. 394 ⁶⁴
—first to be mummified, xii. 181
—flower of life springs from, xii. 112
—followers of, xii. 179, 417 ¹⁷
—four gangways laid down for, xii.
363 ⁴
——sons of, xii. 111–113, 394 ⁶⁷
——sources of Nile as part of or as hostile to, xii. 105
—god of water, xii. 66
—hidden in his pillar, xii. 92 (fig. 83)
—Horus kills Sêth before, xii. 119 (fig.
121)
——reborn as, xii. 102, 117
—hymn addressed by departed to, xii.
184
—identical with Nile, xii. 46
—identification of, with Mnevis bull,
xii. 385 ⁴
—identified with heavenly tree, xii.
36
——Orion, xii. 374 ⁷⁰
—in the basket and in the boat, and Isis,
xii. 117 (fig. 120)
——celestial tree, xii. 93 (fig. 84)
——form of bull, xii. 367 ¹⁰
——Osirian cycle, xii. 92–98, 113–115,
118–120, 122–124
—interpretation of symbolism of four
Meskhenets of, xii. 52
—Isis and Selqet-Nephthys gathering
blood from corpse of, xii. 114 (fig.
118)
——sister and wife of, xii. 122, 123
—legend of, as parallel to deluge-myth,
xii. 76
—Makedon, dog-god, companion of,
according to Greeks, xii. 393 ⁶¹
—master of abysmal depth, xii. 96 (fig.
87)
—member of ennead of Heliopolis, xii.
216
—Mendes soul of, xii. 219

Osiris, Meskhenet governs rebirth of dead for new life with, xii. 52
—Mîn like, xii. 139, 156
——subsequently identified with, xii. 139
—Mont(u)'s sacred bull called soul of, xii. 139
—much praised in the Underworld, worshipped at Dandur, xii. 172
—myth, v. 71
——connexion of Abydos with, xii. 50
————Sothis (Sopdet) with, xii. 56
——later rôle of Horus in, xii. 363 1
— -myths, similarity of, to those of Adonis-Tammuz, xii. 120
——some texts referring to, xii. 122–128
—Nefer-ho(r) epithet of, xii. 140
—Nekhbet watched over, and his resurrection, xii. 143
—Nephthys bewails and cares for body of, xii. 110
—NN., dead addressed as, xii. 178
—not clearly understood in early times as deity of all nature, xii. 425 16
—of Busiris, Mendes ram embodies soul of, xii. 164
—only local divinities attached to cycle of, or cycle of sun, had mythological traits, xii. 20
—pantheistic tendencies attached to, xii. 220
—perhaps confused with Sêth, xii. 109
—personification of the resurrection, xii. 178
—pillar-god of Busiris explained as dying god, xii. 413 12
—plant-life personified in, xii. 66
—Ptah blended with, xii. 145
—rain a manifestation of, xii. 108
—ram of, perhaps represents all nature in, xii. 66
—realm of, xii. 174, 175
—represented as standing on a pillar, xii. 407 76
—restored to life by four sons of himself or Horus, xii. 394 67
—results from first separation of Heaven and earth, xii. 30
—rising to new life in sprouting seed, xii. 94 (fig. 86)
—second life in realm of, xii. 378 98
—self-emasculation of, xii. 398 106

Osiris separated from this world by a serpent, xii. 387 23
—Ser explained as, xii. 147
—Sêth murderer of, xii. 103
—Sêth-Typhon adversary of, xii. 59, 209
—Shwe Pyin Nāts suggest, xii. 353
—situation of realm of, xii. 176, 178, 391 43, 417 18
—Sokar(i) the solarized, xii. 149, 409 102
—solar eye of, torn into many parts in combat with Sêth, xii. 90
—sons of, guard four-fold serpent of abyss, xii. 105 (fig. 101)
—Sop later identified with, xii. 149, 409 104
—Sothis daughter of, xii. 398 105
—soul of, in sacred tree, xii. 166
——revived by Nile, xii. 94 (fig. 85)
—subordinate to late all-god, xii. 222–223
—symbol of, xii. 32 (fig. 14)
——Anubis associated with, xii. 393 62
—symbolized by Morning Star, xii. 54
—" the two maidens " as mothers of, xii. 407 82–408
—" twin sisters " in temples of, xii. 192
—under the vine, xii. 113 (fig. 117)
—Ung later identified with, xii. 151
—watch-dog of, xii. 179, 417 18
—with water and plant of life, xii. 97 (fig. 89)
—Zend(u) compared with, xii. 152
— -Horus, four sons of, interchange with the four baboons of Thout(i), xii. 417 20
——may have had sacred bull at Pharbaethos, xii. 163
——Nile a manifestation of, xii. 90
——Sothis-Venus as mother of, xii. 54
——worshipped under name of Tammuz-Adonis at Byblos, xii. 241, 395 84
— -Serapis retained little more than name and forms of worship in Classical world, xii. 243
— -Sêth, two Orions correspond to myth of, xii. 58
— -Sokar(i), Apis later considered incarnation of, xii. 162
——as cosmic deity, xii. 221
Oskmeyjar (" wish-maids "), ii. 248, 249
Oskopnir, perhaps another name of Vigrid, ii. 343

Osorbuchis, name of Buchis, sacred bull of Mont(u), xii. 163

Osor-ḥap [s] (Osiris-Apis), the Greek Serapis, xii. 98

Osorkon I, v. 43

Ostia, worship of Volcanus at, i. 296

Ostiak family-god, iv. pl. x (2), opp. p. 114

—Samoyeds, iv. xviii, xix

Ostiaks, an Ugrian stock, iv. xvii, xx

Ostius, vii. 380 [7]

Ostrich, vii. 412 [4]

—a demon, v. 131, 281, 283, 352

— -feather as a hieroglyph signifies the goddesses "West" and "Justice," xii. 99, 100, 386 [22]

— -feathers on head of Nuu imply identification with Ptaḥ-Ṭaṭunen, [s] xii. 47

—in prophecy against Babylon, v. 355–356

Otgon, maleficent powers, x. 18, 38

Othensberg, ii. 44

Other-world, ii. 45, 216, 217, 268, 303–323, 334; iii. 14, 16, 21, 93–94, 105, 111, 122–123, 197

——beings interested in heroes, iii. 194

Othinus: see ODIN.

Othrys, Mt., seat of the Titans, i. 8

Oto-hime, viii. 264

Otontecutli similar to Huitzilopochtli, xi. 60

Otos and Ephialtes bound Ares in vase, i. 189, 329 [1] (ch. iv)

—giant, i. 250

—punishment of, in Hades, i. 144

Otr, otter in treasure story, ii. 141

Otshirvani (Vairapani), iv. 319–320, 327, 329, 345, 346, 377, 421, 424

Ottarr, lover of Freyja, ii. 10, 120, 121, 125, 182

Otter, ii. 49

—instructed in mysteries of Medicine Society, x. 40

— -tongue in medicine bag (American Indian) confers knowledge of animal language, iii. 166

Otter's skin to be covered with ransom, ii. 141

Ötükän, iv. 460

Ötygen, Mother-earth, iv. 453

Oualapatou, Wild Men from the West, xi. 340

Oumoara, mythic hero, xi. 342

"Our lady" as term of address among West Semitic people may have been transferred to Virgin Mary, v. 341

Ourania and Amphiaraos reputed parents of Linos, i. 253

—("Heavenly"), epithet of Aphrodite, i. 196, 202, 330 [5] (ch. vi)

——one of the Epic Muses, i. 240

Ouranos and Gaia, Eros son of, i. 203

——founders of "first royal house of gods," i. 5

——parents of Hyperion and Euryphaëssa, i. 242

——Okeanos in Hesiod, i. 256

——Rhea daughter of, i. 274

—("Heaven"), i. 5; v. 66

—married his sister Ge, v. 80

—Melian nymphs born of blood of, i. 258

—mutilated by Kronos, i. 6, 197

—régime of, i. 6

—said to be identified with Varuṇa, vi. 25, 355 [6]

—son and husband of Gaia, i. 5

Ourwanama, tale of, xi. 274–275

Ousōos (probably Esau), inventor of fur clothing, v. 51, 389 [252]

Outcast tribes, vii. 114–115

Outcasts, green-headed, viii. 101

Outside Land: see UTGARD.

Ouvin: see FAROE ISLAND'S BALLAD, ETC.

Ouyan, curlew, ix. 291

Ouydn, Armenian word for ruler of Hades, vii. 97

Ovakuru (ancestral spirits), vii. 124

Ovda, evil spirit, iv. 183

Oven, Kikimoras live behind, and manifestation of their presence portends trouble, iii. 228

—sacrifice on, xii. 195 (fig. 208)

Ovens as dwelling-places of family genii, iii. 228, 246, 247, 251

Over-god, iv. 351, 358, 365, 394, 400, 401, 402

——Yakut, uses tree as tethering post, ii. 334

— -population because no death in world, vii. 163, 171

Owasse, Chief of Underground People, x. 48

Owein and Arthur, chess-game of, iii. 190, 191

Owl, vi. 291; xi. 139, 265, 274

—and eagle, tale of, viii. 334–335

Owl, bird of ill-omen, causes convulsions, vii. 127, 340
—messenger of god of death, vi. 69
——witches, vii. 336, 337, 406 [7]
—sacred bird of witchcraft and its hoot signal call, vii. 340, 428 [13]
Owners or Indwellers, x. 5, 10
Ownership-mark, iv. 261
Ox (as bridge) on whose back men passed from region to region, vi. 289, 298, 303
——judge, vi. 335
—brought to Mag mBreg, iii. 67
—connected with Mars, i. 293
—creator of lakes and rivers, iv. 331
— -fish, cry of, causes fish to become pregnant, vi. 289
—forty-horned, iv. 490
—head of, as religious symbol, xii. 367 [11]
—Nuu only once represented with head of, xii. 47
—primeval, containing germs of all animal species, vi. 286–287
——myths concerning, vi. 287–289, 294, 316
—quarrel over skin of, by first human beings, and determination of colour of their ancestors, vii. 150–151

Ox, skin of newly killed, spotted black and white, as emblem of Anubis, xii. 111
—storm-cloud identified with the, vi. 264
Ox-Leg, constellations around the, xii. 59 (fig. 60)
——guarded by four sons of Horus or Osiris, xii. 112
——name for Ursa Major, xii. 59, 110
Oxen, ii. 179, 181, 182, 234
—ascension of dragon to sky through, vii. 81
—children of water-spirits borne on backs of, iv. 469
—divine origin of ploughing with, iii. 81, 137
—drew an afanc from a pond, iii. 129
—farmers in Punjāb worship, vi. 239
—pulling dragon from lake by means of, vii. 79, 391 [15]
Oxlahun-ti-ku (thirteen gods), xi. 154
Oxomoco, first man, xi. 92, 102, 112, 120, 184
Oxygos, king of the Ektenes, i. 42
Ōye-yama, Mt., viii. 306
Ozruti, wild and gigantic beings, iii. 266

P

Pa sacrifice for good fortune, viii. 61
—Cha, viii. 68
—Hsien, viii. 118
—kua: see DIAGRAMS, EIGHT AND SIXTY-FOUR.
—Kung, viii. 118, 119
—tzŭ, viii. 143, 149
Pabilhursag, Larak city of, v. 206, 207
Pacam, magician, xi. 175
Paccari-Tampu, site of rise of Incas, xi. 248
Pachacamac as creator, xi. 225, 226, 229, 241
—temple of, xi. 215–216, 219, 220, 224
Pachacuti, tale of appearance of sun to, xi. 244–245
Pacha-yachachi, the creator, director of the sun, xi. 247–248
Pacific Coast Indians, x. 212–264
Padan-Aram, v. 80
Padashkhvārgar (Ṭabaristān), vi. 333
Padda, v. 39

Paddan of Syria, v. 41
Padmaḍākinī, vi. 218
Padmanābhi, snake, vi. 155
Padmapāṇi, Bodhisattva, vi. 209, 212, 213
Padmasambhava gave Tibetans decisive impulse to Buddhism, vi. 204, 208–209, 213, 216
Padmāvatī, snake born as, vi. 226
Padmottara, numbers of Buddhas called, vi. 199
Paeōn, name for Eshmun the physician, v. 74, 392 [353]
Pagān, Buddhism brought by Anawrahtā to, xii. 285
—on the Irrawaddy, xii. 271
Pagan civilization of Bolgars, iv. xviii
Paganism, xi. 118–123
—and Christianity, iii. 206–213
—arguments against, ii. 31
—Armenian, lent customs to Urartians, vii. 12

Paganism, dying, ii. 235–236, 242
—Slavic, iii. 222
—trolls represented supernatural powers of, ii. 286
Pagasai, Argo returns to home port of, i. 114
Pagodas, erection of, to decide issue of a struggle, xii. 339
Pagode Balny (temple of Linh-lanh), xii. 310
Pah, moon, x. 108
Pāhlavī, traditions preserved in, vi. 259
Pahuk, animal-lodge, x. 122
Pai Ma Ssŭ, viii. 188
—Shih, viii. 70
Paia, child of Rangi, ix. 8, 34
Paian hymn, purpose of, i. 179
Paiapis Chalia, vii. 67
Paidva, possibly solar horse, vi. 61
Pain guardian of fire, x. 231
Pains, animals may be cause of internal, vii. 314
Paint, identification of secret lover by smearing of, x. xxi
Painting of bodies at end of bear hunt, iv. 88
——face, robe, tipi, etc., x. 80, 86, 92
—origin of, viii. 35
Paintings, mural, of Doura, v. 20
—(scenes from Balder's funeral) in hall in Iceland, ii. 128
Pair (yugalin) period, vi. 225, 226
Pairekse, hero of flood, iv. 363, 366, 394, 409
Pairikā, witch, vi. 327
Pairikās, vi. 261; see also PARIKS.
Pairs, three, in Qat's creation, ix. 106
Pais, chimeras, vii. 91, 92
Pai-tzŭ T'ang, viii. 84
Pajana, creator, iv. 373
Pāka, vi. 154
Pakkatè, cave in which Yatawm and Yatai lived as ogres, xii. 293–294
Pakoti, wife of Tane, ix. 25
Paktolos, waters of, become gold-coloured when Midas bathes in them, i. 220
Palace of Sun, vii. 50
——Waters, viii. 106
Palachucolas and Cussitaws united, x. 72
Palaimon likened to Portunas, i. 290
—(Melikertes), "Storm-Lord," marine god, i. 46

Palamedes entreats aid of Odysseus against Troy, i. 123–124
Palat, Mt., vii. 56
—(or Pashat), Mt., temples of Aramazd and Astλik on, vii. 24, 39
Palaung Bo descended from Min Shwe Thè, xii. 276
Palaungs (of Austro-Asiatic descent), trace origin to dragon source, xii. 275–277
Palenque, xi. 131, 133
—cross-figured tablets of, xi. 56
Pales-murt, Votiak god, iv. 181
Pāli Canon as source for life of Buddha, vi. 187–219
Palladia, bearing of, into battle, x. 101, 191, 306 [59], 307 [61]
Palladion, origin of, i. 118
—stolen from Troy by Odysseus, i. 132
Pallas Athene, statue of, built into a shrine by Ilos, i. 118
—child of Hercules, i. 303
—son of Evander and ally of Aeneas, slain by Turnus, i. 306
——Pandion, i. 68
—sons of, plot unsuccessfully against their cousin Theseus at Athens, i. 100
Pallyan found two females (creation-myth) in water, ix. 274
Palm-branch, hieroglyphic sign of, xii. 146
——offered by goddess to three gods, v. 187–188
——symbolizes time, year, renewal, fresh vegetation, xii. 89
——-tree, mauritia, people grew from seeds of, xi. 271
Palmyra (anc. Tadmar), v. 20, 56
Paluc, children of, nourished demon cat of, iii. 191
Palulukoñ, Palulukoñti, x. 188
Pamaš-oza (" the Spring's master "), iv. 215
Pamelia, origin of festival of, xii. 396 [93]
Pampas to the Land of Fire, xi. 316–344
Pampean, group of South American peoples, xi. 254
Pampeans, El Chaco and the, xi. 319–324
Pamyles educates Horus, xii. 116, 396 [93]
Pan, i. pl. IV (6), opp. p. 1
—as pastoral god, Hermes father of, i. 195

Pan ("Grazier"), i. 267–269
—great, is dead, cry at moment of Christ's Nativity, iii. 213
—Mîn identified with, xii. 139
—native god of Arkadia, i. 22
—sometimes designated twin brother of Arkas, i. 22
—stories of, transferred to Silvanus, i. 294
—survivals of, in modern Greek folk-belief, i. 315
—survives as Pano in modern Romagnola, i. 319
Pan Ku, commentator of Liberal School, viii. 9, 199
P'an Kêng, Emperor, viii. 48
—Ku, first created being and first creator, first epoch inaugurated by, viii. 25, 57, 60, 110–111
P'an t'ao, peach-tree, viii. 104–105, 117–118
Panathenaïc festival celebrated by Aigeus, i. 68
——established by Erichthonios, i. 67
Pañcajana, demon slain by Kṛṣṇa, vi. 173
Pāñcarātra doctrine learned by Nārada, vi. 176
Pandaie said by Megasthenes to be daughter of Herakles, vi. 110
Pandareos, daughters of, endowed with skill by Athene, i. 170
Pandaros, Apollo confers skill in use of bow on, i. 177
—wounds Menelaos and Diomedes, i. 128
Pāṇḍavas connected with Pāṇḍyas of southern India, vi. 110
—Kṛṣṇa goes to the, vi. 225
——supporter of the, vi. 124
—receive honour, vi. 244
—struggles of five seasons represented by the, vi. 130
Pandemos, cult-epithet of Aphrodite, i. 202, 330 [5] (ch. vi)
Pandia, daughter of Selene, i. 245
Pandion, daughters of, i. 70
—grandson of Erechtheus, i. 68
—son and successor of Erichthonios, i. 67
—sons of, i. 68–69
Pandora adorned with garlands by the Horai, i. 238
—("All-giver"), Gaia as, i. 273

Pandora, Athene contributed soul for, i. 171
—box-motif in Spider story, vii. 331
——of, i. 15
——Indian parallel to, x. 140
—creation of, i. 14–15 and fig. 2
—moulded out of clay, i. 208
—said to be wife of Prometheus, i. 12
Pandrosos, i. pl. LVI, opp. p. 266
—("All-bedewing"), daughter of Kekrops and Agraulos, i. 67, 273
—entrusted with chest containing infant Erichthonios, i. 67
—fate of sisters of, i. 67, 325 [3]–326
—union of Hermes with, in Attic legend, i. 329 [5] (ch. v)
—wife of Hermes, i. 70
Paṇḍumahurā (Madurā), vi. 225
Pāṇḍyas identical with Pāṇḍavas, vi. 225
—of southern India worshippers of Kṛṣṇa, vi. 110
Pangaion, Mt., death of Lykourgos at, i. 218
Panhellenios, cult of Zeus, i. 160
Panic ascribed to Pan, i. 268
Pānīpat, ghosts at, vi. 248
Paṇis, vi. 34, 43, 66, 129
Pankaprabhā, vi. 228
Pan-ku, world formed from body of, iv. 372
Panku, Chinese creator-deity and Panggu of New Guinea, similarity between, ix. 325 [25]
Pano, survival of Pan in modern Romagnola, i. 319
Panopeus in Phokis, boulders at, i. 14
Panopolis, Ḥar-khent(i)-merti(?) honoured at, xii. 388 [28]
Panotlan, landing of ancestral Mexicans at, xi. 112
Pan-psychism, Buddhist, viii. 221
Pantaenus, statement of, that Christianity was found in India, vi. 175
Pantheism, iii. 43; vi. 19, 230; viii. 51; 217, 221
—late and rare in Egyptian religion, xii. 9
——manifestations of, xii. 220–224
—wrongly ascribed to Egyptian religion, xii. 15
Pantheon, Araucanian, xi. 325–329
—Armenian, priestly reorganization of, vii. 17, 18

Pantheon, Aztec, xi. 49–57, 354 [6]
—Egyptian, diminution of number of divinities in, xii. 215
——explained by origin from primitive animism, xii. 15
——origins of, xii. 12
——scarcely influenced by African neighbours in historic period, xii. 157
—Inca, xi. 246
Panther connected with west wind, x. 23
— -headed club symbol of Ninurta (Ningirsu), v. 115, 126, 136
Pantibiblos, capital before Flood, v. 207
Pantomime, Marduk, v. 322–324
Panzoism, x. 269 [3]
Pao Ch'ing, viii. 186
—p'ai tso ch'in, marriage by tablet, viii. 149
—P'o-tzŭ, Ko Hung known as, from his book, viii. 145
—Ssŭ, concubine of Yu Wang, viii. 166–167
— -yüeh, viii. 59–60
Pap, King, story of serpents on shoulders teaching divination told of Armenian, vii. 99
Papa (Earth), female of primeval pair, ix. 7, 8, 9, 10, 14, 24, 30, 31, 32, 33, 34, 36, 37, 313 [65]
Papa-tu-a-nuku, Earth mother, ix. 8, 30
Papantzin, sister of Montezuma dies and lives again, xi. 119
Paper articles burned after death, viii. 149
—containing name, dates of birth and death = karsikko in North Savolax, iv. 43
Paphos, Cyprian, temple-home of Aphrodite at, i. 199
—son of Pygmalion and Galateia, i. 200
Pappawadi, marriage of, to Tüng Hkam, xii. 273–274
Paps of Anu (later glossary " Danu "), two hills in Kerry, iii. 39
——Morrígan in Brug na Boinne, iii. 41
Papsukkal, messenger of the gods, v. 332
—Sumerian title of Ilabrat, v. 176, 177
Papuan area, ix. 103
—element in Australia, ix. 302, 303

Papuan element in Melanesian mythology, ix. 103, 148, 149, 304
—mythology, ix. 304, 305
——at best scanty traces of, in Micronesia, ix. 263
Papyri relating to magic, xii. 205–206
Paqok, attacker of women, xi. 141
Paradise, iv. 419; v. 158, 182, 184, 193, 194
—Buddhist, viii. 240–242, 379 [24]
—concept of, crept into Russian Karelia, iv. 79
—Hebrew, v. 183 ff.
—ideas of Iranians, iv. 357–358
—in Genesis of Babylonian origin, v. 73
—life-giving tree some sort of, iv. 351
—of Amitābha, xii. 261
——trees and stones, v. 210
—Sumerian, v. 194 ff.
—tree of, iv. 384
Paradises (" Buddha-lands "), time and number in, viii. 216, 278
Paradisic Age in Cheyenne myth, x. 308 [63]
Parakeets as mortals bathing, ix. 206
Parakyptousa, Aphrodite represented on Assyrian monuments as, v. 32, 33
Paramunca, xi. 220
Parāśara, son of Śakti, vi. 146
Parasol, hieroglyph of, for shadow [soul], xii. 174, 180 (fig. 189)
Paraśurāma annihilated the race of warriors, vi. 111
—avatar of Viṣṇu, vi. 168, 169, 182
Parca, a gloss of Wælcyrge, ii. 253
Parcae, ii. 242, 244, 245, 293–294; iv. 257
Pare and Hutu, tale of, ix. 76–78
Paremheb, Egyptian temple builder, v. 46
Parentalia, feast for souls of dead, v. 122, 162, 334, 398 [105]; vii. 75
Parents, primeval, vi. 16, 18, 21
Pari, charm song, ix. 137
Pariacaca, hero-god, xi. 228, 230, 231, 232, 239
Pārijāta-tree, vi. 174
Pariks (Pairikās), female spirits, vii. 87–88, 91, 394 [43]
Parikṣit cursed to die of snake-bite, vi. 154–155
—marries maiden who must never see water, vi. 147
Paris, i. pl. XXXI, opp. p. 124

Paris and Helen, i. pl. x (1), opp. p. 20
——Menelaos fight duel for Helen, i. 127
—appears on Mt. Ida to judge between beauty of Hera, Athene, and Aphrodite, i. 124–125
—arrow of, slays Achilles, i. 131
—builds ship and sails to Sparta, i. 125
—carries Helen off to Troy, i. 125
—contests of, i. 118–119
—death of, i. 132
—exposed on Mt. Ida, i. 118
—saved by Aphrodite, i. 127–128, 197
—urged by Trojans to give Helen up, i. 128
—yields to spell of Aphrodite, i. 199
Parjanya, ii. 194
—rain-god, vi. 21, 37, 47, 56, 89, 129, 134–135, 143
Parṇaśabarī, vi. 204–205, 217–218
Parnassos, teachings of, in beginnings of civilization, i. 16
Parne, evil spirit, iv. 179, 181
Parnians, vi. 66
Paronomasia in myths, xii. 70, 85, 363 [2], 368 [17], 369 [26], 370 [30], 384 [2], 386 [20]
Paros, Herakles warred on sons of Minos at, i. 85
—sombre character of worship of Charites on, i. 236–237
Paroxene, Gagavitz buried in, xi. 182
Parpara, tale of, ix. 156
Parrot, vii. 286, 418 [35]
—speaking, surrogate for human victim, xi. 199
Parrots as messengers, xii. 276
Parsis, girdle of, vi. 184
—in India, vi. 259
Pārśvanātha, vi. 220, 222, 226
Parthenios ("Maidenhood"), spring, Artemis changed Aktaion into stag at, i. 46
Parthian (Arsacid) Dynasty established in Armenia, vii. 9
Partholan, iii. 137, 206, 207
—(Bartholomew), race of, either died or returned to Spain, iii. 23
Partridge related to cult of Artemis, i. 184
Paruṣṇī, vi. 35
Parvata ("mountain"), vi. 60, 145
Pārvatī, vi. 83, 116, 118, 182, 183, 236
—wife of Lotus Serpent, xii. 271
"Parzival," poem by Wolfram, iii. 203

Pas, Pavas, Mordvin name for God, iv. xix
Pascham (?), torch of race of, vii. 85
Pashat (Palat), Mt., a centre of fire-worship, vii. 63
Pasiphaë aided by Daidalos in her intrigue with bull of Poseidon, i. 65
—bewitches Minos with drug, i. 72
—desire of, for the bull, i. 61
—wife of Minos, i. 61
Passe, Passe-vāra, iv. 101
Passion brought into world by eating of gourd, xii. 289
Passions, gods subject to, ii. 22–23
Passover termed "festival of Zatik," vii. 40
Passwords, vii. 253, 255, 414 [30]
Pastimes of dead, xii. 177
Pastoral god, Hermes as, i. 195
—life, connexion of Pūṣan with, vi. 27
Pāśupata, spear, weapon of Śiva, vi. 111
Paśupati, vi. 81, 82, 111, 112
Patagonian race, xi. 318
Patagonians, xi. 331–338
Pataïk, xii. 64 (fig. 68)
Pataïkoi, Phoenician name of Bês amulets on ships, xii. 64
Pātāla, vi. 151, 154, 157
Pāṭaliputra, vi. 153
Patan, one of lords of Underworld, xi. 173
Patecatl, discoverer of peyote, xi. 77
Patelena, goddess of unfolding of grain, i. 300
Patent, dragon adopted as royal, viii. 102
Path from land of living to land of dead, x. 147–148; see also PERILOUS WAY.
Pathana, nine sons of, slain, vi. 324
Patna, vi. 237
Patollo, Old Prussian deity, ii. 333
Patollus, god of Underworld, worshipped at Romowe, iii. pl. xxxvii, opp. p. 304
Patriarchs, ten, v. 166
Patrick and Brigit in gloss of "Liber Hymnorum," iii. 13
Patrilinear descent, x. 238, 240
Patrinia, grass, grew from grave of woman, viii. 346, 347
Patriotic Militarist, posthumous title of Kuo Tzŭ-i, viii. 96

Patroklos, ashes of Achilles said to be mingled with those of, i. 131
—friend of Achilles, i. 122
—slain by Hektor, i. 129
Patroklos's pyre, flames of, fanned by Boreas and Zephyros, i. 265
Patron of Growth, guardian of south, viii. 243
Patrons, divine, of Corinth, i. 36–37
Patroös, Apollo as, i. 180
Patshak, ghosts in land of living, iv. 82
Paukhkan (Pagān), Thusandi's second egg hatched out at, xii. 277
Paul III issued bull in which Indians pronounced men capable of the Catholic faith, xi. 321
Paulomas, vi. 152
Paurāṇic religion, development of, and influence on theology of the Mahāyāna, vi. 204
Pāurva, ferryman, legend of, vi. 365 4
Pautiwa, lord of dead, x. 210
Pavana, name of Vāyu, vi. 135
Pāvāpurī, Māhavīra was released at, vi. 222
Pavor (" Panic "), i. 299
Pawng, two clans of, xii. 292
Pax (" Peace "), i. 299
—festival honouring war-chief, xi. 138
Paxil, food in place called, xi. 178
Payatamu, god, parallels Pied Piper and Pan, x. 200–201
Paytiti, xi. 194
Pazuzu, lord of wind-demons, v. 371, 372, 417 50 53
Pe, localization of four sons of Horus or Osiris at, xii. 394 67
Peace made by saliva-rite, ii. 53
—of Frodi, ii. 113–114, 282, 283
— -offering to evil spirits, exposure of newborn child as, vii. 89
—Twelve Plans for, viii. 199
Peach, baby boy found in, viii. 313
—men, viii. 105
— -orchard Oath, viii. 174, 176
— -stone, ideographs on, viii. 117
—symbol of immortality, viii. 275
Peaches which ripened once in three thousand years, viii. 104–105, 117–118
Peachling Boy (Momotarō), story of, viii. 313–314
Peacock, heavenly, dance of, viii. 357

Peacock, Sennin riding on mythical, viii. pl. XIX, opp. p. 276
—sometimes associated with Hera in art, i. 168
Peaiman, doctor, priest, or magician, xi. 35, 38, 260, 261, 264, 274, 275, 277, 350 10
Pear-tree, groans of, viii. 177
Pearl Emperor, viii. 196–197
Pearls believed to be tears of Ningyo, viii. 273
Pebble Society, x. 98, 106–107
Peculiar markings on animals, plants, etc., tales of, ix. 144, 288–293, 297
Pe-Dep, Egyptian name of Buto, xii. 365 26
Pedestal, tortoise as, viii. 100
Pediu and Konkel, hero-brothers, xi. 330
Pedu, protégé of the Aśvins, vi. 61
Pegasos associated with the Muses and their arts, i. 40
—Athene gave Bellerophon bit and bridle to guide, i. 172
—bearer of thunderbolt and lightning, i. 34
—created fount of Hippoukrene, i. 213
—derivation of name of, i. 40, 325 16
—development of, as a mythological figure, i. 40–41
—drew thunder-car for Zeus, i. 160
—flew upwards to ancient stables of Zeus and was harnessed to thunder-car, i. 40
—Imgig associated with constellation, v. 119
—leaps forth from severed neck of Medousa, i. 34, 40
—Poseidon father of, i. 213
—winged horse, i. 39, 40
—Zû became, v. 279
Pe-har, Dharmapāla regarded as incarnation of, vi. 209
Peibaw and Nynnyaw transformed into oxen for sins, iii. 71
Pei-chi Chên Chün, viii. 111
— -ling, Monument Grove at Si-ngan-fu, xii. 270
Peiren: see Io.
Peirene, fountain of, at Corinth, i. 258
—spring of, on the Akrokorinthos, i. 40, 41
Peirithoös and Theseus drew lots for Helen, i. 25

Peirithoös and Theseus kidnap Helen of
Sparta, i. 25, 105
—friendship of Theseus with, i. 104
—son of Dia by Zeus, i. 11
—visits Hades to abduct Persephone, i.
145
Péist (Latin bestia), serpents or dragons
infesting lochs, iii. 129, 130–131
Pekhat, vulture-goddess, xii. 407 73
Pekhet, lioness worshipped in Middle
Egypt, xii. 144
—Sekhmet, Tefênet, and Ubastet manifestations of a single deity, xii. 217
Peking, capture of, viii. 181–182
—office of Inspector of Astrology on
eastern wall of; now the Observatory,
viii. 144
—pilgrimage at, viii. 23
—sun ritual reminiscent of, x. 89
—Taoist temples at, viii. pl. ii, opp. p.
22, 23, 135
Pekko (Pellon-), "giver of barley,"
feast of, iv. 244–245, 246
Pelanduk: see MOUSE-DEER, ETC.
Pelasgia, land named from Pelasgos,
i. 20
Pelasgos believed to be first man by
Arkadians, i. 10, 20
—of the Arkadians, teachings of, in beginnings of civilization, i. 16
—sprang from bosom of Gaia, i. 272
Pele, fire-goddess, ix. 39
Pele koleše (" Half dead "), iv. 208
Peleus accidentally kills his father-in-
law and is cleansed of his pollution
by Akastos at Iolkos, i. 121
—and Thetis, i. pl. XXIX (2), opp.
p. 116
—double of Poseidon, i. 212
—Eris causes strife at Thetis's marriage
to, i. 124
—not admitted to Elysion, i. 147
—son of Aiakos, i. 121
—thrown by Atalante in wrestling, i. 57
—took part in hunt of Kalydonian boar,
i. 56
—weds Thetis, i. 122
Pelias, death of, i. 114–115
—dispossesses Aison of throne of Iolkos,
i. 108, 109
—funeral games of, i. 57, 69
—interpretation of myth of, i. 115–
116
—plots against family of Iason, i. 114

Pelias, son of Poseidon and Tyro, i. 106,
107, 211
Pelican and woman, tale of, ix. 279–
280
Pelion, Mt., Kyrene carried off from,
by Apollo, i. 251
—Pelias and Thetis wedded on Mt., in
presence of all the gods, i. 122
Pella, Nektanebos became astrologer at,
i. 223
Pellervo, god of vegetation, iv. 243
Peloponnesos, adventures of Herakles at,
i. 91
—myths of: see MYTHS OF THE PELO-
PONNESOS.
—overrun by Heraklids, i. 95
Pelops bribes Myrtilos, i. 119
—curse of, on Laios, i. 48
—given chariot by Poseidon, i. 213
—killed by his father, i. 161
—served at dinner of gods by Zeus, but
restored by them to life, i. 119
—successful suitor for hand of Hippodameia, i. 119–120
—Telemon married into line of, i. 121
Pelym, god of, iv. 403
Pen Annwfn (" Head of Annwfn"),
cauldron of, iii. 93–94, 95, 111
—Blathaon, Scotland, iii. 190
Pen characterizes office of Sekha(u)it,
xii. 53
—Obelisque of, xii. 304, 305
" Pên Ts'ao Kang Mu," viii. 105
Penalties, God used Kaches to execute,
vii. 83
Penance, x. 12, 124, 135; xi. 62, 70, 78,
86, 94
—imposed on Śukra, vi. 168
—to overcome childlessness, ix. 162–
163
Penates, iii. 228, 239, 240, 241, 244,
309
Peneios River, i. 82
——and Earth, parents of Daphne, i.
180
——worshipped in Thessaly, i. 257
Penelope, daughter of Ikarios, wife of
Odysseus, i. 24, 123, 139
—endowed with skill by Athene, i. 170
—said by some to have been dismissed
by Odysseus on account of her waver-
ing affections, i. 140
P'êng Yü-lin, Hunan General, became
local deity, viii. 65–66

P'êng-lai, viii. 115

Peniēl ("Face of El"), v. 245

Penitential, German, ii. 68–69

—of Baldwin of Exeter, ii. 245

——" Corrector," ii. 69, 244–245, 256, 293

Pensacola, idols on island of, xi. 184

Penthesilea comes to support of Trojans, i. 130

—death of, i. 130, 131 (fig. 5)

Pentheus, contempt of, for rites of Dionysos as practised by women, i. 47

—of Thebes killed for resistance to rites of Dionysos, i. 215

—son of Echion and Agave, i. 47

—torn asunder by Agave, i. 270

——his mother who mistook him for a deer, i. 47, pl. XVI, opp. p. 48

People, Christmas, iv. 67, 68

—sacred, iii. 14

Peoples of Oceania, ix. xii–xiii

Pepper, red, put in eyes to propitiate the spirits of the rapids, xi. 268

Perceval, early hero of Grail story, iii. 196, 198, 202

—Old French poem of Arthurian cycle, iii. 193, 194, 196, 202, 203

Perckun nohl, old Esthonian term for thunderbolt, derived from Letto-Lithuanian source, iv. 228

Per-eb-sen, early king, divine patron of, scarcely identical with Ash, xii. 403 [13]

Peredur (Percival), iii. 129

—Welsh romance, iii. 191, 199

Perekahi, family-beer ceremony, iv. 174

Perfect Ones, viii. 113–114

—the, second grade of supernatural being, viii. 108

Perfume, heavenly, viii. 258, 267

Pergamon, Attalos of, i. 304

Pergrubrius, feast about at St. George's Day, iii. 356 [14]

Per-ḥebet, question whether primitive local cult of Isis was at, xii. 98–99

Periboia received Oidipous from shepherd who found him on Kithairon, i. 48

Perieres, family of, i. 24–28

—(or Pieres), king of Messene, grandson of Amyklas, i. 24

Periklymenos, son of Nereus, receives power of transformation from Poseidon, and is killed by Herakles, i. 92

Perilous Way, x. 132, 257, 273 [8]–274; xi. 81, 330–331

Perimontum, phantom announcing an extraordinary event, xi. 328

Periods, critical, of life, viii. 149

Periphetes, lame son of Hephaistos, i. 207

—Theseus captures club of, and kills, i. 98

Periphrases: see KENNINGS.

Peritios, Macedonian month name, festival on, v. 52

Perjury, hymns of repentance for, xii. 234

Perke ("success"), iv. 258

Perkele, Finnish "devil," derived from Letto-Lithuanian name, iv. 228

Perkuna, Old Prussian deity, ii. 333

Perkúnas, vi. 37

—chief Baltic god, iii. 319, 320, 321, 322, 324, 328, 330, 357 [11], 358 [18] [24]

—cuts moon in two, vi. 316

—god of Heaven and weather, vii. 14

——thunder, worshipped in Romowe, iii. pl. XXXVII, opp. p. 304, 354 [10]

—Lithuanian god, ii. 194

——source of name of Erza thunder-god Pur'gine, iv. 228

—still preserved in Erkir ("earth"), vii. 14

Perkune Tete, mother of thunder and lightning, bathes the sun, vii. 50

——receives sun at night, iii. 319, 357 [11]

Permian linguistic stocks, iv. xvi

Pērōz delared Nestorianism legitimate form of Christianity, vi. 175

Perrhaiboians, Ianus comes from land of, i. 297

Perse ("gleaming"), wife of Helios, i. 242

Persea, xii. 31, 36, 37 and fig. 24

—Amon registers royal name on, xii. 37 (fig. 24)

—of Heliopolis, Phoenix rises over, xii. 166

——Sekha(u)it sometimes localized at, xii. 53

— -tree identified with heavenly tree, xii. 37

Persephone, i. pl. IV (4), opp. p. 1; vii. 97; x. 108

—and Aphrodite carry dispute over possession of Adonis to Zeus, i. 199

Persephone and Demeter, Iroquois story of Onatah parallel of, x. 27
—daughter of Zeus, i. 157, 227
—Ereshkigal occurs with, v. 161
—Gaia as, i. 273
—given pomegranate to eat before release from Underworld, i. 229
—Hekate identified with, v. 369
—in mystic rites at Eleusis, i. pl. L, opp. p. 230
—meaning of seizure of, i. 231
—nature of, i. 230–231
—personified Hel in Saxo, ii. 304
—Proserpina Roman adaptation of, i. 303
—queen of Underworld, i. 142
———Ereshkigal is, v. 335
—redeemed from Hades as personal representative of Eleusinian initiates, i. 220
—represented in marble relief of Eleusinian rites, i. pl. L, opp. p. 230
—search of Demeter for, i. 228
—story of, i. 227
—Theseus and Peirithoös attempt to capture, i. 105
Perses and Asteria, Hekate daughter of, in Hesiod, i. 187
—expelled by Medeia, i. 115
—son of Andromeda and Perseus, parent of Persian people, i. 35
Perseus, i. pl. XIII, opp. p. 32
—Akrisios, and Danaë, i. 33–36
—and Andromeda, i. pl. XIV (2), opp. p. 36
———Irish parallel to story of, iii. 144
—curved sword of, wrought by Hephaistos, i. 207
—fought against Dionysos, i. 215
—legend, theories of origin of, i. 36
—son of Danaë by Zeus, i. 11
———Zeus, i. 157
(Per-)Shentit, temple of, xii. 408 95
Persian dualistic system, v. 373, 374
—Gulf, Himyaritic Minaean culture and religion extended along, v. 4
—influence on African mythology, vii. 121
———Armenia, vii. 17
Persians driven into mad rout at Marathon by Pan, i. 267
—ethnologically closely akin to Aryan races of India, vi. 259
—Perses parent of, i. 35

Persians regarded Sassanian Mihr as helper of " seven gods " (Auramazda and Amesha Spentas), vii. 381 1 (ch. ii)
Personalized parts of nature came to be regarded as animated by spirit, iii. 133
—river or river-god (in form of worms), said to be father of Conchobar, iii. 140
Personification, instances of, viii. 58, 62, 63
—of cosmic powers not found in prehistoric period, xii. 23–24
———death, vii. 117, 172, 173, 174, 177–178
———fate (Dolya) bestowed at birth, iii. 251
———Ireland, Anu perhaps, iii. 39
———misfortune, iii. 252
———nature, iii. 34, 89
——— -powers, vii. 119
Personifications, i. 28, 38, 41, 241, 251, 256, 259, 282, 283, 291, 299, 372 56; ii. 16, 18, 40–44, 56, 74, 81, 91, 93, 154, 160, 171, 190, 191, 192–193, 202, 238, 253–254, 279, 280, 282, 288, 303, 304, 344; iii. 112, 129, 228, 251, 252, 253–254; iv. 447; v. 18, 49, 54, 74, 89, 104, 289, 290; vi. 37, 52, 53, 67, 98, 99, 107, 108, 154, 160, 238; vii. 81, 117, 188, 322, 411 43; viii. 273; ix. 5, 6, 7, 8, 10, 27; x. xxi, 155, 232, 260, 285 28, 289 34, 291 38, 296 45, 308 63; xi. 277, 306; xii. 23, 26, 29–30, 37, 38, 41, 46, 66, 67, 71, 97, 99, 100, 146, 178, 217, 255, 372 56, 378 102, 410 2
—of natural forces, divine or heroic figures in primitive times not, vii. 225
———nature and natural objects, viii. 214, 219, 222, 234, 245, 267, 290, 294
Pe(r)-sopd(u) capital of twentieth nome, xii. 149
Peru, xi. 210–252, 367 6
Perun, chief god of pagan Russians, iii. 293–296, 297
—derivation and local names of, iii. 294–295, 354 13
Pe(r)-uzoit, Buto goddess of, xii. 132
Peshana, Vīshtāspa defeated, vi. 341
Pēshyānsaī, plain of, vi. 327
Pest-god, Nergal the, v. 49
Pestilence, Keeper of Home of the Moon, x. 257

Pestilence sent by Apollo, i. 177
—spread from dead body of Mit-othin, ii. 63–64
Pestilences caused by death of great soul, iii. 14–15
Pestles and mortars, vii. 124, 130
Pêt (Heaven), xii. 37, 367 [10]
Petalesharo put end to human sacrifice for fertilization of grain, x. 76, 303 [58], 306
Petesuchos, late local form of Sobk in the Fayûm, xii. 408 [98]
Petet, a scorpion of Isis, xii. 210, 211
Pe'tiu (" nobles "), a class of mankind, xii. 379 [18]
Petra, v. 16, 18, 20
Petrel wooed Nerrivik, x. 6–7
Petroglyphs, xi. 271
Pewter, casting of, iv. 268, 272
Pe(y), Buto goddess of, xii. 403 [19]
Peyote, adoration of, xi. 123
—(plant), cult of, x. 177
Phaëthon (" Gleaming One " [Helios]), causes drought and heat, i. 243–244
—grieving sisters of, changed into tremulous poplars, i. 16
Phaëthousa, daughter of Helios and Neaira, i. 242
Phaia (wild sow) killed by Theseus, i. 98–99
Phaiakians, Elysion identified with island of the, i. 147
—sojourn of Argonauts among, i. 113
Phaidra, daughter of Minos, i. 61
—wife of Theseus, falls in love with step-son, Hippolytos, i. 104
Phaistos, city of Crete, i. 64
—sistrum pictured on vase of, xii. 241
Phaitakaran, fire-springs in old province of, vii. 56
Phallic aspect of Frey, ii. 29, 115
—cult, iv. 398; vi. 63
—emblem in rites of Dionysos, i. 217, 330 [7] (ch. ix)
—emblems, xi. 75
—features of Hermes cult, i. 195
—theory, iii. 204, 205
—worship, xii. 333, 353
——little trace of, in North America, x. xx
——traces of, in death of Shwe Pyin Nāts, xii. 353
Phallicism, viii. 233, 378 [6]; ix. 330 [7]
Phallus, emblem of Pan, i. 268

Phallus on post before Mongol monastery to frighten female demon, iv. pl. XLV, opp. p. 396
—worship of Śiva connected with, vi. 119
Phantom army, iii. 155
—maiden from egg of wonder-trees, ix. 174
—(or fée), white, Guinevere's name means, iii. 193
—procession headed by Aine, iii. 47
Phantoms, hags as, iii. 169–170, 171
—pale, iii. 16
—(siabhra), Tuatha Dé Danann called, iii. 38, 46
Phaon, story of, i. 200–201
Pharaoh, v. 72
—absolute power of, over life and death, xii. 25
—daughter of, called Thermuthis by Josephus, xii. 397 [94]
—Hophra compared to cedar, v. 189
—of the Israelite captivity in Egypt, account of, not influenced by Gilgamish epic, v. 267
—priesthood of the, xii. 191
Pharaohs claimed divine incarnation, xii. 170
Pharbaethos, sacred bull (perhaps of Osiris-Horus) at, xii. 163
Pha-rmuthi, eighth month, dedicated to Renenutet, xii. 66
Pharos, Proteus king of, i. 261
Phasis, grove sheltering Golden Fleece on bank of river, i. 112
Pheasant and fish-hawk, tale of, ix. 290
Phegeus purified Alkmaion of guilt of shedding kindred blood, i. 54
Phenomena of day and night, vii. 220
Pherai, city built by Pheres, i. 106
Phereklos, builder of ships of Paris, i. 171
Pheres, child of Kretheus and Tyro, i. 106
Philadelphia ('Ammān), v. 19
Philae, temple of Isis at, xii. 99, 244
—Upset identified with Tefênet, Isis, etc., at, xii. 151
Philammon, son of Eosphoros and Philonis, i. 247
Philippines, ape or tortoise as trickster-hero in, ix. 203, 204
—Negritos in, ix. 154

Phillips, Stephen, quotation from the "Marpessa" of, i. 27–28
Philo Byblius quoted, v. 43
Philoktetes, or Poias, lighted pyre of Herakles, i. 94
—possessor of bow of Herakles, healed by Machaon, and slays Paris, i. 132
—receives serpent's bite, i. 126
Philological method of interpreting myths, i. lvii–lviii
Philomele transformed, i. 16, 68, 70
Philonis (or Kleoboia), Eosphoros united in marriage with, i. 247
Philonoë, Bellerophone wedded to, i. 39
Philosopher, Linos a, i. 253
Philosophical systems of divination, three, viii. 137
—thought as influencing Egyptian religion, xii. 24
Philosophy, viii. 13, 14, 16, 17
Philtre, magic, bestowed by Aphrodite upon Phaon, i. 200
Philyra changed into a linden-tree, i. 16, 158
—(Linden-tree), mother of Cheiron by Kronos, i. 11
Phineus, blind seer, tormented by Harpies but rescued by Argonauts, i. 111
—husband of Kleopatra, i. 74
—uncle of Andromeda, disputed right of Perseus to wed her, and was turned into stone, i. 35
Phlachal, elephant-goat, spirit, vii. 92
Phlegethon parallel of Valhall, ii. 314
Phlegyas, father of Koronis, i. 279–280
Phlious, Asopos River worshipped in, i. 257
Phobos, abstract divinity of state of mind, i. 282
—("Fear"), steed of Ares, i. 190
—pronounced in oath of "Seven Generals," i. 190
Phoebe, daughter of Leukippos, i. 24
Phoenicia, v. 132
—bear or boar enemy of young nature-god in, xii. 397 [101]
—influence of Egyptian religion on, xii. 241
—most Semitic deities in Armenia brought from, vii. 36, 38
—supposed connexion of Perseus legend with, i. 36
Phoenician, language of some mythological texts are classical, v. xix

Phoenician ships, amulet figures of Bês on prow of, xii. 64
Phoenix, viii. 21, 33, 35, 42, 43, 98–100
—connexion of, with Morning Star, xii. 54
—of Heliopolis, xii. 165–166
—soul of Osiris, xii. 54
Phoenix-Osiris, Nile-god wakens soul of, to life in new plants, xii. 95
Phoibe and Koios, parents of Leto, i. 174
Phoinikia, Agenor and Phoinix settled in, i. 44
—Menelaos touches at, i. 134
—possible influence of, on Cretan mythology, i. 42
—see also PHOENICIA.
Phoinix, i. pl. XXXII, opp. p. 128
—settled in Phoinikia, i. 44
Phoitos, i. pl. VIII (2), opp. p. 8
Phokos, son of Aiakos, i. 121
Phol, explanations of, ii. 18
—place-names containing, ii. 137
Pholos, Centaur, accidently dies by one of Herakles's poisoned arrows, i. 82
—hospitality of Centaur, i. 270
Phorkys, born of Okeanos and Tethys, i. 5
—represented a phase of the sea, i. 259
—Sirens reputed children of, i. 262
—Skylla daughter of, i. 263
Phoroneus claimed by Argives to have been the discoverer of fire, i. 16
—of Argolis, teachings of, in beginnings of civilization, i. 16, 28
—son of Inachos by an Okeanid, i. 28
Phosphoros and Hesperos, v. 36; xi. 97
—Hekate, i. pl. XLIII, opp. p. 188
—(Light Bearer) = Venus (Latin, Lucifer), i. 247
Phra In: see INDRA (vol. xii).
——Suen, Phra Narai, and Phra Naret = Śiva, Viṣṇu, and Lakṣmī, xii. 327
—Men, Siamese name of Indian Mt. Meru, xii. 259
—Phim (stamped gods) found in Siam counterparts of tablets found in Kaśmīr, Tibet, etc., xii. 327
Phrixos, four shipwrecked sons of, found at Ares, i. 111
—son of Athamas, i. 107–108, 109
Phrygia, Dionysos's connexion as a god of fertility with Zemelo in, i. 216
—Ishtar's cult in, vii. 38

Phrygia, Kybele goddess of, i. 275
—Magna Mater brought to Rome from, i. 304
Phrygian Mother, iii. 98
Phrygians equated with Brig, vii. 385 [8]
—in language and costume, Armenians resembled, vii. 8, 12, 379 [1] (Introd.)
Phthia in Thessaly, Peleus receives portion of land in, i. 121
Phuc-ba, xii. 316, 317
Phyllis marries Demophon and later kills herself, i. 136
Physic, knowledge of, from pygmies, vii. 260
Physician, Eir the best, ii. 186
—methods of Artemis as goddess-, i. 184–185
—of the gods, iii. 174
—see ASKLEPIOS.
Physicians, divine, vi. 31
—I-m-ḥotep patron of, xii. 171
Physiognomy, viii. 139–140
Physiographical divisions of North America, x. 74
Pi, jade tablet, viii. 46, 47
—chung shu, viii. 10
—Kan, heart of, torn out, viii. 40
P'i ku, abstinence from food, viii. 147
Piai, derivation of, xi. 351 [10]
Pi-beseth, Hebrew representation of Egyptian name of Bubastos, xii. 150
Picardy Stone, iii. pl. x, opp. p. 94
Pictographic script invented by Sumerians, v. xvi
Pictographs, v. 90, 92, 113; x. pl. v, opp. p. 18, 124, 128, 216; xi. 23, 99, 100, 101
Picture Island (E-no-shima), viii. 271
Pictures made of bears, stags, and otters killed, iv. 95, 98
Pidba River, iii. 294
Piedras Negras, xi. pl. xx, opp. p. 178
Piegga-oaivi ("Wind fell"), iv. 457
Pien Chi, viii. 190
"Piety, Classic of Filial," viii. 100
Pig, Pigs:
Pig, cat born of a, iii. 191
—dead sometimes take on degrading form of, xii. 180
—head of, given to Niamh, iii. 181
—in sun's eye, xii. 124–125
—last animated sheaf cut called rye-, iv. 247

Pig, origin of offering of, in worship of Demeter, i. 230
—princess changed into, by Bake, ix. 228
—sacred to Ninurta, v. 132, 133
"Pigs of Manannan," iii. 118, 119, 120
—tales of, speared by man, ix. 213–215
Pigeon messenger of god of death, vi. 62, 69
Pigmies, Tung Chün made sacrifice to, viii. 117
Pigsties, reed, placed in way of Bêl, v. 324
Pihuicheñ (Piguchén), vampire-like serpent, xi. 328–329
Pijaos ancestors came from mountain, xi. 200
Pike, water-spirits may appear as, iv. 195, 198, 209
Piker, Esthonian name for Thunderer, iv. 228, 229
Pilgrimages, viii. 23; x. 194; xi. 34, 136
Pili, survivor of flood, ix. 40
Pillan, god of thunder, war, and spirit of fire, xi. 325–327, 329
Pillar as symbol of Osiris, xii. 92–93, 385 [3], 400 [3]
—celestial, xii. 32 (fig. 13)
—copper, a torture, viii. 40
— -god (?) as title of Osiris, xii. 122
——of Busiris fused with Mendes-"spirit," xii. 413 [12]
—golden, iv. 321, 333
—in ground at foot of sacrifice-tree, iv. 266
—of Malcandros's house was tree containing body of Osiris, v. 71
——sky personified as female, xii. 35 (fig. 19), 366 [7]
— -stone, iii. 86, 87, 152, 155
Pillar, stone, of Dusares, v. 16
——symbol of sun-god, v. 51
—support of world, ix. 163
—world-: see WORLD-PILLAR.
—worshipped at Byblos apparently Egyptian symbol of Dêd(u), xii. 399 [111]
Pillars, v. 35
—as supports of sky, xii. 35, 366 [7]
—at cardinal points correspond to cow's four legs, xii. 37
—four, separating heaven and earth, xii. 44 (fig. 39)
—high-seat, Thor engraved on, ii. 83

Pillars of Heaven, viii. 32; x. 132, 250, 254
——four, xii. 363 [4]
——one of the, upheld by Shu, xii. 44 and fig. 39, 366 [7]
——Hel-gate made of bones of dead, ii. pl. XIII, opp. p. 106
——sky, ix. 35
——temple of Thor thrown overboard to guide Rolf to landing-place, ii. 76
—old Irish belief that world or islands rest on, iii. 13
—red, mounds of trolls raised on, on St. John's Eve, ii. 224, 225
—sacrificial, ii. 334
—shaman, representing storeys of heaven, iv. pl. XLVI, opp. p. 400
—two, parallel to night and day, xii. 367 [8]
—wooden, totemism argued from reference to, v. 9
Pilosus, male wood-spirit, ii. 205, 288
Piltzintecutli lover of Xochiquetzal, xi. 78, 93
— -Tonatiuh, lord of princes, the sun, xi. 54
Piman group a possible connexion between Shoshonean and Nahuatlan, xi. 42
Pimentola, gloomy place, iv. 78
Pināka, bow of Śiva, vi. 111
Pinākin, a Rudra, vi. 142
Pinching black and blue by Kaches, vii. 84
Pine insect, people hear voice of departed in, viii. 213
——pines and waits for its friend, viii. 335, 385 [22]
—symbol of longevity, viii. 105; 278, 385 [2]
— -tree, x. 27, 43
—trees, two, at Takasago, viii. 340–341
P'ing-hsiang (ancient Sha-ch'iu), viii. 39
—Ti, Emperor, viii. 62
— -yang, viii. 98
Pīpa, snake-god, vi. 241
Pipe, bestowal of, by Woman-from-Heaven, x. 127–128
—ritual: see CALUMET CEREMONY.
Pipes, musical, connexion of Pan with, i. 267, 268
Pipounoukhe, x. 31, 283 [26]
Pippala-tree, vi. 239

Pipru, demon, vi. 67, 68
Pir'-Shamash (Ashur-bān-apli), fatherhood of god emphasized in name, v. 12
Pirua, royal house, xi. 217, 218, 236
Pisa, capital of Elis, Herakles sacrifices in, i. 92
Piśācas, vi. 227, 248
—closely akin to Rākṣasas, vi. 157, 204, 245
—foes of "the fathers," vi. 67, 98
Piśāci, demon, vi. 67, 108, 217
Pisamar (Bešomar ?), idol, iii. 289
Pisangunuku is name of Ninurta at Kullab, v. 390 [274]
Pisces, fish represents, v. 310
—station of Ishtar-Venus, v. 304, 305
Pīshdādian Dynasty, vi. 339
Pison, river, v. 314–315
Pit guarded by serpents, iii. 132
Pitaona, slain by Keresāspa, vi. 324, 327
Pitazofi, xi. 208
Pitch, cauldron of, containing shamans and officials, iv. 489
Pitfall, first in Ireland, iii. 137
Pitkäinen, Pitkämöinen (from pitkä, "long"), Finnish names for Thunderer, iv. 228, 238
Pitkne, Esthonian name for Thunderer, iv. 228
Pitṛs, Yama king of, vi. 159
Pitṛyāṇa, "Way of the Fathers," vi. 71
Pittheus, father of Aithra and grandfather of Theseus, i. 97
Piye-Tào, creator god, xi. 87
Pizarro conquered Inca empire, xi. 44, 214
Place, holy, Ostiak, iv. pl. XVI, opp. p. 140
— -names containing both Phol and Balder, ii. 137
——English, point to cult of Thunor, ii. 70
——Heimdall occurs in, ii. 156
——Mimir occurs in, ii. 169
——Njord occurs in, ii. 103
——Thor occurs in, ii. 19, 71, 76
——traces of dwarfs in Iceland remain in, ii. 270
——Tyr occurs in, ii. 99
——Ull found in, ii. 157, 158
——Vidarr occurs in, ii. 160
— -where-the-Heavens-stood, xi. 86
Placenta, custom attached to, iv. 261

Places connected with Balder, ii. 134, 138

Placidus (canonized St. Eustathius), legends of, said to have had origin in the Jātakas, vi. 207

Plague, Apollo punishes Argives with, for death of Linos or Psamathe, i. 253

—at Teuthis, i. 22–23

—comes upon Greek invaders of Troy, i. 127

—Ektenes perished by, i. 42

—Guzu Tenno guardian against, viii. 228

—herbs to cure, ii. 206

—peach has powers against, viii. 349

—prayer in time of, xi. 63

—Rutu may have been the spirit of the, iv. 76

—Spirit of, x. 78

Plagues, cat one of three, of Mon, iii. 191

—three, of Britain, iii. 107

—Welsh, occur on Beltane, iii. 108

Plain of High Heaven, viii. 225, 237

——Ill-luck, Cúchulainn crossed, iii. 143

Plains tribes, manner of life of, x. 76

Plan, The Great, viii. 38

Planet-gods, Babylonian, influenced Turco-Tatar cosmology, iv. 405, 410

——Tengeri doubtless signified, iv. 406, 407

Planets, vi. 25, 92, 233; vii. 17; 228, 229; viii. 29, 42, 137, 141, 142–143

—as evil beings, vi. 277, 361 [5]

—colour of, v. 159

—deities of, degraded into demons, vii. 387 [20]

—Five Dragons [epoch] given names of, viii. 25

—Horus associated with, xii. 388 [28]

—no cult of, in prehistoric period, xii. 24

—seven, from teeth of Manzashiri, iv. 372

—spirits of the five, viii. 34

Planks, he who carries Voršud must walk on, iv. 123

Plano Carpini, iv. 390, 395

Plant, aquatic, procreating power, ix. 27

—forms, x. 22

—life, Artemis goddess of, i. 184, 185

——Dionysos embodied in himself power to produce all kinds of, i. 218

Plant life personified in Osiris, xii. 66

—magic, to renew youth, iii. 131

—(magical) of birth, v. 94, 95, 97, 166–174

—names of persons, v. 9

—of birth, vi. 283

——eternal youth, v. 226, 227, 228, 262, 263, 268

——extinguishing poison, v. 302

——healing and rejuvenation, v. 226, 227, 262, 263, 268

——immortality, see IMMORTALITY, PLANT OF.

——rīvās-, primeval pair under form of, vi. 294

—souls, viii. 242

— -spirits, x. 27–28, 289 [35]–290

—(ú-nam-til, "plant of life") used in medicine, v. 187

—Underworld, white-plumed, x. 199, 201

—world, Aphrodite as goddess of, i. 198

Plantains, vii. 130

Planting songs, viii. 370–372

Plants, Ameretāt presides over, vi. 260, 281

—Apollo protector of, i. 180

—aquatic, Meret wore, on her head, xii. 136

—as deities, vi. 60, 96

——symbols of offspring, viii. 105

—born from hairs of Pan-ku, iv. 372

—forage, Pan exerted influence upon, i. 268

—healing, vi. 265, 281, 287

—Khepri came forth from, xii. 69

—leaves of, flat from upholding heavens, ix. 51

—magic in rites and games connected with, xi. 291

—moon affects, vii. 47–48

—new, soul of "Phoenix-Osiris" wakened to life in, by Nile-god, xii. 95

—origin of mankind from, ix. 110, 130

—ritualistic usage of, x. 290 [35]

—see SOMA, DEITY AND PLANT.

—spring from body of earth-god Qêb, xii. 42

—symbolism of, xii. 379 [17]

—trees, flowers, tales of, viii. 316, 338–353

—worship of, vii. 62–63

Plate of gold, signifying creator of Heaven and earth, xi. 246
Platonic ideas, vii. 153
Plato's account of creation, Pawnee analogy to, x. 112
Plays, xii. 342, 345, pl. XVIII, opp. p. 346
Pleasant City, origin of girls in, xii. 75-76
Pleasant Plain, iii. 84, 89
Pleiades, iii. 360 75; iv. 336, 417-418, 427, 430-432, 434, 436; v. 305-306; vii. 228, 229; viii, 34; ix. 295; x. xxii, 26-27, 96, 104; xi. 98, 306-307, 321, 322, 323
—and Hyades, i. 248-249, 250
—borrowed by Egyptians from Asia, xii. 40
—Celtic Apollo harps and dances in sky till rising of, iii. 10
—connected with seven fates, and seven Ḥat-ḥôr cows with bull, xii. 40, 57
—constellation of human fate, xii. 40, 376 78
—foretellers of harvest, xii. 40
— = Kṛttikās, vi. 140
—Sekha(u)it perhaps personification of, xii. 372 56
—seven weapons identified with seven, v. 147
Pleione and Atlas parents of Pleiades and Hyades, i. 248
——daughters pursued by Orion, i. 250
Plenty, Baʽḥet deity of, xii. 378 102
—Horn of, given to Herakles, i. 93, 94
—symbol of, x. 127
—Zefa god of, xii. 66
Pleuron, son of Aitolos, i. 56
Plough and furrow used in purification, iv. 237
——ploughshare divine, vi. 61, 97
—Festival, viii. 64; xii. 328-332
—invented by Athene, i. 171
— -rites, ii. 181, 182, 195
—worship of, at Dasahra festival in Panjāb, vi. 239
—with oxen, divine origin of, iii. 81, 137
Ploughman with goad as tormenter, vi. 134
Ploughs, prayers to Earth for wounds of, iv. 239
Plouto, wife of Zeus, i. 157
Plouton (Hades), i. pl. IV (1), opp. p. 1

Plouton (Pluto) or Plouteus, Hades as, i. 234
—sometimes called Zeus, i. 152
Ploutos, son of Demeter and Iasion, double of Hades, i. 226, 234
Plum-blossom representative of perfume and beauty, viii. 275
— -blossoms, Bloom Lady sometimes genius of, viii. 234
—symbol of longevity, viii. 105
Plutarch identifies Isis with " Justice or Nemesis," xii. 100
—" On Isis and Osiris," as source for knowledge of Osirian cycle, xii. 92, 110, 113-117, 126, 196, 217, 243, 390 34, 392 58, 395 73 75 77 80, 396 85
Pluto, lord of Orcus, ii. 305
—Nyja identified with, iii. 355 44
—parallel of Odin, ii. 314
Pluvialis, Pluvius, names of Iuppiter as rain-god, i. 290
(P)-neb-taui, son of Sonet-nofret, xii. 140, 149
Po, human victims thrown into, in return for knowledge of future, ii. 209
—sacrifice to ancestor of horses, viii. 61
—void, chaos, ix. 5, 6, 11, 26, 72
Po Lang Sha, viii. 93
—Ta Chên Jên, viii. 113
—T'ung, viii. 183-187
—Wu Chih, viii. 70
— -yang, Fu, viii. 167
——Lake, viii. 66
—Yün Kuan, pilgrimage to, viii. 23, 135
Počanya River, iii. 300
Podaga, idol, iii. 289
Podarkes (" Swift Foot "), later called Priamos, granted life by Herakles, i. 91, 118
Podoga, air-god, iii. 355 44
Poem of Ea and Atarhasis, v. 222
Poems divided into mythological and poetic, ii. 9
—divining, viii. 139
—heroic, ii. 11
—meeting of villagers to exchange, viii. 253, 380 7 (ch. ii)
—of skalds deal with deities and myths, ii. 11
Poetical method of interpreting myths, i. lviii
Poetics, ii. 4-5; see also " EDDAS."
Poetry, ii. 52-53, 54-55, 311
—abstract divinities of, i. 283

Poetry, Apollo god of, i. 181
—development of sacred, vi. 11
—divinities of, iii. 21
—early, viii. 214
—Faunus inventor of, i. 293
Pŏhjanael, " nail of sky," iv. 221
Pohjan-akka (or -emäntä), mistress of Pohjola, iv. 79
Pohjola, Finnish home of dead, iv. 78, 79
Poïa (" Scarface "), the Star Boy (Jupiter), legend of, x. 94-95, 113, 278 [14]
Poias induced to light funeral pyre of Herakles by gift of his bow and arrows, i. 94
Poine (" punishment "), a monster created by Apollo in retaliation for death of Linos, i. 253
Poison called Hālāhala, vi. 106
—from which Śiva derives his name " Blue Neck," vi. 212
—pounded gold resource against, ii. 378 [49]
Poisoned robe and garland, i. 37
—spears and javelins, iii. 129, 198
Poisoners (of finger-cutter sect) slain, vii. 371
Poisoning, xi. 39
Poisonous, belief that lizard is, vii. 164
Poisons, viii. 31, 156
—witches have knowledge of, vii. 336
Pokhar, sacred lake, as well as Brahmā's shrine, at, vi. 235
Pokis, mountain in flood-legend, ix. 183
Poko-ha-rua-te-po, wife of Rangi, ix. 8
Pokomo, Buu tribe of, have ancestor who just " appeared," vii. 155, 156
Polabians, goddess of the, iii. 289
Pole, human sacrifice to, and as war standard, x. 63, 295 [42]
—Milky Way as a, x. 249
—Old Man of the Southern, viii. 82
—poor dead must crawl over, iv. 54, 75
—souls of shamans supposed to climb, xi. 307
—spirit of lake bound by a, xi. 272, 273
—Star, iv. 417, 425-428
——Dhruva elevated to position of, vi. 165
——dream of spirit of, viii. 154
——nail of the sky, ii. 335
Poles, barbarians climbing, before Mîn, xii. 138 (fig. 135), 406 [57]
—cannibal, x. 249
—Gilgamish commanded to cut, v. 215

Poles, in ritual, x. pl. XII, opp. p. 56, 89, pl. XVII, opp. p. 90, 295 [42]
—of Tane and Paia placed between Heaven and earth, ix. 34
—sacred, x. 73, 100-101, 269 [4], 277 [13], 307 [61]
—to raise sun, x. 168
—totem-, x. 238, pl. XXX, opp. p. 240
Polevik, field-spirit, iii. 268-269; iv. 242
Polish religion, iii. 222
Political aspects of Zeus, i. 160
Pollen Boy, x. 162
—offered in sacrifice, x. 159, 191
—or fertilization, beard may represent, xi. 68
Pollution of running water, fear of, vii. 59
Pollux and Kastor, Gilgamish wrongly identified with, v. 268
Pölöznitsa, midday-goddess, dweller in rye-fields, iv. 247
Poludnica, Polednica, " midday-spirit," iii. 267-268
Polybotes, giant born of blood of Ouranos, i. pl. VIII (1), opp. p. 8, 9
Polydektes, plan of, to marry Danaë by force, i. 33
Polydeukes, i. pl. IV (1), opp. p. 1
—and Kastor at home, i. pl. XLIX, opp. p. 224
——took part in hunt of Kalydonian boar, i. 56
—kills Amykos in boxing contest, i. 110-111
—son of Tyndareos, i. 24-27
—Zeus bestows immortality on, i. 158
Polydores, son of Kadmos and Harmonia, i. 45
Polydoros king at Thebes, i. 47
Polygamy, xii. 186
Polygonos, son of Proteus, i. 261
Polyidos brings Glaukos back to life, i. 62-63
—solves riddle propounded by soothsayer and Glaukos is found dead, i. 62
Polykaon, son of Lelex, ruler of Messenia, i. 23
Polymnia (" Many Hymns "), one of the Dramatic Muses, i. 240
Polyneikes and Eteokles kill each other in duel, i. 53
——plan of, to rule singly in alternate years unsuccessful, i. 51

Polyneikes exiled and went to Argos, i. 51
—plans of Adrastos to restore rights of, i. 51–53
—son of Oidipous and Iokaste, i. 49
—story, variant of, i. 51
Polynesia, ape or tortoise as trickster-hero in, ix. 204
—composition and mythology of, ix. xi, 3–99
—ethnic composition of, ix. 3, 153
—relationship of Indonesian mythology to, ix. 243, 304
———Melanesian mythology to, ix. 149, 150
———Micronesian mythology to, ix. 263
Polynesian mythology, summary of, ix. 92–99
Polynesians immigrants from Indonesia through Melanesia, ix. 153
Polyphemos, vii. 369
—Aeneas sees blinded, i. 305
—entrapped Odysseus in his cave, i. 136–137
—son of Poseidon, i. 211
Polytheism, vi. 73 ; viii. 51
—Egyptian religion an endless and unsystematic, xii. 21
—in Sumerian and Semitic religions, v. xviii, 231
—taken from Babylonian source, v. 186
Polyxena, Priam's daughter, sacrificed by Greeks at tomb of Achilles, i. 133
Pomegranate associated with Hera in art, i. 168
—attribute of Aphrodite, i. 203
—given to Persephone to eat before release from Underworld, i. 229
—symbolic of offspring, viii. 105
Pomeranian Slavs, iii. 222
Pominki, funeral ceremonies, iii. 237
Pomona, functions of, partly absorbed by Floria in modern Romagnola, i. 319
—Ovid's account of love of Vertumnus for, i. 290
Pôngyi, a mendicant Buddhist monk, is invariably cremated, xii. pl. XIII, opp. p. 326
Pönnäs, prognostications of, xii. 323
Pont de et Village du Papier, xii. 310, 312
Pontic war, vii. 67

Pontos and Gaia, parents of Nereus, i. 260
—(barren " sea "), creation of, i. 6
—represented a phase of the sea, i. 259
Pookonghoya, one of Warrior Brothers, x. 205
Pool claimed human victim, vii. 188, 352
—entrance to abode of dead through, vii. 195, 196, 206
—Jade Lady submerged in, viii. 71
—of water, transformation of Odrus into, iii. 60, 136
Poplar, iv. 494
—(Arm. saus), sacred, tree in divination, vii. 12, 62
Poplars, sisters of Phaëthon changed into, i. 16, 244
Poporo-tree, fruit of, eaten, ix. 86
Pöppä Mountain, abode of manes of Mahāgiri Nāts, xii. 344, 347
Poppy, v. 404 [22]
—may be branches springing from shoulders of Ishtar, v. 187
———plant of life, v. 186, 187
" Popul Vuh," myth-records of primitive America, xi. 157, 158, 159–167, 363 [5]–364
Populona, Samnite epithet of Iuno, i. 291
Porcupine, vi. 91 ; vii. 184, 185, 186, 289
—A-mong wounded by quills of, xii. 283
—asked to bring back sun and moon, iv. 421
—-hunters, guild of, visits ghosts, vii. 186
—moon changes into, x. 114, 115
—(then human being) invents fire, iv. 450
Porcus Troit: see TWRCH TRWYTH.
Porenutius (Poremitius), idol of, iii. 283
Porevit (Puruvit), idol of, iii. 283
Pork, possible origin of religious prejudice of Asia and Africa against, xii. 389 [33]
—quarter of, champion's portion, iii. 146
Porphyrion, i. pl. VIII (3), opp. p. 8
Porpoises, transformation into, ix. 65
Porridge at sacrifice-tree, iv. 267
—boiling of, iv. 471
—meat, at blood-sacrifice, iv. 131
—Norna, first meal eaten after childbirth, iv. 256
— -pans, whittlings of lime-bark in, for omens, iv. 269–275

Porridge placed in smoke-outlet for frost-god, iv. 234
—sacrifice, at cow's-milk feast, iv. 259
—sacrificed for grass, iv. 242
—Sarakka's, iv. 253, 256
—sun-, iv. 224
Pört hozjin, Russian Lapland god, iv. 159
——-ört, bothie soul, iv. 13–14, 168
——-oza, House ruler, iv. 165
Portal, guardian of the, viii. 78
Portents: see OMENS.
Portrait statues, souls may settle in, in case of decay of body, xii. 175
Portraits as guardians of the portal efficacious, viii. 78
Portuguese stories in Angola, vii. 359
Portunas (Roman " Protector of Harbours ") likened to Melikertes, i. 290
Porū Māī of Nadiyā, jungle goddess, vi. 238
Poseidon, i. pl. XLVII, opp. p. 212
—aids Agamemnon against Trojans, i. 129
—alleged by Pittheus to be the father of Theseus, i. 97
—ancestor of Aiolic stock, i. 11
—and Amphitrite parents of Triton, i. 259
——Athene, contest of, for ownership of Attike, i. 172
——Euryale reputed parents of Orion, i. 250
——Gaia, parents of Charybdis, i. 263–264
——Kronos, Olympias, mother of Alexander the Great, traces descent to, i. 223
—Argo dedicated to, at Corinth, i. 114
—Babylonian light-god's spear interpreted by Greeks as trident of, xii. 397 [101]
—born of Kronos and Rhea, i. 6, pl. VIII (1), opp. p. 8, 14 (fig. 2), 274
—conferred power of transformation upon Periklymenos, i. 92
—created spring on the Acropolis, i. 66
—dried up springs and streams in Argos, i. 30
—father of Eumolpos, slays Erechtheus, i. 68
——Harpies, i. 266
——Proteus, i. 261
——Sinis, i. 98

Poseidon, Iason invited to feast of, i. 108
—Isthmus of Corinth awarded to, i. 37
—Kekrops regarded as form of, i. 66
—later identified with Erichthonios, i. 66
—love of, for Skylla, i. 263
—Minos enlists aid of, to obtain crown of Crete, i. 61
—patron deity of Corinth, i. 36–37
—ravishes Tyro, i. 106
—rouses waves against those who incur his anger, i. 153, 328 [4] (ch. i)
—sends monster to devour people of Troy, i. 85
—sent great monster to ravage Aithiopia, i. 34
—supreme divinity of Athenians, i. 66
—survives only in function and attribute in modern Greece, i. 312
—symbols of, i. 7 (fig. 1)
—Theseus son of, i. pl. xxv, opp. p. 96
—trident of, vii. 85
—tutelary deity of Troizen, i. 97
—uncertain relation of rivers to, i. 256
—wooed Hestia in vain, i. 209
Poshaiyanne, magician, x. 204, 210
Positions, vertical and horizontal, assumed by spirit-animals when journeying with shamans, iv. 509
Post, carved animal head, ii. pl. xxx, opp. p. 230
—" fallen stone " fastened to, iv. 397–398
—Heaven-, tethering-place for horses of gods, iv. 337, 340, 349, 351
—lone, is silver, iron, or golden, iv. 333, 334, 340, 408
—of birchwood to which sacrificial horse bound, iv. 268
—sacred, woods to be used for, vi. 239
—sacrificial, vi. 61
—set up at burial-place, vii. pl. XVI, opp. p. 182
—tethering-, of stars, iv. 337
Posts consecrated to Hypsouranios and Ousōos, v. 51
—for climbing into Heaven, vii. 132
—Lapp sacrificial, iv. 108 and fig. 5, 109, pl. IX, opp. p. 110
—of houses, pulling up of, to gain entrance to Underworld, ix. 48
—rope attached to, to uphold earth, iv. 311

Posts, spirit, in Red Karen spring festival, xii. 335–336, pl. xv, opp. p. 336
Pot-carrier, Zulu isitwalambiza means, vii. 418 46
—escape from flood in, x. 178
—half-bow of the, rainbow as, iv. 444
Potala, vi. 210
—residence of Dalai Lama, xii. 262
Potlatch, festival, x. 239
Potniai, town of southern Boiotia, i. 38
Potogogecs, Potawatomi chief, on spirits of cardinal points, x. 23
Potrimpo, Old Prussian deity, ii. 333
Potrympus, god of rivers and springs, worshipped at Romowe, iii. pl. xxxvii, opp. p. 304
Pots-hozjin, Reindeer-master, iv. 176
Potsherds found containing deity with mask and bolts, xi. 235, 368 16–369
Potter-god, Khnûm(u) transformed into, xii. 51
Potter's wheel, all creation made on, xii. 51
Pottery, x. 183, 194, 214
—Gumbas makers of, vii. 259
—of Susa, v. 117, 179, 402 9
Pouch, Chippewa side, x. pl. vi, opp. p. 22
Poultry, children imitate, iii. 309
— -luck, slain hen thrown on coffin in Savolax to prevent dead taking, iv. 18
Pounahou spring, tale of, ix. 88
Pouniu rescued from the flood, ix. 40
Pouring of water in creation-myth, iv. 329
Pourucista, daughter of Zoroaster, vi. 341
Pourushaspa, priest of Haoma sacrifice, vi. 282
—Zoroaster son of, vi. 341, 342
Pou sto, point of the observer (5th of cardinal points), xi. 52, 55
Poverty only want of Land of Opulence, viii. 363
Powamu ceremony, x. 195
Powder to restore life, vii. 358
—used in worship of cemis, xi. 22
Power in magic, xii. 201
—of first female shamans, iv. 505, 506
——owner, hair, nails, etc., contain, ii. 258
——shamans, the costume is the, iv. 519

Power-of-the-Shining-Heavens, a deity, x. 252, 272 6
Powers, x. 77–81
—Above and Below, x. 22, 24, 27–29, 197, 199
—intermediary, xi. 24
—of life and death, xi. 74–84
————generation, iii. 204
——things, x. 18, 226
—preternatural, of gods, ii. 22
Pox, cure for, xi. 32
Poyang Lake, viii. 66
Prabhāsa, a Vasu, vi. 142
—Soma won name of, vi. 137
Pradyumna, son of Kṛṣṇa, vi. 173, 174
Praeneste, cult of Fortuna at, i. 295
Prāgjyotiṣa, vi. 151
Prague, Bishop of, on religion of Czechs, iii. 222
Prahlāda, son of Hiraṇyakaśipu, vi. 123, 164–165
Prahrāda defeated by Indra, vi. 153
—Kāyādhava, an Asura, vi. 84
Praise-name of totem (here a buffalo), vii. 278
— -names, Spider repeats his, vii. 330, 428 26
Praises, Horus of, xii. 382 79
Prajāpati, "Lord of Creatures," vi. 19, 26, 27, 50, 51, 52, 73, 74, 75, 76, 77, 82, 83, 84, 86, 93, 100, 108, 109, 140, 147, 170
—Manu, vi. 142
Prajāpatis, vi. 108, 142
Prakṛti, vi. 74, 75, 184
—Śivā represented by, material out of which universe develops, vi. 180
Pralāda attempts to remove spear of Skanda, vi. 140
Pralamba, Rāma slays, vi. 172
Pramanthas, familiar spirits of Śiva, vi. 181
Pramanthu, myth of, viii. 378 6
Pramarres (Amen-em-ḥêt III) received divine honours near his monument, xii. 171
Pramlocā, an Apsaras, vi. 143
Prāṇa, god, vi. 93
Prāṇata, vi. 227
Pratyūṣa, a Vasu, vi. 142
Pravargya rite, vi. 80
Pravuil, angel, v. 160
Prayer, ii. 24

Prayer, answer to (*yin*), why symbolized by eagle, viii. 104
—by sacrifice, custom of, ii. 113
—Cheremiss sacrificial, iv. pl. xxxiv,
opp. p. 272, 268–281
—for child, ii. 174, 249–250; v. 64
— -houses, Muḥammadan, of Tatar villages, kuala influenced by, iv. 119
—in lud-worship, iv. 151
—later Egyptian attitude towards, xii.
232–233
—of Kintu, vii. 153
——Tan, viii. 47–48
— -plumes, x. 190–191, 193; see also
FEATHER-SYMBOLISM.
—realized by being stated as a fact, xii.
198, 421 ³
— -spire, launched on river at Water
Festival, xii. pl. ix, opp. p. 300
— -sticks, feathers attached to, x. 158,
190, 306 ⁶⁰
—wedding-, iv. 453
Prayers, vi. 19, 24, 78; xi. 63, 73
—for women said to Bugan, ix. pl.
xvii, opp. p. 170
—made to Frigg, ii. 174
—magic, of Mordvins to water-mother,
iv. 211–212
—offered to Thor, ii. 75
—summons to, v. 153
Praying-kuala, iv. 116
Praying Mantis, Koki, wife of Spider,
vii. 323
Precious things, viii. 229
——three, ii. 266
Predestination, vii. 93–94
—in Amen-ḥotep IV's hymn to the sun,
xii. 229, 426 ³⁷
Pre-existence of things in Heaven, v.
192, 308, 310
Pre-Hellenic deity of Peloponnesos, Perseus probably a, i. 36
Pregnancy, miraculous, viii. 6, 27, 111;
see also BIRTHS FROM VARIOUS
CAUSES.
Premieň, changelings, iii. 264
Presents, rule preventing acceptance of,
vi. 144
Pressing stones invoked to drive away
demons, vi. 61
Pret, ghost of cripple or child who
dies prematurely, vi. 247–248
Preta, hungry ghosts, viii. 238, 282
Pretas, ghosts of the dead, vi. 203, 250

Pretas, world of the, vi. 201–202
Priam before Achilles, i. pl. xxix (1),
opp. p. 116
—grandfather of Tror (Thor), ii. 32
—receives body of Hektor from
Achilles, i. 130
—restores Paris to rightful place in his
home, i. 119
—slain by Neoptolemos, i. 133
—uncle of Memnon, i. 130
—wedded Arisbe, i. 118
Priamos: see PODARKES, ETC.
Priapus, Graeco-Roman deity of fertility, iii. 289, 353 ²⁵
Pribyslav, Prince, ordered Triglav destroyed, iii. 285
Pridwen, shield of Arthur, iii. 185
Priest depository of ritual, xi. 350 ¹⁰–
351
—functions of Indian, x. 270 ⁵–271
—in women's clothes served Alcis, ii. 64
—shaman filled post of sacrificing, iv.
282
Priesthood, orders of, xii. 191–192,
419 ¹⁴
Priesthoods, Pueblo, x. 184
Priests, iv. 264–265, 268–281
—and priestly families in the Ṛgveda,
vi. 63
—Christian, sacrificed to Jupiter, and
feasted on sacrifice, ii. 68
—early Spanish, xi. 21
—of surgery and healing attended
Asklepios, i. 281
——Zeus-Aramazd at Ani, vii. 24
—said to be Coyote returning to earth,
x. 143
—sons of Armenian kings become, because of veneration for priesthood,
vii. 19
Primal Source of Being, uhlanga and
umhlanga may refer to some, vii. 145–
146
Primeval pairs, ii. 327; v. 92, 290, 291,
292, 293; vi. 294, 295, 296, 297, 298,
299, 316, 350; vii. 151–152; viii. 222–
224, 225–231, 378 ³ ⁷; ix. 6, 7, 9,
11, 18, 24, 105, 106, 107, 108, 109,
110, 122–124, 157, 159, 161, 166–167,
168, 169, 170, 171, 172, 173, 252, 254;
xi. 120, 184, 244, 248, 249, 250, 251;
xii. 293
Primitive mind demands objectivity in
expression of its thought, i. xlv

Primitive Revelation, vii. 131
Prince, Balder as an appellative for, ii. 18
—evil, of dead, iv. 486
—of Death, iv. 477–478, 491
—— = Kiyamat-tora or Tamek-vui, iv. 75
——Depths, Jewish, iv. 312
——Furnace, viii. 75–76
——O (modern Hupeh), posthumous title of Yo Fei, viii. 66
Princes, lord of, xi. 54
Principle, Babylonians pass over first, and begin with man and woman, v. 290
Principles, active and passive combined in T'ai Yüan, viii. 111
—two, viii. 136
Pripégala compared to Priapus and Ba'al-peor, iii. 289
Prison, narrow, Lludd said to have been confined in, iii. 107
Prisoners, notable, of Britain, iii. 189
—of war sacrificed to Mars, ii. 98
—sacrificed to Odin, ii. 57
Procession through Sweden at end of winter with Frey's image, ii. 24, 115–116
Processions, gods carried in, xii. 194 and figs. 204, 206
Procopius of Caesarea, mentions of religions of eastern and southern Slavs by, iii. 222
Procreation, magic ceremonies connected with cult of, iv. 259–260
Procreative powers, i. 291
—of sky, iv. 397, 398
Procyon, star, Humbaba wrongly identified with, v. 268
Prodigy seen on magic mound, iii. 94
Prohibitions, ceremonial, of totem-clans, vii. 279–281
Proitos and his daughters, i. 32
——Minyas, madness of daughters of, due to ecstasy of Dionysiac ritual, i. 166, 215, 222
—Bellerophon fled to court of, in Argos, i. 39
—corrupted Danaë, i. 33
—sent Bellerophon to Lykia, i. 39
Prokne changed into nightingale, i. 70
——swallow, i. 16
—daughter of Pandion, wife of Tereus, i. 68, 70

Prokris, Artemis rejects, i. 185
—daughter of Erechtheus, wife of Kephalos, i. 68, 71
—receives spear and dog from Artemis, i. 184
Prokroustes (" Stretcher "), brigand who stretched or cut travellers to fit his bed; perhaps death-god, i. 99
Prometheus, vi. 36, 356 ²; vii. 44
—Athene associated with, i. 171
—Cheiron exchanges his immortality for mortality of, i. 82
—(" Forethinker "), son of Iapetos and Gaia (or of Themis), i. 12–14
—Hephaistos associated with, in relation to artificial fire, i. 207
—legends of, vi. 263, 283
—Loki as fire stealer parallel to, ii. 150
—possible Armenian fragment of myth of, vii. 37
—punished by Zeus, i. 158
—rescued by Herakles and given Cheiron's eternal immunity from death, i. 88
—stole fire, v. 228
—varying attitude of, towards Zeus, i. 12
Promise-rope, iv. 70–71
Promises of sacrifice, iv. 69–70, 147, 153, 160, 161, 162, 233
—to dead, iv. 69–70
Pronoia (" Forethought "), abstract divinity of spiritual faculty, i. 282
Pronunciation and transcription, Egyptian, uncertainty of, xii. 3–4
Property burned to supply ghosts, x. 215
—dead prevented by offering from returning for his, iv. 20
—destruction of, evidence of social importance, x. 239
Prophecy, i. 56, 113, 132, 142, 224, 261; ii. 9, 56, 73, 99, 117, 169, 198, 208, 210, 212, 236, 241, 242, 246, 253, 254, 255, 261, 262, 286, 287, 295, 299, 311, 312, 334, 342, 344, 346; iii. 15, 34, 64, 75, 76, 115, 122, 152, 155, 166, 187, 191, 201, 208, 209, 210, 211, 248, 259; 308, 313–314; iv. 367–368; v. 134, 141, 142, 143, 144, 145, 146, 270, 355–356; vii. 159, 175, 340; viii. 41, 43, 44, 100, 101, 158, 167; xi. 35–36, 74, 138, 181, 197, 351 ¹⁰

Prophecy, Apollo endowed with gift of, i. 178, 179
—Proteus and Glaukos skilled in, i. 261
Prophesying from shoulderblade, iv. pl. LIV, opp. p. 470
——stars, iv. 419-420
Prophet, Nereus a, i. 260
—Zeus as, i. 162-163
Prophetic forewarnings, x. 262
Prophets and the ghost-dance, x. 149-153
——wonder-workers, x. 120-124, 169, 173
Prophylactic significance of bonfires in Spring and Midsummer, iv. 237
Propounder of God, iv. 409-410
Props, never falling, iv. 335, 339
Proserpina, i. 303
—may stand for Hel, ii. 17, 134
—myth, lamentation for Xochiquetzal perhaps a, xi. 78
— -Korē, Basilinna equivalent of, v. 19
Prospect Hill, viii. 182
Prosperity-Man (Ninigi), viii. 230
Prosperity, spirit of, viii. 82
Prostitute, first, iv. 380
—see HARLOT.
Prostitution, sacred, v. 386 161
——in honour of Anahit, vii. 26-27, 382 26
Protective ceremonies against wolves, evil spirits, etc., at time of Wandering-night, iv. 62-63
—measures against return of dead, iv. 20-22, 23, 24, 26-27
—trees, ii. 204
Protectors, iv. 503
Protesilaos fell before spear of Hektor at landing at Troy, i. 126
—returns from Hades for a few hours, i. 144
Proteus, iii. 57
—advises Menelaos to sacrifice to gods of the Nile, i. 134
—son of Poseidon, i. 261
Prototypes of ash Yggdrasil, ii. 333
Proven, oak grove sacred to, iii. 295
Providence beliefs, iv. 392-394, 395, 396
Provision-bag of Skrymir, ii. 93
Pṛśni, vi. 38, 39, 53
Pṛthivī, deity of earth, vi. 16, 49, 53
Pṛthu, avatar of Viṣṇu, vi. 168
—birth of, from arm of Vena, vi. 166

Pṛthu Vainya, worship of trees in day of, vi. 158-159
Prussians (ancient) closely akin to Slavs, iii. 317
Pryderi, son of Pwyll, iii. 95, 96, 98, 101, 102, 103, 174, 192, 339 4
Prydwn (Prytwenn), boat of Arthur, iii. 192
Psalter of Cashel, iii. 161
Psamathe exposed her son Linos who was torn to pieces by dogs, i. 253
—wife of Aiakos, changed into a seal, i. 16
Psammetichus, King = the mixer (of drinks), xii. 419 6
Pselchis, in northern Nubia, home of Selqet, xii. 147
Pskov, iii. 317
Psophis, Alkmaion brought sterility to soil of, i. 54-55
—town ravaged by Erymanthian boar, i. 82
Psychic manifestations in shamans, iv. 496-497
Psychology, Haida, x. 262
Ptaḥ and deities identified or associated with; Osiris identified with, xii. 98
—Apis regarded as embodiment of, xii. 162
—archaic character of artistic representations of, xii. 12
—as cosmic deity, xii. 220-221
—Astarte called daughter of, xii. 411 9
—eight forms of, xii. 220
—god of Memphis, xii. 144-145, 220-222
—likeness of Khôns(u) to, xii. 34
—member of ennead at Memphis, xii. 216
—Nefer-ḥo(r) special form of, at Memphis, xii. 140
—of Memphis identified with Hephaistos, xii. 64
—prayer heard by, xii. 232
——that dead may be identified with, xii. 178
——punishment of swearing falsely by, xii. 234
—Sokar(i) identified with, xii. 149
—Tatunen identified with, xii. 47, 145, 150
— -Bês as cosmic universe, xii. 377 90
— -Nuu and Ptah-Nekhbet as parents of Atum, xii. 220

Ptaḥ-Nuu-Sokari, nameless cosmic god partly in form of, xii. 222
— -Sokari, Nuu identified with, as primeval god, xii. 63–64
—(-Tatunen) equated with the Abyss, xii. 47
——identified with Nuu, xii. 47
———pantheistic tendencies attached to, xii. 220
—— -Sokari, Amen-Rêʿ repeatedly identified with, xii. 221
Pteleon, Prokris surrenders herself to, i. 72
Pterelaos, golden hair on head of, i. 77
—war of, with Elektryon and Amphitryon, i. 76–77
Ptolemaïs, Sobk worshipped at, xii. 148
Puberty rites, x. 215–216
Public fire-worship, vii. 56
—speaking, goddess of, viii. 268–269
Pu-chou Mountain miraculously razed, viii. 31–32
Pucu-pucu, bird which sings four times at early dawn, xi. 239
Pueblo Dwellers, x. 182–211
Pueblos in New Mexico discovered, xi. 20
Puellae, ii. 206
Puerperal fever both brought and healed by Artemis, i. 185
Puff-adder, vii. 192, 193
Puges, deity with seven cradles, iv. 260
Puikani, in west, feeds moon, vii. 228
Puirsho ("procreator"), iv. 258
Puiršo-Jumo, iv. 394
Pūitika (Persian Gulf), vi. 278
Pukeheh, x. 180
Pukkasī, vi. 217
Pukkusa clothes Buddha's body in brocade, vi. 193
Pukwudjies, fairies, x. 28, 68, 290 [36]
Pulaha, vi. 108, 144
—a fly in temple of Śiva, reborn as son of Brahmā, vi. 180
Pulastya, vi. 108, 144
Püleh, being who comes to earth at a birth to write fate, iv. 409
Pulkasīs, vi. 204
Pulling up the dragon, vii. 79, 81, 391 [15 21]
Pulomā, vi. 136, 145, 152
Puloman, vi. 132, 136, 145
Pulque, xi. 77, 113
Puma-snake, the deer-god, xi. 86

Pumpkin (calabash) came out of sea with fish in it, xi. 30
—in Lao and Wa creation-myths, xii. 285–286, 288–289
—(or cucumber) grows from a dead mother's grave, vii. 415 [33]
—pursuing, vii. 251
Pumpkins grew on place Zimwi died, and he turned into a, vii. 251, 256, 334, 409 [35]
Pu tao, ten inhuman crimes, viii. 156
P'u-hsien, a Bodhisattva, viii. 196
— -ming, hermit of, viii. 60
— -t'ien district, viii. 72
— -t'o, sacred hill, viii. 71, 193
Puna, shrine where sacrifice to war-god made, xi. 207
Puṇḍarīka Nāga, ancestor of Raja of Chūtiā Nāgpur, xii. 271
Pundjel, creator, ix. 273, 274, 282, 298
Pünegusse, man-eating giant, iv. 386–387
Punishment, iv. 396; x. 160, 282 [21]; xi. 30
—and enmity, divine, iii. 68–77
—of gods, certain offences receive, ii. 24
——Loki, ii. 105
——soul at places where misdeeds occurred, iv. 478
Punishments, i. 119, 158
—and rewards in after life, doctrines of, v. 266
—in hell, vi. 160–161, 180, 186; 345–346
——hereafter, iv. 489, 490, 491–494, 495
—of Hades, i. 144
——primeval pair, vi. 296, 297
Puñjikasthalā, an Apsaras, vi. 143
Puns significant in ancient Orient, xii. 85
Punt, burial in oaken, iv. 32–33
—Mîn patron of incense coast of, xii. 138
Pu-ört, tree-soul, iv. 188
Pupal and son of Tamus, ix. 130–132
Pupils of eyes double, viii. 34, 35
Puppis and Orion, v. 135
—Eridu identified with, v. 310
Purāṇas, mythology of, vi. 163–186
—source of Indian religion and mythology, vi. 13
Purandhi (Pārendi), goddess of plenty, vi. 53
Pürdän-Tura, iv. 394

Pur'gine, Thunderer, iv. 228
Purging, ritual, xi. 26, 33; x. 58
Purification, i. 259; iii. 242; iv. 17, 23, 24, 63, 94, 111, 180, 237, 365; v. 32, 84, 105, 106, 150, 315, 316, 317, 318; vi. 262; vii. 58, 60; viii. 33; 224; x. 21, 58, 63, 196, 234, 247, 282 21, 284 27; xii. 193, 298, 419 17
—after bear hunt, iv. 94, 96
—at birth of humans and animals, iv. 253–254, 256
—bath for, xi. 308
—by leaping over fire, iv. 451
—ceremonies forty days after death, iv. 365
—in ashes, iv. 180
— -meals in honour of Sarakka, iv. 253–254
—of Blessed Virgin, bonfires on, vii. 57
——Herakles refused by Nereus and Spartans, i. 89, 92
—with bull's urine, vi. 302
Purimatāla, Ṛṣabha became a Kevalin at, vi. 221
Purities, The Three, viii. 109
Purity of sky later gave rise to idea of holiness of God, iv. 400
Puron Runa, age of Common Men, xi. 240
Puroshita, domestic priest of the gods, vi. 45
Purple Mountain, viii. 65
Purrunaminari, creator, xi. 259
Purse of divinity, iii. pl. xxv, opp. p. 204
Pursuing pumpkin, vii. 251
"Pursuit of Diarmaid and Grainne," iii. 175–179
Purunpacha, time when all nations at war, xi. 238
Purūravas, vi. 59–60, 95, 147
Puruṣa, all-god, vi. 52, 75, 196
—avatar of Viṣṇu, vi. 168
—Indian first man, differentiated himself into two beings, husband and wife, vi. 294, 316
—Nārāyaṇa saw the human sacrifice and offered with it, vi. 80
—Śiva the eternal, vi. 180
—Sūkta of the "Ṛgveda," vi. 80
—world formed from the body of, iv. 372
Puruṣasiṁha, a Vāsudeva, vi. 225
Puruṣottama, a Vāsudeva, vi. 225

Pūrvas, old Jain scriptures, lost, vi. 220
Pusa, "Spirit," in Mahāyāna Buddhism, xii. 262
Pūṣan ("Nourisher"), vi. 21, 27, 30, 38, 55, 56, 62, 70, 71, 86, 114, 138, 143
Puṣkara, Varuṇa's son, vi. 137, 138
Puṣkarārdha, part of Jain cosmography, vi. 221
Puṣpaka, chariot of Kubera, vi. 158
Putaloka (Potala), original hill-site of Kuan-yin in Southern India, xii. 262
Pūtanā, vi. 172, 185
Puto, island where Kuan-yin takes precedence of all other gods, xii. 262
Puuk = Para, iv. 172
Puzar-Kurgal, "secret of god Enlil," v. 213, 220
Pwyll and Arawn exchange forms, iii. 56, 93–94
—magic cauldron of, iii. 95–96
—Prince of Dyfed, iii. 93–94, 96, 100, 101, 102, 103, 122, 192, 339 4
Pyamma Yek-kha, six clans of, xii. 292
Pydna, Castor and Pollux brought to Romans victory at battle of, i. 302
Pygmalion and Galateia, legend of, i. 200
Pygmies dwell on southern shore of Okeanos, i. 256
Pygmy races, ii. 273
Pylades and Orestes kill Klytaimnestra and Aigisthos, i. 135
Pylos falls before Herakles, i. 92
—Nereus slain at, i. 106
Pyramid Period, several dynasties of, appear to have been of Nubian descent, xii. 157
—small, to put departed in status of early kings in real pyramids, xii. 418 23
Pyramids, xi. 96, 112, 120, 132
Pyramos and Thisbe, i. 201
Pyrasos, Thessalian, sacred field of Demeter, i. 226
Pyriphlegethon, river (of flame) of Hades, i. 143
Pyrrha and Deukalion alone survived from Iron Age and became parents of our race, i. 18
—("Ruddy Earth"), mother of Hellen by Zeus, i. 11
—said to be wife of Prometheus, i. 11

Pyrrha, survival of, in modern Greek folk-belief, i. 313
—wife of Zeus, i. 157
Pyrrhic dance, invention of, i. 171
Pyrrhos (or Neoptolemos), son of Achilles, brought from Skyros and restricts Trojans to their city, i. 132
Pyrshak-Khan, son of creator, iv. 405
Pythian Games instituted by Apollo, i. 177
Pythios, origin of Apollo's epithet of, i. 178

Pythios, title earned by Apollo for killing Python, i. 177
Pytho (Delphoi), old name of shrine of Apollo, i. 178
Python frustrated in killing of Leto by Zeus, i. 177
— -gods, vii. 271, 272
—in beast-fables, vii. 284
—totem, vii. 272, 274
Pyvšan olysa and aika, Siryan gods identical with Bath-house man, iv. 164–165

Q

Qadesh-Astarte, v. 30
Qalanganguasê, myth of, x. 11
Qamaits, x. 253, 273 [7]
Qat, hero, creator of mankind, ix. 106, 111, 113–114, 118, 124–125
Qatabanian inscriptions, v. 3
Qatabanians sons of 'Amm, v. 7
Qati, four youths (sons of Horus or Osiris) sit in shadow of chapel (?) of, xii. 394 [67]
Qatu, tale of sister of, ix. 132–133
Qauš (Qais, Qûs), deity, v. 58, 390 [290]
Qaušgabri, king of Edom, v. 390 [290]
— -malaka, messenger-god found in divine name, v. 58
Qêb and four sons of Osiris or Horus bind 'Apop-serpents, xii. 104
——Nut begotten of Shu and Tefênet, and parents of Osiris, Horus, Sêth, Isis, and Nephthys, xii. 69
——earth and heaven, created by sun, xii. 50
——Osiris child of, xii. 113
—as father of the gods, xii. 371–372 [47]
——serpent and Nut, xii. 42 (fig. 35)
—bearer of vegetation, xii. 42 (fig. 33)
—bids Horus replace his father, xii. 389 [29]
—called into consultation by Rê', xii. 74
—directed by Rê' to bid Nuu guard against reptiles, xii. 78
—divides Egypt between Horus and Sêth, xii. 118
—earliest form of name, xii. 368 [18]
—earth-god, husband of Nut, xii. 42, 369 [22]
—earthly reign of, listed by Turin Historical Papyrus, xii. 399 [108]

Qêb, god of earth, xii. 66
——had no temples in New Empire, xii. 23
—holds down captive Sêth, xii. 390 [39]
—in solar ship, xii. 96
—master of magic, xii. 368 [20]
——snakes, xii. 42, 368 [20]
—member of ennead of Heliopolis, xii. 216
—name of, sometimes written with sign of egg, xii. 71
—Osiris apparently identified with, xii. 385 [7]
—placed over Aker as guardian, xii. 43
—Ptaḥ compared with, xii. 145
—Rê'-Ḥor identified with, xii. 221
—representation of, xii. 42 and figs. 33, 34, 35
—Sobk compared to, xii. 409 [99]
—theologians sought to reconcile existence of Aker and, xii. 43
—watching Aker and extended over him, xii. 43 (fig. 36)
—with hieroglyphic symbol, xii. 42 (fig. 34)
Qebḥet, serpent-goddess, xii. 145
Qebḥ-snêu-f, one of the four sons of Horus or Osiris, xii. 112
Qed, ox-headed deity, xii. 145
Qedesh, xii. 156
——Astarte, Mîn associated with, xii. 139, 156, 406 [60]
Qerery, serpent, assists in watching entrance to lower world, xii. 391 [43]
Qerḥet, serpent-goddess, xii. 146
Qingu (Kingu), monster, v. 295
Quadrupeds, human beings transformed into, i. 16

Quadruplets, xi. 29
Quaigh, Fionn drank from, in old age, iii. 179
Quail, Asteria changed into, i. 15
—related to cult of Artemis, i. 184
—remnants of totemism seen in ritual eating of Artemis under form of a, i. 183
Quarrel, pre-natal, x. 36, 39, 41
Quarters, cult of the, x. 111–112, 275 [11], 311 [67]; xi. 51
—four Bacab deities of the, xi. 137
——beasts of, x. 203
——see Cardinal Points.
——waters of, xi. 71
—gods of water have dominion over, xi. 92, 122
—jewels and colours of, x. 158, 283 [27]–284
—lords of four, xi. 142
—prayer to, x. 101
—see World-quarters.
Quauhtitlan, xi. 70
Qudaid, cult of Manat at, v. 21
Queen of Heaven, Asiatic, xii. 40
——analogies to stellar manifestations of Isis as, xii. 101
——myths of, influence belief in death of Osiris, xii. 119
——Êpet as, xii. 60 (fig. 61)
——hymns to, v. 25, 30
——Semitic, Aphrodite's cult-epithet Ourania borrowed from, i. 202
——eight-rayed star of, xii. 372 [56]

Queen of Heaven surrounded by flames, Asiatic motif of, in Osiris-myth, xii. 395 [84]
——Taoistic, Kuan-yin somewhat resembles, xii. 262
——Venus as, early replaces 'Athtar as morning star in Asia, xii. 54
Queevèt, evil spirit, xi. 324
Questioning deceased, iv. 28
Quetzalcoatl (Green Feather Snake), wind-god, xi. 50, 54, 57, 58, pl. vii, opp. p. 60, 65, pl. ix, opp. p. 70, 66–71, 87, 88, 92, 93, 94, 102, 106–107, 119, 125, 135, 240, 293
—parallels to legend of, x. 204, 311 [69]
Quetzalcohuatl, Pipil worshipped statue of, xi. 184
Quezubû, inferior devils, xi. 333
Quiche and Cakchiquel, xi. 156–159
Quicken-tree, iii. 131
— -trees, Fairy Palace of, iii. 170
Quinquagesima Sunday, winter dziadys on Saturday preceding, iii. 236
Quipus, art of reckoning, xi. 217, 218
Quiqrixgag, Quiqré, Quiqxic, lords of the Underworld, xi. 173
Quirigua, "Dragon" and "Great Turtle" of, xi. pl. i, frontispiece
Quito, Cara established themselves near, xi. 207
—pantheon, xi. 207, 213
Quivira, x. 311 [67]
Quiyauhtonatiuh, Sun of Rains, xi. 94

R

Rå, harmless elfin, ii. 225
Rabbit, x. 40, 143; see also Brer Rabbit; Coyote; Great Hare; Hare; Manibhozo.
—cast upon face of moon darkened it, xi. 57, 89
—in moon makes elixir of life, viii. 103
Rabgaran, Tagtug in, v. 198
Rabisu, Spy, one of the devils, v. 163, 362
Rabû, ghost, v. 355
Race, Finno-Ugric, division of, iv. xv
—of dragon-men, vii. 78–79
—origin of Chinese, viii. 5, 6–7
— -souls of tutelary genii of animals, iv. 187

Race, winning of Atalante by, i. 59
Races, three, of men, x. 124–125, 126
Racing, v. 324
—horse-, Poseidon deity of, i. 213
Rådare (Rå) (Swedish "ruler") corresponds to Finnish Haltia, iv. 12, 171
Rādhā Vallabhīs developed erotic side of cult of Kṛṣṇa, vi. 231
——rites of, vi. 185
Radien-aimo, "Ruler's home," Heaven, iv. 75
Radigast (also god), castle of, contained numerous idols, iii. 286, pl. xxxiii, opp. p. 286, 289
Radishes defended man, viii. 338

Radunica, spring dziadys, ii. 236
Raft in creation-tale, ix. 162
Rafu-sen, female genius of plum-blossom, viii. 275, 348
Rage, giant's, is jötunmodi, ii. 351 [19]
Ragnarok ("twilight of the gods"), ii. 337
—world-destroying, x. 121
Ragnhild, daughter of Hakon, ii. 104, 105
Rahab, v. 133, 134
Râhu, iv. 425
Rāhu, demon, vi. 137, 139, 151, 192, 232, 233
Raiatea, flood-myth from, ix. 39, 40
Rai-jin, genius of thunder, viii. 288, pl. xxx, opp. p. 288
Raikō, warrior, viii. 290, 306, pl. xxxiv, opp. p. 306, 313
Rail and rat, tale of, ix. 144
—desired disease and death for man, ix. 252
Rain, iv. 444; v. 381 [58]; vi. 15, 21, 22, 39, 49, 62, 89, 129, 134, 135, 233, 241; vii. 119, 126, 239–241, 312, 411 [43]; viii. 379 [17]; xi. 121, 209
—arbiter of, viii. 94
—associated with Sêth, xii. 390 [36]
— -bearing clouds, Pegasos may have originally stood for, i. 41
— -belt, iv. 444
— -bird, cuckoo regarded as, i. 166
— -bringers, rain-makers, x. 189–190, 191, 194, 288 [32]
—cause of, iv. 439, 444
—caused by sea Zduhaczs, iii. 227
—ceremonies, iv. 229
——stones in, xi. 24, 350 [9]
— -charm, connexion of Danaïd myth with, i. 30
——drenching with water at festival a, vii. 60
— -clouds, Tefênet not to be compared to, xii. 45
—Dionysos not unqualifiedly a god of, i. 330 [8]
—dragon controls, viii. 102–103
— -dwarfs, xi. 72
—[flood] of Malkôsh, ii. 342
—for blood of phantom maiden, ix. 174
—formed of saliva of Pan-ku, iv. 372
—fructifying summer, Freyja bestower of, ii. 126
— -god, viii. 73
——Aramaic and Canaanite, v. 37, 39

Rain-god, fire festival originally to influence activity of, vii. 57, 388 [11]
—gods of, xi. 25, 29, 34, 54, 68, 81, 137
——related to, vii. 365
—hearts of animals sacrificed for, xi. 137
—human sacrifice for, x. 201
—invoked to quell fire, ix. 47, 49, 115, 316 [33]
— -maker, vii. pl. xxiii, opp. p. 238, 239
——Hare as, vii. 295
— -makers, iv. 447–448
— -making magicians, Salmoneus perhaps belonged to class of, i. 106
——use of frog in, xii. 430 [26]
——without sacrifice, iv. 213
—making of, ix. 123, 179
—manifestation of Osiris, xii. 108
—Mantis praying for, vii. 418 [46]
—master of the, viii. 51
—may fructify human beings and animals, iv. 213
—milk-white, iv. 352
—of blood, ii. 250, 254; xi. 94
——Zeus, i. 159
—omens for, viii. 136
—poetic description of, x. 171–173
— -prayer, xi. 138
—prayers for, xii. 314
——Pueblo religious rites centre about, x. 183, 197, 201
—priesthood, x. 191, pl. xxvi, opp. p. 192
—procured by orphan girl, tale of, vii. 240
—resinous, xi. 164
—Rhea producer of, i. 274
—sacrifice for, iv. 212
—sent by Vahagn, vii. 46
— -serpent goddesses, xi. 122
— -stones, magic, i. 159
—struggles for blessings under form of, vi. 263, 269, 270, 288
— -sun, one of the cosmogonic epochs, xi. 72
—totem, vii. 270
—water-pouring sympathetic magic to ensure, vii. 22
Rainbow, ii. 278, 329, 343; iv. 228, 230; 444; vi. 59; vii. 119, 126, 234, 235, 236, 290; xi. 68, 231, 323, 342; see also BIFROST BRIDGE.

Rainbow as bow (or as drinker of water), arrow as lightning, iv. 443, 444
——divinity, xi. 197, 198, 246
——symbol of hope and success, xi. 203, 249
—ascent to Heaven on, ix. 66, 67
—bride of Hino, x. 24
—bridge, x. 48, 294 [42]
—cannibal-pole sometimes the, x. 249
—Freyja's necklace connected with, ii. 124
—Iris personification of, i. 241
—Izanami and Yasu often interpreted as the, viii. 378 [5] [8]
—made from heart of child of sky-maiden and mortal, ix. 177
—mythic serpent may be personified, x. 139, 300 [50]
—pinned San Juan mountain to earth, x. 162
—Sea-spirit supposed to travel on, ix. 135
—sign of Elōhim's covenant with Noah, v. 233
————promise, xi. 250
—son of sky-deity descended on, and became ancestor of human race, ix. 156
Rainbows, two, in answer to prayer for light, x. 167–168
Rains, Sun of, xi. 94
—tugs of war for, xii. 326
Rairu, xi. 309
Raisin-Eater, tale of, vii. 216–217
Rai-tubu, Sky-producer, ix. 12
Raja-äijä, Boundary-man, iv. 173
Rājā Jaichand of Kanauj, vi. 244
—Kidār, deity of boatmen, vi. 235
—Lākhan, Kol deity, vi. 244
Rājarṣis, royal seers, vi. 145
Raka, deity, ix. 14
Rākā, goddess, vi. 53, 93
Rakhsh, Rustam's steed, vi. pl. xli, opp. p. 332
Raki (Rangi), ix. 6
Rakian and bee-woman, tale of, ix. 218–220
Rākib-El, deity, v. 37, 41, 44, 65–66
Rakkab, deity, v. 37, 39, 44, 55
Rākṣasas, vi. 44, 66, 67, 82, 98, 108, 118, 136, 149, 155–156, 157, 158, 202, 203, 217, 227, 244–245, 356 [4]
Raktākṣa, leader of Daityas, vi. 180

Raleigh, Sir Walter, writes of Amazons, xi. 283
Ram, Amon as, xii. 129, 164 (fig. 170)
—appears on Fox-day, vii. 53
—butts magic calabash, vii. 223
——headed serpents, iii. pl. viii, opp. p. 72, 132
—Khnûm(u) has head of, xii. 50
—later sacred animal of Amon, xii. 129
—of Khnûm(u) has no prominence, xii. 164
—or bull with four heads, north wind as, xii. 65 and fig. 71
—sacred, of city of Mendes in the Delta, xii. 164
—six-headed, refers to monster Yamutbal, v. 129, 134
—with golden fleece, offspring of Poseidon and Theophane, i. 108, 326 [1] (ch. viii)
Rāma, vi. 124, 127–130, 156, 168, 169, 172, 182, 185, 225, 231, 236
— expedition of, to Ceylon, trace of, in story of Momotarō, viii. 383 [13]
Rāmacandra, one of the Baladevas, vi. 225
Rāmānand, footsteps of, revered at Benares, vi. 240
Rāmānanda and Rāmānuja, Vaiṣṇavism gains through reforms of, vi. 231
Ramas (i.e. Ramman = Adad) rendered " Zeus hypsistos " by Hesychius, v. 64
" Rāmāyaṇa," epic of India, vi. 12
—influence of, on Java, ix. 242
Rambhā, an Apsaras, vi. 143
Ramiriqui and Sogamozo, caciques of, fashion men and women from clay and herbs, xi. 200
Ramman-Adad (thunder- and rain-god), close relation of, with sun-god, v. 61
—storm-god, vi. 264
—weather-god, vii. 11
Rammānu, Rāmimu, Rāgimu, names of the Thunderer, v. 39
Ram's head, sun with a, xii. 28
Ramses, Astarte worshipped in city of, xii. 155
Rāmtek, temple at, connected with a Rākṣaṣa, vi. 245
Ran, wife of Ægir, ii. 16, 141, 154, 165, 171, 190–191, 209, 212, 281, 361 [3]
Rana-neidda (" Rana virgin "), iv. 249

Randgrid ("shield-bearer"), Valkyrie, ii. 249

Ranga-hore, wife of Tane, ix. 24

Rangha, vi. 272

Rangi, first king of Mangaia, ix. 39

—potiki, Sky-father, one of primeval pair, ix. 6, 7, 8, 9, 10, 11, 14, 30, 31, 32, 33, 34, 36, 37

Ransom, v. 334, 412 [13]

—from dwarfs cause death, ii. 268

Raodhatakhma: see RUSTAM CONQUERS DRAGON.

Rape of Sītā, vi. 128–129

Raphā in Gath, giants sons of, v. 355

Rapids and whirlpools, birth of goddess of, viii. 226

Rapping in answer to salutation of gods, iv. 170, 172

Rariteshasharu, Pawnee society, x. 96

Ras Shamra, tablets from, v. xix–xx

Rāsa dances, vi. 172

Rasā, mythical stream, vi. 34, 129

Rasātala, seventh layer under the earth, vi. 134

Rashnu, vi. 261

Rastekaise, holy mountain, iv. 103, pl. VIII, opp. p. 104; pl. IX, opp. p. 110

Rat, vi. 182, 237, 242

—and rail, tale of, ix. 144

—sister of Luk, ix. 262

Rata, grandson of Tawhaki, ix. 57, 60–62, 67–69

Ratatosk, squirrel, ii. 332

Rath lulled to sleep by mermaid's song and torn limb from limb, iii. 133–134

Rathakāras, chariot-makers, vi. 58

Rathgrid ("plan-destroyer"), Valkyrie, ii. 249

Rati, vi. 174, 218

—auger, ii. 48, 53

Rationalistic teachings of Confucius, viii. 220

Ratnaḍākinī, vi. 218

Ratnaprabhā, vi. 228

Ratnasambhava, one of the five "Meditative" Buddhas, vi. 211

Rātrī ("Night"), abstract deity, vi. 53

"Rats' Complaint," song of, viii. 370, 373

Ra't-taui, wife of Mont(u), xii. 139, 365 [20]

Rattle, xi. 33, 261

—calabash, god of Tupinambi, xi. 296

Rattle, magic, xi. 276

—sacred, x. 109, 247, 270 [c]; xii. 41

Rattlesnake counsellor of hero-brothers, x. 133

Raudalo, king of snakes, stays flood, ix. 120

Rauhe Else or Rauh Ells, Wood-wife, ii. 205, 206

Rauhina-tree, a relic of the tree of life, iv. 356

Rauni, wife of thunder-god, iv. 230

Raurava Hell, vi. 159

Rāvaṇa, demon, vi. 127, 128, 129, 152, 156, 157, 158, 159

—one of the anti-Vāsudevas, vi. 225

Ravda, wife of thunder-god, iv. 230

Raven, iv. 364–365; x. xvi, 246, 250, 252, 256, 258–262, 275 [10], 299 [48]

—cursed by Apollo for bringing tidings of Koronis's unfaithfulness, i. 280

—given world for dwelling-place, ix. 162

—in flood tale, v. 221, 230

—meat-offering to ancestors changes into, vii. 266

—symbol of messenger-god, v. 177

—to destroy hostile land, v. 126

Ravens, iii. 33, 36, 60

—connected with Valkyries, ii. 255

—of Odin, ii. 65

—Seides as, iv. 106

Ravgga (draugr), fish-god, iv. 191, 192

—water-spirit, iv. 208

Ravi, an Āditya, vi. 143

Ravines, Seven, at Tulan-Zuiva, xi. 166

Ray of sun, first, potency of, x. 87–88, 89, 93

—(or nail) from eye of Ogmios on Gaulish coins, iii. 11

—stellar, symbolism of, xii. 367 [12], 372 [56]

Raymond, Count, of Poitiers, serpent-wife of, vii. 73

Raz, "Bay of Souls" at, in Armorica, iii. 17

Razor between ears of Twrch Trwyth, iii. 187, 188, 189

Razors, bronze, ii. pl. XXVII, opp. p. 204

Ṛbhu (or Ṛbhukṣan), minor god, vi. 57

Ṛbhus, Alfar may be akin to three, ii. 219

—divine artificers, vi. 27, 29, 50, 57, 58, 71, 95, 148

Ṛcīka, father of Śunaḥśepa, vi. 148

Rê', iii. 34; xii. 24, 25, 26, 27, 28, 29, 31, 34, 160

—and Ḥat-ḥôr, attempt to connect myth of lost eye of sun-god with battle of, against rebellious men, xii. 86

——Khepri identified with Osiris, xii. 96

——serpent, myth of, merged with conflict between Horus and Sêth, xii. 107

—Apis connected with, xii. 163

—Buchis, bull of Mont(u), called "living soul" of, xii. 139, 163

—equated with Kronos, xii. 364 [14]

—explained as tomorrow, xii. 219

—followers of, xii. 179

—god of sun and fire, xii. 66

—goddess of justice (or truth) daughter of, xii. 100

—Horus at prow of boat of, xii. 127

—in myth of sun-god's withdrawal from earth, xii. 76–79

—makes Ṭhout(i) his representative to rule the night, xii. 84–85

—Mendes ram occasionally called soul of, xii. 164

—Mi-ḥos son of solar deity, xii. 137

—most local deities ultimately explained as "members" or "souls" of, xii. 28

—name Osiris paronomasiacly connected with, xii. 384 [2]

—(or Osiris), self-emasculation of, xii. 398 [106]

—pantheistic tendencies attached to, xii. 220

—parallel to, in American Indian, x. 89

—punishes mankind's rebellion by flood, xii. 73–76

—see MNEVIS, ETC.

—Sêth associated with, xii. 108

—solarization of, xii. 215, 227

—soul of Nuu, xii. 219

——over whole earth, xii. 220

—(sun) identified with Abyss (Nuu), xii. 220, 221

—wars against 'Apop, xii. 209

Rê'-Ḥor manifests himself in practically all gods, xii. 221

— -Horus as protector, type, ancestor, and soul of king, xii. 215

——Mont(u)'s hawk's head borrowed form, xii. 139

Re-peqer, xii. 98

Rea Silvia forced by Amulius to become Vestal Virgin, i. 307

Ready-to-Give, x. 121, 306 [60]

Realm of Bliss (Gokuraku Jōdo), viii. 241, 242

Reaping "upside down" for dead, iv. 73

Reason, children who die before attaining use of, xi. 83

Rebha rescued from death, vi. 31

Rebirth, i. 275; ii. 11, 105; iii. 62; vi. 100–101, 161, 184, 194–195; x. 78, 91, 99, 275 [10], 280 [18], 289 [34], 302 [55]; xi. 289 [34]

—and immortality of gods ideas survived and utilized for definite purpose, iii. 206, 208

—character of Celtic myths of, iii. 21

—Etain's, iii. 80, 82

—idea of divine shape-shifting combined with Celtic idea of, iii. 56–59

—monthly, of moon, vii. 52

—of Fionn as Mongan, iii. 112

——souls, iv. 481

——Taliesin as Gwion, iii. 109, 111, 112

—Setanta Lug's son and his, iii. 83

Rebirths, bulls as, of semi-divinities, iii. 152

Reckoning, art of, xi. 217, 218

—modes of, vi. 86

Recluses, viii. 275, 299

Recognition of totem, vii. 279

Recompense in Heaven and Hell, vi. 101

"Records of Air and Earth," viii. 245

——Eastern Chow, viii. 166

——the Ten Departments, viii. 117

Re-creation of world, ix. 17

Red, colour of life, x. 93

—Dawn-people dress in, x. 48

——possible meaning of Tsũi || Goab, vii. 157

—heads, how birds gained, ix. 50

—heart, earnest thought or desire called, viii. 387 [9]

—hostel of ("Da Derga's Hostel"), tale of, iii. 74–77

—Karens, Ea-pe supreme deity of, xii. 270

—or brown animals or reptiles symbolize Sêth, xii. 196

—Sea, Ḥat-ḥôr on coast of, xii. 410 [1]

Red Sea, tale of blood of Tiâmat or Adonis may explain, v. 303, 351

Reddening with blood, ii. 50, 226, 244, 295

Reds, three, or Wolves, Conall killed by, iii. 157

Reed, viii. 222

——-beds, vii. 145, 146, 147

—connected with fire-myths, vii. 43–44, 49, 54, 57

—grass in divination, viii. 135, 136, 138

——wards off evil influences, viii. 105

—hollow, x. 161, 203

——-mat, Marduk's creation of world from, v. 312–313

—Vahagn born from, vii. 43, 46

Reeds aid reunion, vii. 247–248

—become forests, iii. 136

—bundle of, set fire to in temple court, v. 319

—Living, xi. 176

—man made from, ix. 176

—or grass, conceal opening to Underworld, ix. 48

—origin from, vii. 145–146, 147, 148; 400 24, 402 9

Rê'et as female sun, xii. 365 20

—representations and worship of, at Heliopolis and other places, xii. 365 20

Ref the skald, ii. 76, 190

Reflexion, deceitful, ix. 227, 338 34

—in water cause of belief in inverted world, iv. 73

—of hidden person in water, ix. 226, 338 33

Regen (perhaps " counsellors "), applied to gods, ii. 20

Regeneration, cauldron of, iii. 100–101, 104, 105, 203

Regia virgo ruled Avalon, iii. 193–194

Regillus, Lake, Castor and Pollux appeared at battle at, i. 302

Regin, dwarf, ii. 267

—(Odin), ii. 44

Reginleif (Companion of gods), Valkyrie, ii. 249

" Reginsmal," ii. 141, 210, 319

Regnator omnium Deus, Semnones sacrificed to, ii. 203

Regulus, v. 317

Rehoboam appointed priests for satyrs, v. 356

Rehoboth-Îr, Nimrod builder of, v. 55

Rehua, child of Ranga, ix. 8, 33, 34, 70

Reidartyr (Thor), ii. 78

Reidgothland (Jutland), Odin came to, ii. 32

Reincarnation, iii. 83, 127, 207; vi. 101, 161, 164, 180; vii. 179, 192; viii. 213, 219; ix. 271; x. 10, 146, 263, 275 10, 281 18 20, 296 46; xi. 39, 61, 82, 185, 279, 302; xii. 309

—in form of animals, totemism confused with idea that dead are concerned in, vii. 272

—sun in procession through sky on way to, vii. 49

Reincarnations, nine, of Heimdall, ii. 154

Reindeer bull, soul of shaman believed to take form of, iv. 42

—bulls, shaman's spirits contested as, iv. 284–285

—escort dead to Underworld, iv. 485

—hide stuffed and turned to east at sacrifice, iv. 111

—Luot-hozjik protectress of, iv. 176

—master, iv. 469

——-skins used by Lapps and Northern Ostiaks for wrapping of dead, iv. 19

—soul of shaman rides on, iv. 508

—spirit-, iv. 506

—stabbing to death or binding alive of, to grave, iv. 483

Rejuvenation, ii. 22, 178, 180; iii. 131, 169; v. 226, 227, 228, 262; vi. 87, 145; viii. 273; x. 38, 91, 157, 164, 296 46–297; xi. 118; see also ESTSANATLEHI, ETC.; FOUNTAIN OF YOUTH.

—by fire, v. 52

—plant of, v. 226, 227, 262, 263, 268

Rek Na = Ploughing Festival, xii. 329–330

Rekh(i)tiu (" knowing ones, wise " ?), a class of mankind, xii. 379 18

Rekub-El, a sun-god, v. 45

Relations of gods and men, ii. 24

Relatives, earlier dead, come to take away corpses, iv. 23

Release, doctrine of, vi. 161

Relics, viii. 200

Religion, aboriginal Yucatec, xi. 136

—agricultural, vii. 15

—ancestral, of Nahuatlan tribes, xi. 120

—ancient, of Armenia, derived from different sources, vii. 5, 12–16

Religion, ancient, of China, doctrines of, viii. 197
—and art, close affinity between, i. lvi
——ceremonies of Pacific coast, x. 215–216
——morality not connected in early religions, i. liv
——myths, close connexion between, i. li–lii, lvii
—Araucanian, xi. 329
—Aztec, xi. 46, 47
—Bantu, amadhlozi central factor of, vii. 117
—currents of, in Semitic lands, v. xvii
—Deukalion founder of, i. 16
—Egyptian, conservatism characteristic of, xii. 11, 12–13
——influenced by dominant worship of sun, xii. 30
————mythology of Asia, xii. 153, 411 [4]
—Fuegian, xi. 339, 341, 377 [18]
—Greek, nature of the, xlviii–xlix
—lack of form of, according to Lalemant, x. 16
—nature of Italic, i. 287
—not to be identified with mythology, x. xvi
—of Isthmians in later times, xi. 192–194
——various peoples, xi. 296–300
——Yamato race, viii. 212
—old Druid, assimilated to that of Rome, iii. 8
—pagan, of Pueblo dwellers sometimes persists, x. 184
—Patagonian, xi. 332–337, 377 [12]
—Persian, vi. 259, 260
—personification of, in vision of Artā-Vīrāf, vi. 344
—Peruvian, xi. 241
—preservation of Phrygo-Thracian stratum in Armenian, vii. 13, 379 [6]–380
—primitive, books on extended discussions of nature and development of, i. 323 [2]
—relation of mythology to, i. xi
—Semitic, must be sought in areas of Arabia, v. 6
—shaman, iv. 282
—spread by bird Karshiptar, vi. 290, 309
—Sumerian, polytheistic, v. 6

Religion, Teutonic, sources of, ii. 12
—value of Egyptian religion in studying origin and growth of, xii. 245
—West Semitic, traces of Marduk legend in, but no ritual, v. 322
Religions, history of, Demeter important figure in, i. 225
—Mongolian and Tatar, books of travel containing accounts of, iv. 304
—Semitic, two large groups of, v. 15
—Spencerian view of, vii. 118
—three monotheistic, born on Semitic soil have belief in devils, v. 353
——national, viii. 13
Religious beliefs, intermixture of early, viii. 46–51
——of the Orinoco and Guiana, xi. 256–259, 260
—matters, Alemanni influenced by Franks in, ii. 38–39
—symbol, Star sign as, v. 93
Remarriage of father after birth of first-born son (Indian), iii. 83
Remi, coins of the, iii. pl. II (4), opp. p. 8, pl. III (3), opp. p. 14
Removal ceremonies, iv. 117, 122–125, 126, 128
—from house by nomads on death, iv. 23
—of corpse, ways of, to prevent return, iv. 22–23
—temporarily, of people to Underworld by ghosts, and restoration, vii. 187
Remus and Romulus, i. pl. LXIII, opp. p. 306, 307
Renaming a living man after dead chief to preserve traits, x. 282 [20]
Renenutet, as nurse-goddess, later confused with harvest-serpent, xii. 378 [98]
—cares for infant Horus, xii. 116, 397 [94]
—connected with birth and education, xii. 52
—divine nurse, xii. 116
—identified with asp on head of sun-god, xii. 378 [98]
—serpent harvest-goddess, xii. 66
—sometimes identified with Nepri, xii. 66
—watches beginning of second life in realm of Osiris, xii. 378 [98]
Renovation of world: see WORLD, RENOVATION OF.
Renowned, guardian of north, viii. 243
Reṇukā beheaded for impurity, vi. 169

Renunciation, god-names in formula of, at baptism, ii. 18
Reochaid, lover of Findabair, iii. 154
Rephâim (giants), may be wandering souls of dead, v. 355, 358
Repit, goddess in the latest period, xii. 146, 408 82, 426 27
Replenishment by magic, x. 307 62
Representative of deceased, iv. 43, 52, 53
Reproduction necessitated by death, vii. 173
Reptiles created by Khepri, xii. 69
—creation of, iv. 315, 320
—Indo-Chinese races claim to be sprung from, xii. 293
—primeval, come from tears of divine eye, xii. 379 17
Rerir prayed for child, ii. 174, 249–250
Reshef (Reşef, Reshep, Resheph, Reshpu), v. 37, 39, 41, 46, 66
—identified with Nergal, v. 49
—Syrian god, xii. 130, 155, 156
—warlike rival of Tammuz-Adonis, xii. 156
—West Semitic god, v. 30, 44–45, 46, 48
Reshef-Mekel in inscription from Cyprus, v. 48, 83
— -Shalamana, war-god on Egyptian stele, almost certainly a sun-god, v. 46
— -Sharamana identified with Shalman or Shalmon, xii. 155
Resin-bowl, iv. 266, 268, 278–279
— -cauldron where wicked souls are tortured, iv. 75
Restitution, realm of dead not place of, iv. 488, 494
Restoration of animals to life, vii. 289, 426 20
—to life: see LIFE, RESTORATION OF.
Resurrection, iv. 372; vi. 293; x. 91; xi. 312
—Egyptian, Osiris personification of, xii. 178
—of Bacab (Yucatec second person of trinity), xi. 143
——Christ, celebrations of death and resurrection of Adonis adopted and identified with, vii. 41
——dead man as boy who is the moon, ix. 278

Resurrection of Marduk, v. 337
——Melqart (sun-god), v. 52
—Osiris as lord of, xii. 93, 97
—spring, v. 75
—symbolized by images of Osiris made of sprouting grain, xii. 399 111
—symbolizes personification of plant-life in Osiris, xii. 66
—Tammuz lord of, v. xvii; see also DYING GODS.
Resurrections of St. George, v. 338
——Tammuz, v. 336, 337
Resuscitation of dead armies each night, ii. 316
Retribution after death, ii. 268, 317–320
—in next world, vi. 100, 161
Return, Arthur declared his, iii. 194
Rêvand, Mt., vi. 306
Revelation, x. 132, 149, 171, 240–241
—account of Satan's binding in, Loki's binding traced to, ii. 150
—birds as transmitters of, vi. 291
Revenge, ghosts may desire, viii. 239
—see YOSHITSUNE, ETC.; SOGA, ETC.
Revengeful and malicious animals, viii. 325–331
Revivification, i. 218; ii. 27; vii. 158–159, 163, 167, 169, 170, 171, 210, 216, 217, 289–290, 337, 338, 339, 358, 407 22; x. 157; xii. 116; see also items s.v. LIFE, RESTORATION OF.
Rewards and punishments in after life, doctrines of, v. 266
"Ṛgveda," vi. 5, 11, 12, 15–72, 73
Rhadamanthys, brother of Minos, assisted him in administration of law, i. 64
—judge in Hades, i. 142, 143–144
—son of Zeus, i. 157
——and Europe, i. 60
—took refuge in Boiotia and wedded Alkmene, i. 61
Rhea and Kronos, Hera daughter of, i. 164
—became sister-spouse of Kronos, i. 6
—born of Okeanos and Tethys, i. 5
—El married, v. 67
—gives stone to Kronos to swallow instead of infant Zeus, i. 155, 159
—Hercules said to be husband of, i. 303
—identification of, with Ops, i. 292
—lent traits to Artemis of Ephesos, i. 183

Rhea, mother of Demeter, i. 225
——Zeus, i. 155
Rhea-Kybele (Great Mother), i. 273–276
——black stone as image of, x. 288 32
Rheneia, Leto at, i. 174–175
Rhetarii worshipped Svaražic, iii. 286
Rhiannon, daughter of Heveidd Hên, iii. 94–95, 101, 102, 103, 121
Rhinoceros, vii. 284
Rhipaean Mountains, iii. 10
Rhode, mother of Phaëthon by Helios, i. 244
Rhodes, Althaimenes killed his father at, i. 63
—centre of sun-cult, i. 242
—connexion of, with legend of Herakles, i. 76
—Herakles sacrifices oxen at, i. 87–88
—worship of Athene in, i. 169
Rhodope Mountains, iii. 296
Rhodos (Rhode), wife of Helios, i. 242
Rhun sent to seduce Elphin's wife, iii. 110
Rhyming competition, viii. 352
Riangabair and Finnabair, castle of, iii. 149–150
Ríb, iii. 56, 73
Rib in creation-myth, ix. 251
—(ribs) of boars and oxen forming arch as gifts, iii. 127
—woman created from man's, iv. 377, 379; ix. 24
Rib-Addi, governor of Gebal, uses title of Tammuz in document, v. 340
Ribbon often found in representations of Resheph, xii. 155, 374 70, 411 7
—or fillet associated with Amon and Mîn, xii. 129, 138, 236
Ribbons, v. 45, 46, 48
Ribera, Hernando de, xi. 282
Ribimbi, vii. 128, 217
Rice brought to bereaved house, vii. 96
— -eating class who came from gourd, xii. 292
— -fields, irrigation of, viii. 225, 226
—furnished from miraculous gourd, viii. 319
—inexhaustible bale of, viii. 315, 381 5 (ch. iv)
—payment for keep in, viii. 13–14
—plant, viii. 232
—planting and harvest, songs of, viii. 369, 370–374

Rice, sacredness of seed, at Ploughing Festival, xii. 331–332
—symbolizes wealth, viii. 279
—thrown into well turns water to wine, viii. 123
Riches gained by thief of spirit fire, iv. 479
—god of, viii. 66, 79, 96
—goddess of, viii. 268–269
—manner of gaining, iv. 244
Riddles, i. 49, 62; ii. 62, 190, 201, 313; vi. 335, 348, 350; vii. 356–357; x. 203
Ride, Hel-, for tidings of dead, ii. 305
Rider Rakkab, sun-god called, v. 44
Riders: see FLIGHT OF WITCHES, ETC.; NIGHT-RIDERS, ETC.; WALRIDERSKE, ETC.
Ridge-pole, song at raising of, viii. 369
Rig, men begotten by, ii. 328
— -Jarl, son of Rig, ii. 155
—Odin said to be, ii. 155
—see HEIMDALL, GOD.
Rigantona (Great Queen) = Rhiannon, iii. 95
Righteousness, Imperial rule based on, viii. 33
—tortoise symbol of power of, in Kuei Shê painting, viii. 100
Rigi came out of a rock, ix. 251
—worm and butterfly in creation-myths, ix. 250
" Rigsthula," ii. 7, 10, 153, 155, 297, 328
Rihamun, Adad identified with, v. 39
Riihitonttu, iv. 171
Rimac, shrine, xi. 219, 224
Rimu, vii. 334
Rind (Rinda), ii. 45–46, 47–48, 49, 64, 65, 134, 135, 165, 174
Ring and sceptre, emblems of rule and justice, v. 150
—Antillean stone, xi. pl. III, opp. p. 28, 350 9
—(Draupnir) of Odin, ii. pl. VI, opp. p. 32, 60, 66, 109, 111, 119, 128, 131, 266
—enclosed in wound to aid in recognition, ii. 104
—from Andvari's treasure, ii. 141
—given to Eri by warrior in silver boat, iii. 26, 27
——son of Cúchulainn with direction to seek his father, iii. 144
—gold, broken and distributed in storm at sea, ii. 191

Ring guarded by warriors would heal him who drank thrice above it, iii. 172
—iron, iv. 337
—oak-sapling twisted by Cúchulainn into, iii. 152
—of brass sacrificed to drum by woman, iv. 289
——Etan, iii. 150
——Fiachna given to Manannan, iii. 63
——Fulla, ii. 130, 184
——son of Conlaoch, iii. 145
——Ull, ii. 156
—produced by Aine, iii. 47
—see DEAD, WASHING OF.
—shot at to determine who shall ride horse of deceased to graveyard, iv. 46
—solar disk, iii. 327
—spirits never form complete, about fire, iv. 479
Ring opponent of Harald, ii. 57
—prayed for Harald to reach Tartarus first, ii. 305
Ringgon, creator-bird, ix. 174
Rings, ix. 163, 164
—fairy, iii. 255, 259
—in sun and moon sacrifices, iv. 222, 224, 225–227
—magic, ii. 267, 308
—on bowl and sieve drums, iv. 289, 290, 291
——images of sister-goddesses, ii. 187, 188
—various, at bear hunt and games, iv. 86–88, 89–99
Rio de la Plata system, xi. 316
—Marañon, xi. 235
Rip Van Winkle cycle, x. 24, 32, 50, 66, 69, 135, 288 33
——motif, ii. 322; viii. 264, 265
Riret, xii. 376 79
Ristaxez ("resurrection"), known to Armenians as proper name (Aristakes), vii. 100
Rita: see RTA.
Rite of blood brotherhood, mythical, iii. 144
Rites and beliefs of Isthmians, xi. 191–192
——symbols, Mayan, xi. 142–146
—begotten by Rangi, ix. 8
—domestic, viii. 74–84
—Indian, x. xvi, 169–175
—magic, performed by Demeter over Demophon, i. 228

Rites of Dionysos orgiastic in character, i. 215, 221
——Pueblos and their myths, x. 196–202
—President of Board of, Wên Ch'ang made, viii. 112
—(tabu to men) women perform, on islands, iii. 117
Ritho, giant whom Arthur fought, iii. 185
Ritual, character of Dionysiac, i. 220, 221, 222
—cleanliness, xii. 192–193, 419 17
—eating, i. 183
—expiatory, i. 73
—importance of corn-spirits in, x. 290 35
—Keeper, x. 304
—method of interpreting myths, i. lviii
—myths, x. 169–175
—of letters on runes, ii. 295–296
—priest with book of, xii. 193 (fig. 201)
—priests, xi. 351 10
—swinging, i. 217
—symbolized in divine help, ii. 24
—vessel on wheels, ii. pl. XXXIII, opp. p. 254
Ritualistic element in cannibalism, xi. 349 5
Rituals, Dionysiac, i. 218
—for New Year's festival, v. 315
—taught people by man who had obtained them in vision, x. 111
Rīvās-plant, first human pair under guise of, vi. 294, 296
River, as creatress, hymn to, v. 105
— -basin of Offering, viii. 239
—Buj, offerings to, iv. pl. XXI, opp. p. 200
—divided and Irimu's wife passed through, vii. 255–256
— -god saves Kwei Chi, viii. 183
— -goddesses, v. 105, 152
—heavenly, iv. 434–435, 490; viii. 225–226
—holy, by which Seides stood, iv. 101
——(Ganges), vi. 234, 235
—man and woman came from bird's eggs laid at source and mouth of, ix. 169
—of fire flowing east and west, iv. 370
——life of paradise, iv. 80
——the Three Routes where soul could decide where to go, viii. 238

River or river-god, lineage from, associated with Belgic Viridomar, iii. 14
—sacrifice of bride to the "mother-," iv. 213–214
—souls ferried over, vii. 419 [4]
—spirit, iv. 208
—survivals of spirits and goddesses of, iii. 133
—Tammuz implored to arise from the, v. 348, 349
—washing of heads in new, iv. 210
—with missiles, ii. 320–321
Rivers, vi. 48–49; viii. 51
—divinity of, i. 256–257
—formed of venom, ii. 318
—four, Asiatic tradition of, xii. 46
——of Paradise, iv. 359–360
—of Erin, hazels of wisdom thought sometimes to grow at heads of, iii. 121
——Slime and Blood, x. 63
——Underworld, i. 143; xi. 170, 173
—or lakes associated with Gargantua, iii. 135
—ruler of water seen at sacrifice to, viii. 73
—sacred, vii. 59
—tears become, iii. 135
—two, Nile divided into, xii. 46
—underground, iv. 487
—usually benevolent deities, vi. 235
—worship of, i. 257; iii. 277
Rjrāśva, sight restored to, vi. 31
rNam-rgyal-c'os-sde, monastery at, vi. 209
Ro Lei, wife of Qat, ix. 125
Roach lake old man, iv. 339
Road, celestial, xii. 25
—Christian's, iv. pl. xxvii, opp. p. 224
—god of, viii. 82
—of Shamash, v. 210
Roads, Five, term Five Brigands originally, viii. 168, 169
—for dead same for a way then branch off, iv. 484
—Peruvian, xi. 212
Roaring Thunder, instructor in sun-dance, x. 123
Roasting, a torture, viii. 40
Robbers sacrificed to sea-gods, ii. 209
Robbery, origin of, iv. 375
Robe gift of Athene to Herakles, i. 80
—poisoned, sent to Glauke by Medeia, i. 115

Robes, Nasca, xi. 222, pl. xxxiii, opp. p. 226
Robin, redbird, origin of red breasts of, x. 66, 231
Robur Jovis dedicated to Donar at Geismar, ii. 203
Roc in Malay Archipelago due to Indian influence, ix. 242
—smith, iii. 175, 177
Rocca leader of Incas, xi. 217
Rock, birth of deities from a, ix. 251
——Lumimu-ut from sweat of, ix. 157–158, 170
— -carvings, ii. 225; xi. 271
— -crystal Boy and Girl, x. 162
—first people came from a, vii. 147, 148
—Forest-master may assume shape of, iv. 466
—from heaven, earth from, ix. 158–159
—in which mead hidden, ii. 53
— -Lady, viii. 233
—miraculous growth of, ix. 277, 278
—Mithra born from, vi. 287, pl. xxxvi, opp. p. 288
—Oisin entered door in, and remained for centuries, iii. 180–181
—pebble thrown becomes, vii. 257
—sacrificial, xi. 59
—skull of burned dog grew into, vii. 253
—with sign of umbilical cord, xi. 185
Rockets used to set fire to pyre of the Pôngyis, xii. pl. xiii, opp. p. 326
Rocks, ii. 202, 204
—as creators, v. 9, 11
——parents, ix. 12, 17
—giants and trolls associated with, ii. 279, 282, 285
—holy, v. 51
—in Arctic dwelling-place of dead, iv. 486
—isolated, frequently associated with Gargantua, iii. 135
—man derived from, in belief of some Hellenic stocks, i. 11
—of Kaua, ix. 91
—origin of mixed colouring of, iv. 387
—sacred, viii. 247, 254
—unusual, tutelary spirits ascribed to, xii. 15–16
—white, believed to mark proximity of Underworld, i. 143

Rod, Rods:
Rod, golden, to mark new site, xi. 249
—magic, of Math, iii. 96
—magical, to transport one to different places, viii. 132
—of brass causes earth to open and close, vii. 202
—Rožanice, etc., genii of fate, iii. 249
Rod, Slavic deity, iii. 293
Rods and rings of twigs, women made of, ix. 107
—three, smeared with blood and holding parts of heart and lungs of sacrifice buried at memorial feast, iv. 38
Rodasī, wife of the Maruts, vi. 39
Roditelskiye suboty, autumnal funeral rites, iii. 237
Roebuck, Ninurta battles against, v. 131
Roga (" Disease "), charioteer of Yama, vi. 160
Rogue, Nikeu surnamed the, ix. 90–91
Rohiṇī, Balarāma (or Baladeva) born from, vi. 171
—constellation, vi. 76, 136
Rohita, god, vi. 93
Rolf (Thorolf), Thor advises, to go to Iceland, ii. 76
Romagnola, survivals of Etruscan and Roman divinities and myths in, i. 316–320
Roman civilization fatal to oral mythology of Druids, iii. 8
—Empire, influence of Egyptian religion on, xii. 242, 243
—mythology, i. 287–320
—Wall, iii. 16
Romantic element in mythology of British Celts, iii. 19
—stories, viii. 293–302
—voyage type of tale, iii. 85
Rome and Venus, temple of, i. 294
—Arthur resolved to conquer, iii. 185
—established by Romulus and Remus, i, 307
—myths of early days of, i. 304–307
Romowe, holy oak at, ii. 333, 335; iii. pl. xxxvii, opp. p. 304, 305, 306, 354 [10]
Romulus and Remus, i. pl. lxiii, opp. p. 306, 307
Rona carried off into sky by moon, ix. 88
Rongo, deity, ix. 8, 9, 14, 26, pl. v, opp. p. 26, 38

Rongo-ma-tane, god of cultivated food, ix. 32
Rongoteus (Rukotivo), giver of rye, iv. 244, 246
Ronpet, xii. 146
Roof, heavenly, supports of, xii. 35
Rook, iv. 364–365
Röönikkä, wife of the thunder-god, iv. 230
Ro'o-nui and Haumea, tale of, ix. 62–63
Root-digger, x. 94–95, 114–115
— -eating class who came from gourd, xii. 292
Roots used to influence weather, iv. 458
Rope as symbol of sea, v. 309
—cotton, means of descent from sky, xi. 271
—living, extending from earth to sky, xi. 153
—promise-, iv. 70
—reaching from earth-supporting fish to Heaven, iv. 311
—three stars of Little Bear called a, iv. 425
Ropes for ascent to Heaven, vii. 135, 136, 140
Roraima, adorations and superstitions of Mt., xi. 276–277
Ros na Rígh, Cairbre Niaper slain at, iii. 155
Rosalia, Roman, possibly related to Armenian Vartavar, vii. 388 [4]
Rosaries, viii. 194
Rose-Sunday: see VARTAVAR, ETC.
Roses and rose-water used in Transfiguration Day rites, vii. 59
—festival of, vii. 370
Ro-setau, temple of Sokari, xii. 149
Rōshan, Mt., Iranian Glory said to be on, vi. 341
Roskva, servant of Thor, ii. 75, 81, 92
Rosses, King of three, iii. 91
Rossitten, Usching worshipped in vicinity of, iii. 330
Rostarus, Odin as, demands souls slain in battle, ii. 44
Rota, Valkyrie, ii. 248
Rõugutaja, deity of birth, iv. 258
Round Table first appears in Wace's " Brut," iii. 186, 187
Rousalia: see RUSALYE.
Route du Ciel, vii. 138, 204

Rowan-berry satisfied hunger, prolonged life, and healed sickness, iii. 131, 176
—protective powers of, iv. 188–189
— -tree, branch taken by Fraoch from, but its guardian attacks him, iii. 130
——called Thor's deliverance, ii. 84
—tree of thunder-god's wife, iv. 230
Rowers of the sun, xii. 26 and fig. 8
—seals as, x. 7
Rožanica, Slavic deity, iii. 293
Rožanice, genii of fate, iii. 249
Ṛṣabha, vi. 168, 221, 222, 225, 226
Ṛṣabhadatta of the family of Koḍāla, vi. 222, 223
Ṛṣis, seers, vi. 144
—seven, vi. 133, 167
Ṛśyaśṛṅga, sage, helps Daśaratha with horse sacrifice, vi. 127
Ṛta, iv. 392, 393, 394
—Lords or Upholders of, vi. 23
—string of Bṛhaspati's bow, vi. 45
Ṛtus, seasons, vi. 95
Ru, raiser of Heaven, ix. 8, 35, 51
Ru Chia, viii. 8, 24
Ruad saw mermaid-like creatures, iii. 133
Ruadan, son of Bres and Brig, iii. 32, 137
Rua-haku, sea-god, causes flood, ix. 39
Rubies, tears of Phaëthon's sisters turned into, i. 244
Rubrics for special days of month, v. 153
Rubruquis, iv. 390
Rucht, herd of Ochall Oichni, iii. 57–58
Ruci, Indra desired, vi. 132
Rūdābah, mother of Rustam, vi. 290, 331
Rudiobus, horse-god, iii. 124
Rudra, storm-god, vi. 18, 21, 27, 29, 37, 38, 39, 53, 54, 56, 73, 76, 81, 82, 83, 84, 93, 106, 109, 112, 114, 116, 118, 179, 216
Rudraige's Wave, iii. 89
Rudras, vi. 56, 81, 89, 94, 142, 149, 181
Rügen, island of, iii. 279, 280, 283
—svatobor on, iii. 305
Rugievit (Rinvit), idol of, at Korenice, iii. 283
Ruins as homes of spirits, vii. 73, 88, 91
—ascribed to giants, ii. 282
Rukmin killed by Baladeva, vi. 174

Rukmiṇī, wife of Kṛṣṇa, vi. 126, 127, 173, 174
Rukotivo: see RONGOTEUS.
Ruku-tia and Tama-nui-a-rangi, tale of, ix. 79–82
Ruler, a god, iv. 169–171, 173
—of fire, iv. 454, 455
——spirits, iv. 479–480
Rulers, seven, of sky = son, moon, five planets, iv. 407
Rumai, or Palaung, women wear costume like skin of Nāga, xii. 277
Rummindei, excavations at, indicate worship of Kṛṣṇa's wife, Rukmiṇī, vi. 126
Rumpelstiltschen, ii. 272
Rún, meaning of Norse, ii. 295
Runes, ii. 10, 25, 42, 45, 46, 47, 48, 50–51, 55, 66, 71, 72, 78, 99, 112, 152, 160, 168, 220, 230, 231, 240, 243, 252, 277, 295–298, 311, 345
—animistic, iii. 44
—ascribed to divinities, iii. 32, 33
—sacrificial, iv. 339
—singing of, in honour of bear, iv. 97
Runic cross in Isle of Man, ii. pl. XIX, opp. p. 152
—monument with troll-wife, ii. pl. XXXVI, opp. p. 286
—stones, ii. pl. XIV, opp. p. 114, 225, pl. XXXI, opp. p. 238
Runner, the, xii. 412 [5]
Running-days, Mongol name for storms, iv. 457
Ruotta, sacrifice to, iv. 67
Rupe as pigeon, ix. 43, 70–71, 82–83
Ruqqû, v. 410 [30]
Rural Dionysia, December festival in honour of Dionysos, i. 221
Ruruti (?), ancient deity associated with Atum, xii. 370 [31]
Ruṣā, Arabian deity, goddess of fate, v. 24
Rusalka, iv. 469
Rusalky (water-nymphs), iii. 254–255, 257
Rusalye, ceremonies at the, iii. 311–312
—Slavic and Macedonian, possibly related to Vartavar, vii. 388 [4]
Rushes to be removed, iii. 81
Russians at Aberdeen example of how myths grow, vii. 348
Rustam and Suhrāb, Irish parallel to story of, iii. 145

Rustam and white demon, vi. pl. XL, opp. p. 328
—conquers dragon, vi. 350
—cured by magic feather, vi. 290
—took place of Keresāspa as the Hercules of Iran, vi. 329–332, 334
Rustam's mace originally thunderbolt of Indra, vi. 351
Rustem Sakjik of Segistān, vii. 86
Rut-aimo where Rutu or Rota tortured dead, iv. 75
Rutja's (or Turja's) rapids, iv. 78–79
Rutu, disease-god, iv. 76, pl. XXVII, opp. p. 224
Rutulians, Turnus king of the, i. 306
Ruwa, Wachaga deity, vii. 116, 138
Ryang'ombe (" Eater of Cattle "), vii. 213, 224, 407 [7]
—miraculous circumstances attending birth of, vii. 213, 407 [7]

Rye, iv. 244, 246
— -god Rongoteus later associated with St. Stephen, iv. 244
— -pig, last animated sheaf cut called, iv. 247
Rynyš-olyša and -aika, Siryan gods identical with Threshing-barn man, iv. 164
Ryōjusen (Skt. Gṛdhra-kūṭa), one of three chief paradises, viii. 241
Ryū-gu, Dragon Palace, viii. 264, 269, 272
— -tō, lanterns of the dragons, viii. 271
— -wō, dragon king, viii. 268
Ryūjin, heavenly maidens and dragon-spirits, viii. 266, 276; see also NĀGAS (vol. viii).
Rzip, mountain of the, Czech rests on the, iii. 240

S

Sà, Nabû translation of old Sumerian title, v. 158
Saar: see SABIA, ETC.
Saattaja (" guide ") same as haltia, iv. 11
Sabaea, map of, v. 377 [8]
Sabaean, Akkadian language allied to, v. 2
—inscription at Warka, v. 377 [10]
Sabaeans sons of Ilmuqah, v. 7
Sabaga (Sakhala), fire-goddess, iv. 454
Śabaras, wild aboriginal tribes of India, vi. 218
Sabazios, Thraco-Phrygian Dionysos called, vii. 12, 97, 364, 390 [14]
—under name of Zagreus, part of sacramental meal, vii. 13, 380 [7]
Šabbāth, institution of Hebrew, v. 152, 153
Sabia, wife of Fionn, the Saar (changed into fawn) of tradition, iii. 168, 174
Sabîtu, woman wine merchant, v. 211
Sable-sacrifice Tōrem, iv. 404
Saboi, part of name of god used in nudity rites, vii. 13
Sâbu, mountain in which Zû lived, v. 102
Sabulana, tale of, vii. 197–198
Sacerdotal privileges in Eridu conferred upon Adapa, v. 181

Śacī, wife of Indra in later mythology, vi. 33, 55, 131, 133, 134, 145
Śacīpati (Lord of Strength), Indra as, vi. 33
Sack containing writings on occultism, viii. 140
Sacks, warriors concealed in, in Bran's house, iii. 101
Sacra, x. 269 [4], 290 [35]
Sacramental meal in which the god became incarnate in his votaries, vii. 13
—rite, eating image of god made of grain as, xi. 60–61
Sacred animals, i. pl. VI, opp. p. lx, 7 (fig. 1), pl. IX, opp. p. 14, 21, 30, 53, 61, 69, 72, 73, 81; ii. 109, 110, 118, 163; v. 132; vii. 428 [11]; viii. 233, 269, 379 [17]; xi. 137; xii. 24, 25, 26, 28, 29, 42, 47, 52, 65, 66, 129, 161, 164, 168, 364 [10] [15], 365 [6] [26] [27], 368 [22], 369 (fig. 221), 378 [98]
——and birds, viii. 98
——probable origin of Classical stories of sexual intercourse of, with women, xii. 164
——significance of, xii. 161, 168
—baetyl: see BAETYL, SACRED.
—birds, iv. 500
—bundle, xi. 90, 167
—cities, vii. 59

Sacred city of West Semitic religion, Gebal is, v. 351
—drum, vii. pl. xxxiii, opp. p. 314
—emblem, paddle a, vii. 129
—fire (caused by lightning), iv. 449, 451, 452
—fountains, ii. 208; v. 20; viii. 247, 251, 252, 267
—friction-drum, vii. pl. xxxiii, opp. p. 314
—garment from Underworld, ix. 73
—groves, ii. 97, 98, 102, 168, 203, 213, 214, 346
——and trees, ii. 203–208; iii. 305–306; iv. 143–158, 184, 189, 262, 281; vii. 190, 191
—hills, ii. 202, 227, 310, 315
—hyena, in East Africa, vii. 428 11
—instruments, xii. 51
—island, Helgoland (Fositesland) is a, ii. 162–163
—islands, iii. 14–15
—lake, vi. 236
—marriage depicted on runic stone, ii. pl. xiv, opp. p. 114, 116
——of Zeus and Hera, i. 165
—mountains, vii. 62–63, 77
—number of Anu is " sixty," v. 99
—object, case with lid as a Votiak, iv. 115; see also SACRIFICE CASE; SACRI-FICE TREE.
—objects in use at mer-festival, iv. 266–281, pl. xxxiii, opp. p. 268
——of shamans transported, during re-movals, on special reindeer not used for profane purposes, iv. 512
——One-Standing-and-moving, earth-supporter, x. 250
—Pack, x. 305–306
—place or person, iv. 445
—places, iv. 101, 103, 104, 139–141, 142, 143–158, 173–174, 184, 189, 231, 232, 262–281; ix. 271; x. 161, 162, 174; xi. 197, 199, 224
——assemblages at, viii. 246–247
——legends of those cutting wood, kill-ing snakes, etc., in, vii. 191–192
——trespass on, iii. 73
—prostitution, v. 386 161; vii. 26, 382 26
—rivers, vii. 59
—springs, vii. 59, 60, 62
—stones, vi. 240
—trees, v. 97, 152; vii. 12, pl. ix, opp. p. 124, 145, 146–147

Sacred trees and groves, ii. 203, 213, 214, 215, 231, 330, 331–336; see also YGGDRASIL, ETC.
——groves, mountains, rivers, and foun-tains, iii. 305
—waters: see WATERS, SACRED.
—woods, vii. 189
Sacrifice, Sacrifices:
Sacrifice, ii. 24, 27, 29, 33, 34, 38, 56, 57, 63, 65, 68, 69, 72, 75, 76, 94, 98, 113, 114, 115, 117, 187, 195, 201, 203, 208, 211, 214, 216, 226, 244, pl. xxxii, opp. p. 246, 248, 310, 333, 334, 335; v. 122, 317, 361, 398 105; vi. 80, 82, 83, 85, 87, 88, 89, 131, 135, 144, 148; vii. 74; viii. 61, 66, 68, 73, 75, 76, 154; ix. 61, 171; x. 82, 85, 111, 158–159, 275 10, 282 21, 287 31
—Agni is himself the, vi. 135, 136
—ancient Slavic, iii. pl. xxxvi, opp. p. 304
—and offerings to gods when Ark stranded, v. 204, 221, 230
——sacrificial fee indissolubly con-nected, vi. 70
—animal, vii. 149, 159; viii. 43, 47, 61
—arrow, xi. 79, 182
—backwards, iv. 73, 152, 245; down-wards, 220; upwards, 152, pl. xxii, opp. p. 204, 220, 262
—before sepulchral chapel, xii. 182 (fig. 192)
—birth, of Pṛthu, vi. 166
— -board, iv. 224, 230 (fig. 8), 231
—bull killed as, and diviner eats its flesh and dreams, iii. 75
—burnt, viii. 43; see also items s.v. BURNT.
——offered by infant Hermes, i. 192, 193
—by Odysseus calls up shades, iii. 16
—case, iv. 115, 119–121, pl. xii, opp. p. 122, 124, 135, 137, 138; see also SAC-RIFICE SHELF.
—collecting of tribute survival (?) of, iii. 27
—Dakṣa's, vi. 114, 179
—days in Babylonian calendar, v. 152–153
—feast to Jengk-tongk, iv. 193
—fire-, at wedding rites, iv. 452
—for rain, iv. 212
—foundation, iii. 271
—Ganges water for use in, vi. 234

Sacrifice, ghosts accept only un-blemished, vii. 186
— -groves, iv. pl. XXXII, opp. p. 262, 262–281
—haoma, v. 282–283, 295
—headless, vi. 80, 87
—horse-, vi. 56, 63, 85, 115, 125, 127, 128, 133
—human, i. 21, 68, 69, 86, 87, 88, 99, 100, 108, 125–126, 133, 183, 218, 324 [1] (ch. ii), 330 [3] (ch. ix); ii. 33, 37, 52, 55, 57, 68, 69, 75, 97, 98, 113, 114–115, 163, 187, 203–204, 208, 209, 211, pl. XXXII, opp. p. 246, 361 [24]; iii. 46–47, pl. XX (A), opp. p. 158; 280, 287, 305; iv. 111, 174, 203, 207; v. 25, 50, 51, 52, 72, 341–342, 343, 361, 389 [244]; vi. 79, 80, 144, 148, 184, 185; vii. 34, 82, 130, 188, 352, 371, 384 [60], 394 [49]; viii. 249, 304; x. 20, 63, 72, 73, 76, 94, 122, 161, 181, 201, 203, 204, 205, 210, 246, 285 [29]–286, 303 [58]–306; xi. 47, 48, 49, 58, 59, 62, 64, 65, 70, 72, 74, 76, 78, 79, 80, 81, 82, 94, 101, 112, 114, 166, 171, 175, 182, 184, 190, 191, 192, 197, 198, 207, 222, 223, 227; xii. 21–23, 177–178, 196; 333, 420 [22]
—instituted, xi. 86, 356 [22]
—kind of wood for implements of, vi. 239
—ladle, iv. 148
—mock, xi. 76
— -money, iv. 147, 193
—of gods of themselves to give motion to sun and moon, xi. 83, 89, 90
——horse in Poseidon cult, i. 213
——snakes, vi. 154–155
——" son of sinless couple " demanded, iii. 72
—offered to dead whose name chosen for child, iv. 15
—on mountains, vi. 299–301, 318
—original theory of, xii. 195
—Ostiak, iv. pl. XXIX, opp. p. 232
—pole of, vi. 41
— -posts, iv. 108, 109; vi. 61
—promise of, by guardian of lud on behalf of sick, iv. 147; see also PROMISES OF SACRIFICE.
—Rākṣasas delight in destroying the, vi. 156
—sexual organs played part in, iv. 250–251

Sacrifice shelf, iv. 115, 119, 124, 131–132, 135, 136, 149; see also SACRIFICE CASE.
—songs, iv. 131
—spring, to Tezcatlipoca, xi. 64–65
— -stumps, iv. 108
—substitutes for humans in: see SURROGATION.
—Sun descends at midday to consume, xi. 138
—teaching of vanity of, vi. 126
—the, avatar of Viṣṇu, vi. 168
—to obtain corn and milk, iii. 46–47
——polar stars of Anu and Antum, v. 94
——spirit of murdered Chên, viii. 193
——Veles, reminiscence of, iii. 300
——wind, vi. 302
—tree, iv. 110, 144, 152, 153, 154, 268–269
—Votiak, at karsikko, at times of illness, iv. 25
—withheld from Indra brings retaliatory storm, vi. 236
Sacrifices at tomb of Ariadne instituted by Theseus, i. 102
—blood of, stained trees in tabued grove, iii. 11
——offered to world-pillar, iv. 333–334, 338, 339
——to the Abasy, iv. 486
—bloodless, iv. 139, 142
—came into existence in Tretā Age, vi. 105
—five, viii. 74, 77
—giving of, to gods, untouched, iv. 456
—human, as food for dead, xii. 177–178
—kuala, iv. 129–135
——must always be performed within one family, iv. 115–116
—not given to cosmic deities in animistic stage, xii. 23
—of captives to nourish Sun, xi. 93
——Chosroës, vii. 17, 18
——food burned to send them to Heaven, xii. 195
——slaves, dogs, horses, and reindeer, iv. 483, 486
—proper to different spirits, xii. 296–297
—Slav, to Vily, iii. 256–260
—to dead man, iv. 25, 38–39
——reason for, xii. 172
——earth, iv. 460

Sacrifices to genii of fate, iii. 249–252
——heaven-god, direction of, and colour of animals for, iv. 399
——" Masters " of animals, iv. 468
——Seides, accounts of, iv. 109
Sacrificer, Manu first, vi. 65
—touched worshippers with honey-whip, vi. 30
Sacrificers, vi. 28, 79, 132
Sacrificial and sacred groves, iv. 143–158; see also SACRED PLACES (vol. iv); also items s.v. GROVES.
—animal, choosing of, to cure sick, iv. 293
—animals, ii. 69, 109, 117, 121, 155, 195, 203, 211, 226; v. 32, 34, 153, 318, 319, 356; vii. 13, 15, pl. II, opp. p. 18, 47, 59, 82, 371, 393 26; viii. 233, 379 17; ix. 118, 119, pl. XIX, opp. p. 198; see also SACRIFICIAL VICTIMS.
—bath, vi. 85
—blood (of swine), ii. 155
—bread: see BREAD, SACRIFICIAL.
—chips, ii. 52
—conception of " Brāhmaṇas," vi. 190
—cow, vi. 134, 169
—cult, Huang Ti reputed founder of the, viii. 21
—cults influenced by old sacred numbers, iv. 407
—feasts in time of trouble, iv. 263–264
—fire, vi. 284
——production of, ii. 83
—flame, Agni represents, vi. 135
—food, iv. 25, 39; vi. 49, 53, 143; xii. 195, 196; see also SACRIFICIAL VICTIMS [AND FOOD].
—god of Sweden, Frey was, ii. 114
—grass and post, vi. 61
—kettle, vi. 80
—meal, iv. pl. xxv, opp. p. 216
—money, ii. 187
—offerings, inversion of idea of, xii. 299
——marriage, war, funeral, and putting up of skull occasion for, xii. 294–295
—ritual, fire in, vi. 76
—Rock, xi. 59
—tree of heaven-god must be white, iv. 220
—vessels, inscriptions on, viii. 7
—victims, i. 45, 102, 184; ii. 109, 203; iii. 233, 234, 235, 238, 242, 271, 277, 281, 295, 296, 305; [and food] iv. 3, 4, 7, 12, 14, 18, 25, 26, 38, 39–70, 40,

44, 46, 47, 48, 49, 53, 54, 55, 56, 57, 58, 64, 67, 69, 70, 75, 76, 109–111, 113, 114, 122, 125, 129, 130, 132, 133–134, 136, 137, 138, 139, 145, 148, 150, 152, 154, 156, 157, 160, 161, 162, 163, 165, 166, 179, 180, 181, 184, 188, 196, 197, 198, 200, pl. xx, opp. p. 204, pl. XXIII, opp. p. 208, 209, 212, 213, 214–215, 220–221, 224, 225, 227, 229, 230, 231, 232, 233, 234, 245, 250–251, 254, 255, 258, 259, 261, 263–264, 267–277, 278; 334, 338, 339, 365, 404, 405, 410, 416, 445, 453, 464, 469; vi. 148; vii. 191; viii. 43; xi. 144, 145; xii. 195–196; 275, 297, 310, 333, 335, 336, 338, 345
Sacrificial vow, iv. 133, 135, 136
Sacrificing in general: see first four chapters of vol. iv.
—to deceased, formula for, iv. 54, 57, 60, 62; see also DEAD MAN, ETC.
—towards the tree, iv. 268, 269, 270, 271, 272
Sacrilege attributed to man who destroyed Thor's hammer, ii. 80
Saʻd, Arabic deity worshipped as stone, v. 24
Sadah, feast of, vi. 301
Sadarnunna, image of, v. 154
" Saddharma-puṇḍarīka," viii. 382 5
Saddle for dead, construction of, iv. 485
Sādhyas, group of deities, vi. 56–57, 94, 144, 149, 157
Sadidus, name derived from Shaddai, the Hebrew title of El, v. 66, 67
Sægr, basket, ii. 184
Sæhrimnir, boar, ii. pl. VI, opp. p. 32, 313
Sæming, ruler of Norway, son of Odin, ii. 33
Sæmund the Wise, ii. 4
Saer, carpenter, iii. 32
—smith (gobán), iii. 133
Säetrold, Norse Näk known as, ii. 210
Safa, Ossete divine smith, iii. 361 90
Saft el-Ḥene, modern name of Pe(r)-sopd(u), xii. 149
Saga, goddess, ii. 15, 50, 183
Sagabin Hills, xii. 276
Sagara, one of the Cakravartins, vi. 225
—sought to perform horse sacrifice, vi. 115–116
Sāgara, Japanese sea-god often identified with Hindu Nāga king, viii. 268

Sāgara serpent, vi. 216
Sagas, Icelandic, contain information on religion and folk-lore, ii. 11–12
Sages of the " Ṛgveda " and " Epic," vi. 99, 145
Saghalie Illahie, Paradise Valley, x. 135
Sagil-bi'di, Aramaic deity, v. 42
Sagittarius, Girtablili ("Scorpion-man "), Sumerian name for, v. 282
—wind-god associated with, viii. 73
Sagunes, a cape named for Saga, ii. 183
Sahadeva, vi. 136, 142
Sahajanyā, an Apsaras, vi. 143
Sahale, creator, x. 134
Šaḥarrat-pot, v. 365
Sahasrāra, vi. 227
Sahime, Mt., viii. 248
Sahirtu, v. 33
Saho-yama Hill, viii. 234
Saho-yama-hime, genius of Spring, viii. 234
Śaibyā, wife of King Śatadhanus, vi. 164
Śaibya Sṛñjaya, vi. 145
—Vṛṣādarbhi given as human sacrifice, vi. 144
Ṣa-i-id nakirim ("Hunter of the foe ") epithet of Ninurta, v. 53
Śailādi, guard of Śiva's palace, vi. 181
Sail-boat sacrifice, iv. 67
Sailors, Ino protectress of, i. 262
Sai-no-kawara, abode of souls of dead children, viii. 239
Sainred, son of Ler, iii. 73
Saint Andrew's cross, xi. 55–56
—Anthony's day, sacrifice on, iv. 137–138
—Artemidoros replaces Artemis in some localities of modern Greece, i. 313
—Athenogene has relation to game and hunting, vii. 365
—Blasius, worship of Veles transferred to, iii. 300
—Boniface put to death by Frisians, ii. 163
——reference of, to were-wolves, ii. 293
—Bran figures as a, iii. 106
—Brendan, Fergus mac Róich recites " Táin " to, iii. 211
—Brigit, sacred fire of, at Kildare, iii. 11
——succeeds to myth and ritual of goddess Brigit (Brigindo; Brigantia), iii. 11, 13
—Bruno, terms Svaražic " Zuarasiz diabolus," iii. 286

Saint Caillin, Fergus mac Róich recites " Táin " to, iii. 211
—Carannog, in Life of, serpent killed by Arthur, iii. 195
—Christopher, stories of, said to be from " Jātakas," vi. 207
—Chrysostom, statement of, that Christian texts were turned into native tongue of India, vi. 175
—Ciaran writes " Táin " to dictation of Fergus mac Róich, iii. 211
—Clement, iii. 211
—Collen, invited to meet the lord of Annwfn on Glastonbury Tor, iii. 212
—Columba, Mongan came to see, iii. 64, 210–211
—Comgall, Liban baptized by, iii. 208
—Cyprian, vii. 27, 383 30
—Demetra, Aphrodite regarded as the daughter of, in modern Eleusis, i. 313–314
—Demetrios replaces in some aspects Demeter in modern Greek folk-belief, i. 313
—Dionysios, i. 313
—Dionysos: see DIONYSOS, ST., ASSUMES, ETC.
—Elmo's fire, Helen sometimes identified with single orb of, i. 246–247
—Ethelbert, church of, iii. 285
—Eustathius, Placidus canonized as, vi. 207
—Fechin of Fore, had power over water-horse, iii. 129
—Fiacc's hymn says men worshipped the síde, iii. 49
—Finnen, " fasts against " Tuan Mac-Cairill and enters his fortress, iii. 207
—George, myth of resurrection of, v. 337–339, 413 5
——slain by a king, v. 340
—George's Day, feast at time of, iii. 356 14
—Graal, Welsh poem of Arthurian cycle, iii. 199
—Helens, x. 134
—Iliya and Perun, blending of, iii. 295, 296, 354 13
——(Elias) as dispenser of good harvests, iii. 296
——oath of Christian Russians in church of, iii. 293, 295
—in certain cases takes place of older pagan personage, iii. 135

Saint John the Baptist, iii. 313
——at end of world dragon will afflict Ireland in vengeance for, iii. 91
——Gregory the Illuminator substitutes festival of, for Navasard, vii. 382 [11]
—John's Eve, ii. 224, 286
——bonfires, vii. 60
——procession on, survival of agricultural ritual, iii. 47
—Justina, martyrdom of, vii. 27, 383 [30]
—Kentigern, iii. 213
—Mary, iv. pl. xxviii, opp. p. 228
—Matthew's Day, sacrifice to Veraldenolmai on, iv. 250
—Michael demanded as guardian angel by Hall, ii. 237
——forced Abyzu to tell her forty names, v. 366
——overcame wind-maids, v. 363
—Michael's Mt., Helena abducted to, iii. 185
—Mochaomhog, iii. 51
—Ninian, iii. 213
—Olaf, ii. 226–227, 277, 286
—Otto, bishop of Bamberg, accounts of Slavic paganism in lives of, iii. 222, 285
—Patrick, iii. 45, 49, 51, 54, 84, 88, 91, 134, 174, 180, 181, 182, 183, 207, 208, 209, 210, 212, 213
—Paul, ii. 138
——New Testament account of, not influenced by Gilgamish epic, v. 266
—Peter, church of, on site of temple of Triglav, iii. 285
—Peter's Eve bonfires, vii. 60
—Stephen, rye-god associated with, iv. 244
—Thomas, xi. 67, 239, 293, 374 [11]
——believed by some to have gone to India and Central Asia, xii. 270
——in India, vi. 175, 206
Saints, vi. 143, 243
—and heroes, meetings of, iii. 208–211
—Celtic, characteristics of Kei recall those of, iii. 198
—destroyed reptiles, iii. 130
—hand, fire from, iii. 137, 198
—have power over water-horses, iii. 129
—old springs placed under patronage of Christian, vii. 59
—Old Testament figures as, in Oriental Churches, iii. 354 [11]

Saints replacing ancient gods among Sir-yans, Russian Karelians, and Orthodox Esthonians, iv. xix
Sairima identified with Sarmatians, iii. 356 [1]
Saïs, Ophoïs wolf-god of, xii. 144
—worship of Neith in, xii. 142
Saiva-neida, Sea-maid, iv. 193
Śaiva system, earth-god or -goddess being taken into, vi. 237
Śaivism, influence of, on Buddhism of Tibet, vi. 211
Śaivite faith, vi. 185, 202, 207, 212, 216, 217, 231, 358 [2]
Saivo-animals, iv. 285–286
—maiden and man, mountain-spirits, iv. 77
—spirits, sacrifices to, near a stone, iv. 104
Saiyamkoob ("the Adjusters"), primitive race of Yucatan, xi. 153
Saka, Bati worshipped in, xii. 131, 393 [60]
—(capital of seventeenth nome), Anubis as god of, xii. 393 [60]
Śākadvīpa, Magas at, vi. 184
Śākapūṇi, three strides of Viṣṇu interpreted by, vi. 29
Sakatabela, woman with seven heads, vii. 358
Saké-beer, Shōjō genius of, viii. 274, 352
Säkhädai, masculine fire-god, iv. 454
Sakkala peasants ate heart of Danish crusader, iv. 5
Sakkut (Etalak), name of Ninurta, v. 134, 135, 316, 399 [141]
Śakra, vi. 131, 143, 186, 226
—corresponds to Indo-Chinese Sek-ya and to Indian Indra, xii. 285
Śākta sects, human sacrifice in, vi. 184
Śakti eaten by Kalmāṣapāda, vi. 146
— -worship, vi. 184, 202, 211, 217, 231
Sakuni, tale of, viii. 337
Śakuntalā, vi. 95, 146
Sakuru, sun, x. 108
Śākya clans of Upper India, Burmese kings claim to be connected with, xii. 271
Śākyamuni, viii. 14, 194
—a Buddha, viii. 241
—one of the Mānuṣibuddhas, vi. 211
Śākyamunis, numbers of Buddhas called, vi. 200
Śala, child of Parikṣit, vi. 147

Sālagrām stone in Gaṇḍak River worshipped, vi. 240

Salamander, vii. 165, 171

Salamānu, king of Moab, v. 45

Salamis, comet seen at battle of, vi. 223
—Telemon took refuge in island of, after murder of Phokos, and became its king, i. 121

Śālāvṛkī (hyena?), Indra changes into, vi. 80

Saligen or salige Fräulein, " blessed maids," ii. 205, 206

Saliva, man created from, ii. 26
—of gods more potent than that of men, ii. 53
——invisible bird or animal poison, xi. 328
——Odin in place of yeast, ii. 121
—poisonous, v. 130
—rain formed from Pan-ku's, iv. 372
— -rite, ii. 26, 53

Salm, son of Farīdūn, vi. 323

Salman = El, v. 46

Salmon, Fionn and the, iii. 111
—inspiration of wisdom obtained by eating, iii. 120, 121
— -leap of Cúchulainn, iii. 143, 149
—Liban changed into a, except for her head, iii. 208
—Loki hid in waterfall as a, ii. 144, 146
—of Inver Umaill, eating of, iii. 127
——knowledge eats of hazels of wisdom, iii. 121, 166
——Fionn ate, iii. 162, 166
—oldest of animals, knew where prison of Mabon was, iii. 189
—red, fire came from, iv. 238
—speckled, iii. 115
— -trout found by boys a Marras, iv. 205
—Tuan MacCairill in form of, eaten by Queen of King Caraill and reborn as child, iii. 207
—with apple containing Cúroi's soul appeared in well every seventh year, iii. 151

Salmoneus, daughter of, ravished by Sisyphos, i. 37
—punished by Zeus, i. 158, 159
—son of Aiolos, i. 106

Salt, ix. 111, 145, 236
—and Pepper Ayars, xi. 249-251
—discovered by Misor and Sydyk, vii. 40

Salt, grain of, placed for each member of family, iv. 66
—how sea became, ii. 283
—obtained from fire and water, ii. 326
—spring produced by Poseidon on the Acropolis, i. 172

Sāl-tree, sacred, vi. 194

Ṣaltu (" Hostility," " Discord ") created to oppose Ishtar, v. 26-27

Salus, same divinity as Hygieia, made wife of Asklepios, i. 301

Sālva, vi. 154

Salvation, attaining of, vi. 105

Salym, sacrifices at sources of, iv. 339

Sām, vi. pl. xxxvii, opp. p. 290, 328, 329, 330, 331, 334

Sama, venerable, viii. 387 3

Samantabhadra, Bodhisattva of Vairocana, vi. 211, 213

Samantapañcaka, altar of Brahmā, vi. 108

Samantapaṅka, lakes in, filled with blood of Kṣatriyas, vi. 169

" Sāmaveda," vi. 11, 73

Sāmba afflicted by leprosy, vi. 183

Sāmbapura, Magas settle in, vi. 183

Śambara, vi. 68, 153, 173, 174, 215

Śambaradeva, vi. 226

Śambuka slain for confusing castes, vi. 177

Same-bito (" shark man "), viii. 381 10

Samem-roumos, descendants of, v. 54, 390 265

Samenkoaner can not kill Olofat, ix. 262

Samera, parent of Buan, iii. 147

Sametaśikhara (Mt. Pārśvanātha), twenty Tīrthakaras obtained release on, vi. 222

Samhain (Hallowe'en), iii. 33, 68

Saṁhlāda, vi. 154

Śamīka, dead snake thrown on neck of the ascetic, vi. 154-155

Samildánach (" possessing many arts "), Lug known as, iii. 29

Śamī-wood, Agni hides in the, vi. 135, 136

Sāṁkhya philosophical system, vi. 162, 179

Sammada, fish, vi. 166

Sammuramat probably Semiramis, vii. 367-368

Samoa, Indonesian myth-incidents in, ix. 96, 97

Samoa, Melanesian myth-elements in, ix. 95, 96, 97

—relation of myths of, to those of Cook Group, New Zealand, and Tonga, ix. 93, 94

Samoan versions of origin-myth, ix. 17, 18–19

Samos, a Pelasgic centre, "sacred marriage" of Zeus and Hera celebrated at, i. 165

Samothrace, Argo arrives at, i. 110

—home of Dardanos and Iasion, i. 117

Samothracian flood, i. 19

Samovila, meaning of, iii. 256

Samoyed family-god, iv. pl. x (1), opp. p. 114

Samoyeds, language of, shows association with Finno-Ugric, iv. xvii

Sämpsä, god of vegetation, iv. 243

Sampula Teng, home of first men on this earth, xii. 291

Saṁsāra, Jain divinities subject to, vi. 227

Samsey (Samsö), witches in, ii. 45, 143

Samson, legend of, v. 82

San Chiao, viii. 189

—Chieh, viii. 93

—Ch'ing, viii. 14, 109, 110

—Hsien Shan, viii. 115

—Huang, viii. 25, 109

—Kuan, viii. 109

—Kung, viii. 109

—Kuo, viii. 94

——Chih Yen I, viii. 174, 179

——Tien Lioh, viii. 169

—Lao, viii. 109

—Pao, viii. 14

—Shêng, viii. 196

San Francisco Mountain in Arizona, x. 162

—Juan Mountain, x. 162

Sanapi, word for sacred number two-thirds, v. 213

Sanatkumāra, vi. 227

Sānchī, sculptures at, vi. 198

Sanchoniatho (Sanchounyathōn), fragments of, regarding Sydyk and Misor, vii. 40–41

—historian of Gebal, v. 15, 43, 51, 54, 66, 67, 68, 74

Sanctity, sign of, viii. 247

Sanctuaries, xii. 189–191

—kuala, iv. 117–119, pl. xi, opp. p. 118, 121

Sanctuaries of Mîn, xii. 138 (fig. 136)

Sanctuary, iii. 305; x. 135

—at Upsala with images of gods, ii. 17

Sand, Perun's, iii. 294

—to prevent demons tormenting Féinn, iii. 183

Śaṇḍa, an Asura, vi. 84, 98, 168

Sanda, god of fertility, identified with Herakles, vii. 379 [1] (ch. i)

——Tarsus, perhaps identical with Sandakos, vii. 41

Sandakos, Syrian hero-god, vii. 41

Sandal of hide, moon once, vii. 227

Sandals, pairs for going forth and for returning, xi. 118

Sandde Bryd-angel, because of his beauty none struck, iii. 189

Sāndīpani, Kṛṣṇa pupil of, vi. 173

Sand-painting, x. 154, pl. xxii, opp. p. 156, 158, pl. xxiii, op. p. 170, 171, 200

——of mythical snake, ix. pl. xxii, opp. p. 270

Sangarios (?), Hekabe daughter of, i. 118

—River and almond-tree parents of Attis, i. 275

Sanga-tree, abode of the Nāts Tin Dè and Thiriwunda, xii. 343, 346

Saṅgha, "Congregation," vi. 189

Sanghavak, sister of Yima, made captive, vi. 311

Sangir Islands, ape or tortoise as trickster-hero in, ix. 203, 204

Sängke, sky-god, iv. 218

Śani, planet Saturn, vi. 182

Sañjñā, Aśvins said to have been born from nose of, vi. 141

Śaṅkara, appellative of Rudra or Śiva, vi. 84, 106, 113, 114, 158

Sänke, heaven-god, iv. 338, 401

Śaṅkhapāla, serpent, vi. 216

Santa Elena, xi. 205, 206

Śāntanu, King, father of the Vasus, vi. 142

Santaramet, corrupt form of Spenta Armaiti, used only in sense of Hades or Hell, vii. 96–97

—goddess of Underworld, vii. 35

Sanuki, viii. 272

Sanzu-no-Kawa ("River of the Three Routes"), viii. 238

Sao Kang, spirit worshipped at July festival in Kēngtūng, xii. 334

Soa Wŏng-ti, ruler of Yün-nan-sen, xii. 273-274
Saoshyant, last man, vi. 274, 293, 339
Saoshyants, prophets, sons of Zoroaster, vi. 343, 344
Šapattu (šabattu), Babylonian, originated in moon worship, v. 153
Sapling, x. 36-38, 296 45 46; see also Twins (vol. x).
Sappho addressed song to Phaon, i. 201
Saqqarah possibly derived from divine name Sokar(i), xii. 149
—tombs of Apis bulls at, xii. 163
Sarajas, Sarantola, iv. 78
Sarakka, deity of birth, iv. pl. xxvii, opp. p. 224, 252-257
Saramā, Indra's messenger, vi. 34, 129
—Yama's dogs offspring of, vi. 62, 69
Šaramana (Šalamana), Reshef identified with, v. 45
Saraṇyū, vi. 30, 50, 53
Sararuma, xi. 313
Sarasvant, water-genius, vi. 49
Sarasvatī, vi. 18, 48, 49, 53, 68, 69, 93, 182, 213, 215, 218
Sardeis, Lydian city, i. 119
——mountain near, reputed birthplace of Zeus, i. 155
Sargon, ancient conquests of, v. 145
——legend of, v. 157
—crossed sea of death, v. 218
—founder of dynasty of Agade, v. 1, 79, 218
—letter of, reference to dogs in, vii. 395 58
—omen of, v. 254
Saritor ("Weeder"), i. 300
Sarjū River, vi. 236
Šarkarāprabhā, vi. 228
Sarpa, a Rudra, vi. 142
Sarpedon attacked Lykia and won its throne, i. 60
—granted life three generations long by Zeus, i. 61, 158
—son of Zeus, i. 157
———and Europe, i. 60
Sarsaok, ox, vi. 289, 298, 303
Sartul family, iv. 499
Sar-uul, Sozun-uul, sons of Nama, iv. 364
Šarva, vi. 81, 82
Sarvakāmadughā (or Nandinī), wish-cow of Indra, vi. 134
Sarvānnabhūti, vi. 97

Sarvārthasiddhas, vi. 227
Sarvitr ("Wound-wight"), ii. 248
Šaryaṇāvant, Indra found head of hidden horse in, vi. 64
Šaryāta Mānava, vi. 87
Šaryāti, vi. 141
Sary-Khan, son of Suilap, iv. 405
Sassun, ancient Tarauntis, vii. 39
Sassû . . . innu, monster with serpent head and fish body, v. 291
Ṣaṣṭhī, cat vehicle of, vi. 242
—sixth, worshipped to avert smallpox, vi. 246
Sata (Zada), iv. 458
Šatadhanus, King, tale of, vi. 164
Satan, ii. 95, 148, 150, 156, 293; v. 136, 139, 353, 354, 373, 374
—constrained men to worship dragon, vii. 82
—in dualistic creation-tales, iv. 313, 316
—(or a ghost) sits in fish and tells him to devour mankind, vii. 244
—Sêth develops into a, xii. 109, 196, 207
"Šatarudriya," Litany to Rudra, vi. 81, 89
Satavĕs, vi. 276
Satem language, Armenian a, vii. 379 1 (introd.)
Saṭet, xii. 20 (fig. 1)
—cataract-goddess, xii. 46
—(Seṭit) worshipped at First Cataract, xii. 146, 408 83
Sathenik, name of, possibly connected with Zaden, vii. 40
—wife of Artaxias, bewitched into love affair with Argavan, chief of dragons, vii. 78
Satī, vi. 184
Sati (Suttee), xii. 343, 345, 346, 347
Satire and humour, tales of, viii. 360-365
—effect of, iii. 27, 31, 60, 137
—in the "Ṛgveda," vi. 62-63
Satīs become saints, vi. 244, 246
Šatrughna, vi. 127
Šatruṁjaya, vi. 97
—in Gujarāt, Aṣṭāpada identified with, vi. 222
Šatšektše, or Šotšen, creator god, iv. 399
Satsuma, personal names compounded with bear occur in, viii. 210
Sättä-Kurö-Džüsägäi-Ai, suite of the over-god Ai-Tojon, and tutelary genii of horses, iv. 402

Saturn (Kronos, Ninurta), seventh day of Harranian week sacred to, v. 154
—grandfather of Latinus, i. 306
—in Plutarch's account of a Celtic island, iii. 15
—Kara-Khan may possibly correspond to, iv. 406, 407
—planet, "Horus the Bull" equals, xii. 388 28
——malicious, vii. 52
——Ninurta identified with, v. 55, 134, 317
——reading of name of, xii. 55
——representative of earth, viii. 142
——represented by black in Ezida, v. 159
——Śani is, vi. 182
——" World's man " compared with, iv. 250
Saturnalia, December festival, i. 292
Saturnus, i. 292
—Ianus banished to Latium with, i. 297
Satyabhāmā, wife of Kṛṣṇa, vi. 174
Satyavant, marriage of Sāvitrī to, vi. 160–161
Satyr, Phrygian, might be set beside Vahagn, vii. 364
—representation of, i. pl. XLVI, opp. p. 206
—type of, influenced by Bês, xii. 63
Satyros said to have been killed by Argos Panoptes, i. 29
Satyrs, i. 267–269; ii. 132
—as goats, v. 355-356
—associated with Dionysos, i. 35
—dance of, i. 14 (fig. 2)
—meet Bacchus (Osiris) with music in Ethiopia, xii. 377 86
—perhaps identified with dwarfs, xii. 377 86
Sa(u), or Sia(u) (" Taste "), one of sense-gods, xii. 66–67
Saubhari, tale of, vi. 166
Saudāsa, vi. 145
Saudharma, vi. 227
Saukavastān, vi. 333
Saul of Benjamin first king (divine appointment) of Israel, v. 42
Saul's body fastened to walls of Beth-Shan and his head placed in temple of Dagōn, v. 30, 83, 385 146
Śauṇḍikeya, vi. 98

Saura sect of Oudh sun-worshippers, vi. 232
—sects, vi. 184
Saus, sausi, vii. 62–63
Sautrāmaṇī rite, vi. 88, 93
Sauvīra, Bharata in service of King, vi. 164
Saviour as an epithet of Great Spirit, x. 283
—Tārā rendered in Tibet as, vi. 217
Savitṛ, form of the sun, vi. 17, 18, 21, 26, 27, 29, 43, 50, 54, 55, 57, 70, 86, 114, 138, 141, 143
Sāvitra, a Vasu, vi. 142
Sāvitrī, marriage of, to Satyavant, vi. 160–161
—wife of Brahmā, vi. 108
Šavoki, iv. 399
Saw feared by Milhoi, vii. 412 4
Saw Mèya, xii. 340
Sawing asunder of Yima, vi. 312, 316
Sawmè-shin, xii. 340
Sawn Hsak Hill, deluge-myth inscription on rock on, xii. 279, 280
Saxa-god (or Saxon-god), Odin the, ii. 29, 59
Saxland, Odin and Frigg came to, ii. 32, 33
Saxnot (Seaxneat), god, ii. 18–19
Saxo Grammaticus on idolatry of Elbe Slavs, iii. 222
Saxons, iii. 62
Sayo-hime metamorphosed into a rock, viii. 254
Sbel Thiourdos, vii. 15
Scaffold used in sacrifice to Morning Star, x, pl. XIV, opp. p. 76, 305
Scaffolding for ascent to heaven, vii. 132
Scald-crows are symbols or incarnations of Irish war-spirits, ii. 255
Scale, Five Dragons [epoch] given names of five notes of musical, viii. 25
Scales, hand-scales, names for Orion, iv. 430
Scalping, x. xx, 117–118, 275 10, 276 12, 291 37, 302 55
—Ostiak belief on, iv. 5
—prevented ghostly walking of enemy, iv. 5
Scandinavia, Finns found in, iv. xv
Scandinavian, likeness of Hawaiian mythology to, ix. 5
Scapegoat, v. 356, 357; vi. 85

Scarab, Khepri associated with, xii. 25
—sun as, accompanied by Isis and Nephthys, xii. 96
Scáth, Cúchulainn's journey to, iii. 131–132, 192
Scáthach, adventures of Cúchulainn with, iii. 143, 144, 145, 153
Sceaf, Danish hero-ancestor, ii. 262
"Scél Mucci Maic Dáthó," iii. 124, 145, 157
Sceptre and ring, emblems of rule and justice, v. 150
—emblem of Demeter and Persephone, i. 233
—of Odin, ii. pl. VI, opp. p. 32
Scheria, Odysseus at, i. 138
Schmidel, Ulrich, tale of adventures of, xi. 282–283
Scholars, I-m-ḥotep patron of, xii. 171
School of Letters (Ju Chia), viii. 24
Schools, Nine, of philosophy, viii. 8
Schrat (Scrato), male wood-spirit, ii. 205, 288
Schretel, small elfin in houses, ii. 205
Science, natural, viii. 28–29
—relation of mythology to, i. x
Sciences, seventy-two, vi. 226
Scimitar and spear, v. 70–71
Scissors between the ears of Twrch Trwyth, iii. 187, 188, 189
Scorpio, v. 317; xi. 98
—constellation, scorpion-man met by Gilgamish wrongly identified with, v. 268
Scorpion and Isis, legend of, xii. 210–211
— -goddess, Selqet a, xii. 99, 147
—infant Horus stung by, xii. 116
— -man, v. 209–210, 262, 278, 279, 280, 282, 283, 316
——met by Gilgamish wrongly identified with constellation Scorpio, v. 268
—sting of, killed Orion, i. 251
Scribe, divine, xii. 32, 33 (figs. 16, 17), 366 [4]
—of Aramazd, Tiur the, vii. 29–30, 31
——gods, Nabû the, vii. 384 [51]
———Sebg(u)-Mercury as, xii. 373 [63]
Scroll presented to Hsi Wang Mu, viii. 129
Sculpture, xi. 130
Scyld, father of Sceaf, ii. 263
Scylla: see SKYLLA.

Scythians settle in Urartu, vii. 12
—Greek view of origin of, vii. 390 [2]
—related to Indo-Iranians, iii. 317
Sea, i. 259–264; viii. 51
—Amphitrite queen of the, i. 214
—as circumambient Great Serpent, xi. 57
——deity, xi. 207, 235
——"Typhonic," xii. 95
—Asuras placed in, in keeping of Varuṇa, vi. 152
— -birds attack Argonauts at Isle of Ares, i. 111
— -bream, fish symbolic of good luck, viii. 279
— -buffaloes in the moon, vii. 52
— -bulls, vii. 91, 92, 396 [62]
— -bursts, three great, iii. 89
—celestial, iii. 329, 360 [80]; vii. 46, 57, 386 [11]
—Cerridwen cast her child into the, iii. 57
—congealed, Breton tradition that church at Kernitou stands on four columns in, iii. 13
— -cows blue, iv. 202
— -dweller, iv. 207
— -eagle, Nisos of Megara changed into, i. 16, 69
——tale of, ix. 141
—eastern, Muireartach may mean, iii. 171
— -god, Dylan perhaps once a, iii. 99
— -goddess, viii. 72–73
——old shrine to a, on Isle of the Temple, viii. 269
— -gods and -demons, offerings to, of robbers, ii. 209
——— -goddesses in pantheon of tribes of Guinea coast, vii. 241
——varying presentments of, iii. 102
—Kalunga used for, vii. 176
—King, viii. 213
——tale of daughter of, viii. 265–266
—Kitunusi of the Swahili lives in, vii. 244
— -lore borrowed from Arabs and from Indonesia, vii. 411 [46]
— -maidens, marriages of, to mortals, viii. 263–264
—(Mama Cocha), xi. 223, 224
—mistress of, Isis as, xii. 387 [26]
— -monster, fire kindled on back of, vii. 57

Sea, mythical fresh water, v. 226
—not personified, vii. 241
—of Dead, iii. 17
——Kahinalii, ix. 39
—on Acropolis of Athens created by Poseidon, i. 212
—origin of, xi. 29–30; see also ORIGINS, MYTHS OF.
—personality of, iii. 133
—personified, ii. 171
—Poseidon god of, i. 210–214
—power of Orion to walk on, i. 250
— -powers, mythic, x. 274 [9]
—primeval, vii. 50; ix. 105, 157, 158, 159, 165, 248–249, 270
—ruled by storm-god, viii. 225
— -shell, chief attribute of Triton, i. 260
— -spirit, iv. 198
——drawing of, ix. 135
—storm-deities born from, vii. 46
—Vahagn son of, vii. 44, 46
—with fish, iv. pl. xxvii, opp. p. 224
—woman of the, taught use of amulets, etc., xi. 32
Seachran, giant, iii. 171–172
Seal and signature of Brahmā demanded by emperor, viii. 358
—of life of Tishpak, v. 288
—(probably talisman), of Anu, v. 316
Seals, v. 4, 48, 49, 60, 68, 69, 89, 90, 93, 98, 119, 131, 132, 133, 159, 187, 237, 244, 245, 278–284, 300, 309
Seal-fat used in shaman-drink, iv. 283
—Psamathe changed into, i. 16
Seals grew from severed fingers of Old Woman of the Sea, x. 6
—Heimdall and Loki as, ii. 142, 155
—lure men to death by drowning, vii. 90
—Proteus herder and guardian of, i. 261
—transformed into rowers, x. 7
Seam of Sky = Milky Way, iv. 336, 434
Seamen, Athene patroness of, i. 172
Searbhan Lochlannach, giant who guarded tree with berries of immortality, iii. 55
Seasons, x. 30–31, 41, 57–59, 61, 78, 87, 105, 138, 193, 225, 246, 247, 253, 254, 264, 292 [39]; xi. 33, 51
—coastal myth may be interpreted as symbol of, xi. 225
—five, of the year, struggle of, vi. 130

Seasons, four, viii. 29
—tale of Amazon and its, xi. 306
Seat of Lethe, Theseus and Peirithoös bound to, i. 105
Seats, stone and wooden, xi. 206, 264, pl. xxxix, opp. p. 264
Seb, worshipped in form of flying hawk, xii. 146
Sebeg, explanation of change of interpretation of, xii. 373 [63]–374
—in the wells, xii. 373 [63] and fig. 224
Sebennytos, Dêdet worshipped at (?), xii. 132
—Onuris localized at, xii. 143
Sebg(u)-Mercury (planet) not connected with Thout(i), xii. 55
Sebit, Asbet perhaps identical with, xii. 131
—goddess, xii. 146
Sechobochobo of Baila brings good luck, vii. 245
Second Advent, x. 1
— -sight, ii. 187, 229, 230, 234, 293
Secret of life betrayed by woman, vii. 171
—Societies and their tutelaries, x. 245–249
Secrets, obtaining of, at instigation of Devil, iv. 361, 362, 363
Sectarianism, development of, in Paurāṇic mythology, vi. 162
Ṣêd ("the Hunter"), sun-god, v. 54, 55, 56, 60
— -Melqart deity at Carthage, Baʿal-Hamman identical with, v. 53
— -Tanit corresponds to Melk-ʿAshtart, v. 53
— -yathon, son of Ger-Sêd, v. 390 [263]
Sedeq, Palestinian deity, vii. 40, 41; see also SYDYK.
Sedes, síd possibly cognate with, perhaps meaning "seats of the gods," iii. 49
Šêdim, class of demons in Hebrew mythology, v. 358–359, 361
Sedit [Coyote] and the Two Brothers Hus [buzzards], x. 234–235
Sedna, x. 5–6, 273 [7]
Šêdu identical with the seven devils, v. 360, 361, 363, 365
Seduction of Enkidu, v. 239–240, 241, 242
Seed, Seeds:
Seed festivals, 241–242

Seed of Gaya Maretan was gold, vi. 294, 316
— -Para, iv. 172
Seeds, forest grew magically from, xi. 313
—men and animals born of, xi. 193, 271
—of all people placed in ship of Manu, vi. 147
Seeing, incantation against, iii. 84
—power of Heaven, iv. 395
Seeland, cult of Nerthus on, ii. 28
—(Selund) sacred grove and lake, ii. 102, 181, 182
Seeress, consultation of, ii. 10
—(in " Voluspa ") remembers first war in world, ii. 27
—speaks the " Voluspa," ii. 9
Seers, iv. 263; vi. 102, 109, 140, 142, 144, 145, 146, 147, 148, 149, 150, 160, 163, 165, 166, 190, 195, 223, 224
—explain dreams, ii. 234, 372 ³
Seesaw (balance of souls), x. 253
Sefkhet 'Abui, meaningless epithet replacing name of Sekha(u)it, xii. 54, 373 ⁵⁹
Segda son of sinless couple, iii. 81
Segen-Sebdek-Tengeri, iv. 411
Segesta, goddess of the sprouting grain, i. 300
Segovesi, Justin's allusion to guidance of the, by birds, iii. 13
Seia, goddess of sowing grain, i. 300
Seides believed dedicated to spirit of famous men, iv. 139
—of Lapps, iv. 100–112, 191
—offerings to, to obtain luck in hunting and fishing, iv. 178, 191
Seimia, title of mother-goddess, as Athene, v. 22, 56, 59
Seimios, Syrian deity, v. 383 ¹⁰⁸
Seirenes (Sirens, " bewitching ones "), i. 262–263
Še'îrim (" Hairy ones " [satyrs as goats]), class of demons, v. 355, 356
Sei-ryo, Japanese name for one of Chinese world-guardians, viii. 379 ²⁸
Seistãn, Rustam hero of, vi. 332
Seizer, devil, v. 362
Sekha(i)t-hor worshipped in third nome, xii. 146
Sekha(u)it, abode of, xii. 53
—(book-goddess), xii. 200
—draws net to capture dragon, xii. 391 ⁵²

Sekha(u)it, epithets of, xii. 52–53, 54
—identifications of, xii. 53, 372 ⁵⁷
—perhaps old local god of Nekhbet, xii. 53
—registers king's name on celestial tree, xii. 53 (fig. 51)
—stellar explanation of, xii. 372 ⁵⁶
—symbols of, xii. 53
Sekhmet, Astarte confused with, xii. 411 ¹⁰
—attacks companions of Sêth, xii. 381 ⁴³
—leontocephalous goddess, xii. 146–147
—overpowers Sêth, xii. 127
—(" Powerful One "), origin of, xii. 75
—regarded as solar goddess, xii. 29
—Tefênet identified with, xii. 87
——Pekhet, and Ubastet manifestations of a single deity, xii. 217
—Ubastet often identified with, xii. 140, 150
Sek-ya Min, Lord of Supernatural Weapons, presented magic drum to Lan-yein and A-mong, xii. 282, 284
—see INDRA OF INDIAN OLYMPOS, ETC.
—(Skt. Śakra) aids Titha-yaza to build Tha-tun, xii. 285
Sela convinced of truth of nature of Buddha by his marks, vi. 196
Sè-lan, Udibwa married daughter of ruler of, xii. 276
Selene, Hekate identified with, v. 369
—lunar divinity, i. 187
—(Moon), i. 244–245
—Sekha(u)it apparently identified with, xii. 372 ⁵⁷
—torch-race in honour of, x. 37
Seleucids, admiration of Tigranes the Great for, vii. 36
Seleukia, Bishop of, vi. 175
Self-emasculation of Osiris or Rê', xii. 398 ¹⁰⁶
— -mutilation of Eshmun, v. 74–75
— -sacrifice, early Greeks had clear idea of, i. 14
Selo-se-Magoma (Rough-hided One), vii. 249
Selqet as a birth-genius of Osiris, xii. 385 ¹²
—goddess, xii. 60, 147, 156 (fig. 166), 157, 158, 412 ¹³
—guards captive 'Apop, xii. 104, 110
—Isis identified with, xii. 99
— -Nephthys gathering blood from corpse of Osiris, xii. 114 (fig. 118)

Selthorir "died" into Thori's hill, ii. 310

Selwanga, python-god, with temple at Budu, vii. 271

Semagumba, descendants of, priests of Bubembe temple, vii. 130

Sema-uêr, old name of celestial bull, xii. 147, 367 [10]

Semdet(i), forgotten stellar deity, xii. 375 [77]

Sĕmĕa, Syrian deity, v. 22, 386 [175]

Semechihi, medicine-men of Arawak, xi. 261

Sĕmĕios, divine symbol, v. 37

Semektet, night ship of sun-god, xii. 27

Semele, daughter of Kadmos, i. 45–46
—ivy at shrine of, i. 217
—liberated by Dionysos from bondage in Underworld, i. 220
—mother of Dionysos in Theban legend, i. 216
—(Pers. Zamin), earth-goddess, vii. 12
—wife of Zeus and mother of Dionysos, i. 157, 217

Semi-celestial beings, viii. 266–267

Semik, summer funeral rites, iii. 237

Semiramis, vii. 68, 69, 367–368, 389 [11]
—Arlez called gods of, in Ara myth, vii. 90

Semites adopted Sumerian culture and religion, v. xvi–xvii
—influenced Iranian thought, vi. 347

Semitic deities in Armenian pantheon, vii. 16, 36–41
—people in Africa, vii. 115
—Queen of Heaven, eight-rayed star of, xii. 372 [56]
—races, geographical and linguistic distribution of, and deities, v. 1–87

Semlicka Mänes, Lettish name for October, iii. 352 [7]

Semnai Theai, i. 277

Semneh in Nubia, Dedun worshipped at, xii. 157

Semnesmâte ("mother of Earth"), ii. 195

Semnones, sacred groves of, ii. 97, 98, 203

Semtet, goddess, xii. 147, 408 [91]

Senach the Unearthly, iii. 36

Sencha, iii. 146

Senchan, poet, iii. 211

Senecherib, king of Assyria, v. 64

Sêng ch'i, life breath, viii. 140

Senik, horse of Sun, vii. 51

Senkyō, meeting-place of Sennins, viii. 278

Sennin, viii. 219, 266, 274–280, 360

Sennins, certain plants associated with, viii. 338

Senones, coin of, iii. pl. III (1 and 7), opp. p. 14

Senotlke, serpent, x. 243

Sen-Serel bird, iv. 500

Senses, four, male personifications of, xii. 66
—lost on seeing Milhoi, vii. 412 [4]

Sentiero, spirit of boundary-stone, survival of Terminus in modern Romagnola, i. 316–317

Šentur dialectic for Nintur, v. 110

Senx, the Sun, x. 253, 254

Senzangakona, King, escaped Spirits by means of a rope to ascend to Heaven, vii. 135

Sepa: see SOP, ETC.

Separation of Heaven and earth, vii. 124; see also SKY, RAISING OF.

Sepharvites, v. 72

Septe Cidade: see CIBOLA, SEVEN CITIES OF.

Sepulchres in fields or at corner of house for converse with devil, suggest ancestral shrines, xi. 224
—of Melqart, Melicertes, Marduk, and Ba'al, v. 52

Seqbet, the leontocephalous goddess, xii. 409 [100]

Sequoya invented Cherokee alphabet, x. 70

Ser, explained as Osiris; localized at Heliopolis, xii. 147

Serapeums, principal temples or burial-places of Osiris, xii. 114

Seraphim, vision of the, v. 98

Serapis chief Graeco-Egyptian deity, xii. 242
—cult of, advanced only slowly among native Egyptians, xii. 239
—(Osor-ḥap, "Osiris-Apis"), origin of, xii. 98, 386 [19], 412 [5]

Series Irra, v. 137

Seriphos, Danaë and her son drift to shores of, i. 33

Serpens and Aquila, close connexion between, v. 170–171

Serpent, xii. 403 [18]
—(Ahi), form of demon Vṛtra, vi. 62

Serpent and eagle, alliance and strife between, v. 168–173
——Rêʿ, myth of, merged with conflict between Horus and Sêth, xii. 107
——tortoise emblems of Huyen-vu, xii. 307, 308
——tree of life, v. 177, 179, 402 [9]
—appeared over head of Abhayākara, vi. 210
—apron, xi. pl. v, opp. p. 46
—around sun-god's spear symbolizes fiery rays of sun, xii. 397 [101]
—as creator of dry land, ix. 105
—emblem of all goddesses, xii. 166, 408 [95]
——rainbow, x. 139; xi. 68
——symbol of earth-goddess, v. 32, 385 [150]
—(Asbet), xii. 131
—associated with Ḥapet and other goddesses, xii. 387 [23]
——late representation of Anubis or Ophoïs, xii. 240
— -ball, legend, iii. 14
— -being, half human, born to woman who released spirit of lake, xi. 272
—bow of Śiva a, vi. 111
—crystal in head of Horned, x. 69, 284 [27], 300 [50]
—cult of household, iii. pl. xxxvii, opp. p. 304
—deities, v. 78, 90
——in Malay Archipelago due to Indian influence, ix. 242
—direct worship of the, vi. 96
—double-headed, xi. 72
— -dragon Tiâmat (female), foe of sun-god, v. 282
—drives heavenly gods from earth, xii. 79, 84
—earth thrown on head of primeval, becomes world, ix. 159–160, 161, 169, 328 [20]
—Erechtheus has feet like, i. 68
—Erwand probably son of, vii. 80
—fed by harvesters, xii. 16
—four sons of Horus united with, xii. 112
—Genius in form of, i. pl. lx, opp. p. 290
— -ghost, vii. 74–76
—Gilgamish associated with, v. 235
—Gitche Manito in Hiawatha myth a, x. 285 [28]

Serpent, God B connected with, xi. 139, 140
—great, Sêth fights against, xii. 107
— -guardians, xii. 166–167, 187 (fig. 194), 188
—guarding tree of life, v. 179
—Ḥar-teḥen sometimes has head of, xii. 388 [28]
—hatched eggs containing boy and girl, ix. 109
— -heads on shoulders of Typhon, i. 9
—hieroglyph of, as class-sign for all goddesses, xii. 102
—in Adam and Eve story, v. 183 ff.
——Glaukos story, i. 62
——hiding for one hundred years, vii. 392 [21]
——various mythologies, xii. 301
—Indra likened to, vi. 41
—Kekrops part man part, i. 66
—killed by Arthur, iii. 195
——cat-god under heavenly tree, xii. 106
——storm-god, viii. 228
— -king, xii. pl. vii (1), opp. p. 272
—King, vii. 30
—magic ring from mouth of, ix. 163
—Midgard-: see MIDGARD-SERPENT.
—motif, Indian origin of, in Indonesian creation-myth, ix. 328 [20]
—mythological, Meḥen the, xii. 135
—numbers, xi. 151, pl. xxii, opp. p. 152
—obtained plant of eternal youth and was rejuvenated, v. 226, 227, 228
—of cedar, v. 316
——Deep (Ahi Budhnya), vi. 37, 89
——Garden of Eden cursed by Yāw, v. 185
——Underworld, xii. 240, 369 [24]
——waters slain by Thunderer, x. 24
—on Gaulish coins and monuments, iii. plate ii (10), opp. p. 8, iii (3)(?), opp. p. 14, v, opp. p. 40, x, opp. p. 94, 158
——Seta bridge, viii. 314
—Osiris connected with a great, xii. 391 [43]
—plumed, x. 188, 243; xi. 68, 161, 226
—Qêb has head of, xii. 42
— -raft, xi. 70
—Renenutet as, xii. 66
—saved by Sun Ssŭ-miao, viii. 106

Serpent: see also items s.v. AZHI
DAHĀKA; ḌAḤḤĀK; DRAGON; NĀGAS;
SNAKE.
—seized magic plant of rejuvenation, iii.
131
—seizing, incantation against, v. 227
—(Śeṣa or Ananta) on which Viṣṇu
rests, vi. 120, pl. XI, opp. p. 120
— -shape frequently chosen by a ghost
for reappearance, vii. 193
—Shay in form of, xii. 52
—shows plant of life, vii. 390 14
—skirt, xi. 74
—sky-, cause of flood, ix. 180–181
—sons, Kadrū received a thousand, vi.
139
—source of fire and bringer of it, ix.
116, 121
—sprang into Conall's belt, iii. 131
—stands in close relation to the ghost,
vii. 72–73
—stays flood, ix. 120
— -steed, x. 24
—stone image of, at Shwe Zīgōn Pagoda, xii. 271
—sun-god, and Isis, myth of, xii. 79–
84
—symbol of Asklepios, i. 281, 301
———deity, xii. 301
———god of medicine, also generative
and healing powers of earth, v. 74,
77
—three-headed, six-mouthed, slain by
Thraētaona, vi. 36
— -torch, xi. 60
—tribes of sea, belief in, viii. 271
—uncanny power of, viii. 325, 331–333
—west wind had head or body of, xii.
65
—White, tale of, viii. 158–160
—whose tail burned like torch, saviour
of fire, ix. 115, 116
— -worship, vi. 155; xii. 270–273, 301–
302, 306, 327
—Zeus assumes form of, i. 223
Serpentarius, Bês corresponds to, xii. 61
—(Ophiuchos), constellation, xii. 61
Serpents, ii. pl. VI. opp. p. 32; 94, 105,
133, 225; iii. 325; v. 77, 78, 89, 90,
103, 111, 127, 130, 151, 179; vii. 148–
149, 169, 412 4, 424 10; viii. 29, 31,
203; x. 52, 114–115, 300 50–301; xii.
25, 29, 131, 132, 136, 137, 141, 151,
301

Serpents and three hearts of son of the
Morrígan, iii. 132
—as ancestral spirits, reside in and protect old home, vii. 73
———fertility emblems, xi. 350 9
—carved on old gravestones, vii. 75
—danger from, averted by declaring
friendship for their various tribes, vi.
203
—destroyer (Thor) of, ii. 75
—destruction of, in relation to Bês, xii.
62, 63, 64
—Devs as, vii. 87
—driven away by leaves of nīm-tree,
vi. 239
—fed on human brains, vi. 320, 322
—fire-spitting, slay dragon, vii. 45
—infesting lochs, etc., and as guardians
of trees, iii. 129–130, 131, 132
—intermediaries communicating with
Powers Below, x. 22
—licked place where soma rested and so
became forked tongued, vi. 140
—Nāgas described as, vi. 154
—on pagodas, xii. 272
———shoulders of Aždahak teaching him
divination, vii. 99
—people turned into, to sleep, ix. 117
—poisonous, in Libya, grew from drops
of blood from Gorgon's head, i. 34
—representations of, at Buddhistic and
Japanese festivals, xii. 301–302
—scales of, marks made by Sun's club,
xi. 273
—sent by Hera to destroy Herakles,
and variant version, i. 79
—signs of earth-goddesses, xi. 74
—soul of every god in, xii. 129
—spirits embodied in, xii. 361 1 (ch. i)
—strangled by Herakles, vii. 45
—swallow souls and carry them to
a land of pleasure, xi. 279
—terra-cotta plaques with, found at
Ānanda, xii. 271
—two, beneath foundations of Vortigern's city, iii. 200
—with rams' heads, iii. 132, pl. VIII, opp.
p. 72
Serungal and Rajah's daughter, tale of,
ix. 216–218
Servants, Hermes divinity of, i. 192
—to gods, men as, xi. 90
Servitors of Huitzilopochtli, young men
as, xi. 61

Śeşa, serpent, vi. 120, 155

Sescind Uairbeoil, three goblins of, iii. 148

Śeşnāg (old Śeşa), worshipped by Nāgas, vi. 241

Sessrumnir, hall of Freyja, ii. 120, 314

Sestos, home of Hero, i. 202

Seta, bridge of, Tōda found serpent on, vii. 314

Setanta (afterwards known as Cúchulainn), iii. 83, 84, 141–142, 157

Setantii, Celtic tribes in Britain, iii. 157

Sètawn Sam, town built by Min Shwe Thè, xii. 276

Setebos, Devil, xi. 332

Śetek (or Śotek), comparable in meaning with Dĕd or Dĕduška, resembling small boy with claws, iii. 244, pl. XXIX, opp. p. 244

Seth = Alagar = Alaparos, Hebrew patriarch, v. 205

Sêth, xii. 155

—and Horus, Isis in combat of, xii. 126–127

—animal, head of, on staves borne by Egyptian gods, xii. 12–13, 389 32

—Anubis son (or, rarely, brother) of, xii. 111

—as a component of proper names, xii. 392 54

—Babi fiend parallel to, xii. 131

—Bebon (Babys) synonymous with, in Greek period, xii. 131

—begotten by Qêb and Nut, xii. 69

—brother of Horus and Osiris, xii. 103, 114, 394 71

——Isis, xii. 210

—comes from " golden city " of Ombos, xii. 365 21

—companions of, attacked by Sekhmet, xii. 381 43

—confused with 'Apop, and serpent of Underworld with Sêth-'Apop, xii. 107, 108–109, 403 18

——Bês, xii. 376 82

—cuts body of Osiris in pieces, xii. 114, 115

—develops into a Satan, xii. 109, 196, 207

—earthly reign of, listed by Turin Historical Papyrus, xii. 399 108

—evil spirit Maga son or double of, xii. 111

—fate of, xii. 72–73

Sêth, god of thunder-storms and clouds, xii. 45, 103–104

—Horus of Hierakonpolis contrasted with, xii. 387 27

—(identified with Sobk), conquest of, by Horus, supposed to be symbolized by feather, xii. 362 8

—in animal form, explanation of, perhaps influenced killing of Adonis by boar, xii. 399 111

——Osirian cycle, xii. 102–104, 107–110, 114–118, 124–125, 126–127

——some prehistoric period god of entire pantheon, xii. 389 32

—member of ennead of Heliopolis, xii. 216

—Nephthys as wife of, xii. 110

—often appears as crocodile, xii. 398 102

—oldest pictures of, xii. 102, 103 (figs. 98, 99)

—perhaps confused with Horus, xii. 391 47

—planet Mercury sometimes dedicated to, xii. 55, 373 63

—solar eye of Osiris torn into many parts in combat with, xii. 90

—sun-god loses one eye in combat with, xii. 29

—symbolized by red or brown animals or reptiles, xii. 196

—variant forms and pronunciations of name of, xii. 389 31

—watchful dragon lurking in the lower world, xii. 141

—wears asp on his head, xii. 88

—worshipped as nome-god and also in Delta, xii. 389 32

——Typhon, adversary of Osiris, xii. 59, 209

——late identification of, with Ursa Major, xii. 59

Set-Sutek, god of thunder and lightning, v. 46

Setting Sun, Village of Souls on Mountains of the, x. 132

Seuēchorus, king of Babylonians, v. 234

—rescued from the flood, ix. 40

Seven decrees of Heaven and earth, v. 159

—deities may have been genii of the seven planets, vii. 17

—demons (devils), v. 106, 361, 364, 373

—devils, šêdu identical with, v. 361

Seven elders assigned to different cities, v. 140
—fates are three Moirae of Greece, v. 22
—gates must be passed to enter Hades, v. 328–329, 330, 331, 334
—gods, vii. 17, 18, 381 [1] (ch. ii)
——are seven weapons of Irra, v. 138, 142, 145, 146, 147
——closed Arallû against the dead, v. 167
——of fates, v. 308
—number, perhaps avoided as unlucky, xii. 384 [115]
—planets, Tammuz summoned king to worship, v. 337
—significance of, in beliefs on world-pillars, iv. 338–339
—Things left by sons of Carman, iii. 36
—winds created, v. 300
—wise men, v. 139, 140, 141, 236
——ones, images of, v. 84
Sevenfold terror decreed for Humbaba, v. 247
Seventy-seven eyes and ears attributed to a cosmic deity, xii. 223
— -two as cosmic number, xii. 395 [75]
Severn, temple of Nodons on, iii. 103
Sewer, Kei a, iii. 199
Sex, x. 187, 206
—changed in womb by Juksakka, iv. 254
—foretold, divination by the means of which, xi. 312
—of deities, v. 4, 5, 14, 36, 108, 115, 202, 381 [58], 381 [108]; viii. 67, 195–196; ix. 48, 275
——sun, ii. 183, 184
———moon, and stars, vii. 226, 227, 228, 229
Sexes, separation of, in world below, x. 160–161, 163, 204
Sexual intercourse of sacred animals with women, probable origin of Classical stories of, xii. 164
—organs play part in sacrifice to Veralden-olmai, iv. 250–251
Sgana quedas is Haida designation of animals as werefolk or man-beings, x. 252
Sgáthach, Fionn offered to wed, iii. 172
Sgathan ripped open caul of Cian, iii. 132
Sgeolan, hound of Fionn, iii. 126, 169, 172
Sgilti Light-Foot, iii. 189

Sha-animal, Egyptian name for animal of Sêth, xii. 389 [33]
Sha-ch'iu (modern P'ing-hsiang), viii. 39
Shaddai, Hebrew title of El of Gebal, v. 66, 67, 70, 392 [325]
Shade, birth of a, ix. 174
—haunts grave or goes to abode of ghosts, vii. 179
—lives in Underworld as long as its predecessor on earth, iv. 73
Shades, by sacrifice Odysseus calls up, iii. 16
—gratified by blood, i. 88
—nature of, i. 141, 142
—of wicked are demons, v. 162
—swimming in Abyss, xii. 180 (fig. 188)
Shadow, abode of, iv. 7
—bhūt has no, vi. 247
—costume of shaman his, iv. 519, 522
—Devil born of God's, iv. 321
—double, soul, three synonyms distinguished, xii. 174
—(in Ostiak song) ascends into heaven, and returns, iv. 6
—lost in dreams, sickness, or death, iv. 472
—of child falling on object conditions its name, iv. 504
——sacrifice, iv. 268
——shaman may go to Underworld to seek aid, iv. 6, 27
—ogres cast no, xii. 294
—or image of sun and moon, iv. 223
——shape of deceased, iv. 5–6, 7
—original meaning of shadow-soul, iv. 12
— = soul, iii. 228
— -soul, iv. 12, 13, 472–482
—soul identified with the, in New Empire, xii. 174
— -souls may be transformed into tutelary genii of persons, iv. 10, 11, 14
— -Swallower, monster judge of dead, xii. 176, 179 and fig. 186, 391 [43], 417 [18]
Shadows, x. 11, 78–79, 146, 190, 262, 276 [12], 306 [60]
—ancestral spirits defined as, vii. 180
—images of shaman, iv. 42
—or images, primal ancestors, shamans, or heroes survive their bodies as, iv. 13

Shadows taken by shamans to other-world, iv. 39
Shaft, air, home of household deity, viii. 80
Shagan, title of Nergal, v. 136
Shahan, fire, title of serpent-god, v. 90, 151; see also s.v. SHAHAN (vol. v, p. 450).
Shahapet of localities, vii. 74–76
Shahar, moon-god, v. 4, 5, 7
Shahdidi, goddess from Libya, xii. 157
"Shāhnāmah," vi. 259–260
Shahrináz, vi. 323
Shai'haqaum, occurrence of Ba'al Sha-mîn with god, v. 63
Shaking releases soul of sacrificial ob-jects, iv. 14
Shakuru, the Sun, x. 87–90, 91
Shala, consort of Adad, v. 67
Shālēm (Salim), ancient name of Jeru-salem, v. 45
Shal-Jime, ruler of infants and those dying happily, iv. 367
Shalmān identical with ancient name of Jerusalem, v. 45
Shalman (Shalmon), Reshpu-Shara-mana identified with, xii. 155
Shalmanassar, v. 388 216
Shalmanassar II, v. 153
Shaman as finder of lost souls, iv. 474
— -bird becomes flame of fire, iv. 495
—continues his calling in hereafter, iv. 483, 488
—dress of, iv. pl. LVIII, opp. p. 494; see also COSTUMES, SHAMAN.
—in form of reindeer carrying dead, iv. 485
——Underworld, iv. 6
—laying of ghost which was changed into a Seide by a, iv. 105–106
—may not be buried in earth, iv. 481
—Mergen-khara first, iv. 477
—must appease spirits to bring back soul, iv. 76–77, 286
——conjure spirit into images, iv. 114
—(noidde) the, iv. 282–295
—Odin in one aspect resembles, ii. 47
—of Heaven and Underworld, iv. pl. XXVII, opp. p. 224
—owl a, iv. 504
—Permian belief that storm arose on death of, iv. 17
— -pillars, iv. 334 (fig. 13), pl. XLVI, opp. p. 400

Shaman, Shamanism, x. 5, 7, 79, 146, 147, 169, 215, 243, 247, 262, 270 5–271
—soul of, travels with Thunderer, iv. 227
—tax paid to, iv. 282
Shamanism, iv. 496–523
Shamanistic or mediumistic rites, x. xvi
—rites at world-tree, iv. 340
Shamans, xi. 121, 122, 256–261, 350 10–351
—as spirit-birds, iv. 494–495, 509
—consulted as to responsibility for storms, iv. 442
—escort dead to otherworld, iv. 39, 286; 484, 485, 510
—images of shadows of, iv. 42
—may see shadow-souls, iv. 473
—only immortal, iv. 70
—power of, to converse with the urt, iv. 11
—sat at entrance to dwelling on Christ-mas night, iv. 66
—spectres of, liable to metamorphosis, iv. 11
—survive their bodies as shadows or images, iv. 13
—trance of, iv. 27, 282, 285–286
Shamash as god of divination, purifica-tion, Light, and patron of law, v. 63, 150
—destruction of, prophesied, v. 141
—Enlil identified with, v. 63
—four-pointed star symbol of, v. 150
—god of divination in Babylonia and Assyria, v. 63, 150
—golden statue of, at Sippar, v. 150–151
—Ishtar twin sister of, v. 36
—Kettu and Misharu are the sons of, vii. 40
—Marduk identified with, v. 155
—plant of birth belongs to, vi. 283
—(sun), vii. 11
— -Sun, Aries station of, v. 304
—sun-god, v. 2, 39, 41, 55, 60, 64, 65, 66, 67, 71, 73, 80, 134, 136, 139, 141, 148, 150, 151, 152, 168, 169, 170, 171, 172, 195, 206, 210, 213, 235, 247, 248, 249, 250, 251, 252, 253, 256, 257, 258, 259, 268, 332, 343, 351, 403 13
Shame, Temple of, xi. 107
Shamshi-Adad I, king of Assyria, built temple to Dagan, v. 80
— -Rammon, inscription of, vii. 389 10

Sham-shu (Shamsu; Šamši), phonetic pronunciation of sun-god, v. 2, 4, 377 [5] [7]

Shan, antecedents of Malay mythology perhaps to be found among, ix. 244

—kings, two first, believed to have descended from the sun, xii. 275

—mouse-deer as trickster-hero among, ix. 204

Shan Hai King, viii. 17, 103

—Hsiao, viii. 150

—Kuei, demon of mountain, viii. 90–91

—T'ung, ninth epoch, viii. 26

—Tung K'ao Ku Lu, viii. 71

Shand (sanda, sandan), "lightning," vii. 379 [1] (ch. i)

Shang, viii. 109

—and Hu sisters, tale of, viii. 156–158

—Ch'ing ("superior"), one of the Three Heavens, viii. 109, 110

—Dynasty, viii. 7, 9, 38–39, 40, 49, 66, 79, 137

—Fu, viii. 96

—Lao, one of the "Three Venerable Ones," viii. 109

—T'ai, stellar deity, viii. 89

—Ti became Yü Huang, viii. 58

——Supreme Ruler, viii. 21, 48–49, 50, 52, 58, 59, 135

Shanghai, temples at, viii. 72, 73

Shannon crossed on Bran's body by his followers, iii. 101

—swineherds as water beasts a year in, iii. 58

Shans drive into hills Chams and remnant of Khas, and occupy their territory, xii. 287–288

—see LAO-TAI CARRY, ETC.

—Siamese, origin of, xii. 277

Shansi, viii. 80, 124

Shantung, viii. 11, 29, 70

Shao Hao, viii. 99

—Lin Temple, viii. 188–189

—Tao, Emperor, viii. 99

—yang, viii. 137

—yin, viii. 137

Shapes of Śiva, vi. 112–113

Shapeshifting, i. 16, 92; ii. 35, 46, 47, 54, 123, 140, 142, 144, 146, 179, 206, 210, 211, 217, 229, 245, 259, 260–263, 266, 277, 279, 287, 291, 292, 293; iii. 13, 40, 56–58, 59, 63, 64, 70, 71, 75, 78–79, 81, 111, 112, 124, 144, 154, 168, 189, 193, 228, 245, 251, 258, 259, 261,
266; iv. 199, 202, 286; 327, 328, 362, 363, 440, 441, 466, 477, 485, 501; vi. 30, 75, 76, 80, 121, 138, 152, 156, 166, 172, 204, 218, 242; 268, 269, 270, 291, 365 [4]; vii. 121, 177, 201, 213, 214, 251, 266, 279, 319, 340, 344, 345, 414 [25]; viii. 158, 159; ix. 45, 47, 55, 56, 60, 76, 79, 117, 138, 141, 206–210, 212, 213, 214, 216, 218–220, 233, 255, 256, 258–259, 261, 262; x. 30, 66, 103, 114, 137–138, 198, 243, 277 [13], 301 [50]; xi. 86, 274, 286, 328–329, 336; xii. 52, 117, 126, 272, 303; see also METAMORPHOSIS; TRANSFORMATION.

Shapeshifting by Nāgas, xii. 272

—divine, combined with Celtic idea of rebirth in Welsh and Irish tales, iii. 56–57

—divinities have gift of, iii. 57, 71, 79

—Merlin's, iii. 201

—of Taliesin, iii. 109, 111, 112

Shara, god who refused to kill Zû, v. 102

—hero, vii. 67

Sharabdâ (slanderer [?]), v. 163

Sharamana (Reshpu-), identified with Shalman or Shalmon, xii. 155

Shargalisharri, king of Agade, seal of, v. 98

Shargaz, weapon of Ninurta called god, v. 115, 128

Sharis (Ishtar), vii. 11, 71, 383 [31]

Shark, ix. 64, 71, 72, 123–124, 258, 259

—and ape, tale of, ix. 193

——man, Same-bito is the, viii. 381 [10]

Sharp-cutting Lord, genius of the weapon, viii. 230

Sharpshooter god, iv. 406

Sharrapu, West Semitic deity, identified with Nergal, v. 49

Sharshar, Mt., devastated, v. 145

Sharur (the cyclone), weapon of Ninurta called god, v. 115, 118, 119, 120, 126, 128

Shas-ḥetep, Khnûm(u) deity of, xii. 135

Shatshektsche, iv. 258

Shavings, motif of discovery through, iii. 178

—of lime-bark, omens from, iv. 270–280

Shawabtiu ("procurers of food"), earlier orthography for ushebtiu, xii. 416 [13]

Shawl, iv. 96

Shay ("Fate"), male counterpart of birth-goddess, xii. 52

—identified with Agathodaimon, takes form of serpent, xii. 52

—of Dandur, xii. 171

—Rê'-Hor identified with, xii. 221

Shaytan crowded out eclipse dragon, vii. 392 21

Shê and Shê chi altars, sacrifices on, viii. 61, 62

Sheaf, emblem of Demeter, i. 233

She-cat probably honoured at Bubastos, xii. 164

Shears of fate, v. 20

Shed, Khaturi Semitic name of, xii. 165

Sheddîm, Lîlith mother of all, v. 363

Shedet(i), xii. 165 (fig. 173)

— -Krokodilopolis, Sobk worshipped at, xii. 148, 408 99

Sheep and goat as messengers, vii. 165

—boys and girls impersonate, at festival for increasing, iv. 259–260

—burning of, v. 156

— -fructifier, iv. 259

—halter, old woman's, rainbow as, iv. 444

—head of, on door of temple of Beltis, v. 323

—of Ntotwatsana, vii. 248

—prohibition against hurting, xii. 362 3

—venomous, loosed by King of Lochlann, iii. 63

—white, viii. 154

——cast into Loch Riach become crimson, iii. 38

—worshipped at full moon, vi. 239

Sheikh Manamana, boatmen make offerings to, vii. 411 46

Shelartish, secondary Urartian moon-god, vii. 11

Shell beads: see COLOUR SYMBOLISM; JEWELS OF THE QUARTERS.

—cowry, lost, vii. 250

— -dust, xi. 208, 209

—universe as a, ix. 14

Shells, xi. 32, 33

Shĕmōna, eight, v. 74

Shemtet, lioness-headed goddess, xii. 147

Shemti as variant of 'Apop, xii. 391 51

"Shên Hsien Chuan," viii. 144, 145

——T'ung Chien, viii. 29, 96, 110, 196

—I, King, viii. 130

—Nung, second Emperor, viii. 25, 26, 27, 28, 29, 30–31, 55, 62, 94

Shemti, Pao popular name of Lao Tzŭ as sovereign of Highest Heaven, viii. 110

Shenazzar, Sumerian name of moon-god occurs in, v. 6

Shenet, goddess probably identical with Shentet, xii. 147–148, 408 95

Shêng, viii. 108, 134

Shensi, viii. 60, 80, 106

Shentet, goddess, xii. 148

Sheol, v. 355

Shepherd and man alternate in liturgical formula, v. 345–346

—Bati-Osiris as, xii. 399 111

—bearing ram, myth of, v. 61

—Boy, viii. 132

—Pan a, i. 268

Sheput, local name of Êpet, xii. 376 79

Sherah, Shahan (Mush), serpent-deity, v. 90

Sherisha, shadows, vii. 180

Shesemtet (Sebshesen, etc.), companion of Sheshmu, xii. 58–59, 375 76

—lion-headed (?) deity, xii. 59, 375 76

—once powerful divinity, later disappears, xii. 59, 375 76

Sheshmu, companion of Shesemtet, xii. 58–59, 375 76

—functions of, xii. 58, 203, 375 75

—representation of, xii. 58

Sheshmu (constellation), old deity of last hour of night, xii. 58

Shesmet, possibly alluded to in hymn on apotheosis of king, xii. 422 17

Shes-Shes, crocodile, in connexion with battle against 'Apop, xii. 109

Sheta (in the Delta?), Khasti worshipped at, xii. 134

Shetani, vii. 250

Shibegeni-Burkhan, creator, iv. 375, 376

Shichi Fukujin, Deities of Good Fortune, viii. 279–280

Shield as ship, ii. 157

— -god, Ull is, ii. 156

— -lay, ii. 181

— -maids, ii. 256

—of Manannan (afterwards of Fionn) made from tree split by Balor's head, iii. 33, 175

—sacred, carried before army, iii. 283

—stone, ii. 82, 83

— -tower, Brynhild bound in a, ii. 251

Shields of Erin, famous, iii. 33

Shih Chi, viii. 7, 31, 62, 66, 145, 199

—Chou Chi, viii. 117

Shih Hu Tz'ŭ, viii. 76
—Huang, Emperor, viii. 10, 70, 81, 89, 93, 114, 115, 134, 145, 146
—Kan, viii. 153
—King, viii. 62
—liu, viii. 105
—P'i, tale of, viii. 171–173
Shiju-gara, tit, viii. 334
Shikoko, such names as "So and So Horse" occur in, viii. 210
Shikoku, Kōbō drove the foxes from island of, viii. 252
Shikomé, viii. 224
Shimbei, heron, viii. 334
Shimti ("Fate"), title of Ishtar, v. 21, 22, 23, 383 [104], 384 [110] [123]
Shimtu, fate, Marduk determines, v. 300
Shin Ne Mi, niece of the Mahāgiri Nāt, xii. 340, 342
Shinab, Sumerian names of moon-god occur in, v. 6
Shindwe Hla: see SHWE MYET-HNA.
Shinto, viii. 212, 215, 216, 221, 222, 247, 256, 264, 267, 279, 316, 341, 342, 381 [1]
Ship, Ships:
Ship assists dead to sail to Heaven, xii. 175
—-building, certain trees in, ii. 204
—Dionysos in the, i. pl. XLIX, opp. p. 224
—in tale of Burkhan and the flood, iv. 361
—-interment, ii. 15, 130, pl. XVI, opp. p. 130, 135
—made from dead men's nails, ii. 159
—magic, of Phaiakians bore Odysseus to his home-land, i. 138
—of Alkinoös turned to stone by Poseidon, i. 211
——Frey: see SKIDBLADNIR.
——sun lifted by Nuu from depths in the morning, xii. 95
——Ull, ii. 157
—on which Balder's pyre is set, ii. 128
—Oseberg (tumulus), ii. pl. XVI, opp. p. 130, pl. XXX, opp. p. 230
—possible meaning of, in the Dionysos-myth, i. 330 [5] (ch. ix)
—-shaped shrine of gods in procession, xii. 194
—symbol of lunar, xi. 235
—winged, of Aśvins, vi. 31

Ships and sailors, Poseidon protector of, i. 212
——warriors on sculptured stone, ii. pl. XVII, opp. p. 138
—Brownies of, ii. 204
—ceremonial, taking great gods to Marduk's temple, v. 157
—figure-heads on, ii. 229
—Odin protects, ii. 42–43
—tossing till sails touch sky, ii. 361 [3]
—two different, of sun-god, xii. 27
Shipololo, "Place of Fog," x. 199, 206
Shippawn Ayawng, first ancestor of southern fringe of Kachins, xii. 264; see also THAGYA MIN.
Shipwreck caused by Thor, ii. 76, 77
Shirak in proverb, vii. 67
Shirt of Dunlaing taken from síd of Cruachan, iii. 69
Shitkur, the devil, iv. 361–362
Shivering in back when lost soul returns, iv. 475
—of sacrificial animal, iv. 14, 148, 211, 264, 269, 270
—releases soul, iv. 14
Shiwanni and Shiwanokia, x. 206
Shizuka, mistress of Yoshitsune, viii. 307, 312
Shka(j)-bavas or Shki-pas, "procreator," Mordvins generally address "god dwelling on high" (Vere-pas) as, iv. 219
Shōbu, flower of boy's doll-festival, viii. 349–350, 386 [12]
Shoe, Hel-, ii. 305
Shoes, iv. 10, 19, 50
—magic, ii. 149, 267
—of Vidarr, ii. 159, 160
—provided for dead, ii. 305
—that were danced to pieces, vii. 358
Shōjō, probably idealized personification of orang-outang, viii. 273–274, pl. XLII, opp. p. 348
Shōki, sort of Japanese archangel Michael, viii. 285–286
Sholmo, Shulmus, Shulman, iv. 315, 320, 376, 420
Shooting star, iv. 395; x. 223
——song of, viii. 373
Shot of Midir's eye in Brug na Boinne, iii. 41
Shotshen, iv. 258
Shou, viii. 150
—Hsing, god of longevity, viii. 81–82

Shou Mountain, viii. 34
—Shih Shu, viii. 142
Shoulder, ivory, of Pelops and his descendants, i. 119
— -soul, xii. 39
Shoulderblade, Mongol seer prophesying from, iv. pl. LIV, opp. p. 470
Showers of water, fire, and gems, iii. 32
Shōzu-ga no Baba, guardian of crossroads of souls, viii. pl. XII, opp. p. 240
Shrew-mouse, xii. 160, 165
Shrimps, ix. 182
Shrine of Semele, i. 217
—small portable, xii. 194 (fig. 205)
Shrines, viii. 246–247, pl. xv, opp. p. 246, 269–271, 279, 304
—for spirits, vii. pl. XVI, opp. p. 182
—in temples, v. 30–31
Shrove Tuesday, straw dolls on, iv. 248
Shtabai, serpentiform demons, xi. 141
Shu, xii. 68, 69, 78 (fig. 77), 87 (fig. 78)
—and Khnûm, Ḥeḥ equated with, xii. 381 [49]
——Tefênet associated with birth of sun-god, xii. 70, 71
——daily restore the sun's eye from ocean to world, xii. 89–90
——space of air between Heaven and earth, created by sun, xii. 50
—as separator of two principal parts of world, xii. 50
——supporter of sky and sun, xii. 44, 366 [7]
—avoidance of leonine form in pictures of cosmic function of, xii. 44
—blended with Ḥeḥ (Infinite Space), xii. 44, 65 (fig. 71), 369 [26]
——Horus, xii. 44
—called into consultation by Rê‘, xii. 74
—causes growth of plants, xii. 45
—celestial lion, xii. 43 and fig. 37, 45
—created by Khepri, xii. 68, 69
—Eri-ḥems-nofer compared with, xii. 133, 404 [27]
—ethereal space separating earth and ocean from Heaven, xii. 44
—etymology of name, xii. 369 [25 26]
—god of air, xii. 66
—Ḥeka identified with, xii. 27 (fig. 10), 44 (fig. 39), 133

Shu identified with An-ḥôret of This, xii. 44
——lunarized god Khôns(u) at Thebes, xii. 44
—in solar ship, xii. 96
—Khnûm soul of, xii. 219
—Leontopolis local place of worship of, xii. 44
—member of ennead of Heliopolis, xii. 216
—Mi-ḥos identified with, xii. 137
—Mîn son of, xii. 139
—Onuris identified with, xii. 143–144
—origin and solarization of, xii. 44, 369 [26]
—perhaps compared with An-ḥôret (Onuris), xii. 383 [103]
—places himself under heavenly cow Nut, xii. 77–78, 381 [47]
—representation of, xii. 44 and fig. 39
—standing on ocean (?), upholds Nut (sky), xii. 43 (fig. 38)
— -Tefênet, Amen-Rê‘ perhaps identified with, xii. 221
—Tefênet's brother, sent to bring her back to Egypt, xii. 86
—Ung treated like, xii. 151
—with four feathers, xii. 369 (fig. 222)
Shu, viii. 82, 94, 139, 174, 175, 179
— -jaku, Japanese name for one of Chinese world-guardians, viii. 379 [28]
—King, viii. 33, 35, 37, 39, 44, 47, 49, 109
—Yü and Yü Lei, guardians of the portal, viii. 78, 105
Shuanna, v. 143
Shubat: see SHVOD.
" Shuh I Chi," viii. 58
Shui Chün, ruler of water, viii. 73
—I, god of waters, viii. 90
—Jung, Ch'êng Huang interpreted as identical with, viii. 67–68, 69
—King, viii. 17, 100, 114
—Kung, viii. 106
—ma, mythic water-horse, viii. 104
—Shên, god of waters, viii. 90
Shullat (Shamash), v. 274
Shulmān, city, v. 45
Shulmanîtu, Ishtar of Assur called, v. 45, 46
Shulmānu (Selamanēs), deity, v. 45
Shulpae (= Enlil) husband of Mah, v. 110, 114
—Marduk called, in Irra myth, v. 144

Shun, Emperor, viii. 20, 33, 34, 35–36, 37, 44, 47, 51, 61, 89, 161
" Shuo Wên," viii. 140
Shuqamuna and Shumaliya, twin gods of battle, v. 115, 397 [77]
Shura (Furious Spirit), viii. 287–288; see also ASURAS.
Shuräle, evil being which can increase or diminish height, iv. 467, 468
Shuruppak, excavations at, v. 1
—(mod. Fara), principal event of Flood at; also city of Aradda, v. 140, 204, 206, 207, 218
—texts containing early Sumerian pantheon come from, v. 92
Shushinak identified with Ninurta, v. 117
Shuswap interpretation of " Old One " and Coyote tales, x. 142–143
Shut, rare name for Tefênet, xii. 148
Shuten Dōji, tale of, viii. 306–307
Shvaz guardian of fields, vii. 75
Shvod, guardian of house, vii. 75, 76, 391 [6]
Shwe Byin, brother-Nāts, xii. 340
—Laung Min, son of an old king of Pagān, xii. 353
—Myet-hna, sister of the Mahāgiri Nāt, xii. 340, 342, 346, 347
—Na Be, wife of the Mahāgiri Nāt, xii. 340, 342
—Pyin-gyi and Shwe Pyin-ngè, children of Byat Ta and a giantess, xii. 349–353
—Pyin Nāts, death of, at Kutywa, xii. 350–351
——Naungdaw Nāt, xii. 348, pl. xix, opp. p. 348
—Zīgōn Pagoda, stone image of serpent and also the thirty-seven Nāts at, xii. 271, 340
Si (Moon), xi. 223
—An, temple of, xi. 235
S(i)a in solar ship, xii. 96
Siabhra, elves, phantoms, iii. 38, 46, 60, 193
Siamese-Chinese legends affect Indo-Chinese mythology, xii. 257
—have no myths essentially their own, xii. 268
Sibú, supreme Being, xi. 192–193, 194
Sibyl, aroused from the dead by Odin to explain dreams, ii. 9

Sibyl of Cumae, i. 305
—prophetess, Tror married, ii. 32
Sibylline oracle causes Romans to turn to Magna Mater, i. 303
Sibzianna, constellation, v. 178
Sicily, herds of Helios located in, i. 242
Sick, ceremonies for, x. 170–171
Sickle, " feeding " of, iv. pl. xxxi, opp. p. 248, 249
—symbol of Saturnus, i. 292
Sickness, iv. 472–482, 496, 505, 507
Síd [home of fairy-folk], division of the, iii. 49–53
—magic mound equivalent of, iii. 94
Ṣîdānu (" fever "), v. 163
Siddhārtha of the Kāśyapa family, vi. 223
—Prince, royal name of the Buddha, xii. 261
Siddhi, Varuṇa's wife, vi. 137
Síde, divine or fairy-folk, iii. 38, 46, 150
Side, wife of Orion, consigned to Hades, i. 250
Sideng, daughter of Mongan, iii. 175
Sidhottr (Odin), ii. 43
Sidon, cult of Reshep in, v. 45
Sidonian Astarte identified with Syrian Kaukabhta, Greek Aphrodite, and Armenian Anahit, vii. 27
Sidskegg (Odin), ii. 161
Sidu-Hall, host of Thorhall, ii. 231
Siduri (West Semitic name of Ishtar), goddess (wine merchant), v. 210, 211, 212, 213, 216
Siegfried, ii. 170, 272
—of Japanese folk-lore, Kintarō the, viii. 290–292
Sieve (leaky vessel), Danaïds had to draw water in, i. 31
—monkey put to fetch water in, xi. 269
—the = the Pleiades, iv. 418, 430
Sif, goddess, wife of Thor, ii. 15, 21, 32, 74, 81, 141, 144, 156, 182, 221; see also SIBYL, PROPHETESS, ETC.
Sigeminne, ii. 206
Sigewîf, ii. 248, 253
Sigfadir (Odin), ii. 58
Siggeir, wolf held to be mother of, ii. 292
Sigh of victory, iii. 149
Sight, Maa (?) deity of, xii. 67
—restoration of, vi. 31; ix. 59, 318 [5]
—second, of Odin and Frigg, ii. 32

Sigi, son of Odin, from whom came the Volsungs, ii. 32, 358 [21]
Sigmund Brestisson, ii. 187
—son of Volsung, ii. 45, 66, 292, 315
Sign given by totem in hunt, vii. 279
— -posts in Underworld directing souls, iv. 77
Signification, social, of family gods, iv. 114
Signs in the sky, iv. 396
Signy, iii. 104
—sister of Sigmund, ii. 292
—wife of Alfrek, ii. 121
Sigrdrifa: see BRYNHILD, ETC.
"Sigrdrifumal," ii. 25, 46, 112, 168, 195, 220, 228, 240, 298, 319
Sigrlin, Atli woos, ii. 189
Sigrmeyjar, ii. 248
Sigrun, ii. 11
—daughter of Hogni, ii. 251, 252, 307
Śigrus, tribal appellation, vi. 63
Sigtun, ii. 29, 33, 58
Sigtyr's (Victory-god's) mountain, ii. 44, 58
Sigu, son of Makonaima, xi. 269, 270
Sigund, Earl, consecrated first cup at banquet to Odin, ii. 77
Sigurd (German Siegfried), ii. 11, 21, 42, 112, 168, 240, 251, 267, 297
—(Norse), obtained wisdom through tasting of roasted heart of Fafnir, iii. 166
Sigvat denied entrance to álfablót, ii. 227
Sigwald fled from demons, ii. 187–188
Sigyn, wife of Loki, collects snake's venom, ii. 139, 144–145, pl. XVIII, opp. p. 146, 150, 174
Sihḷû (cress, mustard), plant of rejuvenation, v. 227
Sihu the brother of Coyote, Montezuma identified with, xi. 119
Sik Sawp, the female spirit representing Heaven, xii. 263
Śikhin, forerunner of Gotama, vi. 211
Sikkūt, corruption of popular name Sakkut, v. 134, 135
Sikor slain by Stone Giant, x. 133
Siksika, x. 14
"Siksiklat," tale of, ix. 221–224
Sikulokobuzuka of the Subiya, vii. 245–246
Sikyon, Aigialeus especially prominent among people of, i. 28

Sikyon, Antiope fled to, i. 43
—Asopos River worshipped in, i. 257
—conference of gods and men at, i. 12–13
—festivals of Dionysos in, i. 221
Śilā, vi. 228
Silence during growing of crops, iv. 246, 247
Silenoi, i. 267–269
—and Maïnads, i. pl. VI, opp. p. lx
Silenos, type of, influenced by Bês, xii. 63
Silk, making of, viii. 26, 28
—never-ending roll of, viii. 315
— -worms, viii. 232, 322
Silvanio modern representative of Silvanus in Romagnola, i. 317
Silvanus, i. 293–294
—represented by Silvanio in modern Romagnola, i. 317
Silver, viii. 38
—bones of Rê', xii. 74
—citadel, vi. 116, 152
—creation of men of, i. 17
—holy pillar, iv. 340
Simeon story may parallel tale of Asita, vi. 206
Siṁhanāda, form of Mañjuśrī, vi. 213
—("Lion's Roar"), form of Dhyānibodhisattva of Gotama, vi. 212
Siṁhavaktrā, a Ḍākinī, vi. 215
Sîmî, daughter of Hadad, fate-goddess, v. 22, 386 [175]
Simmah, swallow star, v. 395 [21]
Simul, pole, ii. 184
Simulacra, dubious meaning of, in Caesar's inscription of Gaulish Mercury, iii. 9, 158, 333 [5]
Sīmurgh (Av. Saēna), bird, vi. 289, 290, pl. XXXVII, opp. p. 290, 330, 331
Sin and Shamash occur in fixed sequence, v. 58
—Ishtar daughter of moon-god, v. 329
—Marduk identified with, v. 155
—(moon), vii. 11
— -Moon, Taurus station of, v. 304, 305
—of Harran distinguished from Babylonian Sin, v. 153
—originally Zu-en, moon-god, v. 5, 6, 92, 97, 141, 150, 151, 152, 153, 154, 172, 265, 287, 329, 377 [12]–378, 378 [13] [16]
—second day of Harranian week sacred to, v. 154

Sin, temple of, at Harran, v. 153–154
Sin, Sins:
Sin, vi. 23, 29, 85
—caused by touch of devil, iv. 378, 380
——departure of fairy-help from man, iii. 257
—doctrine of original, v. 183–184, 223
—human, drives gods from earth, xii. 78
—making light in daytime a, xii. 362 ³
—of Keresãspa, vi. 327, 328
——Yima, vi. 309–311, 317
— -offering, custom of prayer by sacrifice exchanged by Frey for, ii. 113
——goat as, v. 356
——made for killing itonga-snake, vii. 194
—punishment for own or father's, v. 146
—purging of, v. 98
Sins, pardon for, xii. 298–299, 300
—see CONFESSION.
Sin-abu-šu, name emphasizing fatherhood of god, v. 7
Sînai, origin of word, v. 5–6
Sinaitic Peninsula, Ḥat-ḥôr in, xii. 410 ¹
Sinchi Rocca, second [according to one list first], Inca, xi. 249
" Šindãmaṇi," Tamil poem, speaks of a god of Brahmã-like figure, vi. 229
Sindhu (Indus), river, vi. 48, 49
—Maruts' healing-powers brought from river, vi. 39
Sindri, dwarf, maker of Odin's ring and Thor's hammer, ii. 66, 78, 265–266, 318, 319
Sínech, Midir stayed at síd of, iii. 80
Sinend went to see Connla's Well, iii. 120–121
Sinfjotli ferried to other world by Odin, ii. 45
—son of Signy, ii. 292, 315
Sinful souls, moon abode of, iii. 273
Si-ngan-fu, portrait of Ta-mo (St. Thomas ?) at, xii. 270
Singara, v. 19
Singers, Ulua known as, xi. 185
Singing, iii. 238; 307, 308, 311, 313; iv. 86–87, 97, 98, 122, 131; 461
—after death and restoration to life, vii. 210
—at bear hunt and games, iv. 86–99
——creation, x. 110
—maidens, descent of, from sky, x. 290 ³⁶

Singing millstone, vii. 328
—of animals to obtain rain, vii. 313
——fairies, nymphs, and Rusalky, iii. 255, 257, 258, 259, 262
——fire, x. 63
——Gandharvas, vi. 143
——girl in drum of Zimwi, vii. 250
——goddess, iii. 84–85
——Maruts, vi. 39
——shaman and Lapps, iv. 286, 287, 289, 291
—plants, x. 63
—sheep, vii. 248–249
—skull, ii. 169
—to remove stone, vii. 253
Sing-tu' Shrine at Hanoi, xii. 319
Sinhas, snake spirits, dead men often become, vi. 241
Sinis bound to a sapling and killed by Theseus, i. 98
—son of Poseidon, i. 211
—Theseus purified of blood of, i. 100
Sinīvālī, goddess, vi. 53, 93
Sinmora, ii. 331
Sinner condemned to die with Bêl, v. 323, 324, 325
Sinon, Trojan traitor, aids Greeks in taking Trojan citadel, i. 133
Sinope, Argonauts sail to, i. 111
Sinthgunt, goddess, ii. 18, 184
Sioux uprising of 1890, x. 150
Sipapu (Shipapo), place of emergence, x. 185, 203, 205, 210, 289 ³⁴; see also MIDDLE PLACE; ASCENT THROUGH WORLDSTOREYS.
Sippar, a centre of sun-worship, v. 4, 150, 204, 206, 207
Sipylos, Mt., home of Tantalos, i. 119
" Sir Gawayne and the Green Knight," axe game in, iii. 148
Siren (σειρήν) of the Septuagint, Hambaru used to render, vii. 91, 92
Sirens, ii. pl. XXVIII, opp. p. 210; v. 361
—island of, i. 113
—Odysseus and the, i. pl. LV, opp. p. 260
——sails safely past the, i. 137
—Tashōns abandoned village on account of, xii. 267
Siris, Sirash, god of banquets, sometimes defined as goddess, v. 202
Sirius, i. 251, 252; iv. 430; vii. 49

Sirius as dog in the "Story of the Haunted Prince," xii. 153
—cycle of, vii. 65
—dog-star, marks end of rainy season, i. 250
—(Egyptian, Sopdet), queen of fixed stars and of Heaven, xii. 56, 374 66
—identified with Tishtrya, vi. 267, 276, 280
—"measures waters of Tamtu" (Milky Way), v. 317
—Ninurta identified with, v. 135
Sir-šyv-Kudegen or -Kten, land-water deity, iv. 462
Siryans, certain saints replacing ancient gods among, iv. xix
—description of ancient worshipping of heroes, iv. 142–143
—Permian linguistic stock, iv. xvi, xvii, xviii, xix
Sisiri, son of Purrunaminari, xi. 259
Sisiutl, x. 243, pl. xxxi, opp. p. 246, 253, 300 50
Sister, a Vila may become a man's, iii. 258
— -goddesses, cult of, ii. 186
—in personal names, v. 7, 12, 379 22
—title of, for Astarte, v. 13–14
Sisters, female forms, vi. 205
—sun and moon as, iv. 420
—tale of the two, viii. 156–158
—three weird, probably linked to fate-goddesses, ii. 246
—two, temples of, xii. 312–317
Sistrum (sacred rattle) used especially at festivals of Ḥat-ḥôr, xii. 41
—used in religious ceremonies in Crete, xii. 241
Sisyphos, i. 37–38
—derivation of name of, i. 38, 325 14
—instituted Isthmian games in honour of Melikertes, i. 46
—Odysseus said to be son of, i. 123
—punished in Hades by Zeus, i. 158
—said to have founded Corinth, i. 37
—struggles with stone in Underworld, i. 142
Sisythus (Sisythes), legendary Babylonian survivor of Flood, founded Bambyce, v. 37
Sītā ("Furrow"), vi. 60, 96, 97, 127, 128–129, 152, 156
Śītalā, smallpox demon, vi. 245–246

Sītāmarhi in Bengal, aerolite fell at, in 1880, vi. 233
Sitātapattra Aparājitā, vi. 217
Sitconski, trickster, x. 122
Sites for residence of living, fêng shui extended to cover, viii. 141
—ghosts haunt ruins because they are ancient, vii. 73
Sithu became a Nāt, xii. 354
—murdered Kyawzwa, who becomes a Nāt, xii. 354, pl. xxi, opp. p. 354
—son of an old king of Pagān, xii. 353
Śitikaṇṭha, vi. 81
Sitting-on-Earth, x. 245
Sitting out, power of Volva gained by, ii. 299
Siugmall, Midir's grandson, iii. 80, 82
Śiva, vi. 38, 63, 75, 81, 104, 107, pl. ix, opp. p. 108, 109, 110–113, 114, 115, 116, 117, 118, pl. x, opp. p. 118, 119, 120, 121, 131, 140, 141, 142, 147, 151, 153, 157, 158, 163, 168, 170, 174, 178–181, 182, 183, 184, 185, 205, 214, 215, 230, 231, 237, 239, 241, 247
—sacred images of, xii. 327
Śivā, consort of Śiva, vi. 179, 184, 205, 215
Siva: see Živa; Żywie.
Siward's kin put in brothel, ii. 115
—wounds cured by Odin, ii. 44, 57
Six (fourteen, sixty-four) pieces, solar eye of Osiris torn into, xii. 90
—Honoured Ones, viii. 51
—Kingdoms, viii. 163
Sixth and fifteenth day of each month "fill the sacred eye" of sun, xii. 90–91, 238
Sixty-four (six, fourteen) pieces, solar eye of Osiris torn into, xii. 90
Sīyākmak (Siyāmak) and Nashāk, primeval twins, vi. 298, 299
Siyāvakhsh, Garsīvaz murderer of, vi. 338
Siyu-Yacu, mother of Rocca, xi. 217
Size, fairies may increase their, iii. 259
—of silvan spirits, iii. 261
—token of divinity in Celtic myth, iii. 30, 56, 58, 104, 127, 150, 163
Sjællend, ii. 158
Sjen, Sjenovik ("shadow"), among Montenegrins soul personified as, iii. 228
Sjofn, goddess, ii. 15, 185
Sjörå, Swedes knew Ran as, ii. 191

Sjörå, water-spirit, iv. 208
Skaane, island, ii. 182
Skadi, great and mighty man, ii. 358 [21]
—wife of Njord, ii. 16, 101, 102, 103, 104, 105, 106, 110, 141, 144, 157, 186, 244
Skaggi, Grettir killed, ii. 285
Škaj, creator god, iv. 399
Skald, Bragi the divine, ii. 160–162
—he who drinks mead of Suttung becomes a, ii. 51, 53
Skalds, Odin god of the, ii. 55
" Skaldskaparmal," ii. 6, 15, 59, 86, 161–162
Skamandros, Hephaistos consumes raging waters of the, i. 129, 205
—instructed by Artemis in hunting, i. 183
—River in human form, i. 256
Skambha, god, vi. 93
Skanda, vi. 140–141, 153, 156, 159, 174, 181, 182, 183, 185, 238
Škay (" procreator ") sometimes used to denote sky, iv. 219
Skeggjold (" Axe-time "), Valkyrie, ii. 249
Skeleton, dead animals can preserve souls in uninjured, iv. 480
—god of death, xi. 53, pl. XI, opp. p. 80
—Hopi, who lived on earth before emergence, x. 205
—Huitzilopochtli born as a, xi. 92
—Lapp belief that some form of life continues with existence of, iv. 3, 99
Skeletons, animated, forms of dead may appear as, x. 146, 276 [12]
—dancing with spirits which became, x. 230
Skidbladnir, ship of Frey, ii. 108–109, 266
Skidskegg (Odin), ii. 43, 161
Skill, contests of, x. 282 [21]
Skin, Skins:
Skin-changing journey of a wizard Finn, ii. 229–230
Skin, colour of, in origin-myth, ix. 108, 109
—diseases, vii. 235–236
——caused by anger of fire, iv. 235
———offended water, iv. 207, 212
———spirits, iv. 185
—flaying of human, xi. 76, pl. x, opp. p. 76

Skin of Amon, xii. 129
—human sacrifice tribute to Devil, vii. 371
Skins, casting of, as renewal of youth and immortality, ix. 118, 121, 122, 182, 332 [146]
——to regain youth, vii. 169, 170
—of human victims worn by personators of gods, xi. 76
—sky consists of overlapping, iv. 336
Skinfaxi, steed which draws Day, ii. 200
Skirnir, giant, ii. 277, 278, 341
—subordinate god, servant of higher gods, ii. 10, 66, 110, 111, 117, 220
" Skirnismal," ii. 10, 22, 60, 66, 105, 110, 117, 119, 128, 220
Skiron, a robber who threw passers-by over a cliff, slain by Theseus, i. 99
Skironian rocks, Eurystheus slain by Hyllos at, i. 95
Skjold, son of Odin, ancestor of kings of Danes, ii. 32, 65, 181, 182
Skjoldings traced descent from Skjold, son of Odin, ii. 65
Skogsfru, Lady of those pursued by hunters, ii. 205, 206
Skogsjungfru, iv. 185
Skogsman, male wood-spirit, ii. 205
Skogsnufa, forest-maidens, ii. 205
Skogsrå (" wood-goblin "), ii. 205
Skogsrådare, iv. 185
Skogul (" Raging one "), Valkyrie, ii. 249, 250, 251
Skoll, wolf, ii. 199, 201, 279
Skraeling and Norseman, x. 1–3
Škrat (Škratec), Slovenian household genius, iii. 245–246
Škrata or Škriatek, Slovak household genius, iii. 245
Skřítek (" hobgoblin "), family genius, iii. 244–245
Skrymir, giant, ii. 92, 93, 144, 278
Skrzatek, Skrzat, or Skrzot, Polish household genius, iii. 245
Skuld, one of three Fates, ii. 239, 243, 248, 254
Skull, altar made of a buffalo, x. 124
—(head), singing, found by Freysten, ii. 169
—of bear, iv. 98
——burned dog turned into rock, vii. 253
——Closed Man placed on sacred bundle, x. 112

Skull of horse tries to unseat its rider, iv. 464
——Little Star, snake in, x. 114–115
——sacrifice with nose to East left on pole, iv. 221
—Wa worship of, xii. 293, 294, 295
Skulls, xii. 293, 294, 295, 297, 300, 345; see also items s.v. HEADS.
—of sacrificed oxen and buffaloes launched on rafts, xii. 301
—talking, x. 262, 276 [12]
Sky, vi. 16, 17, 18, 19, 24, 29, 30, 34, 74, 80, 91, 94, 96, 146, 148; vii. 116, 126, 127, 132, 133, 137, 149, 151–152; ix. 12, 166, 167; x. xvi, 16, 35, 56, 60, 61, 98, 179; xi. 39
—and air-gods, iv. 217–234
——ocean, little distinction between, xii. 113
——world, previous existence of, ix. 155, 157, 158, 159, 248, 270
—as a god, iv. 391, 392, 393–396, 397, 398
——metal roof, xii. 34
——roof, iv. 335–336, 434
——tent-roof, ii. 335
——tree, xii. 35
——water, xii. 34, 39
—beings descend to earth, ix. 159
—cannibalistic tendencies of, ix. 178
— -cannibals, ix. 57–61, 79
—compared to woman and cow, xii. 37, 39
—conceived as river, lake, or ocean, xii. 25, 39
—cow-shape of, xii. 37–40, 56
— -deity, son of, ancestor of human race, ix. 156
—dwarf of the sacred dances placed in, xii. 377 [86]
— -dwarfs, descent of, in Thonga belief, vii. 269
—eastern, all gods come from, xii. 62
—Elk, x. 26
— -father, ix. 6, 7, 8, 9, 10, 11, 14, 30, 31, 32, 34, 35 (see also RANGI-POTIKI); x. xvi, xvii, 207–209; xi. 24, 373 [7]
—fire originally obtained from, ix. 283
—form of Amen-Rê', xii. 221
—formed by tresses of Ḥat-ḥôr, xii. 39
—four sons of Horus or Osiris correspond to pillars of, xii. 394 [67]
— -god, Aramazd as, vii. 21

Sky-god, Armenak may have been a title of the, vii. 66
——Ba'al Shamîn supreme, vii. 37
——Bag-Mashtu a, and probably older form of Ahura Mazda, vii. 12
——Bagos Papaios a, vii. 12
——oak (in Europe) sacred to, vii. 14
——painting of, xi. pl. xxxvii, opp. p. 240
——Semitic general word for god may have denoted a, v. 65, 93
——Zeus as, i. 159
— -goddess in double form and her consort, xii. 49
——unusual representation of consort of, xii. 49 (fig. 49)
— -goddesses may replace nocturnal sky, xii. 42
— -gods, ii. 97, 194; v. 132; vi. 15–40
——Tsuni ||Goam placed in realm of, vii. 157
—highest god in earliest time merely animated, iv. 218
—Horus male ruler of, xii. 40, 102
—in human, feminine form, xii. 41
—made of Ymir's skull, ii. 325, 326
— -maiden becomes wife of mortal, ix. 60, 63, 319 [12]
—Mordvins sometimes use Škay (" procreator "), name of " god dwelling on high " (Vere-pas), to denote, iv. 219; see also PROCREATION, MAGIC CEREMONIES, ETC.
—most goddesses become personifications of, xii. 217, 410 [2]
—myths of the, vi. 263, 295, 312
—nocturnal, Nut personification of, xii. 41
—Nut mother or daughter of, xii. 45
—of Underworld, Nut explained as, xii. 41
—origin of man from, ix. 274
—Osiris symbolizes, xii. 93, 94
—Osiris's throne later sought in depths of, xii. 97
— -people, x. 97–98
——who come down to fish, ix. 326 [16]
—pillars of, xii. 35 and fig. 19, 366 [7]
— -powers, x. 99
— -producer, ix. 12
—purity of, iv. 400
—raising of, ix. 31–36, 50–51, 178, 317 [51]
—shape of, iv. 308–309

Sky, starry, Argos identified with, i. 30
—storeys in: see STOREYS IN EARTH, ETC.
—subterranean, Sekha(u)it connected with, xii. 53
—sunny, Nephthys mistress of, xii. 110
—support of, iii. 12
—symbol of, borne by Ehet, xii. 71
—tent-like in Old Testament, iv. 336–337
—upheld by Shu and Tefênet, xii. 43–44 and figs. 37, 38, 39, 366 [7]
— -vault rises and falls at regular intervals, x. 250
—winds rise in four corners of, iv. 308
—woman during menstruation must not look at, iv. 400
— -world, x. 114; xi. 271
——man derived from, ix. 167
Skylla, i. 113
—and Charybdis, i. 263–264
——Aeneas endeavoured to avoid, i. 305
—daughter of Nisos, i. 69
—represented a phase of the sea, i. 259
Skyros, Theseus withdraws to, i. 105
Skythia, Io wanders through, i. 29
—Tīr migrates from Iran to, ii. 32
Slagfid, son of Finn king, ii. 259
Slain, Freyja possessor of, ii. 120, 121, 122
—hero's return to life, vii. 395 [58]; see also ARLEZ.
—in their own land, gods are, iii. 55
—way of, ii. 45
Slanderers, Ninkarrak invoked against, v. 182–183
Slaughter, place of, xii. 180
Slaughtering as death ceremony, reason for, iv. 18, 38–39
—for home-sacrifices, iv. 85, 160, 161
—of sacrifice at night, iv. 153, 154
——to lud-spirit, rules for, iv. 148–149
Slav belief in higher being, iii. 249
Slavery, xi. 349 [5]
—of Herakles, i. 90–91
Slaves accompany dead to serve them, iv. 483
—killed and buried or burned near their dead owner, xii. 196–197
—slavery, x. 239, 242, 246, 249, 286 [29]
—swallowed by secret lake after they bathed goddess, ii. 103

Slavic character of things Thraco-Phrygian, vii. 15, 380 [9]
—influence on Magyars, iv. xix
—life, records of ancient, very superficial, iii. 221
—religion, sources for, iii. 221–223
Slavs, relatively small effect of, on modern Greek folk-beliefs, i. 311
Sledge, sacrifice drawn to grave on, xii. 420 [23]
— -ship, Sokar(i) in, xii. 148 (fig. 151), 149, 151–152
Sleep, iii. 89, 107, 117, 121, 134
—charm, iii. 65
— -cure, i. 281
—endless, of Endymion, i. 245
— -goddess, saved seventh child of Devakī, vi. 171
—Heimdall (as watchman) needs little, ii. 153, 154
—Hermes as god of, i. 194
—Hine-maki-moe daughter of troubled, ix. 7
—(Hypnos), i. 6
—induced by dancing, x. 200
——while Tara burnt, iii. 165
—magic, ii. 56, 112, 240, 251
—may not be indulged in while corpse in house, iv. 22, 61
—of Gilgamish, v. 224–225, 251
——three days and nights after bird song of Caer and Oengus, iii. 79
——winds, iv. 457
—people turn into animals during: see WERE ANIMALS.
—personified, xi. 306
—powers acquired through, by Yellow Emperor, viii. 28
—prevented Ailill's keeping tryst, iii. 80
—shown Qat, ix. 113–114
— -strain, magic, on harp, played by Lug, iii. 29
——played by Sgáthach, iii. 172
——sung over Tuag, iii. 89
— -thorn, ii. 56, 251
—town where no one allowed to, vii. 330; 427 [25]
Sleeper must not be awakened suddenly before urt returns, iv. 6
Sleeping in hills, legends of kings or heroes, ii. 316
—One, Buddha about to enter Nirvaṇa, viii. 194
—song of birds, iii. 86

Sleigh of the gods for travelling, iv. 113–114
—see Voršud.
—to convey dead to memorial feast, iv. 56
Sleighs used by Lapps as coffins, iv. 33
Sleipnir born of Loki in form of a mare, ii. pl. vi, opp. p. 32, 43, pl. viii, opp. p. 60, 62, 65, 90, 130, 140, 334
—runes to be written on teeth of, ii. 66
Slid, river with missiles resembles, ii. 321
Slidrugtanni, boar, ii. 109
Sligo, battle of Mag-Tured in, iii. 24
Sling-ball made of brain, iii. 157
Slope, steep, on road to village of dead, iv. 484, 485
"Slovo o pluku Igorevě," old Russian epic, iii. 297, 299, 300
Sluag siabhra, elfin host, iii. 69
Slumber, Keresāspa remains in, until end of world, vi. 327–328
Smallpox, god of, viii. 66
Small-Renown-Man, dwarf-god, viii. 229
Śmaśāna, cemetery, vi. 248
Smeared with clay, feet of spirits, xi. 278
Smearing of ashes and paint for purpose of identification, x. xxii
——blood: see Blood, sacrificial, smearing of, etc.; Blood, smearing of.
——body with oil, xi. 194
——butter as fertility rite, iv. 416
——faces at memorial feasts, iv. 37–38
Smentet, goddess parallel to Isis, xii. 148
Smertullos, deity perhaps of Underworld, iii. pl. v, opp. p. 40, 158
Smierragatto identical with butter-cat, iv. 172
Smintheus, Apollo as, i. 180
Smirgat, wife of Fionn, iii. 179
Smith, celestial, iii. 330, 361 [90]
——of Baltic folk-songs, Svarog may be identical with, iii. 354 [27]
—Culann the, iii. 142
—of Nesjar shoes Odin's horse, ii. 43
—Spider a, vii. 323
— -work Creidne god of, iii. 28, 31, 40
——of dwarfs of magical kind, ii. 266
Smithis, xii. 147, 148
Smiths, i. 129, 207; ii. 170; iii. 30, 31, 168, 175; see also Dwarfs.

Smiths as companions of Horus, xii. 101
—of Zeus originally storm-daemons, i. 267
Smohalla, x. 91, 149
Smok, snake, iii. 247
Smoke, viii. 265; see also Fuji, Mt.
—akin to clouds, x. 194
— -offerings, x. xvi, 20, 271 [6], 286 [30]
— -outlets opened by Finns to allow for passing of dead, iv. 17
—rising to sky in, ix. 209
Smoking Mirror = Tezcatlipoca, xi. 61–66
—out of homes on death, iv. 23, 105
Smyrna changed into a myrrh-tree, i. 16
—(Myrrha), story of, i. 198
Snaefell, Bardar (known as Snaefellsáss), guardian spirit of region about, ii. 20
Snær, snow, ii. 281
Snail could revive dead, vii. 171
Snails born from bones of giant, iv. 388
—sun and moon made from, ix. 250
Snake, iv. 62
—an enemy from beginning, vii. 170
—and heron, fight of, ix. 68
—as guardian at tree of life, iv. 381–382
——messenger, x. 197
—conjuration for person bitten by, xii. 83
—dance, x. 194–195, 197–198, 292 [39], 300 [50]
—fastened over Loki's face, ii. 144–145, 150
— -form may be taken by spirits, xii. 175
—has no legs, vii. 286
—hole of, a subterranean road to roots of sky, xi. 132
—household, cult of, iii. pl. xxxvii, opp. p. 304
—how skin of black-, got its colour, x. 61
—in art and myths, ii. 216, 217, 218, 233
——fertility-rites, i. 172
—lightning as fiery, falling from sky, iv. 445
— -like monster, soul must go through, to village of dead, iv. 485–486
—Man, x. 203
—Master of Forest, appeared at sacrifice to thank descendants, vii. 192

Snake people, x. 198, 301 [50]
—put in drum of Zimwi, vii. 250
—rainbow as kind of giant, iv. 444
——looked on as a, vii. 234
—saivo-, iv. 285
—see KUKULCAN, ETC.
—skins and horns of, worn by underwater people, x. 29
—sky-travelling, x. 188
—sometimes eaten to acquire knowledge
of beast language, iii. 166
—soul (shadow) may assume form of,
iii. 228, 229
—symbol of Hospodáříček and guardian of house, iii. 246–247
——power of evil in Kuei Shê painting, viii. 100
—tears corpses, ii. 318
—three-headed, associated with Charos
in modern Greek folk-belief, i. 314
—water-, Japanese people formerly
worshipped, xii. 301
—who ate shrimps immortal, ix. 182
—with head at each end of body, ix.
299–300
—Youth and Maid, x. 197, 198
Snakes, viii. 158–160
—amadhlozi come back as, vii. 272
—and fire, tales of, ix. 282, 283
—as sea-monsters, iv. 345
—charms against, vi. 96
—feeding of household, xii. 169
—Maboya tutelary of, xi. 38
—messengers of witches, vii. 336, 337
—mythological, iv. 357
—only certain kinds ancestral ghosts,
vii. 193–194
—see NĀGAS; SERPENTS; DRAGONS.
—spirits appear as, vii. 181
—water-spirits conceived of, as, xi. 199
Snares, genii with, xii. 109 (fig. 109)
Snaring of sun, ix. 44–46
Snāvidhka, vi. 324, 326
Sneezing of duck brings rain, iv. 439
—soul jumped out of body during, iv.
476
Sneneik, Cannibal Woman, x. 243–244
Snipe (turi), Tangaloa's daughter in
form of, ix. 29, 44
Snorri, first white child born on American continent, x. 1
—on mythology: see chap. Euhemerism
(vol. ii, 31–36)
Snotra, goddess, ii. 15, 186

Snow, dress of, xi. 231
— -shoe god, Ull is, ii. 156, 157
— -shoes, Skadi goddess of the, ii. 105,
244
— -Woman (Yuki-onne) lures people
to death in snow-storm, viii. 289
Snowland, ii. 216
Snowy Mountain, viii. 23
Snuff-box, magic, dwarfs come from a,
ii. 272
So-at-sa-ki, the Feather Woman, x. 95–
96
Sobdet, Egyptian for Sothis-Sirius, xii.
56
Sobk (crocodile-god), xii. 15, 148, 161,
366 [5], 408 [98] [99]
—fishes out the four sons of Horus or
Osiris, xii. 112
—has no mythological traits, xii. 20
—identified with Sêth, xii. 362 [8]
—sometimes partially portrayed in pic-
tures of nameless cosmic deity, xii.
223
—son of Neith, xii. 142
— -Rê', xii. 148, 408 [99]
Sobket, a crocodile-goddess, xii. 148
Sobks, crocodiles souls of, xii. 219
Social institutions, abstract divinities of,
i. 282–283
—system, xi. 51
Society Islands, Indonesian myth-ele-
ments in, ix. 97
——Melanesian myth-incidents in, ix.
95, 96
——relation of myths of, to those of
Hawaii, New Zealand, and Cook
Group, ix. 93, 94
Soda in shaman drink, iv. 283
Sodem, vii. 67
Sodomy, xi. 205, 206
Sœming, son of Odin and Skadi, from
whence Norwegian kings, ii. 106
" Soga," story of two orphan boys, viii.
313, 383 [12]
Sogamozo and Ramiriqui, xi. 200
" Sogubrot," ii. 256
Soiem tongk (" river-spirits "), iv. 208
Soil a metal according to Burmese, xii.
291
—carrying of, from fertile to sterile field
not practised by Chinese, viii. 63
—cultivation of, unnecessary in " Isle
of Apples," iii. 193
—Demeter goddess of, i. 225, 226

Soil, god of, viii. 62, 66
—Kekrops reputed to have been born of, i. 66
Sōjō-bō, chief of Tengu, viii. pl. xxix, opp. p. 288, 309, 310
Sokar(i), xii. 22 (fig. 2)
—deity of place near Memphis, xii. 148–149
—hawk-god, local deity of necropolis of Memphis, Osiris identified with, xii. 98
—identical with Bês and Nuu-Ptaḥ, xii. 223
—lake of, xii. 364 [11]
—local variant of Ptaḥ, god of Memphis, xii. 63
— -Osiris, pantheistic tendencies attached to, xii. 220
—Ptaḥ perhaps confused with, xii. 145, 407 [77]
—solarization of, xii. 215
Sokhmet and Nefer-têm, wife and son of Ptaḥ, xii. 145
Sokkvabekk, abode of Saga, ii. 50, 183
Sol could hold himself all day on one foot, iii. 190
Sol invictus, v. 99, 115, 119
—sanctissumus, Malak-Bêl identified by Latins with, v. 58
—sun personified as, ii. 16, 183–184, 197
Solar bird, xii. 26
—body as face, eye, or head-ornament of sun, xii. 25
—character often attributed to nome-god, xii. 18
—charm, old, converted into Buddhist spell, vi. 203
—cult in Peru, xi. 242–248
—deity, Dažbog as, iii. 297
—disk, Meneḥtet wore the, xii. 136
—divinities, Shu and Tefênet as, xii. 70
—divinity, god with wheel probably a, iii. pl. iv, opp. p. 20
—god, ram-headed forms of, xii. 364 [15], 402 [4]
—egg, xii. 25, 42
—laid by Qêb, xii. 42, 368 [19]
—eye, xii. 25, 30
—female sun, Rê'et, possibly originated from individualizations of, xii. 365 [20]
—gods come from east or south, xii. 377 [86]

Solar myth, Babylonian Epic of Creation based on, v. 315, 322
—myths dubious in Oceania and Polynesia, ix. xiv, 99
——traces of, vi. 288
—nature of Asklepios, i. 279
——Yima, vi. 313–314, 315
—phenomena, vi. 15
—ship, adventures of, xii. 26–27
——and two celestial trees, xii. 35 (fig. 22)
——as double serpent, xii. 26 (fig. 9)
——dead have place in, xii. 178
——decoration of, in late art, xii. 363 [5]
——description of, xii. 26
——detail on prow of, xii. 25–26, 363 [4] [5]
——drawn by jackals, xii. 364 [10], 371 [45]
——kings alone have right of admission to, xii. 179
——mat hanging from prow of, xii. 363 [4]
——rowed by gods, souls of kings, etc., xii. 26
——sailing over the metal (sky), xii. 35
——sun sails over sky in, xii. 25, 26
——towed by jackals, xii. 364 [10]
——use of, in solemn procession, xii. 31
Solarization, Amon clear instance of, xii. 129
—of most goddesses, as daughter, diadem, or eye of sun, xii. 215
——pantheon, xii. 214–215
" Solarljod," ii. 304
Solbon = Venus, iv. 432–434
Soldiers, Sêth patron of, xii. 103
Solid bodies, power of passing through, xi. 86
Solinus mentions British goddess Sul, iii. 11
Solomon, Jamshīd assimilated to, vi. 319
Solve et coagula of European alchemy, Chinese parallel to, viii. 144
Solymoi, Bellerophon sent against the, i. 39
Soma and Dionysos identified, vii. 380 [11]
—(Avestan Haoma), deity and plant, vi. 15, 18, 19–20, 24, 27, 28, 29, 32, 33, 34, 35, 36, 37, 38, 46–48, 50, 52, 55, 56, 59, 60, 62, 63, 64, 65, 69, 71, 85, 87, 88, 90, 91, 93, 94, 95, 136, 137, 139, 140, 141, 142, 143, 170
— -Dhara (Soma Way), iv. 414

Soma, Goibniu's ale analogous to, iii.
120
—immortality-producing nourishment
of, iv. 356, 447
—sacrifice, vi. 11, 20, 80
—saliva-myth somewhat like myth of
Indian, ii. 54
—see HAOMA.
Somā, daughter of Somila and Soma-
sirī, vi. 224
Sombol-Burkhan, iv. 324, 325
Somila, vi. 224, 225
Somin-Shōrai, viii. 250-251
Son, Sons:
Son, blood of Kvasir collected in vat,
ii. 53, 54
Son of Beach Island (Urashima Tarō),
tale of, viii. 264-265
——God, iv. pl. xxviii, opp. p. 228
——sinless couple, iii. 72, 81, 202
——Sun, x. 112-115, 138, 156, 232, 255
——sun-goddess, birth of, viii. 226
——Three Dogs, iii. 156
—the, vi. 234
—without a father, iii. 200, 202
Sons, dedication of, to Thor, ii. 76
—gods who were, v. 131
—of Elōhim, Sumero-Babylonian devils
correspond to, v. 358
——gods, eighteen, xi. 216
——Heaven and their sister Nambi, vii.
152
——— = rulers and princes in a special
sense, iv. 392
Sónargöltr, atonement boar, ii. 109
Sondergötter, i. 300
Sonet-nofret and Horus, Neb-taui son
of, xii. 140
——deity at Ombos, xii. 149
Song, Songs:
Song and runes, magic, ii. 265
—as medicine, x. 86-87, 269 [4]
—brings birth of first Sia people, x. 203
—connexion of Pan with, i. 268
—death-, x. 133
— -duel, x. 11
—gift of, from singing gourd, xi. 312
—Kenaima, xi. 266
—Llacheu marvellous in, iii. 191
—nightbird's, xi. 31
—Nixe's, ii. 212
—of heaven = thunder, iv. 442
——Igor's Band, fragments of pagan
customs in, iii. 222

Song (of Morrígan) of slaughter between armies, iii. 154
—of Näkk bewitches, iv. 201, 202, 203
——red, white, and black spirits, vii.
209, 210
——spirits, iv. 479
——swans, iii. 51, 59, 60
——the Sun, ii. 304
———Turtle, xi. 305
—popular, at banquets, xii. 185, 418 [4]
Songs, xi. 33, 36
—ancient Hebrew martial, v. 41
—bear, iv. 96
—Bjarka, ii. 314
—ceremonial, x. 88, 93, 151-153, 216,
307 [62]
—death, iv. 79-81
—feast, iv. 151
—folk-, viii. 369-374
—Hamatsa, x. 248-249
—loss of ancient, vii. 64
—magic, ii. 46, 52, 265, 283, 295, 298,
299; iv. 77, 78, 79, 81, 110, 230, 234,
238, 243, 257, 290, 292, 294; vii. 202;
x. 126
—of bon-dancing, viii. 369, 373-374
—sacrifice, iv. 131
—shaman, iv. 349, 389, 403-404, 510,
520, 523
—used in chase of deer, x. 62
—wedding, iv. 69, 122
—weeping-, to memory of dead, iv. 27,
30, 56, 68, 74
—world-making, x. 218-219, 220
Sōngkran, Siamese Spring Festival, xii.
323
So-no-hagahama, viii. 248
Son-tay (Oduyen), xii. 313
Soot, creation from, x. 221
—represented by black on fire-god, iv.
455
Soothsayers, ii. 299
Sop (earlier Sepa), god worshipped in
Heliopolis, xii. 149, 409 [104]
Sopdet-Sothis " mistress of the year,"
xii. 57
Sopd(u), deity of twentieth nome of
Delta, xii. 148 (fig. 152), 149 (fig.
153), 409 [104] [105]
—Khenset wife of, xii. 135, 149
—(" Master of the East ") possibly as-
sociated with Sopdet, xii. 374 [66]
Sophene, unidentified mountain in,
called Throne of Anahit, vii. 28, 63

Sophokles knew Babylonian legend of plant of immortality, v. 228, 229
Sophrosyne (" Temperance "), abstract divinity of virtue, i. 282
Šopšar, stick for sacrifice meat, iv. 273, 274
Ṣor as title of god, v. 9, 11, 379 ³⁵
Sorcerers, vi. 66, 100, 156, 204, 205, 242; 261
—belief that they can change into animals, vii. 343–344
—believed to influence sun and moon, vii. 48
—gathering-place of, iv. 78
—souls of, iii. 231
—theologians of distinction are believed to be, xii. 198
—Wasanye and Yibir tribes reputed to be, vii. 115
Sorceress, gibberish name of, iii. 70
Sorcery, ii. 27, 246, 300; iii. 70, 79, 175; x. 228–229; xii. 200–201, 205
—Hekate in, i. 187, 329 ⁷
—ordeal to determine, v. 161
Sorcha, king of, iii. 173
Sores, Spiders brought, into world, vii. 329, 330–331
" Sorla-thattr," ii. 123, 140, 142
Soshi-mori visited by Susa-no-wo, viii. 228
Sosondowah (" Great Night "), x. 26
Sosva centre, god of the, iv. 403
Sotem: see SOZEM.
Sothic cycle, xii. 56
Sothis and Horus-Osiris connected, xii. 55 (fig. 55)
—associated with Osiris as sister-wife or mother, xii. 94
—comparison of, with planet Venus uncertain in early period, xii. 54
—Isis early connected with, xii. 101
—Orion companion of, xii. 58
— -Orion group described by Daressy, xii. 374 ⁶⁷
— -Sirius and Horus, association of, unexplained, xii. 56
——connected with an archer-goddess, xii. 56, 374 ⁶⁷
——early identified with Isis and Hathôr, xii. 56
——in human form companion of Orion, xii. 56
—sister of Orion, daughter of Osiris, and mother of Horus, xii. 398 ¹⁰⁵

Sothis-star as regulator of time, xii. 56, 146
——husband of, as designation of Dua[-uêr], xii. 132
— -Venus as daughter and wife of sun-god and mother of Osiris-Horus, xii. 54
Sotoba, piece of wood by a tomb in memory of dead, Ono-no-Komachi depicted sitting on, viii. 299
Soul a being distinct from body (which it may leave even in life) in Slavic belief, iii. 227
—accusing animal the reincarnated, vii. 212
—alive, dead buried in standing position because, xi. 279
— -animals, ii. 217; iv. 7, 8, 9, 11, 13, 169, 240, 241, 295; 473; vii. 166
—animating a new body in other-world in Celtic belief in immortality, iii. 14
—as a manikin, ii. 273
—Babylonian explanation of man's immortal, v. 275
—bat as, in Votiak and Vogul belief, iv. 7–8, 11
—belief in, iii. 227–232
—beliefs concerning, viii. 237–240
— -birds, xii. 174 and figs. 181, 182, 183
—bothie, iv. 13–14
—breathed into Diarmaid after death, iii. 178
— -butterfly, iv. 8–9, 241
—child's, comes in shape of bird, iv. 398
—Chinese conception of, based on Yin and Yang, viii. 238
—connexion of, with four winds, xii. 65
—created and carried to child by birth deities, iv. 258, 260
—departing into the west, xii. 99 (fig. 93)
—difficulty of, of finding way to hereafter, iv. 484
—disappearance of, iv. 6
—entering a meteor the Cheremiss remedy against death, iv. 10
—external, of dragon or fairy, sometimes hidden in egg, vii. 391 ⁸
—furnished by Ajysit, iv. 399, 415
——to new-born child by Jajutši, iv. 366
—Greek view of, i. 141–143

Soul, half of man's, lives in animal of his totem species, vii. 279

—(hogi), vii. 94–98

—immortality of, xi. 279

—in Bulgarian tradition, tries to enter corpse on fortieth day to live anew, iii. 230

——teeth, iv. 5

—Inua of the lifeless body, x. 5

—is fled when no reflexion of it can be seen in pupil of eye, xi. 26

— -journeys, x. 7, 146, 262

—led through all lands by a stone, x. 284 27

—magicians used to locate, iv. 6

—man-, belief in a, underlying an animal exterior, x. 244

—may assume many different forms, iii. 227–232

——be in finger-nails, iv. 5

——manifest itself as blue flame, iv. 10

—meaning of term, xii. 220

—mouse as, iv. 7

—must have abode in body, viii. 120

—nailed by hands and feet to tree, iv. 522–523

—objects in contact with man sustain relation to, iv. 5

—of an animal or plant may be saved by power of scripture "Lotus," viii. 242

——Beautiful Land, viii. 229

——both human beings and natural objects, iv. 463

——Carib ascends to Heaven, xi. 39

——child brought from Heaven during birth, iv. 399, 415

——Cúchulainn seen floating over Emain Macha, iii. 209

——dead, vi. 316

——deceased (shaman) rides on reindeer, iv. 508

———supposed to enter memorial doll, iv. 41

——earth, corn, field, iv. 240

——fire may be put out by water, iv. 236

——king lives by cannibalism, xii. 213

——Lapp sometimes called by mountain-spirits causing illness, iv. 76

——life, men created with, v. 192

——mer sacrifice, iv. 271

——murdered lad takes form of bird, vii. 212

Soul of river, digging for, flood legend, ix. 179

——shaman, iv. 284, 285, 286, 292

———protected by thunderbird, iv. 439, 440

——Tanshikai came in form of hail, iv. 398

——threshing-floor, iv. 14

——victims of murder, birds and dogs as avengers connected with, vii. 210, 212

——Waters, Anuanaïtu is the, xi. 268

——witch by charm made to stay in another body, ii. 300

—only, of bloodless sacrifice made over to the god, iv. 142

—or souls which leave body: see FYLGJA, ETC.

—(Ört, Urt), iv. 6

—personified by Montenegrins as Sjen or Sjenovik, iii. 228

—possessed by nearly all inanimate things, iv. 13–14

— -power passes from one body to another by drinking blood, iv. 5

— -powers hidden in important parts of body, iv. 4

—previous existence of, iv. 472–473

—qualities of, acquired by eating organs containing soul, iv. 4–5

—race-, of bear, Leib-olmai, iv. 176

—reincarnated in descendant, vii. 179

—remains where corpse lies, iv. 208

—separable, iii. 151, 187

—serpent-form assumed by escaping, vii. 193

—(shadows), iv. 6

—Tangaroa in one myth a sort of world-, ix. 13, 15

—three words for, x. 262

—to be obtained for newly created, iv. 373–374

—trace of external, in life of clan depending on its totem, vii. 278

— -trees, ix. pl. xviii, opp. p. 182

—Twi and Ewe philosophy of the, vii. 179

—vanishes when body decays, iv. 3–4

—water believed to have, iv. 215–216

——left for cleansing of, iv. 17

—which leaves body to torment sleeper: see MAHR, ETC.

—wind put in mouth of image for a, ix. 176

Soul with material body, iv. 478
Souls, abodes of, vi. 344–345
—and ghosts different, x. 146, 276 [12], 281 [20]
——names, x. 281 [20]–282
——their powers, x. 262
—animal, abode of, at primitive Chaos, x. 106
—as butterflies, viii. 337
—Babi persecutor and butcher of, xii. 131
—(baiu), small distinction between gods and, xii. 16
—balance of, x. 253
—become zemis, xi. 26–27
—belief of Finno-Ugric peoples in, iv. 3–16
—beliefs about, xi. 301
—believed to ascend through an orifice for rebirth, x. 289 [34]
—build cabins at edge of a flat earth, x. 44
—country of, x. 41
—crowded out of isle of dead become birds and fishes, x. 236
—devoured by evil Prince, iv. 486
—different names for, in living and dead bodies, xi. 27
—disembodied, haunt the night, xi. 31
—divine nature of departed, less clear in Egyptian than in other animistic religions, xii. 361 [2] (ch. i)
—each man has three, xi. 39
—fates of human, xi. 336, 337
—feast to, v. 162, 334
—ferried over river by Kipanawazi (hare), vii. 419 [4]
—find concealment in guise of insects, iv. 9
—from Asia judged by Rhadamanthys; from Europe by Aiakos; others by Minos, i. 144
—(gods) of Buto and Hierakonpolis represented with heads of hawks or jackals, xii. 32
—head- and shoulder-, xi. 39
—Hermes as guardian of, i. 194
——marshal of departed, i. 191
—human, the game hunted by spirits in Heaven, iv. 488
—in Jainism, vi. 228
——Tinne belief, x. 78
—interested in fertility of land, vii. 22
—limbo of child-, xi. 83–84

Souls live in Grotto of Caripe, xi. 279
—manner of worship to gods of fruitfulness same as [souls] they were supposed to fructify, iv. 259
—may go to moon or Brahmā, or may be connected with wind, vi. 101, 102
—Milky Way pathway of, xi. 278
—of babes descend from Omeyocan, xi. 53
——battle-slain consecrated to Odin, ii. 44, 58
——buildings, transitions of, iv. 168–169
——children come from Mother-earth, ii. 195, 196
——city equivalent to its gods, xii. 361 [2] (ch. i)
——dead, vi. 69, 71, 215, 249–250; xii. 173–183
———as fairies, iii. 256
———borne on wind, ii. 193
———devoured by Neheb-kau, xii. 141
———feast for, v. 122, 398 [105]
———ferried to " Brittia," iii. 16
———in Arallû, poem on conditions of life of, v. 263–266
———moon abode of, iii. 273
———Roman Junones originally, iii. 249
———Sedna has sovereignty over, x. 6
———snakes of other-world as, ii. 217
———trees and serpents connected with, vi. 239, 241
————associated with, ii. 204
———words for, v. 364
——deities, xii. 160, 164, 166 (fig. 176), 383 [90], 413 [12-14]
——different species of fish contained in water-spirits, iv. 209
——East, xii. 32
——jaguar, boa constrictor, and rattlesnake enter bodies of those who would take vengeance for death of Maconaura, xi. 266
——men made of divine fire, i. 14
——Mexicans cared for by Tezcatepuca, xi. 47
——plants, etc., viii. 338
——righteous appear as white birds, those of wicked as ravens, iii. 60
——self and family, promise of, to Škrat must be signed in own blood, iii. 246

Souls of sick wander in Underworld, iv. 6, 286, 292
—only nobles have immortal, xi. 192, 193
—" owners " of bodies, x. 10
—paths of, xi. 140
—Pharaohs claimed to be souls, etc., of sun-god, xii. 170
—refuges set up for homeless, iv. 512
—seeking an earthly dwelling, x. 98, 99
—serpents swallow, xi. 279
—sometimes in Odin's host, ii. 41
—special, iv. 498, 506
—(spirits), First People were of nature of, xi. 31
—(stars) elect, rowers of the sun by day, xii. 26, 55
—three, iv. 472, 482
—tree-, iv. 14, 188
—village of, x. 49–51, 104, 132
—wandering, may be demons, v. 355
—Yima ruler of, iv. 367
Sounion, Menelaos touches at, i. 134
Sources for Celtic mythology, iii. 19
—of Nile, xii. 46
" Sou Shên Chi," viii. 60, 65, 123
South as the lower world, xii. 53, 374 69, 396 94
—called " that above," iv. 308
—Doctor, x. 178
—door of god's dwelling on, iv. 115
—four sons of Horus or Osiris associated with, xii. 112, 394 67
—guardian of, viii. 243
—homage to, viii. 46, 50
—" left " of the sun, xi. 59
—Lord of the, Sêth as, xii. 102
—man created from fire from, iv. 371
—nine women in white from, ii. 236
—(place of thorns), xi. 60
—Red Sparrow spirit of, xii. 307
—represented by red bird, iv. 360
—(right), x. 287 31
—see COMPASS, COLOURS, ETC.
—Star (Spirit Star or Star of Death), x. 117
—Valkyries said to come from, ii. 252
Southern Cross, xi. 99, 278, 319, 336
—pole stars, Fuku-roku-ju spoken of as an incarnation of, viii. 280
—Sung Dynasty, viii. 76
Sow sometimes symbol of Êpet, xii. 376 79

Sowing, earth-priest determines who shall begin, xii. 338
Sowings, god of, xi. 48
Soyaluña ceremony, x. 194–195
Soychù, god, xi. 333
Soychuhèt, the dead, xi. 333
Sozem (later Sodem, Sotem) (" Hearing "), one of sense-gods, xii. 67
Sozun-uul, iv. 365
Space, vi. 199
—deification of, xii. 48
— -divisions, xi. 52, 56, 58, 97
—infinite, Ḥeḥ deity of, xii. 44
—(Whai-tua), ix. 7
Spade, symbol of Marduk, v. 159
Spades sacrificed to Veralden-olmai, iv. 251
Spadisir (Prophetic women), ii. 237, 244, 255
Spae-wives appear at births, ii. 242, 246
Spain, legendary connexion of Celts with, iii. 23
—perhaps home of giant-children of Ouranos and Gaia, i. 9
—race of Partholan in, iii. 23
Spakona, Norn, prophetic woman, ii. 241, 246, 299
Spananel, spandanotz, vii. 19
Spandaran, Spandunis, place of sacrifice and sacrificial priests, vii. 18–19
Spanish writers on Latin America, xi. 3–5
Spantaramet (Spenta Ārmaiti), vii. 17, 35, 96
Sparks from foot of Gwadyn Odyeith, iii. 190
Sparrow most grateful of Japanese birds, viii. 318–320, 349
—Red (Chu-dieu), xii. 307
Sparta, bride of Lakedaimon, daughter of Eurotas, i. 23
—Eurotas River worshipped in, i. 257
—Helen and Menelaos arrive at, i. 134
—Kastor and Polydeukes fought against Enarsphoros at, i. 26
—Proteus tells Menelaos state of affairs at, i. 261
—Telemachos at, i. 138
—Tyndareos expelled from, i. 24
—worship of Athene in, i. 169
Spartan myth and cult, Kastor and Polydeukes conspicuous figures in, i. 26
Spartoi (" Scattered "), birth of, i. 45

Speaking image, ii. 175
Spear and dog given to Prokris by Artemis, i. 184
—chief weapon of Horus, xii. 103, 104, 109
—fish-, trident, connexion of, with, i. 211
— -head, magic, iii. 198–199
—in Grail romances, iii. 202, 203, 204
—of Odin, ii. 27, pl. VI, opp. p. 32, 43, 56, 60
— -point, Odin at death marked with, ii. 34, 52
—(spear-chain) with line attached, ix. 283, 293, 294, 295; see also ARROW-CHAIN.
Spears dipped in blood, vii. 82, 393 [27]
—magic, iii. 65, 90, 145
—which made many wounds on withdrawal, iii. 200
Speculation, character of Egyptian theological, xii. 218–220
Speech created, ix. 173
—distinct cleavage of, vii. 109
—queer, of Spider emphasized, vii. 324, 427 [11]
Spell as " medicine," x. 269 [4], 307 [62]
—cast over rock, vii. 178
—myth of tears of Isis used as, xii. 126
Spells, i. 59, 114, 166, 199; ii. 26, 54, 64, 82, 143, 195, 205, 220, 222, 251, 295, 299, 300, 311; iii. 28, 30, 32, 36, 42, 52, 55, 58, 60, 62, 72, 79, 84, 88, 110, 132, 140, 148, 149, 153, 156, 168, 169; vi. 217, 249; xii. 205, 208–209
Spenishta fire, vi. 285
Spenjaghrya slain by Vāzishta fire, vi. 285
Spenta Ārmaiti, vi. 260, 294
— -goddess of earth, vi. 306
— -relation of, to Spantaramet, vii. 35
Spentōdāta (Pers. Isfandyār), brother of Zoroaster, vi. 342
—wounds Rustam, vi. 290
Speos Artemidos, Pekhet worshipped near, xii. 144
Spes (" Hope "), i. 299
Spherical form of universe, x. 186, 310 [66]
Sphinx, Great, Harmachis worshipped at, xii. 388 [28]
—interpretation of connexion of, with Theban cycle, i. 55
—on head of the Athene Parthenos, i. pl. IX, opp. p. 14

Sphinx, originally a picture of Ḥu, survived as emblem of royalty, xii. 170
—riddle of, i. 49
—sent to destroy citizens of Thebes, i. 49
—winged, v. 279, 280, 281, 283, 284
Spica, principal star in Virgo, v. 305
" Spider, Ancient " (Areop-Enap), ix. 249, 252, 255
—first Sia being, x. 203
—from sky in creation-myth, ix. 159
—Man, x. 95, 96, 310 [66]
—web for ascent to Heaven, ix. 59, 60, 66
— -sky reached by, x. 94, 96, 113–114
—Woman mythic incarnation of earth, x. 115, 158, 164, 198, 202, 203, 205, 229, 289 [34]
—Young, tale of, born from boil on tortoise, ix. 255
Spiders, vii. 121, 132, 134, 135, 208–211, 213, 284, 286, 309, 321–333, 400 [39]–401, 424 [14], 426 [1]
—associated with ascents to sky, x. 289 [34]
Spiders' webs, boats of, xi. 198
Spindle and distaff of Frigg in constellation Orion, ii. 177
— -sword-handle as ultimate origin of human race, and animals, ix. 159, 176
—descent to sea from thread from, ix. 160–161
Spinners, Three, ii. 245
Spinning, iii. 228, 251, 252, 255; iv. 491, 493
—first taught by Arkas, i. 16
—goddess, Ishtar as, v. 190, 383 [99], 398 [101]
—invented by Athene, i. 171
—see SUŚETKA, ETC.
— -wheel and flax offered to sun-goddess, iv. 225
— -sacrifice, iv. 247, 255, 256
Spirit blown into God's creation, man, by devil, iv. 377
—bringing of the, to new lud, iv. 145–146
— -chariot of Cúchulainn, iii. 209
— -fire, x. 47
— -fish, iv. 209
—forcing of, into dead body, ix. 76
—formed by adding all departed spirits together, vii. 118
—Great, x. xxvii, 5, 19–21, 271 [6]–273, 283 [25], 284 [28]

Spirit helpers, ix. 234, 235
— -hut, vii. pl. xviii, opp. p. 198
—in lud cult, iv. 143–152
—individuals representing totem-ancestors, ix. 271
— -journey, x. 149
—lake in which Thusandi lived, xii. 276
—of holy places and Master of the forest, connexion between, iv. 178
——lake would swallow castle, iii. 148–149
——life, viii. 140
——Long-do appeared to Cao-bien, xii. 318
——lud worshipped even if lud laid waste, iv. 146
—possession, story of, x. 247–248
—(Puruṣa), a name Prajāpati, vi. 75
—quest of, for man, iv. 373–378
—River in which serpent dwelt, ix. 160
—Seide protecting, of family or clan, iv. 104
— -soul disappears on death, iv. 477
—(soul), sky gives the, iv. 397, 398
—stones, ii. 312
— -tablet as proxy in case of death before marriage, viii. 149
—translation of Manito, x. 18, 251
— -walking: see WANDERING NIGHT OF DEAD.
—wood-, iv. 178
— -world, legends of, vii. 195–212
——mythological scenes in, ix. pl. xviii, opp. p. 182
— -worshippers, hill tribes naturally, xii. 293
Spirits, x. 145–149
—ancestor, vii. 55, 387 [4]
—ancestral, vii. 116, 124, 129, 179–194, 195, 274, 288
—and monsters, world of, vii. 72–92
——shamans, xi. 256–261
—associated with Heaven [ruler], viii. 49–50
—at fixed holy places materialized into images, iv. 140, 141, 142, 149
—belief in activity of, viii. 256
—beliefs of Wa hill-tribes concerning, xii. 293
—benevolent, kings of hosts of, viii. 242–243
—[bird-, dog-eating, etc.] patrons of secret societies, x. 246–249

Spirits, Burmese, suggest Vedic gods, xii. 340
—classes of, vs single god, xi. 141
—Corn-, x. 289 [35]–290
—departed, Gaia presided over, i. 273
—eat raw food, ix. 116
—enter into a man and inspire visions, xi. 40
—evil, vi. 69; viii. 105, 149, 150, 152–153, 158–159
——came from six streams of blood, ix. 160
——in shape of birds and insects, iv. 389
——may fly away in form of animal offered to propitiate them, xii. 336
——of Erlik, forty-three kinds of, sent to earth, iv. 411–412, 487
——smoked out of homes in thunder storm, iv. 443
——swords brandished beside hearse to drive away, iii. 235
——vulture sent to protect first creation against, iv. 505
—expelled at Ascension-tide, ii. 231
—field-, iii. 267–269
—forest-, iv. 175–190
—freed at night to haunt earth, xii. 173–175
—good and evil, v. xviii, 352–374; vii. 159
—groves of lower, iv. 152
—have no shadows, iv. 472
—household, iv. 159–174
—in trees, ii. 204–208
—invisible serving-, iv. 493
—journey to land of, x. 273 [8]–274
—local, majority of old local gods originally, xii. 15
—might reveal coming events, iv. 65–66
—mountain-, river-, tree-, etc., vii. 119
—must be conjured into images by shamans, iv. 114
—nature, ii. 192–215
—need felt of appeasing underground, iv. 174
—of ancestors or spirit-powers, Katcinas are, x. 187
——dead relatives usually invisible to man but visible to animals, iv. 24
——deceased, worship of, similar to Voršud cult, iv. 134
——evil and of protection against ill came from purifications of Izanagi, viii. 224

Spirits of nature, viii. 61–73
——night-watch, viii. 191
——the Quarters, x. 23
——seven directions, x. 19
——Wednesday, Friday, and Sunday, vii. 394 [51]
—personal, x. 79
—place of coming-in and going-out of underground, x. 289
—protection against evil, iv. 62–63
—river, viii. 37
—Ryang'ombe chief of departed, vii. 407 [7]
—seeking place where they could come into bodily existence, x. 98
—serving-, iv. 512
—silvan, iii. 261–266
—small distinction between, and gods, xii. 16
—three: red, white, black, vii. 210
—to be procured for people created, iv. 329
—tree-, ii. 205, 207
—tutelary, ascribed to noteworthy objects, xii. 15–16
—two different classes of, in Seide worship, iv. 112
—unclean, iii. 231
—underground, Lapp belief in, iv. 71
——shamans could converse with, iv. 283–284, 285, 291
—universe peopled by, x. 251
—valley, viii. 53
—vampire, iv. 200
—wanderlust of, vii. 95–96
—water-: see WATER-SPIRITS.
—who have never been incarnated, xii. 293
——walk on air and sleep on space, viii. 28
Spiritual faculties, abstract divinities of, i. 282
—power, vii. 128
—powers, definite cult of, grew largely from ancestral ghosts, vii. 179
Spiritualism, x. 262
Spitama family, Zoroaster of the, vi. 341
Spitting, iv. 316, 318, 321, 374
—into fire " wounding " it, or stirring it with unclean stick causes its anger, iv. 235
—juice of alderbark at end of bear hunt, iv. 87–88

Spitting on images in creation, ix. 173
—to east as greeting to sun, vii. 232
Spittle and clay to restore sight, ix. 59, 318 [5]
—creation of stars and Earth-mother from, x. 206–207, 208
—desecrates fire, vii. 54
—man created from, ii. 26
—of devil causes diseases, iv. 374
——gods and red earth used for creation, ix. 24
——Odin in place of yeast, ii. 121
——stars, dew as, xi. 278
—poison to the centipede, viii. 314
Spityura, brother of Yima, vi. 312
Spleen stones, xi. 284
" Spoils of Annwfn," iii. 95–96, 192
Spontaneity, doctrine of, original law of creation, viii. 54–55
Spoon, the silver, iv. 267, 269, 274
Sport of gods to try to harm Balder, ii. 129
Spot, purified, iv. 173–174
" Spring and Autumn Annals ": see " CH'UN CH'IU."
—Armenian Navasard originally celebrated in, vii. 21
—Festival, connexion of Wa with, in Kēngtüng, xii. 281
—goddess, viii. 234
—sowing, pouring of water at, vii. 22
—spirits walk about early in, iv. 63
Spring, Balder created a, ii. 134
—brother and Fire sister, vii. 56, 57, 58
—entrance to hill, x. 127
—Mist- and Cloud-, x. 200
—named for Dirke, i. 43
—of Glauke, i. 41
——Hippoukrene, i. 40
——life, dead at, xii. 36 (fig. 23)
———localized at Abydos, xii. 50–51
——Peirene, i. 40, 41
—(sacred), Fosite's, baptism in, ii. 163
——madness of Glaukos's horses said to be caused by drinking at a, i. 39
—(" sea "), created by Poseidon on the Acropolis, i. 66
—source of four streams in lowest world-storey, x. 159
—used for sacrifices, ii. 333
Springs, ix. 79, 88, 89, 179–180, 221, 233
—and streams, numina of, i. 295
—Corinthian tales of genesis of, i. 41

Springs, cows which Loki milks are warm, ii. 146
—curative, viii. 230, 275
—doorways to Underworld, x. 61
—fairy, iii. 259
—fire-, Persian and Armenian worship of seven, vii. 56
—god of, v. 94
—hot, viii. 252
—Nuu sends his, to " the two mysterious ones," xii. 47–48 and fig. 43, 371 [44]
—(Nymphs), i. 257–259
—of Areia, i. 45
——Lerne, i. 31, 32
——Okeanos, i. 40
—on ladder to Heaven, x. 234
—rain-giving, iv. 213
—sacred, ii. 203–204, 209; vi. 235; vii. 59, 60, 62
—six, in six mountains of cosmic points, x. 190
—warm, presided over by Sul, iii. 11
Springtime, Greek papyrus identifies Isis-Nephthys with, xii. 392 [58]
Sprinkling of rain by means of plumed sticks, x. 190
—water on persons and animals at sacrifice, iv. 212–214, 242, 259, 270
Sprites, ii. 223
Spukdämonen, haunting-demons, vii. 119
Spy, wicked, devil, v. 362
Squash-blossom symbol, x. 199
Squatting divinity, iii. pl. III (3), opp. p. 14, pl. VIII, opp. p. 72, pl. IX, opp. p. 86, pl. XXV, opp. p. 204
Śraddhā (" Faith "), abstract goddess, vi. 54
Śrāddha performed by son for dead, vi. 247, 249
Sraosha, vi. 261, 328, 338, 344
Sṛbinda may be aboriginal name of foe of Aryans, vi. 68
Sreča, Serbian counterpart of Russian Dolya, iii. 252
Sreng, Firbolg warrior, iii. 24, 25
Śrī, goddess, vi. 93–94, 97, 124, 132, 153, 217, 239
Sṛma, an Asura, vi. 84
Sroṅ-btsan-sgam-po, vi. 208, 213, 216
Srvara, dragon, vi. 328, 329, 350
—Keresāspa's fight with, vi. 325
—slain by Keresāspa, vi. 324
Ssabeans worshipped Sin at Harran, v. 154

Ssabeans worshipped Tammuz (Adonî), v. 336
Ssŭ chao (four omens), viii. 135
—hsiang (four heavenly appearances), viii. 136, 142
—K'u Ch'üan Shu, viii. 17
—ling, spiritual animals, viii. 98
— -ma Ch'ien, historian, viii. 7, 145, 199
—Mei Chü (four beautiful objects), viii. 88
—Ming, hero, arbiter of life and death, viii. 86, 89–90
—T'ien T'ai, Inspector of Astrology, viii. 143
——Wang, viii. 14, 110
—Wei, viii. 110
S-symbols, iii. pl. II, opp. p. 8, pl. III, opp. p. 14, pl. IV, opp. p. 20, pl. XIX, opp. p. 152
Stabbing or binding of animals to grave, iv. 483
Staff, goat-herd's, attribute of Pan, i. 269
—Grid's, ii. 84
—lent to Thor, ii. 84
—magic, of hyena, to restore life, vii. 171
—of gold to determine place of settlement, xi. 243, 249
—that kills, vii. 339
Stag, Artemis changed Aktaion into, i. 46
— -divinities, possibly horned gods anthropomorphic forms of, iii. 129
— = Great Bear, Orion, iv. 417, 426–428, 429
—horn moss used as a charm, viii. pl. VIII, opp. p. 226
—six-footed, iv. 435, 436
—Tuan Mac Cairill as, iii. 207
Stage, heroic, Kastor and Polydeukes appeared on, i. 26
Stages, creation in series of eight, ix. 15–16, 18
Stair-design, symbol of earth, xi. 368 [15]
Stairs from earth to sky, iv. 442, 449
—of Osiris and his circle, xii. 97
——the sun, xii. 26, 29, 35 and fig. 20, 97, 98
Staka Pas, god of the Erzä, iv. 157–158
Stake, corpses pinned to ground by, iv. 4
—driven through exhumed corpse of vampire to end its power, iii. 232

Stalk: see REED.
Stallion, white, ridden round stone to call spirit to prevent war, iv. 155, 156
Stamps marking Votiak property, and inheritance of same, iv. 117
Standing-stones, iii. 159
" Stanzas of the Graves," Welsh poem, iii. 189, 191
Star, Stars:
Star, appearance of, viii. 33, 36
—Boy: see POÏA, ETC.
—each mortal has own, iv. 395
—eight-rayed, of Semitic Queen of Heaven, xii. 372 56
—festival of Tana-bata, viii. 235–237, pl. x, opp. p. 236
—four-pointed, symbol of, v. 150
— -gods(?), Babylonian, Kisagan-Tengri and Kudai Jajutshi originally, iv. 406
—Lovers, viii. 235–237
—Morning, 'Athtar as, early replaced in Asia by Venus as Queen of Heaven, xii. 54
——Horus regarded as, xii. 102
——Ishtar and Astarte as, are war goddesses, v. 26
——most important planet, xii. 54
——obscure allusions to birth of or by, xii. 373 61
——Osiris or Horus connected with, xii. 94
——surrounded by female marmosets, xii. 365 27
——symbolizes Osiris, xii. 54
—Nabû as fixed, identified with Aldebaran, v. 160
—of Abundance (Coma Bereneces), v. 317
——the tablet, Aldebaran known as, v. 160
—Plough (Triangulum), v. 29
—polar, layers of Heavens joined by hole under, iv. 310, 487
—seven-rayed, as hieroglyph, xii. 372 56
———between horns on head of Sekha-(u)it, xii. 53
—shooting, sign of death, vii. 94
—Waggon, v. 94, 109
—was ideogram for god An(u), v. 93
— -worship, iii. 273
——in Hispaniola, xi. 32

Stars, ii. 82, 124, 197, 328; iii. 319, 320, 321, 323, 324, 325, 326, 328, 329, 358 22, 359 38 46, 360 75; iv. 417–438; v. 110; vi. 22, 31; vii. 119, 144, 225, 226, 228, 229; viii. 51, 137; ix. 37, 142, 177, 223, 224, 275, 282, 293, 295, 299, 314 103; x. xxii, 8, 25, 26–27, 95–96, 103, 108–112, 116–117, 121, 162–163, 167, 187, 203, 205, 206, 223, 231, 278 14; xi. 60, 98, 138, 169, 176, 240, 246, 304–311, 336
—as fruits and leaves of celestial tree, xii. 35
——holes in sky-roof, iv. 336
——servants and messengers of sun-god, xii. 55
——souls, xi. 39
—associated with divinities, iii. 100
—bands of, v. 306
—Chaldean forecasting from, iv. 407
—circumpolar, xii. 60
—creatures of evil fighting with the, vi. 293
—dead become, xii. 178
—decanal, xii. 139, 405 39
——from Denderah, xii. 56 (fig. 56), 378 94
—explanation of motion of, around holy mountain in the " Bûndahish," iv. 344
—firmament revolves about northern polar, v. 94
—fixed, are all gods or " souls," xii. 55
——divided into three parallel bands, v. 94, 95, 173
——Sothis queen of, xii. 101
—idea that souls are, vi. 102
—in Vedic literature, souls of virtuous men, vi. 314
—Isis as mother of, xii. 99
—lakes and canals depicted in, xii. 416 12
—layers of, iv. 309
—little known of some deities found in, xii. 64, 377 91
—malachite powder falls from, xii. 367 12
—moon grows every month by swallowing, xii. 423 24
—Morning and Evening, had Arabic names in Edessa, v. 35
———in Egyptian religion, xii. 54, 373 60
—never-vanishing, xii. 26, 55, 59

Stars, numbers of rays of, xii. 368 [12], 372 [56]
—Osiris seen in, xii. 124
—prayer and magic assist dead to fly to the, xii. 175
—probably regarded as scattered and reunited fragments of sun, xii. 94, 395 [78]
—scant reference to, in Japanese myths, viii. 235, 237
—shepherded as kine by moon, vi. 233
—shooting, xi. 323, 327
——Leza believed to come in, vii. 133
——Milhoi (or jinn) struck down by, vii. 412 [4]
—Sozun-uul changed into constellation of five, iv. 365
—thought to be fravashis of human beings, vii. 94
—Toltec first to calculate movements of heavens by movements of, xi. 53
—Venus as Morning and Evening, v. 24–25
—vs men, iii. 273
—which fix course of sun as time regulators, v. 306
—worship of, vii. 17, 47–53
Stargard, iii. 305
Starkad, hero and foster-son of Odin, ii. 52, 54, 57, 73–74, 115, 244, 277
State, divine right of kings forms Sumerian and Babylonian theory of, v. 166
—organized by Theseus, i. 103
Stations of gods, Marduk created, v. 304, 305
Statues of Armenian deities, vii. 24, 26, 27, 28, 29, 36, 37
Stature of inmates of lowest Jain hell, vi. 228
Staves, magic, iii. 66, 173
Stealing by ghosts, vii. 186–187
—of earth, iv. 461–462
Steeds of Matholwych mutilated, iii. 100
Steel and flintstone, iv. 450, 453
—origin of, iv. 257
—used to capture water cattle, iv. 205
Stein, son of Thorolf, dedicated to Thor as Thorstein, ii. 76, 190, 208
Steingud, ii. 342
Steinvora, mother of Ref, ii. 76–77
Stelae, sculptured, xi. 149
Stellar deities, forgotten, xii. 375 [77]
—divinity, a lost, xii. 64 and fig. 69

Stellar speculations, xii. 64–65
Stench from hair of Thorkill killed onlookers, ii. 95
Step-mother, cruel, vii. 203
—jealous, ix. 88–89
Steps, flight of, at Abydos represent stairway of sun, xii. 98
Steropes (" Lightning ") born of Ouranos and Gaia, i. 6
Stettin, worship of Triglav at, iii. 284, 285
Sthāṇu, vi. 112, 142
Stheneboia, i. 32
—queen in Argos, made advances to Bellerophon, i. 39
Sthenelos, son of Perseus, i. 76, 77
Stick, black, shaken, causes death; white, a return to life, vii. 339
—cleft: see WOOD, CLEFT.
—divination of length of life of child from, x. 252
—for sacrifice meat, iv. 273, 281
Sticks, fire-, ix. 282
—placed in porridge to determine luck of new born, iv. 253–254, 256
Stilbe (" Flash "), daughter of Philonis and Eosphoros, i. 247
Stilts, ix. 86
Stock, basic, of Japanese, Chinese, and Koreans, viii. 209, 210, 212
Stocks of Andean north, xi. 187–189
——Great Plains, x. 74–77
——Gulf Region, x. 53–54
——Mexico and Central America, xi. 41–43
——mountain and desert, x. 129–181
——North-west Coast, x. 237–240
——Pampas, xi. 316–319
——South America, xi. 255
Stockyards, sacrifice to wind-god on behalf of, iv. 232
Stone aimed at ||Gaunab rebounds and kills thrower, vii. 214
—Amazon, xi. 284, 374 [4]
—and iron, mother and father of fire, iv. 450; see also items s.v. ROCK.
—arch, Heaven as a, iv. 342
—Ariadne turned into, i. 36
—as charm to block approach of Death, vii. 178
—bearded, " Debble " assumes shape of, vii. 414 [25]
—brought by bride to new home, iv. 452

Stone, burning, x. 98
—Calendar-, xi. pl. xiv, opp. p. 100
—canoe, three stone men in, x. 136
—cast in air, divination by, iv. 157
—Choque Suso changed into a, still guarding channel, xi. 231–232
—circles, ii. 282
—claws of, of thunderbird, iv. 439
—creation of earth from, ix. 18, 158–159, 174, 175
——earth-godlings from a, xi. 89
——wife from a, ix. 18
—Dionysos's wife changed into, i. 36
—dragon's or serpent's, vii. 76–77, 391 8
—dwarfs turn to, ii. 197
—embodying Magna Mater brought to Rome, i. 304
—fallen warriors turn into, ii. 316
——worshipped for fruitfulness or rains, iv. 397–398
—fawns conveyed to Heaven by great, x. 233
—fort, Manannan's, iii. 116, 122
—giants: see GIANTS, STONE.
—God commands, to rise from ocean, iv. 317
—gods changed into, xi. 167
—head of Coyolxauhqui, xi. pl. vii, opp. p. 60
—heap into which one must cast stone for luck, iv. pl. li, opp. p. 458, 470
—heated, thrown by Moon to kill his wife, x. 114
—heaven, iv. 342
—hero half of, ix. 89
—implements, vii. 259
—(in Sisyphos myth), allegorical interpretation of, i. 38
—in Thor's head, ii. 82
— -knife god, xi. 54
——birth of the, xi. 89
——pins Mt. Taylor to earth, x. 162
—magic, Grail as a, iii. 203, 204
—man made by Moon from, ix. 273
—memorial, with inscription, iv. pl. xl, opp. p. 302
— -men, sons of, Watwa call themselves in ritual chants, vii. 264
—meteoric, vii. 129–130
—monster ravaging Aithiopia turned into, i. 35
—mother and son turned into, to avoid incest, ix. 172

Stone, names of giants connected with, ii. 279
—Niobe turned into, i. 44, 175
—Odysseus's account of Sisyphos rolling the, i. 38
—of blacksmiths, vii. 27, 28
——Fal, iii. 41, 204
——magic properties found in entrails of animal, iv. 458
——possession of new land, Ayar Auca transformed into a, xi. 251
—old woman who escaped flood turned into, ix. 257
—or metal thrown to Näkk for protection, iv. 203, 206
—origin of mankind from, ix. 110, 111, 170
——world from split open, ix. 158
—Phineus turned into, i. 35
—Polydektes and courtiers turned into, i. 35
—post or pillar, iv. 337–338
—power of Gorgons to turn people into, i. 34
—primitive people turned into, on appearance of Sun, xi. 153
—quest for cure for man turned into, ix. 207–208
—rectangular, Manât represented by, v. 21
—red, used to bring Zada wind, iv. 458
—rolled uphill, i. 38
—sacrifice-, xi. 74
—sacrifices at, near Nemda, iv. 155–156, 174
—seats, perhaps thrones for deities, xi. 206
—see BAETYL, SACRED.
—Seide may be human being or bird turned into, iv. 105–106
— -Shirt slays Sikor, x. 133
—sky vault of, x. 60
—specially consecrated for burnt offering to sun, iv. 238
—square, symbol of Dusares (Dušurā) and Allāt, v. 16
——worshipped as Allāt, v. 16
—stead called, ii. 269
—stretching of, x. 222
—substituted by Rhea for Zeus, history of, i. 7–8
—summoned by Wakanda from waters to be home of animal-souls in primitive chaos, x. 106–107

Stone, sun and moon shaped from, ix.
253
—sunlight turns dwarfs and giants into,
ii. 269, 277
—thrown from Heaven turns to lightning and kills thief, iv. 442
—transformation into, as fulfillment of
wish, x. 50
—wall of Oengus, iii. 41
—with golden chain with which Fionn
slew enemies, iii. 175
— -working, x. 183
—world-bull stands on, iv. 312
—worship, vi. 240
—Zeus changed hound and she-fox at
Thebes into, i. 73
—Zipacna turned into, xi. 169
Stonehenge, iii. 10
—stones of magic and healing virtues
removed to, iii. 201
—Sun ritual reminiscent of, x. 89
Stones, Antillean triangular carved, xi.
23, pl. II, opp. p. 24, 350 9
—(as jewels) x. 138, 188, 288 32, 308 62
—birth, v. 327, 331
—bleeding of, x. 283 27
—boundary and standing, iii. 333 5
—changed into men who supported
Heaven, ix. 252
—creation of men and women from,
i. 19
—fates decreed for, v. 122–124, 129
—for weighing dead, iv. 494
—fragments from body of Chakekenapok cause growth of, x. 41
—gaming- and thunder-, x. 48, 189,
288 32 33
—graven, laid in walls to mark end of
katuns, xi. 149
—heaps of, dedicated to Hermes, i. 194
—heated, put into body of dying man,
xi. 323
—in fields and irrigating channels, worship of, xi. 224
——New Year's festivals, xi. 144
——wailings of Gilgamish, v. 261, 262
—incised, from Scotland, iii. pl. x, opp.
p. 94, pl. XVII, opp. p. 134
—Inue of, especially potent, x. 5
—magic properties in, x. 18, 98, 283 27–
284, 308 62
—moccasins of red-hot, x. 231, 232
—musical, viii. 35, 36
—myth of hostility of, v. 119–120

Stones, naming of, v. 120
—precious, xi. 201; xii. 74, 367 12
——adorning Heavens, v. 94–95
——Gilgamish found, v. 210
—pursuing, x. 290 37–291
—rain of red-hot, xi. 72
—record, discovered, xi. 218
—red-hot, x. 228, 232, 260, 261
——death by, ix. 61, 63, 86, 133
—sacred, vi. 240; xi. 178, 179, 180
—sacrifices on boundary, iv. 173
—slung in war directed by Hero Aren,
iv. 156–157
—soft, ordered to cover grave of Haitsi-
aibeb, vii. 216
—spirit-, ii. 312
—sprang from blood, x. 296 45
—symbolize permanence, long life, wisdom, x. 106
—those of, v. 213, 214
—upshooting, x. 233, 294 42
—venerated, x. 284 27
—why spiders go under large, vii. 328
Stony places as home of spirits: see
MASSIS, SACRED MOUNTAIN.
——Devs in, vii. 87
Stool (chief's seat of honour) in chameleon story, vii. 106
—rose into Heaven with Mrile, vii.
136
—sorcerer's, xi. 264
Stopan, deceased ancestor who guards
house, feast to, iii. 238, 246
Stopanova gozba, festival for Stopans,
iii. 238
Stopper, fiery, iv. 320
Storage-jar of Eurystheus, i. 80, 83
(fig. 3B)
Storehouses for offerings, iv. 140–141,
142, 144, pl. XVII, opp. p. 146
Storeyed house on mountain refuge from
flood, ix. 257
Storeys, earth and sky, how counted,
xi. 52
—in earth, Heaven, sky, Hades, iv. 307,
309, 310, 338, 339, 340, 341, 344, 349,
394, 400, pl. XLVI, opp. p. 400, 404,
405, 486–487, 488
——Tower of Babel, xii. 266
Stork or swan, ii. 363 4
—Peak of Lü Mountains, viii. 123
Storm, viii. 36
— -clouds, Sêth as, xii. 108, 125
— -daemons, i. 267

Storm-divinity, the Chimaira seems to have been a, i. 40
—dragon associated with, vii. 80–81, 392 [21]
—Druidic, iii. 44
—from throwing water on fountain, iii. 191
— -god, vii. 14, 46, 384 [60]
——adventures of, viii. 228–229, 248, 249–251, 381 [1]
——and sun-goddess, contest between, viii. 225–227, 230–231
——born from nostrils of father-god, viii. 224
——brother of sun-goddess, viii. 211
—gods of: see GODS, LESSER.
—malevolent powers of Great Heads personification of, x. 29
— -myth, i. 73
——and story of first man, probability of contamination between, vi. 295
—myths of the, vi. 263, 264, 265, 315, 326; viii. 254–255, 271
—personified, Furious Host the, ii. 40–41
—see HIRA HURRICANE, ETC.; INDRA, ETC.
—Seides had power of raising, iv. 103, 104; see also SHAMAN, PERMIAN BELIEF, ETC.
—terminating Age of Monsters, x. 164
—Thor causes, ii. 80
—with fiery bolts falling, sign of passing of a great soul, iii. 14–15
Storms, iii. 322; iv. 457
—four sons of Horus or Osiris guard blessed against, xii. 394 [67]
—god of, vii. 237
—in Pawnee creation-myth, x. 109–112
——the latter part of the winter release daemons, i. 270
—see SHAMANS CONSULTED, ETC.
Storwolf, skin-changer, ii. 293
" Story of a Chief," vii. 359
Strabo, statements of, regarding cult of Anahit, vii. 17, 26
" Strange Stories of the Liao Studio," viii. 156
Strangers, Erinyes defenders of rights of, i. 277
Strangling of caciques and those named by caciques, xi. 27
Strata, twofold, in Celtic myth, iii. 18–19

Stratagems and sleight of Loki, ii. 139, 140
Straw, belt of, worn at harvest festival by widow of deceased, iv. 58
—burning, carried in procession on St. John's Eve, iii. 47
—cord and papers sign of sanctity, viii. 247
—death, xi. 28
—dolls, iv. 248
—dying moved from bed to litter of, iv. 21
—etc., as fuel, vii. 58, 60
—images, vii. 271
—Vahagn stole, to form Milky Way, vii. 37, 49, 386 [14] (ch. vi)
—wheels set on fire and quenched in river, vii. 60
" Strayings " and darkness brought on Elcmar, iii. 52
Stream, ashes cast into, thereby killing all its creatures, iii. 132
—Feast of the Winding, viii. 352
—may have been personified as a steed, iii. 129
—no one drinks water of, vii. 208
—origin of, and Celtic god-myths mingled, iii. 10
— -spirit, shrine of, xii. pl. VI, opp. p. 268
Streams from mountains are trails to Underworld, x. 61
Strength of Cúchulainn taken by women of síde, iii. 86–87
—Strength-giving deity, xi. 25
—trial of, x. 37, 282 [21]
Stretching contest, ii. 90–91
Striae, ii. 301
Stribog, Slavic deity, iii. 297, 300–301
Stride, triple, of Viṣṇu, vi. 29, 79, 80
Strife, creation of, i. 6
—Homeric, Pawnee analogy to, x. 112
—Odin chooses daily those to fall in, ii. 45
—of gods, iii. 23–41
——powers of light and growth with those of darkness and blight, iii. 35–36
Stringes (" Vampires "), i. 278
Strömkarl, water-elf, lay of, ii. 210–211
Strophades, birds similar to Harpies of the, xi. 191–192
—home of Harpies, i. 266

Strophios brings up Orestes with his own son Pylades, i. 135

Struck-by-Lightning Fraternity, x. 185, 288 [32]

Stump, petrified, used as gnomon of sun priest, x. 193

Stumps: see STOREYS IN EARTH, ETC.

—to mislead dead, iv. 25

Stūpa, Śākyamuni left relics of himself in a, vi. 199

Stupidity of Hubeane, vii. 217–219

Sturgeon: see HIAWATHA.

" Sturlunga-saga," ii. 250, 252

Stylus of metal, Ptaḥ opens mouths of dead with, xii. 407 [77]

Stymphalos, Arkadian, cleared of man-eating birds, i. 84

Styrbjorn prayed Thor for victory, ii. 77

Styx, a tenth part of the waters of Okeanos, i. 256

—Leto's oath by the, i. 174

—river (of hate) of Hades, i. 143

Su Lao-ch'üan Tsi, viii. 83

—Wên, viii. 14, 28

Sualtam, Dechtere affianced to, iii. 84

—Lug called son of, iii. 140–141, 152

Subhadrā, vi. 134

Sucellos, hammer-god, iii. pl. XIII, opp. p. 116, pl. XXVI, opp. p. 208

Sūdābah, vi. 336

Sudanic negroes, speech of, vii. 110

Sudarari, root, song of, xi. 291–292

Sudās, vi. 35

—Bhṛgus foes of historic king, vi. 63

Sudatory, celestial, x. 294 [42]

Sudaung-byi Pagoda at Taung-byōn, xii. 350, 352

Sudeni, a division of Baltic peoples, iii. 317

Sudhanvan (" Good Archer "), vi. 57

Sudharmā, wife of Mātali, vi. 132

Sudice, Sudjenice, etc., givers of fate, iii. 250

Sudika-bambi in Angola, vii. 119

Śūdra, wife of a Brāhman bore Duḥsaha to a, vi. 180

Śūdras, Aśvins were, vi. 141

Sudre (South), dwarf, ii. 265

Sudurmukha of Gāndhāra reincarnation of Duḥsaha, vi. 181

Suegagna (" Demon with Light "), Spaniards called on account of cruelties, xi. 202

Sueje-animal, iv. 285

Sueje, shaman's tutelary genius, iv. 11, 284–285

Sueno, Danish king, offered goblet to Svantovit, iii. 280

Suetiva, a devil, xi. 202

Suffocation, iii. 228; iv. 468

Suga, viii. 249

Sugannunna (" Lord of Seacoast "), title of Ninurta, v. 132

Sugar-cane, origin of humans from the, ix. 110

Sugrīva, Rāma allied with apes under, vi. 128

Suhrāb and Rustăm, Irish parallel to story of, iii. 145

—son of Rustăm, vi. 332, pl. XLI, opp. p. 332

Suhurmashû (" skate-goat "), conception of form of Enki as, v. 105, 106, 396 [52]

Suicide, viii. 346, 347; ix. 77, 89, 226

—of servants and women on graves of kings, vii. 95, 98, 99

Suicides, ii. 42; iv. 493

—burial of, vi. 248

—souls of, iii. 231

Sui-jên, viii. 26

Suilap, son of creator, iv. 405

Suir, swineherds as water beasts a year in, iii. 58

Suitors, Odysseus slaying the, i. pl. XXXIV, opp. p. 136

—test of, viii. 262–263

Sujātā and Buddha, vi. pl. XXIV, opp. p. 190

Sukanyā given to Cyavana, vi. 87, 141

Sukhāvatī, viii. 241–242

—heaven, vi. 200, 211

Sukkal, god, v. 177

Śukra, vi. 153, 168

—(or Mahāśukra), vi. 227

Śukšendal, evil household god, iv. 166

Suku-na-biko, a dwarf god, viii. 229, 381 [5] (ch. iv)

—medicine-man among ancient gods, viii. 252

Sul, British goddess presiding over warm springs, equated with Minerva at Bath, iii. 11

Śūladhara, Śūlapāṇi, Śūlin, names of Śiva, vi. 111

Sulbundu, shepherd-god, iv. 432

Šuldeš, iv. 274, 276, 280

Sultan Darai, tale of, vii. 358
—Majnun, tale of, vii. 358
Sulton (= Sultan), Votiaks and Cheremiss worship a lud-spirit called, iv.
151, 152, 157
Šūlvāṇa, vi. 97
Sumāli, grandfather of Kubera, vi. 157
Sumatra, Indian influence in parts of,
ix. 242, 306
—mouse-deer as trickster-hero in, ix. 203
—possible Indian influence on Battak
in, ix. 243
Sumbur, Sumer, Sumur, world-mountain, iv. 341, 342, 343, 345, 346, 349
Sumer, first South Arabian invasion of,
v. 7
Sumeria, Nana originally a goddess of,
vii. 38
Sumerian, importance of, v. 88
—influence on Iranian and Indian legend, v. 130
—sources for Semitic religion, v. xvi
—texts, philological reasons for arguments and translations based upon,
v. xv–xvi
Sumero-Akkadian pantheon, v. 88–165
Sumeru, world-mountain of India, iv.
344, 355, 356, 410
Sumi-no-ye, home of Urashima, viii.
264
Sumitrā, vi. 127
Sumiyoshi, viii. 286
Sumi-zome-zakura (" cherry tree in
black robes "), viii. 348
Summer lightning sign of ghoulish
spirit, ix. pl. xxiii, opp. p. 284
—son, iv. 243
Sumri, the spirit of man and soul of
life, xii. 264–265
Sumugan, god of cattle, v. 191, 193,
236
Sumukha, husband of Guṇakeśī, vi. 132,
149
Šumundu = kātilu, " slayer," v. 417 41
Sun, ii. pl. v, opp. p. 22, 89, 90, pl. xiii,
opp. p. 106, 124, 196–201, 221, 222,
279, 313, 338, 339, 340, 341, 342, 343,
346, 385 59
—iii. 319, 320, 321, 323, 324, 325, 326,
328–329, 330, 359 38 46 52, 360 75 80 81
—iv. pl. xxvii, opp. p. 224, pl. xxviii,
opp. p. 228; 417, 419–425
—vi. 16, 18, 19, 22, 24, 25, 26, pl. iii,
opp. p. 26, 29, 31, 32, 33–34, 35, 43,
55, 59, 60, 61, 65, 66, 67, 68, 69, 74,
91, 100, 110, 138, 139, 149, 151, 183,
184, 192, 194, 196, 232, 233; 276, 287,
289, 291, 293, 295, 304, 313, 316, 317,
349, 351
—vii. 11, 17, 44, 47–53, 367, 386 2; 116,
133, 144, 220, 225, 226, 227, 232–234,
235, 321
—viii. 29, 42, 51, 84, 99, 137, 142, 143
—ix. 37, 43, 45–46, 110, 111–112, 113,
119, 144, 157, 159, 166, 177, 221–224,
250, 253–254, 274–276, 283, 286, 312 50,
313 63, 314 98 103
—x. xvii, xxii, 8, 16, 22, 25–26, 36, 37,
44, 60, 64, 81, 99, 108, 113–114, 115,
176, 187, 199, 204, 205, 231, 253,
254–258, 275 10 11, 276 13–278, 291 37,
295 44, 296 45, 300 50, 309 65
—xi. 28, 39, 51, 54, 55, 57, 58, 60, 61,
65, 68, 69, 74, 80, 81, 82, 83, pl. xii,
opp. p. 88, 89, 90, 92, 93, 97, 120, 121,
122, 138, 139, 153, 166, 167, 176, 184,
193, 197, 198, 199, 200, 201, 203, 207,
219, 220, 223, 225, 237, 240, 241, 242–
248, 273, 277, 278, 285, 304–311, 313,
319, 329, 330, 333, 342, 356 22, 368 15
—xii. 255
—a form of fire, vii. 44, 49
——man-slayer, x. 138
—address to, v. 317
—Amen-ḥotep IV's hymn to, xii. 227–
231
—and Hekate saw capture of Persephone, i. 228
——moon called " eyes of Horus," xii.
102
——children of Ormazd, vii. 33
——placed in different storeys of
sky, iv. 309, 405
——worship mentioned by Job, v. 6
—other spirits, Kachin worship of,
xii. 296, 297
——sun-god, word for, written with
Sumerian ideogram for sun, v. 2
—animal sacrifice to, vii. 15
—animals and birds symbols of the, x.
293 40
—annual life of, portrayed on altar, v.
60
—Apis incarnation of, xii. 162
—as cosmic deity, xii. 214
——Creator, xii. 50
——eagle, v. 35
——eye of Heaven, xii. 38

Sun as female deity, v. 5
——" god who begat " or " formed himself " grew quite by himself, xii. 49–50, 219, 220
——hawk's egg, xii. 208, 423 [34]
——Khepri in lower world, xii. 43 (fig. 36)
——scarab accompanied by Isis and Nephthys, xii. 96
—astral deity of primitive Semitic religion, v. 6, 11
—Ba'al Shamîn or Mihr probably corresponded to the, vii. 17
—baboons greet the, xii. 32 (figs. 13, 14)
—battles with 'Apop, xii. 364 [11]
— -bearer, xi. 92
—Bês as guardian of, xii. 64
—birth and death of, xii. 96
——of the, witnessed by dead, xii. 35 (fig. 21)
—birthplace of, at Bu-gem(et), xii. 376 [84]
—blending of forms of, xii. 26
—blind, xii. 384 [116]
—born of Nut every morning, xii. 41, 42
—carried on head and body of Ehet, xii. 71
— -carrier, x. 155, 157, 162, 164, 165–166
—cattle of the, i. 113
— -child, snaring of sun attributed to, ix. 46
—children of the, xi. 242–248
—Chors supposed to have been god of, iii. 299
—column of, iii. 12
—creation of, x. 166–169
—daily birth and death of, vii. 49
—dance, x. 89–90, pl. XVII, opp. p. 90, 95, 123, pl. XIX, opp. p. 124, 170, 292 [39], 307 [61]
—daughter of, iii. 328, 329
—description of, at earliest period, xii. 25
—destruction of earth by, x. 139–140
— -disk, i. 332 [9] (ch. xii); v. 47, 69, 377 [9]
——created, x. 162, 166
—divinity and power of, records of Inca doubt of, xi. 247–248
—double occurrence of, in Heliopolitan doctrine, xii. 50

Sun, dragon consumed by, vii. 392 [21]
—drawing up moisture is Loki drinking, ii. 149
—eagle bird of, v. 119
—Êpet appears at birth and death of, each day, xii. 60
—fatal to dwarfs, trolls, and giants, ii. 269, 277, 285
—Father, x. xvii, 81, 200, 206–209
—female personifications of, xii. 29–30
—femininity of, xii. 365 [19] [20]
—fertilization by rays of, ix. 165
—first of cosmic powers to be worshipped generally, xii. 24
—following the, in mer sacrifice, iv. 269, 270, 278
— -girl and Moon-brother, story of, x. 55–56, 280 [17]
—giving of, after Fall, iv. 385
— -god and Hammurabi, v. 149
——Isis, xii. 80–83, 200, 201
——Anubis son (or, rarely, brother) of, xii. 111
——'Apop enemy of, xii. 104
——as archer adapted to Greek mythology, xii. 239
——at night-time, xii. 27 (fig. 10)
——between horns of celestial cow, xii. 38 (fig. 27)
——bitten by serpent, xii. 25
——blind, Ḥar-khent(i)-merti (?) perhaps influenced by, xii. 388 [28]
——celestial arms receiving, xii. 100 (fig. 94)
——child of Nuu and Nut, xii. 49
——daughters (eyes or serpents) of, xii. 29, 30
——dead become members of crew of, xii. 415 [2]
——designs for, v. 381 [63]
——Dušurā a, v. 16
——Egyptian, born of egg or lotus-stalk, vii. 385 [9]
———slays dragon by fire-spitting serpents, vii. 45
——eight parents or ancestors of, connected with Khmun(u) in Middle Egypt, xii. 48
——enemies of, captured in net, xii. 109, 391 [52]
——four youths (sons of Horus or Osiris) watch birth of, and prepare ship of, xii. 394 [67]
——from Amrith, v. 47

Sun-god, hymn concerning origin of, xii. 68–69

——infant, Khepri as, xii. 105

——Isis, and serpent, myth of, xii. 79–84

——Ixion explained as embodiment of, i. 327 [6]

——Lug perhaps a, iii. 40

——made sole deity by Amen-ḥotep IV, xii. 225

——may be accompanied by Ḥeka and Nehes in his ship, xii. 67

——Minos explained as, i. 63

——Monṭ(u) early identified with, xii. 139

——myth of lost eye of, xii. 85–91

——name Eay, Ay of, interpreted as meaning " ass," xii. 108

——Nergal, specialized aspects of, v. 49 50, 68, 69

——of Syria, Adad as, v. 37

——on back of celestial cow, xii. 50, 78

————his stairs, xii. 35 (fig. 20), 365 [18]

——or -hero, Cúchulainn not necessarily a, iii. 141

——parallel with moon, xii. 28

——passes through Aker's body (earth) by night, xii. 43

——personification of four senses frequently accompany, xii. 66

——produces men from his eyes, xii. 30, 50

——Renenutet identified with asp on head of, xii. 378 [98]

——representation of, xii. 24 (fig. 3)

——rises from leaves of celestial tree, xii. 35

————in east, xii. 65

——rising and setting, iv. 223

——rowing departed soul, xii. 26 (fig. 7)

——sculpture of Syrian, at Ferzol, v. 36

——Sothis-Venus as daughter and wife of, xii. 54

——soul of Nuu identified with, xii. 372 [48]

——Syrian, Ba'al Shamîn merged with, vii. 37

——with four ram's heads, theological speculations on, xii. 66

————single eye instead of head, sitting on his stairs, xii. 365 [18]

Sun-god, withdrawal of, from earth, xii. 76–79, 84, 426 [39]

——Zeus as, i. 159

— -goddess, viii. 210, 211, 212, 232, 257, 266

——and storm-god, contest between, viii. 225–227, 230–231

——birth of, from Father-god's left eye, viii. 224

——High-producing-god may have been associated with, viii. 222

——mother-goddess in South Arabia is, v. 15

— -gods, v. 15, 16, 17, 36, 37, 44 ff., 80, 93, 115, 116, 117, 118, 127, 130, 132, 133–134, 146, 148, 150, 151, 155, 160, 162, 204, 208, 210, 219, 235, 256, 257, 281, 286, 294, 322, 342, 343, 350, 391 [322]; vi. 126, 138, 143, 232; xi. 54, 249; xii. 71 (figs. 75, 76), 78 (fig. 77)

——Sydyk and Misōr as, vii. 40

—Greeks see variety of objects in, i. 242–243

—harmonious movement of, philosophically attributed to Apollo, i. 181

—Helios as divinization of, i. 241–243

—Herakles a god of, vii. 45

—hides in body of heavenly cow at night, xii. 38

—Horus as young rising, and Osiris as dying evening, xii. 102

—identified with hawk, xii. 24

—in Cretan myth, i. 325 [1]

——green bed and in green jungles of the Delta, xii. 367 [12]

——lotus flower, xii. 50 (fig. 48)

—interpretations of symbolism of four Meskhenets of, xii. 52

—Isis a daughter of, xii. 90

——as wife and mother of, xii. 99

—jackal falls in love with, vii. 307

—Justice as daughter of, xii. 100, 386 [22]

—kept in heavens nine months, iii. 52

—(Khepri) lifted over eastern horizon, xii. 48 (fig. 45)

—Kyklopes incarnation of disk of, i. 332 [9] (ch. xii)

—Leza (or Nyambe) may represent the, vii. 133

—lost eye of Khepri as, restored by Shu and Tefênet, who hold sun in place, xii. 70

—member of ennead of Heliopolis, xii. 216

Sun, Mîn identified with, xii. 139
—most local deities ultimately explained as manifestations of, xii. 28
—mother, iv. 222
—of, vii. 49
—myth of two eyes of, xii. 87–88
— -myths, x. 48–49, 55–56, 60–61, 87–
90, 276 [13]–277
—nocturnal course of, through realms
of dead, xii. 417 [21]
—ocean enemy of, xii. 237, 428 [77]
—on sieve drums, iv. 288, 289
—one of the Perfect Ones, viii. 113
—only local divinities attached to cycle
of, or cycle of Osiris, had mythological traits, xii. 20
—Osiris as new, xii. 50, 113
—symbolizes, xii. 93, 94, 123
—personified as Sol, ii. 16
—pig in eye of, xii. 124–125
— -pillars at Tyre, v. 51
—pledge (Odin's eye) thought to be
the, ii. 167
—priests, x. 193
—primeval or daily birth of, from blue
lotus, xii. 39
—Ptaḥ equated with, xii. 145
—raising of, x. 56, 60–61, 168
—(Rê') identified with Abyss (Nuu),
xii. 220
—received by arms at evening or sent
forth by them at morning, xii. 99
—represented by gold in Ezida, v.
159
—with four ram's heads, xii. 364 [15]
— -ring and porridge, iv. 224, 225
—rising, faces of sacrificing priest and
victim turned towards, iv. 220, 223
—rituals and shrines, x. 56–57, 88,
287 [31]
— -sacrifices, animals for, iv. 225
—said to have been born on, or by,
" the Great Flood," xii. 39
—salutations of, xii. 32
—seemingly rising in west, radiance
from Lug, iii. 29
—Sekhmet a warlike manifestation of
the, xii. 146
—semi-mythical description of, vii. 51
—setting, shone on dead, vii. 98
—ship of, lifted from depths by Nuu
in the morning, xii. 95
—shrine containing year-counts, x. 195
—síd near rising of the, iii. 80

Sun, Sol drives horses of chariot of, ii.
183
—Spider an alias of, vii. 284
—stairway of, represented by flight of
steps at Abydos, xii. 98
— -star = Saturn, iv. 407–408
—stars probably regarded as scattered
and reunited fragments of, xii. 94,
395 [78]
—sun-goddess's descendants lose battle
facing the, viii. 211
—Sunna may be a personification of
the, ii. 18
—Sūrya god of, vii. 43
—swallowed and disgorged by Sêth, xii.
128, 401 [33]
—by or battling with 'Apop daily,
xii. 106
—Tawyan built tower to capture the,
xii. 267
—Tear given to Loegaire for wife, iii.
37
—temple of, at Ba'albek, v. 54
—totem, vii. 270
—tradition of wolf swallowing, iii. 229
—true Transformer of First People, xi.
31
—two first Shan kings fabled to have
descended from the, xii. 275
—unborn, held by water dragon, xii.
105 (fig. 103)
—Vahagn a god of, vii. 34, 37, 43, 44
—with ram's head during nightly journey through Underworld, xii. 28,
364 [15]
—worn between horns of Ḥat-ḥôr, xii.
38 and fig. 27
— -worship, iii. 273; iv. 224–225; x. 55–
57, pl. xii, opp. p. 56, 87, 276 [13]
—of Gaza, supposed connexion of
Perseus legend with, i. 36
—possible origin of use of barəsman
in, vii. 386 [13]
—two centres of, v. 150
—worship of the, xii. 23–32
—worshipped by a Lithuanian people,
iii. 318–319
— -worshippers, Nabataeans were, v.
381 [67]
—youth of, depicted on altar, v. 61
Sun Ch'üan, Emperor, viii. 95, 100–101,
176
—Ssŭ-miao, encounter of Yo Wang
with, viii. 106

Sunlight, world-bull afraid of, iv. 312
Sunrise and Kokamomako, tale of, ix. 225–227
Suns, early world epochs, xi. 85, 91–96, pl. xiv, opp. p. 100, 104, 151, 153, 164, 357 [7]
—eight, created to dry up sea, ix. 160
—of the cosmogonic period, Chalchiuhtlicue ruled over one of the, xi. 73
—seven original, ix. 178
—several, go up to sky in turns, ix. 275
Sun's eye and Tefênet differentiated, xii. 87
—people descended to earth on spider thread, vii. 400 [38]
—Well, xii. 31
Sunset, sacrifice performed after, by Samoyeds, iv. 39
—Underworld lies towards, iv. 77
Sunä, sunäsun: see Kut, etc.
Śunaḥśepa, tale of, vi. 147–148
Śunāsīra, ploughshare, vi. 61
Sunda and Upasunda obtained boon from Brahmā, vi. 153
Sung, viii. 105
—Dynasty, viii. 56, 68, 70, 72, 82, 88, 95, 97, 100, 112, 128, 134–135, 143, 199
——History, viii. 203
—Imperial house of, viii. 24
—Li Ch'üan Shu, viii. 56
—Mountain, viii. 189
—Shih, viii. 203
Sunīthā, tale of, vi. 165–166
Sunna, goddess, ii. 18, 184, 197
Sūnṛtā ("Bounteousness"), abstract goddess, vi. 54
Šuöje-lodde, bird lamenting at night with human voice, iv. 11
Sunṭ, a lost stellar deity, xii. 64
Supárṇa, vi. 115, 140
"Suparṇādhyāya," Indian poem, iv. 356
Supernatural beings, grades of, viii. 108
—origin of certain tribes, iv. 502
—powers, viii. 72, 178–179
Supernaturalists, schools of, believed Buddha on earth a phantom, vi. 198–199
Superstitions, xi. 276–277
—about Loki, ii. 149
—burial, iv. 17–35
Suppers, Hekates's, i. 187

Supreme Being (Absolute), absorption of all things in the, vi. 193
——belief in, xi. 372 [7], 375 [16]
——Kalunga used for a, vii. 176
——vague notion of, vii. 115–116
—god: Zeus, i. 158
—Ruler, worship of, viii. 48–49, 50, 51, 135
—Wisdom, identification of the Sīmurgh with, vi. 291
Suqe-matua, brother of Tagaro, ix. 126
Sür: see Kut.
— = soul, iv. 498, 499
Sura, vi. 84, 85
Surā, brandy, vi. 87
—Varuṇa's daughter, vi. 106
Surá, good deity to whom seeds of life were entrusted, xi. 193
Surabhi, vi. 134
Sūraj Nārāyaṇ (Sūrya), sun-god, vi. 232
Šurali, Votiak evil spirit, iv. 181, 182, 184
Suras and Asuras, Indra engaged in struggle between, vi. 132
Šuratan-Tura ("Birth-giving Heaven"), iv. 398
Sürem-ceremonies, iv. 246
Sureties of sea, wind, sun, and firmament, iii. 132
Surgery, viii. 107
—priests of, attended Asklepios, i. 281
Sürö Mountain, iv. 343, 402
Śūrpanakhā assisted Rāvaṇa in battle, vi. 156
Surrogation, i. 126, 184; v. 333, 356; vii. 371; xi. 198–199; xii. 175, 196, 296–297
Sursanabu, Sursunabu, v. 214–215
Surt, ii. 110, 279–280, 324, 331, 338, 339, 340, 341, 343
—fire of, ii. 159, 168, 202
Surtarhellir, giant once dwelt in the lava-cave, ii. 280
Suruga, viii. 251, 262
Surūpā, vi. 134
Survival of fittest at creation, ix. 15
Sūrya, vii. 44; xii. 255
—slays Vṛtra, vii. 45
—(sun), Agni (fire), and Indra (lightning) form triad in India, vii. 43
—sun-god, vi. 13, 21, 26, pl. iii, opp. p. 26, 27, 29, 33, 47, 77, 86, 91, 117, 138, 183, 232

Sūryā, sun-maiden, daughter of the Sun, vi. 30, 47, 55

Susa, pottery of, v. 117, 168

—seal from, v. 4

Susa-no-wo, storm-god, viii. 224, 228–229, 230, 248, 249–251, 302

Suśetka, Siryan god identical with House man, iv. 164

Śuṣṇa, struggles of Kutsa with, vi. 65, 67, 98

Suśravas, vi. 337

Sussistinnako, Spider, x. 203

Susuki (Miscanthus), prince, tale of, viii. 347–348

—plant, viii. 346

Sūta ("Herald") brought forth at birth sacrifice of Pṛthu, vi. 166

Sutic, a window through which came the Tampu tribe, xi. 248

Sutlej (Śutudrī) River, vi. 48, 236

Sūtras, rules regarding sacrifice, vi. 12

Suttee: see SATI.

Suttung, giant, ii. 48, 49, 51, 53, 54

—owned poetic mead, ii. 277, 279

Śutudrī (Sutlej) River, vi. 48

Śu-ut abnê, v. 405 19

Suvarcalā, wife of Sūrya, vi. 138

Suvarṇaṣṭhīvin, vi. 145

Šüvö-pieces, ladles, bowls, etc., iv. 272–273, 274, 277

Suwalki, iii. 317

Suwannakhet probably northern limit of Malay invasion of Indo-China, xii. 287

Svadhā, food of fathers and gods, vi. 71

Svadilfari, giant's stallion, ii. 43, 90, 140

Svafnir, serpent, ii. 217

Svafrlami, sword of, ii. 268

Svāhā, call uttered at sacrifice; wife of Agni, vi. 71, 82, 135

Svalin, shield from sun, ii. 196

Svanhit, ii. 136

Svantovit, prominent deity worshipped in Arkona, iii. pl. XXXI, opp. p. 278, 280–283, pl. XXXIV, opp. p. 288, 305

Svar, sky (originally sacred exclamation), vi. 74

Svarang, sons of, stoned Thor, ii. 91

Svaražic, son of Svarog, iii. 286–287

Svarbhānu, demon, vi. 67

—rescued sun, vi. 65, 99

Svarga ("Heaven"), abode of Indra, vi. 131

—Loka, vi. 100

Svarin's mound, ii. 265

Svarog, Baltic celestial smith compared to, iii. 330

—founder of legal marriage according to old Russian chronicle, iii. 298

—(often identified with Hephaistos) probably name of chief Elbe Slav god, iii. 277

Svarožič, Russian god of fire, iii. 277, 298

Svartalfar ("black elves"), ii. 221, 266

Svartalfheim, ii. 141, 221

Svarthofdi, ii. 252

Svaru invoked as sacrificial post, vi. 61

Śvāśva, epithet of Bhairon, vi. 237

Svatobor on Rügen, iii. 305

Svava, beloved of Helgi, ii. 11, 162, 189, 233, 251

Svāyambhuva, Bhūmiya becoming identified with a form of, vi. 237

Svegdir sought homes of gods and Odin, ii. 269

Sveinsson, Brynjolf, bishop of Skálholt, ii. 4, 7

Sventa Ugnele, Lithuanian, bearing title of Visiya, vii. 365

Śveta, Śvetāśva, Śvetaśikha, Śvetalohita, Śiva proclaimed Yoga system to, vi. 177

Śvetadvīpa ("White Island"), vi. 176

Svia-god (or Sweden-god), Frey the, ii. 28–29, 114

Svipdag, bridegroom of Menglod, ii. 11, 112, 124, 241, 243

"Svipdagsmal," ii. 7, 10–11, 112, 165, 168, 186, 243, 252, 298, 331, 346

Swallow, vii. 418 35

—associated with cult of Artemis, i. 184

—Isis mourning for Osiris assumes form of, xii. 115

—People, x. 160

—Philomele changed into, i. 70

—Prokne changed into, i. 16

—Satan as, in creation-myth, iv. 314, 317

—Star, v. 395 21

Swallower, "Debble" as the, vii. 414 25

—of sun, ii. 199–200

Swallowing incidents, i. 170; ii. 103, 132, 322; iii. 131, 148; iv. 522; vi. 173, 302; vii. 119, 198, 199, 200, 220, 221, 223, 224, 236, 244, 249, 313, 319–320, 326, 406 8; ix. 68, 69, 85, 296; x. 44–45, 51, 79, 274 9

Swamps, creation of, iv. 315, 318, 352
Swan, iv. 500, 501, 503, 504
—attribute of Eros, i. 204
— -maiden parallels in Oceanic mythology, ix. 64, 138–139, 206–210,
294–295, 302, 319 12, 326 17
——tale of, viii. 257–260
— -maidens, ii. 11, 24, 206, 212, 258–
263, 289; iii. 79, 121; x. 133
——Valkyries have some traits of, ii.
255
—Nemesis in guise of, i. 24, 284
— -shift type of tale, x. 293 40
—Zeus in guise of, i. 24
Swangi, vampire, tale of, ix. 231–232
Swans, Apollo in chariot drawn by, i.
180
—children of Ler changed into, iii. 51
—Eochaid and Etain escape into air as,
iii. 81
—survivors of flood became black, ix.
280
Swastika, viii. 149; x. pl. xxiii, opp. p.
170, 186, 310 66
—on Gaulish coins, iii. pl. ii (7, 8), opp.
p. 8
Swearing on a ring, ii. 156
Sweat, ix. 37, 157, 250
— -bath, x. xvi, 98, 106, 170, 284 27;
xi. 74
—first man born from, vi. 293, 295
— -house burned by Loon Woman, x.
228–229
——heavenly, picture of Paradise, x.
220, 223
— -lodge, x. 19, 98, 170
Sweating of stone zemis, xi. 29
——stones, etc.: see WEEPING BALDER
OUT OF HEL.
Sweden, Odin came to, ii. 32
—paganism in, ii. 16
Swift, Mabon called the, iii. 189
Swift-impetuous Deity, viii. 224
Swiftness of Medyr, iii. 190
Swine, iii. 51, 58, 95, 96, 98, 118, 124,
125, 126, 127, 208; v. 132, 133
—battle: see HILDISVINI.
—Ninurta connected with, v. 344
—Odysseus's men changed into, i. 137
Swineherds parallel of Tuan Mac Cairill,
iii. 207
Swing Festival at Bangkok, four cele-
brants wear Nāga headdress at, xii.
277

Swing Festival inaugurated in connexion with the Dionysos-cult, i. 217
—golden (the sun), vi. 22
—of the dead, iv. 30
—rope for descent to Underworld
makes, ix. 76, 77
Sword and trough of blood, dream of,
ii. 250
—(Asi), creation of, vi. 109
— -bird, Spider delivers town from, vii.
329, 330
— -bridge, iii. 197
—Brimir, ii. 169, 278
—called "man's fate," ii. 154
—given by Hermes to Herakles, i. 80
—God's, rainbow as, iv. 444
—in Grail romances, iii. 202, 203, 204
—Kusa-nagi the miraculous, viii. 304
—Lake of the Great, xii. 302, 303–309
—magic, viii. 123
——caught in net by Le-Loi, xii. 303
—Mistelteinn, ii. 136
——first plant, then, ii. 361 22
—of Cúroi, iii. 151
——eight-headed dragon in shrine of
Atsuta, viii. 304
——Frey fights of itself, ii. 109, 110,
111
——Miming obtained by Hotherus, ii.
132, 133, 136
——Susa-no-wo, viii. 229
—one of three insignia of ruling family,
viii. 226, 228
— -play of Ushiwaka, viii. 309–311
—see SPINDLE AND SWORD-HANDLE, ETC.
—shrine dedicated to miraculous, viii.
pl. xv, opp. p. 246
—skalds called a, "Heimdall's head,"
ii. 154
—two-handed Sak-ya, given to Hkun
Hsang L'röng to split gourd, xii.
290–291
—with warrior dancing before it, iii. pl.
ii (6), opp. p. 8
Swords, v. 30, 126
—give light instead of fire in Valhalla,
ii. 314
—magic, ii. 62, 79, 109, 110, 111, 132,
134, 136, 267, 268; iii. 29, 33, 65, 90,
136, 199, 204
—snake on, added to strength, ii. 216
Śyāmā colour, vi. 217
Syāvarshan (Pers. Kai Siyāvakhsh), vi.
336

Sydycos begat Asklepios, v. 67, 74

Sydyk (Sedeq), culture-hero, vii. 40–41

—Kittu appears in Phoenician pantheon as, v. 67

Sygä-Tojon, thunder-god, iv. 442

Syiyr-ajak corresponds to " Cow-footed Man," iv. 182

Syleus of Aulis, Herakles at vineyard of, i. 90–91

Symbêtylos, Ashim-Bêthêl appears as, in Greek inscription in Syria, v. 22

Symbol of soul, silhouette of body the, xii. 174

—or object as " medicine," x. 269 4–270

—plant, of Mendes ram, xii. 164 (fig. 169)

—popular, of Ḥat-ḥôr, xii. 38

—Thor's hammer sacred, used in blessings and consecrations, ii. 79–80

Symbols, birds as Celtic, iii. 13

—of gods, iii. 8–9

——Mîn, xii. 137 (fig. 134)

—on monuments, speculation on, iii. 8

—sun, ii. pl. XXIV, opp. p. 196, 198, pl. XXVI, opp. p. 200, pl. XXVII, opp. p. 204

—used for chapters of books, viii. 298, 382 7 (ch. v)

—wheel of sun and gold plate as, vi. 97

Symbolic types, animals assume, x. 293 40

Symbolism, ix. xv, pl. III, opp. p. 10; x. xvii, xx, xxi, 40, 48, 59, 106, 109, 115, pl. XXII, opp. p. 156, 158, 186, 188, 190, 195, 198, 199, 203, 206, 216, 232, 269 4–270, 284 27, 285 29, 290 35, 293 40, 297 74, 300 50, 302 55, 306 60; xi. 24, pl. III, opp. p. 28, 52, 55, 56, 57, 60, 68, 74, 86, 104, 143–144, 145

Symbolism, because of identical sound of words, viii. 104

—egg, xii. 71

—mythical, vi. 349

—of flowers derived from their characteristics and the seasons, viii. 348

——sacrifices, xii. 195–196

—strong tendency towards, in old Indian and Iranian conceptions, vi. 263

Sympathetic magic, vii. 60

——mirror used to welcome sun as, viii. pl. VIII, opp. p. 226

Symplegades, Athene guides the Argo safely past, i. 172

—moving rocks, Athene guides Argonauts between, i. 111

Syn, goddess, ii. 15, 186

Syncretism of divinities in Egypt, xii. 217–218

—tendency towards, xii. 219–220

Synnytär, deity of birth, iv. 257

Synonyms required of Alviss by Thor, ii. 95, 96

Syr (Freyja), ii. 125

Syr Percyvelle, English Grail romance, iii. 202

Syracuse, mistress of the sea, i. pl. IV (4), opp. p. 1

Syria apparently borrowed killing of Adonis by boar from Egypt, xii. 399 111

—Io finds her son in, i. 30

Syrian influence on Armenia, vii. 15–16

—Kaukabhta identified with Sidonian Astarte, Greek Aphrodite, and Armenian Anahit, vii. 27

Syrtes, Argo held by shoals of, i. 113–114

Systems of divination, viii. 137

Szechuan (ancient Shu), viii. 26, 79, 82, 83, 84, 112, 113, 139, 175

T

Ta'annek (anc. Beisan), v. 44

Taaroa, ix. 20, 26–27, 29, 37, 313 57; see also TANGAROA, PRIMEVAL GOD.

Taaut, Phoenician form of Thout(i), xii. 366 2

——name for inventor of writing, xii. 241

Taba, tale of, ix. 201–202

Tabari, Arabic historian, on St. George, v. 338

Table, dead believed to stay at home forty days under the, iv. 48

—of the deceased, iv. 25, 54, 68

Tablecloth, magic, iii. 118

Tables in lud, iv. 144, 148, 149

Tables, genealogy, ix. 6–7, 17

Tablet, ancestral, viii. 47
—awarded the Yellow Emperor, viii. 27
—marriage by, viii. 149
—mystic, Babylonian copy of, v. 295–296
—on back of sea monster, viii. 30
—set up by Shih Huang on T'ai Shan, viii. 70
—written by Chao Mêng-fu, viii. pls. IV, V, opp. pp. 136, 137
Tablets, clay, with names of antediluvian kings, v. 204–205
—divine, written by Nabû, vii. 384 [51]
—genii of trees displayed at weddings on, viii. 341
—in Kaśmīr, Tibet, etc., phra phim counterparts of, xii. 327
—of Arallû, v. 161, 164
——fate: see FATE, TABLETS OF (vol. v).
——Wu Liang Tz'ŭ, mention of Fu Hsi on, viii. 29, 31
—placed on tortoise as pedestal, viii. 100
Tabu, i. 362 [3]; ii. 95, 204, 212, 322; v. 132, 199–200, 232, 336, 356; vii. 120, 125, 132, 147, 190, pl. XXIII, opp. p. 238, 249, 279–281, 407 [20], 419 [4], 428 [11]; ix. 70, 127, 133, 277; x. 58, 66, 94–96, 114, 115, 120, 215, 258, 264, 276 [12], 292 [40], 302 [53]; xi. 38, 76, 261, 291, 293, 294
—breaches of, produce lochs, iii. 136
——punished by gods, iii. 12
—breath, in connexion with fire, where found, iii. 11
—Bres under, to drink what was milked, iii. 26
—oak-sapling ring a, iii. 152–153
—to males, fires of St. Brigit, iii. 11
—water to Fraoch was, iii. 67
—writing of myths, iii. 8
Tabued grove near Marseilles, mythically described by Lucan, iii. 11–12
Tabuerik, primeval divinity, deity of lightning and thunder, ix. 250, 252
Tabus, breaking of personal, causes automatic working out of punishment, iii. 74, 75–77, 82
—(geasa), iii. 75, 76, 152, 156, 176, 177, 181
—local, in each nome, xii. 362 [3]
—of Conaire, iii. 75–77, 82
——Cúchulainn, iii. 156
—see FOOD, RESTRICTIONS ON, ETC.

Tacatecutli, god of merchant-adventurers, xi. 50
Ta-chi, wife of Chou Hsin, viii. 39–40
Ta Chio Chin Hsien, title of Buddha, viii. 194
—Datoe, planting feast of, ix. 212
——hsang Kahsi and Ya-hsang Kahsi: see YATAI AND YATAWM, ETC.
——hsek-khi and Ya-ksek-khi: see YATAI AND YATAWM, ETC.
——shih-chih, one of a Trinity of Three Holy Ones, viii. 196
—T'ang Hsi Yu Chi, viii. 190
—Ti, Emperor, viii. 65, 73
Tacoma, Mt., x. 135
Tacoma, son of Spider, vii. 323
Tadg, a Druid, succeeded to Almha, iii. 164, 165, 175
Tadpole characters, viii. 11
Tadpoles, Wa trace lineage to, xii. 293–294
Tagaro brothers, ix. 118–119, 124–129
——Mbiti, son of Tagaro, ix. 126
—stole wings of swan-maidens, ix. 138–139
Tagaung Min, king of Tagaung, xii. 342–343
Tages, Etruscan divinity, survives as Tago in modern Romagnola, i. 317
—origin of Etruscan religious system attributed to, i. 289
Tagtug (Uttukku, " the Weaver "), legend of, v. 183, 184, 190–192, 196, 197–202, 227
Taguain, Devil, xi. 295
Taguapaca, servant of Viracocha, xi. 240
Tahirussawichi, Pawnee (Chaui) priest, x. pl. xv, opp. p. 80, 93, 276 [11]
Tahit (Taxet), ruler of heaven-world of North, x. 249, 263
Ṭahmūrath (Takhma Urupi), succeeded Hōshang (Haoshyangha), vi. 301–302, pl. xxxvIII, opp. p. 302, 303
Tahuantinsuyu, native name of Peru, xi. 213
Tai Hua Mountain, viii. 67
—Loi, name given to Buddhistic Was by Shans, xii. 296
—Miao, viii. 70
—Po, god, viii. 186
—(Shans), five clans of, xii. 292
—term applied to many different groups in Indo-China, xii. 288
—Tsung, viii. 96

Tai Wang Kung, viii. 42

T'ai (highest), viii. 109

— -an city, tablet in, viii. 70

—chi, finite existence, apex, viii. 56, 136

—Ch'ing (" highest "), one of the Three Heavens, viii. 109, 110

— -fu, one of the " Three Notables," viii. 109

—Hao, Fu Hsi's name as Emperor, viii. 29

—Hsi King, viii. 56

—Hu, viii. 154

—I Ching, viii. 55

—Kung Wang, viii. 9, 70

—Mountain, viii. 51, 70, 71, 153, 154, 156

— -pao, one of the " Three Notables," viii. 109

— -p'ing shih-êrh ts'ê, viii. 199

—Shan, viii. 51, 70, 71

——Shih Kan Tang put over doors, etc., to frighten evil spirits, viii. 153

— -shih, one of the " Three Notables," viii. 109

—Ssŭ, mother of Wu Wang, viii. 42

—Tsung, dynastic title of Li Shih-min, viii. 14, 18, 19, 20, 21, 22, 23, 24, 78, 96, 124, 134, 179, 199

—Yang, viii. 137

—Yin, viii. 137

—Yüan (" the Holy Woman "), viii. 111

— -yüan, city, viii. 167

Taikomol (" He-Who-Goes-Alone "), x. 220

Tail, eight-forked, viii. 325

—fairy with, ii. 223

Tailed demons, vii. 242–243

Tails, cutting off of, for purpose of disguise, vii. 273–274, 416 [9]

—people born with, xi. 19

" Tain Bó Cúalnge," iii. 11, 57, 65, 68, 127, 134, 143, 152–155, 158

——Fráich, iii. 130

——Regamna, iii. 69

—how narrative of the, recovered, iii. 211

Tainaron, entry to lower world, i. 88, 143

Tainaros, Archangel Michael guards, in modern Greek folk-belief, i. 313

Taïno gods, chief of the, regarded as a yucca-spirit, xi. 34

—Taïno-myths, xi. 17, 28–32, 348 [2], 349 [5]

Taira clan, viii. 307, 309, 311, 312, 353, 383 [7]

Taise, daughter of King of Greece, in love with Fionn, iii. 173

Taisen, Mt., viii. 248

Tait, goddess of weaving, xii. 150

Taizhi-Khan, king, iv. 502–503

Tajar, word for temple, vii. 18

Taka-ma-no-hara, viii. 225

— -mi-musubi and Kami-mi-masubi (meaning of kami in latter), primeval couple, viii. 222, 378 [3]

Takaro created mankind, ix. 107, 128

Takaroa, ix. 33

Takasago, genii of pine-trees at, viii. 253, 340

Take-mi-kazuchi, General of sun-goddess, viii. 230

" Taking Off the Lumps," story of, viii. 283–284

Tako, scene of drama of wistaria fairy, viii. 343

Takotsi Nakawe, earth-goddess, xi. 122

Takṣaka, vi. 97, 154–155, 165, 216, 241

Tal Ubaid, v. 117

Talaings bring Buddhism to Indo-China, xii. 285

—held south of Burma for thousand years, xii. 253

Tālajaṅgha, vi. 154

Talar-disir, evil goddesses, ii. 240

Tales and legends of early mediaeval Ireland and Wales, preservation of, iii. 213

—Colombian and Pueblo, parallels between, xi. 200

Taliesin, iii. 101, 103, 109–112, 188

—cycle purely Brythonic, iii. 93

—poems about, valuable as source for myths, iii. 19, 43, 57, 122, 192

Ta-li-fu ancient capital of Nan-chao Kingdom of Shans, xii. 268

Talisman, hieroglyph for, xii. 421 [6]

Talismans, v. 303, 316, 415 [7]; vii. 110; viii. 149; x. 85, 269 [4], 288 [32], 293 [40], 308 [62], 310 [65]; xi. 179, 275–276; xii. 60

—dragon's and serpent's stones or eggs, vii. 76–77, 391 [8]

—Êpet mistress of, xii. 60, 376 [79]

Talk, Moon can, vii. 290

Talos assisted Minos in administration of law, i. 64

Talos, brazen giant, made by Hephaistos, i. 207
—Cretan coast-patrol, i. 114, 326 [4] (ch. vii)
—death of, i. 114
—lame son of Hephaistos, i. 207
Talthybios, i. pl. xxxiii, opp. p. 132
Tamagostad and Çipattoval, perhaps identical with Oxomoco and Cipactonal, xi. 120, 184
Tamaḥprabhā, vi. 228
Tamamo-no-Maye, fox-witch, viii. 325
Tamancu, mountain, xi. 271
Tamanos, powerful, x. 145
Tama-nui-a-rangi, child of Rangi, ix. 9, 79–82
Tama-nui-a-te-ra, name of sun, ix. 46
Tama-nui-ite-Ra, the sun, ix. 52
Tama-pouli-alamafoa (the "King of Heaven"), ix. 19
Tama-shii, appellation of soul, viii. 237
Tama-te-kapua and dog, tale of, ix. 86
Tamarisk, manna from the, v. 97, 98
— -tree sacred to Apollo, i. 180
Tamats, god of wind and messenger of souls, xi. 122
Tamboeja sent to sky to get flame to light fire, ix. 184
Tamek-vui = Prince of Death, iv. 75
Tametomo, epic hero, archer, viii. 307, 308–309, 383 [11]
Tamfana, goddess, temple of, destroyed, ii. 17, 194–195
Tammuz, vii. 69
—a month, v. 131, 160, 342
—and Adonis identified, v. 76
——Gishzida disappeared, v. 178, 180
——Innini children of water-god Enki of Eridu, v. 347–348
——Ishtar, myth of, v. 336–351
——Ninsubur identified with Orion, v. 178
—as dying god, v. 28, 113, 178, 188, 322, 325, 335, 336, 337, 350–351
——Nergal, v. 351
——Orion, v. 178
——shepherd rarely paralleled in Egypt, xii. 399 [111]
——star or constellation, v. 344
—at gate of Heaven, v. 178–180
——Harran, v. 336
—"brother" in personal names may refer to, v. 7
——of Ishtar, v. 326, 340, 344, 350

Tammuz called "my lord," "my hero," v. 76, 335
——the "wanderer," v. 75
—Damu title of, v. 133, 345
—death and resurrection of, v. 322, 326, 335, 342–343
——of, caused by demons, v. 337
—derivation of name, v. 342, 347
—descended in legitimate line of divinely appointed kings, v. 347
—descends to lower world in month of Tammuz, v. 342, 413 [1]
—drowned, v. 348, 349, 350
—dying god, identified with the sun-god, v. 350–351
—equated with Dusares (Dušurā), v. 17
—faithful or true son, legitimate heir, v. 342, 347
—first born son of Ea, v. 344
—god of irrigation, v. 348
—"healer" of sick, v. 75, 152
—husband of Ishtar, v. 344
—hymns, Ishtar in, v. 341
—identified with Adonis of Gebal, v. 335, 339
—in Arallû, v. 334
——West Semitic and Christian sources, v. 339–340
—lord of weeping and the resurrection, v. xvii, 8, 9, 380 [50]
—love of Ishtar for, v. 28, 256, 335
—man tormented by demons prays to, v. 253–254
—Marduk identified with, v. 156
—may have been deified man, v. 341
—mentioned as fourth king of prehistoric dynasty of Erech, v. 341
—myth of birth of, v. 98
——the shepherd, v. 61
—Ninsubur form of, v. 177
—Ninurta originally also, v. 131
—old forms of myth of, v. 113
—(?) on primitive seal, v. 90
—originally a king, v. 341, 343
—plant of earth offered to, v. 188
—recognized deity, v. 235
—shepherd, v. 178, 344, 348, 349
—Shwe Pyin Nāts suggest, xii. 353
—slain by boar, v. 339
—son of Enki, v. 327–328, 344
——mother-goddess, v. 113
—(St. George parallel of), slain by a king, v. 340, 341
—stood at gate of Anu, v. 94

Tammuz, Sumerian dying god, association of Astarte with, v. 14, 17, 75–76,
326
——kings often identified themselves
with, v. 158
—summoned king to worship stars, v.
339
—supposed Celtic parallels of, iii. 204
—wailings, v. 339
——introduced into Temple at Jerusalem, v. 336, 413 [1]
—wept for because he left the earth,
v. 180
—with Shamash, 152
Tammuz-Adonis, Osiris symbolized an-
alogously to, xii. 95
——Osiris-Horus worshipped at Byblos
under name of, xii. 241, 395 [84]
——represented as Mîn, xii. 156
Tammûzî (Dumu-zi), older form of
Tammuz, v. 339
Ta-mo (St. Thomas?), picture of, at
Si-ngan-fu, xii. 270
Tamoanchan, the Paradise of the West,
xi. 77, 82, 112, 113, 356 [24]
Tamoi, hymn to, xi. 297–298
Tamoussicabo, Carib Ancient of Heaven,
not confounded with veyou, the sun,
xi. 278
Tamōzā (Tammuz), hunter and shep-
herd, v. 339, 340
Tampu-Tocco associated with rise of
Incas, xi. 248, 249, 251
——of Inca tradition, ruins at Machu
Piccu identified with, xi. pl. xxx, opp.
p. 212, 216, 217, 218, 219
Tamtu (Tiâmat [salt-sea]), female
dragon of salt sea, v. 288, 317
— -Tehōm, v. 312
Tamus, son of, and Pupal, tale of, ix.
130–132
Tan, cave of, viii. 99
—Duke of Chow, viii. 41, 43, 47–48
—son of Cau, xii. 355
—transformed into mass of limestone at
foot of betel tree which was his
brother, xii. 356
Tana, change of course of, vii. 351,
429 [2]–430
—Valley, vii. 121, 155
Tana-bata festival, songs of, viii. 369,
372–373
——star festival of, viii. 235, pl. x, opp.
p. 236

Tanagra, reputed birthplace of Orion,
i. 250
—Triton raided shipping and herds of,
and was beheaded, i. 260
—women of, attacked at ceremonial
bathing by Triton, i. 260
Tanagran image of Triton headless, i.
260
Tanais River said to divide Europe and
Asia, ii. 33
——Vanaheim said to be situated at
mouth of, ii. 26
Tanaoa, one of primeval pair, ix. 11; see
also TANGAROA, PRIMEVAL GOD.
Tane, deity, ix. 8, 14, 23, 24, 25, 27, 28,
30, 33, 34, 36, 37, 38, 65, 66, 73–74,
165
— -mahuta, father of forests, ix. 32
T'ang (Ch'êng T'ang), Emperor, viii. 9,
38, 48
—Chü, viii. 139
—Dynasty, events in, viii. 5, 14, 18, 19,
67, 68, 69, 70, 76, 81, 82, 96, 105, 134,
143, 199
—Emperor, viii. 16
—Fu-jên (Ts'ui Shih), viii. 163
—History, viii. 143
Tangaloa, ix. 17, 18, 19, 29, 40, 51, 66
— -atu-logo-logo (celestial messenger),
ix. 19
— -eiki (celestial chief), ix. 19
— -tufuga (celestial artisan), ix. 19
" Tanga-lo-mlibo," Xosa tale, vii. 231
Tangaroa, god of fish, ix. 32
—(Taaroa, Tanaoa, Kanaloa), prime-
val god, ix. 6, 8, 11, 12, 13, 14, 15, 20,
24, 26–27, 28, 37, 44, 128, 311 [15], 313 [57]
—Upao Vahu, sea-deity, ix. pl. II, opp.
p. 4
Tängere develops in meaning from
" Heaven " to " god," iv. 217
Tangiia, deity, ix. 14
Tango, deity, ix. 14
Tango, home of Urashima, viii. 264
—story of pine-tree in, viii. 254
Tanks at sacred places objects of rever-
ence, vi. 236
Tanngnjost (" Tooth-gnasher "), goat
of Thor, ii. 77
Tanngrisnir (" Tooth-gritter "), goat of
Thor, ii. 78
Tannim (dragons), v. 361
Ta-no-kami, songs of, viii. 370–372
Tanshikai, soul of, came as hail, iv. 398

Tantalos, father of Niobe, i. 44
—house of, i. 119–121
—kills his son Pelops, i. 161
—punishment of, in Hades, i. 119, 144, 145, 147, 158
—son of Zeus, i. 157
————and Plouto, i. 119
Tantric rites and doctrines, vi. 184, 204, 205, 231
Tanūnapāt, epithet of Agni, vi. 44
Tao, viii. 9, 10, 13, 18, 108, 147, 189
—Chia, viii. 8
—Chiao, popular name of Taoism, viii. 24
—Chih, viii. 168
—Chün, chief of all supernatural beings, viii. 109, 110
—eternal, formed by combination of Yin and Yang, viii. 56
—Teh King, viii. 13, 18, 19, 20, 53, 54, 134, 189
T'ao Jên ("peach men"), viii. 105
—Yüan San Chieh I, viii. 175
Taoism, viii. 13–24, 55, 57, 71, 76, 104, 105, 106, 107, 108, 109, 110–114, 134, 135, 189, 194, 196, 201; 219, 264, 266, 279
Taoist immortals, viii. 274–280
Tap, tapas, vi. 74
Tapa, ix. 88
— -beater, tale of, ix. 141–142
Tapana, feast of, xi. 266
Taparimarru, wife of Purrunaminari, xi. 259
Tapas ("Ardour"), abstract god, vi. 52
Taper-feasts, iv. 60
Taphios, son of Poseidon, i. 76
Taphos, island of, colonized by Taphios, i. 76, 77
Tapio originally meant forest, iv. 189
Tapir, path of, Milky Way signifies, xi. 278
Taquatú, invisible giant in canoe, xi. 341
Tar abitha, Esthonian battle-cry, Thor's name appears in, iv. 228
Tar Baby, vii. 283, 296, 308, 323, 420 15, 421 20, 422 23, 423 32
Tara, Aillén mac Midhna comes out to burn, iii. 72
—Conaire went in tabued direction around, iii. 76
—Cormac found himself in his palace of, iii. 119

Tara, fortress of, burnt every year, iii. 165
—great dynastic family dwelling at, iii. 45
—Kings of, traditional burial-place of, iii. pl. 1, frontispiece
—naked man [Conaire] with sling came to, iii. 75
—Oengus guided Fionn against, iii. 175
Tārā, incarnations of, vi. 208
—rendered as "Saviour" in Tibet, vi. 217
Tarahumare, Mexican tribe, x. 176–177
Tāraka, vi. 116, 132, 140
Tārakākṣa, lord of one of the citadels, vi. 116, 154
Taranos (Gaulish) perhaps identical with Taran, iii. 93
Tarapaca, appellation of servant of Viracocha, xi. 238
Tārās, feminine deities, vi. 202, 217
—five, preside over senses, vi. 205
Tar-'ata, v. 36
Tarauntis, cult of Astλik in, vii. 38, 39
—Meher legendary hero of, vii. 34
Tarbga, tree of, iii. 127
Tarbh Uisge of Western Highlands, vii. 396 62
Targeldeš = Kožla-ia, iv. 182
Targuts, viii. 96
Targyn-nama, one of first seven men, iv. 379
Taria-nui, fishing-god, ix. pl. IV, opp. p. 18
Tārkṣya, sun-horse, vi. 61, 96
Tarkullu, rope, v. 309
Tarnkappe, coat of invisibility, ii. 268, 269
Taro-plant, ghost changed into, ix. 144
Taroba, sacred lake, vi. 236
Tarqu, Hittite god, Torch identified with, vii. 393 33
Tarroo Ushtey of Isle of Man, vii. 396 62
Tartaros, rocks sank with Prometheus into depths of, i. 13
—(Underworld), i. 5; ii. 305
Tartarrax, Indian chief, x. 311 67
Tarvos Trigaranos, iii. 9, 157, pl. XX (B), opp. p. 158, pl. XXI, opp. p. 166
Tashmêtu (Semitic title), wife of Nabû, v. 158
Tashōns abandoned village because of a siren, xii. 267

Tasks accomplished by companions of heroes, iii. 190
—imposed by Gulu on Kintu, vii. 153–154
—performed by dwarfs, ii. 271, 272
—set Midir by Eochaid, iii. 81
—tales of impossible, in Indonesia, due to Hindu contact, ix. 218
Tasmania as part of Oceania, ix. xii
Tasmanian mythology lost, ix. 304
Tasmanians, ethnology of, ix. 268–269, 302
Taso, cannibal, tale of, ix. 132–133
Tassel, iv. 266, 268, 272, 274
Taste, Sa(u) or Sia(u) god of, xii. 66–67
Tata watches over growth of tree of life, iv. 350
Tatars, after 1236, ruling race for a time in Eastern Russia, iv. xviii
—Kitan, territory ceded to, viii. 58
Tate Mukuru, uzera, salutation to tree, vii. 147
Tatet, Taitet, city of Tait, xii. 409 106
Tatevali ("Grandfather Fire"), xi. 121
Tāthryavant, Vīshtāspa defeated, vi. 341
Tátra Mountains, iii. 266
Tatsuta, viii. 234
— -hime, may originally have been a wind-goddess, viii. 213, 234, 379 17
Tatu designs, x. pl. xxxii, opp. p. 256
Tatuing, ix. 53, 72–73, pl. x, opp. p. 76, 80
—dragon on thighs of Princes, xii. 312
—to make invisible, xii. 348
Tatunen: see PTAḤ(-TAṬUNEN).
—usually identified with Ptaḥ and Nuu, xii. 150
Tauaga, mountain of Melanesian flood tale, ix. 119
Taud, Zeret perhaps identical with modern, xii. 139
Taung-byōn, pagoda at, xii. 350, 352
— -nyo Lèma, Sithu and Kyawzwa sent to live at, xii. 353
— -ngu, Sithu and Kyawzwa ordered to, xii. 353
Taurobolos epithet of Anahit, vii. 383 39
Tauroi, Iphigeneia becomes priestess of Artemis among the, i. 126
—sacred image of Artemis to be carried away from, by Orestes, i. 135
Taurus, vii. 225

Taurus, bull of Heaven, v. 28–29, 319
—station of Sin-Moon, v. 304, 305
Tauthe and Apasōn, primeval couple, v. 290
Ta-ūz, festival of, v. 336
—(Tamūz), Tammuz pronounced, at Harran, v. 336
Tava-ajk, forest-spirit, iv. 189
Tavastlanders, one of Finn linguistic groups, iv. xv
Ta-vong, section of Hanoi, xii. 304
Tāwadeinthā, Burmese King of = Tewada King, xii. 323, 341–342
—land of spirits, xii. 341
Tawhaki (Tafa'i), hero-deity, ix. 38, 57, 58–59, 60–62, 64, 65, 66–67
Ta-whiri-ma-tea, ix. 8, 32
Tawiscara (Flint), x. 36–37, 39, 68, 295 45–296, 297 47
Tawyan version of tower legend, xii. 267
Tax paid to shaman, iv. 282
Taxation, exemption from, of those who ferry souls to Brittia, iii. 16
Taxes, ancestral spirits have to pay, vii. 183
Taÿgete, Artemis identified with mountain-nymph, i. 184
—mother of Lakedaimon by Zeus, i. 11
—wife of Zeus, i. 157
Taÿgetos, Artemis hunted over, i. 183
Taylor, Mt., x. 162
Tāzh and Tāzhak, twin children of primeval pair, vi. 298
Tāzīs, Arabs called, vi. 298
Tchakabech, x. 48
Tcoxoltcwedin, x. 221
Te Ao-tu-roa, etc., Day, ix. 7
—Ata, Dawn, ix. 7
—Kore, etc., the Void, ix. 6
—Po, Night, ix. 6–7
Tea, iv. 460
— -leaves, song at picking of, viii. 372
Teacher (shih), why symbolized by lion, viii. 104
Tê Tsung, Emperor, viii. 96
Tê-hua (modern Kiu-kiang), viii. 123
Te-ika-a-maui ("Fish of Maui"), New Zealand, ix. 43
Tear jars, iii. 248
Tears become rivers, iii. 135
—excessive, harm dead, ii. 307
—flood from, ix. 38
—from the eye of Khepri, men created from, xii. 69, 70

Tears of Apollo formed stream, iii. 10
——divine eye, primeval reptiles come from, xii. 379 [17]
——gold and pearls, ii. 27, 125, 126
——Isis bring Nile back from Nubia, xii. 90
——Phaëthon's sisters turned into amber, i. 244
—quench fire, x. 140
—rain is Heaven's, xi. 234
—represented on masks, xi. 199, 234
—river of, vi. 345
—turn to flood, x. 178
Tebi, solarized god, xii. 150
Teçacatetl, xi. 117
Technitēs, inventor of brick building, v. 54
Tecpanec, league of Aztec with, xi. 111
Tecpatl ("Flint"), day-sign, xi. 100
Tecuciztecatl, xi. 88, 89
Tecumbalam, bird, xi. 164
Tecumseh, chief, x. 149
Teeth of cow sacrificed to Athene sown broadcast, thus producing the Spartoi, i. 45
—seven planets from Manzashiri's, iv. 372
—soul in, iv. 5
Tefen, a scorpion of Isis, xii. 210, 211
Tefênet, xii. 44 (fig. 40), 87 (fig. 78)
—and Shu associated with birth of sun-god, xii. 70–71
——daily restore sun's eye from ocean to world, xii. 89–90
——space of air between Heaven and earth, created by sun, xii. 50
——sun's eye differentiated, xii. 87
—as a birth-genius of Osiris, xii. 385 [12]
—association of, with Shu uncertain, xii. 44, 370 [28] [29]
—called into consultation by Rê', xii. 74
—causes growth of plants, xii. 45
—celestial lioness, xii. 43 and fig. 37, 45
—comparisons of, to rain-clouds and dew unfounded, xii. 44–45, 370 [30]
—created by Khepri, xii. 68, 69
—Egyptian popular etymology of name of, xii. 370 [30]
——texts on, xii. 45
—ethereal space separating earth and ocean from Heaven, xii. 44
—identified with Ḥat-ḥôr and Sekhmet, xii. 87
————solarized, xii. 41

Tefênet, lion-form of, never interchanges with human features, xii. 44
—member of ennead of Heliopolis, xii. 216
—Meskhenet sometimes identified with, xii. 137
—regarded as solar goddess, xii. 29
—Sekhmet, Pekhet, and Ubastet manifestations of a single deity, xii. 217
—Shut rare name for, xii. 148
—solar functions of, xii. 45
—Sonet-nofret identified with, xii. 149
—sun's eye as, xii. 86
—upholds sky, xii. 43
Tegea, Athene brings plague upon, i. 173
—city of, founded by Aleos, i. 22
—worship of Athene in, i. 169
Tegid, Lake, iii. 109
Tegid the Bald, iii. 109, 112, 113
Teharonhiawagon, ancient title of Sapling, x. 37, 295 [43], 296 [45]
Tehōm, primeval sea, v. 303, 304
Tehuelche, xi. 331
Teigue's voyage to Elysium, iii. 121
Teika-kazura, ivy, viii. 347
Teima, Nabunidus lived at, v. 5
Teiresias, blind seer of Eteokles, prophecy of, i. 52, 54
—shade of, appears to Odysseus, i. 145
—still prophesies in Underworld, i. 142
—Theban seer in Hades, tells Odysseus his route home, i. 137
Teiro, form of Tīr's name on Indo-Scythian coins, vii. 32
"Tek, Old Man of village," iv. 403
Teka, game, ix. 42
Tekhi, goddess of first month, xii. 150
Telamon accompanied Herakles on expedition against Troy, i. 121
—and Herakles, quarrel between, at Troy, i. 91
—receives Hesione as prize of war, i. 91
—son of Aiakos, i. 121
Telchins, Greek, vii. 85
"Telegonia," i. 139–140
Telegonos, son of Kirke, unknowingly kills his father Odysseus, i. 140
————Proteus, i. 261
Telemachos and Odysseus reunited at hut of Eumaios, i. 138–139
—bidden by Athene to go in search of his father Odysseus, i. 138

Telemachos, son of Odysseus and Penelope, i. 123

Telepathic communication, x. 262

Telephassa, wife of Agenor, settled in Thrace, i. 44

Telephos leads the Greeks to Troy, i. 125–126

—son of Auge, adopted by King Teuthras as his own, i. 22

———wounded at Teuthrania, i. 125

Telete ("Rite of the Mysteries"), abstract deity of social institution, i. 282

Têlîltu ("nun"), title of Ishtar, v. 384 [123]

Telingāna once supposed to have been original home of Mōn, xii. 268

Tell-el-Amarna site of capital built by Amen-ḥotep IV, xii. 225

Tellus, Tellus Mater, Ceres associated with, i. 291–292

—Vediovis invoked in oaths with, i. 296

Telpochtli ("the Youth"), xi. 62

Telyaveli(k), Baltic celestial smith, iii. 330, 361 [90]

Temazcalteci, earth-goddess, xi. 75

Temhit, goddess worshipped in Heliopolis, xii. 150 [8]

Tempellec, king of Lambeyeque, xi. 208–209

Tempers, seven, iv. 378

Tempest, xi. 191–192, 231, 267, 326

—called "Wudes Heer," ii. 41

Temple at Bubembe, vii. 129, 130

———Mutzatzir, golden keys in, vii. 395 [58]

———Throndhjem, ii. 70

—builder, Pelasgos first, i. 20

—circular, in Celtic myth reported by Apollonius, iii. 10

—drawn by oxen, and image, built to Agros, v. 54

—erected by Odin with blood-offerings, ii. 29, 30

—Icelandic, containing god's abode, ii. pl. xxiii, opp. p. 184

—myth in prayer at restoration of a, v. 104

—of Accomplished [and of the Spiritual] Ancestor, viii. 47

———Agriculture in Peking, viii. 63

———Apollo at Delphoi, i. 177–178

———Heaven, viii. 63

———Nodons on the Severn, iii. 103

Temple of Śiva broken into by Duḥsaha, vi. 180

———Thor at Most, ii. 76

—on Isle of the Temple, viii. 269–270

—-priestess, ii. 117

—-priests, ii. 26, 30, 33, 35, 76

—ritual for founding, v. 314

—to Fosite, ii. 162–163

———Kaches in Dsung (Georgia), vii. 84

—words for: Mehyan; Tajar; Bagin, vii. 18

Temples, iii. 278, 279, 280, 284, 286; vii. 16, 17, 18, 23, 24, 26, 28, 29, 31, 34, 38, 39; viii. 14, 23, 65, 68, 71, 72, 97, 111, 113, 135; xi. 46–49, 58–59, 64, 106–107, pl. xv, opp. p. 106, 112, pl. xviii, opp. p. 126, 127, 134, 135–136, 180, 207, 208, 217, 219, 235, 238, 246, 248, pl. xxxviii, opp. p. 248, 250, 354 [5]; xii. 187–197

—birth and memorial, xii. 171

—consecrated fires in, ii. 201

—groves as, ii. 203

—of Frey, ii. 117, 118, 119

———Rê' and Horus, xii. 24

———Venus Genetrix and Venus and Rome, i. 294

—sacred animals in, xii. 167, 414 [21]

—sun, vi. 232

—to sister-goddesses, ii. 187, 188

Temptation of Jesus, v. 353

———saints by trolls, ii. 286

———the woman at the Flood, iv. 361–362, 363

—the, according to Sumerian myth, v. 179, 187

Temptations of Buddha, vi. 196–197, 206

———primeval pair, vi. 297

Tena-ranide, spirit of plague, x. 78, 79

Tencteri regarded Mars as chief of gods, ii. 97

Tenenet adored at Her-monthis, xii. 150 [8]

—patroness of intoxicating drink, xii. 66

Tengeri, Siberian term for gods, iv. 355–356, 406, 410–411, 440, 442, 446, 473

— -Khan, Siberian chief god, iv. 453

Tengri, Siberian Heaven-god, iv. 391–392, 394

Tengu, aerial vampires, viii. 281, 287–288, pl. xxix, opp. p. 288, 309–310

—folk meet in sugi-groves, viii. 341

Tengys (Sea), ruler of earth, iv. 364

Tennes and Kyknos, story of, parallel to that of Bellerophon and Stheneboia, i. 325 15
Tennin, Tennyo, heavenly maidens, viii. 242, 266, 267
Tenoch, xi. 117
Tenochtitlan, xi. 45, 58, 109, 111, 115
Tenskwatawa, prophet, x. 149
Tent of Sarakka, iv. 255
—sacred, made for luminous tree, x. 100
Tentet at Denderah, xii. 165
Teotihuacan, xi. 88, 90, 108, 112
Teoyaoimqui, warrior's death-god, xi. 54
Tepeu, the creator, xi. 160–167
Tepeuh, Quiché king, xi. 182
Tepeyollotl, heart of the mountain, xi. 54, 56, 79
Téquendama, place opened by Bochica for issuance of waters at cataract of, xi. 203
Téramó apparently connected with Turanna, i. 319
—represents Mercurius and Turms in modern Romagnola, i. 318
Teraphim, household gods, v. 34–35
Teredon, vii. 32
Tereus changed into hoopoe, i. 16, 70
—son of Ares, assists Pandion in war between Athens and Thebes, and marries the two daughters of Pandion, i. 70
Terminus, guardian of boundaries between property, Iuppiter as, i. 290
—survives as Sentiero in modern Romagnola, i. 316–317
Terpsichore ("delight in the dance"), one of the Lyric Muses, i. 240
Terra, Jörd parallels, ii. 201
Territory of the Immortals, viii. 114
Terror, panic, ii. 252, 253, 256
—son of Great Fear, giant, iii. 148
Tesana, survival of Etruscan Thesan in modern Romagnola, i. 319
[Tesh]ri-tu, month, v. 219
Teshub, Hittite Adad, v. 64
Teteoinnan, earth-goddess and lunar deity, xi. 75, 79
Tetet, scorpion of Isis, xii. 210, 211
Tethering-post, iv. 337, 340, 349, 351, 408, 444
— -posts, sacred trees as, ii. 334, 335
Tethra, Fomorian king, war-god, iii. 27, 33

Tethys and Okeanos purge Glaukos of imperfections before admitting him as sea-god, i. 261
——Rhea daughter of, i. 274
—grandmother of Hyades, i. 248
—keeps Kallisto from Okeanos, i. 21
—("Nurse"), i. 5
—wife of Okeanos according to Hesiod, i. 256
Teti-(y?)êb, two wives of Sêth, xii. 393 58
Teukros, Apollo confers skill in use of bow on, i. 177
—king, i. 117
—son of Telamon, i. 121
Teuthis (Arkadian village), plague at, i. 22–23
Teuthis commander of the contingent of Arkadians in war against Troy, i. 22–23
Teuthrania attacked by Menelaos under the impression that it was Troy, i. 125
Teuthras, King, made Auge his queen and adopted her son, i. 22
Teutonic peoples, distribution, religion, mythology, and ethnological divisions of, ii. 3–4
Tevennec, souls of drowned conveyed from Raz to, iii. 17
Texcatzoncatl ("Straw Mirror"), xi. 77
Texpi, a priest, preserved from flood, xi. 85–86
Teye, mother of Amen-hotep IV, xii. 224
Teyrnon, Lord of Gwent-is-coed, had mare whose foals disappeared on May Eve, iii. 94–95, 188
Tezcatepuca, god of the lower worlds, xi. 47
Tezcatlipoca, the Great God, xi. 54, 55, 58, pl. VII, opp. p. 60, pl. VIII, opp. p. 64, 61–66, 68, 69, 77, 87, 90, 92, 93, 95, 141, 302
Tezcuco, xi. 65, 109, 112
Thādō, language of, xii. 267
Thags, goddess of the Vindhya once patron divinity of, vi. 236, 239
Thagya Min, king of Nāts, xii. 340, 341, 342, pl. XVI, opp. p. 342
Thagyan or Thingyan festival, xii. 323
Thagyas, Thagya Min representative of king of, xii. 341–342

Thai, antecedents of Malay mythology perhaps to be found among, ix. 244

— -dam, -deng, -hkai, and -nüa, Black, White, Red, and Upper Thai offer sacrifices to the spirits, xii. 300

— -to, king of Le Dynasty, legend of sword of, xii. 302

Thaitōn, king of Ly Dynasty, renewed Dragon Temple and made Cao-bien guardian protector of Thanh-long, xii. 318–319

Thalatd corruption of Thamte for Tamtu, Tiâmat, v. 290

Thaleia ("luxuriant beauty"), one of the Dramatic Muses and one of the Charites, i. 237, 240

Thalesan, flavoured rice, which brought about downfall of original celestial Brahmās, xii. 265, 290

Thallo ("bloom"), one of the Horai, i. 238

Thamudi, v. 379 26

Thanai, first man in Karen myth, xii. 269, 270

Thanatos, abode of, in Underworld, i. 278

—abstract divinity of state of body, i. 282

—(Death), xii. 255

——creation of, i. 6

Thangbrand, ii. 76–77

Thang-long (Blue Dragon), spirit of the East, xii. 307

——City of the Dragon, xii. 311, 318

Thank-offerings to Seides, iv. 101

Thasos settled in Thrace, i. 44

Tha-tun conquered by Anawra-htā, xii. 285

Thaumas father of Harpies, i. 266

The-Chief-Above, x. 272 6

Theatrical tales, viii. 174–187

Theban belief that man was germinated from the dragon's teeth sown broadcast upon earth, i. 10

—gods, long predominance of, xii. 19

Thebans banished Oidipous and he cursed his sons who refrained from helping him, i. 50

—evacuated their city and founded Hestiaia, i. 54

Thebe, child of Prometheus, i. 12

—(spring-nymph), daughter of Zeus and Idama, wife of Ogygos, i. 42, 157

Thebe, Zethos married, according to one account, i. 44

Thebes, Amon, local god of, gains chief position in pantheon, xii. 19

—ancient sanctuary of Ubastet at, xii. 150

—god sometimes had two wives at, xii. 20

—Mont(u) worshipped at, xii. 139

—Opet_s goddess of, xii. 144

—triad of, xii. 34, 362 6

Thebes and Athens, war between, i. 70

—Aphrodite worshipped as ancestress in, i. 196–197

—battle of Adrastos and Eteokles before, i. 52–53

—Dionysos returned to, while Pentheus was king, i. 47

——takes up abode in, i. 219

—dragon of, offspring of Poseidon, i. 211

—early existence of, marked by calamities in ruling families, i. 55

—fate of, to be determined by duel, i. 53

—foes of, denied funeral rites by Kreon, i. 53

—founded by Kadmos, i. 45

—fountain of Kirke at, i. 258

—great antiquity of, as shown by legend of Amphion and Zethos, i. 47

—Kadmos as king, and surviving Spartoi, build up, i. 45

—Pentheus king of, i. 47

—Polydoros king at, i. 47

—ravished by she-fox, i. 73

—reputed birthplace of Orion, i. 250

—settlement of, as shown by myths, i. 47–48

—walls of, charmed into place by lyre of Amphion, i. 44

—wedding-robe and necklace of Harmonia symbol of kingship in, i. 51

Theelgeth, headless, hairy being, x. 163

Theft of children legend, x. 274 9

——fire, sun, or daylight, x. xvii, xxiii, 46–47, 56, 61, 293 40, 301 51

Thegtheg, three-peaked mountain, xi. 330

Theism, vii. 116

Theispas, Khaldian weather-god or Thunderer, vii. 11

Theistic element in Buddhism, vi. 205–206

Themis aids Leto in giving birth to Apollo, i. 175
—and Zeus parents of the Moirai, i. 284
—gives divine food to Apollo, i. 175
—(" Justice "), born of Ouranos and Gaia, i. 6
——Gaia as, i. 273
——second wife of Zeus, i. 156, 237, 238
—said to be mother of Prometheus by Iapetos, i. 12
Theodosius, pagan shrines closed by edict of, xii. 244
Theogony, obscurity of Armenian, vii. 24
Theology, Sumerian pantheon product of, v. 89
Thepla, a variety of Al, vii. pl. v, opp. p. 88, 89
Theravādin School, xii. 261
Theriomorphic, some giants are, ii. 279
Thermuthis (Renenutet) name given by Josephus to Pharaoh's daughter, xii. 397 [94]
Thersandros bribed Eriphyle with Harmonia's robe to secure Alkmaion as leader, i. 54
Thersites and Achilles, i. pl. xxxii, opp. p. 128, 130
—Conan Maol Celtic, iii. 163
—Loki parallel to, ii. 149
Thesan, Etruscan deity, survives as Tesana in modern Romagnola, i. 319
Theseus, i. 96–105
—and Amphitrite, i. pl. xxv, opp. p. 96
——Peirithoös visit Hades to abduct Persephone, i. 145
—by one account, son of Poseidon, i. 211
—departure of, from Crete with Ariadne witnessed by Dionysos, i. 217
—double of Poseidon, i. 212
—gains possession of Helen by drawing lots, i. 25
—gave Oidipous home in which to end his days, i. 50
—helped Adrastos to secure the Argive dead, i. 54
—Medeia plots against life of, i. 115
—released by Herakles in Underworld, i. 88
—slays Cretan bull at Marathon, i. 84
—took part in hunt for Kalydonian boar, i. 56

Thesmophoria, Demeter's power to fructify human beings underlies ceremonies of festival of, i. 331 [3] (ch. x)
Thespiai, Herakles purified of sin of murder at, i. 80
Thesprotians, Odysseus weds queen of, i. 140
Thessaly, Aiolos ruler of certain districts in, i. 37
—Akrisios fled to, i. 35
—Centaurs especially associated with hills of, i. 271
—Nonnos localizes Flood in, i. 19
—Pelias as hero of, i. 115–116
—Peneios River worshipped in, i. 257
Thestios and Oineus supreme in Aitolia's councils, i. 56
—king of Aitolians, Tyndareos takes refuge with, i. 24
—sons of, slain by Meleagros, i. 57, 58
Thetis and Amphitrite lead dances of sea-nymphs, i. 214
——Eurynome, Hephaistos takes refuge with, i. 206
——Okeanos, Philip of Macedon traces descent to, i. 223
——Peleus, i. pl. xxix (2), opp. p. 116
—causes Achilles to yield body of Hektor to Priam, i. 130
—daughter of Nereus, has power of transformation but Peleus captures and weds her, i. 122
—Eris causes strife at Peleus's marriage to, i. 124
—given golden jar by Dionysos, in which she placed ashes of Achilles, i. 217
—gives armour to Achilles, i. 129
—makes Zeus promise to delay Greek victory till Achilles is honoured, i. 127
—takes body of Achilles from pyre to the White Isle, i. 131
Thibaw, King, abandonment of Plowing Festival by, xii. 328
Thickets, green, Horus and other solar divinities born in, xii. 116
Thidrandi, guardian spirits appeared to, ii. 236
" Thidriks-saga," ii. 170, 267, 280
Thietmar, Bishop of Merseburg, gives earliest accounts of religion of Elbe Slavs, iii. 221
—on Svaražic, etc., iii. 286, 289

Thieves, Hermes patron of, i. 191–192, 194–195

Thil, temple of Nane at, vii. 38

Thing, Scandinavian Assembly, ii. 23, 26, 71, 72, 78, 98, 122

"Things," the Nekedzaltara, x. 79

Thingsus, ii. 98

"Thinkers," Cora leaders of ceremonies, xi. 121

Thinle Gyaung, king of Tagaung, builds temple for Mahāgiri Nāts, xii. 343–344

Thiriwunda, sister of Tin Dè, perished in flames with brother, xii. 343

Thirst of soul, iii. 227, 230, 235

—offerings to prevent, in future life, iv. 45

Thirteen of Mexican cosmology, xi. 53, 354 [7]–355

This, Khent(i)-amentiu seems to have received name because of his shrine near necropolis of, xii. 21

—Meḥet worshipped at, xii. 136

—Onuris localized at, xii. 143

—Ophoïs wolf-god of, xii. 144, 407 [72]

—origin of name of, xii. 386 [17]

—Osiris replaces Ophoïs and Khent(i)-amentiu at, xii. 98

Thisbe and Pyramos, i. 201

Thistles and thorns, evil spirits afraid of, iv. 476

Thjalfi, servant of Thor, ii. 75, 81, 82, 84, 91, 92

Thjazi, giant, ii. pl. VI, opp. p. 32, 91, 101, 103, 140, 141, 178, 179, 278, 279, 283, 328

Thjodrörir, dwarf, ii. 46, 201, 220, 265

Thjodvitnir, wolf, ii. 313

Thlawe, Underworld plant plumes, x. 199, 201

Tho, xii. 311

Thobadzistshini, male deity, x. 157, 164

Thokk (Loki), giantess, refuses to weep for Balder, ii. 131

Tholley, Pine Island, ii. 279

Thōn Pan Hla, xii. 340

Thonenli, Water Sprinkler, x. 156

Thonga, traces of survival of totemism among the, vii. 276–278

Thor appears in Esthonian battle-cry "Tar abitha!" and Karelian name Tuuri, iv. 228

—description of sacrifice to, iv. 231

Thor (Donar; Thunaer; Thunaraz; Thunor; Thur), thunder-god, ii. 10, 15, 16, 17, 18, 19, 21, 22, 23, 29, 32, pl. VI, opp. p. 32, 33, 35, 39, 49, 59, 60, 65, 66, 68–96, 100, 103, 115, 121, 123, 125, 130, 133, 139, 140, 141, 144, 145, 146, 153, 158, 172, 177, 179, 182, 187, 193, 202, 203, 229, 265, 266, 267, 268, 269, 270, 277, 278, 281, 285–286, 301, 310, 314–315, 329, 337, 340, 341, 343, 346, 384 [21]

—hammer of, iii. 319

—will kill Midgard snake at end of world, iv. 345

Thora, daughter of king of Finns and Perms, ii. 132, 187

Thord, dream woman, ii. 234, 250

Thordis, wise woman, ii. 226

Thore sacrificed to a grove, ii. 203

Thorfinn, ii. 342

—Karlsefni and Gudrid came to Vinland, x. 1

Thorgerd, daughter of Egil, ii. 122, 180

—Hölgabrud, local goddess, ii. 15, 186–189

—Hölgatroll attends troll-thing, ii. 301

Thorgisl threatened in dreams by Thor, ii. 77

Thorgrim binds Hel-shoes on Vestein, ii. 305

—first settler in Iceland, ii. 76, 201

—see GRIM, SON OF, ETC.

Thorhall, seer, ii. 231, 236

Thori, Selthorir "died" into hill of, ii. 310

Thorir, giant, ii. 286

—saw Fire-demon, ii. 202

Thorket, offering of, to Frey, ii. 117, 285

Thorkill prayed to Thor for food, ii. 75

—sent on mission by Gorm, ii. 94–95, 321

Thorlaf possessed by trolls, ii. 285

Thorleif slain, ii. 188

"Thorleifs Jarlaskald," ii. 188

Thormod, skin-changer, ii. 292

Thorn, enchanted, to split open "Debble," vii. 414 [25]

—see SLEEP-THORN.

—white, given to Carna to banish evil from doorways, i. 297

Thornbush reaching to Heaven, x. 104

Thornbushes, women with naked bodies embrace, iv. 489

Thorny bushes growing out of man's body, vii. 249

Thorod, drowned, comes as ghost to drink Yule-ale, ii. 191

Thorold, viciousness of, survives cremation, ii. 309

Thorolf, one of early settlers in Iceland, ii. 76, 310

—taken by Norns, ii. 240

Thorsness, Thorolf landed at, ii. 76

Thorstad visited barrow at invitation of dead man, ii. 308

Thorstan worships at spirit-stone, ii. 312

Thorstein: see STEIN, ETC.

—went to gandreid, ii. 301, 307, 322

" Thorsteins-saga," ii. 301

Thorsten Ox-foot, Fylgja of, ii. 234

Thortan, statue of Ba'al Shamîn at, vii. 37

Thorward seeks healing, ii. 226

Thôth: see THOUT(I), INSCRIPTIONS, ETC.

Thought, Hugi was, ii. 81, 93, 94

— -runes, ii. 46, 168

Thourioi, Boreas regarded as nearly human at, i. 265

Thout(i) and his cynocephalous baboon, hearts of dead weighed by, xii. 176

——Horus " come from Ptaḥ," xii. 220

—as a baboon, xii. 32 (fig. 12), 428 [85]

——clerk, identified with Khôns(u), xii. 366 [4]

——moon-god, xii. 33 (fig. 17)

——representative of Rê', appointed to rule night, xii. 84–85

——scribe, xii. 33 (fig. 16)

—assists in putting together dismembered body of Osiris, xii. 114

—baboon of, as healer of sun-god's eye, xii. 90

—clerk of sun-god, xii. 30, 32

—divine messenger, xii. 380 [29]

—divides Egypt between Horus and Sêth, xii. 118

—earthly reign of, listed by Turin Historical Papyrus, xii. 399 [108]

—equated with Khôns(u), xii. 34

—first Egyptian month under protection of, xii. 66

Thout(i), four baboons of, as guardians of condemned souls, xii. 365 [27]

—functions of, xii. 33

—heals decapitated Isis, xii. 118, 126

——eye of Horus, xii. 118

——infant Horus stung by a scorpion, xii. 116

—helps to protect and nurse Isis and infant Horus, xii. 116

—ibis-god, moon identified with, xii. 33 and fig. 15

—identified with Mercury (?), xii. 366 [2]

—in baboon form and as scribe, xii. 33 (fig. 17)

——ibis-form, xii. 87 (figs. 78, 79)

——inscriptions from Magharah, v. 378 [14]

——magic text of tears of Isis, xii. 90, 125

—instrumental in depriving 'Apop of limbs, xii. 105

—judge of the dead, xii. 118, 365 [27], 366 [3]

—local divinity of Khmun(u)-Hermopolis, xii. 33

—master of sorcery among male gods, xii. 200

—Mehi perhaps identified with, xii. 136

—member of " little ennead " of Heliopolis, xii. 216

—Nehem(t)-'auit associated with, xii. 141

—prayer to, xii. 233

—protector of Osiris, xii. 123

—reason for yellow skin of, xii. 407 [74]

—registers king's name on celestial tree, xii. 53 (fig. 51)

—sailing heavenly ocean in ship, xii. 34

—sails over sky in form of ibis, xii. 34

—Tekhi substituted for, xii. 150

Thrace, Aeneas at, i. 304

—believed to be home of Dionysos, i. 216

—Io wanders through, i. 29

—Thasos, Kadmos, and Telephassa settled in, i. 44

Thracians, customs of, at birth and death, vii. 397 [4]

—original identity of Armenians with, vii. 12, 364, 379 [1] (introd.)

Thræll, son of Heimdall, ii. 153

Thraētaona and Azhi, myth of, v. 130

—chained dragon, vii. 98, 363, 392 [18]

—conquered Azhi Dahāka, ii. 147

Thraëtaona (Farīdūn), vi. 265, 266, 271, 311, 315, 318, 320, 321, 322, 323, 324, 327-328, 350, 351, 365 [4]
—of the Avesta, Trita Āptya identified with, vi. 36
Thrall, birth of first, ii. 10
Thrand, skin-changer, ii. 293
Thread, Arkas taught Arkadians how to spin, i. 16
—black and grey, sewn into ear of sacrificial reindeer, iv. 38, 231
—blue, spun on blue spindle by Virgin Mary in magic songs, iv. 257
—boat drawn to Isle of Joy by ball of, iii. 115
—bunches of, used to cover eyes, ears, and nostrils of dead, by Chuvash, iv. 21
—laid on corpse, deductions of length of life from, iv. 28
—of life, iii. 251
—snatched from garments of deceased, iv. 29
—spider's, for descent from sky, vii. 321
Threads from staff of Vagneg-imi indicate births, iv. 260
—which enable corpse to climb to Heaven, or child corpse to grow, iv. 30, 31
" Three Deformed Ones," farce, viii. 361
—drops of grief became three lochs, iii. 135
—Emperors (San Huang), viii. 25, 109
—Finns of Emuin, fathers of Lugaid Red-Stripes, iii. 90, 156
—gods of dán ("knowledge" or "fate"), iii. 39
— -headed gods, iii. pl. VII, opp. p. 56, 104, pl. XII, opp. p. 112
——idols, xi. 198
—Heavens frequently identified with the "Three Purities," viii. 109
—Heroes, viii. 93, 175-179
—Holy Ones, Trinity of, viii. 196
— -horned animals, iii. 129
—hundred and sixty(-five) associated with Osiris as god of the year, xii. 94
——Horus in, probably symbolizes the year, xii. 388 [28]
—Kingdoms: Shu, Wei, Wu, viii. 94, 174
—lords of Asgard, ii. 6, pl. III, opp. p. 12 ; see also ODIN.

Three magic harp-strains, iii. 29
—Notables (San Kung), viii. 109
—number, in preparation of weapons, iii. 32, 33
—Officials (San Kuan), viii. 109
—plagues of Britain, iii. 107
—Precious Ones, viii. 14
—Pure Ones, viii. 14, 109, 110
—Venerable Ones (San Lao), viii. 109
—Women, the tale of, vii. 138-139
Threefold disposition of Universe, vi. 15
Threshing-barn man, Votiak god, iv. 163, 167
——prayers for, iv. 275
—dragons, fairies, kaches, and brownies at, vii. 79-80, 83, 391 [17]
— -floor, earliest, built by Keleos, i. 230
——soul of, iv. 14
— -shed father, iv. 248
Thridi (Third), one of lords of Asgard, ii. 6, pl. III, opp. p. 12, 24; see also ODIN.
Thrinakia, island of, herds of cattle of Sun in, i. 113
—Notos and Euros hinder Odysseus's departure from, i. 265-266
—Odysseus meets disaster at island of, i. 137
Thrita Āthwya, vi. 322, 324
—in the Avesta, Trita Āptya associated with, vi. 36, 48
—priest of Haoma sacrifice, vi. 282
Thrivaldi, nine heads of, ii. 81, 91
Throat and mind, same word for, x. 262
Throndhjem, Frey's temple at, ii. 118, 121
Throne, black, of Erlik-Khan, iv. 487
—of Anahit, mountain in Sophene, vii. 28, 63
——metal, Osiris sits on, xii. 97
Thrones, dead sit on, xii. 178
Thronion, in Lokria, Perseus supposed to have been identified with Hermes at, i. 36
Thrud, child of Thor, ii. 74, 95, 182
—("Might"), Valkyrie, ii. 249
Thrudgelmir, son of Vafthrudnir, ii. 275
Thrudheim, Thor to dwell in, ii. 341
Thrudugr, Thrudvald, Thor as, ii. 74
Thrudvang, abode of Thor at, ii. 33, 74, 77
Thrudvangir, Thor's abode, ii. 329

"Thruster-Down": see ||GAUNAB, ETC.

Thrym, giant, ii. 10, 79, 88–89, 123, 139, 153, 186, 193, 276, 278, 281

Thrymheim, home of Thjazi, ii. 104, 105, 179, 279

"Thrymskvitha," ii. 10, 75, 78, 79, 88, 141, 186, 220

Thuêris, xii. 376 [82]

Thule probably Scandinavia according to Procopius, iii. 16

Thum-fish, tale of, ix. 123

Thumb of knowledge, Fionn's, iii. 166–167, 168, 172, 179, 210

Thunaer; Thunor; Thur: see THOR.

Thund, river around Valhall, ii. 313

Thunder, iv. 439–448; vii. 50, 392 [21], 393 [24]; 119, 126, 127, 151, 158, 237, 238, 269, 411 [43]; ix. 57, 88; x. 99–100, 109–112, 138, 139, 171, 231, 232, 306 [59]

—amulet destroyed at clap of, xii. 318

—and thunderbolts, xi. 71, 161, pl. XXXI, opp. p. 218, 237, 241, 246, 295, 296, 369 [16]

— -car of Zeus, i. 160

——Pegasos harnessed to, i. 40

— -clap, Dyfed desolate after, iii. 101–102

—deity of, ix. 250, 260

— -deity, Thor's earliest aspect, ii. 68, 75, 81

—explanation of, xii. 35, 367 [10]

— -god, Aramaic and Canaanite, v. 37, 39

——in shape of oak, iv. 188

— -gods, ii. 193; iv. 158, 217, pl. XXVI, opp. p. 220, pl. XXVII, opp. p. 224, 227, 228, 229, 230–232, 243, 250 (fig. 9); v. 132

—helps stretch the sandstone, x. 222

—made by gaming-stones, x. 288 [32]

—mother usurps place of the Water, iv. 213

—Peak Pagoda, tale of white serpent in, viii. 158–160

—person scared by, receives special shamanic talent, iv. 499

—Perun god of, iii. 294–295, 296

—Rai-jin genius of, viii. 288, pl. XXX, opp. p. 288

—sacrifice to, x. 82

—see PERKÚNAS GOD OF, ETC.

—Semitic Ba'al god of, xii. 155

—Sêth god of, xii. 45, 103–104, 109

Thunder, shapeshifting at crashes of, ix. 117, 255

—Society, x. 288 [32]

— -storm, divergent views of, in Asia and Egypt, xii. 108

— -storms, ii. 78, 79, 80, 82, 83

—Zeus god of, i. 159

Thunderbird, iv. 439 (fig. 17), 448, 449, 510; x. xvii, pl. III, opp. p. 8, 22, pl. VI, opp. p. 22, 24, 25, 42, 43, 45, 46, 48, 61, 62, 68, 81, pl. XVI, opp. p. 84, 99, 100, 138, 228, 244, 281 [19], 287 [32]–288 [33]; xi. 299; see also items s.v. THUNDERERS.

Thunderbolt, vi. 264, 265, 291, 301, 335, 351

—and lightning, Pegasos bearer of, i. 34

—Esthonian perckun nohl (borrowed from Lithuanians), iv. 228

—hammer of Thor a, ii. 79

—Iasion struck dead by, in punishment for crime, i. 117

—Indra wields the, vi. 32, 33, pl. IV, opp. p. 34, 132, 139

—made from bones of the seer Dadhīca, vi. 132, 133

—name of, scares Macedonian dragon, vii. 45

—of Zeus, i. pl. II (1), opp. p. xlii, 8, 9, 90, 280

—personified, iv. 447

—Vajrasattva bearer of the, vi. 213

—Zeus hurls Charybdis into sea by, i. 264

——sends, on Kampaneus, i. 53

Thunderbolts, fingers of Vu-murt resemble, iv. 195

Thunderboy swallowed by horned water-snake, x. 45

Thunderers, iii. 294; iv. 228, 238; v. 39; vii. 11; viii. 357; x. 43; xi. 297; see also THUNDERBIRD.

Thunder's sister, tale of man who married, x. 24

Thunderstones, x. 288 [32]

Thursar, giants, ii. 127

Thusandi, serpent princess, xii. 276

Thuspa (ancient Urartian capital; modern Van), vii. 12

Thyestes, children of, killed and their cooked flesh served to their father, i. 120

—lover of wife of Atreus, i. 120

Thyestes received golden lamb from wife of Atreus and thereby became king at Mykenai, i. 120
—returns throne to Atreus, is first expelled then recalled for purpose of revenge, i. 120
—son of Pelops and Hippodameia, i. 120
Thynias, arrival of Argo at, i. 111
Thyrs, water-giants, ii. 280
Thyrsos (ceremonial wand), emblem of Dionysos, i. 222
Ti, Autumn sacrifice, viii. 61
— -ch'i, viii. 29
—Ch'ing, tale of, regarding use of bamboo slips, viii. 139
— -tsang, Supreme Ruler of Hell, viii. 196
—Wang Shih Chi, viii. 31
— -ya ("Earthly Mute"), a groom of Wên Ch'ang, viii. 113
Ti, meaning of name, vii. 13–14, 383 45
Tiahuanaco in legend place of origin of nations, xi. 215, 216, 235, 240
—monolithic gateway and art at, xi. pl. xxxi, opp. p. 218, 232–233, 240, 248, 368 15
Tiâmat and her brood, iii. 34
——Marduk, battle between, vi. 264
—Babylonian high gods afraid of, iii. 28
——myth of, caused Sêth to evolve into a Satan, xii. 392 54
—female dragon of sea and Chaos, v. 91, 92, 102, 106, 119, 127, 155, 277, 279, 282, 286, 290, 292, 294, 295, 296–297, 298, 300, 302, 303, 317
—Semitic dragon of ocean, xii. 104
—Sumerian original of, v. 288–289
Tiamtu and apsû original watery principles of watery Chaos, v. 289
Tiberinus, son of Ianus and Camese, i. 297
Tibet, Buddhism of, vi. 207–219
—converter of, vi. 204
—yellow races press southwards to Indo-China from, xii. 286
Tibeto-Burman legends affect Indo-Chinese mythology, xii. 257
Tibir, probably original of Tubal-(Cain), v. 190, 403 3
—(Tagtug), v. 198, 199
Tibulon, xi. 127
Ticci Viracocha, xi. 249

Tickling, death by, iii. 253, 255, 262, 264; iv. 181, 183, 189; 467, 468
—image to bring life, ix. 274
—of nose means of driving soul out, iv. 475–476
Tidal wave swamped boats of pirates, viii. 73
Tide caused by moon, iv. 420
—ebb and flow of, viii. 271, 305, 382 3
— -myths, x. 251
—no one dies on rising, iii. 17
—Sisyphos said to have been the, i. 38
Tides, cause of ebb-, ii. 93, 94
Tieholtsodi, water-power, x. 157, 159, 161, 162
Tien, Chinese Heaven-god, iv. 391
— -ming, Chinese "Fate," iv. 393
T'ien, "Heaven," viii. 49, 108
— -ch'i, viii. 29
— -chiu, celestial wine, viii. 130
—fei, viii. 72
—ho, Milky Way, viii. 132
—Hou, sea-goddess, viii. 72
—Hsien Yü Nü Pi Hsia Yüan Chün, viii. 71
—I-hêng, viii. 169
—Li, Yüan Emperor, viii. 23
— -lung ("Celestial Deaf One"), viii. 113
—Pao popular name of Yüan Shih T'ien Tsun, viii. 109
—Shih, viii. 14, 153
— -shu, viii. 59
—Tsu, Father of Husbandry, viii. 62
—Tzŭ, viii. 414
—Wang, viii. 183–187
—Wên, viii. 143
Tiermes, thunder-god, iv. 218, 230
Tiernoglav (Triglav?), iii. 289, 353 27
Tiger, iv. 360
—and mouse-deer, tale of, ix. 186–188, 191–192
—as husband of human, iv. 389
— -cat, Animals and the, tale of, vii. 321
—girl with ears and legs of a, xii. 289
—hatched Hkun Hsak from Nāga egg in teak forest, xii. 292
—man-, vi. 96
—White, xii. 307
Tigernmas, first gold smelter and mythic Irish king, iii. 137
Tigernos ("Chief"); Tigernonos ("Great King"), iii. 95

Tigranes, meaning of name, vii. 33
—the dragon-fighter, vii. 70–71, 77, 390 [16]
——Great introduces Semitic deities into Armenia, vii. 36, 38
——ruler of Armenia, vii. 9
——said to have captured statue of Ba'al Shamîn in Syria, vii. 37
Tigranuhi, wife of Aždahak, vii. 70–71, 77
Tigris, v. 120, 312, 313, 314
—Ea god of, v. 105
—Ninurta conquers lands east of, v. 130
—sources of, worshipped, vii. 59
—Valley, legend of St. George transferred to, v. 338
—waters holy and brought to Babylon for ritual, v. 317, 318
Tii, first-born of mankind, ix. 25, 26, 27, 313 [57]
——maaraatai, men descended from, ix. 25, 27
——tapu, mankind derived from, ix. 26
Tiitii (Maui), raising of sky by, ix. 51
Tikal, ruin of temple 3, xi. pl. xviii, opp. p. 126
Tiki (Tiki-au-a-ha), god, ix. 20, 23–24, 26, 312 [50]; see also Tii, etc.
——kapakapa, female child born for Tane, ix. 25
Till Eulenspiegel, hero resembling the, ix. 199–201
Tilo, Heaven, a place; also spiritual principle, vii. 127
Tilottamā, Śiva tempted by, vi. 110, 134, 153
Tilphossa, story of Saraṇyu similar to that of Erinyes of, vi. 53
Tilth, goddess of the, at Möng Nai, xii. pl. xiv, opp. p. 330, 337
Tima-te-kore, Papa daughter of, ix. 14
Time, vi. 103, 107, 193, 199, 221
—abstract divinities of, i. 282
——conceptions, number-groups react upon, xi. 52, 97
—elapse of, Rip Van Winkle motif, viii. 132
—endless, Zet deity of, xii. 378 [102]
—loss of sense of, iii. 121
——marks, iv. 436–438
—measuring of, by sun, moon, and stars, iv. 417, 422
—obelisks symbolizing, xii. 93 (fig. 84)

Time regulators, Greeks call stellar decans, v. 306
—shift of, x. 24, 50, 288 [33]; see also Rip Van Winkle cycle.
—Sol, Mane, and Mundilfari journey round Heaven to measure, ii. 183
—Toltec first to count, xi. 53–54, 55, 56, 58
Timeless region, iii. 69, 115
Ṭîmî, Jewish souls of departed, v. 364
Timo-taata, primeval god, ix. 20
Tin (Greek This), origin of name of, xii. 386 [17]
Tin Dè, story of the Nāt, xii. 342–343
Tin, molten, as omen, iv. 446
——divination by, iv. 8, 65
Ting kuan, abstraction, viii. 147
—Lan, viii. 165
Tinia in modern Romagnola a survival of Etruscan chief deity Tin(i)a, i. 316
Tinirau, ix. 14, 70, 71, 82–84
Tinne, beliefs of, x. 77–79
Tintagel, Igerna shut up in, iii. 184, 185
Tīr, Iranian deity, vii. 32
—Persian name of Mercury, vii. 384 [54]
—see also Tiur.
Tír fó Thiunn (" Land under Waves "), iii. 173
—na m-Ban (" Land of Women "), iii. 115
—na m-Beo (" Land of Living "), iii. 181
—na nÓg (" Land of Youth "), Oisin went to, iii. 180
Tirawa-atius, x. xx, 80–81, 82, 92, 94, 96, 97, 108, 116, 118, 122, 276 [11]
Tirawahut, x. 108, 276 [11]
Tiri, master of all nature, xi. 314
Ṭirid (" terror "), v. 163
Tiridates characterizes Anahit, vii. 26, 27–28
—I, formerly head of Magi in Parthia, vii. 9
—II, Christianity achieved fuller conquest under, vii. 9
Tîrthakaras of the Jains, vi. 96, 220, pl. xxviii, opp. p. 220, 221, 222, 223, 224, 225, 226, 227, 229
Tîrthas, holy places, vi. 153
Tiryns captured by Proitos with Lykian army, i. 32

Tiryns, Herakles first appears as a hero of, i. 76
—kingdom of, exchanged for Argos by Perseus, i. 35
Tishpak, name of Ninurta in Labbu myth, v. 287, 288, 294, 303
Tishtrya (dog-star [Sirius]), vi. 267–271, pl. XXXIV, opp. p. 272, 276, 280, 281, 289
—dragon fighter, vii. 363
Tisiphone, gloss of Wælcyrge, ii. 253
—one of the Erinyes, i. 277
Tište-kerge, community sacrifice-grove, iv. 262, 263
Tišup (or Tishub, Teshub), principal male deity of Hittites, Sisyphos may have been derived from, i. 325 14
Tiṣya, Aśoka's brother, supposed by some to be Indo-Chinese Titha-yaza, xii. 285
—Bṛhaspati deity of the constellation, vi. 92
Titaness cast down from Heaven, x. 113, 285 28, 289 34
Titanides, daughters of El and Astarte, v. 67
Titans, iii. 34
—battle of, replica of struggle of Giants, i. 9
—born of Okeanos and Tethys, i. 5
——Ouranos and Gaia, i. 6, 272
—conflict of, with Giants, i. 8
—conquered and driven into depths of earth by Zeus and Giants, i. 8
—cosmic, Pawnee analogy to, x. 112
—fought by Poseidon and Zeus, i. 211
—Herakles summoned to support the gods against, i. 91
—Mt. Othrys seat of, i. 8
—overthrown by Zeus, i. 160
—said to have devoured Zagreus, v. 275
—stone-armoured, x. 29
—strife of, with circle of Zeus, i. 8
Titha Kumma and Zaya Kumma, sons of King of Karanaka, become hermits, xii. 284
— -yaza, builder of Tha-tun, supposed by some to be Tiṣya, Aśoka's brother, xii. 285
Tithonos father of Memnon, i. 130
—lover of Eos, i. 246
Titicaca, Lake, xi. 200, 220, 232, 240, 243, 248
Titiko, snake, ix. 120

Titishana, tale of, vii. 276–278
Titlacauan, magician, xi. 65
Titles, father-mother, v. 44
Titthion, infant Asklepios exposed on Mt., i. 280
Titu Yupanqui, King, xi. 217
Tityos and Leto, i. 175
—punishment of, in Hades, i. 144, 145, 147
Tiu (Dyaus = Zeus = *Tiwaz), "day-light," vii. 13, 390 15
Tiuh Tiuh, xi. 178–179
Tiur, scribe of the gods, vii. 14
—patron of writing, vii. 31
—temple of, vii. 17
—(Tīr), vii. 29–33
Tiuz perhaps first sky, ii. 193
—Ull took form of, ii. 158
Tivar ("shining ones"), gods, related to Skt. devas, ii. 21
Tiwaiwaka, a bird, ix. 73
*Tiwaz (equivalent of Dyaus, Zeus, Diespiter), primitive form of Tyr, ii. 97; vii. 13
Tizoc, xi. 111
Tlacaelel, counsellor of first Monte-zuma, xi. 116
Tlacauepan, xi. 65, 66, 354 5
Tlachtli, ball-game, xi. 82, 119, 170, 173, 174, 176, 177
Tlahuicol, Tlascalan chieftain, xi. 59
Tlaik, chief of sky, x. 243
Tlalchitonatiuh, Sun of the Earth, xi. 91
Tlaloc, god of rain, xi. 50, 54, 56, 58, 59, 71–73, 77, 93, 134, 137, 354 5
Tlalocan, terrestrial paradise, xi. 81
Tlaloctecutli, god of water, xi. 92
Tlaloque, x. 201, 286 29
Tlaltecutli, earth as gaping jaws, xi. 54, 75, 80
Tlaltetecuin, xi. 112
Tlapallan, xi. 66
Tlatelolco, temple overlooking, xi. 354 5
Tlatonatiuh, Sun of Fire, xi. 91
Tlauizcalpantecutli, planet Venus, xi. 54, 57, 102
Tlazolteotl, goddess of dirt; earth-god-dess, xi. 54, 56, 78
Tlijevo, Tlinden (St. Iliya's Day) cele-brated, iii. 296
Tlingits, iv. 82
Tloque Nauaque, the Omnipresent, xi. 88

Tlotli (Hawk), messenger, xi. 89–90

Tmolos, former king of Lydia, i. 90

Toad, chalcuitl in shape of, destroyed pyramid, xi. 96

— -master, Gama Sennin is, viii. 276

Toads, iii. 132

Toasts, ii. 106–107, 117, 121, 201, 233, 310, 315

Toba, House of, viii. 188

Tobacco, xi. 29, 35

—as punishment or reward of Chameleon, vii. 161, 164

—ceremonial use of, x. 37, 85; see also CALUMET CEREMONY.

—offering of, x. 58–59, 159

——to tree, xi. 25–26

—origin of, x. 179

—placed on grave, iv. 38

Toboggan, ii. 157

Tōbō-saku ("Prime Man of the East"), viii. 275

Tochipa, x. 179, 180

Tochtli ("Rabbit"), day-sign, xi. 100

Tōda [Tawara] of the Rice-bale, tale of, viii. 314–315

To-dinh, last Chinese Governor of Tongking, xii. 312–313

— -lich River, spirits of, aid Ministers of State in debate, xii. 319

Toe, Aurvandill's, star called, ii. 82, 328

—of Death, people whom he had eaten issue from, vii. 178

——old woman, cows came from, vii. 236

Toeprint of God, pregnancy caused by treading on, viii. 6

Togakushi, Mt., viii. 382 6 (ch. iv)

Tohil, god of Balam-Quitzé, xi. 166, 167

Tohohil, xi. 181

Toi-te-hua-tahi and dog, tale of, ix. 86–87

To-Kabinana and To-Karvuvu, culture-hero brothers and primeval pair, ix. 105, 107–108, 109, 110, 122–124

Tokakami, god of death, xi. 122

Toklok, horse-herd, iv. 432

Tokolotshe, Zulu water-sprite, vii. 244

Tokoyo ("Land of Eternity"), viii. 230

Tōkyō, tale of gingko-tree in Hibiya Park, viii. 342

Tolerance, School of, viii. 8

Tolgom offered by arrow-sacrifice, xi. 182

Tollan, xi. 65, 66, 68, 70, 71, 94, 95, 96, 106, 107, 115, 125, 167, 358 11

Tolpiltzin Quetzalcoatl, last Toltec king, xi. 107

Toltec, civilization of, xi. 106–107

—first to count time, xi. 53

—the, of Nahua tradition, ancestors of Maya, xi. 125–126

Tom Thumb parallel in Africa, vii. 219

Tomb, North Siberian, iv. 480 (fig. 18)

—of shaman, iv. pl. LIII, opp. p. 466, pl. LVI, opp. p. 482

—see GRAVE-HOUSE OF DEAD.

Tombs of Apis bulls, xii. 163

——gods, xii. 166, 169, 414 24

——Melqart, Marduk, and Ba'al, v. 52, 322, 323

——modern English dead sometimes worshipped, vi. 240

——saints said to work miracles, vi. 244

Tombstone, hammer of Thor on, showed consecration to Thor, ii. 80

Tomte: see BROWNIES.

Tona, dwarf-like people, xi. 32

Tonacaciuatl may be identical with goddess of love, xi. 77, 88, 91–92

Tonacatecotle presides over the "thirteen causes," xi. 354 7

Tonacatecutli, a creator god and food-giver, xi. 75, 77, 88, 91–92, 134

"Tonalamatl" calendric period of 260 days, xi. 55, 56, 58, 100, 101, 102, 103, 104, 146, 148

Tonantzin, earth-goddess, xi. 75

Tonapa and Viracocha, xi. 232–242, 293, 370 23; see also TUPA.

Tonatiuh, sun-god, xi. 28, 54, 56, 74, 80, 81

Tonga believed to be land fished up by Maui, ix. 43

— -iti, deity, ix. 14, 37

Tongan mythology has primeval sea, ix. 20

Tongk, Ostiak name for earthly gods and images of same, iv. 12

Tongking, Tran-vu protector of, xii. 309

"Tongue-cut Sparrow," tale of, viii. 319–320

Tongue of Buddha, vi. 196, 199

——flame, soul of Lope de Aguirre haunts savannahs in form of, xi. 279

——giants used to seize victims, iv. 386, 387

Tongue, pricking, with poison, xi. 267, 268

Tongues, confusion of, x. 63, 300 [49]

—giving of, at Heaven-reaching House of God, xi. 132

—protruded, on masks, xi. pl. xxxi, p. 218, 222, pl. xxxii, p. 222, 235

T'on-mi Sambhoṭa sent to India to collect Buddhist books, vi. 208

Tŏnni vakk (case), iv. 137–138

Tonto, iv. 159

Tonttu, guider of house and outbuildings, iv. 171

Tools, magic, xi. 172

Tooth against which thumb of knowledge placed, clairvoyant gift acquired by, iii. 166–167

— -gift, Frey presented with Alfheim as, ii. 108

—of child thrown into fire for exchange by Loki, ii. 149

——Gotama Buddha given to Nawrahtā, xii. 350

—poisonous, v. 129, 130

Topeth, v. 50

Topielec, water-spirit, iii. 270

Topography of Japan, viii. 244–245

Tor, hill at Glastonbury, iii. 194–195, 212

Tora-galles: see HORA-GALLES, ETC.

Torch emblem of Demeter and Persephone, i. 233

— -race dedicated to Prometheus, Hephaistos, and Athene, i. 207

——in honour of Selene, Indian parallel to, x. 37

Torch (Torx) in name and character related to Dvergar, Zwerge, and Telchins, vii. 85, 393 [33] [34]

Torches: see KEREMET SPIRITS, ETC.

Tŏrem, heaven-god, iv. 260

— -Karevel and -Talmas, iv. 404

Tornado-sack of Lightning stolen, x. 116, 121

Tornait, x. 5, 270 [4], 272 [6]

Tornarsuk, ruler of the Tornait, x. 5, 271 [6], 272 [6]

Tornit, Inlanders, legends of, x. 3, 29

Tŏrö, iv. 123, 131

Torone, wrestling match at, between Herakles and the sons of Proteus, i. 261

Töröngöi, first man, iv. 381

Tortoise, vi. 75, 96, 104, 155

Tortoise and serpent emblems of Huyen-vu, xii. 307, 308

—as term of vilification, viii. 101

—ascends altar, viii. 35

—avatar of Viṣṇu, vi. 168

—birth of, xi. 29

—Chinese symbol of Yin, viii. 243

— -crane emblem, meaning of, xii. 307–308

—husbands, ix. 140

—in legend, seizes sword of Thai-to, xii. 302

——trickster tales, ix. 187, 188, 194–196, 204–205

—incarnation, older attribution of, to Brahmā or Prajāpati, vi. 170

—or ape as trickster-hero of Indonesian origin, ix. 204–205

—see HYMN TO HERMES, ETC.

—snake-like head of, ix. 291

—son of a, explanation of, as term of abuse, xii. 307

—spiritual animal, viii. 98, 100–101

—sprang from face of Mañjuśrī, vi. 212

—throne of Ea supports a, v. 396 [52]

—tortoise stories, vii. 121, 135, 144, 284, 309–320, 424 [14]

—used in divination, viii. 135, 138

—wife of crane [Urashima], viii. 265

—writing on, viii. 38

Torture of prisoners unknown on Pacific coast, x. 214

—pillar of copper, viii. 40

—putting to, vii. 370

Tortures devised by Ta-chi, viii. 39

—Sun-dance, x. 89–90, pl. xvii, opp. p. 90, 282 [21]

" Tóruigheacht Dhiarmada agus Ghráinne," iii. 175–179

" Tóruighecht in Ghilla Dhecair," iii. 173

Tös-Khan, son of creator, iv. 405

Tosotsu-ten (Pāli, Tusita), one of three chief paradises, viii. 241

Totem-ancestors of various clans, some human and some animal, ix. 271

— -god, Cagn possibly a, vii. 135, 287

Totemic emblems of the North-west, Peruvian figures reminiscent of, xi. 222–223

Totemism, ii. 258; iv. 496–523; v. xviii, 7, 9, 10, 11; vi. 63, 170, 240–241, 243; xi. 223, 234, 245

Totemism and totemic spirits, x. 238, pl. xxx, opp. p. 240, 240–245, 246, 270 [4], 293 [40]
——totems, vii. 120, 132, 182, 270–290, 288, 322, 416 [1], 418 [40]
—importance of, in Australia, ix. 301, 302
—question of, in Egyptian religion, xii. 362 [4]
—traces of, in Artemis ritual, i. 183
Totems, ix. 116, pl. xii, opp. p. 104
Tou, Empress, viii. 174
Toueyo, name assumed by Tezcatlipoca, xi. 65–66
Towel bound about neck of sacrificial animal, iv. 264
—hung in hut for deceased for forty days, iv. 48
Towels, iv. 148
Tower hidden with magic mist, iii. 201
—of Babel, iv. 367; v. 309, 310, 323
——among Chins, xii. 266, 267
——equivalent, vi. 336, pl. xlii, opp. p. 336
——stands for New Year and fish for end of old, v. 310
—sun imprisoned in, iii. 318
Towers as symbols of earth, v. 90, 94
—colours of stages of, v. 159
—origin of stages of, v. 89–90
Town-pillars, iv. 334–335, 339
Towns, birds inspired heroes to found, iii. 13
—of gods, vii. 19, 387 [5]
Tōyō-tama-hime, tale of, viii. 265–266
Trachis, children of Herakles flee to, i. 95
Trachoma, iv. 136
Trade between Ireland and Spain in pre-historic days, iii. 23
—the silent, ii. 271
Tradition, iii. 8
—Frigg in, ii. 177
—preserves distinct traces of early faith of ancient Slavs, iii. 222–223
Traditions, Chinese, oral and written, viii. 3
—native, xi. 5
" Tragic Death of Sons of Usnech ": see Longes mac nUsnig.
—tales not accepted by Japanese in times of warfare and social disintegration, viii. 265

Trance, artificial stimulants to assist shaman's, iv. 282, pl. xxxvii, opp. p. 282, 285–286, 290–291, 293, 295
Transcription and pronunciation, Egyptian, uncertainty of, xii. 3–4
——Indian, vi. 9
Transfiguration, xi. 197
—Day rites, vii. 59–61
—of Buddha, vi. 193
—roses and rose-water, vii. 381 [5] (ch. ii)
—water-pouring at Feast of, vii. 22
Transformation, i. 15, 16, 20, 21, 29, 35, 36, 44, 46, 68, 69, 70, 73, 122, 137, 158, 175, 181, 195, 211, 246, 257; ii. 10, 22, 125, 141, 142, 143, 144, 146, 151, 155, 181, 197, 240, 269, 277, 293; iii. 31, 40, 51, 60, 66, 71, 72, 75, 80, 89, 96, 97, 100, 102, 124, 125, 126, 127, 129, 136, 155, 168, 169, 171, 172, 174, 175, 177, 187, 188, 207, 208, 229; iv. 105; 365, 374, 409, 480, 481, 503, 504, 506, 507; v. 28, 32, 352; vi. 30, 48, 53, 67, 95, 115–116, 209, 242, 311 ff.; 295, 302; vii. 50; 168, 230, 253; viii. 38, 157; 222, 253, 254, 265, 270, 290, 304–305, 314, 321, 324, 325, 327, 328, 329, 333; ix. 55, 65, 69, 70, 82, 107, 109, 110–111, 144, 172, 208, 229, 252, 271; x. 7, 50, 63, 104, 115, 133, 134, 136, 164, 176, 216, 224–225, 228, 229, 231, 279 [15], 293 [40], 296 [46]–297, 307 [62]; xi. 28–29, 30, 31–32, 61, 66, 69, 83, 91, 93, 94, 95, 153, 167, 169, 171, 172, 174, 194, 201, 202, 225, 228, 231, 239, 249, 250, 251, 269, 271, 275, 276, 301, 304, 310, 311–315; xii. 356; see also Shape-shifting.
—certain medicines produce, iii. 184; vii. 344
—Combat, iii. 56–57, 109, 110
—Flight, iii. 136
—of Niobe and Aëdon, i. 44, 175
——primeval man to woman, ix. 107
—power of, Periklymenos received, i. 92
Transformer: see Hero-transformer-trickster.
Transformers, xi. 62, 85, 88
Translation of man, woman, and child to Heaven, vii. 238–239, 240, 241
——Xisuthros (Ziûsudra; Noah), v. 204, 208, 224

Transliteration, x. 267 ¹–268

Transmigration, iii. 14; vi. 101, 227, 228; viii. 240–241, 281, 316, 317; x. 78, 280 ¹⁸–281, 297 ⁴⁶; xii. 415 ⁵

Transmutation of metals: see ALCHEMY.

Transparency of bodies of Czech genii of fate, iii. 250

Tran-vu (= Huyen-thien, Huyen-vu), Pagoda of (French Grand Buddha), connected with serpent-worship, xii. 306, 308, 309

—(= Huyen-vu), national tutelary deity, xii. 309

—offerings to, xii. 310

—temple of, xii. 309–310

Trap, tale of first, resembles that told of guillotine and its inventor, iii. 137

Trasadasyu, Agni god of, vi. 44

Trātṛ, epithet of Agni or Indra, vi. 50

Trauco, witch appearing in child form, xi. 328

Travel, myth of tears of Isis used as spell for safe, xii. 126

Travelling man, iv. 409

Tray, wooden, Byat Twe and Ta rescued from, xii. 348

Tre, variant form of name Tiur, vii. 383 ⁴⁵

Treasure, ii. 47, 139, 141, 211

—dividing of magical, ii. 272

—snakes guardians of, vi. 241

Treasures, demanded that Kulhwch obtain, iii. 192

—discovered by means of "hand of glory," iii. 107

—magical, to be obtained, iii. 40

—of Britain, Merlin took the, to isle of Bardsey, iii. 201

Treasuries, Brides of, Muslim fairy guardians, vii. 393 ³²

Tree and plant of healing, v. 152, 226

—artificial sacrifice-, iv. 339

—ash-: see YGGDRASIL, ETC.

—bark of, in lieu of human skin, as tribute to devil, vii. 371

—Beach, Lake Biwa, Ōmi, viii. 340

—bending of, to kill person, ix. 231, 321 ⁷¹

—birth of pine-, x. 27

—boat-like trough placed in, at Lapp Christmas festival, iv. 67

—box-, female made from, by Moon, ix. 274

— -burial, iv. 481

Tree, celestial, viii. 339; xii. 32 (fig. 13), 35 (fig. 21), 36, 37 and figs. 22, 23, 24

——associated with sun-myths, vii. 49

——association of Osiris with, xii. 94, 99

——attempts to localize, xii. 36–37

——birth of sun from, xii. 35 (fig. 21)

——dead fed by Ḥat-ḥôr from, xii. 39

———perch on branches of, xii. 178

——divine cat cuts a serpent into fragments at foot of, xii. 106

——Ḥat-ḥôr gives food and drink from, xii. 136

———sitting among green rays identical with, xii. 39

——in relation to the sun, xii. 38, 39

——or cosmic, terrestrial analogies of, xii. 36

——Sekha(u)it, Ṭhout(i), and Atum register king's name on, xii. 53 (fig. 51)

—changing size of, with entrance or exit of spirit, iv. 354

—coins left at sacrifice-, iv. 279–280

—connexion of Yima with a, vi. 315

—containing forbidden fruit, vii. 316–319

—cosmic, xii. 35–36

——or of fate, Isis conceives Horus from, xii. 115

—creation of, iv. 378, 381, 382

—cross carved on memorial, iv. 25–26, 67

—cut by Esus, iii. 9, 157, pl. xx, opp. p. 157, pl. xxi, opp. p. 166

—dedicated to Utumö, promise-rope wound about, iv. 69–70

—fertilized by bird produced mankind, ix. 168

—fire came from, iv. 451

—food offered to, by harvesters, xii. 16

—from Heaven dropped to earth in creation-myth, ix. 159

——which milk is distilled, xi. 83

—Gaokerena, white haoma, vi. 265, 281

—gave rise to gods and men, ix. 167

—Great Oak, song of, iv. 82

—grew from heart of a primeval being, ix. 166

———sword-handle dropped by sun, ix. 159

—head of Hunhun-Ahpu transformed to gourd on, xi. 171

Tree heaven, x. 35, 48–49, 63, 104, 113–114, 136, 174, 221, 233, 234, 255, 257, 260, 294 42, 300 49, 307 62; xii. 31
——and life, Isis identified with, xii. 99
——as aid to passage for dead, xii. 176
——curious legend of a, vii. 137
——see PERSEA-TREE, ETC.
——stellar, Nut united with, xii. 42
—hiding inside of, ix. 119
—holy, iv. 139, 140, 142, 150, 174
——in every nome, xii. 37
—in Loch Guirr, perhaps debased myth of world-tree, iii. 138
———room in, built for Fionn and his grandmother, iii. 167
—one of lower heavens reaching to sky, ix. 160
—iron, iv. 333, 339
—Jumo, iv. 265–280
—kaji-, viii. 237
—karsikko, iv. 25–26, pl. II, opp. p. 26, 43
—katsura-, viii. 232, 378 15
—" killing " of, before chopping down, iv. 187
—kumpong-, man created from, ix. 174
—Lang turned into betel-, xii. 356
—luminous and burning, x. 100
—magic, for healing, v. 152
——restoration of, ix. 59–60, 68, 124–125, 325 14
— -marriage, vi. 238, 239
—mistletoe, ii. 129
—Näkki may appear as, iv. 204
—names of persons, v. 9
—night-, rose-, sun-, iii. 326
—nim-, Nimbāraks worship sun in a, vi. 232
—Odin hung on, for nine nights, ii. 43, 50–51, 52, 354 60
—of all seeds, vi. 281, 289
——death and life, iv. 383
——fate, xii. 36
——knowledge, beneath which Buddha attains Buddhahood, vi. 197
———of good and evil, iv. 381, 382, 383, 490; v. 184–185, 187, 199
————suggestion of, in Wa creation-myth, xii. 289
——life, iv. 349–360, 381–382, 383, 413, 414, 415, 490; xii. 36 and fig. 23
———and nourishment, xi. 70
————serpent, v. 177, 179, 184, 186, 402 9

Tree of life, Biblical conceptions of, influenced Idunn myth, ii. 180
——guarded against mortals, and other marvellous trees, iii. 131
——may have been presented to dying gods, v. 188
——of paradise, iv. 80
——Osiris connected with, xii. 399 111
——Middle Place, xi. pl. IX, opp. p. 70
——Tarbga shaken, iii. 127
—Pārijāta, vi. 174
—Persea-: see PERSEA-TREE, ETC.
—planted at new house, first-fruits and a sheep offered to, iv. 26
——by God (world-pillar), iv. 335, 338
—primeval pair in form of, vi. 295
—rowan, called " Thor's Deliverance," ii. 84
——of the gods resembles quicken-tree of Dubhros, iii. 131
——(quicken), berries of, confer immortality, iii. 54, 55
—sacred, of Heliopolis, local parallels to, xii. 31
——offerings to Leza at, vii. 133
——soul of Osiris in, xii. 166
—sacrifice blood thrown into, iv. 271
——each god has its own, iv. 265–281
——towel from neck of sacrificial animal hung on, iv. 264
—sacrificial animal's bones hung on, iv. 57, 58, 149, 150
—sacrificing towards, iv. 268, 269, 270, 271, 272
—sakaki-, viii. 226, pl. VIII, opp. p. 226
—sanga-: see SANGA-TREE, ETC.
—silk-cotton-, creation by chips from, xi. 271
—song of Shetland woman echo of myth of Odin on the, ii. 354 60
— -soul, iv. 14, 188
—offering to, iv. 188
—speaking, viii. 101
—spirit man and woman descending from, become rulers of branch of Wa race, xii. 281
— -spirit, vi. 238–239; viii. 177
——(as first woman [?]), iv. 352, 353, 358, 359
—shrine of, xii. pl. IV, opp. p. 254, pl. VIII, opp. p. 280
— -spirits, Schrat akin to Teutonic, ii. 205

Tree, splitting of, iii. 322
—sun-god appearing from, v. 133
—ten mythical varieties of men grown on, vi. 298
—that shakes its roots used in making zemis, xi. 25–26, 35
—to wife, Tane took, ix. 25
—transformation into, as fulfilment of wish, x. 50
— -trunks, creation of Ask and Embla out of, ii. 204
——hollowed, used as coffins, iv. 34
—(Ulé) became man, xi. 313–314
—upside down in creation-myth, ix. 249
————sky, whereby men pass back and forth, ix. 38
—water of life confers immortality on, ix. 252–253
—which was origin of all cultivated plants, xi. 269
—with jewelled fruit seen by Gilgamish, iii. 131
—world-: see YGGDRASIL, ETC.; WORLD-TREE.
— -worship, vi. 158–159
——Lithuanian, iii. 356 9
—Yama revels with the Fathers in, vi. 312
—Yaxche, xi. 138
Trees and forests regarded as animate, iv. 187–190
——rocks joining Heaven and earth, xi. 308–309
—ash at which dooms given, ii. 23
—bear's bones hung on, iv. 93
—bending over to carry people to other places, ix. 65, 66, 78
—cacao- and calabash-, grew from buried body of Jáburu, xi. 193
—certain, origins of, i. 16
—cherry-, viii. 213, 233–234
—coniferous, required, if possible, in groves of lower spirits, iv. 152, 158, 220
—different, tutelary genii for, iv. 188
—divine, consisting of pearls and fruits, vi. 138, 144, 201
—dwelling-place of Maruts, Apsarases, and Gandharvas, vi. 89–90, 94
—felling of, by dead man, iv. 55
—fire caught in, ix. 281
—first people came from, vii. 145–146, 401 6

Trees, first people transformed into, xi. 28
—five heavenly, of great sanctity, vi. 159
—forests, as deities, vi. 60–61, 96
—four, which rise into quarters of Heaven perhaps as support, xi. 55, 56
—fruit-bearing, musical, iii. 87, 120
—growing, to escape flood, x. 161
—have lower branches removed in honour of new enterprises or of a bride, iv. 26
—Heaven-supporting, ii. 335
—human sacrifice hung on, iii. pl. xx (A), opp. p. 158
—images carved on, iv. pl. XIX, opp. p. 156, 178
—in divination, vii. 12
—(in nature), ii. 203–208, 213, 214
—kinds of, in sacrifice groves, iv. 152, 158, 262, 266, 281
—lime, associated with Rå and Alf, ii. 226
—linen hung on, iii. 254
—made from Ymir's hair, ii. 326
—magic, iii. 87
——with apples, iii. 195
—magical influence of, viii. 79, 104–105
—man derived from, in belief of some Hellenic stocks, i. 11
—mankind created from, ix. 30, 106, 107, 110, 160, 167, 168, 169; 313 77
—marriage of man and woman who were originally, ix. 160
—memorial, iv. 25–26, 35
—miraculous growth of, ix. 64, 239, 295, 297
—mythic, of Elysium, not unknown on earth, though guarded, iii. 138
—mythical, viii. 339–340
—of Eden, v. 189
——forest sacred to Artemis, i. 184
——Quarters, xi. 56–57
——tabued grove stained with blood of sacrifices, iii. 11
—origins of certain, traced back to human or divine personages, i. 16
—(pine, sugi, camphor, gingko) in legend, viii. 253–254, 341–342, 348
—placenta hung on, at child-birth, iv. 261
—plants, flowers, tales of, viii. 338–353

Trees, preparing Seides from, or sacrificing at, iv. 108, 109–110, pl. IX, opp. p. 110

—progenitors of Pygmies offspring of, vii. 265

—representing the storeys of Heaven erected before sacrificial victims, iv. 400, 487

—sacred, ii. pl. XL, opp. p. 316; vi. 239; 283, 387; viii. 246–247, pl. XV, opp. p. 246, 267

——to Anu, v. 97

—sacrifice, iv. 144, 152, 153, 154, 174, 233; see also KARSIKKO, MEMORIAL TREE, ETC.

—sacrificial victims hung on branches of, ii. 203

—see SHAMAN-PILLARS.

—seeds of fire brought to, ix. 254

—serpents connected with, v. 179

—shaping of humans from, ii. 327

—smeared with blood to support the sky, iv. 222

—soul-, ix. pl. XVIII, opp. p. 182

—spirits appear as tall as, iv. 179, 181, 182, 184–185, 189, 243

——of dead dwell in, ii. 204, 207

——see DRYADS; HAMADRYADS.

—365, typify year; and two, day and night, xii. 35, 38

—tutelary spirits ascribed to, xii. 15–16

—which preserve germ of fire (friction), ix. 47

—wish-, vi. 225

—withered by Mora, iii. 228

—worship of, iii. 273; vii. 62–63

Trelquehuecuve, octopus, xi. 328

Tremyugan, iv. 403

Trench, New Year ceremony at, v. 319, 320

Trespass on a sacred place, iii. 73

Tresses of Ḥat-ḥôr hang across or form sky, xii. 39

——Horus, four sons of Horus or Osiris identified with, xii. 112

Tretā Age, vi. 102, 105

Trèves, altar from, iii. pl. XX, opp. p. 157, pl. XXI, opp. p. 166

Triad, vi. pl. IX, opp. p. 108, 109; x. 220, 221

—earliest form of, in Indian religion, vii. 43

—formed in ancient Persia and in Armenia, vii. 42

Triad formed in India by Indra, Agni, and Sūrya, vii. 43

—Khaldi, Theispas, and Artinis formed a, under Babylonian influence, vii. 11

—of Elephantine, xii. 20 (fig. 1)

——gods existed before Chaos, ix. 16

—original Japanese, viii. 222

—perhaps once formed in Armenia by Aramazd, Anahit, and Mihr, vii. 33

—see TRIMŪRTI.

—Theban, xii. 34, 362 [6]

Triads, ii. 15–16, 23–24, pl. VI, opp. p. 32

—development of, xii. 20, 215

—in Babylonia, xii. 362 [5]

—of gods in Malay Archipelago due to Indian influence, ix. 242

—Welsh poems, iii. 92, 95, 98, 103, 106, 107, 111, 189, 190, 191, 192, 193, 197, 201

Triangular arrangement of army and triangular arrow, vii. 64, 65, 71

Tribal cult of the clan deity, viii. 215

—deities, Ewe totems listed as, vii. 272

Tribe inhabiting foot of mountain, genius of mountain progenitor (or tutelary god) of the, viii. 215

Tribes and lands of the Gulf Region, x. 53–54

—first settling in China, viii. 5

—five, vi. 54, 61, 356 [9]

—forest, x. 13–51

—of men created from body of monster, x. 139

Tribog, triple god (see also TRIGLAV), iii. pl. XXXIV, opp. p. 288

Tribunal, divine, Odin rides to, ii. 23, 43

Tribute, ii. 27, 34; xi. 108

—bound on Ireland may be memory of sacrifice, iii. 27

—double, forced upon Minyans by Thebes, i. 79–80

Trick to gain possession of síd, iii. 50, 52

Trickery, vii. 119, 139–140, 141, 213; ix. 133–134, 136, 146; x. 44–45, 297 [47], 298 [48]

—against spirits, iv. 475–476

Trickster and transformer: see HLAKANYANA, ETC.; also items s.v. the well-known trickster animals.

— -hero, Amalivaca, xi. 259

Trickster tales absent from Micronesian mythology, ix. 263
——Philippines, ix. 240
—and tricksters, ix. 126–128, 186–205, 288–289
——found in Annam, ix. 242
——Indonesian, influenced by Buddhist " Jātakas," etc., ix. 242
Tricksters, vii. 122, 292, 353
—transformers, and wonder folk, x. xvi, 67–69, 81, 120–124, 290 36, 298 48–299, 311 69
Trident, connexion of, with fish-spear, i. 211
—emblem of Nereus, i. 260
—of Poseidon, connexion of, with lightning-bolt of a Mesopotamian divinity, i. 210
——Śiva, vi. 111
—symbol of Poseidon, meaning of, i. 7 (fig. 1)
Triglav, three-headed god at Stettin, iii. pl. xxxi, opp. p. 278, 284–285, 289
Trimūrti (Triad), vi. pl. ix, opp. p. 108, pl. x, opp. p. 118, 183
Trinities, v. 89, 108, 292, 293; viii. 108–109, 110–113, 196; see also various entries s.v. THREE.
Trinity, ii. 24
—Christian, Egyptian and Babylonian triads not comparable with, xii. 362 5
—Yucatec, xi. 143
Triphis and Amon, spell of, against dog-bite, xii. 209
—Greek form of name Repit, xii. 146, 408 82, 426 27
Triple form assumed by Odin, ii. 6, pl. iii, opp. p. 12
—forms, Celtic myths loved, iii. 193
Tripod, sacred, at Delphoi, desecrated by Herakles, i. 90
Tripods, golden, wrought by Hephaistos, i. 206
Tripolemos of Eleusis, teachings of, in beginnings of civilization, i. 16
Triptolemos, a minister of rites of Demeter, i. 230
—judge in Hades, i. 143
—of Syria, Yāw compared to, v. 43
—parentage of, i. 230
—setting forth to bring knowledge of agriculture to mankind, i. 229 (fig. 8), 230
Triṣadhastha, Agni is, vi. 284

Triśalā and Devānandā, foetuses in wombs of, interchanged, vi. 222–223
Triśaṅku, Karamnāśā River represents sins of, vi. 235
—sought to attain Heaven, vi. 148
Triśiras, vi. 153
Tristan, Anglo-Norman poet Thomas wrote concerning, iii. 196
—French poem of Arthurian cycle, iii. 195
Tristram, iii. 104
Triṣṭubh metre, vi. 91
Trita and Viśvarūpa, myth of, v. 130
—Āptya, vi. 36, 48, 67, 89, 176
—(Thrita) in myth, vi. 265
Triton, i. 259–260
—appears to Argonauts and directs them to Sea of Minos, i. 114
—bears Theseus to Poseidon and Amphitrite, i. 101
—holds Theseus in the presence of Amphitrite and Athene, i. pl. xxv, opp. p. 96
Tritonian Lake, Argonauts guided overland by horse to, i. 114
Troan, mother of Tror, daughter of Priam, ii. 32
Troglodyte, Mîn of Koptos not truly, xii. 410 1
Troglodytes, vii. 113
Troia new name of Dardania, i. 117
Troizen, i. 68
—cave believed to lead to Underworld, i. 143
—entrance to Underworld at, i. 89
—oracle at, consulted by Aigeus, i. 97
—Poseidon chief deity of, i. 212
Trojans enveloped in mist by Hera, i. 164, 166
Trold-folk, ii. 223, 224, 231
— -thing, ii. 301
— -wives, ii. 205, 233
— -woman, Helgi's Fylgja, ii. 235
Trolls, ii. 81, 90, 173, 199, 219, 223, 285–287, 301, 302
Trophonios, Hades as earth-god, i. 234
Tror (Thor), ii. 32
Trorhall, host of, ii. 231
Tros, grandson of Dardanos, succeeds to throne, i. 117
—of Ilion, father of Ganymedes, i. 240
Trough as protective covering for dead, iv. 34

Trough, boat-shaped, containing food, put in high pine-tree at Lapp Christmas festival, iv. 67
—burial of food and image in, for dead, iv. 39
—for long-dead placed by door at funeral feasts, iv. 39, 44, 45, 51, 60
Troughs, ghosts seize, vii. 186
Trows of Orkney and Shetland recall trolls, ii. 287
Troy, adventures of Herakles at, i. 91
—afflicted by Apollo and Poseidon, i. 85
—founders of Rome came from, i. 304
—Greek army arrives at, i. 126
—Odysseus entreated by Menelaos and Palamedes to aid in war against, i. 123
—(or Turkland) in Prologue to the "Edda," ii. 32, 33
—sack of, i. 126
—tale of, i. 117–140
—Theseus's children reign in Athens after fall of, i. 105
—thought to have been Asgard, ii. 329
Trumpet, sacred, to which offerings made, xi. 275
Trung sisters, Anh-tong's vision of, xii. 314
——fate of, xii. 314, 315
Trung-nhi and -trac, sisters deified and commemorated in temple at Chua-hai-ba, xii. 312–314
Truxillo, xi. 215, 219, 220, 221
Tryambaka, name of Rudra, vi. 38, 83
Ts'ai and the haunted house, viii. 151–152
—Shên, god of wealth, viii. 66, 79
—Shun, viii. 164
—Yüan-ting, classical scholar of Sung Dynasty, viii. 144
"Ts'an T'ung Ch'i," viii. 144, 145, 146
Tsanahale, creature with feathered back, x. 163
"Tsang Shu," viii. 140
Ts'ang Chieh, viii. 31
Tsao, viii. 74, 76, 77
—Chün ("Prince of the Furnace"), viii. 75–76
—Po, viii. 77
—Shên, god of hearth, viii. 74, 76
—Tzŭ, viii. 105
Ts'ao Kuo-chiu, one of Eight Immortals, viii. 127–128

Ts'ao Ts'ao, viii. 95, 107, 175, 176–177, 178, 179
Tsê, viii. 80
—Shên, household god of brick houses, viii. 81; see also Houses, excavated, etc.
Ts'ê tzŭ, dissection of ideographs, viii. 138
Tsegihi, x. 171, 173
"Tselane," vii. 156, 414 24
Tsên Yü-ying, deified military governor, xii. 260, pl. v, opp. p. 260
Tsêng-ch'êng, viii. 128
—Ts'an, viii. 104, 161–162
Tshaka, vii. 135
Tshembulat, Cheremiss spirit, iv. 155
Tshindi, or devils, evil gods, x. 156
Tshohanoai, Sun-carrier, x. 155
Tsiskagili, red cray-fish, why meat of, inedible, x. 60
Tsisnadzini (Pelado Peak, N. M.), creation and decoration of, x. 162
Tso, commentator, viii. 138
——ch'iu Ming, viii. 199
—Chuan, commentary on "Ch'un Ch'iu" viii. 81, 109, 199
—tao, black art, viii. 155
Tsolob (the Offenders), Age of, xi. 153
Tšon, Cheremiss "life," iv. 4
T-sonet-nofret, xii. 140
Tsoň-k'a-pa, monk of Tibet, vi. 209
Tsonoqoa, Cannibal Woman, x. 243–244
Tšopatsa, Mordvinian "soul," also applied to image of a god, iv. 12
Tsu tien, sacrifice before journey, viii. 61
Ts'ui Chi-shu, viii. 169
—Hao, viii. 189
—Shih, viii. 163
Tsũi ||Goab (or Tsuni ||Goam), supreme Being of Hottentots, discussion of, vii. 157–159, 214, 215
Tsuki-yo-mi, viii. 224
Tsukuba, Mt., viii. 251
Tsukushi (modern Kyūshū), island, viii. 211
—oak of, viii. 339
Tsulkalu, x. 69
Tsuna wounded an ogre, viii. 306
Tsundigewi, dwarfs, x. 68
Ts'ung, jade tube, viii. 46, 47
Tsuraspako, animal-lodge, x. 123
Tsuré-zuré-gusa, viii. 385

Tsutsu-izutsu ("well-curb"), story of, viii. 299–300

Tu, child of Rangi, ix. 8, 9

Tu one of the "Perfect Ones," viii. 113

—Su, hill in Eastern Sea, viii. 117

T'u-drawing, viii. 35, 37

Tuag, drowning of, iii. 72, 89

Tuag's Wave, iii. 89

Tuan MacCairill, long life and transformations of, iii. 206–207

Tuatha Dé Danann, gods and magicians, Nemedian survivors who returned to Ireland, iii. pl. i, frontispiece, 23–24, 25, 26, 27, 29, 30, 31, 34, 35, 36, 38, 39, 40, 42–48, 49, 50, 51, 54, 56, 60–61, 65, 66, 89, 91, 97, 108, 122, 126, 127, 134, 140, 153, 163, 164, 167, 170, 174, 175, 177, 188, 198, 204, 347 [61]

———mythical Irish people, ii. 30

———traditional burial-place of the, iii. pl. i, frontispiece

Tub, iii. 136

—Uzume dances on flat, viii. pl. viii, opp. p. 226

Tubal-Cain, patron of metal-workers, v. 105, 202, 403 [3]

Tubes, drinking-, vii. 169, 403 [23]

Tucuma, an orange-coloured palm, food plant, xi. 309

Tucupacha, creator deity, tale of, xi. 85–86

Tuesday, ploughing, sowing, reaping should be done on a, iii. 33

Tugra, Bhujyu son of, vi. 31

Tugs-of-war, vii. 314–316, 326–327; xii. 326

Tu-huru-huru, son of Tinirau, ix. 82–83

Tuirbe Trágmar forebade sea to come beyond axe, iii. 133

Tuirenn, son of Ogma, iii. 40

Tuirrean transformed into wolf-hound, iii. 169

Tuisto, ii. 24

—and Mannus originators of Germanic race, ii. 328

Tūkarām, divinity of, vi. 244

Tukulti-Ninurta I, v. 145, 400 [155]

Tulala-Madindi, pygmies who sleep in holes, vii. 416 [19]

Tulan-Zuiva, Place of Seven Caves and Seven Ravines, xi. 166

Tulans, four, xi. 178, 179, 180, 181

Tulasī Dās, vi. 231, 244

Tulchainde, Morrígan helped, iii. 67

Tulchuherris, regarded as lightning, x. 232–233

Tulihänd = Money-Para, iv. 173

Tululi, v. 79

Tu-matauenga, god of fierce human beings, ix. 32

Tumbal, war-god, xi. 207

Tumbez, xi. 220

Tumburu, leader of Gandharvas, vi. 143

Tu-metua, deity, ix. 14

Tumo-pas, oak-god, iv. 188

Tumuli, ii. pl. i, frontispiece, pl. xvi, opp. p. 130

—Celtic deities may have been associated with, iii. 49

Tu-mute-anaoa, deity, ix. 14

Tuna, eel lover of Maui's wife and Ina, ix. 55–56

Tunek, the, slain by crystal, x. 3, 284 [27]

Tung Cho, viii. 177

—Chow Lieh Kuo Chih, viii. 166

—Chün, god of sun rising in East, viii. 90, 117

— -fang So called upon at sacrifice to pygmies, viii. 117

—Fu, viii. 114

—Hai ("Eastern Sea"), appearance of daughter of, to Wên Wang, viii. 70

— -hua, abode of male fairies, viii. 114

—Huang T'ai I, hero, viii. 87, 88

—Pien Mên, viii. 155

— -t'ing, lake, viii. 89

———Mountain, viii. 154

—Wang, viii. 114

———Kung, viii. 116

—Yo temple, tablet on, viii. 23, 135

———worshipped by Taoists, viii. 71

—Yung, viii. 162–163

"T'ung Chien," viii. 76

———Kang Mu, viii. 59

———Wai Chi, viii. 58

—Shu, viii. 143

Tüng Hkam, a heavenly deity, xii. 275

———son of Nāga princess and Hkun Ai, marriage of, xii. 273–274

Tungk-Pok, a hunter of six-footed stag, son of god of Heaven, iv. 436

Tunja, Zaque of, xi. 196

Tunkan ("Boulder"), the Earth-power, x. 98

Tunnrida, House-riders, ii. 300, 301

Tuno (magician), iv. 145, 146, 147

Tuonela, home of Tuoni (the dead one), Underworld, iv. 74, 78

Tuonen-portti, Underworld's gate, iv. 75

Tupa (Tupan, Tumpa), cognate form of Tonapa, xi. 293, 294, 295, 296, 297, 299, 375 11

Tupac Yupanqui, Quito subdued by, xi. 207

Tuphion, Ḥemen perhaps hawk-god of, xii. 133

Tūr, son of Thraētaona, vi. 323

Tura, tale of, ix. 78–79

Turachogue (Bachue), xi. 199

Turanian idolatry, Keresāspa became addicted to, vi. 327

Turanna (Etruscan Turan) of modern Romagnola apparently connected with Téramó, i. 319

Turco-Tatar influence on Magyars, iv. xix

Turco-Tatars, contact of Finno-Ugrians with, iv. xviii

Turehu and Mataora, tale of, ix. 72–73

Tūrem mother, soul-giving deity, iv. 260

Turfans, viii. 96

Turisas (? " father Tur "), god of victory, possibly derived from Norse Thor, iv. 228

Turk, the, x. 311 67

Turkey, x. 203, 293 40

Turkish (Seljuk) conquest of Armenia, vii. 8

Turkistan, peoples from, invade Indo-China from India, Yün-nan, and Malaysia, xii. 287

Turms, Etruscan deity, survives as Téramó in modern Romagnola, i. 318

Turnip, forbidden, x. 94, 96

Turnips, deity of, iv. 244

Turnus, betrothal of Lavinia to, annulled; defeated and slain by Aeneas, i. 306

Turones, coins of the, iii. pl. II (5), opp. p. 8

Turquoise Boy, x. 162

—see Colour symbolism; Jewels of the Quarters; Stones as jewels.

—symbolizes blue sky, x. 157, 284 27

Turtle became " Typhonic " animal of Sêth, xii. 390 35

—black = north, iv. 360

Turtle head of Xbalanqué, xi. 174–175

— -shell, origin of, ix. 145–146

—soil on back of, at creation, x. 36, 293 40

—world-bearing, iv. 319–320, 327, 338, pl. XLII, opp. p. 338, 342–343, 346, 366

Turupid, idol, iii. 289

Turuṣkas, vi. 210

Turvaśa, vi. 35

Ṭūs, son of Naotara (Pers. Naudhar), companion of Haosravah, vi. 339

Tushratta, king of the Mitanni, v. 34

Tushup, Hittite weather-god, Sanda may have been tribal variety of, vii. 379 1 (ch. i)

Tuṣita, Buddha-to-be lived in world of the, vi. 194, 198

—one of paradises, viii. 241

Tusser (Trold-folk), ii. 223

T'u-tê, virtue of earth, viii. 27

Tu-te-koro-punga carried off Ruku-tia, ix. 79–80

Tutelaries, xi. 38, 40, 54, 56, pl. VI, opp. p. 56, pl. IX, opp. p. 70, 224, 245, 354 5

Tutelary, x. xvii, 5, 85, 145, 215, 241, 245–249, 270 4, 293 40

—genius of man may precede him, iv. 11

——migratory birds, iv. 176

——shadow-souls may be transformed into, iv. 10, 11, 14

—shaman possessed special, iv. 284–285, 292

—gods, viii. 196

—spirits, xii. 15

——see Vættir, etc.

T'u-ti lao-yeh (feminine: T'u-ti nai-nai), a local deity, viii. 64, 65, 66

—Shên (Hou-t'u Shên), Ko Lung deified as god of soul, viii. 62

Tutul-Xiu formed alliance with Mayapan, xi. 127, 129

Tuture, son of Haumea, ix. 62–63

Tuuri, Karelian name, Thor component of, iv. 228

Tuxtla Statuette, xi. 130

Tvaṣṭṛ, Baltic celestial smith compared to, iii. 330

—" Fashioner," vi. 16, 31, 32, 34, 36, 37, 41, 45, 50, 53, 57, 64, 87, 88, 93, 107, 133, 141, 143

—Goibniu equivalent of, iii. 31

Tveggi, ii. 345

Tver, Finnish Karelians migrated to, iv. xv

Twatahsa, twelve clans of, xii. 292

Twelfth Night, name for Eve of, iii. 307, 309

——water-spirits escorted to water, iv. 196

Twelve-divisioned period, iv. 436–438

Twelve Nights, Furious Host appears during the, ii. 42

" Twenty-four Examples of Filial Piety," viii. 161

Twigs, iv. 24, 31, 55, 56, 67, 86, 87, 88, 92, 93, 100–101, 111, 120–121, 129, 148, 149, 161, 272

——bundle of blood-smeared, on altar to wind-god, iv. 233

——comb, or reeds become forest, iii. 136

——green, stuck in sacred tree, vii. 146

——or leaves which turn to gold given by elves, ii. 206

Twilight, vi. 31

——mother of sun, vii. 49–50

——worship of, iv. 234

Twin-demons, v. 68, 69

— -gods, v. 68, 69, 115–116, 134, 397 [77]

——alternating, ii. 64, 106, 158

——grains, iv. 244

——trees connected with lovers or conjugal fidelity, viii. 253–254

——word Yama means, vi. 357 [6]

Twins, vii. 127; x. 115, 133, 157, 160, 163, 174, 179, 188, 199–200, 204, 205, 209–210, 232, 295 [44], 306 [59]; xi. 25, 30, 82, 83, 86, 168–177, 224, 302, 312; xii. 192

——as ancestors, vii. 156

——born of dead mother, ix. 132

——to Macha at end of her race against chariot, iii. 74

——celestial, two Orions as, xii. 58, 375 [72]

——Chaco first man and woman joined like Siamese, xi. 322

——children born as, who intermarry, vi. 144, 225

——faithful, brought into being, v. 313

——guarding tomb of Bêl, v. 323

——regarded as monstrous, xi. 82

——Warrior, x. 204

Twisting of bark of young tree causes death of a Wood-wife, ii. 207

" Two Brothers, Tale of," Asiatic motifs in, xii. 153, 399 [111]

——Swine-herds, tale of, iii. 57–59

Twofold One (the male-female), xi. 88

Twrch Trwyth, boar, iii. 108, 125, 184, 187

Tychē, vi. pl. xxxiv, opp. p. 272

——Allāt identified with, v. 19

——coin bearing figure of, v. 154

——goddess, v. 18, 19, 20, 21, 22, 23, 68

Tydeus, Diomedes son of, i. 123

——of Aitolia engaged in duel by Polyneikes, i. 51

Tyll Owl-glass, Hubeane recalls Teutonic, vii. 213

Tyndareos at home, i. pl. xlix, opp. p. 224

——of Sparta aided Agamemnon and Menelaos against Thyestes, i. 121

——raised from dead by Asklepios, i. 280

——son of Perieres and Gorgophone, i. 24–27

Types of Africans, vii. 108–109, 398 [1]

——racial, in Melanesian area, ix. 103

Typhon and Echidna, parents of the Chimaira, i. 39

——the Kyklopes, i. 267

——Zeus, i. pl. II (1), opp. p. xlii

——assailed Zeus, i. 9

——daemon of the whirlwind, son of Gaia and Tartaros, i. 8–9

——description of, i. 9

——father of Harpies, i. 266

——Greek name of Sêth, etymology of, xii. 392 [55]

——Hera's son, i. 177–178

——lame doublet of Hephaistos, i. 207

——Mt. Aetna placed upon, i. 9

" Typhonic " animals of Sêth, xii. 390 [35]

——sea as, xii. 95

Typhon's bone, meaning of, xii. 104, 390 [35]

Typhon-Sêth, Thuêris wife of, xii. 376 [82]

Tyr (Tiu, Tiw, Ziu, Zio), god, ii. 15, 17, 18, 19, 21, pl. v, opp. p. 22, 24, 37, 40, 86, 87, 97–100, 143, 277, 341, 384 [21]

Tyre, dirge on destruction of, v. 188

——genealogy of gods of, v. 67

——Herakles equated with Nergal-Malik (Melqart) at, v. 53

——traces of Marduk legend at, v. 322

Tyrfing, sword, ii. 62, 268, 308

Tyro, daughter of Salmoneus, forced to yield to embraces of Poseidon, i. 106

——intrigue of Poseidon with, i. 211

Tys, Tatar loan-word, employed by Cheremiss for shadow-soul, countenance, or image, iv. 12

Tyurun-Muzykay, given birth to by a virgin, iv. 387

Tzental legend of Votan, xi. 131

Tzitzimime, descending stars, xi. 82

Tzontemoc (" He of the Falling Hair "), Mictlantecutli also called, xi. 80

Tzŭ-kung, viii. 168

— -lu, viii. 162

— -t'ung Shên, viii. 112

U

Uac-Mitun-Ahau, god of the centre place, xi. 145

Uaman, síd of, iii. 78

Uaʻ-n-rêʻ (" Only One of the Sun "), a name of Amen-ḥotep IV, xii. 231

Uar-gaeth-sceo Luachair-sceo, gibberish name of giant, iii. 70

Uathach told Cúchulainn how to obtain valour, iii. 143, 144

Uazet possibly a rare form of Buto, xii. 403 ¹⁹

Ubardudu = Opartes = Methusaleh, Sumerian antediluvian king, v. 205

Ubar-Tutu, Ziûsudra son of, v. 209, 218, 262

Ubastet, Bati received honour beside, at Saka, xii. 131

—cat-goddess of Bubastos, xii. 150

—meaning of name, xii. 21

—Mi-ḥos son of, xii. 137

—regarded as solar goddess, xii. 29

—Sekhmet compared with, xii. 140, 147

——Tefênet, and Pekhet manifestations of a single deity, xii. 217

Ubšukkinna, assembly hall of Enlil, Tablets of Fate yearly written in, v. 102, 298, 299, 307

Ububu, name of Tammuz, v. 345, 347, 414 ³³

Ubu-tongo (" sleep "), ama-tongo connected with, vii. 181

Ubyr, blood-drinking god, iv. 173

Ucaijana, one name of Hlakanyana, vii. 219

Uccaiḥśravas, vi. 107, 132, 139

Ucht Cleitich, Oisin went to síd of, iii. 180

Uchtdelbh, Aillén loved, iii. 89

Udagan, female shamans, iv. 499

Udaṅkya, vi. 97

Udayāna, home of magic arts, vi. 208

Udāyin, vi. 192

Uddagubba, messenger of Enlil, v. 100

Udělnicy, genii of fate, iii. 250

Udibwa hatched from first egg of Thusandi found at Man Maw, xii. 276

—Lan-yein chosen as, xii. 284

—title given by Burmese to Emperors of China, xii. 276

Udsar, title of Sin, v. 152

Ŭ-dug-ga, demon, v. 364

Uduntamkur, minor deity, v. 104

Uduntamnag, minor deity, v. 104

Uemac, chief of Toltec, xi. 65

Uenuku and dog, tale of, ix. 86–87

Uêret, xii. 60

— -Êpet, protector of child-birth, companion of Bês, xii. 62

Uetonga engaged in tatuing, ix. 72–73

Ueuecoyotl, god of feasts and dances, xi. 83

Ugallu (probably Leo in astronomy), dragon of Tiâmat, v. 282, 283

Uganda, gods of, vii. 119, 129

Ugarthilocus, being to whom sacrifices made, ii. 94–95

—(Utgard-Loki), Loki may be represented by, ii. 17

Ugga, male dragon Mušḫuššû of Sumeria, became female, v. 289, 410 ¹⁷

Uggerus (Norse Ygg): see ODIN.

Ugliness, none struck Morvran because of, iii. 109, 189

Ugra, vi. 81, 82

Ugrian and Finnish linguistic stocks, early separation of, iv. xvii

Uguisu, Japanese nightingale, viii. 385 ¹¹

Uhlanga, single reed; umhlanga, reed-bed, vii. 128, 145, 146, 400 ²⁴

Ui the Blind, ix. 68

Uí Tarsig, Fionn of sept of, iii. 161

Uicton, xi. 117

Uiracocha: see VIRACOCHA, DEITY.

Uirgreann, opponent of Cumhal, iii. 161, 162, 164, 179

Uitzilopochtli: see HUITZILO-POCHTLI.

Uitztlampa, ("place of thorns"), xi. 60

Uixtociuatl, goddess-wife of victim of sacrifice to Tezcatlipoca, xi. 64

Ujit, forest-folk, vii. 263

Ujjaynī, Kṛṣṇa at, vi. 173

Uke-mochi (food genius), viii. 232

Ukhshyaṭ-ereta (Hūshēṭar), one of three Saoshyants, vi. 343

— -nemah (Hūshēṭar-māh), one of three Saoshyants, vi. 343

——one of Zarathushtra's sons who was to be born in the last millennium, vi. 309

Ukhukh, god worshipped near site of modern Meïr, xii. 152

Ukifune, story of, viii. 302

Ukko(nen) ("grandfather"), Finnish name for Thunderer, worship of, iv. 228–229

Ukkumu ("snatcher"), dog, vii. 395 [58]

Uksakka, deity of birth, iv. 252–257

Uktena, steed of the Thunderers, x. 68

Ukulan Tojon, water-spirit, iv. 469

Ulakhany, fire-god, iv. 454

Ulala, cannibal spirit, x. 247–248

Uldda, underground being who brings cattle to earth, iv. 178

Ulé, xi. 313–314

Ulf, skin-changer, ii. 293

Ulfdalir, ii. 259

Ulfin, confidant of Uther Pendragon, iii. 184

Ulfliot's law, ii. 229

Ulfrun, giantess, ii. 153

Ulfsjar, lake, ii. 259

Ülgen, creator of earth, iv. 310, 314, 316, 342, 364, 366, 377, 378, 379, 401, 402, 405, 406, 411, 449, 450

Ulimgau, serpent husband of, ix. 116

Ull, ii. 156–158, 182

Ullaber, rock on which Midsummer Day gathering held, ii. 158

Ullû: see s.v. ᵈUllu, vol. v, p. 452

Ulster became Mongan's, iii. 63

—heroes, iii. 46

Ulua, xi. 185

Uluken, Heaven-dweller, iv. 453

Ulūkhala, vi. 98

Ulu-Tojon, thunder-god, iv. 442–443, 447, 449, 499

Umā Haimavatī, wife of Śiva in later tradition, vi. 83, 110, 111, 114, 115, 118, 119–120, 158

Umā incited Śiva to take part of the sacrifice, vi. 179

—(or Devī), propitiation of, vi. 117

—Satī reborn as, vi. 184

Umall, suggested reading of name Cumhal, iii. 165

Ūmas, vi. 101

Umbilical cord, rock with sign of, xi. 185

Umé (plum-tree), in love with Yayezakura, viii. 347

Umiarissat, phantom women's boats, x. 7

Umkatshana went to spirit-world, vii. 185, 199

Umkovu, corpse restored to life to become familiar of witches, vii. 338

Umlungu means a white man, vii. 127

Umma (Djokha), v. 117

—(Heat), comrade of Nergal, v. 163

—ummi, ummu, mother, v. 13

Ûmû daprûti (the destructive spirits), a dragon, v. 282

Ûmu (heat), v. 136

Umundara, god, v. 202

Umunesiga also Nergal, Ninurta, v. 397 [80]

—title of hostile Ninurta, v. 116

Umunlua and Umunesiga, names of Mash, v. 116, 397 [80]

Umunmu[zida], Tammuz, v. 345, 346, 347

Umutwa, vii. 262

Unai, tale of maiden of, viii. 295–296

Unakami-aze, another name of Azé, viii. 380 [6] (ch. ii)

"Unanana Bosele," tale of, vii. 198

Unbaptized, ii. 42

—children, iii. 253, 254, 256

Unbinding of hair, belt, or girdle on a death, iv. 27

Uncama in abode of dead, vii. 184–185, 199

"Uncle," iv. 181; vi. 242

—in personal names and as title of gods, v. 7, 378 [21]

—Remus, vii. 283–284, 292

—Sazanami, viii. 377 [6]

Uncleanness, goddess of, xi. 78

Unconsciousness caused by comment on bearded stone, vii. 414 [25]

Underground and underwater peoples, x. 28–29, 105, 274 [9]

—Death took refuge, vii. 172–173

Underground inhabitants of holy mountains, iv. 104, 105, 285; see also MOUNTAINS, HOLY, CUSTOMS OF, ETC.
—spirits, Lapp belief in, iv. 71
Undergrounders, iv. 185, 205
Underwater cities, ix. 117; see also WATER, WORLD BENEATH; WATER-WORLDS; WORLD UNDER WATERS.
—palace or house, ii. 211
—waves, land, iii. 37–38, 120, 173
——of King, iii. 113
Underworld, iii. 9, pl. v, opp. p. 40, pl. VIII, opp. p. 72, 85, 105, pl. XIII, opp. p. 116, pl. XIV, opp. p. 120, pl. xvi, opp. p. 128, pl. XXV, opp. p. 204; iv. pl. XXVII, opp. p. 224; vii. 118, 178, 179, 180, 181, 184, 185, 186, 189, 192, 195, 199–202; ix. 27, 118–119, 165; x. xxii, 6, 7–8, 22, 23, 60, 61, 108, 137, 159, 160, 185, 189, 193, 198, 203, 204, 205, 250, 254, 274 [10]–275, 277 [13], 281 [18], 285 [28], 286 [31], 292 [39], 294 [42], 295 [44], 300 [50]; xi. 54, 61, 68, 81, 83, 102, 103, 170, 173, 174, 200, 324
—account of Sisyphos's punishment in, i. 37–38
—all gods come from, xii. 62
—Babi guards entrance to, xii. 131
—barrows a small, ii. 306
—darkened by creation of earth, ix. 163
—descent to, through following pig, ix. 213–215
—Dioskouroi dwell alternately on Olympos and in, i. 27
—dweller in, may cause illness by obtaining clothing of living, iv. 5
—elders of, iv. 74
—encircled by ocean, xii. 95
——Osiris, xii. 96
—Ethiopia as region or type of, xii. 395 [76]
—ferry of, called " eye of Khnûm," xii. 384 [112]
—fire originally obtained from, ix. 48
— -folk, legendary earliest inhabitants, vii. 266
—food of, fatal to mortals, ix. 321 [70]
—form of Amen-Rê', xii. 221
—four-headed god of, apparently compared with four sons of Horus or Osiris, xii. 394 [67]
——sons of Horus or Osiris near ferryman of, xii. 394 [64]

Underworld, gods and goddesses of, v. 49, 50, 61, 71, 99
—good and evil šêdu a genius of, v. 361
—Hel vague personification of the, ii. 16
—Herakles in, i. 88
—hole in ground at Abydos shown as entrance to, xii. 98
—home of Harpies at gates of, i. 266
—influenced by advent of Europeans into Africa, vii. 183
—jackals associated with, xii. 364 [10]
—Jötuns originally corpse-devouring demons of, ii. 281
—Kara-Khan removed to, iv. 402, 405
—Khnûm guardian of waters coming from the, xii. 28
——lord of, xii. 28
—lies towards north, iv. 77
—magic tree in, v. 152
—Mantus Etruscan god of the, i. 289
—misery of, v. 263–264
—mother-goddess died yearly and descended into, v. 113
—Nephthys associated with, xii. 110
—Nile springs from, xii. 46, 105
—ninefold stream of the, xi. 53, 81
—Odin seeks explanation of Balder's dreams in, ii. 9, 43
—of dead, descent to, ix. 72–73, 74, 75, 77
—one of newly created sons of Batara Guru made his abode in, ix. 163
—Osiris as king of, xii. 93, 94–95, 399 [110]
—Polynesian people of, unacquainted with use of fire, vii. 137
—powers, relation of Mihr to, vii. 35
—preparations of shamans for trip to, iv. 292
—Rê' gives light in, xii. 84, 85
—relation of earth-goddesses and vegetation-gods to, vii. 97
—resurrection (of sun-god) symbolic of sleep of death in, v. 52
—reverse of upper world, iv. 72–73; xii. 41
—rivers of, i. 143
—ruled by Anubis, xii. 364 [10]
—ruler, Sabazios an, vii. 97
—Santaramet goddess of, vii. 35
—second death may be experienced by those in, iv. 72

Underworld: see ARALLÛ, LOWER WORLD; NIFLHEL, ETC.
—Selqet scorpion-goddess from, xii. 99
—serpent of, xii. 240, 369 [24]
—soul of ill and of shamans may go to, and return, iv. 6, 286, 292
—south as the, xii. 397 [94]
—spirits of, drawing solar ship, xii. 27 (fig. 10)
—sun journeys through, by night, xii. 106
—Tellus Mater held to be divinity of, in certain rites, i. 292
—three-storey, of Northern Ostiaks, iv. 77-78
—Tiur guides souls of dead to, vii. 31
—tutelary genius of blacksmiths lives in, iv. 464
—Valhalla extension of, ii. 315, 317
—villages of, iv. 484-485
——strict discipline in, iv. 73
—wife of Heaven deity daughter of divinity of, ix. 162
—Wotan conducts souls to, vii. 384 [50]
Underworlds, twelve, xi. 53-54
Unelanuhi, the sun (feminine), x. 55, 56
Un(en)-nofer (Unnofru), " the Good Being," as name of Osiris, xii. 97, 122
Ung, son of the solar deity, xii. 151
Unhold, harmful spirit, ii. 231
Unicorn, viii. 21, 98
—Ninurta battles against, v. 131, 279
—winged, v. 279, 281, 283
Union of water and fire produces all things, ii. 326
Universe, Eddic conception of, ii. 328
—gods born after creation of, vi. 18
—harmonious movement of, philosophically attributed to Apollo, i. 181
—Ptaḥ god of, xii. 220-222, 407 [79]
Unkulunkulu, vii. 116, 126, 128, 129, 145, 183, 400 [23]
Unlucky animals, vii. 127, 161, 283, 288, 291
—days, guarding idols on, xi. 145
—moon and rainbow, vii. 227, 234, 235
Unmarried dead, i. 324 [9] (ch. ii); iv. 19, 29
Unnerjordiske, Underworld people, ii. 223
Unshorn men consecrated to Yāw, v. 82
Untombi-yapansi, tale of, vii. 199-202

Untsaiyi, the Gambler, x. 68
Unt-tongk (wood-spirit), iv. 178
Un(u?), xii. 31
Unut, goddess worshipped at Denderah, Hermopolis, Menḥet, and Unut, xii. 151
Unyago ceremonies, figures for, vii. 151
Unyandemula, tale of, vii. 417 [23]
Unyengebule, tale of, vii. 210
Unyoro, vii. 220
Üör, spirits who haunt old homes, iv. 479
Upananda, serpent, vi. 216
" Upaniṣads," philosophical treatises attached to the Brāhmaṇas, vi. 12
Uparatāt, vi. pl. XXXII, opp. p. 260
Upaśruti, vi. 98
Upasunda and Sunda obtained boon from Brahmā, vi. 153
Upavīra, vi. 98
U-peqa (U-peqer, Re-peqer), hole in ground at Abydos, shown as entrance to lower world, xii. 98
Upir, Upiór, vampire, iii. 231
Upper Egypt, Mi-ḥos worshipped in tenth nome of, xii. 137
—(or recent) ghosts, vii. 180
Upperworld, x. 7-8, 22, 23, 34-35, 40, 60, 62, 193, 274 [10], 275 [11], 286 [31], 292 [39], 295 [44]
Up-regen, gods above, ii. 21
Upset, identified with Tefênet, Isis, etc., at Philae, xii. 151
Up-uaut, Anubis identified with, xii. 393 [61]
—(Ophoïs), Khent(i)-amentiu seems to be local form of, xii. 21, 98
—wolf-god of Lykopolis, This, and Saïs, xii. 144, 393 [61], 407 [72]
Ur, v. 88, 96, 100, 140, 153, 159, 203, 237, 241
—excavations at, v. 1
—kings of, became dying gods, v. 345
——claimed to be sons of Ninsun, v. 241
—oldest title of Nabû, v. 158
—seat of moon-worship, v. 153
Ur-dumu-zi (servant of Tammuz), v. 346
—Nammu, king, v. 96, 345, 414 [26]
— -Ninurta, v. 327, 346
Uraeus, xii. 25, 26, 29, 88, 135, 150, 378 [98]

Urak (first-milk), iv. 446–447
— -Sagan-Tengeri, iv. 446
Ural, god of the holy, iv. 403
Uranos: see OURANOS.
Urartians, vii. 6, 7, 8, 11, 12
Urashima conducted Musō-Byōye on his travels, viii. 364–365
—Tarō, tale of, viii. 264–265
Urd, personalized fate-goddess, ii. 238, 239, 241, 243, 331
—well of, ii. 23, 43, 167, 239, 243, 262, 329, 331
Urdarbrunn, spring, iv. 357
Urdawl Ben ("Noble Head"), Bran as, iii. 105
Urdun, priest of incantations of Ningirsu, v. 116
Ürgel, Urker = Pleiades, iv. 418, 434
Ur-ḥeka, god in man- or serpent-form, xii. 151
Uridimmû (constellation Lupus), dragon of Tiâmat, v. 282
Urine of horse produced loch, iii. 73, 136
——she-fox, rainbow as, iv. 444
—purification with bull's, vi. 302
Uriseb, son of Haitsi-aibeb, vii. 216, 217, 408 21
Urisnici, genii of fate, iii. 250
Urker, iv. 431
Urn shot off pillar, vii. 348–349
Urpihuachac (Mother of Doves), xi. 229
Ursa Major, i. 251; iv. 339, 417, 426–428, 431, 435, 436; v. 109, 317; vi. 276; viii. 27, 112; x. xxii, 9, 26, 96, 117; xi. 93, 319, 336; xii. 60
——called Charles's Wain, or, in United States, Great Dipper, i. 59
——ill-omened constellation, xii. 59
——late identification of, with Sêth-Typhon, xii. 59, 109, 110
——Van-xoung supposed to live in, xii. 305
Ursa Minor, x. 117; xi. 98
Ursanapi, Sursunabu (old version), boatman of Utnapishtim, v. 213, 214, 215, 216, 225, 226, 227, 262, 263
Urt crying out a portent of death, iv. 10–11
—kuton, Votiak "seeking of the soul," iv. 14
—of Votiak corresponds to ört of Cheremiss, iv. 6

Urt-ḥekau, leontocephalous goddess, xii. 151
Urþr (fate), ii. 238
Uru (urva, urvapast), originally soul, later ghostly apparition, vii. 94
Urubamba, ruins of mountain-seated city in valley of, xi. 218
Urupi, vi. 350
U-ru-sa-lim = Jerusalem, v. 45
Urvākhshaya, brother of Keresāspa, vi. 324, 326
Urvarā, vi. 96
Ūrvas, vi. 101
Urvaśī, an Apsaras, vi. 18, 59, 95, 143
Urvāzishta fire, vi. 285
Urvis, Lake, vi. 278
Ūsā enamoured of Aniruddha, vi. 174
Uśanas, vi. 32, 111, 116, 153
Uṣas, iii. 325
—("Dawn"), only goddess of celestial world, vi. 21, 32, 34, 53, 61, 76, 82, 86, 233
Usching, horse-god, iii. 329–330
Ushebtiu ("answerers"), functions of, xii. 177
Ushindu, Mt., vi. 269
Ushiwaka: see YOSHITSUNE, ETC.
Ushumgalanna, dying god originally called, v. 178
Usilosimapundu, vii. 249, 320, 346
Usilwane, tale of, vii. 200–202
Usilwanekazana, tale of, vii. 200–202
Usir(i) usually assumed to be Egyptian pronunciation of name Osiris, xii. 384 2
Usnech, murder of sons of, iii. 152
Uṣṇīṣavijayā, spell containing name of, vi. 217
Uso-dori, bullfinch, tale of, viii. 334–335
Usret, goddess of fifth nome of Delta; also epithet of many goddesses, xii. 151
Usudsud ("the far away"), v. 414 33
Usukun, xi. 142
Ušumgal, dragon of Chaos, v. 117–118
Ut ("fire"), iv. 453, 456
Uta and Houmea, tale of, ix. 84–86
—Laficho, Galla clan, ancestors of, descended from sky, vii. 152, 402 22
—wa Leza (Bow of Leza), rainbow, vii. 126
Utaṅka rejuvenated, vi. 145

'Uṭārid, Arab deity identified with Mercury, vii. 384 [53]

Utathya dried up waters of earth to induce Varuṇa to return his wife, vi. 137

Utet, deity possibly in the form of a heron, xii. 151

Utgard (Outside Land), ii. 92, 93, 147, 276, 277, 280

— -Loki, lord of Utgard, ii. 85, 92, 93, 94, 139, 147, 277

Uther Pendragon, King of Britain, iii. 52, 184, 185, 201

Uthr Ben ("Wonderful Head") of a Taliesin poem, iii. 105

Utkha, shamanic origin, iv. 499–500, 506, 507

Utnapishtim, Atarhasis as a title used of, v. 270

—(Ziûsudra), v. 38, 209, 210, 213, 214, 215, 216, 218, 219, 221, 222, 223, 224, 225, 227, 230, 232, 262, 263, 265

Utpala, serpent, vi. 216

Utša pijos, iv. 116, 118

Utsarpiṇī, ascending era, vi. 221

Utset, mother of Indians, conjured from magic parcel, x. 203

Utshintsha and the rainbow, vii. 235

Utsushi-kuni-dama, son-in-law of Susa-no-wo, viii. 229, 378 [12]

Uttama, son of Uttānapāda, vi. 165

Uttānapāda, father of Dhruva, vi. 165

Uttara Kurus, vi. 144, 225

Uttukku (Uttuka), Odakōn may be Graecized form of, v. 86

Uttukku ("Weaver"), title of Tagtug, also given to a woman (Ishtar), v. 190, 196

Utu (Shamash), Sippar city of, v. 206

—Sumerian sun-god, v. 4, 93, 148, 152

Utukku, Utukku limnu, demon, v. 106, 362, 364, 365, 372

Utum-sacrifice, single-family sacrifice, iv. 70

— -wedding, memorial feast to Utumö, iv. 70

Utumö, unknown deceased, feast resembling wedding to, iv. 68–70

Uuodan (Wodan), ii. 18

Uvættir, harmful spirit, ii. 231

Uwannami, shadowy rain-makers, x. 190, 194

Uye-minu, eagle, viii. 334

Uyuuyewe and Maasewe, twin warriors, x. 204

Uzava Tumāspana (Pers. Zav), vi. 332, 334

Uz-fish, curse attached to, xii. 125

Uzoit: see BUTO, SERPENT-SHAPED GODDESS.

Uzu, Usū, Ušū, ancient name of Tyre, v. 389 [252]

Uzumā, rope of Heaven and earth, v. 313

Uzume, dance and meaning of name of, viii. 226–227, pl. VIII, opp. p. 226, 378 [9]

Üzüt, spirit long-ago deceased, iv. 479

'Uzzā, goddess, as Venus, v. 24

V

Vāc ("Speech"), abstract deity, vi. 53, 90, 93, 94, 182, 218

Vācaspati, vi. 92

Vaccinium uliginosum, iv. 384

Vacuity, spirit of, viii. 53, 56, 57

Vadgelmir, wading through the, as retribution, ii. 268, 319–320

Vadi, father of Volund, ii. 267

Vaēsaka (Pers. Vīsah), Ṭūs conquered sons of, vi. 339

Vætte-hougar, offering-mounds, ii. 231

Vættir (sing. Vætr), Vætter, Vetter, divine or semi-divine beings, ii. 224, 225, 228–232

Vafthrudnir, giant, ii. 9, 49, 62, 175, 275, 338, 346

"Vafthrudnismal," ii. 6, 9, 25, 26, 27, 54, 62, 101, 102, 107, 128, 159, 168, 175, 183, 199, 200, 241, 275, 313, 325, 329, 330, 336, 339, 341, 346, 347

Vafud (Odin), ii. 42

Vagina, serpent's teeth cut from about, x. 231–232

Vagna-verr (Thor), ii. 78, 95

Vagneg-imi, deity with seven cradles, iv. 260

Vagoniona: see GUAGUGIANA, ETC.

Vague, appellation of Sky-father, xi. 24

Vahagn, corruption of Verethraghna, vi. 271, 320
—eighth deity, vii. 17, 18, 42–46, 49, 54, 55, 63, 78, 363–366, 389 [4]
—Mihr identified with, vii. 34
—myths, storm-god supplants Heaven-god in, vii. 14
—relation of, to Ba'al Shamîn, vii. 36, 37
—storm-god, may have required human sacrifices, vii. 384 [60]
—supersedes Mihr, vii. 33, 34
—temple of, at Ashtishat, vii. 39
—wins love of Astλik, vii. 37, 38–39
Vahram Vardapet, vii. 80
Vahunis, probably priests of temple of Vahagn, vii. 19
Vaijayanta, flagstaff, vi. 132
Vaijayantas, vi. 227
Vaimānika gods, vi. 227
Väinämöinen, iv. 238
Vaipe, language of, xii. 267
Vairapani: see OTSHIRVANI.
Vairocana, one of the five " Meditative " Buddhas, vi. 211
Vairūpas, race of man, vi. 71
Vaiśāleya, vi. 97
Vaiṣṇava system, earth-god or -goddess being taken into, vi. 237
Vaiṣṇavism, vi. 163, 230, 231
Vaiśravaṇa, vi. 215, 218, 229
—see BISHAMON-TEN.
Vaiśvānara, epithet of Agni, vi. 44
Vaiśyas, Maruts became celestial counterparts of the, vi. 40, 89, 90
Vaitaraṇī River in realm of Yama, vi. 159, 160, 235
—souls of dead (in the Epic) said to cross, vi. 69
Vāja, minor god, vi. 57
Vajgat, holy island, iv. 139
Vajra prefixed to names of gods, etc., vi. 205
—thunderbolt, vi. 264
Vajrabhairava, form of Mañjuśrī, vi. 213, 215, 218
Vajrabodhisattvas, Vajrasattva, Vajra-yoginīs, vi. 205, 213
Vajraḍākīnī, vi. 218
Vajradhara derived from Indra, vi. 216
Vajrapāṇi brought into connexion with Buddhas, vi. 204, 213, 214, 216
Vajrasattva, Boddhisattva of Akṣobhya, vi. 211, 213

Vajravarāhī, vi. 218
Vakarĭné, Evening Star of Lithuanians feminine, of Letts masculine, iii. 320
Vakš-oza, watermill-god, iv. 167
Vala, Bṛhaspati appropriates deeds of Indra concerning, vi. 45, 98
—demon, vi. 153
—Indra shatters ridge of, vi. 34, 64, 67
Vāladhi, father of Medhāvin, vi. 159
Valaskjalf, heavenly abode, ii. 61, 329
Valdemar destroyed temple and image of Svantovit, iii. 281
Valdi Kjöla (Thor), ii. 78
Vale of Forgetfulness, Aeneas at, i. 305
Valfadir (Odin), ii. 58
Val-father, Odin was, ii. 314
— -Freyja, chooser of slain, ii. 250
Valgrind, outer gate of Valhalla, ii. 313
Valhalla, ii. pl. IV, opp. p. 16, pl. VI, opp. p. 32, 44, 45, 56, 57, 61, 81, 125, 161, 174, 248, 249, 250, 305, 306, 307, 308, 312–317, 329, 341; iv. 82; x. 275 [10]; xi. 28
Vali (Ali; Voli; Bous; Ran), son of Odin, by Rind, god, ii. 15, 21, 47, 65, 127, 128, 131, 135, 136, 144, 145, 146, 159, 164–165, 166, 346
Valiant, son of Carman, tale of, iii. 35–36
Valiant-August-Thunder, viii. 230
Valichu, souls of wizards are of the number of demons called, xi. 337
Vālin, vi. 128
Valkjosandi (Odin), ii. 45
Valkyries (" Choosers of the slain "), ii. 11, 18, 24, 45, 57, 98, 122, 189, 228, 235, 236, 237, 243, 245, 248–257, 259, 260, 283, 284, 313, 314, 315; viii. 287
Valland, ii. 259
Valley-of-Death-by-Old-Age, x. 232
Valley, spirits of the, viii. 53
Valleys, creation of, iv. 319, 332
—origin of, iii. 136
Valmeyjar (battle-maids), ii. 248
Vālmīki, divinity of, vi. 244
—hermitage, vi. 128
Vålnad and Vård like Fylgja, ii. 237
Vālukāprabhā, vi. 228
Valum-Chivim, journeys to, xi. 132
Vāmadeva, vi. 147
Vampire, Artemisia a, in modern Romagnola, i. 319
—belief, part of Nera tale connected with, iii. 68

Vampire has parallel in vetāla, vi. 247
—jade pendent representing, xi. pl. XXVI, opp. p. 190
—spirits, iv. 200
Vampires, ii. 309; iii. 228, 229, 231, 232; iv. 425; v. 365, 366; ix. 63, 231
—demons, and other ghostly beings, viii. 281–292
—(Stringes), i. 278
Van, vii. 7, 12, 65
—a gate of, still named after Mihr, vii. 384 [59]
—Urarartian works in, ascribed to Semiramis, vii. 368
Van River made from slaver of Fenriswolf, ii. 7, 101, 105, 328
Vanabrudr (Freyja), ii. 120
Vanadis (Freyja), ii. 120, 244
Vanagod (Freyja), ii. 120
Vanaheim, Vanir dwell in, ii. 23, 25, 26
Vanainti (Uparatāt), vi. pl. XXXII, opp. p. 260
Vanakan Vardapet on identifications of Anahit, vii. 27, 39
Vanand, vi. 276
Vanaspati invoked as sacrificial post, vi. 61
—Māī, forest-mother, vi. 238
Vanatur (" Hospitable ") not a separate Armenian deity, vii. 382 [13]
Vandals, ii. 38
Vanir, gods of wealth, fruitfulness, trade, prosperity, ii. 20, 21, 23, 25–30, 35, 55, 89, 165, 166, 185, 220, 337, 341
—group, ii. 101–126
Vanishing suddenly, power of, ii. 22
Vanity, Land of, viii. 363
Vanland, Svegdir's son, tale of, ii. 290, 306
Van-xuong, god of literature, temple of, xii. 305–306
Vapour, Chang Kuo the original, viii. 125
—evil, origin of disease, viii. 29
Vapours, harmonious, viii. 37
Vapreafjord, guardians of, ii. 229
Var, goddess, ii. 15, 186
Vara, vi. 282, 307–309, 312, 315
Varāhāvatāra, vi. pl. XII, opp. p. 122
Varar, compacts made between men and women, ii. 186
Varcin, demon, vi. 67, 68

Vardhamāna (" He that Increases "), name given to Mahāvīra at conception, vi. 223
Vardögr, like Fylgja, ii. 237
Vårdträd, tree confused with karsikko of the dead, iv. 26
—(" Ward-tree "), ii. 333, 334
Vāreghna (Vāregan, Vārengan), bird, vi. 288, 289, 311, 361 [29]
Vare-jielle, forest-dweller, iv. 177
Varena may have corresponded to Gīlān, vi. 266, 300, 363 [22]
Vareshava slain by Keresāspa, vi. 324
Vari-ma-te-takere, female deity, ix. 14
Varjohaltia (" Shadow-ruler ") may foretell events, iv. 11
Varr-lyps, back exit from tent, regarded as holy, iv. 84
Vartanush, vii. 390 [18]
Vartari, thong, ii. 267
Vartavar (" Burning with Roses "), festival, vii. 39, 59–61, 370, 388 [3]
Varuṇa, vi. 16, 18, 19, 20, 21, 22–23, 24, 25, 26, 27, 28, 29, 32, 33, 43, 44, 53, 54, 56, 69, 70, 85, 86, 100, 132, 135, 137–138, 143, 152, 159, 174, 182, 216
—appears in form of Vran, vii. 14
Varuṇānī, wife of Varuṇa, vi. 53
Varuṇapraghāsa, festival of Varuṇa, vi. 85
Vāruṇī, wife of Varuṇa, vi. 138
Vasa (water dweller), iv. 197, 199
Vāsava, vi. 109
Vase of overflowing water, v. 95, 96, 395 [21]
Vases from Susa, v. 117
—see various items s.v. ART.
Vasiṣṭha, child of Mitra and Varuṇa by Urvaśī, vi. 18, 59, 108, 134, 142, 144, 145–146, 147–148
—divinity of, vi. 244
Vāsiṣṭhas, priestly family, vi. 71, 222–223
Vassa, Buddhist, xii. 279, pl. x, opp. p. 302
Vāstoṣpati (" Lord of the Dwelling "), vi. 60, 96
Vasubandhu elevated to rank of Bodhisattva, vi. 210
Vāsudeva ascribed to Viṣṇu, vi. 81
—exchanges Kṛṣṇa and child of Yaśodā, vi. 171, 178
Vāsudevas, nine, vi. 225

Vāsuki, vi. 97, 104, 106, 111, 154, 155, pl. xvii, opp. p. 154, 216, 241
Vasundharā ("Earth"), vi. 216
Vāsupūjya obtained release at Campāpurī, vi. 222
Vasus, vi. 29, 54, 56, 94, 136, 142, 146, 149
Vāta or Vāyu, vi. pl. xxxii, opp. p. 260
—represented by Arm. aud, vii. 14
—the wind, vi. 37, 56, 89, 135
Vātapī, flesh of, eaten by Agastya, vi. 146, 153
Vatchakan, king of Albania, endeavoured to uproot the "finger-cutters," vii. 370
Vatea: see ATEA, ETC.
—sun and moon eyes of, ix. 37
Vatsa ("calf") mark on breast of Viṣṇu, vi. 120, 122
Vatten-elfvor (water-elves), ii. 210
Vätter, spirits, ii. 231
Vava, Night bought at, ix. 113
Vaybrama (Baidrama), xi. 25
Vāyu, vii. 14
—god of wind, vi. 15, 21, 37, 47, 56, 82, 88, 89, 91–92, 100, pl. x, opp. p. 118, 135, 136, 149, 216; vi. 299, 302
—of Vedas and Avesta, Hyas the, vii. 66
Vāzishta fire, vi. 285
Ve, iii. 35
—(Vi) brother of Odin, ii. 15, 24, 61, 63, 143, 175, 176, 324
Vedānta philosophical system, vi. 162, 179
Vedavyāsa, avatar of Viṣṇu, vi. 168, 169
Veden emä, water-spirit, iv. 211
Vedenhaltija (Water ruler) iv. 208, 215–216
Ved-eräj, Vetsa-eräj, water-spirits, iv. 200, 207
Vedic study, verse used to preface all, vi. 27
Vediovis (Veiovis, Vedius), i. 296
Védomec (Slovenian), vampire, iii. 232
Vedrfolnir, hawk, ii. 332
Veeneiu, female water-spirit, iv. 201
Vegavant, vi. 154
Vegdeg, son of Odin, ii. 32
Vegetarianism, viii. 147
Vegetation, x. 81
—and corn, Tammuz as god of, v. 337
——water symbolize life, vii. 382 23
—Aphrodite promotes, i. 198, 199

Vegetation, Aramazd concerned with, vii. 35
——cult, deities, and myth, xi. 25, 75–76, 293
—death of, Phaëthon myth had its roots in the ancient festival celebrated by mourning for, i. 244
—Dionysos god of, i. 218
——god, Esus perhaps a, iii. pl. xx (A), opp. p. 158
——Kṛṣṇa may have been a, vi. 126
——Sedeq a, vii. 41
——Zatik a, vii. 41
——goddess, Ishtar as, vii. 382 23
—male deity of, v. 90, 91
—Menqet produces, xii. 136
—Osiris symbolized by, xii. 95, 124
—rituals, Grail objects may be connected with, iii. 204
Vegtam (Odin), ii. 42, 127
Veil, magic, given Odysseus by Leukothea, i. 262
—of 'Ate, v. 36
——Siduri, v. 211
Veiling of crown of Anu and throne of Enlil, v. 317
——Nabû's chapel, v. 160, 318
Vela, Eridu identified with, v. 310
Vel'-ava, village-mother, iv. 168
Veles, god of flocks, iii. 300–301, pl. xxxv, opp. p. 300
Velint (Volund), ii. 170
Vena, tale of, vi. 165–166
Venedae, iii. 317
Venefica, gloss of Wælcyrge, ii. 253
Venerable Ones, the Three, viii. 109
Vengeance, xi. 266, 323
—divine, iii. 74, 75
—of ghosts, childless man has nothing to fear from, vii. 187
——Yâw, v. 134
Venilia, wife of Ianus, i. 297
Venison, hunt of servants of deity for, led to discovery of opening to sea, ix. 161–162
Venom, giant made from, ii. 275, 326
—rivers formed of, ii. 318
Venus (goddess), Astλik probably corresponded to, vii. 17, 39
——astral deity of primitive Semitic religion, v. 6, 11, 108
——Benten parallel of, viii. 269
——converted into double of Aphrodite, i. 294

Venus (goddess), Dzydzilelya identified
with, iii. 355 [44]

——Freyja's (Frigg's) name glossed as,
ii. 125, 176–177

——lover of, bewailed in a grotto, v.
76

——Prospiciens, v. 32

——sea called Fountain of, iii. 104

——(planet), i. 247, 331 [8] (ch. xi); iii.
323, 325, 329; iv. 432–434; vii. 228;
x. 9; xi. 54, 55, 57–58, pl. VIII, opp.
p. 64, 102–103, 138, 278, 343

——address to, v. 317

——Allāt in Safaitic inscriptions the, v.
381 [63]

——Aphrodite and Astarte represented
by, i. 196

——never identified with, v. 15

——Armenian names for, vii. 17, 39

——as daughter of the sun, xii. 365 [19]

——Morning and Evening Star, v.
24, 35–36, 384 [123]

——Ashdar identified with, v. 2

——'Ashtart not identified with, in Canaanite religion, v. 15

——associated with goddess of love and
war, v. 27

——'Athtar god of, v. 4

——(Balthî, Bêlit), sixth day of Harranian calendar sacred to, v. 154

——beneficent, vii. 52

——called Nahid by Persians, vii. 25

——coin bearing image of, v. 154

——comparison of Sothis with, uncertain in early period, xii. 54

——double, at Edessa, v. 36

——Egyptian misinterpretation of late
cosmic picture of, xii. 373 [61]

——god in South Arabia, v. 3

——in first heaven, v. 172

——Roman period, has two male
heads, xii. 373 [60]

——Innini is, v. 328

——-Ninsianna-Ishtar identified with,
v. 15, 108–109

——Isis associated with, xii. 101, 387 [26]

——-period, computation of a, xi. 97,
358 [10]

——phoenix embodies Rêʿ and Osiris
in, xii. 166

——(Phosphoros), i. 247

——representative of metal, viii. 142

——represented by white gold in Ezida,
v. 159

Venus (planet), South Arabian 'Athtar
identified with, v. 14

——star of Hesperos identified with, i.
248

Venus-Isis as planet very late in Egypt,
xii. 54

Vepses akin to Finns in linguistic and
geographical aspects, iv. xv

Veraldar-god (Frey), ii. 119; iv. 251

——-nagli, "world-nail," iv. 222

Veralden-olmai ("World's man"), sacrifices to, iv. 250–251

——-rade, Lapp "ruler of world," iv. 222

Verdandi, one of three Fates, ii. 239,
243

Vere, ancestor of Buu tribe of Pokomo,
vii. 128, 155–156, 158, 241

Vere-pas (god dwelling on high) generally addressed as "procreator"
(Shka(j)-bavas, Shki-pas) by Mordvins, iv. 219

Verethraghna, vi. pl. XXXII, opp. p.
260, 271–273, 288, 289, 320; vii. 45

——Herakles identified with, vii. 365

——subdued Azhi (= Ahi), v. 130

——Vahagn identified with, vii. 363

Vergil, books of, as aid to magic, iii.
109

——represented Fortuna as incorporate
will of the gods, i. 295

Verona, Castor and Pollux brought victory to Romans at battle of, i. 302

Verse, skaldic, ii. 6

Versipellis, vii. 414 [29]

Vertebrates, earlier, traces of, may have
lingered in Africa after coming of
man, vii. 151

Vertumnus, Italic plant-god, aborigi-
nally a god of changing year, i. 290

Vessel, haltia of, iv. 170

Vesta, i. 298; vii. 55

——fire adored in Rome as, vi. 284

——survives as Esta in modern Romagnola, i. 319

Vestal, Rea Silvia forced to take vows
of, i. 307

——Virgins, i. 298

Vestein, Hel-shoes bound on, ii. 305

Vestre (west), dwarf, ii. 264

Vestrsalir, Rind bears Vali to Odin in,
ii. 127

Vetālas, vi. 217

——enter corpses, vi. 247

Vete-ema (water-mother), iv. 211

Vetehinen, water-dweller and malignant being, iv. 207
Veyou, Carib " sun," xi. 278
Vi: see VE, ETC.
Viaticum, Ganges water as a, vi. 234
Vibhīṣaṇa assisted Rāvaṇa in battle, vi. 156, 157
Vibhvan, minor god, vi. 57
Vices, abstract divinities of, i. 282
Vicitravīrya, vi. 150
Victim at cannibal feast eaten after death or revivified and rekilled, vii. 337
Victims, personal participation of god in battle to obtain, ii. 57
Victory, Agni, Indra, and Vahagn as gods of, vii. 45
—gift of, ii. 38, 56, 57, 58, 77
Vidarbha (Berār), giving of Lopamudrā to king of, explanation of mixed marriages, vi. 146
Vidarr, god, ii. 15, 48, 65, 84, 142, 158–160, 165, pl. XXI, opp. p. 168, 340, 341, 346
Vidarsgarth, name of Vidarr found in, ii. 160
Vidarshof, name of Vidarr found in, ii. 160
Vidblainn, third heaven, ii. 318
Vidblindi, might of giant, ii. 277
Videgha Māthava, vi. 92
Vidfinn, children of, raised from earth by Mane, ii. 184
Vidforull (Odin), ii. 42
Vidhātṛ, epithet of Indra or Viśvakarman, vi. 50, 97
Vidi, plain on which Vidarr dwelt, ii. 159
Vidolf, giant, ii. 280
Vīdrafsh, wizard, vi. 340
Vidura came to life as son of a Śūdra woman, vi. 150
Vidyādharas in Malay Archipelago, ix. 242
—live on Mt. Krauñca, vi. 144
—Sanskrit prototype of swan-maidens, ix. 327 [17]
Vidyunmālin, lord of one of the citadels, vi. 116
" Viga-Glums-saga," ii. 119, 235, 246
Vigdis, dis used of women of higher rank appears in, ii. 244
Vigfuss, Hamingja of, ii. 235
Vigil, x. 58, 132, 135, 171

Vigrid, field, ii. 340, 341, 343
Vigtrold, Norse Näk known as, ii. 210
Vihansa, war-goddess, ii. 255
Vijaya, spear of Indra, vi. 132
Vijayas, vi. 227
Vikar, mock sacrifice of, suggested, ii. 52, 57, 73, 74
Viking Age, growth of culture in, ii. 59–60
Vikings, Norman, offered human victims to Thor, ii. 75
Vikramāditya, iii. 57
Vila, Slavic deity, iii. 293
Vile, iii. 35
Vili, brother of Odin, ii. 15, 24, 61, 63, 143, 175, 176, 324
Vilification, tortoise as term of, viii. 101
" Vilkina-saga," ii. 170
Village deities, vi. 236–237, 240
—du Papier, xii. 312
— -god preceded city-god, xii. 18
—gods of, xii. 17
—Lapp, iv. pl. XXVII, opp. p. 224
—man-eating, iv. 79
—Ovda's, iv. 183
Villages, dead live together in, iv. 73
—of dead, iv. 484–485
Vilna, iii. 317
Vily (fairies), iii. 256–260
Vimāna, vi. 227
Vimur, Thor crossed river, with aid of Grid's staff, ii. 84
Vinatā, vi. 139
Vināyakas, vi. 358 [7]
Vincentius Kadlubek on behaviour of women at graves, iii. 234
Vindalf, dwarf, ii. 266
Vindhjalmsbru, bridge, ii. 329
Vindhya, goddess of the, vi. 236
—prevented from reaching the sky, vi. 146, 159
Vindler, Heimdall also called, ii. 152
Vine as life-token, ix. 234, 235
—connected with Osiris, xii. 374 [70], 385 [8], 399 [111]
—Dionysos afflicted by Hera with frenzy for discovery of, i. 47
——god of, vii. 35
—dropped by moon, mating of, with tree from sun, ix. 159, 164, 169
—Dusares (Dušurā) patron of, v. 17
—emblem of Dionysos, i. 222, pl. XLIX, opp. p. 224

Vine, love and death enter world through fruit of, xii. 36
—or cord for ascent to Heaven, ix. 66
—Osiris teaches cultivation of, xii. 113
——under, xii. 113 (fig. 117)
Vineyards, Spenta Ārmaiti keeper of, vii. 35
Vingi curses himself, ii. 299
Vingnir, Vingthor (Thor), ii. 75
Vingolf abode of goddesses, ii. 314, 327, 329
—(friendly floor), ii. 45, 122
Vingskornir, horse of Brynhild (daughter of Budli), ii. 251
Ving-Thor, ii. 88, 95
Vinili, Lombards called by Paulus, ii. 38
Vinmara, sky-maiden (Leper Island), ix. 327 [17]
Violence, separate abode for those who die by, x. 7, 249, 253, 274 [10]
—those who die by, haunt upper earth, vii. 179
Vipāś (Beas), river, vi. 48, 146
Vipaścit, tale of, vi. 186
Vipaśyin, forerunner of Gotama, vi. 211
Viper, image of, worshipped, ii. 216
Vīra, vi. 154
Vīrabhadra, Śiva created, vi. 179
Viracocha and Tonapa, xi. 232–242, 246, 370 [23]
—deity, xi. 225, 226, 236, pl. xxxvi, opp. p. 236, 245, 247, 249, 369 [17]
Virankannos, tender of oats, iv. 244
Vir-ava, Forest-mother, iv. 184, 185, 189
Virbius, affiliation of Diana with, i. 294
Virgin, a, gave birth to Tyurun-Muzy-kay and Jenghiz Khan, iv. 387, 398
—and God identified with Sun and Moon, x. 176
—Arianrhod pretended to be a, iii. 96, 98
—birth, v. 114; x. 204
—Chaabou mother of Dusares (Dušurā), v. 16
—Charpan buried with young, iv. 29
—conceives by rays of Sun, xi. 201
—conception, festivals celebrating, v. 18
—Dechtere vomited up animal and again became a, iii. 84
—dying at or after giving birth to god or gods, xii. 100

Virgin, earth-goddess, cult of, v. 108, 110
—goddess, Ishtar is, v. 98
——Nanā is a, v. 20
——Sumerian kings frequently proclaim themselves sons of, v. 158
—Goranchacha born of a, xi. 201
—Holy, beauty of, called Hayk-like, vii. 65
—image of, carried on Arthur's shoulder and shield, iii. 184, 185
—Mary, v. 341
——in magic songs given name of Luonnotar, iv. 257
——sky-goddess emerged into, iv. 220
—Rana, iv. 249
—reveals divine decrees on Ascension Eve, vii. 30
— -rock fountain, viii. 252
—sacrificed to Morning Star, x. 76, 286 [29], 303 [58]–306
—second Person of Trinity born of, xi. 143
—Story of the Picture of the, vii. 387 [7]
—sun-, method of sacrifice to, iv. 224
Virgines silvestres resemble Valkyries, ii. 206, 254
Virgins, xi. 228–229, 292
—Coming of the Rhipsimean, vii. 56
—marriage of four, to Sao Kang, xii. 334–335
—of the Sun, xi. 247
Virgo, Hydra, and Orion associated in Asiatic astral myth, xii. 84
—station of Nabû-Mercury, v. 305
Viridomar, Belgic, lineage from river or river-god associated with, iii. 14
Virocana, vi. 154
Virtues, abstract divinities of, i. 282
Virūḍhaka, lord of Kumbhāṇḍas in the south, vi. 215
—(Zōchō-ten), viii. 243
Virunga Volcanoes believed to be abode of dead, vii. pl. xix, opp. p. 206
Virūpākṣa, lord of Nāgas, vi. 215
—(Kōmoku-ten), viii. 243
Virūpas, priestly family, vi. 64
Vis (Earth), xi. 223
Vīsaladeva, turned into a Rākṣasa, vi. 245
Vishap, Armenian (of Persian origin) for dragon, vii. 77, 81, 393 [24]
Vishāpa, vi. 271
—("he whose saliva is poisonous"), connected with Zû, v. 130

Vishapaχaλ, "dragon-reaper," title of Vahagn, vii. 43
Vīshtāspa, vi. 340, 341, 342
Visibility of dead at own funerals, ii. 311
Visible, appearance of gods when, iii. 56
Vision, far, ii. 22
—of Cúchulainn, iii. 86
——Ezekiel, v. 160, 413 [1]
Visions, ii. 254; iii. 143, 152; vii. 125; viii. 273, 358–359; x. 18, 81, 133, 145, 146, 149, 215, 241, 247, 263–264, 275 [11]; xi. 26, 35, 40, 191
—of late Hebrew poets, v. 134
——Triśalā, vi. 223
Visiting old home by corpse, prevention of, iv. 22–23
Visits by bodies of water, iv. 211
—to Other World, ii. 320–323
Viṣṇāpu given back to Viśvaka, vi. 31
Viṣṇu, vii. 17, 21, 27, 29, 30, 56, 73, 75, 78–79, 80, 88, 104, 105, 106, 107, pl. IX, opp. p. 108, 109, 115, 117, 118, pl. X, opp. p. 118, 119, 120, pl. XI, opp. p. 120, 121, 122, 124, 125, 127, 129, 130, 131, 132, 133, 139, 140, 143, 147, 153, 154, 163, 164, pl. XX, opp. p. 164, 165, 166, 167, 168–169, 170, 178, 179, 180, 185, 196, 230, 231, 237, 239, 240, 241, 244
—sacred images of, xii. 327
Viśpalā, leg of, replaced with one of iron, ii. 100; vi. 31
Viśpati, vi. 284
Viśravas, sage, father of Kubera, vi. 157
Vītauru received power to cross the river Vītanguhaiti, vi. 339, 350
Vistula, iii. 317
Viśvabhū, forerunner of Gotama, vi. 211
Viśvācī, an Apsaras, vi. 143
Viśvaka, Viṣṇāpu given back to, vi. 31
Viśvakarman (All-Maker), vi. 16, 26, 50, 52, 74, 93, 138, 152, 153, 158
Viśvāmitra, vi. 144, 145–146, 147–148, 235
Viśvarūpa and Trita, myth of, v. 130
—son of Tvaṣṭṛ, vi. 50, 67, 87, 88, 93
—Triśiras, Indra slays, vi. 133
Viśvāvasu, epithet of the Gandharva, vi. 58, 94, 143
Viśve Devāḥ (All-Gods), vi. 56
Viśveśvara, vi. 112

"Vita Merlini," iii. 193, 194
Vitality, birth of god of, viii. 226
Vītanguhaiti River, vi. 339
Vitebsk, iii. 317
Vithofnir, cock, ii. 331
—Lævateinn (sword) alone could kill, ii. 136
Vitholf, forest-giant, ii. 280
Vit-khan, water-spirit, and his daughter may marry human beings, iv. 194
Vitolfus, forest-giant, ii. 280
Vit'ša-kuguza, -kuva, and -oza, iv. 166, 167
Vīvanghvant (Ind. Vivasvant), priest of Haoma sacrifice, vi. 282, 294, 302, 304, 313, 314
—Vivasvant identical with Avestan, vi. 28, 48
Vivasvant, vi. 18, 28, 30, 36, 48, 53, 85, 86, 138, 143
Viviane, the Chwimbian of Welsh literature, iii. 201
Vivification of newly created, ix. 170, 173, 174, 175, 182, 331 [108]
Vjedogonja, soul which leaves sleeping person or animal, iii. 227
Vladimir, Prince, iii. 293, 300
Vlkodlak (Vukodlak, Vrkolák, Volkun, etc.), [wolf], certain people may become, iii. 228–229
Vocabularies, separate, for men and women, xi. 17, 20, 282, 349 [5]
Vodan (Godan, Gwoden), Voden: see ODIN.
Vodní Panny, water-nymphs, iii. 271
Vodyanik, etc., water-spirit, iii. 270–271
Vodyanoy, water-dweller of Russians, iv. 193, 207
Voguls, an Ugrian stock, iv. xvii, xx
Vohu Fryāna fire, vi. 285
—Manah, vi. 260, 276
Voice, change of, x. 38
Void: see items s.v. CHAOS; TE KORE, ETC.
Vol (Fulla), sister of Frigg, ii. 184
Volcanic birth of universe, x. 221
—fire, vi. 234
—fires of Iceland, Loki may have typified, ii. 149
—forces, red-hot moccasins may be personification of, x. 232
— -god or -demon, Surt as, ii. 202
—spirits of, originally storm-daemons, i. 267

Volcanoes piled upon bodies of giants, i. 9
Volcanus, i. 296
Volga-mother, iv. 210
Volla, goddess, ii. 18
Volor, prophetic woman, ii. 241, 246
Volos, Slavic deity, iii. 293, 300–301
Volsung, child granted, in answer to prayer, to Rerir and, ii. 249–250
" Volsunga-saga," ii. 249, 291, 292
Volsungs, ii. 11
—descended from Sigi, ii. 32
Volsung's sons eaten by she-wolf, ii. 292
Volta, Etruscan mythical monster, i. 289
Volund (Velint), ii. pl. 1, frontispiece, 11, 170, 220, 259, 260, 266, pl. XXXIV, opp. p. 266, 267, pl. XXXV, opp. p. 272; see also WEYLAND THE SMITH.
" Volundarkvitha," Eddic poem, ii. pl. 1, frontispiece, 11, 254, 259
" Voluspa," ii. 6, 9, 10, 15, 20, 27, 28, 29, 46, 55, 61, 127, 128, 136, 146, 147, 151, 152, 164, 167, 168, 169, 197, 199, 200, 220, 241, 243, 249, 264, 265, 300, 318, 319, 320, 321, 325, 326, 327, 329, 330, 331, 337, 338, 339, 341, 342, 343, 344, 347
Völu-Steinn, skald, ii. 194
Volva, or seeress; magic-wielder, ii. 9, 27, 43, 45, 49, 117, 127, 147, 171, 246, 299–300, 346
Vomiting up sun, moon, and stars, vii. 144; see also SWALLOWING INCIDENTS.
Voodoo, vii. 335
Vor, goddess of vows, ii. 89
Voracity chief characteristic of Charybdis, i. 264
Voršud and Votiak wedding, likeness of ceremonies of, iv. 123
—he who carries, must not put foot to bare ground, iv. 123
—(luck protector), iv. 119, 121–122, 123, 124–126, pl. XIII, opp. p. 126, 130, pl. XIV, opp. p. 130, 131, 133, 134, 137
Vortigern's attempt to build a city, iii. 130, 200
Vörys-mort (Forest man), iv. 181
Votan, hero of Tzental legend, xi. 131–133
Votes akin to Finns in linguistic and geographical aspects, iv. xv

Votiaks, a Permian linguistic stock, iv. xvi, xvii, xix
Voting pebbles, i. 194
Votive offerings at fountains, trees, etc., ii. 214
—tablets (of Batavians) to Mercury, ii. 37
Vourukasha Sea, vi. 267, 268, 269, 270, 271, 278, 281, 289, 298, 350
——abode of White Haoma, vi. 59
Vow, Irish, relating to sky, earth, sea, iii. 12
Vows, i. 102; ii. 34, 89, 109, 162, 233, 242; iv. 133, 135; x. 89, 90, 124, 282 21; xi. 282
" Voyage of Bran," iii. 64, 103, 114–116, pl. XXII, opp. p. 176, 211
——Maelduin, iii. 113
Vran in the sense of " tent," vii. 14
Vrātya, god, vi. 93
Vretil, angel, v. 160
Vrindravi (" Rind's sanctuary), ii. 165
Vṛndāvana, vi. 172
V-rod symbol, iii. pl. XVII, opp. p. 134
Vṛṣa, vi. 112
Vṛṣākapi, Indra's ape, vi. 62
Vṛṣaparvan, Uśanas domestic priest of, vi. 153
Vṛtra, vi. 30, 33, 34, 35, 37, 39, 44, 46, 52, 56, 62, 64, 67, 68, 80, 87, 88, 91, 93, 97, 98, 129, 131, 132, 133, 134, 153; 265, 335
—slain by Agni, Indra, and Sūrya, vii. 44, 45
—snake, iv. 444
—spirit of drought, vii. 78, 393 24
Vṛtrahan, Indra called, vi. 265, 271
—title of, survives in that of Vahagn, vii. 46
Vsevolod, Prince, outstripped Chors (the Sun), iii. 299
Vukub-Ahpu, one of hero-brothers, xi. 171, 173
— -Cakix, first of giants, overcome by hero-brothers, xi. 168–169, 177
Vu-kuźo and -murt, Water master and Water man, iv. 195
Vulcan (fire), ii. 197, 201–202
Vulture, vi. 266, 291, 297, 365 4; xii. 167
—'Anuqet appears on rare occasions as a, xii. 131
—gives magic powers to a woman who became a shaman, iv. 505
— -goddess Nekhbet, xii. 132, 142

Vulture, man married a, xi. 274
—no positive knowledge of cult of Nekhbet as incarnate in, xii. 167
—Peak, paradise of, viii. 241–242, 273
—sign of ending of probation, vii. 246
—Tuan MacCairill as, iii. 207
Vushkaparik, vii. 91
Vüt-kuguza and -kuva (Water Old Man and Woman), iv. 200

Vüt-oza (Water master), iv. 199
Vyāhṛtis, the sacred, vi. 74
Vyantaras (wood-dwellers), importance of the, in Jain mythology, vi. 227, 228
Vyāsa, vi. 150
—divinity of, vi. 243–244
Vyatka site of old kuala, iv. 127
Vylep, iv. 82

W

Wa a dwindling race, xii. 295–296
—creation-myth, xii. 288–289
—grades among, xii. 295
—hill tribes, spiritistic beliefs of, xii. 293
—hillmen in Kēngtūng spring feast, xii. 333
—Hpilu Yek-kha, inhabitants of Möng Wa, xii. 291
—Küt (the Wa Who Were Left Behind) probably same race as Hkachè, xii. 296
—possibly represent aborigines of Indo-China, xii. 286
—race sprang from seeds of gourd, xii. 281
—sacred mere of, xii. 291
Wabanunaqsiwok, the Dawn-People: see SUN MYTHS (vol. x).
Wabasso, white rabbit, x. 41, 298 47
Wabilikimo, legendary dwarfs, vii. 259
Wabus, x. 40
Wadd, name of moon-god, v. 5, 7
Wading to Ireland of Bran represented his crossing waters to Hades, iii. 101, 105
Wælcyrge (Valkyries), glosses of, ii. 253
Wager in which Athi (Brahmā) lost his head to Sek-ya (Indra), xii. 323
—of Loki's head, ii. 266
Waggon in sacred grove, ii. 102–103
— -man (Vagna-verr), ii. 78, 95
—of early Iron Age, uses of, ii. pl. xv, opp. p. 122
—Star (Ursa Major), v. 109, 317
Waggons of gods, ii. 22, 24, 41, 71, 77–78, 82, 109, 120, 196, 198, pl. xxv, opp. p. 198, 199
Wahieroa, son of Tawhaki, ix. 60, 67–68
Wahshijja, Arabic writer, on Tammuz, v. 339

Waidelots, priests at sacred oak, iii. pl. xxxvii, opp. p. 304
Wailing at tomb of Bêl, v. 323, 324
—feast of, of all gods in temple Askul, v. 337
—of Enkidu, v. 246
——Gilgamish for Enkidu, v. 260–261, 262
——Ishtar, v. 257, 334
Wailings for Dumu-ê-zi, Enmesharra, and Lugaldukug (Marduk), v. 342
——Tammuz, Innini, and Yanbûshâd, v. 339, 342, 343, 344, 345, 349, 350
—midsummer, v. 347
—Tammuz introduced into Temple at Jerusalem, v. 336, 413 1
—words used in, v. 76
Wail-strain, magic, played on harp by Lug, iii. 29
Wäinämöinen, water-spirit, a mighty hero, iv. 207
Waist, small, of Spider, vii. 323–324
Wak (God), vii. 116, 123, 169, 170
Wakanda, indwelling power of things, x. 18, 22, 82, 83, 84, 98, 106, 269 3
Wakasa, shadow of chestnut-tree over, viii. 339
Wakea: see ATEA.
Wakefulness, Nehes deity of, xii. 67
Wakilengeche, ghosts who turn back, vii. 180, 183
Wakna, culture-hero, xi. 185
Wakonyingo (or Wadarimba), dwarf dwellers on Kilimanjaro have heaven-reaching ladders, vii. 136, 141, 266–269
Wakuluwe tradition of first pair coming from Heaven, vii. 156
Wakyet-wa (or Chinun-way-shun), deity worshipped in Kachin festival, xii. 338

Walad-alat ("child of Alat"), v. 382 [79]
Walala (Ulala), x. 247–248
Waldmännlein, male wood-spirit, ii. 205
Waldminne, forest elf, ii. 205
Walenge, ghosts who have no connexion with the living, vii. 180–181
Walih, son of Etana, v. 167
Walk, Thor said to, when he pronounces dooms, ii. 23
Walkers, night- and day-, vi. 97
Walking-stick for dead, iv. 56
Wall, Roman, iii. 15–16
—running north and south on "Brittia," iii. 16
Wälla Mänes, Lettish name for October, iii. 352 [7]
Wallaby and turtle, tale of, ix. 145–146
Walriderske, "Rider of the dead," ii. 257
"Walum Olum," x. 124
Walumbe, vii. 117, 171
Wan Li, Emperor, viii. 95
Wand, Druidic, causes shapeshifting, iii. 40
—magic, ii. 46; xii. 63, 208 (fig. 213), 366 [6]
——of Cúroi, iii. 151–152
—winged, representing Eagle, x. 92
Wanderlust of spirits, vii. 95
Wander-path of Seide, iv. 107
"Wanderer," Eshmun, v. 75
Wandering-night of dead, iv. 61–62, 66
Wanderings of Chuang-Chu, viii. 362
Wanema, vii. 130
Wang An-shih, viii. 106
—ceremony, viii. 61
—Ch'in-jo, viii. 58
—Hsiang, viii. 163
—P'i, viii. 53
—P'ou, viii. 165
—Tan, viii. 59
—T'ung opponent of all myth, viii. 199, 200
Wanga, wizards, vii. 335
Wanilo, Vali's name derived from, ii. 165
Waning of moon, iv. 424
Wantonness, Land of, viii. 363
War, Wars:
War against Arawak, legend that brave Carib in paradise wage, xi. 39
—Agni, Indra, and Vahagn as gods of, vii. 45
—animal, iv. 507

War, Apollo only incidently god of, i. 177
—beginning of, x. 203
—between Æsir and Vanir, ii. 26, 27, 28, 55
——different divine groups, iii. 38
— -dances, xi. 145
—death in, ensures life in Heaven, iv. 488
—first in world, ii. 337
—god of, viii. 196
War-god, in Sumero-Babylon, Ninurta the, v. 99, 115, 116
——Odin as a, ii. 40, 55–56, 58, 59, 65
——*Tiwaz had become, ii. 97, 98
— -goddesses, i. 172; v. 23, 25, 26, 27, 29, 30
——of Irish mythology, Valkyries resemble, ii. 255
— -gods, v. 99, 115, 116, 132, 136; x. 306 [59]
—gods F and M associated with, xi. 139
—Ḥat-ḥôr sometimes mistress of, xii. 40
—Ishtar a goddess of, vii. 38
— -king, epithet of Caswallawn, iii. 106–107
— -maidens, older, may have degenerated into witches, ii. 253
—Mithra god of, vii. 33
—Northern Ruler sacrificed to in, iv. 156
—Odin brought, into world, ii. 55
— -spirits, Germanic, ii. 255
—task of Ares to wage, i. 189–190
—Thor's aid sought in, ii. 77
—Thunder tutelary of, x. 99, 306 [59]
—Vahagn god of, vii. 42
—Women of western heavens, xi. 82
Wars against enemies of Sumer, v. 126–127
—between giants and race of diviners, ii. 34–35
—Celtic, between divinities, ii. 30
—Mars directs, iii. 9
—of Asuras against gods, vi. 116
——Sumerians, v. 128, 129, 130
—Sun of, xi. 94
Warah, name of moon-god, v. 5
Waranjui, dwellers above the sky, vii. 137
"Ward-tree" (Vårträd), ii. 204, 333, 334
Warimu, ancestral spirits, vii. 180

Warning not to turn back, vii. 154, 172
Warnings, iii. 69
Warring States, viii. 117, 134, 143
Warrior born from bones of monster, first Carib, xi. 272
—Brothers, x. 205
— -spirit, x. 246
—twins, x. 204, 205
Warriors, Age of, xi. 240
—death of, xi. 59, 60, 61, 74, 198
—— -god of, xi. 54
—flesh of, only, men's meat, xi. 349 ⁵
—paradise of, xi. 82
—souls of, in combat when Aurora Borealis appears, iii. 319
—special, chosen by Odin for Valhalla, ii. 57; see also EINHERJAR, ETC.
—who died in battle, Shuras and Tengus reincarnations of, viii. 287, 288
Wart, x. 291 ³⁷
Waruksti, formula of consecration, x. 304, 305
Wasanye tribes reputed to be sorcerers, vii. 115
Washer at the Ford, sight of, prophecy of Cúchulainn's death, iii. 155
"Washerman's Donkey," vii. 353
Washing before prayer, ii. 310
—house of, v. 106
—of goddess in secret lake, ii. 103
"Wa-Sō-Byōye," viii. 362–365
Wasp as soul-animal, iv. 473
—stung God thereby releasing soul, iv. 477
Wasserkopf, a Nix's child, ii. 212
Wasser-mutter, iv. 211–214
Watch of the Lands, guardian of east, viii. 243
Watch-dog of Osiris, xii. 179, 417 ¹⁸
Watchman of the gods, Heimdall is, ii. 152, 153, 154, 156
Watchmen, seven stars of Great Bear as, iv. 425
Wate learned healing art, ii. 205
Water, ii. 208–215; vii. 59–61, 62; x. 22, 81, 98, 140, 186, 299 ⁴⁹
—and bread put on head of dead cacique, xi. 27
—— -fire, theft of, x. 231
—— -vegetation symbolize life, vii. 382 ²³
—as creator, v. 105, 396 ⁵⁰
—— -divine weapon of first man, vi. 295
—— -first principle, v. 104, 109
—at burial preparation, xi. 81

Water becomes object of sacrificial cult, iv. 194, 212
—brought from sea, ritual of, v. 37, 38
— -bull, iv. 470
—— -sea-bull resembles Celtic, vii. 396 ⁶²
—carried in gourd with holes in, ix. 62–63
—cities, etc., under: see items s.v. UNDERWATER.
—Classic, viii. 17
— -clocks for regulating hours of worship, xii. 419 ¹⁷
—could not destroy great shaman, iv. 283
—cow's body covered with lines representing, xii. 39
—Cúchulainn plunged into successive vessels of, iii. 142–143
— -cult, real, connected with agriculture, iv. 212–213
—Daughters of the, x. 180
—dead dragged down into, x. 6
—deities living in, do not represent that element, xii. 15
— -deities, serpentiform, in creation-myth, xi. 199
—dish of, on threshold, aids departure of spirits, vii. 75–76
— -divinities, horses which come from lakes or rivers may be mythic forms of, iii. 129
— -dragon holds unborn Sun, xii. 105 (fig. 103)
—drinking of, of allegiance, xii. 324
— -elfins, ii. 209, 223
—entrance to spirit-world through, vii. 186
—Festival, celebration of, at Luang Prabang, xii. 298
—— of Nāgas, xii. 272; see also items s.v. FESTIVAL, WATER.
— -fetcher, iv. 423
—fire which may not be extinguished by, vii. 387 ²
—first principle, v. 91, 104
—form of Amen-Rê', xii. 221
— -fowl, iv. 317, 318, 321, 322–323, 324, 325, 326, 328
—fresh, came under sway of Poseidon, i. 213
—from Fionn's hands healing, iii. 177–178
— -giants, ii. 280
—god of fresh, v. 102

Water-god, sacrifice to, iv. 99
——see TRITA ĀPTYA.
——Tlaloc, children sacrificed to, xi. 72
— -goddess, Anāhita as, vii. 25
——Artemis as, i. 186
——Ishtar as, vii. 382 23
—goddess of, xi. 54
— -gods: see ENKI; EA.
—Haurvatāt presides over, vi. 260
—hidden by wizards in battles, iii. 25, 30, 76
—holy, vi. 333; see also SACRED PLACES.
— -horse mythic animal, viii. 104
——of France and Scotland, iii. 129
—in Nera tale, iii. 68
——tale of " Gilded Man," xi. 194
—interpreted as " the great god who became by himself," xii. 219
—itself object of sacrificial cult, iv. 194, 210, 211–215
— -jars, v. 110, 111
—journey of dead over, iv. 33, 78
—kept under icons to quench thirst of returning soul, iii. 230
—late speculation of creation from, v. 91
—magic shower of, iii. 32
—man created partly from, iv. 371
— -master and -spirits, iv. 469–470
—may not be crossed without gift to water-spirit, iv. 198
—monster, two of offspring of, stolen by Coyote, x. 161, 162
—mother, iv. 210–214
——prayers to, iv. 210–215
—must be guarded against in choosing grave sites, viii. 141
——put between capturer of serpent ball and serpents, iii. 14
—Nāgas guardians of, viii. 268
— -nymphs, iii. 271–272
——Navky may become, after seven years, iii. 253–255
——of Kyzikos capture Hylas, i. 110
—of death, v. 180
——eternal life, v. 94, 95, 96, 97, 98, 99, 100, 333, 334
——life: see LIFE, ETERNAL, BREAD AND WATER OF; LIFE, WATER OF.
—offended, causes skin diseases, iv. 207, 212
—one of the elements, viii. 29, 142
—origin of, ix. 279

Water, Osiris represents, as life-giving element, xii. 95, 385 10
—placed on window-sill for departed soul to cleanse itself, iv. 17
—poured on sacrificial animal, iv. 130, 211
— -pouring, iv. 41
——at Armenian festivals, vii. 22; see also FESTIVALS, WATER.
——of, in creation-myth, iv. 329
— -powers, x. 99, 156
—rainbow drinker of, iv. 443–444
—relation of Dionysos to, i. 220
—rituals, v. 106
—sacred fire cast into, vii. 57
——extinguished with, vii. 15, 56
—sacrifice of brides to, iv. 213–214
—(sea or basin), near mother of sun, vii. 50
—see ḤA'PI.
—Serpent of the West, xi. 121
—sky compared to, xii. 25, 34
— -soul, iv. 13, 14, 215
— -spirit, Mimir a, ii. 49, 167–170
— -spirits, ii. 208–215; iii. 270–272; iv. 191–216
——human sacrifice to, xi. 197, 198; see also GILDED MAN, ETC.
——serpents as embodiments of, iii. 130
—spirits which do not sink in, viii. 28
— -spouts, sea-spirit supposed to travel on, ix. 135
—sprinkled over crowd at seed festivals, iv. 242; see also items s.v. FESTIVALS, WATER.
—sprinkling of, xii. 299
——at cow's-milk feast, iv. 259
— -sprite, Kitunusi may be a, vii. 244
—Sun's handmaidens descend on spider's thread to draw, vii. 321
—tabu to Fraoch, iii. 67
—to be fetched in basket, vii. 170
—(to quell battle) broke forth from well and formed Loch Riach, iii. 38
— -totem, vii. 280–281, 417 23
—turned to wine, viii. 123
— -vessel, carrying water in leaky, ix. 224, 226
— -Vily, iii. 259
—visits by body of, iv. 211
— -women, three wise, ii. 261
— -world, ii. 330
—world beneath, iii. 112–113, 122

Water-worlds, iii. 109, 112, 113, 128, 194
—worship of, iii. 273
Watercress, plant of rejuvenation a kind of, v. 227
Waterfall, Loki as salmon hid in, ii. 144, 146
Waterfalls, holy, vi. 235
Watermill, marriage of fairies near, vii. 393 ³²
Watermill-god, iv. 167
Waters, vi. 18, 25, 26, 33, 37–38, 46, 47, 48, 63, 67, 85, 94–95, 129, 135–136, 137–138, 147
—bathing in living, of Tane, ix. 88
—celestial, xii. 35
—created, vi. 277–278
—creatures of, as intermediaries with Powers Below, x. 22
—division of, x. 126, 263; xi. 181
—god of, viii. 90
——with overflowing, v. 95, 96, 98, 99
—heavenly, continuation of ocean, xii. 41
—Khnûm guardian of, coming from the Underworld, xii. 28
—of Death, jewelled tree this side of, iii. 131
——four quarters, properties of, x. 71
—origin of all, sought in mythological source of Nile, xii. 50
—Place of Division of the, xi. 165
—prophetic ecstasy effect of drinking, i. 258
—purifying, vi. 82, 115
—pursuing, iii. 121, 138
—quest for, of Ganges, vi. 115
—restore health and life to mortals, iii. 123
—sacred, ii. 163–164, 208, 213, 214, 215, 231, 326, 331, 334; iv. 101; v. 20; vi. 235–236; vii. 59, 60, 62; viii. 247, 251, 252, 267; xii. 31, 194
—said to have been captured by Apaosha, vi. 267
—Sun of the, xi. 91, 95
—tempestuous, Muireartach may be embodiment of, iii. 171
—younger brother sometimes regarded as son of the, x. 295 ⁴⁴
Watery One, Water-Flood, xii. 46
—void before creation, vii. 144
Watsusi and Kowwituma, twins of Sun and Foam, x. 209

Watwa of Urundi consider themselves true aborigines of the country, vii. 264
Wave, Dylan called son of the, iii. 99
—ninth; nine waves have importance in folk-belief, ii. 191
—that drowned Tuag may have been sea-god Manannan, iii. 89
Waves, Ægir's and Ran's daughters personifications of, ii. 190
—fighting of, Celtic ritual of, iii. 133
—give messages to those who can hear them, iii. 133
—were " Son of Ler's horses in a seastorm," iii. 128
Wax Girl: see TAR BABY.
—head-ring, Hare makes, vii. 297
— -legged man, vii. 245–246
—man made from, ix. 175
—tapers in honour of dead, iv. 31, 44, 45, 47, 50, 58, 60, 62, 69, 73; see also CANDLE, CANDLES.
——worship and festivals, iv. 150, 153, 154, 266, 267, 269, 272
——of Peko (Pekko), iv. 245
——sacrifice tree represents, at Seide worship, iv. 110
—used to anoint ears against song of Sirens, i. 263
" Way of the Gods " or " Spirits," meaning of Shinto, viii. 215
—Tao, viii. 108, 128
Wayfarers, Apollo protector of, i. 180
Wayindōk, stocks made of male bamboo, also village, xii. 350
Ways of Anu, Enlil, and Ea, fixed stars as, v. 94, 95, 96, 395 ²¹
Wealth, Bishamon patron of, in later times, viii. 243
—Demeter's connexion with, i. 227
—Dionysos deity of, according to late myth, i. 220
—god of, viii. 66, 79, 96
—goddess of, viii. 268–269
—Hermes giver of, i. 192, 193
—Njord as, ii. 102
—white serpent patron of, viii. 331
Weapon, genius of, viii. 230
—given to Ninurta, v. 126
Weapons, iv. 443, 444, 464
—as insignia comparatively rare, xii. 13
—Celts attacked earthquakes and high tides with, iii. 12
—cult of, iii. pl. II (6), opp. p. 8, 33–34

Weapons, diseases as, vi. 83
—exchanged at parley between Sreng and Bres, iii. 24
—five divine, of first man, vi. 295
—flint, found buried in earth believed thunder-bolts, ii. 79
—given by Odin, ii. 56
—hymn of Ninurta concerning his, v. 127–128
—magic, iii. 31–32, 33, 40, 41, 65, 66, 76, 173, 175
—Odin claimed all who died by, ii. 34, 52
—of demons, vi. 152
——Gilgamish, v. 247
——Indra, vi. 132
——Manannan possessed by Féinn, iii. 65, 173
——Marduk, v. 300
——Śiva, vi. 111
——war divine, vi. 61, 118
———Seven Gods are deified, v. 146
—placed beside the dead, xii. 174
—seven, v. 138, 139
—supernatural, xii. 282
—superstitious use of stone, regarded as supernatural, ii. 80
Wearers of the Leopard's Skin, xii. 134, 405 [39]
Weasel, vii. 219
— -like head, Atum with, xii. 165
Weather, bad, powers of evil in relation to, xi. 339–340
—changes, iv. 417–418, 422, 431, 458
—depends on outcome of battle of land and sea Zduhaczs, iii. 227–228
— -god, vii. 14, 379 [1] (ch. i)
——Pan as a, i. 268
— -goddess, viii. 234
— -gods, warlike character of, vii. 45
—Nāgas often regarded as controllers of, vi. 241
—see ZODIAC, SIGNS OF (vol. vii).
Weaver-maid, constellation, viii. 235, 236
Weavers, v. 190
Weaver's shuttle, sign of Neith misunderstood as, xii. 142
Weaving, x. 183, 238
—fates of warriors, ii. 254–255
—first taught by Arkas, i. 16
—invented by Athene, i. 171
—Neith connected with art of, xii. 142
— -song in vision of Daurrud, ii. 254

Web, spider's, compared with rays of sun, vii. 284
Wechselbalg, a changeling, ii. 212
Wedding ceremonies, kuala ceremonies akin to, iv. 123
——Votiak and Voršud, likeness between, iv. 123
— -dancers, iv. 69
—Finns call bear feast the, iv. 97
—horse-, iv. 57
—house-, iv. 161
— -like ceremonies, earth stolen with, iv. 240
—rites, stealing of earth similar to, iv. 461–462
—see MUDOR WEDDING.
— -songs, iv. 69, 122
— -women at feast to Utumö, iv. 69
Weddings among the dead, iv. 483
—forest-spirits celebrate, iv. 179, 181, 183
—of apes, vi. 237
—water-spirits celebrate, iv. 195, 198
Wedge-shape formation of army, ii. 56
Wedlock, Anahit, Hera, and Ishtar as protectors of, vii. 27
Week, Harranian or Ssabean, v. 154
Weeping at grave, iv. 4, 27–28, 68
—Balder out of Hel, ii. 130, 131, 135, 137
—of goddess: see TEARS OF GOLD, ETC.
—over dead, vii. 95
— -songs, iv. 27, 30, 56, 68, 74
—Tammuz lord of, v. xvii
—women, festival of Ta-ūz known as festival of, v. 336
Wei Chêng, Chancellor, viii. 190, 192
—kingdom, viii. 94, 174
—Po-yang, viii. 144
—T'o, tutelary god, viii. 196
Weighing after death, iv. 494
—in the balance, vi. 100
—of hearts, xii. 176
Weights and measures, Hermes invents, i. 195
Weird, destiny, ii. 246
Weiwōbo (Queen Mother of the West), viii. 275
Wek-wek and giant, contest of, x. 228
Wēlandes geweorc, weapons and ornaments, ii. pl. 1, frontispiece
—Stocc, place in Buckinghamshire, ii. pl. 1, frontispiece
Welderich, forest-giant, ii. 280

Well, animals and the, vii. 297–298, 421 [22], 423 [32]
—Apis only allowed to drink from, xii. 163
—beneath Yggdrasil, wisdom stored in, ii. 49–50
—bursting of sacred, forms lake, iii. 73, 208
— -curb, story of, viii. 300–301
—Cúroi's soul within apple in salmon in, iii. 151
—drinking from, gives inspiration to wisdom, iii. 120–121, 167
—healing, iii. 24, 32
—heavenly, viii. 226
—made from footprint of Balder's horse, ii. 328
—magic, iii. 263
——Fionn drank of, and descended into, iii. 173
—renewal of dry, by magic, iv. 215–216
—sacred ('Ain Shams), xii. 31
—secret, in green of síd Nechtain, iii. 121
—seven streams of wisdom from, iii. 121
Wells, ii. 23, 43, 50, 167, 168, 276, 331, 341; iii. 136
—fairy, vii. 393 [32]
—guardians of crown in, iii. 68
—holy, ii. pl. XLI, opp. p. 320
—protection of, against spirits, iv. 66
—sacred if marked by special feature, vi. 235
—stone-faced, discovered at Cape Santa Elena, xi. 206
Wels (Lettish god of dead), October month of, iii. 352 [7]
Welsh poems and tales, iii. 92, 93
Wemba country, alleged site of creation in, vii. 147
Wên Ch'ang, god of literature, stellar deity, viii. 89, 112, 113
—Hai Po Sha, viii. 143
—Hsien T'ung K'ao, viii. 200
—Ming, personal name of Yü, viii. 37
— -shu, a Bodhisattva, viii. 196
—Ti, viii. 161
—Wang, viii. 9, 16, 40, 41, 42, 43, 44, 70, 137
Weng(i), xii. 409 [110]
Were, some East African tribes call their divinity, vii. 128

Were-animals, vii. 121, 204, 251, 252, 334–347, 413 [23], 414 [29]
— -beasts, imps, cannibals, xi. 260, 300
— -jaguar is a Kenaima, xi. 260, 301–302
Werefolk, x. 252, 296 [46]
Weregild, ii. 49
Werewolves, ii. 291–294; iii. 228, 229
—and witchcraft, vii. 334–347
Wessex, royal families of, traced descent to Bældæg (Balder), ii. 19
West abode of evil spirits, vii. 47
—as a mythological personage, xii. 99, 100, 386 [22]
—Autumn came from, viii. 234, 235
—doors and gates opening towards, iv. 144
—guardian of, viii. 243
—Ḥat-ḥôr divinity of, xii. 42
—head of sacrificial animal turned to, by Samoyeds, iv. 39
—Hesperos associated with, i. 248
—homage to, viii. 46, 50
—Isis and Nephthys originally the two divinities of the, xii. 392 [58]
—Lake, viii. 66
—mouth of earth in the, x. 62
—Osiris lord of the, xii. 122, 399 [110]
—prayers read with face to, iv. 150, 151
—Queen Mother of the (Weiwŏbo), viii. 275
—realm of Varuṇa in the, vi. 137
—represented by white tiger, iv. 360
—river of fire flowing east and, iv. 370
—see COMPASS, COLOURS OF, ETC.
—swallower of the, xii. 179
—" the behind," x. 287 [31]
—turning to, while casting sacrifice into, v. 318
—white tiger spirit of, xii. 307
—wicked turn their faces towards, vii. 97–98
—wind, v. 371
Western Chin Dynasty, events in, viii. 134
—Tengeri, iv. 411, 412
—Travels in the T'ang Dynasty, viii. 190
Westward branches of tree fraught with disaster, iv. 381, 383
Westwards, Heaven moves, viii. 29
Wetting of fingers and smearing of faces at memorial feasts, iv. 37–38

Weyland the Smith, ii. pl. 1, frontis-
piece, 11, 220, 259, 260, 271; see also
VOLUND, ETC.
——(Wieland), Baltic celestial smith
compared to, iii. 330
Whaitari (Whatitiri), female deity, sky-
dweller of cannibalistic tendency, ix.
57, 62
Whai-tua (Space), ix. 7
Whakaturia and dog, tale of, ix. 86–87
Whale, ix. 69, 83
Whales grew from severed fingers of
Old Woman of Sea, x. 6
—Thor caught two, ii. 86
Wheat, Cerridwen swallowed grain of,
and gave birth to child, iii. 57
—strewn on graves, iii. 230
Wheel, vi. 16, 24, 26, 29, 34
—fair, sun called by elves, ii. 197
—following track of, iii. 143
—god with the, iii. pl. IV, opp. p. 20
—icy, x. 6
——marks on Buddha's feet, vi. 191, 195,
196
—of god may be sun, iii. 8
——water-mill, modern Armenians im-
agine sun to be like, vii. 47
——symbol on Gaulish coins, iii. pl. II
(1, 3), opp. p. 8, pl. IV, opp. p. 20
——throwing, iii. 147
—whirling of blades surrounding ambrosia, vi. 139
—winged, of Yāw, v. 43
—with spokes, Jains picture time as,
vi. 221
Whetstone of Hrungnir, ii. 82, 83
Whinnymoor, ii. 305
Whinstone rocks, how formed, ii. 82
Whipping, vivification by, ix. 175,
331 108
Whirling castle caused by spell, iii. 148
Whirlpool at place where water falls
through millwheel, ii. 283, 284
Whirlpools, vi. 235; x. 257
—and Rapids, birth of goddess of, viii.
226
Whirlwind, vi. 233, 236, vii. 81; viii.
70
—carries away Ntotwatsana, vii. 247
—fire-, ii. 280
—forest-spirits move as, iv. 179, 181,
182, 183
—shaman may fly in form of, iv. 286
—souls as the, iv. 9

Whirlwind, two creators carried to sky
by a, ix. 274
—Yin Hung rescued by two Immortals
in a, viii. 67
Whirlwinds believed to be passing spirits, xi. 323
—Wind mother dances in, iv. 232
Whisper, every, heard by Math Hên
and Coranians, iii. 98, 107
Whistle, x. 224, 248
—dragon could enter human being and
cause it to, vii. 77
—for night-signalling invented by
Brigit, iii. 137
——the winds, iv. 457
Whistles made of bones of Hare and
Gazelle, vii. 295, 420 12
Whistling wraiths may represent dead, x.
276 12
White animals as sacrifice, viii. 233
——clad stranger appears to members
of Buu tribe, vii. 349–351
—cloth in burial, ix. 237
——corn Girl, x. 162
—Eagle's account relating to abandon-
ment of human sacrifice, x. 304–306
—Fire-maker of the Night, xi. 167
——Horn: see FINDBENNACH, ETC.
—Isle, Achilles, restored to life, dwells
with Helen in, i. 131
—Ones of Emuin: see THREE FINNS OF
EMUIN, ETC.
——shell Woman of the East, xi. 32
—Tengeri, iv. 411
—Tiger, Chinese, symbolizes Autumn
and metals, viii. 243
—Woman, Etain called, iii. 193
—Women, iii. 271–272
—Youth, iv. 313, 351–352
Whitsunday, summer dziadys on Sat-
urday before, iii. 237
Whitsuntide, feasts at, iii. 306, 311–312
—sacrifice to Rusalky, iii. 254–255
Who (Ka deva), deity, vi. 50, 74
Wichama, second son of first woman,
xi. 225
Wichtlein, Wichtelmann, diminutive be-
ings, ii. 228, 231
Wicked ghost, god, Spy, etc., are de-
mons, v. 362
Widdershins, ii. 302
Wide-gazing, guardian of west, viii. 243
——hearing or Renowned, guardian of
north, viii. 243

Wide (Reaching) Head, an Underworld serpent, xii. 202

Widolt ("Wood-lord"), ii. 280

Widow marked, x. 215

Widows, mourning customs of the, x. 282 21

—sacrifice of, to deceased husbands, iv. 58-59

Wieland: see WEYLAND THE SMITH.

Wieszczy (Polish), vampire, iii. 232

Wife at disposal of guest, iii. 140

—carving of, out of wood, x. 245, 264

—sought in Underworld, ix. 73-75

Wigan and Bugan survived flood, ix. 170-171, 178-179, 180

Wight, ii. 219, 228

Wigit, deity, x. 252

Wikar, son of Geirhild, given to Odin, ii. 121

Wild Boar of Gulban, a transformed child, iii. 125

— -cat messenger of wizards, vii. 336, 337

—Hunt, ii. 316

—Huntsman, ii. 207

—life, Artemis mistress of, i. 183

—Maïnads and Bacchantes feminine spirits of the, i. 269

—Man of Tirol, ii. 280

—Men, iii. 264, 265

——who have no bellies (skeleton men), xi. 341

—Pan chief divine dweller in the, i. 268

—women, woods and mountains home of, iii. 263-265

Wilde Leute, forest-elves, ii. 205

Wilderness, Pan divinity of, i. 267

Wildiu wîp, long-haired forest-spirits, ii. 205, 206

Wildmannel, male wood-spirit, ii. 205

Wildmännlein, caught and intoxicated, imparted knowledge of cures, ii. 206

Wili: see VILY.

William of Scherfenberg, ii. 272

Willow-bush in moon, iv. 423

—Lute, viii. 183

— -tree transformed itself into a woman, viii. 333, 338

— -twigs, man created from, iv. 373

—wards off evil influences, viii. 105

Winalagilis, Warrior of the North, x. 249

Wind, Winds:

Wind and cloud appear to Cao-bien as portent, xii. 317-318

—as breath, ix. 174, 176, 182

—at creation, iv. 328

—ball-, viii. 237

—Bride of, pursuit of Wood-wives resembles, ii. 207

— -demons, v. 371-372

—destroyed Third Age, xi. 91, 93, 94

— -directions, eight, ix. 162

—father of, viii. 51

—fertilization by, ix. 158, 165

—Fū-jin genius of, viii. 288, pl. XXXI, opp. p. 288

— -god, viii. 73; 223; xi. 54, 141

— -goddess, viii. 234

— -godlings, Maruts degenerated into mere, vi. 40

— -horse, iv. 243

— -magic, iv. 233

——blew insect [Etain] about, iii. 79, 80

— -maids, v. 363

— -makers, x. 99

—mother, or woman, or man, iv. 232-233

—of dead, iv. 17

——Elōhim, v. 303-304

—— -the-Nine-Serpents and of -the-Nine-Caves children of deer-god, xi. 86

— -old-man, iv. pl. XXVII, opp. p. 224

—see WHIRLWIND.

—souls of dead borne on, ii. 193

————connected with the, vi. 39, 59, 102

—south, v. 176, 180

—Wodan may originally have been god of dead or of, ii. 40-41, 42, 44, 46, 47

Winds, iv. 457-458; v. 61, 99; vi. 265, 278, 295; viii. 33, 36, 72, 89, 141; x. xvii, 22, 23, 33, 35, 81, 92, 109-112, 250; xi. 121

—all four, with head or shape of ram, an allusion to soul, breath, xii. 65

—Anu begat four, v. 294, 300

—as people, x. 138

—begotten by Rangi, ix. 8

—called grandsons of Stribog, iii. 301

—capture and imprisonment of, ix. 55

—east and west and north and south with heads of animals, xii. 65 (figs. 70, 71)

Winds, Etesian, i. 251, 252
—four, considered divine, xii. 65
—magical practice of playing upon wind-instruments to control, i. 268
—many attributes of quadrupled, xii. 65
—Odysseus given bag containing the, i. 137
—rise in four corners of sky, iv. 308
—rose against Humbaba, v. 253
—tied up in bag, ix. 296–297
—used to combat Labbu and Tiâmat, v. 288, 294, 300, 302
—wrestling, x. 138
Window in sky, x. 95, 96
—ray of sunlight on, worshipped, iv. 223
Windows in coffins, iv. 29, 31, 32
—queen of the, v. 33
—Tavern of the, Tampu-Tocco means, xi. 218, 248, pl. xxxviii, opp. p. 248
Windy Storm a god, x. 78
Wine, vi. 319, 327
—celestial, viii. 130–131
—consecrated with different symbols, ii. 77, 79
—Dionysos mistakenly called god of, i. 218 (cf. 219), 220
—of Dionysos, Goibniu's ale analogous to, iii. 120
——immortality, vii. 393 [32]
——Odin, ii. 60, 65
—sprinkled on grave to prevent thirst, iii. 230
—water turned into, viii. 123
Wing Mai, city founded by Hsö Hkan Hpa, xii. 292
Winged garments, v. 329
—monsters, combats with, v. 279–281, 283
—old man, iv. 227
——— = thunder-god, iv. 441
—sun disk, v. 69, 70
———-god in Hebrew poetry and Bible, v. 69–70
Wings, Egyptian deities later represented with, xii. 114, 212, 392 [58]
—of El, v. 68
——fairies, iii. 258
——mountains, Vedic legends of, vi. 159
Winia and hog came from tree, ix. 168
Winter, ii. 96
— -counts, x. 128

Winter, destructive, foretold to Yima, vi. 307–309
—Flint as a personification of, x. 296 [45]
—mighty, precedes end of world, ii. 338–339, 341, 342, 385 [64]; see also FIMBUL-WINTER.
—myth of, vi. 317, 319
—power of god perhaps wanes in, ii. 64–65
—solstice, vi. 58
—son, iv. 243
—(Zemeka), vii. 86
Wisdom, ii. 9, 49; iii. 109, 110, 112, 120–121, 166
—contest of Vafthrudnir and Odin to prove, ii. 62
—hazels of, iii. 121, 166
—Ḥu god of, xii. 66
—in possession of giants, ii. 54
——solar ship, xii. 27 (fig. 10)
—literature, v. 209
—Nabû god of, vii. 31
—obtained through tasting roasted heart of Fafnir, iii. 166
—of Gilgamish, v. 235
——Utnapishtim, v. 263, 265
—personification of, xii. 26
—secrets of, written, v. 140
—summary of Odin's, in "Havamal," ii. 55
—Thor as seeker of, is unusual, ii. 96
Wise, Vanir called, ii. 25
Wish-drum, xii. 282–283, 284
— -maidens, ii. 45, 251
— -ring, ix. 163
— -sons, ii. 140, 314
— -trees, men received whatever they needed from, vi. 225
Wishes, ii. 267; x. 50
—bordering on magic, xii. 198
—fulfilment of three, granted to Theseus by Poseidon, i. 101, 104
—obtaining of, iv. 336
—three, of Cúchulainn granted, iii. 149
Wishing worms back into tree, ii. 206
Wisiu-wîp, ii. 212
Wistaria, viii. 385 [7]
Witch-doctors, vii. 339, 340, 342
——and witches confused, vii. 335
—head of, brought by Diarmaid to Brug na Boinne, iii. 66
—imprisons daughter-in-law in tree, ix. 137

Witch-society, vii. 339, 340
Witchcraft, ii. 46; vii. 48, 79, 366–
367, 370; viii. 324, 325, 328, 330;
xii. 200
—and werewolves, vii. 334–347
—Mātṛs practise, vi. 156
—see also WITCHES (vols. vii, viii).
Witchery of Sirens, Kirke gives Odysseus direction for escaping, i. 263
Witches, ii. 45, 48, 124, 143, 229, 246,
253, 256, 286, 289, 294, 300, 301,
302; iii. 31, 35, 155; 325; vii. 121,
141, 202, 203, 205, 230, 231, 245,
334–347, 404 ³¹, 406 ⁷, 413 ²³; viii.
154, 156; xi. 328
—and hobgoblins controlled by monkey,
viii. 103
—gathering-place of, iv. 78
—guild of, society to counteract doings
of, vii. 341–342
—last two, from Underworld at the
emergence, x. 201
—nine, in "Peredur," probably of
Gloucester, iii. 191
Wives burned with dead husband, iii.
233, 234
—how men came to be left without, xi.
32
—human, of dwarfs, ii. 272
——elves, ii. 224
—of son of sky-deity, ix. 156
—provided for first creation, xi. 166
Wiyeast, chief, x. 134
Wizard, Byat Twe and Ta ate body of
dead, and acquired his powers, xii.
348
Wizardry, Cúchulainn calls Manannan
his foster-father in, iii. 65
—Dagda called a god of, iii. 40
Wizards, ii. 64, 229; iii. 25, 30, 35, 173;
vii. 200, 324, 335; xi. 337
—may assume animal shapes, vii. 344
—Rākṣasas as, vi. 98, 156
Wloki, old Titanic being who caused
earthquakes, ii. 363 ³⁸
Wo Huang, daughter of Yao, viii. 88–
89
Wodan, vi. 37
—derivations of name, ii. 40, 42; see
also ODIN.
"Wodan's Host," Furious Host connected with, ii. 41
Wôdenesberg, mountain, ii. 44
Wodnesbeorh, mountain, ii. 44

Woi-shun and Chanum, parents of all
things, xii. 263, 264
Wokwuk, x. 224
Wolf, Wolves:
Wolf, iv. 424, 425; x. 39, 106, 121, 122,
133, 143–144, 145, 251
—bean, or pea, or corn, iv. 247
—called Rutu's hound, iv. 76
—connected with Mars, i. 293
—Esdes has head of, xii. 366 ³
—etymology of Greek word for, influences Lykaon-myth, i. 21
—forefather of Bersit clan, iv. 502
—Lykaon changed into, i. 16, 20, 21,
324 ¹ (ch. ii)
—nursed Romulus and Remus, i. pl.
LXIII, opp. p. 306, 307
—of Ophoïs declines in importance, xii.
167
—on Gaulish coins, iii. pl. II (11), opp.
p. 8, pl. III (1) (?), opp. p. 14
—see UP-UAUT, WOLF-GOD, ETC.
——spirit, story of, iv. 187
—Trail (Milky Way), x. 95
—tutelary genius of, iv. 176
—white, with hook in mouth, viii. 38
Wolves, ii. pl. VI, opp. p. 32, 65, 130,
199, 233, 241, 249, 250, 286, 292, 301,
385 ⁵⁹; see also FENRIS-WOLF.
—antediluvian, took off wolf-masks and
became human, x. 261–262
—dead may manifest themselves as, iv.
9
—evil aspect of Norns seen in name for,
ii. 241
—("Reds"), three, kill Conall, iii. 157
—(Vlkodlak), belief that humans may
assume form of, or be turned into, iii.
228–229
Wollin, statue of Triglav in, iii. 285
—summer festival in, iii. 306
Woman, Women:
Woman abandoned, ix. 130, 132, 137,
233, 338 ⁴³
—and giant, tale of, ix. 236–237
——serpent, v. 178
——sugar-cane, tale of, ix. 110
—as Earth Supporter, x. 250
—associated with deity, viii. 66, 69
—corpulent, stops egress of people from
first home, xi. 271, 273
—created from ear of maize, x. 108
—creation of, iv. 373, 377, 378, 381;
v. 184

Woman, duty of, to lead back soul of shaman from trance, iv. 293
—evil comes into world through, i. 15
—first, created by gods, i. 15
— -form, Loki in, gives birth to children, ii. 143
— -from-Heaven, x. 127
—helmeted, from sea, ii. 235
—house, iv. 159, 161, 165, 166, 167
—one only, saved from flood, ix. 180
—primeval man changed into a, ix. 107
—shadow-soul enters sexual organs of, just before confinement, iv. 472
—shaman's drum desecrated by touch of, iv. 289
—sky compared to, xii. 37
—sun as a, ix. 275, 276
—The Holy, viii. 111
—turned into owl for evil teaching, xi. 202
—who climbed to sky, x. 112, pl. XVIII, opp. p. 112
Women (Amazons) of island of Matenino, xi. 19, 281
—appeal directly to Great Spirit, x. 84
—at sacrifices, iv. 130–131, 132, 135
—barren, appealed to Water mother, iv. 214
—birth of cannibals from, x. 204
—creation of: see ORIGINS, MYTHS OF.
—danger of, from Rākṣasas, vi. 98
—derived from maggots of rotting fish and fire, tale of, ix. 254–255
—dream- ii. 250
—dream about blood-stained, ii. 250
—dying in child-birth, xi. 198
—fatherless and husbandless, xi. 154, 285
—Finnish Karelian, kept family name after marriage, iv. 138
—forbidden to have more than two children, one of whom must be sacrificed, xi. 227
—four, uphold sky, xii. 35
—Ḥat-ḥôr patroness of, xii. 40
—have charge of the Lalakoñti, x. 199
—heroic, of mortal birth regarded as Valkyries, ii. 251–254
—illness of, as Seide is approached, iv. 103
—in child-birth, rituals have ceremonies for delivery of, v. 185
——hereafter, iv. 489, 491

Women in labour helped by stone rings, xi. 24, 350 9
—Island of, iii. 117; viii. 364; ix. 140
—kennings for, ii. 255
—Land of Ever-Living, obviously part of divine land, iii. 84–86, 87, 89, 115
—live with other women [as spouses] after taking vow of chastity, xi. 282
—may enter " purified spot " once only after their wedding ceremony, iv. 174
——not enter lud, iv. 143
———walk around tent containing gun (as forest-spirit), iv. 175
—of the clouds, myth of release of, vi. 323
—only take part in feast to birth-goddess, iv. 415–416
—prophetic, ii. 241, 246, 253, 254, 283, 299, 334; see also DREAM-WOMEN; SPADISIR; VOLOR, ETC.
—received after death by Freyja, ii. 121, 122
—represent women and men, men at funeral feasts, iv. 55–56, 122
—Roman Junones protectors of, iii. 249
—rules governing, at hunting, fishing, and worship, iv. 84–85, 87–97, 119
——pertaining to, xii. 186
—saints, vi. 244
—saved by Tortoise swallowing them, vii. 319–320
—sixty, in Etain's form, iii. 82
—sixty-four accomplishments of, vi. 226
—southern, Valkyries called, ii. 252
—Spells of, iii. 84
—status of, in temple worship, xii. 192
—stolen by giants, trolls, and dwarfs, ii. 272, 278, 286
—swans changed into, iv. 501
—tribal rulers, xi. 342
—Trojan, i. 326 3(ch. viii), 327 11
—troll-, ii. 286, 287, 301, 302
—two first Hopi, as creators, x. 204–205
—unmarried, spirits of, wander year after death, iv. 479
——who lived with bachelor warriors, xi. 78, 282
—White, connected with Light-elves, ii. 222
—wild: see WILD WOMEN, ETC.
Women's maturity, four ages of, xi. 79
Womb, four-fold of the World, x. 207

Womb, sacrifice to Ruotta to prevent piercing of, iv. 67

Wombat and kangaroo, tale of, ix. 289–290

Wonder-child, tale of Mongan a myth that might fit any, iii. 64

— -folk, x. 68–69

— -tree, birds, beasts, and fish grew from, ix. 176

——grew from bones of bird, ix. 237–238

— -trees on new-formed earth mated and produced egg from which phantom maid came, ix. 173–174

— -workers, xi. 175

——and prophets, x. 120–124

——(Dasra), vi. 30, 141

Wōng Ti-fang, famous ruler of north country, and his sons, xii. 279–280

Wood, Bragi's, ii. 162

—cleft, a magic method to assist childbirth, iv. 252–253

—dead Osiris concealed in beam or column of, xii. 114–115

—fire born in, vi. 284, 285

—[forest], magic creation of, iii. 136

—in which human pair hidden, ii. 168

— -maidens, ii. 132–133, 135, 242–243, 260

—man made from, ix. 174–175

—manikins of, caused to live and multiply, xi. 163

— -nymph Lesní Ženka, iii. pl. xxx, opp. p. 260

—one of the elements, viii. 142

—sacred to Herakles, cult centre of the Cherusci, ii. 69

— -shavings, motif of discovery through, iii. 178

— -spirits, ii. 205–208

— -wife, ii. 42, 205, 206, 207

Wooden cows, iii. 26

—gods (dolls) of Samoyeds, iv. 113

—Seides, iv. 107–108

—stocks as images, x. 191

Woodmen, viii. 150

Woodpecker connected with Mars, i. 293

Woods, different kinds of, used for fire, ix. 115, 116

—haunted, of Kolelo, vii. 189

—occupants of, ii. 213–215

—used for kindling fires, x. 140

Wooing of Semele by Zeus, i. 46

Word, creative, v. 104, 277

—[of wrath] agent of anger of Enlil and his sons, v. 100

Words, Indo-European religious, and Iranian, in Armenian, vii. 13–14

—School of, viii. 8

Work not performed on day of Jupiter, ii. 68–69

—of dwarfs available to men for offering of metal and money, ii. 271

Workers, skilled, short-lived because Ruler of dead needs their help, iv. 484

World, ages of the, i. 17–18

—and its denizens, x. 135–138

——rulers, x. 249–254

——men, creation of, xii. 68–73

—below world of men, x. 136

—beyond, stories of, viii. 264

— -bull, iv. 311–312

—catastrophes, v. 139, 140, 141, 142, 145, 222, 270–276; see also Fire of Surt, etc.

— -conflagration, iv. 370

—created or organized by sun-god, xii. 30

—creation of, i. 4–5; see also items s.v. Creation and Origins.

—derivation of present, from wreck of former, ix. 15, 16

— -destroyer, dragon as, vii. 392 [18]

—destruction of, ii. 338–344; iv. 361–370; x. 221–225, 228; xi. 84; xii. 72; see also items s.v. Cataclysms.

——and re-creation, ix. 17

——by serpent, ix. 161

——in Dresden Codex, xi. 152, pl. xxii, opp. p. 152, 154

—doctrine of ages of, has affinity to four ages set forth in Hesiod, vi. 103

—domination of, shifted from deity to deity and group to group, xi. 51

— -egg, iv. 330

—end of, iv. 312, 345, 425; vii. 98–100, 397 [9]; x. 60

—Eskimo's, x. 3–8

—evil in, caused by sons of Elōhim marrying daughters of men, v. 358, 373

—fashioning of the, vi. 16–17

—five destructions of, v. 270

——regions of, xi. pl. vi, opp. p. 56

—forecast of new, ii. 346

World formed from body of Manza-shiri, iv. 372
—frame of, x. 21–23, 185
—guardians, vi. 215; viii. 242–247
—heating of, indirectly causes peopling of earth, x. 255
—hymn on creation of, xii. 68–69
—inverted, concept of, comes from reflexions in water, iv. 73
—Kachin beliefs of creation of, xii. 263
—life of, x. 82–85
—Mendes ram pantheistically identified with, xii. 413 [13]
— -mountain, ii. 336; iv. 341–348; see also SUMBUR, ETC.; SUMERU, ETC.
——destiny of men decided on, vii. 384 [51]
— -nail, iron, ii. 335, 336; iv. 222
— -ocean, iv. 345, 346
—of dead reflexion of earthly life, iv. 483–484
——spirits and monsters, vii. 72–92, 93
—pictures, iv. 307–312, 347
— -pillar of Lapps, iv. pl. xxiv, opp. p. 212, 222 (world-pillars are sometimes trees).
——see SACRIFICES, BLOOD OFFERED TO, ETC.
—pillar of, to support sky, iv. 222
— -pillars, ii. 334; iv. 333–340, 344, 349, 401
——constellations as, xi. 99
— -post in " Būndahish," iv. 344
— -powers, x. 5–6, 21, 22, 252, 287 [31]
——orientation of, in space and time, xi. 56
— -protectors, vi. 159
— -quarters, x. 23, 37, 40, 108–112, 185, 186, 286 [31]–287, 290 [35], 310 [66], 311 [67]; xi. 54, 55, 97, 100, 115
—re-forming of, x. 219, 221
—renewal of, ii. 318, 344–347
—renovated (renewed), ii. 131, 137, 152, 165, 168, 318, 344–347
—renovation of, iv. 370; vi. 261, 281, 296, 338, 344
—restoration of, ix. 161, 163
—restored by Manu when his ship comes to rest, vi. 147
—revival of dying, v. 52
—set afire, x. 223–225
——on fire by Mafuike, ix. 47
— -shapers, x. 139-141
—sketch of, x. 148 (fig. 2)

World-soul, ix. 13, 15
— -storeys, x. 22, 23, 60, 105, 159–161, 250, 253, 275 [11]–276; see also items s.v. STOREYS.
—sun swallowed at end of, by Fenriswolf, ii. 199–200
—threatened destruction of, vi. 307–309
— -tree, ii. 168, 331–335, 336, 346; iii. 138; iv. 340, 344, 349, 487, 494, 495, 511, 522; xii. 36; see also MIMAMEID TREE, ETC.; MJOTVID TREE, ETC.; WORLD-PILLARS; YGGDRASIL, ETC.
——like Yggdrasil, debased myth of, found in tree in Loch Guirr, iii. 138
—two human beings survive end of, and from them renovated world peopled, ii. 168
—under waters, iii. 112–113, 122; see also UNDERWATER CITIES, ETC.
—upper, entrance to, blocked by Izanagi, viii. 224
—what primitive man thinks of, i. xliv
Worlds, animal and vegetable, viii. 98–107
—multiplicity of, x. 22
—nine, speculation on, ii. 329–330, 331
——Vanaheim [on earth's surface], one of, ii. 27
—ninety-nine, iv. 411
—separate, for dead, unknown in pagan period, iv. 80
—ten, in Jain system, vi. 220
—three, vi. 71; 116, 121, 132, 138, 140, 152
World's man compared with Saturn, iv. 250
Worm from bird's egg transformed into human shape, ix. 109
——caul of Cian, iii. 132
——sea made from salty sweat of, ix. 250
Worms from tree creep into men's bodies, ii. 206
—in creation-myths, ix. 18, 23, 28, 29, 109, 159, 169, 250, 313 [72]
—swallowed, cause conception, iii. 140
—swineherds as, iii. 58
Worship, x. 84–85, 307 [62]
—in temples, xii. 193–194
—Kachin, xii. 297–299
—of anything having mysterious potency, vi. 158–159
——Kastor and Polydeukes, introduction of, into Athens, i. 25

Worthy, the Holy, and the Heavenly, three grades of, viii. 108

Wotan, human sacrifices required by, vii. 384 [60]

—identified with Mercury as conducting souls to Hades, vii. 384 [50]; see also ODIN.

Woto uttered incantation, trees opened and dwarfs emerged, vii. 265

Wounded Knee, battle between Americans and Indians at, x. 150

——possible meaning of Tsũi ||Goab, vii. 157, 158, 214

Wounding of face expression of sorrow for dead, iv. 27

——fire, or earth, or soul with sharp instruments, iv. 452, 454, 459, 478

Wounds of Arthur break out afresh every year, iii. 195

Wovoka, American Indian prophet, teachings of, x. 150

Wowta, evil frog-woman, xi. 273

Wrappings for dead of birch-bark or skins, iv. 19

Wrath, hymn to Word of, v. 100

Wren and fire, tale of, ix. 283

Wrestlers, two skilled, sent by Kaṁsa to kill Kṛṣṇa, vi. 173

Wrestling, i. 57, 86; v. 244, 245; vii. 245

—death by, iv. 183

—for guardianship of Pekko, iv. 245–246

—of Maui with fire-god, ix. 49

Wristlets, widower's, ix. 136

" Writer " (at time of death), vii. 94

—confused with angel of death, vii. 384 [50]

—epithet of Iranian Tīr and Arab 'Uṭārid, vii. 32, 384 [53]

—man: see PAIREKSE, ETC.

——who writes for the over-god in the Book of Fate, iv. 408, 409, 410

Writers, early, on Antillean religion, xi. 347 [1]–348

Writing, xi. 190

—art of, lost, and reckoning invented, xi. 217

—Chinese, viii. 7, 11, 30, 31

—in air and water, viii. 252–253

—Nabû god of, vii. 31

—of myths tabu, iii. 8

—Tiur patron of, and scribe of Aramazd, vii. 31

Writings, prophetic and oracular, xii. 197, 421 [25]

—Sekha(u)it goddess of, xii. 52

Wu, viii. 65, 73, 94, 101, 165, 174, 176

—chi, great self-existent, viii. 56

——one of the five ancient sacrifices, viii. 76

—Hou, Chinese Empress of T'ang dynasty, viii. 107, 124, 128

—Li T'ung K'ao, viii. 67

—Liang Tz'ŭ, classification of Three Emperors on bas-reliefs of, viii. 29, 31, 32

—Lung, Epoch of " The Five Dragons," viii. 25

— -lung, " black dragon," dog of magician Chang Shan-chün, viii. 107

—Mêng (5th cent.), filial piety of, viii. 163

——(4th cent.), occult arts taught by, viii. 113

—ssŭ day corresponds to element earth, viii. 27

——" five sacrifices," viii. 74

— -t'ai, one of four sacred hills of Buddhistic worship, viii. 72, 194

—Tao, viii. 168

——Chiang Chün, god of brigands, viii. 169

—Ti (B.C. 140–86), Emperor, viii. 75, 105, 117, 118

——(502–550 A.D.), founder of Liang Dynasty, viii. 188

——(265–290 A.D.), patron of occultism, viii. 134, 143, 145

—Tou Mi Tao, name given doctrinal system of Chang Tao-ling, viii. 14

—Wang, founder of Chow Dynasty, viii. 27, 40, 41, 42, 43, 48, 70, 139

—yo, viii. 193

Wuhuu, world above; heaven-clan, vii. 137

Wünschelwybere, women with chain, ii. 261

Wuotunc, name Wodan found in personal name, ii. 40

Wurd, Death, ii. 238

Wurekaddo, wife of Kururumany, xi. 259

Wurruna and seven sky-maidens, ix. 294–295

Wyungare, man made of ordure, tale of, ix. 293

Wyrd (fate), ii. 238, 246

X

Xahila family, xi. 177

Xam, xi. 208

Xaman Ek, North Star, xi. 138

Xan, animal sent to prick legs of Lords of Xibalba, xi. 173

Xanthos and Balios, immortal horses, i. 213

Xbalanqué and Hunahpu, hero-brothers, xi. 164, 168, 169, 172, 174–177

Xecotcovach, bird, xi. 164

Xelua, builder of pyramid at Cholula, xi. 96

Xenophon on his retreat found Armenians sacrificing to sun, vii. 15

Xerxes, v. 323

—army of, Armenians in, vii. 8

—demanded land and water as token of submission, iv. 462

—destruction of fleet of, i. 265

Xibalba, Underworld, challenge to ball-game in, xi. 170–171, 173

— -Okot, " dance of the daemon," xi. 145–146

Xibalbay, one Tulan at, xi. 178

Xich-tich, poetry of, recited, xii. 321

Xilonen, female counterpart of Cinteotl, xi. 75

—goddess-wife of victim of sacrifice to Tezcatlipoca, xi. 64

Xipe Totec, vegetation-deity clothed in human skin, xi. 76, pl. x, opp. p. 76

Xiqiripat, one of lords of Underworld, xi. 173

Xisuthros (Sisythes, Sisythus) = Ziûsudra = Noah, Greek transcription of Sumerian ante-diluvian king, v. 37, 204, 205, 232

—translation of, v. 204, 208, 224

Xiuhcoatl, Fire-snake, xi. 59, 60, pl. vii, opp. p. 60

Xiuhmolpilli, Aztec " Bundle of Years," xi. 146

Xiuhtecutli, god of fire, Fire-snake, x. 53, 54, 55, pl. vii, opp. p. 60

Xius, xi. 127, 128

Xivis, xi. 127

Xmucané, xi. 163, 165

Xoana, x. 191

Xochicauaca, xi. 112

Xochipilli, flower-god as maize-god, god of feasting, xi. 54, pl. vii, opp. p. 60, 77

Xochiquetzal, goddess-wife of victim of sacrifice to Tezcatlipoca, xi. 64, 77, 78, 92, 95

Xochitlicacan (Place of Flowers), xi. 77

Xocotl, similar to, if not identical with, Huitzilopochtli, xi. 60

Xoïs or Athribis, Ḥar-khent(i)-khet(?) worshipped at, xii. 388 28

Xolotl, legends of, xi. 82–83, 89, 90, 108, 122

Xomimitl, xi. 117

Xouthos, Athenian soldier of fortune, husband of Kreousa, i. 71

—consults Delphic oracle regarding offspring, i. 179

Xpiyacoc, xi. 163

Xquiq (" Princess Blood "), mother of Hunahpu and Xbalanqué, xi. 171–172

Xubchasgagua: see CHIE, ETC.

Xue (or Zuhé) culture-hero worshipped as god Bochica, xi. 202

Xulu, magician, xi. 175

Y

Yabme-aimo, common dwelling-place of dead, iv. 75

— -akka, (" old woman of the dead "), iv. 75

Yaccy-ma, immense black man, xi. 341–342

Yachachic, " the Teacher," xi. 236

Yādavas cursed by Nārada, vi. 145

Yādavas, Kṛṣṇa as hero and god among, vi. 110, 125

—establishes the, at Dvārakā, vi. 173

— -Pāṇḍavas, tribe who overthrew the Kurus, vi. 125

Yadu, vi. 35

Yāh: see YĀW.

Ya-hsang Ka-hsi, father of Nang Pyek-kha Yek-khi, xii. 289–290
Yahweh, v. 43; see also Yāw.
Yājñavalkya, worship of planets set forth in the law-book of, vi. 92
" Yajurveda," vi. 11, 73
Yakamouch, equivalent of Angakok, xi. 340–341
Yakṣas, vi. 108, 157, 158, 191, 203, 204, 215, 216, 217, 221, 227, 229
Yakṣī, vi. pl. xviii, opp. p. 156
Yakṣiṇī, vi. 226
Yakumo, Lafcadio Hearn's Japanese name, viii. 249
Yakut Kubai-Khotun, iv. 414
Yama and Bran parallel, iii. 105
——Yamī (Pers. Yima and Yimāka; Pahl. Yim and Yimak), first twins, vi. 294, 312–313, 316
—primeval man, king of departed, vi. 19, 20, 21, 23, 28, 62, 65, 68–70, 99, 100, 135, 138–139, 159–161, 180, 186, 213, 214–215
— -rājā (Skt.), the Japanese Emma, viii. 238
— -uba (Mountain-woman), viii. 289, 290–292, pl. xxxii, opp. p. 288
—Vaitaraṇī flows in realm of, vi. 159, 160, 235
—Vaivasvata, son of Sūrya, vi. 138–139, 159–161
—Yamī, brother and sister of Manu, vi. 18, 24, 50, 53, 59, 68, 215
Yamabuki, flower, viii. 385 [7]
Yamāntaka (or Yamāri), form of Mañjuśrī, vi. 213, 215
Yamato, etymology of word, viii. 377 [3]
—reached by Jimmu Tenno, viii. 211, 212
— -Takeru, story of, viii. 303–305
Yams, origin of good and bad, tale of, ix. 144–145
Yamutbal, six-headed ram, v. 129
Yananamca Intanamca, an idol, xi. 227
Yanbûshâd, wailings for, v. 339
Yanchang, spirit, daemon, etc., xi. 296
Yang, active or male principle corresponding to Heaven and light, viii. 99, 136
—and Yin, viii. 238, 243
——male and female principles, viii. 55, 56, 99, 110, 136, 142, 144
— -chow, viii. 65

Yang Hsiang, viii. 164
—I, viii. 136
—Kuei-fei, Empress, viii. 96
—San-chun, viii. 183–187
— -wu Hsien, viii. 93
—Yung-po, tale of, viii. 171
Yang (Karens), five clans of, xii. 292
Yangtze River, viii. 5
Yao, viii. 20, 33, 35, 37, 38, 41, 47, 66, 68, 69, 86, 88, 98, 99, 124, 135, 161, 168
—Ch'ih (" Lake of Gems "), viii. 117
—Hsiang (Yao appearances), viii. 144
Yard mother, iv. 239
Yāré, joyous exclamation, viii. 387 [2]
Yarhi-Bêl, transcribed Yaribôlos, deity of Palmyra, v. 56
Yar-lun, vi. 208
Yarns, variegated, tied to bamboos, viii. 236
Yāska, grammarian, vi. 53
—" Nirukta " of, vi. 15
Yaśodā, wife of Nanda, Kṛṣṇa exchanged for child of, vi. 171
Yasu, heavenly river, meaning of, viii. 226, 378 [8]
Yatai and Yatawm, ancestors of the Wa, xii. 289, 293–294, 295
——as tadpoles, frog, and ogres, xii. 293–294
Yathā ahū vairyā, powerful prayer, vi. 276
Yatis alone attain to Viṣṇu's abode, vi. 120
—Indra gave, to hyenas, vi. 88
Yatsu-hashi (eight-planked bridge), viii. 349
Yātudhānī, demon, vi. 144
Yātus (sorcerers), vi. 261
—Yātudhānas, demon sorcerers, vi. 67
Yatvyags closely akin to Slavs, iii. 317
Ya-u-bi-'-di (" god Yāw is my help "), v. 42
Yauhahus, evil spirits, familiars of sorcerers, xi. 261
Yāw absorbed character of sun-god El, v. 63
—and Yāh in proper names, v. 42
—created Adam and Eve, v. 183–185
— -Elōhim planted garden in Eden, v. 184–185
—Josiah destroyed images to sun-god at temple of, v. 54

Yāw, myths of war-god of Sumer and Babylonia attached by Hebrews to, v. 133
—see JAHVEH; JEHOVAH, JEWS, GOD OF THE; YAHWEH.
—ṣôr "rock," title of, v. 9, 11
—suggestion that, is ejaculation, v. 393 367
—West Semitic deity, v. xix, 5, 8, 14, 37, 41, 42, 43, 44, 63, 66, 73, 77, 78, 82, 104–105, 132, 133, 134, 135, 144, 156, 200, 229, 230, 233, 353, 356, 357, 363, 364, 387 202, 388 205
Yawng-hwe, lake in Southern Shan States, xii. pl. x, opp. p. 302
Yaxche, tree, xi. 138
Yaye-zakura ("Eight-petalled Cherry"), love-story of, viii. 347–348
Yazatas, vi. 260, 261, 277, 297, 307, 344; vii. 20
Ychdryt Varyvdraws, marvellous beard of, iii. 190
Ychoalay, Dobrizhoffer's conversation with Cacique, xi. 320–321
Ydalir (Yew-dales), dwelling-place of Ull, ii. 157, 158
Year and month, pillars on temple of Sun to measure, xi. 207
— -counts, x. 124–128, 195
—divided amongst the gods, xi. 51
—division of, by the Pleiades and Hyades, i. 249
—lunar, reference to, in herds of Helios, i. 242
—Maya, xi. 147
— -myth, solar, vi. 315
—of twelve months, Gilgamish epic not based on, v. 268
—Osiris as god of the, xii. 94
—Prajāpati is the, vi. 76
—probably symbolized by "Horus in Three Hundred," xii. 388 28
—rite symbolizing death of, x. 58–59
— -signs, rites in connexion with, xi. 144–145
—steeds as, vi. 29
Years, Coatlicamac tied the, xi. 115, 118
Yeast, spittle of Odin in place of, ii. 121
Yega, picture, shadow, x. 78
Yeh Fa-hsi, magician, viii. 134
—Fa-shan, recluse, viii. 125, 134
Yehaw-melek, king of Gebal, v. 69–70
Yehl, demiurge, vii. 322

Yehōwāh, Yăhōwāh, v. 77
Yei, gods, x. 156, 163, 173, 174
Yè-jen ("wild men"), Chinese term for all aboriginal races, xii. 287
Yek, spirits or powers, x. 251
Yelafaz, sky-deity, ix. 249
Yelbegen, nine-headed monster, iv. 490, 491, 492
Yellow as a colour in relation to deities, xii. 144, 407 74
—Corn Boy, x. 162
——Maiden, x. 200
—Emperor: see HUANG TI, ETC.
—River, viii. 5, 100
——god of, viii. 90
—skin of Sêth's animal once represented as, xii. 389 33
—son of Fair, iii. 148
—Turbans, viii. 174, 178
Yemen (Arabia Felix), date of Himyaritic Minaean civilization in, v. 4
Yen Chiu pilgrimage, viii. 23
—Dynasty, incidents in, viii. 96, 155
—Kung, god who calms wind and waves, viii. 73
—Liang, General, viii. 95
—Mei, viii. 156
—Prince of: see YUNG LO.
—Shih-ku, viii. 140
—Tzŭ, viii. 163
— -yüan, viii. 168
Yenisei River: see HOLY WATER.
—Samoyeds, iv. xvii
Yerombalos, priest of Yeuō, v. 44
Yerri Yuppon, good spirit, xi. 342
Yesna identified with Jupiter, iii. 301, 355 44
Yeuō, the god Yāw, v. 44
Yew Glen, three shapes ("phantoms") combat Fionn, Oisin, and Caoilte, iii. 169–170
— -tree, "salmon-leap" to, iii. 144
Yezidis, vii. 393 25
Yezo, Yoshitsune said to have gone to, viii. 383 11
Ygg ("the Terrible"), name of Odin, ii. 17, 43
Yggdrasil, world-tree, tree in Loch Guirr somewhat resembles, iii. 138
—(Ygg's horse), ash (world-tree), ii. pl. IV, opp. p. 16, 23, pl. VI, opp. p. 32, 43, 49, 51, 52, 152, 167, 204, 217, 239, 243, 276, 303, 319, pl. XLII, opp. p. 324, 330, 331–336, 340, 341, 346

"Ygg's (Odin's) ale-bearer," a poet called himself, ii. 54

Yibir tribes reputed to be sorcerers, vii. 115

Yi-dam, guardian deities, vi. 210–211, 213, 214, 215

Yima, vi. 28; 273, 289, 290, 302, 303–319, 320, 321, 322, 327, 338, 342, 350, 351

—first man, iv. 367

—Iranian myth of, parallel of Lif and Lifthrasir, ii. 346–347

Yimak (Yimāka), vi. 310–311, 350

Yimantuwinyai ("Old-One-Across-the-Ocean"), x. 220

Yin, viii. 55, 56, 136–137, 142, 144

—(eagle), viii. 104

—Fu King, viii. 17

—Hung, patron of grain, myth of, viii. 66–67

—I, viii. 136

Ying-chou, viii. 115

Yiyanitsinni, holders up of the heavens, x. 169

Yiyi, Spider, vii. 327–328, 329, 332

Yiyisa, daughter of Spider, vii. 329

Ylfe, Alfar akin to, ii. 219

Ymir, Brimir and Blaenn may be names of, ii. 264

—earth created of flesh of giant, iv. 372

—Eddic cosmic giant, vi. 288

—giant, ii. 275, 276, 324, 325, 328

Ymix-tree, symbol of universal destruction, xi. 154

"Ynglinga-saga " and " -tal," ii. 5, 26, 29, 33, 47, 55, 106, 110, 112, 113, 120, 175, 298, 299

Ynglings at Upsala, Norwegian kings descended from, ii. 5, 33, 112

Yngvi, son of Odin, king of Sweden, ii. 33, 112–113, 114, 126

— -Frey, one of kings of race of, to be chosen to serve Odin, ii. 250

——Frey sometimes called, ii. 28

Yo, viii. 61

—Fei, General, viii. 66, 180–181

——patriot, viii. 97

—Wang, god of healing, viii. 66, 105–106, 107

— -yang, viii. 123

Yoalli Ehecatl (night wind), xi. 62, 87

Yobanua-Borna, rain-deity, xi. 25

Yocahu, appellation of Sky-father, xi. 24

Yocahuguama, "yucca" appears in form, xi. 34, 35

Yoga philosophy, vi. 162–163, 177

Yoginīs, vi. 205

Yogo and the bee, tale of, viii. 323

Yōishta, vi. 335, 350

Yoke (for bearing buckets), Siberian name for Orion, iv. 430

—placing of, taught by divine folk to mortals, iii. 81

Yokes: see STONES, ANTILLEAN TRIANGULAR, ETC.

Yolkai Estsan (Yolaikaiason), White Shell Woman, wife of Moon-carrier, x. 157, 164, 166

Yomi, viii. 248

Yomotsu-kuni, Japanese Hades, viii. 223

Yoni, vi. pl. IV, opp. p. 34

Yorimitsu, general of Minamoto clan, viii. 306

Yoritomo, viii. 383 12

Yorokobu: see KOMBU, ETC.

Yoshi-iye, hero of Minamoto clan, viii. 305

—said to have set free a fountain, viii. 251, 252

Yoshino, Yoshitsune took refuge in, viii. 312

Yoshitsune, epic hero, viii. 307, 308, 309–312

Yoskeha (Sapling), x. 36–37, 295 45–296, 297 47

Young Mother Eagle, Sun's mother, xi. 122

Youth, Apollo protector of, i. 180

—drinking-horn restored, iii. 169

—fountain of: see FOUNTAIN OF YOUTH.

—Hermes god of, i. pl. XLIV, opp. p. 194

—naked, rising from wooded hills, myth of, v. 61

—Sapling retransforms his body to regain, x. 38

—shedding of skins to regain, vii. 169, 170

—symbol of river Orontes, v. 19

Yoyolche, night walkers, xi. 141

Yris, good spirit, xi. 38, 40

Yryn-Ajy[Ai]-Tojon ("White Creator Lord"), iv. 313, 351, 398–399, 400, 449

Yseudydd, swiftness of, iii. 190

Yseult, iii. 104

Yskal-pydo-murt (Cow-footed man), iv. 181

Yskyrdaw, swiftness of, iii. 190

Yspaddaden Penkawr, father of Olwen, iii. 187, 188, 192, 198

Ytzmatul, idol, xi. 133

Yu-ch'ao, viii. 26

— -hsiung the modern Lo-yang, viii. 27, 28

—Wang, viii. 166, 167

Yü Ch'ien-lou, viii. 164

—Ch'ing ("jade"), one of the Three Heavens, viii. 109, 110

—Hsiung, viii. 9

—Hsü Kung, viii. 22

—Huang, Shang Ti became, viii. 58, 59, 60, 110

—Lei and Shu Yü, guardians of the portal, viii. 78, 105

—lin wu, viii. 90

—Nü, statue of, viii. 71

—Po, god of fishes, viii. 90

—sacrifice for rain, viii. 61

—Shih, rain-god, viii. 73

—(Ta-Yü) the Great, founder of Hsia Dynasty, viii. 27, 35, 36-37, 38, 47, 100, 135

—Ti, the Pearl Emperor, viii. 196-197

— -t'ien, "field of jade," viii. 171

Yüan Chuang, adventures of, viii. 190-193

—Dynasty, events in, viii. 22, 23, 24, 56, 71, 110, 112, 113, 117, 119, 135, 142, 161

—Kuei, viii. 100

—Shao, viii. 95

—Shih T'ien Tsun, deity, viii. 80, 109, 110, 111

—Ti, Emperor, viii. 134

Yucatan, xi. 44-45, 124-155

Yucca, xi. 25, 34, 350 9

Yudhiṣṭhira, vi. pl. viii, opp. p. 100, 125, 149-150

—legend like that of Haosravah, vi. 338-339

Yüeh Hsiang, tale of, viii. 172-173

Yufugawo, story of, viii. 301

Yugalin ("pair"), period, vi. 225, 226

Yuki-onne (Snow-Woman), viii. 289

Yule, winter festival of, ii. 96, 109, 191, 233

Yum Cimil, lord of death, xi. 139

—Kaax, god of maize, xi. 137, 139

Yumbalamob, protector of Christians, xi. 141

Yumchakob, lord of rain, xi. 140, 141

Yunca, xi. 44

—pantheons, xi. 220-227

—several successive culture periods of the, xi. 215, 216, 219

—vases, representations of deity of Tiahuanaco on, xi. 235

Yün-ch'i, viii. 29

—Chung Chün, hero, god of clouds, viii. 88

Yung-ch'êng, viii. 26

—K'ang, viii. 101

—Lo, Emperor, viii. 72, 155

Yün-nan, prototypes of Malay perhaps to be sought among wilder tribes of, ix. 244

Yupanqui: see PACHACUTI, ETC.

Yuraks, one of Samoyed group, iv. xvii

Yurará taya, caladium of the turtle, xi. 290

Yurupari festival, xi. 293-294

Yuttoere (that which is on high), x. 82

Yuvanāśva, King, tale of, vi. 166

"Yvain," "Lady of the Fountain" equivalent of, iii. 191

Yzamna, god of the centre, xi. 145

Z

Z-rod symbol, iii. pl. x, opp. p. 94, pl. xvii, opp. p. 134

Zac-Ciui, evil omen of Ix years, xi. 145

— -u-Uayeyab, god of a Quarter, xi. 145

Zactecauh, xi. 178, 179, 181, 182

Zada wind and its spirit Zada-Sagan-Tengeri, iv. 458

Zadan-ulan-shulun, red stone to conjure wind, iv. 458

Zaden, Iberian goddess of unknown functions, vii. 40

Zadušnica, Bulgarian celebration in honour of deceased ancestors, iii. pl. xxvii, opp. p. 236, 237

Zagmuk, Babylonian New Year Festival, vii. 30, 384 [51]
—festival to Marduk (Ashur), v. 156, 157, 315, 322, 411 [44]
Zagreus myth parallel to creation from clay and blood of slain god, v. 275
—see SABAZIOS UNDER NAME OF, ETC.
—title of Dionysos as torn asunder and revived, i. 218
Zagros Mountains, vii. 379 [2]
Zaguaguayu and Abaangui, xi. 297
Zahriel, demoness (Lîlîth), v. 363
Zainigāv, Iran laid desolate by, vi. 336, 350
Zairivairi (Gr. Zariadres; Pers. Zarīr), vi. 340, 341, 342, 350
Zajan, iv. 394, 499
Zakiqoxol, fire-spirit of forest, xi. 182
Zakynthos, Aphrodite still known in, as mother of Eros, i. 314
—traces of Poseidon preserved in modern folk-tale of, i. 312
Zāl, vi. 290, pl. xxxvii, opp. p. 290, 331, 348, 350
Zalmoxis taught of life beyond, vii. 97, 390 [14]
Zamama as war-god, Ninurta's cult under name of, v. 132, 136, 137
—son of Enlil, Bau wife of, at Kish, v. 14
—war-god, Ninurta as, v. 117, 119, 397 [74]
Zambezi, vii. 132
Zambu, Indian tree of life, iv. 356, 357, 359
Zamin (Semele), vii. 12
Zamna, Yucatec hero, xi. 131, 133–134
Zamzummim, v. 355
Zan, Cretan name of Zeus, i. 156
Zanes, bronze images of Zeus, i. 161
Zapatero, idols on island of, xi. 184
Zarathustra, iv. 315, 316
—soul of, comes to earth in stalk of haoma-plant, vii. 45
Zarbanit as Virgo, v. 321, 341
—wife of Marduk, v. 316, 317, 341
Zarvan, vi. pl. xxxiii, opp. p. 264; see also ZRVAN AKARANA.
Zatik, vii. 17, 40–41
Zaya Kumma and Titha Kumma, sons of King of Karanaka, become hermits, xii. 284
Zazen, farce, plot of, viii. 360
Zcernoboch: see ČERNOBOG.

Zduh, Zduhacz ("spirit"), soul which leaves sleeping persons or animals, iii. 227
Zebra, vii. 418 [35]
Zedet, xii. 151, 403 [20]
—Zedut, old pronunciations of Dêdet, xii. 132
Zefa connected with Nile-god, xii. 66
—god of plenty, xii. 66
Zemeka ("winter"), Zoroastrian arch demon, vii. 86
Zemelo, earth-goddess in Phrygia, i. 216
Zemiism, West Indian idolatry, xi. 21–28, 347 [1], 350 [8]
Zemis, xi. 22–26, 34, 35, 36, 261, 350 [9]
Zen, a Mahāyāna School, viii. 189, 219
Zend(u), deity who sat in sledge-ship, xii. 151–152
Zenith, xi. 98
—mask of warrior of the, x. pl. i, frontispiece, 185, 186
Zenjirli, deities of, v. 44
Zephyros, i. pl. v, opp. p. liv, 23, 247, 265
—and Iris, Eros son of, i. 203
Zeret, original bull-headed form of Mon̮t(u) at, xii. 139
Zervanists, Iranian sect, iv. 317; see also ZRVANTISTS.
Zet, god of endless time, xii. 378 [102]
Zetes and Kalaïs free Phineus from depredations of Harpies, i. 111
—son of Boreas and Oreithyia, i. 73
Zethos and Amphion, i. 43–44
—in Farnese Bull group, i. pl. xv, opp. p. 42
—son of Zeus, i. 157
Zeus, i. pl. viii (3), opp. p. 8, 151–163; ii. 97, 100; iii. 35, 53; 322; iv. 391; vi. pl. xxxiii, opp. p. 264; vii. 13, 380 [7]; xii. 255
—abandoned Europe to Asterios, i. 60
—Amon as sun-god identified by Greeks with, xii. 129–130
—and Asteria, Hekate daughter of, in Mousaios, i. 187
——Athene overthrow Giants, i. 9
——Dione, i. pl. iv (5), opp. p. l
——Earth capture Persephone, i. 227–228
——Giants conquer Titans and drive them into depths of earth, i. 8
——Hera wedded, i. 7–8

Zeus and Kallisto parents of Pan, i. 267
——Kouretes, i. pl. xxxviii, opp. p. 158
——Themis parents of the Moirai, i. 284
——Typhon, i. pl. ii (1), opp. p. xlii
—Antiope yielded herself to, i. 43
—Aristaios, reason for epithet, i. 252
—Arotrios, name of Dagōn, v. 80
—Athene defends, from attack of the Titans, i. 172
—Babylonian light-god's spear interpreted by Greeks as thunderbolt of, xii. 397 [101]
—born in Crete, i. 7
——of Kronos and Rhea, i. 5, 6, 14 (fig. 2), 274
—challenged by Giants, i. 9
—changed Dionysos into a kid, i. 46
—changes dog and fox into stone at Thebes, i. 73
—consigned Sisyphos to Hades, i. 37
—coupled with Gaia at Dodona, i. 272
—decree of, on Adonis, v. 335
—Dionysos born from thigh of, i. 46, pl. xliv, opp. p. 194
——reborn from thigh of, i. 217
—directs Hermes to slay Argos, i. 29
—dogs of: see HARPIES.
—Dyaus corresponds to, vi. 21
—eagle of, vi. 48
—enamoured of Europe, assumed form of bull and carried her off, i. 44, 60
—entered chamber of Semele in chariot and so caused her death, i. 46
—equated with Adad, v. 37, 38
—establishment of régime of, i. 8
—Eubouleus, title of Hades, i. 234
—father of Argos, i. 29
———Dardanos, i. 117
———Dionysos, i. 217
———gods and men, i. 11
———Helen by Nike, i. 284
———Hephaistos, i. 206
———Herakles by Alkmene, i. 77–79
———Pelasgos, i. 20, 29
—felled Typhon with thunderbolt, i. 9
—freed the three hundred-handed Giants, i. 8
—gave code of laws to Minos, i. 64
———Harmonia in marriage to Kadmos, i. 45
—granted Sarpedon life three generations long, i. 61
———Tithonos eternal life, i. 246

Zeus grants immortality to Memnon, i. 130
——permission for Odysseus to return to his native soil, i. 138
—Hera sister-spouse of, i. 164
—Herakles explained by some as degenerate, i. 75
—history of, i. xlviii
—hypsistos, rendering of Ramas, v. 64
—Ikmaios, Aristaios raised altar to, i. 252
—infant, nursed by nymphs, i. 258
—Keraunios translation of Ba'al Shamîn, v. 390 [280]
—killed Asklepios by thunderbolt, i. 280
—kills Iasion with thunderbolt because of amour with Demeter, i. 226
—kinship of Muses with, i. 239, 311 [4] (ch. xi)
—lordship of, challenged, i. 9
—makes Hyades a constellation, i. 248
——trial of, and destroys, house of Lykaon, i. 20
—Malak-Bêl identified with, v. 58
—meaning of myth of birth and death of, in Crete, i. 274
—megistos keraunios translation of Ba'al Shamîn, v. 63
—Minos explained as double of, i. 63
—Neoptolemos slays Priam while suppliant at altar of, i. 133
—nymphs usually regarded as daughters of, i. 258
—of the Underworld, Hades known as, in one passage in Homer, i. 233, 234
—Olympios translated Ba'al Shamîn by Syriac writers, v. 64
—Pegasos flew upward to ancient stables of, after death of his master, i. 40
—plea of Kybele to, for restoration of life to Attis, i. 275
—pled with Demeter for people of Eleusis, i. 228
—promise of, to Semele, i. 45–46
—promises Thetis to delay Greek victory till Achilles is honoured, i. 127
—punishes Apollo for slaying Kyklopes, i. 107
—Quetzalcoatl clearly the Toltec, xi. 94
—relation of Moira to, i. 283
—represented by Iuppiter in Roman mythology, i. 288, 289, 299
—river-gods in council of, i. 256

Zeus, rivers sometimes regarded as sons of, i. 256
—sacrifices on mountains to, vi. 318
—saved by Rhea, i. 6–7
—saves Herakles at Kos, i. 91
—seized Aigina and hid her from her father, i. 37
—sends dream upon Agamemnon, i. 127
——thunderbolt on Kampaneus, i. 53, 158
—sent Kadmos and Harmonia to dwell forever in the Elysian Fields, i. 47
—Serapis worshipped in Egypt chiefly under Greek representation of, xii. 386 19
—settles dispute over possession of Adonis for Aphrodite and Persephone, i. 198
—" sire of gods and men," i. 6
—smiths of, originally storm-daemons, i. 267
—smote Phaëthon with a thunderbolt, i. 244
—statue of, in Ani, vii. 24
—strife of, with Titans, i. 8
—strikes Anchises dead for telling of divine descent of Aineias, i. 199
—survivals of, in modern Greek folk-belief, i. 312
—suspends Hera from Heaven, i. 91
—talking oak of, fitted into prow of Argo, i. 109
—thunderbolt of, separates Apollo and Herakles, i. 90
—varying attitude of Prometheus towards, i. 12
—wedded Europe on island of Crete, i. 60
——to Hera, i. 5, 7–8
—with thunderbolt hurled Charybdis into sea, i. 264
—won way to Danaë in form of shower of gold, i. 33
—worship of, established on Mt. Lykaios, i. 20
—wronged Io and changed her into a white heifer, later restoring her to human form, i. 29
—Xenios translated by Vanatur, vii. 382 13
Zhouti, earlier name of Thout(i), xii. 33
Zimwi, kind of demon or ogre, vii. 250–251, 334, 404 4

Zio, Ziu (Tyr), god, ii. 17, 24, 97, 98
Zipacna overcome by hero-brothers, xi. 168, 169
Zis signifies both sun and deity, xi. 278
Ziûsudra = Xisuthros (Sisythes, Sisythus) = Noah, Sumerian antediluvian king, v. 37, 204, 205, 207, 208, 209, 224, 270
Živa, ancient Slav goddess of life, iii. pl. xxxiv, opp. p. 288
Zlota baba: see GOLDEN, THE, ETC.; ZOLOTA BABA.
Zmek, snake, iii. 247
Zōchō-ten (Virūḍhaka), guardian of south, viii. 243
Zodiac, iv. 347, 438; viii. 143; xi. 98, 358 10
—Peruvian, xi. 246
—signs of, iii. 318; v. 305, 306, 319; vi. 233; vii. 52–53, 65, 94
——in Etruscan mythology, i. 289
——Tammuz summoned king to worship, v. 337
——twelve Asiatic, xii. 57
Zodiacal signs, vi. 276; xii. pl. iii, opp. p. 170
——became popular in Graeco-Roman times, xii. 57, 65, 378 94
Zolota Baba (" Golden Gammer "), idol, iii. 354 32; iv. 260–261
Zones, cultural, xi. 2–3
Zoölatry, vii. 276
Zoömorphic pantheon, xi. 190–191
Zor-'addan, ṣor as title of god, v. 379 35
Zoroaster (Zarathushtra), vi. 260, 261, 273, 286, 289, 305, 309, 318, 320–343
Zoroastrian gods of Armenia bear post-classic and pre-Sassanian stamp, vii. 15
Zoroastrianism, vii. 9, 20, 54
Zotz, bat-god, xi. 364 6
Zotzils, xi. 179
Zruty, wild gigantic beings, iii. 266
Zrvan Akarana, Ahura Mazda son of, vii. 23; see also ZARVAN.
Zrvantists, ideas of, reported by Armenian authors, vii. 384 57; see also ZERVANISTS.
—(Magians?) indulged in a triennial worship of the devil, vii. 82
Zû, bird of storm (dragon), who stole Tablets of Fate, v. 40, 101–102, 108, 117–118, 129, 130, 169, 170, 235, 279, 281, 282, 283, 295, 320

Zû, contests of, vi. 264

Zuarasici: see SVARAŽIC.

Zu-en (laterly Sin), Sumerian name of moon-god, used in inscriptions, v. 5, 92, 152

Zuhá, Spaniards termed, xi. 202

Zuhé (Xue), xi. 202

Zuimaco, name of Earth mother, xi. 25

Zuñi beliefs on abode of dead, x. 275 [10]

Zututa, xi. 127

Zuyva, combat with people of, xi. 181

Zwerge, Alfar now has equivalence of German, ii. 223

Zympzymps, Meher lives in cave of, vii. 34

Žywie, deity of life, iii. 355 [44]

—of Polish mythology = Siva, iii. 289